The Wiley-Blackwell Handbook of Infant Development

Wiley-Blackwell Handbooks of Developmental Psychology

This outstanding series of handbooks provides a cutting-edge overview of classic research, current research, and future trends in developmental psychology.

- Each handbook draws together 25–30 newly commissioned chapters to provide a comprehensive overview of a subdiscipline of developmental psychology.
- The international team of contributors to each handbook has been specially chosen for its expertise and knowledge of each field.
- Each handbook is introduced and contextualized by leading figures in the field, lending coherence and authority to each volume.

The *Wiley-Blackwell Handbooks of Developmental Psychology* will provide an invaluable overview for advanced students of developmental psychology and for researchers as an authoritative definition of their chosen field.

Published

Blackwell Handbook of Childhood Social Development
Edited by Peter K. Smith and Craig H. Hart

Blackwell Handbook of Adolescence
Edited by Gerald R. Adams and Michael D. Berzonsky

The Science of Reading: A Handbook
Edited by Margaret J. Snowling and Charles Hulme

Blackwell Handbook of Early Childhood Development
Edited by Kathleen McCartney and Deborah A. Phillips

Blackwell Handbook of Language Development
Edited by Erika Hoff and Marilyn Shatz

Wiley-Blackwell Handbook of Childhood Cognitive Development, 2nd edition
Edited by Usha Goswami

Wiley-Blackwell Handbook of Infant Development, 2nd edition
Edited by J. Gavin Bremner and Theodore D. Wachs

Forthcoming

Blackwell Handbook of Developmental Psychology in Action
Edited by Rudolph Schaffer and Kevin Durkin

Wiley-Blackwell Handbook of Adulthood and Aging
Edited by Susan Krauss Whitbourne and Martin Sliwinski

Wiley-Blackwell Handbook of Childhood Social Development, 2nd edition
Edited by Peter K. Smith and Craig H. Hart

The Wiley-Blackwell Handbook of Infant Development

Second Edition

Volume 1

Basic Research

Edited by J. Gavin Bremner and Theodore D. Wachs

A John Wiley & Sons, Ltd., Publication

This second edition first published 2010
© 2010 Blackwell Publishing Ltd

Edition history: Blackwell Handbook of Handbook of Infant Development, edited by J. Gavin Bremner and Alan Fogel, Blackwell Publishers Ltd (1e, 2001)

Blackwell Publishing was acquired by John Wiley & Sons in February 2007. Blackwell's publishing program has been merged with Wiley's global Scientific, Technical, and Medical business to form Wiley-Blackwell.

Registered Office
John Wiley & Sons Ltd, The Atrium, Southern Gate, Chichester, West Sussex, PO19 8SQ, United Kingdom

Editorial Offices
350 Main Street, Malden, MA 02148-5020, USA
9600 Garsington Road, Oxford, OX4 2DQ, UK
The Atrium, Southern Gate, Chichester, West Sussex, PO19 8SQ, UK

For details of our global editorial offices, for customer services, and for information about how to apply for permission to reuse the copyright material in this book please see our website at www.wiley.com/wiley-blackwell.

The right of J. Gavin Bremner and Theodore D. Wachs to be identified as the authors of the editorial material in this work has been asserted in accordance with the UK Copyright, Designs and Patents Act 1988.

Wiley also publishes its books in a variety of electronic formats. Some content that appears in print may not be available in electronic books.

Designations used by companies to distinguish their products are often claimed as trademarks. All brand names and product names used in this book are trade names, service marks, trademarks or registered trademarks of their respective owners. The publisher is not associated with any product or vendor mentioned in this book. This publication is designed to provide accurate and authoritative information in regard to the subject matter covered. It is sold on the understanding that the publisher is not engaged in rendering professional services. If professional advice or other expert assistance is required, the services of a competent professional should be sought.

Library of Congress Cataloging-in-Publication Data

The Wiley-Blackwell handbook of infant development / edited by J. Gavin Bremner and Theodore D. Wachs. – 2nd ed.
     p. ; cm. – (Blackwell handbooks of developmental psychology)
  Other title: Handbook of infant development
  Rev. ed. of: Blackwell handbook of infant development / edited by Gavin Bremner and Alan Fogel. 2001.
  Includes bibliographical references and index.
  ISBN 978-1-4051-7874-7 (set : hardcover : alk. paper) – ISBN 978-1-4443-3273-5 (v. 1 : hardcover : alk. paper) – ISBN 978-1-4443-3274-2 (v. 2 : hardcover : alk. paper) 1. Infants–Development–Handbooks, manuals, etc. 2. Infants–Health and hygiene–Handbooks, manuals, etc. I. Bremner, J. Gavin, 1949- II. Wachs, Theodore D., 1941- III. Blackwell handbook of infant development. IV. Title: Handbook of infant development. V. Series: Blackwell handbooks of developmental psychology.
  [DNLM: 1. Child Development. 2. Infant Care. 3. Infant. WS 105 W676 2010]
  RJ131.B475 2010
  305.231–dc22

2010016203

A catalogue record for this book is available from the British Library.

Set in 10.5 on 12.5 pt Adobe Garamond by Toppan Best-set Premedia Limited
Printed in Singapore by Markono Print Media Pte Ltd

1   2010

Contents

List of Contributors

Volume 1

Lorraine E. Bahrick, Florida International University.

Rachel Barr, Georgetown University.

John E. Bates, Indiana University Bloomington.

Marc H. Bornstein, Eunice Kennedy Shriver National Institute of Child Health and Human Development.

J. Gavin Bremner, Lancaster University.

Cheryl Bryan, University of New Mexico.

Denis Burnham, University of Western Sydney.

Joseph J. Campos, University of California, Berkeley.

Daniela Corbetta, University of Tennessee.

Alan Fogel, University of Utah.

Sara Harkness, University of Connecticut.

Jennifer A. Harriger, University of New Mexico.

George Hollich, Purdue University.

Mark H. Johnson, Birkbeck College, University of London.

Garene Kaloustian, Lebanese American University.

David J. Kelly, Royal Holloway, University of London.

Kang Lee, University of Toronto.

Andrew Lock, Massey University.

Tessa E. Margett, University of New Mexico.

Karen Mattock, Lancaster University.

Andrew N. Meltzoff, University of Washington.

Olivier Pascalis, University Pierre Mendès-France.

Michal Perlman, University of Toronto.

Germán Posada, Purdue University.

Paul C. Quinn, University of Delaware.

David H. Rakison, Carnegie Mellon University.

Vasudevi Reddy, Portsmouth University.

Patricia Riddell, University of Reading.

Philippe Rochat, Emory University.

Hildy Ross, University of Waterloo.

Carolyn Rovee-Collier, Rutgers University.

Alan Slater, Washington Singer Laboratories.

Ad W. Smitsman, Radboud University.

Dale M. Stack, Concordia University.

Charles M. Super, University of Connecticut.

Catherine S. Tamis-LeMonda, New York University.

Marcia Vickar, University of Waterloo.

Theodore D. Wachs, Purdue University.

Rebecca A. Williamson, Georgia State University.

David C. Witherington, University of New Mexico.

Patricia Zukow-Goldring, University of California, Los Angeles.

Introduction to Volume 1: Basic Research

When plans were made for the first edition of the *Blackwell Handbook of Infant Development*, difficult choices had to be made regarding which topics to include. Despite the fact that the original volume was quite considerably over the agreed length when it went to the publisher, there still were significant gaps in coverage. In the period since its publication in 2001 there have also been continuous gains in our understanding of infant development, making it an even harder task to cover all the major aspects of infant development in one volume. For the second edition it was clear we had to do something to deal with this sheer volume of research and knowledge. Sacrificing depth of coverage did not seem an option. So the solution we arrived at was to move to a two-volume format, with volume 1 covering basic research and volume 2 covering applied and policy issues. We made this decision with some misgivings. After all, it could be argued that by making this split we are reinforcing the relative isolation of applied and basic work. However, we were aware that readers were already selective in what they read within a single volume, so felt that splitting the material into two volumes should not have any major effect, particularly if we took pains to cross-reference chapters between as well as within volumes.

The clear gain of the two-volume format is that we have been able to add 10 new chapters in total. As basic research was most fully represented in the first edition, most of the new chapters are in volume 2. However, volume 1 includes chapters on four topics not covered in the first edition: intermodal perception, perceptual categorization and concepts, imitation, and cultural influences.

The chapters in volume 1 are organized into three parts: perceptual and cognitive development; social cognition, communication, and language; and social-emotional development. These categories very much reflect the groupings of posters and papers at conferences on infancy, but one of the noticeable developments in the field is towards greater integration between research foci that were somewhat isolated in the past. In the case of the present collection of chapters, there are, for instance, links to be seen between face perception (part I, chapter 2) and imitation (part II, chapter 11), face perception and awareness of other minds (part II, chapter 12), and between brain development (part I, chapter 9) and awareness of other minds. These examples by no means form a comprehensive list. The likelihood is that this cross-fertilization will continue, in part through a general tendency for research to cross traditional boundaries within the discipline, but also through the influence of concepts in neuroscience, for instance, research on the mirror neuron system leading to new attempts to integrate cognitive and social development in infancy.

As with the first edition, our aim has been to make the book accessible and informative to a wide audience. Although each chapter addresses current work in a scientifically advanced way, we and the authors have attempted to achieve an approach and writing style that does not rely on prior knowledge of the topic on the part of the reader. Given the relatively high level at which chapters are pitched, we anticipate that the handbook will provide a thorough overview of the field that will be particularly useful to graduate students, advanced undergraduates, and to university staff who teach infancy research but who either do not do research in the field or who are confident only in a limited area. We hope it will also be attractive to academics who are looking for a high-level treatment of current theoretical issues and cutting-edge research.

We open the volume with a chapter by Alan Fogel that sets infancy in theoretical and historical context. This is a revision of his chapter that closed the first edition of the handbook. This time we felt that it was appropriate to place this chapter at the beginning as a scene setter, before the three parts containing the chapters on specific aspects of infant development. Opening with Bronfenbrenner's Ecological Systems Theory, Alan Fogel points out how at each of the four levels of this system (microsystem, mesosystem, exosystem, and macrosystem) there have been important changes through history. Within this framework he indicates how the nature and our images of infancy have changed from prehistoric times to the present, and ends with some speculations regarding the future of infancy. Important changes have occurred across historical time in how infants are thought of, a key factor being the relatively late emergence of the concept of the individual. However, a common theme that exists across time is the constant come and go between romantic and empirical approaches to infancy.

For cataloguing purposes, the editorial order is alphabetic for both volumes. However, Gavin Bremner had editorial responsibility for most chapters in volume 1 and Ted Wachs had editorial responsibility for all chapters in volume 2.

J. Gavin Bremner and Theodore D. Wachs

1

Historical Reflections on Infancy

Alan Fogel

Our daughter was the sweetest thing to fondle, to watch, and to hear. (Plutarch, Rome, second century, BCE)

What is best for babies? Cuddling and indulgence? Early training for independent self-care? The answer depends upon the beliefs that people have about babies. Beliefs about infants and their care differ between cultures and they have changed dramatically over historical time within cultures. The contemporary technology of infant care in Western society, for example, first appears in the eighteenth and nineteenth centuries, with an increase in pediatric medical care, advice books for parents, parental devotion to the individuality of each child, books written especially for young children, and other infant care products and resources.

Why is it important to understand the historical origins and historical pathways of beliefs about infants and their care? Cultural history is vast in its domain, encompassing beliefs and values about human rights, morality, marriage and family, war and peace, love and death. Beliefs about infants are important because to raise a baby is to plant a seed in the garden of culture. We bring up babies in ways that are consistent with responsible childhood and adult citizenship.

Bronfenbrenner's (1979) Ecological Systems theory suggests how infants are embedded in networks of socio-cultural processes and institutions that have both direct and indirect impacts on infant development. Bronfenbrenner defined four levels of system functioning between persons:

The *microsystem* is made up of all the relationships between the person and his or her environment in a particular setting. For example, all of the transactions that take place between the child and the physical and social environment of the family or school form a microsystem.

The *mesosystem* includes the relationships between the major settings in which children are found. An example would be the interaction between the family and the day care center. A child who is experiencing many difficulties in day care is likely to force the family to have more interactions with the center's teachers and administrators, and those family–school interactions should in turn have an effect on the child's functioning.

The *exosystem* extends the mesosystem to include other social systems that do not contain the developing child but have some effect on him or her. The world of work, neighborhood institutions, the media, the government, the economy, and transportation affect the functioning of the family, school, and other social settings in which children are found.

The *macrosystem* contains all of the various subsystems that we have been discussing. It contains all of the general tenets, beliefs, and values of the culture or subculture and is made up of the written and unwritten principles that regulate everyone's behavior. These principles – whether legal, economic, political, religious, or educational – endow individual life with meaning and value and control the nature and scope of the interactions between the various levels of the total social system.

Each of these systems has a history that is embedded within the larger history of a society. The "culture" of infancy, at any particular period in historical time, can be thought of as the complex set of relationships between and within each of these systems. In this chapter, I do not go into details about each of these levels of the system across historical time. Rather, the goal is a more general view of the macrochanges that have occurred across tens of thousands of years.

This chapter is based on research from secondary sources. These include the work of historians and anthropologists who have studied the primary sources of historical evidence, as well as translations into English of original historical documents. For prehistorical data, I rely on evidence from observers of modern hunter-gatherer societies as well as anthropological data. For the historical period, the focus will be on the work of historians and translators of original documents of Western culture (Judeo-Christian, Greek and Roman, and later European and American societies). This research approach may bias my interpretations in favor of the historian or translator who worked with the original documents and artifacts. A different point of view may arise from the work of a scholar who is competent to examine the evidence more directly.

This chapter highlights one major theme that was salient to me in collecting these materials, the historical continuity of a dialectic between *empirical* and *romantic* beliefs about infants. On the *empirical* side are beliefs related to the early education, training, and disciplining of infants to create desired adult characteristics and to control the exploration, shape, and uses of the body. *Romantic* beliefs favor the pleasures of babies and adults. Romantic ideas advocate indulgence in mutual love and physical affection in relationships, they show a respect for the body and its senses and desires, and the freedom of expression of all of the above. Although the terms empiricism and romanticism do not come into the English language until the eighteenth century, the earliest historical records reveal belief systems that will later come to be labeled as empirical or romantic.

The chapter is divided into the following sections: The prehistory of infancy (1.6 million to 10,000 years ago), early civilizations (8,000 BCE to 300 CE), the Middle Ages and Renaissance (third to sixteenth centuries), the Enlightenment (seventeenth to nineteenth centuries), and the recent past (twentieth century). The chapter concludes with a speculative section on the possible future of beliefs and practices about babies.

Prehistory of Infancy: 1.6 Million to 10,000 Years Ago

It is currently thought that all humans are descended from a small population of hunter-gathers who first appeared in Africa during the Pleistocene epoch. The Pleistocene lasted between 1.6 million years ago and 10,000 years ago. Beginning about 10,000 years ago and continuing until the present time, humans gradually abandoned nomadic patterns and began to occupy permanent settlements and to develop agriculture. *Homo sapiens* hunter-gatherer societies first appeared about 100,000 years ago and were descended from a long line of other human species that arose at the beginning of the Pleistocene.

By about 35,000 years ago, *homo sapiens sapiens* hunter-gatherer groups existed in most locations in the old world, in Australia, and in the Americas. Societies of this period were composed of small bands of about 25 humans who sustained themselves by hunting game and gathering wild roots and plants to eat. They would roam typically less than 20 miles (30 kilometers) and it was rare to encounter another group. Generations lived their lives within this small sphere of people and place. Hunter-gatherer societies are believed to have been the only form of human society during the entire Pleistocene epoch. They did not leave artifacts or other documentation of their infant care practices (Wenke, 1990). Relatively few such societies survive today. While there is some controversy about whether surviving hunter-gatherers are similar to prehistorical hunter-gatherers, these contemporary groups are considered to be reasonable approximations to prehistorical lifestyles (Hrdy, 1999; Wenke, 1990).

The human ecology during the Pleistocene is considered to be the *environment of evolutionary adaptedness*, a term devised by John Bowlby the founder of attachment theory (Bowlby, 1969). This is the African Pleistocene environment in which the human adult–infant bond evolved for over a million years, an environment with large populations of predators who could easily kill and eat a baby. In order to protect the infant from this and other dangers, the infant was carried in a sling or pouch at all times, never left alone, and the caregiver responded immediately to fussiness in order not to attract the attention of predators. As a consequence, humans evolved a mother–infant relationship with continuous touch and skin-to-skin contact, immediate attention to infant signals, and frequent breast feeding (Barr, 1990).

The present day !Kung bushmen, a hunter-gatherer group living in the Kalahari desert in Africa, have been observed extensively. !Kung women carry their infants in a sling next to their bodies at all times. They breast feed on demand, as much as 60 times in a 24 hour period. The infant sets the pace and time of breast feeding.

> Nursing often occurs simultaneously with active play with the free breast, languid extension-flexion movements in the arms and legs, mutual vocalization, face-to-face interaction (the breasts are quite long and flexible), and various forms of self-touching, including occasional masturbation. (Konner, 1982, p. 303)

Infants also receive considerable attention from siblings and other children who are at eye-level with the infant while in the sling.

Figure 1.1   Infants in hunter-gatherer societies are in nearly constant skin-to-skin contact with people, as shown with this woman holding a baby in Huli village, Papua New Guinea. *Source*: Photo © Amos Nachoum/Corbis.

> When not in the sling, infants are passed from hand to hand around a fire for similar inter-action with one adult or child after another. They are kissed on their faces, bellies, genitals, are sung to, bounced, entertained, encouraged, and addressed at length in conversational tones long before they can understand words. (Konner, 1982, p. 302)

The high rate of nursing prevents infant crying and has a natural contraceptive effect to prevent the birth of another child while the younger one still requires mother's milk. Births are spaced every 4 or 5 years (Konner, 1982; Wenke, 1990). The present-day Elauma of Nigeria are also hunter-gatherers (Whiten & Milner, 1986). Three-month-old Elauma infants spend almost all their time, whether awake or asleep, in physical contact with an adult or within three feet of the adult. Elauma mothers carry their babies with them while the mothers go about their daily chores (See Figure 1.1).

A similar account is offered from observations of the Fore people of New Guinea, a rain-forest hunter-gatherer group who remained isolated from the outside world until the 1960s. This group displays a "*socio-sensual human organization* [italics added] which began in infancy during a period of almost continuous, unusually rich tactile interaction" (Sorenson, 1979, p. 289). Play with infants includes "considerable caressing, kissing, and hugging" (p. 297).

> Not only did this constant "language" of contact seem readily to facilitate the satisfaction of the infant's needs and desires but it also seemed to make the harsher devices of rule and regimen unnecessary. Infant frustration and "acting out," traits common in Western culture, were rarely seen. (Sorenson, 1979, p. 297)

Because of this indulgence of the senses and a relative lack of overt discipline, hunter-gatherer societies exemplify a primarily romantic culture. Observations of weaning both in the !Kung and the Fore, however, suggest that the training of infants – empirical beliefs and practices – is also important. Although !Kung adults report memories of the difficulty of losing their close contact with their mother during weaning, they also report that these feelings were alleviated by the presence of other adults, siblings, and peers. Weaning occurs when the mother becomes pregnant with the next child. Adults believe that with the onset of pregnancy, the mother's milk will harm the nursing child and must be reserved for the unborn child. In the words of Nisa, a !Kung woman who spoke about her life,

> When mother was pregnant with Kumsa, I was always crying, wasn't I? One day I said, "Mommy, won't you let me have just a little milk? Please, let me nurse." She cried, "Mother! My breasts are things of shit! Shit! Yes, the milk is like vomit and smells terrible. You can't drink it. If you do, you'll go 'Whaagh … whaagh …' and throw up." I said, 'No, I won't throw up, I'll just nurse.' But she refused and said, 'Tomorrow, Daddy will trap a springhare, just for you to eat.' When I heard that, my heart was happy again. (Shostak, 1983, p. 53)

Even here, in the most romantic of human lifestyles, in which the body and its senses are indulged and in which children receive very little discipline or restrictions, empirical beliefs are present in some form. The discourse between the romantic and the empirical may be a law of nature, derived from the simple truth that elders require of children some sacrifice if they are to grow into full coparticipation. If the sacrifice is done in the flow of a balanced dialogue, it will soon be followed by a new and surprising indulgence. The springhare helps Nisa to let go of her tragic loss and gives her a feeling of sharing in the more adult-like ritual of hunting. There is also evidence that hunter-gatherer groups occasionally used infanticide – the deliberate killing of unwanted infants and an extreme form of empiricist practice – for infants who were sick or deformed, those who could not have survived under the rigors of the harsh environment.

For most of human evolution, then, people lived close to the earth, either on open ground, in and near trees, in caves and other natural shelters. They were directly attuned to the earth, its climate, and its cycles. The basic elements of earth, air, fire, and water had enormous practical and spiritual significance. So far as we know, people did not distinguish themselves as separate from their ecology but as part of it, no different or more valuable than the basic elements, the plants, and animals (Shepard, 1998).

For people of the Pleistocene, the environment was not an objective collection of rocks and creatures; it was a form of consciousness in which there was an unquestioned and non-judgmental sense of connection to all things. This has been called a *partnership consciousness* as opposed to the *dominator consciousness* that appeared later (8,000–3,000 BCE) with the formation of towns, social hierarchies, power structures, and warfare (Eisler, 1987).

Beginning about 35,000 years ago, humans developed what has been called *mythic culture*, which saw the origins of symbols, representations, language, and storytelling that served as a way of making sense of the universe. Myths worldwide express the belief that the world, and all its creatures including humans, is sacred. In mythic culture, the universe cannot be changed or shaped. Myths served to integrate and explain the various facets of life and death that were accepted as they were and never questioned (Donald, 1991).

At this time, the first representational art and artifacts began to appear, in the form of cave and rock paintings and small figurines (Wenke, 1990). The paintings depicted animal and human forms, possibly spiritual or mythic figures. The figurines were typically about palm size and represented women with prominent breasts, hips, and vaginas. They were believed by many to represent fertility, while others suggest that they represented a goddess-type deity and a matriarchal social order (See Figure 1.2). These figurines may have conferred fertility on individuals and at the same time celebrated the mysterious life-giving power of the female.

It is probably during this phase of human prehistory that rituals marking the life transitions of birth and death, along with mythical interpretations of their meaning, first appeared. Although there is relatively little archeological evidence, we can learn a great deal about birthing rituals and practices from studies of living tribal societies. In many tribal societies today, for example, birth occurs in the company of women, close female relatives and older "medicine" women, shamans who are expert in the practice of child-birth. Plant and animal extracts are used for the pains of pregnancy and childbirth. In some matriarchal societies, husbands are asked to change their behavior when their wives are pregnant, a practice called *couvade*. Fathers in the Ifugao tribe of the Philippines are not permitted to cut wood during their wives' pregnancy (Whiting, 1974).

Healing practices and prayer rituals were created in prehistory to foster healthy fetal development and childbirth. One common practice, used by the Laotians, the Navaho of North America, and the Cuna of Panama, among others, is the use of music during labor. Among the Comanche and Tewa, North American Indian tribes, heat is applied to the abdomen. The Taureg of the Sahara believe that the laboring mother should walk up and down small hills to allow the infant to become properly placed to facilitate delivery. Taureg women of North Africa deliver their babies from a kneeling position (Mead & Newton, 1967). Many of these practices are ancient in origin, having been passed down between generations of women, perhaps from prehistorical times. The effectiveness of some of these practices is being rediscovered and applied by birthing centers and midwives in Western cultures today. The past 20 years has seen the emergence of profes-sional *doulas*, women who are trained to provide advice, assistance, and emotional support to pregnant and laboring mothers.

Related to the belief system, in which all things in the universe are connected and have equal status, hunter-gatherers have an egalitarian social structure with respect to age and gender differences and have little political hierarchy. An instructive comparative study was done between a hunter-gatherer group (the Aka) and a neighboring agricultural group (the Ngandu) in Central Africa. Both groups live in nearly identical ecologies and have subsistence economies. The Ngandu are sedentary farmers with political hierarchies and inequalities in age and gender roles. The Ngandu use more infant care devices compared to the Aka. Infant care devices – such as cradles, carriers, and toys – are not needed in the Aka due to the constant contact between infants and adults. The Ngandu infants wear more clothing, are more often physically separated from their mothers, and mothers are more likely to let their infants fuss or cry compared to the Aka. Like mothers in the urban cultures, the Ngandu mothers use more objects when playing with their babies (Hewlett, Lamb, Shannon, Leyendecker, & Scholmerich, 1998).

Figure 1.2   The Willendorf "Venus" (ca. 20,000 BCE) is one example of palm-sized statuettes that appeared to celebrate female fecundity. It is not clear whether these figures were used as talismans to promote fertility, as representations of a female goddess, or for some other purpose. *Source*: Photo AKG London/Erich Lessing.

The comparison between the Aka and the Ngandu suggests that there may have been a diversity of early human habits and belief systems related to infancy, even during the Pleistocene. While virtually all humans 100,000 years ago lived in desert and grassland environments, migration patterns eventually led to adaptations for living in less arid climates such as coastal and mountain terrain. In the desert, infants must nurse frequently to prevent dehydration, while this is not the case when the climate is more humid. Desert hunter-gatherers may have had to move frequently, requiring constant physical contact with the infant for safety. Coastal or riverbank hunter-gatherers may have had abundant resources close at hand, which would not have required extensive nomadic activity.

For these reasons, it is unwarranted to use the culture of desert-living hunter-gatherers as the sole basis for making inferences about species-normative patterns of the mother–infant relationship. The desert-living ancestral populations would have had mothers who cared for the infant full-time as well as working full-time. Infants from other hunter-gatherer cultures may not have needed such constant protection and nursing from the mother, allowing her to work while the infant was in substitute care (Hrdy, 1999).

In summary, infancy in prehistory was a very sensual and sensory experience. Infants developed an awareness of other human bodies from which they obtained nourishment, constant touch, affection, warmth, and support. They had the benefit of an extended family of group members. Once they began crawling and walking, infants became familiar with the feel and smell of raw earth and of plants. Living primarily outdoors and in earthen shelters, they became sensitized to changes in light and temperature, to the cycles and rhythms of the earth and its climate. To people living in urban societies today, this ancient way of life may seem primitive and dirty. On the other hand, it would be a primitive form of reasoning to reject the evidence of prehistory and what it has to tell us about human infants and their families.

For 1.6 million years, humans evolved to derive benefit from close touch and connection to other people's bodies, to the naked earth, to heat and cold, and to the smells, sounds, and tastes of the natural world. Humans of all ages perceived no distinctions between self and world, in the same way that young children today view others as extensions of themselves. They saw the world as animated with spirit and with the same kind of partnership consciousness as their own (Abram, 1996; Shepard, 1998).

The past 10,000 years, when humans moved into villages and later began to record their history in writing, is only 0.62% of human evolutionary history. If human evolution began at noon on an imaginary clock, villages and settled life would first appear at 4 minutes before midnight. Civilization, with urban centers, writing, and technologies, would arise about 2 minutes before midnight. The cradle of human consciousness is not a cradle at all. It is the belly of a parent, the loving hands of a brother or grandmother, the taste of milk rising from a teat, the smell of bodies, and a blanket of stars on a summer night. Every baby born today still has the opportunity to experience this "romantic" inheritance.

Early Civilizations: 8,000 BCE–300 CE

The Hebrew people left both archeological and written evidence about their childrearing practices (2000–500 BCE). The biblical Old Testament gives lengthy accounts of the family genealogy of the Hebrew peoples. Childbearing and childbirth were viewed as sacred acts, acts in which God was an active partner (Frymer-Kensky, 1995). When Eve, the mythical original mother, first saw her son Cain, she said, "I have created a man with God." (Gen. 4:1).

There are many stories in the Old Testament about divine intervention in matters of fertility. Hannah, for example, prayed extensively and made vows to God to grant her the ability to conceive and give birth to Samuel. The Bible also gives detailed laws regarding women's behavior during menstruation, pregnancy, and childbirth. Although there are no direct descriptions of infancy in the Bible, it is clear from many of the stories that infants should receive loving care, appropriate blessings for a good and holy life, and that male infants should be circumcised. Parental devotion was also evident in stories about the suffering of parents who were asked to sacrifice their infants. When two mothers claimed to be the parent of the same child, Solomon's threat to kill the child revealed the true mother, whose pain was unmistakable. The Hebrew slave revolt in Egypt, which led to the Exodus and return to the promised land, was precipitated by a Pharonic edict to kill Hebrew first-born sons. The story of Moses, sent floating down the Nile by his heartbroken family and adopted into love by Egyptian royal women, places the concept of human freedom in direct metaphorical alignment with the act of saving a single infant from death (Frymer-Kensky, 1995).

The Bible reminds parents not only to love but to educate their children, a combination of romantic and empiricist views. The importance of teaching children about culture was written in commandments to Abraham to "instruct" his children (Gen. 18:19). Regarding the important facets of Hebrew culture, parents were asked to "teach them intently to your children … when you sit in your home" (Deut. 6:7). Childrearing among the ancient Hebrews involved discipline accompanied by respect for the child, as the following passages illustrate: "Train a child in his own way, and even when he is old, he will not depart from it" (Prov. 22:6); "Foolishness is bound in the heart of the child but the rod of correction shall drive it from him" (Prov. 22:15); and "Chasten your son for there is hope, but set not your heart on his destruction" (Prov. 19:18). While some have interpreted these statements as grounds for justifying corporal punishment, the Old Testament does not specify the type of punishment but makes clear the need for discipline in the context of love. Other Bible stories reveal the undesirable outcomes when discipline is too harsh or nonexistent or when parents fail to educate their children into the stories, rituals, ideals, and history of the culture.

The ancient Egyptians (3000–1000 BCE), while not averse to killing Hebrew babies, expected Egyptian parents to have a large number of children. Parents were expected to take pleasure and pride in their children and to provide love and care. Tomb paintings for the pharaoh Akhenaten and his wife Nefertiti (1378–1362 BCE) show them holding their children on their laps, kissing them, and giving them affectionate hugs. Infants were breast fed until about 3 years of age. Infants and children during this period were constantly in the presence of caring adults, both parents and substitute caregivers, and the whole family spent "quality" time together on walks or picnics. Complex toys from that era have been found in archeological sites including dolls with moving limbs, animal pull toys with moving parts, and puppets. Physicians treated and wrote about common childhood diseases, which were of great concern to parents (French, 2001).

History and literature from ancient Greece and Rome (500 BCE –300 CE) also reveal a mixture of romantic and empiricist sentiments towards infants. The Greeks clearly believed that infants and children were naturally unruly and difficult to control, and therefore needing discipline and guidance. Writers advocated a strict upbringing for the purpose of creating a worthy citizen. Babies were thought to be soft and formless at birth and consequently needed to be hardened and molded. Various devices were used to keep infants' hands open, their legs held straight, and their arms strapped against the body. The right hand was loosened at 2 months to ensure that the child grew up right handed. Swaddling bands were used to mold the infant's head and body shape. Infants were bathed in cold water to prevent them from remaining too soft. Nurses used bath times to further mold the child's skull into a round shape, while attempting to shape other body parts by pulling and stretching (Dupont, 1989). The binding and manipulating of infants was not uncommon in ancient times, as seen in the foot binding of girls in ancient China (which made their feet small but deformed) and head binding in the ancient Maya (Mexico). Head binding of infants can also be found in eighteenth century Europe to give the head an oblong shape (Johnson, 1992).

Roman parents viewed these practices as an expression of their love, so children would grow up strong, their bodies well proportioned and held in appropriate postures. The recognition of the importance of the body for the developing person is salient in Greco-Roman heritage. Exercises for the body were thought to contribute to a strong moral character, a belief that was revived in the eighteenth and nineteenth centuries, following centuries of Christian doctrine that deemphasized the pleasures of the body. People from the educated classes in the Greek and Roman world were expected to hold their bodies in postures appropriate for each occasion and to speak in a dignified way. Gestures were stylized and specific to gender. The nude body was celebrated in real life – clothing was scant and sheer for both gender – and in nude sculptures of both males and females.

Parental devotion to children, especially among the wealthy, is well documented in Roman literature. Fathers and mothers were equally involved in the care of infants. One of the most detailed descriptions of parental love comes from Plutarch in the second century BCE, Plutarch shared childcare with his wife for all their children. They had one daughter, Timoxena, who died when she was 2 years old (French, 2001). Since Plutarch was away at the time of his daughter's death, he wrote these words in a letter to his wife.

> There is a special savor in our affection for children of that age; it likes the purity of the pleasure they give, the freedom from any crossness or complaint. She herself too had great natural goodness and gentleness of temper: her response to affection and her generosity both gave pleasure and enabled us to perceive the human kindness in her nature ... our daughter was the sweetest thing to fondle, to watch, and to hear; and we ought to let the thought of her also dwell in our minds and lives, for there is much more joy in it than sorrow. (Pomeroy, 1999, pp. 59–60)

Although infants were denied affection, older children whose character had begun to form were lavished with hugging and kissing (Dupont, 1989; Gies & Gies, 1987). Toys and games for young children and the values of love and protection for them have been found in artifacts and documents from ancient Egypt (2,000–100 BCE) and Greece (800–200 BCE) (Greenleaf, 1978).

As in the Hebrew culture of the Middle East, Greeks and Romans invoked their own deities for assistance in supporting the baby's health and growth. Prayers and offerings were made for successful childbirth and at each stage of the infant's life. The belief that infants' birth and development was a collaboration with gods or goddesses seems to follow from the partnership consciousness of the Pleistocene. Infants in these ancient cultures were not seen as belonging to the parents or as brought into the world by human choice. Rather, they were seen as part of a divine plan, as one manifestation of the way the universe works either to the favor or disfavor of humans.

Following prehistorical societies, many early civilizations, such as ancient Rome, practiced infanticide. The male head of a Roman family had the duty to decide if a newborn should live or die. This practice eliminated infants who were malformed or sickly. Malformation was thought to be due to an animal nature. Many healthy babies were also left to die because the family was too poor or the child unwanted (Dupont, 1989). Infanticide continued in Europe throughout the Middle Ages, until Christian beliefs diminished the regular use of the practice.

Hebrews did not routinely use infanticide. The story of Moses and the Exodus from Egypt shows that the concept of killing infants was appalling to the Hebrews. Since the Middle Ages, the narrow passage through the Red Sea and to eventual freedom is a central metaphor in Jewish prayers for successful childbirth through the birth canal (Frymer-Kensky, 1995). These ancient Hebrew ideas about the sanctity of childbirth and the creation of new life were later incorporated into Christian beliefs.

In summary, we can never know about the details and diversity of actual infant-care practices during ancient historical times. Documents written by educated leaders may contain more prescriptive and idealistic visions of parenting, visions that the ordinary family may or may not have put into practice. It seems clear, however, that both romantic and empirical beliefs about infants can be found in the earliest written documents of Western Cultures. Roman writings tended to weigh the empirical side more heavily while the Hebrews showed more of a balance between love and discipline. Following the traditions of mythic culture, these ancient historical societies believed that infants were conceived in partnership with a deity that was beyond themselves. Education was required in order to create an adult who was best attuned to the will of the gods or goddesses who were responsible for the mythical foundations of the cultural practices: to cultivate the body and its senses in order to be in more touch with divinity in the human and nonhuman world.

Middle Ages and Renaissance: Third Century to Sixteenth Century

The early Middle Ages in Europe (300–1100 CE), began with the fall of the Roman Empire and the gradual spread of Christianity. Primarily rural populations began to settle in cities and towns. Political boundaries changed during a series of conflicts for power and control over territory. These factors contributed to the growth of an educated urban population living next to a class of urban poor who subsisted in more unhealthy conditions than the poor living in the countryside. As a result of disease, malnutrition, urban pollution, and ignorance, infants of the urban poor were more likely to die or to suffer birth defects than those from rural areas. As disease claimed the lives of both infants and of mothers in childbirth, many destitute or orphaned children walked the streets as beggars, thieves, and prostitutes. The prognosis for children growing up in urban poverty is not much different today.

After 400 CE, the Christian church began having an impact on the beliefs and practices of European childrearing. Christians, following ancient and contemporary Jewish practices, advocated parental love and worked to protect children from infanticide, abortion, and maltreatment. Gravestones for infants began to appear at this time, as well as special penances if a parent had done some wrong to a child (Gies & Gies, 1987).

One of the first written accounts that focuses specifically on infant development and infant care beliefs can be found in the *Confessions* of St. Augustine (354–430 CE). Augustine was from North Africa. He studied in Rome and Milan and later became a priest in Alexandria. His autobiographical account in the *Confessions* (1991) begins with a remarkably detailed and developmentally appropriate reporting of his own infancy. He describes his birth and goes on at length about how he sucked from the breast and his patterns of quieting and crying. He reports that his first smiles occurred during sleep, which can be observed in infants today.

Augustine considers it important to establish the source of his data in the following way. "This at least is what I was told, and I believed it since that is what we see other infants doing. I do not actually remember what I then did." And he goes on, "Little by little, I began to be aware where I was and wanted to manifest my wishes to those who could fulfill them as I could not. For my desires were internal; adults were external to me and had no means of entering into my soul" (Augustine, 1991, p. 8).

Augustine struggled, as he did throughout the *Confessions*, with the moral implications of his "childish" acts. Many of these infantile actions, especially those regarding the pleasures of the body, would have been immoral from his adult Christian perspective. He concluded that what would be wrong for an adult was natural for babies. Since babies could not voluntarily control their behavior, he decided that they were expressing God's will and should therefore be tolerated for the indiscretions of their youth. "Was it wrong that in tears I greedily opened my mouth wide to suck the breasts?" (Augustine, 1991, p. 9). These writings express one of the clearest and earliest statements in the romantic tradition, that the natural tendencies of infants are to be accepted, tolerated, and loved.

Evidence of romantic views and Christian love for infants can be seen in the writings of Gregory of Tours (sixth century), who describes an epidemic of dysentery that killed many infants: "and so we lost our little ones, who were so dear to us and sweet, whom we had cherished in our bosoms and dandled in our arms, whom we had fed and nurtured with such loving care" (Gies & Gies, p. 60). Around the same time, the church developed forms of penance for killing infants: 3 years for abortion and 10 years for infanticide. Other writers of the time report parental mourning of infant death.

We know a great deal about the emotional life of people in the Middle Ages. Events such as the death of an infant would have been marked by deep mourning, benedictions, and ceremonies. One historian of the Middle Ages describes everyday life this way:

> All experience had yet to the minds of men the directness and absoluteness of the pleasure and pain of child-life … Calamities and indigence were more afflicting than at present; it was more difficult to guard against them, and to find solace. Illness and health presented more striking contrast; the cold and darkness of winter were more real evils … All things presenting themselves to the mind in violent contrasts and impressive forms, lent a tone of excitement and of passion to everyday life and tended to produce that perpetual oscillation between despair and distracted joy, between cruelty and pious tenderness which characterize life in the Middle Ages. (Huizinga, 1954, pp. 9–10)

We can infer from Christian art and theology that these heightened emotions occurred at times of both birth and death. In the early Middle Ages, representations of Christ depicted him as an adult engaged in acts of kindness and love. By the late Middle Ages (1100–1300 CE), images of Christ either focused on his death and the deep mourning of his companions, or on his infancy and the joy of the mother–child bond. The paintings of the infant Christ held by Mary continued to evolve during this period. When Christ first appears in paintings as an infant, the posture and body proportions are more adult-like. By the later Middle Ages, Christ looks more like an actual infant. The infant Christ is typically shown in stylized clothing and with adult-like facial features and mannerisms (See Figure 1.3). One painting depicted Christ as an infant making the Catholic gesture of benediction to a group of people kneeling before him. In Renaissance art (after 1400 CE), by contrast, infants and children began to look and behave differently from adults. Children were sometimes shown playing with toys (Koops, 1996). Not only does the infant Christ begin to look more like a real baby (see Figure 1.4) but we also see the emergence of secular paintings of everyday family life and portraits of individual children.

Also appearing in the later Middle Ages were several medical texts giving advice for childbirth and early infant care. Trotola, a female physician in twelfth-century Italy, advised rubbing the newborn's palate with honey, protecting it from bright lights and loud noises, and stimulating the newborn's senses with cloths of various colors and textures, and with "songs and gentle voices" (Gies & Gies, 1987). In England during the same period, birth often occurred in a warm chamber with plenty of bath water, accompanied by the scent of olives, herbs, and roses. It was attended by a female midwife and female friends bringing good fortune and joy (Hanawalt, 1993). During the Middle Ages as in ancient times, the body was viewed as part of God, the earth, the family, and the community. Birth took place in public, attended by female relatives, neighbors, and midwives.

In both Jewish and Christian beliefs of this time, the mother and infant's shared embodied experience were as sacred and important as that shared between husband and wife in the act of love and conception. The great romantic tales of the Middle Ages created the concept of courtship, honor, love, and sacrifice in couple relationships. Trotola's prescriptions for birth – with colorful textiles and captivating aromas – would

Figure 1.3   Cimabue, *Madonna of the Angels*, 1270. In this late medieval painting, Christ is represented in stylized form with adult-like gestures. *Source*: Louvre, Paris/Photo Hervé Lewandowski, RMN.

also have been found on the bodies and in the bedrooms of courting and newly married couples. The romantic view of love and the sacred body did not extend to other sexual or pleasurable acts outside of those reserved human relationships that were deemed by Christians and Jews to be part of the expression of God's love. Christian baptisms – like weddings – were a public ritual welcoming, taking place in the church where ancestors were buried. The biography of Bishop Hugh of Lincoln (1140–1200) describes details of infant action during one baptism led by the Bishop. The infant "bent and stretched out its little arms, as if it were trying to fly, and moved its head to and fro. The tiny mouth and face relaxed in continuous chuckles" (Gies & Gies, 1987, p. 203). Apparently, Bishop Hugh took great pleasure in the baby, who was wrapped in the spiritual significance of the ceremony.

Figure 1.4   Raphael, *The Virgin and Child with St. John the Baptist*, 1507. By the time of the Renaissance, Christ was depicted more like a real baby, with an appearance distinctly different from adults. Around this time, secular paintings of children began to appear, showing an increasing interest in the individual. *Source*: Louvre, Paris/Photo J. G. Berizzi, RMN.

Following the ancient Roman empiricist traditions, infants in the Middle Ages were seen by upper-class families as pliable and soft, needing swaddling and straightening. Wet-nurses began to be used extensively for the wealthy. A wet-nurse was a woman who was paid to nurse the child with her own milk in order to spare wealthy women from the task of nursing the baby themselves. Selection of wet-nurses was important because they were believed to transmit character to the child. Writers, mostly from the church, condemned the practice of giving children to wet nurses from the poorer classes because of the belief that the child could pick up the habits and diseases of the nurse. The Renaissance artist, Michelangelo, half-jokingly claimed that his skill in sculpture was derived from his wet-nurse, the wife of a stonecutter (Gies & Gies, 1987).

Infanticide, however, was still practiced in the late Middle Ages. Although parents had to suffer penances, it was not a crime equivalent to homicide as it is today. By the thirteenth century, some cities in Europe created church-run hospices to adopt orphaned children as an alternative to infanticide, since a child who died unbaptized was barred from heaven for all eternity (Le Goff, 1987). In some countries today, with urban stress and poverty, infants are left in parks and in trash bins. Some cities in the United States and Northern Europe have begun programs that allow mothers to drop unwanted infants at local hospitals without prosecution. Social service agencies then help to find foster homes for these children. Times may have changed but some of the problems still remain.

The European Renaissance (1450–1650) began in Florence, Italy where wealthy patrons funded the development of art and science on a scale not seen since ancient times. This flowering of culture gave rise to the emergence of a philosophy of *humanism*. Paintings of nude figures, of secular themes, and of ordinary people rather than religious figures heralded a reawakening of the values of empiricism and romanticism that were part of classical traditions. As a consequence, the rearing of children took on more importance.

Responsibility for oneself and for one's children was shifted toward the individual. God was still present but people were beginning to feel empowered to make more decisions for themselves and their children. At this time, we begin to see the emergence of written philosophies of childrearing in Western cultures. One example comes from Michel de Montaigne (1533–1592), of France. He condemned violence in education, favored training for honor and freedom, and condemned wet-nursing.

> A true and well-regulated affection should be born and then increase, as children enable us to get to know them; if they show they deserve it, we should cherish them with a truly fatherly love … we feel ourselves more moved by the skippings and jumpings of babyish tricks of our children than by their activities when they are fully formed, as though we loved them not as human beings but only as playthings. Since in sober truth things are so ordered that children can only have their being and live their lives at the expense of our being and of our lives, we ought not to undertake to be fathers if that frightens us. (Screech, 1991, p. 435)

As a result of the spread of Renaissance humanism throughout Europe, by the eighteenth century, a profound shift in Western cultural consciousness coalesced, one that emphasized the importance of individuals in their own right. Up through the seventeenth century, the ancient belief persists that all people, including infants, are part of a larger cosmos of God in partnership with the family. Before the eighteenth century, children were typically given the names of family members, often that of an older sibling who had died, in order to emphasize the historical and sacred connection of one person to another. One sign of the shift toward individuality in the early eighteenth century is that children begin to be given unique names showing their special status as human beings (Stone, 1979). This focus on individuality led gradually to the emergence of private homes, arguments for the freedom of children and of people of all ages, and separate rooms in the house for children. At the same time, we begin to see an increasing distance from nature and from a direct connection with the earth and with God (Gelis, 1989).

In summary, this period in Western culture had two phases. The first was a gradual change in classical ideas about the importance of the body and its senses. Christian empirical beliefs favored innocence, chastity, and denial of the senses as a pathway to God. In contrast, the classical empirical traditions acted to the favor of the gods by shaping the body into a form to be enjoyed and displayed. Augustine could forgive the infant's hungers only until a proper Christian education could begin. This showed that Christians were more romantic in their views about infancy than the Romans, for example, who advocated relatively early and severe discipline of the mind and body.

The second phase of the period from the thirteenth century to the sixteenth century is the emergence of humanism during the Renaissance. This period is a reprise of the classical themes about the body and its senses set against the historical background of 800 years of Christian domination of Western culture. These struggles, begun in the palaces of the most wealthy secular and religious leaders, led eventually to a broader cultural shift in the importance of the individual as distinct from God, family, and society.

The Enlightenment: Seventeenth Century to Nineteenth Century

During the eighteenth century, new ideas about the value of human life, dignity, and freedom began to emerge, a shift of cultural consciousness that is called the "enlightenment." On the one hand, there is a revival of classical romantic beliefs as exemplified in the writings of Jean-Jacques Rousseau (1712–1778). Rousseau, who lived shortly before the period of the French revolution against the monarchy and was a major influence on it, argued that childhood was a time of special privilege, that children bring goodness into the world, and that education should be sensitive to the needs and inclinations of the infant and young child. Rousseau initiated a social movement that, for the first time, acquires the name *romanticism*. Many of Rousseau's ideas, however, had their origins during earlier historical periods. What is new here is the emphasis on the romantic individual, the importance of the child as a person in his or her own right.

Included in this movement are the great English romantic poets, such as William Wordsworth (1770–1850), who wrote of childhood in a way that would have been recognized by members of a hunter-gatherer community.

> Behold the Child among his new-born blisses,
> A six years' darling of pygmy size!
> See, where 'mid work of his own hand he lies,
> Fretted by sallies of his mother's kisses,
> With light upon him from his father's eyes!
> (From "Intimations of Immortality from Recollections of Early Childhood,"
> in Williams, 1952, p. 263)

Other authors, such as William Blake (1757–1827) and Charles Dickens (1812–1870), also wrote about the life and fate of individual children but they had a less than romantic view about them. In Oliver Twist and other famous stories, Dickens courageously exposed the effects of disease, poverty, child abuse, and child labor for all to see. Thus, while the value of the individual was on the rise, people disagreed about what was "natural" compared to what needed to be provided for the child's healthy development. John Locke (1632–1704) believed that children needed more guidance and discipline than the romantics advocated. Locke argued that education should provide the skills to make rational choices. The philosophical movement to which he belonged was for the first time given the name *empiricism*. The origins of Locke's ideas can be found in ancient sources such as the Old and New Testaments and Roman ideas about education. He echoed the contemporary cultural ideals about the importance of the individual. He wrote, "the little and almost insensible expressions on our tender infancies have very important and long-lasting consequences" (as quoted in Clarke-Stewart, 1998, p. 104).

Reversing centuries of Christian doctrine that elevated the spirit above the body, Rousseau and Locke revived the ancient Greek and Roman ideals about the importance of the body in healthy moral development. Locke gave us the now well-known expression, "A sound mind in a sound body, is a short but full description of a happy state in this world." Rousseau suggested that children should "run, jump and shout to their heart's content." Swaddling was abandoned during the eighteenth century because Locke complained that it restricted the infant's freedom of movement and prevented the mother or wet-nurse from hugging and caressing the baby. Parents were advised that infants should exercise early and use their legs. Within a few years, swaddling was being condemned in England as an assault on human liberty.

The eighteenth century, and its rising concern for the individual, also saw a proliferation of advice books for parents. Between 1750 and 1814, 2,400 different child-rearing advice books were published. By 1800, an entirely new concept entered society: books published exclusively for young children. A large range of inexpensive children's books appeared as quickly as the spread of computer games in the late-twentieth century. Around the same time there was an increase in the number of family portraits for the middle and upper classes. The invention of photography and film during the nineteenth century, and digital recording media after another century, continued to expand this tendency to document individual and family lives. The introduction of the Kodak Brownie camera in the early part of the twentieth century brought family documentation even to the poor. The Brownie was easy to use, inexpensive, and users did not have to develop the film themselves.

The rise of the importance of the individual corresponded with an increase in the importance of the nuclear family. There was a shift away from the use of wet-nurses and a move toward the maintenance of a private family home. These two changes had the effect of lessening the duration of breast feeding. Prior to the eighteenth century, infants were breast fed to at least 18 months. Because the value of the individual applied not only to infants but to their mothers and fathers, a conflict began to appear between the rights of parents and the rights of infants. Mothers wanted their own personal time and began to see breast feeding as their responsibility and their burden. The result was that infants were weaned earlier. Husbands wanted their wives to remain sexually available and attractive and became jealous of the infant's monopoly of the breast, which was a factor contributing to the relative increase in the importance of the conjugal bond in relation to the mother-child bond. These historical changes in the family were not seen in all cultures but became the norm for Western families.

During the nineteenth century, the child became an integral part of the definition of the family. What has been called the "discovery" of the child was due to a number of historical currents that flowed through urban Europe and North America. The first current was the segregation of the family from the workplace and the decline of child labor (thanks in part to Dickens). Second, society began to define the mother's role as major supervisor of the home. It may surprise many people that the full-time mother and housewife is a relatively recent historical invention. The final current established love or sentiment (rather than religion, family inheritance, or economic well-being) as the bond holding the family together (Hareven, 1985). This latter current was also coupled with a rise in the significance of the love bond between spouses. As a result, parents became more loving, permissive, and egalitarian with infants and children (Clarke-Stewart, 1998).

The development of this segregated nuclear family and its full-time mother was at first confined to the white middle class. Families from other classes and ethnic and racial groups continued to live in extended families in which love, work, and education all took place within the home and childcare was shared by all family members. Women in these families continued to work in the fields and in the home in the company of their babies, a practice that had been going on for most of human history (Hareven, 1985).

Welfare and medical institutions devoted exclusively to infants and children did not appear in Europe and North America until the 1850s. Around the same time, we see the development of immunization against childhood diseases and the pasteurization of milk. Maternal deaths during childbirth also declined due to the invention of anesthesia and procedures for sterilizing medical instruments (Greenleaf, 1978). These medical advances further solidified the family by reducing infant mortality. On the other hand, they led to a growing trend to move childbirth out of the home and the company of female friends and relatives and into hospitals surrounded by unfamiliar medical (mostly male) and nursing staff.

Empiricist views could be seen in the rise of education for infancy. Infant schools in the nineteenth century were meant for poor children, for early prevention of childhood disorders, for combating urban crime, teaching reading, or to give poor children proper middle-class values and supports (Clarke-Stewart, 1998). Infant schools later became available to middle-class families. In 1840, in Massachusetts, half of all 3-year-olds were enrolled in infant schools. Later in the nineteenth century, however, the practice of sending infants to school was condemned because it put too much pressure on children. The romantic view reemerged in the belief that children should develop naturally instead of being "pushed." Similar ebbs and flows of the value of infant education (schools, musical training, reading, etc.) can be seen throughout the twentieth century.

The nineteenth century was also a period in which science became a new voice of authority, gradually supplanting religion as the sole source of knowledge and guidance. Observations of infants were first recorded by educated European and North American parents during the eighteenth and nineteenth centuries. Their diaries, known as "baby biographies," were partly meant to document the individual child and his or her development and partly meant as observations in the scientific tradition of natural history. One has to put the baby biographies into historical context to understand their significance. Never before had people devoted time and energy to the documentation of the life of a single, individual baby.

Biographers were aware of the distinction between a more empirical approach and a more romantic approach to their recordings. Charles Darwin, for example, recorded the development of his son, William. When William was only a few months old, Darwin was trying to be an objective observer. He added more references to himself as his affections for William grew and as William became more expressive. He thought these references to himself were unscientific, so they were deleted in the versions of his diary that he published (Conrad, 1998). Darwin, like Plutarch, wrote a eulogy for his daughter, Annie, who died at age 10, in which he revealed – more so than in any of his other writings – a romantic side. As if echoing the words of Plutarch almost 2,000 years earlier, he wrote of Annie that she lived "as if she defied the world in her joyousness" (Conrad, 2004).

Female diarists were more generally romantic. Elizabeth Gaskell (1810–1865), a well-known English novelist of the time, wrote a brief biography of her oldest daughter, Marianne, the first of her seven children. Gaskell focuses mostly on moral development in comparison to the male diarists who recorded primarily sensori-motor and expressive development (Wallace, Franklin, & Keegan, 1994). She recognized her stance as participant observer in the following passage describing Marianne at 6 months.

> I should call her remarkably good-tempered; though at times she gives way to little bursts of passion or perhaps impatience … she is also very firm … what I suppose is obstinacy really, only that is so hard a word to apply to one so dear. But in general she is so good that I feel as if I could hardly be sufficiently thankful, that the materials put into my hands are so excellent and beautiful. And yet it seems to increase the responsibility. If I should misguide from carelessness or negligence! (Gaskell, 1996, p. 5)

This passage is enlightening because it gives us a view of the infant–mother relationship and not just of the infant. Diaries were later dismissed by more empirical (i.e. less romantic) scientists in the twentieth century, in part because they could not be verified as scientifically objective.

In summary, the most radical historical change in beliefs about infancy began to unfold during the period between the seventeenth and nineteenth centuries. The rise in the importance of the individual had its roots in earlier Judeo-Christian beliefs about the value of human life and the importance of cultural education. The Renaissance saw a decline in religious art and the emergence of secular themes, texts, and paintings about ordinary people rather than religious or mythical figures. Although these historical roots are unmistakable, the rapid advances in technology, in science, and in education during the Enlightenment created the conditions for a major historical change in cultural consciousness – the emergence of the "individual" – a change that affects every aspect of life in Western societies today. The codification and consolidation of human rights, liberties, and self-enhancement was propelled by people who had unique names, whose identity was founded upon personal accomplishments, and who grew up in a family that respected them as growing individuals (See Figure 1.5). Baby biographies, and the belief in the importance of individual infants, opened a path into a historically unprecedented documentation of infancy during the twentieth century.

Figure 1.5   During the nineteenth century, infants and children became accepted as unique individuals. They received given names that were different from names of other family members, had the benefit of pediatric care, and the opportunity for educational enrichment. Note how this Berlin family (ca. 1896) dressed each of their children, including the infant, with unique and well-tailored clothing. *Source*: Photo AKG London.

The Recent Past: Twentieth Century

Changes in beliefs about infancy seem to have accelerated during the twentieth century, in part because of mass communication about infancy and infant care and because of an increase in scientific studies of infancy. The history of infancy during the twentieth century is characterized by continual debates between romantic and empirical sentiments, as well as shifts every 5 to 10 years between infant care practices favoring one view or the other. It also becomes increasingly difficult to separate the history of infancy research from the history of infants in the family. Infancy research has impacted every facet of infant care. At the same time, scientists as people living during these times were impacted in their own life histories with the beliefs of the larger culture and those beliefs permeated the methods and values of their science.

Earlier debates over romanticism versus empiricism were replaced in part by discussions about the contributions to development of *nature* (genes) versus *nurture* (environments). Arnold Lucius Gesell (1880–1961), the founder of "nativism," following in the romantic tradition, claimed that the orderly changes seen in early development were specified by the genes; developmental stages were "natural." Gesell, who made careful measurements of developmental changes in size, motor skill, and behavior in infants and young children, was the first scientist to use a one-way mirror for unobtrusive observation and the first to use film to record behavior. John B. Watson (1878–1958), an empiricist in contrast to Gesell, believed that, given the right kind of "nurture," infants were entirely malleable. He taught small children to be afraid of cuddly animals by making loud noises whenever they touched the animals, research that would be considered unethical today. Watson was successful, however, in convincing people that even the most basic and innocent of infant behaviors could be shaped by outside forces.

Watson's childrearing advice harkened back to the ancient Romans. Parents were told not to hug and kiss their children, except on the forehead before going to bed, or a pat on the head if they performed well on a task. Mother love was a "dangerous instrument. An instrument which may inflict a never healing wound, a wound which may make infancy unhappy, adolescence a nightmare, an instrument which may wreck your adult son or daughter's vocational future and their chances for marital happiness" (Watson, 1928, *The psychological care of the infant and child*, as quoted in Konner, 1982, p. 311). Watson was especially appealing to immigrants coming to North America, people who believed that they could make a new life for themselves and their children. Anyone could succeed, regardless of past history or genetic heritage.

Given the ancient historical dialectic between empirical and romantic beliefs, Watson's extremism was begging for a romantic counter-argument. It appeared in the work of William James, Karl Jung, John Dewey and Sigmund Freud, all of whom emphasized the emotional and creative aspects of the child, highlighting love, indulgence of infant's needs, and the freedom of the individual. Freud (1856–1939), for example, recognized that all infants experienced emotional highs and lows and that even infants felt the need for love and possessed powerful desires. Freud recognized the importance of the body – the oral, anal, and genital regions – as powerful organizers of the developing psyche. The vicissitudes of infant care led to a more or less repressed adult, one who accepted and enjoyed the body or felt repression about the body and its desires.

These romantic writers were relatively open about their own personal lives and used their experiences in part to inform their work. Watson, on the other hand, had a hidden and repressed romantic side. He was fired from his academic position at Johns Hopkins University in 1920 after it was found out that his research assistant, Rosalie Rayner, who was 21 years younger, was also his mistress. His wife, in the divorce proceedings, made public his letters to Rayner ("My total reactions are positive towards you.") to the newspapers in Baltimore and beyond. *The psychological care of the infant and child*, published 8 years later, when Watson had become an executive at an advertising agency, appears to be a willful act of revenge against academia, women, and probably infants as well (Hulbert, 2004).

Freud's daughter, Anna, following in the tradition of her father, taught parents to hold and cuddle their babies, to indulge their senses and respect their emotions. She counseled parents to be patient in order to allow their babies the time to manage their own desires in appropriate ways (Freud, 1965). On the other hand, Freud's ideas blamed parents who could not meet their children's needs. Parents were considered to be the main cause of neurosis and repression in their children. At the same time, during the 1930s and 1940s, there was an increased demand for infant education in nursery schools. This was meant to counter an overdependence on parents, prevent neurosis, and to give group training (Clarke-Stewart, 1998). It was also a response to the shortage of male workers during World War II and the need for women to join the workforce.

Following the war, the 1950s became a period of the redomestication of women in the United States. Mothers were expected to be the main infant care providers and fathers were meant to be the wage earners (Lamb, Sternberg, & Ketterlinus, 1992). During this decade, there was revival of a more romantic view of relationships. This was the era of Abraham Maslow, Carl Rogers, Fritz Perls, and Willem Reich, each of whom created psychotherapies of caring, warmth, mutuality, responsibility, and affectivity. Reich in particular, a disciple of Freud, emphasized the importance of the body and its full expression of desires, senses, and pleasures, as a key to psychological health.

This is the period in which John Bowlby, mentioned earlier, began to publish his classic studies of mother–infant attachment. Bowlby believed in the importance of a close and affectionate mother–infant bond, a bond he believed to be primarily and exclusively with the infant's biological mother. He based his conclusions in part on observations of hunter-gatherer societies and in part on the evolution of humans during prehistory. A similar approach was taken by reformers of hospital childbirth procedures, who advocated a reduction in maternal anesthesia and a return to more natural and traditional approaches such as controlled breathing, upright postures, and home births. These reformers favored breast feeding over bottle feeding, and looked to Pleistocene practices in order to make childbirth a more satisfying and pleasurable experience for mother and infant. Few mothers and few hospitals of this era, however, adopted these practices.

The dialectic began to swing toward empiricism again in the 1960s and 1970s in the rapid growth of scientific approaches to psychology inspired in part by the Cold War, when Western leaders decided that the education and training of their citizens was the best way to combat the technological threats of advanced weapon systems. Research on infancy turned away from studies of emotion and focused more on infant learning and cognitive development. *The Competent Infant* (Stone, 1979) reflected a desire by scientists to discover early signs of intelligence in infants. Many parents placed their infants into highly structured programs to teach reading, word learning, music, and mathematics before the age of 3 years.

The rise of the women's liberation movement during this period conspired also to create an increased demand for infant day care and nursery schools. Betty Freidan's publication of *Feminine Mystique* in 1963, led to an increase in the numbers of women who sought individual fulfillment in their lives through employment and schooling. A final trend leading to increased demand for infant care during this period was the rise of single mothers who needed to be employed in order to support their children (Lamb et al., 1992).

The work of Jean Piaget from Switzerland and Lev Vygotsky of Russia began to inspire scientific understanding of infant cognitive development and how the infancy period served as a foundation for later intellectual functioning. Both Piaget (1952) and Vygotsky (1978) can also be read as primarily romantic thinkers since they viewed child development as a profoundly creative action, arising in the "natural" discourse between young children and their environments, including the cultural environment. Paradoxically, however, their work was read and applied – in infancy research and in early childhood education – primarily for its empiricist connotations; absorbed into the cultural search to make babies smarter.

This empiricist trend continued in the 1980s by an interest in helping and educating infants who were at risk for developmental difficulties, such as infants who were premature, handicapped, or victims of abuse. This focus on risk was associated with the empiricist idea that all humans can excel, given the right kind of childrearing (Clarke-Stewart, 1998). The same philosophy also brought the ideal of a "supermom" who could be employed, be a great mother, and wonderful and loving wife. The 1980s also saw an increase in the amount of time fathers spent with their babies.

The romantic view returns in the 1990s with a rise in studies of parent–child relationships, emotional development and attachment, and communication and language (Schneider, 1998) while the more empirical approaches to infant development continued to grow in such fields as cognitive neuroscience and behavior genetics. The trends of the 1970s and 1980s, which focused on babies growing up and getting smart as quickly as possible, are currently being replaced by ideas about slowing down and appreciating each phase of a baby's life. Research today has expanded to encompass diversity in parenting and culture: families at risk, substance abusers, handicapped infants, different ethnic groups, gay-lesbian families, fathers, preterm infants, and infantile autism. Meeting an infant's socioemotional needs is seen as important as cognitive and academic growth. There is also a focus on threats to safety such as accidents, abuse, crime, and the origins of psychopathology.

The recent return to romanticism has led to the growth of the holistic health and medicine movement with a focus on body awareness, yoga, massage, meditation, and the healing potential of relationships (Schneider, 1998). These ideas have their origins in ancient non-Western cultural beliefs, such as Chinese, Japanese, Indian, and Native American approaches. In this chapter on Western culture, there is no opportunity to review the history of beliefs about infants in these other cultures. A notable characteristic of these cultures is that, even in the twentieth century, the individual has not become salient in the cultural consciousness. These cultures, like ancient Western culture, were founded upon a mythical belief system in which humans were connected to all things. Their traditions focus on understanding and utilizing relationships between people, relationships between the various systems of mind and body, and between people and their social and physical environments. These cultures tend to be more romantic than empirical, accepting infant behavior in its "natural" form and rejecting early discipline and training of infants (cf. Kojima, 1986).

There is also a recent trend in Western cultures toward using knowledge about infancy to contribute to the healing of older children and adults. Current psychoanalytic traditions advocate a therapist–client relationship that is modeled after what is believed to be the most healthy form of the mother–infant relationship: a balance between love and playfulness on the one hand and encouragement for independence and self-awareness on the other (Ehrenberg, 1992; Stern, 1985; Winnicott, 1971). There has been a partnership between therapists for adults and scientists who observe the mother–infant relationship. Somatic-awareness therapeutic approaches to adult healing are based on the recreation of observed patterns of infant learning through movement and touch. All of these methods are founded upon the view that there is something rejuvenating that occurs when adults reexperience their bodies and their interpersonal relationships in a way similar to being a baby.

Watsu, for example, is an aquatic somatic-awareness method that explicitly attempts to recreate an optimal infant experience. During a Watsu session, clients are moved freely in warm water, stretched gently, and cradled in the practitioner's arms. "By being moved so freely through the water, by being stretched and repeatedly returned to a fetal position, the adult has the opportunity to heal in himself whatever pain or loss he may still carry from that time" (Dull, 1995, p. 65).

In the Rosen Method, clients lie on a padded table while the practitioners' open hands make gentle contact with areas of the body that appear to hold muscular tension and restrict free breathing. Rosen practitioners believe that the body tells its own story shaped by early life experiences, many of them forgotten and unconscious. As a result of either ordinary or traumatic events, people shape themselves through muscular tension in whatever way that helps them to survive. Though the gentle touch of the Rosen Method, people deeply relax and breathe easier and begin to remember the experiences in which they learned to unconsciously contain their tension. Through that knowledge, the individual can regain fuller movement, ease, and a sense of well-being (Wooten, 1995).

Moshe Feldenkrais invented a system of body movement education that reawakens, develops, and organizes capacities for kinesthetic (sensori-motor) learning. Whereas children before the age of three learn movements by relying on their sensori-motor experience, older children and adults in technological cultures often behave according to social expectations, distancing themselves from their bodily feelings. As the Feldenkrais method involves the emulation of how young children learn, its therapeutic value hinges on releasing capacities for learning that had been left behind in childhood (Reese, 1985).

In summary, as in past centuries, the twentieth century continued the historical ebb and flow and romantic and empirical beliefs about babies. Individuality, human rights, and personal freedoms have become such a major component of Western cultures that it is easy to forget the "individual" was a cultural invention that became elaborated during the eighteenth, nineteenth, and twentieth centuries. Yet, from the perspective of the vast time scale of human existence on this planet, the individual is an aberrant form of consciousness. It was invented only a few seconds before midnight on the imaginary clock of human evolution that began at noon. It does not generalize to other cultures from which we have recently borrowed expertise in the healing arts: the Native American and the Chinese, for example.

The individual arose out of the historical and prehistorical romantic traditions respecting the value of the body and its senses. While the romantic view has lasted for as long as humans can remember, it is less clear – since the individual is a relative newcomer to human consciousness – whether the concept of the individual will survive and enhance human life or whether it will die out like many other cultural inventions. Whatever the ultimate significance of the individual for human growth and development, it is uniquely Western in its origin and application. The constitutional governments of most Western nations are founded on the value of the individual. Virtually every law enacted for and about infants and the family in the United States during the twentieth century, for example, is based on the notion of rights. The concept of the individual has spawned new forms of infancy beliefs such as the importance of independence training, a sense of entitlement that pervades early parent–infant discourses about the self, and a sense of fairness and rights that underlie Western conceptions of morality and ethics.

It is difficult to summarize the changes in infancy during the twentieth century. For further reference, I have written a book about what is known and understood about infants (Fogel, 2009). Partly, the difficulty of encapsulating the recent history of infancy is due to the complexity of change and partly to the historically unprecedented extent of documentary evidence. In addition to what has been mentioned, there are currently dozens of scientific journals devoted to prenatal and infant development, many magazines and books for parents, and thousands of Internet sites about infancy, ranging from scientific reports, to advocacy organizations, to infant care advice, and to family photos and videos. At least twice each week I can find a story in my local newspaper about pregnancy, childbirth, or infancy, about the life and death of babies in families, about technological and genetic innovations, or about legal and ethical issues such as harvesting stem cells from aborted fetuses. We are on the threshold of a future in which infancy may change in unknown ways.

The Twenty-First Century and Beyond

The specifics of the future cannot be foreseen but the general pattern, the empirical–romantic dialogue, will continue.

The empirical trends of the future will be related to finding new ways to control reproduction and fetal and infant development: the increasing application of engineering and biotechnology to the end of shaping the infant's body and mind to conform to a cultural ideal.

Speculation about empirical trends in the future comes from current genetic research. Scientists have already shown that replacing, selecting, or cloning genetic material is only part of the developmental story. The environment – its structure and timing – is also crucial to the developmental process. The new science of epigenetics is revealing how experiences become transformed into physiology by means of chemical and physical processes within the cell that regulate gene expression (e.g., Dolinoy, Weidman, & Jirtle, 2007; Feinberg, 2007). We will come to know the precise environmental conditions under which certain genes will be expressed while others are suppressed. Part of the environmental control of the genes could come from within the organism. Scientists are already envisioning transplants of organic computers into the fetus or infant, transplants that will combine developmentally with inherited or altered genetic material to harness the body's power for releasing its own enzymes and transmitters that help regulate gene action for healthy development.

The romantic trends of the future will involve the continued discovery of the rejuvenating aspects of recreating infancy for adults and the revival and preservation of some of the patterns of the Pleistocene parent–infant relationship. The indulgent self-discovery that is the essence of infancy and early childhood today will be extended throughout the life course. The infancy period could thus be elongated in the form of continued playfulness, openness to new experiences, and a life-long commitment to getting up after falling down. All humans will accept and celebrate their differences as part of what is "natural" for the species in order to enhance our ability to adapt to unforeseen changes. Every baby will be an important addition to society, welcomed into a network of love and touch. Perhaps there will be an age in which no one will be unwanted, no one will be poor or hungry, and no one will lack services and supports. Every newborn will be entitled to love, security, shelter, nutrition, self-enhancement, and an extended family. In my romantic vision, we will indeed preserve our humanity. In fact, we will enhance what it means to have a human body that needs touch, love, and adventure. What we hunt and gather will be different but we will not cease wanting to participate in those endeavors.

Another future can be imagined: one that denigrates needs as frailties and that succeeds in eradicating them from the gene pool. Our bodies could be redesigned so that they will no longer be susceptible to heat and cold, hunger and pain. Sensation will become extinct. What would a baby in this future be like? Hard and withdrawn? Sucking power from a global energy grid with wide, vacant eyes? A disembodied mind? Since the romantic pleasures are our million-year inheritance and since they continue to be revived even after centuries of repression, I do not believe that humans could long endure this type of future. Enlightened romanticism requires training in how to use the body, how to develop one's skills at self-discovery and self-expression, how to remain connected with others and the world around us. Without romanticism, empiricism becomes harsh and intolerable. Endurance and indulgence, self and other, separateness and connection, mind and body: these are birthrights.

References

Abram, D. (1996). *The spell of the sensuous.* New York: Vintage Books.

Barr, R. G. (1990). The early crying paradox: A modest proposal. *Human Nature, 1,* 355–389.

Bowlby, J. (1969). *Attachment and loss: Vol. 1. Attachment.* New York: Basic Books.

Bronfenbrenner, U. (1979). *The ecology of human development: Experiments by nature and design.* Cambridge, MA: Harvard University Press.

Clarke-Stewart, K. A. (1998). Historical shifts and underlying themes in ideas and rearing young children in the United States: Where have we been? Where are we going? *Early Development and Parenting, 7,* 101–117.

Conrad, R. (1998). Darwin's baby and baby's Darwin: Mutual recognition in observational research. *Human Development, 41*(1), 47–64.

Conrad, R. (2004). "[A]s if she defied the world in her joyousness": Rereading Darwin on emotion and emotional development. *Human Development, 47*, 40–65.

Dolinoy, D. C., Weidman, J. R., & Jirtle, R. L. (2007). Epigenetic gene regulation: Linking early developmental environment to adult disease. *Reprod Toxicol, 23*(3), 297–307.

Donald, M. (1991). *Origins of the modern mind: Three stages in the evolution of culture and cognition.* Cambridge, MA: Harvard University Press.

Dull, H. (1995). *Watsu: Freeing the body in water* (2nd ed.). Harbin, CA: Harbin Springs Publishing.

Dupont, F. (1989). *Daily life in ancient Rome.* (C. Woodall, Trans.). Oxford: Blackwell.

Ehrenberg, D. (1992). *The intimate edge: Extending the reach of psychoanalytic interaction.* New York: W.W. Norton & Company.

Eisler, R. (1987). *The chalice and the blade: Our history, our future.* San Francisco: Harper Collins.

Feinberg, A. P. (2007). Phenotypic plasticity and the epigenetics of human disease. *Nature, 447*(7143), 433–440.

Fogel, A. (2009). *Infancy: Infant, family and society* (5th ed.). New York: Sloan Publishing.

French, V. (2001). History of parenting: The ancient Mediterranean world. In M. Bornstein (Ed.), *Handbook of Parenting* (Vol. 3, pp. 345–376). Mahwah, NJ: Erlbaum.

Freud, A. (1965). *Normality and pathology in childhood.* New York: International Universities Press.

Frymer-Kensky, T. (1995). *Motherprayer: The pregnant woman's spiritual companion.* New York: Riverhead Books.

Gaskell, E. (1996). Elizabeth Gaskell's diary. In J. A. Chapple & A. Wilson (Eds.), *Private voices: The diaries of Elizabeth Gaskell and Sophia Holland* (pp. 11–71). New York: St. Martin's Press.

Gelis, J. (1989). The child: From anonymity to individuality. In P. Aries & G. Duby (Eds.), *A history of private life* (pp. 309–325). Cambridge, MA: Harvard University Press.

Gies, F., & Gies, J. (1987). *Marriage and the family in the middle ages.* New York: Harper and Row.

Greenleaf, P. (1978). *Children throughout the ages: A history of childhood.* New York: Barnes & Noble.

Hanawalt, B. A. (1993). *Growing up in medieval London: The experience of childhood in history.* New York: Oxford University Press.

Hareven, T. K. (1985). Historical changes in the family and the life course: Implications for child development. *Monographs of the Society for Research in Child Development, 50* (Serial No. *211*), 8–23.

Hewlett, B. S., Lamb, M. E., Shannon, D., Leyendecker, B., & Scholmerich, A. (1998). Culture and early infancy among central African foragers and farmers. *Developmental Psychology, 34*(4), 653–661.

Hrdy, S. B. (1999). *Mother nature: A history of mothers, infants, and natural selection.* New York: Pantheon.

Huizinga, J. (1954). *The waning of the middle ages.* New York: Anchor Books.

Hulbert, A. (2004). *Raising America: Experts, parents, and a century of advice about children.* New York: Random House.

Johnson, D.H. (1992). Body: Recovering our sensual wisdom. In D. Johnson & I. Grand (Eds.), *The body in psychotherapy: Inquiries into somatic psychology* (pp. 1–16). Berkeley, CA: North Atlantic.

Kojima, H. (1986). The history of child development in Japan. In H. Azuma & H. Stevenson (Eds.), *Child development and education in Japan* (pp. 39–54). New York: Academic Press.

Konner, M. (1982). *The tangled wing: Biological constraints on the human spirit.* New York: Holt, Rinehart, & Winston.

Koops, W. (1996). Historical developmental psychology: The sample case of paintings. *International Journal of Behavioral Development, 19*(2), 393–413.

Lamb, M. E., Sternberg, K. J., & Ketterlinus, R. D. (1992). Child care in the United States: The modern era. In M.E. Lamb, K. J. Sternberg, C. Hwang, & A. Broberg (Eds.), *Childcare in context: Cross-cultural perspectives* (pp. 207–222). Hillsdale, NJ: Erlbaum.

Le Goff, J. (1987). *The medieval world.* (L. G. Cochrane, Trans.). London: Collins and Brown Ltd.

Mead, M., & Newton, N. (1967). Cultural patterning of perinatal behavior. In S. Richardson & A. Guttmacher (Eds.), *Childbearing: Its social and psychological aspects* (pp. 142–244). Baltimore, MD: Williams & Wilkins.

Piaget, J. (1952). *The origins of intelligence in children.* New York: International Universities Press.

Pomeroy, S. B. (1999). *Plutarch's advice to the bride and groom and a consolation to his wife.* New York: Oxford University Press.

Reese, M. (1985). Moshe Feldenkrais's work with movement: A parallel approach to Milton Erickson's hypnotherapy. In J. K. Zeig (Ed.), *Ericksonian psychotherapy: Vol. I.: Structures* (pp. 410–427). New York: Brunner/Mazel.

Saint Augustine (1991). *Confessions.* (Henry Chadwick, Trans.). New York: Oxford University Press.

Schneider, K. J. (1998). Toward a science of the heart: Romanticism and the revival of psychology. *American Psychologist, 53*(3), 277–289.

Screech, M. A. (Ed. and Trans.). (1991). *Michel De Montaigne: The complete essays.* Harmondsworth, England: Penguin Books.

Shepard, P. (1998). *Coming home to Pleistocene.* Covelo, CA: Island Press.

Shostak, M. (1983). *Nisa: The life and words of a !Kung woman.* New York: Vintage Books.

Sorenson, E. R. (1979). Early tactile communication and the patterning of human organization: A New Guinea case study. In M. Bullowa (Ed.), *Before speech* (pp. 289–305). New York: Cambridge University Press.

Stern, D. N. (1985). *The interpersonal world of the infant: A view from psychoanalysis and development psychology.* New York: Basic Books.

Stone, L. (1979). *The family, sex and marriage in England 1500–1800.* New York: Harper and Row.

Vygotsky, L. S. (1978). *Mind in society.* Cambridge, MA: Harvard University Press.

Wallace, D. B., Franklin, M. B., & Keegan, R. T. (1994). The observing eye: A century of baby diaries. *Human Development, 37,* 1–29.

Wenke, R.J. (1990). *Patterns in prehistory: Humankind's first three million years.* New York: Oxford University Press.

Whiten, A., & Milner, P. (1986). The educational experiences of Nigerian infants. In H. V. Curran (Ed.), *Nigerian children: Developmental perspectives* (pp. 34–73). London: Routledge & Kegan Paul.

Whiting, B. (1974). Folk wisdom and child-rearing. *Merrill-Palmer Quarterly, 20,* 9–19.

Williams, O. (1952). *Immortal poems of the English language.* New York: Washington Square Press.

Winnicott, D.W. (1971). *Playing and reality.* New York: Basic Books.

Wooten, S. (1995). *Touching the body reaching the soul: How touch influences the nature of human beings.* Santa Fe, NM: Rosen Method Center Southwest.

PART I

Perceptual and Cognitive Development

Introduction

Part 1 reviews current research on development of perception, action, memory for and knowledge of the world. Since the first edition, a large body of new research has emerged on these topics, and the authors of the original chapters have updated their material to take account of this new research. In addition, we have included new chapters on intersensory perception and categorization.

In chapter two Slater and colleagues review current evidence on visual perception in infancy, beginning with consideration of basic sensory and perceptual functioning and then moving on to look at visual organization early in life. Although newborns' visual acuity is poor, Slater et al. present impressive evidence of complex visual organization from birth onwards. And the developments that follow birth, even in very basic aspects of vision, rely very much on visual experience. The chapter then moves on to look at face perception, covering evidence for a crude face template at birth that becomes more sophisticated over time. However, evidence for newborn imitation (chapter 11) indicates that this system is more than a crude perceptual face detector, and one conclusion is that infants' perception is social from birth. Evidence of infants' preferences for attractive faces leads to the possibility that, through experience with faces, infants form and prefer facial prototypes (which are also judged more attractive by adults), though this account is qualified by the existence of such preferences in newborns who have seen few faces. Another central topic in face perception is the *other race effect*. Adults and older children are poorer at discriminating individuals from other races. However, young infants do not show this deficit, and the argument is that, through experience, infants become selectively attuned to the facial features of their own race. This seems very like the phenomenon in language perception (chapter 3), in which infants gradually become selectively attuned to the phonetic distinctions that exist in the language to which they are exposed. The chapter ends with a brief consideration of object perception (which serves as a lead in to the material covered in chapter 6). Although there is evidence for the beginnings of object perception from birth, the ability to segregate objects in contact and to fill in gaps in perception in which one object partly hides another emerges after some months. Thus, the ability to go beyond what is literally visible takes time to develop.

In chapter 3, Burnham and Mattock review what we know about auditory perception and its development. Beginning with a description of the structure and function of the auditory system, they go on to an account of auditory development prior to and around birth. In their account of post-natal auditory development they cover evidence on perception of temporal information, intensity, and frequency. Although young infants are relatively poor at discriminating high frequencies this deficit largely disappears by 6 months. Auditory localization is present from birth but develops to a more sophisticated level by 4 months. The focus of the chapter then shifts to speech perception. One exciting finding in this area was that young infants perceive speech categorically, in the same way as adults. This was taken by some as indication of an innate attunement to language. However, it emerged that categorical perception was not limited to humans, and thus it seems more likely that language evolved to suit basic properties of the auditory system rather than the reverse. Probably a more significant finding is that young infants are sensitive to a wide range of speech distinctions spanning all languages but with increasing age become attuned to the language they are exposed to, losing the ability to distinguish sounds that are not experienced. Much the same picture emerges from research on infants' response to properties such as tempo, rhythm, and harmony, with certain culture-general properties picked up by newborns, and other culture-specific properties emerging 6 to 12 months later. The final part of the chapter considers hearing loss, covering diagnosis, screening, and intervention. Methods of diagnosing hearing defects in infants are now quite sophisticated, providing the potential to provide early intervention which can be seen as highly important for social development.

In Chapter 4, Bahrick reviews evidence on intermodal perception in infancy. From birth infants are sensitive to intersensory correspondences, for instance between location of a sound and a corresponding visual object. In addition to reviewing this evidence, Bahrick makes a case for the centrality of intersensory information in recruiting infants' attention to specific information in their environment. Infants attend selectively to information that is common (redundant) across two or more senses, and this tendency does much to simplify their task of learning about the world, by leading them to focus on this more crucial information. This is particularly true in the case of social development. When people speak they provide information that is redundant across the auditory and visual modalities, and thus the general tendency to attend to information that is redundant across the senses leads infants to respond selectively to people. On this basis the chapter provides a novel account of early social development in which considering infants' response to intermodal information is primary. This applies not just to the case of perceiving others speaking, but also to development of self-perception where redundant proprioceptive and visual information provides information about the self. The chapter ends by presenting an account of the social orienting impairment in autism as a problem in intersensory processing. As such, this section provides a link between basic research and atypical development, complementing the coverage of autism in chapter 9 of volume 2.

In chapter 5 the focus turns from perception to action. Smitsman and Corbetta point out that human action is governed by a complex self-organizing system that is as much emergent from the biodynamics of the skeletal and muscular system as it is due to brain systems. Taking this dynamical systems approach, they lay out the problems infants face in developing the ability to reach out and grasp objects: the problem is not just to execute the reach and grasp, but to maintain body stability during the act. They go on to review evidence on the development of reaching, from early pre-reaching, to goal-directed reaching and grasping. The second focus is the development of walking. Some infants walk unaided at 8.5 months but most walk a good deal later, some as late as 18 months. The authors point out how complex this activity is, involving balance and appropriate timing of gait. Some aspects of the activity can be seen in newborn stepping, formerly thought to be a reflex that was suppressed shortly after birth. More recent evidence indicates that this left-right sequence remains and can be revealed when appropriate support is provided. But beyond this, infants' early attempts at walking are different from adult walking, and the developmental task is considerable. The final focus goes beyond reaching to tool use. By the infant's first birthday, tool use has entered the repertoire. Infants' growing postural control frees their hands to manipulate objects, some of which can be used as tools. Use of a tool extends the infant's reach, but also leads to a greater perturbation of centre of gravity that the infant has to compensate for if stability is to be maintained. Additionally, the use of a tool leads to the need to calculate the relation between tool and target, which in itself is dependent on whether the tool is to be used to push or to pull the target object.

In chapter 6 Bremner provides an account of cognitive development. This literature has its roots in Piagetian theory, according to which knowledge is constructed through action. However, more recent accounts either blur the distinction between cognition and perception, or claim that infants possess innate knowledge of the world and are capable of reasoning about the events they encounter. One body of recent research provides evidence in keeping with perceptual bases for a later developing knowledge. For instance, infants' ability to perceive the unity of an object partly hidden by an occluder, and their ability to perceive the persistence of an object that passes temporarily behind an occluder seem best accounted for in terms of perceptual development. In contrast, a substantial literature interprets infants' responses as based on their reasoning about the events they are exposed to: longer looking at aberrant events is interpreted as detection of a violation of their expectations about the way objects should behave, based on their knowledge of object properties such as their permanence. One of the more striking claims emerging from this literature is that young infants understand simple operations of addition and subtraction, reacting when the numerical outcome of an action sequence is incorrect. Critics interpret the infant's reactions on the basis of more simple perceptual principles, and the debate continues. Finally, the chapter turns to the search errors that Piaget used as evidence of the infant's limited understanding of object permanence. There is a tension here between this literature and that which claims early knowledge of permanence. Various alternative accounts of search errors have been advanced that to an extent avoid this apparent contradiction. The author's favored account draws a distinction between early implicit knowledge and later knowledge that can be used to guide action.

The ability to organize the objects and events we encounter into categories and to form concepts of the world is another topic conventionally treated as an aspect of infant cognition, but which is increasingly investigated as a perceptual process, at least during early infancy. In chapter 7, Rakison reviews current research on this topic. As in the case of other aspects of knowledge, there are opposed views: some argue that infants are innately predisposed to form concepts while others argue that general learning mechanisms can account for the development of concepts. Evidence from early infancy indicates that infants can categorize events and extract prototypes (cf. the claims regarding preference for facial attractiveness, chapter 2), and it seems likely that these early perceptual categories are important precursors for concepts, which many argue emerge in the second year. Certainly, during the second year, infants begin to form categories in terms of the function of objects rather than just their perceptual features. It is still not clear, however, whether progressions such as these indicate the emergence of a different, more cognitive, process, or whether there is continuity in the processes underlying categorization in early and late infancy.

An understanding of infants' memory capacity and learning ability is central to any account of infant development. In chapter 8, Rovee-Collier and Barr describe the methods used to investigate infant memory, ranging from habituation to deferred imitation. Although habituation is harnessed to investigate perceptual discrimination (chapter 2), the fact the phenomenon occurs from birth onwards indicates at least a crude form of learning. And although imitation has importance as a social phenomenon (chapter 11), deferred imitation implies memory of the imitated act. Operant conditioning has been widely used to investigate memory and learning, possibly the best-known work involving reinforcing leg kicks by connecting the infant's leg to a mobile so that it moves when the infant kicks. Memory for the mobile after a delay of one or more days is indicated by kicking reoccurring only when the original mobile is presented. Even at 3 months, infants' memory is very specific, though it declines in specificity over increasing delays. After reviewing this evidence, and much else, including phenomena such as reinstatement and reactivation of memory, the authors turn to theory of infant memory. There is neuropsychological evidence for two distinct forms of memory: implicit memory is an automatic system for remembering information, whereas explicit memory is of a higher level and involves conscious memory of events. The developmental application of this distinction involves the assumption that young infants are limited to implicit memory, whereas older infants have the additional capacity for explicit memory. This conclusion was based largely on the relatively late emergence of deferred imitation, generally taken to measure explicit memory. However, more recent evidence indicates that even 3-month-olds exhibit deferred imitation. Reviewing this and other evidence, Rovee-Collier and Barr conclude that the basic memory systems of young infants and adults are the same, and that differences in memory capacity reflect differences in efficiency of the systems rather than in a maturationally driven shift to a qualitatively different system.

In chapter 9, Johnson rounds off this section by taking a neuroscience perspective on the development of perception and cognition. Until relatively recently our ability to investigate brain processes in infants was limited by the absence of suitable techniques. However, EEG-based methods such as *Event Related Potentials* have become more sophisticated, and fMRI and other more recent imaging methods are now growing in use. One respect in which older neuroscience accounts were disappointing to some developmental theorists was in their tendency to relegate developmental processes to brain maturation. Johnson points out that this *predetermined epigenetic* view is too limited to account for the two-way interaction between brain and behavior at all levels of organization, and favors the *probabilistic epigenetic* approach that recognizes the complex interactions involved. One focus of interest is in the development of functional areas of the cortex and a recent view is that differentiation of these areas emerges at least partly due to neural activity itself. Thus, it is possible to identify a process through which perceptual experience can lead to brain organization. Johnson goes on to indicate how evidence regarding brain processes illuminates our understanding of face processing and language processing, and as such these sections of his chapter complement the accounts developed in chapters 2 and 3. He then considers the likely relationship between development of prefrontal cortex and the emergence of *cognitive control* (often termed *executive function*), reviewing evidence that this is a productive way of explaining search errors made by infants (chapter 6). The evidence to date indicates that the prefrontal cortex is functional rather earlier than previously thought, and thus the account relating development of this brain region to behavior is likely to be complex.

2

Visual Perception

Alan Slater, Patricia Riddell, Paul C. Quinn, Olivier Pascalis, Kang Lee, and David J. Kelly

Introduction

The major characteristic of perception, which applies to all the sensory modalities, is that it is organized. With respect to visual perception, the world that we experience is immensely complex, consisting of many entities whose surfaces are a potentially bewildering array of overlapping textures, colors, contrasts and contours, undergoing constant change as their position relative to the observer changes. However, we do not perceive a world of fleeting, unconnected retinal images; rather, we perceive objects, events and people that move and change in an organized and coherent manner.

For hundreds of years there has been speculation about the development of the visual system and the perception of an organized world; however, answers to the many questions awaited the development of procedures and methodologies to test infants' perceptual abilities. Many such procedures are now available and, since the 1960s, many infant studies have been carried out and the findings from many of these studies are described in this chapter. The chapter is in six main sections. In the first section, Theoretical Overview, an account is given of the theories of visual development that have helped shape our understanding of the infant's perceived world. In order to begin the business of making sense of the visual world, it has to be seen, and considerable research has been carried out to describe the sensory capacities of the young infant. An account of some of this research is given in the section headed Sensory and Perceptual Functioning. In the next section, Visual Organization At and Near Birth, research is described that has investigated the intrinsic organization of the visual world. Several lines of evidence converge to suggest that infants are born with some representation of the human face, and this initially broadly based face-space becomes narrowed with learning and experience, topics that are discussed in the section on Face Perception. Perception of, and learning about, the visually perceived world of objects is the theme of Object Perception, and in the final section, Emerging Questions, Paradigms, Issues, are discussed.

Theoretical Overview

Until recent times the majority of theories of visual perception emphasized the extreme perceptual limitations of the newborn and young infant. For example, the "father of modern psychology" William James claimed (1890, Vol. 1, p. 488), in one of the most memorable phrases in developmental psychology, that "the baby, assailed by eyes, ears, nose, skin and entrails at once, feels it all as one great blooming, buzzing confusion." Hebb (1949), and Piaget (1953, 1954) argued that visual perception is exceptionally impoverished at birth and suggested that its development is a consequence of intensive learning in the months and years from birth. Hebb (pp. 32–33) concluded that "The course of perceptual learning in man is gradual, proceeding from a dominance of colour, through a period of separate attention to each part of a figure, to a gradually arrived at identification of the whole as a whole; an apparently simultaneous instead of a serial apprehension," and he suggested that, "it is possible then that the normal human infant goes through the same process, and that we are able to see a square as such in a single glance only as the result of complex learning." Piaget suggested that infants' vision is limited by their reaching, in that all objects beyond that realm were treated as if they were all at one distance. He also said of the young infant's vision: "Perception of light exists from birth and consequently the reflexes which insure the adaptation of this perception (the pupillary and palpebral reflexes, both to light). All the rest (perception of forms, sizes, positions, distances, prominence, etc.) is acquired through the combination of reflex activity with higher activities" (1953, p. 62). Piaget did not discuss visual development in any detail. However, his constructionist approach suggested that perception becomes structured in a sequence of stages as infancy progresses, and the infant becomes able to coordinate more and more complex patterns of activity. Thus, many perceptual abilities, such as intersensory coordination, size and shape constancy, understanding that hidden objects continue to exist, and understanding of space and objects, develop relatively late in infancy.

The obvious alternative to learning or constructionist/empiricist accounts of visual development is to adopt a nativist view that the ability to perceive a stable, organized visual world is an innate or inherent property of the visual system. A coherent and influential Gestalt theory of perception was developed by three psychologists, Max Wertheimer (1890–1943), Kurt Koffka (1886–1941), and Wolfgang Kohler (1887–1967). The Gestalt psychologists listed rules of perceptual organization that describe how groups of stimuli spontaneously organize themselves into meaningful patterns (research by Quinn and his colleagues into the Gestalt organizational principles and other grouping principles is described later). The Gestalt psychologists believed that the organization of visual perception is the result of neural activity in the brain which, in turn, depends on electro-chemical processes. These physical processes obey the laws of physics, and are a

fundamental characteristic of the human brain. It therefore follows that visual organization is a natural characteristic of the human species and is therefore innately provided.

The distinguished American psychologist J.J. Gibson (1904–1979) was for many years
a leading critic of the empiricist or constructivist position. Gibson (1950, 1966, 1979)
argued that the senses, or "perceptual systems," have evolved over evolutionary time to
detect perceptual invariants directly, and without the need for additional supplementation
by experience. Invariants are higher-order variables of perception that enable observers
to perceive the world effectively, without the need for additional, constructive processes.
Such invariants specify constancy of shape and size of objects, the permanence and properties of objects, the three-dimensional world of space, and so on: "Perception is not a
matter of constructing a three-dimensional reality from the retinal image, either in development or in the perceptual acts of adults. The structure of the environment is "out
there" to be picked up, and perception is a matter of picking up invariant properties of
space and objects" (Bremner, 1994, p. 118). The invariances that infants detect cannot
be easily specified, and perceptual development depends on the distinctive features that
are detected at different ages, an empirical matter that cannot be easily resolved theoretically. However, when researchers began to discover perceptual abilities in young infants
that could not be explained by recourse to empiricist, learning, and constructivist views,
it was appealing to interpret findings in terms of Gibson's views: since perception is direct
and does not need to be enhanced by experience, then Gibson's theory was the only
"grand theory" able to accommodate the findings.

In recent years it has become apparent that Piaget's and Gibson's views both have
much to offer: Piaget because he emphasized the role of action in sensori-motor development, and Gibson because his theory allows for the possibility of perceptual organization
in early infancy. We will touch on these points later in the chapter. No-one would doubt
that considerable learning about the visual world has to take place. However, as soon as
research into infant perceptual abilities began in earnest, from the early 1960s, it became
apparent that extreme empiricist views were untenable. As early as 1966 Bower concluded
that "infants can in fact register most of the information an adult can register but can
handle less of the information than adults can register" (p. 92). Research over the past
40 years has given rise to conceptions of the "competent infant," who enters the world
with an intrinsically organized visual world that is adapted to the need to impose structure
and meaning on the people, objects, and events that are encountered. Subsequent visual
perception soon becomes modified by learning and experience, so that many aspects
of perception are subject to knowledge-based constraints. This research has given rise to
a number of theoretical views, concerned with specific aspects of visual development.
Some of these views are described in the chapter, and an overview of some recent
approaches is given in the final section.

Sensory and Perceptual Functioning

The first, and most obvious, difference between the infant and adult visual system is a
difference in the size of the eye. Figure 2.1 shows schematic horizontal sections through
the eye of an adult (left) and of a neonate (right). This clearly illustrates the differences

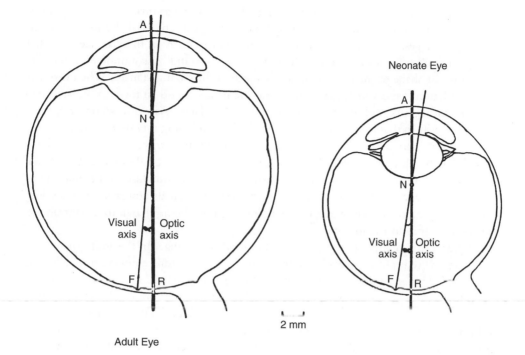

Figure 2.1   Schematic horizontal sections through the (left) eyes of the adult and neonate (to scale), to illustrate differences in gross size, in the shape of the lens, and in the depth of the anterior chamber. (F, fovea; R, retina).

in overall size of the eye. Between birth and maturity, the eye and the brain increase in volume by about three to four times. This is a much smaller increase in volume than is found in the rest of the body between infancy and adulthood (21 times). Thus, with respect to size, the eye and brain are relatively well developed at birth. While this level of development is able to support some visual function at birth, there are also distinct changes in visual ability with age. Mature vision requires the ability to see in fine detail (visual acuity) and to distinguish boundaries on the basis of color, luminance, and texture differences. It also requires the ability to track moving objects, and to pick out objects of interest in a cluttered environment. Excellent recent accounts of the development of infant vision are to be found in Atkinson (2000), Hainline, (1998) and in various chapters in Vital-Durand, Atkinson, and Braddick (1996). A brief account of the development of visual function is given here.

Anatomical differences in the neonatal eye

Since the neonatal eye is smaller, light has to be refracted (bent) to a greater extent in order to be focused appropriately on the retina. This is partially achieved by the greater curvature of the infant cornea (front of the eye) in comparison to the adult. Despite this, many typically developing infants are far-sighted (hyperopic) at birth since the increased steepness of the cornea is not sufficient for the small focal length of the infant eyeball. This might suggest that infants should see objects more clearly in the distance than they do when the object is near, however, this is not what is found. Accommodation refers to changes in the shape of the lens to focus on objects at different distances. When neonatal accommodation is measured, many newborn infants are found to focus at a distance of about 30 cm regardless of where the object is actually placed. Accommodation responses improve rapidly so that by 2 months of age, typically developing infants alter their accommodation appropriately to focus on both near and distant objects (Hainline, Riddell, Grose-Fifer, & Abramov, 1992; Turner, Horwood, Houston, & Riddell, 2002). It has been suggested that the most important visual stimuli are found close to the infant (e.g., the mother's breast and face), so that limiting focusing to near distances early in development might promote development by excluding attention being drawn to distant objects with no relevance to the infant.

Differences also exist between the adult and newborn retinae. In the adult, the central portion of the retina (the fovea) has a greater density of photoreceptors (cones) allowing more detailed vision in this part of the retina. In the newborn, in comparison, the density of photoreceptors is constant across the whole retina (Abramov et al., 1982). Thus, peripheral retina in infants is similar to adult peripheral retina, but in comparison to the adult, the fovea of the infant has a lower cone density. This difference is important since it provides a limit on the ability to see fine detail (see later). Increase in the density of cones in the fovea is substantial over the first 4 years of life, and continues more slowly until the mid teenage years (Yuodelis & Hendrickson, 1986).

In summary, maturation of the eye accounts for improvements in infant focusing and in the ability to see fine detail.

Eye movements, scanning, and fixations

In adults, greatest visual acuity is obtained at the fovea, and so mechanisms have evolved in order to point the fovea at objects of interest and to maintain objects on the fovea despite motion either of the object or the self. This is called foveation, and is most readily accomplished in humans via eye movements, although head and body movements also contribute. The newborn retina, and particularly the fovea, is structurally immature compared to the level of development seen in older children and adults (Hainline, 1998). However, despite its immaturity, even newborn infants foveate small objects, if they are motivated and the object is not too difficult to see (i.e., if it can be distinguished against the background and is close to the eyes). However, there are limitations in very young infants' abilities to successfully produce certain eye movements. For example, until 8 to 10 weeks of age, infants rarely engage in smooth pursuit, or the tracking of a slowly moving target (Aslin, 1981). Saccadic eye movements are rapid movements which point the fovea at targets of interest: when reading a book, such eye movements quickly direct the eye along the line of print. It has been observed that when one target disappears and another reappears, young infants will often "approach" the new stimulus with a series of saccades, rather than just one (Aslin & Salapatek, 1975). These are called "step-like" saccades. However, not all studies have found this apparent immaturity (Hainline & Abramov, 1985). Hainline points out that adults will occasionally produce step-like saccades when they are tired or inattentive, and suggests that perhaps the frequency of such saccades in infants might also be caused by lack of attention to the stimuli that are shown to them in laboratory tests. She says that "We do not regularly observe step-saccades when infants look at natural scenes, so they may be an artefact of the laboratory," and concludes "In general, the saccadic system seems quite mature and ready to function to reorient the fovea at high speeds, even early in life" (p. 36).

In addition to the conjugate eye movements which move both eyes in the same direction, infants also need to develop the ability to make disconjugate (or vergence) eye movements which move the eyes in opposite directions. These eye movements are used, in conjunction with changes in focusing, to follow objects that move towards or away from the infant. During the first two to three months of life, infants have been found to make intermittent errors in their attempts to follow objects in depth (Riddell, Horwood, Houston, & Turner, 1999). When a prism is placed in front of one eye, it bends the light coming into the eye, and so the eye has to turn inwards to refoveate the object of interest. The eye has to return to turn outwards when the prism is removed. This test is a relatively easy way to detect early vergence eye movements. Using this, Riddell et al. showed that infants as young as 2 months were able to make appropriate vergence eye movements, at least when only one target was viewed in an otherwise darkened room. However, before 3 months of age, some infants misinterpreted the movement of the object when the prism was removed from in front of the eye, resulting in an over-convergence (eyes pointing too far inwards). By 4 months of age, this over-convergence was rarely seen.

In summary, neonates seem to be limited in visual scanning skills, although attempts at foveation are readily observed. All types of eye movements are observed in young infants, and the eye movement and fixation systems are mature by around 4 months (Hainline, 1998; Adolph & Joh, 2007).

Visual acuity and contrast sensitivity

In order to test the visual abilities of infants, researchers have had to develop special experimental techniques. One of the most commonly used is the visual preference method, often called preferential looking (PL). This is based on the finding that infants will spend longer looking at objects that they prefer. If the infant is shown a black and white patterned stimulus paired with a blank grey field that is of equal brightness, the infant will look longer at the patterned stimulus, so long as the elements of the pattern are large enough for them to see. Thus, we can measure the level of fine detail seen by an infant (visual acuity) by presenting them with pairs of stimuli only one of which contains black and white stripes, the other being a gray patch. The infant's looking to each side is recorded by an observer watching through a peephole, or on a video monitor. By progressively decreasing the size of the stripes, we can use this technique to determine the smallest stripe width that is reliably preferred to the gray stimulus, and this is taken as the estimate of acuity.

Figure 2.2   A face as it might appear to a newborn (left) and to us.

Preferential looking studies suggest that neonatal visual acuity is poor – about 1 to 2 cycles per degree, which is around 6/180 Snellen acuity. This level of Snellen acuity states that an infant can see clearly an object at 6 meters that an adult can see clearly at 180 meters away! Typical adult vision is 6/6 Snellen acuity. An estimate of the acuity of an infant can be given by looking at the size of your thumbnail when you hold it at arm's length – this is the smallest object the typical newborn infant can resolve. Visual acuity improves rapidly with development, reaching 6/24 Snellen acuity by 6 months of age, and 6/6 Snellen acuity by about 4 years of age (Atkinson, 2000).

In the preferential looking paradigm, infants have to pay attention to the targets in order to be assessed. An alternative method for assessing visual acuity, and other visual functions, is measurement of the visual evoked potential (VEP). In this procedure, small sensors are placed over the visual cortex at the back of the head in order to measure changes in electrical signals in the brain that result from neural activity in response to changes in a visual stimulus. By presenting a striped pattern in which the stripes reverse their phase (i.e., light stripes become dark and dark stripes become light), a response can be measured over the visual cortex at the same rate as the phase reversal – if and only if the stripes are large enough for the visual system to detect. Thus, by decreasing the stripe width, acuity can be measured as the smallest stripe width that will produce a reliable signal from the visual cortex at the same rate as the phase reversal of the pattern. When visual acuity is measured using this technique, infants appear to perform significantly better than when using the PL technique (Riddell et al., 1998). When assessed using the VEP, acuity appears almost adult-like by 6 months of age. The reasons for the discrepancy between the estimates of acuity obtained using different procedures remains unclear (Riddell et al., 1998). Figure 2.2 gives an indication of how the mother's face might look to a newborn infant, and how she might look to us: while the image is degraded and unfocussed for the newborn, enough information is potentially available for the infant to learn to recognize the mother's face.

While measures of visual acuity are useful in providing an assessment of the finest detail that an infant can detect, they do not tell us everything about the visual abilities

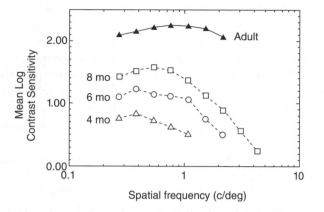

Figure 2.3 Contrast sensitivity functions for 4-, 6- and 8-month-old infants and adults. *Source*: Derived from Peterzell and Teller, 1996.

of the infant. A more complete indication of visual ability is given by measures of contrast sensitivity which gives an indication of how washed out or faded an image can be before it becomes indistinguishable from the background. A black pattern against a white background has a contrast approaching 100%. As the blackness of the pattern is decreased to lighter shades of grey, the contrast of the pattern is decreased. Thus, it is possible to determine, for any stripe width, the degree of contrast required in order to detect the pattern. Again, both PL and VEP techniques have been used to make these measures (Drover, Earle, Courage, & Adams, 2002; Kelly, Borchert, & Teller, 1997; Peterzell & Teller, 1996). Figure 2.3 shows an adult and infant contrast sensitivity function. Note that 100% contrast is shown at the lowest point of the y-axis and that contrast decreases as you move up the y-axis. This figure shows that infants have much lower sensitivity than adults at all stripe widths by a factor of about 100. The difference between infants and adults is not found only at the limit of acuity (point to the furthest right of the x-axis). Thus, in addition to being unable to make out fine details, young infants cannot see low contrast images of any size.

Perception of motion and color

Objects in the world are defined not only by differences in luminance contrast, but also by differences in their reflectance of a range of wavelengths of light (chromaticity). In addition, objects are rarely stationary but move across the retina, as a result of motion of the object, or self-motion. Thus, in order to interpret the visual world, infants also need to develop the ability to perceive motion and color.

Preferential looking techniques have been used to show that very young infants prefer moving over stationary targets (Slater, Morison, Town, & Rose, 1985; Volkmann & Dobson, 1976) but this is not sufficient to demonstrate motion detection, because moving targets result in temporal changes in the response of visual neurones that are similar to those produced by a flickering target with no movement. In order to clearly show that infants can detect motion, it is necessary to show activity in the visual system that discriminates different directions of motion (Atkinson, 2000).

Evidence that infants can detect motion early in life comes from eye movement studies. A full field pattern of stripes that moves in one direction elicits eye movements that follow one stripe, and then move quickly back to follow another stripe. This pattern of eye movements can be seen when people are watching out of a train window, and is called optokinetic nystagmus (OKN). It is used to stabilize a moving image on the retina. Studies of OKN have suggested that early motion perception is controlled by a subcortical route. The evidence for this is that, when infants less than 3 months of age view an OKN target monocularly, eye movements are elicited by a temporal to nasal moving target, but not by a nasal to temporal target (Atkinson & Braddick, 1981). This is thought to be controlled by a pathway which takes information from each retina to a subcortical structure called the Nucleus of the Optic Tract (NOT). This subcortical structure only processes motion in one direction and it is thought that the monocular asymmetry results from its activation in the absence of cortical motion detectors (Hoffman, 1981). This asymmetry in motion detection disappears at about 3 months of age in typically developing infants (although this is later when higher velocity targets are used: Mohn, 1989). The gradual disappearance of the monocular asymmetry has been interpreted as an indication of the onset of cortical motion detection (Atkinson & Braddick).

In support of the suggestion that cortical motion detectors are absent in early infancy Mason, Braddick and Wattam-Bell (2003) tested infants in both a PL and an OKN paradigm with coherent motion targets. These targets consist of moving dots. If the pattern is 100% coherent, all the dots move in the same direction. Coherence can be decreased by making a percentage of dots move in random directions so that the motion signal is carried by a lower percentage of dots. Using these paradigms, Mason et al. (2003) showed that the percentage of dots required to produce reliable OKN was 20–25% at 6 weeks of age, and that this coherence threshold did not change with age. In contrast, the motion coherence threshold measured using PL techniques was always higher than for OKN and improved significantly between 6 and 27 weeks. It was therefore suggested that while OKN measured subcortical motion processing, PL measured cortical motion processing. The absence of cortical motion detectors in early infancy is also implicated in the perception of object unity, as discussed later.

An asymmetry in the response to different directions of motion can also be demonstrated using visual evoked potential (VEP) paradigms (Norcia et al., 1991). In a study that compared motion processing using both VEP and OKN techniques, it was shown that, while monocular OKN shows a stronger temporal to nasal response, the VEP shows a stronger nasal to temporal response (Mason, Braddick, Wattam-Bell, & Atkinson, 2001). Thus, while the subcortical and cortical responses are likely to be related, the relationship between them is not simple.

The ability to detect differences in the wavelength compositions of objects depends on the presence of three photoreceptor types in the retina. These are the long- (L), mid- (M) and short- (S) wavelength-sensitive cones. These are thought to combine subcortically to provide three different channels – one sensitive to changes in brightness or luminance, and two color (chromatic) channels, the red-green and blue-yellow (tritan) opponent channels.

As in motion perception, there is a difficulty in determining the onset of true color vision in infants. Most visual targets are defined both by differences in the reflected wavelengths of light (chromaticity) and in their luminance. Since chromaticity and luminance are detected in separate channels within the visual system, to demonstrate true color perception, the infant has to show the ability to discriminate between targets that are matched on their luminance but vary in their chromaticity. This is a difficult process since individual differences, and/or developmental changes, in the luminance matches require that the exact point of this match be determined before color vision can be tested. Another strategy that can be used with infants is to use a range of targets of different luminance such that the equiluminant point for any individual infant is likely to be included within this range. Thus, if infants are only detecting the difference between targets on the basis of luminance differences, but not chromatic differences, there should be at least one target combination at which these discriminations cannot be made (Atkinson, 2000).

Using a range of targets, Peeples and Teller (1975) showed that infants of 2 months of age could discriminate between a solid white field, and a red target in a white field at all luminances tested. This suggested that, even when the red target was matched for luminance with the white background field, infants could perceive the target on the basis of chromaticity differences. Thus, infants of 2 months of age can be demonstrated to have some form of color vision. This paradigm was extended to test sensitivity to targets with a range of chromatic stimuli (Hamer, Alexander, & Teller, 1982; Clavedetscher, Brown, Ankrum, & Teller, 1988). Infants of 2 months of age were shown to discriminate reds, oranges, blue-greens and blues from white, but were unable to discriminate yellow-greens and mid-purples. This is suggestive of a deficiency in the blue-yellow, or tritan, channel. More recent studies using different methodologies have provided evidence that infants of 2 months of age can make discriminations within this region (Varner, Cook, Schmeck, McDonald, & Teller, 1985), but the sensitivity of the tritan channel might be lower than the red-green channel (Teller, 1997). In comparison, infants of 1 month of age fail to show chromatic discriminations with this paradigm.

Perception of depth

> For those of a creationist bent, one could note that God must have loved depth cues, for He made so many of them. (Yonas & Granrud, 1985, p. 45)

Before 4 months of age, infants are able to fixate accurately on targets placed at different depths and to track objects moving in depth (Hainline & Riddell, 1995; Turner et al., 2002). This probably forms the basis of three dimensional vision (Thorn, Gwiazda, Cruz, Bauer, & Held, 1994). The two eyes are separated in space, and therefore provide slightly different images of the perceived world (retinal disparity). These small differences, or disparities, are interpreted by the visual system as actual depth differences (stereopsis), and so we gain a three-dimensional view of the world. The presence of stereopsis has been tested in infants by placing goggles on the infant which allow presentation of different images to each eye. The infant then views separate stimuli to each eye which contain disparities between the right and the left eyes' images. These are interpreted by adult viewers as depth differences and three-dimensional shapes appear in the image. If the infant has stereopsis and can fuse the two images, then they should also see these shapes. Preferential looking can then be used to see whether the infant prefers a stimulus with the three-dimensional shape over an image in which there is no three-dimensional shape. Increased looking at the image containing the three-dimensional shape indicates that the infant has stereopsis.

Several researchers have reported that infants develop the ability to perceive depth by stereopsis by around 4 months of age (Braddick & Atkinson, 1983; Held, 1985; Teller, 1982). This has a sudden onset in individual infants, and fine stereoacuity (the ability to detect very small differences in the disparity between the images in each eye) develops rapidly, approaching adult levels within a few weeks (Held, 1985; see Birch, 1993 for an overview).

There are many other depth cues. For instance, Slater, Rose, and Morison (1984) showed that newborn infants will selectively fixate a three-dimensional stimulus in preference to a photograph of the same stimulus, even when they are only allowed to view with one eye (removing the retinal disparity information from the image). The main depth cue that is available in a three-dimensional image that is viewed with one eye is motion parallax (near parts of the image move more quickly than far parts as gaze is moved across the image). Thus, even newborn infants appear to be able to use some depth cues. Infants as young as 8 weeks of age perceive three-dimensional object shape when shown kinetic random dot displays in which the three-dimensional image is defined by the relative speed of movement of the dots (Arterberry & Yonas, 2000). Appreciation of pictorial depth cues – those monocular cues to depth that are found in static scenes such as might be found in photographs – has been found from about 5 months. In an early experiment, Yonas, Cleaves and Pettersen (1978) used the "Ames window" – a trapezoidal window rotated round its vertical axis so that the retinal image was rectangular. When adults view the two-dimensional Ames window monocularly, a powerful illusion is perceived of a slanted window with one side (the larger) closer than the other. Yonas et al. reported that 6-month-olds are twice as likely to reach for the larger side of the distorted window than for the smaller side, suggesting that this depth cue is detected by this age. Sen, Yonas and Knill (2001) have described a recently discovered static monocular cue to depth. This illusion is shown in Figure 2.4. In their experiment, Sen et al. found that 7-month-olds, but not 5- or 5.5-month-olds, when tested monocularly, reached for the apparently closer end of the fronto-parallel cylinder. Differences in age of onset of the ability to perceive depth cues (6 to 7 months in some studies, but newborn in others) might partly be influenced by the task used to test the ability. Preferential looking tasks that require the infant to make a choice based on looking behavior suggest earlier development of the ability to use depth cues than tasks involving a motor output such as pointing. This might be due to the later development, or lower sensitivity, of a dorsal visual system that supports action than a ventral system supporting perception (Bruggeman, Yonas, & Konczak, 2007).

Surface Contour Information for Depth

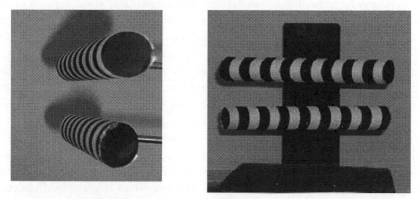

Figure 2.4   A 2-D version of the 3-D illusion used by Sen et al. (2001).

The role of experience in visual development

Studies that have raised animals in artificial visual environments have demonstrated changes in the development of depth perception when animals are raised with vision in only one eye (Hubel & Wiesel, 1965), to the perception of oriented lines when animals are raised in environments that contain lines of only a single orientation (White, Coppola, & Fitzpatrick, 2001) and to color vision when animals are raised in light of only one wavelength (Sugita, 2004). Hence, we can be sure that visual experience is important in development.

While newborn human infants are capable of active vision, there is clearly a great deal of development that takes place during the first 6 months of life and beyond. This could be the result both of maturation of the areas of the visual cortex that support vision in accordance with a genetic program, and of changes in brain areas resulting from visual experience. One way that we can determine which of these processes is more likely to be occurring is to compare healthy preterm infants with healthy full-term infants. Infants can either be matched by age based on time of birth (postnatal age), or on age based on time of conception (gestational age). There are four possible outcomes of such comparisons: 1) delays in development might be found in preterm compared to full-term infants as a result of increased vulnerability due to insufficient maturation in the uterus. Thus, preterm infants would be slower to develop visual functions whether matched by post-natal or gestational age; 2) If the brain is maturing according to a set timetable, premature infants should develop visual functions at the same age as full-term infants when they are matched by gestational age, but should be later than full-term infants when matched by postnatal age (since they are less fully developed when first born); 3) The third possibility, in contrast, is that if visual experience is important, full-term and preterm infants should develop visual functions at the same postnatal age after birth since they are matched for duration of visual experience. In this case, preterm infants should develop functions earlier than full-term infants matched for gestational age since preterm infants will have had ore time since they were born to participate in visual experiences; The fourth possibility is that there may be some interaction between maturation and visual experience.

The onset of a range of visual abilities was compared between healthy preterm and full-term infants (Weinacht, Kind, Schulte Monting, & Gottlob, 1999). They found that, when infants were matched by postnatal age, the age of onset of ocular alignment, convergence, fusion, visual acuity, and OKN symmetry was earlier for the full-term than the preterm infants by between 5 and 7 weeks. However, when the infants were matched for gestational age, these differences in age of onset disappeared. This suggests that the development of these visual abilities is controlled by a genetic timetable rather than being driven directly by visual experience, though abnormal visual experience can alter this timetable.

In summary, newborn infants are capable of many forms of visual processing, as reflected in their ability to produce OKN eye movements to large, striped targets, their visual preferences for some stimuli over others, their ability to discriminate between stimuli as demonstrated by habituation/dishabituation studies (Slater, 1995), and their ability to recognize faces soon after birth (Bushnell, 2003). However, their vision is limited in terms of the fine detail they can see, the contrast required to see targets, and very limited color and depth perception. As Teller (1997, p. 2196) puts it, "Their visual worlds are probably marked less by blooming and buzzing than by the haziness of low-contrast sensitivity, the blurriness of spatial filtering and the blandness of monochrome." Even the poor vision of the very young infant does not hamper their development. Young infants do not need to scrutinize the fine print in a contract or to see things clearly at a distance. The most important visual stimuli are to be found in close proximity. Hainline (1998, p. 9) summarizes it rather nicely: "visually normal infants have the level of visual functioning that is required for the things that infants need to do."

By 2 months, infants are beginning to be able to discriminate color, and can use some depth and motion cues. Visual acuity and contrast sensitivity have also improved. By 3 months, these functions have continued to improve, but the infant still lacks the ability to detect retinal disparity, and so depth perception using this cue is still limited. This appears at about 4 months of age. By 6 months of age, visual perception has improved dramatically in all abilities, and, while some visual functions continue to improve more slowly, even into the teenage years, the visual and perceptual systems of the young infant are mature enough to provide a clear input for cognitive systems.

Visual Organization in Early Infancy

We have seen that scanning abilities, acuity, contrast sensitivity, and color discrimination are limited in neonates. However, despite these limitations, the visual system is functioning at birth. In this section several types of visual organization that are found in early infancy are discussed. Many parts of the brain, both subcortical and cortical, are involved in vision, but it is reasonable to claim that visual perception, in any meaningful sense, would not be possible without a functioning visual cortex, and this is discussed first.

Cortical functioning at birth

The cortex is responsible for humans' memory, reasoning, planning, and many visual skills. The ability to foveate and to discriminate detail is also mediated by the visual cortex, and we presented evidence above, which suggests that newborns can foveate stimuli. However, it has been proposed (Bronson, 1974) that the visual cortex is not functional at birth, and that the visual behaviors of infants for around the first 2 months from birth are primarily mediated by subcortical structures such as the superior colliculus, which is particularly involved in the control of eye movements. Other researchers have also suggested that much of early visual perception is primarily mediated by subcortical structures and that there may be a shift from subcortical to cortical functioning around 2 months after birth (e.g., Atkinson, 1984; Johnson, 1990, 2005; Johnson & Morton, 1991; Pascalis, de Schonen, Morton, Deruelle & Fabre-Grenet, 1995).

A critical test of cortical functioning is discrimination of orientation. In primates, orientation discrimination is not found in subcortical neurons, but it is a common property of cortical cells, and orientation selectivity is therefore an indicator of cortical functioning. Two studies tested for orientation discrimination in newborns (Atkinson, Hood, Wattam-Bell, Anker, & Tricklebank, 1988; Slater, Morison, & Somers, 1988). In these studies, newborn infants were habituated to a black and white stripes pattern (grating), presented in an oblique orientation, and on subsequent test trials they clearly gave a preference for the same grating in a novel orientation (the mirror-image oblique of the familiarized stimulus).

This finding is an unambiguous demonstration that at least some parts of the visual cortex are functioning at birth, as is the VEP evidence for visual acuity, recorded from the visual cortex, described earlier (Riddell et al., 1998). However, there is no doubt that orientation-specific cortical responses develop over the first 3 months (Braddick, Birtles, Wattam-Bell, & Atkinson, 2005). Several accounts have attempted to describe which parts of the visual cortex may be more functional than others (e.g., Atkinson, 1984, 2000; Johnson, 1990). However, even if the visual cortex is immature, it is difficult to know in what ways this imposes limitations on visual perception. As Atkinson and Braddick, (1989, p. 19), have put it, "we do not really have any idea how little or how much function we should expect from the structural immaturity of new-born visual cortex." Certainly, as will be described in the following sections, it has become clear that the newborn infant is possessed of many ways in which to begin to make sense of the visual world.

Shape and size constancy

As objects move, they change in orientation, or slant, and distance, relative to an observer, causing constant changes to the image of the objects on the retina. However, and as indicated in the Introduction, we do not experience a world of fleeting, unconnected retinal images, but a world of objects that move and change in a coherent manner. Such stability, across constant retinal changes, is called perceptual constancy. Perception of an object's real shape regardless of changes to its orientation is called shape constancy, and

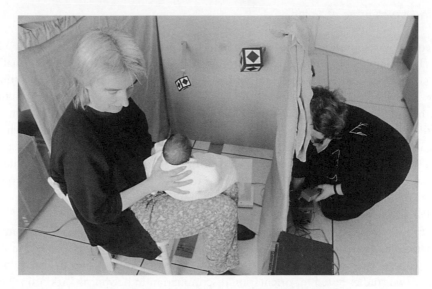

Figure 2.5   A newborn infant being tested in a size constancy experiment.

size constancy refers to the fact that we perceive an object as the same size regardless of its distance from us. If these constancies were not present in infant perception the visual world would be extremely confusing, perhaps approaching James's "blooming, buzzing confusion", and they are a necessary prerequisite for many other types of perceptual organization. However, there is clear evidence that these constancies are present at birth, and this is discussed next.

In a study of size constancy, Slater, Mattock, and Brown (1990) used preferential looking (PL) and familiarization procedures. A newborn infant being tested in a size constancy experiment is shown in Figure 2.5. In the PL experiment pairs of cubes of different sizes at different distances were presented, and it was found that newborns preferred to look at the cube which gave the largest retinal size, regardless of its distance or its real size. These findings are convincing evidence that newborns can base their responses on retinal size alone. However, in the second experiment each infant viewed either a small cube or a large cube during familiarization trials: each infant was exposed to the same-sized object shown at different distances on each trial. After familiarization, the infants were shown both cubes side-by-side, the small cube nearer and the large cube farther, such that their retinal images were the same size (Figure 2.6). The infants looked longer at the cube they were not familiarized with (consistent with the novelty preferences commonly observed in habituation studies). This result indicates that the newborns differentiated the two cube sizes despite the similarities of the retinal sizes, and abstracted the familiar cube's real size over changes in distance. Although it seems that newborn infants might base spontaneous preferential looking on retinal size there is evidence that by 4 months infants attend and respond primarily to real or physical rather than retinal image size (Granrud, 2006).

Slater and Morison (1985) described experiments on shape constancy and slant perception and obtained convincing evidence both that newborn infants detect, and respond

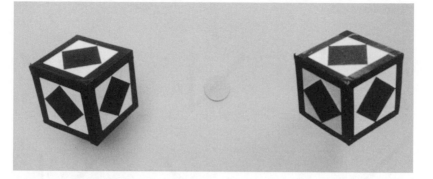

Figure 2.6 The stimuli shown to the infants on the post-familiarization test trials. This photograph, taken from the babies' viewing position, shows the small cube on the left at a distance of 30.5 cm, and the large cube on the right at a distance of 61 cm.

systematically to, changes in objects' slants, and also that they could respond to an object's real shape, regardless of its slant. Their results demonstrate that newborn babies have the ability to extract the constant, real shape of an object that is rotated in the third dimension: that is, they have shape constancy. It is worth pointing out that evidence for size and shape constancy implies some degree of depth perception at birth.

The findings of these studies demonstrate that shape and size constancy are organizing features of perception that are present at birth, although they will show subsequent refinement in infancy. E.J. Gibson (1969, p. 366) seemed to anticipate these findings:

> I think, as is the case with perceived shape, that an object tends to be perceived in its true size very early in development, not because the organism has learned to correct for distance, but because he sees the object as such, not its projected size or its distance abstracted from it.

Form perception

The terms "figure," "shape," "pattern," and "form" are often used interchangeably, and as long ago as 1970 Zusne (p. 1) commented that "Form, like love, is a many-splendored thing ... there is no agreement on what is meant by form, in spite of the tacit agreement that there is." However, the most often used stimuli in studies of form perception are static, achromatic, two- or three-dimensional figures with easily detectable contours that can stand as figures in a figure-ground relationship, and it is primarily with reference to these that most theories of form perception have been concerned.

One of the most intractable issues in the study of form perception in early infancy is whether or not such figures or patterns are innately perceived as parts or as wholes. This can be illustrated with respect to the newborn infant's perception of simple geometric shapes. We know that newborns discriminate easily between the outline shapes of simple geometric forms such as a square, circle, triangle, and cross, but the basis of the discrimination is unclear since these shapes differ in a number of ways, such as the number and

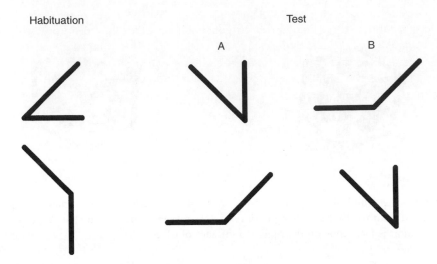

Figure 2.7   Habituation and test stimuli used in experiments on form perception by Cohen and Younger (1984) and Slater et al. (1991). Half of the infants were habituated to the acute angle (upper left), half to the obtuse angle.

orientation of their component lines, and as was mentioned earlier newborns can discriminate on the basis of orientation alone.

One experiment which suggests that there is a change in the way form is perceived in early infancy was by Cohen and Younger (1984). They tested 6- and 14-week-old infants with simple stimuli, each consisting of two connected lines which made either an acute (45°) or an obtuse (135°) angle, similar to those shown in Figure 2.7. Following habituation they found that the 6-week-olds responded to a change in the orientation of the lines (where the angle remained unchanged, test stimulus A in Figure 2.7), but not to a change in angle alone (test stimulus B), while the 14-week-olds did the opposite in that they recovered attention to a change in angle, but not to a change in orientation. Newborn infants have been found to respond to a change in angle if they have previously been familiarized with an angle that changed its orientation over trials (Slater, Mattock, Brown, & Bremner, 1991). These findings suggest that 4-month-olds are able to perceive angular relationships, and hence have some degree of form perception, but that form perception in infants 6 weeks and younger may at times be dominated by attention to lower-order variables such as orientation.

Most, if not all, visual stimuli are stimulus compounds in that they contain separate features that occur at the same spatial location, and which the mature perceiver "binds together" as a whole. With such an ability we see, for example, a green circle and a red triangle, while without it we would see greenness, redness, circularity and triangularity as separate stimulus elements. Evidence suggests that newborn infants perceive stimulus compounds. In an experiment by Slater, Mattock, Brown, Burnham, & Young (1991) newborns were familiarized, in successive trials, to two separate stimuli. For half the infants these were a green vertical stripe and a red diagonal stripe – the other babies were familiarized to green diagonal and red vertical stripes. In the former case there are two novel combinations, these being green diagonal and red vertical, and on post-familiarization test trials the babies were shown one of the familiar compounds paired with one of the novel ones, and they showed strong novelty preferences. Note that the novel compounds consisted of stimulus elements that the babies had seen before (green, red, diagonal, vertical), and the novelty preferences are therefore clear evidence that the babies had processed and remembered the color/form compounds shown on the familiarization trials.

Biomechanical motion

Biomechanical motions are the motions that correspond to the movements of a person (or other biological organism) when the individual is walking or engaging in some other activity. There are several constraints that distinguish biological motion from other types of motion: for example, the foot can move back and forth and side to side relative to the knee, but is always a fixed distance from the knee. Such motions are often depicted as point-light displays (Johannson, 1973) in which points of light that are located at the major joints (shoulder, elbows, wrists, hip, knees and ankles) are used as the stimuli. If observers are shown a single frame of the display (as in Figure 2.8A) they are usually

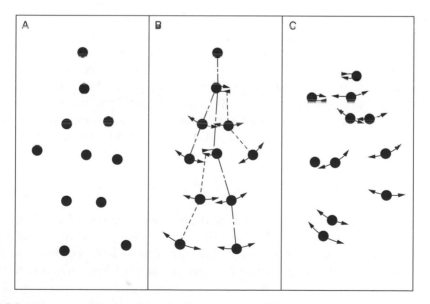

Figure 2.8   Three possible point-light displays. A static display (A) is not usually seen as a human figure. When the display is in motion, as depicted in (B) it is clearly seen as a person walking (the broken lines connecting the points are for illustration only, and not seen by the observer). When the point-light display moves in an incoherent or random motion (C) it is seen as isolated moving dots.

unaware that it represents a human form. However, if the display is in motion (depicted in Figure 2.8B) then adults need as little as 100 ms to identify the movement. Human adults can make an impressive range of discriminations from point-light displays: they can identify different animals by their typical patterns of motion; they can identify different actions (walking, running, dancing, skipping, etc.) and can also specify gender and even the identity of the actor, including their own identity.

Sensitivity to biological motions has been investigated in infants in order to discover the ontogenesis of its detection. Three-month-olds can discriminate between "coherent" and random displays (Figures 2.8B and C, respectively), as do older infants and adults. However, 3-month-olds discriminate between an upside-down point-light walker and a random display, but 5- and 7-month-olds do not! Bertenthal and Davis (1988) interpreted this apparently paradoxical age difference in terms of the experience and accumulated knowledge of the older infants: by 5 months of age infants will have had extensive experience of seeing humans walk in their canonical (upright) orientation and no experience of upside-down walkers, thus, by this age the upside-down and random displays are both equally unfamiliar. This *inversion effect* is similar to that seen in face perception: we can identify hundreds of familiar faces when presented upright but have great difficulty if the faces are shown inverted (e.g., Yin, 1969).

Bertenthal (1993) suggested that it is quite reasonable to suppose that detection of the constraints that distinguish biological motion are part of the intrinsic organization of the visual system, and there is now evidence in support of this. Simion, Regolin, and Bulf (2008) found that 2-day-old human newborns preferred biological to nonbiological point-light displays, leading them to endorse Bertenthal's speculation that detection of biological motion is an intrinsic property of the visual system.

A logical explanation of the age-related changes is that younger infants detect the constraints inherent in biomechanical point-light displays but they do not endow such displays with meaning: thus, they detect them on the basis of *perceptual* information. Older infants, however, imbue such displays with meaning: thus, by 5 months *conceptual* knowledge of humans constrains the interpretation of point-light displays. Some of the ways in which perception interacts with knowledge are particularly evident with changes to face perception in infancy, a topic that is discussed in a later section.

Subjective contours and Gestalt organizational principles

Many organizational principles contribute to the perceived coherence and stability of the visual world. As discussed above, shape and size constancy are present at birth, as is some degree of form perception. Other types of visual organization have been found in young infants, and by way of illustration two of these are discussed here: subjective contours and Gestalt principles.

Subjective contours.   Subjective contours are contours that are perceived "in the absence of any physical gradient of change in the display" (Ghim, 1990). Such contours were described in detail by Kanizsa (1979) and the Kanizsa square is shown in Figure 2.9: the adult perceiver usually "completes" the contours of the figures, despite the fact that

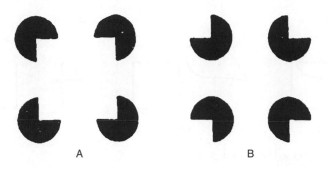

Figure 2.9 Pattern A (a Kanizsa square) produces subjective contours and is seen as a square. Pattern B contains the same four elements but does not produce subjective contours.

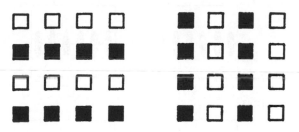

Figure 2.10 Stimuli used by Quinn et al. (1993) with 3-month-olds and by Farroni et al. (2000) with newborns. Infants, like adults, group by similarity and perceive the pattern on the left as rows, and that on the right as columns.

the contours are physically absent. Convincing evidence that 3- and 4-month-old infants perceive subjective contours was provided by Ghim (1990) who described a series of experiments leading to the conclusion that the infants perceived the complete form when viewing the subjective contour patterns. Further evidence of detection of the Kanisza square in 3- to 4-month-olds was provided by Otsuka, Kanazawa, & Yamaguchi (2004), and Kavsek and Yonas (2006) found evidence of detection of a continuously moving subjective Kanisza square in 4-month-olds.

Gestalt organizational principles. One of the main contributions of the Gestalt psychologists was to describe a number of ways in which visual perception is organized. Quinn, Burke and Rush (1993) demonstrated that 3-month-old infants group patterns according to the principle of *lightness similarity*. Two of the stimuli they used are shown in Figure 2.10. Adults reliably group the elements of such stimuli on the basis of brightness similarity and represent the figure on the left as a set of rows, and the other as a set of columns. Three-month-olds do the same, in that those habituated to the columns pattern generalize to vertical lines and prefer (perceive as novel) horizontal lines, while those habituated to the rows prefer the novel vertical lines. In subsequent experiments, using similar stimuli, Farroni, Valenza, Simion, and Umilta (2000) reported that even newborn infants group by lightness similarity.

Stimulus   Possible organizations

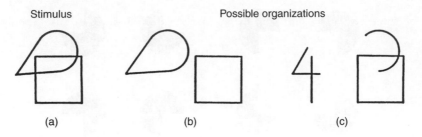

(a)   (b)   (c)

Figure 2.11   Patterns used by Quinn et al. (1997).

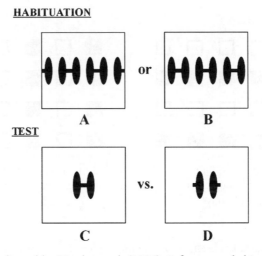

Figure 2.12   The stimuli used by Hayden et al. (2006). Infants were habituated to the connected patterns in A or B and tested with the patterns in C and D.

Quinn, Brown, and Streppa (1997) described experiments using an habituation-novelty testing procedure, to determine if 3- and 4-month-old infants can organize visual patterns according to the Gestalt principles of *good continuation* and *closure*. The stimuli they used are shown in Figure 2.11. Following familiarization to pattern (a) in Figure 2.11, tests revealed that the infants parsed the pattern into a square and teardrop (b) rather than into the "less-good" patterns shown in (c): that is, they had parsed the famil-iarized figure into the two separate shapes of a square and a teardrop in the same way that adults do. Hayden, Bhatt and Quinn (2006) habituated 3-month-old infants to the connected panels A and B shown in the upper part of Figure 2.12 and on subsequent testing the infants displayed a novelty preference for the disconnected elements (Panel D) when paired with the connected elements (Panel C). These findings indicate that the infants were sensitive to the organizing principle of *uniform connectedness* – that is, the tendency to group together elements that are connected. Quinn, Bhatt and Hayden (2008) describe experiments on several Gestalt grouping principles, including *proximity* (grouping together elements on the basis of proximity) and *form similarity* (grouping together elements that are similar in shape) that are also functional in 3- to 4-month-old infants, although the latter required multiple shape contrasts in order to be evidenced (i.e., X-O, square-diamond, H-I), thereby suggesting an important role for perceptual learning in the establishment of perceptual organization, a conclusion that foreshadows a major theme in an upcoming section of the chapter. These several findings lead to the conclusion "that even young infants' interactions with the visual world are guided by a considerable degree of perceptual coherence resulting from adherence to grouping principles that are functional in the first months of postnatal experience" (Quinn et al., p. 142).

Overview

The above is just a sample of the many studies which demonstrate that young infants organize the visually perceived world in a similar manner to that of adult perceivers. But the newborn's and young infant's world is very different from ours: although many perceptual functions are present at or soon after birth "There is also a large literature showing the vital role played by experience in the effective use of perceptual information in *dealing* with the world and learning its meanings" (Gordon, 2004, pp. 38–39). In the next sections some possible ways in which innate (or prefunctional) representations might guide early learning, and some of the ways in which perception is affected and changed by experience and learning in infancy are discussed.

Face Perception

Is there an innate[1] representation of the human face?

We have known for some time that newborn infants have a preference for faces, especially when shown in their canonical upright orientation. Thus, Goren, Sarty, and Wu (1975), and Johnson and Morton (1991) present evidence that newborn infants are more likely to track (follow with their eyes) face-like patterns than non-face-like patterns. These and other findings have led to the view that newborn infants come into the world with some representation of faces: "there does seem to be some representational bias ... that the neonate brings to the learning situation for faces" (Karmiloff-Smith, 1996, p. 10). There have been differing accounts of the nature of this representational bias. One is that there is nothing "special" about faces, and newborns' responses to and preferences for face-like stimuli result from general structural characteristics of the immature visual system, such as a preference for more elements in the upper part of a stimulus (up-down asymmetry) (e.g., Cassia, Turati, & Simion, 2004; Turati, 2004; Turati, Simion, Milani, & Umilta, 2002). Johnson and Morton (1991) argued for the existence of an innate face-detecting device they call "Conspec" (short for conspecifics), which "perhaps comprises just three dark patches in a triangle, corresponding to eyes and mouth" (Pascalis et al., 1995,

Figure 2.13   Two of the patterns presented to newborns by Macchi Cassia et al. (2008): Facelike congruent (left) and Facelike noncongruent (right).

p. 80), and which serves to direct the newborn infant's visual attention to faces. This view is complemented by the finding that newborns also prefer the relationship between this triangular formation of three "blobs" when embedded in a triangular orientation of the external frame to a display where the external frame (but not the "blobs") is inverted (the congruent and incongruent patterns shown in Figure 2.13; Macchi Cassia, Valenza, Simion, & Leo, 2008).

These views suggest that the "face" template at the initial stage of development is rather crude. Other authors (e.g., Quinn & Slater, 2003) have argued that this representational bias is likely to be something more elaborate and face-specific than simply a tendency to attend to stimuli that possess nonspecific perceptual properties, such as three blobs in the location of eyes and mouth, "top-heaviness" or congruency, that is, properties that are not necessarily face-specific. This evidence is reviewed here.

Imitation.   It has been demonstrated that newborn (and older) infants will imitate a variety of facial gestures they see an adult model performing, and it seems probable that "mirror neurons" serve to mediate imitation (e.g., Jackson, Meltzoff, & Decety, 2006). One of the first published reports of imitation by newborn and older infants was by Meltzoff and Moore (1977), and there are now many reports of such imitation including the finding that newborn infants imitate the facial gestures produced by the first face they have ever seen (Reissland, 1988). Meltzoff (1995; see also chapter 11, this volume) suggests that "newborns begin life with some grasp of people" (p. 43) and that their ability to recognize when their facial behavior is being copied implies that "there is some representation of their own bodies" (p. 53). Infants can see the adult's face, but of course they cannot see their own. This means that in some way they have to match their own, unseen but felt, facial movements with the seen, but unfelt, facial movements of the adult. Meltzoff and Moore (1997, 2000) propose that they do this by a process of "active intermodal matching" (AIM) and that they have neural machinery that enables them to code others as "like me" (Meltzoff, 2004), and that this "is the starting point for social cognition, not its culmination" (Meltzoff, 2007, p. 126). A complementary view is that the motive for imitation in the newborn is that babies are born with a deep-seated need to communicate (e.g., Kokkinaki & Kugiumutzakis, 2000). Whatever the motives and mechanisms underlying facial imitation in the newborn the fact that they can imitate specific gestures such as mouth opening and tongue protrusion implies a fairly detailed facial representation.

Infants prefer attractive faces

Beauty provoketh thieves sooner than gold (Shakespeare, *As you like it*)

For thousands of years humans have been attracted to and beguiled by beautiful and attractive faces – "There are few more pleasurable sights than a beautiful face" (Rhodes, 2006, p. 200). Several experimenters have found that infants prefer to look at attractive faces when these are shown paired with faces judged by adults to be less attractive (e.g., Langlois et al., 1987; Langlois, Ritter, Roggman, & Vaughn, 1991; Samuels & Ewy, 1985; van Duuren, Kendell-Scott, & Stark, 2003). The "attractiveness effect" seems to be robust in that it is found for stimulus faces that are infant, adult, male, female, and of different races (African-American and Caucasian), and babies also preferred attractive to symmetrical faces when attractiveness and symmetry were varied independently (Samuels, Butterworth, Roberts, Graupner, & Hole, 1994). The effect has also been found with newborn infants, who averaged less than 3 days from birth at the time of testing (Slater et al. 1998). In newborns the effect is orientation-specific in that it is found with upright, but not inverted, faces (Slater, Quinn, Hayes, & Brown, 2000) and it is driven by attention to the internal features (Slater et al., 2000). Nevertheless, however detailed infants' facial representations may be, from birth on, it appears not to be specific to human faces, at least in early infancy, since 3- to 4-month-old human infants prefer attractive over unattractive domestic cat and wild cat (tiger) faces, as judged by adult humans! (Quinn, Kelly, Lee, Pascalis, & Slater, 2008).

There have been two interpretations of the "attractiveness effect", in terms of either prototype formation or innate representations. When several faces of the same gender, ethnicity and age are averaged or morphed, usually by computer, the resulting average or prototype is always perceived as attractive, and typically more attractive than the individual faces that make up the prototype. This effect was first noted in the early twentieth century (see Slater, 1998) and has since been verified on many occasions (e.g., Langlois & Roggman, 1990; Young & Bruce, 1998). The interpretation of the attractiveness effect that results from this finding is that attractive faces are seen as more "face-like" because they match more closely the prototype that infants have formed from their experience of seeing faces: thus, "Infants may prefer attractive or prototypical faces because prototypes are easier to classify as a face" (Langlois & Roggman, 1990, p. 119).

This interpretation is compromised by the finding that newborn babies, who will have seen very few faces, also show the attractiveness effect, together with the finding that infants younger than 3 months do not form face prototypes, at least in a laboratory setting (de Haan, Johnson, Maurer, & Perrett, 2001). Thus, it is possible that newborn infants' preference for attractive faces results from an innate representation of faces that infants bring into the world with them: Langlois and Roggman (1990) and Quinn and Slater (2003) describe this view, and an evolutionary account of attractiveness preferences is offered by Etcoff (2000).

Overview.   On balance we believe that the evidence supports the view that newborn infants enter the world with a specific representation of faces that is more elaborate than simply a tendency to attend to stimuli that possess three blobs in the location of eyes and mouth ("Conspec"). This view is supported by evidence that newborns imitate the facial gestures produced by the first face they have ever seen, by their preferences for attractive faces, and by their preference to look at faces that engage them in mutual gaze (Farroni, Csibra, Simion, & Johnson, 2002). It is possible that experiences *in utero* (for example, proprioceptive feedback from facial movements) contribute to the newborn infant's representation of faces, which might therefore result from innate evolutionary biases, in interaction with prenatal experiences. Meltzoff and Moore (1998) offer the premise that evolution has provided human infants with innate mental structures that serve as "discovery procedures" for subsequently developing more comprehensive and flexible concepts.

Early experience and learning

Whichever stance one takes about the mechanisms and representations underlying face perception in newborn infants there is substantial evidence that face perception is influenced and tuned by experience throughout infancy and beyond (e.g., Nelson, 2003; Simion, Leo, Turati, Valenza, & Barba, 2007). Experience has an impact within hours from birth: within the newborn period infants come to prefer their mother's face (e.g., Bushnell, 2003). However, neurological and behavioral evidence converge to suggest that the "face-space" is initially broad and becomes more specific or narrowed with development, in the sense that it becomes particularly attuned to the types of faces that are most often encountered. This "perceptual narrowing" is evident at least as early as 3 months: by this age there is evidence that there is some degree of specificity of perceptual and cortical processing of faces (de Haan, Pascalis, & Johnson, 2002; Halit, Csibra, Volein, & Johnson, 2004; Humphreys & Johnson, 2007).

Recent investigations that have focused on how infants respond to gender, species, and race information in faces have produced evidence that illustrates this perceptual narrowing over the first year of life. By 3 months of age infants who have a female as their primary caregiver (the vast majority of them!) prefer to look at female faces when these are shown paired with male faces, and they are also better able to discriminate between individual female faces. The role of experience in inducing this effect is confirmed by the complementary finding that infants reared with a male as their primary caregiver look more at male than female faces! (Quinn, Yahr, Kuhn, Slater, & Pascalis, 2002). Although we do not know for sure, presumably as infants have additional exposure to other-gender faces (usually male) this perceptual bias will diminish and perhaps disappear. Interestingly, this early female preference interacts with the other-race effect (see below) since it is found with own-race but not other-race faces (Quinn et al., 2008). A perceptual narrowing effect also occurs with other-species faces. Six-month-olds are equally adept at discriminating between individuals of own-race and those of a monkey species (*Macaca fascicularis*), see Figure 2.14. However, by 9 months human infants only showed evidence of discrimination between individuals of their own species, as did adults (Pascalis, de Haan, & Nelson, 2002).

Figure 2.14 By 9 months human infants only showed evidence of discrimination between individuals of their own species, as did adults. *Source*: Pascalis et al. (2002).

A similar finding is seen with the other-race effect (ORE) which is the well-established finding that individuals find it easier to discriminate between faces of their own race better than they can discriminate between faces of other races ("why do they all look the same?") The ORE has its origins in early infancy. When shown own-race faces paired with other-race faces newborn infants demonstrated no spontaneous preference for faces from their own ethnic group, however, 3-month-olds demonstrated a significant looking preference for own-race faces, a finding that applies to Caucasian, African, and Chinese infants (Bar-Haim, Ziv, Lamy, & Hodes, 2006; Kelly, Liu, et al., 2007; Kelly et al., 2005). These nascent origins of the ORE become more finely tuned as infancy progresses: 3-month-old Caucasian infants were able to discriminate between faces within their own facial group and within three other-race groups (African, Middle Eastern, and Chinese). However, after extensive continued experience with own-race faces and limited experience with other-race faces, by 9 months their discrimination was restricted to own-race faces (Kelly, Quinn, et al., 2007). A further illustration of perceptual narrowing with respect to the ORE is a study by Anzures, Quinn, Pascalis, Slater, and Lee (2009). They found that 9-month-old Caucasian infants could form discrete categories of Caucasian and Asian faces, each of which excluded instances of the other; however, while the infants could discriminate between different faces from the own-race category of Caucasian faces they could not discriminate between different faces from the other-race (Asian) category of faces.

Both the other-species and other-race effects are readily modified, at least in early infancy: 6- to 9-month-olds who were exposed to different individual same-species monkey faces no longer showed the other-species effect at 9 months (Pascalis et al., 2005); 3-month-old Caucasian infants familiarized with individual Asiatic faces showed a reduced other-race effect (Sangrigoli & de Schonen, 2004).

Collectively, these findings are a clear indication that facial input from the infant's environment shapes the face-processing system early in infancy, resulting in visual preferences for gender ("Ladies first," Ramsey, Langlois, & Marti, 2005), and for own-race faces, followed by greater recognition accuracy with own-race faces. This perceptual narrowing effect in face perception is paralleled by an equivalent native language effect (e.g., Werker, 1989), suggesting a more general change in neural networks involved in early perception and cognition (Pascalis et al., 2002; Scott, Pascalis, & Nelson, 2007; and see also chapters 3 and 14, this volume). The fact that these phenomena can be readily reversed by experience with different types of faces testifies to the remarkable plasticity of the developing visual system.

Object Perception

The visual world that we experience is complex, and one problem confronting the young infant is knowing how to segregate objects, and knowing when one object ends and another begins. Sometimes changes to color, contour, contrast, and so on, are found within a single object. For example, many animals have stripes, spots, different coloring; people wear different colored clothing, and there are natural color and contrast changes, perhaps from hair to forehead, from eyes to face, and so on, but these changes, of course, are all part of the same person.

Sometimes, similar appearance is found for different objects, as when two or more similar objects are perceived. Thus, there is no simple rule that specifies that an abrupt or gradual change in appearance indicates one or more objects. This means that the segregation of surfaces into objects is an important problem confronting the infant, and many of the rules that specify object composition and segregation have to be learned from experience. Object *segregation* is when the perceptual information indicates that two or more objects are present, and object *unity* is where we appreciate that there is only one object, despite breaks in the perceptual display: an example of the latter is where parts of an object are partly occluded by (a) nearer object(s).

Object segregation

The young infant's limitations have been described in studies of *object segregation*. Spelke and colleagues (e.g., Kestenbaum, Termine, & Spelke, 1987; Spelke, Breinlinger,

Jacobson, & Phillips, 1993) have found that 3-month-olds interpret displays in which two objects are adjacent and touching as being a single unit, even though the objects may be very different in their features. Needham and Baillargeon (1998) showed 4-month-olds a stationary display consisting of a yellow cylinder lying next to, and touching, a blue box, and presented them with two test displays. In both events a gloved hand came into view, grasped the cylinder, and moved it to one side, but in one, the move-apart condition, the box remained where it was, while in the other, the move-together condition, the box moved with the cylinder. On these test trials the 4-month-olds looked about equally at the two test events, suggesting that they were uncertain whether the cylinder and box were one or two separate units. Needham and Baillargeon found that if the infants saw either the box or the cylinder alone for as little as 5 or 15 seconds, these brief exposures were sufficient to indicate to the infants that the cylinder-and-box display consisted of two objects.

Needham and Baillargeon (1997) investigated conditions under which 8-month-olds detect objects as separate or interconnected. They found that when the infants saw two identical yellow octagons standing side by side they expected them to be connected: on test trials the infants appeared surprised (as measured by increased looking) when the octagons moved apart, but not when they moved together. Needham and Baillargeon found that this expectation could be readily changed by experience: a nice additional finding was that a prior demonstration that a thin blade could be passed between the identical octagons at the point of contact led the infants to expect them to be two objects. When the objects presented to the infants were a yellow cylinder and a blue box the infants appeared surprised when the objects moved *together*, but not when they moved apart. These findings are a clear demonstration that when the touching objects were identical 8-month-olds expected them to be one object, but when they were different in shape and color they expected them to be two objects.

The developmental story in terms of object segregation seems to be as follows. The young infant applies the rule "adjacency (touching) = a single unit/object"; by 4-months infants are uncertain, and experience plays a critical role in assisting them to parse the events they encounter. By 8 or 10 months the rule "different features = different objects" seems to be applied consistently, and has presumably been learned, or acquired, as a result of experience. One emerging theme from the literature is that very brief experiences can change infants' understanding of particular displays.

Perception of object unity

A clear difference has been found in infants' perception of *object unity* in the age range birth to 4 months. In a series of experiments on infants' understanding of partly occluded objects Kellman and his colleagues (Kellman & Spelke, 1983; Kellman, Spelke, & Short, 1986) habituated 4-month-olds to a stimulus (usually a rod) that moved back and forth behind a central occluder, so that only the top and bottom parts of the rod was visible (as in the upper part of Figure 2.15), and thus providing the Gestalt properties of *good continuation* and *similarity* of shape and color. On the post-habituation test trials the infants recovered attention to two rod pieces, but not to the complete rod (shown

Habituation display

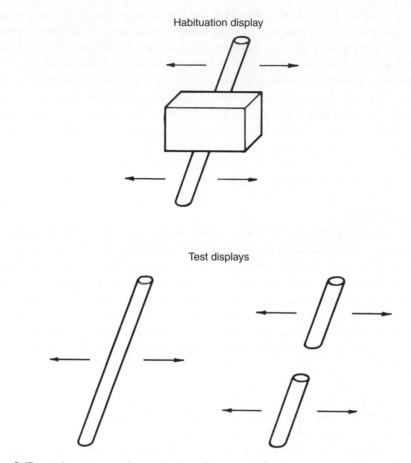

Test displays

Figure 2.15 Habituation and test displays shown to infants to test perception of object unity. During habituation the rod, and during test trials the rod and rod parts, moved back and forth undergoing common motion.

in the lower part of Figure 2.15) suggesting that they had been perceiving a complete rod during habituation and that the rod pieces were novel. However, when newborn babies have been tested with similar displays they look longer on the test trials at the complete rod (Slater, Johnson, Brown, & Badenoch, 1996; Slater, Johnson, Kellman, & Spelke, 1994; Slater et al., 1990). Thus, neonates appear not to perceive partly occluded objects as consisting of both visible and nonvisible portions. Rather, they seem to respond only to what they see directly.

The difference in the response patterns of newborn and 4-month-old infants suggests that some period of development may be necessary for perception of object unity to emerge in infants. Johnson and his colleagues (Johnson & Aslin, 1995; Johnson & Náñez, 1995) presented two-dimensional (computer-generated) rod-and-occluder displays, similar to the habituation display shown in Figure 2.15, to 2-month-olds. Johnson and Náñez found that, following habituation, the infants did not show a preference for either of the test stimuli, suggesting that they were perhaps not fully capable of perceiving object unity. Johnson and Aslin tested the hypothesis that "with additional visual information, infants at this young age would be more likely to perceive the unity of the rod parts" (S.P. Johnson, 1997, p. 10). They did this by testing their infants in three conditions, in each of which more of the rod was shown behind the occluder. In one of these conditions the occluder was simply made smaller in height; in another, a vertical gap was placed in the box; in the third, the occluder contained gaps. In all of these conditions the 2-month-olds now responded like 4-month-olds – that is, they showed preferences for the broken rod on the test trials, thereby indicating early perception of object unity (for further discussion of object unity, see chapter 6 this volume).

One interpretation of these findings is that an understanding of the completeness, or unity, of partly occluded objects begins around 2 months from birth. An alternative interpretation is that the apparent absence of object unity prior to 2 months of age is attributable to infants' inability to detect object motion until around 2 months (e.g., Braddick et al., 2005). Valenza, Leo, Gava, and Simion (2006) provided evidence that if infants were presented with static images of object unity events, that is, separate presentations of rod-and-box with the rod in different locations while the box remained stationary, they then perceived object unity in that they looked longer on test trials at two rod pieces. They suggest (p. 1819) "that newborns' failure to perceive the unity of a partly occluded object in past research may result from limits in infants' motion processing, rather than limits in object processing." These findings offer the intriguing possibility that perception of object unity may be present from birth and, hence, part of the innately provided repertoire of visual organizational abilities available to the immature visual system.

Emerging Questions, Paradigms, Issues

As research into infant visual perception has progressed, there has become less of a reliance on the "grand theories" that were dominant in the middle to late part of the last century. Many theoretical views have emerged which deal with specific areas of development, and these views have often given rise to lively debates and have inspired critical experiments. The aim in this section is briefly to discuss three such areas that are highly interrelated: the relationship between neural structures and visual development; the role of action in visual development; early representation and thinking.

The relationship between neural structures and visual development

Many different neural pathways are developing in the first year from birth (and later), and it is a truism to state that perceptual and conceptual development are constrained and facilitated by their development. There are now many theoretical views which attempt to understand the relationship between neural, perceptual, and cognitive growth. Some of the issues debated include: the role of subcortical and cortical mechanisms in early visual development; hemispheric specialization and its role in face perception; the development of a ventral "what" pathway and its role in object identification and visual recognition, and a dorsal "where" or "how" pathway involved in visually-guided action and spatial location (e.g., Farah, Rabinowitz, Quinn, & Liu, 2000; Johnson, Mareschal, & Csibra, 2008; Nelson, 2003; Milner & Goodale, 1995); the development of the frontal cortex and its role in problem solving. Space does not permit discussion of these, and other issues. An excellent introduction to the subdiscipline of developmental cognitive neuroscience is given by M.H. Johnson (1997), and see also chapter 9, this volume.

The role of action in visual development

All spatially coordinated behaviors, such as visual tracking, visually locating an auditory source, reaching, sitting, crawling, walking, require that action and perceptual information are coordinated. In an excellent review of this topic Bertenthal (1996) quotes J.J. Gibson: "We must perceive in order to move, but we must also move in order to perceive." It has become clear that newborn infants perform many actions that are regulated by perceptual information. These include visual tracking, orienting to sounds, and hand to mouth coordination. However, while perception and action appear coordinated from birth these systems clearly develop as infancy progresses, and new couplings appear. For example, Campos, Bertenthal, and Kermoian (1992) reported that prelocomotor infants show no fear, or wariness, of heights, whereas age-matched crawling infants of the same age showed a significant amount of fear. It seems that experience with crawling changes infants' sensitivity to depth, objects, and surfaces: detailed accounts and synthesis of the role of locomotor experiences in changing infants' perceptual, social, and cognitive development are given by Adolph and Joh (2007) and by Campos et al. (2000). Several researchers have speculated on the relation between perception and action. Bremner (1997) suggests that "development in infancy is very much to do with the formation of links between preexisting objective perception and emerging action, so that knowledge of the world implicit in perception eventually becomes explicit knowledge in the sense that it can be used to guide action."

Several researchers have found evidence of precocious perceptual abilities in young infants. For example, newborn infants have size and shape constancy; infants as young as 3 months can represent the continued existence of invisible objects, they appear to know that solid objects should not pass through each other, their perception and preferences for faces has already been shaped by experience; 2- to 4-month-old infants perceive object unity in that they are aware that a partly occluded object is connected or complete behind the occluder. These findings appear to be in contradiction to Piaget's view, which is that these abilities develop only gradually over infancy, after extensive experience of observing and manipulating objects. For example, he described several observations showing how his own children appeared to acquire concepts of size and shape constancy by observing the effects of objects being moved towards and away from them (Piaget, 1954, observations 86–91). There are at least three possible resolutions to these contradictory claims, all of which appear in the literature. One is simply to argue that Piaget was wrong; certainly "Empirical work over the past 25 years revealed a much richer innate state than Piaget assumed" (Meltzoff, 2004, p. 166). A second is to follow

Bremner and make the distinction between implicit (perceptual) and explicit (in action) knowledge. A third, conceptually related argument, is to suggest that in the perception experiments the infant is a "couch potato" and that "the methods used for studying young infants are inadequate for revealing all of the knowledge and mental processes that are necessary for problem solving." In addition to perceptual abilities "Problem solving also involves coordinating, guiding, monitoring, and evaluating a sequence of goal-directed actions" (Willatts, 1997, pp. 112–113).

Early representation and thinking

Several researchers have argued that infants, from a very early age, possess a core of physical and social knowledge, and they also make use of active representations to reason with this knowledge. For example, newborn infants' ability to imitate facial gestures suggests that they have some innately specified representation of faces. It has been argued that infants possess genetically determined "core knowledge" in five domains that represent objects, actions, number, space, and social partners (Kinzler & Spelke, 2007; Spelke & Kinzler, 2007). With respect to the physical world young infants appear to have knowledge about basic principles such as solidity, causality, trajectory, number, gravity, support, and so on. Research that demonstrates this understanding typically presents infants with "possible" and "impossible" events, where the latter violate one or other physical principle. When the infants look longer at the "impossible" event this is interpreted in terms of the infant *representing* the characteristics (or, e.g., continued existence) of the object(s), *reasoning* about the physical world, *understanding* the physical principle being tested, and being *surprised* at the violation. All the italicized words are characteristics of a conceptual system, and suggest that infants possess considerable physical knowledge from a very early age. Currently, however, these claims are highly controversial. Bogartz, Shinskey, and Speaker (1997), Haith (1998), and Rivera, Wakeley, and Langer (1999) are among those who argue that these sorts of interpretations are too rich, and imbue young infants with too much conceptual ability. Haith argues that "Almost without fail we can account for infants' longer looking at an inconsistent or impossible event ... in terms of well-established perceptual principles – novelty, familiarity, salience, and discrepancy" (p. 173). These conclusions and reinterpretations, of course, have been challenged (e.g., Spelke, 1998; Spelke & Kinzler, 2007). On balance we support a starting state nativist view, most prominently offered by Meltzoff (e.g., 2004), which argues that a capacity for representation is the starting point for infant development, not its culmination, and that the knowledge-base accumulated from learning and experience leads infants to develop coherent visual perceptions of people and things (for further discussion see chapter 6 this volume).

Conclusions

In the first section of this chapter evidence was presented suggesting that scanning abilities, acuity, contrast sensitivity, and color discrimination are limited in neonates.

However, as Hainline and Abramov (1992, pp. 40–41) put it, "While infants may not, indeed, see as well as adults do, they normally see well enough to function effectively in their roles as infants." Thus, despite their sensory limitations, it is clear that newborn infants have several means with which to begin to make sense of the visual world. The visual cortex, while immature, is functioning at birth, and it seems to be the case that newborn infants possess at least rudimentary form perception. Newborn infants can clearly remember what they see, and they demonstrate rapid learning about their perceived world.

One prerequisite for object knowledge is distinguishing proximal from distal stimuli. The proximal stimulus is the sensory stimulation – in this case, the pattern of light falling on the retina. The distal stimulus consists of what is represented by the pattern of stimulation – the object itself. Neonates distinguish proximal from distal stimuli when they demonstrate size and shape constancy: the object is perceived accurately, despite changes to its retinal image. The picture of visual perception in early infancy that is emerging is complex: some aspects of visual perception are very immature, whereas others appear to be remarkably advanced at birth. Several lines of evidence converge to suggest that infants are born with an innate preference for, and representation of, the human face. It is clear that the young infant's visual world is, to a large extent, structured and coherent as a result of the intrinsic organization of the visual system.

However well organized the visual world of the young infant may be, it lacks the familiarity, meaning, and associations that characterize the world of the mature perceiver. Inevitably, some types of visual organization take time to develop. An appreciation of the underlying unity, coherence, and persistence of occluded objects is not present at birth, and a proper understanding of the physical properties of objects emerges only slowly as infancy progresses. As development proceeds, the innate and developing organizational mechanisms are added to by experience and this knowledge base assists the infant in making sense of the perceived world.

Acknowledgments

The authors' research that is described in this chapter has been supported by grants from the ESRC (RC00232466, R000235288, R000237709) and NIH grant RO1 HD046526.

Note

1. The term "innate" refers to behaviors and abilities that are inherited. Thus, visual abilities that are present in the newborn infant are likely to be innate. In the case of face perception it is possible that proprioceptive feedback from its own facial and body movements *in utero* contribute to the newborn infant's facial representation. An alternative term, prefunctional, meaning present in at least some rudimentary form at birth, avoids the potential pitfalls of calling something "innate," but for present purposes the term innate is used without any assumption that we know how the ability(ies) originated.

Further Reading

Research into visual perception is carried out by many thousands of researchers, and in this chapter it is only possible to give a brief outline of its development in infancy. Many related topics are covered in other chapters in this volume, and additional readings that expand on the topics covered in this chapter are given below:

Atkinson, J. (2000). *The developing visual brain.* Oxford: Oxford University Press.

Gordon, I. E. (2004). *Theories of visual perception* (3rd ed.). Hove, East Sussex: Psychology Press.

Kellman, P. J., & Arterberry, M. E. (1998). *The cradle of knowledge: Development of perception in infancy.* Cambridge, MA, London: MIT Press.

Oakes, L. M., Cashon, C. H., Casasola, M., & Rakison, D. H. (Eds.). (2010). *Early perceptual and cognitive development.* Oxford: Oxford University Press.

Pascalis, O., & Slater, A. (Eds.). (2003). *The development of face processing in infancy and early childhood.* New York: Nova Science Publishers, Inc.

Simion, F., & Butterworth, G. (Eds.). (1998). *The development of sensory, motor and cognitive capacities in early infancy.* Hove, UK: Psychology Press.

Vital-Durand, F., Atkinson, J., & Braddick, O. J. (Eds.). (1996). *Infant vision.* Oxford, New York, Tokyo: Oxford University Press.

References

Abramov, I., Gordon, J., Hendrickson, A., Hainline, L., Dobson, V., & LaBossiere, E. (1982). The retina of the newborn human infant. *Science, 5,* 449–452.

Adolph, K. E., & Joh, A. S. (2007). Motor development: How infants get into the act. In A. Slater & M. Lewis (Eds.), *Introduction to infant development* (pp. 63–80). Oxford: Oxford University Press.

Anzures, G., Quinn, P. C., Pascalis, O., Slater, A. M., & Lee, K. (2009). Racial categorization of faces in infancy: A new other-race effect. *Developmental Science,* available at: www3.interscience.wiley.com/search/allsearch?mode=viewselected&product=journal&ID=122544741&view_selected.x=25&view_selected.y=8&view_selected=view_selected

Arterberry, M. E., & Yonas, A. (2000). Perception of three-dimensional shape specified by optic flow by 8-week-old infants. *Perception and Psychophysics, 62,* 550–556.

Aslin, R. N. (1981). Development of smooth pursuit in human infants. In D. F. Fisher, R. A. Monty & J. W. Senders (Eds.), *Eye movements: cognition and visual perception* (pp. 31–51). Hillsdale, NJ: Erlbaum.

Aslin, R. N., & Salapatek, P. (1975). Saccadic localization of visual targets by the very young human infant. *Perception and Psychophysics, 17,* 293–302.

Atkinson, J. (1984). Human visual development over the first six months of life: A review and a hypothesis. *Human Neurobiology, 3,* 61–74.

Atkinson, J. (2000). *The developing visual brain.* Oxford: Oxford University Press.

Atkinson, J., & Braddick, O. (1981). Development of optokinetic nystagmus in infants: An indicator of cortical binocularity? In D. F. Fisher, R. A. Monty & J. W. Senders (Eds.), *Eye movements: Cognition and visual perception* (pp. 53–64). Hillsdale, NJ: Erlbaum.

Atkinson, J., & Braddick, O. (1989). Development of basic visual functions. In A. Slater & G. Bremner (Eds.), *Infant development* (pp. 7–41). Hove, UK: Erlbaum.

Atkinson, J., Hood, B. M., Wattam-Bell, J., Anker, S., & Tricklebank, J. (1988). Development of orientation discrimination in infancy. *Perception, 17*, 587–595.

Bar-Haim, Y., Ziv, T., Lamy, D., & Hodes, R. M. (2006). Nature and nurture in own–race face processing. *Psychological Science, 17*, 159–163.

Bertenthal, B. I. (1993). Infants' perception of biomechanical motions: Intrinsic image and knowledge-based constraints. In C. Granrud (Ed.), *Visual perception and cognition in infancy*. Hillsdale, NJ: Erlbaum.

Bertenthal, B. I. (1996). Origins and early development of perception, action, and representation. *Annual Review of Psychology, 47*, 431–459.

Bertenthal, B.I., & Davis, P. (1998). *Dynamical pattern analysis predicts recognition and discrimination of biomechanical motions*. Paper presented at the annual meeting of the Psychonomic Society, Chicago.

Birch, E. E. (1993). Stereopsis in infants and its developmental relation to visual acuity. In K. Simons (Ed.), *Early visual development: Normal and abnormal* (pp. 224–236). Oxford: Oxford University Press.

Bogartz, R. S., Shinskey, J. L., & Speaker, C. (1997). Interpreting infant looking. *Developmental Psychology, 33*, 408–422.

Bower, T. G. R. (1966). The visual world of infants. *Scientific American, 215*(6), 80–92.

Braddick, O. J., & Atkinson, J. (1983). Some recent findings on the development of human binocularity: A review. *Behavioural Brain Research, 10*, 71–80.

Braddick, O., Birtles, D., Wattam-Bell, J., & Atkinson, J. (2005). Motion- and orientation-specific cortical responses in infancy. *Vision Research, 45*, 3169–3179.

Bremner, J.G. (1994). *Infancy*. Oxford: Blackwell.

Bremner, J.G. (1997). From perception to cognition. In G. Bremner, A. Slater & G. Butterworth (Eds.), *Infant development: Recent advances* (pp. 55–74). Hove: Psychology Press.

Bronson, G. W. (1974). The postnatal growth of visual capacity. *Child Development, 45*, 873–890.

Bruggeman, H., Yonas, A., & Konczak, J. (2007). The processing of linear perspective and binocular information for action and perception. *Neuropsychologia, 45*, 1420–1426.

Bushnell, I. W. R. (2003). Newborn face recognition. In O. Pascalis & A. Slater (Eds.), *The development of face processing in infancy and early childhood* (pp. 41–53). New York: Nova Science Publishers.

Campos, J. J., Anderson, D. I., Barbu-Roth, M. A., Hubbard, E. M., Hertenstein, M. J., & Witherington, D. (2000). Travel broadens the mind. *Infancy, 1*, 149–219.

Campos, J. J., Bertenthal, B. I., & Kermoian, R. (1992). Early experience and emotional development: The emergence of wariness of heights. *Psychological Science, 3*, 61–64.

Cassia, V. M., Turati, C., & Simion, F. (2004). Can a nonspecific bias toward top-heavy patterns explain newborns' face preference? *Psychological Science, 15*, 379–383.

Clavedetscher, J. E., Brown, A. M., Ankrum, C., & Teller, D. Y. (1988). Spectral Sensitivity and chromatic discriminations in 3- and 7-week-old human infants. *Journal of the Optical Society of America, A, 5*, 2092–2105.

Cohen, L. B., & Younger, B. A. (1984). Infant perception of angular relations. *Infant Behavior and Development, 7*, 37–47.

de Haan, M., Johnson, M. A., Maurer, D., & Perrett, D. I. (2001). Recognition of individual faces and average face prototypes by 1- and 3-month-old infants. *Cognitive Development, 16*, 659–678.

de Haan, M., Pascalis, O., & Johnson, M. H. (2002). Specialization of neural mechanisms underlying face recognition in human infants. *Journal of Cognitive Neuroscience, 14*, 199–209.

Drover, J. R., Earle, A. E., Courage, M. L., & Adams, R. J. (2002). Improving the effectiveness of the infant contrast sensitivity card procedure. *Optometry and Vision Science, 79*, 52–29.

Etcoff, N. (2000). *Survival of the prettiest: The science of beauty*. New York: Doubleday.

Farah, M. J., Rabinowitz, C., Quinn, G. E., & Liu, G. T. (2000). Early commitment of neural substrates for face recognition. *Cognitive Neuropsychology, 17*, 117–123.

Farroni, T., Csibra, G., Simion, G., & Johnson, M.H. (2002). Eye contact detection in humans from birth. *Proceedings of the National Academy of Sciences, USA, 99*, 9602–9605.

Farroni, T., Valenza, E., Simion, F., & Umilta, C. (2000). Configural processing at birth: Evidence for perceptual organisation. *Perception, 29*, 355–372.

Ghim, H. -R. (1990). Evidence for perceptual organization in infants: Perception of subjective contours by young infants. *Infant Behavior and Development, 13*, 221–248.

Gibson, E. J. (1969). *Principles of perceptual learning and development.* New York: Appleton-Century-Crofts.

Gibson, J. J. (1950). *The perception of the visual world.* Boston, MA: Houghton Mifflin.

Gibson, J. J. (1966). *The senses considered as perceptual systems.* Boston, MA: Houghton Mifflin.

Gibson, J. J. (1979). *The ecological approach to visual perception.* Boston, MA: Houghton Mifflin.

Gordon, I. E. (2004). *Theories of visual perception* (3rd ed.). New York: Wiley.

Goren, C. C., Sarty, M., & Wu, P. Y. K. (1975). Visual following and pattern discrimination of face-like stimuli by newborn infants. *Pediatrics, 56*, 544–549.

Granrud, C. E. (2006). Size constancy in infants: 4-month-olds' responses to physical versus retinal size. *Journal of Experimental Psychology: Human Perception and Performance, 32*, 1398–1404.

Hainline, L. (1998). The development of basic visual abilities. In A. Slater (Ed.), *Perceptual development: Visual, auditory and speech perception in infancy.* Hove: Psychology Press.

Hainline, L., & Abramov, I. (1985). Saccades and small-field optokinetic nystagmus in infants. *Journal of the American Optometric Association, 56*, 620–626.

Hainline, L., & Riddell, P. M. (1995). Binocular alignment and vergence in early infancy. *Vision Research, 35*, 3229–3236.

Hainline, L., Riddell, P. M., Grose-Fifer, J., & Abramov, I. (1992). Development of accommodation and convergence in infancy. *Behavioural Brain Research, 49*, 33–50.

Haith, M. M. (1998). Who put the cog in infant cognition? Is rich interpretation too costly? *Infant Behavior and Development, 21*, 167–179.

Halit, H., Csibra, G., Volein, A., & Johnson, M. H. (2004). Face-sensitive cortical processing in early infancy. *Journal of Child Psychology and Psychiatry, 45*, 1228–1234.

Hamer, R. D. Alexander, K. R., & Teller, D. Y. (1982). Rayleigh discrimination in young human infants. *Vision Research, 22*, 575–587.

Hayden, A., Bhatt, R. S., & Quinn, P. C. (2006). Infants' sensitivity to uniform connectedness as a cue for perceptual organization. *Psychonomic Bulletin and Review, 13*, 257–261.

Hebb, D. O. (1949). *The organization of behavior.* New York: Wiley.

Held, R. (1985). Binocular vision – Behavioral and neuronal development. In J. Mehler and R. Fox (Eds.), *Neonate cognition: Beyond the blooming, buzzing confusion.* Hillsdale, NJ: Erlbaum.

Hoffman, K. -P. (1981). Neuronal responses related to optokinetic nystagmus in the cat's nucleus of the optic tract. In A. Fuchs and W. Becker (Eds.), *Progress in oculomotor research* (pp 443–454). New York: Elsevier.

Hubel, D. H., & Wiesel, T. N. (1965). Binocular interactions in striate cortex of kittens raised with artificial squint. *Journal of Neurophysiology, 28*, 1041–1059.

Humphreys, K., & Johnson, M. H. (2007). The development of "face-space" in infancy. *Visual Cognition, 15*, 578–598.

Jackson, P. L., Meltzoff, A. N., & Decety, J. (2006). Neural circuits involved in imitation and perspective-taking. *Neuroimage, 31*, 429–439.

James, W. (1890). *Principles of psychology.* New York: Henry Holt.

Johannson, G. (1973). Visual perception of biological motion and a model for its analysis. *Perception and Psychophysics, 14*, 201–210.

Johnson, M. H. (1990). Cortical maturation and the development of visual attention in early infancy. *Journal of Cognitive Neuroscience, 2*, 81–95.

Johnson, M. H. (1997). *Developmental cognitive neuroscience.* Oxford, UK and Malden, MA: Blackwell.

Johnson, M. H. (2005). Subcortical face processing. *Nature Reviews Neuroscience, 6*, 766–774.

Johnson, M. H., Mareschal, D., & Csibra, G. (2008). The development and integration of dorsal and ventral visual pathways in object processing. In C. A. Nelson & M. Luciana (Eds.), *Handbook of developmental cognitive neuroscience* (2nd ed., pp. 467–478). Cambridge: MIT Press.

Johnson, M. H., & Morton, J. (1991). *Biology and cognitive development: the case for face recognition.* Oxford: Blackwell.

Johnson, S. P. (1997). Young infants' perception of object unity: Implications for development of attentional and cognitive skills. *Current Directions in Psychological Science, 6*, 5–11.

Johnson, S. P., and Aslin, R. N. (1995). Perception of object unity in 2-month-old infants. *Developmental Psychology, 31*, 739–745.

Johnson, S. P., & Náñez, J. E. (1995). Young infants' perception of object unity in two-dimensional displays. *Infant Behavior and Development, 18*, 133–143.

Kanizsa, G. (1979). *Organization in vision: Essays on Gestalt perception.* New York: Praeger.

Karmiloff-Smith, A. (1996). The connectionist infant: Would Piaget turn in his grave? *SRCD Newsletter*, Fall, 1–3, 10.

Kavsek, M., & Yonas, A. (2006). The perception of moving subjective contours by 4-month-old infants. *Perception, 35*, 215–227.

Kellman, P. J., and Spelke, E. S. (1983). Perception of partly occluded objects in infancy. *Cognitive Psychology, 15*, 483–524.

Kellman, P. J., Spelke, E. S., and Short, K. R. (1986). Infant perception of object unity from translatory motion in depth and vertical translation. *Child Development, 57*, 72–86.

Kelly, D. J., Liu, S. Y., Ge, L., Quinn, P. C., Slater, A. M., Lee, K., Liu, Q. Y., & Pascalis, O. (2007). Cross-race preferences for same-race faces extend beyond the African versus Caucasian contrast in 3-month-old infants. *Infancy, 11*, 87–95.

Kelly, D. J., Quinn, P. C., Slater, A. M., Lee, K., Ge, L., & Pascalis, O. (2007). The other-race effect develops during infancy: Evidence of perceptual narrowing. *Psychological Science, 18*, 1084–1089.

Kelly, D. J., Quinn, P. C., Slater, A. M., Lee, K, Gibson, A., Smith, M., Ge, L. Z., & Pascalis, O. (2005). Three-month-olds, but not newborns, prefer own-race faces. *Developmental Science, 8*, F31–F36.

Kelly, J. P., Borchert, K., & Teller, D.Y. (1997).The development of chromatic and achromatic contrast sensitivity in infancy as tested with the sweep VEP. *Vision Research, 37*, 2057–2072.

Kestenbaum, R., Termine, N., & Spelke, E. S. (1987). Perception of objects and object boundaries by 3-month-olds. *British Journal of Developmental Psychology, 5*, 367–383.

Kinzler, K. D., & Spelke, E. S. (2007). Core systems in human cognition. *Progress in brain research: From action to cognition, 164*, 257–264.

Kokkinaki, T., & Kugiumutzakis, G. (2000). Basic aspects of vocal imitation in infant-parent interaction during the first 6 months. *Journal of Reproductive and Infant Psychology, 18*, 173–187.

Langlois, J. H., Ritter, J. M., Roggman, L. A., & Vaughn, L. S. (1991). Facial diversity and infant preferences for attractive faces. *Developmental Psychology, 27*, 79–84.

Langlois, J., & Roggman, L. A. (1990). Attractive faces are only average. *Psychological Science, 1*, 115–121.

Langlois, J. H., Roggman, L. A., Casey, R. J., Ritter, J. M., Rieser-Danner, L. A., & Jenkins, V. Y. (1987). Infant preferences for attractive faces: rudiments of a stereoptype? *Developmental Psychology, 23*, 363–369.

Macchi Cassia, V., Valenza, E., Simion, F., & Leo, I. (2008). Congruency as a nonspecific perceptual property contributing to newborns' face preference. *Child Development, 79*, 807–820.

Mason, A. J. S., Braddick, O. J., & Wattam-Bell, J. (2003). Motion coherence thresholds in infants – different tasks identify at least two distinct motion systems. *Vision Research, 43*, 1149–1157.

Mason, A. J. S., Braddick, O. J., Wattam-Bell, J., & Atkinson, J. (2001). Directional motion asymmetry in infant VEPs – which direction? *Vision Research, 41*, 201–211.

Meltzoff, A. N. (1995). Infants' understanding of people and things: From body imitation to folk psychology. In J. L. Bermudez, A. Marcel & N. Eilan (Eds.), *The body and the self* (pp. 43–69). Cambridge, MA, and London: MIT Press.

Meltzoff, A. N. (2004). The case for developmental cognitive science: Theories of people and things. In G. Bremner & A. Slater (Eds.), *Theories of infant development* (pp. 145–173). Oxford: Blackwell.

Meltzoff, A. N. (2007). "Like me": A foundation for social cognition. *Developmental Science, 10*, 126–134.

Meltzoff, A. N., & Moore, M. K. (1977). Imitation of facial and manual gestures by human neonates. *Science, 198*, 75–78.

Meltzoff, A. N., & Moore, M. K. (1997). Explaining facial imitation: A theoretical model. *Early Development and Parenting, 6*, 179–182.

Meltzoff, A. N., & Moore, M. K. (1998). Object representation, identity, and the paradox of early permanence: steps toward a new framework. *Infant Behavior and Development, 21*, 201–235.

Meltzoff, A. N., & Moore, M. K. (2000). Resolving the debate about early imitation. In D. Muir & A. Slater (eds.), *Infant development: The essential readings* (pp. 176–181). Oxford, UK and Malden, MA: Blackwell.

Milner, A. D., & Goodale, M. A. (1995). *The visual brain in action.* Oxford: Oxford University Press.

Mohn, G. (1989). The development of binocular and monocular optokinetic nystagmus in human infants. *Investigative Ophthalmology and Visual Science (Suppl.), 40*, 49.

Needham, A., & Baillargeon, R. (1997). Object segregation in 8-month-old infants. *Cognition, 62*, 121–149.

Needham, A., & Baillargeon, R. (1998). Effects of prior experience on 4.5-month-old infants' object segregation. *Infant Behavior and Development, 21*, 1–24.

Nelson, C. A. (2003). The development of face recognition reflects an experience–expectant and activity-dependent process. In O. Pascalis & A. Slater (Eds.), *The development of face processing in infancy and early childhood* (pp. 79–97). New York: Nova Science.

Norcia, A. M., Garcia, H., Humphry, R., Holmes, A., Hamer, R. D., & Orel-Bixler, D. (1991).Anomolous motion VEPs in infants and in infantile esotropia. *Investigative Ophthalmology and Visual Science, 32*, 436–439.

Otsuka, Y., Kanazawa, S., & Yamaguchi, M. K. (2004). The effect of support ratio on infants' perception of illusory contours. *Perception, 33*, 807–816.

Pascalis, O., de Haan, M., & Nelson, C. A. (2002). Is face processing species-specific during the first year of life? *Science, 296*, 1321–1323.

Pascalis, O., de Schonen, S., Morton, J., Deruelle, C., & Fabre-Grenet, M. (1995). Mother's face recognition by neonates: A replication and an extension. *Infant Behavior and Development, 18*, 79–85.

Pascalis, O., Scott, L. S., Kelly, D. J., Shannon, R. W., Nicholson, E., Coleman, M., & Nelson, C. A. (2005). Plasticity of face processing in infancy. *Proceedings of the National Academy of Sciences, USA, 102*, 5297–5300.

Peeples, D. R., & Teller, D. Y. (1975). Color vision and brightness discrimination in 2-month-old human infants. *Science, 189,* 1102–1103.

Peterzell, D. H., & Teller, D. Y. (1996). Individual differences in contrast sensitivity functions: The coarsest spatial channels. *Vision Research, 36,* 3077–3085.

Piaget, J. (1953). *The origins of intelligence in the child.* London: Routledge and Kegan Paul.

Piaget, J. (1954). *The construction of reality in the child.* New York: Basic Books.

Quinn, P. C., Bhatt, R. S., & Hayden, A. (2008). What goes with what? Development of perceptual grouping in infancy. *Psychology of Learning and Motivation: Advances in Research and Theory, 49,* 105–146.

Quinn, P. C., Brown, C. R., & Streppa, M. L. (1997). Perceptual organization of complex visual configurations by young infants. *Infant Behavior and Development, 20,* 35–46.

Quinn, P. C., Burke, S., & Rush, A. (1993). Part-whole perception in early infancy: Evidence for perceptual grouping produced by lightness similarity. *Infant Behavior and Development, 16,* 19–42.

Quinn, P. C., Kelly, D. J., Lee, K., Pascalis, O., & Slater, A. (2008). Preference for attractive faces extends beyond conspecifics. *Developmental Science, 11,* 76–83.

Quinn, P. C., & Slater, A. (2003). Face perception at birth and beyond. In O. Pascalis & A. Slater (Eds.), *The development of face processing in infancy and early childhood* (pp. 3–11). New York: Nova Science.

Quinn, P. C., Uttley, L., Lee, K., Gibson, A., Smith, M., Slater, A. M., & Pascalis, O. (2008). Infant preference for female faces occurs for same– but not other–race faces. *Journal of Neuropsychology, 2,* 15–26.

Quinn, P. C., Yahr, J., Kuhn, A., Slater, A., & Pascalis, O. (2002). Representation of the gender of human faces by infants: A preference for female. *Perception, 31,* 1109–1121.

Ramsey, J. L., Langlois, J. H., & Marti, N. C. (2005). Infant categorization of faces: Ladies first. *Developmental Review, 25,* 212–246.

Reissland, N. (1988). Neonatal imitation in the first hour of life: Observations in Rural Nepal. *Developmental Psychology, 24,* 464–469.

Rhodes, G. (2006). The evolutionary psychology of facial beauty. *Annual Review of Psychology, 57,* 199–226.

Riddell, P. M., Horwood, A. M., Houston, S. M., & Turner, J. E. (1999). The response to prism deviation in human infants. *Current Biology, 9,* 1050–1052.

Riddell, P. M., Ladenheim, B., Mast, J., Catalano, T., Nobile, R., & Hainline, L. (1998). Comparison of measures of visual acuity in infants: Teller acuity cards and sweep visual evoked potentials. *Optometry and Vision Science, 74,* 702–707.

Rivera, S. M., Wakeley, A., & Langer, J. (1999). The drawbridge phenomenon: Representational reasoning or perceptual preference? *Developmental Psychology, 35,* 427–435.

Samuels, C. A., & Ewy, R. (1985). Aesthetic perception of faces during infancy. *British Journal of Developmental Psychology, 3,* 221–228.

Samuels, C. A., Butterworth, G., Roberts, T., Graupner, L., & Hole, G. (1994). Babies prefer attractiveness to symmetry. *Perception, 23,* 823–831.

Sangrigoli, S., & de Schonen, S. (2004). Recognition of own-race and other-race faces by three-month-olds. *Journal of Child Psychology and Psychiatry, 45,* 1219–1227.

Scott, L. S., Pascalis, O., & Nelson, C. A. (2007). A domain general theory of the development of perceptual discrimination. *Current Directions in Psychological Science, 16,* 197–201.

Sen, M. G., Yonas, A., & Knill, D. C. (2001). Development of infants' sensitivity to surface contour information for spatial layout. *Perception, 30,* 167–176.

Simion, F., Leo, I., Turati, C., Valenza, E., & Barba, B. D. (2007). How face specialization emerges in the first months of life. *Progress in Brain Research, 164,* 169–185.

Simion, F., Regolin, L., & Bulf, H. (2008). A predisposition for biological motion in the newborn baby. *Proceedings of the National Academy of Sciences, USA, 105*, 809–813.

Slater, A. (1995). Visual perception and memory at birth. *Advances in Infancy Research, 9*, 107–162.

Slater, A. (1998). The competent infant: Innate organization and early learning in infant visual perception. In A. Slater (Ed.), *Perceptual development: visual, auditory and speech perception in early infancy* (pp. 105–130). London: Psychology Press.

Slater, A., Bremner, J. G., Johnson, S. P., Sherwood, P., Hayes, R., & Brown, E. (2000). Newborn infants' preference for attractive faces: the role of internal and external facial features. *Infancy, 1*, 265–274.

Slater, A., Johnson, S. P., Brown, E., and Badenoch, M. (1996). The roles of texture and occluder size on newborn infants' perception of partly occluded objects. *Infant Behavior and Development, 19*, 145–148.

Slater, A., Johnson, S. P., Kellman, P. J., & Spelke, E. S. (1994). The role of three-dimensional depth cues in infants' perception of partly occluded objects. *Early Development and Parenting, 3*, 187–191.

Slater, A., Mattock, A., & Brown, E. (1990). Size constancy at birth: Newborn infants' responses to retinal and real size. *Journal of Experimental Child Psychology, 49*, 314–322.

Slater, A., Mattock, A., Brown, E., & Bremner, J. G. (1991). Form perception at birth: Cohen and Younger revisited. *Journal of Experimental Child Psychology, 51*, 395–405

Slater, A., Mattock, A., Brown, E., Burnham, D., & Young, A. W. (1991). Visual processing of stimulus compounds in newborn infants. *Perception, 20*, 29–33.

Slater, A. M., & Morison, V. (1985). Shape constancy and slant perception at birth. *Perception, 14*, 337–344.

Slater, A., Morison, V., & Somers, M. (1988). Orientation discrimination and cortical function in the human newborn. *Perception, 17*, 597–602.

Slater, A., Morison, V., Somers, M., Mattock, A., Brown, E., and Taylor, D. (1990). Newborn and older infants' perception of partly occluded objects. *Infant Behavior and Development, 13*, 33–49.

Slater, A. M., Morison, V., Town, C., & Rose, D. (1985). Movement perception and identity constancy in the new-born baby. *British Journal of Developmental Psychology, 3*, 211–220.

Slater, A., Quinn, P., Hayes, R., & Brown, E. (2000). The role of facial orientation in newborn infants' preference for attractive faces. *Developmental Science, 3*, 181–185.

Slater, A., Rose, D., & Morison, V. (1984). Newborn infants' perception of similarities and differences between two- and three-dimensional stimuli. *British Journal of Developmental Psychology, 2*, 287–294.

Slater, A., von der Schulenburg, C., Brown, E., Badenoch, M., Butterworth, G., Parsons, S., & Samuels, C. (1998). Newborn infants prefer attractive faces. *Infant Behavior and Development, 21*, 345–354.

Spelke, E. S. (1998). Nativism, empiricism, and the origins of knowledge. *Infant Behavior and Development, 21*, 181–200.

Spelke, E. S., Breinlinger, K., Jacobson, K., & Phillips, A. (1993). Gestalt relations and object perception: A developmental study. *Perception, 22*, 1483–1501.

Spelke, E. S., & Kinzler, K. D. (2007). Core knowledge. *Developmental Science, 10*, 89–96.

Sugita, Y. (2004). Experience in early infancy is indispensable for colour perception. *Current Biology, 14*, 1267–1271.

Teller, D. Y. (1982). Scotopic vision, color vision, and stereopsis in infants. *Current Eye Research, 2*, 199–210.

Teller, D. Y. (1997). First glances: The vision of infants. *Investigative Ophthalmology and Visual Science, 38*, 2183–2203.

Thorn, F., Gwiazda, J., Cruz, A. A. V., Bauer, J. A., & Held, R. (1994). The development of eye alignment, convergence and sensory binocularity in young infants. *Investigative Ophthalmology and Visual Science, 35,* 544–553.

Turati, C. (2004). Why faces are not special to newborns: An alternative account of the face preference. *Current Directions in Psychological Science, 13,* 5–8.

Turati, C., Simion, F., Milani, I., & Umilta, C. (2002). Newborn preference for faces: What is crucial? *Developmental Psychology, 38,* 875–882.

Turner, J. E., Horwood, A. M., Houston, S. M., & Riddell, P. M. (2002). The development of the AC/A ratio over the first year of life. *Vision Research, 42,* 2521–2532.

Valenza, E., Leo, I., Gava, L., & Simion, F. (2006). Perceptual completion in newborn human infants. *Child Development, 77,* 1810–1821.

van Duuren, M., Kendell-Scott, L., & Stark, N. (2003). Early aesthetic choices: Infant preferences for attractive premature infant faces. *International Journal of Behavioral Development, 27,* 212–219.

Varner, D., Cook, J. E., Schneck, M. E., McDonald, M., & Teller, D. Y. (1985). Tritan discriminations by 1- and 2-month-old human infants. *Vision Research, 2,* 821–831.

Vital-Durand, F., Atkinson, J., & Braddick, O. (Eds.). (1996). *Infant vision.* Oxford: Oxford University Press.

Volkmann, F. C., & Dobson, V. (1976).Infant responses of ocular fixation to moving visual stimuli. *Journal of Experimental Child Psychology, 22,* 86–99.

Weinacht, S., Kind, C., Schulte Monting, J., & Gottlob, I. (1999).Visual development in preterm and full–term infants: A prospective masked study. *Investigative Ophthalmology and Visual Science, 40,* 346–353.

Werker, J. (1989). Becoming a native listener. *American Scientist, 77,* 54–59.

White, L. E., Coppola, D. M., & Fitzpatrick, D. (2001). The contribution of sensory experience to the maturation of orientation selectivity in ferret visual cortex. *Nature, 411,* 1049–1052.

Willatts, P. (1997). Beyond the "couch potato" infant: How infants use their knowledge to regulate action, solve problems, and achieve goals. In G. Bremner, A. Slater & G. Butterworth (Eds.), *Infant perception: Recent advances* (pp. 109–136). Hove: Psychology Press.

Yin, R. K. (1969). Looking at upside-down faces. *Journal of Experimental Psychology, 81,* 141–145.

Young, A., & Bruce, V. (1998). Pictures at an exhibition – The science of the face. *Psychologist, 11,* 120–125.

Yonas, A., Cleaves, N., and Pettersen, L. (1978). Development of sensitivity to pictorial depth. *Science, 200,* 77–79.

Yonas, A., & Granrud, C. E. (1985). Development of visual space perception in young infants. In J. Mehler and R. Fox (Eds.), *Neonate cognition: Beyond the blooming, buzzing confusion* (pp. 45–67). Hillsdale, NJ: Erlbaum.

Yuodelis, C., & Hendrickson, A. (1986). A qualitative and quantitative analysis of the human fovea during development. *Vision Research, 26,* 847–855.

Zusne, L. (1970). *Visual perception of form.* New York: Academic Press.

3

Auditory Development

Denis Burnham and Karen Mattock

The Nature of the Auditory System

Auditory and visual senses

Vision is often thought to be the most important sense modality for humans, and visual perception is often taken as the model by which to judge all our perceptual systems. Here we draw your attention to the pervasive benefits of audition that transcend those of vision. Consider, for example, that audition does not rely upon the ears being actively orientated to the sense data and human ears cannot be closed, or audition turned off, in any comprehensive manner, so auditory information provides a constant backdrop to our perceptual experience. Moreover, sound waves can permeate solid media, which, along with the early prenatal development of the auditory system (Querleu & Renard, 1981), means that auditory information is the earliest *ex utero* information to be perceived by the fetus, with significant influences on infants' later development (DeCasper & Fifer, 1980; Mehler et al., 1988).

Given this pervasiveness, why might a bias to vision have become established in psychological research? In earlier (precomputer) days, it was difficult to manipulate dynamic stimuli, so researchers tended to concentrate on static stimuli – such as printed nonsense words controlled on various dimensions (Ebbinghaus, 1964), or variations of color using the Munsell (1912) classification system. Such static stimuli were then presented naturally or in a tachistoscope for predetermined short periods, with reaction times measured via participants' responses on mechanical keypads. For auditory stimuli such control was not so easy; sounds are transient – they move through time – so presenting static auditory stimuli has a different connotation than the visual counterpart. Even when behavioral scientists began using experimental environments to present auditory stimuli from file, early computer storage capacities were insufficient to deal with the relatively large auditory (particularly speech) files, especially in contrast to, for example, printed words.

So auditory perception was, but is no longer, more difficult to study than visual perception. Over and above these technical constraints, auditory perception is more ephemeral than visual perception; it is difficult to go back and hear again exactly what a person said, but it *is* possible to go back and see what they look like. Auditory stimulation is dynamic, it moves through time, it provides continuity between one instance and the next (a function that, in vision, relies upon saccadic suppression, e.g., Thilo, Santoro, Walsh, & Blakemore, 2004; Chekaluk & Llewellyn, 1992, so that one snapshot of the world is not interfered with by the previous snapshot). Because audition is temporal, it involves patterns of stimulation over time, and so rhythm, prosody, stress, and tone are integrally involved in auditory perception. It is through these we then reach beat, dancing, and emotion. Audition is truly an omnipresent, dynamic, and evocative sense. In this chapter we investigate how infants' auditory perception develops from conception onwards.

The auditory system

The auditory system is one of the first to develop in the fetus, the only one preceding it being the cutaneous sense (Lasky & Williams, 2005). Auditory information is the only external information available to the fetus, and additionally, pick up of auditory information does not require orientation of the sense organs, so it may be expected that auditory stimulation is available well before birth and may even contribute to the infant's early development. In this section the basic structure of the auditory system is described before a consideration of its anatomical and functional development.

Structure and function of the auditory system.   Here a basic and selective description is given of the structure and function of the auditory system, mainly up to the cochlear level. For further information see: Lasky and Williams (2005); Querleu, Renard, Versyp, Paris-Delrue, and Crepin (1988); and Peck (1994).

Vibrating objects move the air molecules that surround them, and they in turn move other adjacent molecules. The resultant alternating areas of compression and rarefaction that are set up (but not the air molecules themselves) are propagated as longitudinal waves. The human ear transduces pressure waves with frequencies between 20 Hz and 20,000 Hz (though this varies over development) into neural impulses and, if sufficiently intense, these are perceived as sound.

The ear has three main anatomical components, the outer, middle, and inner ear, which together transduce sound into nerve impulses. The main structure of the outer ear is the pinna which helps to localize sound sources, but has little further function in humans. These sound waves are then transmitted along the auditory canal to the middle ear where they produce vibrations on the tympanic membrane. Connected to the tympanic membrane are the three smallest bones in the body, the malleus, incus and stapes, collectively known as the ossicles, whose mechanical movements transmit vibrations at the tympanic membrane to the oval window. The other side of the oval window is fluid filled, rather than air filled, and the size differential of the large tympanic membrane and the much smaller oval window, coupled with the intricate and effective magnification by leverage of the ossicles ensure that the sound waves continue to travel through the higher impedance fluid of the inner ear. Indeed the middle ear system adds about a 30 dB gain (necessary due to the greater impedance of the fluid beyond the oval window) and most of this is due to the size differential of the tympanic membrane and oval window (Lasky & Williams, 2005). In the inner ear the fluid-based waves move along the coiled structure of the cochlea. Running the length of the inside of the cochlea is the basilar membrane. Pressure variations in the cochlear fluid cause vibrations on the basilar membrane which take the form of a traveling wave. Due to the decreasing stiffness and increasing mass of the basilar membrane from its base to apex, the response to high-frequency waves peaks nearer the base and the response to lower-frequency waves nearer the apex. Attached to the basilar membrane is the organ of Corti which contains the inner and outer hair cells. The outer hair cells increase sensitivity by amplifying the peak of the traveling wave. Above the organ of Corti is the tectorial membrane. The movement of the basilar membrane shearing against the tectorial membrane causes the stereocilia on the inner hairs cells to bend and open potassium pathways, causing depolarization of the hair cells and release of neurotransmitters resulting in transmission along the auditory nerve.

Anatomical development of the auditory system.   Inner ear: The ear develops from inside to out. The first embryological evidence of the human ear is at 3 to 4 weeks after conception with the formation of the otic vesicle (Anson & Davies, 1980). Then by 5 weeks the vestibular and cochlear aspects of this are discernable and by 10 weeks the cochlea is near adult like in form (Kenna, 1990). So the full 2.5 turns of the cochlear are formed in the first 2.5 months. Beyond this, the cochlea is said to be mature by 35 weeks (Pujol & Uziel, 1988), although there is still further development of the movement of the outer hair cells (Pujol, Calier, & Lenoir, 1980).

Middle ear: Rudiments of the Eustachian tube are evident at 4 weeks (Ars, 1989) and of the ossicles at 6 weeks (Ars, 1989; Kenna, 1990; Peck, 1994), the latter being recognizable by 10 weeks and near adult size and shape by 15 weeks (Anson & Davies, 1980). Ossification of the ossicles occurs between 16 and 32 weeks (Lasky & Williams, 2005), with the stapes lagging somewhat in fine development, and continuing to develop into adulthood (Kenna, 1990; Lasky & Williams, 2005).

Outer ear: Precursors of the outer ear, the pinna and auditory canal are evident at 5 weeks, and the pinna is close to adult form by 18 weeks (Kenna, 1990). Nevertheless, at birth the auditory canal is still only around 17 mm long, well short of the adult length of 27 mm.

Auditory pathways: The human nervous system begins to develop by 3 weeks postconception, and synaptogenesis is intense from week 28 onwards. Myelination begins after this, and the roots of the 8th (auditory nerve) are completely myelinated by the 5th month, with myelination of the cortical auditory pathway continuing until the 2nd postnatal year (Lasky & Williams, 2005). The radial development of the inner ear means that the inner hair cells mature before the outer hair cells – innervation of the inner hair cells is complete by 14 weeks, but of the outer hair cells some time after 22 weeks (Lasky & Williams, 2005).

Pre- and perinatal auditory function.   There is auditory function by 19 weeks postconception (Hepper & Shahidullah, 1994). However, the pre- and postnatal auditory worlds differ considerably, not least due to the fluidic nature of the intra-uterine environment. Two studies suggest that this precludes outer and middle ear involvement in prenatal hearing. First, human divers have significantly compromised mid- and high-frequency thresholds when water is in the auditory meatus (Hollien & Feinstein, 1975). Second, recordings from the round window of *in utero* fetal sheep show that, compared with a no-treatment fetal head uncovered condition, fetuses are less sensitive to external sound both when their head is completely covered with a sound-attenuating hood *and when* that hood has an aperture cut in to expose the pinna and ear canal (Gerhardt et al., 1996; Gerhardt & Abrams, 1996). These studies show respectively that (a) fluid in the ear canal attenuates auditory response and (b) acoustic access to the fetal ear canal does not facilitate auditory response. They converge on the conclusions that fetal hearing occurs via bone conduction and that prenatal outer and middle ear developments are not functionally relevant until airborne sound is available postnatally.

Thus, the pre- and postnatal auditory environments vary considerably: prenatally there is access *only* to sound via bone conduction and, while newborns would also have access to bone-conducted sound, for example, during feeding, this would be less frequent and dominant than airborne input through the outer and middle ear. Given this basic difference, it is important to set out the perinatal infant's response to the frequency and amplitude of sounds, and the integration of sounds from the two ears. Each is now considered in turn ahead of a snapshot of the prenatal and the newborn's auditory world.

Frequency response: The cochlea develops from base to apex, which might lead one to expect earlier sensitivity to high than to low frequencies (Lasky & Williams, 2005). However, this is in conflict with functional data from mammals, and in fact it appears that the basal cells initially respond to relatively lower frequencies with increasing response to higher frequencies over development (Rubel, Lippe, & Ryals, 1984). In the middle ear, the transmission of low frequencies is impeded somewhat by its stiffness due to middle ear cavities and air cells being much smaller than in the adult (Lasky & Williams, 2005). At term the shorter auditory canal and outer ear resonance characteristics along with the compliance of the canal walls and absorption of low frequencies serve to emphasize high frequencies, with a shift to lower frequency emphasis over age. Thus the prenatal infant appears to have an auditory system that is predisposed to the reception of low-frequency sounds, while in the newborn, with the outer and middle ear now functioning due to the availability of airborne sound, the auditory system also appears to take on greater response to higher frequencies.

Amplitude response: As the inner hair cells mature before the outer hair cells, and as the latter are involved in signal amplification, their progressive development between 20 and 35 weeks should allow progressive decreases in amplitude thresholds (Pujol et al., 1980; Lasky & Williams, 2005) and thus greater auditory stimulation. At the middle ear the relatively immature size of the tympanic membrane (only just over half its diameter when mature) (Lasky & Williams, 2005), means that the mismatch of impedance of airborne sound at the tympanic membrane and the fluid-borne sound at the oval window is not compensated for as much as it is in the adult. Of course, this is of little consequence preterm, due to the fluidic nature of the intra-uterine environment, but at birth it would appear that detection thresholds might be relatively high. Moreover, in the middle ear compliance is about half that in the adult due to smaller middle ear cavities and the immature coupling of the ossicles in the fetus and newborn (Lasky & Williams, 2005). These factors together make for higher intensity thresholds in preterm and newborn infants.

Integration and auditory localization: It has been suggested that prenatal hearing can only be monaural because the speed of sound through the amniotic fluid is too fast to allow temporal discrimination (Querleu et al., 1988), and that due to the transmission of sound prenatally by bone conduction alone (Gerhardt et al., 1996) there is symmetrical input to the central auditory system from the two ears (Gerhardt & Abrams, 1996). Nevertheless, at birth there appears to be rudimentary auditory localization, possibly mainly via intensity differences (Morrongiello & Clifton, 1984), indicating that information from the two ears is integrated as soon as airborne sound is available (see Development of binaural abilities).

The auditory world of the preterm infant. *Influence of the auditory system*: We have seen that the preterm auditory system is most responsive to low-frequency sounds, and that intensity thresholds are high. In accord with this, Hepper and Shahidullah (1994) found a low-frequency bias when they investigated fetal response (movement detected by ultrasound[1]) to pure tones from 19 to 35 weeks gestational age. The first response was at 19 weeks to a 500 Hz tone and by 27 weeks 96% of the fetuses responded to 250 and 500 Hz tones but none to 1,000 or 3,000 Hz tones. By 33 to 35 weeks all infants responded to these higher-frequency tones thus showing a gradual improvement of responses to higher frequencies, presumably reflecting the gradual apical development in the cochlear, coupled with the increasing response of the basal regions of the cochlear to high-frequency sounds over development (Rubel et al., 1984). In a similar vein, Hepper and Shahidullah (1994) also found that the intensity level required for a response decreased by 20 to 30 dB over this time period, presumably reflecting the gradual development of function of the outer hair cells (Lasky & Williams, 2005) (see *Pre- and perinatal auditory function*).

Intra-uterine factors: Besides the state of the auditory system, the other important factor in auditory input to the fetus is the intra-uterine environment. Querleu et al. (1988) provide a good overview: Querleu and Renard (1981) and Versyp (1985) recorded the nature of the fetal environment just before birth using a hydraphone and a prepolarized microphone, and identified both internal and external sound sources. Internally there is low level basal noise (maternal and placental vascular sounds, maternal intestinal noises) from 1 to 1,000 Hz at about 20 dB at 500 Hz, with the mother's heartbeat at about 25 dB above the basal sound, a level not loud enough to mask external sound. External sounds are of course masked by the mother's abdominal wall and the attenuation thereby is greater the higher the frequency of the sounds (2 dB at 250 Hz, 14 dB at 500 Hz, 20 dB at 1,000 Hz, and 26 dB at 2000 Hz, Querleu & Renard, 1981). Thus there is a concentration of input from lower frequencies, although Versyp (1985) has shown that even high-frequency sounds such as that of a musical triangle are transmitted, though possibly not audible.

With respect to voices, the mother's voice in situ emerges at 24 dB above that of the basal noise, and external voices transmitted via loudspeaker 1 m from the womb at around

60 dB are present at levels of around 8 to 12 dB above that of the basal noise. Moreover, when intra-uterine recordings were played to 6 adult listeners for perceptual judgement (Versyp, 1985), they were able to identify 30% of the 3,120 French phonemes presented. Nevertheless, Querleu et al. (1988) observe that the recordings reveal greater low- than high-frequency components, and opine that any intra-uterine perception of speech would be highly concentrated on the low-frequency prosodic components. Indeed, consonant with, but not proof of, this observation Versyp (1985) showed that *in utero* recordings of a French lullaby sung by the mother (directly recorded) and by the mother, a female, or a male (at 60 dB via an external loudspeaker), revealed exactly the same fundamental frequency (F0) patterns as recordings *ex utero* of the same renditions. Thus, the low-frequency components of speech permeate the abdominal wall and F0 is transmitted intact. Moreover, as we will see in the next section, these low-frequency components are perceived and remembered by the infant.

Postnatal auditory development

Once the child is born, airborne sound waves are transmitted along the auditory canal and through the middle ear. This, in addition to the absence of the low-pass filter of the uterine wall, will result in greater response to higher frequencies post- than prenatally. The absence of the uterine wall between the sound source and the ear allows access to more sound energy, although the addition of the outer and middle ear to the overall auditory system function does nothing to change amplitude thresholds. The addition of transmission of airborne sounds gives the newborn access to time, phase, and amplitude differences between the two ears, cues used in localizing sounds.

Over and above the structure of the auditory system, and the information retained from the early prenatal experience (see *Spotlight on perception of speech*), there is now evidence that certain cortical predilections may facilitate patterns of learning useful in language development. Gervain, Macagno, Cogoi, Peña, and Mehler (2008) used near-infrared spectroscopy (NIRS) to examine newborns' response to repetitive sequences. They found increased response to ABB sequences such as "mubaba" and "penana" compared with random ABC sequences such as "mubage" and "penaku" in initial presentations, and this enhanced response increased over time for ABB repetitions but not ABC control sequences. Similar results were *not* found for ABA patterns, for example, "bamuba" and "napena" compared to the control sequences. Together these results show that there is both a perceptual predisposition to detect certain types of repetitions, and also to learn about these repetitions. It can be seen that such an ability could profitably facilitate later language development.

Thus, the newborn comes armed with a well-developed auditory system, certain cortical predispositions, a low-frequency bias, and raised amplitude thresholds. In the following sections, we consider the world of the newborn in terms of their basic auditory abilities, both monaural (see below) and binaural (see later). Later, in the 3rd section, we will consider how these basic abilities plus infant postnatal pick up of auditory information combine in the perception of particularly salient auditory information – speech and music.

Monaural abilities are those that do not require the registration of inter-aural differences and so are evident with either monaural or binaural hearing, such as the pick up of temporal, intensity, and frequency variations. Binaural abilities are those that require and rely on two ears, and the perception of certain inter-ear differences that typically underlie spatial auditory perception.

Development of monaural abilities

In this section the concern is with infants' monaural abilities, the discrimination of temporal, amplitude (perceived as loudness), and frequency (perceived as pitch), all of which are important for perceiving speech and music (see Growing Up in an Auditory World); and finally and more generally sound detection.

Infants' sensitivity to temporal information.   Good temporal processing is needed for distinguishing between-category differences in speech sounds, such as the brief 10 ms difference that changes /ba/ to /pa/. We know that infants can do this from very early in life (e.g., Eimas, Siqueland, Jusczyk, & Vigorito, 1971). Tallal and Piercy (1973) found that difficulties with processing rapidly changing acoustic stimuli are linked to poorer performance in speech discrimination and comprehension tasks, and there is some evidence that temporal processing can be improved with training (e.g., Tallal et al., 1996).

A number of methods have been employed to investigate infants' temporal processing of nonspeech sounds, including temporal grouping tasks (Chang & Trehub, 1977; Demany, McKenzie, & Vurpillot, 1977), changes in duration of stimulus, changes in duration of gap between successive stimuli (Morrongiello & Trehub, 1987), and the precedence effect[2] (Morrongiello, Kulig, & Clifton, 1984).

In grouping tasks Demany et al. (1977) found that infants as young as 2.5 months discriminate tone sequences with different temporal groupings, for example, a 3-9-3-9 grouping from a 3-6-3-12 grouping, and even different temporal groupings which incorporate the same intervals, 1-3-6 from 1-6-3. In addition, Chang and Trehub (1977) found that 5-month-olds reliably discriminate tone sequences with different temporal groupings, for example, 2-4 from 4-2. However, Morrongiello (1984) demonstrated that while 6- and 12-month-old infants reliably discriminate a 3-3-3 from a 5-4 and a 9-element tone grouping, indicating sensitivity to an absolute timing change, only 12-month-olds could discriminate changes in relational timing information, for example, a change from 3-3 to 4-1-4.

Data from gap detection tasks highlight that 6-month-olds discriminate white noise bursts and silence duration differences of 20 ms following training in a head-turn procedure (Morrongiello & Trehub, 1987). Moreover, 11-month-olds succeed in making finer discriminations of pulse trains of 0.5 versus 1.2 s, but fail when more similar pulse rates of 0.2, 0.3 and 0.4 s are presented (Ferland & Mendelson, 1982). A gap detection method has also been used to measure listeners' segmentation of tone cues on the basis of duration and intensity. For both infant and adult listeners, silent gaps at segmentation boundaries were more difficult to perceive than gaps within perceived groupings, suggesting that longer tones mark the boundaries of perceived groupings (Trainor & Adams, 2000) (see also *The influence of the language environment on speech perception* and *Temporal relations*, below).

Infants' sensitivity to intensity variations.   Neonates are less sensitive to variations in intensity (perceived as loudness) than adults (see earlier), but are nevertheless quite well-developed; they respond to intensity changes as small as 6 dB (Tarquinio, Zelazo, & Weiss, 1990). The amplitude threshold for 1-month-olds at 4,000 Hz is approximately 35 dB higher than that of adults, with further improvement to 30 dB at 3 months, and improvement to a 15 dB infant–adult difference by 6 months.

Seven- to nine-month-old infants also detect 6 dB intensity differences between repeating 1,000 Hz tones (Sinnott & Aslin, 1985) but need greater differences of 9 dB for broadband noise (Kopyar, 1997). The ability to detect intensity changes improves across the 1st year, as indicated by the improvement of thresholds from 6 dB to 4 dB between 6 and 12 months (Sinnott & Aslin, 1985). Similar intensity estimates in the order of 2 to 2.5 dB to 6 to 6.5 dB have been reported for infants' detection of intensity increments of syllables embedded within multisyllabic units (Bull, Eilers, & Oller, 1984), and for detection of tone intensity increments in broadband noise (Schneider & Trehub, 1985). By comparison, adults' difference limens are 1 to 2 dB (Miller, 1947; Sinnott & Aslin, 1985). Seven-month-old infants' intensity increments (in range of 28 to 58 dB) in 400 Hz continuous noise is inferior for low frequencies at lower intensities and decreases with increases in intensity up to 30 dB (Berg & Boswell, 1998).

For intensity discrimination of more complex speech sounds, Nozza, Rossman and Bond (1991) found that infants need around 25 to 28 dB more signal intensity than adults to reach criterion level of performance. While there are improvements in intensity discrimination across infancy, the development of intensity discrimination continues into the preschool years where it approaches adult thresholds of 1 dB (Jensen & Neff, 1993; see also Maxon & Hochberg, 1982).

Infants' sensitivity to frequency variations.   In accord with pre- and perinatal auditory system developments (see above), converging evidence from a number of studies shows that young infants have difficulties with the higher frequencies; 3- and 6-month-olds have similar low-frequency discrimination thresholds (Olsho, Koch, & Halpin, 1987), but 3-month-olds have higher high-frequency discrimination thresholds than 6-month-olds (Tharpe & Ashmead, 2001; Werner & Gillenwater, 1990). Thus infants have difficulty detecting higher-frequency sounds initially, but this is largely resolved by 6 months of age. At the other end of the spectrum, low-frequency discrimination is not mature until later in childhood: Soderquist and Moore (1970) report that 5-year-olds' discrimination of low-frequency tone (Yip, 2002) is significantly poorer than that of 7- and 9-year-olds; and converging evidence from 4- and 5-year-olds tested in an "odd one out" procedure shows that despite improvements across age children's discrimination of a 440 Hz tone from comparison stimuli differing by 1 to 400 Hz was poorer and more variable than adults' discrimination (Jensen & Neff, 1993).

Moving to more environmental sounds, infants' pitch perception has been studied from a number of perspectives, including discrimination of tone sequences, sensitivity to the pitch of syllables (e.g., Kuhl & Miller, 1982; Morse, 1972), and rising versus falling intonation contour (Kaplan, 1970) and pitch differences in /ra/ vs /la/ syllables

(Karzon & Nicholas, 1989). In general these studies show that infants have good pitch perception.

Infants' detection of sound using frequency and intensity cues.   Newborn infants are generally less sensitive in detecting sounds than adults and this is especially the case for higher frequencies. For example, 6- and 7-month-olds' thresholds at the mid and higher frequencies are more mature than low-frequency thresholds (Olsho, Koch, Carter, Halpin, & Spetner, 1988; Trehub, Schneider, & Endman, 1980; Berg & Boswell, 1998).

Infants' initial difficulty with detecting higher-frequency sounds is due in part to immature frequency resolution. Frequency resolution is the ability to detect a frequency-specific sound, the target, in the presence of a competing sound, the masker, that activates the same auditory nerve fibers as the signal, making it difficult to separate the competing signals. Infants' poorer sensitivity to high-frequency sounds may also be due to immaturity of the middle ear (Keefe & Levi, 1996, see also *Pre- and perinatal auditory function*), or to poor transmission of auditory signals through the brainstem contributing to a loss of information, and initially poor frequency resolution (Abdala & Folsom, 1995; Folsom & Wynne, 1987; Werner, Folsom, & Mancl, 1994). In terms of infant–adult differences in frequency discrimination, 3-month-olds require a 120 Hz differential to detect a change between two tones around 4,000 Hz (~3%), whereas adults require a difference of only 40 Hz (~1%), and these relative percentages (3% and 1%) also hold for adults and 6-month-olds respectively for frequency changes around 1,000 Hz (Aslin 1989).

Six-month-old infants' masked thresholds are elevated in comparison to adults by between 5 and 15 dB, and are not adult-like until approximately 10 years of age (Allen & Wightman, 1994; Bargones, Werner, & Marean, 1995; Berg & Boswell, 1999; Leibold & Werner, 2006; Nozza & Wilson 1984; Schneider & Trehub, 1992; Werner & Boike, 2001), but observer-based procedures reveal that infants experience less difficulty detecting broadband noise than narrowband sounds, possibly because of the multiple frequencies available in broadband noise. There is some debate about whether difficulty in separating simultaneous sounds stems from problems with (a) intensity coding, that is, an inability to determine the addition of a tone to noise, (b) actually separating out the sound, or (c) attending selectively to one sound when two sounds are detected. Infants may also have problems with selective attention. For example, Bargones and Werner (1994) found that when adults are expecting to hear a low-intensity tone at one frequency they do not detect the presentation of a tone at another frequency, whereas infants respond to both the expected and irrelevant frequencies, indicating a problem with selectively attending to relevant sounds (see also Gomes, Molholm, Christodoulou, Ritter, & Cowan, 2000). However, infants do show selective attention when trained to respond to a particular temporal event. For example, when infants learn to respond to a tone presented 500 ms after another tone, they detect this tone, but not others presented at different duration intervals (Parrish & Werner, 2004).

Development of binaural abilities – auditory localization in infancy

Auditory localization depends both upon monaural and binaural cues. Monaurally, the shape of the pinna affords differential amplification patterns of sounds of different frequencies, and this allows some degree of sound localization, which is especially useful in resolving back/front confusions and in localization in the up/down sagittal plane. There appears to be no research on how infants may use such cues. Binaural cues are based on inter-aural differences of a particular distal sound due to the spatial dislocation of the two ears and the various effects this dislocation has as a function of the position of the sound source. There are differences in the time of arrival of a sound to the two ears, and this temporal difference can result in phase differences in the waveform at time of arrival. Moreover, the inter-aural distance means that the sound will be softer at the ear opposite to the sound location and this, coupled with the sound shadow of the head, neck and shoulders results in inter-aural intensity differences. Thus the binaural cues to auditory localization are inter-aural time, phase, and intensity differences, and adult humans indeed use these to localize sound (Moore, 1997). We will return to these cues after consideration of infants' auditory localization abilities.

Newborns reliably localize single source broadband sounds if sufficient time is allowed for their typically long latency responses (Clifton, Morrongiello, Kulig, & Dowd, 1981; Field, Muir, Pilon, Sinclair, & Dodwell, 1980; Muir & Field, 1979). This early localization is thought to be reflexive in nature (Field et al., 1980; Muir, Abraham, Forbes, & Harris, 1979), although following habituation of head turns to a repeated sound, there is recovery of localization to a novel sound perhaps reflecting interaction with some higher processes (Zelazo, Weiss, Papageorgiou, & Laplante, 1989). Despite this, the frequency and accuracy of head turns to a sound reduces markedly over early development particularly between 1 and 3 months; evidence that is consistent with the waning of an early reflex (Field et al., 1980; Muir & Clifton, 1985; Muir, Clifton, & Clarkson, 1989). More robust localization re-emerges around 4 months with head turns that are both faster and more accurate than those of newborns (Muir et al., 1989) and it has been suggested that these later responses are more cognitively based than they were in neonates; that older infants may take into account the visual source of sounds, for example, look for an object if one is not apparent at the supposed position after a head turn (Field et al., 1980; Muir et al., 1979). This is consistent with behavioral evidence for the perception of auditory-visual events around 4 months (e.g., Spelke, 1976) and the beginning of the development of the association areas around the same time (Gibson, 1981; Yakovlev & Lacours, 1967).

The Precedence Effect (PE) occurs when two identical sounds of equal intensity are played to a listener through separate laterally-placed loudspeakers with a short delay (about 4 to 40 ms) between their onsets (Clifton, 1985; Saberi & Antonio, 2003; Wallach, Newman, & Rosenzweig, 1949). Under such conditions, listeners perceive only the sound from the leading loudspeaker to the exclusion of the sound from the lagging speaker. As the delay between the onsets is increased, both sound sources are perceived. For adults the threshold is about 9 ms for simple clicks, 23 ms for more complex broadband rattle sounds (Clifton, 1985; Morrongiello et al., 1984), and probably even longer for more complex sounds such as human speech (Wallach et al.). The PE may be a manifestation of an echo-suppression device which enhances the true location of the source of a sound, especially in cases when an original sound is multiply reflected from many spatially disparate surfaces (Clifton, 1985; Mills, 1972; Wallach et al., 1949; but see Perrott, Marlborough, & Merrill, 1989), so its occurrence serves as a good index of whether the perceiver is integrating information from two spatially disparate events.

In contrast to their single source localization ability, newborns do not locate PE at the leading speaker; in fact they appear completely unresponsive to PE stimuli (Clifton et al., 1981). The PE is still not evident at 2 months, but it is at 5 months (Clifton, Morrongiello, & Dowd, 1984, see also Litovsky & Ashmead, 1997). In a fine-grained developmental study Muir et al. (1989) showed that the PE emerged around 4 months, just the time when single source localization re-emerges. This coincidence of the emergence of the PE and the reemergence of the more sophisticated single source localization is thought to be maturationally based (Clifton, 1985; Muir & Clifton, 1985) and to index the onset of cortical function (Muir et al.). In support of this maturational hypothesis Burnham, Taplin, Henderson-Smart, Earnshaw-Brown, and O'Grady (1993) tested full-term 7-month-olds and 10-month-olds, and a preterm group of infants who were 7 months corrected age but 10 months chronological age and found that PE thresholds for the preterms and the 7-month-olds were equivalent and together higher than those for the 10-month-olds. These results suggest that PE thresholds, and thus the PE itself, are a function of maturation rather than experience.

Given that (a) PE thresholds are a product of maturation, (b) both nonhuman ablation studies (Cranford & Oberholtzer, 1976; Cranford, Ravizza, Diamond, & Whitfield, 1971; Whitfield, Cranford, Ravizza, & Diamond, 1972; Whitfield, Diamond, Chiveralls, & Williamson, 1978) and studies of children with temporal lobe epilepsy (Hochster & Kelly, 1981) show that the auditory cortex is necessary for the PE, then the late emergence of the PE in human infancy may be taken to be an index of auditory cortex development. PE thresholds decrease from 5 months to 5 years (Morrongiello et al., 1984), and this is consistent with the development of myelinization of primary auditory cortex which begins around 3 months of age, extends throughout the layers of the cortex around 2 years (Gibson, 1981) and is complete around 3 to 4 years of age (Yakovlev & Lacours, 1967). Thus it appears that auditory cortex maturation has behavioral manifestations in infancy and childhood. Later reductions of PE thresholds into adulthood (Morrongiello et al., 1984), would presumably index further binaural development, such as increased sensitivity to inter-aural differences (Nozza, 1987) rather than auditory cortex maturation.

Thus we can conclude that there is basic auditory localization in neonates and a more sophisticated form of it in 4-month-olds. However, we can not be certain what binaural or even monaural cues infants might use to achieve this. Of the different cues for binaural localization, it has been suggested that the inter-aural intensity differential is possibly the most potent (Morrongiello & Clifton, 1984), with sensitivity to inter-aural time differences perhaps improving by 5 months (Morrongiello & Clifton). Sensitivity to inter-aural phase differences in 5-month-olds is quite immature compared to that of adults (Nozza, 1987). In the vertical plane, pinna cues are important for localization by adults. By at least 6 months infants localize sounds deviating in large vertical shifts, with acuity increasing over age (Morrongiello, 1987). Importantly for the issue of the mechanisms involved, as for adults, vertical localization by infants is better for high frequencies, suggesting that young infants, like adults, use pinna cues for vertical localization. The continued age-related improvement in vertical localization up to at least 18 months suggests improvements as the pinna gets longer (Morrongiello, 1987). Further, more detailed research on the relative use of these cues in infancy is indicated, and in addition how infants might cope with the anatomical changes to head size and thus inter-aural distance (Clifton, Gwiazda, Bauer, Clarkson, & Held, 1988), and pinna size and shape (Morrongiello, 1987).

Growing Up in an Auditory World

We now have a good understanding of prenatal structural and functional development, and of the basic monaural and binaural abilities of the very young infant. Audition is an active sense that allows us to pick up information that moves through time as we move through the environment. Two significant sources of such information for humans are speech and music, both of which have been created by humans. All human societies have developed speech and music. Due to certain anatomical and cognitive constraints there are similarities in the speech and music developed by each culture, but equally, due to various historical, geographical, emotional, and social factors the speech and music systems that have evolved in each culture differ. Thus, it is important that we understand auditory perception of speech and music not only because they are significant auditory events for humans, but also because they form mini-laboratories in which the joint influence of, on the one hand, anatomical and cognitive givens, and on the other emotional, social, and developmental factors may be determined. In this section the spotlight is turned onto the development of speech perception and music perception.

Spotlight on perception of speech

To perceive speech, sensitivity to temporal, intensity, and frequency aspects of sound are paramount. Perceiving consonants relies on sensitivity to more transient energy, and to the amplitude (level) of that energy. For example, voiceless [h] and [f] have less spectral energy than voiced [b] and [g], but the strident fricative [s] has a higher amplitude level than the nonstrident [f]. Consonants can be broadband, such as fricatives, or they can be largely concentrated in a single frequency region, such as the low-frequency resonance of nasals with energy near the floor of the spectrogram (e.g., [m] and [n]). Stop consonants such as [b] and [p] have the additional acoustic cues of release burst (abrupt release of air) and transition from the burst to the formants (Ladefoged & Maddieson, 1996). Perceiving vowels relies on the ability to respond to differentials in bands of energy in multiple, relatively invariant frequency regions (formants) and to do so over temporal variations in the energy bands. Finally, perceiving lexical tones (which occur in more than 70% of the world's languages to distinguish otherwise phonetically identical sound sequences, Yip, 2002) relies mainly on the detection of variations in pitch height, and also of pitch contour, although in some languages there is also some involvement of other cues, such as duration and voice quality. Research on the perception of these segments (consonants, vowels, and tones) is considered both in early infancy and as the result of linguistic experience over the 1st year.

Speech perception in newborns; special mode or determined by the auditory system?   Newborns retain some important legacies from prenatal auditory input – specific linguistic preferences that are evident before (Kisilevsky et al., 2003) and at birth (DeCasper & Fifer, 1980) for their mother's voice and their native language (Mehler et al., 1988). These preferences appear to be based on prosodic (rhythmic and intonational) aspects of speech because: (a) newborn preference for the mother's over a stranger's voice is enhanced when speech is low-pass filtered (Moon & Fifer, 1986), and disrupted in 1-month-olds by mother and stranger reading a passage backwards (Mehler, Bertoncini, Barrière, & Jassik-Gerschenfeld, 1978); and (b) the native language preference is actually a preference for the rhythm class of the language, for example, stress-defined units in English, syllable-defined units in Italian, and mora-defined units in Japanese (Nazzi, Bertoncini, & Mehler, 1998; Ramus, Hauser, Miller, Morris, & Mehler, 2000). Indeed it has been suggested that infants' perceptual attention is biased to steady state periodic information (such as vowels, tones, and intonation), which assists infants in parsing the surrounding language (Cutler & Mehler, 1993), and that the prosodic aspects of speech actually bootstrap language development (Nazzi & Ramus, 2003).

The initial impetus for investigating infants' perception of phones (speech segments), arose out of an attempt to understand adult speech perception and to determine whether infants display the same kind of categorical speech perception as had been found for adults (Liberman, 1957). Categorical perception is the tendency to perceive a physical continuum discontinuously, that is, for the relevant perceptual system to group stimuli on a continuum such that discrete categories are perceived.

Eimas et al. (1971) conducted the first study to investigate infants' speech perception of voicing onset time (VOT) contrasts. Using the high-amplitude sucking procedure, they tested 1-month-old infants for discrimination of bilabial stops, [b] versus [pʰ], using stimuli differing along a continuum of voice onset time (VOT). Following the presentation of stop consonants from one phonetic category, infants showed greater sucking rates to a new stimulus from a contrasting phonetic category (between-category contrasts, [ba] vs. [pʰa]) but not from the same phonetic category (within-category contrasts, [ba1] vs. [ba2]), even though the physical distance between the members of each pair was equivalent in terms of VOT. Eimas et al. concluded that (a) mechanisms underlying such perception may well be innate specifically in humans, (b) infants are tuned to perceive speech categorically, and (c) human infants perceive speech in a linguistic mode. Converging evidence from 2-month-old infants' categorical discrimination of a variety of phonetic contrasts, for example [m] vs. [n] (Eimas & Miller, 1980), [w] vs. [j] (Jusczyk, Copan, & Thompson, 1978), [v] versus [f], (Levitt, Jusczyk, Murray, & Carden, 1988) [b] versus [d] (Eimas, 1974) and from categorical perception data obtained from even younger, newborn infants (Bertoncini, Bijeljac-Babic, Blumstein, & Mehler, 1987) strengthened these claims.

The suggestion that categorical perception is unique to humans was quashed by the discovery that chinchillas (Kuhl & Miller, 1975, 1978), macaque (Kuhl & Padden, 1982, 1983) and rhesus monkeys (Morse & Snowdon, 1975) also perceive speech sounds categorically. Moreover, contrary to the "speech is special" implication of Eimas' first and third conclusions, it has been found that music-like sounds which vary continuously in rise-time are categorized into "plucks" and "bows" both by adults (Cutting & Rosner, 1974) and infants (Jusczyk, Rosner, Cutting, Foard, & Smith, 1977, but see also Rosen & Howell, 1981; Cutting, 1982), and that two-tone complexes which vary continuously in tone onset time (TOT) are perceived categorically both by adults (Pisoni, 1977) and by infants (Jusczyk, Pisoni, Walley, & Murray, 1980). However, in assessing infants' discrimination for speech sounds and nonspeech sounds (chirps – isolated presentations of second-formant transitions in speech, reflecting acoustic information for backness of tongue in the oral cavity) of equal complexity, Mattingly, Liberman, Syrdal, and Halwes (1971) found that infants discriminated within- and between-category pairs of nonspeech sounds indicating continuous discrimination, whereas the discrimination of speech stimuli was heightened at the category boundaries. In contrast, Jusczyk, Rosner, Reed, and Kennedy (1989) report categorical perception of both speech and nonspeech sounds in infants.

Together these studies show (a) that categorical speech perception depends not on the species, but rather on the nature of the auditory system, and (b) that for young infants (and even adults), it is the acoustic nature of an incoming stimulus rather than its linguistic status that is important in the perception of speech and nonspeech. Thus it appears that, rather than there being a linguistic mode of perception in early infancy that is the product of autoplastic evolution of human hardware, there has been alloplastic evolution of the software (the phonologies of languages) such that these take advantage of the particular characteristics of the auditory system. Thus infants begin their speech perception career with an acoustically based advantage for speech simply because human languages have evolved to make maximal use of their auditory system, rather than the other way around. Now we will see how the speech environment affects this initial state.

The influence of the language environment on speech perception.   In the 1980s Werker, Gilbert, Humphrey, and Tees (1981) conducted a series of conditioned head turn studies that showed for the first time age-related changes in speech perception, specifically consonants, as a product of native language experience. They tested English-learning infants at several ages, on several nonnative consonant contrasts, the Hindi retroflex/dental stop contrast, [ʈ] vs. [t̪], the Hindi voiceless aspirated breathy voiced contrast, [dʰ] vs. [t̪ʰ], and the Salish (Nthlakampx) glottalized velar versus uvular ejective stop contrast, [k̓] vs. [q̓], and found that 6- to 8-month-old English-learning infants differentiate these nonnative contrasts (Werker et al.); in contrast to 10- to 12-month-old infants (Werker & Tees, 1984), 4-year-old children (Werker & Tees, 1983), and English-speaking adults (Werker et al.), who find discrimination much more difficult. However, this age-related decline in discrimination performance was not observed in three Salish learning and three Hindi-learning (11- to 12-month-old) infants for whom the test contrasts are native, thus showing that there is a language-specific perceptual reorganization that occurs around this period – the second half of the first year (Werker & Tees, 1984). The pattern of reorganization across the first year of life is robust – it has also been shown using a habituation–dishabituation procedure for English infants tested on the Salish contrast (Best, McRoberts, LaFleur, & Silver-Isenstadt, 1995), and for Japanese infants tested on the English /r-l/ distinction, a discrimination that is especially difficult for Japanese speaking adults (Tsushima et al., 1994). In contrast, there is reported to be no attenuation in the ability to perceive certain other nonnative consonant contrasts in the first year of life. For example, Best, McRoberts, & Sithole, 1988) showed that both English-learning infants between 6 and 14 months *and* English-speaking adults successfully discriminated nonnative Zulu click consonant contrasts. Best and colleagues suggest that the Zulu clicks are not discriminated in a language-specific manner because they sound unlike any English speech sound, and in fact were not even perceived to be speech by the English-speaking adults.

Turning to vowels, Kuhl, Williams, Lacerda, Stevens, and Lindblom (1992) have shown that there are language-specific influences on the internal structure of vowel categories by 6 months of age in the form of a perceptual magnet effect; their vowel discrimination is superior when a poor exemplar of a vowel category is used as a background stimulus and a good exemplar as the target, than when the reverse is the case because the more prototypical vowel category member acts as a magnet, attracting other more peripheral members and rendering them less discriminable (Grieser & Kuhl, 1989; Kuhl, 1991). This magnet effect appears to be a product of language experience as indicated by the finding that Swedish-learning 6-month-olds show a magnet effect for Swedish but not English vowels, and English-learning 6-month-olds show a magnet effect for English but not Swedish vowels (Kuhl et al.). Decline in perceptual discrimination in the first year has also been shown in English-learning infants for several nonnative vowel contrasts, including the Norwegian /y-u/ (Best et al., 1997) and the German /u-y/ and /U-Y/ (Polka & Werker, 1994) contrasts, but the decline occurs earlier than for consonants and tones, from 4 months of age.

Perceptual reorganization for lexical tones has also been found – between 6 and 9 months. Both 4- and 6-month-old English and French infants discriminated nonnative Thai lexical tone contrasts, while older 9-month-olds fail to do so (Mattock & Burnham, 2006; Mattock, Molnar, Polka, & Burnham, 2008), whereas Chinese-language infants, for whom tone is phonologically relevant, successfully discriminated the lexical tone contrasts at both 6 and 9 months of age. In addition Mattock and Burnham (2006) showed that for English and Chinese infants there was no decline in discrimination performance for the tones transformed into violin sounds with the same F0 patterns.

Thus, by 6 months of age for vowels, and by around 9 months for consonants and tones there is a decline in discrimination performance for nonnative speech contrasts. The specificity of this for nonnative speech suggests that it is an index of a general language-specific perceptual reorganization. Moreover, the results for the violin sounds with tones (Mattock & Burnham 2006), indicates that perceptual reorganization is specific to speech or, in the case of Zulu clicks, what is perceived to be speech by listeners in the particular language environment (Best et al., 1988).

Newborn infants' preference for their native language and their mother's voice rests on a basic auditory ability – the perception of rhythm and to some extent intonation. This "periodicity bias" as it has been called (Cutler & Mehler, 1993) may bootstrap sensitivity to other properties of the native language later, between 6 and 10 months, such as intonational markings of phrases (Jusczyk, Pisoni, & Mullennix, 1992) and native stress patterns that assist infants to recognize words, (e.g., Jusczyk, 1993; Jusczyk, Cutler, & Redanz, 1993; Jusczyk, Houston, & Newsome, 1999).

Spotlight on perception of music

Just as the early studies by Eimas et al. (1971) predisposed researchers to favor a "speech is special" position, some studies on music perception appear to suggest a modular domain-specific account of music perception (Peretz & Coltheart, 2003; Trehub & Hannon, 2006). However, certain basic aspects of music perception appear to rely on a biological substrate. This is no better demonstrated than by the fact that, as for speech, there is categorical perception of musical sounds (Jusczyk et al., 1977; but see Cutting, 1982; Rosen & Howell, 1981). In addition, for both speech and music this early categorical perception is based on the available hardware, but gives way to culture-specific perception after the age of about 6 months. In the case of speech, specific linguistic experience results in selective perception of just those consonants, vowels, tones, and prosody that are used in the native language; in the case of music, Western 6-month-old infants detect rhythmic variations in both native and nonnative (Balkan nonisochronous meters) (Hannon & Trehub, 2005a) whereas 12-month-olds and adults do not (Hannon & Trehub, 2005b) and Western 6-month-old infants detect note variations in both native and nonnative (Indonesian pelog scales) whereas adults do not (Lynch, Eilers, Oller, & Urbano, 1990). So, just as categorical speech perception (Eimas et al., 1971) appears to be a by-product of the particular auditory system we humans have (Kuhl, 1978), music may also be a system that has developed alloplastically to make use of certain biological givens.

The above example points to the two broad aspects of the structure of music: its temporal (rhythm, tempo, meter), and its melodic (pitch, consonance, harmony) qualities. The development of each of these is now discussed in turn.

Temporal relations: Tempo, rhythm, and meter.   It was highlighted above that infants are able to discriminate absolute and relational temporal groupings, that is, discriminate rhythms, as young as 2.5 months (Demany et al., 1977). In addition, 2- and 4-month-old infants discriminate between sequences of tones that differ in tempo by being 15% faster in habituation than test, but only in intermediate tempo ranges around 300 ms and 600 ms inter-onset-interval (IOI) between tone elements, not lower (100 ms) or higher (750, 1,500 ms) IOIs (Baruch & Drake, 1997). It is of interest that these intermediate tempi are just those at which adults' tempo discrimination is optimal (Drake & Botte, 1993). Nevertheless, there are differences in tempo perception in adults, children, and infants: while adults prefer those tempi that they best discriminate, 6- to 10-year-olds prefer the faster of tempi that are presented, and 4-month-old infants show no tempi preferences (Baruch, Panissal-Vieu, & Drake, 2004), despite their better performance at the same intermediate tempi at which adults also excel. Thus, it appears there is a biological predisposition for humans to respond best to particular tempi, but that tempi preferences in infancy and childhood are driven by different factors both to those that determine optimal discrimination, and that determine adult tempo preferences. The notion of a biological determination of tempo preference is supported by findings that by adulthood it appears that preferred tempo (beat rate) is related to anthropomorphic variables, such that people with greater body mass, shoulder width, and so forth, prefer slower tempos (Todd, Cousins, & Lee, 2007). In commenting on the Todd et al. study, Trainor (2007) suggests that preferred beat rate may be a species-general phenomenon (Fitch, 2005) related to locomotion, and indeed it has been found that even nonhuman animals perceive rhythm (Trehub & Hannon, 2006): starlings (Hulse, Humpal, Cynx, 1984a) and dolphins (Harley et al., 2003) discriminate patterns distinguished only by rhythm (not interval duration) and do so despite transformations involving tempo frequency (Hulse, Humpal, & Cynx, 1984b; Harley et al., 2003). The pervasiveness of rhythm can be seen if we recall that languages fall into relatively distinct rhythm classes (e.g., stress-timed Germanic languages, syllable-timed Romantic languages, and the mora-timed Japanese), and that infants' early preference for their native language appears to be based on perception of these rhythms (Nazzi et al., 1998; Ramus et al., 2000; see *Speech perception in newborns*) learned prenatally. It is interesting to speculate about the way in which these rhythmic differences in languages may have evolved. Over and above any species-general preferred beat rate, as individual tempo rate preferences in humans are inversely related to body mass and shoulder width, it may be that tempo differences between human languages have evolved due to the tempo preferences of the speakers of the language, which in turn are based on their general anatomical structure, namely, decreasing prosodic unit size from stress-timed Germanic languages, to syllable-timed Romance languages, and to mora-timed languages such as Japanese.

Recently another temporal phenomenon has been discovered which, thus far, appears to be more human-specific. Phillips-Silver and Trainor (2005) familiarized 7-month-old infants with an unaccented rhythm and simultaneously bounced infants in one group on every second beat (duple rhythm) and those in another on every third beat (triple rhythm). When then tested with auditory-only accented versions of the previously unaccented rhythms, infants preferred the one that was familiar due to the earlier bimodal presentation (see Bahrick, this volume, for further discussion of intersensory effects). (This response to underlying meter is consistent with findings that infants respond to a novel rhythm more if it also entails a novel meter – Hannon & Johnson, 2005). Further experiments with infants (Phillips-Silver & Trainor, 2005) and adults (Phillips-Silver & Trainor, 2007) show that visual information is not necessary for this beat entrainment effect, but movement is. On these bases Phillips-Silver and Trainor (2007) conclude that early in life there is a strong relationship between audition and movement, or more generally perception and action, and Trainor (2007) posits that this beat entrainment is a human-specific quality, as opposed to the more species-general biometrically based beat rate preferences (Todd et al., 2007).

Further investigating the issue of culture specificity, Hannon and Trehub (2005a, 2005b) have shown that Western adults can detect rhythmic variations that disrupt a familiar Western isochronous meter, but not ones that disrupt an unfamiliar (Balkan) nonisochronous meter, whereas Western 6-month-olds act in a culture-general mode like both Western and Balkan (Bulgarian and Macedonian) adults; they detect both. By 12 months, however, Western infants move from this culture-general to a more culture-specific mode and act like their adult Western counterparts, although unlike Western adults they can still learn the foreign discrimination after appropriate exposure.

Finally, moving to a higher level of rhythmic structure, Krumhansl and Jusczyk (1990; Jusczyk & Krumhansl, 1993) investigated 4.5-month-old infants' perception of the phrase structure of music. In a result reminiscent of that with speech (Jusczyk et al., 1993; Jusczyk et al., 1992, see above) infants were found to prefer Mozart minuets in which pauses were inserted at natural boundaries rather than ones in which pauses were inserted at unnatural boundaries. Investigation of the critical cues for this preference revealed that it is decrease in pitch height and lengthening of tone duration in the melody line before pauses that drive this preference. While there are, as yet, no cross-cultural studies to test the effect of the presence of specific structures in the infant's music environment, it is likely that this is experientially based.

In summary, newborn infants have good rhythm and tempo perception, and these basic auditory abilities pave the way for what appear to be: *species-general* mechanisms that alert young infants to a particular tempo range; a more *species-specific* mechanism by which infants listening to a particular beat rate can entrain to particular tempi, for example, to hear every second or every third beat as accented; and finally a *culture-specific* mechanism emerging between 6 and 12 months by which music perception becomes influenced by and specialized for the particular musical structures they hear around them.

Spectral properties: consonance/dissonance, harmony.   As for adults across many cultures (Hannon & Trainor, 2007), both newborn (Masataka, 2006) and 2- and 4-month-old (Trainor, Tsang, & Cheung, 2002) infants strongly prefer consonant sounds (those with fundamental frequencies differing in small integer intervals) to dissonant sounds. Nonhuman animals, for example, sparrows (Watanabe, Uozumi, & Tanaka, 2005) also *discriminate* consonant and dissonant sounds, but do not *prefer* either. This, plus the fact that cortical responses to consonance and dissonance are very similar in monkeys and humans (Fishman et al., 2001), has led to the suggestion that early sensitivity to consonance/dissonance may be due to peripheral auditory system properties. In particular, because pitches with complex ratios have harmonics with similar frequencies, frequency resolution on the basilar membrane is degraded such that beating and a perception of roughness occurs (Fishman et al.). Despite this species-general platform human infants and nonhuman animals differ in that infants *prefer* consonance whereas nonhuman primates do not (McDermott & Hauser, 2004), and in fact prefer no music to music (McDermott & Hauser, 2007). This difference has led Hannon and Trainor (2007) to suggest that infants' preference for consonance might provide an entrée into more culture-specific aspects of harmony.

In concert with this, sometime between 8 months (Trainor & Trehub, 1992) and 5 years of age (Dowling, 1999) children develop the music-general system-specific ability to respond to changes in key (Trainor, 2005). Moreover, there appear to be musical enculturation processes at work, as it has been found that: 6-month-old Western environment infants discriminate note changes in Western major and minor scales *and* in Indonesian pelog scales, whereas Western adults only discriminate within the Western scales (Lynch et al., 1990); 8-month-olds respond both to a 4-semitone within-key melody change and a 1-semitone between-key change, whereas adults respond only to the between-key change (Trainor & Trehub, 1992); and by 6 years North American, French, and Australian children make more accurate and faster judgments about the nature of a target sound in a Western scale when the target is more rather than less stable harmonically, showing that children exposed to Western culture music develop the culture-specific ability to respond to harmony based on Western conventions (Schellenberg, Bigand, Poulin-Charronnat, Garnier, & Stevens, 2005).

A final aspect of melody and pitch perception in music concerns whether judgments are made on the basis of absolute or relative pitch. Most adults perceive pitch in a relative manner, but between 0.01 and 0.05 % of the population only perceive pitch in an absolute manner and even name isolated notes in the absence of context (Levitin & Rogers, 2005). The question thus arises regarding relative versus absolute pitch perception in infancy. Using a statistical learning paradigm, in which both absolute and relative pitch cues were available, Saffran (Saffran, 2003; Saffran & Griepentrog, 2001) found that 8-month-olds readily use absolute pitch cues to solve a three-tone recognition task whereas adults more readily use relative cues. These results led to consideration of the possibility that infants initially have absolute pitch and then, in a period of reorganization similar to that for phonological development, revert to a relative pitch mode (Saffran, 2003; Saffran & Griepentrog, 2001). However, more recent studies have found that 6- to 7-month-old infants respond to either absolute or relative pitch depending on which is the most effective to solve the task at hand (Plantinga & Trainor, 2005; Saffran, Reeck, Niebuhr, & Wilson, 2005; Volkova, Trehub, & Schellenberg, 2006). In addition recent investigations have shown that there is a form of memory for absolute pitch (e.g., for familiar instantiations of particular tunes) that is widespread in children and adults (Schellenberg & Trehub, 2003), and that nonhuman primates, while very proficient at relational tasks, tend to use absolute in preference to relative pitch cues (Wright, Rivera, Hulse, Shyan, & Neiworth, 2000), while nonprimates appear to prefer to use absolute pitch (Hauser & McDermott, 2003; Hulse & Page, 1988). Together these results suggest that the judicious task-specific use of relative and absolute pitch codes is a quality that human, but not nonhuman, animals have and possibly one that – along with other species-specific qualities, such as infants' preference for consonance – underlies the human appreciation of music.

In summary, as in the case of temporal properties of music, there appear to be species-general, species-specific, and culture-specific mechanisms in perceptual development for the spectral qualities of music. Infants show an initial discrimination of consonant versus dissonant sounds, which appears to be *species-general*, and a *species-specific* preference for consonant sounds which gives way to *culture-specific* appreciation of key changes and harmonic structure.

Hearing Loss, Diagnosis, Screening, and Intervention

We have seen that the infant auditory system matures early, allowing perception of a rich array of auditory information at birth. This is then augmented by infants' fine-tuned ability to learn about and direct their attention to the specific characteristics of the ambient environment – especially speech and music. Thus hearing loss that goes unnoticed in infants and young children can compromise speech, language, and music development. Given that speech and music input determines the organization of systems upon which language ability and music appreciation will be built, it is important to understand what can go wrong when the quality or quantity of speech or music input is either degraded due to sensori-neural loss or inconsistent due to conductive hearing loss. Moreover, understanding the effects of hearing impairment on speech perception is important for managing the condition and fitting an amplification device. In this section we discuss the risk factors for hearing loss, and point out the problems that can occur as a result of undetected hearing loss. We then show how hearing in infants is measured and discuss benefits of universal hearing screening and early intervention. The reader is directed to a complementary account of auditory and other sensory deficits by Preisler (volume 2, chapter 4).

Hearing loss

Hearing impairment mainly affects the adult population (Davis & Hind, 1999). One in 5 adults in the UK (Davis, 1997) and 1 in 3 adults in the USA (Campbell, Crews, Moriaraty, Zack, & Blackman, 1999) and 39% Australians aged over 55 have a hearing loss (Sindhusake et al., 2001). However, in the United Kingdom 1 in 750 children have a permanent hearing impairment (Fortnum & Davis, 1997). Prevalence estimates of child hearing loss are <1.1 and 2 per 1,000 in the USA and Australia (Van Naarden, Decouflé, & Caldwell, 2000; Wake et al., 2006). The major effect of a hearing impairment is loss of ability to hear some or all acoustic information including speech and music cues. Even mild hearing loss, around 15 to 30 dB, can have an impact on the perception of speech sounds, and prosodic cues such as stress and linguistic boundaries. Moderate losses of 30 to 50 dB are debilitating to the extent that infants and children with such loss miss almost all conversational speech (Northern & Downs, 1991). For *infants* with a hearing impairment, such audibility problems are compounded by the fact that infants have not yet built up stable phonemic representations, nor learned the phonotactic or prosodic patterns of their language.

The fitting of hearing aids within the infant's first 6 months has been shown to substantially improve hearing, particularly speech intelligibility (Markides, 1986). Furthermore, children whose hearing loss is identified by 6 months of age and who receive intervention (typically hearing aids) within approximately 2 months, show significantly better receptive and expressive vocabulary outcomes at 31 to 36 months of age compared to infants identified for hearing loss after 6 months of age and who receive intervention within approximately 2 months (Yoshinaga-Itano, Sedey, Coulter, & Mehl, 1998). Thus, it has been suggested that there is a sensitive period for optimal hearing development between birth and 6 months (Brookhouser, 1996).

Risk factors and classification of hearing loss. In addition to family history of hereditary childhood hearing loss, a number of neonatal complications increase the risk of neonatal hearing disorders. Low birthweight (1,500 to 2,999 grams) is a major risk factor for hearing loss (Van Naarden & Decoufle, 1999; Clarke & Conry, 1978), and premature infants are more likely to comprise this risk group. Delayed oxygenation is hypothesized to lead to deafness, however deafness may be associated with comorbid congenital *in utero* infections such as jaundice, rubella, measles, mumps, cytomegalovirus (Bradford et al.,

2005), or meningitis (Bedford et al., 2001) and to 5 min postpartum Apgar scores less than or equal to 6 (Meyer et al., 1999). Other risk factors for deafness include admission of the neonate to the neonatal intensive care unit (NICU) for 2 or more days (Halpern, Hosford-Dunn, & Malachowski, 1987) and/or mechanical ventilation lasting 5 days or more. Some publications recommend all infants in NICUs be comprehensively screened for hearing disorder (Jacobson & Morehouse, 1984). Furthermore, infants born with fetal alcohol syndrome (Church & Gerkin, 1988), neonatal sepsis (Feinmesser & Tell, 1976) and aberrant ear canal or pinna structures (Meyer et al., 1999) are also at higher risk of hearing impairment or deafness.

Auditory disorders can be classified as exogenous – those caused by toxicity, noise, or injury – and endogenous – arising from within the individual (genes). Congenital hearing loss, hearing loss present at birth, may or may not be hereditary, and is usually a sensori-neural loss. Endogenous disorders can be dominant (one parent has a loss and this is transmitted to the offspring), recessive (both parents of the child with hearing loss have normal hearing, yet the child has received one atypical gene from each parent) or sex-linked (the mother is a carrier of a hearing loss gene and this is manifested in male off-spring phenotypically, but in female offspring genotypically).

Conductive hearing losses occur when there is a problem with the outer ear, for example, a deformity of the pinna (outer ear) or with the middle ear, for example, otitis media. Otitis media with effusion (OME) is the most frequently diagnosed illness among infants and young children in the United Kingdom (Midgley, Dewey, Pryce, Maw, & Alspac Study Team, 2000). In OME, fluid accumulates in the middle ear as a result of negative pressure that alters Eustachian tube function. An episode of OME lasts on average 1 month, though in cases in which effusion is present following an acute infec-tion, the effusion may persist for a few months (Klein, 1983). Hearing thresholds during an OME episode are a function of the amount of fluid in the ear and vary from as low as 10 to as high as 50 dB (Fria, Cantekin, & Eichler (1985), compared with typical thresholds at or below 10 dB in infants without OME (Gravel & Wallace, 2000). The mild-to-moderate hearing loss associated with an episode of OME is hypothesized to impede children's ability to perceive language. It has been shown that many children with long-term or recurrent bouts of OME have later speech, language, and learning difficul-ties, although this claim is controversial. For example, studies of school-aged children's language abilities show that recurrent bouts of OME in infancy can have a negative impact on auditory processing (Updike & Thornburg, 1992), at brainstem and cortical levels (Maruthy & Mannarukrishnaiah, 2008) and impacts upon auditory attention (Asbjørnsen et al., 2005), speech perception and verbal working memory (Mody, Schwartz, Gravel, & Ruben, 1999), phonological awareness and literacy (Winskel, 2006; Rvachew & Grawburg, 2006). Other studies have revealed no influence of OME on language skills in childhood (Grievink, Peters, Vanbon, & Schilder, 1993; Harsten, Nettleblandt, Schalén, Kalm, & Prellner, 1993). Perhaps these differences are due to the uncertainty stemming from the retrospective methods employed in the majority of these studies, that is, only when school-aged children present with language difficulties is their OME history traced. A recent study by Polka and Rvachew (2005) was the first to dem-onstrate the impact of otitis media on speech perception as it is happening in infancy. Six- to 8-month-old infants were tested for discrimination of the native /bu/ vs /gu/

contrast using the conditioned head turn procedure and with a tympanometry posttest. Those infants with presenting OME on the day of testing and/or history of OME were more likely to fail to discriminate the syllables than infants with no history of OME. These results show that OME certainly affects hearing, and may indeed have long-term consequences.

Hearing screening and intervention

Hearing screening is designed to differentiate those individuals who exhibit an auditory disorder from those who do not, and to allow correction if necessary in a timely and economical manner. Many developed countries have established universal hearing screening programs for neonates with the aim of identifying sensori-neural hearing loss before 6 months of age. This allows early intervention in the form of amplification (where necessary) and educational management. Early identification and intervention is cost-effective, as a deaf infant who receives educational and audiological intervention in infancy or toddlerhood is more likely to be mainstreamed into a regular classroom at school (Bess & Humes 2003). No prospective controlled study has directly investigated the efficacy of newborn hearing screening results for improving language, speech, music, or educational performance. However, it has been shown that children who receive intervention after age 1 show poorer language and speech outcomes at 5 years of age than children who received early intervention – hearing aids (Bubbico, Di Castelbianco, Tangucci, & Salvinelli, 2007) or cochlear implants (Nicholas & Geers, 2006). There are a number of intervention strategies for hearing loss in infants and children, including fitting of hearing aids or cochlear implants, sign language or speech-language therapy. All are aimed at improving language outcomes, although this is debated by Preisler (1999) who claims that such interventions are disability-focused and that alternative interventions focusing on competencies such as nonverbal communication and joint attention between parent and infant will be more beneficial to language acquisition in hearing-impaired infants. In a series of studies, Yoshinaga-Itano and her colleagues compared language outcomes in infants diagnosed with hearing loss before (early) or after (late) 6 months of age. Hearing impaired infants who were identified early had better expressive and receptive vocabulary scores on the Minnesota Child Development Inventory at 13 to 40 months of age than later-identified infants (Apuzzo & Yoshinaga-Itano, 1995; Yoshinaga-Itano & Apuzzo, 1998a, 1998b; Yoshinaga-Itano et al., 1998). Moreover, multiple regression studies reveal that age at diagnosis explains 23% of the variance in expressive language at 24 and 36 months of age (Mayne, Yoshinaga-Itano, Sedey, & Carey, 2000), age of entry into intervention programs explains 44 to 50% of the variance in receptive and expressive language at 3 years (Calderon & Naidu, 2000), and family involvement in intervention explains 57% of the variance in vocabulary at 5 years of age (Moeller, 2000).

The Joint Committee on Infant Hearing (USA) endorsed the goal of Universal Hearing Screening in June 1994, primarily because even mild hearing loss can interfere with the development of speech and language. Many countries have since followed suit, for example, the UK in 2001, and Australia in 2006. However, universal hearing screening of newborns may not be viable because of the overall costs and the practicality of implementing hearing screening programs in rural communities where there are significantly fewer births (Bess & Humes, 2003). A more practical solution has been proposed, that is to only screen infants at risk for hearing impairment, such as infants in neonatal intensive care units who are 10 to 20 times more likely to be diagnosed with moderate to severe permanent hearing loss (White, Vohr, & Behrens, 1993). In support of this proposal Fortnum and Davis (1997) argue that 10 to 30% of newborns are exposed to risk factors for hearing loss, and thus, if only these infants were screened, then 50 to 75% of all cases of moderate to profound bilateral hearing loss would be captured. Many neonatal hearing screening programs use a two-step screening method – otoacoustic emissions and the auditory brainstem response (e.g., Wessex Universal Hearing Screening Trial Group, 1998; Kanne, Schaefer, & Perkins, 1999; Doyle, Burggraaff, Fujikawa, Kim, & Macarthur, 1997), and we now turn to consideration of these and other measures.

Behavioral observation audiometry and visual reinforcement audiometry.   Behavioral Observation Audiometry (BOA), and Visual Reinforcement Audiometry (VRA) are commonly used for determining the presence versus the absence of auditory function, as opposed to assessing responsivity to particular levels of loudness, frequency, or pitch. BOA is best suited to infants aged 6 to 24 months. Typically, an external auditory stimulus is played to the infant and reflexive and orienting responses such as eye blink "startle" responses are recorded by multiple observers, or an auditory stimulus is presented to the infant without the observer's knowledge and the observer is required to judge whether or not the sound was presented. Reinforcement is given to the infant in the form of a mechanical dancing toy if the infant produces a response that leads to a correct observer judgment (Werner, 1995). A downfall of BOA methods is that infants may quickly habituate to the auditory stimulus such that the same response may not be achieved after repeated presentations.

By 5 to 6 months of age infants are able to localize sound (see *Development of binaural abilities* above), and make head turns reliably. Visual Reinforcement Audiometry (VRA) uses stimulus response reinforcement to elicit head turn responses to a change in sound. In an initial phase, conditioned head turns to the presentation of an auditory stimulus are shaped by a visual reinforcer contingent on sound presentation. Once the infant reliably produces head turns to a preestablished criterion they enter the test phase. Here, signal intensity is decreased by 10 dB following correct head turns and increased by 10 dB when no head turn is produced. This staircase procedure continues until a criterion number of reversals with the threshold calculated by averaging across the reversal point values. This procedure yields good test-retest reliability within children across multiple sessions and is suitable for 6-month-olds to 2.5-year-olds.

Delays in speech and language development are often good indicators of hearing impairment in older infants and preschoolers; failure to reach key milestones, including no differentiated babbling or vocal imitation at 12 months, no single word production at 18 months, fewer than 10 words at 24 months and fewer than 30 words at 30 months are all likely covariates of hearing loss (Matkin, 1984). The Early Language Milestone parental checklist (Coplan, 1987) is commonly used to screen for disorders in expressive, receptive, and early visual language skills that may be related to hearing loss in children up to 3 years of age (Leung & Kao, 1999). However, using behavioral and parent report measures to assess hearing loss and speech communication disorders is often too late, and other tests can be used for earlier detection of hearing problems.

Measures of hearing: Otoacoustic emissions, and auditory brainstem responses.   Otoacoustic emissions (OAE) are sounds generated from hair cells of the cochlear as a by-product of acoustic stimulation of a functional auditory system. Typically broadband clicks or two continuous tones at a rate of 50 per second are used to measure OAEs, "transient evoked OAEs" or "distortion product OAEs," respectively. The sounds are presented to the ear via a probe and the OAE response is measured in the external ear canal. Absence of OAEs suggests damage to the hair cells of the cochlear and hearing loss of approximately 40 dB. OAE tests are easy to conduct, however, many infants are referred for further screening because the presence of ear canal vernix, in 1 to 2-day-old newborns, can interfere with the reading (see Cavanaugh, 1996).

Auditory evoked potentials are obtained by placing electrodes on the scalp and recording electrical activity of the brain that is phase-locked to a particular stimulus. The earliest components of the waveform are associated with responsiveness of the subcortical regions of the auditory system to sound – the brainstem. Known as the auditory brainstem response (ABR), this component is measured from two-channel electrodes in vertex-to-nape of neck and vertex-to-mastoid configuration. Clicks or tone bursts can be used: ABRs to clicks allow measurements of thresholds across the frequency range, while ABRs to tone burst stimuli are better suited for determining thresholds at specific frequencies (within the 500 to 4,000 Hz range). The ABR is a reliable measure of hearing sensitivity and is particularly advantageous for the infant population because it (a) uses near-threshold stimuli thus allowing detection of mild hearing losses, (b) does not require a behavioral response from the infant, so can be obtained in sleep or waking states, and (c) reduces tester bias because the screening tool gives a pass or fail result – and thus can be performed by nonprofessionals (Doyle et al., 1997). The ABR has also been used to assess hearing aid effectiveness (Davidson, Wall, & Goodman, 1990) but may not give a reliable indication of amplification because the use of brief clicks/tones does not activate hearing aid circuitry in the same manner as speech does (Brown, Klein, & Snydee, 1999).

Tympanometry.   Tympanometry is an objective measure of middle ear status (ear canal volume) that determines acoustic admittance (how easily a probe tone flows through the middle ear) as the air pressure within the ear canal is varied. Infant tympanograms are typically recorded using a 226 Hz probe tone and ipsilateral acoustic reflexes at 1,000 Hz allowing peak pressure (in ear canal pressure, daPa), static compliance (in ml), and ear canal volume (in ml) to be determined. Abnormal middle ear function is inferred when there is either a flat tympanogram or peak pressure below −100 daPa combined with an absent ipsilateral acoustic reflex at 1,000 Hz (Silman & Silverman, 1991). Flat tympanograms are a cause for concern, as they indicate the presence of middle ear fluid (Sprague, Wiley, & Goldstein, 1985). The screening guidelines of the American Speech and Hearing Association (1997) recommend tympanometry from 7 months of age. Both OAEs and ABRs can be influenced by the status of the middle ear, and thus tympanometry is a useful resource for identifying middle ear as opposed to cochlear or brainstem pathology (Fowler & Shanks, 2002).

Intervention and amplification considerations for infants with hearing loss

It is widely accepted that children diagnosed with hearing loss must receive adequate auditory stimulation and appropriate intervention as soon as possible to maximize the potential for learning language. The introduction of neonatal screening has meant that children with hearing loss are more likely to be identified and fitted with hearing aids or cochlear implantation at a very early age. The advantages of early amplification have long been recognized (Pediatric Working Group, 1999; Yoshinaga-Itano et al., 1998). For example, prelingually deafened children with cochlear implants demonstrate the capacity to learn language at an equivalent rate to their hearing peers (Balkany, Hodges Miyamoto, Gibbin, & Odabassi, 2001; McConkey-Robbins, Burton Koch, Osperger, Zimmerman-Phillips, & Kishon-Rabin, 2004). Moreover, children who receive cochlear implants show improvements in their perception of stress and words in a closed-set context within 1 year of implantation (Tyler et al., 1997). Similar gains are reported for open-set speech perception where recipients of a cochlear implant prior to 2 years of age achieve open-set speech perception equal to or faster than children implanted after age 2 (Waltzman & Cohen, 1998).

Much headway has been made over the past two decades in understanding how the communication needs of infants differ from those of older children and adults (e.g., Allen & Wightman, 1994; Clarkson & Rogers, 1995). For example, in an investigation of 7- to 8-month-old infants' perception of harmonic tonal complexes, Clarkson and Rogers (1995) found that infants were able to categorize low-tone complexes on the basis of the pitch of the missing fundamental, but were unable to categorize high-frequency energy this way. Adults, however, successfully categorized tonal complexes with both low and high-frequency energy. These findings highlight the importance of low-frequency amplification for infants. Traditionally, it has been viewed that there is little benefit of low-frequency amplification for adults with mild to severe hearing loss for perceiving speech in noise (Skinner & Miller, 1983). However, for the infant acquiring language the low-frequency features of speech such as rhythm, intonation, pitch, and stress are important and sought after by young hearing infants to differentiate word boundaries (Jusczyk & Aslin, 1995), phrasal boundaries in speech (Jusczyk et al., 1992) and music (Jusczyk & Krumhansl, 1993; Krumhansl & Jusczyk, 1990), and in the linguistically and emotionally rich form of speech spoken to young infants – infant-directed speech (Kuhl et al., 1997; Burnham, Kitamura, & Vollmer-Conna, 2002).

Developmental changes in infants' communication environment have implications for microphone technology used in communication devices such as hearing aids. For example, for very young infants who are not yet crawling, incoming aural communication emanates from directly in front of the infant, at close range, and so a directional microphone is most suitable (Stelmachowicz, 1996), and, where appropriate, binaural directional amplification is optimal (Hawkins & Yacullo, 1984). For the older, more mobile infant who is crawling or walking, language spoken to them will not always come from the forward direction, and thus omnidirectional microphone devices may be more suitable. As sound waves are received by both the left and right ears, and the resultant auditory signals are used to localize and perceive sound, there are a number of benefits of wearing two hearing aids: (a) the brain more accurately processes sounds making it easier to perceive speech, especially speech in noise; (b) there is decreased risk of distortion as the volume level of each hearing aid can be set lower (as compared to a higher volume level for one hearing aid); and (c) sounds are localized more easily (see Development of binaural abilities above) with binaural amplification.

Cochlear implants are prostheses designed to provide hearing to individuals with severe to profound sensori-neural hearing loss, and according to Valencia and colleagues (Valencia, Rimell, Friedman, Oblander, & Helmbrecht, 2008) are safe to insert in infants as young as 6 months of age. Implants are surgically fitted in the mastoid of the temporal bone and have an electrode array that extends from the implant to the cochlea where it is inserted. A microphone, speech processor, cable, and transmitting coil are worn externally. Fitting techniques depend on the age and cognitive abilities of the individual recipient but can incorporate both behavioral testing of sound detection, and objective methods.

The use of a hearing aid and a cochlear implant in opposite ears can improve binaural speech perception, sound localization, and communicative functioning relative to the use of cochlear implants alone. In a study of 16 children, all children showed binaural benefits on at least one measure (Ching, Psarros, Hill, Dillon, & Incerti, 2001). Studies with adults highlight how speech perception of sentences and words in the presence of noise is improved with combined use of cochlear implant and hearing aid (Armstrong, Pegg, James, & Blamey, 1997).

Conclusions and Future Directions

In this chapter we have shown that the auditory system develops early; that the infant is born with a number of auditory abilities and preferences, some learned in the womb; and that there are developmental influences of species-general auditory experience and culturally and linguistically specific auditory experience. Auditory competence underlies the understanding of speech and the appreciation of song and music, rich sources of communication that enhance our enjoyment of the world and our fellows. There are a number of factors that may put intact hearing at risk, and hearing loss is not as uncommon as we would wish. Given the early emergence of auditory abilities, if there is early deprivation in the auditory sphere, there can be significant later consequences. Fortunately, there are now quite sophisticated means of both early screening and early intervention for hearing loss. Nevertheless, further research is required so that the mechanisms of hearing loss are better understood and the technology of hearing prostheses improved. To achieve this research goal, further understanding of the development of normal hearing is necessary. Such research will not only aid the impairment area, but also help us to understand the delicate interplay of species-general aspects of the auditory system we share with other animals, species-specific predilections of humans, and culture-specific influences of speech and music, that make up the richness of human auditory experience. At a more general level, the world's variety of speech and music systems provides a natural collection of mini-laboratories in which the age-old question of nature and nurture may be investigated.

Notes

1. Shahidullah and Hepper (1993) have shown that fetal response to sound stimulation (using a bright light as a control stimulation) and the lack of such movement specifically to sound, as measured by movement recorded by ultrasound, is a reliable predictor of intact hearing versus hearing impairment tested at birth.
2. The precedence effect is the phenomenon of perceiving two sounds delivered in quick succession from different sources, as one sound emanating from the first source. See also Development of binaural abilities.

References

Abdala, C., & Folsom, R. C. (1995). The development of frequency resolution in humans as revealed by the auditory brain-stem response recorded with notched-noise. *Journal of the Acoustical Society of America*, 98(2), 921–930.

Allen, P., & Wightman, F. (1994). Psychometric functions for children's detection of tones in noise. *Journal of Speech and Hearing Research*, 37, 205–215.

American Speech & Hearing Association. (1997). *Guidelines for audiologic screening*. Rockville, MD: American Speech-Language-Hearing Association.

Anson B. J., & Davies, J. (1980). Embryology of the ear. Developmental anatomy of the ear. In M. M. Paparella & D. A. Shumrick (Eds.), *Otolaryngology* (2nd ed., pp. 3–25). Philadelphia: WB Saunders.

Apuzzo, M. -R. L., & Yoshinaga-Itano, C. (1995). Early identification of infants with significant hearing loss and the Minnesota Child Development Inventory. *Seminars in Hearing*, 16, 124–139.

Armstrong, M., Pegg, P., James, C., & Blamey, P. (1997). Speech perception in noise with implant and hearing aid. *The American Journal of Otology*, 18(Suppl. 6), S140–S141.

Ars, B. (1989). Organogenesis of the middle ear structures. *Journal of Laryngology and Otology*, 103, 16–21.

Asbjørnsen, A. E., Obrzut, J. E., Boliek, C. A., Myking, E., Holmefjord, A., Reisaeter, S., et al. (2005). Impaired auditory attention skills following middle-ear infections. *Child Neuropsychology*, 11(2), 121–133.

Aslin, R. N. (1989). Discrimination of frequency transitions by human infants. *Journal of the Acoustical Society of America*, 86, 582–590.

Balkany, T. J., Hodges, A., Miyamoto, R. T., Gibbin, K., Odabassi, O. (2001). Cochlear implants in children. *Otolaryngology Clinic of North America*, 34(2), 455–467.

Bargones, J. Y., & Werner, L. A. (1994). Adults listen selectively; infants do not. *Psychological Science*, 5(3), 170–174.

Bargones, J. Y., Werner, L. A., & Marean, G. C. (1995). Infant psychometric functions for detection: Mechanisms of immature sensitivity. *Journal of the Acoustical Society of America*, 98(1), 99–111.

Baruch, C., & Drake, C. (1997). Tempo discrimination in infants. *Infant Behavior and Development*, 20, 573–577.

Baruch, C., Panissal-Vieu, N., & Drake, C. (2004). Preferred perceptual tempo for sound sequences: Comparison of adults, children, and infants. *Perceptual and Motor Skills*, 98(1), 325–339.

Bedford, H., de Louvois, J., Halket, S., Peckham, C., Hurley, R., & Harvey, D. (2001). Meningitis in infancy in England and Wales: Follow up at 5 years. *British Medical Journal*, 323, 1–5.

Berg, K. M., & Boswell, A. E. (1998). Infants' detection of increments in low- and high-frequency noise. *Perception & Psychophysics*, *60*, 1044–1051.

Berg, K. M., & Boswell, A. E. (1999). Effect of masker level on infants' detection of tones in noise. *Perception & Psychophysics*, *61*(1), 80–86.

Bertoncini, J., Bijeljac-Babic, R., Blumstein, S. E., & Mehler, J. (1987). Discrimination in neonates of very short CVs. *Journal of the Acoustical Society of America*, *82*, 31–37.

Bess, F. H., & Humes, L. E. (2003). *Audiology: the fundamentals* (3rd ed.). Philadelphia, PA: Lippincott Williams & Wilkins.

Best, C. T., McRoberts, G., LaFleur, R., & Silver-Isenstadt, J. (1995). Divergent developmental patterns for infants' perception of two nonnative consonant contrasts. *Infant Behavior and Development*, *18*, 339–350.

Best, C., Singh, L., Bouchard, J., Connelly, G., Cook, A., & Faber, A. (1997, April). *Developmental changes in infants' discrimination of non-native vowels that assimilate to two native categories.* Poster presented at the Meeting of Society of Research in Child Development, Washington, DC, April 3–6.

Bradford, R. D., Cloud, G., Lakeman, A. D., Boppana, S., Kimberlin, D. W., Jacobs, R. et al. (2005). Detection of Cytomegalovirus (CMV) DNA by Polymerase Chain Reaction is associated with hearing loss in newborns with symptomatic congenital CMV infection. *Journal of Infectious Diseases*, *191*, 227–233.

Brookhouser, P. E. (1996). Sensorineural hearing loss in children. *Pediatric Clinics of North America*, *43*, 1195–1216.

Brown, E., Klein, A. J., & Snydee, K. A. (1999). Hearing-aid-processed tone pips: electroacoustic and ABR characteristics. *Journal of the American Academy of Audiology*, *10*(4), 190–197.

Bubbico, L., Di Castelbianco, F. B., Tangucci, M., & Salvinelli, F. (2007). Early hearing detection and intervention in children with prelingual deafness, effects on language development. *Minerva Pediatrica*, *59*(4), 307–313.

Bull, D., Eilers, R. E., & Oller, D. K. (1984). Infants' discrimination of intensity variation in multisyllabic stimuli. *Journal of the Acoustical Society of America*, *76*(1), 13–17.

Burnham, D., Kitamura, C., & Vollmer-Conna, U. (2002). What's new pussycat? On talking to babies and animals. *Science*, *296*, 1435.

Burnham, D., Taplin, J., Henderson-Smart, D., Earnshaw-Brown, L., & O'Grady, B. (1993). Maturation of precedence effect thresholds: Full-term and pre-term infants. *Infant Behavior and Development*, *16*, 213–232.

Calderon, R., & Naidu, S. (2000). Further support for the benefits of early identification and intervention for children with hearing loss. *Volta Review*, *100* (5), 53–84.

Campbell, V., Crews, J., Moriarty, D., Zack, M., & Blackman, D. (1999). Surveillance for sensory impairment, activity limitation, and health related quality of life among older adults – United States, 1993–1997. *MMWR. CDC Surveillance Summaries: Morbidity and Mortality Weekly Report. CDC Surveillance Summaries/ Centers for Disease Control*, *48*(8), 131–156.

Cavanaugh, R. M. J. (1996). Pneumatic otoscopy in healthy full-term infants. *Pediatrics*, *79*, 520–523.

Chang, H. W., & Trehub, S. E. (1977). Auditory processing of relational information by young infants. *Journal of Experimental Child Psychology*, *24*, 324–331.

Chekaluk, E. U., & Llewellyn, K. R. (1992). Saccadic suppression: A functional viewpoint. In E. U. Chekaluk & K. R. Llewellyn (Eds.), *The role of eye movements in perceptual processes* (pp. 171–192). Oxford: Elsevier.

Ching, T. Y. C.; Psarros, C., Hill, M., Dillon, H., Incerti, P. (2001). Should children who use cochlear implants wear hearing aids in the opposite ear? *Ear & Hearing*, *22*(5), 365–380.

Church, M. W., & Gerkin, K. P. (1988). Hearing disorders in children with fetal alcohol syndrome – findings from case-reports. *Pediatrics*, *82*(2), 147–154.

Clarke, B. R., & Conry, R. F. (1978). Hearing impairment in children of low birthweight. *Journal of Auditory Research*, 18(4), 277–291.

Clarkson, M. G., & Rogers, E. C. (1995). Infants require low-frequency energy to hear the pitch of the missing fundamental. *Journal of the Acoustical Society of America*, 103, 1128–1140.

Clifton, R. K. (1985). The precedence effect: Its implications for developmental questions. In S. E. Trehub & B. Schneider (Eds.), *Auditory development in infancy* (pp. 85–99). New York: Plenum.

Clifton, R. K., Gwiazda, J., Bauer, J. A., Clarkson, M. G., & Held, R. M. (1988). Growth in head size during infancy: Implications for sound localization. *Developmental Psychology*, 24, 477–483.

Clifton, R. K., Morrongiello, B., & Dowd, J. (1984). A developmental look at an auditory illusion: The precedence effect. *Developmental Psychobiology*, 17, 519–536.

Clifton, R. K., Morrongiello, B., Kulig, J., & Dowd, J. (1981). Newborns' orientation toward sound: Possible implications for cortical development. *Child Development*, 52, 833–838.

Coplan J. (1987). *ELM scale: The early language milestone scale*. Austin, TX: Pro-Ed.

Cranford, J. L., & Oberholtzer, M. (1976). Role of the neocortex in binaural hearing in the cat. II The "precedence effect" in sound localization. *Brain Research*, 111(2), 225–239.

Cranford, J., Ravizza, R., Diamond, I. T., & Whitfield, I. C. (1971). Unilateral ablation of the auditory cortex in the cat impairs complex sound localization. *Science*, 172, 286–288.

Cutler, A., & Mehler, J. (1993). The periodicity bias. *Journal of Phonetics*, 21, 103–108.

Cutting, J. E. (1982). Plucks and bows are categorically perceived sometimes. *Perception & Psychophysics*, 31, 462–476.

Cutting, J. E., & Rosner, B. S. (1974). Categories and boundaries in speech and music. *Perception & Psychophysics*, 16, 564–570.

Davidson, S. A., Wall, L. G., & Goodman, C. M. (1990). Preliminary studies on the use of an abr amplitude projection procedure for hearing-aid selection. *Ear and Hearing*, 11(5), 332–339.

Davis, A., & Hind, S. (1999). The impact of hearing impairment: A global health problem. *International Journal of Pediatric Otorhinolaryngology*, 49, S51–S54.

DeCasper, A. J., & Fifer, W. P. (1980). Of human bonding: Newborns prefer their mothers' voices. *Science*, 208, 1174–1176.

Demany, L., McKenzie, B., & Vurpillot, E. (1977). Rhythm perception in early infancy. *Nature*, 266, 718–719.

Dowling, W. J. (1999). The development of music cognition. In D. Deutsch (Ed.), *The Psychology of Music*, (2nd ed. pp. 603–625), San Diego, CA: Academic.

Doyle, K. J., Burggraaff, B., Fujikawa, S., Kim, J., & Macarthur, C. J. (1997). Neonatal hearing screening with otoscopy, auditory brain stem response, and otoacoustic emissions. *Otolaryngology – Head and Neck Surgery*, 116(1), 597–603.

Drake, C., & Botte, M. -C. (1993). Tempo sensitivity in auditory sequences: Evidence for a multiple look model. *Perception & Psychophysics*, 54, 277–286.

Ebbinghaus, H. (1964). *Memory: A contribution to experimental psychology*. New York: Dover.

Eimas, P. D. (1974). Auditory and linguistic processing of cues for place of articulation by infants. *Perception and Psychophysics*, 16, 513–521.

Eimas, P. D., & Miller, J. L. (1980). Discrimination of the information for manner of articulation. *Infant Behavior and Development*, 3, 367–375.

Eimas, P. D., Siqueland, E. R., Jusczyk, P., & Vigorito, J. (1971). Speech perception in infants. *Science*, 171, 303–306.

Feinmesser, M., & Tell, L. (1976). Neonatal screening for detection of deafness. *Archives of Otolaryngology*, 102(5), 297–299.

Field, J., Muir, D., Pilon, R., Sinclair, M., & Dodwell, P. (1980). Infants' orientation to lateral sounds from birth to three months. *Child Development*, 51, 295–298.

Fishman, Y. I., Volkov, M., Noh, D., Garell, C., Bakken, H., Arezzo, J. C. et al. (2001). Consonance and dissonance of musical chords: neural correlates in auditory cortex of monkeys and humans. *Journal of Neurophysiology, 86*, 2761–2788.

Fitch, T. (2005). The evolution of music in comparative perspective. In G. Avanzini, L. Lopez, S. Koelsch & M. Mzanjno (Eds.), *The Neurosciences and Music II: From Perception to Performance* (pp. 29–49). New York: New York Academy of Sciences.

Folsom, R. C., & Wynne, M. K. (1987). Auditory brain stem responses from human adults and infants: Wave V tuning curves. *Journal of the Acoustical Society of America, 81*(2), 412–417.

Fortnum, H., & Davis, A. (1997). Epidemiology of permanent childhood hearing impairment in Trent region, 1985–1993. *British Journal of Audiology, 31*, 409–446.

Fowler, C. E., & Shanks, J. E. (2002). Tympanometry. In J. Katz (Ed.), *Handbook of clinical audiology* (5th ed., pp. 175–204). Baltimore: Lippincott, Williams, & Wilkins.

Fria T. J., Cantekin E. I., & Eichler J. A. (1985). Hearing acuity of children with otitis media with effusion. *Archives of Otolaryngology – Head and Neck Surgery, 111*(1), 10–16.

Gerhardt, K. J., & Abrams, R. M. (1996). Fetal hearing: Characterization of the stimulus and response. *Seminars in Perinatology, 20*, 11–20.

Gerhardt, K. J., Huang, X., Arrington, K. E., Meixner, K., Abrams, R., & Antonelli, P. J. (1996). Fetal sheep in utero hear through bone conduction. *American Journal of Otolaryngology, 17*, 374–379.

Gervain, J., Macagno, F., Cogoi, S., Peña, M., & Mehler, J. (2008). The neonate brain detects speech structure. *Proceedings of the National Academy of Science, 105*, 14222–14227.

Gibson, K. R. (1981). Comparative neuro-ontogeny: Its implications for the development of human intelligence. In G. Butterworth (Ed.), *Infancy and epistemology* (pp. 52–82). Brighton, England: Harvester Press.

Gomes, H., Molholm, S., Christodoulou, C., Ritter, W., & Cowan, N. (2000). The development of auditory attention in children. *Frontiers in Bioscience, 5*, 108–120.

Gravel, J. S., & Wallace, I. F. (2000). Effects of otitis media with effusion on hearing in the first 3 years of life. *Journal of Speech Language and Hearing Research, 43*(3), 631–644.

Grieser, D. L., & Kuhl, P. K. (1989). Categorization of speech by infants: Support for speech-sound prototypes. *Developmental Psychology, 25*, 577–588.

Grievink, E. H., Peters, S. A. F., Vanbon, W. H. J., & Schilder, A. G. M. (1993). The effects of early bilateral otitis-media with effusion on language ability – a prospective cohort study. *Journal of Speech and Hearing Research, 36*(5), 1004–1012.

Halpern, J., Hosford-Dunn, H., & Malachowski N. (1987). Four factors that accurately predict hearing loss in "high risk" neonates. *Ear & Hearing, 8*(1), 21–25.

Hannon, E. E., & Johnson, S. P. (2005). Infants use meter to categorize rhythms and melodies: Implications for musical structure learning. *Cognitive Psychology Science, 50*, 354–377.

Hannon, E. E., & Trainor, L. J. (2007). Music acquisition: Effects of enculturation and formal training on development. *Trends in Cognitive Sciences, 11*, 466–472.

Hannon, E. E., & Trehub, S. E. (2005a). Metrical categories in infancy and adulthood. *Psychological Science, 16*, 48–55.

Hannon, E. E., & Trehub, S. E. (2005b). Tuning in to rhythms: Infants learn more readily than adults. *Proceedings of the National Academy of Science USA, 102*, 12639–12643.

Harley, H. E., Odell, K., Fellner, W., Putnam, E., Clark, D., Goonen, C., et al. (2003, December). *Rhythm discrimination by the bottlenose dolphin*. Presented at the 15th biennial conference on the biology of marine animals. Greensboro, NC.

Harsten, G., Nettelbladt, U., Schalén, L., Kalm, O., & Prellner, K. (1993). Language development in children with recurrent acute otitis media during the first three years of life:

Follow-up study from birth to seven years of age. *The Journal of Laryngology & Otology, 107*(5), 407–412.

Hauser, M. D., & McDermott, J. (2003). The evolution of the music faculty: A comparative perspective. *Nature Neuroscience, 6,* 663–668.

Hawkins, D., & Yacullo, W. (1984). Signal-to-noise advantage of binaural hearing aids and directional microphones under different levels of reverberation. *Journal of Speech and Hearing Disorders, 49,* 279–286.

Hepper, P. G., & Shahidullah, B. S. (1994). Development of fetal hearing. *Archives of Disease in Childhood, Fetal and Neonatal Edition, 71,* F81–F87.

Hochster, M. E., & Kelly, J. B. (1981). The precedence effect and sound localization by children with temporal lobe epilepsy. *Neuropsychologia, 19,* 49–55.

Hollien, H., & Feinstein, S. (1975). Contribution of the external auditory meatus to auditory sensitivity underwater. *Journal of the Acoustical Society of America, 57,* 1488–1492.

Hulse, S. H., Humpal, J., & Cynx, J. (1984a). Discrimination and generalization of rhythmic and arrhythmic sound patterns by European starlings (Sturnus vulgaris). *Music Perception, 1*(4), 442–446.

Hulse, S. H., Humpal, J., & Cynx, J. (1984b). Processing of rhythmic sound structures by birds. *Annals of the New York Academy of Sciences, 423,* 407–419.

Hulse, S. H., & Page, S. C. (1988). Toward a comparative psychology of music perception. *Music Perception, 5,* 427–452.

Jacobson, J. T., & Morehouse, C. R. (1984). A comparison of auditory brain stem response and behavioral screening in high risk and normal newborn infants. Electrophysiologic techniques in audiology and otology. *Ear & Hearing, 5*(4), 247–253.

Jensen, J. K., & Neff, D. L. (1993). Development of basic auditory discrimination in preschool children. *Psychological Science 4*(2), 104–107.

Jusczyk, P. W. (1993). How word recognition may evolve from infant speech perception capacities. In G. T. M. Altmann & R. Shillcock (Eds.), *Cognitive models of speech processing: The second sperlonga meeting.* Hillsdale: Erlbaum.

Jusczyk, P. W., & Aslin, R. N. (1995). Infants' detection of the sound patterns of words in fluent speech. *Cognitive Psychology, 29,* 1–23.

Jusczyk, P. W., & Krumhansl, C. L. (1993). Pitch and rhythmic patterns affecting infants' sensitivity to musical phrase structure. *Journal of Experimental Psychology-Human Perception and Performance, 19*(3), 627–640.

Jusczyk, P. W., Copan, H., & Thompson, E. (1978). Perception by two-month-olds of glide contrasts in multisyllabic utterances. *Perception and Psychophysics, 24,* 515–520.

Jusczyk, P. W., Cutler, A., & Redanz, N. J. (1993). Infants' preference for the predominant stress patterns of English words. *Child Development, 64,* 675–687.

Jusczyk, P. W., Hirsh-Pasek, K., Kemler Nelson, D. G., Kennedy, L. J., Woodward, A., & Piwoz, J. (1992). Perception of acoustic correlates of major phrasal units by young infants. *Cognitive Psychology, 24,* 252–293.

Jusczyk, P. W., Houston, D. M., & Newsome, M. (1999). The beginnings of word segmentation in English-learning infants. *Cognitive Psychology, 39*(3–4), 159–207.

Jusczyk, P. W., Pisoni, D. B., & Mullennix, J. (1992). Some consequences of stimulus variability on speech processing by 2-month-old infants. *Cognition, 43,* 253–291.

Jusczyk, P. W., Pisoni, D. B., Walley, A., & Murray, J. (1980). Discrimination of relative onset time of two-component tones by infants. *Journal of the Acoustical Society of America, 67,* 262–270.

Jusczyk, P. W., Rosner, B. S., Cutting, J. E., Foard, G. F., & Smith, L. B. (1977). Categorical perception of nonspeech sounds by 2-month-old infants. *Perception & Psychophysics, 21,* 50–54.

Jusczyk, P. W., Rosner, B. S., Reed, M., & Kennedy, L. J. (1989). Could temporal order differences underlie 2-month-olds' discrimination of English voicing contrasts? *Journal of the Acoustical Society of America, 85,* 1741–1749.

Kanne, T. J., Schaefer, L., & Perkins, A. (1999). Potential pitfalls of initiating a newborn hearing screening program. *Archives of Otolaryngology and Head and Neck Surgery, 125,* 28–32.

Kaplan, E. (1970). The role of intonation in the acquisition of language. *Dissertation Abstracts International, 30,* 3407.

Karzon, R., & Nicholas, J. (1989). Syllabic pitch perception in 2- to 3-month-old infants. *Perception & Psychophysics, 45*(1), 10–14.

Keefe, D. H., & Levi, E. (1996). Maturation of the middle and external ears: Acoustic power-based responses and reflectance tympanometry. *Ear and Hearing, 17*(5), 361–373.

Kenna, M. A. (1990). The ear and related structures. Embryology and developmental anatomy of the ear. In C. D. Bluestone, S. E. Stool, & M. D. Scheetz, *Pediatric otolaryngology* (pp. 77–87). Philadelphia, PA: W. B. Saunders & Co.

Kisilevsky, B. S., Hains, S. M. J., Lee, K., Xie, X., Huang, H., Ye, H. H., et al. (2003). Effects of experience on fetal voice rendition. *Psychological Science, 14,* 220–224.

Klein, J. O. (1983). Epidemiology and natural history of otitis media. In *Workshop on effects of otitis media on the child.* [Special article; C. D. Bluestone, J. O. Klein, J. L. Paradise, et al.] *Pediatrics, 71,* 639–640.

Kopyar, B. A. (1997). *Intensity discrimination abilities of infants and adults: Implications for underlying processes.* Unpublished doctoral dissertation, University of Washington, Seattle.

Krumhansl, C. L., & Jusczyk, P. W. (1990). Infants' perception of phrase structure in music. *Psychological Science, 1,* 70–73.

Kuhl, P. K. (1978). Predispositions for the perception of speech sound categories: A species specific phenomenon? In F. D. Minifie & L. L. Lloyd (Eds.), *Communicative and cognitive abilities: Early behavioural assessment* (pp. 229–255). Baltimore: University Park Press.

Kuhl, P. K. (1991). Human adults and human infants show a "perceptual magnet effect" for the prototypes of speech categories, monkeys do not. *Perception and Psychophysics, 50*(2), 93–107.

Kuhl, P., Andruski, J., Chistovich, I., Chistovich, L., Kozhevnikova, E., Ryskina, V. et al. (1997). Cross-language analysis of phonetic units in language addressed to infants. *Science, 277,* 684–686.

Kuhl, P. K., & Miller, J. D. (1975). Speech perception by the chinchilla: Voiced-voiceless distinction in alveolar plosive consonants. *Science, 190,* 69–72.

Kuhl, P. K., & Miller, J. D. (1978). Speech perception by the chinchilla: Identification functions for synthetic VOT stimuli. *Journal of the Acoustical Society of America, 63,* 905–917.

Kuhl, P. K., & Miller, J. D. (1982). Discrimination of auditory target dimensions in the presence or absence of variation in the second dimension by infants. *Perception and Psychophysics, 31*(3), 279–292.

Kuhl, P. K., & Padden, D. M. (1982). Enhanced discriminability at the phonetic boundaries for the voicing feature in macaques. *Perception & Psychophysics, 32,* 542–550.

Kuhl, P. K., & Padden, D. M. (1983). Enhanced discriminability at the phonetic boundaries for the place feature in macaques. *Journal of the Acoustical Society of America, 73,* 1003–1010.

Kuhl, P. K., Williams, K. A., Lacerda, F., Stevens, K. N., & Lindblom, B. (1992). Linguistic experience alters phonetic perception in infants by 6 months of age. *Science, 255*(5044), 606–608.

Ladefoged, P., & Maddieson, I. (1996). *The sounds of the world's languages.* Oxford: Blackwell.

Lasky, R. E., & Williams, A. L. (2005). The development of the auditory system from conception to term. *NeoReviews, 6,* e141–e152, DOI: 10.1542/neo.6-3-e141. Retrieved February 24, 2010, from: http://neoreviews.aappublications.org/cgi/content/full/neoreviews;6/3/e141

Leibold, L. J., & Werner, L. A. (2006). Effect of masker-frequency variability on the detection performance of infants and adults. *Journal of the Acoustical Society of America, 119*(6), 3960–3970.

Leung, A. K. C., & Kao, C. P. (1999). Evaluation and management of the child with speech delay. *American Family Physician, 59*(11), 3121–3128, 3135.

Levitin, D. J., & Rogers, S. E. (2005). Absolute pitch: Perception, coding, and controversies. *Trends in Cognitive Science, 9*, 26–33.

Levitt, A., Jusczyk, P. W., Murray, J., & Carden, G. (1988). The perception of place of articulation contrasts in voiced and voiceless fricatives by two-month-old infants. *Journal of Experimental Psychology: Human Perception and Performance, 14*, 361–368.

Liberman, A. M. (1957). Some results of research on speech perception. *Journal of the Acoustical Society of America, 29*, 117–123.

Litovsky, R., & Ashmead, D. (1997). Development of binaural and spatial hearing in infants and children. In R. H. Gilkey and T. R. Anderson (Eds.), *Binaural and spatial hearing* (pp. 571–592). Hillsdale, NJ: Erlbaum .

Lynch, M. P., Eilers, R. E., Oller, D. K., & Urbano, R. C. (1990). Innateness, experience, and music perception. *Psychological Science, 1*, 272–276.

Markides, A. (1986). Age at fitting of hearing aids and speech intelligibility. *British Journal of Audiology, 20*, 165–167.

Maruthy, S., & Mannarukrishnaiah, J. (2008). Effect of early onset otitis media on brainstem and cortical auditory processing. *Behavioral and Brain Functions, 4*, 17.

Masataka, N. (2006). Preference for consonance over dissonance by hearing newborns of deaf parents and hearing parents. *Developmental Science, 9*, 46–50.

Matkin, N. D. (1984). Early recognition and referral of hearing-impaired children. *Pediatrics in Review, 6*(5), 151–156.

Mattingly, I. G., Liberman, A. M., Syrdal, A. K., & Halwes, T. (1971). Discrimination in speech and non speech modes. *Cognitive Psychology, 2*, 131–157.

Mattock, K., & Burnham, D. (2006). Chinese and English infants' tone perception: Evidence for perceptual reorganization. *Infancy, 10*(3), 241–265.

Mattock, M., Molnar, M., Polka, L., & Burnham, D. (2008). The developmental course of lexical tone perception in the first year of life. *Cognition, 106*, 1367–1381.

Maxon, A. B., & Hochberg, I. (1982). Development of psychoacoustic behavior: Sensitivity and discrimination. *Ear and Hearing, 3*, 301–308.

Mayne, A. M., Yoshinaga-Itano, C., Sedey, A. L., & Carey, A. (2000). Expressive vocabulary development of infants and toddlers who are deaf or hard of hearing. *Volta Review, 100*, 1–28.

McConkey Robbins, A., Burton Koch, D., Osperger, M. J., Zimmerman-Phillips, S., & Kishon-Rabin, L. (2004). Effect of age at cochlear implantation on auditory skill development in infants and toddlers. *Archives of Otolaryngology: Head and Neck Surgery, 130*(5), 570–574.

McDermott, J., & Hauser, M. D. (2004). Are consonant intervals music to their ears? Spontaneous acoustic preferences in a nonhuman primate. *Cognition, 94*, B11–B21.

McDermott, J., & Hauser, M. D. (2007). Nonhuman primates prefer slow tempos but dislike music overall. *Cognition, 104*, 654–668.

Mehler, J., Bertoncini, J., Barrière, M., & Jassik-Gerschenfeld, D. (1978). Infant recognition of mother's voice. *Perception, 7*(5), 491–497.

Mehler, J., Jusczyk, J., Lambertz, G., Halsted, N., Bertoncini, J., & Amiel-Tison, C. (1988). A precursor of language acquisition in young infants. *Cognition, 29*, 143–178.

Mendelson, M., & Ferland, M (1982). Auditory-visual transfer in four-month-old infants. *Child Development, 53*(4), 1022–1027.

Meyer, C., Witte, J., Hildmann, A., Hennecke, K. H., Hennecke, H., Schunck, K. U., et al. (1999). Neonatal screening for hearing disorders in infants at risk: Incidence, risk factors, and follow-up. *Pediatrics, 104*(4), 900–904.

Midgley, E. J., Dewey, C., Pryce, K., Maw, A. R., & Alspac Study Team (2000). The frequency of otitis media with effusion in British pre-school children: A guide for treatment. *Clinical Otolaryngology & Allied Sciences, 25*(6), 485–491.

Miller, G. A. (1947). The masking of speech. *Psychological Bulletin, 44,* 105–129.

Mills, A. (1972). Auditory localization. In J. V. Tobias (Ed.), *Foundations of modern auditory theory* (Vol. 2, pp. 301–348). New York: Academic Press.

Mody, M., Schwartz, R. G., Gravel, J. S., & Ruben, R. J. (1999). Speech perception and verbal memory in children with and without histories of otitis media. *Journal of Speech Language and Hearing Research, 42*(5), 1069–1079.

Moeller, M. P. (2000). Early intervention and language development in children who are deaf and hard of hearing. *Pediatrics, 106,* E43.

Moon, C., & Fifer, W. (1986, November). *Newborn infants prefer the sound of mother's voice as experienced in the womb.* Paper presented at the International Society for Developmental Psychobiology, Toronto, Canada.

Moore, B. C. J. (1997). *An introduction to the psychology of hearing.* San Diego, CA: Academic Press.

Morrongiello, B. (1987). Infants' localization of sounds in the median sagittal plane: Effects of signal frequency. *Journal of the Acoustical Society of America, 82,* 900–905.

Morrongiello, B., & Clifton, R. (1984). Effects of sound frequency on behavioral and cardiac orienting in newborn and five-month-old infants. *Journal of Experimental Child Psychology, 38,* 429–446.

Morrongiello, B., Kulig, J., & Clifton, R. (1984). Developmental changes in auditory temporal perception. *Child Development, 55,* 461–471.

Morrongiello, B. A., & Trehub, S. E. (1987). Age-related changes in auditory temporal perception. *Journal of Experimental Child Psychology, 44,* 413–426.

Morse, P. A. (1972). The discrimination of speech and nonspeech stimuli in early infancy. *Journal of Experimental Child Psychology, 14*(3), 477–492.

Morse, P. A., & Snowdon, C. (1975). An investigation of categorical speech discrimination by rhesus monkey. *Perception and Psychophysics, 17,* 9–16.

Muir, D., Abraham, W., Forbes, B., & Harris, L. (1979). The ontogenesis of an auditory localization response from birth to four months of age. *Canadian Journal of Psychology, 33*(4), 320–233.

Muir, D., & Clifton, R. K. (1985). Infants' orientation to the location of sound sources. In G. Gottlieb & N. A. Krasnegor (Eds.), *Measurement of audition and vision in the first post-natal year of life: A methodological overview* (pp. 171–194). Norwood, NJ: Ablex.

Muir, D., Clifton, R. K., & Clarkson, M. G. (1989). The development of a human auditory localization response: A U-shaped function. *Canadian Journal of Psychology, 43,* 199–216.

Muir, D., & Field, J. (1979). Newborn infants orient to sounds. *Child Development, 50,* 431–436.

Munsell, A. H. (1912). A pigment color system and notation. *American Journal of Psychology, 23,* 236–244.

Nazzi, T., Bertoncini, J., & Mehler, J. (1998). Language discrimination by newborns: Toward an understanding of the role of rhythm. *Journal of Experimental Psychology: Human Perception & Performance, 24*(3), 756–766.

Nazzi, T., & Ramus, F. (2003). Perception and acquisition of linguistic rhythm by infants. *Speech Communication, 41*(1), 233–243.

Nicholas, J. G., & Geers, A. E. (2006). Effects of early auditory experience on the spoken language of deaf children at 3 years of age. *Ear and Hearing, 27*(3), 286–298.

Northern, J. L., & Downs, M. P. (1991). *Hearing in children* (4th ed.). Baltimore: Williams & Wilkins.

Nozza, R. J. (1987). The binaural masking level difference in infants and adults: Developmental change in binaural hearing. *Infant Behavior and Development, 10*, 105–110.

Nozza, R. J., Rossman, R. N., & Bond, L. C. (1991). Infant-adult differences in unmasked thresholds for the discrimination of consonant-vowel syllable pairs. *Audiology, 30*(2), 102–112.

Nozza, R. J., & Wilson, W. R. (1984). Masked and unmasked pure-tone thresholds of infants and adults. *Journal of Speech and Hearing Research, 27*, 613–622.

Olsho, L. W., Koch, E. G., Carter, E. A., Halpin, C. F., & Spetner, N. B. (1988). Pure-tone sensitivity of human infants. *Journal of the Acoustical Society of America, 84*(4), 1316–1324.

Olsho, L. W., Koch, E. G., & Halpin, C. F. (1987). Level and age effects in infant frequency discrimination. *Journal of the Acoustical Society of America, 82*(2), 454–464.

Parrish H. K., & Werner, L. A. (2004). Listening windows in infants and adults. *Paper presented at the American Auditory Society*, Scottsdale, AZ.

Peck, J. E. (1994). Development of Hearing. Part II: Embryology. *Journal of the American Academy of Audiology, 5*, 359–365.

Pediatric Working Group (1999). Amplification for infants and children with hearing loss. *Seminars in Hearing, 20*, 339–350.

Peretz, I., & Coltheart, M. (2003). Modularity of music processing. *Nature Neuroscience, 6*, 688–691.

Perrott, D. R., Marlborough, K., & Merrill, P. (1989). Minimum audible angle thresholds obtained under conditions in which the precedence effect is assumed to operate. *Journal of the Acoustical Society of America, 85*, 282–288.

Phillips-Silver, J., & Trainor, L. J. (2005). Feeling the beat: Movement influences infant rhythm perception. *Science, 308*, 1430.

Phillips-Silver, J., & Trainor, L. J. (2007). Hearing what the body feels: Auditory encoding of rhythmic movement. *Cognition, 105*, 533–546.

Pisoni, D. B. (1977). Identification and discrimination of the relative onset time of two component tones: Implications for voicing perceptions in steps. *Journal of Acoustical Society of America, 61*, 1352–1361.

Plantinga, J., & Trainor, L. J. (2005). Memory for melody: Infants use a relative pitch code. *Cognition, 98*, 1–11.

Polka, L., & Rvachew, S. (2005). The impact of otitis media with effusion on infant phonetic perception. *Infancy, 8*(2), 101–117.

Polka, L., & Werker, J. F. (1994). Developmental changes in perception of nonnative vowel contrasts. *Journal of Experimental Psychology: Human Perception and Performance, 20*(2), 421–435.

Preisler, G. (1999). The development of communication and language in deaf and severely hard of hearing children: Implications for the future. *International Journal of Pediatric Otorhinolaryngology, 49*(1), S 39–S43.

Pujol, R., Calier, E., & Lenoir, M. (1980). Ontogenetic approach to inner and outer hair cell functions. *Hearing Research, 2*, 423–430.

Pujol, R., & Uziel, A. (1988). Auditory development: peripheral aspects. In E. Meisami & P. S. Timiras (Eds.), *Handbook of human growth and developmental biology* (Vol. 1B, pp. 109–130). Boca Raton, FL: CRC Press.

Querleu, D., & Renard, X. (1981). Bruit Intra-Uterin. Perceptions auditives et reactivité foetale aux simulations sonores. *Medicine & Hygiene, 39*, 2102–2110.

Querleu, D., Renard, X., Versyp, F., Paris-Delrue, L., & Crepin, G. (1988). Fetal hearing. *European Journal of Obstetrics & Gynecology and Reproductive Biology*, *28*, 191–212.

Ramus, F., Hauser, M. D., Miller, C., Morris, D., & Mehler, J. (2000). Language discrimination by human newborns and cotton-top tamarin monkeys. *Science*, *288*, 349–351.

Rosen, S. M, & Howell, P. (1981). Plucks and bows are not categorically perceived. *Perception & Psychophysics*, *30*, 156–168.

Rubel, E. W, Lippe, W. R., & Ryals, B. M. (1984). Development of the place principle. *Annals of Otology, Rhinology and Laryngology*, *93*(6), 609–615.

Rvachew, S., & Grawburg, M. (2006). Correlates of phonological awareness in preschoolers with speech sound disorders. *Journal of Speech, Language and Hearing Research*, *49*(1), 74–87.

Saberi, K., & Antonio, J. V. (2003). Precedence-effect thresholds for a population of untrained listeners as a function of stimulus intensity and interclick interval. *Journal of the Acoustical Society of America*, *114*(1), 420–425.

Saffran, J. R. (2003). Absolute pitch in infancy and adulthood: The role of tonal structure. *Developmental Science*, *6*, 35–45.

Saffran, J. R., & Griepentrog, G. J. (2001). Absolute pitch in infant auditory learning: Evidence for developmental reorganization. *Developmental Psychology*, *37*, 74–85.

Saffran, J. R., Reeck, K., Niebuhr, A., & Wilson, D. (2005). Changing the tune: The structure of the input affects infants' use of absolute and relative pitch. *Developmental Science*, *8*, 1–7.

Schellenberg, E. G., Bigand, E., Poulin-Charronnat, B., Garnier, C., & Stevens, C. (2005). Children's implicit knowledge of harmony in Western music. *Developmental Science*, *8*, 551–566.

Schellenberg, E. G., & Trehub, S. E. (2003). Good pitch memory is widespread. *Psychological Science*, *14*, 262–266.

Schneider, B., & Trehub, S. (1985). Behavioral assessment of basic auditory abilities. In S. Trehub & B. Schneider (Eds.), *Auditory development in infancy* (pp. 101–114). New York: Plenum.

Schneider, B. A., & Trehub, S. E. (1992). Sources of developmental change in auditory sensitivity. In L. A. Werner & E. W. Rubel (Eds.), *Developmental psychoacoustics* (pp. 3–46). Washington DC: American Psychological Association.

Shahidullah, S., & Hepper, P. G. (1993). Prenatal hearing tests? *Journal of Reproductive and Infant Psychology*, *11*(3), 143–146.

Shahidullah, S., & Hepper, P. G. (1994). Frequency discrimination by the fetus. *Early Human Development*, *36*, 13–26.

Silman, S., & Silverman, C. A. (1991). *Auditory diagnosis: Principles and applications*. Academic Press: San Diego.

Sindhusake, D., Mitchell, P., Smith, W., Golding, M., Newall, P., Hartley, D., et al. (2001). Validation of self-reported hearing loss. The Blue Mountains Hearing Study. *International Journal of Epidemiology*, *30*, 1371–1378.

Sinnott, J. M., & Aslin, R. N. (1985). Frequency and intensity discrimination in human infants and adults. *Journal of the Acoustical Society of America*, *78*, 1986–1992.

Skinner, M. W., & Miller, J. D. (1983). Amplification bandwidth and intelligibility of speech in quiet and noise for listeners with sensorineural hearing loss. *Audiology*, *22*, 253–279.

Soderquist, D. R., & Moore, M. J. (1970). Effect of training on frequency discrimination in primary school children. *Journal of Auditory Research*, *10*, 185–192.

Spelke, E. (1976). Infants' intermodal perception of events. *Cognitive Psychology*, *8*, 53–60.

Sprague, B. H., Wiley T. L., & Goldstein, R. (1985). Tympanometric and acoustic-reflex studies in neonates. *Journal of Speech and Hearing Research*, *28*, 265–272.

Stelmachowicz, P. G. (1996). Current issues in pediatric amplification. *The Hearing Journal*, *49*(10), 10.

Tallal, P., Miller, S. L., Bedi, G., Byma, G., Wang, X., Nagarajan, S. N., et al. (1996). Language comprehension in language-learning impaired children with acoustically modified speech. *Science*, *271*, 81–83.

Tallal, P., & Piercy, M. (1973). Developmental aphasia: Impaired rate of non-verbal processing as a function of sensory modality. *Neuropsychologia*, *11*, 389–398.

Tarquinio, N., Zelazo, P. R., & Weiss, M. J. (1990). Recovery of neonatal head-turning to decreased sound pressure level. *Developmental Psychology*, *26*, 752–758.

Tharpe, A., & Ashmead, D. H. (2001). A longitudinal investigation of infant auditory sensitivity. *American Journal of Audiology*, *10*, 104–112.

Thilo, K. V., Santoro, L., Walsh, V., & Blakemore, C. (2004). The site of saccadic suppression. *Nature Neuroscience*, *7*, 13–14.

Todd, N. P. McA., Cousins, R., & Lee, C. (2007). The contribution of anthropomorphic factors to individual differences in the perception of rhythm. *Empirical Musicology Review*, *2*, 1–13.

Trainor, L. J. (2005). Are there critical periods for musical development? *Developmental Psychobiology*, *46*, 262–278.

Trainor, L. (2007). Do preferred beat rate and entrainment to the beat have a common origin in movement? *Empirical Musicology Review*, *2*, 17–20.

Trainor, L. J., & Adams, B. (2000). Infants' and adults' use of duration and intensity cues in the segmentation of tone patterns. *Perception and Psychophysics*, *62*, 333–340.

Trainor, L. J., & Treub, S. E. (1992). A comparison of infants' and adults' sensitivity to Western musical structure. *Journal of Experimental Psychology: Human Perception and Performance*, *18*, 394–402.

Trainor, L. J., Tsang, C. D., & Cheung, V. H. W. (2002). Preference for sensory consonance in 2- and 4-month-old infants. *Music Perception*, *20*, 187–194.

Trehub, S. E., & Hannon, E. E. (2006). Infant music perception: Domain-general or domain-specific mechanisms? *Cognition*, *100*, 73–99.

Trehub, S. E., Schneider, B. A., & Endman, M. (1980). Developmental changes in infants' sensitivity to octave-band noises. *Journal of Experimental Child Psychology*, *29*(2), 282–293.

Tsushima, T., Takizawa, O., Sasaki, M., Shiraki, S., Nishi, K., Kohno, M., et al. (1994, September). *Discrimination of English /r-l/ and /w-y/ by Japanese infants at 6–12 months: Language-specific developmental changes in speech perception abilities* Paper presented at the International Conference on Spoken Language Processing, Yokohama, Japan, pp. 1695–1698.

Tyler, R. S., Fryauf-Bertschy, H., Kelsay, D. M. R., Gantz, B. J., Woodworth, G. P., & Parkinson, A. (1997). Speech perception by prelingually deaf children using cochlear implants, *Otolaryngology – Head and Neck Surgery*, *117*(3), 180–186.

Updike, C., & Thornburg, J. D. (1992). Reading-skills and auditory processing ability in children with chronic otitis-media in early-childhood. *Annals of Otology Rhinology and Laryngology*, *101*(6), 530–537.

Valencia, D. M., Rimell, F. L., Friedman, B. J., Oblander, M. R., Helmbrecht, J. (2008). Cochlear implantation in infants less than 12 months of age. *International Journal of Pediatric Otorhinlaryngology*, *72*, 767–773.

Van Naarden, K., & Decoufle, P. (1999). Relative and attributable risks for moderate to profound bilateral sensori-neural hearing impairment associated with lower birth weight in children 3 to 10 years old. *Pediatrics*, *104*, 905–910.

Versyp, F. (1985). Transmission intra-amniotique des sons et dex voix humaines. Thèse de Médecine, Lille. In D. Querleu, X. Renard, F. Versyp, L. Paris-Delrue & G. Crepin, (Eds.). (1988). Fetal hearing. *European Journal of Obstetrics & Gynecology and Reproductive Biology*, *28*, 191–212.

Volkova, A., Trehub, S., & Schellenberg, E. G. (2006). Infants' memory for musical performances. *Developmental Science, 9*, 583–589.

Wake, M., Tobin, S., Cone-Wesson, B., Dahl, H.-H., Gillam, L., McCormick, L., Poulakis, Z., Field, W., Rickards, K. S. (2006). Slight/mild sensorineural hearing loss in children. *Pediatrics, 118*, 1842–1851.

Wallach, H., Newman, E. B., & Rosenzweig, M. R. (1949). The precedence effect in sound localization. *American Journal of Psychology, 62*, 315–336.

Waltzman, S. B., & Cohen, N. L. (1998). Cochlear implantation in children younger than 2 years old. *American Journal of Otololaryngology, 19*(2), 158–162.

Watanabe, S., Uozumi, M., & Tanaka, N. (2005). Discrimination of consonance and dissonance in Java sparrows. *Behavioral Processes, 70*, 203–208.

Werker, J. F., Gilbert, J. H. V., Humphrey, K., & Tees, R. C. (1981). Developmental aspects of cross-language speech perception. *Child Development, 52*, 349–355.

Werker, J. F., & Tees, R. C. (1983). Developmental changes across childhood in the perception of nonnative speech sounds. *Canadian Journal of Psychology, 37*, 278–286.

Werker, J. F., & Tees, R. C. (1984). Cross-language speech perception: Evidence for perceptual reorganisation in the first year of life. *Infant Behavior and Development, 7*, 49–63.

Werner, L. A. (1995). Observer-based approaches to human infant psychoacoustics. In G. M. Klump, R. J. Dooling, R. R. Fay, & W. C. Stebbins (Eds.), *Methods in comparative psychoacoustics* (pp. 135–146). Boston: Birkhauser Verlag.

Werner, L. A., & Boike, K. (2001). Infants' sensitivity to broadband noise. *Journal of the Acoustical Society of America, 109*, 2103–2111.

Werner, L. A., Folsom, R. C., & Mancl, L. R. (1994). The relationship between auditory response latencies and behavioral thresholds in normal hearing infants and adults. *Hearing Research, 77*(1–2), 88–89.

Werner, L. A., & Gillenwater, J. M. (1990). Pure-tone sensitivity of 2- to 5-week-old infants. *Infant Behavior and Development, 13*, 355–375.

Wessex Universal Hearing Screening Trial Group (1998). Controlled trial of universal neonatal screening for early identification of permanent childhood hearing impairment. *The Lancet, 32*, 1957–1964.

White, K. R., Vohr, B. R., & Behrens, T. R. (1993). Universal newborn hearing screening using transient evoked otoacoustic emissions: Results of the Rhode Island Hearing Assessment Project. *Seminars in Hearing, 14*, 18–29.

Whitfield, I. C., Cranford, J., Ravizza R., & Diamond, I. T. (1972). Effects of unilateral ablation of auditory cortex in cat on complex sound localization. *Journal of Neurophysiology, 35*, 718–731.

Whitfield, I. C., Diamond, K., Chiveralls, K., & Williamson T. G. (1978). Some further observations on the effects of unilateral cortical ablation on sound localization in the cat. *Experimental Brain Research, 31*, 221–234.

Winskel, H. (2006). The effects of an early history of otitis media on children's language and literacy skill development. *British Journal of Educational Psychology, 76*(4), 727–744.

Wright, A. A., Rivera, J. J., Hulse, S. H., Shyan, M., & Neiworth, J. J. (2000). Music perception and octave generalization in rhesus monkeys. *Journal of Experimental Psychology: General, 129*, 291–307.

Yakovlev, P. I., & Lecours A.-R. (1967). The myelogenetic cycles of regional maturation of the brain. In A. Minkowski (Ed.), *Regional development of the brain early in life* (pp. 3–64). Oxford: Blackwell Scientific.

Yip, M. (2002). *Tone*. Cambridge: Cambridge University Press.

Yoshinaga-Itano, C., & Apuzzo, M. L. (1998a). Identification of hearing loss after 18 months is not nearly enough. *American Annals of Deafness, 143*, 380–387.

Yoshinaga-Itano, C., & Apuzzo, M. L. (1998b). The development of deaf and heard of hearing children identified through the high-risk registry. *American Annals of Deafness, 143*, 416–424.

Yoshinaga-Itano, C., Sedey, A. L., Coulter, D. K., & Mehl, A. L. (1998). Language of early- and later-acquired children with hearing loss. *Pediatrics, 102*(5), 1161–1171.

Zelazo, P. R., Weiss, M. J., Papageorgiou, A. N., & Laplante, D. P. (1989). Recovery and dishabituation of sound localization among normal-, moderate-, and high-risk newborns: Discriminant validity. *Infant Behavior and Development, 12*, 321–340.

4

Intermodal Perception and Selective Attention to Intersensory Redundancy: Implications for Typical Social Development and Autism

Lorraine E. Bahrick

Introduction

The world of objects and events floods our senses with continuously changing multimodal stimulation, but we can attend to only a small portion of this stimulation at any time. The organization of our senses plays a fundamental role in guiding and constraining what we attend to, perceive, learn, and remember from this flux of multimodal stimulation. A fundamental challenge for the infant is to develop economical skills of attentional shifting that maximize the pick-up of relevant information, coherent across time and space, and minimize the pick-up of information that is irrelevant and incoherent across time and space (E. J. Gibson, 1969). It is critical that we process multimodal stimulation from single, unitary events and follow their flow of action. For example, we must selectively attend to a single person speaking and follow the flow of dialogue, rather than attending to disconnected streams of auditory and visual stimulation from unrelated but concurrent events. How do we accomplish these challenging tasks?

In this chapter, I review what is known about how these skills emerge and develop across infancy. I argue that the overlap across unique forms of stimulation from the different senses plays a powerful role in this developmental process. This overlap provides "amodal" redundant information (such as temporal synchrony, rhythm, or intensity, common across more than one sense modality) which guides and constrains what we attend to, perceive, learn, and remember, particularly in early development when attentional resources are most limited. Detection of amodal information effectively simplifies and organizes incoming sensory stimulation and provides a basis for perceiving unitary objects and events rather than the "blooming, buzzing, confusion" postulated long ago by William James (1890, Vol. 2, p. 488).

Most perception is "intermodal" (also referred to as intersensory or multimodal) and includes perception of social and nonsocial events, the self, and stimulation from all the senses and their combinations. In order to reduce the scope of this chapter, I focused on some topics at the expense of others. I include primarily the development of auditory-visual perception (a topic of much infant research) at the expense of tactile, gustatory, and olfactory perception. I also focus on the development of intermodal perception of the self and social events, at the expense of nonsocial events, because the self in interaction with the social world provides a foundation for the majority of infant learning (see Bahrick, 2004; Kellman & Arterberry, 1998; Lewkowicz & Lickliter, 1994, for additional reviews of intermodal perception). Since research has demonstrated that even areas previously considered "unimodal", such as face discrimination, are profoundly influenced by intersensory redundancy from multimodal stimulation, this chapter has a somewhat different emphasis and scope from prior reviews of this topic. Here, I examine the effects of intersensory redundancy on the development of perception and learning about all types of event properties, both amodal and modality-specific.

Three important themes that call for the integration of research and theory across traditionally separate areas are emphasized throughout this chapter. The first highlights the need for conducting and integrating research on the nature of selective attention into developmental accounts of perception, learning, and memory. Attention provides the input for all that is perceived, learned, and remembered and these processes are inextricably interconnected, forming a system of reciprocal influences. The second theme calls for enhancing ecological validity of developmental research by integrating studies of unimodal functioning (e.g., auditory perception, visual perception) with studies of multimodal functioning (e.g., audiovisual perception). The modalities are typically studied separately yet exploratory behavior typically results in stimulation to multiple sense modalities and gives rise to important interactions not observable through studying one sense alone. Finally, the third theme emphasizes the need for cross-fertilization between basic research on typical and atypical development, particularly disorders of development such as autism. Typical and atypical development are generally studied separately, yet considerable insight into typical development can be gained though understanding how developmental processes go awry, and conversely, identifying atypical patterns of development hinges on clearly articulating the course of typical development. The present chapter provides a starting point for integration along these three critical dimensions.

Selective Attention: The Underappreciated Foundation for Perception, Learning and Memory in a Dynamic, Multimodal Environment

The natural environment provides a flux of changing, concurrent stimulation to all our senses, far more than can be attended to at any given time. However, adults are exquisitely skilled at selectively attending to unitary multimodal events, picking out information that is relevant to their needs, goals, and interests, and ignoring irrelevant stimulation from this vast array. For example, we easily pick out a friend in a crowd, follow the flow of action in a ball game, and attend to the voice of the speaker at a cocktail party in the context of competing conversations. Moreover, we long ago learned to pick out figure from ground, signal from noise, human speech from nonspeech sounds, parse continuous speech into meaningful units such as syllables and words, and ignore variations across speakers, accents, and differing intonations to identify words. Similarly, we learned to parse the visual array into coherent objects and surfaces despite variation due to lighting and shadow, and interruption of surfaces due to occlusion. These remarkable skills, easily taken for granted by experienced perceivers, develop rapidly across infancy through experience interacting with objects and events. They entail systematic changes in selective attention across time – increasing attention and economy of information pick-up for relevant aspects of the environment, honing in on useful and economical levels of analysis, and attending to meaningful variability while ignoring meaningless variability (E. J. Gibson, 1969, 1988; E. J. Gibson & Pick, 2000; Ruff & Rothbart, 1996). A great deal of research and theory has been devoted to accounts of how perception and learning develop. In contrast, little research effort has focused on the processes that guide selective attention to relevant aspects and levels of stimulation in the first place. This process itself is the result of much learning and at the same time, it provides the basis for further learning and exploratory activity. Figure 4.1 depicts the central role of selective attention in relation to processes of perception, learning, and memory.

Selective attention can be considered the gateway to information pick-up and processing (e.g., Broadbent, 1962; Neisser, 1976; Triesman, 1964). As depicted in Figure 4.1, selective attention to stimulation generated from our exploratory activity provides the basis for all that is perceived, learned, and remembered. In turn, what is perceived, learned, and remembered, influences what is attended to next, in continuous cycles of attention → perception → learning → memory → attention, and so forth. Moreover, action is tightly coupled with these processes, as exploratory activity constantly provides new stimulation for attention, perception, learning, and memory (Adolph & Berger, 2005, 2006; E. J. Gibson, 1988; E. J. Gibson & Pick, 2000; Thelen, 1995; Von Hofsten 1983, 1993). Attention entails exploratory behavior such as orienting, eye movements, and active interaction with the environment (e.g., reaching, head turning) and these ongoing behaviors in turn provide continuous and contingent feedback to multiple senses. This cycle may be characterized as a system of dynamic, interactive influences that evolve over time (see Adolph & Berger, 2006; E. J. Gibson, 1988; Thelen & Smith, 1994, for a discussion of such systems). Figure 4.1 depicts the integral role of attention in two interrelated feedback loops. One loop highlights the role of attention in the processes of perception, learning, and memory, and their reciprocal interactions. The other, highlights the role of attention in perception-action cycles, and the reciprocal interactions among these processes. Selective attention (honed and shaped by learning and memory) operates on stimulation from action, and determines what we perceive versus ignore, and in turn the nature of our next exploratory activities.

Across infancy, we develop and establish patterns for selectively attending to aspects of our environment. These patterns become increasingly more efficient with experience

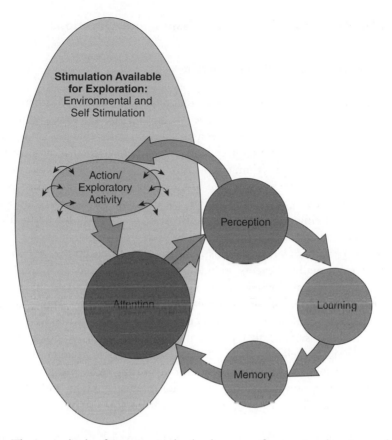

Figure 4.1   The integral role of attention in the development of perception, learning, and memory is depicted through two interrelated, concurrent, feedback loops, (a) the attention → perception → learning → memory system, and (b) the attention → perception → action system. The arrows represent the primary direction of the flow of information. Selective attention to stimulation that results from our exploratory activity provides the basis for what is perceived, what is perceived provides the basis for what is learned, and in turn what is remembered. This in turn affects what we attend to next and in subsequent encounters with similar stimulation. Perception is also tightly coupled with action via selective attention to the stimulation generated from exploratory activity in a continuous feedback loop.

and evolve into the expert patterns of adult selective attention. What rules govern this process and how does such uniformity evolve across individuals in the way adults attend to people, faces, voices, objects, and events? Little scientific effort has been devoted to the study of attentional selectivity in infancy (see Ruff & Rothbart, 1996 for a review) despite its obvious importance for providing the input for cognitive, social, perceptual, and linguistic development. In the remainder of this chapter, I address this gap by considering the fundamental role of selective attention in the development of perception and learning about multimodal events.

Intermodal Perception: Definitions, Issues, and Questions

Amodal versus modality-specific information

Objects and events provide both amodal and modality-specific information. Amodal information is information that is not specific to a particular sense modality, but is common or redundant across multiple senses. This includes changes along three basic dimensions of stimulation – time, space, and intensity. In particular, amodal properties include temporal synchrony, rhythm, tempo, duration, intensity, and colocation common across auditory, visual, and proprioceptive stimulation, and shape, substance, and texture common across visual and tactile stimulation. For example, the same rhythm and tempo can be detected by seeing or hearing the pianist strike the notes of the keyboard, and the same size, shape, and texture can be detected by seeing or feeling an apple.

Since events occur across time, are distributed across space, and have a characteristic intensity pattern, virtually all events provide amodal information. For example, speech is comprised of changes in audiovisual synchrony, tempo, rhythm, and intonation (intensity changes) that are common to the movements of the face and the sounds of the voice. Self-motion produces continuous proprioceptive feedback (information from the muscles, joints, and vestibular system) that is synchronous and shares temporal and intensity changes with the sight of self-motion (e.g., seeing and feeling one's hand move). Perception of amodal information is critically important for organizing early perceptual development and for accurate perception of everyday events, for infants, children, and adults alike (see Bahrick & Lickliter, 2002; Lewkowicz & Lickliter, 1994; Calvert, Spence, & Stein, 2004, for reviews).

All events also make modality-specific information available. Modality-specific information is information that can be specified through only one sense modality. For example, color and visual pattern can be detected only through vision, pitch and timbre can be detected only though audition, and temperature can be detected only through touch. Most events that can be seen and heard typically provide information that is specific to vision and audition. For example, perception of modality-specific information allows us to differentiate between the faces and between the voices of different individuals of the same gender, between sounds of a guitar versus a harp, between letters of the alphabet, and between a ripe versus a green apple.

Selecting relevant, cohesive, multimodal events

Because we can attend to only a small portion of the available stimulation at a time, the infant faces a significant developmental challenge: to become increasingly economical and efficient at selecting multimodal stimulation that is unitary (coherent across the senses and originating from a single event) and relevant to their needs and actions, while ignoring stimulation that is less relevant and discordant with the focus of their attention.

All events, whether enjoying a family dinner, watching television, or playing basketball, provide a continuously changing array of both modality-specific and amodal information across time. They also provide variations in incoming stimulation that are meaningful and relevant (e.g., speech sounds, goal-directed human actions) and other variations that are relatively meaningless and must be ignored or categorized as similar (differences in lighting and shadow across cohesive objects, changes in retinal size of objects across observer or object movement, variations in accent, speaker voice, or intonation across the same phoneme). What determines which information is selected and attended to and which information is ignored? In early development, it is thought, selective attention is more stimulus-driven and with experience attention becomes increasingly endogenous and modulated by top-down processes such as prior goals, plans, and expectations (see Colombo, 2001; Haith, 1980; Johnson, Posner, & Rothbart, 1991; Ruff & Rothbart, 1996, for reviews). Thus, for experienced perceivers, prior knowledge, categories, goals, plans, and expectations guide information pick-up (Bartlett, 1932; Chase & Simon, 1973; Neisser, 1976; Schank & Ableson, 1977). What we learn, know, and expect influences where we look and, in turn, what information we pick-up in present and future encounters. What guides this learning process in infants who have little prior knowledge to rely on, such that perception becomes rapidly organized and aligned with adult categories?

One important skill that fosters perception of unitary multimodal events is the infant's early coordination and calibration of audiovisual space. Typically, there is visual information about an event at the locus of its sound, such as a person speaking or an object falling and breaking. Even newborns turn their head and eyes in the direction of a sound, promoting the early coordination of audiovisual space and providing a basis for further processing of unitary multimodal events (Muir & Clifton, 1985; Wertheimer, 1961). Over time, the perception of audiovisual space is further calibrated and refined. However, in the typical environment, there are many objects and events in one's field of view and sound localization is not precise enough to specify which of many visible objects goes with the sound one is hearing. What guides this process so that attention is efficiently and reliably directed to the source of a sound and can then follow the flow of action?

Consistent with J. J. Gibson's (1966, 1979) ecological view of perception, research has revealed that detection of amodal information such as temporal synchrony, rhythm, tempo, and intensity is a cornerstone of this developmental process (see Bahrick, 2004; Bahrick & Lickliter, 2002 for reviews). J. J. Gibson proposed that the different forms of stimulation from the senses were not a problem for perception, but rather provided an important basis for perceiving unitary objects and events. Our senses, he proposed, work together as a unified perceptual system. They pick up "amodal" information that is "invariant" or common across the senses. By attending to and perceiving amodal information, there was no need to learn to integrate stimulation across the senses in order to perceive unified objects and events, as proposed by constructivist accounts of development (e.g., Piaget, 1952, 1954). Perceiving amodal relations ensures that we attend to unified multimodal events. Temporal synchrony, the most global type of amodal information, has been described as the "glue" that binds stimulation across the senses (see Bahrick & Pickens, 1994; Bahrick & Lickliter, 2002; Lewkowicz, 2000). For example, by attending to audiovisual synchrony, the sounds and sights of a single person speaking would be perceived together, as a unified event. Detecting this information prevents the accidental association of unrelated but concurrent sensory stimulation, such as a nearby conversation. The "ventriloquism effect" (Alais & Burr, 2004; Radeau & Bertelson, 1977; Warren, Welch, & McCarthy, 1981) illustrates the powerful role of this amodal information in guiding attention and perception. The ventriloquist moves the dummy's mouth and body in synchrony with his own speech sounds, thus, he creates the illusion that the dummy is speaking, despite the fact that the sound emanates from a slightly different location. Amodal information such as temporal synchrony, rhythm, tempo, and intensity changes common across the visual and acoustic stimulation promote the perception of a unitary event, the dummy speaking, and override information about the location of the sound. Infants show this effect even in the first months of life (Morrongiello, Fenwick, & Nutley, 1998). Once attention is focused on the "unitary" audiovisual event, further differentiation of the unitary event is promoted. In this way, detection of amodal information such as audiovisual synchrony then guides and constrains further information pick-up.

Increasing specificity in the development of intersensory perception: Synchrony as the gatekeeper for intermodal processing

Objects and events can be characterized as having nested or hierarchically organized properties, with global amodal information (such as temporal synchrony and collocation), nested levels of amodal structure, and more specific, "modality specific" information (E. J. Gibson, 1969). According to E. J. Gibson's theory of perceptual development, based on J. J. Gibson's ecological theory of perception, differentiation of perceptual information proceeds in order of increasing specificity. Research has demonstrated that the domain of intersensory perception is no exception. Detection of amodal relations proceeds in order of increasing specificity with infants first differentiating synchrony between an object's motions and its sounds, and later detecting more specific, embedded temporal information ("temporal microstructure") such as that specifying the object's composition or substance (Bahrick, 2000, 2001, 2004; E. J. Gibson, 1969). Further, there is a developmental lag between detecting amodal and modality-specific information in the same events (Bahrick, 1992, 1994, 2004). This lag is adaptive since knowledge of amodal relations can be meaningfully generalized across events and contexts, can constrain perception of modality-specific information, and can provide a framework for organizing more specific details. For example, when objects striking a surface are presented in synchrony with their impact sounds, synchrony promotes rapid differentiation of sound–sight relations and differentiation progresses to the specific nature of the sound, the specific appearance of the object, and the relation between them (Bahrick, 1988, 1992; Bahrick, Hernandez-Reif, & Flom, 2005). In contrast, after experiencing asynchronous impact sounds along with objects striking a surface, infants show no evidence of differentiating the sound, the appearance of the object, or learning the relations between them (Bahrick, 1988). Similarly, in the domain of speech, infants who are too young to understand that speech sounds refer to objects, detect the arbitrary relation between a verbal label and the object to which it refers when there is temporal synchrony between naming and showing the object, but not when the object is static or moved out of synchrony with naming (Gogate & Bahrick, 1998). Thus, in early development, synchrony functions as a "gatekeeper" for further processing of unitary events (see Bahrick & Lickliter, 2002; Lewkowicz, 2000; 2002). That amodal properties of multimodal stimulation are salient and detected developmentally prior to other properties is critically important for optimal perceptual development (Bahrick, 2000, 2001; Bahrick & Lickliter, 2002, Bahrick & Pickens, 1994). Sensitivity to amodal properties promotes attention to unified multimodal events in the presence of competing stimulation from other sounds and motions, and guides subsequent knowledge acquisition by allowing general perceptual information to precede and constrain the acquisition of details. What makes this important type of information so salient to infants?

Intersensory redundancy

When the same amodal information occurs together, and in synchrony across the senses, this is called "intersensory redundancy" (Bahrick & Lickliter, 2000). The argument developed here is that intersensory redundancy makes amodal information stand out with respect to other types of stimulation. "Intersensory redundancy" is provided by an event when the same amodal information (rhythm, tempo, intensity changes) is simultaneously available and temporally synchronized across two or more sense modalities. For example, when the same rhythm and tempo of speech can be perceived by looking and by listening, the rhythm and tempo are said to be redundantly specified (as illustrated by a typical speaker, or artificially created by a ventriloquist). Intersensory redundancy is highly salient to both human and animal infants (Lickliter & Bahrick, 2000, 2004). Its salience also appears to have a neural basis (see Calvert et al., 2004, for a review). It promotes heightened neural responsiveness as compared with the same information in each modality alone (Stein & Meredith, 1993) and promotes attention to and perceptual processing of the event and its redundant properties. Most naturalistic, multimodal events provide intersensory redundancy for multiple properties (e.g., tempo, rhythm, duration, intensity). By definition, only amodal properties (rather than modality-specific properties) can be redundantly specified across the senses. Typically, a given event (such as a person speaking) also provides nonredundant, modality-specific information such as the appearance of the face and clothes, and the specific quality of the voice.

What guides selective attention to these various properties of events? Research indicates that redundancy across the senses promotes attention to redundantly specified properties at the expense of other (nonredundantly specified) properties, particularly in early development, when attentional resources are most limited (e.g., Bahrick & Lickliter, 2000, 2002). Later, attention extends to less salient nonredundantly specified properties. Factors such as the length of exploratory time, complexity, familiarity, and the level of expertise of the perceiver affect the speed of progression through this salience hierarchy. The intersensory redundancy hypothesis, a model of early selective attention, provides a framework for understanding how and under what conditions attention is allocated to amodal versus modality-specific aspects of stimulation in a world providing an overabundance of concurrent, dynamic multimodal stimulation, and how this guides perceptual development.

The Intersensory Redundancy Hypothesis (IRH)

Bahrick, Lickliter, and colleagues (Bahrick & Lickliter, 2000, 2002; Bahrick, Flom & Lickliter, 2002; Lickliter, Bahrick, & Honeycutt, 2002, 2004) proposed and provided empirical support for the Intersensory Redundancy Hypothesis (IRH). The IRH consists of a fundamental set of principles that are thought to guide information pick-up. It is a model of selective attention developed to explain under what conditions perceivers attend to and process different properties of events, redundantly specified versus nonredundantly specified. The IRH provides a framework to address the question of how infants with no knowledge of the world, learn to perceive unitary events and attend to stimulation that is relevant to their needs and actions. Moreover, because environmental stimulation far exceeds our attention capacity, particularly during early development, these principles of information pick-up should have a disproportionately large effect on perception in early development when attention is most limited. Although the IRH is primarily thought of as a framework for describing the early development of attention and intermodal perception, the principles also apply across development. The IRH also integrates into a single model, perception of unimodal and multimodal events, bridging the long-standing gap in the literature between these areas.

The IRH consists of four specific predictions. Two predictions address the nature of selective attention to different properties of events and are depicted in Figure 4.2. The remaining two are developmental predictions that address implications across the life

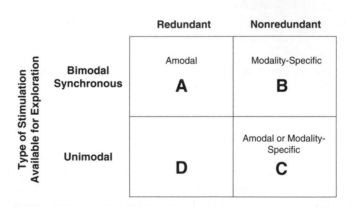

Specification of Event Property

Figure 4.2   Facilitation versus attenuation of attention and perceptual processing for a given event property is a function of whether the property is redundantly versus nonredundantly specified and whether the type of stimulation available for exploration is bimodal, synchronous versus unimodal. Predictions of the IRH: Intermodal facilitation *of AM properties* (A > C): detection of a redundantly specified AM property in bimodal stimulation (A) is greater than when the same property is nonredundantly specified in unimodal stimulation (C); Unimodal facilitation *of MS properties* (C > B): detection of a nonredundantly specified MS property in unimodal stimulation (C) is greater than when the same property is nonredundantly specified in bimodal stimulation (B). Note: Quadrant D reflects *intra*sensory redundancy *not discussed here*.

span. These predictions have been supported by empirical studies with human and animal infants. Below I review the four predictions and the original research findings that support each.

Prediction 1: Intersensory facilitiation (A > C, figure 4.2)

> Redundantly specified, amodal properties are highly salient and detected more easily in bimodal synchronous, stimulation than the same amodal properties in unimodal stimulation (where they are not redundantly specified).

According to the IRH, intersensory redundancy (the synchronous alignment of stimulation from two or more senses), makes amodal properties of events such as tempo, rhythm, and intensity highly salient. Redundancy recruits infant attention to redundantly specified properties, causing them to become "foreground" and other properties to become "background". In fact, this redundancy is so salient that it allows young infants to selectively attend to one of two superimposed events while ignoring the other. When the soundtrack to one film, such as a person striking the keys of a toy xylophone, is played, 4-month-old infants can selectively follow the flow of action, even when it is superimposed with another film such as a hand-clapping game. The sound event appears to "pop out" and become attentional foreground while the silent event becomes background. Infants then treat the background event as novel in a novelty preference test (Bahrick, Walker, & Neisser, 1981). Detecting intersensory redundancy leads to early processing and learning about unitary events by focusing attention on properties that are specified in more than one sense modality concurrently. Research has demonstrated that intersensory redundancy promotes enhanced attention and perceptual processing in both human and non-human animal infants (Bahrick & Lickliter, 2000, 2002; Bahrick, Flom, et al., 2002; Lickliter & Bahrick, 2000; Lickliter et al., 2002, 2004).

For example, young infants detected the rhythm and tempo of a toy hammer tapping when they experienced the synchronous sights and sounds together (providing intersensory redundancy) but not when they experienced the rhythm or tempo in one sense modality alone or when the sights and sounds were out of synchrony (providing no intersensory redundancy) (Bahrick & Lickliter, 2000; Bahrick, Flom, et al., 2002). Research from other laboratories has also found support for this hypothesis. For example, 4-month-old infants detected the serial order of events in synchronous audiovisual but not unimodal auditory or unimodal visual stimulation (Lewkowicz, 2004). Seven-month-old infants detect numerical information in audiovisual sequences of faces and voices developmentally earlier than in auditory or visual sequences alone (Jordan, Suanda, & Brannon, 2008). Finally, this hypothesis has also received clear support from studies of nonhuman animal infants. Following redundant audiovisual prenatal stimulation (where synchronized lights and call were presented to embryos), quail chicks learned an individual maternal call four times faster and remembered it four times longer than when they had only heard the call alone, or when the call and light were presented out of synchrony (Lickliter et al., 2002, 2004).

Taken together these studies have shown that intersensory redundancy available in bimodal stimulation plays a critical role in organizing selective attention and, in turn, perception, learning, and memory. It facilitates attention to redundantly specified properties such as the rhythm, tempo, and temporal patterning of audible and visible stimulation, as compared with the same properties experienced in one sense modality alone. Moreover, the facilitation observed in bimodal synchronous but not bimodal asynchronous conditions (where the overall amount and type of stimulation are equated), rules out alternative hypotheses such as arousal or receiving stimulation in two different modalities as the basis for facilitation. Thus, it appears that the redundancy across the senses serves as a basis for heightened attention and processing of certain aspects of multimodal events.

Prediction 2: Unimodal facilitation (C > B, figure 4.2)

> Nonredundantly specified, modality-specific properties are more salient and detected more easily in unimodal stimulation than the same properties in bimodal, synchronous stimulation (where redundantly specified, amodal properties compete for attention).

In unimodal stimulation, where intersensory redundancy is not available, attention is selectively directed to nonredundantly specified properties such as color, pattern, pitch, or timbre, to a greater extent than in multimodal stimulation. This "unimodal facilitation" occurs in part because there is no competition for attention from salient intersensory redundancy. Particularly in early development, a given event typically provides significantly more stimulation than can be attended to at any one time, and thus redundantly and nonredundantly specified properties within the same event compete for attention. Because redundantly specified properties are more salient, they capture attention at the expense of modality-specific properties. For example, a young infant exploring a person speaking, might selectively attend to amodal properties such as the prosody of speech (composed of rhythm, tempo, and intensity patterns) at the expense of modality-specific properties such as the appearance of the person, color of their clothing, or specific nature of their voice. In contrast, when salient redundancy is unavailable, as when the person is silent, attention is free to focus on nonredundant, modality specific properties available in unimodal visual stimulation. Under these conditions we would observe unimodal facilitation and enhanced attention to the appearance of the individual. (This attentional tradeoff as a function of modality of stimulation will be elaborated further using social events as an example, in The Role of Intersensory Redundancy in Social Development below).

Consistent with this prediction, research has shown that, in early development, unimodal stimulation selectively recruits attention and promotes perceptual processing of nonredundantly specified, modality-specific properties more effectively than does redundant, audiovisual stimulation. Studies assessing infant discrimination of faces, voices, and the orientation of a toy hammer tapping (Bahrick et al., 2006; Bahrick, Lickliter, et al., 2005; Bahrick, Lickliter, Vaillant, Shuman, & Castellanos, 2004) have demonstrated that young infants discriminate these properties in unimodal visual and unimodal auditory stimulation, but not in synchronous audiovisual stimulation. For example, Bahrick et al. (2006) found that 3- and 5-month-olds discriminated a change in the orientation of a toy hammer tapping (upward against a ceiling vs. downward against a floor) when they could see the hammer tapping (unimodal visual stimulation) but not when they could see and hear the natural synchronous audiovisual stimulation from the hammer. This latter condition provided intersensory redundancy which presumably attracted attention to redundantly specified properties such as rhythm and tempo and interfered with attention to visual information such as the direction of motion or orientation of the hammer. Further, research has also shown that infants' failure to discriminate in the redundant, bimodal condition was due to competition from salient redundant properties and not to other factors such as bimodal stimulation providing a greater amount of stimulation or being more distracting than unimodal stimulation. We tested the possibility that these factors, rather than intersensory redundancy per se, drew the infant's attention away from the visual information, attenuating detection of orientation. To address this issue, an asynchronous control condition was presented which eliminated intersensory redundancy but equated overall amount and type of stimulation with the bimodal synchronous condition. Instead of impairing perception of orientation, this bimodal but asynchronous condition *enhanced* infant perception of orientation of the hammer tapping as compared with the bimodal, synchronous condition. Consistent with predictions of the IRH, asynchronous sights and sounds resulted in heightened discrimination on a par with that of the unimodal, visual condition. Thus, unimodal facilitation occurs when salient intersensory redundancy is eliminated and attention is free to focus on information conveyed by a single sense modality at a time.

Predictions 1 and 2 integrated: Attentional biases and salience hierarchies as mechanisms of developmental change

In sum, these findings reveal an attentional trade-off in early development such that in multimodal stimulation, amodal properties are more salient and modality-specific properties less salient, whereas in unimodal stimulation, modality specific properties are more salient and amodal properties less salient. Together, studies of intersensory and unimodal facilitation using the same toy hammer events (Bahrick & Lickliter, 2000; Bahrick, Flom, et al., 2002) indicate that synchronous, bimodal stimulation attenuates attention to modality-specific properties of events because salient redundancy directs attention elsewhere – to amodal, redundantly specified properties such as rhythm and tempo. Multimodal stimulation appears to impair attention to modality-specific and nonredundantly specified properties (such as orientation, pitch, timbre, color, pattern, and facial configuration) when it is synchronous and provides intersensory redundancy (as in most natural stimulation). In fact, synchronous, bimodal stimulation appears to be "unitized" (perceived as one event) by infants (e.g., Spear, Kraemer, Molina, & Smoller, 1988). This unitization simplifies the event and effectively reduces the overall amount of stimulation experienced, as infants are adept at detecting organization and pattern in stimulation.

It should be noted that testing predictions 1 and 2 of the IRH (intermodal versus unimodal facilitation) entails comparing detection of a given property of an event under conditions of redundant stimulation (bimodal, synchronous) versus conditions of nonredundant stimulation (unimodal or asynchronous). Tests of these predictions have typically not involved comparing detection of one property (e.g., amodal) versus another (e.g., modality specific), a comparison with inherent task difficulty confounds. Instead, by focusing on detection of a particular property of an event (e.g., tempo) in one modality versus another, we can hold constant the nature of the information to be detected, and can then generalize findings appropriately to the particular modalities tested (e.g., audio-visual vs unimodal visual).

Because most events are multimodal, and intersensory redundancy is highly salient to infants, on balance there is a general processing advantage for amodal over modality-specific properties in early development. This is adaptive and ensures coordinated perception by allowing infants to process visual, auditory, and tactile stimulation from unitary events. This provides a viable explanation for the "developmental lag" described above and promotes development in order of increasing specificity. Moreover, it may have a cascading effect on cognition, language, and social development, which emerge from multimodal learning contexts, by establishing initial conditions that favor processing of amodal information from unitary, multimodal events (Bahrick & Lickliter, 2002; Gogate & Bahrick, 1998; Lickliter & Bahrick, 2000).

Furthermore, the general processing advantage for amodal over modality-specific information exerts a greater influence on early development than later development for another important reason. Salience hierarchies have the greatest impact when resources are most limited, as is the case in early development. We (Bahrick, Gogate, & Ruiz, 2002; Bahrick & Lickliter, 2002; Bahrick, Lickliter, Castellanos and Vaillant-Molina, in press; Bahrick & Newell, 2008) have proposed that properties of objects and events are processed in order of attentional salience, with properties that are most salient attracting attention initially, and as exploration continues attention is then allocated to less salient properties as well. Thus, during longer bouts of exploration and with faster processing of information, the likelihood of processing the less salient modality-specific information along with the more salient amodal information increases. However, on average (across episodes of exploration), the more salient aspects of objects and events receive substantially greater attention and processing than less salient aspects. Effects of salience hierarchies are most pronounced in early development when attentional resources are most limited. In this case only the most salient aspects of stimulation are likely to be processed. For example, a given bout of exploratory activity may terminate before attention can shift to less salient aspects. In contrast, when greater attentional resources are available, processing of both the less salient and more salient aspects is promoted. For this reason, salience hierarchies should have a much greater impact on attention and processing in early development than later development. They should also exert a greater influence when tasks are difficult or attentional capacities of perceivers are taxed, for example, under conditions of high attentional and cognitive load (see Bahrick et al., 2010 for discussion). Predictions 3 and 4 build upon this logic.

Prediction 3: Developmental improvement in attention: Attenuation of facilitation effects

Across development, infants' increasing perceptual differentiation, efficiency of processing, and flexibility of attention lead to detection of both redundantly and nonredundantly specified properties in unimodal, nonredundant and bimodal, redundant stimulation.

The IRH thus provides a basis for describing developmental change in attention and perceptual processing. Salience hierarchies exert the greatest effect on perceptual development during early infancy. As infants become older and more experienced, processing speed increases, perceptual differentiation progresses, and attention becomes more efficient and flexible (see E. J. Gibson, 1969, 1988; Ruff & Rothbart, 1996). Infants habituate more quickly to stimuli, show shorter looks, more shifting between targets, and can discriminate the same changes in objects and events with shorter processing times (e.g., Colombo, 2001, 2002; Colombo & Mitchell, 1990, 2009; Colombo, Mitchell, Coldren & Freeseman, 1991; Frick, Colombo, & Saxon, 1999; Hale, 1990; Hunter & Ames, 1988; Rose, Feldman, & Jankowski, 2001). These changes, along with experience differentiating amodal and modality-specific properties in the environment, allow infants to detect both redundantly and nonredundantly specified properties in unimodal and bimodal stimulation. As perceptual learning improves, greater attentional resources are available for detecting information from multiple levels of the salience hierarchy. Attention progresses from the most salient to increasingly less salient properties across exploratory time. Improved economy of information pick-up and increased familiarity with events and their structure through experience, frees attentional resources for processing information not detected earlier when attention was less economical and cognitive load was higher.

For example, infants show developmental shifts from detection of global to local (more detailed) information (Frick, Colombo, & Allen, 2000), from detection of actions and information about object function to more specific information about the appearance of objects (Bahrick, Gogate, et al., 2002; Bahrick & Newell, 2008; Oakes & Madole, in press; Xu, Carey, & Quint, 2004), and from detection of global, amodal audiovisual relations to more specific amodal audiovisual relations across exploration time and across development (Bahrick, 1992, 1994, 2001; Morrongiello, Fenwick, & Nutley, 1998). These examples characterize progressions in order of attentional salience both across development and during a given sustained period of exploration within a single point in development. These developmental progressions also illustrate the principle of increasing specificity proposed by E. J. Gibson (1969) as a cornerstone of perceptual development. Differentiation of information is thought to progress from abstract and global, to increasingly more specific levels of stimulation across development.

Studies testing predictions of the IRH reveal findings consistent with the developmental improvements described above. Research demonstrates that with only a few months additional experience, infants viewing the toy hammer events used in the prior studies detect both redundantly specified properties such as rhythm and tempo (Bahrick, Lickliter & Flom, 2006), and nonredundantly specified properties such as orientation (Bahrick & Lickliter, 2004) in both unimodal visual and bimodal synchronous stimulation. Thus, patterns of facilitation (described by Predictions 1 and 2 of the IRH) that were apparent in early development became less apparent in later development as infants gained experience with objects and events in their environment.

Moreover, research indicates that one avenue for developmental improvement is "education of attention" (see E. J. Gibson, 1969; Zukow-Goldring, 1997 for discussions of this concept). Multimodal stimulation elicits selective attention to amodal properties of stimulation at the expense of other properties. By focusing on amodal properties in multimodal stimulation, we can "educate" attention to those same properties in subsequent unimodal stimulation, much like transfer of training effects. Comparative studies of bobwhite quail chicks illustrate this process. Lickliter, Bahrick, & Markham (2006) found that prenatal redundant audiovisual exposure to a maternal call followed by unimodal auditory exposure (bimodal → unimodal) resulted in a significant preference for the familiar auditory maternal call 2 days after hatching, whereas the reverse sequence did not (unimodal → bimodal). Intersensory redundancy (in bimodal stimulation) apparently highlighted the temporal features of the call and then "educated attention" to these features, generalizing to the subsequent unimodal stimulation. This conclusion was also supported by additional control conditions showing that asynchronous followed by unimodal stimulation and unimodal-only stimulation were also insufficient to lead to a preference for the familiar call 2 days later. Remarkably, education of attention to amodal temporal properties was effective even after delays of 2 or 4 hours between initial bimodal stimulation and subsequent unimodal stimulation. Recent studies of human infants assessing their sensitivity to the tempo of action in the toy hammer events using combinations of redundant audiovisual, asynchronous audiovisual, and unimodal visual presentations, showed parallel findings (Castellanos, Vaillant-Molina, Lickliter, & Bahrick, 2006). Thus, education of attention appears to be a viable potential mechanism for developmental change in human infants.

Do the patterns of unimodal and intermodal facilitation of attention disappear across age as infants become more skilled perceivers? The answer depends on the nature of the task, and in particular its difficulty in relation to the skills of the perceiver. Patterns of intersensory and unimodal facilitation do become less evident across development as discrimination capabilities improve and the events presented become more familiar and relatively simple to perceive. However, attentional facilitation may depend on relative task difficulty. The simple discrimination tasks used with younger infants would not sufficiently challenge older infants and thus their performance may be at ceiling. The logic underlying the IRH suggests that if measures of discrimination were more sensitive or tasks were made sufficiently difficult to challenge older perceivers, intersensory and unimodal facilitation predicted by the IRH should be apparent across the life span. Thus, patterns of facilitation described by the IRH should not disappear across age. Rather, they should simply become less evident as perceiving the world of objects and events becomes easier with experience. Prediction 4, below, describes the rationale and conditions under which intersensory and unimodal facilitation should be most evident in later development.

Prediction 4: Facilitation across development: Task difficulty and expertise

> Intersensory and unimodal facilitation are most pronounced for tasks of relatively high difficulty in relation to the expertise of the perceiver, and are thus apparent across the lifespan.

Attentional salience is thought to lead to longer, deeper processing and greater perceptual differentiation of events and their salient properties (Adler & Rovee-Collier, 1994; Craik & Lockhart, 1972; E. J. Gibson, 1969). Continued exposure to an event promotes perceptual differentiation, likely in order of salience, such that more salient properties are differentiated first and differentiation of less salient properties requires longer processing time. Further, perceptual differentiation of event properties may, in turn, enhance efficiency and flexibility of attention by fostering more rapid detection of previously differentiated properties in subsequent encounters and more flexible attentional shifting among familiar properties (see Ruff & Rothbart, 1996). Thus, the degree of intersensory and/or unimodal facilitation observed should be, in part, a function of familiarity and task difficulty in relation to the expertise of the perceiver. In early development, perceivers are relatively naïve and events are relatively novel, and therefore perceptual processing of most events is likely rather difficult and effortful, entailing a higher cognitive load. Thus, effects of intersensory redundancy should be most pronounced in early development. However, because perceptual learning and differentiation progress throughout the lifespan, effects of intersensory facilitation should also be evident in later development, as well. Perceivers continue to develop expertise through interaction with new information or by learning to perceive finer distinctions in familiar stimuli. For example, children and adults may learn a new language, learn to play a musical instrument, or become skilled at identifying birds. Under these conditions, in early stages of learning, expertise is low in relation to task demands. Therefore, older perceivers should experience intersensory and unimodal facilitation when learning new material.

Research findings are consistent with this view. Studies in a variety of domains including motor and cognitive development, indicate that under conditions of higher cognitive load, performance of infants and children reverts to that of earlier stages of development (Adolph & Berger, 2005; Berger, 2004; Corbetta & Bojczyk, 2002). Research generated from predictions of the IRH has also directly tested this hypothesis. By the age of 5 months, infants no longer showed intersensory facilitation for discrimination of simple tempo changes, as their performance was at ceiling in both the unimodal and bimodal audiovisual conditions (Bahrick & Lickliter, 2004). However, by increasing task difficulty, we reinstated intersensory facilitation in 5-month-olds. They showed intersensory facilitation in the more difficult tempo discrimination task, comparable to that shown by 3-month-olds in a simpler version of the task (Bahrick et al., in press). Data collection with adults is currently in progress and findings thus far indicate intersensory facilitation (Bahrick et al., 2009). If findings of intersensory and unimodal facilitation hold up across studies of adults, the IRH will provide a useful framework for understanding the nature of selective attention and perceptual processing of various properties of events across development. This will have important applications, particularly when children or adults are attending to new or difficult information or when cognitive load is high.

Significance and broader implications of the IRH for development

The IRH provides a model of selective attention addressing how attention is allocated in early development to dimensions of stimulation that are fundamental for promoting veridical perception of objects and events. Because selective attention provides the basis for what is perceived, learned, and remembered, patterns of early selectivity can have longterm, organizing effects on the development of knowledge across the lifespan. Together, current findings indicate that (a) attentional trade-offs such that amodal properties are more likely to be detected in multimodal stimulation and modality-specific properties in unimodal stimulation, (b) these processing biases lead to general salience hierarchies in attentional allocation, (c) salience hierarchies exert a disproportionately large effect on early development when attentional resources are most limited and cognitive load is highest, and (d) they also exert some influence on later development when cognitive load and task difficulty are high.

Given that initial conditions have a disproportionately large effect on development, particularly because they can constrain what is learned next (Smith & Thelen, 2003; Thelen & Smith, 1994), these principles of early attention have a profound impact on the emergence of typical perceptual, cognitive, and social development. However, there has been little research on the development of selective attention in infancy (see Ruff & Rothbart, 1996) and no prior model that integrates attention to unimodal and multimodal stimulation. Given that environmental stimulation is primarily experienced multimodally, this focus is critical for making research and theory more ecologically relevant (see Lickliter & Bahrick, 2001). The IRH provides a viable starting point for this integration. By examining how detection of redundant, amodal information is coordinated with detection of nonredundant, modality-specific information across development, we can observe interactions between unimodal and multimodal functioning not otherwise accessible to scientific study. Further, an understanding of these interactions will provide a basis for specific educational applications or interventions such as more appropriate matching of learning tasks (whether they require knowledge of amodal or modality-specific properties) with their mode of presentation (multimodal vs. unimodal) to enhance learning outcomes. It will also provide an important basis for comparisons between children of typical versus atypical development.

The following sections examine the development of perception and learning about social events in a multimodal environment, using principles of the IRH as a framework for achieving a more ecological and integrated approach. First, I review what is known about the development of perception of multimodal social events in typically developing infants, and later how this developmental process might go awry in atypical development, such as autism.

The Role of Intersensory Redundancy in Social Development: Perception of Faces, Voices, Speech, and Emotion

"Social orienting" in infancy promotes typical development

Social events are arguably the most important form of stimulation for guiding and shaping infant perceptual, cognitive, social, and linguistic development. Consequently, "social orienting" or selective attention to social events on the part of infants is critically important for fostering typical developmental outcomes. It is therefore fortunate, but no accident, that the developmental requirements of the infant fit so well with the stimulation typically provided by the social environment – social events are prevalent, highly salient, and readily capture infant attention. Typically developing infants prefer faces over many other stimuli, pick out the sounds of speech even *in utero*, and orient to voices and faces in the first days of life. Social events are one of the first and most frequent events encountered by infants, and it appears that perceptual learning occurs rapidly in this domain. Indeed, even newborns can discriminate their mothers' face (Bushnell, 2001; Field, Cohen, Garcia, & Greenberg, 1984), her voice (DeCasper & Fifer, 1980), and the prosody of speech (DeCasper & Spence, 1986) in unimodal stimulation. Rather than being "innate", these early capabilities arise from a complex system of organism–environment interactions that guide and shape early social orienting (Gogate, Walker-Andrews, & Bahrick, 2001; Harrist & Waugh, 2002; Mundy & Burnette, 2005). Much infant learning takes place during face-to-face interactions with adults. Adults provide a rich source for learning about the world of objects, events, and language, as well as a forum for social interaction and for the infant's developing sense of self and other. Adults guide and direct infant attention, scaffold learning about the affordances of people, objects, and the structure of language (e.g., Gogate, Walker-Andrews, & Bahrick 2001; Moore & Dunham, 1995; Mundy & Burnette, 2005; Rochat & Striano, 1999; Zukow-Goldring, 1997). Unfortunately, in developmental disorders such as autism, young children do not respond to this structure in the same way as typically developing children, and they show social orienting impairments (e.g., Dawson, Meltzoff, Osterling, Rinaldi, & Brown, 1998; Dawson et al., 2004), paying little attention to faces, voices, speech, and people, and focusing more attention on nonsocial events. It is not known how these children develop such deficits in social attention and the resulting impairments in cognitive and communicative functioning. However, it is clear that understanding how typically developing infants come to selectively attend to social events such as faces, voices, and emotions, is critical to answering this question, as well as for constructing more viable theories of perceptual and cognitive development. What makes social events so salient to infants and why do they typically show "social orienting"?

The salience of intersensory redundancy promotes social orienting in infancy

Social events are widely known to be highly salient to infants, and there are many theories regarding the basis for their attractiveness to infants, ranging from innate mechanisms (Goren, Sarty, & Wu, 1975; Johnson & Morton, 1991; Morton & Johnson, 1991), to their contingent responsiveness (Harrist & Waugh, 2002; Watson, 1979), and to familiarity, experience, and their general perceptual qualities (Diamond & Carey, 1986; Gauthier & Tarr, 1997; Nelson, 2001). There is currently no consensus regarding which perspectives are more correct or most fundamental. The basis for social orienting and interaction clearly involves a complex system of interactive influences, and identifying more fundamental and influential components of this system is critical for understanding the mechanisms underlying typical and atypical development. Recent advances in the field of neuroscience (see Mareschal et al., 2007) have generated promising neurodevelopmental models of autism and social orienting (e.g., Akshoomoff, Pierce, & Courchesne, 2002; Brock, Brown, Boucher, & Rippon, 2002; Dawson et al., 2002; Mundy, 2003; Mundy & Burnette, 2005; Mundy & Newell, 2007). In conjunction with behavioral models such as the IRH, important strides can be made toward identifying underlying mechanisms and fundamental components of this social orienting system. Here, I propose that a fundamental basis for "social orienting", or the attentional salience of social events to infants, starting in the first months of life, is the salience of intersensory redundancy (see Bahrick & Lickliter, 2002; Flom & Bahrick, 2007 for discussions).

Social events, in particular, provide a great deal of rapidly changing, amodal, redundant stimulation. For example, audiovisual speech is rich with intersensory redundancy uniting the tempo, rhythm, and intensity shifts across faces and voices. Social agents are also contingently responsive, providing cycles of reciprocal communicative exchanges with infants characterized by distinctive amodal temporal and intensity patterning common across auditory, visual, and tactile stimulation. These important forms of multimodal and redundant stimulation can serve as a basis for social orienting in early development by attracting and maintaining selective attention to faces, voices and audiovisual speech. Because detection of intersensory redundancy focuses and maintains attention on social events and their amodal properties such as temporal synchrony, rhythm, and intensity, this promotes perception of integrated multimodal social events and serves as the gatekeeper to further perceptual processing of cohesive social events. Prolonged attention leads to detection of modality-specific information, in order of increasing specificity. Detection of amodal information is particularly important in social contexts, where multiple individuals speak and interact concurrently, and one must selectively attend to the sights and sounds of a particular individual and separate them from those of other individuals. Communication involves engaging in reciprocal, well-synchronized social interaction involving coordination of gaze, vocalization, movement, and touch with a social partner. Thus, detection of intersensory redundancy for amodal temporal and spatial information in social exchanges plays an important role in parsing the stream of social stimulation into meaningful social events, initiating and maintaining infant attention to these events, and regulating interaction with a social partner.

The IRH provides a framework for exploring the development of infant perception of social events ranging from detection of specific faces and voices (based on modality specific information) to emotion and the prosody of speech (based on amodal information), in both unimodal and multimodal dynamic social stimulation. What do infants abstract from this diverse array of changing stimulation? As highlighted in the sections above, all aspects of events, be they social or nonsocial, are not equally salient, and in the context of limited attentional resources, differences in attentional salience have a pronounced effect on what is attended to and perceived from a single event, such as a person speaking. When and under what conditions do infants attend to different properties of social events, from discrimination of faces and voices, to selectively attending to a single speaker in the context of concurrent speech, and perceiving and recognizing emotional expressions?

Intersensory redundancy: A foundation for typical social development

It is clear that to foster optimal social development, young infants must look at faces, listen to voices, coordinate what they see with what they hear, and engage in reciprocal social interactions with adults. Developmental disorders such as autism highlight that these basic processes, often taken for granted in typical development, sometimes go awry. This presents a clear challenge to developmental psychologists: How and under what conditions do young infants come to perceive different aspects of this social stimulation as salient? What is the typical course of development of interest in faces, voices, speech, and emotion in multimodal everyday events and on what basis does it emerge? Developmental science is making progress in addressing these important questions, but it is far from providing a complete picture of these developmental processes. This is due, in part, to a lack of research focus on development in a multimodal, dynamic environment as well as a scarcity of studies assessing developmental change across a number of ages under uniform conditions; methods, measures, and research questions have differed widely across studies. For all of these reasons it is difficult to piece together an integrated developmental account of each of these skills. However, a more complete and integrated account of these developmental processes is central to developmental theories of attention, perception, learning, and memory as well as being critically important for identifying atypical developmental patterns for the early detection of children at risk for developmental delay and autism. The IRH provides a framework that can guide this process and suggests that an important mechanism for promoting typical social development is detection of intersensory redundancy which promotes attention to some aspects of stimulation (amodal) and attenuates attention to other aspects (modality-specific) in early development. The sections below review what is known about social development and orienting to social events across the first half year of life and the role of interrersensory redundancy in this developmental process.

Prenatal origins of intersensory responsiveness   Prenatal development has a profound effect on postnatal behavioral organization (see Fifer & Moon, 1995; Gottlieb, 1997; Lickliter, 2005; Smotherman & Robinson, 1990, for reviews). Although little is known about the development of intersensory functioning during the prenatal period, it is clear that fetuses are exposed to intersensory redundancy across a wide range of stimulation to auditory, vestibular, and tactile senses. During fetal development, the functioning of the senses emerges in an invariant sequence (common across mammals and birds), with tactile/vestibular functioning emerging first, the chemical senses of smell and taste next, followed by auditory functioning early in the third trimester, and finally visual functioning becomes available at birth (Gottlieb, 1971). The successive emergence of sensory function raises the important question of how the senses and their respective stimulation histories influence one another during the prenatal period. Turkewitz & Kenny (1982) proposed that sensory limitations during early development both reduce overall stimulation and mediate the timing of the introduction of stimulation, thereby reducing the amount of competition between sensory systems. Thus, auditory perception typically develops without competition from visual stimulation during fetal development, and provides a context for the emergence of visual functioning at birth.

The developing fetus is likely to experience a diverse array of redundancy across the senses, particularly accompanying self-movement and the sounds of the mother's voice. Moving one's body produces proprioceptive feedback that is correlated with tactile and vestibular consequences of the motion. Thus, sucking, kicking, and turning produce patterns of proprioceptive, tactile, vestibular, and even auditory stimulation that covary and share amodal temporal, spatial, and intensity patterning. This activity and the multimodal stimulation it generates in turn affect neural development in a continuous and complex pattern of mutual influence. Altering the amount and/or timing of stimulation to one sense modality affects responsiveness and neural development in other modalities (Lickliter, 2005; Gottlieb, 1997). Neural development is activity-dependent, in the sense that it is continuously shaped by the nature of our actions and the stimulation we experience across development (see Edelman, 1987; Mareschal et al., 2007, for reviews). The prenatal period is one of strikingly rapid neural development (some 250,000 new neurons are generated each minute during some stages) and thus the activity of the fetus has a particularly large effect on neural development. Fetal activity and the multimodal stimulation it generates foster the development of neural architecture which supports further development of intersensory perception.

Auditory stimulation from sources such as the mother's voice is detected beginning in the 6th month of fetal development (see Fifer, Monk, & Grose-Fifer, 2001 for a review). Stimulation from the mother's voice is the loudest and most frequently heard sound (Fifer & Moon, 1995) and is also likely to be accompanied by a range of stimulation to various senses, providing a rich source of intersensory redundancy during the fetal period. For example, the mother's voice produces vibrations of her spinal column, synchronous movements of her diaphragm, and is often accompanied by movements of her body, as well as physiological changes (Abrams, Gerhardt & Peters, 1995; Fifer & Moon, 1995; Mastropieri & Turkewitz, 1999; Turkewitz, 1994). This multimodal synchrony may be detected by the fetus, causing the temporal patterning and prosody of the mother's voice to become particularly salient. This is likely to provide an important basis for the neonate's preference for the mother's voice and the prosody of her speech (DeCasper & Fifer, 1980; DeCasper & Spence, 1986; Moon & Fifer, 2000), as well as her face (Sai, 2005) shortly after birth.

Sai (2005) found evidence that newborns' preference for their mother's face results from intermodal perception and familiarity with her voice during prenatal development. Neonates' preference for their mother's face over that of a female stranger disappeared if they were prevented from hearing their mother's voice while observing her face from birth until the time of testing. Preferences for the mother's face were shown only by neonates who received postnatal experience with the mother's face and voice together. This remarkable finding suggests that the newborn's preference for the mother's face is a product of intermodal perception, probably due to experiencing her face moving in synchrony and collocated with her voice, a highly familiar stimulus which, itself, has been accompanied by intersensory redundancy. This provides a viable developmental explanation for an early preference that has puzzled scientists for decades.

Animal models of intersensory development have provided direct evidence of intersensory functioning during prenatal development and the links between sensory experience and neural development. These studies can manipulate the experience of the embryo by augmenting or decreasing typical sensory stimulation, or substituting one type of sensory stimulation for another (see Lickliter, 2005 for a review). Research indicates that altering stimulation to one sense modality can result in changes in other senses, affecting both behavioral and neural development. For example, studies with bobwhite quail embryos have shown that unusually early visual experience interferes with typical auditory responsiveness following hatching (Lickliter, 1990). Moreover, providing avian embryos with augmented auditory stimulation while the visual system is developing (rather than just before or after) results in impaired visual responsiveness and modified neural development in multimodal areas of the brain (Markham, Shimuzu, & Lickliter, 2008). Further, there is clear evidence that intersensory redundancy experienced *in ovo* can promote learning and memory for temporal properties of events in quail embryos, just as it does in human infants (Lickliter et al., 2002, 2004). For example, chicks who received redundant audiovisual exposure to a maternal call learned the call with one fourth of the exposure time and remembered it four times longer than chicks who received unimodal auditory exposure, and chicks who received asynchronous exposure showed no learning at all. The convergence of findings across species highlighting the important role of intersensory redundancy in directing learning and memory suggests that this is a fundamental process shaping fetal development across species. A direct test of human fetal sensitivity to intersensory redundancy awaits future research.

Intermodal proprioceptive-visual information and self-perception.   Self-exploration results in one of the earliest and most potent sources of intersensory redundancy (see Rochat, 1995; Rochat & Striano, 1999). Infants engage in active intermodal exploration of the self, starting during fetal development and increasing dramatically after birth and across the first months of life (Butterworth & Hopkins, 1988; Rochat, 1993; Van der Meer, Van der Weel, & Lee, 1995). At birth, vision becomes functional and provides a new, and particularly powerful, channel for detecting amodal, redundant stimulation, both about events in the world, and also about the self. Visual stimulation specifying self-motion is continuously available, and provides redundancy across auditory, tactile, and proprioceptive stimulation. Infants experience continuous and ongoing proprioceptive feedback from their muscles, joints, and vestibular system resulting from their own motion. For example, when the infant observes his own hand move, he experiences congruent information across vision and proprioception for self-motion. This amodal, proprioceptive-visual information is temporally synchronous, perfectly contingent, and characterized by common patterns of temporal, spatial, and intensity variation across the senses. Similarly, when the infant vocalizes, he experiences the covariation between his sounds and the feedback from his articulatory movements. This multimodal self-exploration provides infants with access to a great deal of controllable intersensory redundancy and contributes to the early emergence of the "ecological" self (Neisser, 1991; Rochat 1995) – the infant's sense of self as a separate entity and an agent of action.

Research demonstrates that infants of 3 to 5 months detect intersensory redundancy across visual and proprioceptive feedback from their own motions and can differentiate self from social stimulation in the first months of life (Bahrick & Watson, 1985; Rochat & Morgan, 1995; Schmuckler, 1996). Bahrick & Watson (1985) developed a procedure to directly assess infants' ability to perceive intersensory redundancy from self-motion. Infants were presented with a live video image of their own legs kicking (which provides perfect contingency or intersensory redundancy between felt and seen motions), along side that of another infant's legs kicking, or a prerecorded video of their own legs kicking (which provides only accidental contingency or intersensory redundancy). Results indicated that 5-month-old infants detected the intersensory redundancy provided by the live video feedback and preferred to watch the nonredundant videos of the peer's legs and their own prerecorded legs. Because only stimulation from the self is perfectly redundant with proprioceptive feedback, we proposed this perfect redundancy or contingency provided an early basis for distinguishing self from social stimulation. Five-month-olds prefer the social stimulation from a peer over the perfectly contingent and redundant stimulation from the self. At 3 months, however, infants showed bimodally distributed preferences, suggesting they were in transition from a preference for self to social stimulation. Subsequent studies have replicated the preference for noncontingent social stimulation over the perfectly redundant stimulation from the self and extended these findings across a variety of contexts (e.g., Rochat & Morgan, 1995; Schmuckler, 1996: Schmuckler & Fairhall, 2001). Taken together with other findings reviewed in this chapter, there appears to be a shift in early development, around the age of 3 months, from attention to self and the perfect intersensory redundancy it provides, to greater attention to social partners and the partially contingent, turn-taking structure of social interaction. In other words, there is a transition to greater "social orienting" in early infancy. Interestingly, a recent study using Bahrick & Watson's (1985) task to compare children with autism and mental age-matched children of typical development (Bahrick, Castellanos, et al., 2008) found that 2- to 5-year-old children with autism had not made this important transition. It is not yet clear whether these children failed to detect the redundancy across proprioceptive stimulation and the visual display of their own motion or whether they had no preference for social stimulation over self generated stimulation.

Further evidence of this transition comes from data showing that young infants also discriminate a video image of their own face from that of another infant, based on its visual appearance (Bahrick et al., 1996). Here, too, infants show a preference for the social partner over the self, and consistent with findings above, this appears to emerge between 2- and 3-months of age (Bahrick, 1995; Bahrick et al. 1996). Parents of children in this study reported that their infants received regular mirror exposure. Most likely, this allowed them to detect the correspondence between visual transformations and proprioceptive feedback, making their own facial images not only familiar, but distinct from other facial images.

Infants also detect intermodal relations between self-motion and external events, allowing them to discover the effects of their own behavior on the environment, promoting a sense of competence and self-efficacy (e.g., Watson, 1972, 1979). Infants who discover that they control the movements of an overhead crib mobile though detecting proprioceptive-visual contingency show positive affect and social behaviors such as smiling and cooing (Watson, 1972). Infants also remember the contingency between their own motion and the movement of a crib mobile even after delays of 24 hours or more (Bhatt & Rovee-Collier, 1994; Greco, Rovee-Collier, Hayne, Griesler, & Earley, 1986; Rovee-Collier & Barr, 2001). Even newborns show evidence of early intermodal coordination and self-perception. They appear to distinguish between the self and other objects by showing a rooting response to touch from objects but not to self touch (Rochat & Hespos, 1997; Rochat & Striano, 2000). This is likely to have its roots in prenatal intersensory exploration. Neonates are also able to imitate facial expressions (Meltzoff & Moore, 1977, 1983). In order to do this, they must relate their own production of the expression with the visual appearance of the adult model. This is most likely guided by proprioceptive feedback and shows evidence of active intermodal mapping (Meltzoff & Moore, 1983, 1994). Meltzoff (2007) argues that detection of self–other equivalence is a starting point for social cognition and through self-perception infants come to understand the actions of others.

Intermodal coordination of self-motion with external visual information is also evident by the rapid development of posture control and "visually guided reaching" across the first year of life (see Bertenthal, 1996; Butterworth, 1992; von Hofsten, 1993 for reviews). Visually guided reaching involves the prospective control of motion, and is present even in newborns (von Hofsten, 1980, 1993). Young infants can adapt the trajectory of their reach to contact a moving target and this involves continuous adjustments in reaching as a function of visual input about the size, shape, and position of the object (von Hofsten, 1983, 1993). Infants, like adults, also use visual feedback to maintain an upright posture and adapt their posture to changes in the environment (e.g., Bertenthal, Rose, & Bai, 1997; Butterworth & Hicks, 1977; Lee & Aronson, 1974). Older infants show prospective control of locomotion, adapting their posture, locomotion, and exploratory behavior to visual information about the slant and solidity of the surface (see Adolph & Berger, 2006 for a review).

Infants also detect auditory-proprioceptive/vestibular patterns. Bouncing to a rhythm results in listening preferences for rhythmic patterns that match the infant's own movement patterns (Phillips-Silver & Trainor, 2005). Even neonatal learning benefits from self-contingent stimulation. Infants receiving audiovisual stimulation contingent upon their looking behavior learned an arbitrary sound-sight relation, whereas those who received noncontingent stimulation did not (Slater, Quinn, Brown, & Hayes, 1999). This illustrates the principle of increasing specificity and the powerful role of intersensory redundancy in guiding attention to contingent events and promoting further processing of those events.

Identifying speakers, differentiating speech, and learning words: The critical role of intersensory redundancy. Infant sensitivity to intersensory redundancy is critically important for the development of speech perception and language. As discussed earlier, intersensory redundancy attracts and maintains attention to the face of a speaker, allowing the infant to perceive coordinated visual and vocal stimulation emanating from a unitary multimodal event – audiovisual speech. When adults speak to infants, it is well known that they use a special form of speech (infant-directed speech, or "motherese"; see Fernald, 1984, 1989) which exaggerates the amodal information and intersensory redundancy across face, voice, and gesture, providing one of the most important bases for social orienting (see Perceiving Emotion and Prosody below for more detail).

What about perception of speech in the natural environment, which is often "noisy", providing a dynamic flux of concurrent events and multiple speakers? Like adults, infants make extensive use of intersensory redundancy in order to localize speakers and follow the flow of speech (e.g., Gogate et al., 2001; Hollich, Newman, & Jusczyk, 2005). Young infants prefer to look at faces that are synchronized with speech sounds as compared with those that are not (Lewkowicz, 1996) and they match faces and voices on the basis of speech sounds. For example, 2-month-olds can determine which woman is producing an /a/ sound and which is producing an /i/ sound, when both are articulating in synchrony, by relating the shape of the mouth and its movement with the "shape" of the sound (Kuhl & Meltzoff, 1982, 1984).

Moreover, like adults, infants rely on intersensory redundancy between auditory and visual speech to separate two concurrent speech streams (as in the "cocktail party phenomenon," Cherry, 1953). Hollich et al., (2005) found that infants were able to use face–voice synchrony to separate a target speech stream from concurrent background speech of equal intensity. This allowed infants to identify individual words (segment the speech stream) in the target speech. Even a synchronized oscilloscope pattern was equally effective, demonstrating the critical role of intersensory redundancy. In a similar study, providing infants with the synchronized face of one woman speaking against concurrent speech of another woman, allowed infants to selectively attend to the synchronized voice, ignore the nonsynchronized voice, and discriminate between the two voices (Bahrick, Shuman, et al., 2008). These findings illustrate how intersensory redundancy in the form of synchronous audiovisual stimulation, serves as a basis for localizing speakers in noise, selectively attending to one voice while ignoring another, and differentiating individual words in continuous speech in the context of concurrent events.

Infants also learn speech sound–object relations on the basis of intersensory redundancy. In contrast to nativist views of language development (e.g. Chomsky, 1980; Fodor, 1983) research on intersensory perception indicates that general perceptual processes rather than language-specific mechanisms account for early word–object mapping (see Gogate et al., 2001). For example, infants as young as 7 months can detect the relation between a speech sound and an object, only when the sound is temporally synchronized with a movement of the object (such as lifting and showing the object) and not when it is spoken while the object is still, or when the object is moved out of synchrony with the speech sound (Gogate & Bahrick, 1998). Detection of temporal synchrony fosters coordinated perception of word–object relations, highlighting which of many visible objects is the referent of the sound, eventually contributing to the understanding that sounds refer to things, and that a particular sound refers to a particular object (see Gogate et al., 2001). This learning is embedded in a mutually contingent social interaction between the infant and caregiver, described in more detail in the section below.

Intermodal dyadic synchrony and social development.   Successful social and communicative development also depends on engaging in reciprocal social interactions that are temporally and spatially intercoordinated. Detection of amodal information and intersensory redundancy is the foundation for this process and infants quickly become skilled at this exchange. For example, in the first months of life, infants learn to participate in reciprocal exchanges and turn-taking interactions with their adult caretakers – their movements and vocal rhythms are intercoordinated with the temporal patterning of adult communication and this relies on intermodal perception of proprioceptive-visual-auditory relations (Beebe et al., 2010; Jaffe et al., 2001; Sander, 1977; Stern, 1985; Trevarthen, 1993; Tronick, 1989). Dyadic synchrony (the continuous, bidirectional, temporal, intensity, and spatial coordination of gaze, touch, vocalization, and affect) has been found to promote a wide range of fundamental developmental processes, including the early regulation of arousal and internal rhythms, as well as fostering caregiver–infant affective attunement and later attachment, joint attention, communicative competence, and a sense of self-efficacy (see Harrist & Waugh, 2002; Tarabulsy, Tessier, & Kappas, 1996, for reviews).

Dyadic synchrony between caregivers and infants functions as part of a well-honed intermodal developmental system that promotes cognitive, social, and communicative development (see Thelen & Smith, 1994, for discussion). For example, when teaching infants novel names for objects, mothers embed words in multimodal events and tailor their use of temporal synchrony between naming and showing an object to their infants' level of lexical development (Gogate, Bahrick, & Watson, 2000). Temporal synchrony attracts and maintains attention to the object-referent relations, and mothers make most use of synchrony for infants in early stages of lexical development, when they can most benefit from it. Infant phonological development is also the product of bidirectional, multimodal, mother–infant interactions. The development of babbling and the produc-tion of more canonical speech sounds is shaped by the contingent responsiveness of the mother/caregiver (Goldstein, King, & West, 2003). Similarly, birdsong of juvenile males is also shaped by interactive, reciprocal exchanges with adult females who selectively reinforce more adult forms with behaviors such as wing strokes (West & King, 1988). These mutually contingent, social interactions involve a host of complex, multimodal skills. The infant must selectively attend to amodal, redundant, temporal, spatial, and intensity patterns from continuously changing multimodal social stimulation, discrimi-nate and track visual, proprioceptive, and auditory stimulation generated by the self as distinct from that of the social partner, and intercoordinate their multimodal behaviors with those of the adult. This complex dance provides a cornerstone for social and com-municative functioning in typical development.

Perceiving emotion and prosody: The critical role of intersensory redundancy.   Intersensory redundancy between audible and visible speech makes emotion and prosody particularly salient in communicative exchanges. Detection of emotion and prosody of speech is primarily supported by amodal information and is thus promoted in synchronous stimu-lation from face, voice, and gesture. Emotion is conveyed by a complex combination of amodal properties including changes in tempo, temporal patterning, and intensity of facial and vocal stimulation (see Walker-Andrews, 1997, for a review). Prosody of speech provides information about communicative intent (such as prohibition, comfort, or approval) and is conveyed by amodal information such as rhythm, tempo, and intensity shifts (see Cooper & Aslin, 1990; Fernald, 1984).

Adults typically speak to infants using infant-directed speech and this stimulation is highly attractive to infants and preferred over adult-directed speech (Cooper & Aslin, 1990, Fernald, 1984, 1989; Nazzi, Bertonicini, & Mehler 1998, Werker & McLeod, 1989; see Cooper, 1997 for a review). Natural infant-directed speech contains a great deal of intersensory redundancy such as exaggerated prosody (rhythm, tempo, and inten-sity shifts), longer pauses, more repetition, and wider pitch excursions (Fernald, 1984, 1989) that can be experienced in the sounds of speech as well as the facial movements and gestures (see Gogate, Walker-Andrews & Bahrick, 2001). The salience of redundant, amodal stimulation appears to underlie the well-established infant preference for infant-directed speech over adult-directed speech. Infant-directed speech also conveys informa-tion about language identity, communicative intent such as comfort versus prohibition, and helps infants parse and detect meaning-bearing parts of the speech stream (Cooper, 1997; Cooper & Aslin, 1990; Moon, Cooper, & Fifer, 1993; Nazzi et al., 1998; Spence & Moore, 2003).

Consistent with predictions of the IRH, research has found that detection of prosody in speech is facilitated by intersensory redundancy. For example, infants of 4 and 6 months were habituated to a woman reciting phrases using prosodic patterns conveying approval versus prohibition in unimodal auditory speech, synchronous audiovisual speech, or asynchronous audiovisual speech. Infants discriminated a change in prosody only in the synchronous audiovisual speech condition at 4 months of age. By 6 months, they discriminated the change in unimodal auditory speech as well (Castellanos, Shuman, & Bahrick, 2004). These findings demonstrated that prosody specifying approval versus prohibition is initially perceived by detecting amodal information in the multimodal stimulation from faces and voices, and a few months later, detection of prosody is extended to unimodal auditory and visual speech. Moreover, intersensory redundancy in audiovisual speech was also found to educate attention to prosodic changes specifying approval and prohibition in the unimodal auditory speech that followed, for infants as young as 4 months. This provides a potential basis for the developmental improvement observed between 4 and 6 months (Castellanos et al., 2006).

Perception and discrimination of emotion follow a similar developmental trajectory. Infants become skilled at discriminating emotional expressions such as happy, sad, and angry, under a variety of conditions between the ages of 3 and 7 months (see Walker-Andrews 1997 for a review). Discrimination of emotions appears to emerge prior to matching faces and voices on the basis of emotion (Walker-Andrews, 1997). The ability to match facial and vocal expressions of emotion in unfamiliar individuals appears to develop between the ages of 5 and 7 months, whereas detection of emotion in familiar individuals, such as the mother, appears to emerge earlier, by the age of 3 months (Montague, & Walker-Andrews, 2002). From an extensive review of the literature, Walker-Andrews (1997) concluded that emotion is perceived and discriminated in multimodal, naturalistic stimulation early in development and later in development is extended to unimodal stimulation from vocal expressions and from facial expressions alone.

We recently tested this hypothesis directly. Flom and Bahrick (2007) habituated infants of 3, 4, 5, and 8 months with films of a woman speaking in a happy, angry, or sad manner, under a variety of conditions, and then assessed discrimination of the woman displaying a different emotion. Consistent with predictions of the IRH, infants discriminated the emotion in multimodal stimulation (synchronous audiovisual speech) by 4 months of age; however, discrimination in unimodal stimulation was not evident until later. By 5 months of age, infants discriminated the emotions in unimodal auditory speech, and by 8 months, discrimination was extended to unimodal visual speech. This trend from multimodal emotion perception, to unimodal auditory, to unimodal visual emotion perception parallels that found by Walker-Andrews (1997) from her survey of the literature and reflects the critical role of intersensory redundancy in guiding and organizing perceptual development.

Discriminating faces and voices relies on detection of modality-specific information.   The need for more ecologically relevant research is particularly apparent in the domain of face and voice perception. Face perception has become a "hot topic" of investigation and debate regarding origins of knowledge in infancy in recent years. It has been described by some scientists as "special" in the sense that faces are thought to be innately preferred over other stimuli by young infants, and mediated by special-purpose mechanisms rather than general perceptual processes (Bruyer et al, 1983; Farah, Wilson, Drain, & Tanaka, 1995; Goren et al., 1975; Johnson & Morton, 1991; Morton & Johnson, 1991). Others argue that although face processing is "special", it differs in degree, not kind, from processing of complex nonsocial objects (Diamond & Carey, 1986; Farah Wilson, Drain, & Tanaka, 1998; Gauthier & Tarr, 1997; Gauthier & Nelson, 2001; Nelson, 2001; Turati, 2004). From this view, the development of expertise through experience with faces underlies our remarkable ability to perceive faces. This expertise view is most compatible with predictions of the IRH and with research findings generated from ecological, multimodal face events.

In contrast to the development of skills reviewed earlier such as detection of prosody, emotion, dyadic synchrony, and localization of speakers, which all rely on detection of amodal information in multimodal stimulation, discriminating faces and voices relies primarily on detection of modality-specific information in unimodal stimulation, and is thus impaired by intersensory redundancy (see Figure 1: Prediction 2 of the IRH, Bahrick & Lickliter, 2002; Bahrick, Lickliter, & Flom, 2004). Voice recognition is primarily based on sensitivity to pitch and timbre (although individuals also show distinctive prosodic patterns), whereas face recognition is primarily based on detection of facial features and their configuration. Thus, although not yet widely appreciated, face and voice perception are enhanced in unimodal face or voice presentations and impaired in multimodal presentations, particularly in early development. This is evident in studies directly comparing face perception in unimodal versus multimodal conditions. Given that the vast majority of face discrimination studies have been conducted using unimodal visual facial stimuli where infant attention is drawn to facial features, findings of these studies are likely to present an exaggerated view of the salience of faces to infants in the typical dynamic, multimodal environment where faces and voices occur as a unified multimodal event and individuals speak in synchrony with facial movement. In fact, research has found that everyday actions, such as brushing hair or teeth, are much more salient, discriminable, and memorable to infants than the faces of the women engaging in these activities (Bahrick, Gogate, & Ruiz, 2002; Bahrick & Newell, 2008; Walker-Andrews & Bahrick, 2001). That being said, the vast proliferation of studies of unimodal visual face perception (where there is no competition from intersensory redundancy) have shown adept face processing skills in the first half year of life.

For example, newborns show recognition of the mother's face in visual displays within hours of birth (Bushnell, 2001; Bushnell, Sai, & Mullin, 1989; Field et al., 1984; Sai, 2005; Slater & Quinn, 2001) and by 1-month, they show recognition of her face when external features such as the hair have been masked (Pascalis, de Schonen, Morton, Dereulle, & Fabre-Grenet, 1995). Infants of 2 to 5 months also differentiate faces of strangers in unimodal static visual conditions (Cohen & Strauss, 1979; Cornell, 1974; de Haan, Johnson, Maurer, & Perrett, 2001; Fagan, 1972; 1976). Between 3 and 6 months infants differentiate between their own face and that of an age-matched peer in static and dynamic conditions, and discriminate somewhat better in dynamic displays (Bahrick et al., 1996). However, it cannot be determined how these excellent face processing skills in unimodal visual events compare with those of multimodal events. Direct comparisons are needed.

Much less research has focused on perception and discrimination of individual voices in infancy. However, it is clear that following a history of fetal experience with voices, infants discriminate the mother's voice from that of a female stranger and the father's voice from a male stranger, and even between the voices of two strangers shortly after birth (DeCasper & Fifer, 1980; DeCasper & Prescott, 1984; Floccia, Nazzi, & Bertoncini, 2000). Further, studies of intermodal face–voice matching demonstrate that following synchronous audiovisual exposure, by 4 months of age infants can discriminate adult female faces, voices, and match the women's faces with their voices (Bahrick, Hernandez-Reif, et al., 2005). Between 4 and 6 months, infants also match faces and voices on the basis of amodal properties such as those specifying gender (Walker-Andrews, Bahrick, Raglioni, & Diaz, 1991) and age (Bahrick, Netto, & Hernandez-Reif, 1998), and classify voices on the basis of gender (Miller, 1983; Miller, Younger & Morse, 1982).

The superiority of face and voice perception in unimodal stimulation over multimodal stimulation has been tested in a few studies to date. Bahrick, Hernandez-Reif, et al. (2005) found that 2-month-olds could discriminate the faces and voices of two unfamiliar women in unimodal visual and unimodal auditory speech, respectively. However, it was only by 4 months of age that infants could discriminate the faces and voices and detect a relation between them in natural, audiovisual speech, where intersensory redundancy was available and most likely competed for attention. More direct tests of the interfering effects of intersensory redundancy and the resulting superiority of face perception in unimodal stimulation as compared with multimodal stimulation have also been conducted (Bahrick, Lickliter, Vaillant, et al., 2004; Vaillant-Molina, Newell, Castellanos, Bahrick, & Lickliter, 2006). Two- and 3-month-old infants were habituated with faces of unfamiliar women speaking in unimodal visual, audiovisual synchronous, and audiovisual asynchronous speech, and were then tested for discrimination of the familiar from a novel face. Consistent with predictions of unimodal facilitation (Prediction 2 of the IRH), at 2 months, infants discriminated the faces in unimodal visual but not bimodal synchronous, audiovisual speech where intersensory redundancy apparently interfered with face discrimination. They also discriminated the faces in an asynchronous audiovisual speech control condition. This condition eliminated intersensory redundancy but the amount and type of stimulation was equal to that of synchronous audiovisual speech. Only by 3 months of age, did infants discriminate the faces in the context of intersensory redundancy from natural, synchronous audiovisual speech. Thus, discrimination of faces appears to emerge first in unimodal visual stimulation (where there is no competition from intersensory redundancy and attention is free to focus on visual properties) and later in development it extends to multimodal contexts where there is attentional competition from redundantly specified properties. A parallel study of voice perception also revealed a similar developmental pattern (Bahrick, Lickliter, et al., 2005). Discrimination among voices of unfamiliar women emerged first in unimodal auditory stimulation at 3 months, and was later extended to bimodal, audiovisual speech at 4 months of age.

Thus, the developmental progression for discriminating faces and voices is consistent with predictions of the IRH and parallels the pattern found for nonredundantly specified aspects of nonsocial events described earlier (e.g., Bahrick et al., 2006, orientation of motion). This developmental shift from detection of visual and acoustic information in nonredundant, unimodal stimulation to detection of this same information in the context of competition from redundant audiovisual stimulation becomes possible as infants increase their speed and efficiency of information processing, gain attentional flexibility, and gain experience with similar classes of events. This allows them to detect both the most salient and somewhat less salient aspects of stimulation in an episode of exploration. This developmental progression appears to occur more rapidly in the social domain (across a period of only 1 month for face and voice perception) than the nonsocial domain. This may be due to the high frequency of exposure, salience, and degree of familiarity with faces and voices.

These findings thus support the view that the development of face perception is governed by general perceptual processes as a result of perceptual experience and contrast with the position that face perception is the result of specialized face processing mechanisms that function differently from object processing. From the present view, faces become especially salient to infants because they are frequently encountered and typically the source of a great deal of intersensory redundancy. Their attentional salience would promote rapid processing and perceptual learning in order of salience and increasing specificity (Bahrick, 2001; E. J. Gibson, 1969), first facilitating detection of amodal properties such as prosody, affect, rhythm, and tempo of audiovisual speech in multimodal stimualtion. Later, with further exploration, more specific properties such as the configuration and specific facial features and the pitch and timbre of voices would be promoted. In contrast, in unimodal stimulation, visual features of the face become especially salient, consistent with newborn recognition of the mother's face in silent unimodal conditions (e.g., Field et al, 1984; Bushnell, 2001) and this promotes the development of face expertise. Similarly, voice perception, is promoted by unimodal auditory exploration where vocal qualities such as pitch and timbre are more easily differentiated. Converging findings across the literature (Bahrick, Hernandez-Reif, et al., 2005; see Walker-Andrews, 1997 for a review) show improvement in face and voice processing across early infancy, with detection in unimodal contexts and for familiar individuals emerging first, and sensitivity to specific faces and voices in bimodal contexts emerging somewhat later, and finally, intermodal matching of faces and voices, and memory for these relations emerging later.

Lessons from Atypical Development

Social orienting impairments in autism

In contrast to typical development, in atypical development characterizing autism spectrum disorder, children show a "social orienting impairment" (Dawson et al, 1998, 2004; Landry and Bryson, 2004; Mundy & Burnette, 2005). They exhibit reduced attention and orienting to social as compared with nonsocial events, avoid interaction and eye contact with others, and fail to respond to their own name. Because autism is a disorder that appears to emerge and worsen across early development, affecting a wide variety of areas, including social, communicative, and cognitive functioning, it is generally agreed that identifying developmental precursors or symptoms that are "primary" and have the potential for explaining a range of later developing symptoms is critical to early diagnosis, theory, and intervention (e.g., Volkmar, Lord, Bailey, Schultz, & Klin, 2004; Sigman, Dijamco, Gratier, & Rozga, 2004). This poses a challenge for researchers for a number of reasons. First, we cannot reliably identify which infants will develop autism and its relatively low incidence, occurring in approximately one in 150–200 individuals (Frombonne, 2005), makes longitudinal or prospective studies difficult and impractical. Second, although there is a major emphasis on the need for early diagnosis, autism is not typically diagnosed until 18 to 24 months of age, when significant delays in social and communicative functioning have become apparent and entrenched. Thus scientists have had to rely on indirect methods such as using home videos and questionnaires to learn about the infant behaviors of children who were later diagnosed with autism (e.g., Maestro et al, 2002; Osterling & Dawson, 1994). We now have more promising prospective methods including studies of siblings of children with autism who tend to have a higher incidence of either developing autism or showing symptoms of the "broad phenotype", symptoms that fall along the spectrum of behaviors associated with autism (e.g., Cassel, Messinger, Ibanez, Haltigan, Acosta & Buchman, 2007; Yirmiya et al., 2006). Finally, autism presents a wide variety of symptoms with a great deal of individual variability, so no one pattern fits all cases.

Given recent research indicating that neurodevelopmental anomalies occur even in prenatal development (see Akshoomoff et al., 2002, for a review), it is clear that research should focus on early developing skills, particularly those that emerge within the first 6 months of life. Early disturbances of attention such as the "social orienting impairment" (Dawson et al., 1998, 2004) are excellent candidates for the study of potential primary symptoms. The neurodevelopment of attention is shaped during prenatal development, attention develops rapidly across the first 6 months of life, and social orienting is seen in typical development even at birth (Bushnell, 2001; DeCasper & Fifer, 1980; Mondloch et al., 1999; Sai, 2005; Simion, Valenza, & Umilta, 1998). Further, the development of attention has been the subject of well-controlled studies in early infancy (as reviewed in this chapter; see Bahrick & Lickliter, 2002; Ruff and Rothbart, 1996 for reviews). Given that attention provides the input for all that is perceived, learned, and remembered it provides the foundation for the rapid development of a wide range of skills, both social and cognitive, in infancy and childhood.

In particular, the early disturbance of attention to social events may contribute to impairments in a host of other skills that depend on heightened attention to social events, including joint visual attention (sharing attention by coordinating eye gaze with a social partner on an object of mutual interest), face recognition, the development of reciprocal interactions, responding to emotional signals, and language development (Dawson et al., 1998; Mundy & Burnette, 2005; Mundy, 1995; Volkmar, Chawarska, and Klin, 2005). The development of autism has been described as a developmental cascade where impairments in early systems such as joint attention, reciprocal interactions, and social orienting, lead to increasing social, communicative, and neurological disturbance (Mundy & Burnette, 2005). Symptoms become evident and worsen across development, in part because deficits in basic building blocks of social and communicative functioning in infancy lead to further amplification of disturbances in more complex, derivative skills and associated neurodevelopment (Akshoomoff et al, 2002; Dawson et al., 2002 Mundy & Burnette, 2005). Thus, a failure of social stimulation to become salient and preferentially attended over other stimulation in early infancy would lead to a drastic decrease in the flow of social information that provides the input and interaction necessary for typical developmental gains in cognitive, social, emotional, and linguistic development. It seems reasonable that even a small deficit in social orienting could lead to an ever widening gap between typical and atypical development.

In this light, I have made a case (see *The salience of intersensory redundancy promotes social orienting in infancy*) hat a fundamental basis for social orienting in typical infant development is the salience of intersensory redundancy. As reviewed in this chapter, social events are multimodal and provide an extraordinary amount of rapidly changing intersensory information which infants rely on for differentiating self from other, identifying speakers in noisy environments, differentiating speech from nonspeech, learning words, perceiving emotion and communicative intent, and engaging in reciprocal communicative exchanges. The salience of intersensory redundancy is a primary mechanism for promoting social orienting and for guiding and constraining acquisition of knowledge about the social world. Impairment to this system would lead to a wide range of atypical developmental outcomes.

Intersensory processing impairment: An hypothesis for autism

In light of the above logic and the growing literature on intersensory impairments in autism, I propose that a fundamental basis for the development of social-communicative and cognitive impairments characterizing autism is an "intersensory processing impairment", in particular, a reduced sensitivity to amodal information in the context of inter sensory redundancy (see also Bebko, Weiss, Demark, & Gomez, 2006; Brock et al., 2002; Iarocci & McDonald, 2005; Mundy & Burnette, 2005). A slight deficit in intersensory functioning, evident in infancy, could lead to early social orienting impairments and, in turn, promote a cascade of impairments to social, cognitive, and communicative functioning, typical of autism spectrum disorders.

Moreover, the Intersensory Redundancy Hypothesis (Bahrick & Lickliter, 2000, 2002) can provide a new perspective regarding the nature and basis of impairments in autism. In particular, if intersensory processing is impaired, in addition to reduced attention to social events, the typical salience hierarchies and critical balance between attention to amodal versus modality-specific properties of events as a function of type of stimulation (unimodal vs. multimodal, see Figure 4.2) would be disrupted. This disruption of salience hierarchies would alter the typical developmental pattern where amodal properties guide and constrain the detection of modality-specific details, in order of increasing specificity. This, in turn, could result in more piecemeal information processing, a greater emphasis on local than global information, processing modality-specific information prior to perceiving unitary multimodal events, heightened attention to visual and acoustic detail disconnected from context, and less generalization of learning across domains, all characteristics of individuals with autism. Future research will be needed to map the nature of intersensory processing impairments in autism by evaluating each of the four predictions of the IRH in children with autism and those of typical development. If intersensory processing is intact but somewhat reduced, interventions may build on existing intersensory skills to train attention, rebuild intersensory processing, and promote typical attentional salience hierarchies.

Evidence of impaired intersensory processing in autism is now mounting, supporting "intersensory processing impairment" as a hypothesis for autism. Individuals with autism show impaired intersensory integration of audiovisual speech (Smith & Bennetto, 2007; Magnee, de Gelder, van Engeland, & Kemner, 2008). Smith & Bennetto (2007) demonstrated that adolescents with autism showed less benefit from visual information in identifying speech in noise than do typically developing adolescents (matched for IQ), and this impairment could not be explained by auditory or visual processing deficits alone. Both adults and children show a reduced susceptibility to the McGurk effect, an index of audiovisual speech integration (de Gelder, Vroomen, & van der Heide, 1991; Mongillo et al., 2008; Williams, Massaro, Peel, Bosseler, & Suddendorf, 2004). Moreover, even young children with autism show impaired intersensory processing of audiovisual temporal synchrony in simple and complex audiovisual speech events, but no evidence of impairment in nonsocial events (Bebko et al., 2006). The mirror neuron system (Williams, Whiten, Suddendorf, & Perrett, 2001), an intersensory system thought to show similar neural activity to both observed and performed actions, is also thought to be compromised in autism, contributing to impaired empathy, imitation, and speech perception (e.g., Dapretto et al., 2006; Oberman et al., 2005; Oberman & Ramachandran, 2008). However, there is still debate as to the nature and basis of intersensory impairments in autism (e.g., Hamilton, Brindley, & Frith, 2007; van der Smagt, van Engeland, & Kemner, 2007). Some studies find no evidence of impairment to specific intersensory skills (Haviland, Walker-Andrews, Huffman, Toci, & Alton, 1996; van der Smagt et al., 2007), some find impairments are related to cognitive ability (e.g., Loveland et al., 1997), others find intersensory processing is limited by unimodal sensory impairments, particularly to social stimuli (e.g., Boucher, Lewis, & Collis, 1998; Williams et al., 2004), whereas others find intersensory impairments independent of these factors (e.g., Bebko et al., 2006; de Gelder et al., 1991; Smith & Benetto, 2007). Nevertheless, it appears that intersensory impairments are most pronounced for social and speech events, which are relatively complex and provide a particularly high level of intersensory redundancy. These findings suggest that the IRH and proposed intersensory processing impairment may provide a viable hypothesis for guiding future investigations of impairments in autism.

Benefits of integrating basic research across typical and atypical development

It is clear that a more profound understanding of the nature and basis of social orienting in typical development, at both the behavioral and neural levels, will have important pay-offs in terms of earlier and more accurate identification of atypical patterns of social development and the development of interventions. Moreover, understanding patterns of atypical development also has important benefits for the study of typical development. The challenge of understanding the developmental cascades that characterize the emergence of autism spectrum disorders highlights a critical lack of knowledge about typical development. Scientists have yet to clearly identify basic building blocks of social and communicative functioning in typical infant development, identify primary versus derivative skills, and articulate the nature of developmental cascades that lead to optimal developmental patterns. Studying the critical role of intersensory redundancy for guiding and shaping social attention and social interaction, outlined in this chapter, is one clear starting point for this endeavor. Understanding the nature of attentional biases is critical to understanding the typical and atypical emergence of social orienting and the host of other skills that emerge from attention to social stimulation. The cross-fertilization of typical and atypical developmental perspectives will provide significant benefits to developmental science for understanding the typical trajectories, mechanisms, and bases for developmental processes.

Conclusions and Future Directions: Toward a More Integrated, Ecologically Relevant Model of Perceptual Development

This chapter has highlighted three themes, each stressing the benefits of greater integration across typically separate areas of inquiry in developmental science. The first theme emphasizes the need to integrate selective attention with studies of perception, learning, and memory, as attention provides the foundation for what is perceived, learned, and remembered. This review illustrated the benefits of such an approach for developmental science by applying the Intersensory Redundancy Hypothesis, a theory of selective attention, to understanding perceptual development. The second theme emphasizes the importance of integrating the study of both multimodal (e.g., audiovisual) and unimodal (visual or auditory) functioning in understanding what drives development and in making our investigations more ecologically relevant. This chapter thus highlighted how the attentional salience of intersensory redundancy, available in multimodal but not unimodal stimulation, promotes perceptual processing of some properties of events at the expense of others, creating general salience hierarchies that can impact development across the life span. In multimodal stimulation, attention is selectively focused on redundantly specified amodal properties such as synchrony, rhythm, tempo, and intensity, which support perception of emotion, prosody, and localization of speakers. Development of these skills emerges in multimodal stimulation and is later extended to unimodal contexts. In contrast, in unimodal (visual or auditory) stimulation, selective attention focuses first on modality-specific properties of events such as visual pattern, form, color, or auditory pitch and timbre, supporting perception of individual faces and voices and the appearance of objects and the specific nature of their sounds. Development of these skills emerges in unimodal contexts and later extends to multimodal contexts. Since most events are multimodal, these attentional biases promote general salience hierarchies for amodal over modality specific properties of events, and thus can have a profound effect on development, particularly when there is competition for attentional resources and processing capacity is most limited, as in early development.

Just as sensory limitations in prenatal development are adaptive for promoting healthy differentiation of the senses in an environment of competition for developmental resources, sensory limitations in early postnatal development may be adaptive for promoting optimal perceptual and cognitive development in an environment of competition for attentional resources. Salience hierarchies, like sensory limitations of the fetus, limit the amount and type of incoming stimulation during a time when development is particularly plastic and the system is particularly vulnerable to outside influence (Turkewitz & Kenny, 1982). Thus, the salience of intersensory redundancy in combination with sensory limitations limits the amount of modality-specific detail that can be processed in early development. This effectively buffers the young infant against a flood of disorganized and specific information until a more general organizational framework has begun to emerge. These early emerging patterns of perceiving the world of objects and events in turn support later developing skills such as joint attention, language, and social interaction patterns, promoting subsequent social and cognitive developmental cascades. It is likely that even a relatively slight modification of the typical salience hierarchy could result in an ever widening gap between typical and atypical development, such as that observed in the neurodevelopmental disorder of autism. Although salience hierarchies are likely to have their most profound effects on early development when attentional resources are most limited, they also appear to persist across development and affect performance primarily in tasks that are difficult.

Future research should assess the implications of these and other attentional biases for promoting developmental change, in an atmosphere of competition for attentional resources, for both typical and atypical perceptual development. Attentional biases are likely to affect processing across exploratory time as well as across age and cumulative experience. A relatively unexplored hypothesis is that perceptual processing proceeds in order of attentional salience across exploratory time (similar to a levels of processing view, e.g., Craik & Lockhart, 1972), with processing of the most salient aspects of events first, and later progressing to the less salient aspects. Cumulative experience from such a processing hierarchy in turn may provide a basis for the developmental progressions in order of attentional salience reported here.

The third theme of this chapter stressed integration across studies of typical and atypical development, highlighting the benefits of cross-fertilization for each. Not only does knowledge of typical development provide a foundation for understanding and identifying atypical development such as autism, but developmental disorders such as autism also have a great deal to teach us about typical development. For example, appreciating the importance of identifying developmental precursors to later emerging abilities and understanding the nature of developmental cascades in autism highlights both the relative lack of knowledge and the value of understanding these processes in typical development. There is a critical need for systematic studies of developmental change across multiple ages, under uniform conditions, in the study of typical perceptual development.

In particular, this review highlighted the need for articulating the developmental processes that lead to social orienting in typical infants and toddlers. This seemingly simple phenomenon turns out to be quite rich, complex, and multiply determined, with factors ranging from prenatal determinants, infant-directed speech, dyadic synchrony, and emotional communication playing fundamental roles. The present review suggests that a common denominator across these varied contexts that attracts and maintains attention to social events is the high degree of intersensory redundancy they provide, coupled with the salience of intersensory redundancy to young infants. An intersensory processing impairment in autism was proposed as a basis for social orienting impairment and the resulting cascade of disturbance to social and communicative functioning.

In this chapter, we have seen how significant processes that shape the nature and direction of development originate from the interaction of our limited capacity attentional system and the overabundance of dynamic, multimodal stimulation provided by the environment. It is strikingly clear that the "messiness" of natural, dynamic, multimodal stimulation, in combination with attentional competition from overlapping multimodal events is a key to the typical development of perception, learning, and memory. An important conclusion of this review is the need for developmental science to take seriously the rich and complex structure and conditions of the natural environment for fostering development. Thus, the study of the emergence of skills, whether they be face perception, speech perception, categorization, or language should be conducted in both *unimodal and multimodal* contexts, and in the *dynamic stimulation* of naturalistic events. This effort will promote more integrated, ecologically relevant theories of development, and bring us closer to solving critical applied issues such as the early identification of atypical patterns of development in disorders such as autism.

Acknowledgments

The research and theory development reported here were supported by NIH grants RO1 HD 053776, RO1 MH 62226, and RO3 HD052602, NSF grant SBE 0350201, and Autism Speaks grant #1906. Correspondence should be addressed to Lorraine E. Bahrick, Department of Psychology, Florida International University, Miami, FL 33199, bahrick@ fiu.edu.

References

Abrams, R. M., Gerhardt, K. J., & Peters, A. J. M. (1995). Transmission of sound and vibration to the fetus. In J. P. Lecannuet, W. P. Fifer, N. A. Krasnegor, & W. P. Smotherman (Eds.), *Fetal development: A psychological perspective* (pp. 315–330). Hillsdale, NJ: Erlbaum.

Adler, S. A., & Rovee-Collier, C. (1994). The memorability and discriminability of primitive perceptual units in infancy. *Vision Research, 34,* 449–459.

Adolph, K. E., & Berger, S. E. (2005). Physical and motor development. In M. H. Bornstein & M. E. Lamb (Eds.), *Developmental science: An advanced textbook* (5th ed., pp. 223–281). Hillsdale, NJ: Erlbaum.

Adolph, K. E., & Berger, S. E. (2006). Motor development. In W. Damon & R. Lerner (Series Eds.), & D. Kuhn & R. S. Siegler (Vol. Eds.), *Handbook of child psychology: Vol 2: Cognition, perception, and language* (6th ed., pp. 161–213). New York: Wiley.

Akshoomoff, N., Pierce, K., & Courchesne, E. (2002). The neurobiological basis of autism from a developmental perspective. *Development and Psychopathology. Special Issue: Multiple levels of analysis, 14,* 613–634.

Alais, D., & Burr, D. (2004). The Ventriloquist Effect results from near-optimal bimodal integration. *Current Biology, 14,* 257–262.

Bahrick, L. E. (1988). Intermodal learning in infancy: Learning on the basis of two kinds, of invariant relations in audible and visible events. *Child Development, 59,* 197–209.

Bahrick, L. E. (1992). Infants' perceptual differentiation of amodal and modality-specific audio-visual relations. *Journal of Experimental Child Psychology, 53,* 180–199.

Bahrick, L. E. (1994). The development of infants" sensitivity to arbitrary intermodal relations. *Ecological Psychology, 6,* 111–123.

Bahrick, L. E. (1995). Intermodal origins of self-perception. In P. Rochat (Ed.), *The self in early infancy: Theory and research* (pp. 349–373). Amsterdam: North Holland/Elsevier.

Bahrick, L. E. (2000). Increasing specificity in the development of intermodal perception. In D. Muir &. A. Slater (Eds.), *Infant development: The essential readings* (pp. 117–136). Oxford: Blackwell.

Bahrick, L. E. (2001). Increasing specificity in perceptual development: Infants' detection of nested levels of multimodal stimulation. *Journal of Experimental Child Psychology, 79,* 253–270.

Bahrick, L. E. (2004). The development of perception in a multimodal environment. In G. Bremner, & A. Slater (Eds.), *Theories of infant development* (pp. 90–120). Malden, MA: Blackwell.

Bahrick, L. E., Castellanos, I., Shuman, M., Vaillant-Molina, M., Newell, L. C., & Sorondo, B. M. (2008, May). *Self-perception and social orienting in young children with autism.* Poster presented at the annual meeting of the International Meeting for Autism Research, London, UK.

Bahrick, L. E., Flom, R., & Lickliter, R. (2002). Intersensory redundancy facilitates discrimination of tempo in 3-month-old infants. *Developmental Psychobiology, 41,* 352–363.

Bahrick, L. E., Gogate, L. J., & Ruiz, I. (2002). Attention and memory for faces and actions in infancy: The salience of actions over faces in dynamic events. *Child Development, 73,* 1629–1643.

Bahrick, L. E., Hernandez-Reif, M., & Flom, R. (2005). The development of infant learning about specific face–voice relations. *Developmental Psychology, 41,* 541–552.

Bahrick, L. E., & Lickliter, R. (2000). Intersensory redundancy guides attentional selectivity and perceptual learning in infancy. *Developmental Psychology, 36,* 190–201.

Bahrick, L. E., & Lickliter, R. (2002). Intersensory redundancy guides early perceptual and cognitive development. In R. Kail (Ed.), *Advances in child development and behavior* (Vol. *30,* pp. 153–187). New York: Academic Press.

Bahrick, L. E., & Lickliter, R. (2004). Infants' perception of rhythm and tempo in unimodal and multimodal stimulation: A developmental test of the intersensory redundancy hypothesis. *Cognitive, Affective and Behavioral Neuroscience, 4,* 137–147.

Bahrick, L. E., Lickliter, R., Castellanos, I., & Vaillant-Molina, M. (in press). Increasing task difficulty enhances effects of intersensory redundancy: Testing a new prediction of the Intersensory Redundancy Hypothesis. *Developmental Science.*

Bahrick, L. E., Lickliter, R., & Flom, R. (2004). Intersensory redundancy guides infants' selective attention, perceptual and cognitive development. *Current Directions in Psychological Science, 13,* 99–102.

Bahrick, L. E., Lickliter, R., & Flom, R. (2006). Up versus down: The role of intersensory redundancy in the development of infants' sensitivity to the orientation of moving objects. *Infancy, 9,* 73–96.

Bahrick, L. E., Lickliter, R., Shuman, A., Batista, L. C., Castellanos, I., & Newell, L. C. (2005, November). *The development of infant voice discrimination: From unimodal auditory to bimodal audiovisual presentation.* Poster presented at the annual meeting of the International Society for Developmental Psychobiology, Washington, DC.

Bahrick, L. E., Lickliter, R., Vaillant, M., Shuman, M., & Castellanos, I. (2004, May). *Infant discrimination of faces in the context of dynamic, multimodal, events: Predictions from the intersen-*

sory redundancy hypothesis. Poster presented at the biennial meetings of the International Conference on Infant Studies, Chicago, IL.

Bahrick, L. E., Moss, L., & Fadil, C. (1996). The development of visual self- recognition in infancy. *Ecological Psychology, 8,* 189–208.

Bahrick, L. E., Netto, D., & Hernandez-Reif, M. (1998). Intermodal perception of adult and child faces and voices by infants. *Child Development, 69,* 1263–1275.

Bahrick, L. E., & Newell, L. C. (2008). Infant discrimination of faces in naturalistic events: Actions are more salient than faces. *Developmental Psychology, 44,* 983–996.

Bahrick, L. E., & Pickens, J. N. (1994). Amodal relations: The basis for intermodal perception and learning. In D. Lewkowicz and R. Lickliter (Eds.), *The development of intersensory perception: Comparative perspectives* (pp. 205–233). Hillsdale, NJ: Erlbaum.

Bahrick, L. E., Shuman, M. A., & Castellanos, I. (2008, March). *Face-voice synchrony directs selective listening in four-month-old infants.* Poster presented at the biennial meetings of the International Conference on Infant Studies, Vancouver, Canada.

Bahrick, L. E., Todd, J. T., Shuman, M., Grossman, R., Castellanos, I., & Sorondo, B. M. (2009, April). *Intersensory facilitation across the life-span: Adults show enhanced discrimination of tempo in bimodal vs. unimodal stimulation.* Poster presented at the Society for Research in Child Development, Denver, CO.

Bahrick, L. E., Walker, A. S., and Neisser, U. (1981). Selective looking by infants. *Cognitive Psychology, 13,* 377–390.

Bahrick, L. E., and Watson, J. S. (1985). Detection of intermodal proprioceptive-visual contingency as a potential basis of self-perception in infancy. *Developmental Psychology, 21,* 963–973.

Bartlett, F. C. (1932). *Remembering: A study in experimental and social psychology.* Cambridge, UK: Cambridge University Press.

Bebko, J., Weiss, J., Demark, J., & Gomez, P. (2006). Discrimination of temporal synchrony in intermodal events by children with autism and children with developmental disabilities without autism. *Journal of Child Psychology and Psychiatry, 47,* 88–98.

Beebe, B., Jaffe, J., Markese, S., Buck, K., Chen, H., Cohen, P., Bahrick, L. E., Feldstein, S., Andrews, H., & Moore, M. S. (2010). The origins of 12-month attachment: A microanalysis of 4-month mother-infant attachment. *Attachment and Human Development, 12,* 3–141.

Berger, S. E. (2004). Demands on finite cognitive capacity cause infants' perseverative errors. *Infancy, 5,* 217–238.

Bertenthal, B. I. (1996). Origins and early development of perception, action, and representation. *Annual Review of Psychology, 47,* 431–459.

Bertenthal, B. I., Rose, J. L., & Bai, D. L. (1997). Perception–action coupling in the development of visual control of posture. *Journal of Experimental Psychology: Human Perception & Performance, 23,* 1631–1643.

Bhatt, R. S., & Rovee-Collier, C. (1994). Perception and 24-hour retention of feature relations in infancy. *Developmental Psychology, 30,* 142–150.

Boucher, J., Lewis, V., & Collis, G. (1998). Familiar face and voice matching and recognition in children with autism. *Journal of Child Psychology and Psychiatry, 39,* 171–181.

Broadbent, D. E. (1962). Attention and the perception of speech. *Scientific American, 206,* 143–151.

Brock, J., Brown, C. C., Boucher, J., & Rippon, G. (2002). The temporal binding deficit hypothesis of autism. *Development & Psychopathology, 14,* 209–224.

Bruyer, R., Laterre, C., Seron, X., Feyereisen, P., Strypstein, E., Pierrard, E., & Rectem, D. (1983). A case of prosopagnosis with some preserved covert remembrance of familiar faces. *Brain and Cognition, 2,* 257–284.

Bushnell, I. W. (2001). Mother's face recognition in newborn infants: Learning and memory. *Infant and Child Development, 10,* 67–74.

Bushnell, I. W., Sai, F., & Mullin, J. T. (1989). Neonatal recognition of the mother's face. *British Journal of Developmental Psychology, 7*, 3–15.

Butterworth, G. (1992). Origins of self-perception in infancy. *Psychological Inquiry, 3*, 103–111.

Butterworth, G., & Hicks, L. (1977). Visual proprioception and postural stability in infancy: A developmental study. *Perception, 6*, 255–262.

Butterworth, G., & Hopkins, B. (1988). Hand–mouth coordination in the newborn baby. *British Journal of Developmental Psychology, 6*, 303–314.

Calvert, G., Spence, C., & Stein, B. E. (2004). *Handbook of multisensory processes.* Cambridge, MA: MIT Press.

Cassel, T., Messinger, D. S., Ibanez, L., Haltigan, J. D., Acosta, S., & Buchman, A. (2007). Early social and emotional communication in the infant siblings of children with Autism Spectrum Disorders: An examination of the broad phenotype. *Journal of Autism and Developmental Disorders, 37*, 122–132.

Castellanos, I., Shuman, M., & Bahrick, L. E. (2004, May). *Intersensory redundancy facilitates infants' perception of meaning in speech passages.* Poster presented at the biennial meetings of the International Conference on Infant Studies, Chicago, IL.

Castellanos, I., Vaillant-Molina, M., Lickliter, R., & Bahrick, L. (2006, October). *Intersensory redundancy educates infants' attention to amodal information in unimodal stimulation.* Poster presented at the annual meeting of the International Society for Developmental Psychobiology, Atlanta, GA.

Chase, W. G., & Simon, H. A. (1973). Perception in chess. *Cognitive Psychology, 4*, 55–81.

Cherry, E. C. (1953). Some experiments on the recognition of speech with one and two ears. *Journal of the Acoustical Society of America, 25*, 975–979.

Chomsky, N. (1980). *Rules and representations.* New York: Columbia University Press.

Cohen, L. B., & Strauss, M. S. (1979). Concept acquisition in the human infant. *Child Development, 50*, 419–424.

Colombo, J. (2001). The development of visual attention in infancy. *Annual Review of Psychology, 52*, 337–367.

Colombo, J. (2002). Infant attention grows up: The emergence of a developmental cognitive neuroscience perspective. *Current Directions in Psychological Science, 11*, 196–199.

Colombo, J., & Mitchell, D. W. (1990). Individual and developmental differences in infant visual attention: Fixation time and information processing. In J. Colombo & J. W. Fagen (Eds.), *Individual differences in infancy: Reliability, stability, and prediction* (pp. 193–227). Hillsdale, NJ: Erlbaum.

Colombo, J., & Mitchell, D. W. (2009). Infant visual habituation. *Neurobiology of learning and memory, 92*(2), 225–234.

Colombo, J., Mitchell, D. W., Coldren, J. T., & Freeseman, L. J. (1991). Individual differences in infant visual attention: Are short lookers faster processors or feature processors? *Child Development, 62*, 1247–1257.

Cooper, R. P. (1997). An ecological approach to infants' perception of intonation contours as meaningful aspects of speech. In C. Dent-Read & P. Zukow-Goldring (Eds.), *Evolving explanations of development: Ecological approaches to organism-environment systems* (pp. 55–85). Washington, DC: American Psychological Association.

Cooper, R. P., & Aslin, R. N. (1990). Preferences for infant-directed speech in the first month after birth. *Child Development, 61*, 1584–1595.

Corbetta, D., & Bojczyk, K. E. (2002). Infants return to two-handed reaching when they are learning to walk. *Journal of Motor Behavior, 34*, 83–95.

Cornell, E. (1974). Infants' discrimination of faces following redundant presentations. *Journal of Experimental Child Psychology, 18*, 98–106.

Craik, F. I., & Lockhart, R. S. (1972). Levels of processing: A framework for memory research. *Journal of Verbal Learning and Verbal Behavior, 11*, 671–684.

Dapretto, M., Davies, M., Pfeifer, J., Scott, A., Sigman, M., Bookheimer, S., et al. (2006). Understanding emotions in others: Mirror neuron dysfunction in children with autism spectrum disorders. *Nature Neuroscience, 9*, 28–30.

Dawson, G., Meltzoff, A. N., Osterling, J., Rinaldi, J., & Brown, E. (1998). Children with autism fail to orient to naturally occurring social stimuli. *Journal of Autism and Developmental Disorders, 28*, 479–485.

Dawson, G., Munson, J., Estes, A., Osterling, J., McPartland, J. & Toth, K. (2002). Neurocognitive function and joint attention ability in young children with autism spectrum disorder versus developmental delay. *Child Development, 73*, 345–358.

Dawson, G., Toth, K., Abbott, R., Osterling, J., Munson, J., Estes, A., et al. (2004). Early social attention impairments in autism: Social orienting, joint attention, and attention to distress. *Developmental Psychology, 40*, 271–283.

Dawson, G., Webb, S., Schellenberg, G. D. Dager, S., Friedman, S., Aylward, E. et al. (2002). Defining the broader phenotype of autism: Genetic, brain, and behavioral perspectives. *Development and Psycopathology, 14*, 581–611.

DeCasper, A. J., & Fifer, W. P. (1980). Of human bonding: Newborns prefer their mothers' voices. *Science, 208*, 1174–1176.

DeCasper, A. J., & Prescott, P. A. (1984). Human newborns' perception of male voices. Preference, discrimination, and reinforcing value. *Developmental Psychobiology, 5*, 481–491.

DeCasper, A. J., & Spence, M. (1986). Newborns prefer a familiar story over an unfamiliar one. *Infant Behavior and Development, 94*, 133–150.

de Gelder, B., Vroomen, J., & van der Heide, L. (1991). Face recognition and lip-reading in autism. *European Journal of Cognitive Psychology, 3*, 69–86.

de Haan, M., Johnson, M. H., Maurer, D., & Perrett, D. I. (2001). Recognition of individual faces and average face prototypes by 1- and 3-month-old infants. *Cognitive Development, 16*, 659–678.

Diamond, R., & Carey, S. (1986). Why faces are and are not special: An effect of expertise. *Journal of Experimental Psychology: General, 115*, 107–117.

Edelman, G. M. (1987). *Neural Darwinism: The theory of neuronal group selection*. New York: Basic Books.

Fagan, J. F. (1972). Infants' recognition of memory for faces. *Journal of Experimental Child Psychology, 14*, 453–476.

Fagan, J. F. (1976). Infants' recognition of invariant features of faces. *Child Development, 47*, 627–638.

Farah, M. J., Wilson, K. D., Drain, M., & Tanaka, J. N. (1995). The inverted face inversion effect in prosopagnosia: Evidence for mandatory, face-specific perceptual mechanisms. *Visual Research, 14*, 2089–2093.

Farah, M. J., Wilson, K. D., Drain, M., & Tanaka, J. N. (1998). What is "special" about face perception? *Psychological Review, 105*, 482–498.

Fernald, A. (1984). The perceptual and affective salience of mother's speech to infants. In L. Feagans, C. Garvey, & R. Golinkoff (Eds.), *The origins and growth of communication* (pp. 5–29). Norwood, NJ: Ablex.

Fernald, A. (1989). Intonation and communicative intent in mothers' speech to infants: Is the melody the message? *Child Development, 60*, 1497–1510.

Field, T. M., Cohen, D., Garcia, R., & Greenberg, R. (1984). Mother–stranger face discrimination by the newborn. *Infant Behavior and Development, 7*, 19–25.

Fifer, W., Monk, C., & Grose-Fifer, J. (2001). Prenatal development and risk. In G. Bremner & A. Fogel (Eds.), *Blackwell handbook of infant development* (pp. 505–542). Cambridge, MA: Blackwell.

Fifer, W. P., & Moon, C. M. (1995). The effects of fetal experience with sound. In J. P. Lecannuet, W. P., Fifer, N. A., Krasnegor, & W. P. Smotherman (Eds.), *Fetal development: A psychobiological perspective* (pp. 351–366). Hillsdale, NJ: Erlbaum.

Floccia, C., Nazzi, T., & Bertoncini, J. (2000). Unfamiliar voice discrimination for short stimuli in newborns. *Developmental Science, 3*, 333–343.

Flom, R., & Bahrick, L. E. (2007). The development of infant discrimination of affect in multimodal and unimodal stimulation: The role of intersensory redundancy. *Developmental Psychology, 43*, 238–252.

Fodor, J. (1983). *Modularity of mind.* Cambridge, MA: MIT Press.

Frick, J. E., Colombo, J., & Allen, J. R. (2000). Temporal sequence of global–local processing in 3-month-old infants. *Infancy, 1*, 375–386.

Frick, J. E., Colombo, J., & Saxon, T. F. (1999). Individual and developmental differences in disengagement of fixation in early infancy. *Child Development, 70*, 537–548.

Frombonne, E. (2005). *Epidemiological studies of pervasive developmental disorders.* Hoboken, NJ: Wiley.

Gauthier, I., & Nelson, C. A. (2001). The development of face expertise. *Current Opinion in Neurobiology, 11*, 219–224.

Gauthier, I., & Tarr, M. J. (1997). Becoming a "greeble" expert: Exploring mechanisms for face recognition. *Vision Research, 37*, 1673–1682.

Gibson, E. J. (1969). *Principles of perceptual learning and development.* East Norwalk, CT: Appleton-Century-Crofts.

Gibson, E. J. (1988). Exploratory behavior in the development of perceiving, acting, and the acquiring of knowledge. *Annual Review of Psychology, 39*, 1–41.

Gibson, E J., & Pick, A. D. (2000). *An ecological approach to perceptual learning and development.* New York: Oxford University Press.

Gibson, J. J. (1966). *The senses considered as perceptual systems.* Boston: Houghton-Mifflin.

Gibson, J. J. (1979). *The ecological approach to visual perception.* Boston: Houghton-Mifflin.

Gogate, L. J. and Bahrick, L. E. (1998). Intersensory redundancy facilitates learning of arbitrary relations between vowel sounds and objects in seven-month-old infants. *Journal of Experimental Child Psychology, 69*, 1–17.

Gogate, L., Bahrick, L. E., & Watson, J. D. (2000). A study of multimodal motherese: The role of temporal synchrony between verbal labels and gestures. *Child Development, 71*, 878–894.

Gogate, L., Walker-Andrews, A. S., & Bahrick, L. E. (2001). Intersensory origins of word comprehension: An ecological-dynamic systems view (Target Article). *Developmental Science, 4*, 1–37.

Goldstein, M. H., King, A. P., & West, M. J. (2003). Social interaction shapes babbling: Testing parallels between birdsong and speech. *Proceedings of the National Academy of Sciences, 100*, 8030–3035.

Goren, C., Sarty, M., & Wu, P. (1975). Visual following and pattern discrimination of face-like stimuli by newborn infants. *Pediatrics, 56*, 544–549.

Gottlieb, G. (1971). Ontogenesis of sensory function in birds and mammals. In E. Tobach, L. Aronson, & E. Shaw (Eds.), *The biopsychology of development* (pp. 67–128). New York: Academic Press.

Gottlieb, G. (1997). *Synthesizing nature–nurture: Prenatal origins of instinctive behavior.* Mahwah, NJ: Erlbaum.

Greco, C., Rovee-Collier, C., Hayne, H., Griesler, P., & Earley, L. (1986). Ontogeny of early event memory: I. Forgetting and retrieval by 2- and 3-month-olds. *Infant Behavior and Development, 9*, 441–460.

Haith, M. M. (1980). *Rules that babies look by: The organization of newborn visual activity*. Potomac, MD: Erlbaum.

Hale, S. (1990). A global developmental trend in cognitive processing speed. *Child Development, 61*, 653–663.

Hamilton, A. F., Brindley, R. M., & Frith, U. (2007). Imitation and action understanding in autistic spectrum disorders: How valid is the hypothesis of a deficit in the mirror neuron system? *Neuropsychologia, 45*(8), 1859–1868.

Harrist, A. W., & Waugh, R. M. (2002). Dyadic synchrony: Its structure and function in children's development. *Developmental Review, 22*, 555–592.

Haviland, J. M., Walker-Andrews, A. S., Huffman, L. R., Toci, L., & Alton, K. (1996). Intermodal perception of emotional expressions by children with autism. *Journal of Developmental and Physical Disabilities, 8*, 77–88.

Hollich, G. J., Newman, R. S., & Jusczyk, P. W. (2005). Infants' use of visual information to segment speech in noise. *Child Development, 76*, 598–613.

Hunter, M. A., & Ames, E. W. (1988). A multifactor model of infant preferences for novel and familiar stimuli. In C. Rovee-Collier & L. P. Lipsitt (Eds.), *Advances in infancy research* (Vol. 5, pp. 69–95). Norwood, NJ: Ablex.

Iarocci, G., & McDonald, J. (2005). Sensory integraton and the perceptual experience of persons with autism. *Journal of Autism and Developmental Disorders, 36*, 77–90.

Jaffe, J., Beebe, B., Feldstein, S., Crown, C. L., & Jasnow, M. D. (2001). Rhythms of dialogue in infancy. *Monographs of the Society for Research in Child Development, 66*(Serial No. 265).

James, W. (1980). *The principles of psychology* (Vol. 2). New York: Holt.

Johnson, M. H., & Morton, J. (1991). *Biology and cognitive development: The case of face recognition*. Oxford: Blackwell.

Johnson, M. H., Posner, M. I., & Rothbart, M. K. (1991). Components of visual orienting in early infancy: Contingency learning, anticipatory looking, and disengaging. *Journal of Cognitive Neuroscience, 3*, 335–344.

Jordan, K. E., Suanda, S. H., & Brannon, E. M. (2008). Intersensory redundancy accelerates preverbal numerical competence. *Cognition, 108*, 210–221.

Kellman, P. J., & Arterberry, M. E. (1998). *The cradle of knowledge: The development of perception in infancy*. Cambridge: MIT Press.

Kuhl, P. K., & Meltzoff, A. N. (1982). The bimodal perception of speech in infancy. *Science, 218*, 1138–1141.

Kuhl, P. K., & Meltzoff, A. N. (1984). The intermodal representation of speech in infants. *Infant Behavior and Development, 7*, 361–381.

Landry, R., & Bryson, S. (2004). Impaired disengagement of attention in young children with autism. *Journal of Child Psychology and Psychiatry, 45*, 1115–1122.

Lee, D. N., & Aronson, E. (1974). Visual proprioceptive control of standing in human infants. *Perception and Psychophysics, 15*, 529–532.

Lewkowicz, D. J. (1996). Infants' response to the audible and visible properties of the human face: I. Role of lexical syntactic content, temporal synchrony, gender, and manner of speech. *Developmental Psychology, 32*, 347–366.

Lewkowicz, D. J. (2000). The development of intersensory temporal perception: An epigenetic systems/limitations view. *Psychological Bulletin, 126*, 281–308.

Lewkowicz, D. J. (2002). Heterogeneity and heterochrony in the development of intersensory perception. *Cognitive Brain Research, 14*, 41–63.

Lewkowicz, D. J. (2004). Perception of serial order in infants. *Developmental Science, 7*, 175–184.

Lewkowicz, D. J., & Lickliter, R. (Eds.). (1994). *Development of intersensory perception: Comparative perspectives*. Hillsdale, NJ: Erlbaum.

Lickliter, R. (1990). Premature visual stimulation accelerates intersensory functioning in bobwhite quail neonates. *Developmental Psychobiology, 23,* 15–27.

Lickliter, R. (2005). Prenatal sensory ecology and experience: Implications for perceptual and behavioral development in precocial birds. *Advances in the Study of Behavior, 35,* 235–274.

Lickliter, R., & Bahrick, L. E. (2000). The development of infant intersensory perception: Advantages of a comparative convergent-operations approach. *Psychological Bulletin, 126,* 260–280.

Lickliter, R., & Bahrick, L. E. (2001). The salience of multimodal sensory stimulation in early development: Implications for the issue of ecological validity. *Infancy, 2,* 451–467.

Lickliter, R., & Bahrick, L. E. (2004). Perceptual development and the origins of multisensory responsiveness. In G. Calvert, C. Spence, & B. E. Stein (Eds.), *Handbook of multisensory processes* (pp. 643–654). Cambridge, MA: MIT Press.

Lickliter, R., Bahrick, L. E., & Honeycutt, H. (2002). Intersensory redundancy facilitates prenatal perceptual learning in bobwhite quail (colinus virginianus) embryos. *Developmental Psychology, 38,* 15–23.

Lickliter, R., Bahrick, L. E., & Honeycutt, H. (2004). Intersensory redundancy enhances memory in bobwhite quail embryos. *Infancy, 5,* 253–269.

Lickliter, R., Bahrick, L. E., & Markham, R. G. (2006). Intersensory redundancy educates selective attention in bobwhite quail embryos. *Developmental Science, 9,* 605–616.

Loveland, K. A., Tunali-Kotoski, B., Chen, Y. R., Ortegon, J., Pearson, D. A., Brelsford, K. A., & Gibbs, M. C. (1997). Emotion recognition in autism: Verbal and nonverbal information. *Development and Psychopathology, 9,* 579–593.

Maestro, S., Muratori, F., Cavallaro, M. C., Pei, F., Stern, D., Golse, B., et al. (2002). Attentional skills during the first 6 months of age in autism spectrum disorder. *Journal of the American Academy of Child & Adolescent Psychiatry, 41,* 1239–1245.

Magnee, M. J. C. M., de Gelder, B., van Engeland, H., & Kemner, C. (2008). Audiovisual speech integration in pervasive developmental disorder: Evidence from event-related potentials. *Journal of Child Psychology and Psychiatry, 49,* 995–1000.

Mareschal, D., Johnson, M. H., Sirois, S., Spratling, M. W., Thomas, M. S. C., & Westermann, G. (2007). *Neuroconstructivism: How the brain constructs cognition* (Vol 1.). Oxford University Press: New York.

Markham, R. G., Shimuzu, T., & Lickliter, R. (2008). Extrinsic embryonic sensory stimulation alters multimodal behavior and cellular activation. *Developmental Neurobiology, 68*(13), 1463–1473.

Mastropieri, D., & Turkewitz, G. (1999). Prenatal experience and neonatal responsiveness to vocal expressions of emotion. *Developmental Psychobiology, 35,* 204–214.

Meltzoff, A. N. (2007). "Like me": A foundation for social cognition. *Developmental Science 10,* 126–134.

Meltzoff, A., & Moore, M. K. (1977). Imitation of facial and manual gestures by human neonates. *Science, 198,* 75–78.

Meltzoff, A. N., & Moore, M. K. (1983). Newborn infants imitate adult facial gestures. *Child Development, 54,* 702–709.

Meltzoff, A. N., & Moore, M. K. (1994). Imitation, memory, and the representation of persons. *Infant Behavior & Development, 17,* 83–99.

Miller, C. L. (1983). Developmental changes in male/female voice classification by infants. *Infant Behavior and Development, 6,* 313–330.

Miller, C. L., Younger, B. A., & Morse, P. A. (1982). The categorization of male and female voices in infancy. *Infant Behavior and Development, 5,* 143–159.

Mondloch, C. J., Lewis, T. L., Budreau, D. R., Maurer, D., Dannemiller, J. L., Stephens, B. R., & Kleiner-Gathercoal, K. A. (1999). Face perception during early infancy. *Psychological Science, 10,* 419–422.

Mongillo, E. A., Irwin, J. R., Whalen, D. H., Klaiman, C., Carter, A. S., & Schultz, R. T. (2008). *Journal of Autism and Developmental Disorders, 38*, 1349–1358.

Montague, D. P., & Walker-Andrews, A. S. (2002). Mothers, fathers, and infants: The role of person familiarity and parental involvement in infants' perception of emotion expressions. *Child Development, 73*, 1339–1352.

Moon, C., Cooper, R. P., & Fifer, W. P. (1993). Two day olds prefer their native language, *Infant Behavior and Development, 16*, 495–500.

Moon, C., & Fifer, W. P. (2000). Evidence of transnatal auditory learning. *Journal of Perinatology, 20*, S37–S44.

Moore, C., & Dunham, P. (1995). *Joint attention: Its origins and role in development.* Hillsdale, NJ: Erlbaum.

Morrongiello, B. A., Fenwick, K. D., & Nutley, T. (1998). Developmental changes in associations between auditory-visual events. *Infant Behavior and Development, 21*, 613–626.

Morton, J., & Johnson, M. H. (1991). CONSPEC and COLEARN: A two-process theory of infant face recognition. *Psychological Review, 98*, 164–181.

Mundy, P. (1995). Joint attention and social-emotional approach behavior in children with autism. *Developmental and Psychopathology, 7*, 63–82.

Mundy, P. (2003). The neural basis of social impairments in autism: The role of the dorsal medial-frontal cortex and anterior cingulated system. *Journal of Child Psychology and Psychiatry, 44*(66), 793–809.

Mundy, P., & Burnette, C. (2005). Joint attention and neurodevelopment: In F. Volkmar, A. Klin, & R. Paul (Eds.), *Handbook of autism and pervasive developmental disorders* (Vol. 3, pp. 650–681). Hoboken, NJ: John Wiley.

Mundy, P., & Newell, L. (2007). Attention, joint attention, and social cognition. *Current Directions in Psychological Science, 16*, 269–274.

Muir, D., & Clifton, R. (1985). Infants' orientation to the location of sound sources. In G. Gottlieb & N. Krasnegor (Eds.), *Measurement of audition and vision in the first year of postnatal life: A methodological overview* (pp. 171–194). Bethesda, MD: Ablex.

Nazzi, T., Bertoncini, J., & Mehler, J. (1998). Language discrimination by newborns: Toward an understanding of the role of rhythm. *Journal of Experimental Psychology: Human Perception and Performance, 24*, 756–766.

Neisser, U. (1976). *Cognitive psychology.* Englewood Cliffs, NJ: Prentice Hall.

Neisser, U. (1991). Two perceptually given aspects of the self and their development. *Developmental Review, 11*, 197–209.

Nelson, C. A. (2001). The development and neural bases of face recognition. *Infant and Child Development, 10*, 3–18.

Oakes, L. M., & Madole, K. L. (in press). Function revisited: How infants construe functional features in their representation of objects. In R. Kail (Ed.), *Advances in child development and behavior* (pp. 135–185). New York: Academic Press.

Oberman, L. M., Hubbard, E. M., McCleery, J. P., Altschuler, E. I., Ramachandran, V. S., & Pineda, J. A. (2005). EEG evidence for mirror neuron dysfunction in autism spectrum disorders. *Cognitive Brain Research, 24*, 190–198.

Oberman, L. M., & Ramachandran, V. S. (2008). Preliminary evidence for deficits in multisensory integration in autism spectrum disorders: The mirror neuron hypothesis. *Social Neuroscience, 3*, 348–355.

Osterling, J., & Dawson, G. (1994). Early recognition of children with autism: A study of first birthday home videotapes. *Journal of Autism and Developmental Disorders, 24*, 247–257.

Pascalis, O., de Schonen, S., Morton, J., Dereulle, C., & Fabre-Grenet, M. (1995). Mother's face recognition by neonates: A replication and an extension. *Infant Behavior and Development, 18*, 79–85.

Phillips-Silver, J., & Trainor, L. J. (2005). Feeling the beat: movement influences infant rhythm perception. *Science, 308,* 1430–1430.

Piaget, J. (1952). *The origins of intelligence in children.* New York: International Universities Press.

Piaget, J. (1954). *The construction of reality in the child.* New York: Basic Books.

Radeau, M., & Bertelson, P. (1977). Adaptation to auditory-visual discordance and ventriloquism in semirealistic situations. *Perception & Psychophysics, 22,* 137–146.

Rochat, P. (1993). Hand-mouth coordination in the newborn: Morphology, determinants, and early development of a basic act. In G. Savelsbergh (Ed.), *The development of coordination in infancy* (pp. 265–288). Amsterdam: Elsevier.

Rochat, P. (1995). Early objectification of the self. In P. Rochat (Ed.), *Advances in psychology: Vol. 112. The self in infancy: Theory and research* (pp. 53–71). Amsterdam: Elsevier.

Rochat, P., & Hespos, S. J. (1997). Differential rooting responses by neonates: Evidence for an early sense of self. *Early Development and Parenting, 6,* 105–112.

Rochat, P., & Morgan, R. (1995). The function and determinants of early self-exploration. In P. Rochat (Ed.), *Advances in psychology: No. 112. The self in infancy: Theory and research* (pp. 395–415). Amsterdam: Elsevier.

Rochat, P., & Striano, T, (1999). Social-cognitive development in the first year. In P. Rochat (Ed.), *Early social cognition: Understanding others in the first months of life* (pp. 3–34). Mahway, NJ: Erlbaum.

Rochat, P., & Striano, T. (2000). Perceived self in infancy. *Infant Behavior and Development, 23,* 513–530.

Rose, S. A., Feldman, J. F., & Jankowski, J. J. (2001). Attention and recognition memory in the 1st year of life: A longitudinal study of preterm and full-term infants. *Developmental Psychology, 37,* 135–151.

Rovee-Collier, C., & Barr, R. (2001). Infant learning and memory. In G. Bremner, & A. Fogel (Eds.), *Blackwell handbook of infant development: Handbooks of developmental psychology* (pp. 139–168). Malden, MA: Blackwell.

Ruff, H. A., & Rothbart, M. K. (1996). *Attention in early development: Themes and variations.* New York: Oxford University Press.

Sai, F. Z. (2005). The role of the mother's voice in developing mother's face preference: Evidence for intermodal perception at birth. *Infant and Child Development, 14,* 29–50.

Sander, L. (1977). The regulation of exchange in the infant-care taker system and some aspects of the context-content relationship. In M. Lewis and I. Rosenblum (Eds.), *Interaction, conversation, and the development of language* (pp. 133–156). New York: Wiley.

Schank, R., & Ableson, R. (1977). *Scripts, plans, goals, and understanding.* Hillsdale, NJ: Erlbaum.

Schmuckler, M. J. (1996). Visual-proprioceptive intermodal perception in infancy. *Infant Behavior and Development, 19,* 221–232.

Schmuckler, M. A., & Fairhall, J. L. (2001). Visual-proprioceptive intermodal perception using point light displays. *Child Development, 72,* 949–962.

Sigman, M., Dijamco, A., Gratier, M., & Rozga, A. (2004). Early detection of core deficits in autism. *Mental Retardation and Developmental Disabilities Research Reviews, 10,* 221–233.

Simion, F., Valenza, E., & Umilta, C. (1998). Mechanisms underlying face preference at birth. In F. Simion and G. Butterworth (Eds.), *The development of sensory, motor and cognitive capacities in early infancy: From perception to cognition* (pp. 87–102). Hove, UK: Psychology Press.

Slater, A., & Quinn, P. C. (2001). Face recognition in the newborn infant. *Infant and Child Development, 10,* 21–24.

Slater, A., Quinn, P. C., Brown, E., & Hayes, R. (1999). Intermodal perception at birth: Intersensory redundancy guides newborns' learning of arbitrary auditory-visual pairings. *Developmental Science, 2,* 333–338.

Smith, E. G., & Benetto, L. (2007). Audiovisual speech integration and lipreading in autism. *Journal of Child Psychology and Psychiatry, 48,* 813–821.

Smith, L. B., & Thelen, E. (2003). Development as a dynamic system. *Trends in Cognitive Sciences, 7,* 343–348.

Smotherman, W. P., & Robinson, S. R. (1990). The prenatal origins of behavioral organization. *Psychological Science, 1,* 97–106.

Spear, N. E., Kraemer, P. J., Molina, J. C., & Smoller, D. E. (1988). Developmental change in learning and memory: Infantile disposition for "unitization". In J. Delacour & J. C. S. Levy (Eds.), *Systems with learning and memory abilities: Proceedings of the workshop held in Pris, June 1-5-19, 1987.* Amsterdam: Elsevier/North Holland.

Spence, M. J., & Moore, D. (2003). Categorization of infant-directed speech: Development from 4 to 6 months. *Developmental Psychobiology, 42,* 97–109.

Stein, B. E., & Meredith, M. A. (1993). *The merging of the senses.* Cambridge, MA: MIT Press.

Stern, D. (1985). *The interpersonal world of the infant.* New York: Basic Books.

Tarabulsy, G. M., Tessier, R., & Kappas, A. (1996). Contingency detection and the contingent organization of behavior in interactions: Implications for socioemotional development in infancy. *Psychological Bulletin, 120,* 25–41.

Thelen, E. (1995). Motor development. A new synthesis. *American Psychologist, 50,* 79–95.

Thelen, E., & Smith, L. B. (1994). *A dynamic systems approach to the development of cognition and action.* Cambridge, MA: MIT Press.

Trevarthen, C. (1993). The self born of intersubjectivity: The psychology of an infant communicating. In U. Neisser (Ed.), *Ecological and interpersonal knowledge of the self* (pp. 121–173). New York: Cambridge University Press.

Triesman, A. M. (1964). Selective attention in man. *British Medical Bulletin, 20,* 12–16.

Tronick, E. (1989). Emotions and emotional communication in infants. *American Psychologist, 44,* 112–119.

Turati, C. (2004). Why faces are not special to newborns: An alternative account of the face preference. *Current Directions in Psychological Science, 13,* 5–8.

Turkewitz, G. (1994). Sources of order for intersensory functioning. In D. J. Lewkowicz & R. Lickliter (Eds.), *The development of intersensory perception: Comparative perspectives* (pp. 3–18). Hillsdale, NJ: Erlbaum.

Turkewitz, G., & Kenny, P. A. (1982). Limitations on input as a basis for neural organization and development. *Developmental Psychobiology, 15,* 357–368.

Vaillant-Molina, M., Newell, L., Castellanos, I., Bahrick, L. E., & Lickliter, R. (2006, July). *Intersensory redundancy impairs face perception in early development.* Poster presented at the biennial meetings of the International Conference on Infant Studies, Kyoto, Japan.

Van de Meer, A. L., Van der Weel, F. L., & Lee, D. N. (1995). The functional significance of arm movements in neonates. *Science, 267,* 693–695.

Van der Smagt, M. J., van Engeland, H., & Kemner, C. (2007). Brief report: Can you see what is not there? Low-level auditory-visual integration in autism spectrum disorder. *Journal of Autism and Developmental Disorders, 37,* 2014–2019.

Volkmar, F., Chawarska, K., & Klin, A. (2005). Autism in infancy and early childhood. *Annual Review of Psychology, 56,* 315–336.

Volkmar, F. R., Lord, C., Bailey, A., Schultz, R. T., & Klin, A. (2004). Autism and pervasive developmental disorders. *Journal of Child Psychology and Psychiatry, 45,* 135–170.

Von Hofsten, C. (1980). Predictive reaching for moving objects by human infants. *Journal of Experimental Child Psychology, 30,* 369–382.

Von Hofsten, C. (1983). Catching skills in infancy. *Journal of Experimental Psychology: Human Perception and Performance, 9,* 75–85.

Von Hofsten, C. (1993). Prospective control: A basic aspect of action development. *Human Development, 36,* 253–270.

Walker-Andrews, A. S. (1997). Infants' perception of expressive behaviors: Differentiation of multimodal information. *Psychological Bulletin, 121,* 437–456.

Walker-Andrews, A., & Bahrick, L. E. (2001). Perceiving the real world: Infants' detection of and memory for social information. *Infancy, 2,* 469–481.

Walker-Andrews, A., Bahrick, L. E., Raglioni, S. S., and Diaz, I. (1991). Infants' bimodal perception of gender. *Ecological Psychology, 3,* 55–75.

Warren, D., Welch, R., & McCarthy, T. (1981). The role of visual-auditory "compellingness" in the ventriloquism effect: Implications for transitivity among the spatial senses. *Perception & Psychophysics, 30,* 557–564.

Watson, J. S. (1972). Smiling, cooing, and "the game". *Merrill-Palmer Quarterly, 18,* 323–339.

Watson, J. S. (1979). Perception of contingency as a determinant of social responsiveness. In E. B. Thoman (Ed.), *The origins of social responsiveness* (pp. 33–64). New York: Erlbaum.

Werker, J. F., & McLeod, P. J. (1989). Infant preference for both male and female infant directed talk: A developmental study of attentional and affective responsiveness. *Canadian Journal of Psychology, 43,* 230–246.

Wertheimer, M. (1961). Psychomotor coordination of auditory-visual space at birth. *Science, 134,* 1692.

West, M. J., & King, A. P. (1988). Female visual displays affect the development of male song in the cowbird. *Nature, 334,* 244–246.

Williams, J. H. G., Massaro, D. W., Peel, N. J., Bosseler, A., & Suddendorf, T. (2004). Visual-auditory integration during speech imitation in autism. *Research in Developmental Disabilities, 25,* 559–575.

Williams, J. H. G., Whiten, A., Suddendorf, T., & Perrett, D. I. (2001). Imitation, mirror neurons and autism. *Neuroscience and Biobehavioral Reviews, 25,* 287–295.

Xu, F., Carey, S., & Quint, N. (2004). The emergence of kind-based object individuation in infancy. *Cognitive Psychology, 49,* 155–190.

Yirmiya, N., Gamliel, I., Pilowsky, T., Feldman, R., Baron-Cohen, S., & Sigman, M. (2006). The development of siblings of children with autism at 4 and 14 months: Social engagement, communication, and cognition. *Journal of Child Psychology and Psychiatry, 47,* 511–523.

Zukow-Goldring, P. (1997). A social ecological realist approach to the emergence of the lexicon: Educating attention to amodal invariants in gesture and speech. In C. Dent-Read & P. Zukow-Goldring (Eds.), *Evolving explanations of development* (pp. 199–249). Washington, DC: American Psychological Association.

5

Action in Infancy – Perspectives, Concepts, and Challenges

Ad W. Smitsman and Daniela Corbetta

The Study of Action

This chapter concentrates on the development of action in the first years of life and the challenges that infants must overcome to function effectively in the environment. After introducing themes and definitions in the study of action, we focus on the development of reaching, grasping, walking, and object manipulation.

The study of action, broadly defined, addresses the emergence and refinement of goal-directed behaviors over seconds, minutes, days, and years of recurring activities, as new forms of action evolve with accumulated experience. Action is never static. It is fundamentally dynamic and time-dependent. It is also embodied and situated in the environment. Scientists study the development of action to infer hypothetical mental organizations – which we often use in psychology to explain behavior – but also to understand the body, its biological and dynamic characteristics, and the environment in which it resides.

Action involves the cooperation of several body segments, from simple to complex forms. In development, these bodily organizations adapt increasingly to changing environmental circumstances; they are molded by them and take advantage of them.

Action is not just movement. Inanimate objects may move, but living organisms such as hominids and human neonates act (see e.g., Reed, 1982, 1996). Also, action has a meaning that is embedded in a sequence of movements (Bernstein, 1996). This succession of movements is governed by its future end state and influenced by its prior history. In this progression, any movement state that is sensed over milliseconds and seconds contributes to anticipation and preparation for the future end state.

Future end states may be called goals. Goals can be social (e.g., sharing experiences with friends) or nonsocial (e.g., grasping a cup for drinking). Actions directed at the physical world or social environment may be similar. For instance, one may reach for a cup to quench one's own thirst, or to hand it to another thirsty person. In this movement sequence, the reach can be the same, but the grip may differ slightly; instead of transporting the cup directly to one's own mouth, the cup will be held such that the other person can grasp it and transport it to their mouth. This example also highlights a fundamental aspect of action; that action is intimately connected to its environment.

Ecological psychologists (E. J. Gibson, 1988, 1994, 1997; J. J. Gibson, 1979; E. J. Gibson & Pick, 2000) have coined the term *affordance* to denote this intrinsic connection of action to the environment. Affordances are goals an actor can realize because of the match existing between what the environment provides for action and the bodily resources and capabilities the actor has for taking advantage of what the environment provides (E. J. Gibson & Pick, 2000; Reed, 1996). Thus, action is the realization of a *potential* that is situated both within the actor's body and the environment. The realization of this potential can take different forms throughout one's day and over the many days one lives because of the various goals one needs to achieve to function in the physical and social world. For example, bipedal locomotion can serve several goals; that is, going up or down stairs, moving forward or backward, jumping, running, and even expressing different emotional states while doing so, or communicating social values to others, as is the case in (ritual) dancing. These goals may involve small or large changes in the organization of gait and may lead to varied forms of locomotion. Regardless, these forms are always intimately linked to the environment and its characteristics. Locomotion continuously takes advantage of gravity, the surface upon which the pattern is performed, or even the atmospheric conditions. Furthermore, the highly flexible characteristics of the locomotor system allow the actor to continuously adapt to these environmental circumstances as they change over time.

Five reasons to study action

Why is action so interesting to study? And what is peculiar about infants acting in the world? Perhaps the most general answer to the above questions is that living organisms regulate their daily existence through action. To live, humans have to relate themselves to the surrounding world in various ways, by getting food, communicating, and cooperating with others.

Studying action can also shed new light onto an organism's relation to its environment. The environment is a reality for any acting organism and needs to be known in order for the organism to survive. The study of action helps establish what this knowledge entails, how it is attained in the course of daily actions, and how it changes over the course of a lifetime when the experience and skill to act develop.

A *third* reason why action is so interesting concerns its complexity, flexibility, and dynamic nature. Action's complexity and flexibility rest in the astonishing number of degrees of freedom (i.e., range of possible movement combinations) that need to be organized to achieve many functions and goals for living. Its dynamic nature lies in the ever changing forms of action. Even for organisms with bodies that are much simpler than that of humans, the number of degrees of freedom that need to be organized in a coherent way far surpasses that of any artificial system or machine. Thus, understanding how actions can become complex, flexible, and dynamic over time is a core question in developmental science and learning.

A *fourth* reason for interest is that actions are complex systems. This realization has led to a fascinating new branch of science, recently brought into the arena of developmental psychology by action researchers such as Thelen and Smith (1994), and Goldfield (1995). Nature and human beings are formed by and rest on a complex web of relationships between multiple elements. This web of relationships self-organizes and is maintained by continuous processes of exchange taking place within the web and between the web and other systems in the environment. The study of such complex systems is relevant for development. In particular, the study of the development of action as it takes place in infancy enables researchers to unravel the principles of change over time, and therefore to understand better what development means and entails.

A final motivation for studying action and its development is the acknowledgement that many core areas of development such as cognition, social interaction, and social understanding are grounded in infants' action development (e.g., Overton, Müller, & Newman, 2008). The relation between action and the development of cognition has long been acknowledged by Piaget. Recently however, the link between action and cognition has taken a new meaning in the so-called dialogue on embodied cognition. Researchers who embrace this new view of cognition depart from the traditional Piagetian perspective, which conceived action as a lower form of cognition being progressively liberated from its bodily roots by a process of abstraction. Rather, they see action with the body and its intrinsic properties as fundamental constituents of cognition (e.g., Corbetta, 2009; Cox & Smitsman, 2008; Thelen, 2000, 2008). Furthermore, from an embodied cognition view, the formation and growth of human intelligence is no longer seen as the product of brain activity alone; instead, human intelligence is considered an emergent property of the continuous exchanges between brain, other body parts, and the environment (Chiel & Beer, 1997).

The Action Problem

Within 1 year of birth, most healthy infants attain two important motor milestones: object manipulation and upright locomotion. Attaining these milestones is a monumental task. Only recently, psychologists have begun to understand their scope and complexity. To imagine how colossal these infant achievements are, think of how difficult it is, even today with all our technical knowledge, to design an infant robot that can walk flexibly and intelligibly avoiding all kinds of obstacles. How do infants become skillful actors in their first year?

Nowadays, we recognize that, to become skillful actors, infants have to overcome a number of difficult challenges. But in the past, action development was not understood in terms of problem solving. In their early pioneering work, motor developmentalists such as Gesell and Amatruda (1945) and McGraw (1935) believed that infants could not start performing skills such as grasping, reaching, and walking until the appropriate neural structures had developed. This belief emerged because they observed much regularity in the order in which new forms of behavior developed across the first years of life. They assumed that maturational processes, especially the ones affecting the brain, followed a regular and predefined timetable and were the main cause driving motor development. Other developmental psychologists (e.g., Piaget, 1952) who were more cognitively oriented, completely ignored the action problems that infants had to surmount, or assumed that the kernel of the problem resided in the development of an appropriate cognitive scheme or motor program needed to coordinate and control the movements of the limbs voluntarily. Finally, behaviorists believed that action could be decomposed into simple responses that only needed to be connected by association and reinforcement (see Reed and Bril, 1996, for a discussion of this issue). Yet, by reducing action formation to such associations, they still ignored the challenges infants faced.

It has become clear in recent years that even fundamental motor skills such as reaching and walking, which have for long been taken for granted and assumed to emerge as the product of a genetic blueprint, are, in fact, the result of a long learning process. Infants need to solve a number of action problems when transforming seemingly purposeless activities of the limbs into organized goal-directed behaviors. What are these action problems?

To answer this question we need to take a closer look at young infants' movement patterns. When we observe newborns that are awake, we notice that their movements usually involve the whole body. Infants become easily excited especially when looking at moving objects and faces. This excitement not only leads to gazing, but also to mouthing, protruding the tongue, kicking, and waving both arms. One major problem that infants face when so active, is to discover how to regulate the flow of energy running through the whole body such that movements of the limbs, head, and trunk can be goal-directed (Bertenthal & von Hofsten, 1998). For example, to stay attuned to interesting moving objects and direct the hand toward them, infants need to energize both head and arm, but also stabilize the movements of these particular body segments against a background of ongoing activities from the other limbs. This is not a trivial task if we consider that early gaze control can easily be disrupted by widespread lack of body control and that reaching and grasping alone take months to develop (Konczak, Borutta, Topka, & Dichgans, 1995; Thelen, Corbetta, & Spencer, 1996; von Hofsten, 1991). So, what is involved in solving such an action problem?

The pioneering work of Bernstein (1967), a Russian physicist, made scientists aware of the need to look more carefully at the human body – its neuromuscular system and skeleton – in answering questions about the development of action (for an excellent discussion of the Bernstein perspective, see Fitch, Tuller, & Turvey, 1982; Tuller, Fitch, & Turvey, 1982; Turvey, Fitch, & Tuller, 1982). Bernstein identified the degrees of freedom (DFs) of the joints interconnecting the different body segments and the nearly unlimited number of movement trajectories they make available for action (Turvey, 1990). DFs reflect the number of movement variations that can be performed by a single joint. For instance, if we consider the three major joints of the arm, the wrist contains 3 DFs, the elbow contains 1 and the shoulder has 3. Indeed, the arm can move up and down, left and right, and both shoulder and wrist can be rotated, while the elbow can only flex and extend in one direction. Thus, the arm has a total of 7 DFs to control movement if we consider only its kinematics. However, when we include the several muscles and multiple neuromotor units needed to activate the muscle fibers of each limb segment, the DF number becomes extremely large. For example, the muscles alone have 2 DFs. A muscle can become shorter or longer and less or more stiff. Moreover, muscles are present in antagonistic pairs, that is, each muscle can only pull, but the pulling movement of a flexor muscle can be counteracted by the antagonistic pulling of an extensor muscle and vice versa.

A fundamental question for researchers in motor development is to understand how infants discover the trajectory that will bring their hand towards a wanted object given the large number of DFs available for action. Again, this is not a trivial task. For a 1 DF-system there is only one trajectory available, but for a 2 DF-system there are already a large number of possible trajectories in 2-D space. What about a 7 DF-system such as the arm? Clearly, in such a system the number of possible trajectories in the 3-D space is unlimited. Given this large number of possibilities, the question becomes how infants manage to reduce or freeze the DFs to control the movement and prevent unwanted motion. But, the control problem does not stop with the control of the arm. It becomes even more complicated when we realize that any action of the arm is not confined to the arm itself. Because the body forms an interconnected network of many segments, the activation of one segment (i.e., one arm) affects other body segments (i.e., trunk and other arm) and these effects feed back onto the segment that is being activated. Thus, controlling the movement of one body segment requires also being able to control other body parts. This task is immense given that the body contains 800 muscles and 100 DFs at the joints. Additionally, for each body segment, 2 sets of values always need to be specified: for each joint, angle and velocity are needed, and for each related muscle, stiffness and length are needed.

Another puzzle Bernstein (1967) identified is the *context conditioned variability within the movement apparatus*. In skilled actors, the transport of the hand toward an object for the purpose of grasping it forms a smooth trajectory and velocity profile. However, a closer look at the joints and muscles involved in the movement reveals a huge amount of variability. Indeed, the smooth hand trajectory of a skilled actor is actually the product of many nonlinear linkages between the different elements involved in the movement. For example, one pattern of muscle activation can lead to different hand movement profiles depending on the local circumstances. Likewise, different patterns of muscle activity may lead to similar movement trajectories. Such variability arises from the way muscle contractions at the different joints set the arm in motion. This involves coordinating the DFs of the different joints to make the movement smooth and in the intended direction. To make each joint flex or extend one needs torques. Torques result from muscle contraction. Passive forces combined with gravity add to the torques acting on the joints. Body segments have a mass and the motion from these segments creates passive forces of magnitude that depend on the mass of the segment and how forcefully the movement is performed (force = mass x acceleration). Note that the segment mass can include the mass of a carried object. Finally, the muscles *per se* have spring-like properties. Muscles do not pull directly on the joint segments, but on tendons connected to the joints which have a smoothing effect. Both the spring-like properties of muscles and the smoothing effect of tendons make the relation between muscle activity and muscle force even more nonlinear (Latash, 1996). Nonlinearity is also present at the linkage between joint rotation and hand movement, and between motor units and motor neurons.

As one moves, these nonlinearities between multiple levels of the system arise continuously. Furthermore, nonlinearities also occur during the ongoing exchanges between the system and its environment. Given that upcoming events can only partly be foreseen, and that earlier experiences do not always contribute to foreseeing them, the actor is left with a challenge. For infants, the situation seems even more challenging, because they lack experience.

Given the level of complexity and nonlinearity involved in forming and controlling an action, it is quite astonishing to think of the great level of behavioral flexibility and adaptability that humans acquire over developmental time. This shows that the body is quite smart in achieving the immensely complex task of acting, but it also reveals how little we know about the body's intelligence. One question related to this action problem, is how the brain manages to control the body with all its DFs. How do we maintain movement flexibility with such a complex body? A groundbreaking answer to this question is that the brain cares little about what happens at the lower levels of the individual joints, muscles, and neuromotor units involved in action. Rather, the brain takes advantage of the properties emerging from the assembly of these components in interaction with the environment. This leads us to discuss complex systems.

Complex Systems

Complex systems are systems composed of many, often heterogeneous, elements that continuously interact with each other. For the body, these elements are the limbs, joints, various types of muscles, tendons, smaller motor units, sensors, and muscle fibers connected to the motor neurons, and so on. One characteristic of complex systems is that new properties, not present in any of the elements of the system, emerge as the result of the interconnections and exchanges between elements of the system and the environment. The newly interconnected system as a whole is a much simpler system to control because it only has a few degrees of freedom compared to the original system of unconnected elements. Such an interconnected system can be described as organized complexity, and the system of unconnected elements as disorganized complexity. In its organized complexity, the system and its emergent properties form as the product of a self-organized process between elements and show an astonishing potential for new behaviors, with an amazing variety of new goals, and huge flexibility to adapt to upcoming circumstances when realizing these goals. In short, the self-organization between the different elements of the system creates highly intelligent systems capable of adaptive behavior.

We can illustrate the most important properties of complex systems by looking at a real-life example such as windsurfing. Windsurfing is immensely complex in terms of its DFs and the number of elements involved in it: air, water, sail's materials, mast, board, plus the body segments contributing to the movements and postures of the surfer. Clearly, windsurfing cannot be controlled at the level of the individual elements. However, the interactions between the board and water, board and sail, sail surface and airflow, and body reduce this complexity into an interconnected system which, as a whole, possesses entirely new properties, not present in any of the single elements, and reduces to a few DFs to control. For example, orienting the sail at the right angle creates an air pressure system around the sail, which acts as a pulling force on the sail and board. Pulling on the board at the same time creates a streaming pattern of water under the board that lifts the board to the water surface and, with the sail correctly oriented in the wind, the board will surf over the waves. These exchange processes between parts provide not only the pushing force and lift, but also stability for the board, the surfer's posture and movement, and the sail. As a result, the aerodynamics and hydrodynamics that underlie windsurfing are coupled and can be regulated by only a few parameters. Setting the sail at the proper angle against the wind is the most important parameter; but the postures and movements of the surfer are also important as they contribute directly to keeping the system stable amid the continuously changing conditions of the wind and waves. Indeed, a slight change in wind or waves can perturb the system leading to an instantaneous loss of stability and pulling force.

The example of windsurfing also highlights important characteristics of the development of action and skills. One does not learn windsurfing by learning appropriate postures and movements. The surfer's postures and movements form as a function of the energetic properties emerging from the interconnected system and need to be modulated constantly to keep the system going amid the continuously changing air and water environment. Learning to surf involves discovering the free parameters regulating the system. This discovery also arises by self-organization and by learning how to regulate the task parameters through posture and movement (see also Reed & Bril, 1996).

Similar processes underlie the organization of more mundane activities such as walking, reaching, grasping, and object manipulation. In windsurfing, posture and movement serve to keep the sail and board going. In walking, posture and movement serve to keep the body upright and going for various purposes. In reaching, they serve to transport the hand to another location in space for purposes as diverse as touching, grasping, and manipulating objects. The goals may endlessly change, but the general process by which these goals are attained is similar. In all cases, a new system arises reducing the amount of DFs from each individual components to a few, and, the newly assembled system, as a whole, provides the means that is needed to attain an intended goal (see Goldfield, 1995; Kelso, 1995; Kugler, Kelso & Turvey, 1980; Thelen & Smith, 1994, for more details on complex systems).

Mass Spring Systems

Some other complex systems that arise from single or multiple joint movements are known as mass spring systems and pendulums (Berthouze & Goldfield, 2008; Goldfield, Kay, & Warren, 1993; Hogan, 1985; Kelso & Holt, 1980; Lussanet, Smeets, & Brenner, 2002). For the sake of clarity, we will confine our discussion to single joint movements.

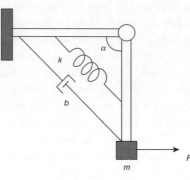

Figure 5.1   Schematic drawing of a single joint mass spring system with spring-stiffness k, damping b and (limb-)masses m_1 and m_2.

There is a huge variety of mass spring systems, but each of them can be controlled by a small number of parameters: mass, spring stiffness, and spring damping. Each is the composite of several variables at a lower level of the system (see Figure 5.1). When we consider single joint movements, we notice that the joint can oscillate like a pendulum, or can end its swing at a fixed endpoint as when reaching. Both types of movements are typical for a mass spring system and depend on the parameter settings of the system. The most important parameter for making a joint spring back or end its movement is the damping of the system. Suppose one stretches a spring to a certain amplitude by pulling its mass and then letting the spring go. If the system were undamped, the spring would return to its original position, overshoot this point by about the same distance it has been pulled out, and continue oscillating with this amplitude forever, which, in reality, never occurs. In a damped system, the oscillations progressively die out and the spring settles into a neutral position, which is an equilibrium point for the system. At critical damping, however, the spring will no longer oscillate, but return to its neutral position and reach this point irrespective of where and how far it has been stretched out. The frequency of oscillation of the pendulum can be manipulated by the stiffness of the system; the stiffer the system, the higher the frequency. And the amplitude of the oscil-lations depends on the pulling force exerted on the spring. A mass attached to the system will lower the oscillating frequencies.

What does all this mean for the control of movement toward a certain end point? Joints are much more flexible than actual springs. A spring has only one neutral point, fixed by its design. Joints, however, can have equilibrium points throughout their range of motion, which, for instance, is 150° for the one DF of the elbow. The location of the neutral point depends on the stiffness and length of the muscle. Suppose one reaches from a momentarily fixed initial position by using the DF of the elbow and freez-ing the DFs of the shoulder and wrist. To ensure the hand will reach a new endpoint in space and stop at that endpoint, one needs to change the existing equilibrium state of the muscle into one corresponding to the new endpoint and joint angle. To do this, the relative stiffness and length of the extensor and flexor muscles corresponding to the new endpoint have to be reset. The newly set relative stiffness of the extensor and flexor muscles creates a state of disequilibrium the system dissolves by reaching the new equilibrium state. With sufficient damping, the hand reaches the endpoint from its initial location without overshooting and the movement reflects the trajectory to the new point of equilibrium.

Propensities for Solving the Action Problem

We have seen that joints and limbs have the potential to behave as complex systems (mass spring systems and pendulums), the behaviors of which can be regulated by a few parameters. The appropriate setting of these parameters enables a performer to attain a nearly unlimited set of goals. How do infants manage to discover these appropriate parameters? Recall that mass spring systems are not confined to single joints but span several joints. This increases the potential for fine-tuning the system, but the high DFs of a multijoint system makes the problem more challenging to solve.

A set of important fundamental properties, inborn abilities, and developmental changes, enable infants to explore and discover their body, with its articulating joints, and movement capabilities. Important ones are: the motivation to explore and be active, inbuilt strategies for solving the action problem when exploring the body's potential for action, and the coupling between perception and action, which is morphologically pre-structured at birth (von Hofsten, 2007).

We understand nowadays that newborns come to life with a set of organized behavioral patterns that have developed and settled prenatally (Kurjak et al., 2004). Some of these neonatal patterns, often called reflexes, such as eye blinking, grooming, sucking, and swallowing, are profitable for the child. Some can be astonishingly flexible and goal specific. Others, do not serve a clear goal, or no longer serve such a goal after birth, such as the stepping reflex, some whole body neonatal behavioral patterns such as the symmetrical and asymmetrical tonic neck reflexes (STNR/ATNR) may complicate the development of action. They must disappear for action to develop. In the ATNR, the side head turn leads to the stretching of the arm and leg on that same side of the body while the contralateral limbs flex. Although the coupling between head movement and arm might be beneficial for the development of eye–hand coordination, it compromises the discovery and regulation of the mass spring system of the arm. This problem is enhanced for infants with cerebral palsy, but, in normal development, most of these synergies disappear during the first 2 to 3 months after birth, which frees the movement apparatus for exploring and discovering new functional linkages, and promotes the attainment of new goals (Thelen & Spencer, 1998; van der Fits & Hadders-Algra, 1998).

Note that this discovery occurs during a period of rapid growth when body mass, muscle stiffness, length, and existing neuromuscular linkages are changing. To solve the action problem, an initial strategy infants use is freezing the DFs and exploring the parameter settings for single joint movements. This is followed later by freeing the DFs, such that more joints get involved. This process usually begins with the joints most central to the trunk and head and then extends to more distant joints (Gesell, 1956).

Perception–Action Coupling

Researchers agree that regulating neuromuscular activities to turn limb movements into goal-directed actions requires a coupling between perception and action. They, however, disagree about how this coupling should be conceived. A recent proposal stems from James' old ideomotor principle (James, 1890). This principle assumes a direct coupling between the conscious aim to move and the body that generates the intended movement. Researchers who embrace this view maintain that infants learn to control their body by exploring, discovering, and recollecting the consequences of their goal-directed behaviors. They agree that associations are formed but, unlike the behaviorists, they see these associations forming between behaviors and their consequences, not between stimuli and responses (e.g., Elsner & Hommel, 2001; Hommel, 2003, 2006; Prinz, 1997).

In our view, this theory understates the problem infants face for several reasons. First, the relation between movements and their consequences is equivocal. Depending on the environmental circumstances, the same movement can lead to different outcomes (see previous discussion about context conditioned variability). Second, movements need to be geared toward the future to transform them into actions (von Hofsten, 1997, 2003, 2004, 2007; von Hofsten & Gibson, 1993). Infants need to anticipate the different consequences when planning an action. Finally, whether the movement swings like a pendulum or ends at a fixed endpoint depends on the particular parameter settings of the system. Thus, what is important is not the relation between movements and their consequences, but the relation between the projected parameter settings, from which movements result, and their consequences for the child's interactions with the environment.

A related, albeit different, approach to the above questions is J. J. Gibson's (1979) affordance concept (E. J. Gibson & Pick, 2000). Affordances also refer to action outcomes but these outcomes reside in the environmental characteristics that enable the individual to attain an intended outcome. More specifically, affordances concern environmental dimensions that fit the dimensions of an action system. For example, the distance and size of an object fits the length of the arm and size of the hand when reaching for it. Affordances denote goals of action that can be attained depending on the fit between a person's bodily potential for action and the environment, and the person's capability to organize the action accordingly. Consequences, on the other hand, denote events and outcomes that have taken place because of the way the person organized the action with respect to an environment. Affordances point to future states, whereas experienced consequences point to past states. This fact leads to another important difference, particularly to the learning and development of actions. It is obvious that to develop, infants should take advantage of past experiences. But, it is also important to direct activities as a function of future states – the goals and outcomes they intend to attain – when the goals cannot be attained immediately (Adolph & Berger, 2006; Reed & Bril, 1996). Infants have to try repeatedly to develop new skills. It seems plausible to assume that their motivation to persist when current outcomes fail must be fuelled by the ability to direct attention to future states afforded by environmental features beyond their capacity to attain. Ecological psychologists (E. J. Gibson & Pick, 2000) have pointed to *prospectivity*:

the capacity to perceive what will happen ahead of time and *prospective control*, the ability to guide actions towards future states. According to them, the origin of *prospectivity* is grounded in infants' capacity to perceive affordances. This capacity is morphologically prestructured by the functional anatomy and physiology of the infant's body at birth (von Hofsten, 2003) and becomes differentiated as skills develop. Of course, later on, as the infant's memory develops (see chapter 8 this volume), past experiences will increasingly become part of this capacity.

The problem infants need to solve in perceiving affordances is to discern whether a set of environmental features is within the boundaries of their action, that is, the bodily organization they select to attain a goal and skill (Adolph & Berger, 2006). Adolph's research offers a good illustration of this. In one study, infants were followed longitudinally as they crawled and walked on sloped surfaces that varied in steepness (Adolph, 1997). Two measures were of major interest: (a) infants' motor strategy choices used to climb up or go down sloped surfaces when steepness varied, and (b) successful attempts. Infants were observed biweekly, throughout the transition from crawling to walking. From the very first visit to the laboratory, they were selective in their attempts to go up or down the slopes depending on their steepness, although many infants greatly overestimated their locomotor capacity. Infants' decision to traverse or refuse to traverse the slopes was defined by a clear boundary in slope steepness. However, this boundary was higher than that of the slopes infants could successfully perform. Over the weeks of crawling experience, infants' choices increasingly approximated their actual slope traversal success, and even underestimated their skill. At the onset of walking, when they switched to this new form of locomotion, the affordance of slope steepness changed. Interestingly, they again attempted slopes that were too steep to traverse successfully. These results clearly indicate that infants perceived slope steepness relative to their manner of locomotion. Over the months they did not learn to associate steepness with positive or negative outcomes, but to refine their perception of the consequences of slope steepness for their postural stability when crossing the slopes.

Reaching and Grasping

Reaching, grasping, and object manipulation are key functions of the hand. However, the human hand does not do only that: it points, pounds, explores by touch, and even performs symbolic functions such as gesturing and counting. How do infants learn to use their hands in such diverse ways? The answer to this question encompasses the activity of the hand itself. As for many behaviors, using the hands involves the whole body. Hands and arms have to be coordinated with the head and trunk, and with sight and perception. A bright object or a ringing bell, for example, will elicit a head turn and a leaning of the trunk before the arm is extended toward the object. Once attained, the object can be shaken, brought to the mouth, or thrown away, all behaviors that continue to require a simultaneous head, trunk, and arm coordination. To perform these actions successfully, infants need to discover how to activate their arm such that the posture of the head and trunk form a stable platform to support the movement (Bertenthal & von Hofsten, 1998).

This is not a given, because any extension of the arm away from the body will displace the center of mass outward. Plus, any movements of the torso will further aggravate this, making coordination a really challenging task. Stability of the head and trunk are particularly needed to compensate such mass displacement effects. Stability of the head is also crucial to keep the gaze focused on the target. How do infants manage to develop such complex and sophisticated goal-directed actions, when as newborns they begin with a limited set of coordinated and somewhat rigid behaviors? Here we address this question in the context of basic manual functions such as reaching and grasping.

Prereaching

Before voluntary reaching for objects emerges at about 4 months of age, infants display a rudimentary form of the behavior called prereaching. Prereaching is a full arm and hand extension toward an object that can be observed in newborns when they are provided with full support of the head and trunk (Grenier, 1981). These early arm extensions are called prereaches because it is unclear whether they correspond to a movement guided by the sight of the object, or to a movement elicited by other activities such as gazing at the object or turning the head. Von Hofsten (1982) considered them more as orienting responses than reaching responses *per se*, because these arm extensions never lead to successful contacts with the object. Nonetheless, despite failure to attain the toy, he observed that 5- to 9-day-old infants extended their arm closer to an object if the object was fixated than not. And, if the extension was well aimed, arm movements tended to slow down in the vicinity of the fixated object, suggesting some form of anticipation of an encounter with the object.

During the first 4 months following birth, important changes take place in the organization and muscular synergies that underlie the visual and manual activities of infants. These changes set the stage for the development of goal-directed reaching. From 1 to 7 weeks, prereaching attempts decrease. The hand – fully extended in the original neonatal response – becomes gradually fisted during arm extension, and the number of object fixations increases. Then, from 9 to 17 weeks of age, the fist reopens, apparently in preparation for the onset of voluntary reaching (von Hofsten, 1984). Presumably, during the first 7 weeks of life, the head, shoulders, arm, and hand muscle synergies used in prereaching reorganize, freeing the infants from the ATNR configuration (Goldfield, 1995). This reorganization enables infants to explore visually, haptically, and proprioceptively the newly freed degrees of freedom of the arms. Consistent with this hypothesis, White, Castle, and Held (1964) found that the decline in the ATNR at the end of the second month freed the arms from their initial asymmetrical-unilateral organization and gave rise to bilateral movements with greater haptic and visual exploration of both hands at midline. Finally, by 4 months, unilateral reaching reappeared with the head oriented at midline.

Recent studies provided further support to the hypothesis that the transition from prereaching to goal-directed reaching is accompanied by a change in muscle synergies (Thelen & Spencer, 1998; van der Fits & Hadders-Algra, 1998). Thelen and Spencer (1998) reported that the transitions occurring between prereaching and goal-directed reaching movements were linked to the use of very different muscle combinations. Other researchers revealed that the organization of purposeful reaching begins weeks before infants are actually able to reach successfully (Bhat & Galloway, 2006; Bhat, Heathcock, & Galloway, 2005; Bhat, Lee, & Galloway, 2007). This group of researchers investigated how the presence or absence of a toy influenced the kinematics of infants' upper arm movements prior to the onset of voluntary reaching. They found that 8 to 10 weeks before the onset of reaching infants slowed down their movement in presence of a toy. Four to 6 weeks before the onset of purposeful reaching, they sped up their movement and brought their hand much closer to the toy, activating mainly their shoulder joint. Finally, by the time they were close to developing reaching, they began to make more frequent contacts with the toy.

Goal-directed reaching

Goal-directed reaching – the ability to attain a wanted toy successfully – emerges around 3 to 4 months. How are those patterns performed at first and what action problems do infants have to solve to make progress? Mainly due to Piaget's (1952) influence, a long-standing assumption was that vision was crucial for monitoring the hand step-by-step to the aimed target. Eye–hand coordination was considered a fundamental prerequisite for reaching development. Today, research has shown that vision is not so crucial in guiding early reaching. Instead, the emergence and development of goal-directed reaching is the product of complex dynamic organizations involving the arms, head, trunk, vision, and other senses. In order to reach, infants need to regulate the exchange of energy between muscles, limbs, and surroundings when one or both hands extend outward to approach the desired target and grasp it.

The argument used to stress the role of vision in the development of reaching was based mainly on the characteristics of the hand trajectory to the toy. Infants' first hand trajectories to the target are very discontinuous. Then, toward the end of the first year, they smooth out, become straighter and more direct (Thelen et al., 1996; von Hofsten, 1979, 1991; von Hofsten & Rönnqvist, 1993). The old assumption was that those dis-continuities in trajectory were the product of continuous visual corrections of the hand in order to guide it progressively closer to the toy (Bushnell, 1985). But Clifton, Muir, Ashmead, and Clarkson (1993) testing 6- to 25-week-old infants while reaching for glowing objects in the dark, revealed that infants do not need to see their hand to contact the object. This is clear evidence that vision is not needed to guide the hand to the target.

If early discontinuities in trajectory are not the product of visual guidance, why do they occur? An appealing explanation could be that they are the product of infants' poor motor planning abilities. However, one may question whether motor planning alone is the cause of irregularities in trajectory. Highly discontinuous movements also arise in neonates, at an age when arm extensions are unlikely to be planned (von Hofsten & Rönnqvist, 1993). Moreover, modeling work by Out, Savelsbergh, van Soest, and Hopkins (1997) in 12- to 20-week-old infants indicated that movement distortions may arise from the lower level of the biomechanics of the articulated arm, instead of being the result of higher-level planning. This later finding is consistent with the complex systems theory, according to which smooth trajectories and consequently adequate planning may result from the ability to regulate the intrinsic dynamics (i.e., muscle stiffness) of the arms and shoulders in relation to muscle activation. Cognitive/motor planning alone would be of little help to the infant without the ability to regulate those bodily characteristics. A longitudinal study by Thelen et al. (1993) illustrated how trajectory discontinuities in early reaching are the product of the biomechanical and dynamic characteristics of the arm in motion. These investigators used what they called a multileveled approach to study the development of reaching in 4 infants from age 3 to 52 weeks. They measured the space-time characteristics of the movement, such as its trajectory, velocity, and their change over time, in relation to the underlying patterns of muscle activation that the infants used to generate and control their arm movement. They called these underlying patterns intrinsic dynamics. Consistent with the complex systems view, and the view conceiving the arm as a mass spring device, they found that the development of smoother trajectories with age resulted from the improved ability to coregulate muscle activation with muscle stiffness. During the first weeks of reaching, however, infants differed greatly in the strategies they adopted to solve this action problem. Two infants, who were very active, used too much muscle force to set the arm into motion and relatively too little muscle stiffness to damp the oscillatory flapping motions of the arm toward the target. This introduced huge distortions in the trajectory of the arm and hands, which ultimately lead to the discontinuous hand trajectories typically observed in infants' first weeks of reaching. The two other infants were much calmer and displayed much smoother and better controlled trajectories than those of the two active infants. The smoothness of their movement was a direct result of the lower energy level those infants used to activate their arm, but this was not a reflection of better arm control. Less muscle activation made it more challenging to lift the arm against gravity. Thus, learning to move an arm toward an endpoint and regulating its trajectory was not simply done by visual monitoring or cognitive planning; it involved being able to coregulate the level of muscle coactivation and muscle stiffness in order to lift the arm against gravity and prevent excessive force momentum, arising from the movement itself, throwing the arm off trajectory.

A simpler way to look at this action problem is to reason in term of the movement speed that arises from muscle activation. When young infants move their arms vigorously before initiating a reaching movement, high movement speed results. High movement speed, in turn, will perturb the infant's ability to properly regulate the forces generated by this motion and stabilize the reach. To understand how infants' arm control in reaching developed in the first year, Thelen et al. (1996) further analyzed the reaches of those 4 infants in terms of movement speed. Analyses showed that irregularities of the reaching trajectory were consistently related to fast movements. The relationship existed for reaches and spontaneous nonreaching movements, and was most clearly shown during periods when infants were particularly active. These active periods all occurred before infants were able to control the reach adequately. According to Thelen et al. (1996), during those active and nonactive periods, infants explored the range and boundaries of their arm movement, which, in turn, allowed them to fine-tune their arm system and regulate movement speed better once they discovered how to configure the reach. The timing and length of the active periods varied among infants, but arm control considerably improved for all infants after the last active period, which occurred between 30 and 36 weeks of age. Interestingly, by that time, infants can sit alone (Rochat, 1992), begin to crawl (Goldfield, 1993), and perceive that they can reach further away by extending the arm and leaning forward (Rochat & Goubet, 1995). By 12 months, they begin extending their reaching distance using an implement such as a spoon (McKenzie, Skouteris, Day, Hartman, & Yonas, 1993) and by 15 months, they have developed precision reaching, which is the age and kind of task for which vision begins to play a more critical role (Carrico & Berthier, 2008).

The improved postural stability acquired by the end of the first year, due to the discovery of new synergies for the trunk, arms, and shoulders, is likely to underlie the development of each of these skills (van der Fits & Hadders-Algra, 1998). We also know that, by this time, infants are quite able to organize their body and arm movements in a flexible manner such that changing body orientations and gravitational forces will not perturb their movement. The muscle organization needed to reach forward when sitting up is quite different from that required when reaching upward from a supine position. A number of studies (Carvalho, Tudella, & Savelsbergh, 2007; Out, van Soest, Savelsbergh, & Hopkins, 1998; van der Fits, Klip, van Eykem, & Hadders-Algra, 1999) found that, at the onset of reaching, young infants are more successful at contacting the target when seated than when supine, because moving their arm against gravity makes arm control more challenging. By the age of 5 to 6 months these differences in performance disappear. Over time, infants learn to modulate their head, neck, trunk, and arm muscle synergies to respond to the different ways postural orientation and gravitational force interact with arm movements (Carvalho, Tudella, Caljouw, & Savelsbergh, 2008; van der Fits et al., 1999).

Bimanual coordination

In many tasks, one hand may be used to hold an object, say, a cup, while the other hand is performing some other joint activity on the object, say, stirring the coffee in the cup with a spoon. In other tasks, both hands may perform very similar actions such as clapping. In the first year of life, infants perform more similar than dissimilar actions when activating both hands at the same time. For example, they often reach for and grasp small objects with two hands even though they could grasp them with one hand, or they often extend both arms symmetrically toward the object along the midline despite making contact with the object with one hand only (Corbetta & Thelen, 1996; Corbetta et al., 2000; Fagard & Jacquet, 1996). Typically, infants do not begin to scale their bimanual activity to the size of objects until the second half of the first year (Corbetta et al.), and sometimes this ability does not appear until the beginning of the second year (Fagard & Jacquet). Early forms of bimanual activities involving a division and complementary coordination of hand roles also do not begin to emerge until the mid to end of the first year (Bojczyk & Corbetta, 2004; Kimmerle, Mick, & Michel, 1995; Fagard & Pezé, 1997). Why does it take so long for infants to adapt bimanual activity to the task at hand?

According to Corbetta and Thelen (1996), unimanual or bimanual patterns are carved out from a substrate of coordination tendencies that are prevalent in the system and often associated with other existing behaviors. For example, in neonates, unimanual arm movements occur by exploiting the ATNR when this response is prevalent in the system. Then, symmetrical bilateral movements emerge after the ATNR dissolves. Changes in interlimb patterning follow a similar principle. Patterns of interlimb coordination alternate frequently between bimanual and unimanual movements over the first year (Corbetta & Thelen, 1996; Gesell & Ames, 1947), although the precise timing between hands may vary depending on age (Goldfield & Michel, 1986). This alternation in patterning was also found to occur in nonreaching behaviors, though each infant follows an individual developmental time scale (Corbetta & Thelen, 1996). Despite developmental variations, Corbetta & Thelen always found a strong match between reaching and nonreaching movements. During the periods of bimanual reaching, high synchronous bimanual activity was also found in the nonreaching arm movements. When unilateral reaches predominated, synchronous activity in nonreaching movements was not found. It appeared that the forms of reaching exploited underlying patterns of interlimb coordination that were prevalent at the different times.

What makes some forms of coordination more prevalent at certain times of development? Several factors may operate on different time scales (Corbetta & Thelen, 1996). One factor is the energetic status of the infant. When young babies become excited, they channel a lot of energy to all their limbs, which makes it difficult to break movement coupling and move one arm only. Other factors include the particular gross motor skills that infants are developing (i.e., sitting, crawling, walking), the complexity of the bimanual skills being performed, and the task constraints such as the shape and size of the objects wanted. A study by Rochat (1992), for example, showed that independent sitters reached more frequently for small objects with one hand while same age nonsitters used more bimanual responses to reach for the same objects. The emergence of hands-and-knees crawling has also been shown to break infants' early bimanual reaching tendencies (Corbetta & Thelen, 2002; Goldfield, 1993), while the development of walking or scooting in a seated posture are associated with more two-handed reaching (Corbetta & Bojczyk, 2002; Corbetta, Williams, & Snapp-Childs, 2006). The explanation for these shifting tendencies in reaching seems to have its root in the upper arm pattern activities that infants are practicing when developing these locomotor skills (Corbetta et al., 2006). For example, when infants begin to crawl on hands and knees – activity that breaks the coupling patterns of the limbs to alternate movements – they begin to reach more with one hand and also begin to use either hand alternately, which temporarily hinders hand preference (Goldfield, 1993; Corbetta & Thelen, 1996). When infants learn to walk upright, or begin scooting on their buttocks using their arms in a coupled fashion to control balance and help create forward momentum, they also tend to use two hands for reaching (Corbetta & Bojczyk, 2002; Corbetta et al., 2006).

Gross motor skills learning are not the only factors affecting interlimb coordination. Fagard and Pezé (1997) showed that increase in bimanual reaching by the end of the first year of life coincides with success in bimanual tasks, such as taking a toy out of a container while lifting the lid with the other hand. Thus, bimanual reaching may have different origins at 6 months than at 11 and 12 months of age when bimanual responses become prevalent again (Corbetta & Bojczyk, 2002; Fagard & Pezé, 1997). Six-month-old infants may experience different motor constraints than 12-month-old infants when resorting to more coupled reaching (Corbetta et al., 2000). But, a recurrent theme is that bimanual reaching and the organization of the upper arm system is not independent from the head, trunk, and whole body organization.

Grasping

Grasping and object manipulation are important goals of reaching. Before infants can grasp objects, they traverse a short period between 15 and 18 weeks where they reach and touch objects but are unable to grasp them (von Hofsten & Lindhagen, 1979; Wimmers, Savelsbergh, Beek, & Hopkins, 1998). Wimmers et al., using catastrophe theory, demonstrated that the transition from touch to grasp involves a qualitative shift in behavior. The reason why infants only touch objects instead of grasping them at the onset of goal-directed reaching might be due to their difficulty in adjusting the hand to the target while controlling arm trajectory in approaching it. Grasping objects requires timed adjustments of the hand and grip configuration to the shape, size, and orientation of an object, all of which demand anticipatory abilities.

To study infants' anticipatory hand adjustments for grasping, Lockman, Ashmead, and Bushnell (1984) presented 5- and 9-month-old infants dowels oriented either vertically or horizontally. They found that 9-, but not 5-month-olds, adjusted the hand to the orientation of the dowel before touching it. Von Hofsten and Fazel-Zandy (1984), on the contrary, observed such adjustments at 18 weeks. In a subsequent study, von Hofsten and Rönnqvist (1988) discovered that 5-month-old infants started to close the hand around the object just before the hand encountered the object, while for 9- and 13-month-olds, the closing of the hand started much earlier during the movement approach. At the older ages, the opening of the hand was scaled to the size of the target, whereas this was not the case in the younger group. Finally, to test grasp anticipation more readily, Savelsbergh, von Hofsten, and Jonsson (1997) displaced a target to the side suddenly during reaching in 9-month-olds. They reasoned that a sudden change of target position would be more perturbing if the infants are anticipating the grasp because they would have to modify both the trajectory and the hand configuration. On the other hand, if infants are not anticipating the grasp, a change in object location would not be so detrimental because, in this case, the grasp is only planned after the reach has ended and the hand is touching the target. Their results confirmed their hypothesis. When the target was displaced, 9-month-olds who anticipate their grasp during the reach took more time to execute a reach and made more errors in touching an object. Witherington (2005) confirmed that prospective grasping control develops progressively from 5 to 7 months old. Like McCarty, Clifton, Ashmead, Lee, and Goubet (2001), Witherington contends that change in grasp control transitions from an initial tactual control toward a more prospective visual control, meaning that at 5 months, infants need to rely on touch once in contact with the object to orient their hand for grasping a rod, while by 7 months they can anticipate hand orientation based on visual information before touching the object.

This issue of how infants learn to adjust their grip to the shape, size, and orientation of objects based on changing sensory information is, however, controversial. Newell and colleagues (Newell, McDonald, & Baillargeon, 1993; Newell, Scully, McDonald, & Baillargeon, 1989) claim that infants can adapt their grip configurations to object size from the age of 4 months. Along the same lines, Barrett, Traupman, and Needham (2008) claim that such an ability exists even before infants are able to form a full grasp to pick up objects. Newell et al. (1989) showed that the grip patterns and number of fingers used to pick up cups of different sizes varied systematically in 4- to 8-month-olds. At all ages, infants used only a few fingers to pick up very small cups and proportionately increased the number of fingers used to grasp cups of increasing size, using up to 10 digits (2 hands) for cups that could not be picked up with one hand. These findings contrast dramatically with the research on bimanual reaching reported above and more classic reports showing that infants initially only touch or reach objects using undifferentiated palmar grasps (Halverson, 1931; von Hofsten & Lindhagen, 1979). Newell et al. (1989) contend that infants as young as 4 months old can differentiate their grip configuration because they rely essentially on haptic information to adjust their hand once in contact with the target. As they become older, infants rely more and more on visual information to anticipate their grasp before contacting the object. Newell and his colleagues see object size as a task constraint that affects the selection of a grip in a way that is similar for infants and adults.

This interpretation has, however, been challenged by Corbetta and colleagues (Corbetta & Snapp-Childs, 2009; Corbetta et al., 2000). These authors used solid objects and soft pompoms made of yarn of different sizes to assess infants' ability to rely on haptic information to adjust their grip configuration. They reasoned that if infants truly rely on touch to adjust their grip, they should always grasp the pompoms with one hand regardless of their size (pompoms, like pieces of cloth, can be handled with one hand), while they should show differentiated one and two-handed grips for the solid objects depending on their size. Their results did not support Newell's interpretation. They found that the young infants' reaching and grasping patterns were seemingly stereotyped – they either used bimanual or unimanual patterns consistently regardless of object solidity and size – and could not find evidence that they relied on touch for grasping. Only the older infants, the 8- and 9-month-olds, revealed the ability to scale their response to the object's physical properties and relied on touch occasionally to modify their grip. Corbetta et al.'s interpretation was that task constraints alone do not suffice to drive the selection of a motor response in young infants. Infants also bring to the task their own intrinsic motor constraints which can interfere with motor planning, as we discussed earlier in this chapter. According to these authors, increase in perceptual-motor mapping and the ability to scale movement to object properties evolves as infants become increasingly able to control and modulate these intrinsic motor tendencies. Taken together, these findings show that orientation of the hand and preparation of the grip based on visual information develops progressively as infants learn about their own action on objects. Part of this improvement may also result from better control of hand trajectory during reaching. And, as mentioned before, control of the movement of the hand goes along with stabilization of the head and torso for reaching, which in turn will facilitate picking up information to anticipate grasping (Bertenthal & von Hofsten, 1998).

Walking

As early as 6 months, infants may take their first assisted steps with a caretaker. At about 7 months, they may begin to stand alone, and at 8.5 months, they may take their first unaided steps (see Figure 5.2). Few infants reach these motor milestones at this early age. There is enormous variation among children. Some begin to walk with assistance as late as 14 months, stand alone at 17 months and take their first independent steps at 18 months (WHO Multicentre Growth Reference Study Group, 2006).

Humans are not the only species walking on two feet. Birds do too and apes sometimes walk upright. But the way humans walk is unique. The gait pattern consists of a long period, the stance, in which one leg supports the body, followed by a short period, the double support phase, in which both legs support the body. When one leg supports the body, the other leg swings forward like a regular pendulum, while the stance leg behaves like an inverted pendulum transporting the body's center of mass (COM) in the forward anterior-posterior direction (see Figure 5.3 and Figure 5.4). When the COM moves in the sagittal plane (a plane running from top to bottom dividing the body into a right and left side), it goes up and down, first against and then along the direction of gravity. The short double support phase begins when the heel of the swing leg strikes the ground, with the foot dorsi-flexing just before landing. This phase ends when the stance leg pushes

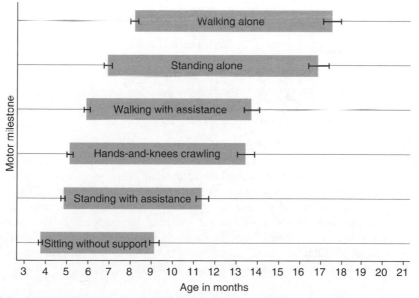

Reference: WHO Multicentre Growth Reference Study Group. WHO Motor Development Study: Windows of achievement for six gross motor development milestones. Acta Paediatrica Supplement 2006;450:86–95.

Figure 5.2   Overview of the development of locomotion from "sitting without support" to "walking alone." *Source*: WHO (2006).

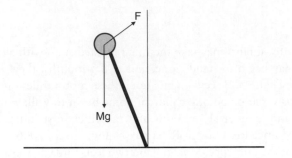

Figure 5.3 Schematic drawing of a simplified inverted pendulum system. Mg = mass x gravitational acceleration, F = muscular driving force; other parameters such as stiffness and damping are not presented in the figure. *Source*: Ulrich & Kubo (2005).

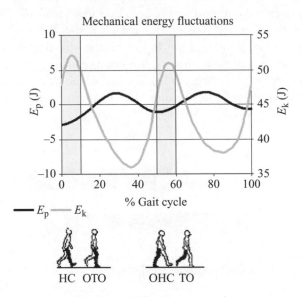

Figure 5.4 Schematic drawing of walking: different phases and energy recovery. Adult E_p and E_k oscillations are plotted as a function of gait cycle duration. The shaded area indicates the periods of double support. The IP mechanism, as observed in adult gait, shows an out-of-phase oscillation of kinetic and potential energy, allowing energy exchange to occur from Ep to Ek and partially from Ek to Ep. Though 70% of the required mechanical energy can be recovered due to this energy-saving mechanism, 30% of energy is lost and must be resupplied by the muscles. It is primarily used to redirect the centre of mass from one pendular arc to the next. HC, heel contact; OTO, opposite toe-off; OHC, opposite heel contact; TO, toe-off. *Source*: Adapted with permission from Hallemans, Aerts, Otten De Deyn, & De Clercq (2004).

off the ground by plantar-flexion of the foot at the ankle. The dorsi-flexion of the landing foot at the start of the double support period and the plantar-flexion of the other foot at the moment of push-off, make the COM roll over the new supporting foot. Overall, this is energetically a very economic way of transporting the body's COM in the sagittal plane.

The gait pattern of infants at the onset of independent walking bears some similarities to that of adults. Infant gait patterns also entail a 180° out of phase alternation between swing and stance legs, and the stance phase is also interspersed by a double support phase (see Figure 5.4). This pattern can already be observed in neonates when they are held upright allowing the feet to touch the ground. However, this early response resembles a reflex because it dissipates after about 2 months and returns later when aided stepping appears. Although the stepping looks automatic and rigid, some researchers surmised that the pattern was not quite a reflex. In a first study, Thelen and Fisher (1982) discovered that 3-month-old infants, who apparently had stopped stepping, were able to generate the pattern when immersed to the waist in a water basin which made the legs less heavy. In another assessment with younger infants who displayed the response, they found that stepping was hindered when they put a piece of lead under the infant's feet, making the leg heavier. The lead was of about the same amount of weight the body would have gained by the time stepping would have normally disappeared (Thelen, Fisher, & Ridley-Johnson, 1984). Both assessments demonstrated that the stepping reflex did not disappear as believed for a long time, but was temporarily hindered by the increasing mass of the body. The research also showed that the stepping pattern was not specific to the stimulation of the feet touching the ground. The same pattern occurred in infants kicking behavior when supine on a steady surface (Thelen & Fisher, 1983). Finally, in a longitudinal study, the pattern never disappeared during the whole first year of life when infants were held standing upright upon a treadmill (Thelen & Ulrich, 1991). The same pattern was shown to be present even when aided stepping appeared (Forssberg, 1985), but by then, the pattern occurred voluntarily, whereas in neonates it arose involuntarily.

Despite the fact that elicited stepping in neonates, on a treadmill or during aided walking, shows an alternation in leg patterning interspersed by short double support phases, this pattern differs significantly from the adult gait pattern, especially following the onset of independent locomotion (Bril & Brenière, 1989, 1992; Brenière, Bril & Fontaine, 1989; Forssberg, 1985; Ivanenko et al., 2004; Kimura et al., 2005; Kubo & Ulrich, 2006a). It takes 4 to 6 years of walking experience before children walk the way adults do (Brenière & Bril, 1998). During the first month of independent walking, step length is short, step frequency and progression velocity are low, step width is large, and the cadence or rhythm at which successive steps follow one another is irregular. The foot shows no heel strike on landing and no toe-off on push-off. Typically, infants' swing leg lands on the ground either with a flat foot or toes first. During the double support phase, infants keep the feet on the ground for a much longer period before generating the next step, and they walk leaning forward. In addition, the movements of the shank and thigh are slow, short, and irregular, and their relative phasing is different from that of infants who have 4 to 5 weeks of walking experience (Clark & Phillips, 1993). In walking, both the shank and thigh oscillate forward and backward. A major difference is that, in adults, the thigh leads the shank at the start of the step cycle at toe-off, and then the relative phasing changes during the cycle such that, at heel strike, the shank leads the thigh. When infants begin to walk, the phasing of the shank and thigh stays the same over the whole cycle. Although the movement and coordination of the shank and thigh change during the first weeks of independent walking, their angular displacement in relation to their angular velocity still shows the typical, albeit unstable profile of a limit cycle attractor seen at walking onset (Clark & Phillips, 1993). Also, during the first weeks of walking experience, the arms are maintained in a high guard position, with the hands up at or above the shoulder level, and the head and trunk both sway sideways as well as backward and forward (Ledebt, Bril, & Wiener-Vacher, 1995, Kubo & Ulrich, 2006b).

After the first month of walking experience, there is considerable improvement in each of the above described behavioral characteristics. Walking develops following two phases (Bril & Brenière, 1992; Clark & Phillips, 1993; Ledebt et al., 1995; Kimura et al., 2005). The first is a short phase spanning 1 to 2 months from the onset of upright locomotion and displays the most dramatic changes with respect to the above mentioned gait characteristics. The second is much longer and only at the age of 4 to 6 years does the gait pattern become similar to that of adults. In this phase, changes with respect to gait parameters are much more gradual.

What underlies developmental changes in gait and what causes the transition from the first to the second phase? Some researchers have attributed this to maturational changes in the neural circuits that control the behavior. According to Forssberg (1985), up to the emergence of independent stepping, a central pattern generator, at or below the brain stem and present at birth, controls stepping. After that, changes in walking are driven by infants' improved upright postural stability, increased muscular strength, and gradual neuronal changes.

Posture plays a central role in infants' gait development. Postural changes in gait occur within weeks of the onset of locomotion, the most readily observable being the lowering of the arms from a high guard position to the sides of the body. Maybe by keeping their arms in high guard during early walking, infants may freeze the degrees of freedom of the arms so as not to compromise their already unstable upright posture further by arm sway (Ledebt, 2000). On the other hand, the high guard posture of the arms raises the center of mass of the body, which ultimately can have a detrimental effect on the stability of the posture. This negative effect may be counteracted because raising the arms also reduces the sideways oscillations of the upper body and helps stabilize the posture (Ledebt et al., 1995; Kubo & Ulrich, 2006b). This effect is similar to more experienced walkers, such as children or adults, who raise their arms when walking on a beam to stabilize their posture and control balance.

Another important postural change occurring after walking onset is linked to the oscillations of the upper body. The upper part of the body sways in the fronto-parallel plane during walking, but also, the hips and upper part of the body show considerable up and down movements (Ledebt et al., 1995). Particularly, when the COM is transferred from one leg to the other, extra muscle forces from the knees and hips are needed to prevent the body from falling. Bril and Brenière (1989) discovered that during the first 5 months of independent walking, infants actually "walk by falling" (Bril & Brenière, 1989, 1992; Brenière & Bril, 1998). They concluded that infants need a relatively long double support period to regain stability before the next step is initiated. After 1 month of walking experience, gait velocity increases considerably, steps become longer, less wide, and stepping frequency is higher. Despite these changes, children still lack the muscular strength to counteract gravitational forces sufficiently when transferring the COM from one leg to the other. This lack of sufficient muscular force in the legs lasts approximately until the age of 5 (Brenière & Bril).

Other factors linked more specifically to the cooperation between the different sensory systems (visual, proprioceptive, and vestibular systems) also play a critical role. In particular, the sensory systems need to be tuned such that they can contribute to the control of the spatiotemporal relation between body segments and the environment (Ledebt et al., 1995).

As we know, from a complex systems perspective, when we try to understand how the body achieves functional goals, and how it changes over developmental time, we cannot find the answer by looking only at one single factor or by attributing a privileged status to one factor (Thelen & Smith, 1994). Walking emerges as a behavior because of the multiple interconnections between contributing factors. How do infants assemble such a system? How do they discover its parameter settings? And how do they fine-tune it over developmental time? The key to these issues rests in the energy that needs to be delivered to move the body mass and walk. This energy arises from the cooperation of the many body parts (arms, trunk, legs, muscles, brain, sensory systems) that work together in interaction with the environment (surface characteristics, gravity, atmospheric conditions, etc.) to accomplish the task. The energy for walking is delivered by two systems working in concert. The first is an inverted pendulum system over the stance leg (Cavagna, Saibene, & Margaria, 1963, Cavagna, Thys, & Zamboni, 1976; see Figure 5.3). After heel strike, the leg becoming the stand leg, moves in an anterior-posterior direction. This movement displaces the COM over the foot in an arc. Thus, the movement of the leg displaces the COM forward and also upward during the first half of the stance period and downward during the second half. In a gravity field, the upward movement of the COM converts kinetic energy into potential energy. This potential energy can be used for the second half of the stance, as in a pendulum, to swing the other leg further forward, which in turn, converts potential energy back into kinetic energy because the COM goes back downward (see Figure 5.4). This conversion of energy reduces the amount of work that needs to be delivered by the muscles. Experienced walkers can recover up to 60–70% of the total energy, depending on the speed of walking. The amount of energy recovery forms an inverted U-shaped function of the speed of walking. Most of the energy loss arises when the COM is shifted from one leg to the other (Kuo, Donelan, & Ruina, 2005). To compensate for the loss of energy, the muscular system needs to provide an impulse at each new step. This is provided by the inverted pendulum system at the end of the double support period when the COM is transferred to the other leg (Holt, Hamill, & Andres, 1990; Holt, Jeng, & Fetters, 1991).

The second system is the muscular system which behaves as an oscillatory spring system. Together, the inverted pendulum and the muscular systems form a spring-loaded inverted pendulum system (SLIP). From biomechanics and ordinary experience with playground swings we know that the timing of a push is an important factor allowing a pendulum swing of maximum amplitude with the least amount of energy. The push is most effective when it is given at the right time. Only a tiny push is needed when the swing reaches the highest point of its trajectory to increase the amplitude of the swing. This, in physics, is called the *resonance frequency* of the swing and it requires a minimum amount of energy. Pushes that are faster or slower in time will lead to smaller arcs, no matter how forceful the push may be. The same principles work for the inverted pendulum. The muscular spring system has to deliver its push at the resonance frequency of the inverted pendulum, which depends on the pendulum length. How do both systems get attuned to each other? The length of the leg cannot be adapted, but the muscles that deliver the push during foot contact can adapt their springiness by modifying their stiffness. To ensure that the inverted pendulum and the muscle spring system cooperate in time, the stiffness of the muscles should be adapted to the natural frequency of the inverted pendulum system.

Insight into the principles of the SLIP system that deliver the means for walking has led researchers to investigate several interesting questions about walking and its development. One general question relates to mechanical energy recovery as a function of walking experience. Other questions that dig more deeply into the system, concern children's developing sensitivity to the SLIP system and its parameter setting, in particular their timing of the push and their ability to adapt muscular stiffness to the resonance frequency of the inverted pendulum. We confine the discussion to these two.

It takes much walking experience before children's recovery of energy approximates that of adults. Several studies report recovery rates of about 40% in toddlers compared to 60–70% in adults (Hallemans, Aerts, Otten, De Deyn, & De Clercq, 2004; Ivanenko et al., 2004; Kimura et al.. 2005; Kubo & Ulrich, 2006a), although the variation is high. Recovery rates do not become similar to those of adults until children are 4 to 5 years of age. Holt, Saltzman, Ho, Kubo and Ulrich (2006) showed that 1 month of walking experience was sufficient for infants to discover how to supply the pendulum system with new energy at each step. They investigated infants' discovery of the timing of the push at landing of the foot from the onset of walking and over the next 6 months of walking experience. Single-peaked accelerations of the COM in the anterior-posterior plane first appeared after infants had 1 month of walking experience. They occurred within 200 ms of initial foot contact. But, fine-tuning of the stiffness of the muscular system that delivers the impulse to the pendulum-system did not occur until the 7th month of independent walking (Holt, Saltzman, Ho, & Ulrich, 2007). According to Holt et al. (2007), below the age of 3 years, toddlers are unable to fine-tune the muscular system to the pendulum system. Holt et al.'s study involved 7 infants during their first 7 months of independent walking and also addressed gait parameters such as walking speed, stride length, and stride frequency in addition to stiffness. Consistent with earlier studies, results revealed a considerable increase in walking speed, stride length, and stride frequency after 1 month of walking experience. During the first month of independent walking, stiffness was low. It increased during the second month, which also contributed to the increase in stride frequency and gait velocity, but remained too high over the subsequent months of walking. Together, these results confirm earlier conclusions of a two-stage process in which infants first discover the pendulum system and how to energize it (Ivanenko et al., 2004; Kubo & Ulrich, 2006a), and then work on how to fine-tune it. But it takes a few more years before they are able to make the different oscillatory systems cooperate smoothly with each other.

During the first months of walking, children explore different strategies before they discovery the pendulum mechanism (McCollum, Holroyd, & Castelfranco, 1995; Snapp-Childs & Corbetta, 2009). A reason for this delay might be linked to insufficient dynamical postural stability, which may result from several interacting factors. Among these are: insufficient muscular strength; a relatively high location of the COM, which becomes less critical during the first months of independent walking due to a rapid growth of the lower trunk segments compared to the upper trunk, neck, and head segments (Chester & Jensen, 2005); and the gait pattern itself. Ulrich, Haehl, Buzzi, Kubo, and Holt (2004) found a relation between insufficient muscle strength and stiffness when they compared walking of normal children and children with Down syndrome. Children walked over ground at a self-selected pace, and on a treadmill at speeds slower and faster than their normal speed over ground. To compensate for their hypotonic muscles which generate less force and jeopardize stability, children with Down syndrome (DS) reacted to the faster speed of the treadmill with higher muscle stiffness than normal children. Children with DS also face more problems in stabilizing their limbs at the early stage of walking than normally developing children. Independent walking develops approximately a year later in children with DS (Henderson, 1986). Moreover, their development shows large discrepancies relative to that of normally developing children after 1 month of walking experience. At the onset of walking, all children show a relatively large COM-displacement in the mediolateral direction (Hallemans et al., 2004; Ivanenko et al., 2004; Kubo & Ulrich, 2006a). Thus, presumably, children prefer a larger step width to compensate for this threat on stability. Kubo and Ulrich (2006a) discovered that, after approximately 1 month of walking experience, step width decreased considerably in normally developing children but did not or did so less in children with DS. Moreover, the COM-displacement in the mediolateral, compared to the anterior–posterior, direction remained high in children with DS compared to the other group of children, and the ability to recover mechanical energy in the forward direction was low. The weaker limbs of children with DS increase their problem of exploring and discovering the mechanisms of walking and their parameter settings.

Object Manipulation: Tool Use

By the end of the first year, tool use plays a central role in children's developing action repertoire. It offers them unique ways to expand their capacity to act and enables transference of cultural knowledge and skills. How does this expansion take place? We answer this question by focusing mainly on the theoretical perspective offered by the complex systems view.

In the past, cognitive theorists have attributed the development of tool use to the emergence of means–end abilities and various cognitive competences underlying them. Among these competences are physical knowledge of objects (Baillargeon, 1993; Tomasello, 1998; Willatts, 1999), representational skills (Piaget, 1954), attention (Boudreau & Bushnell, 2000; Bushnell, 1985), and the ability to resolve conflicts between goals and subgoals (Baillargeon, 1998; Willatts, 1999). Action-oriented developmental psychologists, on the other hand, have pointed to children's growing manual skill and dexterity (E. J. Gibson & Pick, 2000; Lockman, 2000; Smitsman, 1997; Smitsman & Bongers, 2003). Similarly to the manual behaviors described in the previous sections, tool use is fueled by the attainment of motor milestones such as sitting, standing alone, and object manipulation. Improved sitting balance, for example, enables infants to lean forward and sideways which expands the reaching space (Rochat & Goubet, 1995).

Postural balance when sitting and standing also considerably improves children's flexibility in manipulating objects (Bertenthal & von Hofsten, 1998), which is essential for tool use. Furthermore, postural control when standing and walking frees the hands for manipulating objects and further expands the manual capacity.

The complex systems view has shed new light on how the above developments give rise to the emergence and progression of tool use (Lockman, 2000; Smitsman, 1997; Smitsman & Bongers, 2003; Smitsman, Cox, & Bongers, 2005; Smitsman & Cox, 2008). It addresses how geometrical, dynamical, and information gathering resources for action underlie tool use and also points to the new behavioral patterns that emerge when a person discovers these resources and learns to take advantage of them. Change can occur instantaneously when an object is held, but it also requires some insights. Choosing and using a tool involves understanding what resources arise from holding the tool and what new goals can be attained with them. It also involves knowing how to take advantage of those resources to attain these goals by setting appropriate parameters for the new action system (Smitsman & Cox, 2008). New resources arise, for example, when a stick is held to form a new "arm + stick" system. Holding the stick instantaneously extends the arm in space and changes the biomechanical resources of the arm system. The length of the stick and its own mass and inertia add to the geometrical and dynamical properties of the limb carrying the stick. Together, these changes enable the stick-holder to access and act on objects and surfaces over a longer distance, and with greater impulse. Thus, tool use changes the boundaries between the body and its environment (Smitsman, 1997) and the change of action potential it encompasses entails opportunities for the discovery of new affordances.

The means–end insight, and accordingly the parameter setting that is needed to mobilize and take advantage of the new tool-related resources, involves two reciprocal relations (Smitsman & Cox, 2008). These are key elements in the new child, tool, and target system. Whether a child will transform a potential tool object into an effective means to an end depends on the parameters that are set for two relations and their control (Smitsman et al., 2005). The first one concerns the *tool-to-target* relation and forms the connection of the tool object with the target object. The second one is the *actor-to-tool* relation and forms the connection of the body and tool.

Control of the tool-to-target relation requires physical knowledge of the objects concerned. However, to guide the action, this knowledge does not exclusively concern the objects *per se* (i.e., their sizes, shapes, and material properties). Rather, it needs to be related to the events themselves and the physical relations between objects that unfold when objects of certain sizes, shapes, and material properties interact with one another (Smitsman, DeJonckheere, & de Wit, 2009). Some researchers coined the term topology to qualify the functional tool-to-target relation (Smitsman & Bongers, 2003; Smitsman, Bongers, & Cox, 2005). Other researchers use the term tool–environment interface to denote the same relation (Wagman & Carello, 2004; Wagman & Taylor, 2004). This relation is critical and constrains fundamentally the possibilities for tool use. A change of topology can change a tool into a different tool. For instance, a change in the location of a target-object from being enclosed inside the hook of a cane to being located outside of the hook turns the cane from a pulling instrument into a pushing instrument. The

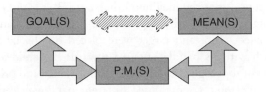

Figure 5.5 Schematic drawing of the interconnection of goals, means, and parameter settings. The dashed arrow indicates a relation of potential means to goals. Appropriate parameter settings transform potential means into actual means.

knowledge also has to be embodied because of the reciprocity between the tool-to-target and actor-to-tool relation. The tool-to-target relation constrains the actor-to-tool relation and the actor-to-tool relation determines which tool-to-target relation can be realized. Therefore, for realizing an intended tool-to-target relation, the child needs to foresee these constraints prospectively and control the actor-to-tool relation in grasping and holding a tool object. For instance, hitting a ball with the side of a stick, or poking the tip of the stick into a hole are different tool-to-target relations that put different constraints on the grip, arm, and body postures. The feel of a tool object in the hand needs to be an intrinsic part of the tool-to-target relation that can be accomplished and should constantly be focused on this relation.

A question central to the study of the development of tool use concerns the evolution of the actor, tool, and target system as a function of various tool uses, children's growing experiences with objects, events they are involved in, and control of those events by manipulation of objects. This question concerns the interconnection of end states, potential means for modifying the action system objects furnish, and parameter settings that turn potential means into effective means. It is our guess that means–end insights involve the system as a whole, and not just particular components of it, such as physical knowledge of objects per se (see Figure 5.5). The discovery of new means objects may furnish depends on the parameters the child sets for both relations the objects are involved in: the tool-to-target relation as well as the actor-to-tool. A different parameter setting for each of these relations can lead to new and unexpected end states for the same objects.

Several studies show that toddlers attend to the tool-to-target relation, the actor-to-tool relation, and their parameter setting when manipulating objects to change the state of another object (Cox & Smitsman, 2006a, 2006b, McCarty, Clifton, & Collard, 1999, 2001). However, sometimes both relations are in conflict due to the multiple sources of information that are available at the same time and can affect children's choices. That is, the actor-to-tool relation may afford a parameter setting, due, for instance, to a tool-object's position, shape, and size, that conflicts with that of the tool-to-target relation that needs to be established after the tool-object has been grasped. Such a conflict may lead to awkward tool uses or even a loss of sight of the tool function an object affords. Support for this assertion has already come from earlier studies on tool use such as the famous primate studies of Köhler (1925), Richardson (1932), Bates, Carlson-Luden, and Bretherton (1980), and more recently van Leeuwen, Smitsman, and van Leeuwen (1994).

Van Leeuwen et al. found that the likelihood that 1- to 3-year-old children would grasp a rake to bring a target object nearby depended on the distance and orientation of the rake to the target object. Tool and target were placed on the table in front of them, the rake within reach with its handle oriented towards the child and the target object beyond reach. Different topological combinations of distance and orientation of the hook of the rake to the target object represented different parameter settings of the tool-to-target relation. When the rake's hook enclosed or nearly enclosed the target object, children easily grasped the rake by its handle and pulled the target closer. However, when the topology needed to be changed by rotating the hook and/or displacing the rake over a larger distance to enclose the target with the rake's hook, children seemed to be unable to identify its function. They leaned forward as far as possible and unsuccessfully tried to grasp the target by hand. Cox and Smitsman (2006a, 2006b) further confirmed that children's attention is directed to the topology. Their movement of the tool-object directly derived from the topology they intended to realize. When the goal changed and they had to switch to a different topology and parameter setting, this complicated the task. In another hook use study (Smitsman & Cox, 2008), 3-year-old children correctly placed a target object either within or beyond a hook when they had to either pull the object near or push it away (like a croupier). When, however, after a few trials, the target destination changed from further away to nearby or vice versa and they had to switch the topology, they persevered in the original topology. In another task, similar perseverative behaviors occurred when the choice concerned the hand for grasping the tool.

Tool use is a multistep process. Choices about the actor-to-tool relation need to prepare control of the tool-to-target relation. McCarty, Clifton, and Collard (1999, 2001) showed that prospective control imposes problems on infants and toddlers. Their task required 9-, 14-, and 19-month-old children to unimanually grasp a spoon filled with food and subsequently transport it to and empty it into the mouth. The spoon was placed on a support in front of the child at midline, and in the fronto-parallel plane. On some trials the handle pointed to the right, on other trials it pointed to the left. When the handle pointed away from the preferred hand, 9-month-olds, mostly choose the preferred hand for grasping the spoon, leading to grips on the bowl instead of the handle, or awkward ulnar grips (the little finger close to the bowl instead of the thumb), but, at 19 months, children selected a hand and grip that allowed them to adequately control the orientation of the spoon's bowl when transporting the food to the mouth. Hand choices and grips of 14-month-old children were in between those of the 9 and 19 months.

Control of the tool-to-target relation may also be achieved by changing the parameter setting for the tool-to-actor relation when control of the tool-to-target relation requires such a change. Grasping and holding a tool changes the task situation and furnishes new information for how to set the tool-to-target relation. Cox and Smitsman (2006a, b) found that 3-year-old children flexibly switched the parameter setting for the actor-to-tool relation such that it more adequately prepared the parameter setting for the tool-to-target relation by switching the hand choice. Such a switch was hardly found in 2-year-old children, who persevered in their hand choice and grip. These results show that planning is a dynamical affair and that with age children become more flexible in sequencing activities to attain an intended goal.

Final Remarks

Recently, the significance of action for children's development has been appraised by researchers from various disciplines (e.g., Thompson, 2007). Studies on action, perception, imitation, and discovery of the mirror neuron system among others have shown that the meaning of action for development extends well beyond that of reaching motor milestones or attaining physical skills *per se*. Action is also intrinsically social. From birth onwards, by collaborative action, children learn to understand and appreciate the world, other people, and themselves. Although this chapter focused mainly on the action problems that infants must solve in relation to learning to reach, grasp, walk, and manipulate objects, it is clear that these patterns develop within a social context. Here, we briefly touch on this issue.

Imitation is one of the first forms of collaborative action with others (see chapter 11 this volume). It is present at birth, and develops in concert with perception, action skills, and the understanding of the causal structure of tasks and events. Meltzoff (2007) nicely phrased the meaning of being engaged in the same action as the discovery of another person as one that is "like me" and myself as one that is "like him or her." Action is the primary form of communication before language develops and continues to be an important means for relating to others after language develops in infancy and childhood. Action also forms the underpinning of language development and leads to physical understanding and symbolic thought. Further elaborating the relation between action development, communication, social and physical understanding, and symbolic thought extends far beyond the scope of this chapter. We hope, however, that the concepts, research, and insights we have presented will stimulate new questions and foster research in these important areas.

Another topic of interest which deserves more discussion is the planning of action. Reaching an intended end state involves much more than performing a single movement such as extending an arm, or sequencing movements such as stepping. Often multiple actions need to be interconnected over time to attain a goal, where the earlier actions prepare for the later ones. The time-dependent organization of these actions requires anticipation and planning. In our foregoing discussion, we have shown that the future directedness of action is already present in the early often jerky activities of infants. When action skills develop, future directedness develops. What we lack are theories and research on how this development takes place. We doubt that traditional theories that conceive planning as a static affair will suffice. Such theories face the paradox of how a system that is static (goal) can gear another system (action) to a future that is fundamentally dynamic. This will make them inadequate to address how behavioral sequencing can adequately take advantage of upcoming and sometimes unforeseeable circumstances without losing sight of the goal the system intends to attain. In our view, one promising avenue is to theorize on the action choice process we mentioned earlier when discussing tool use. As we explained, this involves decisions about goals, means, and parameter settings. A few years ago, Thelen and her colleagues (Thelen, Schöner, Scheier, & Smith, 2001) presented a dynamical field approach, which conceptualized planning as a dynamic affair and revealed that the action outcome was influenced by multiple sources of information (see Schöner & Dineva, 2007, for a recent overview). Their research concerned the planning of a reach in the Piagetian A-not-B task and the perseverative tendencies of 8- to 12-month-old infants to continue reaching to A on B trials (the so called A-not-B error; see chapter 6 this volume). This approach has been extended since to other tasks (i.e., tool use, Smitsman & Cox, 2008). Tool use offers a rich platform to study action planning as a multistep problem. Using the dynamical field approach, one can study the dynamics of planning in actions that encompass several steps and capture how the system can maintain its intended end state, while at the same time switching parameter settings or means in response to upcoming circumstances (see Smitsman, Cox, & Bongers, 2005; Smitsman & Cox, 2008).

References

Adolph, K. E. (1997). Learning in the development of infant locomotion. *Monographs of the Society for Research in Child Development, 62*, 1–140.

Adolph, K. E., & Berger, S. (2006). Motor development. In D. Kuhn, R. Siegler, S. Robert, W. Damon, & R. M. Lerner (Eds.), *Handbook of child psychology: Vol. 2, Cognition, perception, and language* (pp. 161–213). Hoboken, NJ: Wiley.

Baillargeon, R. (1993). The object concept revisited: New directions in the investigation of infants' physical knowledge. In C. E. Granrud (Ed.), *Visual perception and cognition in infancy* (pp.265–315). Hillsdale, NJ: Erlbaum.

Baillargeon, R. (1998). Infants' understanding of the physical world. In M. Sabourin & F. Craik (Eds.), *Advances in Psychological Science, Vol 2: Biological and Cognitive Aspects* (pp. 503–529). Hove, England: Psychology Press/Erlbaum.

Barrett, T. M., Traupman, E., & Needham, A. (2008). Infants' visual anticipation of object structure in grasp planning. *Infant Behavior and Development, 31*, 1–9.

Bates, E., Carlson-Luden, V., & Bretherton, I. (1980). Perceptual aspects of tool-using in infancy. *Infant Behavior and Development, 3*, 181–190.

Bernstein, N. (1967). *The co-ordination and regulation of movements.* Oxford: Pergamon Press.

Bernstein, N. (1996). On dexterity and its development. In M. L. Latash & M. T. Turvery (Eds.), *Dexterity and its development* (pp. 3–244). Mahwah, NJ: Erlbaum.

Bertenthal, B. I., & von Hofsten, C. (1998). Eye, head and trunk control: The foundation for manual development. *Neuroscience and Biobehavioral Reviews, 22*, 515–520.

Berthouze, L., & Goldfield, E. C. (2008). Assembly tuning and transfer of action systems in infants and robots. *Infant and Child Development, 17*, 25–42.

Bhat, A. N., & Galloway, J. C. (2006). Toy-oriented changes during early arm movements: Hand kinematics. *Infant Behavior and Development, 29*, 358–372.

Bhat, A. N., Heathcock, J., & Galloway, J. C. (2005). Toy-oriented changes in hand and joint kinematics during the emergence of purposeful reaching. *Infant Behavior and Development, 28*, 445–465.

Bhat, A. N., Lee, H. M., & Galloway, J. C. (2007). Toy-oriented changes in early arm movement: II. Joint kinematics. *Infant Behavior and Development, 30*, 307–324.

Bojczyk, K. E., & Corbetta, D. (2004). Object retrieval in the first year of life: Learning effects of task exposure and box transparency. *Developmental Psychology, 40*, 54–66.

Boudreau J. P., & Bushnell, E. W. (2000). Spilling thoughts: Configuring attentional resources in infants' goal-directed actions. *Infant Behavior and Development, 23*, 543–566.

Brenière, Y., & Bril, B. (1998). Development of postural control of gravity forces in children during the first 5 years of walking. *Experimental Brain Research, 121,* 255–262.

Brenière, Y., Bril, B., & Fontaine, R. (1989). Analysis of the transition from upright stance to the steady state locomotion in children with under 200 days of autonomous walking. *Journal of Motor Behavior, 21,* 20–37.

Bril, B., & Brenière, Y. (1989). Steady-state velocity and temporal structure of gait during the first six months of autonomous walking. *Human Movement Science, 8,* 99–122.

Bril, B., & Brenière, Y. (1992). Postural requirements and progression velocity in young walkers. *Journal of Motor Behavior, 24,* 105–116.

Bushnell, E. W. (1985). The decline of visually guided reaching during infancy. *Infant Behavior and Development, 8,* 139–155.

Carrico, R. L., & Berthier, N. E. (2008). Vision and precision reaching in 15-month-old infants. *Infant Behavior and Development, 31,* 62–70.

Carvalho, R. P., Tudella, E., Caljouw, S. R., & Savelsbergh, G. J. P. (2008). Early control of reaching: Effects of experience and body orientation. *Infant Behavior and Development, 31,* 23–33.

Carvalho, R. P., Tudella, E., & Savelsbergh, G. J. P. (2007). Spatio-temporal parameters in infant's reaching movements are influenced by body orientation. *Infant Behavior and Development, 30,* 26–35.

Cavagna, G. A., Saibene, F. P., & Margaria, R. (1963). External work in walking. *Journal of Applied Physiology, 18,* 1–9.

Cavagna, G. A., Thys, Z. A., & Zamboni, A. (1976). The sources of external work in walking and running. *Journal of Physiology, 262,* 639–657.

Chester, V. L., & Jensen, R. K. (2005). Changes in infant segment inertias during the first three months of independent walking. *Dynamic Medicine, 4,* 9.

Chiel, H. J., & Beer, R. D. (1997). The brain has a body: Adaptive behavior emerges from interactions of nervous system, body and environment. *Trends in Neurosciences, 20,* 553–557.

Clark, J. E., & Phillips, S. J. (1993). A longitudinal study of intralimb coordination in the first year of independent walking: A dynamical systems analysis. *Child Development, 64,* 1143–1157.

Clifton, R. K., Muir, D. W., Ashmead, D. H., & Clarkson, M. G. (1993). Is visually guided reaching in early infancy a myth? *Child Development, 64,* 1099–1110.

Corbetta, D. (2009). Brain, body, and mind: Lessons from infant motor development. In J. P. Spencer, M. Thomas, & J. McClelland (Eds.), *Toward a unified theory of development? Connectionism and dynamic systems theory re-considered* (pp. 51–66). New York: Oxford University Press.

Corbetta, D., & Bojczyk, K. (2002). Infants return to two-handed reaching when they are learning to walk. *Journal of Motor Behavior, 34,* 83–95.

Corbetta, D., & Snapp-Childs, W. (2009). Seeing and touching: The role of sensory-motor experience on the development of infant reaching. *Infant Behavior and Development, 32,* 44–58.

Corbetta, D., & Thelen, E. (1996). The developmental origins of bimanual coordination: A dynamic perspective. *Journal of Experimental Psychology: Human Perception and Performance, 22,* 502–522.

Corbetta, D., & Thelen, E. (2002). Behavioral fluctuations and the development of manual asymmetries in infancy: Contribution of the dynamic systems approach. In S. J. Segalowitz & I. Rapin (Eds.), *Handbook of neuropsychology, Vol. 8: Child neuropsychology, part I* (pp. 309–328). Amsterdam: Elsevier.

Corbetta, D., Thelen, E., & Johnson, K. (2000). Motor constraints on the development of perception–action matching in infant reaching. *Infant Behavior and Development, 23,* 351–374.

Corbetta, D., Williams, J., & Snapp-Childs, W. (2006). Plasticity in the development of handedness: Evidence from normal development and early asymmetric brain injury. *Developmental Psychobiology, 48,* 460–471.

Cox, R. F. A., & Smitsman, A. W. (2006a). Action planning in young children's tool use. *Developmental Science, 9,* 628–641.

Cox, R. F. A., & Smitsman, A. W. (2006b). The planning of tool-to-object relations in young children. *Developmental Psychobiology, 48,* 178–186.

Cox, R. F. A., & Smitsman, A. W. (2008). Towards an embodiment of goals. *Theory and Psychology, 18,* 317–339.

Elsner, B., & Hommel, B. (2001). Effect anticipation and action control. *Journal of Experimental Psychology: Human Perception and Performance, 27,* 229–240.

Fagard, J., & Jacquet, A. Y. (1996). Changes in reaching and grasping objects of different size between 7 and 13 months of age. *British Journal of Developmental Psychology, 14,* 65–78.

Fagard, J., & Pezé, A. (1997). Age changes in interlimb coupling and the development of bimanual coordination. *Journal of Motor Behavior, 29,* 199–208.

Fitch, H., Tuller, B., & Turvey, M. T. (1982). The Bernstein perspective: III. Tuning of coordinative structures with special reference to perception. In J. S. A. Kelso (Ed.), *Human motor behavior: An introduction* (pp. 271–281). Hillsdale, NJ: Erlbaum.

Forssberg, H. (1985). Ontogeny of human locomotor control. I. Infant stepping, supported locomotion and transition to independent locomotion. *Experimental Brain Research, 57,* 480–493.

Gesell, A. (1956). The ontogenesis of infant behavior. In L. Carmichael (Ed.), *Manual of child psychology* (pp. 295–331). New York: Wiley.

Gesell, A., & Amatruda, C. S. (1945). *The embryology of behavior.* New York: Harper.

Gesell, A., & Ames, L. B. (1947). The development of handedness. *Journal of Genetic Psychology, 70,* 155–175.

Gibson, E. J. (1988). Exploratory behavior in the development of perceiving and acting, and the acquiring of knowledge. *Annual Review of Psychology, 39,* 1–41.

Gibson, E. J. (1994). Has psychology a future? *Psychological Science, 5,* 69–76.

Gibson, E. J. (1997). An ecological psychologist's prolegomena for perceptual development: A functional approach. In C. Dent-Read & P. Zukow-Goldring (Eds.), *Evolving explanations of development: Ecological approaches to organism-environment systems* (pp. 413–443). Washington, DC: American Psychological Association.

Gibson, E. J., & Pick, A. D. (2000). *An ecological approach to perceptual learning and development.* Oxford: University Press.

Gibson, J. J. (1979). *The ecological approach to visual perception.* Boston: Houghton Mifflin.

Goldfield, E. C. (1993). Dynamic systems in development: Action systems. In L. B. Smith & E. Thelen (Eds.), *A dynamic systems approach to development: Applications* (pp. 51–71). Cambridge, MA: MIT Press.

Goldfield, E. C. (1995). *Emergent forms: Origins and early development of human action and perception.* New York and Oxford: Oxford University Press.

Goldfield, E. C., Kay, B. A, & Warren, W. H. (1993). Infant bouncing: The assembly and tuning of action systems. *Child Development, 64,* 1128–1142.

Goldfield, E. C., & Michel, G. F. (1986). Spatiotemporal linkage in infant interlimb coordination. *Developmental Psychobiology, 19,* 259–264.

Grenier, A. (1981). La "motricité libérée" par fixation manuelle de la nuque au cours des premières semaines de vie. *Archive Françaises de Pédiatrie, 38,* 557–561.

Hallemans, A., Aerts, P., Otten, B., De Deyn, P. P., & De Clercq, D. (2004). Mechanical energy in toddler gait. A trade-off between economy and stability? *The Journal of Experimental Biology, 207,* 2417–2431.

Halverson, H. M. (1931). An experimental study of prehension in infants by means of systematic cinema records. *Genetic Psychology Manuscripts*, *10*, 107–286.

Henderson, S. E. (1986). Some aspects of the development of motor control in Down's syndrome. In H. T. A. Whiting & M. G. Wade (Eds.). *Themes in motor development*, (pp. 69–92). Boston, MA: Martinus Nijhoff.

Hogan, N. (1985). Mechanics of multi-joint posture and movement control. *Biological Cybernetics*, *52*, 315–331.

Holt, K. G., Hamill, J., & Andres, R. O. (1990). The force-driven harmonic oscillator as a model for human locomotion. *Human Movement Science*, *9*, 55–68.

Holt, K. G.., Jeng, S. F., & Fetters, L. (1991). Walking cadence of 9 year olds is predictable as the resonant frequency of a force-driven harmonic oscillator. *Pediatric Exercise Science*, *3*, 121–128.

Holt, K. G., Saltzman, E., Ho, C. L., Kubo, M., & Ulrich, B. D. (2006).Discovery of the pendulum and spring dynamics in the early stages of walking. *Journal of Motor Behavior*, *38*, 206–218.

Holt, K. G., Saltzman, E., Ho, C. L., & Ulrich, B. D. (2007). Scaling of Dynamics in the Earliest Stages of Walking. *Physical Therapy*, *87*, 1458–1467.

Hommel, B. (2003). Planning and representing intentional action. *The Scientific World Journal*, *3*, 593–608.

Hommel, B. (2006). How we do what we want: A neuro-cognitive perspective on human action planning. In R. J. Jorna, W. van Wezel, & A. Meystel (Eds.), *Planning in intelligent systems: Aspects motivations and methods*. New York. Wiley.

Ivanenko, Y. P. Dominici, N., Capellini, G., Dan, B., Cheron, G., & Lacquaniti, F. (2004). Development of the pendulum mechanism and kinematic coordination from the first unsupported steps in toddlers. *Journal of Experimental Biology*, *207*, 3797–3810.

James, W. (1890). *The principles of psychology*. New York: Dover Publications.

Kelso, J. A. S. (1995). *The self-organization of brain and behavior*. Cambridge, MA: MIT Press.

Kelso, J. A. S., & Holt, K. G. (1980). Exploring a vibratory system analysis of human movement production. *Journal of Neurophysiology*, *43*, 1183–1196.

Kimmerle, M., Mick, L. A., & Michel, G. F. (1995). Bimanual role-differentiated toy play during infancy. *Infant Behavior and Development*, *18*, 299–307.

Kimura, T., Yaguramaki, N., Fujita, M., Ogiue-Ikeda, M., Nishizawa, S., & Ueda, Y. (2005). Development of energy and time parameters in the walking of healthy human infants. *Gait and Posture*, *22*, 225–232.

Köhler, W. (1925). *The mentality of apes* [Intelligenzprüfungen an Menschaffen]. New York: Harcourt and Brace.

Konczak, J., Borutta, M., Topka, H., & Dichgans, J. (1995). Development of goal-directed reaching in infants: Hand trajectory formation and joint torque control. *Experimental Brain Research*, *106*, 156–168.

Kubo, M., & Ulrich, B. D. (2006a). Early stage of walking: Development of control in mediolateral and anteroposterior Directions. *Journal of Motor Behavior*, *38*, 229–237.

Kubo, M., & Ulrich, B. D. (2006b). A biomechanical analysis of the high guard position of arms during walking. *Infant Behavior and Development*, *29*, 509–517.

Kugler, P. N., Kelso, J. A. S., & Turvey, M. T. (1980). On the concept of coordinative structures as dissipative structures: I. Theoretical lines of convergence. In G. E. Stelmach and J. Requin (Eds.), *Tutorials in Motor Behavior* (pp. 3–47). Amsterdam: North-Holland.

Kuo, A. D., Donelan, J. M., & Ruina, A. (2005). Energetic consequences of walking an inverted pendulum: Step-to-step transitions. *Exercise & Sport Science Review*, *33*, 88–97.

Kurjak, A., Stanojevic, M., Wiku, A., Salihagic-Kadic, A., Carrerra, J. M., & Azumendi, G. (2004). Behavioral pattern continuity from prenatal to postnatal life: A study by four-dimensional (4D) ultrasonography. *Journal of Perinatal Medicine*, *32*, 346–353.

Latash, M. L. (1996). The Bernstein Problem: How does the central nervous system make its choices. In M. L. Latash & M. T. Turvery (Eds.), *Dexterity and its development* (pp. 277–305). Mahwah, NJ: Erlbaum.

Ledebt, A. (2000). Changes in arm posture during the early acquisition of walking. *Infant Behavior and Development, 23*, 79–89.

Ledebt, A., Bril, B., & Wiener-Vacher, S. (1995). Trunk and head stabilization during the first months of independent walking. *Neuro Report, 6*, 1737–1740.

Lockman, J. J. (2000). A perception–action perspective on tool use development. *Child Development, 71*, 137–144.

Lockman, J. J., Ashmead, D. H., & Bushnell, E. W. (1984). The development of anticipatory hand orientation during infancy. *Journal of Experimental Child Psychology, 37*, 176–186.

Lussanet, M. H., Smeets, J. B., & Brenner, E. (2002). Relative damping improves linear-mass models of goal directed movements. *Human Movement Science, 21*, 85–100.

McCarty, M. E., Clifton, R. K., Ashmead, D. H. Lee, P., & Goubet, N. (2001). How infants use vision for grasping objects. *Child Development, 72*, 973–987.

McCarty, M. E., Clifton, R. K., & Collard, R. R. (1999). Problem solving in infancy: The emergence of an action plan. *Developmental Psychology, 35*, 191–1101.

McCarty, M. E., Clifton, R. K., & Collard, R. R. (2001). The beginnings of tool use by infants and toddlers. *Infancy, 2*, 233–256.

McCollum, G., Holroyd, C., & Castelfranco, A. M. (1995). Forms of early walking. *Journal of Theoretical Biology, 176*, 373–390.

McGraw, M. B. (1935). *Growth: A study of Johnny and Jimmy.* New York: Appleton-Century-Crofts.

McKenzie, B. E., Skouteris, H., Day, R. H., Hartman, B., & Yonas, A. (1993). Effective action by infants to contact objects by reaching and leaning. *Child Development, 64*, 415–429.

Meltzoff, A. N. (2007). "Like me": A foundation for social cognition. *Developmental Science, 10*, 126–134.

Newell, K. M., McDonald, P. V., & Baillargeon, R. (1993). Body scale and infant grip configurations. *Developmental Psychobiology, 26*, 195–205.

Newell, K. M., Scully, D. M., McDonald, P. V., & Baillargeon, R. (1989). Task constraints and infant grip configurations. *Developmental Psychobiology, 22*, 817–832.

Out, L., Savelsbergh, G. J. P., van Soest, A. J., & Hopkins, B. (1997). Influence of mechanical factors on movement units in infant reaching. *Human Movement Science, 16*, 733–748.

Out, L., van Soest, A. J., Savelsbergh, G. J. P., & Hopkins, B. (1998). The effect of posture on early reaching movements. *Journal of Motor Behavior, 30*, 260–272.

Overton, W. F., Müller, U., & Newman, J. L. (2008). *Developmental perspectives on embodiment and consciousness.* New York: Erlbaum.

Piaget, J. (1952). *The origins of intelligence in children.* New York: International Universities Press.

Piaget, J. (1954). *The construction of reality in the child.* New York: Basic Books.

Prinz, W. (1997). Perception and action planning. *European Journal of Cognitive Psychology, 9*, 129–154.

Reed, E. S. (1982). An outline of a theory of action systems. *Journal of Motor Behavior, 14*, 98–134.

Reed, E. S. (1996). *Encountering the world: Toward an ecological psychology.* New York: Oxford University Press.

Reed, E. S., & Bril, B. (1996). The primacy of action in development. In M. L. Latash & M. T. Turvery (Eds.), *Dexterity and its development* (pp. 431–453). Mahwah, NJ: Erlbaum.

Richardson, H. M. (1932). The growth of adaptive behaviour in infants: An experimental study at seven age levels. *Genetic Psychology Monographs, 12*, 195–359.

Rochat, P. (1992). Self-sitting and reaching in 5- to 8-month-old infants: The impact of posture and its development on early eye-hand coordination. *Journal of Motor Behavior, 24,* 210–220.

Rochat, P., & Goubet, N. (1995). Development of sitting and reaching in 5- to 6-month-old infants. *Infant Behavior and Development, 18,* 53–68.

Savelsbergh, G. J. P., von Hofsten, C., & Jonsson, B. (1997). The coupling of head, reach and grasp movement in nine-months-old infant prehension. *Scandinavian Journal of Psychology, 38,* 325–333.

Schöner, G., & Dineva, E. (2007). Dynamic instabilities as mechanisms for emergence. *Developmental Science, 10,* 69–74.

Smitsman, A. W. (1997). The development of tool use: Changing boundaries between organism and environment. In C. Dent-Read & P. Zukow-Goldring (Eds.), *Evolving explanations of development: Ecological approaches to organism-environment systems* (pp. 301–329). Washington, DC: American Psychological Association.

Smitsman, A. W., & Bongers, R. M. (2003). The development of tool use and tool making: A dynamical developmental perspective. In J. Valsiner & K. J. Connolly (Eds.), *Handbook of developmental psychology* (pp. 172–194). London: Sage.

Smitsman, A. W., & Cox, R. F. A. (2008). Perseveration in tool use: A window for understanding the dynamics of the action-selection process. *Infancy, 13,* 249–269.

Smitsman, A. W., Cox, R. F. A., & Bongers, R. M. (2005). Action dynamics in tool use. In V. Roux & B. Bril (Eds.), *Stone knapping: the necessary conditions for a uniquely hominid behavior* (pp. 129–147). Cambridge: McDonald Institute Monograph Series.

Smitsman, A. W., DeJonckheere, P. J. N, & de Wit, T. C. J. (2009). The significance of event information for 6–16-month-old infants' perception of containment. *Developmental Psychology, 45,* 207–223.

Snapp-Childs, W., & Corbetta, D. (2009). Evidence of early strategies in learning to walk. *Infancy, 14,* 101–116.

Thelen, E. (2000). Grounded in the world: Developmental origins of the embodied mind. *Infancy, 1,* 3–28.

Thelen, E. (2008). Grounded in the world: Developmental origins of the embodied mind. In W. F. Overton, U. Müller, & J. L. Newman (Eds.), *Developmental perspectives on embodiment and consciousness* (pp. 99–129). New York: Erlbaum.

Thelen, E., Corbetta, D., Kamm, K., Spencer, J. P., Schneider, K., & Zernicke, R. F. (1993). The transition to reaching: Mapping intention and intrinsic dynamics. *Child Development, 64,* 1058–1098.

Thelen, E., Corbetta, D., & Spencer, J. P. (1996). Development of reaching during the first year: Role of movement speed. *Journal of Experimental Psychology: Human Perception and Performance, 22*(5), 1059–1076.

Thelen, E., & Fisher, D. M. (1982). Newborn stepping: An explanation for a "disappearing" reflex. *Developmental Psychology, 18,* 760–775.

Thelen, E., & Fisher, D. M. (1983). The organization of spontaneous leg movements in newborn infants. *Journal of Motor Behavior, 15,* 353–377.

Thelen, E., Fisher, D. M., & Ridley-Johnson, R. (1984). The relationship between physical growth and a newborn reflex. *Infant Behavior and Development, 7,* 479–493.

Thelen, E., Schöner, G., Scheier, C., & Smith, L. B. (2001). The dynamics of embodiment: A field theory of infant perseverative reaching. *Behavioral and Brain Sciences, 24,* 1–34.

Thelen, E., & Smith, L. B. (1994). *A dynamic systems approach to the development of cognition and action.* Cambridge, MA: MIT Press.

Thelen, E., & Spencer, J. (1998). Postural control during reaching in young infants: A dynamic systems approach. *Neuroscience and Biobehavioral Reviews, 22,* 507–514.

Thelen, E., & Ulrich, B. D. (1991). Hidden skills. *Monographs of the Society for Research in Child Development, 56*, 1–106.

Thompson, E. (2007). *Mind in Life: biology, phenomenology, and the sciences of mind.* Cambridge, MA: Belknap.

Tomasello, M. (1998). Uniquely primate, uniquely human. *Developmental Science, 1*, 1–32.

Tuller, B., Fitch, H., & Turvey, M. T. (1982). The Berstein perspective II. The concept of muscle linkage or coordinative structure. In J. S. A. Kelso (Ed.), *Human motor behavior: An introduction* (pp. 253–270). Hillsdale, NJ: Erlbaum.

Turvey, M. T. (1990). Coordination. *American Psychologist, 45*, 938–953.

Turvey, M. T., Fitch, H., & Tuller, B. (1982). The Bernstein perspective: I. The problems of degrees of freedom and context-conditioned variability. In J. S. A. Kelso (Ed.), *Human motor behavior: An introduction* (pp. 239–252). Hillsdale, NJ: Erlbaum.

Ulrich, B. D., Haehl, V., Buzzi, U. H., Kubo, M., & Holt, K. G. (2004). Modeling dynamic resource utilization in populations with unique constraints: preadolescents with and without Down syndrome. *Human Movement Science, 23*, 133–156.

Ulrich, B. D., & Kubo, M. (2005). Adding pieces to the puzzle: A commentary. *Infant and Child Development, 14*, 519–522.

van der Fits, I. B. M., & Hadders-Algra, M. (1998). The development of postural response patterns during reaching in healthy infants. *Neuroscience and Biobehavioral Reviews, 22*, 521–526.

van der Fits, I. B. M., Klip, A. W. J., van Eykern, L. A., & Hadders-Algra, M. (1999). Postural adjustments during spontaneous and goal-directed arm movements in the first half year of life. *Behaviourial Brain Research, 106*, 75–90.

van Leeuwen, L., Smitsman, A. W., & van Leeuwen, C. (1994). Affordances, perceptual complexity, and the development of tool use. *Journal of Experimental Psychology: Human Perception and Performance, 20*, 174–191.

von Hofsten, C. (1979). Development of visually directed reaching: The approach phase. *Journal of Human Movement Studies, 5*, 160–178.

von Hofsten, C. (1982). Eye–hand coordination in the newborn. *Developmental Psychology, 18*, 450–461.

von Hofsten, C. (1984). Developmental changes in the organization of prereaching movements. *Developmental Psychology, 20*, 378–388.

von Hofsten, C. (1991). Structuring of early reaching movements: A longitudinal study. *Journal of Motor Behavior, 23*, 280–292.

von Hofsten, C. (1997). On the early development of predictive abilities. In C. Dent-Read & P. Zukow-Goldring (Eds.), *Evolving explanations of development: Ecological approaches to organism-environment systems* (pp. 163–195). Washington, DC: American Psychological Association.

von Hofsten, C. (2003). On the development of perception and action. In J. Valsiner & K. J. Connolly (Eds.), *Handbook of developmental psychology*. London: Sage.

von Hofsten, C. (2004). An action perspective on motor development. *Trends in Cognitive Science, 8*, 266–272.

von Hofsten, C. (2007). Action in development. *Developmental Science, 10*, 54–60.

von Hofsten, C., & Fazel-Zandy, S. (1984). Development of visually guided hand orientation in reaching. *Journal of Experimental Child Psychology, 38*, 208–219.

von Hofsten, C., & Gibson, E. J. (1993). Prospective control: a basis aspect of action development, Comment. *Human Development, 36*, 253–273.

von Hofsten, C., & Lindhagen, K. (1979). Observations on the development of reaching for moving objects. *Journal of Experimental Child Psychology, 28*, 158–173.

von Hofsten, C., & Rönnqvist, L. (1988). Preparation for grasping an object: A developmental study. *Journal of Experimental Psychology: Human Perception and Performance, 14*, 610–621.

von Hofsten, C., & Rönnqvist, L. (1993). The structuring of neonatal arm movements. *Child Development, 64,* 1046–1057.

Wagman, J. B., & Carello, C. (2004). Haptically creating affordances: The user-tool interface. *Journal of Experimental Psychology: Applied, 9,* 175–186.

Wagman, J. B., & Taylor, K. R. (2004). Chosen striking location and the user-tool-environment system. *Journal of Experimental Psychology: Applied, 10,* 267–280.

White, B. L., Castle, P., & Held, R. (1964). Observations on the development of visually directed reaching. *Child Development, 35,* 349–364.

WHO Multicentre Growth Reference study Group (2006). *Acta Paediatrica, Supplement, 450,* 86–95.

Willatts, P. (1999). Development of means–end behaviour in young infants: pulling a support to retrieve a distant object. *Developmental Psychology, 35,* 651–657.

Wimmers, R. H., Savelsbergh, G. J. P., Beek, P. J., & Hopkins, B. (1998). Evidence for a phase transition in the early development of prehension. *Developmental Psychobiology, 32,* 235–248.

Witherington, D. C. (2005). The development of prospective grasping control between 5 and 7 months: A longitudinal study. *Infancy, 7,* 143–161.

6

Cognitive Development: Knowledge of the Physical World

J. Gavin Bremner

Theoretical Overview

The term *cognition* is generally used to describe psychological processes that in some way go beyond straightforward perception. Conventionally, there are two respects in which cognition has been identified as vital for a full awareness of the world. First, it has been claimed that cognitive processes are required to interpret and organize perception: although perception may provide rich information about the physical world, at least until recently the notion has been that meaning and other types of high-level structuring can only be attached to perceptual experience through the functioning of cognitive interpretative processes. Second, there is the argument that cognition involves the process of *mental representation*, a process that supports mental activity in the absence of relevant perceptual input. Thus, cognitive processes are seen as structuring and interpreting perception, and function both in the presence and absence of perceptual subject matter.

Piaget's (1954) account of the development of *sensori-motor intelligence* in infancy is based on the principle that cognitive development occurs through a process of construction in which individuals develop progressively more complex knowledge of the world through their actions in it. The crowning achievement of sensori-motor intelligence is the emergence of mental representation, making possible the awareness that objects remain permanent even when out of sight, and although from the middle of the period onwards evidence for representational ability begins to emerge, it is only at the end of the period that representational processes become truly independent of perception and action.

There have been a growing number of challenges to *constructionist* accounts of this sort. These have been based on growing evidence for sophisticated awareness of the world in very young infants, and have been in two quite distinct forms. First, based on Gibsonian theory of *direct perception* (J. J. Gibson, 1979), investigators have argued that perception of environmental structures and even their meanings is objective: the structure is out there and can be directly perceived in relation to the individual's acts (E. J. Gibson, 1977). This account leaves no place for representational processes in everyday awareness of the world: perception *is* knowing, and there is no need to invoke representational processes to explain development during infancy. In contrast, *nativist* theorists see cognitive processes as central, but rather than see them as constructed from scratch, postulate innate mental structures and processes which they believe are necessary to explain the impressive abilities of young infants (Baillargeon, 1993; Spelke, Breinlinger, Macomber, & Jacobson, 1992).

In the following sections, I shall review compelling evidence that young infants respond to high-level properties of perceptual input. Most of the evidence pointing to psychological precocity arises from what are generally called *violation of expectancy* tasks, in which infants are familiarized with lawful events and are then presented with test events, one of which violates certain physical rules of object movement, stability, and so forth. Longer looking at the violation event is interpreted as indication that infants have noted the violation and are thus aware of the principle in question. Recently, however, there has been a serious challenge to cognitive interpretations of this sort, it being argued that positive results from violation of expectation studies can actually be interpreted in terms of low-level properties of attention and perceptual memory (Bogartz, Shinskey, & Speaker, 1997; Cohen & Marks, 2002; Haith, 1998). Given the crucial importance of establishing an appropriate level of interpretation of these data, this controversy will be a major focus of this chapter.

A further important objective in relation to claims about early cognitive competence is to explain why early awareness of properties like object permanence and causality is not revealed in the infant's actions until much later. Although Piaget's constructivist theory has suffered growing criticism, the data on which he based it, revealing limitations in infants' actions towards objects, replicate readily. For instance, we are left to explain why, if young infants understand the continuing existence of hidden objects (object permanence), they do not reveal this understanding in their manual search for hidden objects until the age of 9 months or later. Recently, there has been a renewed focus on deficits in search by infants around 9 months of age and older, and various accounts have emerged to explain why these errors exist. In one way or another, all these accounts lay stress on the developing relationship between perception and action, and here a recent theoretical orientation has gained popularity. According to *dynamical systems theory*, psychological development is the outcome of self-organization; complex systems progress naturally through states of instability followed by new relatively stable states, and very subtle and often simple factors are capable of triggering highly complex changes (see chapter 5). In many respects, this approach to development is similar to Piaget's constructionism. But in replacing construction with self-organization, it shifts the emphasis away from mentalistic theorizing towards theorizing about organization that is distributed across the system rather than situated in hypothetical mental structures.

However, there are other viable candidate accounts of errors in action. Diamond (1985; Diamond & Goldman-Rakic, 1989) suggests that immaturity of the frontal cortex leads to the inability to both represent hidden objects and inhibit past actions. This account is a good example of a cognitive science approach to developmental questions, with its interdisciplinary emphasis on coordinating evidence about development of brain and behavior. A related approach is neural network and connectionist modeling, in which the primary base for model building is computer modeling of hypothetical neural systems connecting perception and action. Munakata, McClelland, Johnson, and Siegler (1997) have developed a neural network model that explains object search errors in terms of relative strengths of active memory for the object and latent memory based on past experiences. Finally, and in contrast, Topál, Gergely, Miklósi, Erdőhegzi, and Csibra (2008) explain errors in terms of infants' pragmatic misinterpretation of the experimenter's acts.

As we shall see, to a greater or lesser extent each of the above models manages to explain search errors without being challenged by the evidence of earlier object knowledge revealed by violation of expectancy tasks. However, there remains considerable doubt as to which of these accounts is more appropriate, and indeed whether they are mutually exclusive. In the following sections of this chapter I review research evidence bearing on these points, and in the final section I revisit the theoretical issues outlined here and propose a developmental account that takes account of both the evidence for early competence and later emerging skill in self-guided action.

Research on young infants' object knowledge

Some of the evidence argued by some to relate to object permanence arises from habituation-novelty studies of infant perception (see chapter 1 this volume), specifically, perception of object unity and object trajectory continuity.

Perception of object unity

The initial study on which much recent work has been based was by Kellman and Spelke (1983). Four-month-old infants were habituated to a rod that moved back and forth behind a box, and were then tested for novelty preference on two displays in which the box was absent: (a) the two rod parts (what they had literally seen of the rod during habituation); and (b) a complete rod (Figure 6.1). Infants showed a novelty preference for the two rod parts, indicating that, during habituation, they had perceived a complete rod moving behind the box. This phenomenon, in which infants are apparently "filling in" the absent part of the rod, may be compared to object permanence, in which the infant represents the whole absent object. This work has been extended to show that infants rely on a variety of perceptual information to segregate surfaces and perceive object unity (Johnson & Aslin, 1996, Johnson & Náñez, 1995). For instance, depth information provided by a background texture is necessary if 4-month-olds are to detect object unity in computer-generated versions of the rod and box display.

Evidence for object unity is only obtained if the occluded object is in motion, pointing to the possibility that common motion is an important factor in perception of unity. However, the fact that background texture is also necessary has led to the view that

Habituation display

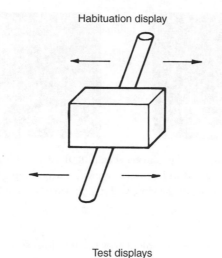

Test displays

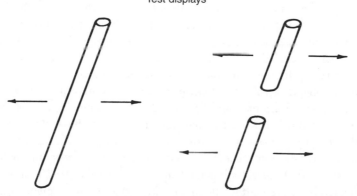

Figure 6.1 A subset of the stimuli used by Kellman and Spelke (1983) to investigate young infants' perception of object unity.

motion is necessary because of the accompanying accretion and deletion of background texture, but it appears that common motion is not a sufficient factor for detection of object unity. Johnson and Aslin (1996) showed that 4-month-olds did not perceive object unity in displays in which the rod was a dog-leg form with unaligned differently oriented visible parts or if the visible parts, although parallel, were out of alignment. Thus, alignment of parts as well as common motion appears to be important. However, other higher-level stimulus properties appear to be important too. Johnson, Bremner, Slater, and Mason (2000) showed that 4-month-olds perceived object unity in displays in which the occluded object was a circle or a cross (see Figure 6.2). In both cases, although there was no alignment of figure elements immediately on each side of the occluding box, infants were apparently using the principle of overall figural "goodness" to perceive object unity.

Interestingly, perception of object unity in these displays appears to develop between birth and 2 months. When newborns were tested on the Kellman and Spelke display,

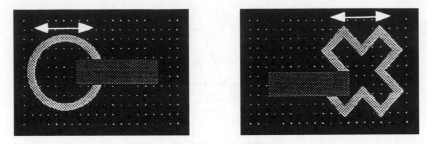

Figure 6.2   Habituation stimuli used by Johnson et al. (2000). After habituation to either the circle or cross display, infants are presented with test displays with the occluding bar removed, consisting of either a complete cross or circle, or the same with the previously occluded part omitted.

they showed a preference for the complete rod (Slater, Johnson, Brown, & Badenoch, 1996), indicating that during habituation they perceived what was visible, the two rod parts, treating the complete rod as novel. However, by 2 months, infants have been found to perceive object unity, provided the occluding box is narrow (Johnson & Aslin, 1995).

Strangely, these effects do not appear to apply to all forms of object movement. Although positive results are also obtained for vertical translations and movements in depth (Kellman, Spelke, & Short, 1986), negative results are obtained at 4 months for rotational movements (Eizenman and Bertenthal, 1998). There is a developmental progression here, however, because Eizenman and Bertenthal showed that 6-month-olds perceived object unity in both the rotating and translating rod tasks. Interestingly, the way in which relative motion is generated between occluded object and its occluder also determines perception of unity: Kellman, Gleitman, and Spelke (1987) found that relative motion generated by movement of the infant rather than by movement of the occluded object did not lead to perception of unity.

In summary, although perception of object unity appears to imply something about the permanence of the hidden parts of an object, the processes leading to it may have more to do with Gestalt-like perceptual processes than with awareness of object permanence. The likelihood remains, however, that there is a developmental link between perception of unity and object permanence.

Perception of trajectory continuity

Another indicator of object perception of object persistence may be found in infants' responses to the temporary disappearance of a moving object behind an occluder. Recent work on infants' perception of trajectory continuity uses two main methods. First, a series of studies has been carried out using habituation-novelty methods very much like those used in the object unity literature (Bremner et al., 2005; Bremner et al., 2007; Johnson, Bremner, Slater, Mason, Foster, & Cheshire, 2003). Second, several studies have used eye-tracker measures to identify the conditions under which infants anticipate reemergence of a moving object from behind an occluder that it has been seen to disappear behind (Gredebäck, & von Hofsten, 2004; Johnson, Amso, & Slemmer, 2003; Rosander & von Hofsten, 2004; von Hofsten, Kochukhova, & Rosander, 2007).

The habituation-novelty work involves habituating infants to an event in which a ball cycles back and forth across a display, disappearing behind an occluder on the middle part of its trajectory. Following habituation, infants view two test displays (presented in alternation three times each). In both, the occluder is absent, and in one (the continuous test display) the ball moves continuously back and forth, whereas in the other (the discontinuous test display) only the parts of the trajectory visible during habituation are presented (see Figure 6.3). If infants processed the trajectory presented during habituation as continuous they should treat the discontinuous test display as novel and hence look longer at it, whereas if they processed the habituation trajectory as discontinuous, they should treat the continuous test display as novel and hence look longer at it.

In our first study (Johnson, Bremner, et al., 2003) initially 4- and 6-month-olds were tested as indicated above. Four-month-olds showed a looking preference for the continuous test display, whereas 6-month-olds did the opposite, looking longer at the discontinuous test display. This suggested that 4-month-olds perceived the trajectory as discontinuous, whereas 6-month-olds perceived it as continuous. However, a second experiment presented 2- and 4-month-olds with the same displays but with a much narrower occluder. In this case, 4-month-olds perceived trajectory continuity but 2-month-olds showed no preference for either test display. A third study with 4-month-olds showed an orderly relationship between occluder width and the direction of preference on test trials. Thus, it was concluded that 4-month-olds perceived trajectory continuity provided the " gap" in perception was small.

When the occluder is narrow, the object is out of sight for a shorter time and also over a smaller distance, and the question arises as to whether it is the size of the spatial gap or the size of the temporal gap that matters (or indeed whether both matter). The second series of studies (Bremner et al., 2005) set about teasing apart these variables. Our first manipulation was to change the speed of the ball, thus manipulating time out of sight with distance out of sight held constant. However, this proved ineffective, probably because infants' processing of trajectories is highly sensitive to object speed (Mareschal, Harris, and Plunkett, 1997; Muller & Aslin, 1978). In another experiment, we used a much larger ball than previously, such that it was out of sight for a very short time behind the wide occluder. This resulted in perception of trajectory continuity at 4 months. A final method involved using a similar visible ball speed to previous work, but slowing down or speeding up the ball while it was out of sight. Speeding up the ball behind a wide occluder led to perception of continuity. Interestingly, however, slowing down the ball behind a narrow occluder also resulted in perception of continuity. Apparently either a short temporal gap or a short spatial gap was sufficient to support perception of trajectory continuity by 4-month-olds.

In a third series (Bremner et al., 2007), we looked at how changes in trajectory direction affected perception of continuity, finding that changing either the height or the angle of the trajectory between sides of the occluder led to perception of discontinuity, and that this was the case even when the display gave the impression of a ball bouncing on a surface behind the occluder. We also found that 4-month-olds have difficulty processing linear oblique trajectories, only perceiving continuity when the trajectory was a shallow

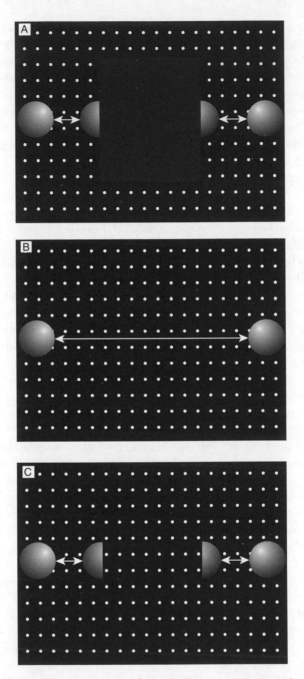

Figure 6.3 Habituation and test stimuli used by Johnson et al. (2003). Infants were habituated to an event in which a ball travelled back and forth horizontally, disappearing behind and reemerging from an occluder. Test trials omitted the occluder and consisted of the ball moving back and forth on a continuous trajectory, or on a trajectory with a gap in the middle where the occluder had been.

oblique 22° from horizontal, and the occluder was narrow and rotated so that the occluding edge was at right angles to the direction of motion. Further recently completed work (Bremner, Johnson, Slater, Mason, & Spring, in preparation) indicates that infants process vertical trajectories in much the same way as horizontal ones, so this limitation does truly appear to relate to oblique trajectories.

In summary, although 4-month-olds perceive trajectory continuity, they only do so when the processing load required to fill in the gap in perception is fairly low. And although they perceive discontinuity under predictable conditions (specifically, when the object's trajectory changes) they show a quite surprising limitation in relation to oblique trajectories.

Eye tracking work indicates growing accuracy of anticipatory tracking (fixating the predicted point or reemergence before reemergence) with age (Gredebäck & von Hofsten, 2004; Rosander & von Hofsten, 2004). Probably the best use of eye tracking evidence is in conjunction with habituation–novelty work of the sort reviewed above. Johnson, Amso, et al. (2003) obtained data in keeping with the first experiment in the habituation–novelty work. In a wide occluder tracking task, 4-month-olds showed little predictive tracking whereas 6-month-olds showed a high level of prediction. They also showed that 4-month-olds (but not 6-month-olds) benefited from prior exposure to a continuous trajectory with no occluder. Basically, the predictive tracking literature agrees quite well with the habituation–novelty literature. It is possible that the habituation–novelty work gets more directly at the question of whether and when infants perceive trajectories as continuous across gaps in perception, since anticipatory tracking could be anticipation of an event sequence rather than of object reemergence (Goldberg, 1976). However Bertenthal, Longo, and Kenny (2007) found that predictive tracking was more frequent when the object disappeared lawfully by progressive occlusion rather than by instantaneous disappearance or implosion, and argue that predictive tracking reflects knowledge of the object's continuing existence following disappearance by gradual occlusion.

Violation of expectancy as a measure of infant knowledge

The technique used in many recent studies of object knowledge involves familiarizing infants with an event sequence and then presenting them with test events that either do or do not violate the physical principle under test. The procedure here is similar to habituation studies of perception, with an important difference. Increased looking at a new event sequence indicates more than surface discrimination: it indicates not just that something is different but that something is wrong with the new event. If this interpretation is appropriate it is possible to diagnose the level of infants' awareness of object permanence or the rules by which one object moves relative to another, because if they note a violation they must be aware of the principle that has been violated. One of the first studies to use this technique was carried out by Baillargeon, Spelke, and Wasserman (1985). In what is often called the *drawbridge task*, 5-month-old infants were familiarized with a repeated event in which a flap rotated from flat on the table through 180°. From the infant's perspective, this would look like the raising of a drawbridge, except that the rotation went through a full 180°. After familiarization, two types of test event were

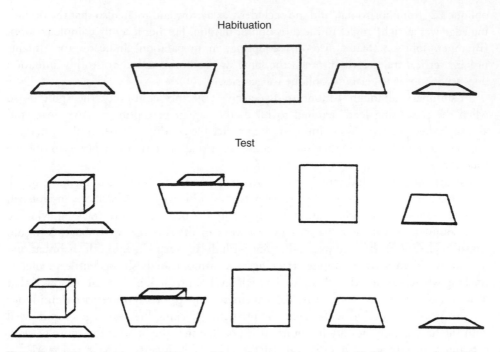

Figure 6.4   The infant's view of the possible and impossible events in Baillargeon et al. (1985)

presented, in both of which a cube was placed in the path of the flap (Figure 6.4). In a "possible" test event, the flap rotated but came to a stop on making contact with the cube, whereas in an "impossible" test event, it rotated through 180° as usual, appearing to annihilate the cube in the process. Note that this comparison nicely creates an opposition between surface event similarity, in which the impossible event (full 180° rotation) is more similar to the familiarization event than is the possible event (less than 180° rotation), and event lawfulness, in which only the impossible event presents a violation of physical reality. Thus, if infants were simply showing recovery of looking on the basis of perceptual dissimilarity, we would expect more looking at the possible event where there is both a new object (the block) and a different rotation. However, they actually looked more at the impossible event, with the conclusion that infants of this age both understand object permanence and know that one object cannot move through another.

This initial finding was later replicated with infants as young as 3.5 months old (Baillargeon, 1987a). Additionally, Baillargeon (1987b) used the same technique to investigate the accuracy with which older infants could anticipate events of this sort. She found that 7-month-olds had quite precise expectations about such collisions, expecting that the occluder would stop rotating sooner if the cube was larger or closer to the occluder, but expecting it to stop later if the object in its path was compressible.

Figure 6.5 illustrates another application of this approach (Baillargeon, 1986). Infants were familiarized with an event sequence in which a toy truck rolled down a ramp and

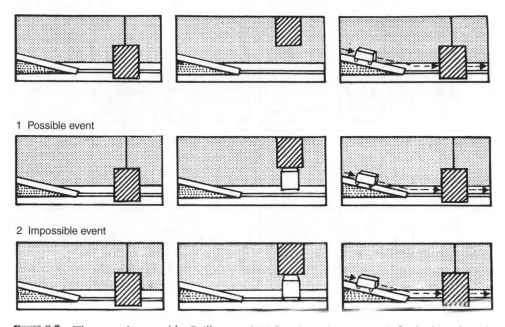

1 Possible event

2 Impossible event

Figure 6.5 The procedure used by Baillargeon (1986) to investigate young infant's object knowledge. The familiarization event is at the top and the two test events are shown below.

passed behind an occluder (prior to each trial the occluder was raised, revealing nothing behind it, and lowered again). After familiarization, infants saw one of two test events. In the possible event, a block was placed behind the occluder, but behind the track so that it did not obstruct the path of the truck. In the impossible event, the block was placed behind the occluder on the track, so that it presented an obstruction. In both cases, the occluder was raised to reveal the block and lowered again, whereupon the truck rolled down the track and reemerged from behind the occluder as usual. Baillargeon found that 6- to 8-month-olds looked longer at the impossible event, a finding replicated by Baillargeon and DeVos (1991). Apparently, infants not only appreciate the continued existence of the block but also can use precise memory for its position to reach a conclusion about whether or not the truck event is possible.

Spelke et al., (1992) used modified versions of this task to test even younger infants. In one case, they familiarized 2.5-month-olds to an event in which a ball rolled behind an occluder, whereupon the occluder was lifted to show that the ball had come to rest against an end wall. On test trials, a box was placed in the path of the ball so that when the occluder was lowered only the top part of the box was visible. Two events followed, a possible event, in which removal of the occluder revealed the ball resting against the box having collided with it, and an impossible event in which the object was revealed resting against the end wall, having apparently passed through the box to come to rest in its usual place. Infants looked longer at the impossible event, suggesting that 2.5-month-olds can detect the position of the whole box from perception of a visible part, and understand that one object cannot move through another in its path.

Habituation events

Short-carrot event   Tall-carrot event

Test events

Possible event   Impossible event

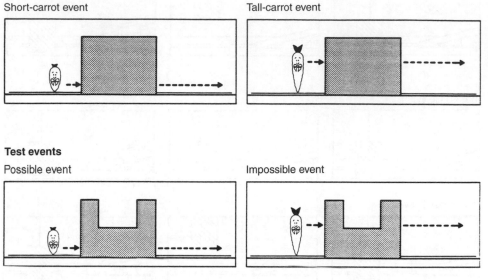

Figure 6.6   The stimuli used by Baillargeon and DeVos (1991) to investigate how infants' knowledge of how the size of an object affects its visibility.

This approach can be used to investigate infants' understanding of a wide range of object properties. For instance, Baillargeon and DeVos (1991) investigated infants' awareness of how the dimensions of an object affect its visibility as it passes behind an occluder. They used the arrangement shown in Figure 6.6, first to familiarize infants with an event in which either a tall or a short carrot moved behind an occluder, to reemerge at the opposite side. Test trials followed with a new occluder with a window cut in it. The size of the window was such that the small carrot would not appear there, whereas the top of the large carrot would appear. But neither the small nor the large carrot appeared at the window on these test trials, making the small carrot event sequence lawful and the large carrot event sequence unlawful. Three-and-a-half-month-old infants looked more at the unlawful test event, leading to the conclusion that they have a good awareness of the conditions under which one object will occlude another.

More recent work indicates that Baillargeon and DeVos's (1991) finding marks the end of a developmental sequence in the early months during which infants' understanding of conditions for reemergence becomes gradually more sophisticated (Baillargeon, 2004). Aguiar and Baillargeon (1999, 2002) investigated the conditions under which very young infants expected objects to emerge in gaps in or between occluders, finding that there was a developmental sequence in this over the early months. Two-and-a-half-month-olds expect an object to reappear between two separate occluders (Aguiar & Baillargeon, 1999). However, by 3 months they predict reappearance in a gap in a single occluder, though only if this gap extends from the bottom of the occluder rather than from the top (Aguiar & Baillargeon, 2002). Finally, as indicated above, 3.5-month-olds extend this prediction to gaps extending from the top of the occluder (Baillargeon & DeVos, 1991; Baillargeon & Graber, 1987).

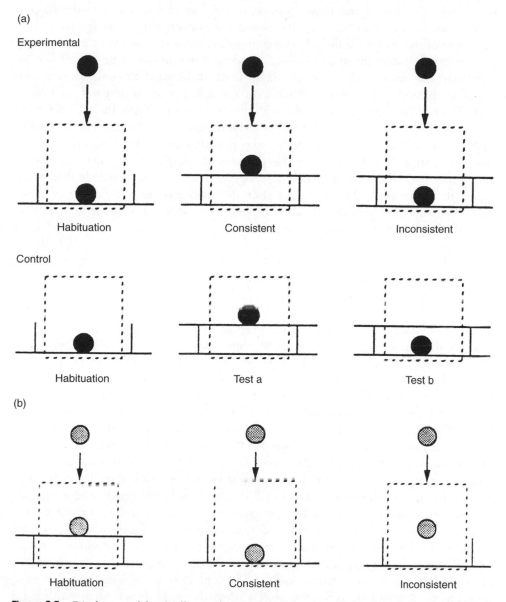

Figure 6.7 Displays used by Spelke et al. (1992) to investigate infants' understanding of how objects move under the effect of gravity.

Two studies (Spelke et al. 1992) indicate that young infants have general problems in understanding movement under gravitational force. In the first, 4-month-old infants were habituated to a sequence in which an object fell behind an occluder, which was subsequently lifted to reveal it at rest on a surface (see Figure 6.7a). On test trials, a higher shelf was introduced (still behind the occluder when it was down), the object was dropped, and infants either saw an end result of the object resting on the shelf, or the object resting on the original (lower) surface. Infants looked longer at the latter (impossible) outcome, suggesting that they understood movement under gravity and the solidity constraint of the interposed shelf. However, this conclusion is shown to be premature by the results of a follow-up study in which the same 4-month-olds were presented with, effectively, the initial study in reverse. Infants were habituated to events in which an object fell behind an occluder, on removal of which it was revealed at rest on a raised shelf (Figure 6.7b). Test trials were done with the shelf removed. Again the ball fell behind the occluder and the occluder was lifted to reveal it either at rest on the lower surface or suspended in mid-air just where the shelf had previously supported it. Under these conditions, 4-month-olds looked longer at the first outcome, despite the fact that this was the appropriate end point of a movement under gravity. Spelke et al. conclude that young infants do not understand *inertia* (that objects do not change direction or rate of movement suddenly or without the operation of some external force) or *gravity* (that objects move downwards in the absence of support).

Numerical identity and numerical knowledge

Numerical identity.   Several studies have investigated knowledge of number in an indirect way that ties in directly with work on object identity. For instance, Xu and Carey (1996) investigated 10- to 12-month-olds' use of featural versus spatiotemporal knowledge to decide whether one or more than one object was involved in the tested events. In a *discontinuous* condition, infants were shown events in which one object was seen to emerge and then disappear behind one occluder, followed by emergence of an identical object from a second occluder, whereas, in a continuous condition, the events were the same except that a single object contributed to the event, travelling between the occluders. After repetitions of these events, the occluders were lowered to reveal either one or two objects (see Figure 6.8). Infants in the *discontinuous* condition looked significantly longer at the one-object outcome, whereas those in the *continuous* condition looked marginally significantly longer at the two-object display. These results were taken as evidence that infants use continuity/discontinuity of movement as a means of estimating the number of objects involved: when the occluders were removed infants in the discontinuous condition expected two objects and those in the continuous condition expect one object. However, in a similar study with a single occluder and distinct objects, infants showed no evidence of expecting to see two objects when the occluder was removed. Xu and Carey therefore proposed that 10-month-olds do not use featural information to individuate objects.

Working with much younger infants, Spelke, Kestenbaum, Simons, and Wein (1995) obtained rather similar results to those of Xu and Carey in their first experiment. Following a two-occluder task, 3- and 4-month-olds showed different looking preferences for one or two objects dependent on whether they had seen no object between occluders or a continuous movement past both occluders. However, when two occluders were replaced by one, and events corresponded to a single object moving back and forth on a constant trajectory, 3- to 4-month-olds provided no evidence of using this constant

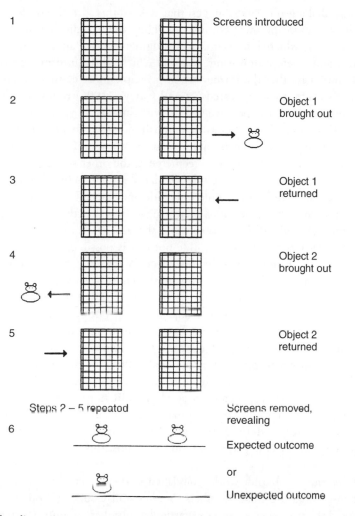

Figure 6.8 The discontinuous movement event used by Xu and Carey (1996) to investigate infants' knowledge of numerical identity. After familiarization with the event sequence, the occluders are removed to reveal either one or two objects. The continuous event sequence differs only in the respect that a single object is involved, which thus appears between the occluders as well as to left and right.

trajectory information (what Spelke et al. called smoothness of motion) to determine that only one object was involved. In a subsequent experiment, Spelke et al. found that infants showed no evidence of using violation of smoothness of motion (early reemergence) to conclude that two objects were involved. In contrast, Wilcox and Schweinle (2003) showed that young infants take violations of smoothness as indication that two objects (and hence two separate trajectories) are involved. It is possible that the different findings here emerged because Wilcox and Schweinle used a very extreme "acceleration" such that reemergence was virtually instantaneous.

Wilcox and Baillargeon (1998) suggest that tasks of this sort may underestimate young infants' ability because of their complexity. They draw a distinction between "event mapping" tasks, in which infants make a judgment about an end event in terms of earlier events, and "event monitoring" tasks, in which all the information is based in the event itself, and claim that the former are in principle more complex than the latter. In support of this claim, they replicated Xu and Carey's (1996) results in a similar event-mapping task, but obtained positive results with infants as young as 7 months in an event-monitoring task. This task was ingeniously designed to investigate infants' inferences about the number of objects involved in the event. Infants saw one object move behind an occluder and a distinct one reemerge at the other side under two conditions. In a wide-occluder condition, the occluder was large enough to hide both objects, whereas in a narrow-occluder condition, it could only hide one object. Infants aged 7- to 9-months looked longer at the narrow-occluder event, suggesting that they knew that the change in object form indicated a different object and that this was an impossible sequence only when the occluder was too narrow to hide both. It is possible, however, that the difference in occluder width might explain this effect. Wilcox and Baillargeon controlled for this by testing infants again with the narrow occluder, using smaller objects both of which could be concealed behind it, and finding that infants treated this event in the same way as the wide-occluder event with larger objects. Note, however, that the use of smaller objects meant that the time between one disappearing and the other appearing was longer than in the narrow-occluder large-object condition. Remembering how crucial time out of sight is in trajectory perception (Bremner et al., 2005) we must wonder whether longer looking in the original narrow-occluder condition arose because infants noticed the object change across the very small temporal gap but not otherwise. Thus in this case longer looking may have a simple perceptual basis and, using a different form of event-monitoring task, Krøjgaard (2007) found that use of property–kind information to individuate objects only emerged at 9.5 months. Thus, this issue remains contentious.

Numerical knowledge.   Earlier work established evidence that quite young infants were capable of discriminating small numbers. Starkey and Cooper (1980) habituated 4- to 7-month-old infants to patterns of a particular number of dots (two or three) and tested for dishabituation to the other number (three or two). They also included a large-number condition in which there were either four or six dots. Infants dishabituated to number change in the small number but not in the large-number condition. This supported their supposition that infants' number discrimination was based on *subitizing*, an ability to enumerate number perceptually that is limited to small numbers. Additionally, the negative result with larger numbers serves to make unlikely discrimination on the basis of lower-level stimulus properties such as contour density or brightness differences, because these differences were actually greater in the large-number arrays. Starkey, Spelke, and Gelman (1990) reduced further the possibility that discrimination between arrays could be based on lower-order perceptual properties by habituating infants to pictures of sets of different objects in different spatial arrangements which were always in groups of the same number, testing them on sets of novel objects in novel arrangements that were either the same or different in number. Despite the fact that all test arrays contained novel objects in novel arrangements, 6- to 9-month-olds looked longer at arrays containing a novel number of objects. In addition to confirming the earlier work, this result suggests that infants' discrimination of number is not limited to comparisons between sets of identical objects, a limitation that had at one time been assumed to apply to young children's enumeration of sets. And results of this sort are not limited to infants of 4 months and over, because Antell and Keating (1983) replicated Starkey and Cooper's results with newborn infants.

There is also evidence that 6-month-olds are capable of discriminating large-number arrays, such as 8 versus 16 (Xu & Spelke, 2000). However, discriminations of this sort are conditional on the ratio being large. That is, infants discriminate between 8 and 16, but not between 8 and 12. Thus, Xu and Spelke conclude that what is being uncovered here is an ability to represent approximate numerosity, probably subserved by a different system from the one supporting small-number discrimination. Feigenson, Dehaene, and Spelke (2004) argue that infants have two core number systems, one that deals with precise number, limited to very small numbers and overlaid by judgments of total (non-numerical) amount when number exceeds 3, and another approximate system dealing with large numbers and based on ratio difference. Interestingly, while the small-number discrimination system is easily disrupted by variations in continuous variables such as overall amount (Feigenson, Carey, & Spelke, 2002), the large-number system is robust relative to continuous variables. For instance, 6-month-olds discriminated a 2:1 change in number with surface area held constant, but failed to discriminate a 2:1 difference in surface area with number held constant (Brannon, Abbott, & Lutz, 2004).

Perception of number does not appear to be limited to the visual modality, or indeed to one modality. Starkey et al. (1990) also showed that infants were capable of detecting the numerical equivalence between sets of objects and groups of sounds. Six- to 8-month-olds were presented with pairs of visual arrays, one containing two and the other three objects, while a drum beat pattern of either two or three beats was presented. They found that infants looked longer at stimuli containing the same number of objects as the number of drum beats presented.

These are striking results, particularly because the abilities attributed to infants are greater than have so far been shown in preschool children. However, they have not gone unquestioned. For instance, Moore, Benenson, Reznick, Peterson, & Kagan (1987) and Mix, Levine, and Huttenlocher (1997) obtained the opposite auditory–visual matching result, finding that infants looked longer at the display that was not numerically equivalent to the sound pattern. This in itself is not a fatal problem, because the opposite effect still implies detection of a consistent relationship between auditory and visual numerosity. There is also no reason to assume that infants should look at the pattern with the same number rather than the pattern with a different number. However, the inconsistency of results raises concern about the reliability of the techniques used. In addition, Mix et al. point out that the auditory–visual correspondence could be based on an imprecise match in quantity between visual array and sound. Furthermore, in previous work, auditory numerosity was always confounded with either pattern frequency or pattern duration, and, when Mix et al. randomized these variables within the task, they found no significant preference for either the corresponding or different number visual array. However, randomly altering these variables may add an attention-getting factor to the task that distracts infants from the numerical correspondence. So it may be that this test is too strong. The positive results, despite their inconsistency, suggest that at least some rather global notion of quantity is present in the first year of life. If it does not constitute numerical competence, it is probably one of its important developmental precursors.

Wynn (1992, 1995) carried out a number of ingenious studies designed to go beyond research on numerical correspondence, to establish whether infants possess a number system as such, that is, whether they understand numerical operations such as addition and subtraction. Her basic method is illustrated in Figure 6.9. In the addition task, infants are presented with a single object, an occluder is raised to hide it, whereupon a hand appears with a second object and places it behind the occluder (the addition operation). The occluder is then lowered for the test trial to reveal either one object (original array

Sequence of events: 1 + 1 = 1 or 2

| 1 Object placed in case | 2 Screen comes up | 3 Second object added | 4 Hand leaves empty |

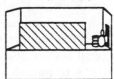

Then either (a) Possible outcome   **Or (b) Impossible outcome**

| 5 Screen drops … | 6 Revealing two objects | | 5 Screen drops … | 6 Revealing one object |

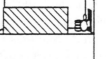

Sequence of events: 2 – 1 = 1 or 2

| 1 Objects placed in case | 2 Screen comes up | 3 Empty hand enters | 4 One object removed |

Then either: (a) Possible outcome   **Or (b) Impossible outcome**

| 5 Screen drops … | 6 Revealing one object | | 5 Screen drops … | 6 Revealing two objects |

Figure 6.9   Displays used by Wynn (1992) to investigate infants' knowledge of addition and subtraction. The addition event sequence is above and subtraction event sequence below.

but impossible given addition of the second object) or two objects (novel array but correct given addition). In the subtraction task, two objects are presented initially, and the hand removes one once they are screened. Thus in this case on the test trial the single object outcome is correct and the two object outcome is incorrect. Four- and 5-month-olds looked longer at the single object in the addition case and longer at the double object in the subtraction case. Wynn concluded that infants have an understanding of addition and subtraction, but recognized that this could be a very approximate system in which any larger or smaller number would be accepted as the result of addition and subtraction respectively. Thus she conducted a further study in which 4-month-olds were exposed to the 1 + 1 addition task and on test trials were presented with either two or three objects. Infants looked longer at the three-object outcome, and Wynn concluded that their knowledge of addition was quite precise, to the extent that they expected precisely two objects and just not more objects to result from a 1 + 1 operation. To explain these abilities, she proposes an accumulator mechanism (originally developed by Meck & Church, 1983, to account for discrimination of number by rats) through which discrete pulses for each object "counted" are passed into an accumulator, and relative numerosity judgments are then based on the fullness of the accumulator between the two sets of objects "counted."

Some recent neuroscientific evidence supports the notion that infants are detecting incorrect outcomes. Berger, Tzur, and Posner (2006) found that when infants saw an incorrect outcome they exhibited ERP activity similar in brain location and form to that exhibited by adults faced with incorrect outcomes. However, there is controversy regarding whether infants' responses to Wynn's task reveals awareness of violation of addition and subtraction as such. Feigenson et al. (2002) point out that number and continuous extent are confounded, since the objects are of constant size. They replicated Wynn's result with constant size objects, but found that when object size was manipulated between addition/subtraction operation and outcome, infants looked longer at unexpected outcomes in terms of continuous extent rather than number. Although this is in keeping with their work on discrimination of changes in number versus physical extent, in which the latter dominates, one must wonder whether in this task the change in object size between operation and outcome destroys the identity of the objects involved in the operation. And perception of identity is likely to be a condition for understanding addition and subtraction.

In conclusion, there is evidence that young infants can discriminate small numbers, both within and across modalities, and that they are aware of the outcome of simple addition and subtraction operations. Additionally, they appear to predict the number of objects involved in certain events. All this evidence relates to very small numbers of objects, and it appears likely that perceptual processes such as subitizing support this early ability. However, this appears to be a fragile capability that is quite hard to separate from perception of overall stimulus extent. There is also evidence for discrimination of relatively large numbers, provided the ratio is sufficiently large. This appears to be an approximate system based on ratios, which is, somewhat paradoxically, independent of overall stimulus extent. Interestingly, the ratio difference required for discrimination of large numbers is similar to that in discriminating stimulus duration (Brannon, Suanda, & Libertus, 2007; vanMarle & Wynn, 2006) and area (Brannon, Lutz, & Cordes, 2006), and Feigenson (2007) suggests that this work is tapping into a general system for processing quantity.

Interpreting the Evidence: Innate Cognitive Structures?

Object identity

Taken alone, the results of some of the earlier studies by Baillargeon and Spelke suggest that very young infants have an awareness of the world that virtually matches that of adults. However, although young infants do appear to possess a good basic understanding of physical principles, this becomes more sophisticated as they get older, and Baillargeon and colleagues (Baillargeon, 2007; Baillargeon, Needham and De Vos 1992) and Spelke et al. (1992) argue that initial core knowledge becomes elaborated through experience. As Baillargeon et al. (1992, p. 77) put it: "in their first pass at understanding physical events, infants construct all-or-none representations that capture the essence of the events but few of the details. With further experience, these initial, core representations are progressively elaborated."

The picture emerging from this literature is radically different from the conventional Piagetian constructionism. It is argued that infants are endowed with innate knowledge and psychological processes. They possess core knowledge concerning fundamental physical principles of *continuity* (that objects move on continuous paths) and *solidity* (that objects occupy space and no two objects can occupy the same space simultaneously). This theory of core knowledge is not limited to object knowledge, but extends to actions, number, and space (Spelke & Kinzler, 2007). Early knowledge, however, is limited as indicated by the evidence that young infants do not understand principles of gravity or inertia, and development of further knowledge is based on experience. A good example of this is found in the case of understanding of the conditions under which one object supports another. At 4-months-old infants treat any contact between supporting and supported objects as sufficient for support (Needham & Baillargeon, 1993), whereas by 6 months they distinguish between sufficient and insufficient contact (Baillargeon et al., 1992), and by 8 months they begin to understand gravity as a factor in support relationships (Huettel & Needham, 2000). It is suggested that this gradual refinement in part results from infants' experience, in this case, their experience of stacking objects.

There are, however, growing criticisms of these approaches. First, it is not clear whether the data demand interpretation in terms of cognitive processes, in particular the notion of infant reasoning. The only factor in moving object studies that appears to demand interpretation in terms of reasoning, or indeed representation, is the presence of an occluder concealing part of the object's trajectory. Supposedly, to produce positive results, the infant must have represented the continuing existence of the screened object and reasoned about its continued history on the basis of knowledge of physical reality. However, alternative conceptualizations exist. Other, more modest, accounts rely on at least the notion that young infants form mental representations of objects. For instance, as a first stage in their account of the development of object permanence, Meltzoff and Moore (1998) argue that young infants form representations of objects that serve to specify their continued existence over breaks in sensory contact. More radically, however, the ecological approach to perception (Gibson, 1979) questions the need for the concept of mental representation. According to this account, perceptual input is dynamic and continuous over time, and movement of an individual through the world generates a continuous flow of information that specifies the relationship between objects in world and their changing relationship to the individual. True, there are gaps in perception as one object is temporarily occluded by another but the information flow before and after occlusion serves to specify the object continuously over this gap: perceptual information specifies the occlusion of a further object by a near one, not its annihilation, and the same applies on its reappearance. Thus, according to ecological theorists, detection of an object's spatiotemporal history arises directly from perpetual information and does not require representational processes or reasoning. In other words, perceptual extrapolation fills breaks in sensory contact, and there is no need to invoke representational processes. It may be that there is a parallel here with the work on object unity and trajectory continuity, where in both cases there is evidence for persistence of perception across small spatial and temporal gaps. Similarly, in the case of a stationary object temporarily hidden from view, there may be persistence of perception across a temporal gap.

Another form of criticism of nativist interpretation gets more to the roots of the tasks themselves. Investigators such as Bogartz et al. (1997) and Haith (1998) argue that it is at least premature to apply interpretations of these recent data, it being possible to explain much of the evidence in terms of much more basic properties of perception and memory. One of the puzzles regarding recent studies is why there is a need for initial familiarization trials prior to tests trials. After all, if we are tapping into innate knowledge and reasoning processes, violation tests trials should be detected as discrepant without prior familiarization. Yet, it is apparent that positive results depend on prior familiarization. Possibly, this is because early knowledge is sufficiently weak to require prior repeated experience of an event to bolster judgment. Alternatively, infants' responses in these tasks may reflect detection of a departure from an expectation built up over the series of familiarization trials rather than violation of a core principle of physical reality.

Bogartz et al. (1997) point out how the detection of disparity between familiarization and test event can be at quite a low level, tapping into basic attentional or perceptual processes. As already noted, Baillargeon and deVos (1991) habituated infants either to a short or a tall rabbit passing behind an occluder, and test trials were identical except that a gap was cut in the top of the occluder which should reveal the tall but not the short rabbit. However, in neither test trial did a rabbit appear in the gap. Their interpretation is that infants can reason about visibility on the basis of the height of the rabbit. In contrast, Bogartz et al. (1997) suggest that in the short rabbit display, infants' attention is attracted to the rabbit's face and they scan across the occluder at that height. Thus they do not notice the change in the top of the occluder. Infants in the tall rabbit condition, however, scan at the higher level of the rabbit's face, and note the gap on test trials. Thus, increased looking is due solely to the change in the occluder, and whether or not this change is detected is determined by the attentional focus built up during familiarization. Like many alternative interpretations, however, their account only explains performance in a specific case, and does not explain infants' responses to nonreappearance of an object between two separate occluders (Aguiar & Baillargeon, 1999) or in a gap in the bottom edge of an occluder (Aguiar & Baillargeon, 2002).

Other studies also appear to be open to alternative interpretations. For instance, investigating the drawbridge task (Baillargeon et al. 1985), Rivera, Wakeley, and Langer (1999) suggest that infants' longer looking at the impossible event in which the drawbridge rotates apparently through the position of the block may be due to a simple preference for a longer rotation involving as it does greater perceptual change. Baillargeon (1987a) dismisses such an interpretation because she found no preference for 180° degree rotation over 112° rotation in a control task in which no block is placed in the path of the drawbridge. However, these test trials followed normal habituation trials with the 180° rotation, and as Rivera et al. point out, under these circumstances one would expect a novelty preference for the 112° rotation. They hypothesize that infants actually have a preference for the larger rotation that is lost due to exposure to this event during habituation and test this possibility by replicating the Baillargeon technique omitting prior habituation trials. Under these circumstances, infants show a preference for the 180° rotation the strength of which is unaffected by whether there is a block in the path of the drawbridge or not.

It does appear that the incomplete designs used in much of this work limit the conclusions that can be drawn. Also, it is true that some of the findings are open to alternative interpretations that rely on quite simple processes. Typically, however, each of the findings requires a different low-level interpretation, which leads to the question of whether such interpretations are really more parsimonious or plausible. Additionally, it is very hard to explain some findings in these terms, in particular, the effect obtained by Baillargeon (1986, Figure 4), in which the difference between possible and impossible test events lay in whether the block lay on or behind the track of the train. It seems inescapable that, at some level, perceptual or cognitive, infants registered whether the block obstructed the track or not, and that looking duration was determined by a combination of this information and the fixed outcome of object reemergence.

Numerical knowledge

It should be noted that, despite the apparently high levels of control in studies of number discrimination, some workers question whether discrimination of number is really at the root of the findings. For instance, Clearfield and Mix (1999) point out that number was often confounded with total contour (three objects have more total contour than two objects of the same size). In a study investigating this, they found that infants dishabituated to changes in contour but not to changes in small number (2 vs. 3) with contour held constant. Thus, they conclude that when the appropriate controls are applied, evidence for number discrimination disappears. In contrast, however, Xu and Spelke (2000) obtained positive results for large numbers with total contour controlled. The problem is that technical detail is probably critical; certain ways of applying controls may actually suppress an ability that is really there. Clearfield and Mix presented a block of test trials each one of which involved either a change in total contour or a change in number.

The change in contour that they used looks to adult eyes more striking than the change in number, and this may have led infants to operate at the level of contour rather than number. In contrast, Xu and Spelke varied contour during habituation trials, holding number constant, a technique that is more likely to lead infants to focus on number as the constant variable during habituation.

Haith (1998) criticizes the conclusions that Wynn draws from her work, on the basis that her results can be interpreted at a simple perceptual level. He bases his argument on a "thought experiment" in which Wynn's procedures are carried out exactly the same way but with the occluder absent. In this scenario, impossible outcomes are manifested in the sudden appearance or disappearance of an object seen to have been removed or added. His claim is that if one assumes a lingering (though decaying) sensory trace, the two situations become comparable, and all that infants are responding to is something strange in the outcome.

Cohen and Marks (2002) suggest that Wynn's results can be explained on the basis of simple perceptual variables. First of all, they suggest that infants may have a spontaneous preference for more numerous arrays, which they claim may explain longer looking in Wynn's 1+1 = 3 condition. Second, they point out that when infants are not fully habituated, they may exhibit a familiarity preference rather than the usual novelty preference (Hunter & Ames, 1988). Thus, they suggest that longer looking at the incorrect numerical outcome in Wynn's 1+1 and 2–1 events is actually a familiarity preference for the original array, and they provide evidence in keeping with this interpretation in a task in which no object is added or subtracted, and hence where the same number outcome is correct. There are, however, two problems for this account. First, Wynn provided prior baseline trials in which infants saw one or two objects in alternation. Thus, when they started test trials, one and two object events were more or less equally familiar. Second, in a task that replicated Wynn's exactly but in which no object was actually added or removed, Slater, Bremner, Johnson, and Hayes (in press) found no evidence for familiarity preferences.

Slater et al. (in press) also used an eye-tracker to obtain more precise information regarding where infants looked when presented with test trials. The clearest effect was that when two objects were present, infants looked longer at the left-hand object when it should not be present (subtraction incorrect outcome) than when it should be present (addition correct outcome). Such an effect is not predicted on the basis of a general familiarity preference, and is in keeping with Wynn's account. However, it is also in keeping with object-tracking accounts that do not make the same assumptions regarding numerical ability (Cheries, Wynn, & Scholl, 2006; Simon, 1997). Infants may attend primarily to the locus of the most recent event, and thus longer looking may reflect registration that an object is occupying a location that it was seen to leave, or that an object should occupy a location that it was seen to go to. Put simply, the left-hand object could be irrelevant, and infants' responses may be based on identifying whether the right-hand location is correctly or incorrectly occupied or vacant. Although Koechlin, Dehaene, and Mehler (1997) set out to test spatially specific accounts of this sort by moving the objects to new locations while they were out of sight, they replicated Wynn's result for the case of subtraction alone, raising issues regarding the interpretation of their results. Given the importance of this issue, future work should be directed at investigating the role of lower level spatial "place holder" or object file processes (Cheries et al., 2006; Simon, 1997) as possible precursors of numerical knowledge.

Summary

Research based on violation of expectancy tasks has yielded a wealth of evidence regarding young infants' reactions to a variety of events embodying different physical principles governing the persistence and movement of objects. However, there is a healthy controversy over the interpretation of these results, nativists arguing that they reveal innate core knowledge and the ability to reason about physical reality, and direct perception theorists arguing that the phenomena can be explained on the basis of simpler perceptual principles through which the structure of events is picked up directly and without the need for mediating cognitive processes. Other workers even question whether the phenomena relate to awareness of the assumed physical principles, suggesting that the results are effectively artifacts that can be explained in terms of underlying preferences for particular events or attentional biases to certain parts of displays. It appears, however, that these latter accounts struggle to explain the breadth of evidence, and it seems likely that many of these studies reveal important information about infants' early awareness of physical reality. Even if they do not reveal innate knowledge structures, they are probably the developmental precursors of the knowledge individuals use to guide action later in infancy.

Object Search and Object Knowledge

Whatever the final interpretation of work focusing on knowledge of the world in early infancy, we are left with the problem of explaining the negative evidence regarding rather older infants' knowledge revealed in tasks in which infants have to search for hidden objects. If the evidence from early infancy does indicate innate knowledge, there is a real problem to be faced in explaining why this knowledge is not revealed in action, even several months later. If, on the other hand, the evidence from early infancy reveals some lower-level developmental precursor of mature object knowledge, there is less of a problem in reconciling this evidence with the object search phenomena, but it is still vital to provide a developmental model that integrates the two bodies of evidence, showing how early awareness develops into a form of knowledge that can be used to guide action.

Piaget's account

Piaget's view was that it was only through developing and coordinating sensori-motor schemes that infants began to construct a representation of hidden objects. Initially, there is no objective awareness of a separate world of objects, and infants treat objects as sensations arising from their own actions. As they construct more complex sensori-motor schemes, infants begin to build the precursors of mental representation, the beginnings of which can be seen at around 8 months when infants begin to search for hidden objects. Search requires the coordination of separate schemes directed to occluder and object, and it is in coordinating these that infants construct the spatial relationship between object and occluder and hence begin to represent the hidden object. Even at this point, however, object representation is not fully independent of action, and it is only by the end of the sensori-motor period that infants have a well-developed representational ability that is independent of action.

Two of Piaget's findings provide persistent problems for accounts that portray the young infant as aware of object permanence. First, infants fail to search for hidden objects until they are about 8 months old. Second, once they begin to search for objects they make systematic errors in search. If the object is first hidden in one place and then another, they retrieve it successfully from the first place but continue to search there when it is hidden in the new place.

Search failure

One obvious possibility is that infants below 8 months fail to search for a hidden object because they are unable to organize the response required to retrieve the hidden object. In effect, this was a central point in Piaget's sensori-motor theory; it is only through coordinating action schemes directed to cover and uncover an object in the correct sequence that infants construct the relationship between them and thus come to represent the invisible object. However, it is possible that they understand permanence but cannot organize the necessary actions for retrieval. Rader, Spiro, and Firestone (1979) found that infants were more likely to search if the cover was easily manipulable. However, this result may have been artifactual, because the more manipulable the cover was the more likely it was to be dislodged by swiping movements. Bower and Wishart (1972) showed that although 6-month-old infants would not lift an opaque upturned cup to retrieve a hidden object, they retrieved the object successfully if it was placed under a transparent cup, a result replicated by Shinskey, Bogartz, and Poirier (2000) for the case of an object hidden behind a vertical curtain. Also, Moore and Meltzoff (2008) demonstrated that infants were more likely to retrieve a partially hidden object than a fully hidden one, even though the action required was the same in each case. Thus, it is clear that infants are capable of the necessary actions, and that invisibility of the object is the primary determinant of search failure. It may be, however, that limitations in infants' understanding or perception of the specific occluder–object relationship may be part of the reason for their difficulty. Although Moore and Meltzoff found infants were no more successful searching behind vertical occluders than under horizontal ones, Neilson (1977) showed that the presence of a clear separation in depth between object and occluder as it went out of sight enhanced search behind a vertical occluder. Six-month-olds failed to search when an object disappeared immediately behind an occluder, but searched successfully when there was a clear separation in depth at the point of disappearance. It is interesting to speculate on the possibility that this effect may be related closely to object segregation phenomena discussed earlier.

The A not B search error

The A not B or stage IV search error is a tantalizing phenomenon that to date has eluded convincing explanation. The fascination of this phenomenon is that it is so unexpected. An attentive 9-month-old infant searches accurately at the first place (A) and will do so almost without error over a series of trials. When the object is then hidden in the new position (B) the infant, without hesitation, searches again in position A – in strong examples of the error, no attempt at correction occurs and errors of a similar sort recur over a series of further hidings at B. Not all infants show such a convincing pattern, possibly because in any cross-sectional sample infants are bound to be at different developmental levels, but the convincing cases make the phenomenon a real explanatory puzzle.

Piaget's explanation of this phenomenon was that infants had only a limited awareness of the hidden object's continued existence. They were beginning to represent the absent object, but they could only do this in a limited way, imagining it to be present in the hiding place where it had previously been found. Thus, a move to a new hiding location led to error. Not all investigators accepted this interpretation, however, and in the 1970s and 1980s a substantial body of work accumulated investigating possible explanations of the phenomenon.

The role of action.   According to Piaget, the infant's ability to represent the object was dependent on action: the error involved repeating the action that had been successful in the past. However, it turned out that action was not necessary for error: infants who had simply seen the object hidden and revealed at the first location, made errors when permitted to search on B trials (Butterworth, 1974; Evans, 1973; Landers, 1971). These data also appear to rule out a simpler account of the error, namely that it is no more than response perseveration.

Memory interference?   At first sight, it is tempting to guess that the error is due to forgetting the location of the object. However, the phenomenon cannot be due to global forgetting, because infants are highly successful from the first A trial. The problem is why they should encode the object's location accurately on A trials but fail to do so on B trials. Harris (1973) suggested that this arose through memory interference: when the object is hidden at A, search is successful, but when the new location is used, interference takes place between memory for the past location and memory for the present location, such that infants often search back at the old location. In support of this account, Harris found that errors were infrequent when infants were allowed to search immediately on B trials. Gratch, Appel, Evans, LeCompte, and Wright (1974) found that a delay of only a second was sufficient to produce errors at the normal rate, but that delays above 1 second did nothing to increase error, so if interference is at the root of things, it has its effect very quickly. Gratch et al. interpret their results differently, suggesting that the lack of error with delays less than a second is due to the maintenance of a postural orientation (and possibly a partial reach) towards the correct location. Infants are fortuitously correct because they simply continue an act that began when the object was in view.

There is, however, a major problem for all memory accounts. Piaget noted that the error still occurs when the object was visible at the new location. This finding has been replicated by Butterworth (1974) and Harris (1974) in versions of the task using transparent covers, and by Bremner and Knowles (1984) who did not even cover the object on B trials. It is not clear how memory accounts can explain this, since there should be no need to hold the visible object in memory. Additionally, there is now clear evidence that search failure and errors are not due to a simple lack of awareness of where the object has gone. Wilcox, Nadel, and Rosser (1996) presented infants of between 2.5 and 6.5 months with event sequences in which an object disappeared at one of two locations and after a delay either reappeared at the opposite location (impossible event) or in the same location (possible event). All age groups looked reliably longer at the impossible event, suggesting that they were capable of holding the location of the hidden object in memory, and noting a violation when it reappeared in the wrong place. If such young infants have well-developed location memory, it seems unlikely that this would be a major aspect of the problem 6 or 7 months later. This is confirmed by Ahmed and Ruffman (1998), who made a direct comparison between 8- to 12-month-olds' performance on an A not B search task and a comparable violation of expectation task in which, after concealment and reappearance at A, the object was hidden at B and revealed either at B (possible) or at A (impossible). Infants who made search errors nevertheless anticipated reemergence at B, even after delays of 15 seconds. Additionally, Hofstadter and Reznick (1996) found that infants were more likely to make manual search errors than looking errors in an A not B task, again suggesting that infants have a better memory of object position than their search suggests.

Spatial analyses.   One possible explanation of the error is that infants have difficulty updating the spatial location of the object when it is moved from A to B. A number of workers have investigated the spatial demands of the stage IV task. Harris (1973) and later Butterworth (1975) pointed out that when the object is moved from the A location to the B location, both its absolute position in space changes and its relative position changes, that is, it goes from, say, the left-hand to the right-hand container. By changing the position of the containers between A and B trials Butterworth made it possible to hide the object either in the same relative location but a different absolute position, or in the same absolute position but a different relative location. The finding was that a change in location according to either of these spatial reference systems led to error at about the same rate as if object location changed relative to both reference systems at once. So apparently infants use both ways of coding the position of the hidden object and have difficulty if its position changes relative to either.

Bremner and Bryant (1977) pointed out that because infants remained stationary throughout the task, it was impossible to tell if they were coding the object's position in absolute terms, or through self-reference, in relation to their own body. However, the confound between these two types of coding is removed if the infant is moved to the opposite side of the table. We found that on B trials following such a movement, infants searched at the same position relative to self as before, and hence at a different absolute position. This happened despite the fact that the two locations lay on clearly different backgrounds. However, Bremner (1978) found that if differently colored covers were used, the effect was reversed: infants now searched at the same absolute location after movement, and hence at a different self-referent location. Thus, it appears that absolute position coding is possible if the alternative locations are clearly distinguished.

It may well be that these studies, while telling us a good deal about how infants code spatial locations, tell us little about the reasons for the A not B error. Elsewhere (Bremner, 1985) I have suggested that these manipulations do not reduce the error but rather affect the way infants define the single place to which they direct their search efforts. However, Butterworth, Jarrett, and Hicks (1982) did find that differentiating the covers reduced errors in a standard A not B task, and claim that knowledge of object identity is intimately linked to keeping track of the spatial history of the object. It is only through linking the successive positions of an object that infants perceive its identity over the move, and it is because infants encounter difficulties in doing this that search errors occur.

Locations as places of concealment.   Two things happen when an object is hidden: it disappears and a place takes on the function of container or place of concealment. Most previous accounts have assumed that object search phenomena tell us about object permanence. It is possible, however, to develop an account based on knowledge of places as containers (Bremner, 1985). During the early years, infants spend a good deal of time removing objects from containers (for instance taking toys from toy boxes) but they very rarely put them back: as Piaget noted, the act of putting one object inside another is a relatively late development. It is thus plausible that they have semi-magical notions about containers as sources of objects, notions that are based more on finding objects there than on seeing them go there. Admittedly, seeing an object disappear at a place must be a sufficient cue to lead to search at that place, otherwise infants would never search for an object on the first trial. And even the perceptual features of the container may cue its function. But my hypothesis was that object retrieval or revelation is a much more potent cue to a place as a container. Thus, once an object has been retrieved (or has been revealed) at A, that place is firmly established as a container where an object will be found. When the object is hidden at B, there is a conflict between object disappearance at B and the newly established function of A as a container, and the greater salience of the latter normally wins that day. This account does not make assumptions about limited object representation as the basis of error, an advantage given the evidence that some form of object knowledge is well developed in the early months. In relation to this account, Topál et al. (2008) add a social dimension to the A not B task, arguing that infants interpret the experimenter's acts as indication that position A is a place where objects are to be found, and finding that errors are reduced when the experimenter does not engage in direct interaction with the infant.

Action history.   Despite earlier dismissals of the action perseveration explanation, Smith, Thelen, McLin, and Titzer (1999) revisit the notion that the error is due to motor history of reaching to A. They obtained evidence that infants made search errors even when no objects were hidden. Instead of hiding an object at A and later at B, they simply attracted infants' attention to A (by waving and tapping the container lid) and later to B in the same way. They found that infants made "search" errors with the same incidence as in the standard task, and concluded that the phenomenon was due to establishment of a reaching habit, and nothing to do with memory or representation of the object at A.

Although this is a plausible possibility, it encounters the same difficulty as previous action perseveration accounts. As already mentioned, infants make search errors even if they have only seen the object hidden and revealed at the A location. Smith et al. (1999) rightly point out that most procedures involve warm-up trials in which the infant is encouraged to retrieve a partially hidden object from A prior to full hiding there, and this is enough to establish the reaching habit. However, Butterworth (1974) took care to avoid such a problem by giving warm-up trials at the midline. Thus, on commencement of B trials infants had no prior experience of reaching to A, but erred nonetheless. Additionally, the account contains a logical difficulty. If similar "errors" occur when no object is hidden, it does not follow that the hiding of the object in the standard A not B task is irrelevant; superficially similar behaviors can have quite different bases. In short, their research does not provide conditions in which different performance is predicted dependent on whether or not an object is hidden, whereas experimental logic depends on showing significant effects of different manipulations. Additionally there is evidence that the presence of an object does affect behavior. Munakata (1997) compared infants' reaching in two tasks, one of which replicated that of Smith et al. (1999) in which no object was hidden on A or B trials, and another in which no object was hidden on A trials, but an object was hidden on B trials. In the replication condition, just as Smith et al. (1999) found, infants made errors, but on the version in which the object was introduced and hidden on B trials, they made few errors, despite the fact that up to that point the motor history of both groups was identical. The object had no prior history at A, and they searched correctly when it was hidden for the first time at B. Munakata concludes that the hiding of an object has an effect and so is an important factor in the standard task. Other work confirms this conclusion, Bremner and Bryant (2001) showed that cover differentiation had opposite effects on error rate depending on whether an object was hidden or not. When an object was hidden, cover differentiation led to a reduction in error, the same result as obtained by Butterworth, et al. (1982). In contrast, when no object was hidden, cover differentiation increased error rate. It seems likely that when no object is hidden, cover differentiation simply helps infants to individuate the cover that becomes the focus of action during A trials, and there is no real reason to change this focus when the experimenter turns their attention to the new location. However, when an object is hidden, the hidden object is the focus of action, and cover differentiation helps infants to identify its new location on B trials.

A neurophysiological account.   Diamond (1988) has suggested that the error can be explained by the fact that the frontal cortex becomes fully functional only rather late in infancy, an account that is based in part on the finding that rhesus monkeys with lesions of frontal cortex perform poorly on the stage IV task (Diamond, 1990). She proposes that a primary function of frontal cortex is to support two capacities, the maintenance of an object representation in memory and inhibition of incorrect responses, and her claim is that although infants are capable of these singly, the load becomes too great when they have to do both. There is some evidence that there is a link between error and frontal cortex development. For instance, Bell and Fox (1992) showed that infants who did not make the stage IV error showed more developed frontal EEG patterns than those who erred. We must note, however, that this is correlational evidence that does not allow us to assume a direct causal link.

A key aspect of Diamond's evidence is that there is a clear relationship between a delay between hiding and search and error. Errors are more likely after longer delays, and older children tolerate longer delays without error than younger ones. This certainly suggests a memory factor. However, this evidence is rather different from the result obtained by Gratch et al. (1974), namely that the increase in error occurred entirely between zero and one second delay. There are two reasons why Diamond's results may be different. First, she employed a distraction procedure, in which the infant's attention was drawn from the correct location after the object had been hidden. This procedure is unnecessary, because infants make errors even when fully attentive, but any distraction is likely to increase or introduce memory load. Second, she adopts a multitrial reversal procedure in which the B location becomes the A location for the next test. Under such circumstances, once some way into a test session, infants have a complex and probably confusing past search history. Thus again the task may become more about the real problem of simply remembering the last location acted on than understanding the sequence of hidings as an integrated whole. There is thus reason to question whether Diamond's task taps into the same factors as a more conventional A not B task.

Despite these question marks, by presenting a multifactor explanation Diamond's account is an advance over previous accounts that have tried to explain the error in terms of a single factor. However, there is reason to doubt the detail of the argument. It does not appear that failure to inhibit a previous response can explain the error, either alone or in conjunction with a memory factor. Remember that early studies (Butterworth, 1974; Evans, 1973; Landers, 1971) obtained errors after observational trials. In this case, no prior response had been established. Additionally, the problem for the memory component of her account is that, although she recognizes that errors sometimes occur when the object is visible, the prediction is that these should be very occasional. However, using transparent covers, Butterworth (1977) obtained errors at much the same rate as when using opaque covers and a similar rate of error occurred when the object was not even covered on B trials (Bremner & Knowles, 1984). There is no evidence from these sources that errors were significantly reduced by object visibility.

A connectionist model of search errors.   Munakata has developed a connectionist model to account for the data regarding the stage IV error (Munakata et al., 1997; Munakata, 1998a). This is based on the notion that infants' search is determined by the interaction of two factors, "latent" and "active" memory traces. Latent traces are reflected in the experience-based strengthening of connections between units in the system, leading to certain responses being likely in the presence of certain inputs (comparable to long-term memory) and active traces are reflected in the level of ongoing activity maintained within the system (comparable to working memory). Thus, when faced with concealment of the object at B, infants' responses are determined by the relative dominance of latent traces specifying place A and active traces specifying place B. Working from this basic assumption, Munakata develops a sophisticated model which accounts for much of the data on infant search and makes new predictions, such as the counter intuitive one that, during development, errors should increase gradually before decreasing again.

This is an important approach, because it allows precise specification of predicted effects on search of different factors such as delay, number, and distinctiveness of locations. However, models of this sort run into difficulties over some of the more subtle aspects of the error. In particular, errors are significantly reduced if differently colored covers are used (Butterworth et al., 1982) whereas they are not significantly reduced when the object is visible at B. One would have thought that a visible object would serve to differentiate locations in a most salient way, yet it does not have the effect that cover differentiation has. Munakata (1998b) claims that errors with the object visible are occasional random errors, citing evidence from a study by Sophian and Yengo (1985), which suggested that errors with a visible object at B were due to lapses of attention rather than real problems locating the object. However, in contrast to Butterworth (1974) and Bremner and Knowles (1984), Sophian and Yengo obtained very few errors when the object was visible. Bremner and Knowles' data provide no support for the notion that these errors are random, because they obtained errors under very precise conditions, when the object was uncovered at B but the A location was covered. Virtually no errors were obtained when there was no covered location, and when the objects were uncovered at A but the B location was covered. In this study it is clear that the presence of a covered location at A was as strong a determinant of search as was the visible presence of the object at B. Such a finding fits with Bremner's account of the stage IV error in terms of place knowledge, and calls for the need to consider the infant's notions about locations as hiding places as well as their notions about hidden objects.

Problem-solving analyses.   Baillargeon, Graber, DeVos, and Black (1990) argue that by the age of 5 months infants are both able to represent hidden objects and can identify the actions necessary to recover them. Evidence for the second claim comes from ingenious experiments in which infants watch possible and impossible object retrieval events; as in other work of this nature, infants look longer at the impossible sequences. Baillargeon et al. thus conclude that the infant's difficulty lies in certain aspects of problem solving. Failure to search can be explained by inability to plan means–ends sequences, and even once infants are capable of this, the stage IV error arises due to a tendency to repeat old means–ends solutions. In addition to explaining manual search failure and later errors in the face of apparently contrary evidence revealed in violation of expectation tasks, this sort of analysis can also explain superior object localization reflected in looking (Hofstadter & Reznick, 1996). Looking does not involve problem solving in the way that manual search does. This, however, is only one possible analysis in terms of problem solving. Willatts (1997) questions whether the evidence presented by Baillargeon et al. really indicates that infants can identify the necessary retrieval actions, pointing out that recognition of possible versus impossible retrievals does not imply awareness of how to execute retrieval. Again, we are back to the point that studies based on violation of expectation cannot really tell us about the infant's ability to construct solutions in action. Willatts also questions whether early examples of search really involve means–ends problem solving, suggesting instead that success initially arises from trial and error. Thus, although bearing a number of similarities to the account presented by Baillargeon et al., Willatts' account presents the infant as more fundamentally lacking in problem-solving skills. It alerts us to the fact that there is more to correct object search than simply having a sufficiently strong representation of the object, and he cites evidence from other problem-solving tasks involving retrieval of visible but inaccessible objects through use of supports to show that infants' difficulties have a generality that extends beyond hidden object problems.

Conclusion. These recent accounts of search failure and search errors have made considerable progress in (a) identifying factors that influence search; and (b) in modeling possible underlying processes. More than ever, it becomes clear that several factors underlie behavior, including memory arising from past history of events at A and active memory of the most recent event. Furthermore, there is value in attempts to localize the neural substrate supporting different functions as well as modeling the processes involved. There is a good deal in common between Diamond's account and Munakata's model, and much may be gained by incorporating aspects of both. However, probably something has to be added as well. Just as the model developed by Smith et al. (1999) may be accused of laying too much stress on action and action history, the other accounts may be criticized for relying too much on relatively simple memory processes. Arguably as a result, every account has difficulty in accounting for all the phenomena, and it may be that further progress will only result from recognizing that infants are in the process of making sense of the world, not just acting on it and forming memories about it. Sure enough, during infancy making sense of the world is probably inseparable from action, but it involves more than strengthening simple connections and forming memories. This is where models of the infant as an active problem-solver become valuable, and where it becomes difficult to proceed without recognizing the presence of active mental representations. One model that goes some way towards reconciling all three of the above accounts, and which also treats the infant as possessing knowledge of the world is the *competing systems* account (Marcovitch & Zelazo, 1999: Zelazo, Reznick, & Spinazzola, 1998). According to this account, two potentially separate systems determine search in the A not B task, a response-based system the activity of which is determined by past motor history, and a representational system linked to the infant's conscious representation of the location of the hidden object. The more searches that have been directed to A the stronger the effect of the response-based system in directing search back to location A on B trials. Support from this aspect of the model comes from a meta-analysis of A not B results indicating that the number of A trials is a determinant of error on B trials. However, this aspect of the model is also its weakness, because it fails to explain errors following observational A trials, and it may be necessary to add other components to the representational side of such a model, including infants' representations of places as containers, and also to extend the model to recognize the infant as an active problem-solver.

Challenges for Future Work

The evidence reviewed in the early sections of this chapter indicate that, by the middle of their first year, infants have a fairly sophisticated basic awareness of the world, including object permanence and the physical rules governing object motion and stability. However, controversy remains regarding the appropriate interpretation of this work and the literature concerning infants' numerical abilities. Future research may benefit from being framed more in terms of Gibsonian ecological theory and concepts (such as object files) emerging from cognitive science than in terms of infants' capacity for reasoning.

Additionally, it would appear that infants are not initially able to use this information to guide action. Munakata (1998) concludes that manual search demands a stronger object representation than simple detection of an unlawful outcome in a violation of expectation task, and Shinskey and Munakata (2005) obtained evidence that in contrast to the usual novelty preference when objects are in view, infants searched more for the more strongly represented familiar object. Guidance of action may require a self-maintained active representation of the hidden object that may be beyond the infant's capabilities, and, beyond that, the ability to plan means–ends solutions. Given this state of affairs, infants have to use other means to guide action, which are liable to relate to visible objects in the scene and what they offer for action and also the cues provided by the experimenter's acts (Topál et al., 2008). Thus, initial search and retrieval at A may be, as Willatts (1997) suggests, the result of accident or trial and error, but it leads to knowledge of place A as a container of things, knowledge which may subsequently guide action even in the visible presence of the object at another location. Alternatively, in the lack of action guidance based on object knowledge, infants may be particularly likely to use the experimenter's acts as a guide to where to search and what the task is about (Topál et al., 2008) Whatever the appropriate interpretation, this analysis has links with notions about the development of executive functions (Hughes, 1998; Russell, 1996), and it may be argued that a large part of what is happening while infants develop the ability to use object knowledge to guide action has to do with the development of basic executive functions.

In the sense that infants possess awareness of the world but are unable to use it to guide action, we may consider early perceptual capacities *implicit knowledge*, because although they involve detection of information vital for action guidance, they do not yet qualify as *explicit knowledge* at the most basic level of "knowing how." One suggestion (Ahmed & Ruffman, 1998; Bremner, 1997, 1998; Bremner & Mareschal, 2004) is that a vital developmental process in early infancy involves the transformation of knowledge implicit in perception into explicit knowledge that can be used to guide action.

Some investigators apply this distinction to knowledge revealed through action versus knowledge revealed through language. For instance, Gibson (1979, p. 260) defines explicit knowledge as information that can be linguistically expressed. Karmiloff-Smith (1992) defines implicit knowledge more generally as a form of representation not available to guide the mental activities of the individual, and proposes that this is transformed into explicit knowledge through a process of representational redescription. There is also a tendency to relate the distinction to conscious versus unconscious processes, with implicit learning conceptualized as the result of unconscious processing (Cleeremans, 1993) and *tacit knowledge* the outcome of such learning (Reber, 1993). However, the present definition need not be at variance with other uses of the distinction provided we define the level of psychological activity to which we are applying it. Thus, it becomes acceptable for a form of knowledge to be explicit with respect to manual activity, while at the same time being implicit (procedural) knowledge with respect to linguistic activity. The key assumption is that there is a set of levels (principally perceptual, procedural, and declarative) at which knowledge becomes available to guide the activities of the individual, and this progression may be repeated during development of successively higher levels of psychological activity.

Links between theories and pointers to developmental processes

The implicit–explicit distinction is descriptive because, in itself, it does not illuminate the processes underlying development. However, we may look to other theories to identify some possible developmental processes. Gibsonian theory generates some straightforward predictions and dynamic systems analysis (see chapter 5 this volume) that may in time provide a detailed account of some of the processes involved. In particular, important predictions emerge in relation to the concept of affordances. As Adolph, Eppler, and Gibson (1993, p. 51) state, "An affordance is the fit between an animal's capabilities and the environmental supports that enable a given action to be performed." A given feature of the environment will hold one type of affordance for one species and a different one for another. This has the important developmental parallel that the affordances detected will depend on the infant's ability to act. To say that a particular object affords grasping or that a particular surface affords crawling only makes sense in relation to infants who can grasp and crawl respectively. Thus, as new motor achievements come on the scene, new affordances emerge. Since these affordances are essentially relationships between environmental structure and the structure of action, it is here that dynamic systems theory may help us to understand the process by which new affordances are developed, through the meshing of the organism and environmental components of the system. Before the emergence of a new affordance, the relevant environmental feature was available to perception. Thus, the environmental information specifying the affordance was implicit in perception. However, it is not until this information is meshed in as part of a system including both perception and the appropriate action that we can say that the affordance has been detected. And because an affordance is a relationship between perception and action that in itself may be sufficient to guide action it is appropriately labeled explicit knowledge.

The claim of the dynamic systems approach is that there is no need to go beyond consideration of the environmental, mechanical, and biological constraints in the system in order to reach an adequate developmental explanation. On the one hand, through its denial of the need to rely on mentalistic concepts, this approach has some clear advantages: reliance on mentalistic terminology (such as knowledge, understanding, and reasoning) in explanations of infants' ability often seems inherently inappropriate. However, it seems evident that there is more to infant development than the natural emergence of functions that link behavior to the environment. Although in time the dynamic systems approach may help to explain many of the basic activities of infants, activities which both emerge and are exercised at a relatively automatic unconscious level, this approach will have greater difficulties in dealing with the infant as an active problem-solver engaged in means–ends analysis (Willatts, 1997).

We can describe the outcomes of development through these processes in terms of different forms of implicit-to-explicit shift. As already mentioned, detection of perceptual variables specifying an affordance make that affordance implicit in perception, but this cannot be called explicit knowledge until the infant can use it to guide action. In relation to object search, it seems likely that this transformation occurs largely through the infant's efforts as a purposive problem-solver, discovering through this activity certain ways in which perception and action fit together. It should be noted that this shift from implicit to explicit involves more than a formation of a simple connection between implicit knowledge and the action system. Problem-solving analyses demonstrate that the connections between perception and action are liable to be quite complex, including processes connected with both knowledge of objects and causality. The task of future research is to identify both the form of these connections and the processes leading to their formation. It is here that both dynamic systems analysis and connectionist modeling are liable to have important roles in providing precise specifications of the conditions for development. Additionally, this endeavor is liable to be informed by neuropsychological analyses (see chapter 9 this volume). Some quite detailed analyses of frontal cortex function already exist that are highly relevant to developmental questions, specifically development of links between perception and action. For instance, Thatcher (1992) identifies a parallel between functioning of the lateral and medial frontal cortex and Piagetian concepts of assimilation and accommodation, and Goldberg (1985) identifies another region of frontal cortex, the *supplementary motor area*, as having an important role in control of intentional action. Thus, rather than limiting the analysis to the role of frontal cortex in inhibition of past responses (Diamond, 1985), it should be possible to broaden the analysis to identify this brain region as intimately involved in the control of executive functions. In this respect, there may be close links between the development of frontal cortex and the development of explicit knowledge for the guidance of intentional action.

References

Adolph, K. E., Eppler, M. A., & Gibson, E. J. (1993). Development of perception of affordances. In C. Rovee-Collier & L. P. Lipsitt (Eds.), *Advances in infancy research* (Vol. 8, pp. 51–98). New Jersey: Ablex.

Aguiar, A., & Baillargeon, R. (1999). 2.5-month-old infants' reasoning about when objects should and should not be occluded. *Cognitive Psychology, 39,* 116–157.

Aguiar, A., & Baillargeon, R. (2002). Developments in young infants' reasoning about occluded objects. *Cognitive Psychology, 45,* 267–336.

Ahmed, A., & Ruffman, T. (1998). Why do infants make A not B errors in a search task, yet show memory for the location of hidden objects in a nonsearch task? *Developmental Psychology, 34,* 441–453.

Antell, S. E., & Keating, D. P. (1983). Perception of numerical invariance in neonates. *Child Development, 54,* 695–701.

Baillargeon, R. (1986). Representing the existence and the location of hidden objects: Object permanence in 6- and 8-month-old infants, *Cognition, 23,* 21–41.

Baillargeon, R. (1987a). Object permanence in 3.5- and 4.5-month-old infants. *Developmental Psychology, 23,* 655–664.

Baillargeon, R. (1987b). Young infants' reasoning about the physical and spatial properties of a hidden object. *Cognitive Development, 2,* 179–200.

Baillargeon, R. (1993). The object concept revisited: New directions in the investigations of infants' physical knowledge. In C. E. Granrud (Ed.), *Carnegie-Mellon Symposia on Cognition: Vol. 23. Visual perception in infancy* (pp. 265–316). Hillsdale, NJ: Erlbaum.

Baillargeon, R. (2004). Infants reasoning about hidden objects: Evidence for event-general and event-specific expectations. *Developmental Science, 7*, 391–424.

Baillargeon, R. (2007). Detecting impossible changes in infancy: A three-system account. *Trends in Cognitive Sciences, 12*, 17–23.

Baillargeon, R., & DeVos, J. (1991). Object permanence in young infants: Further evidence. *Child Development, 62*, 1227–1246.

Baillargeon, R., & Graber, M. (1987). Where's the rabbit? 5.5-month-old infants' representation of the height of a hidden object. *Cognitive Development, 2*, 375–392.

Baillargeon, R., Graber, M., DeVos, J., & Black, J. (1990). Why do young infants fail to search for hidden objects? *Cognition, 36*, 255–284.

Baillargeon, R., Needham, A., & DeVos, J. (1992). The development of young infants' intuitions about support. *Early Development & Parenting, 1*, 69–78.

Baillargeon, R., Spelke, E. S., & Wasserman, S. (1985). Object permanence in five-month-old infants, *Cognition, 20*, 191–208.

Bell, M. A., & Fox, N. A. (1992). The relations between frontal brain electrical activity and cognitive development during infancy. *Child Development, 63*, 1142–1163.

Berger, A., Tzur, G., & Posner, M. (2006). Infant brains detect arithmetic errors. *Proceeding of the National Academy of Sciences, 103*, 12649–12653.

Bertenthal, B. J., Longo, M. R., & Kenny, S. (2007). Phenomenal permanence and the development of predictive tracking in infancy. *Child Development, 78*, 350–363.

Bogartz, R. S., Shinskey, J. L., & Speaker, C. (1997). Interpreting infant looking. *Developmental Psychology, 33*, 408–422.

Bower, T. G. R., & Wishart, J. G. (1972). The effects of motor skill on object permanence. *Cognition, 1*, 165–172.

Brannon, E. M., Abbott, S., & Lutz, D. J. (2004). Number bias for the discrimination of large visual sets in infancy. *Cognition, 93*, B59–B68.

Brannon, E. M., Lutz, D., & Cordes, S. (2006). The development of area discrimination and its implications for number representation in infancy. *Developmental Science, 9*, F59–F64.

Brannon, E. M., Suanda, S., & Libertus, K. (2007). Temporal discrimination increases in precision over development and parallels the development of numerosity discrimination. *Developmental Science, 10*, 770–777.

Bremner, A. J., & Bryant, P. E. (2001). The effect of spatial cues on infants' responses in the AB task, with and without a hidden object. *Developmental Science, 4*, 408–415.

Bremner, A. J., & Mareschal, D. (2004). Reasoning … what reasoning? *Developmental Science, 7*, 419–421.

Bremner, J. G. (1978). Spatial errors made by infants: Inadequate spatial cues or evidence for egocentrism? *British Journal of Psychology, 69*, 77–84.

Bremner, J. G. (1985). Object tracking and search in infancy: A review of data and a theoretical evaluation. *Developmental Review, 5*, 371–396.

Bremner, J. G. (1997). From perception to cognition. In G. Bremner, A. Slater, & G. Butterworth (Eds.), *Infant development: recent advances* (pp. 55–74). Hove: Psychology Press.

Bremner, J. G. (1998). From perception to action: The early development of knowledge, In F. Simion and G. Butterworth (Eds.), *Perceptual, motor and cognitive abilities in early infancy* (pp. 239–255). Hove: Psychology Press.

Bremner, J. G., & Bryant, P. E. (1977). Place versus response as the basis of spatial errors made by young infants. *Journal of Experimental Child Psychology, 23*, 162–171.

Bremner, J. G., Johnson, S. P., Slater, A. M., Mason, U., Cheshire, A., & Spring, J. (2007). Conditions for young infants' failure to perceive trajectory continuity. *Developmental Science, 10*, 613–624.

Bremner, J. G., Johnson, S. P., Slater, A. M., Mason, U., Foster, K., Cheshire, A., & Spring, J. (2005). Conditions for young infants' perception of object trajectories. *Child Development, 74,* 1029–1043.

Bremner, J. G., Johnson, S. P., Slater, A. M., Mason, U., & Spring, J. (in preparation). Four-month-old infants' perception of horizontal, vertical, and oblique trajectories.

Bremner, J. G., & Knowles, L. S. (1984). Piagetian stage IV errors with an object that is directly accessible both visually and manually. *Perception, 13,* 307–314.

Butterworth, G. (1974). *The development of the object concept in human infants.* Unpublished DPhil thesis, University of Oxford, UK.

Butterworth, G. (1975). Object identity in infancy: The interaction of spatial location codes in determining search errors. *Child Development, 46,* 866–870.

Butterworth, G. (1977). Object disappearance and error in Piaget's stage IV task. *Journal of Experimental Child Psychology, 23,* 391–401.

Butterworth, G., Jarrett, N., & Hicks, L. (1982). Spatio-temporal identity in infancy: Perceptual competence or conceptual deficit. *Developmental Psychology, 18,* 435–449.

Cheries, E. W., Wynn, K., & Scholl, B. J. (2006). Interrupting infants' persisting object representations: An object-based limit? *Developmental Science, 9,* F50–F58.

Clearfield, M. W., & Mix, K. S. (1999). Number versus contour length in infants' discrimination of small visual sets. *Psychological Science, 10,* 408–411.

Cleeremans, A. (1993). *Mechanisms of implicit learning: connectionist models of sequence processing.* Cambridge, MA: MIT Press.

Cohen, L. B., & Marks, K. S. (2002). How infants process addition and subtraction events. *Developmental Science, 5,* 186–212.

Diamond, A. (1985). Development of the ability to use recall to guide action, as indicated by infants' performance on A not B. *Child Development, 56,* 868–883.

Diamond, A. (1988). Abilities and neural mechanisms underlying A performance. *Child Development, 59,* 523–527.

Diamond, A. (1990). The development and neural bases of memory functions as indexed by the A and delayed response tasks in human infants and infant monkeys. In A. Diamond (Ed.), *The development and neural bases of higher cognitive functions* (pp. 267–317). New York: New York Academy of Sciences Press.

Diamond, A., & Goldman-Rakic, P. S. (1989). Comparison of human infants and rhesus monkeys on Piaget's A task: Evidence for dependence on dorsolateral prefrontal cortex. *Experimental Brain Research, 74,* 24–40.

Eizenman, D. R., & Bertenthal, B. I. (1998). Infants' perception of object unity in translating and rotating displays. *Developmental Psychology, 34,* 426–434.

Evans, W. F. (1973). *The stage IV error in Piaget's theory of object concept development.* Unpublished dissertation, University of Houston, TX.

Feigenson, L. (2007). The equality of quantity. *Trends in Cognitive Sciences, 11,* 185–187.

Feigenson, L., Carey, S., & Spelke, E. (2002). Infants' discrimination of number vs. continuous extent. *Cognitive Psychology, 44,* 33–66.

Feigenson, L., Dehaene, S., & Spelke, E. (2004). Core systems of number. *Trends in Cognitive Sciences, 8,* 307–314.

Gibson, E. J. (1977). How perception really develops: A view from outside the network. In D. LaBerge and S. J. Samuels (Eds.), *Basic processes in reading: perception and comprehension.* Hillsdale, NJ: Erlbaum.

Gibson, J. J. (1979). *The ecological approach to visual perception.* Boston, MA: Houghton Mifflin.

Goldberg, G. (1985). Supplementary motor area structure and function: Review and hypotheses. *The Behavioral & Brain Sciences, 8,* 567–616.

Goldberg, S. (1976). Visual tracking and existence constancy in five-month-old infants. *Journal of Experimental Child Psychology, 22,* 478–491.

Gratch, G., Appel, K. J., Evans, W. F., LeCompte, G. K., & Wright, N. A. (1974). Piaget's stage IV object concept error: evidence of forgetting or object conception. *Child Development, 45,* 71–77.

Gredebäck, G., & von Hofsten, C. (2004). Infants' evolving representations of object motion during occlusion: A longitudinal study of 6- to 12-month-old infants. *Infancy, 6,* 165–184.

Haith, M. M. (1998). Who put the cog in cognition? Is rich interpretation too costly? *Infant Behavior & Development, 21,* 167–179.

Harris, P. L. (1973). Perseverative errors in search by young infants. *Child Development, 44,* 28–33.

Harris, P. L. (1974). Perseverative search at a visibly empty place by young infants. *Journal of Experimental Child Psychology, 18,* 535–542.

Hofstadter M., & Reznick, J. S. (1996). Response modality affects human infant delayed-response performance. *Child Development, 67,* 646–658.

Huettel, S. A., & Needham, A. (2000). Effects of balance relations between objects on infants' object segregation. *Developmental Science, 3,* 413–427.

Hughes, C. (1998). Executive function in preschoolers: Links with theory of mind and verbal ability. *British Journal of Developmental Psychology, 16,* 233–253.

Hunter, M. A., & Ames, E. W. (1988). A multifactor model of infant preferences for novel and familiar stimuli. In C. Rovee-Collier & L. P. Lipsitt (Eds.), *Advances in Infancy Research* (Vol. 5, pp. 69–95). Norwood, NJ: Ablex.

Johnson, S. P., Amso, D., & Slemmer, J. A. (2003). Development of object concepts in infancy: Evidence for early learning in an eye-tracking paradigm. *Proceedings of the National Academy of Sciences (USA), 100,* 10568–10573.

Johnson, S. P., & Aslin, R. N. (1995). Perception of object unity in 2-month-old infants. *Developmental Psychology, 31,* 739–745.

Johnson, S. P., & Aslin, R. N. (1996). Perception of object unity in young infants: The roles of motion, depth, and orientation. *Cognitive Development, 11,* 161–180.

Johnson, S. P., Bremner, J. G., Slater, A. M., & Mason, U. C. (2000). The role of good form in infants' perception of partly occluded objects, *Journal of Experimental Child Psychology, 76,* 1–25.

Johnson, S. P., Bremner, J. G., Slater, A. M., Mason, U. C., Foster, K., & Cheshire, A. (2003). Infants' perception of object trajectories, *Child Development, 74,* 94–108.

Johnson, S. P., & Náñez, J. E. (1995). Young infants' perception of object unity in two-dimensional displays. *Infant Behavior and Development, 18,* 133–143.

Karmiloff-Smith, A. (1992). *Beyond modularity: A developmental perspective on cognitive science.* Cambridge, MA: MIT Press.

Kellman, P. J., Gleitman, H., & Spelke, E. (1987). Object and observer motion in the perception of objects by infants. *Journal of Experimental Psychology: Human Perception & Performance, 13,* 586–593.

Kellman, P. J., & Spelke, E. R. (1983). Perception of partly occluded objects in infancy. *Cognitive Psychology, 15,* 483–524.

Kellman, P. J., Spelke, E., & Short, K. R. (1986). Infant perception of object unity from translatory motion in depth and vertical translation, *Child Development, 57,* 72–76.

Koechlin, E., Dehaene, S., & Mehler, J. (1997). Numerical transformations in five-month-old human infants. *Mathematical Cognition, 3,* 89–104.

Krøjgaard, P. (2007). Comparing infants' use of featural and spatiotemporal information in an object individuation task using a new event-monitoring design. *Developmental Science, 10,* 892–909.

Landers, W. F. (1971). The effect of differential experience on infants' performance in a Piagetian stage IV object concept task. *Developmental Psychology, 5,* 48–54.

Marcovitch, S., & Zelazo, P. D. (1999). The A-not-B error: Results from a logistic meta-analysis. *Child Development, 70,* 1297–1313.

Mareschal, D., Harris, P., & Plunkett, K. (1997). Effects of linear and angular velocity on 2-, 4-, and 6-month-olds' visual pursuit behaviors. *Infant Behavior & Development, 20,* 435–448.

Meck, W. H., & Church, R. M. (1983). A mode control model of counting and timing processes. *Journal of Experimental Psychology: Animal Behavior Processes, 9,* 320–334.

Meltzoff, A. N., & Moore, M. K. (1998). Object representation, identity, and the paradox of early permanence: Steps toward a new framework. *Infant Behavior and Development, 21,* 201–235.

Mix, K. S., Levine, S. C., & Huttenlocher, J. (1997). Numerical abstraction in infants: Another look. *Developmental Psychology, 33,* 423–428.

Moore, D., Benenson, J., Reznick, J. S., Peterson, M., & Kagan, J. (1987). Effect of auditory numerical information on infants' looking behavior: Contradictory evidence. *Developmental Psychology, 23,* 655–670.

Moore, M. K., & Meltzoff, A. N. (2008). Factors affecting infants' manual search for occluded objects and the genesis of object permanence. *Infant Behavior & Development, 31,* 157–332.

Muller, A. A., & Aslin, R. N. (1978). Visual tracking as an index of the object concept. *Infant Behavior & Development, 1,* 309–319.

Munakata, Y. (1997). Perseverative reaching in infancy: The roles of hidden toys and motor history in the A not B task. *Infant Behavior & Development, 20,* 405–416.

Munakata, Y. (1998a). Infant perseveration and implications for object permanence theories: A PDP model of the AB task. *Developmental Science, 1,* 161–184.

Munakata, Y. (1998b). Infant perseveration, rethinking data, theory, and the role of modelling. *Developmental Science, 1,* 205–211

Munakata, Y., McClelland, J. L., Johnson, M. J., & Siegler, R. S. (1997). Rethinking infant knowledge: Toward as adaptive process account of successes and failures in object permanence tasks. *Psychological Review, 104,* 686–713.

Needham, A., & Baillargeon, R. (1993). Intuitions about support in 4.5-month-old infants. *Cognition, 47,* 121–148.

Neilson, I. (1977). *A reinterpretation of the development of the object concept in infancy.* Unpublished PhD thesis, University of Edinburgh, UK.

Piaget, J. (1954). *The construction of reality in the child* (M. Cook, Trans.). New York: Basic Books (originally published 1936).

Rader, N., Spiro, D. J., & Firestone, P. B. (1979). Performance on a stage IV object-permanence task with standard and nonstandard covers. *Child Development, 50,* 908–910.

Reber, A. S. (1993). *Implicit learning and tacit knowledge: An essay on the cognitive unconscious.* Oxford: Oxford University Press.

Rivera, S. M., Wakeley, A., & Langer, J. (1999). The drawbridge phenomenon: Representational reasoning or perceptual preference? *Developmental Psychology, 35,* 427–435.

Rosander, K., & von Hofsten, C. (2004). Infants' emerging ability to represent occluded object motion. *Cognition, 91,* 1–22.

Russell, J. (1996). *Agency: Its role in mental development.* Hove: Erlbaum/Taylor & Francis.

Shinskey, J. L., Bogartz, R. S., & Poirier, C. R. (2000). The effects of graded occlusion on manual search and visual attention in 5- to 8-month-old infants. *Infancy, 1,* 323–346.

Shinskey, J. L., & Munakata, Y. (2005). Familiarity breeds searching: Infants reverse their novelty preferences when reaching for hidden objects. *Psychological Science, 16,* 596–600.

Simon, T. J. (1997). Reconceptualizing the origins of number knowledge: A "non-numerical" account. *Cognitive Development, 12,* 349–372.

Slater, A. M., Bremner, J. G., Johnson, S. P., & Hayes, R. A. (in press). The role of perceptual processes in infant addition/subtraction experiments. In L. M. Oakes, C. H. Cashon, M. Cassaola, & D. H. Rakison (Eds.), *Early perceptual and cognitive development.* Oxford: Oxford University Press.

Slater, A., Johnson, S. P., Brown, E., & Badenoch, M. (1996). Newborn infants' perception of partly occluded objects. *Infant Behavior and Development, 19,* 145–148.

Smith, L. B., Thelen, E., McLin, D., & Titzer, R. (1999). Knowing in the context of acting: the task dynamics of the A-not-B error. *Psychological Review, 106,* 235–260.

Sophian, C., & Yengo, L. (1985). Infants' search for visible objects: Implications for the interpretation of early search errors, *Journal of Experimental Child Psychology, 40,* 260–278.

Spelke, E. R., Breinlinger, K., Macomber, J., & Jacobson, K. (1992). Origins of knowledge. *Psychological Review, 99,* 605–632.

Spelke, E. S., Kestenbaum, R., Simons, D. J., & Wein, D. (1995). Spatiotemporal continuity, smoothness of motion and object identity in infancy. *British Journal of Developmental Psychology, 13,* 113–142.

Spelke, E. S., & Kinzler, K. D. (2007). Core knowledge. *Developmental Science, 10,* 89–96.

Starkey, P., & Cooper, R. G. (1980). Perception of number by human infants. *Science, 210,* 1033–1035.

Starkey, P., Spelke, E. S., & Gelman, R. (1990). Numerical abstraction by human infants. *Cognition, 36,* 97–128.

Thatcher, R. W. (1992). Cyclic cortical reorganization during early childhood. *Brain & Cognition, 20,* 24–50.

Topál, J., Gergely, G., Miklósi, A., Erdőhegzi, Á., & Csibra, G. (2008). Infants' perseverative search errors are induced by pragmatic misinterpretation. *Science, 321,* 1831–1833.

vanMarle, K., & Wynn, K. (2006). Six-month-old infants use analog magnitudes to represent duration. *Developmental Science, 9,* F41–F49.

von Hofsten, C., Kochukhova, O., & Rosander, K. (2007). Predictive tracking over occlusions by 4-month-old infants. *Developmental Science, 10,* 625–640.

Wilcox, T., & Baillargeon, R. (1998). Object individuation in infancy: The use of featural information in reasoning about occlusion events. *Cognitive Psychology, 37,* 97–155.

Wilcox, T., Nadel, L., & Rosser, R. (1996). Location memory in healthy preterm and full-term infants. *Infant Behavior & Development, 19,* 309–324.

Wilcox, T., & Schweinle, A. (2003). Infants' use of speed information to individuate objects in occlusion events. *Infant Behavior & Development, 26,* 253–282.

Willatts, P. (1997). Beyond the "couch potato" infant: How infants use their knowledge to regulate action, solve problems, and achieve goals. In G. Bremner, A. Slater, & G. Butterworth (Eds.), *Infant development: Recent advances* (pp. 109–135). Hove: Psychology Press.

Wynn, K. (1992). Addition and subtraction by human infants. *Nature, 358,* 749–750.

Wynn, K. (1995). Origins of numerical knowledge. *Mathematical Cognition, 1,* 35–60.

Xu, F., & Carey, S. (1996). Infants' metaphysics: The case of numerical identity. *Cognitive Psychology, 30,* 111–153.

Xu, F., & Spelke, E. S. (2000). Large number discrimination in 6-month-old infants. *Cognition, 74,* B1–Bll.

Zelazo, P. D., Reznick, J. S., & Spinazzola, J. (1998). Representational flexibility and response control in a multistep multilocation search task. *Developmental Psychology, 34,* 203–214.

7

Perceptual Categorization and Concepts

David H. Rakison

The ontogenetic origins of knowledge have been at the core of a trenchant debate that began with the Socrates and Plato over 2,000 years ago and persists unabated today among developmental scientists. The modern adaptation of this debate has been recently been played out by those studying one of the most complex and daunting challenges faced during early development, namely, when and how infants acquire knowledge about the wide range of objects and entities that surround them. This task is particularly challenging for infants because not only do things in the world look different on the surface but they are capable of a wide range of behavioral (e.g., self-propulsion) and psychological actions (e.g., goal-directedness) and may possess distinctly different internal parts (e.g., a heart vs. an engine). Moreover, animate entities (i.e., people, animals, insects) and inanimate objects (e.g., plants, furniture, vehicles) vary considerably along these dimensions, and many of the crucial features that infants must learn about them are not immediately or continually available in the perceptual input.

In light of the highly disparate perspectives presented by the Greek philosophers at the genesis of this debate, it is perhaps not surprising that radically different views currently exist about when and how concepts are first formed, how they are used, and how they change over developmental time. Indeed, perhaps no other area of developmental science is as polarized as that involving the study of concepts. At stake is not just the establishment of developmental milestones in knowledge acquisition but the nature, content, and origins of such knowledge. Specific questions that are posed in this debate relate to whether infants possess innate concepts for objects or acquire them through experience, and whether infants have general or specialized mechanisms or modules for learning about things in the world.

As this chapter will demonstrate, considerable headway has been forged in elucidating the answers to these questions but many important issues remain unresolved. In this chapter, I hope to highlight the key questions that remain central to the study of concept development and describe the different answers that have been generated by various researchers. The format of the chapter is as follows. I will begin with definitions of key terms and then outline a number of prominent yet diverse theoretical perspectives on how infants develop concepts. I will then discuss the principal methods for studying concept development in the first years of life – many of which were developed in the last 20 years – and summarize the key empirical findings that have emerged during this time. I will conclude by evaluating how far developmental science has come in the study of concepts and speculate about how far it still has to go and how that destination can be reached.

What Are Concepts and Categories?

The human mind, as well as that of nonhuman animals, is designed mentally to group things that exist in the world. Infants as young as 3 months of age – though perhaps younger – can categorize as different perceptually similar groups such as cats and dogs (Quinn, Eimas, & Rosenkrantz, 1993), and many of the first words that infants learn denote individual exemplars that belong to a group of things such as "ball" and "dog" (Gershkoff-Stowe & Smith, 2004). At the centre of this process, and cognitive development more broadly, is the ability to categorize or classify. Categorization is defined as the ability to group discriminable properties, objects, or events into classes by means of some principle or rule and to respond to them in terms of their class membership instead of as individuals (see Bruner, Goodnow, & Austin, 1956). Thus, categorization refers to things in the world: animals, vehicles, brothers, things that are red, and so on. More formally, we can specify categorization in the form:

if X_1 is a P then X_2 is also a P

Thus, if a certain animal is a dog, then a similar animal is also a dog. More informally, as Neisser (1987) put it, categorization is to "to treat a set of things as somehow equivalent: to put them in the same pile, or call them by the same name, or respond to them in the same way (p. 1)." Clearly, then, categorization involves grouping multiple objects as equivalents and as different from other things. In a related but similar process, called *discrimination* or *differentiation*, a single object is judged to be different from another object case.

A process related to categorization is *induction* or *inductive inference*. This is the ability to use prior experience to decide how far to generalize or extend a particular observation to a novel instance, or, more formally:

if X_1 has property P then X_2 also has property P

Thus, if the family dog is observed to bark, have fur, and chase squirrels, one might infer that another dog will also have these properties or abilities. Thus, inductive inference, as with categorization, tends to refer to objects and things in the world.

Finally, the term *concept* refers to mental representations in the brain that encapsulate or summarize the properties, features, and structures that exist among items within categories in the world. Concepts are a means of storing information about the objects and entities that we experience in the world, and they allow us to determine how to group things together into categories and to generalize from one instance to other, novel things that we encounter in the world. There is considerable evidence that humans' concepts vary in their structure and content. For example, research has indicated that human adults – as well as infants – store information as individual exemplars (e.g., your mother's face; Medin & Schaffer, 1978), as a list of necessary features (e.g., cats have whiskers; Bruner, Olver, & Greenfield, 1966), as *prototypes* or averages of a category (e.g., an equilateral triangle), and as a probabilistic cluster of correlated features (e.g., things with wings have feathers and claws; Rosch, 1975; Rosch & Mervis, 1975).

The utility of concepts

Clearly, concepts allow humans to categorize and perform induction inference. These processes themselves are fundamental to human cognition. The ability to form categories reduces considerably the information-processing demands on inherently limited memory storage and perceptual processes. Moreover, if things in the world were not grouped representationally then it would be necessary to remember independently similar information about every individual member of a category. For instance, we would have to store in memory the information that every individual cat that we encounter "meows" and purrs. Likewise, inductive inference is vital to cognition because it is possible to experience only a small proportion of the entities, objects, features, and events in the world. By generalizing from our experience, we can infer many things about the properties, features, and behaviors of objects and entities in the world.

Categorization and inductive inference, via concepts, are also inextricably linked to language. Words often refer to categories of objects and events, or properties of those things, and if we did not mentally group objects then we would have to refer to – and have names for – everything in the world as an individual exemplar. Thus, concepts make it possible to talk about "dogs," "knives," and "cars" rather than having an individual label – essentially a proper noun – for every instance of these categories.

In summary, human cognition would not be possible without concepts or mental representations. They are the means by which we mentally represent the world, which in turn allows us, among other things, to categorize, perform induction, reason, solve problems, and use a complex language system. Although few theorists would disagree with the role of concepts in human cognition, the next section will show that there is considerable debate about how and when concepts for objects and entities in the world are formed in infancy.

Theoretical Views on Early Concept Formation

Broadly speaking, there are two contrasting views on how infants form concepts and subsequently categorize and perform inductive inferences. Elsewhere, I have labeled these two perspectives the *Smart Infant view* and the *Dumb Infant view* (Rakison & Hahn,

2004), although the specifics of those grouped under each label differ considerably. Those who support the Smart Infant view claim that innate specialized mechanisms or modules underpin early concept formation (Gelman, 1990; Leslie, 1995; Mandler, 1992; Premack, 1990). A corollary of this view is that infants are precocious concept formers who rapidly learn about, and rely on, the less obvious properties of objects as the basis for categorization and induction (e.g., these things go together because they are animates). Those who support the Dumb Infant view propose that general learning mechanisms such as habituation, conditioning, and associative learning are foundations for how infants learn about the world (Oakes & Madole, 1999; Quinn & Eimas, 1997; Rakison & Lupyan, 2008; Smith, Jones, & Landau, 1996). According to this perspective, infants are certainly not "dumb" but they are relatively slow concept formers, and consequently properties in the perceptual input (e.g., features such as shape or parts) play an important role in categorization and induction early in life and beyond. In this section, I outline the details of these theoretical perspectives, discuss predictions about infants' behavior from the views, and outline potential criticisms that each one faces.

The Smart Infant view: Specialized mechanisms for learning

There are three main arguments for why infants possess specialized mechanisms for acquiring concepts for things in the world. The first is that the problem space is too complex for so-called simple general mechanisms to account for how infants acquire concepts. For instance, it has been proposed that information that pertains to motion cues, psychological cues, and biological cues cannot be learned by a general mechanism because they are only intermittently or never available in the perceptual input or are misleading and ambiguous (Gelman, 1990; Mandler, 1992). The second is that associations between perceptual cues for motion – as well as psychological cues such as goal-directed action and spatial information such as support and containment – cannot give rise to accessible concepts that support inference, categorization, thought, or recall (Mandler, 2003). The third is that there is an *insufficiency of constraints* inherent in general (but not specialized) learning mechanisms (Keil, 1981); that is, there is so much information in the world to which one could attend that there is no way to know what is relevant for category membership and what is not.

A number of prominent researchers have presented theories that address and overcome these issues due to their reliance on domain-specific mechanisms for learning. Leslie (1984, 1988, 1995), for example, proposed that infants are born with three distinct modules that facilitate rapid learning about the properties of animates and inanimates. He suggested that one module processes the physical or mechanical properties of objects and entities (*theory of body*), a second processes psychological or intentional properties (*theory of mind*), and a third processes their cognitive properties. A similar view of early concept development was proposed by Rochel Gelman (1990; Gelman, Durgin, & Kaufman, 1995). She suggested that infants possess innate skeletal causal principles that allow them to form conceptual schemes for things by directing attention to aspects of their motion and composition. Specifically, Gelman (1990) posited that these cues lead infants to develop knowledge about the energy sources and materials of objects (e.g., people have a renewable energy sources and balls do not). Gelman (1990; Gelman et al., 1995) highlighted that these early skeletal causal principles are far from fully fledged concepts about a domain but rather that they contain some initial knowledge that directs later learning.

Finally, the most prominent and comprehensive domain-specific theory of early concept development was proposed by Jean Mandler (1992, 2000, 2003). Mandler (1992) argued that the first concepts encapsulate the surface appearance of things, and these concepts support *perceptual categorization* whereby infants group, for example, animals as different from vehicles on the basis of how they look. Infants also, however, possess an innate specialized process called *perceptual analysis* that recodes what they see and converts it into an abstract and accessible format. This process generates *image-schemas*, or *conceptual primitives*, that sum up critical characteristics of objects' spatial structure and movement. These schemas provide infants by 9 or 10 months of age with an understanding of the *meaning* of things or what Mandler called *conceptual categorization*. As a result, by the end of the first year of life infants start to categorize, for example, animals as different from vehicles not on the basis of their appearance but because of category membership (i.e., knowledge that animals are a "different kind of thing" from vehicles) or different motion characteristics (e.g., caused to start vs. self-propelled). Thus, Mandler proposed that "what holds a class such as animals together so that membership can be assigned to it is neither overall perceptual similarity nor a common perceptual features, but instead a notion of common kind" (Mandler & McDonough, 1996, p. 314).

The Dumb Infant view: General mechanisms for learning

In contrast to the Smart Infant view, a number of researchers have proposed that domain-general learning mechanisms are sufficient for infants to form object concepts (e.g., Jones & Smith, 1993; Oakes & Madole, 2003; Quinn & Eimas, 1997; Rakison & Lupyan, 2008). The general arguments for this view – and against a domain-specific approach – are as follows. First, the problem space is rich in statistical regularities that specify category membership, and infants are adept at attending to such regularities across a range of domains (e.g., Fiser & Aslin, 2002; Saffran, Aslin, & Newport, 1996; Younger & Cohen, 1986). Second, it is tricky, if not impossible, empirically to test whether infants possess innate specialized mechanisms or modules or core principles. Third, specialized mechanisms are considered unparsimonious because they create a heavy biological burden in that they require a dedicated brain region and, in the case of categorization, two mental mechanisms (one perceptual and one conceptual) rather than one. Moreover, there is little in the way of evidence or argument of selection pressure during evolution for the emergence of such mechanisms (Quinn & Eimas, 2000; Quinn, Johnson, Mareschal, Rakison, & Younger, 2000; Rakison, 2005a). Fourth, a domain-general approach is inherently developmental in that – in contrast to the Smart Infant view – it explains how or why infants' ability to form concepts changes over time. Finally, and perhaps most importantly, the domain-general view is more consistent with the available empirical evidence.

The specifics of the various domain-general theories differ considerably. Yet, they have in common the idea that concept acquisition is a gradual process whereby information is continuously added – via habituation, associative learning, conditioning, and imitation – to existing concepts over developmental time. In addition, many, if not all, of these approaches share the notion that information available in the perceptual input – even that which is intermittently available such as motion information – is initially and throughout development at the core of concepts.

One of the first and most forceful advocates of this view was Linda Smith (Jones & Smith, 1993; Smith, Colunga, & Yoshida, 2003; Smith & Heise, 1992). Smith and Heise (1992), for instance, proposed that the insufficiency of constraints argument is moot because infants' experience with correlations in the world causes them to attend to the features that are a part of those correlations. In other words, infants' initial attention to the features that characterize or define categories causes them to pay attention to those features in the future. Thus, innate mechanisms are not necessary to direct attention to the significant physical, psychological, or cognitive aspects of a category.

A similar view was proposed by Oakes and Madole (1999, 2003) who outlined a principled, three-part developmental trajectory in infants' ability to form concepts. First, infants' general development in cognitive, motor, and linguistic skills allows them access to an increasingly wide range of features on which to base their category membership decisions. Second, over developmental time infants have access to information in a broader set of contexts, and they are better able to take advantage of this information with their improving cognitive skills. Third, infants increase their background knowledge over time about the likely and plausible relations that exist among features, and they use this knowledge to determine which features predict category membership.

A comparable account for the development of object concepts was presented by Quinn and Eimas (Eimas, 1994; Quinn & Eimas, 1996a, 1997, 2000). They proposed that concept acquisition is a process of continuous representational enrichment that relies on a sensitive perceptual system that is robust enough to allow infants to form categories that cohere because of similarity relations. Thus, infants use a variety of surface features to categorize the different objects and entities they encounter in the world; they may categorize on the basis of shape and texture (e.g., Jones & Smith, 1993), functional parts (e.g., Rakison & Cohen, 1999), or facial features (e.g., Quinn and Eimas, 1996b).

Finally, Rakison (Rakison & Lupyan, 2008; Rakison & Poulin-Dubois, 2001) has presented a similar domain-general framework of object concept development called *constrained attentional associative learning* (CAAL). This account explains how infants form concepts that include not only static features of category members but also the dynamic cues involved in motion. In line with Quinn and Eimas (1997), Rakison and Lupyan (2008) proposed that associative processes are the fundamental mechanism for learning with representations continuously augmented over developmental time. In addition, however, they argued that infants possess a number of inherent attention biases (e.g., for dynamic over static features) and that development is propelled by advances in information-processing abilities as well as neurological maturation.

Summary and predictions of the two views of concept development

The two perspectives of category and concept development in infancy have in common the idea that very early concepts are grounded in the perceptual features of objects, or how they look. At the same time, they differ considerably in one important aspect; the domain-specific view posits that innate specialized mechanisms, a module, or core principles underpin early concept formation whereas the domain-general view posits that universal mechanisms such as associative learning, habituation, and condition play this role. A number of key predictions stem from this commonality and difference. Both views predict that very young infants – those in the first half year of life – should categorize on the basis of the perceptual appearance of things; that is, they use perceptual categorization. For example, infants might categorize cats as different from dogs on the basis of their shape, their facial features, and so on.

According to the Dumb Infant view, infants and older children continue to use such features for categorization and induction. However, those in the Smart Infant camp predict that infants approximately aged 9 months or older categorize on the basis of deeper, less obvious properties such as category relatedness, motion cues, or psychological properties. For example, by 12 months of age infants categorize animals as different from vehicles because they know that animals are a "different kind of thing" from vehicles or that animals – but not vehicles – are self-propelled entities that have goals, drink, and sleep (Mandler, 1992; Mandler & McDonough, 1996).

In the following sections, I outline the methods used to test infants in the first and the second year of life as well as the evidence used by both camps to support their view of infant concept development.

The First Year of Life: Perceptual Categorization

As discussed in the previous section, it is generally assumed that infants in the first year of life categorize on the basis of perceptual features – those that can be readily seen in the input. Here I outline a number of key findings on how and when young infants are able to use such features to categorize.

Methods for studying categorization in the first year of life

A considerable challenge for researchers who study the development of early categories is to create procedures that assess accurately those cognitive abilities. These researchers must find a way to allow infants without language skills to show how they perceive a certain stimulus or whether they group one thing with another. In this section, I briefly outline the most common of the ingenious solutions that researchers have devised to assess the development of categories and concepts in prelinguistic babies.

Without doubt, the primary methods for studying category and concept development in infants under 12 months of age are the habituation and familiarization paradigms. These procedures rely on infants' visual fixation or looking time to a stimulus. In this general procedure, infants are presented with a number of items from the same category and their looking time is recorded. They are then presented with a novel item from a different category as well as a novel item from the familiar category, and their looking times to these items are compared. In the familiarization procedure, infants are shown images of category items for a set duration. For example, infants might be shown 12 pictures of different cats for 10 seconds each – in many cases with two images presented side-by-side – and then their looking at a novel dog and a novel cat is assessed. Longer looking to the novel dog relative to the novel cat would be taken as evidence that infants formed a category of dogs that excludes cats (Quinn et al., 1993).

One shortcoming of the familiarization paradigm is that it cannot always be predicted that infants will look longer at the novel category member; that is, following familiarization infants sometimes show a preference for the familiar item over the novel item (Hunter & Ames, 1988). The habituation paradigm overcomes this issue because infants are shown images serially – that is, one at a time – but the duration of each presentation lasts only as long as the infant looks at the image and the test phase starts when looking time decreases to a preset percentage of the original looking time. The rationale for this method is that the length of infants' visual fixations will decrease as their mental representation or concept for the presented category of items matches what they see (Sirois & Mareschal, 2002). In this sense, the habituation paradigm is controlled by the infant and is sensitive to individual differences in learning rates. During the test phase, the infant is presented with a novel category stimulus and a familiar category test stimulus and "looking time" times to the two are compared. The assumption is that because infants have habituated to a set of category members they will look longer at the novel stimulus than the familiar stimulus.

Finally, Rovee-Collier, Hayne, and collaborators (Rovee-Collier & Hayne, 1987, 2000) have pioneered the use of operant conditioning to study categorization in very young infants between 3 and 7 months of age. Infants in these studies are trained with their leg attached to a mobile via a piece of string such that every time a leg is kicked the mobile moves. In a categorization study, infants are trained with a number of different mobiles – that perhaps share a common feature such as, for example, color – and the rate of their kicking is measured. The experimenter then evaluates whether infants generalize their kicking response to other mobiles. Thus, infants would be tested with a mobile of the same color and of a different color.

Basic mechanisms for concept formation in the first year of life

Infants' ability to form prototypes (e.g., shapes, faces, animals).   Eleanor Rosch and Carolyn Mervis proposed that the categories formed in early childhood fall into one of three hierarchical classes (e.g., Rosch, 1975, 1978; Rosch & Mervis, 1975; Rosch, Mervis, Gray, Johnson, & Boyes-Braem, 1976). According to Rosch and her colleagues, categories develop first at the "psychologically privileged" basic level (e.g., dogs, cars), and then later at the superordinate level (animals, vehicles) and subordinate level (Rottweilers, pickup truck). Rosch and her associates argued that these categories – and in particular the basic level – have a nonarbitrary structure in that they take advantage of correlations in the attributes of real-world objects. For example, things with wings and beaks tend to have feathers, and things with wheels and seats tend to have engines. Rosch found also that the category members that possess more attributes common to the category are considered better examples and are therefore more *prototypical*. For example, an Alsatian or Labrador is considered more typical of the concept of dog than a Great Dane or Rottweiler, and it is therefore more likely, or probable, to be a member of the category of dogs. More formally, a prototype can be considered a mathematical average of the attributes of category members.

There is now considerable empirical evidence that even very young infants are capable of forming prototypes for a wide range of stimuli. Bomba and Siqueland (1983), for example, presented 3- and 4-month-old infants with randomly generated distortions of triangles in the habituation paradigm. During the test phase, they showed infants a prototypical triangle (e.g., an equilateral triangle) as well as a previously seen distorted triangle. As outlined earlier, infants usually prefer a novel stimulus over a familiar one. The authors surmised that if infants had formed a mental prototype of triangles they would look longer at the distorted triangle than the prototypical one because the latter would be familiar. This is exactly what they found. Using a similar design, Younger and Gotlieb (1988) tested 3-, 5-, and 7-month-olds in a similar design but used more abstract shapes (e.g., a "y" shape") as well as more common, symmetrical ones (e.g., a cross). They found that infants at all ages were able to form prototypes but the younger group could do so only for the simpler shapes whereas the older group could do so for all of the shapes (see also Quinn & Bomba, 1986).

Infants' ability to form prototypes is not limited to simple shapes, however. It is well established that infants at 2, 3, and 6 months of age prefer to look at attractive rather than unattractive faces (as rated by adults) when such images are presented side-by-side (Langlois et al., 1987; Langlois, Roggman, & Musselman, 1994). According to one view, this early preference results from infants' ability to form prototypes for faces. The reasoning behind this argument is that attractive faces tend to be average, or prototypical, and humans may possess a central tendency preference for prototypical exemplars over nonprototypical exemplars (Halberstadt & Rhodes, 2000). In support of this view, it has been shown that adults find a composite face (generated by averaging features across multiple faces) more attractive than nearly all the individual faces from which it was formed (Langlois & Roggman, 1990). Moreover, infants as young as 6 months of age show a preference for a composite face as well as the ability to extract the central tendency from a set of faces (Rubenstein, Kalakanis, & Langlois, 1999; see also Strauss, 1979).

Finally, research by Quinn et al. (1993) implied that very young infants form prototypes for animals such as cats and dogs. Infants at 3 and 4 months of age were familiarized with pictures of cats or dogs and then shown a novel cat and a novel dog. Interestingly, 3- and 4-month-olds who were familiarized with cats looked longer at the novel dog relative to the novel cat whereas those familiarized with dogs did not look longer at the novel cat relative to the novel dog. This suggests that infants' category of dogs may subsume, in some respect, the category of cats; that is, based on surface features alone a cat is a feasible dog but a dog is not a feasible cat. Moreover, Quinn et al. reported that they found it harder to familiarize infants with dogs when the exemplars were variable (as defined by adults), which they interpreted to mean that category representations structured around prototype members develop earlier than representations for less tightly structured categories.

Thus, infants are capable of forming prototypes for a range of stimuli and probably do so for a number of real-world categories. These prototypes are at the centre of category representations and in all likelihood facilitate classification because they act as a central instance to which novel instances can be compared. Note, however, that in many cases the prototype may not be a "real" exemplar but rather an average of all the category members that infants experience. Thus, although prototypes may facilitate categorization, it is not always the case that they represent a specific exemplar in the world.

Infants' sensitivity to correlated features.   As outlined earlier, Rosch and Mervis (1975) suggested that category members tend to share the same clusters of correlated attributes. It is now well established that infants are sensitive to such statistical regularities across a broad range of perceptual inputs (e.g., Kirkham, Slemmer, & Johnson, 2002; Saffran et al., 1996). For instance, infants as young as 8 months of age can use the transitional probability between sounds to identify word boundaries (Saffran et al.). Thus, it is important to determine whether infants are able to form categories on the basis of correlations – or bundles – of features.

There is compelling evidence that even neonates are sensitive to correlated features. Slater, Mattock, Brown, Burnham, and Young (1991) conducted an experiment in which newborns were familiarized with stimulus compounds such as a green vertical stripe and a red diagonal stripe (see Figure 7.1). Infants could encode the stripes in terms of their color, their orientation, or both their color and orientation. In the test trials, the infants were shown a new combination of the two elements – for example, a green diagonal stripe – as well as one of the familiar stimuli. The newborns' pattern of looking revealed that they preferred to look at the new combination of elements, which suggests that they had processed the color and orientation of the stripes together rather than independently. Using the mobile conjugate reinforcement procedure, Bhatt and Rovee-Collier (1994, 1996) tested whether 3-month-old infants could learn and remember feature relations. Infants were trained to kick a mobile of which the color of the blocks was correlated with the figure displayed on them and with the color of the figures; thus, all three features that varied were correlated. Bhatt and Rovee-Collier (1994, 1996) found that infants encoded the color–form feature relations and remembered them for up to 3 days. Interestingly, they also found that individual features and feature relations were dissociated in memory such that the relations among the features were forgotten before the individual features.

These studies are informative about whether infants are capable of learning that one feature is correlated with another. However, they do not clarify whether infants can extract such correlated features in a category context; that is, when two or more instances can be grouped together because of correlated features in the presence of other varying features. One of the first studies of infants' ability to form categories on the basis of correlated features was conducted by Younger and Cohen (1986). Infants at 4, 7, and 10 months of age were habituated to line-drawings of novel animal stimuli that possessed a cluster of correlated attributes (e.g., legs and tails). Examples of the stimuli are illustrated in Figure 7.2. In the study, infants were habituated to two stimuli with a long neck and a "fan" tail and two stimuli with a short neck and a stubby tail. Importantly, a third feature varied within the category and all other features of the four stimuli were identical.

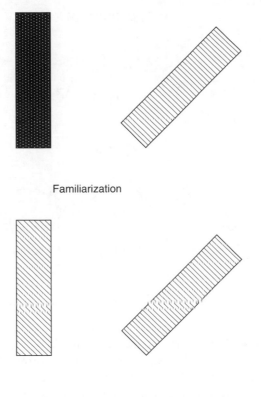

Familiarization

Switched features   Familiar Features

Figure 7.1   Examples of the stimuli used by Slater et al. (1991). Neonates looked longer at the stimulus with the new combination of elements (switched features) relative to the familiar stimulus following familiarization with the two shapes at the top of the figure. *Source*: Adapted with permission from Slater et al. (1991).

Following habituation, infants were tested with a familiar correlated stimulus as well as a "switch" uncorrelated stimulus that paired one neck and one tail from each of the habituation categories. The rationale for this kind of *switch design* is that if infants are capable of learning correlated features, they should look longer at the switch test stimulus than the familiar test stimulus. Note that longer looking to the switch test stimulus could not result from the novelty of the individual features because no new feature was introduced in the test trial.

Younger and Cohen (1986, experiment 2) found that infants at 4 months of age did not learn the correlated attributes embedded in a category context whereas those at 10 months of age did. Infants at 7 months of age showed a somewhat unusual pattern of behavior in that they failed to habituate, which leaves it difficult to interpret whether they were able to form categories based on correlated features. This basic result is informative about 10-month-old infants' ability to attend to and learn correlated features in a category context; however, a key aspect of categories is that they allow for generalization

HABITUATION STIMULI

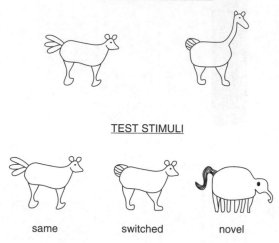

TEST STIMULI

same   switched   novel

Figure 7.2   Examples of stimuli in Younger and Cohen (1986).

to a novel instance. Thus, in a follow-up study, Younger and Cohen (1986, experiment 3) habituated infants to only three of the four stimuli used previously; that is, they omitted one category member that was to be used as the correlated stimulus in the test phase. This change in design meant that the "uncorrelated" or switch test stimulus was more similar overall to the set of habituation stimuli than was the "correlated" test stimulus. Longer looking to the uncorrelated stimulus relative to the correlated stimulus – which is what was found for 10-month-olds in this later experiment – could not result purely from its similarity to the habituation stimuli but instead suggested that infants attended to the correlations among the objects' features. This basic result – showing that 10-month-olds are sensitive to correlated attributes in a category context – has since been replicated and extended in habituation studies with realistic color photographs of animals (Younger, 1990) as well as in object-examining studies with three-dimensional wooden animals (Younger & Fearing, 1998).

These studies suggest that infants are able to use correlated features to form categories and can do so for a variety of stimuli. In all likelihood, this ability acts as a powerful mechanism for extracting the regularities of categories and may be at the core of infants' – and perhaps adults' – concepts.

Infants' ability to form categories for real-world stimuli.   Earlier I outlined classic work by Quinn et al. (1993) that showed that 3- to 4-month-old infants can form perceptually based basic-level categories for cats and dogs. This finding is particularly noteworthy because it highlights that even very young infants can form categorical representations for highly similar categories. In this section, I describe a large body of research, much of it conducted by Quinn and colleagues, which illustrates how surface features alone are sufficient for infants to form categories for animate and inanimate objects that we encounter in our environment. Moreover, if infants are capable of forming fine-grained categorical distinctions on the basis of perceptual features alone, then it is plausible that such features continue to play an important role in categorization beyond the first years of life (Quinn & Eimas, 1997; Rakison, 2003).

Quinn et al. (1993) showed that 3-month-old infants form categories for cats that exclude dogs but form a category for dogs that includes cats. In a series of follow-up experiments, Eimas and Quinn (1994) used the same familiarization methodology to examine the exclusivity of basic-level representations of horses and cats. They found that 3- and 4-month-olds developed representations for horses that excluded cats, giraffes, and zebras, and they developed representations for cats that excluded horses, tigers, but not female lions.

Quinn and Eimas (1996b) investigated the perceptual basis of infants' categories of cats and dogs, and in particular, the role of facial information. Infants aged 3 and 4 months were familiarized to one of three sets of stimuli. In the control condition infants were familiarized with the same cats used by Quinn et al. (1993), and then tested with a novel cat paired with a novel dog. In the second condition, the bodies of the cats were obscured and infants were familiarized only with the faces of the cat stimuli and tested with the face of a novel cat paired with the face of a novel dog. In the third condition, the faces of the cats were obscured and infants were familiarized only with the bodies of the cat stimuli and tested with the body of a novel cat paired with the body of a novel dog. The results showed that infants in the control condition performed similarly to those in Quinn et al. (1993). However, infants who were familiarized with the faces of cats preferred to look at the face of a novel dog than at the face of a novel cat, but infants who were familiarized with the body of cats divided their attention between the body of a novel cat and the body of a novel dog. Thus, facial information is sufficient to form a category of cats that excludes dogs but body information is not. However, it remains to be seen whether facial information is necessary for infants to form a category of cats, or whether another body part alone such as leg or tail might suffice equally well. Indeed, it could be that the large amount of information given in the body-only condition – at least relative to the face-only condition – made it harder for infants to extract a single basis for categorization.

Quinn and colleagues have also examined whether very young infants can use perceptual cues to categorize at a broader, global or superordinate level. Behl-Chadha, Eimas, and Quinn (1995) used the familiarization paradigm to explore whether young infants can form representations for superordinate-like categories. The studies showed that 3- and 4-month-old infants will form a representation for mammals that includes giraffes, cats, dogs, deer, and horses, but excludes birds, fish, and furniture. In a later study by Behl-Chadha (1996) infants at 3 and 4 months of age were found to form representations of furniture at multiple levels. Thus, not only did the infants form categorical representations of chairs and couches that excluded beds, but they also formed a categorical representation of beds, chairs, couches, cabinets, and tables that excluded mammals. Moreover, Quinn and Johnson (2000) found that 2-month-olds can form category representations at this global level but they cannot do so at the basic level. They found that 2-month-olds formed category representations for mammals that excluded furniture but could not form category representation for cats that excluded elephants, rabbits, or dogs.

In more recent investigations, Quinn (2004) tested whether young infants can also form representations for more specific classes called subordinate categories. This task is particularly difficult because many subordinate categories are highly similar at a perceptual level and consequently it can be accomplished only via extremely fine-grained distinctions. Quinn (2004) familiarized 3- to 4-month-olds as well as 6- and 7-month-olds with exemplars of subordinate-level classes of either cats and dogs and then tested them with a different subordinate exemplar. For instance, if infants were familiarized with Siamese cats they were tested with a novel Siamese cat and a Tabby cat or if they were familiarized with a Beagle they were tested with a novel Beagle and a Saint Bernard. Results showed that the 6- to 7-month-olds were able to form subordinate categories for the stimuli but that the younger age group was not. It is quite possible, however, that 3- to 4-months-olds would be able to form categories for more distinct subordinate classes (e.g., Great Danes vs. Chihuahuas) and that 6- to 7-month-olds would fail to form categories for more similar subordinate classes (e.g., Australian Shepherds vs. Border Collies). Thus, it may be presently premature to claim that infants are capable (or incapable) of subordinate categorization.

Quinn and colleagues' research is important because it shows that infants in the first years of life can form categories at the superordinate, basic, and subordinate level on the basis of perceptual cues alone. It is worth noting, however, that this line of research demonstrates what has been called "superordinate-like" or "basic-like" categorization (Rakison, 2000); that is, these categories resemble those formed by older children and adults but they are considerably impoverished versions of them because they do not include category relation information (e.g., these things are cats, these things are animals). At the same time, Mandler and colleagues (e.g., Mandler & Bauer, 1988; Mandler & McDonough, 1993) have argued that not all categorization in the first 12 months of life is based on perceptual features. For instance, Mandler and McDonough (1993) used an *object-examination* task to investigate superordinate categorization in 7-, 9- and 11-month-olds. This task is similar to the visual habituation procedure except that instead of looking at images of objects, infants play with scale-model toys. In one task, for example, infants played with a series of animals and were then presented with a novel animal and a novel vehicle. Infants at 9 and 11 months, though less so infants at 7 months, responded with increased playing with the novel vehicle relative to the novel animal. Moreover, Mandler and McDonough (1993) found that infants' categorization of animals and vehicles was not influenced by the degree of between-category similarity; for example, infants categorized birds as different from airplanes despite the fact that exemplars from both categories had similar shapes.

Based on these findings, Mandler and McDonough (1993) claimed that infants' categorization of perceptually similar objects implies that they must possess a conceptual understanding of animals and vehicles as "different kinds of things." It is worth noting, however, that within their tasks the majority of the exemplars within each category possessed the same parts; that is, four of the five animal exemplars possessed legs and all the vehicle exemplars possessed wheels, and the birds and planes differed in a number of perceptual attributes (e.g., the planes had tail wings and the birds did not). Moreover, Mandler and McDonough (1993) reported that their results were not replicated with the standard picture-looking technique; that is, 9- and 11-month-olds did not categorize the superordinate domains of animals and vehicles when a different methodology was used. Indeed, Van de Walle and Hoerger (1996) examined whether Mandler and McDonough's (1993) results might have been caused by overall perceptible differences. They found that

9-month-old infants, following a period of familiarization, discriminated between novel animal-like and novel vehicle-like stimuli on the basis of overall part structure; that is, curvilinearity versus rectilinearity (the objects were otherwise matched for size, overall shape, texture, and color). Thus, whether Mandler and McDonough's (1993) study demonstrates conceptual categorization, as they argue, remains to be seen.

The Second Year of Life: Going Beyond the Immediate Input?

The previous section illustrated that between birth and 12 months of age infants' categorization is predominantly underpinned by attention to perceptual cues; that is, it relies on the surface features of objects. Indeed, most theorists from both the Smart and Dumb Infant camps agree this to be the case, at least for the first 7 or 8 months of life (Mandler, 2003; Quinn & Eimas, 1996a). There is considerably more debate, however, about the basis for categorization as infants reach their second year. Recall that those in the Dumb Infant camp propose that infants at 12 months of age and beyond continue to use the surface features of objects to categorize but also start to incorporate other less perceptually available features into their already existing concepts. Crucially, these theorists argue that infants rely on the same mechanisms for learning about this less perceptible information as they did for the more obvious static surface features in the first year of life. In contrast, those in the Smart Baby camp posit that conceptual categorization begins in earnest during the second year of life (Gelman, 1990; Mandler 2003; Mandler, Bauer, & McDonough, 1991; Pauen, 2002). According to this view, infants start to categorize and perform inductive inference on the basis of nonobvious properties (e.g., animacy, self-propulsion) and category relations (e.g., this is an animal). In this section, I will address the evidence for both of these views.

Methods for studying categorization in the second year of life

As one might expect, many of the same challenges arise for those who study categorization – and induction – in the second year of life as for those who study the same area in younger infants. Between 12 and 24 months, infants' and toddlers' language ability remains insufficient for linguistically based measures of categorization. As a result, experimental methods for the study of concept development in the second year of life continue to rely on nonverbal responses, and many studies that examine categorization after 12 months of age rely on the visually based habituation and familiarization procedures. However, because infants' motor skills are more finely developed by 12 months of age, a number of additional paradigms exist in which infants manipulate objects. One such method – the object-examining technique – was outlined in the previous section. The other methods that are available to researchers are outlined in this section.

A primary method used to study categorization in the second year of life is called *sequential touching* or *object manipulation* procedure (e.g., Mandler et al., 1991; Mandler & Bauer, 1988; Mandler, Fivush, & Reznick, 1987; Nelson, 1973; Rakison, 2007;

Rakison & Butterworth, 1998a, 1998b; Rakison & Cohen, 1999; Ricciuti, 1965; Starkey, 1981). In this paradigm, a number of objects – typically scale model toys – are placed in front of an infant and their spontaneous touching of the objects is coded. Typically, infants are presented with eight objects at a time, four of which are drawn from one category and four from another. If infants either come to the task with knowledge of the objects or if they can observe a basis for categorization, they tend to touch sequentially the objects from the same category. For instance, infants will categorize cubes as different from spheres by touching a number of the cubes and then touching a number of the spheres.

Finally, the inductive generalization or generalized imitation method was developed to study how infants generalize from one instance, or category, to another (Mandler & McDonough, 1996, 1998; Rakison, 2005b; Rakison, Cicchino, & Hahn, 2007; Younger & Johnson, 2004). This method has three phases: baseline, modeling, and test. During the baseline phase infants are presented with two exemplars from different categories – for instance, a dog and car – and often (though not always) a prop that is connected to one (or sometimes both) of the exemplars; for instance, a key (Mandler & McDonough, 1996). Infants are allowed to play spontaneously with the toys and prop and the toys are then withdrawn. During the modeling phase, an experimenter introduces a novel model exemplar – for the key it would be a vehicle such as a truck – and then performs an action with the exemplar and the prop (e.g., "starting the truck with the key"). In the test phase, the model exemplar is withdrawn and infants are presented with the prop and the two category exemplars from the baseline condition; they are then encouraged to repeat the observed action.

Primary Findings on Categorization in the Second Year of Life

Infants' ability to use function to categorize

It has been suggested that a cue to which infants might attend to form categories is *function*. There is no set definition that applies universally to the term function, in part because the correlation between form and function confounds any attempt at a pure definition, and in part because function is related to the purposes which an object serves and is therefore defined by intentions. The Dictionary of Psychology (Reber, 1985) defines function as the proper activity or appropriate behavior of a person, object, structure, or part which is achieved by the specific behavior on the part of an actor. Similarly, Madole and Cohen (1995) define functional properties as "those involving the reaction of a thing to an action upon it" (p. 646). More recent formulations, however, consider function not only as a feature of objects that infants can attend to and encode but as an emergent property of the combination of a number of different features (e.g., actions performed on the object and the resulting effects) (Horst, Oakes, & Madole, 2005; Madole & Cohen, 1995; Madole et al., 1993; Madole, Oakes, & Rakison, in press).

Studies that examined the effects of function on early categorization initially compared infants' and children's attention to perceptual attributes with their attention to functional attributes. In an early study by Nelson (1973), 12- to 24-month-old infants were presented with a set of ball-like objects that differed in functional or perceptual qualities to a prototypical ball (a rubber ball). Nelson (1973) found that when infants were asked to give the experimenter a "ball" they tended to hand over an object that was functionally similar but perceptually dissimilar to the prototype (e.g., a plastic "whiffle" ball with holes) rather than one that was perceptually similar and functionally different (e.g., a cork sphere on a stand with holes). Nelson (1973, 1974, 1985) concluded that categories based on functional properties emerge prior to categories based on perceptual properties.

A study by Benelli, D'Odorico, Levorato, and Simion (1977) presented evidence that function plays a role in category formation but that classes are initially determined by physical similarity. They found that 10- to 13-month-old infants initially chose objects as "balls" or "pacifiers" on the basis of their physical similarity to previously encountered balls or pacifiers, but they continued to classify only those objects that functioned like balls or pacifiers. A similar conclusion was made by Mervis (1985) who found that her 8-month-old son categorized objects as a "horn" depending on their physical resemblance to a well-known exemplar, but that he only continued to include objects in the category if they actually functioned like a "horn."

Further evidence that infants attend to function after form in recognition and categorization came from two impressive studies with the object-examination paradigm by Madole and her colleagues (Madole et al., 1993; Madole and Cohen, 1995). In one series of experiments performed by Madole et al. (1993) infants were familiarized – through exploratory manipulation – with a number of real objects that either differed or correlated in form and function (e.g., rolling, shaking). The infants were then tested with a novel object that did not embody the properties of the training exemplars. The results showed that 10-month-olds attend to form, 14-month-olds attend to form and function as independent properties, and 18-month-olds attend to the relation between an object's form and its function. The authors concluded that infants in the first year categorize by form alone and infants in the second year develop sensitivity to form-function correlates.

These conclusions were confirmed in a follow-up study by Madole and Cohen (1995) that showed that 18-month-olds, but not 14-month-olds, will learn only form and function relationships that make sense in the real world (i.e., when an object part predicted its function) and not form–function relations that do not make sense (i.e., when an object part predicted another part's function). Madole and Cohen (1995) concluded that 18-month-olds attend to the relationship between form and function as the basis for categorization and are constrained in the kinds of form–function correlates they will recognize. However, there is evidence that this behavior does not continue into the third year of life. For instance, a number of studies showed that 2- to 5-year-old children label objects by form rather than function (e.g., Anderson & Prawat, 1983).

More recently, Oakes and colleagues (Horst et al., 2005; Perone & Oakes, 2006) have shown that the origins of infants' ability to attend to features involved in function may be present at the end of the first year of life. Horst et al. habituated 10-month-old infants with four events in which an object had the same appearance on each trial (e.g., always a purple round object) but four different "functions" (e.g., squeezing that produced squeaking on some trials, rolling that produced clicking on some trials). Infants in a separate condition were habituated to four events in which the same function was presented on each trial, but it was performed on four different objects (e.g., squeezing produced clicking on a purple round object and a pink oblong object). Infants' looking times revealed that when habituated with four different items – regardless of whether those items shared a common function or a common appearance – function was the most salient feature. In other words, infants who were shown four different objects and one function dishabituated when shown a new event involving a familiar appearance and a new function. Similarly, infants who were shown four different functions and a single appearance dishabituated when shown a new event involving a familiar appearance and a new function. This result suggests that even though infants start to use function actively as a basis for categorization in the second year of life, the origins of this knowledge may be in play toward the end of the first year.

The global to basic-level shift

As outlined earlier, the basic level (e.g., dogs, cars) is thought to be *psychologically privileged*. Children's first object words are often at the basic level and when asked to name pictures of objects 3-year-olds tend to use those at the basic level rather than any other (Anglin, 1977; Clark, 1973; Rosch et al., 1976). Adult labeling is also consistent with this pattern such that naming occurs more frequently at the basic level (e.g., frog) than the superordinate level (e.g., amphibian) or the subordinate level (e.g., tree frog). The ubiquity of basic-level labels was initially supported by research on early categorization: in sorting and match-to-sample studies in which children were asked to put objects that are alike together, 3-, 5-, and 6-year-olds sorted poorly at the superordinate level but performed almost perfectly at the basic level (Rosch et al., 1976), while infants as young as 22 months made basic-level matches more easily than superordinate matches (Daehler, Lonardo, & Bukatko, 1979). These findings led researchers to believe that children form categories at the basic level (e.g., lions vs. pigs) before they form categories based on superordinate groups (e.g., animals vs. vehicles) (e.g., Mervis & Rosch, 1981; Rosch et al., 1976). Basic-level categorization was thought to be particularly easy for children because exemplars belonging to the same basic-level category are highly similar to one another (e.g., dogs share many perceptual features with one another) and at the same time differ substantially from members of neighboring categories (e.g., dogs and giraffes look different).

An alternative view of categorization was presented Mandler and colleagues (Mandler et al., 1991; Mandler & McDonough, 1993) who rejected Rosch's claim that basic-level categories are primary and instead proposed that infants' first conceptual categories are at a *global* level. Although these global categories resemble superordinate domains (e.g., animals), they differ from superordinates in that they have no distinctions of basic-level classes nested within them. In one study by Mandler and Bauer (1988) that supported this view, 16- and 20-month-old infants were presented with basic-level contrasts from either a single superordinate domain (e.g., dogs and horses) or from distinct superordinate categories (e.g., dogs and cars). Categorization was assessed through sequential touching.

Infants at both ages were successful in forming categories based on different superordinate domains – that is, they categorized dogs as different from cars. In contrast, only the 20-month-olds formed basic-level categories within the same superordinate domain – that is, by categorizing dogs as different from horses. The results, then, reveal a global-to-specific trend in categorization – one that opposes the view that children initially categorize at the basic level before the superordinate level.

Further support for this claim came from a later series of studies by Mandler et al. (1991) that used the object-manipulation paradigm. In one experiment 18-, 24-, and 30-month-olds were presented with different levels of contrast of basic-level categories drawn from the same superordinate (e.g., animals). Thus, a low contrast of animal exemplars was judged to be dogs and horses, and a high contrast was considered to be dogs and fish. In addition, the same infants were presented with a superordinate contrast of animals and vehicles. The results indicated that 18-month-old infants categorized the superordinate-level domains of animals and vehicles but did not categorize basic-level contrasts within these domains when the contrast between the object sets was low or moderate (e.g., dogs versus horses, dogs versus rabbits). Although 24-month-olds' performance was superior to that of the 18-month-olds, they did not categorize basic-level categories when the contrast between the two object sets was considered to be low (e.g., dogs versus horses). Mandler et al. (1991) took this finding, in conjunction with the results of the earlier study by Mandler and Bauer (1988), as confirmation that basic-level categories are not the first to develop in young infants. In other words, they interpreted infants' success in superordinate level categorization tasks and failure in many basic-level categorization tasks to mean that concepts for the former emerge developmentally earlier than the latter.

Although the primacy of the superordinate level has become less of a controversial issue, the factors responsible for early global categorization are still a matter of contention. According to Mandler and colleagues, global categories are based on conceptual knowledge of nonobvious properties (e.g., animacy, support). The argument for this is that members of a superordinate category share few perceptual properties but they do share a number of deeper nonobvious properties. Consequently, if infants group together a diverse set of superordinate members this cannot be done on the basis of perceptual features and must instead be based on their nonobvious properties. For example, rabbits, giraffes, parrots, and whales do not share many perceptual features but they are all self-propelled agents that are goal-directed. In this sense, categorization is thought to be driven by knowledge of the "kinds of things" objects are (Mandler & McDonough, 1993).

There are a number of studies, however, that suggest that perceptual cues are sufficient for infants to categorize at the global level. Recall that Behl-Chadha (1996) and Quinn and Johnson (2000) found that infants as young as 3 months of age could form global-level categories for animals that excluded, for example, furniture. Although it is possible that 3-month-old infants understand that animals are the "same kind of thing," most researchers – including Mandler (2003) – believe it unlikely. This suggests that surface features alone can act as the basis for categorization at the global level. But what about infants in the second year of life? Rakison and Butterworth (1998a, 1998b) analyzed the stimuli used by Mandler and colleagues (Mandler & Bauer, 1988; Mandler et al., 1991) and found that the animals and furniture exemplars they used mostly possessed legs and the vehicles possessed wheels. They subsequently hypothesized that infants' categorization of animals, vehicles, and furniture was based not on a conceptual understanding of category relations or other nonobvious properties but rather the shared parts that are possessed by members of each class. Thus, animals tend to have legs, heads, and facial features whereas vehicles tend to have wheels, a windscreen, and lights. To test this idea, Rakison and Butterworth (1998a) used the object-manipulation paradigm with 14- to 22-month-olds. They found that infants categorized objects from superordinate domains with different parts (i.e., legs and wheels) at 14 months of age but were unable to categorize objects from superordinate domains with the same parts (i.e., legs) until 22 months of age.

In a second experiment by the same authors (Rakison & Butterworth, 1998a), sequential touching behavior towards novel versions of toy animals and toy vehicles was explored. The novel stimuli were generated by removing or attaching parts such as legs and wheels. In such a way, infants were presented with two tasks in which parts were matched within and between the categories – that is, all the stimuli possessed legs and wheels or all of the stimuli possessed no legs or wheels – and one task in which parts were balanced across the categories; that is, half the animals had legs and half had wheels and likewise half the vehicles had legs and half had wheels. The results revealed that infants at 14, 18, and 22 months of age categorized normal animal and normal vehicle, but they did not categorize when the available stimuli had the same parts (both legs and wheels) or possessed no salient parts at all (legs or wheels removed). In the final condition, infants at 14 and 18 months of age classified on the basis of parts (objects with legs and objects with wheels) instead of category relations (animals and vehicles) when presented with a choice to categorize on either basis. By 22 months, however, a single part was no longer sufficient as the basis for categorization. These results were interpreted to mean that 14- and 18-month-old infants categorize on the basis of surface features such as object parts. Finally, these findings were extended by Rakison and Butterworth (1998b) who found that 14- to 22-month-olds in the sequential touching paradigm do not attend to parts per se, but rather they are sensitive to the structural configuration of objects which is given by parts.

In sum, it is now well established that infants first form categories at the superordinate – or global – level and then later form categories at the basic level. However, the basis for these categories remains hotly debated. According to one view, the global-to-basic trend indicates that infants use knowledge about category relations or nonobvious properties to categorize at the superordinate level and that this knowledge does not facilitate categorization at the basic level (e.g., Mandler et al., 1991; Pauen, 2002). According to an alternative view, this developmental trend follows from infants' use of perceptual features to categorize; superordinate categories, which can be categorized on the basis of object parts whereas basic-level categories (e.g., cats and dogs) cannot.

Using concepts for induction

Recall that a process related to categorization is *induction* or *inductive inference*. Children and adults can use their concepts to categorize objects into groups but they can also use them to decide whether to generalize or extend a particular observation to a novel instance. For instance, based on my knowledge of dogs I can predict that a novel dog I have never previously seen will bark and chase squirrels. Although this is an important cognitive process, there is relatively little research on when and how this ability develops in infants. However, evidence from the handful of studies that exist mirrors in some ways that found of the global-to-basic shift in infancy.

In a now classic series of studies, Mandler and McDonough (1996, 1998; McDonough & Mandler, 1998) used the generalized imitation technique to investigate whether infants between 9 and 14 months of age use inductive inference to show that they understand that animals are capable of specific actions (e.g., drinking from a cup, going to bed) and that vehicles are capable of different actions (e.g., starting with a key, giving a ride). The rationale for these studies was to test the top-down or Smart Infant view of early induction developed by Mandler (1992; Mandler & McDonough, 1996); that is, Mandler and McDonough aimed to show that infants can use their conceptual knowledge to generalize a property of animals or vehicles to a novel instance. Mandler and McDonough (1996) found that infants between 9 and 14 months of age generalize animal properties to novel animals but not to novel vehicles, and they generalize vehicle properties to novel vehicles but not to novel animals. For example, infants generalized going to bed to a dog but not a truck and giving a ride to a car but not a dog.

These studies were extended by Mandler and McDonough (1998) who used the same four actions as the modeled properties but in some conditions presented infants with two members of the appropriate category for the action (e.g., after seeing a dog drink from a cup infants were allowed to imitate with a dog and a cat or a dog and a rabbit). Mandler and McDonough (1998) predicted that if infants have conceptual knowledge that animals drink or go to bed then they should enact the action they observe with both of the category-appropriate exemplars. Indeed, this is what they found: infants imitated animal actions with a cat and a rabbit, and a cat and a dog, and they were just as likely to imitate the vehicle actions with a car, a truck, and a motorcycle.

In a series of more recent studies, Poulin-Dubois, Frenkiel-Fishman, Nayer, & Johnson (2006) used the generalized imitation procedure with 14-, 16-, and 20-month-olds to investigate whether they would generalize properties such as going to bed, looking in a mirror, and jumping over a wall from animals to other animals, from people to animals, and from a monkey to people and animals. Their results indicated that 14-month-olds generalized bodily and sensory properties from an animal to another animal and not to a vehicle, and that 16- and 20-month-olds extended motion and sensory properties from a person to other mammals instead of vehicles. Finally, they found that 20-month-olds extended motion properties from a monkey to people, cats, and tigers, but that they were more likely to generalize sensory properties to people than to animals.

The results of Mandler and McDonough (1996, 1998) as well as Poulin-Dubois et al. (2006) have been interpreted to mean that by the beginning of the second year infants possess an abstract concept of animals and vehicles that underpins inductive generalization. However, the interpretation of these data has been questioned as overly rich. For one thing, it has been proposed that the model exemplar used by the experimenter may influence infants' choice of object to demonstrate an action. For example, infants may observe which exemplar the experimenter uses in the modeling phase and then choose the one of the two test objects that is perceptually similar to that exemplar (Rakison, 2003). To test this hypothesis, Furrer, Younger, and Johnson (2005) presented infants at 14 and 16 months of age with the same events used by Mandler and McDonough (1996, 1998) except that they also modeled the events with an inappropriate exemplar (e.g., a dog starting with a key). Their results supported the *perceptual matching* hypothesis: infants in both age groups imitated events with the appropriate category exemplar when they observed an experimenter model with a con-ventional object (e.g., a bus starting with a key) but enacted events with an inappropriate category exemplar when the event was modeled with an unconventional item (e.g., a dog starting with a key).

A second issue with the results of Mandler and McDonough (1996, 1998) is that category relatedness in their studies was confounded with the object features of the stimuli. For example, infants tended to generalize to objects with the same object parts (e.g., cats, rabbits, and dogs all have legs whereas cars, trucks, and buses all have wheels). If infants brought knowledge to the research about the actions or motions of animals and vehicles, it is unclear from their data alone whether this was in an abstract form – as Mandler and McDonough (1996, 1998) proposed – or grounded in the typical perceptual features of the members of those categories.

To test these alternative explanations, Rakison (2005b) used the inductive generaliza-tion procedure to examine 18- and 22-month-old infants' knowledge about the path of land motions typical of animals (i.e., nonlinear) and vehicles (i.e., linear). In contrast to previous experiments with the inductive generalization task, Rakison (2005b) presented infants with four test stimuli instead of two during the baseline and testing phases of the experiments. For example, if the experimenter modeled nonlinear "walking" with a cat, one test object was a dog (correct category, correct parts), another was a dolphin (correct category, incorrect parts), another was a table (incorrect category, correct parts), and another was a car (incorrect category, incorrect parts). It was predicted that if infants' induction is based on abstract conceptual knowledge they should generalize to the objects from the correct category regardless of parts; however, if their knowledge is grounded in perceptual features they should generalize to objects with the appropriate parts for the motion irrespective of category membership. The results of two experiments were consist-ent in their findings: 18-month-olds generalized to objects on the basis of object parts whereas 22-month-olds generalized to objects on the basis of category membership. These data, in conjunction with those of Furrer et al. (2005; see also Cicchino & Rakison, 2008), suggest that infants' inductive generalizations may continue to be based on the perceptual features of objects until toward the end of the second year. Clearly, however, considerably more research on infants' ability to generalize object properties is required before strong conclusions can be drawn either way.

Summary and Conclusions

The ability to form concepts for the categories that exist in the world is undoubtedly one of the cornerstones of cognitive development. Without this ability, memory would be overstretched, language would be unworkable, and each new object encountered would have no reference point. It is perhaps not surprising, then, that infants' ability to develop concepts – and use them to categorize – begins early in the first year of life. Before infants reach their first birthday they possess considerable categorizing skills. There is strong evidence that infants can form categories on the basis of correlated clusters of features (e.g., Younger & Cohen, 1986) and can form prototype-like category structures for realistic images as well as geometric categories (e.g., Bomba & Siqueland, 1983; Quinn et al., 1993). There also exists a considerable database on infants' ability to form perceptually based categories at the superordinate, basic, and subordinate level. These early perceptually based categories, however, are unlikely to match those formed by older children in that they do not encapsulate the relations that typically exist among members of class (e.g., "these things are animals", "these things eat"). In conjunction, the extant literature reveals that perceptual cues are sufficient for infants to form categories for a wide range of stimuli and that the basic mechanism for category formation is present at birth if not shortly thereafter.

Infants' categorization and induction abilities develop considerably between 1 and 2 years of age. They learn to use function to form categories, can group objects at the superordinate, basic, and subordinate level, and can generalize what they know about the members of a category to a novel exemplar. These abilities, which emerge prior to the development of language, signify that infants' concepts for objects in the world continue to incorporate ever more detailed information, much of which is not always present in the perceptual input. It remains an open question, however, whether infants undergo some kind of shift from a reliance on perceptual information to a reliance on conceptual knowledge. As this section demonstrates, in many cases the basis for categorization and induction in the second year of life remain hotly disputed.

In light of the importance of category and concept development to human cognition, research continues apace on when and how infants' abilities emerge. Researchers have only recently begun to apply new methodologies, including ERP (Quinn, Westerlund, & Nelson, 2006) and computational modelling (Rakison & Lupyan, 2008), to these issues and it is in all likelihood only a matter of time before there exists a more coherent and concise understanding of infants' developing concepts. For instance, computational modeling is an excellent technique for testing theoretical assumptions, which in many cases cannot be addressed by empirical research (see e.g., Quinn & Johnson, 2000). Likewise, clever application of infant-appropriate imaging techniques can clarify whether the same or different categorization processes are involved in, for example, basic- and superordinate-level categorization (Quinn et al.).

It is only by applying these converging methodologies that researchers can shed illumination on many of the classic philosophical questions raised by the Greeks over 2000 years ago: Where does knowledge come from? In what way is information about the world stored in the mind? And how does this knowledge change over time? The importance of these questions, and the unique window into the mind that is available only to infancy researchers, mean that research will continue to study in depth early category and concept development. Thus, although the answers to these questions remain some way off, this chapter illustrates that in a relatively short period of time developmental scientists have made, and continue to make, considerable progress toward them.

References

Anderson, A. L., & Prawat, R. S. (1983). When is a cup not a cup? A further examination of form and function in children's labeling responses. *Merrill-Palmer Quarterly*, *29*, 375–385.

Anglin, J. M. (1977). *Word, objects, and conceptual development*. New York: W. W. Norton.

Behl-Chadha, G. (1996). Basic-level and superordinate-like categorical representations in early infancy. *Cognition*, *60*, 105–141.

Behl-Chadha, G., Eimas, P. D., & Quinn, P. C. (1995, March). *Perceptually-driven superordinate categorisation by young infants*. Paper presented at the meeting of the Society for Research in Child Development, Indianapolis, IN.

Benelli, B., D'Odorico, L., Levorato, C., and Simion, F. (1977). Formation and extension of the concepts of a prelinguistic child. *Italian Journal of Psychology*, *3*, 429–448.

Bhatt, R. S., & Rovee-Collier, C. (1994). Perception and 24-hour retention of feature relations in infancy. *Developmental Psychology*, *30*, 142–150.

Bhatt, R. S., & Rovee-Collier, C. (1996). Infants' forgetting of correlated attributes and object recognition. *Child Development*, *67*, 172–187.

Bomba, P. C., & Siqueland, E. R. (1983). The nature and structure of infant form categories. *Journal of Experimental Child Psychology*, *35*, 294–328.

Bruner, J. S., Olver, R. R., & Greenfield, P. M. (1966). *Studies in cognitive growth*. New York: Wiley.

Bruner, R., Goodnow, J. J., & Austin, G. A. (Eds.). (1956). *A study of thinking*. New York: Wiley.

Cicchino, J. B., & Rakison, D. H. (2008). Producing and processing self-propelled motion in infancy. *Developmental Psychology*, *44*, 1232–1241.

Clark, E. V. (1973). What's in a word? On the child's acquisition of semantics in his first language. In T. E. Moore (Ed.), *Cognitive development and the acquisition of language* (pp. 65–110). New York: Academic Press.

Daehler, M. W., Lonardo, R., & Bukatko, D. (1979). Matching and equivalence judgements in very young children. *Child Development*, *50*, 70–179.

Eimas, P. D. (1994). Categorisation in infancy and the continuity of development. *Cognition*, *50*, 83–93.

Eimas, P. D., & Quinn, P. C. (1994). Studies on the formation of perceptually based basic-level categories in young infants. *Child Development*, *65*, 903–917.

Fiser, J., & Aslin, R. N. (2002). Statistical learning of higher-order temporal structure from visual shape-sequences. *Journal of Experimental Psychology: Learning, Memory, and Cognition*, *28*(3), 458–467.

Furrer, S. D., Younger, B. A., & Johnson, K. E. (2005, April). *Do planes drink? Generalized imitation following modeling with an inappropriate exemplar*. Poster presented at the Society for Research in Child Development Biennial Conference, Atlanta, GA.

Gelman, R. (1990). First principles organize attention to and learning about relevant data: Number and the animate-inanimate distinction as examples. *Cognitive Science*, *14*, 79–106.

Gelman, R., Durgin, F., & Kaufman, L. (1995). Distinguishing between animates and inanimates: Not by motion alone. In D. Sperber, D. Premack, & A. J. Premack. (Eds.), *Causal Cognition* (pp. 150–184). Oxford: Clarendon.

Gershkoff-Stowe, L., & Smith L. B. (2004). Shape and the first hundred nouns. *Child Development*, *75*, 1–17.

Halberstadt, J., & Rhodes, G. (2000). The attractiveness of nonface averages: Implications for an evolutionary explanation of the attractiveness of average faces. *Psychological Science*, *11*, 285–289.

Horst, J. S., Oakes, L. M., & Madole, K. L. (2005). What does it look like and what can it do? Category structure influences how infants categorise. *Child Development, 76*, 614–631.

Hunter, M. A., & Ames, E. W. (1988). A multifactor model of infant preferences for novel and familiar stimuli. In C. Rovee-Collier & L. P. Lipsitt (Eds.), *Advances in infancy research* (Vol. 5, pp. 69–95). Norwood, NJ: Ablex.

Jones, S. S., & Smith, L. B. (1993). The place of perception in children's concepts. *Cognitive Development, 8*, 113–139.

Keil, F. C. (1981). Constraints on knowledge and cognitive development. *Psychological Review, 88*, 197–227.

Kirkham, N. Z., Slemmer, J. A., & Johnson, S. P. (2002). Visual statistical learning in infancy: Evidence of a domain general learning mechanism. *Cognition, 83*, 35–42.

Langlois, J. H., & Roggman, L. A. (1990). Attractive faces are only average. *Psychological Science, 1*, 115–121.

Langlois, J. H., Roggman, L. A., Casey, R. J., Ritter, J. M., Rieser-Danner, L. A., & Jenkins, V. Y. (1987). Infant preferences for attractive faces: Rudiments of a stereotype? *Developmental Psychology, 23*, 263–369.

Langlois, J. H., Roggman, L. A., & Musselman, L. (1994). What is average and what is not average about attractive faces? *Psychological Science, 5*, 214–220.

Leslie, A. M. (1984). Infant perception of a manual pick-up event. *British Journal of Developmental Psychology, 2*, 19–37.

Leslie, A. M. (1988). The necessity of illusion: Perception and thought in infancy. In L. Weiskrantz (Ed.), *Thought without language* (pp. 185–210). New York: Oxford University Press.

Leslie, A. M. (1995). A theory of agency. In D. Sperber, D. Premack, & A. J. Premack (Eds.), *Causal cognition* (pp. 121–141). Oxford: Clarendon.

Madole, K. L., & Cohen, L. B. (1995). The role of object parts in infants' attention to form–function correlations. *Developmental Psychology, 31*, 637–648.

Madole, K. L., Oakes, L. M., & Cohen, L. B. (1993). Developmental changes in infants' attention to function and form–function correlations. *Cognitive Development, 8*, 189–209.

Madole, K. L., Oakes, L. M, & Rakison, D. H. (in press). Information processing approaches to infants' developing representation of dynamic features. In L. M. Oakes, C. H. Cashon, M. Casasola & D. H. Rakison (Eds.), *Infant perception and cognition: Recent advances, emerging theories, and future directions*. New York: Oxford University Press.

Mandler, J. M. (1992). How to build a baby II. Conceptual primitives. *Psychological Review, 99*, 587–604.

Mandler, J. M. (2000). Perceptual and conceptual processes in infancy. *Journal of Cognition and Development, 1*, 3–36.

Mandler, J. M. (2003). Conceptual categorisation. In D. H. Rakison & L. M. Oakes (Eds.), *Early category and concept development: Making sense of the blooming, buzzing confusion* (pp. 103–131). New York: Oxford University Press.

Mandler, J. M., & Bauer, P. J. (1988). The cradle of categorisation: Is the basic level basic? *Cognitive Development, 3*, 247–264.

Mandler, J. M., Bauer, P. J., & McDonough, L. (1991). Separating the sheep from the goats: Differentiating global categories. *Cognitive Psychology, 23*, 263–298.

Mandler, J. M., Fivush, R., & Reznick, J. S. (1987). The development of contextual categories. *Cognitive Development, 2*, 339–354.

Mandler, J. M., & McDonough, L. (1993). Concept formation in infancy. *Cognitive Development, 8*, 291–318.

Mandler, J. M., & McDonough, L. (1996). Drinking and driving don't mix: Inductive generalization in infancy. *Cognition, 59*, 307–335.

Mandler, J. M., & McDonough, L. (1998). Studies in inductive inference in infancy. *Cognitive Psychology, 37*, 60–96.

McDonough, L., & Mandler, J. M. (1998). Inductive generalization in 9- and 11-month-olds. *Developmental Science, 1*, 227–232.

Medin, D. L., & Schaffer, M. M. (1978). Context theory of classification learning. *Psychological Review, 85*, 207–238.

Mervis, C. B. (1985). On the existence of prelinguistic categories: A case study. *Infant Behaviour and Development, 8*, 293–300.

Mervis, C. B., & Rosch, E. (1981). Categorisation of natural objects. *Annual Review of Psychology, 32*, 89–115.

Neisser, U. (1987). From direct perception to conceptual structure. In U. Neisser (Ed.), *Concepts and conceptual development* (pp. 11–25). London: Cambridge Press.

Nelson, K. (1973). Some evidence for the cognitive primacy of categorisation and its functional basis. *Merrill-Palmer Quarterly, 19*, 21–39.

Nelson, K. (1974). Concept, word, and sentence: Interrelations in acquisition and development. *Psychological Review, 4*, 267–285.

Nelson, K. (1985). *Making sense: Development of meaning in early childhood.* New York: Academic Press.

Oakes, L. M., & Madole, K. L. (1999). From seeing to thinking: A reply to Mandler. *Developmental Review, 19*, 307–318.

Oakes, L. M., & Madole, K. L. (2003). Principles of developmental change in infants' category formation. In D. H. Rakison & L. M. Oakes (Eds.), *Early category and concept development: Making sense of the blooming buzzing confusion* (pp. 159–192). New York: Oxford University Press.

Pauen, S. (2002). Evidence for knowledge-based category discrimination in infancy. *Child Development, 73*, 1016–1033.

Perone, S., & Oakes, L. M. (2006). It clicks when it is rolled and squeaks when it is squeezed: What 10-month-old infants learn about object function. *Child Development, 77*, 1608–1622.

Poulin-Dubois, D., Frenkiel-Fishman, S., Nayer, S., & Johnson, S. (2006). Infants' inductive generalization of bodily, motion, and sensory properties to animals and people. *Journal of Cognition and Development, 7*, 431–453.

Premack, D. (1990). The infants' theory of self-propelled objects. *Cognition, 36*, 1–16.

Quinn, P. C. (2004). Development of subordinate-level categorization in 3- to 7-month-old infants. *Child Development, 75*, 886–899.

Quinn, P. C., & Bomba, P. C. (1986). Evidence for a general category of oblique orientations in 4-month-old infants. *Journal of Experimental Child Psychology, 42*, 345–354.

Quinn, P. C., & Eimas, P. D. (1996a). Perceptual organization and categorisation. In C. Rovee-Collier & L. Lipsitt (Eds.), *Advances in infancy research* (Vol. 10, pp. 1–36). Norwood, NJ: Ablex.

Quinn, P. C., & Eimas, P. D. (1996b). Perceptual cues that permit categorical differentiation of animal species by infants. *Journal of Experimental Child Psychology, 63*, 189–211.

Quinn, P. C., & Eimas, P. D. (1997). A reexamination of the perceptual-to-conceptual shift in mental representations. *Review of General Psychology, 1*, 171–187.

Quinn, P. C., & Eimas, P. D. (2000). The emergence of category representations during infancy: Are separate perceptual and conceptual processes required? *Journal of Cognition and Development, 1*, 55–61.

Quinn, P. C., Eimas, P. D., & Rosenkrantz, S. L. (1993). Evidence for representations of perceptually similar natural categories by 3-month-old and 4-month-old infants. *Perception, 22*, 463–475.

Quinn, P. C. and Johnson, M. H. (2000). Global before basic category representations in connectionist networks and 2-month old infants. *Infancy*, *1*, 31–46.

Quinn, P. C., Johnson, M., Mareschal, D., Rakison, D., & Younger, B. (2000). Response to Mandler and Smith: A dual process framework for understanding early categorisation? *Infancy*, *1*, 111–122.

Quinn, P. C., Westerlund, A., & Nelson, C. A. (2006). Neural markers of categorisation in 6-month-old infants. *Psychological Science*, *17*, 59–66.

Rakison, D. H. (2000). When a rose is just a rose: The illusion of taxonomies in infant categorisation. *Infancy*, *1*, 77–90.

Rakison, D. H. (2003). Parts, categorisation, and the animate–inanimate distinction in infancy. In D. H. Rakison, & L. M. Oakes, (Eds.), *Early category and concept development: Making sense of the blooming buzzing confusion* (pp. 159–192). New York: Oxford University Press.

Rakison, D. H. (2005a). Infant perception and cognition: An evolutionary perspective on early learning. In D. Bjorkland, & B. Ellis (Eds.), *Origins of the social mind: Evolutionary psychology and child development* (pp. 317–353). New York: Wiley.

Rakison, D. H. (2005b). Developing knowledge of motion properties in infancy. *Cognition*, *96*, 183–214.

Rakison, D. H. (2007). Inductive categorisation: A methodology to examine the contents of concepts in infancy. *Cognition, Brain, Behavior*, *4*, 773–790.

Rakison, D. H., & Butterworth, G. (1998a). Infants' use of parts in early categorisation. *Developmental Psychology*, *34*, 49–62.

Rakison, D. H., & Butterworth, G. (1998b). Infant attention to object structure in early categorisation. *Developmental Psychology*, *34*, 1310–1325.

Rakison, D. H., Cicchino, J. B., & Hahn, E. R. (2007). Infants' knowledge of the identity of rational goal-directed entities. *British Journal of Developmental Psychology*, *25*, 461–470.

Rakison, D. H., & Cohen, L. B. (1999). Infants' use of functional parts in basic-like categorisation. *Developmental Science*, *2*, 423–432.

Rakison, D. H., & Hahn, E. (2004). The mechanisms of early categorisation and induction: Smart or dumb infants? In R. Kail (Ed.), *Advances in Child Development and Behavior* (Vol. 32, pp. 281–322). New York: Academic Press.

Rakison, D. H., & Lupyan, G. (2008). Developing object concepts in infancy: An associative learning perspective. *Monographs of the Society for Research in Child Development*, *73*, 1–110.

Rakison, D. H., & Poulin-Dubois, D. (2001). Developmental origin of the animate–inanimate distinction. *Psychological Bulletin*, *127*, 209–228.

Reber, A. S. (1985). *The Penguin Dictionary of Psychology*. New York: Penguin.

Ricciuti, H. (1965). Object grouping and selective ordering behaviour in infants 12- to 24-months-old. *Merrill-Palmer Quarterly*, *11*, 129–148.

Rosch, E. (1975). Cognitive representations of semantic categories. *Journal of Experimental Psychology General*, *104*, 192–233.

Rosch, E. (1978). Principles of categorisation. In E. Rosch, and B. Lloyd (Eds.), *Cognition and categorization* (pp. 27–48). Hillsdale, NJ: Erlbaum.

Rosch, E., & Mervis, C. B. (1975). Family resemblances: Studies in the internal structure of categories. *Cognitive Psychology*, *7*, 573–605.

Rosch, E., Mervis, C. B., Gray, W. D., Johnson, D. M., & Boyes-Braem, P. (1976). Basic objects in natural categories. *Cognitive Psychology*, *8*, 382–439.

Rovee-Collier, C., & Hayne, H. (1987). Reactivation of infant memory: Implications for cognitive development. In H. W. Reese (Ed.), *Advances in child development and behavior* (Vol. 20, pp. 185–238). New York: Academic.

Rovee-Collier, C., & Hayne, H. (2000). Memory in infancy and early childhood. In E. Tulving & F. I. M. Craik (Eds.), *The Oxford handbook of memory* (pp. 267–282). New York: Oxford University Press.

Rubenstein, A. J., Kalakanis, L., & Langlois, J. H. (1999). Infant preferences for attractive faces: A cognitive explanation. *Developmental Psychology, 35*, 848–855.

Saffran, J. R., Aslin, R. N., & Newport, E. L. (1996). Statistical learning by 8-month old infants. *Science, 274*, 1926–1928.

Sirois, S., & Mareschal, D. (2002). Models of habituation in infancy. *Trends in Cognitive Sciences, 6*, 293–298.

Slater, A. M., Mattock, A., Brown, E., Burnham, D., & Young, A. W. (1991). Visual processing of stimulus compounds in newborn babies. *Perception, 20*, 29–33.

Starkey, D. (1981). The origins of concept formation: Object sorting and object preference in early infancy. *Child Development, 52*, 489–497.

Strauss, M. S. (1979). Abstraction of prototypical information in adults and 10-month-old infants. *Journal of Experimental Psychology: Human Learning and Memory, 5*, 618–632.

Smith, L. B., Colunga, E., & Yoshida, H. (2003). Making an ontology: Cross-linguistic evidence. In D. H. Rakison, & L. M. Oakes, (Eds.), *Early category and concept development: Making sense of the blooming buzzing confusion* (pp. 275–372). New York: Oxford University Press.

Smith, L. B., & Heise, D. (1992). Perceptual similarity and conceptual structure. In B. Burns (Ed.), *Percepts, Concepts, and Categories*. Amsterdam: Elsevier.

Smith, L. B., Jones, S. S., & Landau, B. (1996). Naming in young children: A dumb attentional mechanism? *Cognition, 60*, 143–171.

Van de Walle, G. A., & Hoerger, M. L. (1996). *Perceptual foundations of categorisation in infancy.* Poster presented at the International Conference on Infant Studies, Providence, RI.

Younger, B. A. (1990). Infants' detection of correlations among feature categories. *Child Development, 61*, 614–620.

Younger, B. A., & Cohen, L. B. (1986). Developmental change in infants' perception of correlations among attributes. *Child Development, 57*, 803–815.

Younger, B. A., & Fearing, D. (1998). Detecting correlations among form attributes: An object-examining test with infants. *Infant Behavior and Development, 21*, 289–297.

Younger, B. A., & Gotlieb, S. (1988). Development of categorisation skills: Changes in the nature or structure of infant form categories? *Developmental Psychology, 24*, 611–619.

Younger, B. A., & Johnson, K. E. (2004). Infants' comprehension of toy replicas as symbols for real objects. *Cognitive Psychology, 48*, 207–242.

8

Infant Learning and Memory

Carolyn Rovee-Collier and Rachel Barr

Introduction

Since Freud first proposed that adult behavior is rooted in the infancy period, the experiences of infants have been viewed as the cornerstone of behavioral and cognitive development. Most psychologists have assumed that the effects of early experiences gradually accrue and that later learning builds on what was learned before. Implicit in this assumption, however, is a capacity for long-term memory – some means by which a relatively enduring record of those early experiences is preserved. Paradoxically, this is a capacity that infants are thought to lack – a belief that also originated with Freud (1935), who thought that early memories are forced into an unconscious state where they motivate subsequent behavior but cannot be recalled. The phenomenon of infantile amnesia – that people usually cannot remember what occurred before the age of 2 or 3 – supports Freud's view.

During the infancy period (birth to 2 years), infants undergo rapid physical, social, and cognitive change (see Figure 8.1). What young infants remember about their prior experiences is difficult to study. Not only can they not verbalize what they remember, but also younger infants lack the motoric competence to perform most of the nonverbal tasks that have been used with older infants and children to study memory. In addition, factors such as the presence or absence of the caregiver, the familiarity or novelty of the training and/or test setting, and the infant's momentary state of arousal radically affect their learning and memory differently at different ages. In describing the major experimental procedures that have been applied to the study of learning and memory development, we will also describe how some of the problems associated with conducting research with human infants have been overcome.

The first part reviews what and how infants learn, how long they remember it, and the effect of reminder procedures on retention. The second part considers recent challenges to maturational models of memory development.

Figure 8.1   From left to right, infants are 2, 3, 6, 9, 12, 15, and 18 months of age. Note the dramatic physical and behavioral differences between the youngest and oldest infant.

Research on Infant Learning and Memory

For many years, the notion that ontogeny recapitulates phylogeny was thought to describe the progressive development of learning abilities during the infancy period. The evolutionary continuum of learning extends from habituation, the simplest form of learning that is exhibited by single-celled organisms, to deferred imitation, a form of observational learning that is exhibited by new world primates (Buss, 1973). Today, however, this notion has been refuted by evidence that infants have exhibited every form of learning along the entire continuum within the first 3 months of life. This chapter presents a "broad brush" picture of what is currently known about what young infants can learn and remember. As the bulk of systematic research on infant learning and memory has used habituation, conditioning, and imitation procedures, we have focused on them.

Habituation

Habituation is a stimulus-specific response decrement that results from repeated exposures to a stimulus that elicits orienting toward or away from it. This definition excludes response decrements resulting from constant exposure (e.g., swaddling), one-stimulus exposure, fatigue, sensory adaptation, circadian rhythms, and physiological processes.

These are the defining characteristics (examples italicized) of habituation (Thompson & Spencer, 1966):

1   Repeated stimulus presentations result in decreased responding (usually, a negative exponential function of presentation number) to an asymptote or zero. *A new object is repeatedly presented for 10 s. Initially, the infant fixates it continuously. Over successive presentations, she fixates it progressively less until she stops fixating it altogether.*

2   When the stimulus is withheld, responding recovers over time ("spontaneous recovery"). *The next day, the infant fixates the object again.*

3   Over repeated series of habituation and spontaneous recovery trials, habituation is progressively more rapid. *When the same object is presented on successive days, the infant's fixation declines to asymptote after fewer and fewer trials.*

4   Other things being equal, the more rapid the stimulation, the more rapid and/or pronounced is habituation. *The shorter the interval between successive presentations, the faster the infant ceases fixating the object.*

5   The weaker the stimulus, the more rapid and/or pronounced is habituation. *The simpler the object, the faster the infant ceases fixating it.*

6   The habituation process can continue below the observable baseline level ("sub-zero habituation") if the stimulus continues to be presented after overt responding to it has ceased. Evidence of sub-zero habituation is seen when the subsequent level of spontaneous recovery is lower than if presentation of the stimulus terminated when responding to it ceased. *Presenting the object after the infant had stopped fixating it reduces the magnitude of the infant's renewed fixation the next day.*

7   Habituation to one stimulus generalizes to another stimulus to the extent that they share common elements. How similar the infant perceives a novel stimulus to be to the habituating stimulus is inferred from the magnitude of generalized habituation: The smaller the response (i.e., the greater the generalized habituation) to the novel stimulus, the greater is the inferred subjective similarity. *Infants fixate a green square less after habituating to a green triangle than after habituating to a red triangle.*

8   When an extraneous (usually strong) stimulus occurs during habituation trials, responding to the original habituating stimulus increases ("dishabituation"). Responding to the distractor temporarily disrupts the active inhibitory process of habituation, so that the previously habituated response is stronger on the next habituation trial.
     Developmental psychologists frequently confuse "dishabituation" with increased responding to a novel stimulus (see 7, above). *If a fire alarm sounds after the sixth presentation of an object, then the infant will fixate that object longer on its seventh presentation.*

9   Over repeated presentations of the extraneous stimulus, responding to it habituates. *When the alarm sounds periodically, the infant habituates to it, and its excitatory effect on fixation diminishes correspondingly.*

Sokolov's (1963) model of habituation of the orienting reflex was exploited by researchers to assess infants' perceptual and cognitive abilities. In this model, an internal representation of a stimulus is formed during each encounter, and the discrepancy between the representation and the physical stimulus determines how long subjects fixate the stimulus on the next encounter. As the representation becomes progressively fleshed out by new information that participants notice in the physical stimulus, they attend to it progressively less. When the discrepancy disappears, looking ceases. Because the internal representation decays over time (i.e., forgetting), looking will be renewed to the extent that the internal representation and the physical stimulus no longer match. When the delay is such that looking is as long as when the stimulus was novel, forgetting is complete.

Fantz (1964) obtained habituation to a repeated visual stimulus with infants between 2 and 6 months of age, and older infants habituated faster. Graham, Leavitt, Strock, and Brown's (1978) finding that an anencephalic infant habituated to an auditory stimulus that normal infants did not revealed that habituation is controlled at multiple levels of the central nervous system, with the functions of newly developing structures superimposed on more primitive ones.

Using a habituation procedure, Stinson (1971, cited in Werner & Perlmutter, 1979) obtained the first forgetting function with infants. Each high-amplitude suck of 4-month-olds on a nonnutritive nipple produced the brief illumination of a visual stimulus on a screen, and the faster infants sucked, the more continuously the stimulus remained visible. As infants habituated (satiated) to the visual stimulus, their rate of sucking decreased until it was only a fraction of its original rate. At this point, the nipple was removed for an interval of 0, 15, 30, or 75 s. When it was reinserted, infants' rate of sucking to produce the visual stimulus was increasingly faster when more time had elapsed since infants last saw it. After just 15 s, infants had begun to suck as fast as they had initially, when the visual stimulus was novel. These data were taken as evidence that infants forgot the visual stimulus within 15 s.

There are both individual and age-related differences in habituation. Infants who habituate faster exhibit better visual recognition memory (i.e., they look longer at a novel test stimulus) than slow habituators (for review, see Colombo & Mitchell, 1990). Also, infants typically remember the habituating stimulus for 5 to 15 s at 3 to 4 months, 1 min at 6 months, and 10 min at 9 to 12 months (for review, see Rose, Feldman, & Jankowski, 2007).

Classical (Pavlovian) conditioning

Like habituation, classical conditioning occurs at all phyletic levels and involves repeated stimulus presentations, but the correlation between the repeated stimulus and a given subsequent environmental event is 1 instead of zero. Because events in nature often occur in an orderly fashion, classical conditioning permits organisms to exploit this orderliness by anticipating (preparing for) the succeeding event instead of simply reacting to it, as in habituation. The classical conditioning procedure initially requires two basic components – an unconditional stimulus (US) that reliably elicits a reflex (the unconditional response, UR) and a stimulus (the eventual conditional stimulus, CS) that does not initially elicit the same reflex as the US. After repeated and contiguous CS–US pairings, the CS elicits a response (the conditional response, CR) that is similar to the UR, either before the US is actually presented or on trials when it is omitted. In essence, in classical conditioning, subjects do not learn a new response but a new occasion for the old response.

Pavlov thought that conditional reflexes were exclusively cortical. Early Soviet researchers, therefore, viewed the timing of the appearance of the first conditional reflex to stimuli from different modalities as a reflection of the functional maturation of the cortex. In 1913, Krasnogorski (Pavlov's student) failed to obtain conditioning with infants younger than 6 months and concluded that the cortex was too primitive for the formation of cortical connections before then. Much later, Soviet researchers obtained conditioned sucking in 3-week-olds (Koltsova, 1949) and conditioned eyeblinks in 6-week-olds who were 2.5 months premature (Irzhanskaia & Felberbaum, 1954).

Early western studies of classical conditioning traced the conditioning performance of single subjects over time, thereby providing evidence of long-term memory as well. In a famous study (Watson & Rayner, 1920), a loud gong (the US) that produced crying and hand withdrawal (the UR) was sounded each time 11-month-old Albert touched a white rat (the CS). One week later, Albert withdrew his hand (the CR) from the rat and, after several CS-US pairings, responded 5 days later to the rat and other stimuli that were somewhat similar (a rabbit, dog, fur coat, Santa Claus mask, cotton swatch, and Watson's beard). Ten days later, his weak CR was "freshened" by pairing the gong with the rat, rabbit, and dog. One month later – 2 months after his initial conditioning experience – Albert still exhibited CRs to the rat, dog, mask, and fur coat. This study demonstrated that CRs are established rapidly, maintained by occasional CS–US repetitions, and generalized to physically similar stimuli. In another single-subject study, Jones (1930) repeatedly presented a tapping sound (CS) followed by an electrotactual stimulus (US) to a 7-month-old over 5 days. Without more CS–US pairings, the CR was still exhibited 7 weeks later.

Many classical conditioning studies were successfully conducted with newborns between 1959 and 1970 (for review, see Siqueland, 1970), but skeptics continued to challenge the evidence (Sameroff, 1971). Blass, Ganchrow, and Steiner (1984) laid all challenges to rest by demonstrating classical conditioning in newborns as young as 2 hours. Between scheduled feedings, the experimental group received forehead stroking (CS) immediately followed by sucrose (US) delivered through a pipette; the explicitly paired control group received the same number of CS–US trials but received sucrose after longer and variable delays; and the sensitization control group received sucrose only. In acquisition, only the experimental group exhibited CRs (head-orienting, puckersucks) during the CS. In extinction, the experimental group exhibited a classic decrease in CRs during the CS, with the sharpest decline occurring between trials 1 and 2.

In heart-rate conditioning studies, immature and compromised infants often cannot respond during the CS-US interval, so whether the two stimuli have been associated is determined by interspersing US-omission trials among CS–US trials. Researchers infer that an association was formed if a heart-rate change occurs during the US-omission trial. Omitting an aversive US (e.g., a loud noise) produces *heart-rate acceleration*, and omitting an appetitive US (e.g., sucrose) produces *heart-rate deceleration*. These changes are interpreted as defensive (protective) and orienting (where-is-it?) responses, respectively. There is an important exception to this rule: Premature and decerebrate infants exhibit heart-rate acceleration on US-omission trials.

The optimal CS–US interval (ISI, interstimulus interval) is substantially longer for infants than for adults of all species. At 10 to 30 days of age, a 1500-ms ISI yields classical eyeblink conditioning, but a 500-ms ISI does not (Little, Lipsitt, & Rovee-Collier,

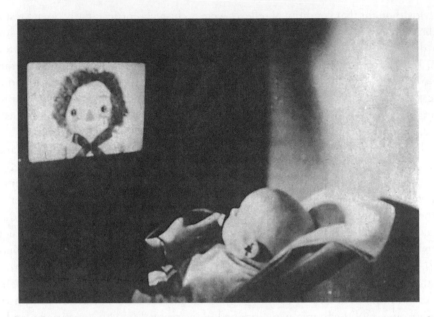

Figure 8.2   A 4-month-old infant producing illumination of a visual target by means of high-amplitude sucks. *Source*: Photograph courtesy of E. R. Siqueland.

1984). Thereafter, the optimal ISI decreases to 650 ms for 5-month-olds (Herbert, Eckerman, & Stanton, 2003) and 500 ms for young adults. Numerous failures to obtain classical conditioning with infants younger than 6 months undoubtedly resulted from selecting an ISI that was optimal for adults.

Operant conditioning

Classically conditioned responses are reflexive and elicited; operantly conditioned responses are voluntary and emitted. Infants must spontaneously perform the response at a low or moderate rate in order for the response to be followed by a reinforcer (reward) that increases its rate. There is no biological relation between the reinforcer and the response it influences. Sucking increases as readily whether it produces the mother's voice, a computer-generated speech sound, a colored slide (see Figure 8.2), or milk. Early operant conditioning studies had very brief baselines and did not demonstrate that increased responding was attributable to the response-reinforcement contingency (operant control) instead of behavioral arousal. Studies of "social reinforcers" (reinforcers administered by humans, such as smiling, eye contact, touching, vocalizing), for example, were criticized because the adult's auditory/visual reinforcement might have elicited the infant's reciprocal social or affective behavior, thereby mimicking conditioning (Bloom, 1984).

Brackbill (1958) asked whether 4-month-olds' smiling behavior was sensitive to the reinforcement schedule. Infants' baseline level of smiling was determined while the experimenter stood motionless and expressionless above each infant. During acquisition, after every smile, the continuous-reinforcement (CRF) group was smiled at, picked up, jostled, patted, and talked to for 30 s by the experimenter; the partial-reinforcement (PRF) group was initially treated the same but eventually had to emit three smiles per reinforcer. Although their responding did not differ during baseline or the initial phase, the response rate after PRF increased with the reinforcement schedule. As with adults of all species, PRF led to a higher response rate and more total responses in extinction. Although Brackbill's study lacked noncontingent-reinforcement controls, and the CRF group received more total reinforcing stimulation, correction of these problems yielded the same results, and the same finding was obtained with other tasks and ages (Siqueland, 1970).

Other operant studies used constant-magnitude, simple, and discrete reinforcers that rapidly became ineffective. In most, therefore, training lasted only a few minutes. Because critics doubted that young infants could be operantly conditioned (Piaget, 1952), such short sessions obviously worked against obtaining positive results. These problems were overcome in conjugate reinforcement procedures, in which the intensity of reinforcing stimulation varies from 0 to 100%, depending on the intensity and rate of responding. In the mobile conjugate reinforcement task (Rovee & Rovee, 1969), 10-week-olds' kicks produced movement (the reinforcement) in a crib mobile via a ribbon strung from one ankle to an overhead suspension hook (Figure 8.3a). Small foot movements slightly jiggled the mobile, whereas vigorous and/or rapid kicks made it bounce and swing back and forth. During acquisition, infants' kicking doubled or tripled within a few minutes and remained under operant control throughout sessions lasting 15 to 46 min. Ironically, Piaget had recorded in his diary that Laurent, his 3-month-old, increased hand movements after his hand hit and moved an object hanging over the bassinet. Piaget had called this an "elicited joy reaction." He thought that infants could not initiate "interesting spectacles" until they were several months older.

The mobile procedure has been standardized to assess infants' capacity for long-term memory. Infants are trained at home for two 15-min sessions 24 hr apart. In session 1, the ankle ribbon and mobile are connected to different hooks, and operant level (*baseline*) is recorded for 3 min. Next, the ribbon is switched to the same hook as the mobile, and kicks conjugately moved the mobile for 9 min (*acquisition*). Finally, the baseline condition is reinstated for 3 min. Session 2 is identical, but in the final 3-min nonreinforcement period (*immediate retention test*), the infant's final level of learning and retention after zero delay is measured. After a delay of 1 or more days, infants receive a 3-min *long-term retention test* with the original mobile or one that differs in some way (Figure 8.3b). Infants kick robustly if they recognize the mobile and respond at baseline if they do not. Because the retention test occurs during a nonreinforcement period, responding reflects only prior learning and not savings. At 6 months, sessions are one-third shorter, infants are seated inside a playpen, and the mobile is suspended from a modified floor microphone stand.

Three-month-olds' memories are highly specific. For example, they do not recognize a pink block mobile displaying black +s that are 25% smaller or larger than the +s that were on the training mobile, which they had not seen for 1 day (Figure 8.3). With longer delays, as infants gradually forget the specific details of their training mobile, they

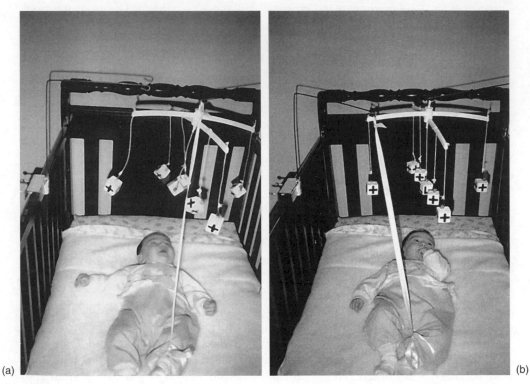

(a)   (b)

Figure 8.3 The experimental arrangement in the mobile task, shown with a 3-month-old. (a) *Acquisition*. The ribbon and mobile are attached to the same hook so kicks move the mobile. (b) *Baseline* and *Long-term recognition test*. The ribbon and mobile are attached to different hooks so kicks cannot move the mobile.

increasingly respond to ("recognize") a novel test mobile until they finally treat them equivalently (Rovee-Collier & Sullivan, 1980).

Because infants outgrow the mobile task after 6 months, an upward extension of the mobile task is used with older infants. Instead of kicking to move a mobile, infants press a lever to move a miniature train (Figure 8.4); during nonreinforcement periods, the lever is deactivated. Combining these two tasks reveals that the duration of retention increases linearly over the first 18 postnatal months (Figure 8.5; Hartshorn et al., 1998).

Latent learning

Latent learning epitomizes the learning–performance distinction: It is behaviorally "silent." Unlike habituation and conditioning, its acquisition is not accompanied by a change in responding; in fact, there is no observable evidence of learning when it takes place. Moreover, latent learning is not available to scrutiny by the outside world until

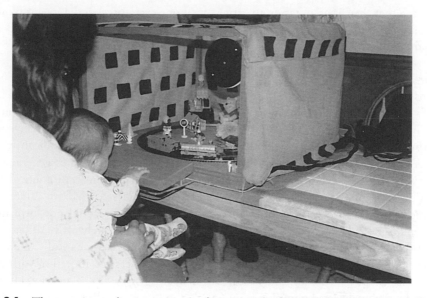

Figure 8.4 The experimental arrangement in the train task, shown with a 6-month-old. During baseline and all retention tests, the lever is deactivated so presses cannot move the train. Note the complex array of toys in the train box.

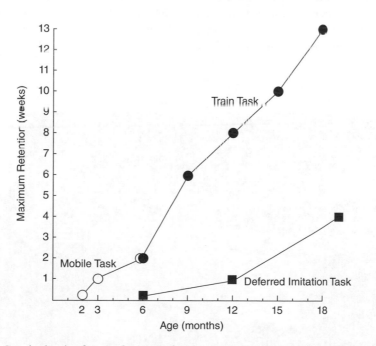

Figure 8.5 Standardized reference functions for the maximum duration of retention (in weeks) of infants trained and tested in the operant mobile and train tasks and the deferred imitation (puppet) task using standardized procedures with age-calibrated parameters. Slope differences reflect different training parameters.

such time that there is an occasion to express it (if one ever arises) and a means by which to do so. All learning, latent or not, is relatively permanent and is incorporated in an individual's knowledge base.

Deferred imitation.   In deferred imitation tasks, infants observe a sequence of target actions and then receive an opportunity to reproduce them after a delay. In elicited imitation, a variant of deferred imitation, infants imitate the actions immediately (and also sometimes during the retention interval) as well as after a delay, and they receive verbal prompts during modeling and testing. These procedural differences significantly affect infants' deferred imitation. Immediate imitation, for example, facilitates generalization, whereas both interpolated imitation and verbal cues independently promote deferred imitation after long delays (for review, see Hayne, 2004; Jones & Herbert, 2006a, b).

Piaget (1962) believed that before 18 months of age, infants could not form mental representations and hence could not exhibit deferred imitation. Meltzoff's (1988a) report that 9-month-olds imitated a novel action after a 24-hr delay dramatically altered this conception and motivated the current surge of studies of deferred imitation with young infants (see chapter 11 this volume). Barr, Dowden, and Hayne (1996) developed a single task to document deferred imitation from 6 to 24 months of age. In their task, a sequence of three target actions is modeled on a hand-puppet wearing a same-colored mitten on one hand. Infants who observe a demonstration lasting 60 s at 6 months or 30 s at 9 to 24 months exhibit deferred imitation 24 hr later. An infant's imitation score is the number of target actions (remove the mitten, shake it, attempt to replace the mitten) performed within 90 to 120 s of touching the puppet (Figure 8.6). Although older infants have higher imitation scores, some 6-month-olds imitate all three actions. Age-matched con-

Figure 8.6   The experimental arrangement used with 6- to 24-month-old infants in the deferred imitation (puppet) task. A 6-month-old is removing the puppet's mitten – an action that was modeled 24 hours earlier. *Source*: Barr, Dowden, & Hayne (1996).

trol groups who have not seen the modeling event rarely produce the target actions spontaneously.

Retention of deferred imitation also increases linearly with age (Figure 8.5), but the retention function is shallower than the operant retention function because of differences in the training parameters of the two tasks. At all ages, however, the duration of retention is significantly affected by the number of times the memory of the demonstration has been retrieved and the time between successive retrievals. At 6 months, for example, infants remembered the demonstration for at least 10 weeks when they retrieved its memory on multiple occasions that were widely spaced (Barr, Rovee-Collier, & Campanella, 2005). Six-month-olds who watched a second 30 s demonstration 24 hr after the original demonstration (one retrieval) exhibited deferred imitation 7 days later. Further, all of the 6-month-olds who actually imitated the modeled actions 24 hr later (also one retrieval) exhibited deferred imitation 10 days later, and all of these infants also exhibited deferred imitation both 30 days after modeling (two retrievals), when the test delay was doubled from 10 to 20 days, and 70 days after modeling (three retrievals), when the test delay was doubled again, from 20 to 40 days. This result was replicated with a new experimental group whose final deferred imitation test was 60 days after modeling. A control group that received the same regimen of tests as the experimental group but did not see the target actions modeled performed at baseline throughout. Because 6-month-olds otherwise remember the same target actions for only 1 day whether they imitate immediately after the demonstration or not (Barr et al., 1996; Barr, Vieira, & Rovee-Collier, 2001), this study documented the dramatic effect of retrieval on how long infants remember.

Sensory preconditioning (SPC). During SPC, an association is formed between two stimuli or events that occur together, such that what is eventually learned about one of them generalizes to the other. "Preconditioning" refers to the fact that the association is formed between two contiguous external ("sensory") stimuli or events in the absence of reinforcement, before formal conditioning occurs. Because associations are latent, however, the subsequent conditioning (training) procedure provides an overt means of expressing it. The SPC paradigm has three phases: (1) two neutral stimuli are paired (S1 + S2); (2) a specific response (R1) is trained to one of the stimuli (S1 $\Rightarrow$ R1); and (3) subjects are tested with the other stimulus (S2). If the trained response (R1) is produced to S2 (S2 $\Rightarrow$ R1), then it can be concluded that transfer of responding from one stimulus to the other was mediated by an association between S1 and S2 that had been formed when they were paired in phase 1. This conclusion is dependent on a finding of no response transfer between two stimuli that were preexposed separately (unpaired) in phase 1.

Barr, Marrott, and Rovee-Collier (2003) used SPC and a deferred imitation task to study associative learning and memory with 6-month-olds. In phase 1, the experimental group was preexposed to two paired hand puppets (A + B) for 1 hr/day on 7 consecutive days, and the control group saw the puppets equally long, but unpaired, at different times of day. In phases 2 and 3, paired and unpaired groups were treated identically. In phase 2 (1 day later), an adult modeled the target actions on one puppet (A $\Rightarrow$ R$_A$); in phase 3 (1 day after modeling), infants were tested with the other puppet (B). They found that the paired group imitated the target actions on the other puppet (B $\Rightarrow$ R$_A$), but the unpaired group did not. The transfer of learning from A to B indicated that an A $\Leftrightarrow$ B association had been formed in phase 1. Barr et al. (2003) also found that infants associated the paired puppets after a 1-hr preexposure on each of 2 consecutive days.

Giles (2008) found that infants could also associate puppets A and B if exposed to them for 1 hr on a single day. To determine how long infants could remember the association, she inserted a delay between the preexposure phase (phase 1) and the demonstration of the target actions on puppet A (phase 2), testing for deferred imitation (phase 3) on puppet B after increasing delays until infants failed to imitate on puppet B. The longest interval after which infants could successfully transfer responding from puppet A to B was 7 days after a 1-hr preexposure on 2 consecutive days or 3 days after a single, 1-hr preexposure session.

The basis of the retention benefit following two spaced sessions, however, was unclear. Two sessions entailed both twice as much exposure time and one memory retrieval at the outset of session 2. To deconfound the effects of exposure time and retrieval, Giles (2008) administered 1 hr of preexposure time in two 30-min sessions that were 5 hr apart. In this way, the total exposure duration was the same for one session as for two, but a retrieval was required at the outset of session 2. They found that the single retrieval produced a five-fold increase in infants' retention; 6-month-olds now remembered the association (i.e., imitated the actions on the second puppet) for 14 days instead of 3 days. Notably, 14 days is the same duration for which 6-month-olds remember the operant train and mobile tasks after two training sessions. This finding reveals that when and how often the memory was retrieved determines how long infants remember – not the type of task or the duration of preexposure beyond some minimum amount.

Using a variant of the puppet SPC procedure, Townsend (2007) preexposed 6-month-olds to a different pair of puppets (instead of repeating exposure to the same pair) on successive days. One member of each new pair overlapped with the pair that was preexposed the day before, while the other member was novel. His results suggested that infants had formed an associative chain in which the successive puppet–puppet associations were linked by the common member. When one member of the chain was activated, the activation spread along the chain to more remote members, allowing responding to transfer from the training stimulus to other stimuli that had not been directly paired with it.

In phase 1, Townsend preexposed 6-month-olds to a different pair of puppets each day (day 1: A + B; day 2: B + C). In phase 2, he modeled the target actions on either puppet C or puppet A. In phase 3, he administered a deferred imitation test with either puppet A or puppet C, respectively. When puppet A was the retrieval cue during testing, infants exploited a forward associative chain and imitated the actions that had been modeled on puppet C (A $\Rightarrow$ B $\Rightarrow$ C). When puppet C was the retrieval cue, infants exploited a backward associative chain and imitated the actions that had been modeled on puppet A (A $\Leftarrow$ B $\Leftarrow$ C). When another puppet pair (C + D) was added to the chain, and the actions were modeled on puppet D, infants imitated them on puppet A as well, but they did not imitate on a novel puppet (puppet E).

Finally, infants who saw either puppets A and B unpaired on the first day of phase 1 or puppet B alone after the A + B association was formed (an extinction procedure), failed to imitate the modeled actions on puppet A, confirming that the integrity of the A $\Rightarrow$ B link of the chain was critical. These data reveal that by 6 months of age, infants form relational representations of new associations that enter into a mnemonic network, where they are linked to existing memory representations and participate in the establishment of new associations. As the network expands and becomes increasingly interconnected and complex, memory performance becomes increasingly flexible.

Potentiation.   When a response to one stimulus is learned better in the presence of another stimulus, the enhancement is called *potentiation*. A cognitive account of associative learning holds that one member of an association (S1) evokes a memory representation of the second member (S2), which then enables the participant to produce the response that was originally made to S1. This cognitive representational account has important implications for memory. Any operation that will strengthen the memory of S1 (e.g., retrieving it) will also potentiate, or strengthen, all learning that occurs in its presence. The potentiation effect will be expressed in the duration of retention: members of stronger associations are remembered longer.

In studies with laboratory animals, potentiation has been studied almost exclusively in conditioned taste or odor aversion paradigms. The development of an associative learning paradigm in which operant conditioning and deferred imitation tasks were linked, however, permitted the first opportunity to study potentiation with human infants. A potentiation effect was seen in the duration of deferred imitation, for example, when the demonstration of the target actions on the puppet was associated with the previously learned operant train task. At 6 months of age, infants can exhibit deferred imitation of actions modeled for 60 s on a hand puppet for 24 hr. In contrast, they can remember the operant train task for 2 weeks. When the target actions were modeled on the puppet in the presence of the train immediately after operant training ended, however, 6-month-olds exhibited deferred imitation on the puppet for 2 weeks – the same duration that they remembered the train task (Barr et al., 2001). How did this happen? The memory of the train and the demonstration were associated when they simultaneously occupied primary (active) memory. Theoretically, the strength of the memory of the train task transferred to the demonstration via the association, potentiating the encoding of the demonstration to the same degree as the train task and thus enabling infants to remember the two tasks for an equal length of time.

We have found that retrieving the memory of an event increasingly later along its forgetting function actually strengthens that memory increasingly more and protracts its future retention increasingly longer (Galluccio & Rovee-Collier, 2006; Hsu & Rovee-Collier, 2009). When the target actions were demonstrated on the puppet in the presence of the train 7 days after operant training, for example, the mere sight of the train cued retrieval of the train memory, which was strengthened and associated with the demonstration because the two representations were simultaneously active in primary (short-term) memory. The stronger memory of the train task potentiated the strength of the associated demonstration and enabled infants to exhibit deferred imitation after 4 weeks instead of only 24 hr. Finally, when the demonstration occurred in the presence of the train 14 days after operant training, the train memory was strengthened even more, and the potentiation effect was even stronger. Now, 6-month-olds remembered the train task for 8 weeks after its memory was retrieved, and they exhibited deferred imitation after 6 weeks instead of only 24 hr (Rovee-Collier & Barr, 2007). These data reveal that the length of time young infants remember what they see depends on the meaningfulness of the context in which they see it. These findings have major implications for the important role of varied experience and enriched environments in early learning and memory.

Video deficit effect.   Although additional stimulation benefits learning and memory, the source of that stimulation affects the benefit. Researchers using a number of different experimental paradigms have demonstrated that infants, toddlers, and preschool children learn less from television and still 2D images than from face-to-face interactions (for review, see Anderson & Pempek, 2005). The *video deficit effect* refers to the fact that infants' ability to transfer learning from television to real-life situations is poor relative to their ability to transfer learning from a live demonstration. The video deficit effect is nonapparent at 6 months of age, peaks around 15 months of age, and persists until at least 36 months of age (Barr & Hayne, 1999; Barr, Muentener, & Garcia, 2007; Hayne, Herbert, & Simcock, 2003; Meltzoff, 1988b). Recently, research using event-related potentials has found that 18-month-olds recognize familiar 3D objects significantly earlier in the attentional process than familiar objects depicted in 2D digital photos (Carver, Meltzoff, & Dawson, 2006). The slower processing of 2D information that then must be transferred to 3D test conditions might contribute to the video deficit effect. Because the video deficit effect can be partially offset by additional repetitions of the target actions (Barr, Muentener, & Garcia, 2007; Barr, Muentener, Garcia, Fujimoto, & Chavez, 2007), it is possible that more repetitions strengthen the representation of the event in much the same way that additional repetitions enabled 6-month-olds to exhibit deferred imitation of a live demonstration after 24 hr (Barr et al., 1996). Given the prevalence of 2D materials – including books, television, touch screens, and computers – in homes and daycare centers, understanding the basis of the video deficit effect and its amelioration has obvious practical consequences for early education.

Reminders

Most psychologists assume that early experiences have a critical influence on later behavior. Yet, arguments that the infant brain is too immature to encode and maintain early memories over the long term has cast doubt on this assumption. Recent evidence that *reinstatement* and *reactivation* reminders can maintain early memories over significant periods of development, however, has removed this doubt. Reminders have now been successfully used with infants in all paradigms (for review, see Rovee-Collier & Cuevas, 2008).

Reinstatement.   Reinstatement is a small amount of periodic, partial practice throughout the retention interval (Campbell & Jaynes, 1966). The experimental group, is both trained and given periodic reminders, exhibits significant retention at the end of the interval. A *reinstatement control group* receives the same reminders but is not trained and a *forgetting control group* is trained but not reminded and exhibits no retention during the long-term test. The control groups are necessary to demonstrate that the reminders themselves did not produce new learning and that forgetting would have been complete without reminders.

Even very young infants can remember after long delays if periodically reminded. For example, 2-month-olds learned the mobile task, were reminded every 3 weeks (six reminders total), and received a final retention test at 7.25 months of age, when the study ended. Although 2-month-olds typically forget the task after 1 to 2 days, all remembered it for 4.5 months after periodic reminding, and four of six infants remembered it for more than 5.25 months. Control groups exhibited no retention after any delay (Rovee-Collier, Hartshorn, & DiRubbo, 1999). As most infants still remembered the mobile task when the study was terminated, Hartshorn (2003) repeated the study using the train task beginning at 6 months of age. After only five reminders, infants trained at 6 months still exhibited significant retention when they were 2 years old – 1.5 years after they were originally trained. Furthermore, infants had received only one reminder in the preceding year – at 18 months. Control groups exhibited no retention after any delay.

Reactivation.   Reactivation is a priming procedure in which an isolated component of the original event is presented once at the end of the retention interval – after forgetting has occurred but before the long-term test. Concluding that the original memory was reactivated requires that subjects who were both trained and primed exhibit renewed retention and that control groups that were only primed or only trained exhibit none.

In the first reactivation study with human infants, 3-month-olds learned the mobile task, forgot it, and were primed 13 or 27 days after training. During priming, the experimenter moved the mobile. After both delays, conditioned responding was restored to its original level, and infants forgot the reactivated memory at the same rate as the original one. Although reactivating the memory within 1 week of forgetting doubles the duration of retention throughout the infancy period, reactivating it after the longest delay possible quadruples it through 12 months of age (Hildreth & Hill, 2003). Fifteen- and 18-month-olds remember for so long, however, that they outgrow the task before the upper limit of reactivation is reached. When the forgotten training memory is primed after infants reach 2 years of age, most children simply quit lever pressing when the train does not move during the test and tell the experimenter that the train is "broken" or "needs batteries" (Hsu & Rovee-Collier, 2006). Although their verbal behavior confirms that the forgotten memory had been reactivated, their rate of lever pressing (the "official" retention measure) does not. Obviously, the operant measure underestimates the upper limit of reactivation when infants are tested at older ages. Although a single reactivation can dramatically increase the duration of retention, repeated reactivations can have an even greater effect (Hayne, 1990; Hitchcock & Rovee-Collier, 1996).

The memory-preserving effect of reactivation is not unique to studies of infant conditioning but has also been reported in studies of deferred imitation (e.g., Barr et al, 2003; Hayne, Barr, & Herbert, 2003; Campanella & Rovee-Collier, 2005). Campanella and Rovee-Collier, for example, used SPC and repeated reactivations to document deferred imitation with 3-month-olds, who are motorically incapable of performing the target actions. Infants were exposed to puppets A + B paired for 1 hr/day for 7 days, and on day 8 the experimenter modeled the three target actions on puppet B for 60 s. On day 9 and five more times over the next 3 months, the infants were shown puppet B for 30 s on the experimenter's stationary hand (a reactivation treatment). At 6 months of age, when infants had become sufficiently coordinated to perform the target actions, they were tested with puppet A. Despite not seeing the target actions or puppet A for 3 months, infants exhibited significant deferred imitation. In contrast, both the unpaired A-B control group and the reactivation control group responded at baseline during the deferred imitation test. This result confirms that repeated reactivations maintain early memories over long periods of behavioral development and that doing so is not task-specific.

Maturational Models of Infant Memory

Most developmental and cognitive psychologists assume that young infants suffer a maturational deficiency in the ability to encode, store, and retrieve memories over the long term. It is commonly thought that infant memory capacity undergoes a transition beginning late in the first year of life that is made possible by the progressive maturation of the hippocampal region and adjacent cortex (for review, see Bauer, 2008; Bauer, DeBoer, & Lukowski, 2007). Currently, maturational models of infant memory face serious challenges. In this part we review these challenges and their implications.

Multiple memory systems

Maturational models of memory development are rooted in the assumption that the memories of adults are supported by two neuroanatomical memory systems (implicit and explicit memory), and the memories of young infants are supported by only one (implicit memory). Implicit memory is characterized as a primitive system that processes perceptual information automatically and mediates memories of skills and procedures, whereas explicit memory is characterized as a higher-level system that supports the conscious recollection of specific prior episodes. Since adult amnesics performed normally on priming (implicit memory) tests but failed recall and recognition (explicit memory) tests, their brain damage was thought to impair explicit memory but not implicit memory. Schacter and Moscovitch (1984) likened the memory capacity of young infants to that of amnesics and concluded that the higher-level (explicit) memory system matured late in the first year of life.

Graf, Squire, and Mandler (1984) found that the same memory dissociations that amnesics exhibited on recall/recognition and priming tests were also exhibited by healthy adults who were instructed to "say the first word that comes to mind" (a priming test) or to "circle the words that were on the list you studied a few minutes ago" (a recognition test). Since then, researchers have identified more than a dozen independent variables (e.g., the retention interval, trial spacing, interference, amount of training) that produce functional memory dissociations on recognition and priming tests. In all instances, different levels of these variables had a major effect on recognition but none on priming.

The first challenge to a maturational account of infant memory development came from evidence that 2- to 6-month-old infants, who presumably possess only one memory system, exhibit the same functional memory dissociations in response to all of the same independent variables on priming (implicit memory) and recognition (explicit memory) tests as adults, who presumably possess two memory systems (Rovee-Collier, 1997; Rovee-Collier, Hayne, & Colombo, 2001). For example, infants' magnitude of retention on a recognition test declines as a function of the length of the retention interval, but their retention on a priming test is high and stable over retention intervals ranging from 1 day to 1 month. These findings suggested that if memory dissociations are diagnostic of two memory systems, then two memory systems must be present in early infancy.

Other challenges to maturational models of infant memory development have come from studies of deferred imitation, which is widely regarded as an explicit memory task (McDonough, Mandler, McKee, & Squire, 1995). The report that infants exhibited reliable 24-hr deferred imitation at 9 months but not before (Carver & Bauer, 2001) was taken as evidence that the explicit memory system becomes functionally mature late in the first year of life (Bauer, 2008; Carver & Bauer, 2001). However, more recent reports that 6-month-olds with no practice exhibited significant deferred imitation 7 days after the demonstration (Barr et al., 2005) and that 3-month-olds, also with no practice, exhibited significant deferred imitation 3 months after the demonstration (Campanella & Rovee-Collier, 2005) significantly advances the age at which infants can first exhibit reliable deferred imitation. Second, evidence that 3- and 6-month-olds form artificial categories (Greco, Hayne, & Rovee-Collier, 1990; Hayne, Rovee-Collier, & Perris, 1987) and acquire relationships between arbitrary pairs of objects (Barr et al., 2001, 2003; Cuevas, Rovee-Collier, & Learmonth, 2006; Giles, 2008; Rovee-Collier & Barr, 2007; Townsend, 2007) also pose a significant challenge to neuromaturational models of infant memory development. If there are two independent memory systems, then they do not mature hierarchically but instead develop simultaneously from early infancy.

Maturation or experience.   Prior neuroanatomical studies of adult memory fostered speculation that infants undergo a developmental transition in memory capacity that corresponds to the progressive maturation of the hippocampal region and adjacent cortex, which are critically implicated in adult declarative memory (e.g., Bauer, 2008; Nelson, 1995). Currently, however, a growing number of age-related changes in infant memory that were previously attributed to maturation of the neural structures that support explicit memory in adults have been found to be experientially determined in young infants. Although on the precipice, developmental researchers currently lack the technology necessary to study the maturation of different brain regions in infants directly, and therefore they must infer it from infants' behavior. Even so, positive behavioral evidence of a given memory capacity in very young infants is totally silent about the neural mechanisms that underlie it.

A major impact of experience on infant memory capacity pertains to the formation of long-term memories. Amnesics, for example, can form short-term but not long-term memories. Additionally, the duration of retention in operantly trained infants increases linearly between 2 and 18 months of age (Figure 8.5), as predicted by a neuromaturational account. At all ages, however, infants can remember twice as long if they are given two sessions instead of only one, and their retention is prolonged exponentially – by weeks or months – if the interval between the two sessions is increased (Hsu & Rovee-Collier, 2009). As a result, even the youngest infants can remember for as long as infants 2 to 3 times older. Thus, the maturational status of the infant brain does not limit their ability to form long-term memories.

Parallel effects have been found in studies of deferred imitation (Figure 8.5). As discussed above (see Potentiation), if 6-month-olds associated the target actions with the train task, then they subsequently remembered both actions for an equal length of time, For example, they exhibited deferred imitation and retention of the train task for 2 weeks when the association was formed immediately after operant training, 4 weeks when the association was formed 1 week after operant training, and 6 weeks when the association was formed 2 weeks after operant training (Rovee-Collier & Barr, 2007), Otherwise, 6-month-olds can exhibit deferred imitation for only 24 hr after the demonstration (Barr et al., 1996, 2001).

Prior priming experience also increases the duration of long-term memories when infants are primed again. At 3 months, for example, a second prime increases retention from 1 week to 2 weeks (Hayne, 1990) – the same duration of retention exhibited by once-primed 6-month-olds. Similarly, the speed of responding to a memory prime increases logarithmically over the first year of life (Hildreth & Rovee-Collier, 1999), but after prior priming, 3-month-olds respond to the second prime as rapidly as 6-month-olds had responded to the first (Hayne, Gross, Hildreth, & Rovee-Collier, 2000). Also, the minimum duration for which an effective prime can be exposed 1 week after forgetting and still be effective decreases from 2 min at 3 months to 1.8 s at 18 months (Hsu, Rovee-Collier, Hill, Grodkiewicz & Joh, 2005). Priming the forgotten memory before, however, cuts the minimum duration of 3-month-olds' second prime in half, regardless of when the first prime was presented or for how long it was exposed (Bearce & Rovee-Collier, 2006).

Finally, Hitchcock and Rovee-Collier (1996) primed the forgotten memory of 3-month-olds twice, using a novel cue or novel context during the second prime. The second prime reactivated the memory when the context was novel – just as the first prime reactivates the memory of 12-month-olds when the context is novel (DeFrancisco, 2008). During priming a third time, either a novel cue or a novel context reactivated the memory. The fact that prior priming eliminates the hyperspecificity that is a hallmark of implicit memory is a stark example of the pervasive contribution of experience to memory performance.

Clearly, models of infant memory development that cast neuroanatomical maturation as the *determinant* of infant memory capacity are fundamentally flawed. Currently, mounting evidence indicates that the basic memory capacities of adults and young infants are the same and that a higher-level memory system does not simply come online at a given age as previously conceived. If the late-maturing development of neuroanatomical mechanisms does not initially *permit* particular memory capacities, then what does it do? We propose that it *facilitates the efficiency of memory processing* by providing multiple and more direct routes of access to critical memory structures.

Infantile amnesia.   Most adults cannot remember what occurred before the age of 2 or 3. This phenomenon, *infantile amnesia*, is popularly attributed to the functional immaturity of the neurological mechanisms responsible for maintaining memories over the long term (Nelson, 1995).

Recently, however, even very young infants remembered a prior event after very long delays when they were periodically exposed to multiple reminders in the interim (Hartshorn, 2003; Rovee-Collier et al., 1999). Taken together, these studies provide unequivocal support for the hypothesis that periodic reminding can maintain early memories over a significant period of development. Moreover, because periodic nonverbal reminders maintained the memories of two comparable events (the mobile task and the train task) over an overlapping period between 2 months and 2 years of age, it is highly likely that appropriate periodic nonverbal reminders could also maintain the memory of a single event from 2 months through to 2 years of age, if not longer. This period encompasses the entire time span thought to be characterized by infantile amnesia.

How might these experiential factors contribute to infantile amnesia? First, the memory attributes that represent contextual information (i.e., when and where an event happened) are fragile and lost with repeated reactivation (Hitchcock & Rovee-Collier, 1996); as a result, older children and adults may actually remember early-life events but be unable to pinpoint their origins. Second, because memories encoded early in life have probably been modified or updated many times, their original source would be impossible to identify.

Conclusions

In most current models, memory is viewed as being composed of two independent and functionally distinct systems that mature at different rates. These models are based on data that were originally obtained from amnesic adults and are at odds with data obtained directly from infants themselves. The infant data, gathered with a variety of tasks, reveal that young infants and adults possess the same basic memory capacities. Most of the age-related changes in infant memory that have been attributed to maturation can be reproduced in very young infants by merely giving them additional experience with the manipulation. Very young infants also encode the relations between events (a late-maturing capacity), which can remain latent for a relatively long periods. These new associations can be linked to what was learned before in a rapidly expanding memory network, also called the *knowledge base* – because only the tiniest fraction of this knowledge will ever be expressed, it is impossible to guess its extent.

Evidence of the sophistication of young infants' learning and memory capacities marks a sharp departure from prior views and raises the question of their adaptive significance. In fact, from their earliest moments, all organisms must learn the structure of the niche into which they are born. Meeting this evolutionary imperative requires building stable representations of the physical and functional relations in their environment by either passively inspecting or actively interacting with it. Recurring associations are strengthened, becoming increasingly accessible, while one-time relations are eventually culled or forgotten and cannot be reactivated (Hsu & Rovee-Collier, 2009; Richardson, Wang, & Campbell, 1993).

Future Directions

Current insights into infant learning and memory have come from asking new questions and using new paradigms and technologies to answer them. In the future, two lines of research hold great promise. First, it is critical to understand the mechanisms that increase the accessibility of target information as well as the mechanisms that reduce the accessibility of potentially useless or interfering information. Additionally, it is important to examine the organization of the developing associative network and how changes in the strengths of existing links affect it. Second, the application of noninvasive technologies (e.g., eye tracking, electroencephalography, event-related potentials, magnetoencephalography, near infrared spectroscopy) are poised to shed new light on the relationship between infant behavior and neurobiological functioning during tests administered both after different delays and after priming. It would also be important to know what neurobiological changes are produced by the provision of additional experience that produces behavioral changes that mimic maturational changes (cf. Casey & de Haan, 2002; Jones & Herbert, 2006a, b; Spelke, 2002). Until advances in neuroimaging techniques permit the direct study of infants' brain structures, however, we have to make do with what we have – behavioral evidence and inferences from indirect measures. Meanwhile, there is plenty of exciting work to keep us busy!

Further Reading

The following list expands upon the topics reviewed in the present chapter. The list includes seminal papers on habituation, conditioning, deferred imitation, latent learning, and reminder procedures.

Barr, R., Dowden, A., & Hayne, H. (1996). Developmental changes in deferred imitation by 6- to 24-month-old infants. *Infant Behavior and Development, 19*, 159–170. This is the first report of deferred imitation in infants as young as 6 months and also of developmental changes in deferred imitation across a wide age range using the same task.

DeCasper, A. J., & Fifer, W. P. (1980). Of human bonding: Newborns prefer their mothers' voices. *Science, 208*, 1174–1176. This paper reports that infants within a day or so of birth will learn an operant response that gives them selective access to the voice that they had heard in the womb.

Fantz, R. L. (1964). Visual experience in infants: Decreased attention to familiar patterns relative to novel ones. *Science, 46*, 668–670. This classic study showed that infant attention habituates during repeated exposures to the same pattern but is maintained at a high level during repeated exposures to changing patterns.

Meltzoff, A. N., & Moore, M. K. (1977). Imitation of facial and manual gestures by human neonates. *Science, 198*, 75–78. This important report of imitation by infants only hours old initiated a storm of controversy over the imitative capacity of young infants.

Rovee, C. K., & Rovee, D. T. (1969). Conjugate reinforcement of infant exploratory behavior. *Journal of Experimental Child Psychology*, 8, 33–39. This was the first report of free operant conditioning using a nonbiological reinforcer with very young infants. It is notable for the unusual character of the reinforcer, its long sessions, its robustness, and its arousal controls.

Rovee-Collier, C. (1997). Dissociations in infant memory: Rethinking the development of implicit and explicit memory. *Psychological Review*, 104, 467–498. This article reviews numerous parallels between memory data from infant and adults. It concludes that infants and adults possess the same memory systems.

References

Anderson, D. R., & Pempek, T. (2005). Television and very young children. *American Behavioral Scientist*, 48, 505–522.

Barr, R., Dowden, A., & Hayne, H. (1996). Developmental changes in deferred imitation by 6- to 24-month-old infants. *Infant Behavior and Development*, 19, 159–170.

Barr, R., & Hayne, H. (1999). Developmental changes in imitation from television during infancy. *Child Development*, 70, 1067–1081.

Barr, R., Marrott, H., & Rovee-Collier, C. (2003). The role of sensory preconditioning in memory retrieval by preverbal infants. *Learning and Behavior*, 31, 111–123.

Barr, R., Muentener, P., & Garcia, A. (2007). Age-related changes in deferred imitation from television by 6- to 18-month-olds. *Developmental Science*, 10, 910–921.

Barr, R., Muentener, P., Garcia, A., Fujimoto, M., & Chavez, V. (2007). The effect of repetition on imitation from television during infancy. *Developmental Psychobiology*, 49, 196–207.

Barr, R., Rovee-Collier, C., & Campanella, J. (2005). Retrieval facilitates retrieval: Protracting deferred imitation by 6-month-olds. *Infancy*, 7, 263–284.

Barr, R., Vieira, A., & Rovee-Collier, C. (2001). Mediated imitation in 6-month-olds: Remembering by association. *Journal of Experimental Child Psychology*, 79, 229–252.

Bauer, P. J. (2008). Toward a neuro-developmental account of the development of declarative memory. *Developmental Psychobiology*, 50, 19–38.

Bauer, P. J., DeBoer, T., & Lukowski, A. F. (2007). In the language of multiple memory systems. In L. M. Oakes & P. J. Bauer (Eds.). *Short- and long-term memory in infancy and early childhood* (pp. 240–270). Oxford: Oxford University Press.

Bearce, K. H., & Rovee-Collier, C. (2006). Repeated reactivation increases memory accessibility in infants. *Journal of Experimental Child Psychology*, 93, 357–376.

Blass, E. M., Ganchrow, J. R., & Steiner, J. E. (1984). Classical conditioning in newborn humans 2–48 hours of age. *Infant Behavior and Development*, 7, 223–235.

Bloom, K. (1984). Distinguishing between social reinforcement and social elicitation. *Journal of Experimental Child Psychology*, 38, 93–102.

Brackbill, Y. (1958). Extinction of the smiling response in infants as a function of reinforcement schedule. *Child Development*, 29, 115–124.

Buss, A. (1973). *Psychology: Man in perspective*. New York: Wiley.

Campanella, J., & Rovee-Collier, C. (2005). Latent learning and deferred imitation at 3 months. *Infancy*, 7, 243–262.

Campbell, B. A., & Jaynes, J. (1966). Reinstatement. *Psychological Review*, 73, 478–480.

Carver, L. J., & Bauer, P. J. (2001). The dawning of a past: The emergence of long-term explicit memory in infancy. *Journal of Experimental Psychology: General*, 130, 726–745.

Carver, L. J., Meltzoff, A. N., & Dawson, G. (2006). Event-related potential (ERP) indices of infants' recognition of familiar and unfamiliar objects in two and three dimensions. *Developmental Science, 9,* 51–62.

Casey, B. J., & de Haan, M. (2002). Introduction to new methods in developmental science. *Developmental Science, 3,* 265–268.

Colombo, J., & Mitchell, D. W. (1990). Individual differences in early visual attention: Fixation time and information processing. In J. Colombo & J. W. Fagen (Eds.), *Individual differences in infancy* (pp. 193–227). Hillsdale, NJ: Erlbaum.

Cuevas, K., Rovee-Collier, C., & Learmonth, A. E. (2006). Infants form associations between memory representations of stimuli that are absent. *Psychological Science, 17,* 543–549.

DeFrancisco, B. S. (2008). The specificity of priming effects over the first year of life. *Developmental Psychobiology, 50*(5), 486–501.

Fantz, R. L. (1964). Visual experience in infants: Decreased attention to familiar patterns relative to novel ones. *Science, 46,* 668–670.

Freud, S. (1935). *A general introduction to psychoanalysis.* New York: Clarion.

Galluccio, L., & Rovee-Collier, C. (2006). Nonuniform effects of reinstatement within the time window. *Learning and Motivation, 37,* 1–17.

Giles, A. D. (2008). *Long-term memory of preconditioned associations at 6 and 9 months of age.* Unpublished Master's thesis, Department of Psychology, Rutgers University, New Brunswick, NJ.

Graf, P., Squire, L. R., & Mandler, G. (1984). The information that amnesic patients do not forget. *Journal of Experimental Psychology: Learning, Memory, and Cognition, 10,* 164–178.

Graham, F. K., Leavitt, L., Strock, B., & Brown, H. (1978). Precocious cardiac orienting in a human anencephalic infant. *Science, 199,* 322–324.

Greco, C., Hayne, H., & Rovee-Collier, C. (1990). Roles of function, reminding, and variability in categorization by 3-month-old infants. *Journal of Experimental Psychology: Learning, Memory, and Cognition, 16,* 617–633.

Hartshorn, K. (2003). Reinstatement maintains a memory in human infants for 1½ years. *Developmental Psychobiology, 42,* 269–282.

Hartshorn, K., Rovee-Collier, C., Gerhardstein, P., Bhatt, R. S., Wondoloski, T., Klein, P., et al. (1998). The ontogeny of long-term memory over the first year-and-a-half of life. *Developmental Psychobiology, 32,* 1–31.

Hayne, H. (1990). The effect of multiple reminders on long-term retention in human infants. *Developmental Psychobiology, 23,* 453–477.

Hayne, H. (2004). Infant memory development: Implications for childhood amnesia. *Developmental Review, 24,* 33–73.

Hayne, H., Barr, R., & Herbert, J. (2003). The effect of prior practice on memory reactivation and generalization. *Child Development, 74,* 1615–1627.

Hayne, H., Gross, J., Hildreth, K., & Rovee-Collier, C. (2000). Repeated reminders increase the speed of memory retrieval by 3-month-old infants. *Developmental Science, 3,* 312–318.

Hayne, H., Herbert, J., & Simcock, G. (2003). Imitation from television by 24- and 30-month-olds. *Developmental Science, 6,* 254–261.

Hayne, H., Rovee-Collier, C., & Perris, E. E. (1987). Categorization and memory retrieval by three-month-olds. *Child Development, 58,* 750–767.

Herbert, J. S., Eckerman, C. O., & Stanton, M. E. (2003). The ontogeny of human learning in delay, long-delay, and trace eyeblink conditioning. *Behavioral Neuroscience, 117,* 1196–1210.

Hildreth, K., & Hill, D. (2003). Retrieval difficulty and retention of reactivated memories over the first year of life. *Developmental Psychobiology, 43,* 216–229.

Hildreth, K., & Rovee-Collier, C. (1999). Decreases in the response latency to priming over the first year of life. *Developmental Psychobiology, 35*, 276–289.

Hitchcock, D. F. A., & Rovee-Collier, C. (1996). The effect of repeated reactivations on memory specificity in infants. *Journal of Experimental Child Psychology, 62*, 378–400.

Hsu, V. C., & Rovee-Collier, C. (2006). Memory reactivation in the second year of life. *Infant Behavior and Development, 28*, 91–107.

Hsu, V. C., & Rovee-Collier, C. (2009). The time window construct in early memory development. In F. Columbus (Ed.). *New directions in developmental psychobiology* (pp. 1–22). Hauppauge, NY: Nova Science.

Hsu, V. C., Rovee-Collier, C., Hill, D. L., Grodkiewicz, J., & Joh, A. S. (2005). Effects of priming duration on retention over the first 1½ years of life. *Developmental Psychobiology, 47*, 43–54.

Irzhanskaia, K. N., & Felberbaum, R. A. (1954). Conditioned reflex activity in premature children. Reprinted in Y. Brackbill & G. T. Thompson (Eds.). (1967). *Behavior in infancy and early childhood* (pp. 246–249). New York: The Free Press.

Jones, H. E. (1930). The retention of conditioned emotional reactions in infancy. *Journal of Genetic Psychology, 37*, 485–498.

Jones, E. J., & Herbert, J. S. (2006a). Exploring memory in infancy: Deferred imitation and the development of declarative memory. *Infant and Child Development, 15*, 195–205.

Jones, E. J., & Herbert, J. S. (2006b). Using deferred imitation to understand the process of change in infant memory development. *Infant and Child Development, 15*, 215–218.

Koltsova, M. M. (1949). On the rise and development of the second signal system in the child. *Research of the Laboratory of I. P. Pavlov, 4*, 49–102.

Little, A. H., Lipsitt, L. P., & Rovee-Collier, C. (1984). Classical conditioning and retention of the infant's eyelid response: Effects of age and interstimulus interval. *Journal of Experimental Child Psychology, 37*, 512–524.

McDonough, L., Mandler, J. M., McKee, R. D., & Squire, L. R. (1995). The deferred imitation task as a nonverbal measure of declarative memory. *Proceedings of the National Academy of Sciences, 92*, 7580–7584.

Meltzoff, A. N. (1988a). Infant imitation and memory: Nine-month-olds in immediate and deferred tests. *Child Development, 59*, 217–225.

Meltzoff, A. N. (1988b). Imitation of televised models by infants. *Child Development, 59*, 1221–1229.

Nelson, C. A. (1995). The ontogeny of human memory: A cognitive neuroscience perspective. *Developmental Psychology, 31*, 723–738.

Piaget, J. (1952). *Origins of intelligence in children.* New York: International Universities Press.

Piaget, J. (1962). *Play, dreams and imitation in childhood* (C. Gattegno & F. M. Hodgson, Trans.). New York: Norton.

Richardson, R., Wang, P., & Campbell, B. A. (1993). Reactivation of nonassociative memory. *Developmental Psychobiology, 26*, 1–23.

Rose, S. A., Feldman, J. F., & Jankowski, J. J. (2007). Developmental aspects of visual recognition memory in infancy. In L. M. Oakes & P. J. Bauer (Eds.), *Short- and long-term memory in infancy and early childhood* (pp. 153–178). New York: Oxford University Press.

Rovee-Collier, C. (1997). Dissociations in infant memory: Rethinking the development of implicit and explicit memory. *Psychological Review, 104*, 467–498.

Rovee-Collier, C., & Barr, R. (2007, October). *Deferred imitation at 6 months: Potentiation by an associatively-activated memory representation.* Presentation at the meeting of the International Society for Developmental Psychobiology, San Diego, CA.

Rovee-Collier, C., & Cuevas, K. (2008). Infant memory. In H. L. Roediger, III. (Ed.), *Cognitive psychology of memory: Vol. 2. Learning and memory: A comprehensive reference* (pp. 687–715). Oxford: Elsevier.

Rovee-Collier, C., Hartshorn, K., & DiRubbo, M. (1999). Long-term maintenance of infant memory. *Developmental Psychobiology, 35*, 91–102.

Rovee-Collier, C., Hayne, H., & Colombo, M. (2001). *The development of implicit and explicit memory*. Amsterdam: John Benjamins.

Rovee, C. K., & Rovee, D. T. (1969). Conjugate reinforcement of infant exploratory behavior. *Journal of Experimental Child Psychology, 8*, 33–39.

Rovee-Collier, C., & Sullivan, M. W. (1980). Organization of infant memory. *Journal of Experimental Psychology: Human Learning and Memory, 6*, 798–807.

Sameroff, A. J. (1971). Can conditioned responses be established in the newborn infant: 1971? *Developmental Psychology, 5*, 1–12.

Schacter, D. L., & Moscovitch, M. (1984). Infants, amnesics, and dissociable memory systems. In M. Moscovitch (Ed.), *Advances in the study of communication and affect: Vol. 9. Infant memory* (pp. 173–216). New York: Plenum.

Siqueland, E. R. (1970). Basic learning processes. I. Classical conditioning. In H. W. Reese & L. P. Lipsitt (Eds.), *Experimental child psychology* (pp. 65–95). New York: Academic Press.

Sokolov, E. N. (1963). Higher nervous functions: The orienting reflex. *Annual Review of Physiology, 25*, 545–580.

Spelke, E. S. (2002). Developmental neuroimaging: A developmental psychologists' look ahead. *Developmental Science, 3*, 392–396.

Thompson, R. F., & Spencer, W. A. (1966). A model phenomenon for the study of neuronal substrates of behavior. *Psychological Review, 73*, 16–43.

Townsend, D. (2007). *The transitivity of preconditioned infantile associative memories during deferred imitation*. Unpublished doctoral dissertation, Rutgers University, New Brunswick, NJ.

Watson, J. B., & Rayner, R. R. (1920). Conditioned emotional reactions. *Journal of Experimental Child Psychology, 3*, 1–14.

Werner, J. S., & Perlmutter, M. (1979). Development of visual memory in infants. In H. W. Reese & L. P. Lipsitt (Eds.), *Advances in child development and behavior* (Vol. *14*, pp. 1–56). New York: Academic.

9

Functional Brain Development during Infancy

Mark H. Johnson

Theoretical Overview

What is development? Many introductory biology textbooks define development as an "increasing restriction of fate." What this means is that as the biological development of an individual (ontogeny) proceeds, the range of options for further specification or specialization available to the organism at that stage decreases. Structural or functional specialization is an end state in which there are few or no options left to the organism. By this view, plasticity can be defined as a developmental stage in which there are still options available for alternative developmental pathways (Thomas & Johnson, 2008). Another dimension of ontogenetic development is that it involves the construction of increasingly complex levels of biological organization, including the brain and the cognitive processes it supports. As we will see later in this chapter, organizational processes at one level, such as cellular interactions, can establish new functions at a higher level, such as that associated with overall brain structure. This characteristic of ontogeny means that a full picture of developmental change requires different levels of analysis to be investigated simultaneously. The developmentalist, I suggest, needs to go beyond statements such as a psychological change being due to "maturation," and actually provide an account of the processes causing the change at cellular and molecular levels. Thus, as distinct from most other areas of psychology, a complete account of developmental change specifically requires an interdisciplinary approach.

Despite the above considerations, it is only recently that there has been renewed interest in examining relations between brain and cognitive development. Biological approaches to human behavioral development fell out of favor for a variety of reasons, including the widely held belief among cognitive psychologists in the 1970s and 1980s that the "software" of the mind is best studied without reference to the "hardware" of the brain. However, the recent explosion of basic knowledge on mammalian brain development makes the task of relating brain to behavioral changes considerably more viable than previously. In parallel, molecular and cellular methods, along with theories of self-organizing dynamic networks (see chapter 5 this volume), have led to great advances in our understanding of how vertebrate brains are constructed during ontogeny. These advances, along with those in functional neuroimaging, have led to the recent emergence of the interdisciplinary science of *developmental cognitive neuroscience* (see Johnson, 2005a).

There are a number of assumptions commonly made about the relation between brain development and behavioral change which stem from the adoption of a "predetermined epigenesis" view of development. Epigenesis refers to the process through which genes interact with their environment (at various levels, inside and outside the organism) to produce new structures. Gottlieb (1992) has distinguished between *predetermined epigenesis* and *probabilistic epigenesis*. Predetermined epigenesis is the view that there is a one-way causal pathway from genes to proteins to brain to cognition. In other words, there is a "genetic blueprint" which imposes itself on the developing organism in a direct way. In contrast, probabilistic epigenesis is the view that there are two-way interactions through all levels of organization. While most people would acknowledge that there are complex interactions between genes and environment and back at the molecular, genetic, and cellular level involved in development, the predetermined epigenesis view still tends to dominate assumptions about the relation between brain development and cognition. Specifically, it is often assumed that brain development involves a process of unfolding of a genetic plan, and that "maturation" in particular regions of the brain causes or allows specific advances in cognitive, perceptual, or motor abilities in the infant or child. This overly static view of brain development fails to capture the importance of two-way inter-actions between brain and behavior, and the importance of activity-dependent processes in neural development. Brain development is not just a genetic process, but is an *epigen-etic* one crucially dependent on complex interactions at the molecular, cellular, and behavioral levels. Indeed, later I will suggest that attentional biases in human infants contribute to their subsequent patterns of brain specialization.

Three different perspectives on human postnatal functional brain development are currently being explored. The first of these approaches, the maturational perspective, has the goal to relate the maturation of particular regions of the brain, usually regions of the cerebral cortex, to newly emerging sensory, motor, and cognitive functions. This approach is based on the predetermined epigenesis assumption mentioned earlier. Evidence concerning the differential neuroanatomical development of cortical regions is used to determine an age when a particular region is likely to become functional. Success in a new behavioral task at this same age is then attributed to the maturation of a newly functional brain region, with maturation often assumed to be an "all or none" phenomenon, or at least to have a sudden onset. Typically, comparisons are then made between the behavioral performance of adults with acquired lesions and behaviors during infancy. One example of this approach comes from the neurodevelopment of visual orienting and attention, where several researchers have argued that control over visually guided behavior is initially by subcortical structures, but with age and development posterior cortical regions, and finally anterior regions, come to influence behavior.

In contrast to the maturational approach in which behavioral developments are attributed to the onset of functioning in one region or system, an alternative viewpoint assumes that postnatal functional brain development, at least within the cerebral cortex, involves a process of organizing interregional interactions: "interactive specialization." One of the assumptions behind this view is that of probabilistic epigenesis mentioned earlier. Recent trends in the analysis of adult brain imaging data have proceeded on the assumption that the response properties of a specific region may be determined by its patterns of connectivity to other regions and their current activity states. Extending this notion to development means that we should observe changes in the response properties of cortical regions during ontogeny as regions interact and compete with each other to acquire their role in new computational abilities. The onset of new behavioral competencies during infancy will be associated with changes in activity over several regions, and not just by the onset of activity in one or more additional region(s). In further contrast to the maturational approach, this view predicts that during infancy patterns of cortical activation during behavioral tasks may be more extensive than those observed in adults, and involve different patterns of activation. Within broad constraints, even apparently the same behavior in infants and adults could involve different patterns of cortical activation.

A third perspective on human postnatal functional brain development has been termed the skill-learning hypothesis. Recent neuroimaging evidence from adults has highlighted changes in the neural basis of behavior that result as a consequence of acquiring perceptual or motor expertise. One hypothesis is that the regions active in infants during the onset of new perceptual or behavioral abilities are the same as those involved in skill acquisition in adults. This hypothesis predicts that some of the changes in the neural basis of behavior during infancy will mirror those observed during more complex skill acquisition in adults.

Methods

Part of the reason for the recently renewed interest in relating brain development to cognitive change comes from advances in methodology which allow hypotheses to be generated and tested more readily than previously (see also the *Handbook of Developmental Cognitive Neuroscience*, Nelson and Luciana, 2008). One set of tools relates to brain imaging – the generation of "functional" maps of brain activity based on either changes in cerebral metabolism, blood flow, or electrical activity. Some of these imaging methods, such as positron emission tomography (PET), are of limited utility for studying transitions in behavioral development in normal infants and children due to their invasive nature (requiring the intravenous injection of radioactively labeled substances) and their relatively coarse temporal resolution (of the order of minutes). Two brain imaging techniques are currently applied to development in typically developing children – event-related potentials (ERPs), and functional and structural magnetic resonance imaging (MRI/fMRI).

ERPs involve using sensitive electrodes on the scalp surface to measure the electrical activity of the brain generated as groups of neurons fire synchronously. These recordings can either be of the spontaneous natural rhythms of the brain (EEG), the electrical activity induced by the presentation of a stimulus (Event-Related Potentials – ERP), or adjustments of the oscillatory rhythms of the brain in response to stimulus or task demands (Event-Related Oscillations – ERO). Normally the ERP from many trials is averaged, resulting in the spontaneous natural rhythms of the brain that are unrelated to the stimulus presentation averaging to zero. With a high density of electrodes on the scalp, algorithms can be employed which infer the position of the brain sources of electrical activity (dipoles) for the particular pattern of scalp surface electrical activity. Recent developments of the ERP method allow relatively quick installation of a large number of sensors thus opening new possibilities in the investigation of infant brain function.

Functional MRI allows the noninvasive measurement of cerebral blood flow (Kwong et al., 1992), with the prospect of millimeter spatial resolution and temporal resolution in the order of seconds. Structural and functional MRI has been conducted with infants, particularly in auditory and language paradigms. However, it remains extremely challenging to conduct visual paradigms with infants in this method unless they are under sedation for clinical reasons. Most recently, a new method is being developed for studying brain function in infants – Near InfraRed Spectroscopy (NIRS). This method uses optodes and diodes to measure the scatter or bending of low-intensity light beams as they permeate brain tissue, and can yield a measure of regional blood oxygenation very similar to that derived from fMRI.

Finally, the emergence of connectionist neural network models offers the possibility of assessing the information-processing consequences of developmental changes in the neuroanatomy and neurochemistry of the brain. For example, O'Reilly and Johnson (1994) demonstrated how the microcircuitry of a region of vertebrate forebrain could lead to certain self-terminating sensitive period effects. Such models promise to provide a bridge between our observations of development at the neural level and behavioral change in childhood.

Postnatal Brain Development: The First Two Years

While some developmental processes can be traced from pre- to postnatal life, in postnatal development there is obviously more scope for influence from the world outside the infant. This need not be a passive process, but rather may reflect the actions of the infant within the environment. A striking feature of human brain development is the comparatively long phase of postnatal development, and therefore the increased extent to which the later stages of brain development can be influenced by the environment of the child.

A number of lines of evidence indicate that there are substantive changes during postnatal development of the human brain. At the most gross level of analysis, the volume of the brain quadruples between birth and adulthood. This increase comes from a number of sources such as more extensive fiber bundles, and nerve fibers becoming covered in a fatty myelin sheath which helps to conduct electrical signals. Perhaps the most obvious manifestation of postnatal neural development, as viewed through a standard microscope, is the increase in size and complexity of the dendritic tree of many neurons. The extent and reach of a cell's dendritic tree may increase dramatically, and it often becomes more specific and specialized. Less apparent through standard microscopes, but more evident with electron microscopy, is a corresponding increase in density of functional contacts between neurons and synapses.

Huttenlocher (1990) has reported a steady increase in the density of synapses in several regions of the human cerebral cortex. For example, in parts of the visual cortex, the generation of synapses (synaptogenesis) begins around the time of birth and reaches a peak around 150% of adult levels toward the end of the first year. In the frontal cortex (the anterior portion of cortex, considered by most investigators to be critical for many higher cognitive abilities), the peak of synaptic density occurs later, at around 24 months of age (but see Goldman-Rakic, Bourgeois, & Rakic, 1997). Although there is variation in the timetable, in all regions of cortex studied so far, synaptogenesis begins around the time of birth and increases to a peak level well above that observed in adults.

Somewhat surprisingly, regressive events are commonly observed during the development of nerve cells and their connections in the brain. For example, in the primary visual cortex the mean density of synapses per neuron starts to decrease at the end of the first year of life (e.g., Huttenlocher, 1990). In humans, most cortical regions and pathways appear to undergo this "rise and fall" in synaptic density, with the density stabilizing to adult levels at different ages during later childhood. The postnatal rise and fall developmental sequence can also be seen in other measures of brain physiology and anatomy. For example, PET studies of children can measure the glucose uptake of regions of the brain. Glucose uptake is necessary in regions of the brain that are active, and because it is transported by the blood is also a measure of blood flow. Using this method, Chugani, Phelps, and Mazziotta (1987) observed an adult-like distribution of resting brain activity within and across brain regions by the end of the first year. However, the overall level of glucose uptake reaches a peak during early childhood which is much higher than that observed in adults. The rates return to adult levels after about 9 years of age for some cortical regions. The extent to which these changes relate to those in synaptic density is currently the topic of further investigation.

A controversial issue in developmental neuroscience concerns the extent to which the differentiation of the cerebral cortex into areas or regions with particular cognitive, perceptual, or motor functions, can be shaped by postnatal interactions with the external world. This issue reflects the debate in cognitive development about whether infants are born with domain-specific "modules" for particular cognitive functions such as language, or whether the formation of such modules is an activity-dependent process (see Elman, Bates, Johnson, & Karmiloff-Smith, 1996; Karmiloff-Smith, 1992). Brodmann (1912) was one of the first to propose a scheme for the division of cortex into structural areas assumed to have differing functional properties. A century of neuropsychology has taught us that the majority of normal adults tend to have similar functions within approximately the same regions of cortex. However, we cannot necessarily infer from this that this pattern of differentiation is intrinsically prespecified (the product of genetic and molecular interactions), because most humans share very similar pre- and postnatal environments. In developmental neurobiology this issue has emerged as a debate about the relative importance of neural activity for cortical differentiation, as opposed to intrinsic molecular and genetic specification of cortical areas. Supporting the importance of the latter processes, Rakic (1988) proposed that the differentiation of the cortex into areas is due to a protomap. The hypothesized protomap either involves prespecification of the tissue that gives rise to the cortex during prenatal life or the presence of intrinsic molecular markers specific to particular areas of cortex. An alternative viewpoint, advanced by O'Leary (1989) among others, is that genetic and molecular factors build an initially undifferentiated "protocortex," and that this is subsequently divided into specialized areas as a result of neural activity. This activity within neural circuits need not necessarily be the result of input from the external world, but may result from intrinsic, spontaneous patterns of firing within sensory organs or subcortical structures that feed into the cortex, or from activity within the cortex itself (e.g., Katz & Shatz, 1996).

Although the neurobiological evidence is complex, and probably differs between species and regions of cortex, most recently a middle ground view of cortical specification has emerged (Kingsbury & Finlay, 2001; Ragsdale & Grove, 2001). According to this view, large-scale regions of cortical tissue are defined by gradients of gene expression forming a "hyperdimensional plaid" rather than a "mosaic quilt" of areas (Kingsbury & Finlay, 2001). Within these large-scale regions smaller-scale functional areas emerge at least partly as a result of neural-activity-dependent processes. With several exceptions, it seems likely that activity-dependent processes contribute to the differentiation of the smaller-scale functional areas of the cortex, especially those involved in higher cognitive functions in humans. During prenatal life, this neural activity may be largely a spontaneous intrinsic process, while in postnatal life it is likely also to be influenced by sensory and motor experience. However, it is unlikely that the transition from spontaneous intrinsic activity to that influenced by sensory experience is a sudden occurrence at birth, for in the womb the infant can process sounds and generate movement, and in postnatal life the brain maintains spontaneously generated intrinsic electrical rhythms (EEG).

As just one of many examples of the effect of experience on cortical specialization, PET studies of word recognition in adults have identified a localized region of the left visual cortex as being involved in English word recognition, while not responding to other stimuli such as random letter strings (Petersen, Fox, Posner, Mintun, & Raichle, 1988). It seems implausible to suggest that we are born with a region of cortex prespecified for English word recognition, so we are forced to conclude that at least some cortical functional specialization is experience-dependent. Other lines of evidence also support this conclusion. For example, studies of scalp-recorded event-related potentials in congenitally deaf subjects show that regions of the temporal lobe which are normally auditory, or multimodal, become dominated by visual input (Neville, 1991). Despite these examples it is clear that there are also limits on the plasticity of cortex. Analyzing normal and abnormal processes of postnatal cortical specialization will be one of the major challenges for developmental cognitive neuroscience over the next decade.

Postnatal Brain Development and Behavioral Change

Researchers have begun to investigate relations between brain, perceptual, and cognitive development in several different domains. In this introduction I have chosen to select three domains in which the most progress has been made, but readers are referred to Johnson (2005a), Nelson and Ludemann (1989), and Nelson and Luciana (2008) for related research in other domains.

Developing a social brain

One of the major characteristics of the human brain is its social nature. As adults, we have areas of the brain specialized for processing and integrating sensory information about the appearance, behavior, and intentions of other humans. A variety of cortical areas have been implicated in the "social brain" including the superior temporal sulcus (STS), the fusiform "face area" (FFA), and orbitofrontal cortex. One of the major debates in cognitive neuroscience concerns the origins of the "social brain" in humans, and theoretical arguments abound about the extent to which this is acquired through experience.

Johnson and Morton (1991; Morton & Johnson, 1991) reviewed much of the existing behavioral literature on face recognition in infants and found two apparently contradictory bodies of evidence. While most of the evidence supported the view that it takes the infant 2 or 3 months of experience to learn about the arrangement of features that compose a face (for reviews see Maurer, 1985; Nelson & Ludemann, 1989), one team of researchers (Goren, Sarty, & Wu, 1975) suggested that even newborns would track, by means of head and eye movements, a face-like pattern further than various "scrambled" face patterns. This latter study has now been replicated several times (see Johnson, 2005b for review).

The apparent conflict between the results of the newborn studies and those with older infants raised a problem for existing theories of the development of face recognition that involved only one process. Johnson and Morton (1991) proposed a two-process theory of infant face preferences that, to some extent, was built on contemporary theories of the development of visually guided behavior (a closely related account was provided by de Schonen & Mathivet 1989). They argued that the first system is accessed via the subcortical visuo-motor pathway (but likely also involves some cortical structures) and controls the preferential orienting to faces in newborns. However, the influence of this system over behavior declines (possibly due to inhibition by later developing cortical systems) during the second month of life. The second process depends upon cortical functioning, and exposure to faces over the first month or so, and begins to influence infant orienting preferences from around 2 months of age. The newborn preferential orienting system biases the input to circuitry on the ventral cortical pathway that is still specializing. This circuitry is configured through processing face input, before it comes to control the infant's actions around the second month. At this point the cortical system is sufficiently specialized for faces to ensure that it continues to acquire further information about this class of stimulus. Thus, a specific, early developing brain circuit acts in concert with the species typical environment to bias the input to later developing brain circuitry. In this sense, the young infant actively selects appropriate inputs for her own further brain specialization.

Turning to the neurodevelopment of face processing during infancy and early childhood, several laboratories have examined developmental changes in event-related potentials (ERPs) during infancy (see de Haan et al. 2003 for review). When viewing faces an ERP component, termed the "N170" (a negative-going deflection that occurs after around 170 milliseconds), has been strongly associated with face processing in a number of studies on adults. Specifically, the amplitude and latency of this component vary according to whether or not faces are present in the visual field of the adult volunteer under study. An important aspect of the N170 in adults is that its response is highly selective. For example, the N170 shows a different response to human upright faces than to very closely related stimuli such as inverted human faces and upright monkey faces. While the exact underlying neural generators of the N170 are currently still debated, the specificity of response of the N170 can be taken as an index of the degree of specialization of cortical processing for human upright faces. For this reason we undertook a series of studies on the development of the N170 over the first weeks and months of postnatal life.

The first issue we addressed in these developmental ERP studies is when does the face-sensitive N170 emerge? In a series of experiments, a component in the infant ERP that has many of the properties associated with the adult N170, but that is of a slightly longer latency (240–290 ms), was identified (de Haan, Johnson, & Halit, 2003). In studying the response properties of this potential at 3, 6 and 12 months of age it has been discovered that (a) the component is present from at least 3 months of age (although its development continues into middle childhood); and (2) the component becomes more specifically tuned to respond to human upright faces with increasing age. To expand on the second point, it was found that while 12-month-olds and adults show different ERP responses to upright and inverted faces, 3- and 6-month-olds do not. Thus, the study of this face-sensitive ERP component is consistent with the idea of increased specialization of cortical processing with age, a result also consistent with some behavioral results (see below).

While we still await definitive functional imaging studies on face processing in infants and young children, evidence for increased localization of cortical processing of faces comes from several recent fMRI studies of the neural basis of face processing in children compared to adults (see Cohen-Kadosh & Johnson, 2007). In some of these studies, even when children and adults were matched for behavioral ability, children activated a larger extent of cortex around face-sensitive areas than did adults. These changes fit with the "interactive specialization" view mentioned earlier.

Converging evidence about the increasing specialization of face processing during development comes from a behavioral study that set out to test the intriguing idea that, as processing "narrows" to human faces, then infants will lose their ability to discriminate nonhuman faces. Pascalis, de Haan, and Nelson (2002) demonstrated that while 6-month-olds could discriminate between individual monkey faces as well as human faces, 9-month-olds and adults could only discriminate the human faces. These results are particularly compelling since they demonstrate a predicted competence in young infants that is not evident in adults.

Moving beyond the relatively simple perception of faces, a more complex attribute of the adult social brain is processing information about the eyes of other humans. There are two important aspects of processing information about the eyes. The first of these is being able to detect the direction of another's gaze in order to direct your own attention to the same object or spatial location (eye gaze cueing). Perception of averted gaze can elicit an automatic shift of attention in the same direction in adults, allowing the establishment of "joint attention." Joint attention to objects is thought to be crucial for a number of aspects of cognitive and social development, including word learning. The second critical aspect of gaze perception is the detection of direct gaze, enabling mutual gaze with the viewer. Mutual gaze (eye contact) provides the main mode of establishing a communicative context between humans, and is believed to be important for normal social development. It is commonly agreed that eye gaze perception is important for mother–infant interaction, and that it provides a vital foundation for social development.

In a series of experiments with 4-month-old infants using a simple eye gaze cueing paradigm (in which a stimulus face looked left or right), Farroni and colleagues (Farroni, Mansfield, Lai, & Johnson, 2003; Farroni, Menon, & Johnson 2006) have established that it is only following a period of mutual gaze with an upright face that cueing effects are observed. In other words, mutual gaze with an upright face may engage mechanisms of attention such that the viewing infant is more likely to be cued by subsequent motion of facial features. In summary, the critical features for eye gaze cueing in young infants are (a) lateral motion of elements of facial features and (b) a brief preceding period of eye contact with an upright face.

Following the surprising observation that a period of direct gaze is required before cueing can be effective in infants, the authors investigated the earliest developmental roots of eye contact detection. It is already known that human newborns have a bias to orient toward face-like stimuli (see earlier), prefer faces with eyes opened, and tend to imitate certain facial gestures. Preferential attention to faces with direct gaze would provide the most compelling evidence to date that human newborns are born prepared to detect socially relevant information. For this reason Farroni and colleagues (2002) tested healthy human newborn infants by presenting them with a pair of stimuli, one a face with eye gaze directed straight at the newborns and the other with averted gaze. Results showed that the fixation times were significantly longer for the face with the direct gaze.

In a further experiment, converging evidence for the differential processing of direct gaze in infants was obtained by recording event-related potentials (ERPs) from the scalp as infants viewed faces (Farroni, Csibra, Simion, & Johnson, 2002). Four-month-old babies were tested with the same stimuli as those used in the previous experiment with newborns, and a difference was found between the two gaze directions at the same time and scalp location as the previously identified face-sensitive component of the infant ERP discussed earlier. The conclusion from these studies is that direct eye contact enhances the perceptual processing of faces in infants during the first months. This conclusion has been further strengthened by converging evidence from an analysis of EEG bursting (Grossman, Johnson, Farroni, & Csibra, 2007).

Beyond face processing and eye gaze detection there are many more complex aspects of the social brain such as the coherent perception of human action and the appropriate attribution of intentions and goals to conspecifics. Investigating the cognitive neuroscience of these abilities in infants and children will be a challenge for the next decade.

Developing a linguistic brain

Is language biologically special? This motivating question refers to the extent to which the human infant is predisposed to process and learn about language, and the extent to which the underlying neural circuits are "prewired" to process language input. Two cognitive neuroscience approaches to this question have been taken. The first approach has been to attempt to identify neural correlates of speech processing abilities present from very early in life, before experience is thought to have shaped cortical specialization. The second approach addresses the issue of whether there are particular parts of the cortex critical for primary language acquisition, or whether a variety of cortical areas can support this function.

The first approach to investigating the extent to which language is biologically special involves attempting to identify language-relevant processes in the brains of very young infants. One example of this concerns the ability to discriminate speech-relevant sounds such as phonemes. Behavioral experiments have demonstrated that young infants show enhanced (categorical) discrimination at phonetic boundaries used in speech such as /ba/- /pa/ (for a full treatment of this topic see chapter 3, this volume). That is, like adults, a graded phonetic transition from /ba/ to /pa/ is perceived as a sudden categorical shift by infants. This observation was initially taken as evidence for a language-specific detection mechanism present from birth. However, over the past decade it has become clear that other species, such as chinchillas, show similar acoustical discrimination abilities, indicating that this ability may merely reflect general characteristics of the mammalian auditory processing system, and not a an initial spoken language specific mechanism.

In a further line of behavioral experiments, Werker and Polka (1993) reported that, although young infants discriminate a wide range of phonetic contrasts including those not found in the native language (e.g., Japanese infants, but not Japanese adults, can discriminate between "r" and "l" sounds), this ability becomes restricted to the phonetic constructs of the native language around 12 months of age. If brain correlates of this process could be identified, it may be possible to study the mechanisms underlying this language specific selective loss of sensitivity. Dehaene-Lambertz and Dehaene (1994) presented their infants with trials in which a series of four identical syllables (the standard) was followed by fifth that was either identical or phonetically different (deviant). They recorded high-density ERPs time-locked to the onset of the syllable and observed two voltage peaks with different scalp locations. The first peak occurred around 220 ms after stimulus onset and did not habituate to repeated presentations (except after the first presentation) or dishabituate to the novel syllable. Thus, the generators of this peak, probably primary and secondary auditory areas in the temporal lobe, did not appear to be sensitive to the subtle acoustical differences that encoded phonetic information. The second peak reached its maximum around 390 ms after stimulus onset and again did not habituate to repetitions of the same syllable, except after the first presentation. However, when the deviant syllable was introduced the peak recovered to at least its original level. Thus, the neural generators of the second peak, also in the temporal lobe but in a distinct and more posterior location, are sensitive to phonetic information.

Researchers have used functional imaging methods with greater spatial resolution to investigate early correlates of speech perception. Dehaene-Lambertz, Dehaene, and Hetz-Pannier (2002) measured brain activation with fMRI in awake and sleeping healthy 3-month-olds while they listened to forwards and backwards speech in their native tongue (French). The authors assumed that forward speech would elicit stronger activation than backward speech in areas related to the segmental and suprasegmental processing of language, while both stimuli would activate mechanisms for processing fast temporal auditory transitions. Compared to silence, both forwards and backwards speech activated widespread areas of the left temporal lobe, which was greater than the equivalent activation on the right for some areas (planum temporale). These results provide converging evidence for the ERP data discussed earlier. Forwards speech activated some areas that backwards speech did not, including the angular gyrus and mesial parietal lobe (precuneus) in the left hemisphere. The authors suggest that these findings demonstrate an early functional asymmetry between the two hemispheres. However, they acknowledge that their results cannot discriminate between an early bias for speech perception, or a greater responsivity of the left temporal lobe for processing auditory stimuli with rapid temporal changes.

Adopting the second approach to establishing whether language is special concerns studies designed to investigate the extent to which particular cortical areas, such as Broca's and Wernicke's areas, are "prewired" to support specific functions. Two main lines of research have been pursued, with one set of studies examining the extent to which language functions can be subserved by other regions of the cortex, and another line of research concerned with whether other functions can "occupy" regions that normally support language. The first of these approaches has been pursued through investigations of whether children suffering from perinatal lesions to the classical "language areas" of cortex can still acquire language. The second approach has involved the testing of congenitally deaf children to see what, if any, functions are present in regions of cortex that are normally (spoken) language areas.

If particular cortical regions are uniquely prewired to support language, then it is reasonable to assume that damage to such regions will impair the acquisition of language regardless of when the insult occurs. This implicit hypothesis has motivated a good deal of research, the conclusions of which still remain somewhat controversial. Lenneberg (1967) argued that, if localized left hemisphere damage occurred early in life, it had little effect on subsequent language acquisition. This view contrasted with the effect of similar lesions in adults or older children, and to many congenital abnormalities in which language is delayed or never emerges. This view lost adherents in the 1970s, as evidence accumulated from studies of children with hemispherectomies suggesting that left hemisphere removal commonly leads to selective subtle deficits in language, especially for syntactic and phonological tasks. Similar results have also been reported for children with early focal brain injury due to strokes. These findings were compatible with studies of normal infants showing a left hemisphere bias at birth in processing speech and other complex sounds, and led some researchers to the conclusion that functional asymmetries for language in the human brain are established at birth, and cannot be reversed. This view was reinforced by a number of neuroanatomical studies that have shown differences between parts of left and right cerebral cortex in adults. For example, Geschwind and Levitsky (1968) reported that the left planum temporale (an area associated with language processing) was larger than the right planum temporale in 65% of adult brains studied. A number of groups have looked for similar differences in infant brains as evidence for prespecified language abilities. As early as the 29th week of gestation, the left planum temporale is usually larger than the right in human infants. It is important to remember, however, that (a) this asymmetry is probably not specific to humans and (b) gyral and sucal measures only tell us about the quantity of cortical tissue within a region, and cannot therefore be used to argue for the detailed specific prewiring assumed by some to be necessary for language-specific processing. In addition to these reservations about the neuroanatomical evidence, many of the secondary sources that summarized the work on hemispherectomies and/or early focal injury failed to note that the deficits shown by these children are very subtle – far more subtle in fact than the aphasic syndrome displayed by adults with homologous forms of brain damage. Significantly, most of the children with left hemisphere injury who have been studied to date fall within the normal range, attend mainstream schools, and certainly do better than adults with equivalent damage.

The other approach to studying the extent to which the cortical areas supporting language-related functions are prespecified is to see whether other functions can occupy such regions. This issue has been investigated in a recent fMRI study in which hearing and deaf participants were scanned while reading sentences in either English or American Sign Language (ASL) (Newman, Bavelier, Corina, Jessard, & Neville 2001). When hearing adults read English, there was robust activation within some of classical left hemisphere language areas, such as Broca's area. No such activation was observed in the right hemisphere. When deaf people viewed sentences in their native ASL they showed activation of most of the left hemisphere regions identified for the hearing participants. ASL is not sound based, but because it does have all of the other characteristics of language, including a complex grammar, these data suggests that some of the neural systems that mediate language can do so regardless of the modality and structure of the language acquired. Having said this, there were also some clear differences between the hearing and deaf activations, with the deaf group activating some similar regions in the right hemisphere. One interpretation of the right hemisphere activation is that it is evoked by the biological motion inherent in sign, but not spoken, language. A third condition addressed the issue of whether there is a sensitive period for the establishment of left-hemisphere language. In this condition, deaf people read English (their second language, learned late) and did not show activation of the classical left hemisphere language regions, suggesting that, if a language is not acquired within the appropriate developmental time window, the typical pattern of adult activation does not occur.

In summary, therefore, a reasonable working hypothesis is that regions of the left temporal lobe are most suitable for supporting speech recognition. This suitability likely comes from a combination of spatial and temporal factors that may predispose this region to the processing of rapid temporal stimuli. Other regions of cortex are probably also important for the acquisition of language, and can substitute for the left temporal region if required. Language is only "biologically special" in the broadest sense in which the human species' typical environment interacts with the architecture of cortex and its developmental dynamics to generate representations appropriate for the domain.

Frontal cortex development and the emergence of "cognitive control"

The region of the frontal lobe anterior to the primary motor and premotor cortex, the prefrontal cortex, accounts for almost one-third of the total cortical surface in humans and is considered by most investigators to be critical for many higher cognitive abilities. In adults, types of cognitive processing that have been associated with the frontal cortex concern the planning and execution of sequences of action, the maintenance of information "online" during short temporal delays, and the ability to inhibit a set of responses that are appropriate in one context but not another. The frontal cortex shows the most prolonged period of postnatal development of any region of the human brain, with changes in the density of synapses (electrical contacts between cells) detectable even into the teenage years, and for this reason it has been the region most frequently associated with developments in cognitive abilities.

Two alternative approaches to the relation between frontal cortex structural development and advances in cognitive ability in childhood have been taken. One of these is the attempt to relate structural developments in the frontal cortex at a particular age to changes in certain cognitive abilities. This refers to the "maturational approach" outlined earlier. A refinement of this approach is that the frontal lobes are composed of a number of regions that subserve different functions and show a different timetable of maturation. The alternative approach is based on the assumption that the frontal cortex is involved in acquisition of new skills and knowledge from very early in life, and that it may also play a key role in organizing other parts of cortex (skill learning or interactive specialization approaches). According to this latter view, regions of frontal cortex are important in many cognitive transitions primarily because of their involvement in the acquisition of any new skill or knowledge. A corollary of this is that frontal cortex involvement in a particular task or situation may decrease with increased experience or skill in the domain. There is currently evidence consistent with both of these approaches.

One of the most comprehensive attempts to relate a cognitive change to underlying brain developments has concerned marked behavioral changes around 8 to 10 months of age. In particular, Diamond (1985, 1991) argued that the maturation of the prefrontal cortex during the second half of the human infant's first year of life accounts for a number of transitions observed in the behavior of infants in object permanence and object retrieval tasks. One of the behavioral tasks they have used to support this argument comes from Piaget (1954) who observed that infants younger than 8 months often fail to accurately retrieve a hidden object after a short delay period if the object's location is changed from one where it was previously and successfully retrieved: out of sight is out of mind. Infants often made a particular perseverative error in which they reach to the hiding location where the object was found on the immediately preceding trial. This characteristic pattern of error was cited as evidence for the failure to understand that objects retain their existence or permanence when moved from view. By around 9 months, infants begin to succeed in the task at successively longer delays of 1–5 s, although their performance remains unreliable up to about 12 months if the delay between hiding and retrieval is incremented as the infants get older.

Diamond and colleagues (Diamond and Goldman-Rakic, 1989) tested monkeys in a modification of the above object permanence task. Consistent with the observations on human infants, infant monkeys failed to retrieve the hidden object. Further, adult monkeys with damage to the dorsolateral region of the prefrontal cortex (DLPC) were also impaired in this task. Damage to some other parts of the brain (parietal cortex, or the hippocampal formation) did not significantly impair performance, suggesting that the DLPC plays a central role in tasks that require the maintenance of spatial or object information over temporal delays.

Further evidence linking success in the object permanence task to frontal cortex maturation in the human infant comes from two sources. The first of these is a series of EEG studies with normal human infants, in which increases in frontal EEG responses correlate with the ability to respond successfully over longer delays in delayed response tasks (Bell and Fox, 1992). The second source is work on cognitive deficits in children with a neurochemical deficit in the prefrontal cortex resulting from Phenylketonuria (PKU) (Diamond et al., 1997). Even when treated, this inborn error of metabolism can have the specific consequence of reducing the levels of a neurotransmitter, dopamine, in the dorsolateral prefrontal cortex. These reductions in dopamine levels in the dorsolateral prefrontal cortex result in these infants and children being impaired on tasks thought to involve parts of the prefrontal cortex such as the object permanence task and object retrieval tasks, and being relatively normal in tasks thought to depend on other regions of cortex such as the DNMS task mentioned earlier.

Having established a link between prefrontal cortex maturation and behavioral change in a number of tasks, Diamond has speculated on the computational consequence of this aspect of postnatal brain development. Specifically, she suggested that the DLPC is critical for performance when (a) information has to be retained or related over time or space *and* (b) a prepotent response has to be inhibited. Only tasks that require both of these aspects of neural computation are likely to engage the DLPC. In the case of the object permanence task, a spatial location has to be retained over time and the prepotent previously rewarded response inhibited. Recent findings suggest that the prefrontal cortex maturation hypothesis is not the whole story, however, and that some modification or elaboration of the original account will be required. Gilmore and Johnson (1995) observed that infants succeed on a task that requires temporal spatial integration over a delay at a much younger age than is indicated by the object permanence tasks. In addition, studies by Baillargeon (1987, 1993) and others entailing infants viewing "possible" and "impossible" events involving occluded objects have found that infants as young as 3.5 months look longer at impossible events indicating that they have an internal representation of the occluded object. In order to account for the apparent discrepancy between these results and those with the reaching measures, some have provided "means–ends" explanations, arguing that infants are unable to coordinate the necessary sequence of motor behaviors to retrieve a hidden object. To test this hypothesis, Munakata, McClelland, Johnson, and Siegler (1997) trained 7-month-olds to retrieve objects placed at a distance from them by means of pulling on a towel or pressing a button. Infants retrieved the objects when a transparent screen was interposed between them and the toy, but not if the screen was sufficiently opaque to make the object invisible. Since the same means–ends planning is required whether the screen is transparent or opaque, it was concluded that means–ends explanations cannot account for the discrepancy between the looking and the reaching tasks. Munakata et al. (1997) proposed an alternative "graded" view of the discrepancy implemented as a connectionist model.

An alternative approach to understanding the role of the prefrontal cortex in cognitive development stems from the view that the region plays a critical role in the acquisition of new information and tasks. By this account the prefrontal cortex involvement in the object retrieval tasks is only one of many manifestations of prefrontal cortex involvement in cognitive change. From this perspective, the challenge to the infant brain in, for example, learning to reach for an object, is equivalent in some respects to that of the adult brain when facing complex motor skills like learning to drive a car. A concomitant of this general view is that the cortical regions crucial for a particular task will change with the stage of acquisition. Three lines of evidence indicating the importance of PFC activation early in infancy have given further credence to this view: (1) fMRI studies, (2) psychophysiological evidence, and (3) the long-term effects of perinatal damage to PFC.

The limited number of fMRI studies that have been carried out with infants have, often surprisingly, revealed functional activation in PFC, even when this would not be predicted from adult studies. For example, in the fMRI study of speech perception in 3-month-olds discussed earlier, Dehaene-Lambertz and colleagues (2002) observed a right dorsolateral prefrontal cortex activation that discriminated (forward) speech in awake, but not sleeping, infants. While this is evidence for activation of at least some of the PFC in the first few months, it remains possible that this activation is passive and does not play any role in directing the behavior of the infant. Two other recent lines of evidence, however, suggest that this is not the case.

While developmental ERP studies have often recorded activity changes over frontal leads in infants, some recent experiments suggest that this activity has important consequences for behavioral output. These experiments involve examining patterns of activation that precede the onset of a saccade. In one example, Csibra, Tucker, and Johnson (1998) observed that presaccadic potentials that are usually recorded over more posterior scalp sites in adults are observed in frontal channels in 6-month-old infants. Since these potentials are time-locked to the onset of an action, it is reasonable to infer that they are the consequence of computations necessary for the planning or execution of the action.

Further evidence for the developmental importance of the PFC from early infancy comes from studies of the long-term and widespread effects of perinatal damage to PFC. In contrast to some other regions of cortex, perinatal damage to frontal and PFC regions often results in both immediate and long-term difficulties. For example, infants with perinatal focal lesions to parts of cortex in a visual attention task have been studied (Johnson et al., 1998). Damage to parietal cortical regions would be expected to produce deficits in this task in adults, but only infants with perinatal lesions to the anterior (frontal) regions of cortex were impaired suggesting that these regions were involved to a greater extent in the task in infants than in adults.

In conclusion, the prolonged anatomical development of the frontal cortex has led some to characterize the functional development of this region in terms of the differential maturation of different areas. However, increasing evidence indicates that at least parts of PFC are functional in the first few months, and that these regions may be important for the acquisition of new skills and the structuring of other parts of the cortex.

Emerging Issues

The lines of research reviewed in this chapter illustrate the potential of the new inter-disciplinary field of developmental cognitive neuroscience. While this field is still young, there are already a number of themes emerging across different domains. One of these concerns the importance of activity-dependent processes at a number of levels in both prenatal and postnatal life. It is apparent that at least some aspects of specialization of the cerebral cortex are due to intrinsic activity-dependent processes. This is continued into postnatal life with the primitive biases of the newborn (such as its tendency to look toward faces and process speech sounds) serving to bias the input to later develop-ing circuits. In this sense infants can be said to be actively contributing to the later stages of their own subsequent brain specialization. It is also possible that parts of the prefrontal cortex play a role in the specialization of other (posterior) parts of the cortex. Later in infancy, social experience and interaction with caregivers may contribute further to the specialization of later developing parts of the cerebral cortex. Much of later postnatal brain development, therefore, can be viewed as an active process to which both the child and its caregivers contribute. Thus, studying the postnatal emergence of cortical specialization for different cognitive functions offers the possibility of new per-spectives not only on the study of perceptual and cognitive development in healthy human infants, but also for social development, education, and atypical developmental pathways.

With regard to atypical development, the perspective outlined above suggests that an early abnormality in brain function, or in environmental factors, could be greatly com-pounded by subsequent interactions with the environment which are abnormal. Thus, a slight deviation from the normal developmental trajectory early on could become more severe with subsequent development (see Karmiloff-Smith, 1998). However, the positive side of this approach to understanding developmental disorders is that it suggests hope for early remediative strategies.

Some domains of cognition, such as language, appear plastic in the sense that regions of cortex are not exclusively dedicated to them from birth, while other domains, such as face processing, may have fewer options. Less extensive plasticity does not necessarily imply strict genetic determinism, however, because functions more closely tied to sensory input or motor output are likely to be more restricted to the cortical regions that have the appropriate information in their input. For example, face recognition is necessarily restricted to structures on the visual "what" (ventral) pathway because it requires both visual analysis and encoding of particular items within a category. Language may be less constrained in the sense that it is less restricted to particular information processing routes within the cortex. Thus, a key point about the emergence of localization of functions within the cortex is that the restrictions on localization may be more related to which cortical routes of information processing are viable for supporting the functions, rather than being due to prewired intrinsic circuitry within regions of cortex.

The study of functional brain development in infancy is still just beginning. However, the insights into this process gained so far suggest that further study of this topic will be rewarded with a deeper understanding of how the specificity of function observed in adults' cognitive abilities is attained. The next few decades promise some exciting breakthroughs.

Acknowledgments

Sections of text in this chapter are adapted from Johnson (2005a, 2008), and I am grateful to my various colleagues and collaborators who commented on those works for their indirect contribution to the present chapter. The preparation of this chapter was funded by the UK Medical Research Council.

Further Reading

Johnson, M. H. (2005a). *Developmental cognitive neuroscience: An introduction* (2nd ed.). Oxford: Blackwell. An introductory survey of facts and theories about the relation between brain development and the emergence of cognitive abilities in humans.

Johnson, M. H., Gilmore, R. O., & Munakata, Y. (2002). *Brain development and cognition: A reader* (2nd ed.). Oxford: Blackwell. Contains a number of "classic" and new readings by various authors on the relation between brain development and cognition.

Mareschal, D., Johnson, M. H., Sirois, S., & Spratling, M. (2007). *Neuroconstructivism: How the brain constructs cognition: Vol. I.* Oxford: Oxford University Press. This book presents a new perspective on the relation between the developing brain and cognition, emphasizing the importance of dynamic interactions and context.

Nelson, C. A., & Luciana, M. (2008). *Handbook of developmental cognitive neuroscience* (2nd ed.). Cambridge, MA: MIT Press.

References

Baillargeon, R. (1987). Object permanence in very young infants. *Cognition, 20*, 191–208.

Baillargeon, R. (1993). The object concept revisited: New directions in the investigation of infant's physical knowledge. In C. E. Granrud (Ed.), *Visual perception and cognition in infancy* (pp. 265–315). Hillsdale, NJ: Erlbaum.

Bell, M. A., & Fox, N. A. (1992). The relations between frontal brain electrical activity and cognitive development during infancy. *Child Development, 63*, 1142–1163.

Brodmann, K. (1912). Neue Ergebnisse über die vergleichende histologische Lokalisation der Grosshirnrinde mit besonderer Berücksichtigung des Stirnhirns. *Anatomischer Anzeiger, 41*(Suppl.), 157–216.

Chugani, H. T., Phelps, M. E., & Mazziotta, J. C. (1987). Positron emission tomography study of human brain functional development. *Annals of Neurology, 22*, 487–497.

Cohen Kadosh, K., & Johnson, M. H. (2007). Developing a cortex specialized for face perception. *Trends in Cognitive Sciences, 11*, 9, 367–369.

Csibra, G., Tucker, L. A., & Johnson, M.H. (1998). Neural correlates of saccade planning in infants: A high-density ERP study. *International Journal of Psychophysiology, 29*, 201–215.

de Haan, M., Johnson, M. H., & Halit, H. (2003). Development of face-sensitive event-related potentials during infancy: A review. *International Journal of Psychophysiology, 51,* 45–58.

de Schonen, S., & Mathivet, H. (1989). First come, first served: A scenario about the development of hemispheric specialization in face recognition during infancy. *European Bulletin of Cognitive Psychology, 9,* 3–44.

Dehaene-Lambertz, G., & Dehaene S. (1994). Speed and cerebral correlates of syllable discrimination in infants. *Nature, 370,* 292–295.

Dehaene-Lambertz, G., Dehaene, S., & Hertz-Pannier, L. (2002). Functional neuroimaging of speech perception in infants. *Science, 298*(5600), 2013–2015.

Diamond, A. (1985). Development of the ability to use recall to guide action, as indicated by infants' performance on AB. *Child Development, 56,* 868–883.

Diamond, A. (1991). Neuropsychological insights into the meaning of object concept development. In S. Carey and R. Gelman (Eds.), *The epigenesis of mind: Essays on biology and cognition* (pp. 67–110). Hillsdale, NJ: Erlbaum.

Diamond, A., Hurwitz, W., Lee, E. Y., Bockes, T., Grover, W., Minarcik, C., et al. (1997). Cognitive deficits on frontal cortex tasks in children with early-treated PKU: results of two years of longitudinal study. *Monographs of the Society for Research in Child development* Monographs No. *252*(4), 1–207.

Elman, J., Bates, E., Johnson, M. H., & Karmiloff-Smith, A. (1996). *Rethinking innateness: A connectionist perspective on development.* Cambridge, MA: MIT Press.

Farroni, T., Csibra, G., Simion, F., & Johnson, M. H. (2002). Eye contact detection in humans from birth. *Proceedings of the National Academy of Sciences, USA, 99,* 9602–9605.

Farroni, T., Mansfield, E. M., Lai, C., & Johnson, M. H. (2003). Infants perceiving and acting on the eyes: Tests of an evolutionary hypothesis. *Journal of Experimental Child Psychology, 85*(3), 199–212.

Farroni, T., Menon, E., & Johnson, M. H. (2006). Factors influencing newborns' face preferences for faces with eye contact. *Journal of Experimental Child Psychology, 95,* 298–308.

Geschwind, N., & Levitsky, W. (1968). Human brain: Left–right asymmetries in temporal speech region. *Science, 161,* 186–187.

Gilmore, R. O., & Johnson, M. H. (1995). Working memory in infancy: Six-month-olds' performance on two versions of the oculomotor delayed response task. *Journal of Experimental Child Psychology, 59,* 397–418.

Goldman-Rakic, P.S., Bourgeois, J-P., & Rakic, P. (1997). Synaptic substrate of cognitive development: Life-span analysis of synaptogenesis in the prefrontal cortex of the nonhuman primate. In N.A. Krasnegor, G.R. Lyon, & P.S. Goldman-Rakic (Eds.), *Development of the prefrontal cortex: Evolution, neurobiology, and behavior* (pp. 27–67). Baltimore, MD: Paul H. Brookes.

Goren, C. C., Sarty, M., and Wu, P. Y. (1975). Visual following and pattern discrimination of face-like stimuli by newborn infants. *Pediatrics, 56,* 544–549.

Gottlieb, G. (1992). *Individual development and evolution.* New York: Oxford University Press.

Grossmann, T., Johnson, M. H., Farroni, T., and Csibra, G. (2007). Social perception in the infant brain: Gamma oscillatory activity in response to eye gaze. *Social Cognitive & Affective Neuroscience, 2,* 284–291.

Huttenlocher, P. R. (1990). Morphometric study of human cerebral cortex development. *Neuropsychologia, 28,* 517–527.

Johnson, M. H. (2005a). *Developmental cognitive neuroscience: An introduction* (2nd ed.). Oxford: Blackwell.

Johnson M. H. (2005b). Sub-cortical face processing. *Nature Reviews Neuroscience, 6,* 766–774.

Johnson, M. H. (2008). Cognitive neuroscience. In M. Haith and J.B. Benson, (Eds.), *Encyclopaedia of Infant and Early Childhood Studies* (Vol. *1,* pp. 309–318). Oxford: Elsevier.

Johnson, M. H., & Morton, J. (1991). *Biology and cognitive development: The case of face recognition*. Oxford: Blackwell.

Johnson, M. H., Tucker, L. A., Stiles, J., & Trauner, D. (1998). Visual attention in infants with perinatal brain damage: Evidence of the importance of anterior lesions. *Developmental Science*, *1*, 53–58.

Karmiloff-Smith, A. (1992). *Beyond modularity: A developmental perspective on cognitive science*. Cambridge, MA: MIT Press/Bradford Books.

Karmiloff-Smith, A. (1998). Development itself is the key to understanding developmental disorders. *Trends in Cognitive Science*, *2*(10), 389–398.

Katz, L. C., & Shatz, C. J. (1996). Synaptic activity and the construction of cortical circuits. *Science*, *274*, 1133.

Kingsbury M. A., & Finlay, B. L. (2001). The cortex in multidimensional space: Where do cortical areas come from? *Developmental Science*, *4*, 125–142.

Kwong, K. E., Belliveau, J. W., Chesler, D. A., Goldberg, I. E., Weisskoff, R. M., Poncelet, B. P., et al. (1992). Dynamic magnetic resonance imaging of human brain activity during primary sensory stimulation. *Proceedings of the National Academy of Sciences*, *89*, 5675–5679.

Lenneberg, E. H. (1967). *Biological foundations of language*. New York: Wiley.

Maurer, D. (1985). Infants' perception of facedness. In T. N. Field and N. Fox (Eds.), *Social perception in infants* (pp. 73–100). New York: Ablex.

Morton, J., & Johnson, M. H. (1991). CONSPEC and CONLERN. A two-process theory of infant face recognition. *Psychological Review*, *98*(2): 164–181.

Munakata, Y., McClelland J. L., Johnson, M. H., & Siegler, R. S. (1997). Rethinking infant knowledge: Toward an adaptive process account of successes and failures in object permanence tasks. *Psychological Review*, *104*(4), 686–713.

Nelson, C. A., & Ludemann, P. M. (1989). Past, current and future trends in infant face perception research. *Canadian Journal of Psychology*, *43*, 183–198.

Neville, H. J. (1991). Neurobiology of cognitive and language processing: Effects of early experience. In K. R. Gibson and A. C. Petersen (Eds.), *Brain maturation and cognitive development: Comparative and cross-cultural perspectives* (pp. 355–380). Hawthorn, NY: Aldine de Gruyter.

Newman, A. J., Bavelier, D., Corina, D., Jessard, P., & Neville, H. J. (2001). A critical period for right hemisphere recruitment in American Sign Language processing. *Nature Neuroscience*, *5*, 76–80.

O'Leary, D. D. M. (1989). Do cortical areas emerge from a protocortex? *Trends in Neuroscience*, *12*, 400–406.

O'Reilly, R., & Johnson, M. H. (1994). Object recognition and sensitive periods: A computational analysis of visual imprinting. *Neural Computation*, *6*, 357–390.

Pascalis, O., de Haan, M., and Nelson, C. A. (2002). Is face processing species-specific during the first year of life? *Science*, *14*, 199–209.

Petersen, S. E., Fox, P., Posner, M., Mintun, M., & Raichle, M. (1988). Positron emission tomographic studies of the cortical anatomy of single-word processing. *Nature*, *331*, 585–589.

Piaget, J. (1954). *The construction of reality in the child*. New York: Basic Books.

Ragsdale C. W., & Grove, E. A. (2001). Patterning in the mammalian cerebral cortex. *Current Opinions in Neurobiology*, *11*, 50–58.

Rakic, P. (1988). Specification of cerebral cortical areas. *Science*, *241*, 170–176.

Thomas, M. S. C., & Johnson, M. H. (2008). New Advances in understanding sensitive periods in brain development. *Current Directions in Psychological Science*, *17*, 1–5.

Werker, J. F., & Polka, L. (1993). Developmental changes in speech perception: New challenges and new directions. *Journal of Phonetics*, *21*, 83–101.

PART II

Social Cognition, Communication, and Language

Introduction

Part II reviews current evidence on social cognition, communication, and language. Since the first edition there have been considerable advances in knowledge in these areas. Original authors have updated and restructured their chapters to reflect this, and we have new authors writing chapters on imitation and language.

In chapter 10, Rochat writes on the emergence of the self-concept, arguing that from the early months of life infants detect information specifying the self. This implicit self-knowledge is picked up from perception of the physical world, infants' actions in it, and from social interaction. Intermodal perception (chapter 4) is important here, since one of the sources of perceptual specification of the self is the synchrony between propriocep-tive information and visual information for body movements such as leg movements. The big developmental question is how infants progress from this initial embodied self to an objective awareness of self, and the author suggests that an important factor in this process is infants' active contemplation of their own effects on the world. However, rather than suggesting that an objective awareness of self replaces the embodied self, the view is that later in infancy both exist in parallel. The interesting point is made that explicit knowledge of self (Me) leads to understanding of possession (Mine) reflected in increasing and very determined use of the term "mine" towards the end of the second year. Rochat sees this as an area for further research, with potential links to social negotiation and development of ethical regarding treatment of others.

Piaget treated the emergence of imitation as another form of evidence regarding infants' developing representations. However, demonstration of neonatal imitation changed the account radically, and in chapter 11, Meltzoff and Williamson review current evidence and theory regarding the role of imitation. They argue that imitation serves social-communicative functions, cognitive functions, and that it is a foundation for the understanding of other minds. The social-communicative function arises because copying the acts of others is a form of social engagement. The cognitive function concerns the fact that imitation helps infants to master new strategies and to use tools. Finally, because imitation leads to formation of mappings between self and others, it provides a platform from which to develop an understanding of others. Neonatal imitation can be interpreted as a form of social engagement. Also, it is argued that infants use imitation to identify others by reenacting their acts. Older infants will imitate novel and complex actions. Additionally, they are capable of deferred imitation after delays of at least 4 months. This is likely to be a valuable tool in learning from adult demonstrations. In addition, infants reveal sensitivity to the other as an intending agent. For instance, when faced with a failed act, rather than literally imitating they model what they assume was the intended act. One emerging approach to imitation is based on the concept of mirror neurones. However, the evidence for mirror neurones is strongest in monkeys, who are poor imitators, so this theory may only partially contribute to a full account.

In chapter 12, Reddy focuses on infants engaging with the minds of others. Her topic relates closely to aspects of the two preceding chapters and she advances a strong view that to move forward we have to abandon the notion of the disembodied mind. Her argument is that minds and interactions between minds are embodied and as such are not observable "from a distance." As a consequence, she argues that, to understand mind engagement, rather than observe from the sidelines the scientist must engage fully with the infant. The chapter has two main foci: attention and intention. Reddy argues that young infants are sensitive to others' attending to them, even newborns preferring to look at faces in which gaze is directed to them. Additionally, it has long been known that breaking eye contact leads to a negative emotional response in 2-month-olds. Adult attention acts as a cue to interact and also leads to emotional responses. At around 4 months there is a shift from awareness of others' attention to self to awareness of their attention to things, and accurate identification of the target of others' attention is a considerable spatial problem in itself. However, it is now evident that at least a crude awareness of direction of gaze is present by 3 months. Awareness of intentions is commonly detected in terms of identification of goals of others' acts, and this appears to emerge around 14 months. There is little direct evidence regarding infants' awareness of intentions directed to self, but it is possible that, in neonatal imitation, the infant recognizes intention in the adult's act. A further likely example can be seen in 4-month-old infants' accommodative responses to adults' attempts to pick them up. Then there is the question of infants' awareness of others' intentions to objects. Here the finding that older infants imitate the intended act rather than a failed version is suggestive, but there is also evidence of this form of awareness within the first year.

Interest in prelinguistic communication only began in the 1970s. In chapter 13, Lock and Zukow-Goldring identify three major transitions during the prelinguistic period. First, at around 3 months, infants begin to engage in communication with their parents. Then, at around 5 months, they shift their primary interest from direct interaction to an interest in objects. Finally, at around 9 months, they coordinate their interest in objects with communication with parents. This is identified as "real" communication and is accompanied by infants' use of gestures to achieve goals. The authors point to certain difficulties in analyzing communication. For instance, it is not clear whether the focus of interest should be the individuals or the communicative group they constitute, and problems arise from the fact that communication occurs at different levels, some more easily defined and measured than others. Lock and Zukow-Goldring go on to review the now considerable evidence, ordered in terms of the three transitions summarized above, and extending their review into the second year as gestures are gradually overtaken by words. Prelinguistic communication clearly relates closely to the other topics covered in this part of the book, and the reader will see a number of points of contact between this chapter and the others. The authors are of the view that the field is now at a point where development has been quite fully described and there is a need for a paradigm shift. They are skeptical that the answers lie in a disembodied mirror neurone theory and instead conclude (like Reddy, chapter 12) that development should be treated as a process of educating attention and that the unit of interest should be the enmeshed relationship between two or more mutually responsive embodied individuals.

Unlike prelinguistic communication, investigation of the origins of language has a very long history. In chapter 14, Hollich outlines current knowledge of the processes through which children come to recognize sounds of language, learn word meanings, and learn how to combine words to produce new meanings. First, however, he identifies four prerequisite abilities. Intermodal perception (chapter 4) is necessary if sounds are to relate to things seen, touched, or tasted. Second, social understanding is needed in the sense that language is entwined with others' intentions and goals. Third, the capacity for statistical learning is required: language is a complex pattern from which it is necessary to extract regularities, and recent work on statistical learning indicates that infants have these capabilities from an early age. Finally, and probably most obviously, memory is important if the infant is to learn and retain new words. As chapter 3 indicated, infants distinguish speech sounds categorically, a basic principle of speech perception. Quite young infants are also able to segment continuous speech, and this appears to relate to their ability to identify common patterns in sounds. As early as 6 months, infants begin to show understanding of the relationship between words and referents in the world. Intermodal perception is likely to be important in the beginning of this process, with social processes taking a more important role later in development. The author points out that there are very large individual differences in the number of words understood at a given age. In large part these differences relate to the language environment the individual is immersed in. Moreover, language-learning style also seems to be important, *referential* infants having larger vocabularies than *expressive* infants. When it comes to grammatical understanding, concrete grammatical constructions appear to be more easily understood, suggesting the importance of being able to form links between words and objects. Despite the complexity of the problem, there is evidence that infants learn some grammatical constructions before they are 2 years old. The final focus of the chapter is language production. Production of words emerges as the culmination of developments from first attempts at sounds, to babbling, to babbling that contains many of the prosody and tone patterns of language, and finally to recognizable words. Finally, at around 2 years of age words become combined as telegraphic speech.

10

Emerging Self-Concept

Philippe Rochat

Questions regarding the origins and nature of self-knowledge are arguably the most fundamental in psychology. What is knowledge about oneself made of and where does it come from? The aim of this chapter is to discuss recent progress in infancy research that sheds a new light on these questions. The issue of whether self-knowledge finds its root in language development is first considered. On the basis of recent empirical evidence, I will then assert that self-knowledge does not depend exclusively on language development. Infancy research demonstrates that self-knowledge is expressed at an *implicit* level long before children become symbolic and competent talkers. The main idea running through the chapter is that at the origin of explicit and conceptual self-knowledge (i.e., self-concept) is an implicit knowledge about the self developing in the preverbal child. My focus is on the nature of early implicit self-knowledge and its link to later emerging explicit self-knowledge.

In general, I will try to show that infants from birth, and particularly from 2 months of age, develop two types of implicit self-knowledge. On one hand, infants develop implicit knowledge about their own body via self-exploration and self-produced action on objects. On the other, they develop specific knowledge about their own affective dispositions via interaction and reciprocation with others. The origins of these two types of implicit self-knowledge are respectively *perceptual* and *social*.

Prior to this presentation, let me briefly situate the origins of self-knowledge in relation to language and the emergence of symbolic functioning by the second year of life.

Self and Language

We all have some notions of who we are and what distinguishes us from others. We know what we look like, have some sense of our relative power, the personality we project onto the world, including individuated and abstract things we claim as "ours." We have a sense of what belongs to us and what does not, the things we excel in and those we do not. In short, we all have some explicit conception of ourselves, a so-called explicit *self-concept*. The explicit self-concept of adults is to a large extent articulated in words as we frequently engage in talking about ourselves, perform silent monologues, and display a universal compulsion for internal speech, adopting the self as audience and as sole witness of ... ourselves.

An explicit, hence reflective conception of the self is already apparent at the early stage of language acquisition. As argued by Bates (1990, p. 165) "the acquisition of any natural language requires a preexisting theory of self – a theory of the self as distinct from other people, and a theory of the self from the point of view of one's conversational partners." By 18 months, infants start to mark contrasts between themselves and other people in their verbal production. They express semantic roles that can be taken either by themselves or by others (Bates, 1990). Does that mean, however, that the nature of self-concept is primarily linguistic? In other words, does it imply that the roots of an explicit sense of self are to be found in language and its development?

It is feasible that self-concept emerges under the pressure of growing linguistic competence, and is essentially a linguistic epiphenomenon. With language would come self-marking and labeling, with children somehow compelled to become explicit about who they are in terms of their own desires (e.g., "Candy!"), beliefs (e.g., "Katy nice!"), feelings (e.g., "Happy!"), and other states of mind (e.g., the unfortunately too typical "Mine!"). Communicating verbally does indeed require much explicit reference to the self as the subject of action, intentions, and beliefs.

The idea that the emergence of self-concept is linked to the development of language finds corroboration in the roughly synchronous developmental timing of mirror self-recognition in the young child. By the time children start to utter their first conventional words, using arbitrary sounds that are acknowledged by their community as standing for things in the world, in particular possessives like "mine!" at around 21 months of age (Tomasello, 1996), they also start to show clear signs of self-recognition in mirrors and photographs. It is also by the middle of the second year, around the time children typically start to show some fluency and their vocabulary tends to explode that they start to show self-referencing (e.g., pointing to themselves) and self-conscious emotions (e.g., embarrassment) in front of mirrors (Lewis & Brooks-Gunn, 1979). In the context of the famous mirror "rouge task", this is evident when children perceive their own reflection, noticing that a stain of rouge has been surreptitiously smeared over their face (as an illustration, see Figure 10.1 below).

From the perspective of evolution, formal and generative language is a cardinal aspect differentiating humans from other animal species. Interestingly, self-concept is also a trademark of humans, with the exception of only a few other species, including some of our close great ape primate relatives who demonstrate mirror self-recognition in the context of the "rouge" task (i.e., orangutans and chimpanzees, see the thorough review by Tomasello and Call, 1997). Thus, if language and self-concept are connected in child development, they also appear to be linked as major cognitive trademarks in primate evolution (Gallup, 1982; Povinelli, 1993).

In child development, although language and explicit self-concept appear connected in the timing of their emergence, this does not mean that they are mutually dependent.

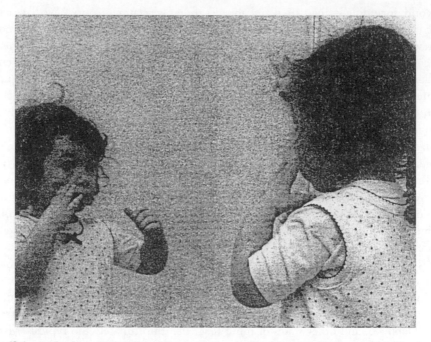

Figure 10.1   Self-referencing and embarrassment manifested by an 18-month-old infant in front of a mirror during the rouge test. *Source*: Photo Pascale L. R.

On one hand, there are good grounds for assuming that language acquisition and the learning of word meanings rest on an understanding of self as intentional. When children hear a new word and learn that *this* particular word stands for *that* specific object or event in the world, they connect the intention of others with their own to communicate about objects and events in the environment (Tomasello & Akhtar, 1995). Children clearly show a distinct notion of others and of themselves as intentional communicators (Tomasello, 1995). On the other hand, children do not wait until they are symbolically competent to express some *implicit* or *preconceptual* self-knowledge. As proposed by William James over a century ago, it is necessary to distinguish implicit and explicit levels of self-knowledge.

Self-Knowledge without Language

In his seminal writing on the self, James (1890) distinguishes the "Me" and the "I" as two basic aspects of the self: The "Me" corresponds to the self that is identified, recalled, and talked about. It is the conceptual self that emerges with language and which entails explicit recognition or representation. It is beyond the grasp of infants, who by definition are preverbal, not yet expressing themselves within the conventions of a shared symbol system. On the other hand, there is the self that is basically implicit, not depending on any conscious identification or recognition. The "I" is also referred to as the *existential self* (Lewis & Brooks-Gunn, 1979) or the *implicit self* (Case, 1991). It is, for example, the sense of their own body expressed by young infants when they start to reach and grasp objects around them. Infants implicitly express a sense of themselves as agent (reachers) as well as a sense of their own physical situation in the environment (objects around them are perceived by the infant as reachable and graspable depending on size and distance, see Rochat, 1997). Infancy research shows that the "I" is expressed long before any signs of a conceptual (explicit) sense of self (the "Me").

If we accept James's distinction, the question is what kind of relation these two fundamental aspects of the self entertain, and in particular, how do they relate in their development? One possibility is that they develop independently of each other and that somehow their functioning is parallel and unrelated. Another possibility, proposed here and supported by infancy research, is that the development of the conceptual self emerging by the second year is *rooted in* and *prepared by* an implicit sense of self already present at birth and developing from the outset (the early sense of an existential self or "I" following James distinction).

In the tradition set by James but expanding his work, Neisser (1991) further distinguishes two kinds *of implicit self* or *Is* manifested in early infancy, long before the developmental emergence of a conceptual self. Neisser proposes that from the outset of development, infants have two kinds of selves within either the social or physical domain. Each domain provides the infant with specific perceptual information specifying different aspects of the self: the *interpersonal* self in the social domain, and the *ecological* self in the physical domain.

The interpersonal self grows out of the infant's transactions with others, in particular the developing sense of shared experience and reciprocity. In the physical domain, infants develop a sense of their own body in relation to other objects, what Neisser labels the ecological self. The ecological self is the sense infants develop of their own physical body as a differentiated, situated agent in relation to other objects furnishing the environment. The ecological self develops as infants interact with physical objects and also as they perceive their own body directly via self-exploration (see below, Rochat, 1998; Rochat & Morgan, 1995).

Neisser's conceptualization of the self in infancy is justified based on a growing body of observations provided by infancy research (see Butterworth, 1995). We will see next that this research demonstrates that at the origin of development, infants manifest a sense of the ecological as well as the interpersonal self.

The Self in Infancy

Infants, from a very early age differentiate perceptually between self and nonself stimulation, namely between themselves and other entities in the environment. Early on, for example, infants differentiate between their own movements in the environment, whether passively or actively produced, and the independent movements of objects observed from a stationary point in space (Kellman, Gleitman, & Spelke 1987). Young infants and even newborns respond with markedly different postural adjustments (e.g., straightening of the trunk or head movements) when they are surreptitiously set in motion, or if their surrounding is set in motion with them maintaining a stationary position (Bertenthal & Rose, 1995; Jouen & Gapenne, 1995).

Apart from being situated in the environment, infants also manifest an implicit sense of their own effectivity in the world. From birth, infants learn to be effective in relation to objects and events. For example, within hours after birth, neonates are capable of learning to suck in certain ways and apply specific pressures on a dummy pacifier to hear their mother's voice or see their mother's face (DeCasper & Fifer, 1980; Walton, Bower, & Bower, 1992). This remarkable instrumental learning capacity testifies to the fact that early in their lives infants manifest a sense of themselves as an *agent* in the environment, an important aspect of the (implicit) ecological self (Neisser, 1995; Rochat, 1997).

As we will see, in the social domain there is also good evidence of implicit self-knowledge. From at least 2 months of age infants start to reciprocate with others, smiling, gazing, and cooing in face-to-face exchanges with a social partner. They show some signs of what Trevarthen (1979) coined "primary intersubjectivity", the sense of shared experience infants manifest in dyadic face-to-face interactions. When social partners adopt a sudden still-face, staring at the infant with a neutral, frozen facial expression, infants from 2 months of age react with strong negative facial expressions: they gaze away, smile markedly less, and even cry (Toda & Fogel, 1993; Tronick, Als, Adamson, Wise, & Brazelton, 1978). This robust phenomenon suggests that infants already have an implicit sense of others, as well as of themselves, as reciprocating (social) agents. They expect social partners to reciprocate in certain ways to their *own* emotional displays. If they smile, they expect others to reciprocate with analogous emotional expressions.

Early on, others are social mirrors in which infants contemplate and learn about themselves via imitation (Meltzoff, 1995) and the behavioral mirroring provided by caretakers who tend to feedback to the infant what they just did. Adult mirroring of the infant contains rich information about the self, characterized by systematic exaggeration of infants' emotions and precise marking of such mimicking by the adult (Gergely & Watson, 1999). In short, there is now good evidence for the early development of an implicit sense of self as *social agent*, reciprocating with people in systematic ways and developing social expectations (Rochat, Querido, & Striano, 1999; Rochat & Striano, 1999a; Striano & Rochat, 1999, 2000).

The abundance of findings supporting the existence of both an ecological and interpersonal self at the origin of development contrasts sharply with the theoretical assertions that have been traditionally put forth by developmentalists. Current research has radically changed the traditional view of an originally confused infant devoid of any implicit sense of self. Infants do not appear to start off in a state of fusion and confusion in regard to their situation in the environment. James (1890) famous account of the world of newborns as a "blooming, buzzing confusion" does not fit well with current infancy research.

In general, the view of an initial state of undifferentiation between the infant and the environment (e.g., Wallon, 1942/1970; Piaget, 1952; Mahler, Pine, & Bergman, 1975) needs to be revised in light of evidence of remarkable abilities in newborns for instrumental learning, social attunement, as well as differential responding to self and nonself stimulation (DeCasper & Fifer, 1980; Rochat & Hespos, 1997; Walton et al., 1992). What remains unclear, however, is how various kinds of implicit sense of self might develop to become explicit beyond infancy, when, for example, infants start explicitly to label and to recognize themselves in mirrors. If we accept Neisser's assertion of an implicit sense of the ecological and interpersonal self that would develop prior to language, questions remain as to how they develop and relate to each other. Do they develop independently? Does one precede the other? Do they need to be integrated for infants eventually to become explicit about themselves, such as through self-recognition in mirrors or starting to label themselves as *persons*?

Different Views on the Origins of Self-Knowledge

For some infancy researchers like Fogel (1993, 1995) or Lewis (1999), the implicit sense of self in infancy develops primarily through *relationships with others*. An implicit sense of the interpersonal self is viewed as central to infant psychological development and as having some developmental precedence over others. In the tradition of George Herbert Mead (1934), the emphasis is on an early sense of self molded into the adult state via social interaction (see also Meltzoff, 1995; chapter 11 this volume).

Although focusing on the interpersonal world of infants, Stern (1985) proposes that infants in the first 2 months of their life develop an implicit sense of themselves that is somehow presocial, not yet based on reciprocation with others per se. For Stern, during the first 2 months of life, infants develop an implicit sense of what he calls the *emergent self*. The emergent self precedes the development of the *core self* corresponding to Neisser's interpersonal self (Neisser, 1991, 1995). In Stern's view, during the first 2 months, infants primarily experience their own behavioral organization in terms of fluctuating states, growing sensori-motor organization, and in terms of learning about the relations between various sensory experiences: simultaneous sounds and sights, smells and touch stimulation, proprioceptive and visual sensations. The sense of an emergent self would correspond to both a sense of the process and of the product of growing intermodal and sensori-motor integration (Stern, 1985, p. 45). As a by-product of early sensori-motor learning and experience, the sense of an emergent self would be primary, developing in relative independence of social interactions.

Between 2 and 6 months, when infants start to reciprocate with people and view others as differentiated entities with distinct histories, Stern proposes that infants then develop the sense of a *core self* that is interpersonal, based on the relationship with others as emphasized by Fogel (1993). Once again, in Stern's view, there is a developmental precedence of a sense of self as a functioning entity that feels, acts, and develops, over a sense of self (the core or interpersonal self) that is revealed to infants exclusively in social interactions.

Other infancy researchers emphasize the importance of an implicit sense of the self infants develop by interacting with their environment, without putting a particular emphasis on either physical or social objects (people). Eleanor J. Gibson (1988, 1995) construes self-knowledge within the general context of infants learning about what the physical and social objects afford for action, so-called *affordances* (J.J. Gibson, 1979).

In the process of exploring and detecting affordances, E.J. Gibson (1988) suggests that infants learn first about their own *effectivities* as perceivers and actors in a meaningful environment. For example, by detecting mouthable objects, sucking on them and eventually extracting food from them, infants come to grasp their own capacities for perception and action. This is, according to Gibson, a primary sense of self developing from birth, long before children can start to talk about or recognize themselves in mirrors.

In summary, to account for the implicit sense of self infants appear to manifest from the outset of development, infancy researchers distinguish different kinds of preconceptual knowledge pertaining to the self: knowledge infants develop in the physical domain (i.e., the ecological self) and social domain (i.e. the interpersonal self). Different theories are proposed as to how these kinds of selves might relate in development, some emphasizing the primacy of the interpersonal self (e.g., Fogel, 1993; Meltzoff, 1995), and others considering them as emerging in succession (Stern, 1985; but also Neisser, 1991), or on a more equal footing (Gibson, 1995). The problem of their integration and the extent to which this integration might contribute to the development of the conceptual self that emerges by the second year remains an open question. What research shows, however, is that both perceptual and social factors need to be considered in trying to capture the developmental origins of self-concept. These two factors are reviewed next.

Perceptual Origins of Self-Knowledge

The body is a primary object of perceptual exploration in infancy. As infants move and act, they perceive their own body moving and acting, hence detect its own organization, its physical characteristics, as well as its own vitality. As proposed by Gibson (1979), perceiving and acting always entail coperceiving oneself, perception and action being inseparable. When, for example, we perceive and act on objects, we situate ourselves in relation to these objects, coperceiving ourselves as perceivers and actors. In an analogous way, when newborns move about, kick, cry, suck, or systematically bring their hand to the mouth (Butterworth & Hopkins, 1988; Rochat, Blass, & Hoffmeyer, 1988), they pick up perceptual information that *specifies their own body as a unique entity in the environment* (e.g., double touch information in the case of hand-mouth contacts, Rochat, 1995; see below).

Self-produced action comes with the experience of uniquely contingent and analog perception across modalities. This is an important feature of what infants gain from engaging in self-exploration. This experience specifies the body as differentiated from other objects in the environment. When my hand crosses my visual field, for example, I perceive that it is my hand and not someone else's, because I both feel it proprioceptively and see it moving at exactly the same time and by a commensurate amount. The experience of the body entails proprioception with contingent and analog inputs from other sense modalities.

The robust propensity of infants from birth, and even prenatally, to bring their hand in contact with the mouth and face provides a perceptual experience that specifies the body in a unique way. This experience, in addition to proprioception, entails a "double touch," a specific self-experience. When the hands of infants touch their face or mouth, the tactile sensation goes both ways in reference to their own body: the hand feels the face and at the same time, the face feels the hand. Again, this double touch experience uniquely specifies their own body as opposed to other objects in the environment.

In one study Rochat & Hespos (1997) tested newborn infants within 24 hours of birth to see whether they would manifest a discrimination between double touch stimulation specifying themselves, and external (one-way) tactile stimulation specifying nonself objects. For testing, we used the robust rooting response all healthy infants manifest from birth and by which tactile stimulation at the corner of the mouth is followed by the infant's head turn with mouth opening toward the stimulation. Following a simple procedure, we recorded the frequency of rooting in response to either external tactile stimulation, the experimenter stroking the infant's cheek, or in response to tactile self-stimulation when infants spontaneously brought one of their hands in contact with their cheek. We found that newborns tended to manifest rooting responses almost three times more often in response to external compared to self-stimulation. These observations suggest that already at birth, infants pick up the intermodal invariants (single touch or double touch combined with proprioception) that specify self versus external stimulation, showing evidence of an early sense of their own body, hence an early perceptually based sense of themselves.

The early sense of the body developed by infants from birth does not only pertain to the physical body, but also to the dynamics of their own affectivity. The intermodal experience of the body is inseparable from feelings about their own vitality (Stern, 1985, 1999). Suppose that an infant engages in exploring his own hands by raising and moving them in front of his eyes. Suppose now that in a sudden burst of excitement, he claps them together. Besides the intermodal perception of joint touch and proprioception, as well as the double touch experience we discussed above, the infant perceives the dynamic of his own vitality: from calm to being excited, then calm again. This dynamic is perceived both privately and publicly. It is privately experienced because the infant feels from within a state change, from being calm to being excited with specific waxing and waning of tensions. It is publicly experienced because the hands move accordingly in front of the infant's eyes. In a way, the movement of the hands is a choreography of what the infant feels from within. Self-exploratory activity thus provides infants with an opportunity to objectify the feelings of their own vitality via perceived self-produced action of the body (Rochat, 1995).

By at least 3 months of age and as a result of self-produced action and perception, infants manifest an intermodal calibration of their own body. Recent evidence shows that young infants develop a sense of perfect contingency and invariant covariations across modalities that specify the body as a dynamic entity with particular characteristics. This calibration is necessary not only to provide the perceptual foundations of self-knowledge, but also for infants to use their body in order to act on objects in the environment (see chapter 5, this volume).

Daniel Stern (1985) reports some striking observations made with particular conjoined twins. These infants were congenitally attached on the ventral surface, facing one another. They shared no organs and were surgically separated at 4 months. Stern and colleagues noticed that often they would suck one another's fingers. A week before separation, Stern and his colleagues conducted a series of tests to assess the extent to which these infants, despite their odd situation of forced binding, differentiated what was part of their own body and what belonged to the attached sibling. In one of the tests, they compared each infant's reactions to the gentle removal from their mouth of either their own fingers they were sucking, or the fingers of their sibling. They found that the twins responded differentially depending whether it was theirs or the other's hand that was removed.

These observations corroborate our own with healthy newborns who showed differential rooting responses to their own hand touching their face compared to the finger of an experimenter (Rochat & Hespos, 1997). In these observations, infants show that they differentiate between two basic categories of perceptual information: one category pertaining to the own body and the other to surrounding entities. This information is intermodal and in most instances involves a sense of self-produced action via proprioception.

If young infants appear capable of perceiving their own body as a differentiated entity, the question is what exactly do they perceive of their own bodies as physical and acting entities. Some years ago, we performed research demonstrating that from at least 3 months of age, infants are aware of complex aspects of their own body as a dynamic and organized entity with particular featural characteristics (Morgan & Rochat, 1998; Rochat, 1998; Rochat & Morgan, 1995). We measured 3- to 5-month-old infants' preferential looking to different views of their own body. For example, facing two television screens, infants saw on each of them their own body videotaped from the waist down. Both views were on-line, thus perfectly contingent. When infants moved their legs, they saw them moving simultaneously on either of the screens (see Figure 10.2).

Within this experimental set-up, we measured infants' preferential looking for either view. One of the views presented their own legs as they would be specified via direct visual-proprioceptive feedback, for example by bringing them in the field of view while laying supine in their crib. The other view provided an experimentally modified on-line view of their own legs.

In general, what we found is that from 3 months of age, infants tend to look significantly longer at the view of the legs that is unfamiliar, namely that violates the visual-proprioceptive calibration of the body in terms of general movement directionality, relative movement of the limbs, as well as overall leg configuration in relation to the rest of the body (Rochat, 1998). In particular, infants are shown to look significantly longer as well as to move their legs more, while looking at a view of their legs that reverses by 180° the seen and felt directionality of movement, or that reverses the way legs move in relation to each other. In all, this research suggests that by moving and acting, infants from at least 3 months of age manifest an intermodal calibration of the own body, developing an intermodal body schema. This body schema is an implicit, perceptually based "protorepresentation" of the body as specified by the intermodal redundancy accompanying perception and action. This body schema is not yet the objectified bodily representation or body image expressed by young children recognizing themselves in a mirror by claiming this is "Me" or showing embarrassment or shame (see the conceptual distinction

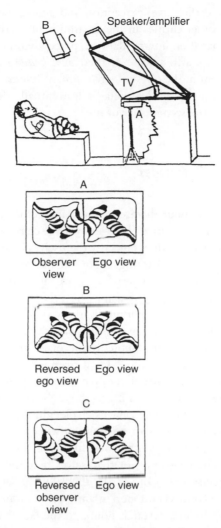

Figure 10.2   A Apparatus and experimental set-up of the infant wearing black and white socks while reclined in front of the large television monitor projecting an on-line view of the legs from the waist down. Camera Λ provided a close-up of the infant's face for the analysis of gazing at the display as Camera B and C provided each a particular view of the legs (i.e., ego vs. reversed ego view). **B** The two views of their own legs as seen by the infant on the television in the three experimental conditions studied in Rochat and Morgan (1995): (A) Observer view vs. ego view (Experiment 1); (B) Reversed ego view vs. ego view (Experiment 2); (C) Reversed observer view vs. ego view (Experiment 3).

between body schema and body image introduced by Gallagher, 1986, see also Gallagher & Meltzoff, 1996; Rochat, 2003, 2009). The intermodal redundancy specifying the body is experienced and explored by infants from birth. Considering the rich behavioral repertoire of fetuses 20 weeks and older, it may also be experienced in the confines of pregnancy (e.g., Prechtl, 1984).

In summary, from the earliest age, perception and action specify the body as a differentiated entity among other entities in the environment. Early on, infants appear to calibrate their own body based on intermodal (i.e., perceptual) invariants that specify the sense of their own ecological self: a sense of their *own bodily self* that is differentiated, situated, and acts as an agent in the physical environment (Neisser, 1991; Rochat, 1997). This may form the perceptual origins of what will eventually develop as an explicit or conceptual sense of self by the second year of life.

Social Origins of Self-Knowledge

Alongside what infants learn about themselves by being actors in the physical world of inanimate objects, another major source of self-knowledge comes from social interactions. Not unlike adults, very early on children objectify themselves in reciprocating with others, searching for social approval and learning about themselves as differentiated, unique entities. As adults, we use others to reveal who we are, as a sort of social mirror. Much of how we perceive ourselves is measured against how we think others perceive us. Self-perception is inseparable from our perception of others as *onlookers of us* (Rochat, 2009). This is what being "self-conscious" means and it is close to impossible to escape the so-called "audience effect". People are undoubtedly the main source of feedback by which we objectify ourselves. This process is also evident from the outset of development.

As mentioned above, the first words of children are mainly oriented toward attracting attention of others to objects, but also mainly to themselves. When children keep calling parents to watch them doing what they view as challenging feats, such as jumping off a diving board or riding their bicycle with no training wheels, they seek confirmation of who they think they are: courageous, outrageous, funny, or smart, aside from attempting to impress an audience. The perception of themselves becomes essentially social. They project and recognize themselves in others. In this process, self-knowledge and social knowledge are inseparable. But what about infants, prior to any explicit expression of such process via language? Infancy research points to the fact that from a very early age infants learn about themselves by monitoring others and the way they respond to their own behavior.

The most common way parents interact with their young baby is by reciprocating and *mirroring* their emotions. There is much parental imitation of their infant in early face-to-face interaction. In this process the emotions displayed by infants are fed back to them, amplified and clearly demarcated with exaggerated gestures and intonations (Gergely & Watson, 1999). This emotional mirroring is certainly a source of self-knowledge for the infant as it provides them with a perceptual scaffolding for the objectification of their own affects: what they feel from within and project to the outside is externalized as it is reflected back to them by the social partner. In this process, infants are exposed to an explicit, analyzable form of what they feel privately at an implicit level (Rochat, 1995, 2009).

As adults, we are strongly compelled to empathize with babies. When, for example, they start to show signs of distress and start to cry, we typically comfort them by providing physical proximity, stroking their back while adopting a sad voice with lowered brows and inverted U shaped mouth. In doing so, we actually provide infants with an emotional *simulation* of what they are supposed to feel, a simulation of their subjective life.

When infants monitor people's faces and begin to reciprocate in face-to-face interaction, they lay down the foundations of both social and self-awareness. As a result of the strong propensity of adults to engage in mirroring and affective attunement, they also learn about themselves being somehow simulated or *reenacted*. From the earliest age, caretakers present infants with a social mirror that reflects back to them their own vitality and affective life in a sort of running commentary they are compelled to produce, like sportscasters verbalizing and mimicking actions back to an audience. Aside from the sense of the ecological self infants develop by acting and perceiving the physical environment, this emotional simulation by caretakers is probably also at the origin of explicit *self-consciousness*, clearly manifested by infants once they pass the symbolic gateway marking the end of infancy, referring to themselves verbally and identifying themselves in mirrors.

Prior to the symbolic gateway, the idea of an implicit self-knowledge gained by young infants in their interaction with others is supported by numerous studies demonstrating sophisticated social attunement of the infant from birth, in particular their propensity to pay special attention to faces (De Haan, Pascalis, & Johnson, 2002), and to imitate social partners (see chapter 11, this volume). The early propensity to imitate is probably a major mechanism by which infants start objectifying their own actions and affective dispositions. In matching the behavior of others, one could say that they simulate themselves as others. In this process and what appears to be a developmentally deeply rooted inclination to reproduce the action and emotion of others, young infants from birth acquire knowledge about themselves. Social mirroring is a two-way phenomenon from the very beginning of life. On the one hand, caretakers tend to have the uncontrollable proclivity to reproduce infants' actions and affects, as they compulsively scaffold face-to face exchanges with babies (Gergely & Watson, 1999). On the other hand, infants from birth do the same by reciprocating via emotional resonance and imitation (Field, Woodson, Greenberg, & Cohen, 1982).

The combination of adults' systematic scaffolding of face-to-face exchanges and young infants early proclivity to imitate others is an important aspect of what constitutes the developmental origins of self-knowledge. In the context of protoconversations and play games initiated by caretakers (e.g., peek-a-boo games, see below), infants specify themselves as a function of how others respond to them, in particular how contingent and attuned they are to their *own* behavior (Trevarthen, 1979).

By imitating each other, the infant–adult pair engages primarily in reciprocating affects and feelings. Such reciprocation is at the origin of intersubjectivity, itself a foundation of early social cognition and, I propose, an important source of implicit self-knowledge, in particular of the self as a *communicative agent* (the interpersonal self according to Neisser, 1991). Via mutual imitation adults and infants can probe the degree to which they communicate with one another.

Evidence of a developing interpersonal self in early infancy is now extensive. By the second month, when starting to reciprocate by smiling and engaging in long bouts of gazing toward others (Wolff, 1987), infants are shown to become increasingly sensitive to specific timing in social interaction and develop expectations regarding the behavior of others in relation to the self (Rochat & Striano, 1999a). Such timing indexes the quality of communicative flow, and in particular the level of relative matching between their own dispositions and those displayed by the social partner. The social expectations developing by the second month are inseparable from the developing sense of the inter-personal self or social self of infants.

As an illustration, we explored the sensitivity of 2- to 6-month-old infants to the rela-tive structure of the interactive frame offered by an adult stranger (Rochat, Querido, & Striano, 1999). The rationale for this study was to capture how infants aged from 2 months on refine their ability to detect regularities in ongoing social interaction and develop specific expectations based on a sensitivity to the structure of the interaction. We hypothesized that between 2 and 6 months infants develop specific expectations in the dyadic context based on cues specifying the *quality* of response of a social partner to their own behavior, in other words *the relative attunement of the social partner to the self*.

We videotaped 2-, 4-, and 6-month-old infants interacting with a female stranger in a face-to-face situation that did not include any touching. Apart from the baseline periods, in two different experimental conditions the experimenter introduced the infant to a peek-a-boo routine that was either structured or unstructured. In the structured condi-tion, the peek-a-boo routine was strictly organized into three phases articulating a total of 8 subroutines. In the unstructured condition, the experimenter was wearing an ear piece connected to a tape recorder playing instructions of subroutines to be performed in a random, disorganized way. In other words, in the unstructured condition, the experi-menter engaged in a *scrambled* peek-a-boo game, with unrelated subroutines that did not coalesce to form a compelling, socially attuned script.

The scoring of infants' smiling and gazing at the experimenter revealed that 2 month-olds looked towards the experimenter and smiled equally in both the structured and unstructured peek-a-boo conditions. In contrast, 4- and 6-month-olds looked signifi-cantly more toward the experimenter and smiled markedly less in the unstructured compared to the structured peek-a-boo condition.

In all, these results illustrate how, from a diffuse sense of others' attunement to the self, by 4 months of age infants begin to monitor social partners in the way they relate to them. Based on such monitoring, infants develop an implicit sense of an interpersonal or social self, expecting not only that others pay attention and smile at them, but also that they relate to them in ways that are attuned or contingent with their own behavior (Murray & Trevarthen, 1985; Stern, 1985).

Origins of Self-Recognition and the Overcoming of the Mirror Paradox

From an implicit sense of their own physical, behaving body, and an implicit sense of themselves as social entities, how do infants develop an *explicit sense of themselves* as indexed by mirror self-recognition? What are the origins of the conceptual self manifested by children when they start to speak and pass the symbolic threshold that separates infancy from childhood? In this section, I discuss mirror self-recognition as one of the first signs of explicit self-concept that originates from the fusion of implicit self-knowledge developed in the physical and social domains over the first months of life. The rationale for such discussion is that, although mirror self-recognition is limited to one particular experience (i.e., the specular or mirror image of the self), it informs us about what it takes for infants to become explicit about themselves, hence to have a conceptual sense of self as "Me" in addition to the existential sense of self as "I".

Three-month-old infants placed in front of mirrors spend much time exploring their reflection, staring at themselves in the eyes and moving their limbs often with smiles and cooing (Amsterdam, 1972). They are attracted by their specular image but that does not mean that they yet *recognize* themselves in it. They are using the opportunity offered by the mirror to experience and explore the perfect contingency and spatial calibration between proprioception and vision. This opportunity is unique and particularly attractive to infants because it also offers the visual-proprioceptive experience of larger portions of the body, much larger than the hands and feet perceivable directly in certain postures. As adults, we also use the optical affordance of mirrors to work on our appearance, except that the behavior of fixing hair and making up is to a large extent an explicit expression that we know it is us in the mirror.

Clearly, the behavior of young infants in front of mirrors does not imply the same level of awareness of either adults applying lipstick or toddlers showing embarrassment and manual contact with the face because they discover some rouge has surreptitiously stained their nose, as in the classic rouge task already mentioned at the beginning of this chapter (Gallup, 1982; Lewis & Brooks-Gunn, 1979).

Bahrick, Moss, & Fadil (1996) reported that infants as young as 3 months show some discrimination between viewing a frontal prerecorded view of themselves or viewing an analogous view of another infant wearing the same bib. Infants were carefully matched for age and gender. In general, infants are reported to spend significantly more time looking at the image of the other child compared to their own. The question is whether this apparent visual discrimination actually means that they *recognize* themselves on the television? In other words, does this discrimination entail some rudiments of self-concept? It is certainly not a direct demonstration of self-concept. This discrimination, although remarkable, probably means that from an early age, infants are familiarized with their own featural (i.e., facial) characteristics and vitality based on previous mirror experiences. In the context of the Bahrick et al. experiment, the feature characteristics of the other child are newer, therefore more interesting to the infant, so explaining their visual preference. The observations reported by Bahick and her collaborators are no evidence that infants as young as 3 months "know" it is them on the television.

So, from the early sensitivity to intermodal contingency (Amsterdam, 1972), the early intermodal calibration of the body as a schema, as opposed to an image (Gallagher & Meltzoff, 1996; Rochat, 1998), and early perceptual learning (Bahrick et al., 1996), how do infants develop the ability to eventually recognize and identify themselves in mirrors?

First, let me stress that although revealing something about self-recognition, the mirror test should be considered with caution to account for the origins of self-concept. Mirrors are unusual objects in the environment, carrying with them the experience of a fundamental paradox: the *"self–other paradox."* As mentioned above, when you look at your own mirror reflection, you perceive aspects of your body that you cannot experience directly, in particular a full view of your face. Considering that eye contact in social exchanges is an important determinant of social interaction from the outset of development, the specular image of a full face with eyes gazing toward the self specifies what is normally experienced with others, not in relation to the self. Therefore, self-recognition in a mirror requires the *suspension* of the normal social experience of others facing you with eye contact. Mirror reflection of the self is paradoxical in the sense that what is seen in the mirror is the self as another person: it is you where what is normally perceived is another person. As the self in disguise of the other, the specular image reflects what can be called the fundamental *you but not you* or *self–other paradox*. On the one hand, the specular image reflects the self via the perfect contingency and spatial analog of visual-proprioceptive information (i.e., the ecological self). On the other hand, it does reflect another (nonself) person as specified by past experience (face-on view with potential eye contact).

The self reflected by mirrors does not match the embodied self infants experience directly from birth, namely the self situated in the body. Rather, it reflects back to the infant the implicit sense of an *interpersonal* or *social self* (i.e., themselves interacting with what appears to be someone else).

To some extent, inspecting oneself in a mirror and recognizing that it is "Me" out there is very much an "out-of-the-body experience." What mirror self-recognition and other video and picture self-recognition tasks measure is primarily the ability of individuals to suspend what they normally experience of themselves, step back, and literally reflect on the new, out-of-the-body aspects the mirror reveals about themselves. Mirror images are indeed physical reflections of the body on a polished surface that call for mental reflection to be *recognized*, hence *conceptualized*. This conceptualization requires the suspension of perceptual experiences typically specifying self *or* others, not self as others.

Observations made by anthropologists introducing reflecting devices to adult individuals who presumably never experienced their own mirror reflection are particularly telling of the fundamental paradox attached to the experience of self in mirrors. Edmund Carpenter (1975) introduced mirrors to members of an isolated tribe (the Biami) living in the Papuan plateau where neither slate or metallic surfaces exist, and where rivers are murky, not providing clear reflections (see also Priel & deSchonen, 1986, for the same kind of empirical observations on young nomadic children from Palestine living without mirrors). Recording the initial reaction of adults confronted for the very first time with a large mirror reflection of themselves, Carpenter reports:

> They were paralyzed: after their first startled response – covering their mouths and ducking their heads – they stood transfixed, staring at their images, only their stomach muscles betraying great tension. Like Narcissus, they were left numb, totally fascinated by their own reflections: indeed, the myth of Narcissus may refer to this phenomenon. (Carpenter, 1975, pp. 452–453)

We might add that Narcissus, aside from falling in love with himself, probably became fascinated with the existential experience of the "self–other" paradox that reflecting surfaces offer.

Despite the intrinsic paradox attached to mirrors, mirror self-recognition tests remain a valid instrument to assess self-knowledge at a conceptual and recognitive level. It is particularly valid to assess the ability of children to *objectify* themselves and eventually get over the "self–other" paradox. This requires stepping back and reflectiveness in the sense of mental reflection, beyond direct perception and action.

In relation to mirrors, two questions are of particular interest from a developmental perspective. The first is, when do infants start to become contemplative in the exploration of themselves, not merely experiencing their embodied self via direct perception and action? The second is, what might be the process enabling infants to adopt a contemplative, reflective stance when exploring themselves? These are important "how" and "why" questions regarding the origins of self-concept. These questions are wide open for speculation (i.e., "reflect") on the developmental origins of self-recognition, hence self-concept.

In the last section of this chapter, I would like to stress the fact that self-concept, from the origins, extends far beyond the polished surface of mirrors. It encompasses more than the recognition of the body and the objectification of embodied self-experience. It includes also objects of possession, physical things that are incorporated to the self as "belongings" or self-extensions. This is rarely considered and would deserve much more research scrutiny.

With the emergence of *Me*, comes the possessive *Mine*, and in development, *Me* and *Mine* are inseparable, two sides of the same coin. This aspect is stressed in the writings of both William James (1890) and John Dewey (1922) about the self, often overlooked in recent years by developmental psychologists who tend to treat the early development of self-concept almost exclusively in reference to body schema and body image, not of possession.

Me and Mine: Coorigins of Self-Concept and Property Sense

William James in his seminal discussion about the self insists on the inseparability of the *Me* (conceptual sense of self) and the *Mine*, the fact that what I am is also what I own. He writes:

> The self of a man is the total sum of all that he can claim as his, not only his body and his psychic power, but his clothes and his house, his wife and his children, his ancestors and his friends, his reputation and his accomplishments, his land, his sailboat and his bank account. All these things give him the same emotions. If they grow and prosper, he feels triumphant. If they disappear and come to vanish, he feels diminished and from this concludes: It is clear that between what someone calls "ME" and what he calls "MINE," the line is difficult to draw. We feel and act in relation to certain things that are ours in the same way that we feel and act in relation to ourselves. (James, 1890, p. 291)

In James' footsteps, pragmatist and functionalist philosopher John Dewey adds: "the 'Me' cannot exist without the 'Mine.' The self gets solidity and form through an appropriation of things which identifies them with whatever we call myself ... Possession shapes and consolidates the 'I' " (John Dewey, 1922, p. 116).

Following Dewey's intuition that the appropriation of things gives shape and contributes to the objectification of the self (i.e., the conception of Me), there is good empirical evidence that the emergence of an explicit inclination to possess and the emergence of self-concept are strongly correlated in early development.

By 21 months, as children become proficient speakers and as the volume of their vocabulary explodes, their mouth also becomes full of personal pronouns and adjectives like "I," "Me," and "Mine" (Bates, 1990; Tomasello, 1996). Not only does the child recognize or identify himself as author of his own action (objectified self-agency), he also begins to recognize himself as proprietor of particular things. In the same way that he experiences himself as the author of what he does (the I and Me stance), by the end of the second year the child becomes forcefully explicit about what belongs to the self, *de facto* to nobody else (the Mine stance). When the child begins to claim "that is mine!," it is also to say "that is not yours!," and not just to bring attention to the object or just the forceful ostentation of a request for it (Tomasello, 1998). The first claim of possession is an assertion of power over objects in relation to others. It is an ostentatious act of incorporation whereby the mine (the object of possession) becomes Me, hence gives it solidity as suggested by Dewey.

The claim of possession emerging by 21 months does indeed give solidity to the self in relation to others. It is primarily an expression of social self-assertiveness (Rochat, 2009), being first and foremost *self-elevating* and *self-magnifying* in relation to others. There is an absolutist connotation in the first identification of the young child with objects and their forceful claims as proprietor, a typical trait of the so-called "terrible twos." In stating that it is "Mine!," children tell whoever wants to hear that it belongs to nobody else, is thus absolutely *nonalienable*. However, this first inclination changes rapidly in the context of social exchanges and reciprocation.

The young child eventually learns the central notion that objects that are possessed by the self can be *alienable*, brought into a space of exchange that is guided by principles of fairness and reciprocity. Recent research on sharing in children from various cultures and socio-economic backgrounds show that this development appears to occur universally between 3 and 5 years of age (see Rochat et al., 2009).

The notion of property from being primarily a claim of unalienability and self-edification (end of second year and in parallel to self-recognition), becomes also alienable or shareable. From this point on, children discover the social power of property in the context of exchanges (Faigenbaum, 2005). If they show an original trend for self-maximizing gains, consistent with an absolutist *unalienable* sense of property, research shows that from 36 months on children begin to develop a complex sense of equity and fairness in sharing, developing a sense of justice that tends to favor protagonists based on ethical principles (e.g., relative wealth, Rochat, 2009). During the preschool years (3- to 5-year-olds), the ability to apply rules of equity in sharing desirable goods with others emerges, overriding the strong self-maximizing propensities (i.e., self-assertiveness in relation to others) that prevail in 2-year-olds. Preschoolers develop an ethical stance in relation to possession, a notion now defined by its alienability in the context of balanced social exchanges increasingly guided by principles of reciprocity and inequality aversion, the basic ingredients of human sociality (Fehr, Bernhard, & Rockenbach, 2008; Olson & Spelke, 2008; Rochat, 2009).

Reciprocity requires a concept of self that is enduring in a moral space made of consensual values and norms, a space in which the child becomes accountable and in which reputation starts to play a central role. Self-consciousness, in particular the valued (ethical) sense of self in relation to others does develop in parallel to the early development of reciprocal exchanges (Rochat, 2009). Changes in self-concept accompany the development of reciprocal exchanges and the alienable sense of property. Reciprocal exchanges constrain children to project themselves, as well as what they perceive of others, in the context of ongoing social transactions. Exchanges based on reciprocation require that the protagonists keep track and agree on who owns what and when, at all times. Engaging in such exchanges forces children to objectify themselves not only in the here and now of perception and action, but also in past and future social situations. Indirect evidence supporting such interpretation is, for example, provided by the work of Povinelli & Simon (1998) on early self-concept development.

The careful empirical work of Povinelli and colleagues (see Povinelli, 2001 for a review) on delayed self-recognition shows that it is later than approximately 3 years of age that children begin to grasp the temporal dimension of the self. From this age on, they develop a concept of self that does not pertain only to what is experienced here and now, but also to what was experienced then: what can be seen in a mirror now, but also in a movie tomorrow or days later. From 3 years old, children begin to express the notion of a self that is enduring over time. They will recognize themselves on a prerecorded video, taken days ago, wearing a sticker on their forehead. However, they will not reach for it on their own body while watching the video of themselves. Younger children tend to do so, not differentiating past and present self, thus not yet expressing an enduring sense of who they are in time, the self projected into the past or into the future, beyond the here and now of bodily experience. Povinelli reports, for example, the commentary of a 3-year-old viewing herself on a prerecorded video with a sticker on her forehead. She says: "It's Jennifer ... it's a sticker" and then adds: "but why is she wearing my shirt?" (Povinelli, 2001, p. 81). The paradox of seeing oneself as an other is expressed by the child, who clearly identifies that what she sees on the TV relates to her, but trying, with confusion, to construe that it is not in the present.

There is a noticeable synchrony between the developmental emergence of the notion of alienable possession brought into a space of reciprocal exchanges with others, and the notion of a self that is permanent and enduring over time. Much more research is needed to document this synchrony, in particular the mechanisms of cross-fertilization and mutual determination of the *Me* and of the *Mine* starting at 2 years of age.

Conclusion: Developing Objectification of the Self and Its Belongings

We have seen that infants appear to be born with an ability to pick up perceptual information that specifies themselves as differentiated from other physical and social entities in the environment. The development of self-knowledge does not start from an initial state of confusion. Infants are born with the perceptual means to discriminate themselves from other objects and people. Early on, they express an implicit sense of themselves as embodied, differentiated, situated, and effective in the physical and social environment. This sense of self corresponds to the ecological and interpersonal selves of infants described by Neisser (1991, 1995).

These implicit kinds of selves are determined by direct perception and action, not mental reflection or conception. The early propensity of infants to engage in self-exploration when, for example, watching their own legs moving on a TV screen (Rochat, 1998) does not entail any awareness that it is their own legs on the screen. If, as some studies show, infants prefer to look at the view displaying the legs of another baby rather than an on-line view of their own (see for example, Bahrick & Watson, 1985; Schmuckler, 1995), it is because the visual perception of these legs does not correspond to the proprioceptive perception of their own legs moving. It is not because they recognize that it is another infant kicking on the television. For infants to recognize that the legs are their own legs or, on the contrary, that they are the legs of someone else, would take an additional reflective step, namely the step towards an *objectification of the self*. Such a process would entail the ability to integrate the sense of the embodied (ecological) self, and the representation of the disembodied "Me" projected on the television screen.

The question, of course, is how such an integration might come about. To conclude, I propose that an important determinant of this development might be young infants' propensity to explore their own actions and their consequences via repetition or so-called "circular reactions" (Baldwin, 1884/1925; Piaget, 1952).

By the second month, infants become inquisitive and start reciprocating with others as indexed by the emergence of smiling and eye contact (Wolff, 1987; Rochat & Striano, 1999a). They also become playful in relation to themselves. They start to spend a lot of time self-entertaining, exploring their own body by repeating visually controlled actions either on themselves or on objects. They grab their hands and feet, bringing them in the field of view for long bouts of inspection. They seize any opportunity to reproduce actions that are accompanied by interesting consequences. In addition to perceiving and acting in the context of highly organized action systems (e.g., sucking, rooting, tracking), 2-month-olds compared to newborns express behavioral novelty by engaging in the *contemplation of their own effectivity* based on a sense of the own body (i.e., proprioception) that can be linked to perceived events: the auditory event of self-activating the vocal system, the proprioceptive-visual event of moving a hand in the visual field, of kicking a mobile (Rochat & Striano, 1999b). In this new process, infants manifest much repetition of actions for the apparent sake of exploring how they feel in their execution and how they are linked to particular perceptual consequences.

This active contemplation of self-produced perceptual consequences (e.g., self-produced sounds or object motion) is probably an important factor in the progressive objectification of the self. Infants need to break away from the direct perception of the embodied self as specified by intermodal invariants and the contingency of others' behavior in order to start *representing* or conceptualizing themselves as objects of reflection. That does not mean that the implicit sense of the embodied ecological and social self vanish to be replaced by a conceptual self. Rather, the sense of the ecological and social self, bearing no traces of anything that looks like conscious or intentional processes, is complemented with a new stance on self-perception that allows for explicit representation, as evidenced by mirror self-recognition.

There is certainly an important development, yet largely unspecified, occurring from the time infants seem to show the first signs of breaking away from the direct perception of the embodied self, to explicit self-recognition. The original process that might trigger this development is the propensity of infants by 2 months of age to engage with and start paying particular attention to the result of their own playful and repetitive actions. With such engagement, they start to probe their own vitality, systematically reproducing certain effects, and discovering themselves as a dynamic system with means to achieve goals (Baldwin, 1884/1925). This process determines a new sense of self as *intentional* or planful, in parallel to the direct sense of the embodied self (ecological self) and social self they develop early on in their interaction with objects and people. By intentional (a semantically loaded term), what is meant here is a sense of self as a planning entity that can anticipate future events and relate to past ones, whether physical or social. It is a sense of self which, in contrast to the embodied ecological and interpersonal selves, is not linked to the immediacy or "here and now" aspect of direct perception and action in physical or social contexts. It is actually a sense of self that cuts across the ecological and interpersonal self, transcending them and resting on their integration as suggested by mirror self-recognition.

Finally, it is important to link the emerging self-concept to the development of possession, particularly the sense of alienable property in the context of reciprocal exchanges with others. Following the theoretical intuition of John Dewey discussed earlier, the conceptual sense of "Me" gets solidified by the developing sense of "Mine" within a normative moral space in which children have increasingly to situate themselves. The coemergence of Me and Mine in development would deserve much more research scrutiny if we want to unveil further the nature and determinants of early self-concept.

In conclusion, at the origin of an explicit sense of self, there might be the early ability to contemplate and repeat actions in order to explore their consequences, beyond the immediate, embodied sense of the self infants experience from birth in their interaction with physical objects and people. This process, I propose, contributes to an early objectification of the self which eventually develops into an explicit self-concept by the middle of the second year. Explicit self-concept dramatically expands in span by including objects of alienable possession in the following months.

Aside from this general process, questions remain as to what factors lead infants toward self-conceptualization, and what the actual content of self-concept is when it emerges by the second year of life. These questions are particularly important from a developmental perspective, when considering that the content of self-concept dramatically changes by the third year, becoming principled and moral in the context of reciprocal exchanges of alienable belongings (things incorporated as self, or "self-owned," in other words: "proper-ties").

Future directions for research would be to consider the link between emerging self-concept and the developing sense of possession, ownership, and sharing in children. Self-concept does exist primarily, if not only, in relation to others (see Rochat, 2009 for further treatment of the argument). It does not emerge in either a social or ethical vacuum. This is particularly evident as children, by the end of the second year, begin to assert who they are through their claims of possession (e.g., my toy, my initiative, my prerogative, my turn, etc.). From then on, the issue of self-concept is inseparable from social negotiation and exchanges of things owned, either physical things or psychological possessions including trust, prerogative, admiration, respect, beliefs, attention, or recognition. All become major aspects of self-concept in development. As I have tried to show, from at least 3 years of age, children become increasingly "principled" or righteous in the construal of themselves in relation to others, developing an ethical stance toward others. It would be of theoretical interest to further investigate the relation between the developing ethical stance taken by children in the preschool years and the development of self-concept. The relation between self-concept and moral development remains generally underinvestigated. In this respect, research on self-concept would benefit from borrowing procedures, experimental paradigms, and methodologies currently used in the domains of moral development, behavioral economics, and comparative and cross-cultural studies on issues such as the sense of ownership, possession and the notion of property as well as altruism, selfishness, and fairness in the sharing of personal resources (see for example such an attempt in Rochat et al., 2009).

Related Issues

Some theories emphasize the role of social frames from which infants develop a sense of self that is primarily interpersonal (Fogel, 1993; Kaye, 1982). Other theories emphasize the role of active interaction between infants and their environment, whether physical or social (Baldwin, 1884/1925; Piaget, 1952, 1954). Furthermore, some theorists suggest that infants develop first a sense of the core (intermodal) self that eventually grows into an interpersonal and conceptual self (Stern, 1985). By contrast, other theories state that the concept of self is inseparable from social relationships and the relational narratives infants create in interaction with people (Fogel, 1995).

The debate is still very much open, and it is only with more empirical data that we will make progress in approximating what counts in the early development of self-concept, namely the development of the self recognized in a mirror or objectified in action on physical objects, but also the self that is conceptualized and develops in relation to others. The question of the origins of self-concept is indeed inseparable from issues regarding the origins of physical knowledge, as well as the origins of social knowledge (Rochat, 1999), emotional development (Lewis, 1992), and theories of mind (Hala, 1997).

Further Reading

Fogel, A. (1993). *Developing through relationships: Origins of communication, self and culture.* Hemel Hempstead: Harvester Press. A theoretical view on the essentially social nature of self-knowledge, developing from the outset in relation to others.

Lewis, M. (1992). *Shame: The exposed self*. New York: The Free Press. An account of self-development in infancy and early childhood as it relates to emotional development, in particular the emergence by the second year of life of secondary (self-conscious) emotions such as embarrassment, guilt, and shame.

Rochat, P. (1995). *The self in infancy: Theories and research*. Advances in Psychology Book Series. Amsterdam: Elsevier. An edited volume assembling chapters by major infancy researchers and theorists on the issue of developing self-knowledge in the first year of life.

Rochat, P. (1999). *Early social cognition*. Hillsdale, NJ: Erlbaum. An edited volume assembling chapters on the issue of understanding others, but also indirectly on the issue of developing an understanding of the self in interaction with others during the first year of life.

Rochat, P. (2003). Five levels of self-awareness as they unfold early in life. *Consciousness and Cognition, 12*(4), 717–731. A short article outlining major developmental steps leading infants toward self-objectification and conception.

Rochat, P. (2009). *Others in mind – Social origins of self-consciousness*. New-York & Cambridge, UK: Cambridge University Press. A social constructionist view on the origins of self-consciousness considered as a unique human trait. The book deals with the irreconcilable gap between what one represents of himself and what he construes of others' evaluation and representation of the self.

References

Amsterdam, B. (1972). Mirror self-image reactions before age two. *Developmental Psycholobiology, 5*, 297–305.

Bahrick, L., Moss, L., & Fadil, C. (1996). Development of visual self-recognition in infancy. *Ecological Psychology, 8*(3), 189–208.

Bahrick, L. E., & Watson, J. S. (1985). Detection of intermodal proprioceptive-visual contingency as a potential basis of self-perception in infancy. *Developmental Psychology, 21*(6), 963–973.

Baldwin, J. M. (1884, 1925). *Mental development of the child and the race: Methods and processes*. London: Macmillan.

Bates, E. (1990). Language about me and you: Pronominal reference and the emerging concept of self. In D. Cicchetti & M. Beeghly (Eds.), *The self in transition: Infancy to childhood* (pp. 165–182). Chicago: University of Chicago Press.

Bertenthal, B. I., & Rose, J. L. (1995). Two modes of perceiving the self. In P. Rochat (Ed.), *The self in infancy: Theory and research*, (pp. 303–326). Amsterdam: Elsevier.

Butterworth, G. E. (1995). The self as an object of consciousness in infancy. In P. Rochat (Ed.), *The self in infancy: Theory and research* (pp. 35–52). Amsterdam: Elsevier.

Butterworth, G., & Hopkins, B. (1988). Hand-mouth coordination in the new-born baby. *British Journal of Developmental Psychology, 6*, 303–314.

Carpenter, E., (1975). The tribal terror of self-awareness. In P. Hikins (Ed.), *Principles of visual anthropology* (pp. 56–78). The Hague, Netherlands: Mouton.

Case, R. (1991). Stages in the development of the young child's first sense of self. *Developmental Review, 11*, 210–230.

DeCasper, A. J., & Fifer, W. P. (1980). Of human bonding: Newborns prefer their mother's voices. *Science, 208*, 1174–1176.

De Haan, M., Pascalis, O., & Johnson, M.H. (2002). Specialization of neural mechanisms underlying face recognition in human infants. *Journal of Cognitive Neuroscience, 14*(2), 199–209.

Dewey, J. (1922). *Human nature and conduct. An introduction to social psychology*. New York: Carlton House.

Faigenbaum, G. (2005). *Children's economic experience: Exchange, reciprocity, and value*. Buenos Aires: Libros EnRed.

Fehr, E., Bernhard, H., & Rockenbach, B. (2008). Egalitarianism in young children. *Nature, 454*, 1079–1084.

Field, T., Woodson, R., Greenberg, R., & Cohen (1982). Discrimination and imitation if facial expression by neonates. *Science, 218*(4568), 179–181.

Fogel, A. (1993). *Developing through relationships: Origins of communication, self and culture*. Hemel Hempstead, UK: Harvester Press.

Fogel, A. (1995). Relational narratives of the prelinguistic self. In P. Rochat (Ed.), *The self in infancy: Theory and research*, (pp. 117–140). Amsterdam: Elsevier.

Gallagher, S. (1986). Body image and body schema: A conceptual clarification. *Journal of Mind and Behavior, 7*, 541–554.

Gallagher, S., & Meltzoff, A. N., (1996). The earliest sense of self and others: Merleau-Ponty and recent developmental studies. *Philosophical Psychology, 9*(2), 213–236.

Gallup, G. G. (1982). Self-awareness and the emergence of mind in primates. *American Journal of Primatology, 2*, 237–248.

Gergely, G., & Watson, J.S. (1999). Early social-emotional development: Contingency perception and the social-biofeedback model. In P. Rochat (Ed.), *Early social cognition* (pp. 101–136). Hillsdale: Erlbaum.

Gibson, E. J. (1995). Are we automata? In P. Rochat (Ed.), *The self in infancy: Theory and research*, (pp. 3–16). North-Holland: Elsevier.

Gibson, E. J. (1988). Exploratory behavior in the development of perceiving, acting, and the acquiring of knowledge. *Annual Review of Psychology, 39*, 1–41.

Gibson, J. J. (1979). *The ecological approach to visual perception*. Boston: Houghton-Mifflin Co.

Hala, S. (Ed.). (1997). *The development of social cognition*. Hove: Psychology Press.

James, W. (1890). *The principles of psychology*. New York: Henry Holt & Co.

Jouen, F., & Gapenne, O. (1995). Interactions between the vestibular and visual systems in the neonate. In P. Rochat (Ed.), *The self in infancy: Theory and research*, (pp. 227–302). Amsterdam: Elsevier.

Kaye, K. (1982). *The mental and social life of babies*. Chicago: Chicago University Press.

Kellman, P. J., Gleitman, H., & Spelke, E. S. (1987). Object and observer motion in the perception of objects by infants. *Journal of Experimental Psychology: Human Perception and Performance, 13*, 586–593.

Lewis, M. (1992). *Shame: The exposed self*. New York: The Free Press.

Lewis, M. (1999). Social cognition and the self. In P. Rochat (Ed.), *Early Social cognition: Understanding others in the first months of life* (pp. 81–100). Mahwah, NJ: Erlbaum.

Lewis, M., & Brooks-Gunn, J. (1979). *Social cognition and the acquisition self*. New York: Plenum Press.

Mahler, M. S., Pine, F., & Bergman, A. (1975). *The psychological birth of the human infant: Symbiosis and individuation*. New York: Basic Books.

Mead, G. H. (1934). *Mind, self and society*. Chicago: University of Chicago Press.

Meltzoff, A. N., & Moore M. K. (1995). A theory of the role of imitation in the emergence of self. In P. Rochat (Ed.), *The self in infancy: Theory and research* (pp. 73–94). North-Holland: Elsevier.

Morgan, R., & Rochat, P. (1998). Two functional orientations of self-exploration in infancy. *British Journal of Developmental Psychology, 16*, 139–154.

Murray, L., & Trevarthen, C. (1985). Emotional regulation of interactions between two-month-olds and their mothers. In T.M. Field & N.A. Fox (Eds.), *Social Perception in Infants* (pp. 177–197). Norwood, NJ: Ablex.

Neisser, U. (1991). Two perceptually given aspects of the self and their development. *Developmental Review, 11*, 197–209.

Neisser, U. (1995). Criteria for an ecological self. In P. Rochat (Ed.), *The self in infancy: Theory and research* (pp. 222–231). Amsterdam: Elsevier.

Olson, K.R., & Spelke, E.S. (2008). Foundations of cooperation in young children. *Cognition, 108*, 222–231.

Piaget, J. (1952). *The origins of intelligence in children.* New York: International Universities Press.

Piaget, J. (1954). *The child's construction of reality.* New York: International Universities Press.

Povinelli, D. J. (1993). Reconstructing the evolution of mind. *American Psychologist, 48*, 493–509.

Povinelli, D. J. (2001). The self: Elevated in consciousness and extended in time. In Moore, C., & Lemmon, K. (Eds.), *The self in time: Developmental perspectives* (pp. 75–95). Mahwah, NJ: Erlbaum.

Povinelli, D. J., & Simon, B. B. (1998). Young children's reactions to briefly versus extremely delayed images of the self: Emergence of the autobiographical stance. *Developmental Psychology, 43*, 188–194.

Prechtl, H. F. R. (Ed.). (1984). *Continuity of neural functions from prenatal to postnatal life.* Oxford: Blackwell.

Priel, B., & deSchonen, S. (1986). Self-recognition: A study of a population without mirrors. *Journal of experimental child psychology, 41*(2), 237–250.

Rochat, P. (1998). Self-perception and action in infancy. *Experimental Brain Research, 123*, 102–109.

Rochat, P. (1995). Early objectification of the self. In P. Rochat (Ed.), *The self in infancy: Theory and research* (pp. 53–71). Amsterdam: Elsevier.

Rochat, P. (1997). Early development of the ecological self. In C. Dent-Read & P. Zukow-Goldring (Eds.), *Evolving explanations of development: Ecological approaches to organism environment systems* (pp. 91–122). Washington, DC: American Psychological Association.

Rochat, P. (1999). *Early social cognition.* Hillsdale, NJ: Lawrence Erlbaum.

Rochat, P. (2003). Five levels of self-awareness as they unfold early in life. *Consciousness and Cognition, 12*(4), 717–731.

Rochat, P. (2009). *Others in mind – The social origins of self-consciousness.* New York & Cambridge, UK: Cambridge University Press.

Rochat, P., Blass, E. M., & Hoffmeyer, L. B. (1988). Oropharyngeal control of hand-mouth coordination in newborn infants. *Developmental Psychology, 24*, 459–463.

Rochat, P., & Hespos, S. J. (1997). Differential rooting response by neonates: Evidence for an early sense of self. *Early Development & Parenting, 6*(2), 105–112.

Rochat, P., & Morgan, R. (1995). Spatial determinants in the perception of self-produced leg movements by 3–5 month old infants. *Developmental Psychology, 31*, 626–636.

Rochat, P., Querido, J., and Striano, T. (1999). Emerging sensitivity to protoconversation narratives by 2- to 6-month-old infants. *Developmental Psychology, 35*(4), 950–957

Rochat, P., & Striano, T. (1999a). Social cognitive development in the first year. In P. Rochat (Ed.). *Early social cognition* (pp. 3–34). Hillsdale, NJ: Erlbaum.

Rochat, P., & Striano, T. (1999b). Emerging self-exploration by 2-month-olds. *Developmental Science, 2*(2), 206–218.

Rochat, P., Dias, M. D. G., Guo, L. Broesch, T. Passos-Ferreira, C., & Winning, A. (2009). Fairness in distributive justice by 3- and 5-year-olds across 7 cultures. *Journal of Cross-Cultural Psychology, 40*(3), 416–442.

Schmuckler, M. A. (1995). Self-knowledge of body position: Integration of perceptual and action system information. In P. Rochat (Ed.), *The self in infancy: Theory and research* (pp. 221–242). Amsterdam: Elsevier.

Stern, D. (1985). *The interpersonal world of the infant.* New York: Basic Books.

Stern, D. (1999). tern, ity contoursooks.d, Elsevier Science Publishers.nd action system information. autobiographi's social experience. In P. Rochat (Ed.), *Early social cognition* (pp. 67–80). Hillsdale, NJ: Erlbaum.

Striano, T., & Rochat, P. (1999). Developmental link between dyadic and triadic social competence in infancy. *British Journal of Developmental Psychology, 17*(4), 551–562.

Striano, T., & Rochat, P. (2000). Emergence of selective social referencing. *Infancy, 1*(2), 253–264.

Toda, S., & Fogel, A. (1993). Infant response to the still-face situation at 3 and 6 months. *Developmental Psychology, 29,* 532–538.

Tomasello, M. (1995). Joint attention as social cognition. In C. Moore & P. Dunham (Eds.), *Join attention: Its origins and role in development* (pp. 103–130). Hillsdale, NJ: Erlbaum.

Tomasello, M. (1998). One child early talk about possession. In J. Newman, Ed. *The linguistics of giving* (pp. 349–373). Amsterdam: John Benjamins.

Tomasello, M., & Akhtar, N. (1995). Two-year-olds use pragmatic use to differentiate reference to objects and actions. *Cognitive Development, 10,* 201–224.

Tomasello, M., & Call, J. (1997). *Primate cognition.* New York: Oxford University Press.

Trevarthen, C. (1979). Communication and cooperation in early infancy: A description of primary intersubjectivity. In M. M. Bullowa (Ed.), *Before speech: The beginning of interpersonal communication* (pp. 321–347). New York: Cambridge University Press.

Tronick, E. Z., Als, H., Adamson, L. Wise, S., & Brazelton, T. B. (1978). The infant's response to entrapment between contradictory messages in face-to-face interaction. *Journal of the American Academy of Child Psychiatry, 17,* 1–13.

Wallon, H. (1942/1970). *De l'acte à la pensée: Essai de psychologie comparée.* Collection Champs Flammarion.

Walton, G. E., Bower, N. J. A., & Bower, T. G. R. (1992). Recognition of familiar faces by newborns. *Infant Behavior and Development, 15,* 265–269.

Wolff, P. (1987). *The development of behavioral states and the expression of emotions in early infancy.* Chicago: The University of Chicago Press.

11

The Importance of Imitation for Theories of Social-Cognitive Development

Andrew N. Meltzoff and Rebecca A. Williamson

Humans are inherently social. We live in complex societies, navigate intricate social interactions, and rapidly learn from those around us. We have a special adaptation that supports this – the ability to learn from observing others. Instead of having to rely on trial and error learning (which can be dangerous) or on independent invention (which can be slow), we profit from others' examples, including their actions, goals, intended efforts, and mistakes. Humans carefully study what others are doing in their transactions with the physical and social world and learn by observing their behavior. Anyone who has visited a foreign culture or attended a dinner party with a formal place setting has felt the need for rapid learning. In such cases we turn to others and imitate what they do. This powerful form of social learning is rare in the animal kingdom. There is a wide consensus among developmental psychologists and primatologists that humans are the most imitative creatures on the planet, imitating more prolifically than other species, including our closest living evolutionary relative, the chimpanzee.

In this chapter we will examine imitation from a developmental perspective, focusing particularly on preverbal imitation. We will show that imitation serves three important functions in infancy: (a) social-communicative, (b) cognitive, and (c) as a foundation for understanding other minds.

Imitation serves a social-communicative function, because copying the actions of others facilitates social engagement. Imitation serves a cognitive function because copying acts on objects helps infants learn how to use tools and cognitive strategies that are used by experts in the culture. Imitation is foundational for children's understanding of other minds because it provides opportunities for mapping the similarities and differences between self and other, what Meltzoff (2007a) calls the "Like-Me" aspect of imitation. A developmental pathway has been described for how infants progress from the recognition of shared acts to an understanding of shared minds (Meltzoff, 2007b), thereby jumpstarting "mentalizing" and "theory of mind."

Early Bodily Imitation and Social Interaction

There is evidence that even the earliest forms of imitation are connected to infants' social-communicative development. In 1977, Meltzoff and Moore reported that 12- to 21-day-old infants imitate simple body acts. These infants responded to an adult's tongue protrusion by sticking out their own tongues and responded to an adult's mouth opening/closing by duplicating that action themselves. Subsequent studies conducted in a hospital setting (Meltzoff & Moore, 1983, 1989) showed facial imitation in newborns as young as 42 minutes old. Imitation in early infancy has now been replicated in more than two dozen studies across a variety of cultures (for a review see Meltzoff & Moore, 1997), and there is preliminary evidence concerning the evolutionary bases of behavioral matching in other primate species (Bard, 2007; Ferrari et al., 2006; Myowa, 1996).

Importantly, human newborns' responses are specific in ways that have not yet been documented in other primates. Human infants show differential matching responses to two types of lip movements (mouth opening versus lip protrusion), two types of protrusions (lip versus tongue), and they differentially respond to straight tongue protrusions and to tongue protrusions to the side (Meltzoff & Moore, 1977, 1994, 1997). This type of specific mapping has yet to be established in nonhuman primates. The response specificity is important because it indicates that human infants are not merely showing increased activity due to the presence of a social agent or the arousing properties of a dynamic visual display. These results also show that human infants are not restricted to imitating one gesture (for example tongue protrusion and nothing else, as was previously argued by some theorists), but rather have a more general imitative capacity.

Human neonates are not only specific, they are flexible in their imitation. The imitative response can be *temporally decoupled* from the adult demonstration itself. Infant facial imitation does not depend on the dynamic display being in the perceptual field, and thus cannot be explained away as arousal or motor resonance. Young infants will reproduce a behavior after a delay period. In Meltzoff & Moore's (1977) original experiments, the infants had a pacifier in their mouths during the adult's demonstration and later produced the behavior while looking at a passive face. In more recent studies, the adult showed the gesture on one day and returned the next. The infant stared at the same adult who now was showing a passive face, and then reproduced the gesture that the adult had shown the day before. They imitated from memory (Meltzoff & Moore, 1994).

Several researchers have proposed that infant imitation serves as a way to socially engage other people (Carpenter, 2006; Meltzoff, Kuhl, Movellan, & Senjowski, 2009; Meltzoff & Moore, 1995; Nadel-Brulfert & Baudonniere, 1982; Nadel, Guérini, Pezé, & Rivet, 1999; Uzgiris, 1999). There is evidence that the earliest bodily imitation serves a social function. In research by Nagy and Molnar (1994, 2004) newborns were observed while engaging in an imitative exchange with an experimenter. Infants were shown to match the adult's behaviors over several turns and to manifest variations in their heart rate depending on their current role in the interaction, showing different patterns when initiating a behavior versus when reproducing another's act. The authors argue that both the infants' matching behaviors and their physiological reactions suggest that they were socially engaged during these imitative exchanges.

Meltzoff and Moore presented other evidence that infant imitation serves a communicative function. They found that imitation is connected to identity. Infants use imitation to identify the people around them, as a kind of social-communicative probe. For example, if one adult systematically shows tongue protrusion and a second adult systematically shows mouth opening, 6-week-old infants differentially imitate the facial gestures made by two separate people (Meltzoff & Moore, 1992). However, if the adults surreptitiously switch places – that is if the first adult leaves without the infant tracking him, and a second adult takes his place and shows the opposite gesture – the infants make an interesting error. They carefully stare at the new adult and then produce the previous person's gesture! Without clear spatiotemporal information that the old person left and a new one has entered and taken the old person's place (i.e., without monitoring the identity switch), the infant is uncertain about which person this is. The person looks different (visual appearances) but is in the place of the previous person (spatial location). Given this conflicting information about the person's identity, infants test the individual's behavior. It is as if they are "nonverbally testing" the person and checking which person it is by probing how the person responds in action. This finding supports the theory that infants use imitative interactions to tell people apart or, more technically, as a way of establishing the numerical identity of people (Meltzoff & Moore, 1992, 1995, 1998). In sum, there is evidence that imitation is a social act and it is used as a tool in social cognition starting from the earliest periods of infancy – even young infants are deploying the imitative response flexibly and with a social-communicative purpose. The use of reciprocal imitation games as a powerful force for establishing social rapport has been well documented in older infants and young children (e.g., Nadel et al., 1999; Meltzoff 1999, 2007a).

Instrumental Imitation: Learning and Memory for Object-Directed Acts

Infant imitation consists of more than the duplication of bodily acts. As early as the second half-year of life, they begin to imitate instrumental acts on objects and soon thereafter learn how to use tools through watching others. For example, by 6 months of age, infants begin to duplicate simple acts such as removing a puppet's glove and shaking it to produce a sound (e.g., Barr, Dowden, & Hayne, 1996; Collie & Hayne, 1999). Throughout the next year infants become more adept at storing multiple behaviors over increasing delays (Barr & Hayne, 2000; Meltzoff & Moore, 1998).

One study of 14-month-old infants that investigated imitation of actions on objects had three important features: (a) 14-month-olds were required to remember multiple different demonstrations, (b) novel acts were used, (c) imitation was tested after a 1-week delay (Meltzoff, 1988b). One of the acts, for example, was to bend forward from the waist and touch a panel with one's forehead, which made the panel illuminate. The infants were not allowed to touch or handle the objects; they were confined purely to watching the adult's behaviors. They were then sent home for a 1-week delay. Upon returning to the laboratory, the infants were presented with the objects to assess imitation.

The details of the control groups are interesting, because they show that the child's manipulation of the objects after the week delay was based on their memory and imitation. Let us examine more closely what these test groups witnessed in session 1, before the delay. In the imitation group, infants were shown six distinct acts on different objects. In a baseline control group, the adult met the infants in session 1 but did not present the test objects. This control assessed the spontaneous likelihood of the infants producing the target acts after the delay. In a second control group, the adult-manipulation control, the adult played with the same objects during session 1 for the same length of time as in the imitation group; but he did so using different movement patterns. For many stimuli, such as the head-touch gesture, the end-state (the panel light turning on) occurred but was activated through different means than were used in the imitation group. All three groups experienced the same delay and then returned to the laboratory where they were presented with the objects and had their behavior videotaped. The results showed significantly more target acts in the imitation group than in each of the controls, providing clear evidence for imitation of thoroughly novel acts from memory.

Subsequent research has demonstrated that 14-month-olds possess an ability to defer their imitation for a period of at least 4 months (Meltzoff, 1995b). Imitation has been used as a cognitive marker to track the development of infants' recall memory (e.g., Barr & Hayne, 2000; Bauer, Wenner, Dropik, Wewerka, & Howe, 2000; Carver & Bauer, 2001; Herbert, Gross, & Hayne, 2006; Meltzoff & Moore, 1998). Researchers have also begun to connect findings of imitation-after-delay to measures of infant neural activity (e.g., Bauer, Wiebe, Carver, Waters, & Nelson, 2003; Carver, Bauer, & Nelson, 2000). Results from both deferred imitation and event-related potential (ERP) measures on the same infants indicate that by about 10 months of age there is a correlation between the memory measured via behavioral imitation and the brain (ERP) measures (e.g., Carver et al., 2000). Factors known to improve adult recall memory have also been shown to improve infants' abilities to imitate after a delay. Reminders and additional exposures to a demonstration improve imitation of a sequence of acts after a delay (Bauer, Wiebe, Waters, & Bangston, 2001; Hayne, Barr, & Herbert, 2003), and hearing a verbal narration of a set of acts has been shown to improve 18-month-olds' later imitation of those behaviors (Hayne & Herbert, 2004).

Whether or not the adult actions have salient, causal effects also appears to influence infants' and young children's imitation of those acts. In a study by Hauf, Elsner, & Aschersleben (2004), 12- and 18-month-olds saw an adult act in different ways on an object (e.g., shake versus place it). The infants were more likely to imitate each of these behaviors when it led to an effect (the production of a sound). Young children are also better able to imitate the steps and sequence of a series of actions when the acts build upon one another to achieve an outcome, such as putting soap on a sponge before washing, so-called "enabling" versus "arbitrary" action sequences (e.g., Barr & Hayne, 1996; Bauer, 1992; Bauer & Mandler, 1989).

In summary, infants have been shown to imitate multiple acts, including novel acts, after lengthy delays. As we will see, this is a cognitive ability that infants deploy in many social situations. Human parents engage in purposeful pedagogy, often demonstrating a new skill at a time and place far removed from when the infant has an opportunity or reason to imitate. Taken as a whole, the studies on the imitation of object-related acts suggest that infants are well equipped to take advantage of these pedagogical lessons – learning and remembering the observation and deploying the skill at another time.

Imitation from Television

Infants are not limited to imitating live models. They have also been shown to imitate televised acts. In a study by Meltzoff (1988a), 14- and 24-month-olds viewed a video in which an adult demonstrated an action on an object. When given the objects to manipulate after either a brief or a 24-hour delay, the infants reproduced the target act. Even though the infants had never handled the real object before, they were able to remember and transfer what they witnessed in the televised display to govern their own motor plans in the real world with the 3-D object. Repacholi (2009) replicated and extended this finding of infant imitation from TV, finding that infants were less likely to imitate an act if the adult on TV adopted a negative as opposed to a positive or neutral expression upon completing the demonstration.

Although infants can learn from televised displays, they show lower rates of imitation compared to when they observe the behaviors of live models (e.g., Barr & Hayne, 1999; Barr, Muentener, & Garcia, 2007; Barr, Muentener, Garcia, Fujimoto, & Chávez, 2007; Hayne, Herbert, & Simcock, 2003; Klein, Hauf, & Aschersleben, 2006). Scientists are investigating the reasons for this so-called "video-deficit effect."

One possible account of the video-deficit effect may be the transformation between two-dimensional (2D) and three-dimensional (3D), real-world objects. Perhaps infants have difficulty using the 2D depiction as a guide for what to do in the real world. This was explored in a study using 15-month-old infants using a novel touch-screen technology (Zack, Barr, Gerhardstein, Dickerson, & Meltzoff, 2009). In one cross-dimension condition, the infants were first shown how to activate a toy via a television presentation and then given the chance to reenact this on a 3D version of what had been shown on the television. This is the standard test. In the novel cross-dimension condition infants were shown how to activate a toy by pushing a button on a real (3D) object and subsequently were tested using a television representation of the toy with a sensitive touch screen button. All possible combinations of information transfer were tested (3D to 3D, 2D to 2D, 2D to 3D, and 3D to 2D). The infants exhibited significantly higher levels of imitation on the within-dimension tests (3D to 3D or 2D to 2D) than on the cross-dimension tests (2D to 3D or 3D to 2D). This suggests that one reason infants show poor performance on standard televised imitation tasks is that they require infants to generalize across dimensions. It is not simply that they cannot learn acts from television, because they do well on tests involving a 2D to 2D assessment. Transferring information across dimensions presents them with a special problem.

A second likely contributor to the video-deficit effect is the lack of social interaction involved in many studies using televised displays (this is not necessarily a concomitant of television, but it is a correlate if interactive television is not used). Meltzoff et al. (2009) argued that this social interactivity is important for learning and imitation and that this too contributes to the video-deficit effect. Nielsen, Simcock, & Jenkins, (2008) used a closed-circuit system to allow an adult viewed on television to act contingently with 24-month-olds. The toddlers in this study were more likely to imitate these interactive displays than a traditional noncontingent video model.

Imitation of Peers

Peers can be important sources of information about how to manipulate objects and interact with others. Many infants spend a great deal of time interacting with other children. Families often have multiple siblings, and increasingly, infants attend day care and socialize with peers. In a recent study, preschoolers have been shown to prefer peers over adults as informants in some situations (VanderBorght & Jaswal, 2009). Studies of imitation suggest that peers' and siblings' acts are also important examples of appropriate social behavior for infants (e.g., Abramovitch & Grusec; 1978; Barr & Hayne, 2003; Hanna & Meltzoff, 1993).

In an experiment by Hanna and Meltzoff (1993) 14-month-old naïve infants observed "tutor infants" who had been previously trained to play with toys in novel ways. After observing the peer play with five objects, the naïve infants left the test room. When they later returned and were presented with the test objects in the absence of the peer, the (previously) naïve infants imitated the actions that had been demonstrated by the peer tutors. Further research extended this investigation to a day-care setting in which the tutor infant played with objects as part of a large group rather than in a one-to-one peer setting. The naïve infants were not allowed to approach or touch the toys in this setting. After a 2-day delay, a new experimenter (not the one who had accompanied the tutor) brought a bag of objects to the infants' homes and presented them to the infant as their behavior was video-recorded. Neither the parent nor the new experimenter had been present in the day-care center 2 days earlier. Correct imitation could only derive from the memory of the once naïve infant. The results showed significant imitation relative to control infants (who had not seen the model's act in the day-care center), providing evidence that infants can learn from peers and transfer the information they have learned across contexts, for example, from daycare to home. Such cross-context generalization is crucial if imitation is to serve important pedagogical functions in infant learning and development.

Recent studies using techniques borrowed from the animal literature have simulated the role that peer-to-peer tutoring and imitation can play in the transmission of behaviors across generations of learners (Flynn & Whiten, 2008; Horner, Whiten, Flynn, & de Waal, 2006). In these studies, a novel tool-use behavior was initially taught to a 3- or 5-year-old child, who then served as a tutor to a second child, and so on, through five children. Children who participated in the peer-to-peer learning chains showed striking consistency in their manipulation of the tools. Taken together with the earlier studies of infants, we can conclude that imitation is a useful means for transmitting information from one infant or child to the next over long delays both inside and outside of laboratory settings (for example in day-care centers and preschools).

Regulating Imitation: Social and Causal Information

Infants do not imitate indiscriminately, automatically, or compulsively. Studies show that infants are more likely to imitate a model that engages them socially. In an experiment by Brugger, Lariviere, Mumme, & Bushnell (2007) an adult varied the cues she gave to 15-month-olds by modifying her posture, attention, and vocalizations. For one group of children the model looked at and spoke to the child before demonstrating the target behavior. For the other group, she did not engage the children, but instead looked at a wall while speaking. The results showed that the infants were less likely to reproduce the demonstrated behaviors when the adult did not look at or speak directly to them. Similarly, Nielsen (2006) found that 18-month-olds showed more faithful imitation when an experimenter engaged them versus acting aloof.

Csibra & Gergely (2006) suggested that human demonstrations involve many cues, including eye-gaze and purposeful actions that set up an expectation of a pedagogical exchange. Such cues allow the adult to indicate to the child that instruction is being given and to isolate what is being taught. The social engagement and intentional production of a behavior may also be a cue for young children that the act is purposeful (e.g., Gergely, Bekkering, & Király, 2002) and causally relevant for completing a task (Lyons, Young, & Keil, 2007) and therefore ought to be copied rather than skipped over.

Studies have isolated important parameters that seem to control imitation. For example, Meltzoff (2007b, experiment 3) discovered that infants vary their imitation depending on whether or not they understand that a person is causally involved in producing an outcome. Infants are more likely to reenact the event if they think that a person has caused an outcome as opposed to the same event happening by itself with no human intervention. This work has been replicated and extended using more complex tests of causal reasoning (Bonawitz, Saxe, Gopnik, Meltzoff, Woodward, & Shulz, 2010). In related work examining particular stimulus conditions that maximize imitation, Slaughter and Corbett (2007) found that 12- and 18-month-old infants produced more target acts after watching a person or human hands, versus hands with mittens or mechanical pincers produce the outcome on an object (see also Meltzoff 1995a for further work on mechanical pincers). However, we also know that under some circumstances infants imitate acts shown by nonhuman agents such as puppets (Johnson, Booth, & O'Hearn, 2001). One active line of research on infant imitation is directed at discovering how animate or human the display must be in order for infants to imitate and infer intention, and what constitutes an "agent" that motivates imitation (Meltzoff, 2007b). A related line of work examines how infants integrate imitation of others with their own independent problem-solving and prior knowledge about the physical outcomes and endpoints (Huang & Charman, 2005; Want & Harris, 2002; Williamson, Meltzoff, & Markman, 2008; Williamson, Jaswal, & Meltzoff, 2010).

Young children will sometimes reproduce behaviors they see even in cases where such precision in copying the model is irrelevant or counterproductive to reaching an instrumental end (Horner & Whiten, 2005; McGuigan, Whiten, Flynn, & Horner, 2007; Nagell, Olguin, & Tomasello, 1993; Nielsen, 2006; Tennie, Call, & Tomasello, 2006; Whiten, Custance, Gomez, Teixidor, & Bard, 1996). For example, Nielsen found that 18- and 24-month-olds (though not 12-month-olds) imitated an act they observed even though it was not, strictly speaking, necessary for achieving the desired outcome. This tendency to reproduce irrelevant behaviors has been shown to persist and even increase through early childhood and is sometimes called "over-imitation" (McGuigan et al., 2007). One hypothesis is that young children are more likely to imitate an irrelevant act or over-imitate if they are unsure about what aspect of the display is causally necessary, or unsure what the adult intends to communicate by acting in the way she does. In such cases of ambiguity children might adopt the strategy of copying "everything the adult does." When children have their own ideas or prior knowledge about how to best reach the outcome, research shows they are less likely to over-imitate (e.g., Williamson et al., 2008).

Regulating Imitation: Emotional Eavesdropping and Beyond the Dyad

It is not necessary for children to be directly involved in an interaction to learn and imitate. They can learn as a bystander – as a third party who is watching the interactions of others. This is adaptive because infants can learn the ways of the culture and the likely emotional consequences of acting in specific ways simply by watching the social dynamics of others. Other people's emotional responses also play a role in regulating imitation.

In an imitation-eavesdropping procedure designed to test infants' learning from watching the emotional interchange between others, 18-month-olds seated at a table observed an interaction between two adults (Repacholi & Meltzoff 2007; Repacholi, Meltzoff, & Olsen, 2008). When one adult performed a seemingly ordinary act, such as pushing a button to make a sound, the second adult responded with an angry outburst saying, "that is so irritating!" while looking at the first adult and speaking in an angry tone of voice. The results showed that infants were less likely to imitate the act that caused the adult's anger if the previously angry adult was watching them; but, interestingly, if that adult left the room, infants were as likely to imitate as when the adult had not displayed anger. The imitation of the act was regulated by a combination of the adult's gaze and her previous emotional reactions.

In a further study, the emoter stayed in the room in all conditions. After her emotional display, the emoter adopted a passive expression and either (a) turned her back so that she was not looking at the child or (b) faced the child with a neutral expression. The infant was then given the object to manipulate. The infants in the anger-back condition displayed significantly higher levels of imitation relative to those in the anger-face group. Repacholi et al. (2008) next zeroed in on the role of adult gaze. The studies followed the same general procedure but in the critical condition the previously angry emoter either:

(a) stayed facing the child but picked up a magazine to read (so not looking at the child); or (b) stayed facing the child but closed her eyes (so not looking at the child). Children were significantly more likely to imitate the demonstrator's act when the emoter could not visually monitor their behavior than in comparison groups that were identical except that the emoter could see them. If the previously angry adult was visually monitoring their behavior, they did not tend to imitate, but as long as the adult was not able to see them (reading a magazine, eyes closed), they quickly grabbed the toy and reproduced the act.

These results are important for theory because they go beyond classical social referencing paradigms (e.g., Feinman, Roberts, Hsieh, Sawyer, & Swanson, 1992) and cannot be explained by emotional contagion. In these eavesdropping studies the child had the chance to "catch" the adult's emotion equally well in all of the conditions in which the emoter became angry. If the children simply caught the adult's angry emotion and were frozen and loathe to imitate, they would not have imitated in any of the angry conditions. That is not what happened. They were perfectly happy to imitate in the conditions where the adult had been angry and then left the room, turned her back, and even when she was facing them but was looking at a magazine or sitting with eyes closed. Children's actions were influenced by their memory of the adult's past emotions. The infants' behavior varied as a function of whether that previously angry adult could see the children's actions.

Taken together this work shows that infants regulate their behavior based on whether or not the previously angry person has *visual access* to their own actions. This contributes to a growing body of research demonstrating that infants and young children do not blindly or automatically imitate others' actions (e.g., Bekkering, Wohlschläger, & Gattis, 2000; Carpenter, Call, & Tomasello, 2005; Gleissner, Meltzoff, & Bekkering, 2000; Schulz, Hooppell, & Jenkins, 2008; Williamson & Markman, 2006; Williamson et al., 2008). Children *regulate* their imitative responses depending on a number of factors, including the emotional reactions of others and whether their acts are being monitored. This establishes that children's imitation is flexible and selective, rather than fixed, automatic, and compulsory. We have learned a great deal about the factors governing when, what, and whom children imitate; this continues as an active line of inquiry, with the aim of utilizing imitation research to address fundamental questions about early emergence of executive functions in toddlerhood.

Imitation, Goals, and Intentions

Infants do not always see successful and well-formed behavior. In the everyday world, people make mistakes. They fail to fulfill their intentions. Adults are able to identify a person's intended goal from unsuccessful behaviors; a batter does not have to hit a ball in order for an adult to recognize that intention. Even these unsuccessful attempts present opportunities for learning. Developmental research suggests that infants also have abilities to understand and utilize the behaviors of others in this sophisticated way; they read into adults' unsuccessful behaviors and reproduce intended outcomes.

Initial demonstrations of infants' abilities to understand the intentions underlying adults' acts used the "behavioral reenactment procedure." In one such study, 18-month-olds saw an adult perform an unsuccessful act (Meltzoff, 1995a, 2007b). For example, the adult pulled on both ends of a barbell-shaped object as if to pull it apart, but one of his hands slipped off the end. The adult repeated the pulling and slipping several times, but the infants never saw the actor complete the underlying goal of separating the toy. The experimental question was what they would take from the adult's demonstration. Would they copy the adult's physical actions and slip their fingers from the toy, or would they infer the intended, but never seen act by separating the pieces of the object?

When given the barbell during the test phase of the experiment, the infants demonstrated their understanding of the adult's intended goal by deliberately pulling the object apart. In fact, their rates of separating the object were comparable to those of a group of infants who saw an adult successfully complete that act and significantly above both those of a baseline group and a second control group who saw the adult manipulate the object but not demonstrate the intention or target act. These results show that toddlers are able to look beyond the surface form of the movements and reproduce what the adult intended to do.

An additional manipulation using the behavioral reenactment procedure further supports the proposal that infants' interpretation of actions is related to their understanding of underlying goals. In this experiment, 18-month-old infants saw a set of mechanical pincers manipulate the barbell-shaped object. The ends of the object were each held in a pincer, and each pincer was mounted on a pole. This contraption did not look human (or even animate), but it closely matched the spatiotemporal movements that adults used when acting on the barbell. The infants watched as the poles moved apart and a pincer slipped off of one end of the object, providing a good match for the spatiotemporal movements made by the adult in the unsuccessful demonstration condition (Meltzoff, 1995a).

In contrast to when the adult was unsuccessful, the infants who saw the inanimate device slip off the end of the barbell rarely pulled the object apart when given an opportunity to act on it. They readily picked up and handled the object, but they were no more likely to complete that target act than a baseline control group of infants who did not see a demonstration at all. The infants did not identify any overarching goal from the movements of this mechanical device. These results suggest that infants make different attributions to people than to clearly inanimate devices.

Using a much simpler type of task, younger infants have also been shown to profit from others' incomplete behaviors. In a simplified case of "act completion" where the target did not have to be mentally created (as in the foregoing work), but rather was an endpoint object in the visual field or at the end of the reach trajectory, infants who saw an adult strain to reach one of two toys are more likely to reach to and choose that specific object to play with versus the other object (Hamlin, Hallinan, & Woodward, 2008; see also Brandone & Wellman, 2009).

Toddlers can also distinguish ill-formed, accidental acts from purposeful action sequences, especially when these are accompanied by verbal markers. Carpenter, Akhtar, and Tomasello (1998) showed that 18-month-olds are more likely to imitate actions that are verbally and behaviorally marked as purposeful ("There!") versus accidental ("Woops!"). Additionally, when an adult fails to complete a behavior using specific means, infants and young children use that information to guide how they approach the task (Carpenter, Call, & Tomasello, 2002; Nielsen, 2006; Want & Harris, 2001). For example, Nielsen found that 12-month-olds were more likely to use a tool when an adult's failure without the tool suggested that the tool was necessary. Overall, this line of research suggests that infants are adept at learning from others' behaviors, even their unsuccessful acts, which they use as a basis for inferring the adults' underlying goals and intentions.

Enduring Theoretical Questions in Developmental Science

Infant imitation addresses enduring theoretical issues in developmental science and psychology more generally. We here consider five enduring issues: (a) self–other mapping and the sense that others are "Like Me," (b) the equivalence between perception and production, (c) neural mirroring systems, (d) roots of "theory of mind," and (e) the early identification and treatment of autism.

Others "like me"

There is now substantial evidence that infants are able to detect similarities between their own acts and those produced by others, what Meltzoff (2007a) calls the "Like-Me" aspects of imitation. This is demonstrated, for example, by studies in which 14-month-old infants are presented with two adults who are sitting side-by-side and acting on toys. Only one of the adults is imitating the infant's own actions, and the other is performing control actions on a matching toy (Meltzoff, 2007a). The results show that infants systematically choose to look longer and smile more at the adult who is imitating their own acts. They prefer the adult who is acting "Like Me", probably because of a feeling of kinship and rapport with others who act like they do. Reciprocal imitation provides a kind of social bond between the self and like-minded (or at least like-acting) others. It is a key foundation for the development of more sophisticated forms of social cognition, because imitation and reciprocal imitation exchanges "highlight" social agents in the world to which infants direct attention and from whom they learn.

Perception–production equivalence

Studies of infant imitation directly inform theories about perception and action coupling. In order for infants to imitate, they must at some primitive level recognize equivalence between the acts they see others do and the acts they do themselves. Meltzoff and Moore (1997) proposed the AIM (active intermodal mapping) theory to account for facial imitation. According to this idea, infants map information about human acts into a common *supramodal* framework. The representation of others' behavior is used as the model against which infants compare the state of their own body. When there is a mismatch, infants are able to create an action plan to bring the self and other into congruence. Infants are able to observe the act of another, store a representation of it, and to use this internal model to correct and refine their matching acts at a later time. Such correction of the imitative reactions has been documented in numerous studies (Meltzoff & Moore, 1997), underscoring that the imitative response involves active mapping between self and other. Of course, this does not mean that the infant's sense of self is like the adult's – it is not. It does mean, however, that the infant has a metric of equivalence between perception and production. There is a connection between self and other at the level of *shared acts* right from the earliest periods of infancy. This basic connection to other people, and the capacity to accelerate one's own learning by observing the acts of others, has cascading developmental consequences.

Neural mirroring systems and developmental social-cognitive neuroscience

A third enduring issue is the neural basis of imitation and the representation of action. This topic has garnered increased attention due to the report of "mirror neurons" in the brain of the monkey. Animal researchers using single-cell recording measures with monkeys found cells that respond both at the observation and execution of certain behaviors and dubbed them mirror neurons (e.g., Gallese, 2003; Rizzolatti, Fogassi, & Gallese, 2001). Noninvasive brain imaging techniques (fMRI, MEG) have since found evidence for shared neural circuitry for the observation and execution acts in adult humans (e.g., Chaminade, Meltzoff, & Decety, 2005; Hari & Kujala, 2009; Iacoboni, 2005; Iacoboni et al., 1999; Jackson, Meltzoff, & Decety, 2006; Meltzoff & Decety, 2003; Rizzolatti, Fadiga, Fogassi, & Gallese, 2002). To date, the origins of the neural mirroring system is not well understood in any species (Lepage &Théoret, 2007). Neuroscience studies with newborn monkeys would be valuable (equivalent to what has been carried out in human newborn imitation), but this has yet to be done.

At the present time, the behavioral evidence about human infant imitation goes beyond what can be explained by canonical mirror neurons alone. For one thing, monkeys have mirror neurons but are poor imitators, so this immediately suggests that something more is needed to account for the imitative effects in humans. Second, mirror neurons are more compatible with direct resonance than with the details reported about infant imitation. There are five pieces of empirical evidence showing that human infants go beyond direct motor resonance when imitating. Human infants imitate from *memory* often overriding what they currently see; they *actively correct* their behavior rather than immediately resonating with it; they reenact *goals* and intentions (even when the goal goes beyond simple effects of filling in the endpoint); they imitate *novel* acts where prior associations and resonances do not apply; and they *selectively imitate and regulate* their imitative actions indicating control and flexibility. Such effects go beyond a mirror neuron account taken in isolation, and imply a more complex neural system including top-down influences.

The time is ripe for work examining the neural underpinnings of infant imitation and perception–action coupling more generally. Developmental social-cognitive neuroscience work is beginning to emerge using imitation and other tasks to examine infant neural responses. The results show EEG desynchronization (mu rhythm suppression), particularly at central scalp sites, when 9- to 14-month-old infants either watch someone else perform an act or perform the act themselves (e.g., Marshall, Young, & Meltzoff, 2010;

Southgate, Johnson, Osborne, & Csibra, 2009). Such EEG approaches will be useful in examining the neural mechanisms underlying perception–production parity in infancy, and how imitation and neural mirroring systems co-develop.

Roots of "theory of mind"

A fourth enduring issue concerns the developmental origins of understanding others' minds, sometimes called "mentalizing" or "theory of mind." In order to imitate behaviors, infants have to link their own and another's body parts. This seems difficult enough, but the studies on inferring others' goals and intentions go a step further. In this case, the infant must infer the intended act without seeing the outcome. Meltzoff's (2007a, b) "Like-Me" theory proposes that infants can use self-experience as a framework for understanding others, because they recognize the *equivalence* in the acts of self and other.

The "Like-Me" theory provides a mechanism of change in early mentalizing (Meltzoff & Brooks, 2008). For example, infants develop experience with their own bodies and their own wants, goals, and intentions. When they want something, they reach for it. This first-person experience then allows infants to recognize that when another acts "Like Me" that person has the same underlying mental states that the child has when the child acts that way. Infants can act as the other does (imitation) and can also project to others who act like them what they themselves feel when acting that way. The fundamental similarity at the level of acts allows infants to realize other deeper similarities between self and other – including that others have goals, intentions, perceptions, and emotions that underlie their behaviors just like the infant does. In this view, "mentalizing" and "theory of mind" starts from more primitive beginnings – the recognition of *equivalence between the acts* of self and other, as first manifest in action imitation.

Imitation and autism

A fifth enduring issue raised by infant imitation concerns clinical psychology. Making links between self and other is crucial for smooth functioning in our social world (e.g., Beebe, Rustin, Sorter, & Knoblauch, 2003; Beebe, Sorter, Rustin, & Knoblauch, 2003). This is dramatically exemplified by the behavior of individuals with autism. This disorder is characterized by impaired abilities to interact and communicate with others. Autism has been described as a kind of "mind-blindness" (Baron-Cohen, 1995), because individuals with this disorder do not seem to understand others as mental agents. Individuals with the disorder have been shown to have deficits in a cluster of social competencies including imitation, gaze following, and understanding emotions (e.g., Dawson, Meltzoff, Osterling, & Rinaldi, 1998; Hobson & Meyer, 2005; Mundy, 2009; Mundy & Newell, 2007; Nadel, 2006; Rogers, 1999, 2006; Toth, Munson, Meltzoff, & Dawson, 2006). Advances in understanding infant imitation promise to help in two ways. First, imitation provides a sensitive preverbal measure for identifying children with this disorder at earlier ages. Second, training on imitation may provide efficacious treatment that boosts children's understanding of social cognition more generally (Rogers & Williams, 2006).

The Future: Imitation and an Interdisciplinary Science of Learning

Humans are distinguished from other species by their remarkable ability to teach and learn in social situations (Csibra & Gergely, 2006; Meltzoff et al., 2009; Tomasello, 1999). Imitation contributes to these accomplishments in several ways. For one, imitation provides a mechanism for even young infants to socially engage the people around them. Shared body movements allow infants to take turns interacting with and identifying the people around them. Second, through imitation infants can learn the specific behaviors, customs, and practices of their culture, including techniques for using simple tools. Infants learn about these things in a variety of situations, including through overt pedagogy, by overhearing exchanges and, to some extent, from observing the acts of others through cultural artifacts such as television and other media. From the viewpoint of philosophy of mind, however, perhaps the fundamental insight emerging from infant imitation concerns the growth of social cognition and intentionality. Infants' representation of other people's acts as something that *can be imitated* is a key ingredient to their coming to appreciate that they share something deeper with humans: An understanding of shared minds develops from a prior understanding of shared acts. Infant imitation is thus not only a window into infant social-cognitive development it is a mechanism by which infants learn about themselves, other people, and the relationship between the two. Through imitation infants become full-fledged, practicing members of their individual culture.

A number of disciplines are beginning to take advantage of the findings and theories regarding infant imitation. Evolutionary biologists and primatologists are using imitation to investigate the social learning abilities of other species to determine what is or is not uniquely human. Computer scientists and engineers are being inspired by infant imitation to design robots that can learn from observing the skilled actions of experts. Educators are increasingly paying closer attention to how children learn through observation, role-modeling, and informal apprenticeship. These mechanisms, which start in infancy, are highly motivating and emotionally satisfying for children as they learn a wide variety of skills and practices. Educators see the value of capitalizing on the natural power of observational and imitative learning and are beginning to make use of it in learning technologies and designed environments to motivate student learning both inside and outside school (Bell, Lewenstein, Shouse, & Feder, 2009). In summary, imitation is emerging as a topic that unites developmental science, clinical psychology, evolutionary biology, neuroscience, artificial intelligence, and education. Infant imitation is thus playing a key role in galvanizing interdisciplinary research on a "new science of learning" (Meltzoff et al., 2009) connecting brain, development, education, and technology.

Acknowledgments

The order of authorship is alphabetical; the authors shared equally in the writing of this chapter. We gratefully acknowledge financial support from grants from the National Science Foundation LIFE Center (SBE-0354453) and the National Institutes for Health

(HD-22514). The views expressed in this chapter are the authors' and do not necessarily represent those of NSF or NIH. We thank Calle Fisher and Craig Harris for assistance in preparing this chapter, and K. Moore, A. Gopnik, P. Kuhl, and the LIFE Center team for helpful discussions on the issues raised here.

References

Abramovitch, R., & Grusec, J. E. (1978). Peer imitation in a natural setting. *Child Development*, *49*, 60–65.

Bard, K. A. (2007). Neonatal imitation in chimpanzees (Pan troglodytes) tested with two paradigms. *Animal Cognition*, *10*, 233–242.

Baron-Cohen, S. (1995). *Mindblindness: An essay on autism and theory of mind*. Cambridge, MA: MIT Press.

Barr, R., Dowden, A., & Hayne, H. (1996). Developmental changes in deferred imitation by 6- to 24-month-old infants. *Infant Behavior & Development*, *19*, 159–170.

Barr, R., & Hayne, H. (1996). The effect of event structure on imitation in infancy: Practice makes perfect? *Infant Behavior & Development*, *19*, 253–257.

Barr, R., & Hayne, H. (1999). Developmental changes in imitation from television during infancy. *Child Development*, *70*, 1067–1081.

Barr, R., & Hayne, H. (2000). Age-related changes in imitation: Implications for memory development. In C. Rovee-Collier, L. P. Lipsitt, & H. Hayne (Eds.), *Progress in infancy research* (Vol. *1*, pp. 21–67). Mahwah, NJ: Erlbaum.

Barr, R., & Hayne, H. (2003). It's not what you know, it's who you know: Older siblings facilitate imitation during infancy. *International Journal of Early Years Education*, *11*, 7–21.

Barr, R., Muentener, P., & Garcia, A. (2007). Age-related changes in deferred imitation from television by 6- to 18-month-olds. *Developmental Science*, *10*, 910–921.

Barr, R., Muentener, P., Garcia, A., Fujimoto, M., & Chávez, V. (2007). The effect of repetition on imitation from television during infancy. *Developmental Psychobiology*, *49*, 196–207.

Bauer, P. J. (1992). Holding it all together: How enabling relations facilitate young children's event recall. *Cognitive Development*, *7*, 1–28.

Bauer, P. J., & Mandler, J. M. (1989). One thing follows another: Effects of temporal structure on 1- to 2-year-olds' recall of events. *Developmental Psychology*, *25*, 197–206.

Bauer, P. J., Wenner, J. A., Dropik, P. L., Wewerka, S. S., & Howe, M. L. (2000). Parameters of remembering and forgetting in the transition from infancy to early childhood. *Monographs of the Society for Research in Child Development*, *65*(4, Serial No. 263), 1–213.

Bauer, P. J., Wiebe, S. A., Carver, L. J., Waters, J. M., & Nelson, C. A. (2003). Developments in long-term explicit memory late in the first year of life: Behavioral and electrophysiological indices. *Psychological Science*, *14*, 629–635.

Bauer, P. J., Wiebe, S. A., Waters, J. M., & Bangston, S. K. (2001). Reexposure breeds recall: Effects of experience on 9-month-olds' ordered recall. *Journal of Experimental Child Psychology*, *80*, 174–200.

Beebe, B., Rustin, J., Sorter, D., & Knoblauch, S. (2003). An expanded view of intersubjectivity in infancy and its application to psychoanalysis. *Psychoanalytic Dialogues*, *13*, 805–841.

Beebe, B., Sorter, D., Rustin, J., & Knoblauch, S. (2003). A comparison of Meltzoff, Trevarthen, and Stern. *Psychoanalytic Dialogues*, *13*, 777–804.

Bekkering, H., Wohlschläger, A., & Gattis, M. (2000). Imitation of gestures in children is goal-directed. *The Quarterly Journal of Experimental Psychology*, *53A*, 153–164.

Bell, P., Lewenstein, B., Shouse, A. W., & Feder, M. A. (Eds.). (2009). *Learning science in informal environments: People, places and pursuits*. Washington, DC: National Academy Press.

Bonawitz, E. B., Saxe, R., Gopnik, A., Meltzoff, A. N., Woodward, J., & Shulz, L., (2010). Just do it? Investigating the gap between prediction and action in toddlers' causal inferences. *Cognition, 115*, 104–117.

Brandone, A. C., & Wellman, H. M. (2009). You can't always get what you want: Infants understand failed goal-directed actions. *Psychological Science, 20*, 85–91.

Brugger, A., Lariviere, L. A., Mumme, D. L., & Bushnell, E. W. (2007). Doing the right thing: Infants' selection of actions to imitate from observed event sequences. *Child Development, 78*, 806–824.

Carpenter, M. (2006). Instrumental, social, and shared goals and intentions in imitation. In S. J. Rogers & J. H. G. Williams (Eds.), *Imitation and the social mind: Autism and typical development* (pp. 48–70). New York: Guilford.

Carpenter, M., Akhtar, N., & Tomasello, M. (1998). Fourteen- through 18-month-old infants differentially imitate intentional and accidental actions. *Infant Behavior & Development, 21*, 315–330.

Carpenter, M., Call, J., & Tomasello, M. (2002). A new false belief test for 36-month-olds. *British Journal of Developmental Psychology, 20*, 393–420.

Carpenter, M., Call, J., & Tomasello, M. (2005). Twelve- and 18-month-olds copy actions in terms of goals. *Developmental Science, 8*, F13–F20.

Carver, L. J., & Bauer, P. J. (2001). The dawning of a past: The emergence of long-term explicit memory in infancy. *Journal of Experimental Psychology: General, 130*, 726–745.

Carver, L. J., Bauer, P. J., & Nelson, C. A. (2000). Associations between infant brain activity and recall memory. *Developmental Science, 3*, 234–246.

Chaminade, T., Meltzoff, A. N., & Decety, J. (2005). An fMRI study of imitation: Action representation and body schema. *Neuropsychologia, 43*, 115–127.

Collie, R., & Hayne, H. (1999). Deferred imitation by 6- and 9-month-old infants: More evidence for declarative memory. *Developmental Psychobiology, 35*, 83–90.

Csibra, G., & Gergely, G. (2006). Social learning and social cognition: The case for pedagogy. In Y. Munakata &. M. H. Johnson (Eds.), *Processes of change in brain and cognitive development: Attention and performance XXI* (pp. 249–274). New York: Oxford University Press.

Dawson, G., Meltzoff, A. N., Osterling, J., & Rinaldi, J. (1998). Neuropsychological correlates of early symptoms of autism. *Child Development, 69*, 1276–1285.

Feinman, S., Roberts, D., Hsieh, K., Sawyer, D., & Swanson, D. (1992). A critical review of social referencing in infancy. In S. Feinman (Ed.), *Social referencing and the social construction of reality in infancy* (pp. 15–54). New York: Plenum.

Ferrari, P. F., Visalberghi, E., Paukner, A., Fogassi, L., Ruggiero, A., & Suomi, S. J. (2006). Neonatal imitation in rhesus macaques. *PLoS Biology, 4*, 1501–1508.

Flynn, E., & Whiten, A. (2008). Cultural transmission of tool use in young children: A diffusion chain study. *Social Development, 17*, 699–718.

Gallese, V. (2003). The manifold nature of interpersonal relations: The quest for a common mechanism. *Philosophical Transactions of the Royal Society of London. Series B, Biological Sciences, 358*, 517–528.

Gergely, G., Bekkering, H., & Király, I. (2002). Rational imitation in preverbal infants. *Nature, 415*, 755.

Gleissner, B., Meltzoff, A. N., & Bekkering, H. (2000). Children's coding of human action: Cognitive factors influencing imitation in 3-year-olds. *Developmental Science, 3*, 405–414.

Hamlin, J. K., Hallinan, E. V., & Woodward, A. L. (2008). Do as I do: 7-month-old infants selectively reproduce others' goals. *Developmental Science, 11*, 487–494.

Hanna, E., & Meltzoff, A. N. (1993). Peer imitation by toddlers in laboratory, home, and day-care contexts: Implications for social learning and memory. *Developmental Psychology, 29,* 701–710.

Hari, R., & Kujala, M. (2009). Brain basis of human social interaction: From concepts to brain imaging. *Physiological Reviews, 89,* 453–479.

Hauf, P., Elsner, B., & Aschersleben, G. (2004). The role of action effects in infants' action control. *Psychological Research, 68,* 115–125.

Hayne, H., Barr, R., & Herbert, J. (2003). The effect of prior practice on memory reactivation and generalization. *Child Development, 74,* 1615–1627.

Hayne, H., & Herbert, J. (2004). Verbal cues facilitate memory retrieval during infancy. *Journal of Experimental Child Psychology, 89,* 127–139.

Hayne, H., Herbert, J., & Simcock, G. (2003). Imitation from television by 24- and 30-month-olds. *Developmental Science, 6,* 254–261.

Herbert, J., Gross, J., & Hayne, H. (2006). Age-related changes in deferred imitation between 6 and 9 months of age. *Infant Behavior & Development, 29,* 136–139.

Hobson, R. P., & Meyer, J. A. (2005). Foundations for self and other: A study in autism. *Developmental Science, 8,* 481–491.

Horner, V., & Whiten, A. (2005). Causal knowledge and imitation/emulation switching in chimpanzees (*Pan troglodytes*) and children (*Homo sapiens*). *Animal Cognition, 8,* 164–181.

Horner, V., Whiten, A., Flynn, E., & de Waal, F. B. M. (2006). Faithful replication of foraging techniques along cultural transmission chains by chimpanzees and children. *Proceedings of the National Academy of Sciences, 103,* 13878–13883.

Huang, C.-T., & Charman, T. (2005). Gradations of emulation learning in infants' imitation of actions on objects. *Journal of Experimental Child Psychology, 92,* 276–302.

Iacoboni, M. (2005). Neural mechanisms of imitation. *Current Opinion in Neurobiology, 15,* 632–637.

Iacoboni, M., Woods, R. P., Brass, M., Bekkering, H., Mazziotta, J. C., & Rizzolatti, G. (1999). Cortical mechanisms of human imitation. *Science, 286,* 2526–2528.

Jackson, P. L., Meltzoff, A. N., & Decety, J. (2006). Neural circuits involved in imitation and perspective-taking. *NeuroImage, 31,* 429–439.

Johnson, S. C., Booth, A., & O'Hearn, K. (2001). Inferring the goals of a nonhuman agent. *Cognitive Development, 16,* 637–656.

Klein, A. M., Hauf, P., & Aschersleben, G. (2006). The role of action effects in 12-month-olds' action control: A comparison of televised model and live model. *Infant Behavior & Development, 29,* 535–544.

Lepage, J.-F., & Théoret, H. (2007). The mirror neuron system: Grasping others' actions from birth? *Developmental Science, 10,* 513–523.

Lyons, D. E., Young, A. G., & Keil, F. C. (2007). The hidden structure of overimitation. *Proceedings of the National Academy of Sciences, 104,* 19751–19756.

Marshall, P. J., Young, T., & Meltzoff, A. N. (2010). Neural correlates of action observation and execution in 14-month-old infants: An event-related EEG desynchronization study. *Developmental Science,* in press.

McGuigan, N., Whiten, A., Flynn, E., & Horner, V. (2007). Imitation of causally opaque versus causally transparent tool use by 3- and 5-year-old children. *Cognitive Development, 22,* 353–364.

Meltzoff, A. N. (1988a). Imitation of televised models by infants. *Child Development, 59,* 1221–1229.

Meltzoff, A. N. (1988b). Infant imitation after a 1-week delay: Long-term memory for novel acts and multiple stimuli. *Developmental Psychology, 24,* 470–476.

Meltzoff, A. N. (1995a). Understanding the intentions of others: Re-enactment of intended acts by 18-month-old children. *Developmental Psychology, 31*, 838–850.

Meltzoff, A. N. (1995b). What infant memory tells us about infantile amnesia: Long-term recall and deferred imitation. *Journal of Experimental Child Psychology, 59*, 497–515.

Meltzoff, A. N. (1999). Origins of theory of mind, cognition and communication. *Journal of Communication Disorders, 32*, 251–269.

Meltzoff, A. N. (2007a). "Like me": A foundation for social cognition. *Developmental Science, 10*, 126–134.

Meltzoff, A. N. (2007b). The "Like me" framework for recognizing and becoming an intentional agent. *Acta Psychologica, 124*, 26–43.

Meltzoff, A. N., & Brooks, R. (2008). Self-experience as a mechanism for learning about others: A training study in social cognition. *Developmental Psychology, 44*, 1257–1265.

Meltzoff, A. N., & Decety, J. (2003). What imitation tells us about social cognition: A rapprochement between developmental psychology and cognitive neuroscience. *Philosophical Transactions of the Royal Society of London. Series B, Biological Sciences, 358*, 491–500.

Meltzoff, A. N., Kuhl, P. K., Movellan, J., & Sejnowski, T. J. (2009). Foundations for a new science of learning. *Science, 325*, 284–288.

Meltzoff, A. N., & Moore, M. K. (1977). Imitation of facial and manual gestures by human neonates. *Science, 198*, 75–78.

Meltzoff, A. N., & Moore, M. K. (1983). Newborn infants imitate adult facial gestures. *Child Development, 54*, 702–709.

Meltzoff, A. N., & Moore, M. K. (1989). Imitation in newborn infants: Exploring the range of gestures imitated and the underlying mechanisms. *Developmental Psychology, 25*, 954–962.

Meltzoff, A. N., & Moore, M. K. (1992). Early imitation within a functional framework: The importance of person identity, movement, and development. *Infant Behavior & Development, 15*, 479–505.

Meltzoff, A. N., & Moore, M. K. (1994). Imitation, memory, and the representation of persons. *Infant Behavior & Development, 17*, 83–99.

Meltzoff, A. N., & Moore, M. K. (1995). Infants' understanding of people and things: From body imitation to folk psychology. In J. L. Bermúdez, A. Marcel, & N. Eilan (Eds.), *The body and the self* (pp. 43–69). Cambridge, MA: MIT Press.

Meltzoff, A. N., & Moore, M. K. (1997). Explaining facial imitation: A theoretical model. *Early Development and Parenting, 6*, 179–192.

Meltzoff, A. N., & Moore, M. K. (1998). Object representation, identity, and the paradox of early permanence: Steps toward a new framework. *Infant Behavior & Development, 21*, 201–235.

Mundy, P. (2009). Lessons learned from autism: An information-processing model of joint attention and social-cognition. In D. Cicchetti & M. R. Gunnar (Eds.), *Minnesota symposia on child psychology: Vol 35. Meeting the challenge of translational research in child psychology* (pp. 59–113). Hoboken, NJ: Wiley.

Mundy, P., & Newell, L. (2007). Attention, joint attention, and social cognition. *Current Directions in Psychological Science, 16*, 269–274.

Myowa, M. (1996). Imitation of facial gestures by an infant chimpanzee. *Primates, 37*, 207–213.

Nadel, J. (2006). Does imitation matter to children with autism? In S. J. Rogers & J. H. G. Williams (Eds.), *Imitation and the social mind* (pp. 118–137). New York: Guilford Press.

Nadel, J., Guérini, C., Pezé, A., & Rivet, C. (1999). The evolving nature of imitation as a format for communication In J. Nadel & G. Butterworth (Eds.), *Imitation in infancy* (pp. 209–234). Cambridge: Cambridge University Press.

Nadel-Brulfert, J., & Baudonniere, P. M. (1982). The social function of reciprocal imitation in 2-year-old peers. *International Journal of Behavioral Development, 5,* 95–109.

Nagell, K., Olguin, R. S., & Tomasello, M. (1993). Processes of social learning in the tool use of chimpanzees (*Pan troglodytes*) and human children (*Homo sapiens*). *Journal of Comparative Psychology, 107,* 174–186.

Nagy, E., & Molnar, P. (1994). Homo imitans or homo provocans? *International Journal of Psychophysiology, 18,* 128.

Nagy, E., & Molnar, P. (2004). Homo imitans or homo provocans? Human imprinting model of neonatal imitation. *Infant Behavior & Development, 27,* 54–63.

Nielsen, M. (2006). Copying actions and copying outcomes: Social learning through the second year. *Developmental Psychology, 42,* 555–565.

Nielsen, M., Simcock, G., & Jenkins, L. (2008). The effect of social engagement on 24-month-olds' imitation from live and televised models. *Developmental Science, 11,* 722–731.

Repacholi, B. M. (2009). Linking actions and emotions: Evidence from 15- and 18-month-old infants. *British Journal of Developmental Psychology, 27,* 649–667.

Repacholi, B. M., & Meltzoff, A. N. (2007). Emotional eavesdropping: Infants selectively respond to indirect emotional signals. *Child Development, 78,* 503–521.

Repacholi, B. M., Meltzoff, A. N., & Olsen, B. (2008). Infants' understanding of the link between visual perception and emotion: "If she can't see me doing it, she won't get angry." *Developmental Psychology, 44,* 561–574.

Rizzolatti, G., Fadiga, L., Fogassi, L., & Gallese, V. (2002). From mirror neurons to imitation, facts, and speculations. In A. N. Meltzoff & W. Prinz (Eds.), *The imitative mind: Development, evolution, and brain bases* (pp. 247–266). Cambridge: Cambridge University Press.

Rizzolatti, G., Fogassi, L., & Gallese, V. (2001). Neurophysiological mechanisms underlying the understanding and imitation of action. *Nature Reviews Neuroscience, 2,* 661–670.

Rogers, S. J. (1999). An examination of the imitation deficit in autism. In J. Nadel & G. Butterworth (Eds.), *Imitation in infancy* (pp. 254–283). Cambridge: Cambridge University Press.

Rogers, S. J. (2006). Studies of imitation in early infancy: Findings and theories. In S. J. Rogers & J. H. G. Williams (Eds.), *Imitation and the social mind: Autism and typical development* (pp. 3–26). New York: Guilford Press.

Rogers, S. J., & Williams, J. H. G. (Eds.). (2006). *Imitation and the social mind: Autism and typical development.* New York: Guilford Press.

Schulz, L. E., Hooppell, C., & Jenkins, A. (2008). Judicious imitation: Children differentially imitate deterministically and probabilistically effective actions. *Child Development, 79,* 395–410.

Slaughter, V., & Corbett, D. (2007). Differential copying of human and nonhuman models at 12 and 18 months of age. *European Journal of Developmental Psychology, 4,* 31–45.

Southgate, V., Johnson, M. H., Osborne, T., & Csibra, G. (2009). Predictive motor activation during action observation in human infants. *Biology Letters, 5,* 769–772.

Tennie, C., Call, J., & Tomasello, M. (2006). Push or pull: Imitation vs. emulation in great apes and human children. *Ethology, 112,* 1159–1169.

Toth, K., Munson, J., Meltzoff, A. N., & Dawson, G. (2006). Early predictors of communication development in young children with autism spectrum disorder: Joint attention, imitation, and toy play. *Journal of Autism and Developmental Disorders, 36,* 993–1005.

Uzgiris, I. (1999). Imitation as activity: Its developmental aspect. In J. Nadel & G. Butterworth (Eds.), *Imitation in infancy* (pp. 186–206). Cambridge: Cambridge University Press.

VanderBorght, M., & Jaswal, V. K. (2009). Who knows best? Preschoolers sometimes prefer child informants over adult informants. *Infant and Child Development, 18,* 61–71.

Want, S. C., & Harris, P. L. (2001). Learning from other people's mistakes: Causal understanding in learning to use a tool. *Child Development*, *72*, 431–443.

Want, S. C., & Harris, P. L. (2002). How do children ape? Applying concepts from the study of non-human primates to the developmental study of "imitation" in children. *Developmental Science*, *5*, 1–13.

Whiten, A., Custance, D. M., Gomez, J.-C., Teixidor, P., & Bard, K. A. (1996). Imitative learning of artificial fruit processing in children (*Homo sapiens*) and chimpanzees (*Pan troglodytes*). *Journal of Comparative Psychology*, *110*, 3–14.

Williamson, R. A., Jaswal, V. K., & Meltzoff, A. N. (2010). Learning the rules: Observation and imitation of a sorting strategy by 36-month-old children. *Developmental Psychology*, *46*, 57–65.

Williamson, R. A., & Markman, E. M. (2006). Precision of imitation as a function of preschoolers' understanding of the goal of the demonstration. *Developmental Psychology*, *42*, 723–731.

Williamson, R. A., Meltzoff, A. N., & Markman, E. M. (2008). Prior experiences and perceived efficacy influence 3-year-olds' imitation. *Developmental Psychology*, *44*, 275–285.

Zack, E., Barr, R., Gerhardstein, P., Dickerson, K., & Meltzoff, A. N. (2009). Infant imitation from television using novel touch screen technology. *British Journal of Developmental Psychology*, *27*, 13–26.

12

Engaging Minds in the First Year: The Developing Awareness of Attention and Intention

Vasudevi Reddy

Ten years ago in the first edition of this handbook I began this chapter with a statement that, while the field of developmental psychology had shifted in the past two decades to recognize the awareness of people as well as things in children, it had not yet extended this recognition to infancy. The barrier to this recognition, I argued, was a conception of mind as something that lies "behind" behavior and that needs to be inferred rather than perceived. Such a definition of mind prohibits its use with reference to prereflective and preinferential infants. This conception of mind invokes a "mind–behavior" dualism which underpins, paradoxically, both behaviorism and cognitivism (Coulter, 1979; Costall & Leudar, 2009). In fact, it comfortably posits a behaviorist stage as a developmental precursor to a cognitivist one (see Reddy, 2008a and Reddy & Morris, 2004 for discussions). Any theories which posit the need for a theoretical route (such as a theory of mind) for awareness of various aspects of mentality often explicitly exemplify this sequence of first merely perceiving behavioral movements and later inferring mind (Perner, 1991).

The empirical picture today is a very different one from that of 10 years ago. Reports of infant reactions to others' gaze and others' goal-directed actions drip from every relevant journal and reach into the earliest points in the first year. Arguments about the age of emergence of infants' awareness of dyadic engagements have started to shift from 3 months to birth and about the age of emergence of triadic engagements from 9 months to 3 months. However, the discovery of these startlingly early phenomena has not yet changed our discussions about the recognition of mind in infancy. In general, mind is still firmly categorized as opaque to perception and frequently identified with (and sometimes confounded with) inferential capacities. Discussions about grades of "mind-reading," evident 10 years ago in the nonhuman primate literature (e.g., Whiten, 1994), are now more common in the infant literature. The mind–behavior distinction has become a more elaborated one, for instance, differentiating between the recognition of animacy, of goal-directedness, and of fully-fledged intentions without abandoning the assumptions of the internality and invisibility of mind at all (Tomasello, Carpenter, Call, Behne, & Moll, 2005). For some theorists, unobservability is actually an explicit definitional feature of anything that is to be classified as mental (Penn & Povinelli, 2007). Perhaps the situation today, with its contrast between empirical dynamism and meta-theoretical stagnation, illustrates the wisdom of Warnock's dictum that metaphysical systems (such as the assumptions about the hiddenness of mind) are citadels never taken by storm but quietly discovered one day to be no longer inhabited (Warnock, 1969, cited by Costall, Leudar, & Reddy, 2006).

Does It Matter If We Have a Disembodied and Disembedded Conception of Mind?

An internalist conception of mind leads not only to an assumed disembodiment, that is, to mind as separate from the body and what it does, but also leads to an assumed disembeddedness from relations with the world, most significantly from relations with other minds. But does it matter? It could be argued that whether we call something mind or not is merely a matter of labels, and cannot fundamentally affect the empirical facts that our science uncovers. For instance, empirical studies from various laboratories continue to uncover earlier and earlier demonstrations of infant awareness of others' perceptions, intentions, and emotions, despite general beliefs about the impossibility of these abilities in infancy. Science does stride ahead despite its theories. However, theories – and especially meta-theories – do matter. They affect not only our methodologies but also our construal of the evidence we gather. Our conceptions of mind do influence our appraisal of the phenomena we observe, and therefore also influence our responses – as parents and as scientists.

As parents, for instance, if we adopt "behaviorist" beliefs, our emotional responses to infants' reactions and initiatives are likely to come under strong pressure for suppression. If we believe that our mentality is a largely closed book for the very young infant, it is unnecessary for us to seek to engage psychologically with the infant. Paradoxically, this is a strong argument for the power of a "theory of mind" to influence (but not completely determine) our actions in relation to minds! It has not been long since parents were advised by the medical profession about the perceptual and emotional inadequacies of their newborns – for instance to justify invasive medical procedures without anesthesia or to justify the "rational" abandonment of handicapped infants.

As scientists too, our theories constrain us – although fortunately never completely. On the one hand, we can be caught in definitional traps which influence our evaluation of the evidence. For instance, if we define mind as invisible and therefore in need of inference, no matter how sensitive or complex the infant's discrimination of our gaze and goal-directed behavior, we cannot but see them in just these terms – as sensitive and clever behavioral discriminations – rather than as involving any kind of mental or psychological awareness. It is ultimately impossible (given the assumptions of this theory, which also rules out a concordance between behavior and mind) to test whether these discriminations involve mental or behavioral awareness: both explanations must remain equally tenable and require developments in other domains to decide between them (for a more detailed discussion of this issue see Reddy, 2005).

On the other hand, and more seriously, our meta-theories about mind affect our methodology: internalist conceptions of mind specifically encourage us to adopt either first-person methods (such as having and exploring self-experience) or third-person methods (such as experimentation and detached observation), and discourage us from considering second-person methods (such as engagement and participatory awareness). Adopting methods in which the "knower" is a bystander rather than a participant already skews the findings of the research we undertake and seriously impedes scientific progress[1] (see Markova, 1982 for a discussion of the contrasting Hegelian argument about the fundamental relatedness of the knower and the known). If mind is conceptualized as an internal entity, it is by definition conceived of as a property of individuals, disembedded from other individuals, and visible from the outside in the form of behavioral movements. Mind, from a bystander theory, through inferences made from behavior, can be studied from a distance. It can be observed, looked at, and analyzed "in the head." It does not need engagement to reach it or to understand it. This, I will show in the course of this chapter, is a problem for our understanding of how infants understand our attention and our intentions. I will argue that first- and third-person approaches to infant mind knowledge cannot lead us to an adequate understanding: we need to build the second-person directly into both our theories and our methods. It is *only* within second-person engagement (principally with other minds) that infants can develop as minds, and come to understand others; and it is only by exploring minds in engagement that we can understand infant capacities. This means, of course, that in scientific studies of infant social cognition, we need to have an equally engaged scientific partner in order to get good data.

In this chapter I will show that engagement with young infants is crucial, both for their understanding of our minds, and for our understanding of their understanding. The empirical evidence I report is organized on the basis of the expanding scope of engagements – starting with infant–person engagements, moving to infant–action/body–person engagements and then to infant–world–person engagements. I will focus on two key aspects of psychological engagement: attention and intention. I choose these because most theorists in this area would agree that they are the most basic psychological phenomena demanding understanding in early infancy. One could argue that affect is a phenomenon that is even more basic. But precisely because affect is so central to attention and intention that any separate consideration of it would lead to a spurious separation, I focus here only on these two "domains." The separation between these domains is ultimately a problematic one. Although some have suggested a distinct modularity in the origins of both domains (e.g., Baron-Cohen, 1995, 1997), most theorists today would argue against this. Tomasello, in fact suggests that attention can be thought of as intentional perception (e.g., Tomasello et al., 2005). The difficulty evident later in this chapter, in trying to separate the categories of "directing attention towards the self" from "directing intentions towards the self" is evidence of this point and of their phenomenological integration. It is more than likely that not only is the empirical distinction between attention and intention muddied and constantly overlapping, but that the conceptual distinction between the two is a mere habit of psychological thought – a temporary theoretical contrivance which will eventually disappear.

What is Attention?

What does an embodied, noninternalist, and nondualist conception of attention look like? Maurice Merleau-Ponty's approach to attention (and indeed to intention too) is refreshingly embodied and firmly embedded in a real (rather than imagined) world. He takes serious issue with the standard Cartesian approach in which attention – or in this case, seeing – is conceived of as an activity that happens *inside* someone's head. It is not, he argues a private, hidden phenomenon, but one that *acts* in a shared perceivable world.

> I discover vision, not as a "thinking about seeing," to use Descartes" expression, but as a gaze at grips with a visible world, and that is why for me there can be another's gaze. (Merleau-Ponty, 1961, p. 410)

Understanding attention happens not by thinking about it, but by seeing "seeing" engage with, or come to grips with, a world of things that can be seen. Merleau-Ponty's depiction of the nature of attention (as gaze which moves around and grips the world) resonates closely with that of one school of modern-day attention theorists who argue that attention itself is fundamentally object-based[2] (Scholl, 2001) and not a "spotlight" moving about in empty space (Posner & Cohen, 1984).[3]

Issues in the study of attention awareness

1 Conceiving of attention as a "spotlight" (Baldwin & Moses, 2001) *versus* as object-based (Scholl, 2001)
2 Conceiving of attention as perceivable (Gibson & Pick, 1963; Reddy, 2003, 2008a) *versus* as something that needs inference (Bates, Camaioni, & Volterra, 1976; Tomasello, 1999; Tomasello et al., 2005)
3 Theorizing that attention is discovered by infants with the onset of "joint attention" (i.e., with triadic attentional engagements between infant, other person, and an external object, Bates et al., 1976; Tomasello, 1999, Tomasello et al., 2005) *versus* that attention is already known as attention within mutual attention (i.e., dyadic attentional engagements between infant and other person, Adamson & Bakeman, 1991; Reddy, 2003, 2005, 2008a; Trevarthen, 1980)
4 Favoring top-down explanations of the developing awareness of attention (e.g., explanations based on socio-cognitive revolutions, Tomasello, 1999) or on domain-general cognitive changes *versus* bottom-up and gradualist explanations such as conditioning

(Corkum & Moore, 1994, 1998), social engagement and increasing complexity (Adamson & Bakeman, 1991; Amano, Kezuka, & Yamamoto, 2004; Reddy, 2003, 2008a)

A "spotlight" view of attention assumes a degree of disembeddedness of attention from the world of things to attend to. It also allows the possibility of disembodiment in two ways: in terms of a disconnection between the spotlight and whatever it is inside the organism that moves the spotlight, and in terms of a disconnection between the spotlight and the things it alights on. From an object-based approach, it is objects that are seen as grabbing the attention and actions of organisms. There is considerable evidence in the literature on adult visual attention that in fact people do not attend to space – they attend to specific *things* in space (Neisser & Becklen, 1975; Simons & Chabris, 1999) and they are faster at organizing their percepts on the basis of object identity than spatial identity (Duncan, 1984; Egly, Driver, & Rafal, 1994). Attention, by these accounts, is an engagement with things, an activity, better conceived of as a verb: attending, than as a noun: attention. By the same token, if we accept that attending is fundamentally and intimately related to object-hood (Scholl, 2001), so we may argue that the awareness of attending is fundamentally and intimately bound up with the awareness of its objects (Reddy, 2003, 2008a). In other words, by an object-based account we can perceive others' attentional relations with objects and therefore we can also perceive how infants perceive (and relate attentionally to) these attentional relations.

Adopting an object-based account I argue that infant awareness of attention is a perception of others attending to things, especially things that are potentially meaningful to the infants themselves. The first such perception of attending is to the self. Adapting Merleau-Ponty's image, I argue that it is the other's gaze at grips with the *self* that makes gaze first (and properly) meaningful to infants. Attending exists for infants because it is first *felt* in direct emotional response to another's attention to oneself. This is a "second-person" view of attending which suggests that experiencing attention to the self is quite different from "observing" another person attend to the world (a third-person view of attending) and from attending to something else oneself (a first-person experience of attending).

Relating to others attending to oneself

Ten years ago I was struggling to find evidence to support the argument that the awareness of gaze to self is present by 2 months of age. Today evidence is available to support this claim even for neonates. In a dramatic series of studies Teresa Farroni and colleagues (Farroni, Csibra, Simion, & Johnson, 2002) have found that newborns (up to 5 days of age, with a mean age of 72 hours) presented with pairs of photographs of faces, look longer at those with direct gaze than at those with averted gaze, a difference that was shown in 15 of the 17 infants studied. All 17 infants also oriented more frequently to the face with direct gaze than to the face with averted gaze. What does this neonatal preference for faces which look at the self mean? Given the impoverished nature of any engagement with these static images of gaze to the self, it is both impressive that neonates nonetheless prefer it, and potentially puzzling that this should be the case.

In a successful replication, Farroni, Menon, and Johnson (2006) found, further, that this preference for direct gaze in newborns only holds for faces presented upright. They discuss three possible contenders for exploring early eye contact preference: (a) the Baron-Cohen (1995) theory of an innate Eye Direction Detector where gaze "pops out" as salient regardless of context and experience; (b) the Vecera and Johnson (1995) view that eye contact becomes meaningful with facial context and perceptual experience – thus that it is the face that makes the eyes mean something; and (c) the Johnson and Morton (1991) theory of two mechanisms for face perception – an early subcortical one which is highly context dependent (called ConSpec) and a later cortical mechanism (called ConLern). Farroni and colleagues favor the last explanation on the grounds that experience *per se* may not be necessary for detecting gaze to self in newborns, but that context appears to be crucial.

Do newborns prefer direct gaze *before* any engagement with people looking at them? There is some indirect support for the view that detecting gaze to self in primates may be experience-independent: monkeys reared for up to 6 to 24 months without exposure to faces nonetheless prefer faces (human or monkey) to nonfaces (Sugita, 2008). However, in the above-mentioned studies with human neonates, the preference for direct gaze was found in a group whose mean age was 72 hours (Farroni et al., 2002). Given the intensity of newborns' interest in the face (Fantz, 1965, Goren, Sarty, & Wu, 1975; Johnson & Morton, 1991; Johnson, Dziurawiec, Ellis, & Morton, 1991), and their rapid learning abilities, a considerable amount of engagement with other people's gaze is likely to have already occurred by 72 hours of age. The idea that it is only the high-contrast elements of the eyes in direct gaze (supposedly less so in averted gaze) which lead to the early preference for direct gaze, rather than experience of engagement with direct gaze (Farroni et al., 2006) is yet to be proven.

Evidence of orientation discrimination at 6 weeks has led to the suggestion that some form of orientationally tuned detectors are present even at birth (Atkinson, Hood, Wattam-Bell, & Anker, 1988). Several studies have shown that 3-month-olds can detect head orientation, responding with less gaze and smiling to adults with averted heads and to shut eyes (Caron, Caron, Mustelin, & Roberts, 1992). More naturalistically, Wolff (1987) showed that making and breaking eye contact affected infants emotionally even from 8 weeks of age. Three-month-olds smile less when adults look away from them, with a 20° deflection of the eyes (Muir & Hains, 1999), or even a 5° horizontal deflection (i.e., to the ears rather than the eyes), but not to a 5° vertical deflection (i.e., to the forehead or chin, Symons, Hains, & Muir, 1998).

Direct gaze leads to enhanced neural activity in 4-month-olds. In an ERP study Farroni, Johnson, Brockbank, and Simion (2002) found higher amplitude of activity in a component (N170) known to be sensitive to faces in adults, when 4-month-old infants were shown photos with direct gaze versus photos with averted gaze. This difference was present in 12 of the 15 infants in their study. However, similar to their finding about preference for direct gaze in newborns, the increased neural processing of direct gaze in 4-month-olds only occurs for upright faces (Grossman, Johnson, Farroni, & Csibra 2007). In a more detailed exploration of the neural processing of faces with direct and averted gaze, this study also showed that 4-month-olds not only responded with increased gamma activity to direct gaze[4] (in upright faces only) but also found such activity in similar cortical regions to that found in adults. Interestingly, direct gaze also seems to lead to enhanced processing of other stimuli at 4 months – such as of emotional expressions (Striano, Kopp, Grossman, & Reid, 2006) of objects (Parise, Palumbo, Handl, & Frederici, 2008; Hoehl, Reid, Mooney, & Striano, 2008) of language (Parise et al., 2008) and the enhanced likelihood of gaze following (Farroni, Pividori, Simion, Massaccesi, & Johnson, 2004). However, the importance of methodological variations between studies (e.g., using photos, vs. videos vs. real persons) leaves many questions as yet unanswered. In adults at least, the significant neural effects of direct gaze appear to be pronounced when facing real persons, but not when looking at photographs (Hietanen, Leppanen, Peltola, Linna-aho, & Ruuhiala, 2008).

Adult attention does not merely act as a cue to the infant to interact, but allows subtle engagement and the organized play of many "prespeech" behaviors in addition to gaze and smiling (Trevarthen, 1977), and leads to complex affective responses. Reddy (2000) described shy or coy smiles (consisting of smiling with gaze and head aversion and sometimes curving arm movements in front of the face) in 2- and 3-month-olds in response to attentional contact with adults, and especially following the renewed onset of mutual attention. There is anecdotal evidence of even 2-month-olds using unemotional head and gaze aversion to avoid mutual gaze with adults when the adult repeatedly tries to gain eye contact, and of negative responses to mutual gaze when the infant cannot disengage, perhaps for reasons of neurological immaturity (Brazelton, 1986). For infants as for adults, the attention of others is arousing and inducing of multiple emotional reactions (i.e., positive, negative, neutral, and ambivalent).

Evidence of infant responses to attention comes also from studies which create inappropriate attention, showing that by 2 months of age infants are sensitive not just to the presence of attention but also to the quality of attentive behavior. When adults change from interactive attention to still-faced attention even 6-week-olds become distressed (Cohn & Tronick, 1989; Murray, 1980), showing either a sensitivity to the abnormal quality of attention in the still face condition or to the change from a dynamic to a static display. Some aspects of the still face effect have recently been shown, startlingly, even in newborns. Following a period of face to face contact, when the adult experimenter held a still face, neonates of between 4 and 96 hours showed decreased eye contact, increased negative affect (actual distress in some cases), and more sleepiness (Nagy, 2008).

Murray and Trevarthen's ground-breaking study in 1985 showed that even watching video-replays of their mothers in which the mothers were expressing positive and interactive behaviors led to 2-month-old infants becoming perturbed, alternating between attempts to reengage interactive attention and gaze aversion and frowning. This finding was replicated with 9-week-olds by Nadel and Tremblay-Leveau (1999) who also showed that during a second live condition (to control for fatigue effects) infants showed a clear recovery with a significant increase in gaze to the mother, as if in scrutiny. This is strong evidence for concluding that 2-month-olds not only detect attention and inattention, but detect and respond appropriately to the appropriateness of the attention they receive. It could be argued that this pattern might reveal merely a preference for temporal contingencies rather than any awareness of attention (Gergely & Watson, 1996, 1999; Gergely, 2002). However, findings that responses to such perturbations of communication differ depending on the prior emotional relations between the mother and the infant, in particular the mother's affective mirroring or attunement (Markova & Legerstee, 2006), suggest that the contingent responsiveness sought by the infant is more than just a temporal pattern – its meaning is already "psychological."

Infants of 2 and 3 months are clearly capable of responding with appropriate affect and reciprocity when they are already the targets of others' attention. However, can infants *seek* such attention? The studies using still-face or video-replay disruptions in the adult's communicative behavior also show that, when deprived of adult responsiveness, even 6-week-old infants attempt a series of other-directed acts including vocalizations and arm movements with gaze to the other's face. These have been interpreted as attempts to regain adult attention to the self (Cohn & Tronick, 1989; Murray, 1980) and are at the very least, attempts to reengage interaction. Further, in the presence of an inadequately responsive adult, infants can increase the intensity of their normal vocal and facial expressions (Trevarthen, 1990; Reddy, Hay, Murray, & Trevarthen, 1997). There is some evidence that after about 3 or 4 months of age infants take on a more active initiating role in interaction, with different kinds of shrill, "calling" vocalizations and initiating of interactions when adults are absent or naturally inattentive (Kopp, 1982, 2002; Reddy et al., 1997). This could imply a growing confidence in adult responsiveness in the context of dyadic interactions, as well as a developing ability to engage in varied vocalizations and facial expressions. Intriguing studies from Fivaz-Depeursinge and colleagues show that triangular bids for attention, for example, addressing both parents by alternating gaze and communication from one to the other, are present even in 3- and 4-month-olds (Fivaz-Depeursinge, Favez, Lavanchy, de Noni, & Frascarolo, 2005; Fivaz-Depeursinge & Corboz-Warnery, 1999). However, as they grouped both responsive and initiated actions as "triangular bids" it is difficult to draw conclusions about the infants' attempts to direct attention to the self. To date, we lack studies showing clear evidence of such abilities until the second half of the first year.

What do emotional reactions to, and attempts to reengage mutual attention indicate? Traditionally, evidence of triadic attention has been seen as necessary to conclude that infants not only feel something for attention but know what that attention is *about*. However, several studies suggest that attention to self has already come to mean, within the first few months, something powerfully relevant to the outside world.

Relating to others attending to actions and body parts

We know very little as yet about infant awareness of others' attention to actions and body parts. It is evident that such awareness must be significant. The middle of the first year is the "period of games" (Stern, 1985; Trevarthen & Hubley, 1978) where there is a huge amount of attention directed to hands and actions, both the adults' in their demonstrations of games, and to the infants' in their increasing participation in these games. An intriguing study looking at micro-shifts in infant gaze during engagements at 4 months suggests an explanation for just how infants develop from the awareness of others' attention to self towards the awareness of others' attention to other things. They found that infants started to look at mothers' hands primarily when the mother's gaze was turned away from the infant's face. Thus, the temporary withdrawal of mutual gaze within participation might start to cue the infant at 4 months to look at other salient intentional actions – such as the mother's hands – thus gradually expanding the infant's awareness of other aspects of maternal attentionality (Amano et al., 2004).

Within naturalistic interactions infants from around 7 months of age engage in attention-seeking behaviors that go beyond simply trying to regain the other's attention to the self in simple face-to-face communication. Infants now seek to gain it for specific acts performed by the self. They start to do things for effect, which at the simplest level involves a breaking of the flow of the interaction in some way, and at more complex levels involves a repetition of acts which have previously received adult attention (Bates et al., 1976).

Infants from this age produce two different kinds of attention-directing acts – "showing-off" and "clowning" (Bates et al., 1976; Reddy, 1991; Reddy, 2001; Trevarthen & Hubley, 1978), showing a developing awareness of being an actor (Reddy et al., 1997). Both involve the repetition of acts for re-eliciting responses from the other; showing-off can involve "clever" acts for praise or "silly" acts for attention and clowning involves exaggerated or rule-violating acts for laughter. The commonest forms of clowning at 8 months involve repetitive movements of particular parts of the body, such as shaking the head vigorously, making odd facial expressions, odd movements of the body, putting odd things such as pajamas on the head, and blowing raspberries. Showing-off (through the performance of silly acts) and clowning are commonly reported by parents at 8 months of age. While the prevalence of silly acts for attention is not reported to change with age (some children do it and some not) the prevalence of clowning and of showing-off through the repetition of clever acts (such as clapping or waving or saying a word) does increase with age: it is not until after 11 months of age that 50% of children engage in clever showing-off. The broad finding of deficits in such actions in preschool children with autism lends further support to the interpretation that these acts are significant milestones in the developing awareness of attention (Reddy, Williams, & Vaughan, 2002). Such acts show not just an awareness of simple attentiveness, but an awareness that others can and do attend to specific aspects of the self, and to actions performed by the self.

Relating to others attending to the external world

Scaife & Bruner (1975) first suggested that infants of 2 months could follow others' gaze to an external target and that this was dramatic evidence of infant ability to understand the mental significance of others' gaze. Following several decades of controversy about when this ability might actually emerge (see Moore, 1999) and several contending explanations of how it emerges (e.g., Moore, 1999; Butterworth, 1995) the story today seems to converge more or less in support of the Scaife and Bruner findings. Explanations of the process of emergence of the ability to follow others' gaze seem to occupy the full theoretical range between internal cognitive revolutions (Tomasello, 1999), ecological "mechanisms" (Butterworth, 1995; Butterworth & Jarrett, 1991), behaviorist modeling and reinforcement (Moore, 1999) and a socially led expansion of dyadic awareness into triadic attentionality (Bakeman & Adamson, 1984; Trevarthen, 1980).

Evidence of gaze-following abilities today has shifted dramatically downwards in infant age from the safe 10 months suggested by Corkum and Moore (1994, 1998). Several studies show evidence of gaze following at around 9 months (Senju, Csibra, & Johnson, 2008; Tomasello et al., 2005), at 7 months (Flom & Pick, 2005), at 6 months (Morales, Mundy, & Rojas, 1997; Morisette, Ricard, & Gouin-Decarie, 1995), at 6 months (Luo & Johnson, 2009[5]), at 5 months (Striano & Bertin, 2005; Gredeback, Theuring, Hauf, & Kenward, 2008), at 3 months (D'Entremont, Hains, & Muir, 1997;[6] Striano, Stahl, Cleveland, & Hoehl, 2007) and at 10 weeks (Willen, Hood, & Driver, 1997). This last study manipulated eye direction independent of head turning and showed that infants as young as 10 weeks could process changes in gaze alone. When the pupils of the eyes in an animated face shifted to the periphery of the field and were followed by a target at that side, infants turned to look at the target significantly more often than if the peripheral target were not preceded by shifting gaze. While it is not yet clear whether the shifting of any stimulus might have the same effect on infant gaze, it is evident that even before 3 months infants can be sensitive to shifts in gaze direction. This sensitivity, however, appears evident only when the shift is preceded by a period of mutual gaze (Farroni, Mansfield, Lai, & Johnson, 2003). Most strikingly, Farroni and colleagues have shown that even in newborns (of between 2 and 5 days) gaze can be an effective cue for directing attention. They showed not only that newborns were able to differentiate direct from averted gaze in schematic faces as well as photographs, but that they were faster to make saccades to peripheral targets if they were cued by the visible pupil motion (only visible in direct gaze) of the eyes (Farroni et al., 2004).

The relation between gaze following and the presence of objects in the environment is evident in a number of different ways, showing also the close link between attention and intention: first, infants turn their heads to look where adults look and tend to stop at the nearest likely object, even if inaccurate (Butterworth, 1995). Second, at 9 months, infants will not only follow adult gaze to targets, but look longer at adult faces if the gaze shift is congruent with the presence of a target to look at (Senju et al., 2008). Intriguingly, this effect of congruence between gaze and object was present in this study only if there was a preceding period of eye contact. Third, seeing other people's gaze to things in the world seems to change the way adults perceive the world (Becchio, Bertone, & Castiello, 2008). Another person's gaze can lead to objects developing the properties of the looker's perception of it (novelty, familiarity, graspability, emotional valence), transferring to the objects the intentionality of the person looking at it in a form of "intentional imposition" (Becchio et al., 2008). This appears to be the case not only in adults (Bayliss, Frischen, Fenske, & Tipper, 2007) but also in very young infants, at least from around 4 months of age. Parise and colleagues showed infants photographs of faces with direct or averted gaze coupled with forward or backward spoken words. By 4 or 5 months of age, when facing direct gaze, neurologically infants reacted quicker (in the Nc component on frontal-central EEG channels) to normal words. When presented with normal words, infants reacted earlier to averted than direct gaze. In other words, infants at this age were perceiving words in conjunction with gaze; backward-spoken words appear to be per-ceived as novel or strange only when accompanied by direct gaze, and forward-spoken words appear to be perceived as novel or strange when accompanied by averted rather than direct gaze (Parise et al., 2008). In other studies Hoehl, Reid, Mooney, and Striano

(2008) have found, also at around 4 months of age, enhanced neural processing of objects when those objects were being looked at by others. These studies are striking not only for the remarkably early age of this linkage between others' gaze and objects, but for its early relevance to the learning of language (Baldwin, 1995).

There are a variety of ways in which infants take a more active role in triadic engagements involving not just their own acts but also external targets. They begin to develop their own "primitive marking system for singling out the noteworthy" (Bruner, 1983, p. 77) which includes vocalizations, gestures, and even making contact with an object a potential partner is manipulating (Adamson & Bakeman, 1991). And even 9-month-old infants can use communicative signals that make reference to the toy and to the adult when the adult suddenly misses a turn in a game (Ross & Lollis, 1987). Bates (Bates et al., 1976) found that the first signs of the "protodeclarative" (early, nonverbal forms of telling someone something) involved the directing of attention to an external target and were seen in giving/showing an object – at around 10 months of age. Research in this area has focused primarily on protodeclarative pointing, which emerges on average between 12 and 14 months of age (Franco & Butterworth, 1998; Perucchini & Camaioni, 1993).

There is an old debate about the ontogeny of pointing with the Vygotskian view suggesting that pointing emerges from the parents' attribution of intentional reference to acts of simple reaching (Vygotsky, 1926/1962). However, recent evidence suggests that pointing is rarely confused with reaching (Franco & Butterworth, 1996) and that pointing is not dependent on the adult's social scaffolding, emerging simultaneously with adults and with peers (Franco, Perucchini, & Butterworth, 1992). Some suggest that protodeclarative pointing may be merely a conditioned response or experimental test of others' reactions (Perner, 1991), but this is not consistent with evidence about the social significance of pointing (Franco & Butterworth, 1998), and its communicative purposes, from several recent experimental studies showing that pointing in infants is clearly linked to the attentional states of the adult. For instance, Legerstee and Barillas (2003) found that 12-month-olds who were rewarded for pointing, did so in a more coordinated fashion if they were pointing at a person rather than an object and also pointed more and vocalized more when the target was not in the adult's attentional field than when it already was. Similarly, showing the 12-month-old's sensitivity to adult attentional state, Liszkowski, Albrecht, Carpenter, and Tomasello (2008) showed that, even at 12 months, infants initiated more pointing when the adult was attending to them than when not, and attempted repairs when the adult was attending but did not respond. Pointing may serve other functions too: it appears not only to be declarative or imperative, but also deliberately "informative," with the giving of news even in the absence of referents (Liszkowski, Carpenter, & Tomasello, 2007; Liszkowski, Striano, Carpenter, & Tomasello (2006). We have yet to explore the intriguing identification of a "protointerrogative" gesture in infants at this age (Rodriguez, 2009).

Thus far, we have seen that responding to the visual attention of others is a complex and coordinated process even in the first few months of life. Within days of birth infants prefer direct gaze and reveal a potential to follow gaze to other targets. Evidence of appropriate emotional responses to others' attention, inattention, and inappropriate attention to the self is present from around 2 months of age. From as early as 3 months of age we may see the beginnings of appropriate responses to others' attention directed to external targets, a skill more robustly evident from the middle of the first year. The ability to direct others' attending appears to begin at least from around 3 months of age. The targets to which infants can bring others to attend change with age. The initial target being the self (at around 3 months) differentiates into different aspects of the self's acts (from around 7 or 8 months) to targets distant from the self (from 11 months). To some extent the significance of others' attending, especially its referential significance, involves an understanding of the intentionality of the attentional act. This aspect of attending has received much recent attention from psychological research on infants' understanding of intentions, which we will now consider.

What are Intentions?

Most approaches to the awareness of intentions in infancy and childhood tend, either explicitly or implicitly, to define intention as comprising mental representations of goals; in other words, as internal "ideas" about goals and not themselves observable by others. This focus on goal-directedness, by and large, would require some kind of evidence of inferential abilities in infants before their responses to or engagements with others' intentional actions can be accepted as indicating awareness of intentionality. The risk of adopting an inferential definition is that the perceivable features of intentional actions (e.g., their directedness, shape, singularity) can be either neglected or dismissed as low-level information thus precluding adequate exploration of the crucial developmental phenomena, and portraying others' intentional actions as "stimuli" to be observed rather than engaged with by the infant.

Issues in explaining the developing awareness of intentions

There are a number of issues which currently preoccupy the literature in this area. These issues crisscross between theorists so that it is often difficult to identify clear-cut divisions in position. Nonetheless, despite the rapidly shifting panorama of arguments, the following issues broadly reflect current controversies in the field.

1   The importance in development of *top-down* influences (such as a conceptual/ theoretical grasp of intentions (Astington, 1991) or of mentalistic inferences about intentional capacities of humans, Legerstee, Barna, & DiAdamo, 2000) versus *bottom-up* influences (such as of lower-level features of actions, Woodward, 1998, 1999); and, related to this, the perceivability of intentions versus the need for inference
2   The importance in development of *experience* – the relevance of general action observation (Baldwin, Andersen, Saffran, & Meyer, 2008; Baldwin & Baird, 2001) and of specific action experiences (Somerville, Woodward, & Needham, 2005) versus the presence of an *experience-independent* mechanism (using efficiency/rationality) for attributing goals (Southgate, Johnson, & Csibra, 2008)

3   The *modularity* of early intention awareness (Baron-Cohen, 1995, 1997) versus the *integratedness* of the development of intention awareness (with, for instance, the awareness of perceiving; Tomasello et al., 2005)

4   The relevance of *human-like features* for perceiving movements as goal-directed (Kamewari, Kato, Kanda, Ishiguro, & Hiraki, 2005; Legerstee, 1991, 1997, 2005; Legerstee, Barna, & DiAdamo, 2000) versus the presence of *domain-specific representational systems* (e.g., focusing on efficiency) specialized for interpreting actions as being intentional (Kiraly, Jovanovic, Prinz, Aschersleben, & Gergely, 2003; Southgate et al., 2008)

5   The specific need for *second-person engagement* with others' intentions directed to self for an appropriate awareness of intention (Hobson, 1999; Reddy, 1996, 2008a, 2008b; Trevarthen, 1980) versus the synthesizing of *third-person observations* of others' and *first-person experience* of own intentions (Barresi & Moore, 1996; Elsner & Aschersleben, 2003; Somerville et al., 2005)

Two major theories emphasize infants' inferences about "goal-directedness" as being key to the awareness of intentions and each argues for slightly different stages in the development of intention awareness. Tomasello et al. (2005) posit a distinction between infant awareness of animate action (from around 6 months of age), the understanding of goals and persistence in the pursuit of goals (from around 9 months), the understanding of "full-fledged intentional action" including the rational choice of action plans and selective attention to the situation (from around 14 months). Also adopting an interpretive approach, Csibra and Gergely argue for the importance of an experience-independent mechanism or principle – the "rationality" or "efficiency" principle – which is used to interpret movement (human or inanimate) as "intentional" (Southgate et al., 2008). They place the emergence of intention awareness at around the end of the first year.

In contrast to the latter, strongly experience-independent, position and to the inferential emphasis in both of these theories, other theorists focus on specific features of intentional actions, and on the infant's detection of and appropriate responses to, these features. Woodward, for instance, has shown the importance of features such as the perceived animacy of a hand versus the movement of a claw (Woodward, 1998), and the direction of a grasp (back of hand versus front of hand, Woodward, 1999) as being important in the perception of goal-directedness. Somerville, Woodward, and Needham (2005) emphasize the importance of experience with specific actions (especially the production of the actions) as being vital to the grasping of goal-directedness when observing others' actions. Using a Chomskyan notion of action-parsing and proposing an intriguing analogy to the infants' discovery of phonetic segments in unfamiliar speech, Baldwin et al. (2008) also focus on the detailed and perceivable features of intentional actions. They too emphasize experience, and argue that the observation of the statistical structure of actions allows the perception and combination of action segments. With detailed analyses of infants' parsing of dynamic movements seen on video, Baldwin et al. suggest that infants can parse intentional action segments by 10 months of age (Baldwin & Baird, 2001; Baldwin, Baird, Saylor, & Clark, 2001), an ability which could combine with a more top-down awareness of intentions (Baldwin et al., 2008).

In keeping with the latter theorists' emphasis on the perceivable features of intentional actions, I adopt in this chapter the phenomenological alternative to defining intentions as "goal-directed" actions (where intentions are defined by directedness towards the mental representations of a target) namely "object-directedness" (where intentions are defined by directedness towards the targets themselves; Merleau-Ponty, 1961, Vedeler, 1994). This definition brings intentions into the perceivable world rather than keeping them locked "inside the head." Adopting such a definition allows us to explore infant awareness in greater detail, and allows us to understand exactly how it is embedded in contexts of action and interpersonal engagement. It allows us, in other words, to explore how an awareness of others' and one's own intentional actions can emerge, be contained in and engaged with, in second-person, direct engagements. Intentionality in a philosophical sense is often seen as involving "aboutness," that is, as having an intentional (or mental) object, and thus being "about" something. Adopting an object-directed approach to intentions could involve not an analysis of the mental objects, but of the manifest objects of intentional action. Such an approach also allows us to consider situations where infants themselves are potential objects of others' intentional actions, and allows us to explore possible differences between their engagements with others' intentions towards themselves and their perceptions of others' intentions towards other objects in their field.

Relating to intentions directed towards the self

There is little direct evidence about infants' responses to intentional actions directed towards them in the early months of life. Most studies focus on infants' reactions to others' actions on objects. The evidence that we have available, therefore, does not so far come with an intentionality label. The earliest evidence of interactions of this nature, involving actions towards the infant, comes from studies of neonatal imitation (Kugiumutzakis, 1998, 1999; Meltzoff & Moore, 1977; see chapter 11 this volume). In these studies, typically, the adult faces the infant directly, and with mutual gaze, directs some gesture physically toward the infant – a tongue protruded forward to the infant (or even sideways in one intriguing study, albeit with gaze toward the infant, Meltzoff & Moore, 1994), a mouth opening wide with gaze and body oriented to the infant's face, a finger being raised somewhere between the adult's and the infant's face with continuing mutual gaze (Nagy & Molnar, 2004), or a vocalization "aaa" directed toward the infant with mutual gaze (Kugiumutzakis, 1998). Neonates imitate these facial, manual, and vocal gestures. That this imitation is in some sense intentional is supported circumstantially by evidence of intentional arm movements in 4 week-olds (Van der Meer, Van der Weel, & Lee 1995) and by the nonautomaticity of the imitations and the variations in imitative patterns – some infants engage in successive approximations, others do single-shot imitations, some repeat the imitation but less effortfully each time, and some do not imitate at all despite being alert and attentive (Kugiumutzakis, 1998, 1999). In addition, the identification of provocative "imitation" of finger movements with decelerating (i.e., attentive) heart rate rather than the accelerating pattern typically accompanying neonatal imitation (Nagy & Molnar, 2004) argues against the claim that neonatal imitation is reflexive (Anisfeld,

1996) or simple oral exploration (Jones, 1996). Whatever the intentionality in these actions, does the neonate recognize, in some sense, the intentionality in the *adult's* act? The studies have not yet been done to test the effects of either the directedness of the model's act (e.g., modeling an action without face and body oriented to the infant) on infant responses or whether infants dishabituate differently depending on the orientation of the act. Further indirect evidence comes from infant responses to adult attempts to pick them up. Infants from about 4 months of age are reported to accommodate their bodies to the reaching movement of others' arms and hands, a reaction which children with autism are reported not to show (Lord, 1993). Such accommodation suggests infant recognition of the adult's intention to "pick-me-up." In the context of infant recognition at 5 and even 3 months of age (given the right experience) of the intentional directedness of adults reaching out to pick up objects (Woodward, 1998; Somerville et al., 2005), the recognition of pick-me-up intentions is not surprising.

When we consider infant responses to the intentionality of communicative acts the interconnectedness of intention and attention becomes evident. Do infants recognize the intentionality of communication directed to them, or more specifically of the cessation of communication? The still-face and replayed video studies reported in the discussion of attention suggest an early sensitivity to intentional acts of inattention. A third perturbation condition in the Murray and Trevarthen (1985) study involved the adult interrupting the face-to-face conversation with the infant to turn to talk to someone who had entered the room – a condition which, unlike the noncontingent replay condition, did not cause any distress to infants. Replications of this finding have been contradictory: Striano (2004) failed to replicate this difference in 3-month-olds, while Legerstee and Markova (2007) did replicate it in 3-, 6-, and 9-month-olds.

Infants respond to the playful intentions of others from at least around 4 months of age, as evidenced by their laughter and participation in games, especially those involving potentially risky acts by others such as tickling, chasing (although this does not start eliciting laughter until they *can* be chased!), and looming. There is little evidence, as yet, of early discrimination between playful and serious intentions in different contexts. One study explored infant reactions to mothers' playful "threats" with a mask in a free play context and showed that 9-month-old infants reacted with laughter to this action, while 18-month-olds reacted with anxiety (Nakano & Kanaya, 1993). Different interpretations are possible of this intriguing developmental shift; Nakano suggests that playful intentions are perceivable as such and do not need a knowledge of meta-intentions as suggested by Bateson (1973), in order for the infant to distinguish them from serious acts.

If the neonatal provocations (Nagy & Molnar, 2004) are seen as simple attempts to reelicit an act from another person towards themselves, then this ability to direct/seek acts towards the self is present from birth and develops in complexity over the next months.

Infants also selectively direct their communicative attempts to people and their actions (such as reaching) to objects even at 3 to 4 months (Legerstee, Pomerleau, Malcuit, & Feider, 1987). Two-month-olds (Legerstee, 1991) and also 18-month-olds (Meltzoff, 1995) imitate people, but not objects. Legerstee (1994) found that when precrawling 4-month-olds are confronted with either a person or an object disappearing behind an occluder, they *reach* for the occluder in the case of the disappearing object but *call* to the person in the case of the disappearing person. These findings suggest that infants are capable of calling others' acts and attention to themselves from the early months.

Overall, however, we know very little about infants' attempts to direct others' intentional actions toward themselves. Early anticipatory responses to others' actions (such as arching the back towards another's reach) may develop into acts which are performed as an expression of need (i.e., arching the back *in order to be* picked up). While such acts occur in the first 6 months, it is not until about 9 months of age that they are used with any degree of specificity for others' intentions (see Service, 1984 for a discussion of developments in the hands-raised pick-me-up gesture). Further research is needed for understanding how such intentional engagements develop.

Relating to intentions directed towards actions

The first context for understanding of others' intentions towards actions appears to be an understanding of the other's instructions for the infant's own actions. This can be seen in episodes where the mother provides incomplete demonstrations of actions which she wants the infant to complete – such as showing the place where the doll is to be placed. Rather than copy the exact demonstration (which, being incomplete, would be inappropriate), infants display an understanding of the intent by obeying the instruction (Trevarthen & Hubley, 1978). This conclusion is also drawn by Tomasello, Kruger, and Ratner (1993) showing that infants from around the end of the first year engage in selective inferential imitation rather than exact "mimicking" of others' acts.

It is also in the last quarter of the first year that parents begin to give commands to their infants and that infants begin to comply with instructions (Stayton, Hogan, & Ainsworth, 1971). It is likely that the onset of parental commands at this age is partly the result of their sensing that their infants are capable of responding to such directive intentions. From around 7 or 8 months of age infants become capable of responding with some compliance to positive directives such as: "Put the dolly there," "Wave bye-bye," "Clap hands," "Come to Mummy," and "Give me the biscuit." All of these directives are usually delivered through partial demonstrations, open palm invitations, and so on. Infants also start responding (not necessarily with compliance) to prohibitions concerning their actions and incomplete intentions in ways that suggest that they are detecting both the presence of others' intentions for infant action as well as the level of seriousness of the intentions.[7]

In a longitudinal analysis of parental reports about infant compliance I found (Reddy, 1998) that some sensitivity to prohibitions (other than simply being startled by them) was present in 50% of 8-month-olds; occasional compliance to verbal prohibitions was present in less than one-third of the children at this age, but in over two-thirds of the children by 11 months and in all children by 14 months. There were some instances of apparent regression between 8 and 11 months, where infants who had previously shown sensitivity and even compliance to verbal commands started to ignore them either with laughter or with sober-faced unresponsiveness. Provocative noncompliance (i.e., noncompliance for its effect on the other rather than just from desire for the prohibited goal) was rare at 8 months, but present in 50% of the infants by 11 months. Infants distinguished between serious and nonserious issues, probably through tone of voice and other signs of playfulness in the parents, and early provocative noncompliance was limited primarily to nonserious issues.

Other forms of teasing involving playful offer and withdrawal of objects and playful disruption of others' acts, were more prevalent at 8 and 11 months. Disruptions of others' acts usually involved acts which were directed to the infant rather than acts between the other and an external target. For instance, one infant at 11 months showed several instances of false requests, repeatedly asking for a drink and then refusing it until his mother realized that he was teasing her. Similarly, another infant at 11 months developed a game where he refused his mother's kiss until she was nearly out of the door. There were a few instances of teasing which involved a disruption of the other's acts towards another target such as tipping the toy box out as soon as his sibling had tidied it up, or throwing the cushions back down on the floor while the mother was tidying up preparatory to vacuuming the floor (Reddy, 1991). These reflect some understanding of the other's goal-directed actions towards external targets. Suggestions that at least by 8 to 9 months of age, infants are aware of some "central" or holistic intentionality in the teasing person's act comes from evidence that when teased by being offered something which is then withdrawn or by some action of theirs being obstructed, infants gaze straightaway to the person's face rather than at their obstructing or teasing hands (Phillips, Baron-Cohen, & Rutter, 1992; Carpenter, Akhtar, & Tomasello, 1998).

A recent cross-cultural study suggests more support for the experience-dependent nature of infants' awareness of others' intentions-for-intentions and for a considerably earlier development of this awareness than hitherto reported (Reddy, Hicks, Jonnalagadda, Liebal, & Beena, in preparation). Following specific cultural experiences with directives, infants from as young as 6 months of age respond with occasional compliance even to purely "distal" directives, that is, with no physical support and encouragement. Such compliance occurs to commands for simple actions such as "sit," "stand," "throw the ball," "don't scratch the eczema," and so on, the frequency of which differs between cultures.

Relating to others' intentions directed towards external targets

When do infants detect the intentionality of others' actions directed towards external targets? There is considerable evidence from the second year of the detection of intentional looking at, and intentional action towards, external targets. Infants of 24 months learn novel verbs only when preceded by an intentional action (Tomasello & Barton, 1994), 18-month-olds (Baldwin, 1991, 1993) and even 12-month-olds (Baldwin, Bill, & Ontai, 1996) use gaze direction to interpret adult labeling of objects. Infants of 18 months imitate unsuccessful adult actions on the basis of the intention rather than the actual act (Meltzoff, 1995), and 14- to 18-month-olds successfully distinguish intentional actions on objects (followed by a verbal "There!") from accidental actions (followed by a "Whoops!") (Carpenter et al., 1998). Infants and toddlers (between 9 and 18 months of age) distinguish between adult unwillingness and inability to cooperate in a game, showing more impatience towards the former than the latter (Tomasello et al., 2005).

By the end of the first year, infants appear to be adopting what Gergely calls "the intentional stance" in relation to others' actions on objects which do not involve the infant, discriminating between "sensible" or "efficient" detours made on screen by a moving ball, versus detours made for no apparent reason (Gergely, Nadasdy, Csibra, & Biro, 1995). From the middle of the second year there is evidence that infants try to fix other people's problems – 15-month-olds try out new ways to help someone achieve what they are unable to do (Bellagamba & Tomasello, 1999) and 14- and 18-month-olds clearly go out of their way to help complete intentions which adults cannot complete (Warneken & Tomasello, 2007).

However, the detection of others' intentions towards the world appears to be robustly evident even in the first year. Twelve-month-olds appear to understand the relevance of the sequentiality of actions to the presence of overarching goals, construing ambiguous actions (such as an adult's hand touching the lid of a box) as relevant to the overall goal only if the subsequent action is causally related to it (to removing the lid and grasping the toy inside) and not if the action is temporally but not causally linked to it (i.e., the toy is outside the box) (Woodward & Somerville, 2000). Even 5-month-olds (although not as strongly as 9-month-olds) differentiate between a behavior that seems to be goal-directed (grasping an object) and one that seems unintentional (dropping the back of the hand in front of an object) (Woodward, 1999). Infants of 7 and 5 months appear to detect the intention to reach for a specific object and distinguish this intention from the specific path taken by a moving arm (Woodward, 1998). Most strikingly, even infants of three months, if given specific experience of producing the reaching and "grasping" action (with the aid of Velcro-enhanced mittens) appear to discriminate between the intention to reach for a specific object and the action itself (i.e., the path taken in the action) (Somerville et al., 2005). When dealing with familiar actions such as reaching, infants as young as 7 or 8 months of age imitate adults' rational actions or complete (in their imitations) the adult's incomplete goal-directed actions (Hamlin, Hallinan, & Woodward, 2008; Hamlin, Newman, & Wynn, 2009). Such evidence supports reports from naturalistic studies that infants from around 6 months of age not only seem to understand others' intentions towards things in the environment, but start to comply with others' intentions for the infants to do something; in other words, to comply with others' intentions for the infant's own intentions (Reddy et al., in preparation).

The debate about whether the features of intentionality detected by infants pertain to their human-like-ness continues and is still inconclusive. A series of studies by Maria Legerstee has shown that infants discriminate the communicative attempts of animated dolls and people from 2 months of age (Legerstee, 2005), and that 6-month-olds respond differently to people who disappeared behind an occluder (calling them) than to objects which did the same (reaching for them) (Legerstee, 1994). In line with this suggestion, Woodward (1998, 1999) focused on the specific humanoid features of actions (although at a more detailed level of specification) which infants responded to as intentional. For example, reaching and grasping actions carried out by a mechanical claw were not distinguished as goal-directed, while those done by a human hand were (Woodward, 1998), although this finding is now under challenge (Jovanovich et al., 2007). Most strikingly, in support of the "efficiency" principle, Southgate, Johnson, and Csibra (2008) have shown that 6- to 8-month-olds appear to be unbothered by (i.e., they do not dishabituate to) biomechanically impossible events (which are definitely not human-like and could not have been seen before) but do notice as unusual the very ordinary but inefficient actions of an arm doing something redundant. In contrast, Kamewari and colleagues (2005) support the humanoid features claim. Using real videos rather than the computer-generated images of Gergely and colleagues (1995), they showed that 6.5 month olds notice as unusual (dishabituate to) the inefficient (redundant) walking of people and humanoid robots, but not the inefficient movements of a box, suggesting that they did not expect intentional or rational action from the box.

Towards the end of the first year, at around the same time as infants are able to comply with others' intentions, infants also demonstrate an ability to *direct* others' intentions towards the external world. There is some debate about whether the ability to direct others' *intentions* (through protoimperatives or early, nonverbal commands) develops prior to or at the same time as the ability to direct others' *attention* (through protodeclaratives) to external targets. A Piagetian analysis of protoimperatives sees them as developmentally equivalent to protodeclaratives, with both emerging at the same time and from the same underlying cognitive advance in the understanding of means–ends relations and tool use (Bates et al., 1976). However, protoimperative pointing may in fact predate protodeclarative pointing by about 2 months (Perucchini & Camaioni, 1993) and may be the result of a simpler instrumental perception of others' actions than the understanding of attentionality implied in protodeclaratives (Camaioni, 1993). The mere presence of protoimperatives need imply no understanding of others' intentionality as has been shown in a subtle analysis of the development of a protoimperative act in a gorilla (Gomez, 1991). In order to obtain one's own goal, one can use the other as an object, as a tool, as an agent, or as an intentional being. Treating the other as an intentional being in protoimperatives can be observed through an indicative rather than forceful expression of the intention for the other's act, and the presence of eye contact following this. In human infants, imperative pointing is evident by 11 months (Perucchini and Camaioni, 1993), with gaze to the face at some point during the act. Even earlier than this, human infants appear to indicate needs through, for example, reaching for an object and waiting for adults to come to their help (Bates et al., 1976). However, confusions between various divisions abound and the conceptual and empirical links between attention and intention are as yet unclear. For instance, in "social referencing" (Sorce, Emde, Campos, & Klinnert, 1985) and "attentional referencing" (Reddy, 2005) infants from the middle of the first year show sensitivity to others' emotional and attentional reactions towards aspects of the world. The relation between these phenomena and those involving the seeking of intentional actions from others remains to be clarified.

The language we use in talking about intention and attention is revealing. Why do I talk about attention in the singular but of intentions in the plural? Why do I argue for a shift to the term attending, but not for the term intending? Perhaps the answer to the former question lies in seeing attending as one kind of intentional action (as suggested by Tomasello's "intentional perception," (Tomasello, Carpenter, Call, Behne, & Moll, 2005), whereas when we talk about intentions we talk of many different kinds of action. To the latter question, perhaps the answer lies in the way in which English casts the word "attending" as an activity while it casts "intending" very much as a prior, nonactive state.

This is unlikely to be the case in all languages, but the impact of different conceptions of these terms on our theorizing remains for future research to explore.

Conclusion

There is considerable evidence from studies with adults that second-person engagement (Buber, 1937) matters. The importance for psychological understanding of being "addressed" or of being treated as a "Thou" (i.e., spoken to or addressed directly in dialogue) rather than of being cast in the social role of observer or experimenter has recently received striking empirical support. Studies with adults show how crucial the personal directedness of an experimental "stimulus" is for neural processing of the stimuli and for influencing various aspects of behavior (Mojzisch et al., 2006; Schilbach et al., 2006). Being addressed activates specific brain regions (Kampe, Frith, & Frith, 2003) and enhances activity in dopaminergic regions of the brain (linking interpersonal engagement to rewardingness) upon meeting an attractive stranger's eyes (but only when there is eye contact, Kampe, Frith, Dolan, & Frith, 2001). "Other" people, it seems clear, do not provide us with identical "stimulus" features independent of our involvement with them. At any given time there are at least two kinds of "others": those whose minds are directed towards us (as if they were addressing us, and we them, as a "You") and those who relate to us only indirectly (as if each saw the other as a "he" or "she"; Reddy, 2008b). There is very good reason to argue that in order to understand how infants understand other minds, we should focus first on early phenomena within second-person engagement.

Of the two domains of mind knowledge considered in this chapter – attention and intention – the latter seems to currently be under greater pressure to adopt third-person methodologies than the former. Studies in the domain of intention awareness primarily adopt third-person or spectator methods in which the infant passively observes the actions of other agents on objects and draws inferences from this observation, and, alternatively but less frequently, first-person experience methods in which the infant's own prior experience of these actions is prioritized. In contrast, in the domain of attention awareness there are now several studies using a second-person method, where the other's attention is directed to the infant herself. These studies reveal dramatic results even from birth, but have not yet been conducted with intention awareness.

Some studies have explicitly attempted to relate the infant's own experience of intentional action on objects with their grasp of the intentionality of similar actions by others (e.g., the whole range of impressive studies by Amanda Woodward and colleagues) and have based their explanations of the development of intentional understanding on this similarity (Somerville et al., 2005; Meltzoff & Moore, 1999). There has also been an explicit attempt to experimentally test the impact of third-person observation on first-person experience of the effects of actions on objects (e.g., Elsner & Aschersleben, 2003). However, there are almost no studies to date explicitly focusing on the infant's awareness of intentions in second-person engagements. In a review of the literature in 2000, identifying different categories of experimental findings about intention awareness, Susan Johnson (2000) labeled awareness within active interaction as one such category, but could only find studies of gaze following or pointing as evidence – not much was available on intention awareness. The problem and its solutions continue to be phrased and explored in first-person versus third-person terms rather than with any recognition of second-person engagements as offering different opportunities for awareness (Reddy, 2008a, b). That is, the problem is seen in terms of a clash between first- and third-person awareness and resolved through some synthesis of third-person perception (i.e., from the "outside") of the characteristics of others' actions and first-person proprioception (i.e., from inside) of one's own actions (Baldwin, 1909; Olson, Astington, & Zelazo, 1999; Barresi & Moore, 1996). Second-person engagements shatter this boundary between perception and proprioception, making all intention-awareness both a perceptual and responsive process, and making affective experience central in this experience (see Reddy, 2008a, 2008b).

Overall, we have come a long way towards developing a participant rather than a bystander psychology. However, this is not yet far enough. Psychological phenomena are fundamentally participatory. They are participatory in a developmental sense – they cannot come into existence without someone to participate with them. But they are also participatory in an epistemic sense. As John MacMurray put it: I can know another person as a person only by entering into personal relation with him. Without this I can know him only by observation and inference, only objectively (MacMurray, 1961, p. 28).

For any awareness of others' attention or intentions, therefore, engaging with them is primary, and this must apply to the psychologist as well as the infant.

Notes

1. While science legitimately seeks to disentangle the separate knowledge of each participant, this might be better done through contrasting different kinds of participatory situations than through setting up nonparticipatory experimental situations.
2. Such an approach highlights the intentionality of attentional acts (Tomasello et al., 2005) and thus their inseparability from the development of intentionality.
3. Given the paucity of data on other modalities of attention this discussion will be limited to visual attention alone.
4. Taken by the authors as indicative of detecting eye contact and communicative intent.
5. Luo and Johnson (2009) showed in a remarkable demonstration that 6-month-olds not only appeared to grasp the intentional choice in adult reaching and grasping of objects (and took adult choice as indicative of preference), but did so only when the adult actually could see both objects. When the adult's orientation or a screen blocked one of the objects from their view, their reaching and grasping of one of the two objects appeared not to be seen as a choice.
6. D'Entremont et al. (1997) investigated infant eye turning behavior when an adult with whom they were interacting turned to look at one of two puppets on either side of her. They found that, even at 3 months, infants spontaneously turned their eyes to look at the correct puppet (significantly more often than at the incorrect puppet), with no age differences in accuracy between 3-, 5- and 6-month-olds. Interestingly, this adult distraction (turning 4 times in 4 minutes to talk to one of the puppets for 10 seconds) had an overall distracting effect on the infants, with infant gaze frequently alternating between the adult and the puppet. Infant head

turns to the correct object had a surprisingly long latency of 2 seconds, suggesting that the turn is not simply an automated tracking but possibly the result of an appreciation that the adult is *looking at* something else, as well as recognition of the direction of the look.

7. See also studies of motionese – Brand, Baldwin, and Ashburn (2002).

8. Differentiates early detection of communication (i.e., of ostension) from early "mind reading." The former happens and allows learning about the world, while the latter may simply be the researcher's overattribution. But this raises the question of why he prioritizes learning about the world over learning about people, and how one deals with ostension or communicative intention without being able to understand people as mental beings.

References

Adamson, L. B., & Bakeman, R. (1991). The development of shared attention during infancy. In R. Vasta (Ed.), *Annals of child development* (Vol. 8, pp. 1–41). London: Jessica Kingsley.

Amano, S., Kezuka, E., & Yamamoto, A. (2004). Infant shifting attention from an adult's face to an adult's hand: A precursor of joint attention. *Infant Behavior and Development, 27,* 64–80.

Anisfeld, M. (1996). Only tongue protrusion modelling is matched by neonates. *Developmental Review, 16,* 149–161.

Astington, J. (1991). Intention in the child's theory of mind. In D. Frye & C. Moore (Eds.), *Children's theories of mind.* Hillsdale, NJ: Erlbaum.

Atkinson, J., Hood, B., Wattam-Bell, J., & Anker, S. (1988). Development of orientation discrimination in infancy. *Perception, 17*(5), 587–595.

Bakeman, R., & Adamson, L. B. (1984). Co-ordinating attention to people and objects in mother–infant and peer–infant interaction. *Child Development, 55,* 1278–1289.

Baldwin, D. (1991). Infants' contribution to the achievement of joint reference. *Child Development, 62,* 875–890.

Baldwin, D. (1993). Early referential understanding: Infants' ability to recognise referential acts for what they are. *Developmental Psychology, 29,* 832–843.

Baldwin, D. (1995). Understanding the link between joint attention and language. In C. Moore, & P. Dunham (Eds.), *Joint attention: its origins and development* (pp. 131–158). Mahwah, NJ: LEA.

Baldwin, D., Andersen, A., Saffran, J., & Meyer, M. (2008). Segmenting dynamic human action via statistical structure. *Cognition, 106,* 1382–1407.

Baldwin, D., & Baird, J. (2001). Discerning intentions in dynamic human action. *Trends in Cognitive Sciences, 5,* 171–178.

Baldwin, D., Baird, J., Saylor, M., & Clark, A. (2001). Infants parse dynamic human action. *Child Development, 72,* 708–717.

Baldwin, D., Bill, B., & Ontai, L. L. (1996, April). *Infants' tendency to monitor others' gaze: Is it rooted in intentional understanding or a result of simple orienting?* Paper presented at the International Conference on Infant Studies, Providence, RI.

Baldwin, D., & Moses, L. (2001). Links between understanding and early word learning: challenges to current accounts. *Social Development, 10,* 309–329.

Baldwin, J. M. (1909). The influence of Darwin on theory of knowledge and philosophy. *Psychological Review, 16,* 207–218.

Baron-Cohen, S. (1995). The Eye Direction Detector (EDD) and the Shared Attention Mechanism (SAM): Two cases for evolutionary psychology. In C. Moore & P. Dunham (Eds.), *Joint Attention* (pp. 41–59). Hillsdale, NJ: Erlbaum.

Baron-Cohen, S. (1997). *Mindblindness: An essay on autism and theory of mind.* Cambridge, MA: MIT Press.

Barresi, J., & Moore, C. (1996). Intentional relations and social understanding. *Behavioral and Brain Sciences, 19*, 107–154.

Bates, E., Camaioni, L., & Volterra, V. (1976). Sensorimotor performatives. In E. Bates (Ed.), *Language and context: The acquisition of pragmatics.* New York: Academic Press.

Bateson, G. (1973). *Steps to an ecology of mind.* London: Paladin Books.

Bayliss, A. P., Frischen, A., Fenske, M. J., & Tipper, S. P. (2007). Affective evaluations of objects are influenced by observed gaze direction and emotional expression. *Cognition 104*, 644–653

Becchio, C., Bertone, C., & Castiello, U. (2008). How the gaze of others influences object processing. *Trends in Cognitive Sciences, 7*, 254–258.

Bellagamba, F., & Tomasello, M. (1999). Re-enacting intended acts: comparing 12- and 18-Month-Olds, *Infant Behavior and Development 22*(2), 277–282.

Brand, R. J., Baldwin, D. A., & Ashburn, L. A. (2002). Evidence for "motionese": Modifications in mothers' infant-directed action. *Developmental Science, 5*(1), March, 72–83.

Brazelton, T. B. (1986). The development of newborn behaviour. In F. Faulkner & J. M. Tanner (Eds.), *Human growth: A comprehensive treatise* (Vol. 2, pp. 519–540). New York: Plenum Press.

Bruner, J. (1983). *Child's talk: learning to use language.* New York. Norton.

Buber, M. (1937). *I and thou.* Edinburgh: T & T Clark, Ltd.

Butterworth, G. (1995). Origins of mind in perception and action. In C. Moore & P. Dunham (Eds.), *Joint attention: Its origins and role in development* (pp. 29–40). Hillsdale, NJ: Erlbaum.

Butterworth, G., & Jarrett, N. L. M. (1991). What minds have in common is space: Spatial mechanisms serving joint visual attention in infancy. *British Journal of Developmental Psychology, 9*, 55–72.

Camaioni, L. (1993). The development of intentional communication: A re-analysis. In J. Nadel & L. Camaioni (Eds.), *New perspectives in early communicative development* (pp. 82–96). London: Routledge.

Caron, A., Caron, R., Mustelin, C., & Roberts, J. (1992). Infant responding to aberrant social stimuli. *Infant Behaviour and Development, 19*, 335.

Carpenter, M., Akhtar, N., & Tomasello, M. (1998). Fourteen through eighteen-month-olds differentially imitate intentional and accidental actions. *Infant Behaviour and Development, 21*, 315–330.

Cohn, J. F., & Tronick, E. Z. (1989). Specificity of infants' response to mothers' affective behavior. *Journal of the American Academy of Child and Adolescent Psychiatry, 28*, 242–248.

Corkum, V., & Moore, C. (1994). Development of joint visual attention in infants. In C. Moore & P. Dunham (Eds.), *Joint attention: Its origins and role in development* (pp. 61–83). Hillsdale, NJ: Erlbaum.

Corkum, V., & Moore, C. (1998). The origin of joint visual attention in infants. *Developmental Psychology, 34*, 28–38.

Costall, A., & Leudar, I. (2009). *Against theory of mind.* London: Ashgate.

Costall, A., Leudar, I., & Reddy, V. (2006). Failing to see the irony in "mind-reading." *Theory & Psychology, 16*(2), 163–167.

Coulter, J. (1979). *The social construction of mind.* London: Macmillan.

D'Entremont, B., Hains, S. M. J., & Muir, D. (1997). A demonstration of gaze following in 3- to 6-month-olds. *Infant Behaviour and Development, 20*, 569–572.

Duncan, J. (1984). Selective attention and the organisation of visual information. *Journal of Experimental Psychology: General, 113*, 501–517.

Egly, R., Driver, J., & Rafal, R.D. (1994). Shifting visual attention between objects and locations: Evidence from normal and parietal lesion subjects. *Journal of Experimental Psychology: General, 123,* 161–177.

Elsner, B., & Aschersleben, G. (2003). Do I get what you get? Learning about the effects of self-performed and observed actions in infancy. *Consciousness and Cognition, 12,* 732–751.

Fantz, R. L. (1965). Visual perception from birth as shown by pattern selection. *Annals of the New York Academy of Sciences, 118*(21), 793-814.

Farroni, T., Csibra, G., Johnson, M., & Simion, F. (2002). Eye contact detection at birth. *PNAS, 99*(14), 9602–9605.

Farroni, T., Johnson, M. H., Brockbank, M., & Simion, F. (2000). Infants' use of gaze direction to cue attention: The importance of perceived motion. *Visual Cognition, 7,* 705–718.

Farroni, T., Mansfield, E. M., Lai, C., & Johnson, M. H. (2003). Infants perceiving and acting on the eyes: Tests of an evolutionary hypothesis. *Journal of Experimental Child Psychology, 85,* 199–212.

Farroni, T., Menon, E., & Johnson, M. (2006). Factors influencing newborns' preference for faces with eye contact. *Journal of Experimental Child Psychology, 95,* 298–308.

Farroni, T., Pividori, D., Simion, F., Massaccesi, S., & Johnson, M. H. (2004). Eye gaze cueing of attention in newborns. *Infancy, 5.*

Fivaz-Depeursinge, E., & Corboz-Warnery, A. (1999). *The primary triangle.* New York: Basic Books.

Fivaz-Depeursinge, E., Favez, N., Lavanchy, S., de Noni, S., & Frascarolo, F. (2005). Four-month-olds make triangular bids to father and mother during trilogue play with still face. *Social Development, 14*(2), 361–378.

Flom, R., & Pick, A. (2005). Experimenter affective expression and gaze following in 7-month-olds. *Infancy, 7*(2), 207–218.

Franco, F., & Butterworth, G. (1996). Pointing and social awareness: Declaring and requesting in the second year. *Journal of Child Language, 32*(2), 307–336.

Franco, F., & Butterworth, G. (1998). *The social origins of pointing in human infancy.* Paper presented at the Annual Conference of the Developmental Section of the BPS, Coleg Harlech, Wales.

Franco, F., Perucchini, P., & Butterworth, G. (1992, September). *Referential communication between babies.* Paper presented at the Fifth European Conference on Developmental Psychology, Seville, Spain.

Gergely, G. (2002). The development of an understanding of self and agency. In U. Goswami (Ed.), *Blackwell's handbook of childhood cognitive development* (pp. 26–46). Oxford: Blackwell.

Gergely, G., Nadasdy, Z., Csibra, G., & Biro, S. (1995). Taking the intentional stance at 12 months of age. *Cognition, 56,* 165–193.

Gergely, G., & Watson, J. (1996). The social biofeedback theory of parental affect mirroring: The development of emotional self-awareness and self-control in infancy. *International Journal of Psychoanalysis, 77*(6), 1181–1212.

Gergely, G., & Watson, J. (1999). Early socio-emotional development: contingency perception and the social-biofeedback model. In P. Rochat (Ed.), *Early social cognition* (pp. 101–136). Mahwah, NJ: Lea.

Gibson, J. J., & Pick, A. D. (1963). Perception of another person's looking behavior. *American Journal of Psychology, 76,* 386–394.

Gomez, J.-C., (1991). Visual behavior as a window for reading the mind of others in primates. In A. Whiten (Ed.), *Natural theories of mind* (pp. 195–207). Oxford: Blackwell.

Goren, C. G., Sarty, M., & Wu, P. Y. K. (1975). Visual following and pattern discrimination of face-like stimuli by newborn infants. *Paediatrics, 56,* 544–549.

Gredeback, G., Theuring, C., Hauf, P., & Kenward, B. (2008). The microstructure of infants' gaze as they view adult shifts in overt attention. *Infancy, 13*(5), 533–543.

Grossman, T., Johnson, M., Farroni, T., & Csibra, G. (2007). Social perception in the infant brain: Gamma oscillatory activity in response to eye gaze. *SCAN, 2,* 284–291.

Hamlin, J. K., Hallinan, E. V., & Woodward, A. L. (2008). Do as I do: 7-month-old infants selectively reproduce others' goals. *Developmental Science, 11,* 487–494.

Hamlin, J. K., Newman, G. E., & Wynn, K. (2009). Eight month-old infants infer unfulfilled goals despite ambiguous physical evidence. *Infancy, 14*(5), 579–590.

Hietanen, J., Leppanen, J., Peltola, M., Linna-aho, K., & Ruuhiala, H. (2008). Seeing direct and averted gaze activates the approach–avoidance motivational brain systems. *Neuropsychologia, 46,* 2423–2430.

Hobson, R. P. (1999, June). *Intersubjective foundations for joint attention: Co-ordinating attitudes (rather than actions).* Paper presented at the workshop on Joint Attention, University of Warwick, UK.

Hoehl, S., Reid, V., Mooney, J., & Striano, T. (2008). What are you looking at? Infants' neural processing of an adult's object-directed eye gaze. *Developmental Science, 11*(1), 10–16.

Johnson, M. H., & Morton, J. (1991). *Biology and cognitive development: The case of face recognition.* Oxford: Blackwell.

Johnson, M. H., Dziurawiec, S., Ellis, H., & Morton, J. (1991). Newborns' preferential tracking of face-like stimuli and its subsequent decline. *Cognition, 40*(1 2), 1–19.

Johnson, S. (2000). The recognition of mentalistic agents in infancy. *Trends in Cognitive Sciences, 4*(1), 22–28.

Jones, S. (1996). Imitation or exploration? Young infants' matching of adults' oral gestures. *Child Development, 67*(5), 1952–1969.

Jovanovich, B., Kiraly, I., Elsner, B., Gergely, G., Prinz, W., & Aschersleben, G. (2007). The role of effects for infant's perception of action goals. *Psychologia, 50*(4), 273–290.

Kamewari, K., Kato, M., Kanda, T., Ishiguro, H., & Hiraki, K. (2005). Six-and-a-half-month-old children positively attribute goals to human action and to humanoid-robot motion. *Cognitive Development, 20,* 303–320.

Kampe, K., Frith, C., Dolan, R., & Frith, U. (2001). Psychology: Reward value of attractiveness and gaze. *Nature, 413,* 589.

Kampe, K. W., Frith, C. D., & Frith, U. (2003). "Hey John": Signals conveying communicative intention toward the self activate brain regions associated with "mentalizing," regardless of modality. *Journal of Neuroscience, 23,* 5258–5263.

Kiraly, I., Jovanovic, B., Prinz, W., Aschersleben, G., & Gergely, G. (2003). The early origins of goal attribution in infancy. *Consciousness and Cognition, 12*(4), 752–769.

Kopp, C. (1982). Antecedents of self-regulation: A developmental perspective. *Developmental psychology, 18*(2), 199–214.

Kopp, C. (2002). The co-development of attention and emotion regulation. *Infancy, 3*(2), 199–208.

Kugiumutzakis, G. (1998). Neonatal imitation in the intersubjective companion space. In S. Braten (Ed.), *Intersubjective communication and emotion in early ontogeny* (pp. 63–88). Cambridge: Cambridge University Press.

Kugiumutzakis, G. (1999). Genesis and development of early infant mimesis to facial and vocal models. In J. Nadel & G. Butterworth (Eds.), *Imitation in infancy* (pp. 36–59). Cambridge: Cambridge University Press.

Legerstee, M. (1991). The role of person and object in eliciting early imitation. *Journal of Experimental Child Psychology, 51,* 423–433.

Legerstee, M. (1994). Patterns of 4-month-old infant responses to hidden silent and sounding people and objects. *Early Development and Parenting, 20,* 71–80.

Legerstee, M. (1997). Contingency effects of people and objects on subsequent cognitive functioning in three-month-old infants. *Social Development, 6*, 307–321.

Legerstee, M. (2005). *Infants' sense of people.* Cambridge: Cambridge University Press.

Legerstee, M., & Barillas, Y. (2003). Sharing attention and pointing to objects at 12 months: Is the intentional stance implied? *Cognitive Development, 18*(1), 91–110.

Legerstee, M., Barna, J., & DiAdamo, C. (2000). Precursors to the development of intention at 6 months: Understanding people and their actions. *Developmental Psychology, 36*(50), 627–634.

Legerstee, M., & Markova, G. (2007). Intentions make a difference: Infant responses to still-face and modified still-face condition. *Infant Behavior and Development, 30*, 232–250.

Legerstee, M., Pomerleau, A., Malcuit, G., & Feider, H. (1987). The development of infants' responses to people and a doll: Implications for research in communication. *Infant Behavior and Development, 10*, 81–95.

Liszkowski, U., Albrecht, K., Carpenter, M., & Tomasello, M. (2008). Infants' visual and auditory communication when a partner is or is not visually attending. *Infant Behaviour and Development, 31*(2), 157–167.

Liszkowski, U., Carpenter, M., & Tomasello, M. (2007). Pointing out new news, old news, and absent referents at 12 months of age. *Developmental Science, 10*(2), F1–F7.

Liszkowski, U., Striano, T., Carpenter, M., & Tomasello, M. (2006). Twelve- and eighteen-month-olds point to provide information for others. *Journal of Cognition and Development, 7*(2), 173–187.

Lord, C. (1993). The complexity of social behaviour in autism. In S. Baron-Cohen, H. Tager-Flusberg, & D. Cohen (Eds.), *Understanding other minds: Perspectives from autism* (pp. 292–316). New York: Oxford University Press.

Luo, Y., & Johnson, S. (2009). Recognising the role of perception in action at 6 months. *Developmental Science, 12*(2), 264–271.

MacMurray, J. (1961). *Persons in relation.* New York: Humanity Press.

Markova, G., & Legerstee, M. (2006). Contingency, imitation and affect sharing: foundations of infant social awareness. *Developmental Psychology, 42*(1), 132–141.

Markova, I. (1982). *Paradigms, thought and language.* Chichester, UK: Wiley.

Meltzoff, A. (1995). Understanding the intentions of others: Re-enactment of intended acts by 18-month-old children. *Developmental Psychology, 31*(5), 838–850.

Meltzoff, A., & Moore, K. (1977). Imitation of facial and manual gestures by human neonates. *Science, 198*(4312), 75–78.

Meltzoff, A., & Moore, K. (1994). Imitation, memory and the representation of persons. *Infant Behavior and Development, 17*(1), 83–99.

Meltzoff, A., & Moore, K. (1999). Persons and representation: Why infant imitation is important for theories of human development. In J. Nadel & G. Butterworth (Eds.), *Imitation in infancy.* Cambridge studies in cognitive perceptual development (pp. 9–35). New York: Cambridge University Press.

Merleau-Ponty, M. (1961). *The phenomenology of perception.* London: Routledge.

Mojzisch, A., Schilbach, L., Helmert, J. R., Pannasch, S., Velichkovsky, B., & Vogeley, K. (2006). The effects of self-involvement on attention, arousal, and facial expression during social interaction with virtual others: A psychophysiological study. *Social neuroscience, 1*(3–4), 184–195.

Moore, C. (1999). Gaze following and the control of attention. In P. Rochat (Ed.), *Early social cognition* (pp. 241–256). Mahwah, NJ: Erlbaum.

Morales, M., Mundy, P., & Rojas, J. (1997). Gaze following and language development in 6 and 8 month-olds. *Infant Behaviour and Development, 21*, 349–372.

Morisette, P., Ricard, M., & Gouin-Decarie, T. (1995). Joint visual attention and pointing in infancy: A longitudinal study of comprehension. *British Journal of Developmental Psychlogy, 13*, 163–175.

Muir, D., & Hains, S. (1999). Young infants' perception of adult intentionality. In P. Rochat (Ed.), *Early social cognition* (pp. 155–188). Mahwah, NJ: Erlbaum.

Murray, L. (1980). *The sensitivities and expressive capacities of young infants in communication with their mothers*. Unpublished PhD thesis, University of Edinburgh.

Murray, L., & Trevarthen, C. (1985). Emotional regulation of interactions between two-month-old infants and their mothers. In T. Field & N. Fox (Eds.), *Social perception in infancy* (pp. 177–197). Norwood, NJ: Ablex.

Nadel, J., & Tremblay-Leveau, H. (1999). Early perception of social contingencies and interpersonal intentionality: Dyadic and triadic paradigms. In P. Rochat (Ed.), *Early social cognition* (pp. 189–212). Mahwah, NJ: Erlbaum.

Nagy, E. (2008). Innate intersubjectivity: Newborns' sensitivity to communication disturbance. *Developmental Psychology, 44*(6), 1779–1784.

Nagy, E., & Molnar, P. (2004). Homo imitans or homo provocans? The phenomenon of neonatal imitation. *Infant Behaviour and Development, 27*, 57–63.

Nakano, S., & Kanaya, Y. (1993). The effects of mothers' teasing: Do Japanese infants read their mothers' play intention in teasing? *Early Development and Parenting, 2*, 7–17.

Neisser, U., & Becklen, R. (1975). Selective looking: Attending to visually specified events. *Cognitive Psychology, 7*, 480–494.

Olson, D., Astington, J., & Zelazo, P. (1999). Introduction: Actions, intentions and attributions. In P. D. Zelazo, J. W. Astington, & D. R. Olson (Eds), *Developing theories of intention* (pp. 1–13). Mahwah, NJ: Erlbaum.

Parise, E., Palumbo, L., Handl, A., & Frederici, A. (2008, September). *Gaze direction influences word processing in 4- to 5-month-old infants: An ERP investigation*. Poster presented at the Developmental Section Conference of the British Psychological Society, Oxford.

Penn, D. C., & Povinelli, D. J. (2007). On the lack of evidence that nonhuman animals possess anything remotely resembling a "theory of mind." *Philosophical Transactions of the Royal Society, B, 362*(1480), 731–744.

Perner, J. (1991). *Understanding the representational mind*. Harvard: MIT Press.

Perucchini, P., & Camaioni, L. (1993). *Proto-declarative and proto-imperative pointing*. Poster presented at the Annual Conference of the Developmental Section of the BPS, Birmingham.

Phillips, W., Baron-Cohen, S., & Rutter, M. (1992). The role of eye contact in goal-detection. Evidence from normal toddlers and children with autism or mental handicap. *Development and Psychopathology, 4*, 375–384.

Posner, M., & Cohen, Y. (1984). Components of visual orienting. In H. Bouma & D. Bouwhuis (Eds.), *Attention and performance X* (pp. 531–554). Hillsdale, NJ: LEA.

Reddy, V. (1991). Playing with others' expectations: Teasing and mucking about in the first year. In A. Whiten (Ed.), *Natural theories of mind* (pp. 143–158). Oxford: Blackwell.

Reddy, V. (1996). Omitting the second-person in mind knowledge. *Behavioral and Brain Sciences, 16*, 140–141.

Reddy, V. (1998). *Person-directed play: Humour and teasing in infants and young children*. Research on Grant No. R000235481 received from the Economic and Social Research Council.

Reddy, V. (2000). Coyness in early infancy. *Developmental Science, 3*(2), 186–192.

Reddy, V. (2001). Infant clowns: The interpersonal creation of humour in infancy. *Enfance, 3*, 247–256.

Reddy, V. (2003). On being an object of attention: Implications for self–other consciousness. *Trends in Cognitive Sciences, 7*(9), 397–402.

Reddy, V. (2005). Before the "third element": Understanding attention to self. In N. Eilan, C. Hoerl, T. McCormack, & J. Roessler (Eds.), *Joint attention: communication and other minds* (pp. 85–109). Oxford: Clarendon Press.

Reddy, V. (2008a). *How infants know minds*. Cambridge, MA: Harvard University Press.

Reddy, V. (2008b). Experiencing the social: A second person approach. In U. Muller, J. Carpendale, N. Budwig & B. Sokol (Eds.), *Social life and social knowledge: Toward a process account of development* (pp.123–143). Mahwah, NJ: Erlbaum.

Reddy, V., Hay, D., Murray, L., & Trevarthen, C. (1997). Communication in infancy: Mutual regulation of affect and attention. In G. J. Bremner, A. Slater, & G. Butterworth (Eds.), *Infant development: Recent advances* (pp. 247–273). Hove, UK: Psychology Press.

Reddy, V., Hicks, K., Jonnalagadda, S., Liebal, K., & Beena, C. (in preparation). The emergence of compliance in infancy.

Reddy, V., & Morris, P. (2004). Participants don't need theories. *Theory and Psychology*, *14*(5), 647–665.

Reddy, V., Williams, E., & Vaughan, A. (2002). Sharing humour and laughter in autism and Down's syndrome. *British Journal of Psychology*, *93*(2), 219–242.

Rodriguez, C. (2009). The "circumstances" of gestures: Proto-interrogatives and private gestures. *New Ideas in Psychology*, *27*(2), 288–303.

Ross, H. S., & Lollis, S. P. (1987). Communication within infant social games. *Developmental Psychology*, *23*, 241–248.

Scaife, M., & Bruner, J. (1975). The capacity for joint visual attention in the human infant. *Nature*, *253*, 265–266.

Schilbach, L., Wohlschlaeger, A. M., Kraemer, N. C., Newen, A., Shah, N. J., Fink, G. R., & Vogeley, K. (2006). Being with virtual others: Neural correlates of social interaction. *Neuropsychologia*, *44*, 718–730.

Scholl, B. (2001). Objects and attention: The state of the art. *Cognition*, *80*, 1–46.

Senju, A., Csibra, G., & Johnson, M. (2008). Understanding the referential nature of looking: Infants' preference for object-directed gaze. *Cognition*, *108*, 303–319.

Service, V. (1984). Maternal styles and communicative development. In A. Lock & E. Fisher (Eds.), *Language development* (pp. 132–140). London: Croom Helm.

Simons, D.J., & Chabris, C.F. (1999). Gorillas in our midst: Sustained inattentional blindness for dynamic events. *Perception*, *28*, 1059–1074.

Somerville, J.A., Woodward, A.L., & Needham, A. (2005). Action experience alters 3-month-old infants' perception of others' actions. *Cognition*, *96*(1), B1–B11.

Sorce, J., Emde, R., Campos, J., & Klinnert, M. (1985). Maternal emotional signalling: Its effect on the visual cliff behaviour of one-year-olds. *Developmental Psychology*, *21*, 195–299.

Southgate, V., Johnson, M., & Csibra, G., (2008). Infants attribute goals even to biomechanically impossible actions. *Cognition*, *107*(3), 1059–1069.

Stayton, D. J., Hogan, R., & Ainsworth, M. (1971). Infant obedience and maternal behaviour: The origins of socialization reconsidered. *Child Development*, *42*, 1057–1070.

Stern, D. (1985). *The interpersonal world of the infant*. New York: Basic Books.

Striano, T. (2004). Direction of regard and the still face effect in the first year: Does intention matter? *Child Development*, *72*, 468–479.

Striano, T., & Bertin, E. (2005). Coordinated affect with mothers and strangers: a longitudinal study of joint attention between 5 and 9 months of age. *Cognition and. Emotion 19*, 781–890.

Striano, T., Kopp, C., Grossman, T., & Reid, V. (2006). Eye contact influences neural processing of emotional expressions in 4-month-old infants. *SCAN*, *1*, 87–94.

Striano, T., Stahl, D., Cleveland, A., & Hoehl, S. (2007). Sensitivity to triadic attention between 6 weeks and 3 months of age. *Infant Behaviour and Development*, *30*, 529–534.

Sugita, Y. (2008). Face perception in monkeys reared with no exposure to faces. *PNAS*, *105*(1), 394–398.

Symons, L. A., Hains, S. M. J., & Muir, D. W. (1998). Look at me: 5-month-olds' sensitivity to very small deviations in eye-gaze during social interactions. *Infant Behaviour and Development*, *21*(3), 531–536.

Tomasello, M. (1999). Social cognition before the revolution. In P. Rochat (Ed.), *Early Social Cognition* (pp. 301–314). Mahwah, NJ: Erlbaum.

Tomasello, M., & Barton, M. (1994). Learning words in non-ostensive contexts. *Developmental Psychology*, *30*, 639–650.

Tomasello, M., Carpenter, M., Call, J., Behne, T., & Moll, H. (2005). Understanding and sharing intentions: The origins of cultural cognition, *Behavioural and Brain Sciences*, *28*, 675–735.

Tomasello, M., Kruger, A., & Ratner, H. (1993). Cultural learning. *Behavioural and Brain Sciences*. *16*, 495–552.

Trevarthen, C. (1977). Descriptive analyses of infant communication behaviour. In H.R. Schaffer (Ed.), *Studies in mother-infant interaction: The Loch Lomond Symposium*, (pp. 227–270). London: Academic Press.

Trevarthen, C. (1980). The foundations of intersubjectivity: Development of interpersonal and cooperative understanding in infants. In D. Olson (Ed.), *The social foundations of language and thought: Essays in honor of J. S. Bruner*. New York: Norton, 316–342.

Trevarthen, C. (1990). Signs before speech. In T. A. Sebeok & J. Umiker-Sebeok (Eds.), *The semiotic web* (pp. 689–755). Berlin: Mouton de Gruyter.

Trevarthen, C., & Hubley, P. (1978). Secondary intersubjectivity: Confidence, confiding and acts of meaning in the first year. In A. Lock (Ed.), *Action, gesture and symbol*, (pp.183–229). London: Academic Press.

Van der Meer, A., Van der Weel, F., & Lee, D. N. (1995). The functional significance of arm movements in neonates. *Science*, *267*, 693–695.

Vecera, S. P., & Johnson, M. H. (1995). Gaze detection and the cortical processing of faces: evidence from infants and adults. *Visual Cognition*, *2*, 59–87.

Vedeler, D. (1994). Infant intentionality as object-directedness: A method for observation. *Scandinavian Journal of Psychology*, *35*(4), 343–366.

Vygotsky, L. (1926/1962). *Thought and language*. Cambridge, MA: MIT Press. Warneken, F., & Tomasello, M. (2007). Helping and cooperation at 14 months of age. *Infancy*, *11*(3), 271–294.

Whiten, A. (1994). Grades of mind reading. In C. Lewis & P. Mitchell (Eds), *Children's early understanding of mind* (pp. 47–70). Hove: LEA.

Willen, J. D., Hood, B. M., & Driver, J. R. (1997). An eye direction detector triggers shifts of visual attention in human infants. *Investigative Opthalmology and Visual Science*, *38*, 313.

Wolff, P. H. (1987). *The development of behavioral states and the expression of emotions in early infancy: New proposals for investigation*. Chicago: University of Chicago Press.

Woodward, A. (1998). Infants selectively encode the goal of an actor's reach. *Cognition*, *69*, 1–34.

Woodward, A. L. (1999). Infants' ability to distinguish between purposeful and non-purposeful behaviours. *Infant Behaviour and Development*. *22*(2), 145–160.

Woodward, A. L., & Somerville, J. A. (2000). Twelve-month-olds interpret action in context. *Psychological Science*, *11*(1), 73–77.

Warneken, F., & Tomasello, M. (2007). Helping and cooperation at 14 months of age. *Infancy*, *11*(3), 271–294.

13

Preverbal Communication

Andrew Lock and Patricia Zukow-Goldring

Successful communication requires the continuous coordination of the attention of self and others to meanings carried by actions, gestures, and/or words, as the participants unceasingly negotiate a shared understanding. Thus, for the infant-novice, the process of becoming adept at participating in everyday life entails becoming able to engage in interaction and to negotiate sufficient shared meaning to maintain a practical consensus that permits interaction to continue in a mutually intelligible way.

Are these abilities preadaptations, autonomously learned, guided (Fogel, 1993, p. 85), or some combination of all these things? Is communication the individual achievement of either the "sender" or the "receiver" (Papoušek, 2007)? Or is it co-constructed? Should we expect the same course of development across cultures or do different cultures nurture different paths (De León, 2000; Keller, 2007)? There are two broad frameworks available for approaching these questions. The first is the traditional cognitive science approach ordered around the concept of internal representations. Here, meanings, intentions, and so on are regarded as not directly observable, since they are processes that are internal to an organism, and, thus, can only be inferred from the behaviors that they produce. Therefore, development is conceived as a process of becoming better able to interpret the behaviors of others through the construction of more and more complex systems of representations of the world and others. The second framework, which can be characterized as embodied, situated, distributed (ESD) interactionism (see Lock & Hill, forthcoming), is quite wary of this representational account. In contrast, this perspective regards organisms as embodied actors. The body that is observed does not express the results of internally computed plans. Intentions and meanings are not hidden away internally, needing to be theorized and interpreted. Rather, they are directly available to observation because they are a constitutive component of what is observed. This approach goes back to Wundt in his (1900) critique of Darwin's (1872) work on the expression of the emotions: actions and gestures are not *expressions* of emotions, but rather an *integral part* of an emotion or experience. For example, shivering is not something which *expresses* having a fever: it is a *component* of having a fever. Thus, development is conceived as a process of differentiation in which infant-novices' attention is educated during interaction as well as solitary action, so that they become better able to detect what the physical and social environment affords for action (e.g., E. J. Gibson, 1969; J. J. Gibson, 1979; Zukow-Goldring, 1997, 2006).

Despite these macro differences in perspectives, investigations of this early period can now be formulated much more coherently than in previous decades. Interest in preverbal communication only really began in the 1970s. The early work was characterized by two issues. The first was establishing the general lie of the land through largely naturalistic work, made possible with the advent of affordable and portable video technology (a technology that is now much more powerful and still a bedrock vehicle for work on this topic). The second was an intellectual audacity on the part of mainly postgraduate students looking at this period for the purpose of their PhD theses. This audacity comprised a simultaneous adoption and rejection of key planks in the insights of generative linguists, particularly Chomsky (1965). The adopted point was that, for understanding language, the behaviorist paradigm was unproductive. Similarly, a stimulus–response framework could not handle preverbal communication. Finally, mentalistic terms, such as "understanding," "intention," and "meaning" needed to be used to describe the course of development as it was being revealed through a participant observer standpoint (Goffman, 1981; DeWalt, DeWalt, & Wayland, 1998). While it is now commonplace to find papers investigating how the ability to *understand* another's perspective develops, or to specify the conditions under which "very young infants *interpret actions as referential* [italics added]" (Tremblay & Rovira, 2007, p. 376), the rehabilitation of these terms remains a gradual process. The rejected point was Chomsky's insistence on the uniqueness of language and that its appearance in the second year of life was based on the possession of innately given knowledge of the possible grammatical structures of human languages. This view trivialized developments prior to that age as irrelevant to language acquisition. While the development of grammar is still not adequately explained today, the view that prelinguistic communication is irrelevant to becoming able to talk has long gone.

Three factors have subsequently contributed to a sharpening up of the investigative terrain: data; theoretical interpretation; and the practical demands of robotics researchers. Data and theoretical interpretation now interpenetrate and inform each other. This was not initially the case. One of the most important early studies is that of Bates, Benigni, Bretherton, Camaioni, & Volterra (1979). Their pioneering longitudinal work was motivated by curiosity rather than hypotheses. The basic aim was to measure as many parameters as possible in a longitudinal cohort of infants from 9 to 13 months (with some followed up at 18 months) to reveal associations and dissociations among the measures made across age and time. Their results provided some of the basic data for understanding early communicative development: that measures of means–ends analysis – as indexed by tool use – as well as imitation and communicative gesturing were predictive of later symbolic communication, whereas object permanence scores, for example, were not. These findings were the motivation for asking "why?" questions – why tool use?, and why not object permanence?, for example – as well as "how" questions – how is imitation done? This basic research plan has subsequently been successfully adopted with more theoretically motivated objectives so as to tease out the component skills that feed into the transition to language, such as individual differences in memory abilities, temperament, joint attention, pattern recognition, and so forth. (e.g., Camaioni, Aureli, Bellagamba, & Fogel, 2003; Greenspan & Shanker, 2007; Heimann et al., 2006; Morales, Mundy, Delgado, Yale, Messinger, et al., 2000; Mundy & Gomes, 1998; Slater, 1995; Smith, Fagan, & Ulvund, 2002). These longitudinal studies have been supplemented with cross-sectional ones that are similarly motivated (e.g., Jones & Hong, 2001). Longitudinal and cross-sectional research designs have also been extended to include intra- and cross-cultural studies (e.g., de León, 2000; Keller, 2007; Morales, Mundy, Delgado, Yale, Neal, et al., 2000; Zukow-Goldring, 2006 – see below) and other species (e.g., Gomez, 2005; Masataka, 2003b – see below). At the same time, the general developmental schedules and frameworks that these studies enable have come under an increasing spotlight of experimental work in which robustly grounded hypotheses are put to the test (e.g., Amano, Kezuka, & Yamamoto, 2004; Butterworth, 2003; Striano, Stahl, Cleveland, & Hoehl, 2007; Tremblay & Rovira, 2007).

Theory has come to the fore in the past decade, in the sense of how best to interpret what is going on such that infants do develop the social and cultural understanding that underwrites their beginning to talk in their second year of life. The debate is healthy, because the issues at stake are so crucial to a wider grasp of the fundamental question: what is it that enables the species of *Homo sapiens* to become persons? On this issue, the nature of prelinguistic development and the transition to symbolic communication is where the action is. As befits its status, this developmental period is characterized by differences in theoretical orientations that range from micro to macro. Understanding the process of joint attention and its contribution to development can be used as an example of both ends of the scale. "Joint attention" is a category of interactive activity in which caretaker and infant are able to coordinate their attention simultaneously on a common focus. Researchers agree that shared attention is centrally important to most facets of social and language development and most concur regarding the course of its emergence over time. However, as Racine & Carpendale (2007a, p. 4) note "there is an ongoing debate about the theoretical explanation for the development of these abilities and what such abilities reveal about infants' understanding." They list three broad areas of interpretation: *biologically driven theories*, which come in three varieties – starting-state nativism (e.g., Meltzoff & Brooks, 2001), modular maturation (e.g., Baron-Cohen, 1999), and an evolutionary-ecological approach (e.g., Butterworth, 2003); *cognitively driven theories*, which come in two varieties – secondary subjectivity (e.g., Trevarthen & Hubley, 1978) and intentional insight, the inferring of subjective states of others or "mind-reading" (e.g., Tomasello, Kruger, & Ratner, 2007); and *socially driven theories*, which come in four varieties – mental state matching (e.g., Barresi & Moore, 1996, Moore, 1999), Piagetian (e.g., Piaget, 1963/1936); emotional engagement (e.g., Hobson, 1993, 2004; see also Greenspan & Shanker, 2004, 2007); and we add the embodied, situated, and distributed approach adopted here.

Overlaid on these approaches are further theoretical variations. First, there is the isolated Cartesian child with a disembodied, representational mind running algorithms laid down in the Pleistocene who somehow deduces the knowledge and rules that are being played out by those with whom she interacts, and uses these to generate her own behavior. Second, there is the embodied infant (e.g., Merleau-Ponty, 1964) whose shared understandings emerge while engaged in social practices (e.g., Cowley, 2004, Racine and Carpendale, 2007b; Zukow-Goldring, 1997, 2006) or "utterance activities" (e.g., Spurrett & Cowley, 2004). Partaking in language games cultivates and thereby assembles a "form of life" or shared context (Wittgenstein, 1953). The problematics of these two positions also arise in robotics (below), where similar tensions of interpretation also exist.

Robotics researchers aim to design intelligent agents that can focus on, engage in, and eventually communicate about the "same" aspects of ongoing events. To do this requires very articulated analyses of the abilities that underlie such accomplishments. Kaplan and Hafner's review (2006) leads them to propose four skills necessary for attaining joint attention: attention detection – tracking where the other is looking; attention manipulation – directing the other's attention; social coordination – interacting cooperatively with the other; and intentional understanding – appreciating that the self and the other are attempting to reach particular goals. This same set of skills may also be key to designing robots that can learn new behaviors via imitation (e.g., Breazeal & Scassellati, 2002; Dautenhahn & Nehaniv, 2002). Using infant development as a basis for designing robots capable of joint attention highlights gaps in developmental theory and research (e.g., how the dynamic coupling of attention and action in embodied agents leads to a shared understanding, Zukow-Goldring, 2006, Zukow-Goldring & Arbib, 2007). The aim is a feedback loop in which data on infants' abilities might be decomposed to enable their use in robotics; and work in robotics might point to missing elements in the developmental literature, motivating new avenues of infant research. Such reverse engineering may specify the likely component skills that eventually enable symbolic communication.

Before turning to recent research and theoretical perspectives, we summarize some changes in the field as well as persistent methodological issues. On the positive side, the last decade of work by and large confirms the "developmental milestones" that were previously apparent. That is, there are some major reorganizations observable in infants' communicative abilities at around 3, 6, and 9 months of age. What we have now, though, is a much finer grain to these observations. There has been, for example, that well-known phenomenon in infant research of abilities thought to occur in older infants, and be characteristic of, say 9-month-old infants, now being found within the gamut of much younger infants (in the case of joint attention, see Amano et al., 2004; for gaze following, D'Entremont, Hains, & Muir, 1997).

We are using the term "by and large" above in a cautionary way. In experimental studies, most researchers hone in on *what* infants "know" at what age, whereas, in more naturalistic settings, others investigate *how* they come to "know." Many recent studies are laboratory-based, with experimental designs that control variables between different subjects and settings, so as to tease out, in the classical way, what is "really going on." There are plusses and minuses for the experimental paradigm in psychology in general. But, in the case of studies of interaction and those involving infants in particular, the situation is particularly confusing. For example, if, as Vygotsky (1978) argued, the crucial developmental situation is acting within an apprentice's zone of proximal development, what can one learn or infer by seeing what an infant does or does not do when bereft of social support in an impoverished, unfamiliar environment? Although laboratory results may be dramatic and significant, researchers too often inadvertently test rare or never-occurring activities that have little relation to what people actually do in the physical and sociocultural environments in which they usually do them (Bronfenbrenner, 1979; Brunswick, 1947). Conversely, naturalistic, observational studies may rate well for eco- logical validity, but they suffer from other problems. Many infant communicative actions may be produced with very low frequencies in everyday life. This drawback is more pronounced as younger infants are observed. In addition, anyone with experience in testing or observing an infant in the morning and afternoon of the same day will appreci- ate a "different" infant can show up on each occasion. In sum, methodological issues are endemic when investigating preverbal communication.

Coding "the data" is also problematic, because what counts as a category of action, to be assigned to this column rather than that as particular data, always needs an interpretive decision. Like words, preverbal gestures are highly context-dependent in their ability to convey meaning; and this is no doubt even more the case with the components of their precursor abilities. Even such apparently clear-cut examples as episodes of pointing and joint attention are actually not fully transparent and ostensively definable. A hand may extend an index finger, but that does not make it a point; similarly, eyes making contact do not by themselves mean either person is looking at the other. Interobserver reliability checks are never perfect, but in practice are generally adequate.

Overview of Prelinguistic Period

The course of preverbal communicative development is punctuated by 3 major transitions during the first year of life. The timing of these transitions shows some variability in age of occurrence across different infants, thus the ages we give here must be taken as approxi- mate. The *first* of these occurs at around 3 months of age, when infants begin to engage communicatively with caregivers. This change is sudden – "almost as clear a boundary as birth itself" (Stern, 1985, p. 37). The *second* transition occurs late in the fifth month of age. Infants, again quite suddenly, appear to lose their interest in face-to-face interac- tions with caregivers who, instead, begin to redirect infants' attention to objects that they can manipulate (Lamb, Morrison, & Malkin, 1987; Messer & Vietze, 1984; Stern, 1985). The *third* transition is less clear-cut, but occurs around 9 to 10 months of age, arising from and building on infants' nonverbal understanding of everyday events (Greenfield & Smith, 1976). As infants' interest in objects connects with their emerging grasp of the agentive abilities of other people (Trevarthen & Hubley, 1978, pp. 221–222; see also Barresi & Moore, 1996; Carpendale & Lewis, 2004), "real" communication emerges at this time, with infants starting to use gestures to achieve their goals (Bates et al., 1979). Note that the course that any particular infant now takes in moving forward to verbal communication will vary as the different areas of this grasp and their emerging referential abilities are elaborated by the caregiving environment and subsequently feed back into the differentiation of the particular skills that enable language. Perhaps the increasing multideterminedness of development has an immediate effect that leads to this transi- tional point being a little less clear-cut than the two previous ones. In all cases, however, changes in cognitive abilities and interactional skill – as new biologically determined "bits of kit" come online – suggest that perceptual factors and the general course of growth are major underwriters of the changes we see in infant behaviors and actions.

The least certain temporal point in "preverbal communication" is when it might be said to end. There are two issues involved here. First, the individual differences between infants as to when they begin to "talk" are large, such that any time during the second year of life could be regarded as "normal." Second, when does a communicative episode or item stop being "preverbal" and become "verbal"? How one answers this question is important. On the one hand, a clear, operational definition could be regarded as an important topic to settle, for if the "data" being studied are ill-defined, then the first stage of a scientific investigation is stymied. On the other hand, though, clear definitions can create artifactual developmental Rubicons that then obscure the very processes of change that scientific investigations are seeking to understand. These are problems that we will return to later in this chapter. What needs to be borne in mind until then, however, is that all of the phenomena being dealt with here are at root *transitional*, rather than *categorical*, ones. At the outset, infants are "without speech"; but by the age of 2 years, small increments in the different strands of their development have fed back and forth among themselves to endow them with the qualitatively different ability of being able to "talk."

This qualitative change in the status of early communication is a major complicating factor in the way this period of infancy is understood and reported in the literature. Psychology still lacks an explanatory theoretical framework in which to locate the key components of "how to make meanings in a human world." As a result, the research to date on preverbal communication is very difficult to summarize in a coherent way, given the biological, cognitive, and/or social frameworks used by different researchers.

There are three main problems to be faced. First, as will be obvious when dealing with the development of communication, at least two partners have to be involved in the process. Thus, it is not immediately apparent what the most appropriate "unit of analysis" is: individuals or the groups they constitute. Second, "communication" is a quite variable phenomenon. Some aspects of communication can be handled by a purely objective approach, and we can talk sensibly, for example, of communicative *signals* produced by individual animals that have become chained together to produce patterns of behaviors in which each stimulates the other to produce the stimulus for the next act, and so on (see, for example, almost any ethological study of animal courtship behaviors). Communication, at this level, may simply be the coordination of the activities of two individuals, and the question "what does animal A *mean* when it does X?" is not one that need be asked. This is not the case, though, with respect to gestural and linguistic communications, which, at least, have intentional and meaningful aspects that go beyond a purely objective level of description and explanation. Which is the most appropriate strategy with respect to early human infant communication – dealing with infant "behaviors and their functional significance for later communication" or "communicated meanings?" Masataka's ethological studies with monkeys and investigations of human caregiver–infant interaction (2003b) suggest an answer. He proposes that the precursors of the human ability to communicate with each other derive from behaviors shared with nonhuman primates, such that coordinating action becomes a stepping stone to later exchanges of information. His research confirms that monkeys engage in vocal turn-taking, modulate natural vocalizations to match those of kin and group, produce particular vocalizations in appropriate contexts, and exchange information that identifies individual, group, "internal" states (such as "lost"), location, etc. In monkeys and humans, such behaviors do not appear fully formed, but are refined during social interaction. However, monkeys display these abilities adeptly only as adults, whereas human infants become proficient during the first years of life. These (remarkable) parallels underscore the significance of caregiver–infant interaction, both phylogenetically and ontogenetically (see below), to the subsequent emergence of communication and eventually language.

Third, and related to this dilemma, are the issues of subjectivity and intersubjectivity. Mutual eye contact is one of the most emotionally charged and satisfying forms of interchange caregivers participate in with their young offspring, but what does the infant make of it? Is it similarly a satisfying sharing or communion of being for them, or are caregiver eyes just very interesting things to look *at*, rather than *into*? We return to these issues in our concluding section.

The Course of Development

To assess the perceptual, cognitive, and social interactive aspects of development, we summarize important achievements related to preverbal communication from a variety of theoretical perspectives. We present research that has investigated these aspects of development during periods following key developmental transitions: neonatal, 3, 6, and 9 to 10 months as well as developments in the second year.

Birth to 3 months

The first of four major achievements attained during this period is that caretakers and infants come to share increasing amounts of time "staring at each other." There appear to be a number of developmental strands that contribute to this. Newborn infants periodically, but briefly, show a transitory state of quiet or inactive alertness, which is a "fragile and easily disrupted condition" (Wolff, 1987, p. 66). Infants have been reported to spend about 10% of their waking time in this state during their first week of life (Berg, Adkinson, & Strock, 1973). These periods increase in both frequency and length until they occupy around half of daylight waking hours in the third month (Wolff, 1987). Being able to maintain this state is self-evidently crucial to the infant and caregiver subsequently sharing and modulating their mutual attention.

Second, an increasing "control" by the infant over the "components" of its states of arousal becomes apparent. Crying by newborns, for example, is not just a vocal activity, but a whole package of facial distortions, limb movements, changes in skin coloration and muscle tone, breathing patterns, and hand-clenching (Wolff, 1987; Papoušek & Papoušek, 1977). The activity appears to be a species-specific response to distress, and the amplitude of crying conveys information about the infant's level of distress rather than any more specific information as to what the nature of that distress is. Anything more specific about what a cry might mean is a construction on the part of caregivers (see, for example, Frodi, 1985; Gustafson & Harris, 1990; Zeskind, 1985). The early developmental course of crying follows what Barr (1990) has termed a *normal cry curve*: its frequency rises from birth to a peak during the second month, and then declines to a low level around 4 months of age. This turns out to be true even in cultures where, because of differences in care in comparison to those Western societies from which most of the data come, infants cry much more rarely (Barr, Konner, Bakeman, & Adamson, 1991). Periods of infant alertness come to overlap more and more with the caregiver routines of holding and talking to them (Chappell & Sander, 1979; Sander, 1977). Sander comments (1977, p. 147) that it is through these early interactions that "unique and idiosyncratic characteristics of exchange" develop that increasingly regulate the inter-actions of caregivers and infants: endogenous rhythms become restructured around social ones, providing a patterned framework within which development proceeds. For instance, infants begin to notice that caregivers respond contingently to their behavior. Caregivers reflect back positive displays of affect and react differentially to negative affect, say, with soothing caresses or vocalizations (Papoušek, 2007). As early as 5 weeks of age, infants of highly attuned mothers "answer" by gazing, smiling, and vocalizing more, contributing to an exchange of affect (Markova & Legerstee, 2006). Thus, affect-arousal regulation (Kaye, 1982) emerges near the end of this period, giving rise to a potent combination of skills that have functional significance for communication (Stern, 1999), including responding contingently and in kind to the other.

The infant's interest in mutual gaze as opposed to faces more generally would appear to be present from birth (e.g., Farroni, Csibra, Simion, & Johnson, 2002). Again, ingen-ious experimental work suggests that the precursors of an ability to follow another's gaze may well be present at birth (Farroni, Johnson, & Csibra, 2004). Similarly sophisticated investigations (e.g., Hood, Willen, & Driver, 1998) reveal a sensitivity to the cues of another's changes in gaze by 3 months of age. Note, however, that gaze following may be socially responsive, but that is not evidence that the infant understands or notices what the other sees (even in infants of 9 to 11 months) (Brune & Woodward, in press). Further, in this early period there is no evidence that infants under naturalistic conditions are able to follow the gaze of another if they break away from eye-contact to look elsewhere (Striano et al., 2007). The reasons for these differences in performance are informative. Hood (1995) demonstrated the difficulty young infants have in disengaging their interest from salient cues, such as an adult's face interacting with them. They are thus "stuck" with what they see. To move on from here requires two changes. The first is the infant gaining voluntary control over her attention. The second is that the caregiver socially engineers something interesting enough that the infant "wants" to see what it is somebody else is looking at and in so doing experiences joint attention. Once achieved, shared attention provides the foundation for negotiating a shared understanding of ongoing events so crucial to successful communication.

Third, neonates can be described as being variously "preadapted" to having their atten-tion drawn to different components of the communicative systems they are immersed in. For instance, emerging perceptual systems are *selectively tuned* (to use Richards' phrase, 1974) to dimensions that form the characteristic constellations of objects and events in their social worlds. Stern (1977, p. 37) has termed this "innateness once removed." Thus, for example, infants may not initially be specifically attracted to human faces *per se*, but adult human faces presented to them in the real time of everyday life may be sites that condense the varied perceptual dimensions that are individually attractive to infants: contrast, organization, movement, and multimodality. In addition, adults tend to modify their social actions towards infants in ways that exaggerate those dimensions that infants already find attractive, thus making them even more attractive to infants (e.g., Fernald, 1991, for the characteristics of speech directed to infants; Stern, 1977, for facial expression and its rhythmic integration with sound and touch).

Fourth, unlike older infants who are most attracted to novelty, young infants are most attracted to familiar social events: 2-week-old breast-fed infants prefer the smell of their own mothers; within two days of birth neonates prefer their mothers' faces to those of others (Walton, Bower, & Bower, 1992; Field, Cohen, Garcia, & Greenberg, 1984); and because of what they will have heard most often in the womb before birth, they prefer the characteristic sounds and tempos of their mother's voice from the outset (De Casper and Spence, 1986). Note, though, that these kinds of familiar events are always varying in their specific occurrences and manifestations. If they did not, then infants would probably habituate to them, rather than find them so attractive.

From 3 months to 6 months

Infants change quite dramatically at the end of their second month: they begin to become intensely interested in people, and they become very rewarding "human" partners in the eyes of those who care for them (see, for details, Emde, Gaensbauer, & Harmon, 1976; Fischer & Hogan, 1989). While this change is most probably rooted in perceptual development, it has a qualitative rather than purely quantitative flavor: infants present a different interactive "feel" to those who engage with them. This "presence" arises quickly. The quantifiable changes that accompany it fall into four areas: alertness, gaze control, smiling, and cooing. Infants are now in a state of alert awareness for around 80% of their waking time (Wolff, 1987). They give the impression of being able to both select objects in their environment to attend to as well as initiate interpersonal actions, rather than have their attention captured by external events. Eye movements are under better control (e.g., Aslin, 1987); the caretaker's eyes can be focused on so that periods of sustained mutual regard become possible; and the distance over which coordinated interchanges can occur extends continuously outward, no longer occurring only while infants are held (Papoušek & Papoušek, 1977).

Facial expressions become more animated, and their timing synchronizes with the shared properties of the visual and physical interactions in which they are engaged. These behaviors leave the caregiver in no doubt that these expressions are part of their joint interaction with a human partner, rather than being merely random activities on the infant's part. Smiling, in particular, shifts from what has been termed endogenous to exogenous control, and is often directed to the adult with whom mutual gaze is being sustained (Emde et al., 1976; Wolff, 1987). Trevarthen (1979) has called attention to the increasing movements of the tongue and lips of the infant during interactions, terming it *prespeech*. In addition, Fogel and Hannan (1985) have noted how such prespeech can be accompanied by hand movements that adults also read as having an expressive content.

Overall, infants of this age become much more attuned to the finer details of the adult's vocal and facial expressions, and especially so to their temporal patterning. These tempos increasingly moderate the interpersonal meshing of affect for those involved. Further, these properties of their interaction begin to be clearly exploited by caregivers so as to maintain mutually enjoyable interactions with infants. For instance, "baby talk," exaggerated facial expressions, and the captivating of the infant's attention by exaggerating the temporal characteristics of "conversation" are prime aspects of the flowering of what Papoušek and Papoušek (1987) term "intuitive parenting" (see also Papoušek, 2007).

At the same time, infants become increasingly active participants in determining the course of interactions. Thus, the patterning of social interchanges results from the moment-to-moment responsiveness of each partner to the other, rather than being imposed by one or the other. There is evidence that 3- to 4-month-old infants can follow another's gaze, but as D'Entremont et al. (1997, p. 572), point out, "given the brevity of the ... shift in gaze, it should only be considered a precursor of a joint attention mechanism." This ability is more pronounced when the gaze shift in question is to another person and an interaction takes place between the two (termed "triangular" abilities) than when it is to an object (termed "triadic" abilities) (Tremblay and Rovira, 2007). Early attention to other persons is common in subsistence cultures as infants are in near constant body contact with their caregivers who hold them turned outward toward others, rather than in the face-to-face arrangement typical of technological cultures (Keller, 2007). Thus, caregiver and infant share the same visual field much of the time. For instance, among the Tzotzil Maya of Chiapas, Mexico, when a neighbor passing by called out, the caregiver turned to respond. As a result, her 4-month-old infant saw-and-heard the greeting at adult eye-level (de León, 2000).

Active participation in turntaking, a fundamental communicative pattern, requires proficient, socially contingent behavior. Masataka (2003b) argues that this most basic unit of interpersonal signaling in the vocal mode arises at about 3 months during nursing, rather than late in the first year, when infants begin to produce intonation contours, as previously claimed. When infants spontaneously coo after bouts of nursing (Kaye, 1982), caregivers respond contingently with behavior that evokes further nursing as well as exchanges of vocalizing and facial expression. Given the effectiveness of their contingent cooing behaviors, infants gradually come to modulate and control vocalizing. Thus, a protoconversational framework arises as old forms (spontaneous cooing) take on new communicative functions (turntaking) (Slobin, 1973; Werner & Kaplan, 1963; cf. Snow, 1977). Cooing plays another role as the first step in vocal learning at 3 to 4 months, when infants acquire the ability to produce speech-like sounds (Masataka, 2003b). Infant vocal quality changes from more nasal *vocalic sounds* to *syllabic sounds*. Adults prefer the latter and "echo" back, imitating most often the vowels /a/, /i/, and /u/ which appear in all the world's languages. This contingent responding may facilitate infants' perceptual development and ensuing ability to match the caregivers' vocalizations. As the infants become proficient imitators, caregivers gradually decrease their echoic responding. The basics of human communicative "dancing" are thus in place by about 6 months of age. Then infants head off on a new tack: they become dominated by an interest in "things" rather than people.

From 6–9 months to 10 months

Piaget (e.g., 1963/1936) was one of the first investigators to emphasize the importance of this three-month period in an infant's life. At the beginning of this time, what he calls "secondary schemes" – aimed at objects rather than the infant's body itself (primary schemes) – make their first appearance. These actions become coordinated around three months later to produce what he considered as the first truly intelligent and intentional behaviors: infants begin to act in ways that strongly suggest they are doing one thing *in order* that a particular end might be achieved. What Piaget did not emphasize in his classic account was the impact this interest in objects has for the development of communication. This shift to objects initially ruptures the episodes of mutual regard (Kaye & Fogel, 1980; Trevarthen & Hubley, 1978). However, this change simultaneously sets infants a new and crucially important problem: how to incorporate and recruit people to share in their interest in objects, or, more generally, the world that exists beyond the boundaries of their previous absorption in the microcosm of faces and voices. The new challenges are to coordinate these separate attentions on the world outside the dyad's immediate horizons; to initiate these coordinations; and to tell when these have not been achieved.

From a communicative perspective, these are very important challenges. Mastering them must in some way underpin the eventual move to achieving *reference* and to being able to talk *about* a common world, which is a primary characteristic of human language. At the root of these challenges is a complicated problem of imaginative interpersonal geometry: to come to understand, for example, that another's emotional expression can be a comment about something that is happening outside of the expression itself; to be able to "read" where another is looking so as to be able to locate and share in the event they are communicating about, rather than to be clueless as to what is going on; and to grasp that actions of self and other can "point to" something beyond themselves, such that one does not look *at* another's fingers and hands when they point with them (Carpenter, Nagel, & Tomasello, 1998; Morisette, Ricard, & Gouin-Decarie, 1995). Instead, one needs to follow the path indicated by the moving finger and then extend that path to where it intersects with the other's target of attention (Butterworth & Jarrett, 1991). These are not easy problems to solve, and human infants are almost the only organisms known to be able to master them (see below). This mastery is very much a joint achievement rather than individual one, with caregivers providing a framework for it. Caregivers, adult and sibling, provide a "scaffolding context" (Bruner, 1975; de León, 2000; Wood & Middleton, 1975; Zukow-Goldring, 2002) whereby they engage and sustain their involvement with infants-and-objects-and-others before infants can do this for themselves.

The intense research focus on joint attention probably arises from evidence that its achievement is a step toward *reference*: An infant's ability to detect the target of another's attention correlates with early word learning (Baldwin, 1995; Morales, Mundy, Delgado, Yale, Messinger, et al., 2000; Tomasello, 1988, 2003). However, what infants can actually do at this point in their lives is currently unclear. Butterworth (2003; see also Scaife & Bruner, 1975), for example, argues that there is evidence that 6- to 9-month-olds act on the assumption that their own visual space is held in common with those they are interacting with. That is, infants can use the visual information from the caregivers' looking to guide their own as a general strategy, but what they look at when they turn to follow another's gaze is not something infants can work out from just observing the caregiver. Rather, they end up looking at something that "stands out" as worth looking at when they orient in the direction of their caregivers' gaze. These "ecological" features of the environment capture attention, completing the message that the caregiver is signaling. In contrast, Corkum & Moore (1995) find no evidence that infants of this age can follow another's line of regard, and that, while this ability begins to come in around 12 months of age, it is still rudimentary and not fully formed until at least 15 months. Nevertheless, by 12 months most comprehend many words and produce somewhat fewer (Benedict, 1979; Fenson et al., 1994). Given this disjunction, how do infants learn the relation between word and referent (object) before they are skilled at detecting another's target of attention? Surprisingly, an important link between attention and early word learning may be the often disregarded fact that looking at some target of attention is not enough: People *talk* about what they are looking at and *look at and monitor the attention of* the person to whom they are talking. Thus, someone else, a caregiver, directs and educates an infant's attention from at least 6 months of age (Zukow-Goldring, 1997). In particular, caregivers in a variety of cultures "say-*and*-do" by synchronizing the onset/offset, tempo, and rhythm of saying a word and dynamically gesturing as they show objects, embody actions, or demonstrate properties in their infants' line of sight (Zukow-Goldring, 1997). These practices lead to learning early word–object associations in infants of 8 to 15 months (Gogate, Walker-Andrews, & Bahrick, 2001) and learning the correspondence between word and referent (Rader & Zukow-Goldring, in press/under review).

While it is important to gather more data on what infants can actually do in this period, we want to suggest that at this age it is the actions of the *caregiver* that are of the prime developmental significance as the findings from early word learning confirm. What we mean is this: if we take the central point from Piaget that infants learn through their actions on the world, then how the world they are learning about is structured becomes of major significance as to what they learn. During the last quarter of the first year of their lives, a number of new capabilities come "online" (see below). How these abilities are structured as they emerge is crucially dependent on the raw material they both work on and are forged through. That is, it is not just the case that infants act on the world, but that the world itself is *transacted* to them in the way another presents it.

Consider how a caregiver can interact with an infant whose interests are focused on object-manipulation when the objects are part of a form board into which the pieces can be fitted. If the pieces are in their places, then they can be difficult for a 7-month-old to extract. If the pieces are not in their places, then getting them there is even more difficult (shapes have to be oriented and matched to forms, for example). Putting pieces in places is not a goal these infants are likely to be able to formulate. However, they can achieve it, if the caregiver places the piece in such a way that just by touching it, the piece is likely to fall into its place. Further, their hands and grip can be embodied or put through the motions by caregivers, enabling them to achieve their aim. During such "assisted imitation," infants "see and feel what to do," as caregivers narrow the search space, so that infants learn the body's work as well as what objects afford for action (Zukow-Goldring, 2006). Infants have the opportunity to perceive that the self is "like others" as they act in tandem with others (Zukow-Goldring, in press): only much later can infants observe and then do what they see others doing. There are numerous other reports in the literature that draw attention to the ways caregivers, often seamlessly, structure the opportunities infants have for attending to and manipulating their environments (e.g. Adamson & Bakeman, 1984; Bruner, 1983; Trevarthen & Hubley, 1978). As they do so, infants gradually become "cultural beings" who notice and can participate in every-day activities. With this nonverbal, shared understanding, infants take a step closer to communicating about them (de León, 2000; Greenfield & Smith, 1976; Zukow-Goldring, 2002). Moreover, it is important to remember that the actions of caregivers are them-selves not just opportunistically forged in the changing possibilities their infants offer, as they act on objects that afford different canonical actions (balls are for rolling and blocks are for stacking – not just sucking, for example). Rather, the momentary possibili-ties for where-to-go-next are themselves embedded in the form-conserving practices, techniques, plans, formats of the cultural sphere within which caregivers structure their own plans and intentions: "the very essence of cultural development is in the collision of mature cultural forms of behavior with the primitive forms that characterize the child's behavior" (Vygotsky, 1981, p. 151). While Vygotsky's point applies equally to earlier periods, its importance is more apparent and critical as infants of this age begin to act with objects.

Toward the end of this period, we begin to see glimpses of infants being able to show the first stirrings of a coordination between their previous person-oriented communica-tion skills and at least their "reactions" with respect to objects and events. For example, Trevarthen & Hubley (1978, p. 200) report on a 38-week-old infant called Tracey: "Tracey and her mother banged hands on the table in alternation and Tracey, while looking at her mother, grinned at the effect they produced." To begin with, as these indications of an emerging awareness of the agency of others become apparent, there are few indications that infants can properly integrate action on objects into their commu-nicative interactions with caregivers (Tomasello, 1995, pp. 107–108).

From 9–10 months to 12 months

> At 40 weeks, Tracey's mother became an acknowledged participant in actions. Tracey repeat-edly looked up at her mother's face when receiving an object, pausing as if to acknowledge receipt. She also looked up to her mother at breaks in her play, giving an indication of willingness to share experiences as she had never done before. (Trevarthen & Hubley, 1978, p. 200)

Nine- to 12-month-old infants also seem to be in a transitional phase. Beginning around this time, their actions on the world and the staged integration of these into their social interactions with their culture that intrude on their otherwise individual "obsessions," start to bear fruit. This shift enables an active integration of infant, caregiver, object, and intention into more deliberate actions. There is a lot going on during this time. The changes that are reported in the infant's abilities are important in that, *first*, they evidence a qualitative shift in the character of their performance. *Second*, they appear in a number of abilities – for example, imitation (Meltzoff, 1988), conventionalized gesturing (Bates et al., 1979); social referencing (e.g., contributors to Feinman, 1992); giving and taking objects (Clark, 1978; Griffiths, 1954). Either severally or individually, these abilities contribute to the infant coming to understand that others are separate beings whose attention and goals may differ from those of their own. These different perspectives need to be brought into line with one another. Interactions become increasingly coordinated (Adamson & Bakeman, 1985), such that by the end of their first year infants undergo "a revolution in their understanding of persons ... that is just as coherent and dramatic as the one they undergo at around their fourth birthday" (Tomasello, 1995, p. 104; see also Bates, Bretherton, & Snyder, 1987; Bretherton, 1992; Tomasello et al., 1993).

The general course of development at this time is now quite well established in the literature. Around 9 months of age, infants begin to change their pattern of attention when interacting with objects and people simultaneously. Prior to this time, an infant will focus his or her attention exclusively on an object that they either want or have. In the first case, infants give the appearance of being "frustrated" at their lack of success in reaching for an object, for example, and express that frustration while continuing to look at the object. The participating caregiver may act to give the object to the infant. But, at around 9 months, infants begin to break their gaze, in such situations, away from the object to look back and forth between it and the caregiver: assistance in the pursuit of intentions is recruited rather than fortuitously received (Bates, Camaioni, & Volterra, 1975, Bates et al., 1979; Lock, 1978, 1980). That is, their communicative intent becomes more explicit as infants develop a number of, often idiosyncratic, gestures that can convey their desires (*protoimperatives*) – for example, objects can be "requested" by whining and reaching towards them, and interests or targets/topics of attention (*protodeclaratives*), can be pointed to (Bates, 1976; Volterra, Caselli, Caprici, & Pizzuto, 2005).

A nonverbal understanding of daily activities grounds the emergence of gestures. For example, requests, at first, are usually excerpts from direct actions: a stylized reach or upturned palm in the recruitment of assistance in obtaining an object (e.g. Clark, 1978; Bruner, Roy, & Ratner, 1982), or a raising of both arms so as to be picked up (Service, 1984). To begin with, these gestures are tied very closely to their immediate context of occurrence and only later extend beyond this as the infant's ability to predict events increases. Thus, when someone approaches with arms extended, a 9-month-old might arm-raise to be picked up. In contrast, a 13-month-old might anticipate being picked up because a meal is imminent, indicating the need to be moved by arm-raising to a nearby caregiver. Similarly, the distance over which objects can be requested also increases (Bruner et al., 1982; Werner & Kaplan, 1963). Infants of about 12 months are reported to request both objects (more water from a pitcher) and actions (opening a window) with (proto-) imperative pointing gestures (Tomasello et al., 2007). However, the main function of pointing appears to be declarative (attention-directing). At the end of the first year, the means of directing attention or referring to what is being requested or noticed is no longer limited to excerpts from action or pointing (*indexical signs*, see Peirce, 1955). Referring gestures now include *icons* which resemble or have a likeness to the topic of attention, extending referring beyond the immediate context to events experienced in the past. For instance, infants may use a twisting motion of the wrist and hand to specify "open this jar for me."

Returning to the topic of pointing, there is now evidence that chimpanzees and other great apes point to request as well, but rarely, if ever, point declaratively (to direct attention). Consequently, pointing is not truly a unique species characteristic of humans (Gomez, 2007; cf. Butterworth, 1995). However, those nonhuman-primates who do point have had a great deal of experience with human social interaction. Both human infants and captive chimpanzees experience environmental (cages, high chairs) and/or physical barriers (locomotor capacities) to obtaining desirable but unobtainable food or objects. Both are dependent on human caregivers to retrieve these (chimpanzees foraging in the wild do not experience such pressures). Leavens, Hopkins, & Bard, (2005) argue that the act of pointing arises during development in response to this referential problem which is solved by incorporating distant objects into the relationship between an individual sending a message and the one receiving it. Gomez (2007, p. 733) argues that the ability to "read" behavior *without implying the understanding and use of multi-layered mind-reading* underlies this accomplishment in both species. That is, detecting the visual appearance and orientation of the other's body and face, direction of gaze, and the target or aim of another's action within a particular physical environment narrows the search space, contributing to understanding someone's actions (Boesch, 1993; Povinelli, Bering, & Giambrone, 2000; Sterelny, 2002). In addition, D'Entremont and Seamons (2007) argue persuasively that human infants under 18 months use third-person cues to monitor attention and behavior, not an understanding of the subjective, first person, perspective of others. In contrast to nonhuman primates, the prolonged loco-motor immaturity of human infants as well as the degree to which they are physically restrained created, so Leavens et al. (2005, pp. 188–189) speculate, a referential problem space that may have had a causative influence on "'our species' evolutionary trajectory into referential communication."

Declarative pointing becomes productive later than imperative pointing to make requests, at around 12 months. Despite an increasing number of studies of this gesture, its actual developmental origins are still unclear. Some have argued (e.g., Vygotsky, 1966; Werner & Kaplan, 1963) that it is an abbreviated reach. Bates (1976) and Leung & Rheingold (1981) have claimed that it is originally an action for the self, enabling an infant to keep their own attention on an object out of reach and that this only later becomes imported into directing the attention of others. Still others contend that its origins are to be found in direct object exploration using the index finger and all that happens developmentally is that this exploratory action is called into play with respect to objects that are just out of reach (Masataka, 2003a). Whichever way, at first, pointing's unintentional social function is to direct another's attention, only later becoming controlled by the infant for this purpose.

The fact, however, that even imperative (requestive) pointing among nonhuman primates has taken nearly 30 years to be reported, and that so little evidence exists for declarative pointing, suggests that declarative pointing does not come easily to nonhuman primates. Apparently, then, the ability to divorce "desires" from objects and shift to wanting to "communicate something" about an object, event, or where one is looking is just that much more difficult to achieve than requesting. Declarative pointing does appear to have a separate origin from request gestures. For humans, then, pointing is most probably rooted in attention directing, rather than trying to gain contact with objects. Still other factors contribute to the mature performance of the act. For example, the anatomical configuration of the human hand predisposes the use of the index rather than any other finger for the actual performance of a point (see, Lock, Young, Service and Chandler, 1990; Povinelli & Davis, 1994). Cultural variability exists as well, favoring lip-, hand-, and head-pointing (Wilkins, 2003; Zukow-Goldring, 2006). Recently, several longitudinal studies link action, gesture, and word. Compelling evidence documents that adeptly engaging in everyday activities not only leads to "content-loaded" gestures in those activity settings, but eventually to producing words with corresponding meaning (Bavin et al., 2008; Camaioni et al., 2003; Caprici, Contaldo, Caselli, & Volterra, 2005; Volterra et al., 2005). As Camaioni et al. (2003, p. 25) noted "'true' symbolic communication and language do not arise as a sudden burst of words and sentences (something like a 'language organ'), but rather are grounded on social conventions constructed within communicative frames." Caregivers provide opportunities to relate word and referent for a range of semantic functions (objects, animate beings, actions, properties, and so on) in a variety of ways (Greenfield & Smith, 1976). They unceasingly "say-and-do" as they integrate talk about their own and their infants' ongoing actions (Zukow-Goldring, 1997). And, as infants become more adept at communicating, they create an environment for word learning. Caregivers talk about their infants' focus of attention (Carpenter et al. 1998; Rollins, 2003), the targets of their pointing (Brooks & Meltzoff, 2008) as well as translate their infants' gestures into words (Goldin-Meadow, Goodrich, Sauer, & Iverson, 2007). Communicating is not a one-way street: the perceiving and acting (behavior) of one continuously affects that of the other.

Developments during this time have been theorized as arising in different ways. Cognitive explanations have tended to be either inspired by the Piagetian notion of a fundamental reconfiguration of cognition that informs action in many different spheres (e.g., Adamson, Bakeman, & Smith, 1990; Fischer & Farrar, 1988). Others propose that developments occurring separately in different domains in concert establish a base for a new emergent ability that capitalizes on the achievements in the developmental strands that enable it. To repeat, Bates and colleagues (1979) found that measures of an infant's abilities with respect to imitation, tool use (an index of the infant's understanding of means-end relations) and conventionalized communicative abilities at earlier ages were predictive of the time of emergence of productive symbolic communicative abilities at a later age. Evidence from longitudinal, naturalistic studies conducted in subsistence as well as technological cultures suggest an answer to the "why" question regarding these three abilities we posed earlier. De León (2000) argues that nonverbal interaction plays a central role in socializing children to engage in communicative acts. Unpacking "nonverbal interaction" has documented that assisted imitation cultivates the use of cultural objects to achieve various ends and nurtures a shared understanding of daily life fundamental to communication (Zukow-Goldring, 2006). As infants interact, their use of stylized actions and gestures suggests they comprehend that these signs are tools which have an instrumental effect on others. Additionally, to use a conventional "word" requires one to know how to communicate, know how to reproduce (imitate) a conventional sound, and to have abstracted that sound out of the flow of speech one is immersed in (abstraction being integral to the mastery of means–end relations).

By contrast, Trevarthen (1988) argues for a genetic base to the emergence of intentional communication, taking the view that there is a real difference in the nature of understanding the causal world of objects and the intentional nature of people. The basis for this latter understanding is built into the design of the developing human brain which is anatomically partitioned from birth into three modes:

> These modes are probably three real systems of the brain that achieve functional differentia-
> tion by interaction with each other and with the environment. Forms of action and percep-
> tual processing appropriate for (1) knowing and using objects (praxic mode), for (2)
> communicating with the human world (communicative mode), and for (3) acting in a self-
> directed or thoughtful manner (reflective mode) appear as distinct rudiments in the newborn
> (Trevarthen & Hubley, 1978, p. 213).

The functional differentiation of action and perception during interactions with each other and the environment, plus the opportunities for the integration of the developing "contents," may account for the timing of the emergence of new levels of communicative competence. The evidence consistent with this claim is that there are detectable changes in cortical functioning that correlate with the timing of the changes noted thus far in the first year of life (e.g., Thatcher, Walker, & Giudice, 1987); cortical maturation correlates with the onset of new, apparently modular, abilities (e.g., Baron-Cohen, 1995); and the universality of the timing of these shifts cross-culturally (e.g., Bakeman, Adamson, Konner, & Barr, 1990; Trevarthen, 1988).

It would seem most likely that both cognitive achievements and perceptual differentia-
tion are integral to these changes in infant abilities, and that the course of development in any particular child is determined by the unique constellation of events that child's maturing "wetware" has available to it in the course of its structural – and hence func-
tional – differentiation. One such account is the *dynamic systems perspective* (e.g. Fogel, 1990; Thelen, 1989; Thelen & Smith, 1994; van Geert, 1991). Clearly, one thing that we do know beyond doubt from the intensive work on infancy in the past 40 years is that single factor explanations are wide of the required mark. This realization enriches our conception of these early developmental processes, but at the same time makes the "telling of a normative tale" as to the actual course of development that much more difficult, for there is no one way in which infants might go on to "crack the symbolic code." Rather, there are many individual trajectories that can be traversed to reach a successful outcome (Nelson, 1996).

Developments in the second year

Consider the episodes captured in Figures 13.1 and 13.2, which portray a 12-month-old infant deploying all the skills she has amassed during her first year of life so as to very clearly convey to another what she wants: in one case an apple, in the other "more to drink." How does she go from here into "language?" The major development beginning around 12 months of age happens in two modalities, and marks a "freeing of meaning from context" in, first, gesture and, second, vocalization. Deictic gestures such as pointing rely on the context in which they occur to specify the object that is being "commented on," as in Figure 13.1. Animate beings and objects can be specified using iconic gestures, for example, "walking fingers" to indicate a spider. Similarly, desired actions can be speci-

Figure 13.1   Unable to reach the apple (1), the child turns to attract the adult's attention by vocalizing (2). Having established eye contact with the adult (3), the child uses a pointing gesture to direct the adult's attention to the apple (4), thereby identifying the object implied as being wanted by the tonality of the vocalization. *Source*: Lock (1980), p. 98.

fied: a twisting motion of the hand to request opening a jar or door. Single element action or gestural communications predominate until around 16 months of age; words gradually become more numerous thereafter (Iverson, Caprici, & Caselli, 1994). Using sounds to convey such messages can "decontextualize" meanings a bit further than iconic gestures: "woof" refers as a familiar part of a dog's behavioral repertoire, whereas saying "dog" is an arbitrary social convention.

Infants begin to use single words around the start of their second year of life (Bates et al., 1979; Lock, 1978; Nelson, 1973). Their vocabularies increase slowly at first, with only a few items added each month. During this single-element period, infant communications express semantic functions, such as agents, actions/states, objects, recipients of action, locations, instruments, and more (Greenfield & Smith, 1976). From about 17 to 18 months of age, gestures begin to cooccur with utterances. They seem to act in concert with each other, referring to the same thing (Greenfield & Smith, 1976; Volterra et al., 2005; Zinober & Martlew, 1986): a point, for example, serves to identify the object that is simultaneously named. Later, gestures and words begin to be used in a complementary or supplementary relationship that is functionally similar to early sentences or propositions: the infant may point at an object and say "mine" (Greenfield & Smith, 1976; Özçalişkan & Goldin-Meadow, 2005; Zinober & Martlew, 1986). Gesture–word

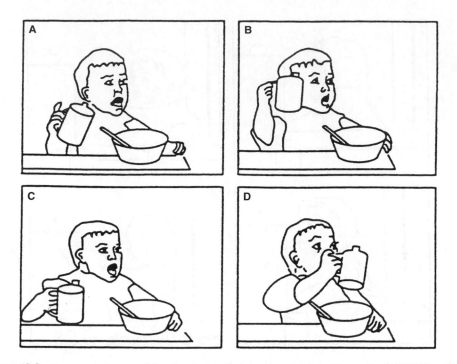

Figure 13.2   Incorporating an object into preverbal communication. *Source*: Lock (1980), p. 98.

combinations precede word-word combinations. The age at which complementary gesture–word productions appear is strongly predictive of the subsequent age at which two-word utterances appear, whereas redundant combinations of word and gesture are not (Butcher & Goldin-Meadow, 2000; Iverson & Goldin-Meadow, 2005). These two-element messages may be transitional forms that underpin syntactic development (Greenfield and Smith, 1976; Greenfield, Reilly, Leaper, & Baker, 1985). Both Greenfield and Volterra and their colleagues have investigated the ways that dialogue with the care-giver nurtures the transition to syntax. Multiword utterances and question–answer sequences about ongoing events may set the stage for subsequent messages on the "same" topic by eliciting contributions from both caregiver and infant.

Gestures tend to outnumber words in the first part of the second year, but after that vocal signs become more dominant (Goodwyn & Acredolo 1993; Iverson et al., 1994). The shift from gesture to words is probably the result of the verbal envelope of everyday social life in which infant development is immersed (Greenfield & Smith, 1976). There is little evidence that infants are predisposed to favor vocal over manual production, or vice versa (Bates et al., 1979), once they have attained the symbolic level. However, there is a clear developmental edge/precedence for the gestural modality being elaborated before the spoken one (Acredolo & Goodwyn, 1988; Goodwyn & Acredolo, 1993; Goodwyn, Acredolo, & Brown, 2000; Iverson & Goldin-Meadow, 2005; Özçalişkan & Goldin-Meadow, 2005; Rodríguez, 2009).

Somewhere towards the middle of the second year, a rapid increase in the rate of development sets in (e.g., Halliday, 1975; Nelson, 1973). A number of the early investigators (e.g., Stern & Stern, 1907; Moore, 1896) as well as more recent ones (e.g., McShane, 1980) argue that it is at this point that infants gain the *insight* that words name or refer to things. Armed with this principle, infants can learn new words more rapidly than by building up more laborious individual sound–object associations. By the end of their second year, children (they are not infants anymore) are combining words together in predictable and regular ways, and these regularities can be captured in simple rule systems. Whether these rule systems are productive or descriptive of the child's output is not settled at this point; neither is the question of whether the regularities found in child speech at this age arise from the same mechanisms that have been claimed to later generate grammar. Gestures become much less frequent in the language activities of hearing children from the age of two, and the burden of "making meaning" falls on words, their ordering, their intonation, and their emphases. However, gestures do not disappear (Guidetti, 2002), but are integral to adept communication throughout the lifetime across language communities. Gestures continue to express information left unspoken, such as the targeted "it" or "that" of a point, the path of action, manner, and more, (Kendon, 2004; Kita, 2003; McNeill, 1992). Most researchers would probably accept this story as a reasonable generalization of developments in the second year. In support, there are both studies with large numbers of subjects (e.g., Bates, O'Connell, & Shore, 1987; Caselli et al., 1995) and also compilations across studies of the period (e.g., McCarthy, 1954; Reich, 1986) that do suggest a set of average milestones. There are, however, quite marked individual differences between the rates of development between different children.

Concluding Remarks

It is necessary for psychologists to understand the nature of the child's experience at different points in development. This requires in part the specification of the environment, as in ethological and ecological studies; it requires as well, and specifically, an effort to understand the perspective of the experiencing individual. (Nelson, 1996, p. 10)

Recent work on preverbal communication has confirmed, and thus filled in, the general developmental timetable of emerging abilities that was first outlined in the 1970s. We suggest that the field is now at the point that, important as empirical data are, the real challenge to properly understanding the development of human interactions, the establishment of mutually comprehensible gestures, the role of imitation, and so on, is at the theoretical, or interpretive, level: and here we believe a paradigm shift – and a radical one at that – is required. It is possible to trace an implicit interpretive shift in characterizing infant capabilities back to the early work in the 1970s – the attempt we noted among many of the pioneers to introduce notions such as "intentionality" and "understanding" as legitimate topics of enquiry. In one sense, this shift has been adopted in much of the contemporary vocabulary so as to become commonplace rather than heretical. Thus, presently, it is not unusual to find infants being described, in no uncertain terms, as "persons" (albeit immature ones), who, at around 9- to 12-months-old "understand other persons as intentional agents" (Carpenter et al., 1998, p. 5; see also Legerstee & Barillas, 2003; and Racine & Carpendale, plus commentators, 2007a).

Claims regarding the Mirror Neuron System (MNS), however, require further scrutiny. Rizzolatti & Arbib (1998) proposed that the MNS suggests a strong link between action and communication. That is, a *shared understanding of action* grounds the emergence of gesture and leads eventually to language, both phylogenetically and ontogenetically. The core of this understanding is knowing that the actions of others are analogous to that of the self. So far, so good – however, according to Rizzolatti and Craighero (2004, pp. 173–174), the monkey mirror neuron system provides the basis for "understanding the meanings of observed actions." Researchers from a variety of disciplines (Hurford, 2002; Immordino-Yang, 2008, Zukow-Goldring, 2006, Zukow-Goldring & Arbib, 2007) note that there is a large gap between matching behavior already in a creature's repertoire to that of a conspecific (the work of mirror neurons) and achieving an understanding of self–other equivalence. The gap widens further with respect to learning and understanding new behaviors from observing others. Thus, this changing use of terminology from persons to neurons constitutes, we suggest, a very peculiar practice that obscures the range of abilities such learning entails.

It is people, not neurons, brains, or cognitive models, who "understand" meanings, and who perform them through their bodies within particular traditions and social practices. We propose that the field needs to shift to a postCartesian approach to develop an adequate psychological account of early human infancy. There are four central issues. First, mainstream psychological theory leaves out the fact that highly encephalized organisms have a subjective – and in the case of humans, intersubjective – experience of being in their worlds (Nagel, 1974, pp. 435–436). Infants and their caregivers quite clearly have separate, and different, perceptual experiences, and share these with each other in their interactions (Zukow-Goldring, 1997). To ignore either view is to guarantee an inadequate account of communicative development.

Second, the dominant Cartesian approach in psychology applies psychological predicates to "the mind," and thus only derivatively to the human person. This view leaves an explanatory gap to be bridged between person and mind – and this same gap exists with the new, neuroscience trend to apply these predicates to the brain instead (for a critique of such fallacious applications, see Bennett and Hacker, 2003, p. 72). Neither, then, are "infants" an appropriate subject for psychological predicates when they are conceptually treated without reference to understanding their own as well as shared experiences.

Third, most branches of psychology ignore that brains are contained in bodies which are immersed in a "lived-in" environment. Bodies, even if they are taken into account, are reduced to vehicles for systems that input environmental information to a mind that processes it. Thus, the world is reduced to a source of problems or a space in which to perform the solutions the mind computes, rather than a resource that can be physically manipulated as a component in the act of problem solving. Few take into account that intelligent action rests in processes that interconnect embodied actors and their world. In ignoring this, culture comes to be viewed as merely an environment that provides a developing human with the knowledge he or she needs to acquire so as to act properly (e.g., Goodenough, 1957 in D'Andrade, 1984, pp. 89). Once development becomes a problem of acquiring something, the parameters of a mechanism that enables this acquisition need to be established, as does its origin. These origins are generally accounted for by some vague and ill-founded hand-waving toward biology as providing an evolved and innate architecture.

Thus, fourth, we believe psychological development should be characterized quite differently, and more in line with J. J. Gibson's point that this process is one of "educating attention" (1979, p. 254). This education involves two or more persons who are embodied and spontaneously "responsive to each other" (cf. Shotter, 2008). In their joint activities, they provide a context for the nurturing, and hence emergence, of socially mediated performance of cultural skills. This education occurs in real time (Zukow-Goldring, 1997, 2006) and makes prominent the affordances – opportunities for action – that are jointly available in the course of continuing, repeating, and varying interaction:

> the world becomes a meaningful place for people through being *lived in*. … Meanings are not attached by the mind to objects in the world, rather these objects take on their significance – or in Gibson's terms, they afford what they do – by virtue of their incorporation into a characteristic pattern of day-to-day activities. (Ingold, 2000, p. 168)

Three challenges follow for research on preverbal communication from making this paradigmatic shift. First, new projects of inquiry are delineated. At least one has been foreshadowed in the work of, for example, Garfinkel (1967, p. 49):

> Despite the interest in social affects that prevails in the social sciences, and despite the extensive concern that clinical psychiatry pays them, surprisingly little has been written on the socially structured conditions for their production. The role that a background of common understandings plays in their production, control, and recognition is, however, almost *terra incognita*. This lack of attention from experimental investigators is … remarkable.

Infancy is that point where this "background" of common understandings is initially negotiated. Caregivers, peers, and infants begin to establish an ongoing history of interaction through which they can develop "expectations" of each other – a grasp of "what comes next" in the perceivable, continuous unfolding of their embodied intertwinings. The investigation of this "background" promises to clarify an understanding of how words come to be comprehended through their use *in situ* (Zukow-Goldring, 1997). Here, Wittgenstein, quite remarkably and presciently, sets out a summation of this period of prelinguistic communication:

> The origin and primitive form of the language game is a reaction; only from this can more complicated forms develop. Language – I want to say – is a refinement, "in the beginning was the deed." (1980, p. 31)
>
> The primitive reaction may have been a glance or a gesture, but it may also have been a word. (1953, pp. 217–218)

Elsewhere he further adds: "But what is the word 'primitive' meant to say here? Presumably that this sort of behavior is *prelinguistic*: that a language-game is based *on it*, that it is the prototype of a way of thinking and not the result of thought" (1980, no. 541). Pursuing questions such as these is to enter a challenging investigative territory.

Second, then, we suggest that traditional empirical modes of investigation – both experimental and observational – need to be supplemented (if not replaced) by other methodological stances, in particular that of participant observation. Cultural anthropologists have long recognized the importance of conducting their studies as participant observers (DeWalt et al., 1998; Goffman, 1981). Newson argued early on for this stance for infancy research:

> We must shift perspective … so as to look at the process of communication from the point of view of a participant observer. … Furthermore we, as observers, must use an effort of imagination so as to share with the baby's caretaker the general feeling of what it is to engage in an ongoing dialogue with him: otherwise we will not be in a position to describe the evolution of those shared understandings which subsequently begin to develop through this intricate process of interpersonal involvement and negotiation. (1978, pp. 36–42)

His prescience was largely ignored in infancy research. This is unfortunate. Reddy & Trevarthen (2004, p. 15) point out:

> If we did not engage with infants, they would not learn very much at all about us, just as we would not learn very much about them. We draw their knowledge into existence and they draw ours. That is how infants, and we too, "learn how to mean" from each other.

The reality in which babies develop is one of mutual participant interacting agents and observers. To ignore this is to leave little hope of understanding development. So as to fully appreciate the characteristics of real-time interaction and communication with infants, investigators need to engage with infants in the ways they observe caretakers doing it. Development occurs in real-time performance, and an expressive performance at that.

> If you allow yourself to be engaged with a two-month-old infant, … especially if it is an infant you know well, and who knows you, it is impossible to resist becoming involved and talkative. It is absurd then to doubt the communicative intent of the baby, or to argue that the baby's acts merely *appear* to be responses to yours, that they are merely some kind of biologically preprogrammed reflex behaviour without appropriate feelings, or that what the baby is doing is just appreciating and testing the "mechanical" contingency of your behaviour in time, and having no appreciation of its affective or companionable content. (Reddy & Trevarthen, 2004, p. 10)

Consequently, the third challenge facing work in this field is to develop an adequate explanatory account of the epigenetic pathways that make such episodes of shared engagement possible as a matter of course among humans.

References

Acredolo, L. P., & Goodwyn, S. W. (1988). Symbolic gesturing in normal infants. *Child Development, 59,* 450–466.

Adamson, L. B., & Bakeman, R. (1984). Mothers' communicative acts: Changes during infancy. *Infant Behavior and Development, 7,* 467–478.

Adamson, L. B., & Bakeman, R. (1985). Affect and attention: Infants observed with mothers and peers. *Child Development, 56,* 582–593.

Adamson, L. B., Bakeman, R., & Smith, C. B. (1990). Gestures, words, and early object sharing. In V. Volterra & C. Erting (Eds.), *From gesture to language in hearing and deaf children* (pp. 31–41). New York: Springer-Verlag.

Amano, S., Kezuka, E., & Yamamoto, A. (2004). Infant shifting attention from an adult's face to an adult's hand: A precursor of joint attention. *Infant Behavior & Development, 27,* 64–80.

Aslin, R. N. (1987). Visual and auditory development in infancy. In J. D. Osofsky (Ed.), *Handbook of infant development* (2nd ed. pp. 5–97). New York: Wiley.

Bakeman, R., Adamson, L. B., Konner, M., & Barr, R. G. (1990). !Kung infancy: The social context of object exploration. *Child Development, 61,* 794–809.

Baldwin, D. (1995). Understanding the link between joint attention and language. In C. Moore & P. J. Dunham (Eds.), *Joint attention: Its origins and role in development* (pp. 131–158). Mahwah, NJ: Erlbaum.

Baron-Cohen, S. (1995). The eye direction detector (EDD) and the shared attention mechanism (SAM): Two cases for evolutionary psychology. In C. Moore & P. J. Dunham (Eds.), *Joint attention: Its origins and role in development* (pp. 41–59). Hillsdale, NJ: Erlbaum.

Baron-Cohen, S. (1999). The evolution of a theory of mind. In M. C. Corballis & S. E. G. Lea (Eds.), *The descent of mind: Psychological perspectives on hominid evolution* (pp. 261–277). Oxford: Oxford University Press.

Barr, R. G. (1990). The normal crying curve. What do we really know? *Developmental Medicine and Child Neurology, 32,* 369–374.

Barr, R. G., Konner, M., Bakeman, R., & Adamson, L. B. (1991). Crying in !Kung San infants: A test of the cultural specificity model. *Developmental Medicine and Child Neurology, 32,* 601–611.

Barresi, J., & Moore, C. (1996). Intentional relations and social understanding. *Behavioral and Brain Sciences, 19,* 107–154.

Bates, E. (1976). *Language and context: The acquisition of pragmatics.* New York: Academic Press.

Bates, E., Benigni, L., Bretherton, I., Camaioni, L., & Volterra, V. (1979). *The emergence of symbols: Cognition and communication in infancy.* New York: Academic Press.

Bates, E., Bretherton, I., & Snyder, L. (1987). *From first words to grammar: Individual differences and dissociable mechanisms.* Cambridge: Cambridge University Press.

Bates, E., Camaioni, L., & Volterra, V. (1975). The acquisition of performatives prior to speech. *Merrill-Palmer Quarterly, 21,* 205–226.

Bates, E. O'Connell, B., & Shore, C. (1987). Language and communication in infancy. In J. D. Osofsky (Ed.), *Handbook of infant development* (2nd ed. pp. 149–203). New York: Wiley.

Bavin, E. L., Prior, M., Reilly, S., Bretherton, L., Williams, J., Eadie, P., et al. (2008). The early language in Victoria study: Predicting vocabulary at age one and two years from gesture and object use. *Journal of Child Language, 35,* 687–701.

Benedict, H. (1979). Early lexical development: Comprehension and production. *Journal of Child Language, 6,* 183–200.

Bennett, M. R., & Hacker, P. M. S. (2003). *Philosophical foundations of neuroscience.* Oxford: Blackwell.

Berg, W. K., Adkinson, C. D. P., & Strock, B. D. (1973). Duration and frequency of periods of alertness in neonates. *Developmental Psychology, 9,* 434.

Boesch, C. (1993). Aspects of transmission of tool-use in wild chimpanzees. In K. R. Gibson & T. Ingold (Eds.), *Tools, language, cognition in human evolution* (pp. 171–183). Cambridge: Cambridge University Press.

Breazeal, C., & Scassellati, B. (2002). Robots that imitate humans. *Trends in Cognitive Science, 6,* 481–487.

Bretherton, I. (1992). Social referencing, intentional communication, and the interfacing of minds in infancy. In S. Feinman (Ed.), *Social referencing and the social construction of reality in infancy* (pp. 57–77). New York: Plenum.

Bronfenbrenner, U. (1979). *The ecology of human development*. Cambridge, MA: Harvard University Press.

Brooks, R., & Meltzoff, A. N. (2008). Infant gaze following and pointing predict accelerated vocabulary growth through two years of age: A longitudinal, growth curve modeling study. *Journal of Child Language, 35*, 207–220.

Brune, C. W., & Woodward, A. L. (in press). Social cognition and social responsiveness in 10-month-old infants. *Journal of Cognition and Development, 2*(8), 3–27.

Bruner, J. S. (1975). From communication to language: A psychological perspective. *Cognition, 3*, 255–287.

Bruner, J. S. (1983). *Child's talk: Learning to use language*. New York: Norton.

Bruner, J. S., Roy, C., & Ratner, N. (1982). The beginnings of request. In K. E. Nelson (Ed.), *Children's language* (Vol. 3, pp. 91–138). Hillsdale, NJ: Erlbaum.

Brunswick, E. (1947). *Systematic and representative design of psychological experiments*. Berkeley: University of California Press.

Butcher, C., & Goldin-Meadow, S. (2000). Gesture and the transition from one- to two-word speech: When hand and mouth come together. In D. McNeill (Ed.), *Language and gesture* (pp. 235–257). Cambridge, UK: Cambridge University Press.

Butterworth, G. E. (1995). Origins of mind in perception and action. In C. Moore & P. J. Dunham (Eds.), *Joint attention: Its origins and role in development* (pp. 29–40). Hillsdale, NJ: Erlbaum.

Butterworth, G. (2003). Pointing is the royal road to language for babies. In S. Kita (Ed.), *Pointing: Where language, culture, and cognition meet* (pp. 9–33). Mahwah, NJ: Erlbaum.

Butterworth, G. E., & Jarrett, N. L. M. (1991). What minds have in common is space: Spatial mechanisms serving joint visual attention in infancy. *British Journal of Developmental Psychology, 9*, 55–72.

Camaioni, L., Aureli, T., Bellagamba, F., & Fogel, A. (2003). A longitudinal examination of the transition to symbolic communication in the second year of life. *Infancy & Child Development, 12*, 1–26.

Caprici, O., Contaldo, A., Caselli, M. C., & Volterra, V. (2005). From action to language through gesture: A longitudinal perspective. *Gesture, 5*, 155–177.

Carpendale, J. I. M., & Lewis, C. (2004). Constructing an understanding of mind: The development of children's social understanding within social interaction. *Behavioral & Brain Sciences, 27*, 79–151.

Carpenter, M., Nagel, K., & Tomasello, M. (1998). Social cognition, joint attention, and communicative competence from 9–15 months. *Monographs of the Society for Research in Child Development, 63* (Serial No. 255).

Caselli, M. C., Bates, E., Casadio, P., Fenson, J., Fenson, L. Sanderl, L. et al. (1995). A cross-linguistic study of early lexical development. *Cognitive Development, 10*, 159–199.

Chappell, P. F., & Sander, L. W. (1979). Mutual regulation of the neonatal-maternal interactive process: Context for the origins of communication. In M. Bullowa (Ed.), *Before speech: The beginning of interpersonal communication* (pp. 89–109). Cambridge: Cambridge University Press.

Chomsky, N. (1965). *Aspects of the theory of syntax*. Cambridge: MIT Press.

Clark, R. A. (1978). The transition from action to gesture. In A. J. Lock (Ed.), *Action, gesture, and symbol: The emergence of language* (pp. 231–257). London: Academic Press.

Corkum, V., & Moore, C. (1995). Development of joint visual attention in infants. In C. Moore & P. J. Dunham (Eds.), *Joint attention: Its origins and role in development* (pp. 61–84). Hillsdale, NJ: Erlbaum.

Cowley, S. J. (2004). Contextualizing bodies: Human infants and distributed cognition. *Language Sciences, 26,* 565–591.

D'Andrade, R. G. (1984). Cultural meaning systems. In R. A. Shweder & R. A. LeVine (Eds.), *Culture theory: Essays on mind, self and emotion* (pp. 88–119). Cambridge: Cambridge University Press.

Darwin, C. (1872). *The expression of emotions in man and animals.* London: John Murray.

Dautenhahn, K., & Nehaniv, C. L. (2002). The agent-based perspective on imitation. In K. Dautenhahn & C. L. Nehaniv (Eds.), *Imitation in animals and artifacts* (pp. 1–40). Cambridge, MA: MIT Press.

De Casper, A. J., & Spence, M. J. (1986). Prenatal maternal speech influences newborns' perception of speech sounds. *Infant Behavior and Development, 9,* 133–150.

de León, L. (2000). The emergent participant: Interactive patterns in the socialization of Tzotzil (Mayan) infants. *Journal of Linguistic Anthropology, 8,* 131–161.

D'Entremont, B., Hains, S. M. J., & Muir, D. W. (1997). A demonstration of gaze following in 3- to 6- month-olds. *Infant Behavior and Development, 20,* 569–572.

D'Entremont, B., & Seamons, E. (2007). Do infants need social cognition to act socially? An alternative look at infant pointing. *Child Development, 78,* 723–728.

DeWalt, K. M., DeWalt, B. R., & Wayland, C. B. (1998). Participant observation. In H. R. Bernard (Ed.), *Handbook of methods in cultural anthropology* (pp. 259–299). Walnut Creek, CA: AltaMira Press.

Emde, R. N., Gaensbauer, T. J., & Harmon, R. J. (1976). Emotional expression in infancy: A biobehavioral study. *Psychological Issues* (Monograph No. 37).

Farroni, T., Csibra, G., Simion, F., & Johnson, M. H. (2002). Eye contact detection in humans from birth. *Proceedings of the National Academy of Sciences, USA. 99,* 9602–9605.

Farroni, T., Johnson, M. H., & Csibra, G. (2004). Mechanisms of eye gaze perception during infancy. *Journal of Cognitive Neuroscience, 16,* 1320–1326.

Field, T. M., Cohen, D., Garcia, R., & Greenberg, R. (1984). Mother–stranger face discrimination by the newborn. *Infant Behavior and Development, 7,* 19–25.

Feinman, S. (Ed.). (1992). *Social referencing and the social construction of reality in infancy.* New York: Plenum.

Fenson, L., Dale, P. S., Reznick, J. S., Bates, E., Thal, D. J., & Pethick, S. J. (1994). Variability in early communicative development. *Monographs of the Society for Research in Child Development, 59* (5, Serial No. 242).

Fernald, A. (1991). Prosody in speech to children: Prelinguistic and linguistic functions. In R. Vasta (Ed.), *Annals of Child Development* (Vol. 8, pp. 43–80). London: Jessica Kingsley.

Fischer, K. W., & Farrar, M. J. (1988). Generalizations about generalizations: How a theory of skill development explains generality and specificity. In A. Demetriou (Ed.), *The neo-Piagetian theories of cognitive development: Toward and integration* (pp. 137–171). Amsterdam: Elsevier.

Fischer, K. W., & Hogan, A. E. (1989).The big picture for infant development: Levels and variations. In J. J. Lockman & N. L. Hazen (Eds.), *Action in social context: Perspectives on early development* (pp. 275–305). New York: Plenum.

Fogel, A. (1990). The process of developmental change in infant communicative action: Using dynamic systems theory to study individual ontogenies. In J. Colombo & J. Fagen (Eds.), *Individual differences in infancy: Reliability, stability, prediction* (pp. 341–358). Hillsdale, NJ: Erlbaum.

Fogel, A. (1993). *Developing through relationships*. Chicago: Chicago University Press.

Fogel, A., & Hannan, T. E. (1985). Manual actions of nine- and fifteen-week-old human infants during face-to-face interaction with their mothers. *Child Development, 56*, 1271–1279.

Frodi, A. M. (1985). When empathy fails: Aversive infant crying and child abuse. In B. M. Lester & C. F. Z. Boukydis (Eds.), *Infant crying: Theoretical and research perspectives* (pp. 217–277). New York: Plenum.

Garfinkel, H. (1967). *Studies in ethnomethodology*. Englewood Cliffs, NJ: Prentice Hall.

Gibson, E. J. (1969). *Principles of perceptual learning and development*. New York: Appleton-Century Crofts.

Gibson, J. J. (1979). *The ecological approach to visual perception*. Boston, MA: Houghton Mifflin.

Goffman, E. (1981). *Forms of talk*. Philadelphia: University of Pennsylvania Press.

Gogate, L. J., Walker-Andrews, A. S., & Bahrick, L. E. (2001). The intersensory origins of word comprehension: An ecological-dynamic systems view. *Developmental Science, 1*, 1–18.

Goldin-Meadow, S., Goodrich, W., Sauer, E., & Iverson, J. (2007). Young children use their hands to tell their mothers what to say. *Developmental Science, 10*, 778–785.

Gomez, J. - C. (2005). *Apes, monkeys, children and the growth of the mind* (pp. 61–80). Cambridge: Cambridge University Press.

Gomez, J. - C. (2007). Pointing behaviors in apes and human infants: A balanced interpretation. *Child Development, 78*, 729–734.

Goodenough, K. (1957). Cultural anthropology and linguistics. In P. Garvin (Ed.), *Report at the 7th Annual Round Table Meeting on Linguistics and Language Study* (pp. 167–173). Washington, Georgetown University Press.

Goodwyn, S. W., & Acredolo, L. P. (1993). Gesture versus word: Is there a modality advantage for the onset of symbol use? *Child Development, 64*, 688–701.

Goodwyn, S. W., Acredolo, L. P., & Brown, C. A. (2000). Impact of symbolic gesturing on early language development. *Journal of Nonverbal Behavior, 24*, 81–103.

Greenfield, P. M., Reilly, J., Leaper, C., & Baker, N. (1985). The structural and functional status of single-word utterances. In M. D. Barrett (Ed.), *Children's single-word speech* (pp. 233–267). Chichester, UK: Wiley.

Greenfield, P. M., & Smith, J. H. (1976). *The structure of communication in early language development*. New York: Academic Press.

Greenspan, S., & Shanker, S. (2004). *The first idea: How symbols, language and intelligence evolved from our primate ancestors to modern humans*. Boston, MA: Da Capo Press, Perseus.

Greenspan, S., & Shanker, S. (2007). The developmental pathways leading to pattern recognition, joint attention, language and cognition. *New Ideas in Psychology, 25*, 128–142.

Griffiths, R. (1954). *The abilities of babies*. London: London University Press.

Guidetti, M. (2002). The emergence of pragmatics: forms and functions of conventional gestures in young French children. *First Language, 22*, 265–285.

Gustafson, G. E., & Harris, K. L. (1990). Women's responses to young infants' cries. *Developmental Psychology, 26*, 144–152.

Halliday, M. A. K. (1975). *Learning how to mean*. London: Arnold.

Heimann, M., Strid, K., Smith, L., Tjus, T., Ulvund, S. E., & Meltzoff, A. N. (2006). Exploring the relation between memory, gestural communication, and the emergence of language in infancy: A longitudinal study. *Infant and Child Development, 15*, 233–249.

Hobson, R. P. (1993). *Autism and the development of mind*. Hove: Erlbaum.

Hobson, R. P. (2004). *The cradle of thought*. Oxford: Oxford University Press.

Hood, B. M. (1995). Visual selective attention in infants: A neuroscientific approach. In L. Lipsitt & C. Rovee-Collier (Eds.), *Advances in infancy research* (Vol. 9, pp. 163–216). Norwood, NJ: Ablex.

Hood, B. M., Willen, J. D., & Driver, J. (1998). Adult's eyes trigger shifts of visual attention in human infants. *Psychological Science, 9*, 131–134.

Hurford, J. R. (2002). Language beyond our grasp: What mirror neurons can, and cannot, do for language evolution. In K. Oller, U. Griebel, & K. Plunkett (Eds.), *The evolution of communication systems: A comparative approach.* Cambridge MA: MIT Press.

Immordino-Yang, M. H. (2008). The smoke around Mirror Neurons: Goals as sociocultural and emotional organizers of perception and action in learning. *Mind, Brain, and Education, 2,* 67–73.

Ingold, T. (2000). *The perception of the environment: Essays on livelihood, dwelling and skill.* London: Routledge.

Iverson, J. M., Caprici, O., & Caselli, M. C. (1994). From communication to language in two modalities. *Cognitive Development, 9*, 23–43.

Iverson, J. M., & Goldin-Meadow, S. (2005). Gesture paves the way for language development. *Psychological Science, 16*, 367–371.

Jones, S. S., & Hong, H-W. (2001). Onset of voluntary communication: Smiling looks to mother. *Infancy, 2*, 353–370.

Kaplan, F., & Hafner, V. V. (2006). The challenges of joint attention. *Interaction Studies, 2,* 135–169.

Kaye, K. (1982). *The mental and social life of babies: How parents create persons.* Chicago: University of Chicago Press.

Kaye, K., & Fogel, A. (1980). The temporal structure of face to face communication between mothers and infants. *Developmental Psychology, 16*, 454–464.

Keller, H. (2007). *Cultures of infancy.* Mahwah, NJ: Erlbaum.

Kendon, A. (2004). *Gesture: Visible action as utterance.* Cambridge: Cambridge University Press.

Kita, S. (2003). *Pointing: Where language, culture, and cognition meet.* Mahwah, NJ: Erlbaum.

Lamb, M. E., Morrison, D. C., & Malkin, C. M. (1987). The development of infant social expectations in face-to-face interaction: A longitudinal study. *Merrill-Palmer Quarterly, 33*, 241–254.

Leavens, D. A., Hopkins, W. D., & Bard, K. A. (2005). Understanding the point of chimpanzee pointing. *Current Directions in Psychological Science, 14*, 185–189.

Legerstee, M., & Barillas, Y. (2003). Sharing attention and pointing to objects at 12 months: Is the intentional stance implied? *Cognitive Development, 18*, 91–110.

Leung, E. H. I., & Rheingold, H. L. (1981). Development of pointing as a social gesture. *Developmental Psychology, 17*, 215–220.

Lock, A. (Ed.) (1978). *Action, gesture and symbol: The emergence of language.* London: Academic Press.

Lock, A. (1980). *The guided reinvention of language.* London: Academic Press.

Lock, A., & Hill, S. R. (forthcoming). *Out of our heads: The second cognitive revolution.* Oxford: Oxford University Press.

Lock, A., Young, A. W., Service, V., & Chandler, P (1990). The origins of infant pointing gestures. In V. Volterra & C. Erting (Eds.), *From gesture to language in hearing and deaf children* (pp. 42–55). New York: Springer-Verlag.

Markova, G., & Legerstee, M. (2006). Contingency, imitation, and affect sharing: Foundations of infants' social awareness. *Developmental Psychology, 42*, 132–141.

Masataka, N. (2003a). From index-finger extension to index-finger pointing: Ontogenesis of pointing in preverbal infants. In S. Kita (Ed.), *Pointing: Where language, culture, and cognition meet* (pp. 69–84). Mahwah, NJ: Erlbaum.

Masataka, N. (2003b). *The onset of language.* Cambridge: Cambridge University Press.

McCarthy, D. (1954). Language development in children. In L. Carmichael (Ed.), *Manual of child psychology* (2nd ed. pp. 492–630). New York: Wiley.

McNeill, D. (1992). *Hand and mind: What gestures reveal about thought.* Chicago: University of Chicago Press.

McShane, J. (1980). *Learning to talk.* Cambridge: Cambridge University Press.

Meltzoff, A. N. (1988). Infant imitation and memory: Nine-month-olds in immediate and deferred tests. *Child Development, 59,* 217–225.

Meltzoff, A. N., & Brooks, R. (2001). Like me as a building block for understanding other minds: Bodily acts, attention, and intention. In B. F. Malle, L. J. Moses, & D. A. Baldwin (Eds.), *Intentions and intentionality* (pp. 171–191). Cambridge, MA: MIT Press.

Merleau-Ponty, M. (1964). The child's relations with others. In W. Cobb (Trans), & J. M. Edie, (Ed.), *The primacy of perception* (pp. 96–155). Evanston: Northwestern University Press. (Original work published 1960).

Messer, D. J., & Vietze, P. M. (1984). Timing and transitions in mother-infant gaze. *Infant Behavior and Development, 7,* 167–181.

Moore, C. (1999). Gaze following and the control of attention. In P. Rochat (Ed.), *Early social cognition* (pp. 241–256). Mahwah, NJ: Erlbaum.

Moore, K. (1896). The mental development of a child. *Psychological Review, Monograph Supplements, 1,* 115–145.

Morales, M., Mundy, P., Delgado, C. E. F., Yale, M., Messinger, D., Neal, R., et al. (2000). Responding to joint attention across the 6- through 24-month a period and early language acquisition. *Journal of Applied Developmental Psychology, 21,* 283–298.

Morales, M., Mundy, P., Delgado, C. E. F., Yale, M., Neal, R., & Schwartz, H. K. (2000). Gaze following, temperament, and language development in 6-month-olds: A replication and extension. *Infant Behavior & Development, 23,* 231–236.

Morisette, P., Ricard, M., & Gouin-Decarie, T. (1995). Joint visual attention and pointing in infancy: A longitudinal study of comprehension. *British Journal of Developmental Psychology, 13,* 163–175.

Mundy, P., & Gomes, A. (1998). Individual differences in joint attention skill development in the second year. *Infant Behavior and Development, 21,* 469–482.

Nagel, T. (1974). What is it like to be a bat? *Philosophical Review, LXXXIII,* 435–450.

Nelson, K. (1973). Structure and strategy in learning to talk. *Monographs of the Society for Research in Child Development, 38* (1–2, Serial No. 149).

Nelson, K. (1996). *Language in cognitive development.* Cambridge: Cambridge University Press.

Newson, J. (1978). Dialogue and development. In A. J. Lock (Ed.), *Action, gesture and symbol: The emergence of language* (pp. 32–42). London: Academic Press.

Özçalişkan, S., & Goldin-Meadow, S. (2005). Gesture is at the cutting edge of early language development. *Cognition, 96,* B101–B113.

Papoušek, M. (2007). Communication in early infancy: An arena of intersubjective learning. *Infant Behavior & Development, 30,* 258–266.

Papoušek, H., & Papoušek, M. (1977). Mothering and the cognitive headstart: Psychobiological considerations. In H. R. Scaffer (Ed.), *Studies in mother-infant interaction* (pp. 63–88). London: Academic Press.

Papoušek, H., & Papoušek, M. (1987). Intuitive parenting: A dialectic counterpart to the infant's integrative competence. In J. D. Osofsky (Ed.), *Handbook of infant development* (2nd ed. pp. 669–720). New York: Wiley.

Piaget, J. (1963/1936). *The origins of intelligence in children.* New York: Norton.

Peirce, C. S. (1955). *Philosophical writings of Peirce.* In J. B. Buchler (Ed.), New York: Dover.

Povinelli, D. J., Bering, J. M., & Giambrone, S. (2000). Toward a science of other minds: Escaping the argument by analogy. *Cognitive Science, 24,* 509–541.

Povinelli, D. J., & Davis, D. R. (1994). Differences between chimpanzees (Pan troglodytes) and humans (Homo sapiens) in the resting state of the index finger: Implications for pointing. *Journal of Comparative Psychology, 108*, 134–139.

Racine, T. P., & Carpendale, J. I. M. (2007a). The role of shared practice in joint attention. *British Journal of Developmental Psychology, 25*, 3–25.

Racine, T. P., & Carpendale, J. I. M. (2007b). Response to commentaries: Shared practices, understanding, language, and joint attention. *British Journal of Developmental Psychology, 25*, 45–54.

Rader, N. de V., & Zukow-Goldring, P. (under review/in press). Caregivers' gestures direct infant attention during early word learning: The importance of dynamic synchrony. In B. Hodges, J. Martin, & S. Steffensen (Eds.), Caring and conversing: The distributed dynamics of dialogue. *Language Sciences.*

Reddy, V., & Trevarthen, C. (2004). What we learn about babies from engaging with their emotions. *Zero to three, 24*, 9–15.

Reich, P. (1986). *Language development.* Englewood-Cliffs, NJ: Prentice-Hall.

Richards, M. P. M. (1974). First steps in becoming social. In M. P. M. Richards (Ed.), *The integration of a child into a social world* (pp. 83–97). Cambridge: Cambridge University Press.

Rizzolatti, G., & Arbib, M. A. (1998). Language within our grasp. *Trends in Neuroscience, 21*, 188–194.

Rizzolatti, G., & Craighero, L. (2004). The mirror-neuron system. *Annual Review of Neuroscience, 27*, 169–192.

Rodríguez, C. (2009). The "circumstances" of gestures. Proto-interrogatives and private gestures. *New Ideas in Psychology, 27*, 288–303.

Rollins, P. R. (2003). Caregivers contingent comments to 9 month old infants: Relationships with later language. *Journal of Applied Psycholinguistics, 24*, 221–234.

Sander, L. W. (1977). The regulation of exchange in the infant–caretaker system and some aspects of the context-content relationship. In M. Lewis & L. A. Rosenblum (Eds.), *Interaction, conversation, and the development of language* (pp. 133–156). New York: Wiley.

Scaife, M., & Bruner, J. S. (1975). The capacity for joint visual attention in the infant. *Nature, 253*, 265–266.

Service, V. (1984). Maternal styles and communicative development. In A. Lock & E. Fisher (Eds.), *Language development.* (pp. 132–140). London: Croom Helm.

Shotter, J. (2008). *Conversational realities revisited. Life, language, body and world.* Chagrin Falls, OH: Taos Institute Publications.

Slater, A. (1995). Individual differences in infancy and later IQ. *Journal of Child Psychology and Psychiatry and Allied Disciplines, 36*, 69–112.

Slobin, D. I. (1973). Cognitive prerequisites for the development of grammar. In C. A. Ferguson & D. I. Slobin (Eds.), *Studies of child language development* (pp. 175–208). New York: Holt, Reinhart & Winston.

Smith, L., Fagan, J. F., & Ulvund, S. E. (2002). The relation of recognition memory in infancy and parental socioeconomic status to later intellectual competence. *Intelligence, 30*, 247–259.

Snow, C. (1977). The development of conversation between mothers and babies. *Journal of Child Language, 4*, 1–22.

Spurrett, D., & Cowley, S. J. (2004). How to do things without words: Infants, utterance-activity, and distributed cognition. *Language Sciences, 26*, 443–466.

Sterelny, K. (2002). Primate worlds. In C. Heyes & L. Huber (Eds.), *The evolution of cognition* (pp. 143–162). Cambridge, MA: MIT Press.

Stern, D. N. (1977). *The first relationship: Infant and mother.* Cambridge, MA: Harvard University Press.

Stern, D. N. (1985). *The interpersonal world of the infant: A view from psychoanalysis and developmental psychology*. New York: Basic Books.

Stern, D. S. (1999). Vitality contours: The temporal contour of feelings as a basic unit for constructing the infant's social experience. In P. Rochat (Ed.), *Early social cognition: Understanding others in the first months of life* (pp. 67–80). Mahwah, NJ: Erlbaum.

Stern, W., & Stern, C. (1907). *Die Kindersprache*. Leipzig: Barth.

Striano, T., Stahl, D., Cleveland, A., & Hoehl, S. (2007). Sensitivity to triadic attention between 6 weeks and 3 months of age. *Infant Behavior and Development, 30*, 529–534.

Thatcher, R. W., Walker, R. A., & Giudice, S. (1987). Human cerebral hemispheres develop at different rates and ages. *Science, 236*, 1110–1113.

Thelen, E. (1989). Self-organization in developmental processes: Can systems approaches work? In M. R. Gunnar & E. Thelen (Eds.), *Systems and development* (Vol. 22, pp. 77–117). Hillsdale, NJ: Erlbaum.

Thelen, E., & Smith, L. (1994). *A dynamic systems approach to the development of cognition and action*. Cambridge, MA: MIT Press.

Tomasello, M. (1988). The role of joint attentional processes in early language development. *Language Sciences, 10*, 69–88.

Tomasello, M. (1995). Joint attention as social cognition. In C. Moore & P. J. Dunham (Eds.), *Joint attention: Its origins and role in development* (pp. 103–130). Hillsdale, NJ: Erlbaum.

Tomasello, M. (2003). *Constructing a usage-based theory of language acquisition*. Cambridge: Cambridge University Press

Tomasello, M., Carpenter, M., & Liszkowski, U. (2007). A new look at infant pointing. *Child Development, 78*, 705–722.

Tomasello, M., Kruger, A. C., & Ratner, H. H. (1993). Cultural learning. *Behavioral and Brain Sciences, 16*, 495–552.

Tremblay, H., & Rovira, K. (2007). Joint visual attention and social triangular engagement at 3 and 6 months. *Infant Behavior and Development, 30*, 366–379.

Trevarthen, C. (1979). Communication and cooperation in early infancy: A description of primary intersubjectivity. In M. Bullowa (Ed.), *Before speech: The beginning of interpersonal communication* (pp. 321–347). Cambridge: Cambridge University Press.

Trevarthen, C. (1988). Universal cooperative motives: How infants begin to know the language and culture of their parents. In G. Jahoda & I. M. Lewis (Eds.), *Acquiring culture: Cross cultural studies in child development* (pp. 37–90). London: Croom Helm.

Trevarthen, C., & Hubley, P. (1978). Secondary intersubjectivity: Confidence, confiding and acts of meaning in the first year. In A. Lock (Ed.), *Action, gesture and symbol: The emergence of language* (pp. 183–229). London: Academic Press.

Van Geert, P. (1991). A dynamic systems model of cognitive and language growth. *Psychological Review, 98*, 3–53.

Volterra, V., Caselli, M. C., Caprici, O., & Pizzuto, E. (2005). Gesture and the emergence and development of language. In M. Tomasello & D. Slobin, (Eds.), *Beyond nature-nurture: Essays in honor of Elizabeth Bates* (pp. 3–40). Mahwah, NJ: Erlbaum.

Vygotsky, L. S. (1966). Development of the higher mental functions. In A. Leontiev, A. Luria, & A. Smirnov (Eds.), *Psychological research in the USSR* (Vol. 1, pp. 11–46). Moscow: Progress.

Vygotsky, L. S. (1978). *Mind in society*. (Eds. and Trans. M. Cole, V. John-Steiner, S. Scribner, & E. Souberman). Cambridge, MA: Harvard University Press.

Vygotsky, L. S. (1981). The genesis of higher mental functions. In J. V. Wertsch (Ed.), *The concept of activity in Soviet psychology* (pp. 144–188). Armonk, NY: Sharpe.

Walton, G. E., Bower, N. J. A., & Bower, T. G. R. (1992). Recognition of familiar faces by newborns. *Infant Behavior and Development, 15*, 265–269.

Werner, H., & Kaplan, B. (1963). *Symbol formation*. New York: Wiley.

Wilkins, D. (2003). Why pointing with the index finger is not a universal (in sociocultural and semiotic terms). In S. Kita (Ed.), *Pointing: Where language, culture, and cognition meet* (pp. 171–215). Mahwah, NJ: Erlbaum.

Wittgenstein, L. (1953). *Philosophical investigations*. Oxford: Blackwell.

Wittgenstein, L. (1980). *Culture and value*. Introduction by G. Von Wright (P. Winch, Trans). Oxford: Blackwell.

Wolff, P. H. (1987). *The development of behavioral states and the expression of emotions in early infancy*. Chicago: University of Chicago Press.

Wood, D., & Middleton, D. (1975). A study of assisted problem-solving. *British Journal of Psychology, 66*, 181–191.

Wundt, W. (1900). *Völkerpsychologie, Vol. 1*. Translation of parts of Vols. 1 and 2: *The language of gesture* (1973). The Hague: Mouton.

Zeskind, P. S. (1985). A developmental perspective on infant crying. In B. M. Lester & C. F. Z. Boukydis (Eds.), *Infant crying: Theoretical and research perspectives* (pp. 159–185). New York: Plenum.

Zinober, B., & Martlew, M. (1986). The development of communicative gestures. In M. D. Barrett (Ed.), *Children's single-word speech* (pp. 183–216). Chichester, UK: Wiley.

Zukow-Goldring, P. G. (1997). A social ecological realist approach to the emergence of the lexicon: Educating attention to amodal invariants in gesture and speech. In C. Dent-Read & P. Zukow-Goldring (Eds.), *Evolving explanations of development: Ecological approaches to organism-environment systems* (pp. 199–250). Washington, DC: American Psychological Association.

Zukow-Goldring, P. (2002). Sibling caregiving. In M. Bornstein (Ed.), *Handbook of Parenting: Vol. III, Status and social conditions of parenting* (2nd ed., pp. 253–286). Hillsdale, NJ: Erlbaum.

Zukow-Goldring, P. (2006). Assisted Imitation: Affordances, effectivities, and the Mirror System in early language development. In M. A. Arbib (Ed.), *From action to language via the mirror neuron system* (pp. 469–500). New York: Cambridge University Press.

Zukow-Goldring, P. (in press). Assisted imitation: Caregiver gestures embody infants' shared understanding of ongoing events. In B. Hodges, J. Martin, & S. Steffensen (Eds.), Caring and conversing: The distributed dynamics of dialogue. *Language Sciences*.

Zukow-Goldring, P., & Arbib, M. A. (2007). Affordances, effectivities, and assisted imitation: Caregivers and the directing of attention. *Neurocomputing, 70*, 2181–2193.

14

Early Language

George Hollich

Gradually from naming an object we advance step by step until we have traversed the vast distance between our first stammered syllable and the sweep of thought in a line of Shakespeare. (Helen Keller, 1903)

Over the first 3 years of life, children move quickly from hearing the sounds of language, to recognizing the meanings of words, to combining those words to produce unique and original utterances. They go from being cute mutes to expressing themselves in ways that are illuminating and ultimately transforming. Anyone who has tried to learn a second language later in life appreciates the difficulty of this task. To a nonnative speaker, language cuts against natural tendencies and is anything but reflexive or automatic. From wrapping one's tongue around a new accent, to finding the right word, to remembering the correct word endings; the difficulty experienced by second language learners helps demonstrate the complexity of native language learning by children. Further complicating matters, children do not have the luxury of already knowing a language, so they cannot use native words to learn new ones (as in the Spanish word for "hello" is "ola").

This chapter gives a roadmap of the progress of the language-learning infant. The coming sections review what the latest research has discovered about how children recognize the sounds of language (*phonology*), learn the meanings of words (*semantics*), and learn how words combine to produce new and original meanings (*grammar*). Along the way, some of the predominant theories and methods applied in each of these areas will be covered, as well as longstanding debates and questions, including "What are the evolutionary origins of language?," "What learning mechanisms are necessary?," and "How much do children understand before they speak?" This chapter concludes by considering talking (*production*): discovering how infants move from indecipherable babbling to producing words and sentences. Before delving into language-specific skills, the next section examines how language learning may be partially based on foundational skills of intermodal perception, social understanding, statistical learning, and memory.

Foundational Skills

Bates (2004) described language as a "new machine ... constructed out of old parts" (p. 250). While this statement is not without controversy, clearly, language results from the combined interaction of multiple abilities, some relevant only to language, others relevant to a whole range of human behaviors (Hollich, Hirsh-Pasek, Golinkoff, 2000). While previous views of language acquisition (e.g., Chomsky, 1965) focused on language as a separate system, unique and as different in form and function from other cognitive faculties as an elephant's trunk is different from a rhino's tusk, modern language research increasingly considers how foundational skills such as intermodal perception, social understanding, statistical learning, and memory play a role.

As the word "foundational" suggests, these skills are considered the building blocks upon which language understanding is based. While no one is claiming that these skills alone can account for all of language, it is nonetheless critical to understand how these abilities relate to language. In essence, without an understanding of how the "old parts" work, our knowledge of language development is limited. With this in mind, let us turn to four skills researchers have suggested as foundational to language: intermodal perception, social understanding, statistical learning, and memory.

Intermodal perception

Language operates across multiple modalities. We do not just see a rose. We feel the softness of its petals, and we smell its perfume. Likewise, language is not just about hearing or seeing the lone word "rose." One immediately relates that word to a rose's sight, touch and smell, even the sight of a person saying that word. As such, language involves *intermodal perception* (see chapter 4 this volume). Intermodal perception occurs whenever information is present across multiple inputs. For language, this includes connecting face to speech, sight with sound, symbol with object, concept to arbitrary index, and it is especially relevant when information is common (or *amodal*) across inputs, as when rhythm can be both seen and heard, or location in space is indicated by both visual and auditory information.

Bahrick, Lickliter, & Flom (2004) suggest that such *intersensory redundancy* is one of the most salient and transformative types of information early in development and is preferred to virtually all unimodal inputs (see chapter 4 this volume). This preference for amodal information leads infants to quickly connect lip movements with the sounds of a person talking (Dodd, 1979), to learn to connect particular sights (e.g., ball bouncing, glass breaking, balloon popping) with their attendant sounds (e.g., boing, crash, pop) and may also help them connect word to object. Gogate and Bahrick (1998) found that infants will associate a word with an object at an earlier age if that word is spoken simultaneous with movement of that object rather than if the spoken word and the movement are unrelated.

They further suggest that such intermodal input may get the process of word learning started by helping infants discover their first (admittedly concrete) connections between sight and sound (Gogate, Walker-Andrews, & Bahrick, 2001). Consistent with this hypothesis, parents not only instinctively move objects simultaneous with labels during play, but they do this most often early in development and less as their child's vocabulary grows (Gogate, Bahrick, & Watson, 2000). Similarly, even blind individuals seem to require some crossmodal relationship to spark the process of language understanding. Helen Keller famously grasped the point of language when her teacher spelled out "water" on her hand while holding that hand under a stream of water. The simultaneous combination of two modalities (text: as represented by the spelling of the word "water" in her hand, and touch: the feel of the actual water) led to a critical insight. This is similar to the insight that occurs when young readers discover the connection between the printed word "cup" and a picture of a cup or when deaf individuals discover the connection between the sign for "cookie" and the actual object. In this manner, intermodal learning could be a critical first step to language understanding: giving infants a gateway through which they discover connections between language and objects in the world.

Social understanding

Language takes two. While people can (and do) often talk to themselves, a principle benefit of language is the opportunity it provides for a more sophisticated channel of social interaction and communication. Thus, just as children might point to the sink to request a glass of water or raise their hands in a plea to be carried, language allows those same children to request a glass of water even when the sink can not be seen, and to tell mommy where they would like to be carried. Language thus allows for a degree of specificity and abstraction not possible with other means of communication, although the kinds of things that children and their parents talk about have nonverbal analogues long before speech comes into play (Bruner, 1981). Indeed, work by McCune (2008) suggests a link between grunts used as communication (as in the child who grunts while pointing toward the refrigerator) and the onset of their first recognizable words. Taking this idea to logical extension, some theorists (Bloom, 2000; Tomasello, 2000) have suggested that language and advanced social abilities (including the concept of a theory of mind) are part of the same series of evolutionary adaptations towards a greater (and more sophisticated) cooperation between individuals.

Many aspects of language learning clearly depend on infants' understanding of social intentions and conventions. For example, correctly inferring the referent of a label seems to require the ability to follow eye gaze or an understanding of the goals of another's action. Indeed, infants will not connect a new word to a novel object unless the speaker indicates, in some way, that they intended to label it (Baldwin, 1993; Tomasello & Barton, 1994). Likewise, Tomasello and Akhtar (1995) found that infants can use pragmatic cues to decide whether a speaker was labeling a noun or a verb. Autistic children, in contrast, hear a great deal of language, yet never quite grasp its significance. Indeed, the more difficulty autistic infants have in following social cues, the harder it is for them to learn spoken language (Kuhl, Coffey-Corina, Padden, & Dawson, 2005).

Without the social component, learning language appears to have no relevance. Thus, children do not learn to recognize sounds of a foreign language through simply watching television (Kuhl, Tsao, & Liu, 2003). In addition, Tamis-LeMonda, Bornstein, and Baumwell (2001) have found that maternal responsiveness is strongly connected to children meeting certain language milestones, such as first 50 words or the emergence of combinatorial speech. Social pragmatics and language are thus intertwined. All available evidence indicates that advances in language development seem to closely follow measures of infant abilities to understand the intentions and thoughts of others (Bloom & Tinker, 2001).

Nowhere is the tight connection between social skills and language development more apparent than in children's abilities to imitate and learn from the actions of others, a process coined *observational learning* by Bandura (1977) and which has been associated with the mirror neuron system within the brain (Rizzolatti & Arbib, 1998; see also chapters 11 and 19 this volume). In learning a language, infants imitate even the smallest details of rhythm, action, and social expression, and they do so from the earliest ages tested. For example, by 9 months, infants will imitate the sounds that their parents (and objects) make (Bruner, 1993). While this is initially confined to nonverbal expressions and animal/object noises, with time, such imitative skill leads infants' speech productions to closely mirror the expressions of the adults around them, copying not just the words but also the accent and vocal characteristics of the speaker, as when a child adopts a deeper voice and formal manner when saying "all aboard!"

This is not to say that observational learning alone is responsible for learning a language, but imitation filtered through limited linguistic understanding and gross performance deficits would seem to provide a fruitful theoretical viewpoint from which to explore the beginnings of infant language (see Speidel & Nelson, 1989). Thus, just as one could see a professional tennis player hit the perfect serve yet be unable to (imitate) reproduce that same serve, so might infants attempt to copy the properties of language that they hear, but, due to lack of experience or immaturity, fail in this attempt miserably. Under this view, many of the unique properties of infant language (e.g., telegraphic speech, over-regularization of verbs, etc.) represent the inevitable compromise between infants' linguistic skill and the richness of their social representations.

Statistical learning

Language is pattern recognition. While it goes under different names in each of the core areas (phonology: normalization, semantics: induction, grammar: rules), a surprising amount of language learning involves the detection of regularities. Why would a child say something like "mous*es*" instead of mice? One answer could be that infants have discovered (or think they have discovered) certain regularities within language (e.g., add an "s" to make plurals). This discovery of regularities (sometimes termed *invariance detection* or *statistical/Bayesian learning*) has received new emphasis as a possible mechanism for how infant learn aspects of speech perception (Saffran, Aslin, & Newport, 1996;

Pierrehumbert, 2003), word learning (Xu & Tenenbaum, 2007), and grammar (Elman, 1993; Gomez & Gerken,2000) and will be discussed more extensively in those sections. For now, it is enough to note that pattern detection is a fundamental property within the brain and other neural networks (Rolls & Treves, 1998), and that a substantial contingent of researchers (Elman et al., 1996; Gogate & Hollich, in press) has been examining how domain general mechanisms of statistical learning and invariance detection might play a role in language acquisition.

Memory

Rounding out the list of skills that infants need prelinguistically is memory (see chapter 8 this volume). Clearly, the task of learning a language (with some 40,000 words and billions of combinations places enormous demands on memory. Some estimates of infant vocabulary suggest that they could be learning as much as nine new words a day (Clark, 1983, 2003), not to mention the vast numbers of combinations for those words. Indeed, it was the virtually limitless combinatorial possibility of language that lead Chomsky (1965; see also Gold, 1967) to propose that learning the language presents such a difficult task that it could not be achieved without some kind of innate module.

Furthermore, limitations in memory could also account for many of the strange behaviors characteristic of child language. For example, the context specificity observed in early word recognition and learning (e.g., the child who uses the word duck only for their rubber duck in the bathtub but not for live ducks at the pond) also seems to be a general property of any new memory – it takes time and experience to ascertain what aspects of any situation are worth encoding into memory and which are not. This holds true whether one is trying to remember which berries are OK to eat (not the ones with the dark spots) or remember which acoustic differences are meaningful (cat and cap are different but cat said in a high voice is no different, from a linguistic standpoint, than cat said in a low voice, even though the difference between /p/ and /t/ is the more subtle of the two acoustic differences). In this manner, any fully realized theory of language must connect with the literature on infant's memory abilities.

In sum, despite differences between language and other learned behaviors, many aspects of language acquisition depend on general mechanisms of intermodal perception, social understanding, statistical learning, and memory. These general skills probably interact with infants' developing understanding of the specifics of language, including knowledge of language sounds (phonology), word meanings (semantics), and the ways in which words are combined (grammar).

Phonological Perception

For most, language is sound. It starts with the warbles, pops, and clicks of our lips and tongue combined with vibrations that begin inside our throats. These sounds resonate through our heads, drift across the cavernous spaces of rooms, and finally, come to rest and resonate in the minds of the listener.

Infants' exposure to the sounds of language begins in the womb, where they hear enough to recognize, from birth, the rhythm (Nazzi, Jusczyk, & Johnson, 2000) and pitch contours (Nazzi, Floccia, & Bertoncini, 1998) of their native language as well as the melody inherent in a passage of Dr. Seuss (DeCasper & Spence, 1986). Newborns also appear to be particularly focused on frequencies and sounds within the range of human speech (Vouloumanos & Werker, 2004). Unfortunately, the womb muffles much of the high frequency acoustics necessary to learn other equally crucial distinctions between specific sounds. For example, the acoustic difference between "bat" and "pat". Nonetheless, despite not hearing such distinctions in the womb, when it comes to hearing even these subtle sound differences, 7-month-olds are more competent than adults, being "universal perceivers" (Hollich & Houston, 2007). Adults and older infants, specialized for their native language, literally cannot hear phonological contrasts that are not used in their language. For example, Japanese-speaking adults have a hard time hearing the difference between /r/ and /l/, while English-speaking adults cannot hear the difference between the Hindi /ta/ and /tʰa/ (a t-type sound that is made by placing the tongue at the roof of the mouth rather than the tip of the teeth). In both cases, adults' difficulty in hearing these distinctions occurs because their native languages only use one of the these sounds, and, as native speakers, they have learned to ignore the sound differences between these subtle distinctions, while infants appear to have developed this "learned ignorance" by 12-months (Werker and Richard Tees, 1984).

Similarly, infants appear to hear some differences in a categorical manner, something called *categorical perception* (see chapter 7 this volume). That is, certain acoustic changes lead to dramatic changes in infant performance from the earliest ages tested, apparently with little or no experience, while other changes, of similar size, are virtually ignored. For example, Eimas, Siqueland, Jusczyk, and Vigorito (1971) demonstrated that infants paid more attention to the difference between /ba/ and /pa/ rather than a similar-sized acoustic difference between one /pa/ and another /pa/ with increased *voice onset time* (more time between the onset of the /p/ sound and when the /a/ sound begins, something like /pʰa/). Infants also seem to notice individual phonemes, but ignore the difference between *allophones*, different versions of the same phoneme (but see Jusczyk, Hohne, & Bauman, 1999). Kuhl and Miller (1975) subsequently demonstrated that even chinchillas make the same categorical distinction, suggesting that this ability is not specific to speech and may relate to hardwired abilities of the nervous system.

In summary, even though infants can hear all the sounds of the world's languages from the youngest ages tested, some sounds are easier to hear than others, and over the first year of life, infants begin to specialize in hearing just those distinctions used by their native language.

Speech Stream Segmentation

Another of the linguistic tasks faced by infants is to segment words from the fluent stream of speech (Jusczyk, 1997). Again, anyone who has ever been in a foreign country can relate to this issue. To the nonnative speaker, language is one long stream of unending sound without obvious breaks between words, phrases, or sentences. Indeed, as auctioneers have proven, one can talk very long and fast, without breaking breath. Speaking without pauses is not confined just to auctioneers; it is estimated that less than 7% of the speech directed toward children consists of isolated words (Van de Weijer, 1998).

So just how are infants supposed to find where one word ends and a new word begins? For that matter, *can* infants even do this? In 1995, Jusczyk and Aslin provided the first evidence that infants are capable of findings words (at least some words) in the fluent stream of speech, using a method called the head turn preference procedure. In this procedure, infants sit on their parent's lap in the center of a three-sided booth with lights on each side. The lights flash while a passage written about a particular word is played. For example, infants might hear: "The cup was bright and shiny. The clown drank from the red cup. His cup was filled with milk …" After this familiarization phase, the target word from the passage they heard was played. So, for example, when the passage was talking about a cup, 7.5-month-old infants looked more when the word "cup" was played. Naturally, this ability was tested many times with many different words and passages to be sure it was not something about the specific words or passages that allowed them to succeed.

This head turn preference procedure has since been used by hundreds of different labs to test the situations under which infants succeed in segmentation. Through this work, it has become apparent that while infants are not yet speaking during the first year of life, they make good use of what they know about the properties of their language to help them succeed in the segmentation task. This includes paying attention to word and sound statistics, listening to where words are stressed and taking copious advantage of the redundancies inherent in infant-directed speech.

The first way that infants seem to discover words in a fluent stream of speech is through the use of statistics. That is, infants notice when the same sounds or syllables appear together. So in the previous study, infants appeared to notice that /cu/ and /p/ go together. While this is true for familiar words, infants can also do this with limited exposure to a made-up language in which the "words" consist of three syllables that always go together. To demonstrate this, Saffran et al. (1996) played a "passage" made up of an continuous string of three syllable nonsense words, such as "pigola," "bikuti," "pabiku," and discovered that infants noticed that "pi," "go," and "la" always went together: distinguishing between "pigola," and "golati," a three syllable pairing that never went together. This suggests that when adults use the same word multiple times in a phrase (e.g., "Do you see the ball?," "Look at the ball," "It is a ball!," infants recognize that /ba/ and /l/ always go together and can use this information to discover the word (Mattys, Jusczyk, Luce, & Morgan, 1999).

This ability to discover common patterns of sound is not specific to speech, but appears to extend to tone sequences (Saffran, Johnson, Aslin, & Newport, 1999) and even sequences of visual shapes as well (Kirkham, Slemmer, & Johnson, 2002). Such findings support the idea that statistical learning is a domain general property of the nervous system which is used in the service of language learning, rather than specific to it.

This work also suggests that the first words infants should discover in speech are the most frequent, and this appears to be true. Infants can recognize their own name as early as 4.5 months (Mandel, Jusczyk, & Pisoni, 1995). Infants can even use their familiarity with their name to discover adjacent words (Bortfeld, Morgan, Golinkoff, & Rathbun, 2005). So if Julien, the infant, hears "Julien's cup was bright and shiny. A clown drank from Julien's cup ..." then even at 6 months, Julien can pick out the word, cup, from the passage – a full month and a half earlier than if just the word cup is used without his name proceeding it.

Parents seem to recognize the need for repetition and modification of their speech. For example, mothers are 44% likely to repeat an utterance when speaking to their infants (younger than 26 weeks). In contrast, strangers' utterances were longer and far less repetitive (Kaye, 1980). Those same mothers were also less repetitive by the time the child was 2-years-old. Likewise, adults the world over tend to adopt a higher register of speaking when talking to infants and become more extreme in their amplitude and pitch modifications, something called *infant-directed speech* (Fernald, 1985). These exaggerated tendencies apparently make it easier for infants to segment the speech stream (Thiessen, Hill, & Saffran, 2005). How?

One possibility is stress – where words are accented. That is, many languages tend to use particular stress patterns. So for example, English tends to accent the first syllable of nouns (e.g., *bar*bie, *sci*ence, *doc*tor). If infants "knew" this then they could assume a new word begins whenever they hear a stressed syllable. Not only do English-learning infants prefer words with the stress on the first syllable (Jusczyk, Cutler, & Redanz, 1993; Morgan, 1996), but by 9 months of age, they adopt exactly this type of strategy (segmenting words at the accented syllable, called the *Metrical Segmentation Strategy*; Jusczyk, Houston, & Newsome, 1999), although their use of this strategy appears to depend partially on statistics (Johnson & Jusczyk, 2001). Research has shown that infants also have an easier time discovering a word if it is at the end or beginning of a phrase (Seidl & Johnson, 2006).

To summarize, infants come to segment the fluent stream of speech using statistics, location in the phrase, and the stress on the words, which is one of many things exaggerated in infant-directed speech.

Semantic Understanding

It is not enough just to discover a word within the speech stream. After all, repeating words and whole phrases is something that even parrots can do. Children often repeat words and phrases that they do not truly understand, to many a parent's chagrin. In practice, it's somewhat difficult to know when children accurately understand meaning. Just as a stranger in a strange land may nod and smile when someone speaks, similarly, infants often react to the spoken language addressed to them and use social context to correctly respond to requests, despite later evidence that they did not truly comprehend what was being said. Thus, careful control of external cues and possible confounds is critical to ascertaining if the infant has truly connected word and object. In general, there are at least three ways to test comprehension with a high level of scientific rigor:

1   The most obvious and incontrovertible means of assessing understanding is verbal behavior. If children say "ball" when a ball is present and not otherwise, then they have clearly made some connection between the sight and sound. Most early studies of infant vocabulary did exactly this: scientists wrote down words as they were spoken by the child, noting whether those words corresponded to actual entities or circumstances in the environment (Darwin, 1887; Dromi, 1987; Stern & Stern, 1928; Tomasello, 1992). More recently, researchers simply ask the parents to select the words their child currently says using a standardized checklist, such as the MacArthur-Bates Communicative Development Inventories (Fenson et al., 1994) or the Language Development Survey (Rescorla, 1989). These checklists result in data that are similar in their growth curves to more detailed diary studies (Robinson & Mervis, 1999), but by being much easier to administer, the checklists provide an excellent way to track language across large samples of children. Unfortunately, infants seem to understand many words before they say them, so a means other than verbal behavior is often necessary. While checklists often ask parents to report the words their child understands, again there is some question as to accuracy and what type of evidence the parents are using.

2   Researchers sometimes request that the child point or act out instructions, as in: "Get me the ball," or "Point to the ball!," while showing the child a selection of possible items. This method is very popular when teaching children new words. Using it, researchers have discovered that some older infants (approximately 2 years of age) can learn a new word in as little as one repetition, a process often called "*fast mapping*" (Dollaghan,1985). This method has also been used to test the ways in which children extend the meanings of the words they know (Waxman & Booth, 2001) or to assess which of several possible objects children think received a label (Tomasello & Barton, 1994). However, shy children may be reluctant to respond, and very young infants may have difficulty coordinating a point or indicating an object, despite some level of understanding.

3   The last and most controversial method of testing comprehension is to simply observe where the child is looking. This is the rationale underlying the *intermodal preferential looking procedure*. The logic is that, if, when presented with a ball and a doll, and the child looks at a ball when the experimenter asks "where is the ball?" but not when the experimenter asks "where is the doll?" this indicates some degree of comprehension.

Using this method, Tincoff & Jusczyk (1999) discovered that infants have made some word-to-world connections as early as six months of age. Thus, six-month-olds looked longer at Mommy when asked "where's Mommy?" and longer at Daddy when asked "where's Daddy?" Other studies have used preferential looking to demonstrate that 15-month-olds can learn a new word in as few as 12 repetitions (Schafer & Plunkett, 1998) and that 19-month-olds notice even subtle differences in pronunciation, such as the difference between "baby" and the mispronunciation, "vaby" (Swingley & Aslin, 2007).

However, while successful preferential looking indicates some connection between sight and sound, controversy exists with regard to the degree of that connection and whether such early sight–sound associations are developmentally linked to later word learning. Tomasello (2000) asserts that, from the earliest ages, language connects to the social world of the infant. That is, even for the very young, language is used to talk about things which are in the head, not the world. Under this view, connecting sight to sound has as much to do with mature language and word learning as playing with toy blocks has to do with building the pyramids. That is, many creatures can make "word-like" associations, including chimps with sign language (Savage-Rumbaugh et al., 1993; Seidenberg & Pettito, 1979), dogs that fetch specific objects (Kaminski, Call, & Fischer, 2004), and even parrots that talk in response to real world objects and events (Pepperberg, 1999). Yet mature word learning appears fundamentally different from even these impressive examples of associative learning. Consider the findings of Tomasello and Barton (1994). They found that children do not associate a label with just any object, but rather use social cues to determine the correct referent. So if an experimenter says, "Where's the toma?" and then pulls out a novel object from a bucket but then looks at it disapprovingly and puts it back, two-year-olds almost never select this distractor object when "toma" is requested. Likewise, Hollich et al. (2000; see also Baldwin, 1993) found that 20-month-olds do not misattach a label to an interesting object presented at the same time an experimenter is looking at, and labeling, a boring object. Thus, the argument goes, the connections that children make during "true" word learning are always socially informed and have little to do with the paired associations demonstrated by preferential looking tasks on very young infants or by the clever tricks performed by our animal friends.

Of course, not everyone asserts the primacy of social knowledge during word learning, at least in early stages. As the first section indicated, others assert that intermodal perception may help get word learning started (Gogate et al., 2001). My colleagues and I (Hollich et al., 2000) have suggested that word learning could be conceived as developing from a combination of factors: some social, some linguistic, and some perceptual. These factors rise and fall in prominence throughout language acquisition. Thus, perceptual factors, including intermodal perception, may be critically important early in development (as children learn their first concrete connections between word and object). Social and linguistic factors may be weighted more heavily, or even discovered, at a later age. In support of this idea, 10-month-olds seem to rely solely on perceptual salience in deciding the referent for a novel word (Pruden, Hirsh-Pasek, Golinkoff, & Hennon, 2006). In contrast, as mentioned above 18-month-olds seem to recognize the primacy of social cues, such as eye gaze, during labeling (Hollich et al., 2000). Thus, the debate seems to be whether social factors are *the* foundation for all language or merely an important component of mature language understanding.

Another obvious and potentially powerful way for children to learn the correct meaning of a word is to see/hear it used across multiple contexts. For example, if children hear the word "dog" used to refer to dalmatians, beagles, dachshunds, and greyhounds, they should develop a good idea of the variation and commonalities inherent in the concept. This helps them avoid *overgeneralizing*, referring to cats as dogs, or *undergeneralizing*, not recognizing a chihuahua as a dog. This phenomenon is sometimes called cross-situational learning (Akhtar, & Montague, 1999). Work by Xu (1999) and colleagues (Xu, & Tenenbaum, 2007) demonstrates that the size and nature of the familiarization set determines how broadly children interpret meaning. She found that, if children see a restricted set of exemplars (e.g., multiple instances of beagles for the word "dog"), they do not extend that word to include more unusual members, such as a poodle. In contrast, if the familiarization set is broad (e.g., beagles, dachshunds, dalmatians), children are much more likely to recognize diverse members.

Finally, in the process of learning their first words, infants appear to have (or develop) certain predispositions which lead them to prefer certain interpretations of meaning over others. Indeed, a focus of the literature in the 1990s was listings and classifications of the many biases (sometimes called *constraints*) possessed by infants (Golinkoff, Mervis, & Hirsh-Pasek, 1994; Markman, 1990; Nelson, 1988; Waxman & Kosowski, 1990, Woodward & Markman, 1997). Some of the many biases that children seem to develop over the first 2 years of life include the *whole object bias*, that words tend to label whole objects (Macnamara, 1972; Markman, 1989) rather than actions or parts (Hollich, Golinkoff, Hirsh-Pasek, 2007; Saylor & Sabbagh, 2004); the *shape bias*, that words tend to extend based on similar shapes rather than colors (Smith, 2000); and *mutual exclusivity* that objects tend to have one, and only one, label in discourse (Markman & Wachtel, 1988; Merriman & Bowman, 1989; also called *contrast*, Clark, 1983).

With the advent of the new century, the theoretical accounts of constraints took on a more developmental flavor: suggesting that constraints may be products of word learning rather than drivers. For example, an infant may learn the word cup, and from this experience make an educated guess about what parents are talking about in subsequent learning episodes. Linda Smith (2000, Colunga & Smith, 2005; Smith, Jones, & Landau, 1996) has championed this viewpoint for some time and has called this "an associative crane." Through laborious statistical learning of a few words, infants discover regularities which lead to apparent systematic biases in subsequent word learning. Just as children make inferences about what individual words mean through a number of examples, so they infer how certain classes of words work and extend these findings to interpret the meaning of new words.

Even these learned biases may develop: beginning as general tendencies exhibited by younger infants, which quickly become more sophisticated over time to apply in specific situations and only under certain conditions (see Hollich et al., 2007 for a discussion). For example, infants may first learn that labels apply to similarly shaped objects. With additional experience, infants learn that words preceded by "the" typically label similar shaped objects while words with an "ing" ending label actions (Echols & Marti, 2004) and words used as prepositions label particular spatial relations (Fisher, Klinger, & Song, 2006). Biases represent infants' best guess at any given time about the meaning of a word. Given more experience, context, and/or social support, these guesses become more sophisticated.

Consider infants' ability to pay attention to grammatical morphology. Waxman and colleagues (Waxman & Booth, 2001; Waxman & Markow, 1995) have carried out a series of studies looking at children's developing understanding of morphological endings. In one, Waxman and Booth (2001) labeled a series of four pink horses saying "These are blicke*ts*," (implying the speaker was talking about horses), or "These are blick*ish*," (implying the speaker was referring to some common property, such as pink-ish). The difference between these two utterances is only a single phoneme, yet it led 14-month-olds to pay more attention to the shape (horse) in the "blicket*s*" case and the color of the objects (pink) in the "blick*ish*" case. Thus, even the subtle difference between blicket*s* and blick*ish* was enough to direct infants' attention to the appropriate dimension.

So how do infants learn the meanings of words? In sum, across the second year of life, infants are learning a great number of words based on the many contexts in which they hear those words, their developing understanding of social intent, and in their growing knowledge of the ways in which words work (even connecting morphology to grammatical classes and dimensions of categorization). Clearly, infants are very sophisticated in learning meaning.

Individual Differences in Vocabulary Understanding

While virtually all children learn language, there is tremendous individual variability in how fast, how much language, and what types of words any given child will learn. In a landmark study, Fenson et al. (1994) tracked the developing production and comprehension abilities of 1,803 children between 8 and 30 months of age. They found vast differences between the top 10% and the bottom 10% of children. By way of example, at 16 months, the top 10% were saying as many as 347 words (possibly more given that checklists often underestimate the total number of words). The bottom 10% said none. By age 2, spoken vocabulary ranged from 7 to 675 words. These differences are so extreme in effect size that they dwarf effects of gender, birth order, and even socioeconomic status.

What can account for such variability? The most likely candidate would seem to be children's linguistic environments. The more opportunities and situations under which a child hears a word used, the more likely it is that the child will discover the meaning. This is not to say that children are implicitly counting the number of times they have heard a word in relationship with a referent (although such a mechanism could exist; see Yu & Smith, 2007), but more words equals more opportunity to learn: a larger sample set from which to draw conclusion about the nature and subtleties of language.

Unfortunately, differences in children's linguistic environments are as striking as their variability in understanding. Hart and Risley (1995) carried out a large-scale longitudinal study looking at the linguistic environment surrounding 42 children in different socioeconomic classes (including children whose parents were on welfare). They calculated that by 48 months of age, children in professional families had heard approximately 40 million more utterances, on average, than children in welfare families. Not surprisingly, given this dramatic difference in the amount of language heard by the children, the professionals' children in their sample had much larger vocabularies at 48 months, more than 1000 words, while the welfare children had vocabularies of just over 500 words. Furthermore, regardless of socioeconomic status, greater speech in the environment was strongly correlated with vocabulary size. Similarly, Hoff and Naigles (2002) found that in addition to sheer quantity, the diversity and syntactic complexity of the input is strongly correlated with lexical development (with correlations ranging from .21 to .55).

In addition to environmental effects, even within the same families (and presumably the same linguistic environment), there appear to be at least two different types, or styles, of language learners: *Referential* learners tend to have very large vocabularies and seem to be focused on objects and attributes. In contrast, *expressive* learners tend to have slightly smaller vocabularies and tend to be focused on social words (Nelson, 1973). This tendency toward being one type or the other may have something to do with genetic tendencies toward social behavior and/or the well-known person–thing orientation found in children's play preferences and occupational preferences along a person–thing dimension (Lippa, 2002; Prediger, 1982), or it may also be linked to difference in parental style (Pine, Lieven, & Rowland, 1997).

One other finding that comes out of the literature on individual differences is the discovery that the learning of grammar follows in step with children's initial successes in learning words. Indeed, the variation in children's grammatical skill at 28 months is perfectly predicted by measures of lexical knowledge at 20 months, and strongly predicted by lexical measures taken even as young as 13 months (Bates, Bretherton, & Snyder, 1988). Furthermore, work with atypical populations and with brain-damaged children and adults also points to a strong link between the size of vocabulary and grammatical skill (Bates & Goodman, 1997). Such a link would seem to suggest that the mechanisms of word learning are similar, if not identical to, the mechanisms that support grammatical understanding. At minimum, these mechanisms seem closely linked.

Grammatical Understanding

The last, and most controversial, language skill to be acquired is *grammar*: an understanding of how words and word parts, called *morphemes*, combine to form meaning. This skill is controversial because theorists have long contended that grammar must be innate: suggesting that grammatical phrases and rules could not be learned from the input alone (AKA the *poverty of the stimulus* argument). That is, without some initial starting knowledge of grammar, the input itself is too ambiguous to allow infants to quickly guess the correct grammatical rule. To a naïve observer, this argument might seem odd. After all, we know that humans are very good pattern detectors, and grammatical regularities or "rules" would seem to make excellent candidates for statistical learning based on input (Elman et al., 1996, Gogate & Hollich, in press). Why is grammar so hard?

One answer to this apparent contradiction is provided by a clever series of simulations by Gillette and colleagues (Gillette, Gleitman, Gleitman, & Lederer, 1999). In brief, the meaning of many verbs (e.g., transitive verbs, which need an argument) and other grammatical words is far less obvious from the input. In their studies they showed college students videos of mothers talking to their children (with the audio turned off). They then asked the students to guess what word the mother was using at any given moment. Students were most successful at guessing when concrete nouns were being used. Performance on concrete nouns was followed by highly concrete verbs that require no argument (a verb like bake) while students were least successful for transitive and non-concrete verbs (e.g., "Mommy is thinking about dinner").

Gleitman (1990) suggests (similar to an argument by Gentner, 1982), that things which are easily pictured/heard/smelled (i.e., concrete) are easily mapped to real world events, and thus require fewer iterations in order to be learned. Thus, although the word "think" might be very frequent, its meaning is far more elusive than the word "hammer," for example. Furthermore, there are aspects of meaning which are only contained in the structure of the sentence. For example, what does "do" do in the phrase, "we do like him"? In this manner, because grammar is defined by the relationships among words rather than any relationship to the external environment, it becomes a special kind of learning that is much more difficult than connecting the word "apple" to the object. Thus, while both word learning and grammar may involve pattern detection, the patterns at play during grammatical learning are often more abstract and, as a result, more difficult to perceive. Indeed, a disproportionate number of infants' early words tend to be concrete nouns rather than verbs (Bornstein et al., 2004).

In general, this hypothesis also seems to be borne out by research on infants' early understanding of grammar. If the grammatical construction being tested is relatively concrete then very young infants seem to be able to ascertain the meaning. For example, Seidl, Hollich, & Jusczyk (2003) found that even 20-month-old infants looked at the correct answer when asked "What hit the apple?" (Note that the verb "hit" is very concrete and an all too frequent word in a speech addressed to young children, especially those with siblings). Likewise, Hirsh-Pasek and Golinkoff (1996) found that 13- to 15-month-old infants looked at the correct picture when they heard "She is kissing the keys" (in one picture a girl was kissing a pair of keys while she was also moving a ball; in the other picture the girl was kissing a ball while moving the keys). Note that the "is __ing" is a very frequent frame which often corresponds to a clear action. Mintz (2003) has suggested that in any language there are numerous frequent frames such as these which uniquely correspond to verbs and nouns, and which could help children disambiguate parts of speech.

While it might be tempting to conclude that infants understand something about word order from these studies, it appears infants are simply adopting an "agent, action, patient" interpretation. Thus, if an intransitive (and infrequent) sentence form is presented such as "Watch Big Bird and Cookie Monster bending!" infants still interpret it as "Big Bird bends Cookie Monster." Not until 24 months do children look at the correct answer in such a case (Hirsh-Pasek & Golinkoff, 1996). Similarly, Naigles (1990) found that it is not until at least 24 months that infants can use syntax to learn meaning: correctly mapping new verbs based on whether the verb is presented with transitive or intransitive syntax. Thus, the more abstract, infrequent, or distal the grammatical relationship, the older the child must be for correct performance. Indeed, infant performance very strongly follows frequency and experience with particular verbs – a phenomenon Tomasello (1992) calls the "verb island hypothesis." In this manner, children are laboriously learning how a few frequent verbs (and, one could add, verb frames) work and only later extending this to less frequent or novel verbs. Using computational modeling, Elman (1993) has demonstrated that, under some situations, grammar learning is better if children confine their focus to smaller grammatical units.

Another difficulty with grammar learning is that grammar is productive. While a child is unlikely to say a word they have never heard before, they often will produce word combinations which they have not heard before. With a word, the challenge is to match the word to the situation, which may be new: old words to new exemplars. In contrast, with grammar, the challenge is to apply "rules" and combine words to fit the new situation: new word combinations for new situations. One famous example of this is the "wug" test, originated by Jean Berko Gleason (1958). In this test, infants are given an unfamiliar object and told that it is a "wug." Next, a second example of the same object is introduced: "Look, now there is another one, there are two ___." While 3- and 4-year-olds will say "wugs," even 24-month-olds infants will look at multiples when they hear "these *are* blicks" and 36-month-olds do so even if it is just the "s" at the end (Kouider, Halberda, Wood, & Carey, 2006). These results suggest that infants are productive in their grammar and can apply the "rules" even in unfamiliar situations.

Thus, grammatical learning presents some unique problems in comparison to word learning including: (a) the meaning of verbs, morphemes, and even frequent grammatical structures is not as obvious from input because the regularities specified often lie in the relationships between words rather than between words and an obvious external referent; and (b) grammar is productive, leading children to produce a continuing stream of new thoughts and sentences. Nonetheless, it appears that infants are learning some aspects of grammar (particularly concrete and verb-specific aspects) before their second birthday.

Speech Production

At 12 months of age, my son, Sebastien said his first word. I could tell you that this word was "dada," but I would be lying. His mother would like to tell you that his first word was "mama," but it was not. In fact, Sebastian's first word was "Victor," the name of the family dog. It makes sense, with all the "Victor get away from the baby!" and "Victor, no jumping!" and "Victor, stop eating the baby's diaper!" While his choice of words might be surprising, what was more surprising was the realization that he'd been saying this word for several weeks before we could figure out that "Victor" was what he was trying to say.

Sebastien's difficulty being understood illustrates an important point in learning to speak: It is much like learning a musical instrument. Only with time and experience does the musician move from being competent to proficient and perhaps even talented at producing the intricate melodies, moving phrasings, and clever ornamentations that mark the expert. Similarly, infants move from trying to produce sounds to speaking these sounds in words and longer phrases, increasing their diversity and gaining control until they are confidently producing complex forms.

First attempts (around 4 to 6 months) are often clumsy: concerned with making any noise at all, much less a recognizable one. This is why many of the first utterances of children tend to be explosives sounds or coos: /bu/ or /aaa/, perhaps even a raspberry or two: the coordination of the tongue, lips, with exhaling, is, at this stage, daunting – not unlike the difficulty posed by walking, which involves the coordination of stepping with maintaining balance, among other skills. Years of research on motor behavior tell us the coordination of any two complex skills is problematic early in development (see chapter 5, this volume). Thus, is not surprising that it should take some time for infants to learn how to correctly produce the words that they already understand, although they might attempt to produce these words quite early.

With practice (around 6 to 8 months), the language learner is happily producing a range of animal sounds and phoneme combinations (some more word-like than others). Especially prevalent at this stage is the tendency to repeat consonant vowel combinations (Oller & Eilers, 1982), something called *reduplicative* babbling, (e.g., /bababa/ or /dada/). It is interesting to note that virtually all of the worlds nicknames for the primary caregivers (e.g., "mama" and "papa") involve reduplication of syllables (perhaps those caregivers simply wanted the child to be able to call them easily, or perhaps those caregivers like the conceit of thinking their child's first words involve them).

Some reports of this stage have also suggested that the melody of the babbling distinctly matches that of the contour of the child's native language (DeBoysson-Bardies, Sagart, & Durand, 1984). Thus, from 6 to 8 months infants seem to markedly imitate the prosody of their native language, leading trained phoneticians (at 6-months) and even naive listeners (by 8-months) to reliably identify French-learning babies from Arabic- or Cantonese-learning babies. Thus, infants babble in a way that distinctly sounds like the native language, at least until they try to produce individual words.

From 8 to 12 months, babbling changes and becomes variegated (e.g., "madabaga") and children appear to be focusing on producing a range of consonants along with the prosody, tone patterns and even vowels of their native language. It is at this stage when one could comment that "she's talking, we just don't understand her." These longer language sounding utterances are called *jargon*. In addition to jargon, infants will also begin what Dore (1974) has called *primitive speech acts*, using a single sound or "word" to request, protest, question, affirm, or label. Each sound is thus *holophrastic*: children are using it to convey a full utterance (e.g., "da!" translates to "I would like that!"). Intonation further allows the listener to determine the child's meaning (e.g., "da?" "da." "da!").

Finally, around 11 to 13 months, after months of practice, it is possible to string sounds into recognizable words. Even then, there is much modification that takes place (including *reduplication* of vowels and *reduction* of the full word). For example, a young child might say "mama" instead of "mommy," "ca" instead of "cat," and an older child might say "basketti" instead of "spaghetti." In all of these utterances, it is common for infants to be slower and more variable in their productions than older children and adults (Goffman & Smith, 1999; Goodell & Studdert-Kennedy, 1993).

Somewhere around 2 years of age (20 to 24 months), infants begin systematically combining words productively in a form of speech known as telegraphic speech. Even these apparently primitive utterances reveal a fairly sophisticated grammatical understanding, expressing the full range of concepts including noun–verb combinations such as "he fall," adjective–noun combinations such as "tiny train," and even possessives such as "my train."

Even at this stage, spoken language is not error-free: consonant clusters such as "str" and other constructions which require an extra degree of dexterity on a child's part are often simplified. Thus "string" becomes "ting," and "that" becomes "dat." Interestingly, recent work on something called *covert contrast* indicates that while a child might say "dat," they are actually trying to say the "th" sound. Fine-grained acoustic analysis indicates subtle differences between their production of the /d/ in dat versus the /d/ in dad, for example (Macken & Barton, 1980). Despite these imperfections, it is clear that in the first 2 years of life children make a great deal of progress in speaking their language.

Early Language: Lessons Learned

Lesson 1

Repetition matters. The single largest factor in determining the size and complexity of a child's language is the language environment. One can not learn something if not exposed to it, and it holds that the more one is exposed to a thing, the more likely that the thing will be learned. This is true for recognizing familiar sounds, finding familiar words in the fluent stream of speech, learning meaning, and even discovering aspects of grammar. For sounds, this means that infants quickly come to recognize and prefer the sounds and rhythm of their native language, even noticing frequently repeated words, such as their own name. For word learning, this implies that children are more likely to learn the meaning of and say frequent words. Indeed, infant vocabulary very closely matches the words they hear in the surrounding environment. Finally, for grammar this implies that the more frequent a verb or verb frame, the sooner it is acquired, and the more quickly infants come to use that construction in their own production.

Lesson 2

Competence is not performance. In many ways, Chomsky (1965) was right to emphasize the distinction between competence and performance. Competence defines the learner's understanding of language while performance is the echo of that understanding as filtered through "memory limitations, distractions, shifts of attention and interest, and errors" (Chomsky, 1965, p. 3). This idea suggests that infants might understand a great deal about language that is limited in their performance. The past 20 years of language research have revealed a multitude of infant competencies in the understanding of phonology, semantics, and even grammar that had previously been hidden by performance limitations. Through careful design, researchers have found that infants understand aspects of speech perception at birth, comprehend words well before their first birthday, and understand aspects of grammar before the age of two. Children are even trying to produce complex words and sentences well in advance of recognizable utterances. In short, children's performance limitations in attention, memory, or motor skills can often prevent them from demonstrating their language competencies.

Given that infants do process aspects of grammar well before they string words together or that they understand the meanings of some words well before their first birthday, a more holistic approach to early language is needed. The straightforward timeline of infants proceeding from sounds, to words, to word meanings, to grammar must give way to a richer conception of infants making some early concrete word-to-world pairings which may strengthen phonetic representations, and cases where infants can use concrete grammatical forms to learn more abstract concepts. In short, early capabilities necessitate new avenues for development.

Lesson 3

Language is emergent. In the first handbook chapter on language development, Bates, O'Connell, and Shore (1987) suggested that "Language development depends crucially on skills from a variety of domains including perception, cognition, motor development, and socialization." This interactionist perspective has only been further validated in the years since. From finding the sounds and units in the speech stream (Jusczyk, 1997; Christiansen, Allen, & Seidenberg, 1998), to learning the meanings of words (Hollich et al., 2000), and even to discovering grammar (Hirsh-Pasek & Golinkoff, 1996), language has proven a prototypical example of a complex dynamical system with a multitude of parts working in concert to produce a whole that is more than the sum of those parts.

The idea that language is the emergent result of multiple systems interacting has profound implications for the direction of future research. Emergentist ideas insist that we at least consider the possibility that many of the difficulties of language may have more to do with connections and interactions between language-specific skills and foundational abilities then specific impairments in language itself. Autism, late talkers, selective mutism, and even Down syndrome may have significant language impairments that may not be due to flaws in language-specific skills per se (phoneme detection, speech segmentation, grammatical sequencing, etc.), but rather result from impairments in skills such as social savvy, memory, and intermodal perception.

In this manner, the coming decades should prove a challenging time for the study of language, as researchers leave their comfortable niches within language domains and begin the rough task of figuring out how infants' abilities work together to produce language. For example, Saffran (2001) examined how infants' developing speech segmentation abilities affected their ability to learn the meaning of new words, and found a strong facilitative relationship between segmenting a word from speech and learning a meaning for that word. Similarly, Kuhl, Coffey-Corina, Padden, and Dawson (2005) found that autistics' difficulty with social cues was strongly correlated to their learning of new words. As a final example, consider the case of specific language impairment (Leonard, 1989). In this disorder, despite relatively normal scores on others measures of cognition, subjects seem unusually impaired on aspects of grammar (including grammatical morphology and use of ambiguous pronouns). Recent computational simulations (Joanisse & Seidenberg, 2003) suggest that such difficulty may result from impairments in phonological perception – in each of these cases, factors outside the traditional domain had significant effects on infants' performance within the domain. Thus, new lines of research are needed that look at interactions within and among domains (perception and word learning, semantics and grammar, etc.).

Such research may be vitally important to the discovery of new therapies and interventions: For just as the cause of a problem may lie outside a domain, the solution to the problem may come from outside as well. Thus, word learning may be helped by additional experience with segmentation or social skills, and grammar learning may be helped by training on the meanings of words and increasing phonological awareness. In the past, researchers carved up language into component areas of study (phonology, word learning, grammar, etc.), yet, disorders know no boundaries, and it is possible that the largest beneficial effects need not lie solely within a given domain.

References

Akhtar, N., & Montague, L. (1999). Early lexical acquisition: The role of cross-situational learning. *First Language*, *19*, 347–358.

Bahrick, L. E., Lickliter, R., & Flom, R. (2004). Intersensory redundancy guides infants' selective attention, perceptual and cognitive development. *Current Directions in Psychological Science*, *13*, 99–102.

Baldwin, D. (1993). Early referential understanding: Young children's ability to recognize referential acts for what they are. *Developmental Psychology*, *29*, 832–843.

Bandura, A. (1977). *Social learning theory*. Englewood Cliffs, NJ: Prentice Hall.

Bates, E. (2004). Explaining and interpreting deficits in language development across clinical groups: Where do we go from here? *Brain and Language*, *88*, 248–253.

Bates, E., Bretherton, I., & Snyder, L. (1988). *From first words to grammar: Individual differences and dissociable mechanisms*. Cambridge: Cambridge University Press.

Bates, E., & Goodman, J. (1997). On the inseparability of grammar and the lexicon: Evidence from acquisition, aphasia, and real-time processing. *Language and Cognitive Processes*, *12*, 507–586.

Bates, E., O'Connell B., and Shore, C. (1987). Language and communication in infancy. In J. Osofsky, (Ed.), *Handbook of infant development* (pp. 149–203), New York: Wiley.

Berko Gleason, J. (1958). The child's learning of English morphology. *Word*, *14*, 150–177.

Bloom, P. (2000). *How children learn the meanings of words*. Cambridge, MA: MIT Press.

Bloom, L., & Tinker, E. (2001). The intentionality model and language acquisition. *Monographs of the Society for Research in Child Development*, *66* (Serial No. 267).

Bornstein, M. H., Cote, L. R., Linda, R., Maital, S., Painter, K., Park, S., et al. (2004). Cross-linguistic analysis of vocabulary in young children: Spanish, Dutch, French, Hebrew, Italian, Korean, and American English. *Child Development*, *75*, 1–25.

Bortfeld, H., Morgan, J. L., Golinkoff, R. M., & Rathbun, K. (2005). Mommy and me: Familiar names help launch babies into speech stream segmentation. *Psychological Science*, *4*, 298–304.

Bruner, J. S. (1981). The social context of learning language. *Language and Communication*, *1*, 155–178.

Bruner, J. S. (1993). *Child's talk: Learning to use language*. New York: Norton.

Chomsky, N. (1965). *Aspects of the theory of syntax*. New York: MIT Press.

Christiansen, M. H., Allen, J., & Seidenberg, M. S. (1998). Learning to segment speech using multiple cues: A connectionist model. *Language and Cognitive Processes*, *13*, 2–3.

Clark, E. (2003). *First language acquisition*. Cambridge: Cambridge University Press.

Clark, E. V. (1983). Meanings and concepts. In J. H. Flavell & E. M. Markman (Eds.), *Handbook of child psychology: Vol. III, Cognitive development* (pp. 787–840). New York: John Wiley & Sons.

Colunga, E., & Smith, L. B. (2005). From the lexicon to expectations about kinds: A role for associative learning. *Psychological Review*, *112*, 347–382.

Darwin, C. (1887). A biographical sketch of an infant. *Mind, 2,* 285–294.

DeBoysson-Bardies, B., Sagart, L., & Durand, C. (1984). Discernible differences in the babbling of infants according to target language. *Journal of Child Language, 11,* 1–15.

DeCasper, A. J., & Spence, M. (1986). Newborns prefer a familiar story over an unfamiliar one. *Infant Behavior and Development, 9,* 133–150.

Dodd, B. (1979). Lip reading in infants: attention to speech presented in-and-out of synchrony. *Cognitive Psychology, 11,* 478–484.

Dollaghan, C. (1985). Child meets word: "Fast mapping" in preschool children. *Journal of Speech and Hearing Research, 28,* 449–454.

Dore, J. (1974). A pragmatic description of early language development. *Journal of Psycholinguistic Research, 3,* 343–350.

Dromi, E. (1987). *Early lexical development.* Cambridge: Cambridge University Press.

Echols, C., & Marti, C. N. (2004). The identification of words and their meanings: From perceptual biases to language specific cues. In D. G. Hall & S. Waxman (Eds.), *Weaving a lexicon* (pp. 41–78). Cambridge, MA: MIT Press.

Eimas, P. D., Siqueland, E. R., Jusczyk, P., & Vigorito, J. (1971). Speech perception in infants. *Science, 171*(968), 303–306.

Elman, J. (1993). Learning and development in neural networks: The importance of starting small. *Cognition, 48,* 71–99.

Elman, J., Bates, E., Johnson, M., Karmiloff-Smith, A., Parisi, D., & Plunkett, K. (1996). *Rethinking innateness. A connectionist perspective on development.* Cambridge, MA: MIT Press.

Fenson, L., Dale, P. S., Reznick, J. S., Bates, E., Thal, D., & Pethick, S. (1994). Variability in early communicative development. *Monographs of the Society for Research on Child Development, 59* (Serial No. 242).

Fernald, A. (1985). Four-month-old infants prefer to listen to motherese. *Infant Behavior and Development, 8,* 181–195.

Fisher, C., Klinger, S. L., & Song, H. (2006). What does syntax say about space? Two-year-olds use sentence structure to learn new prepositions. *Cognition, 101,* B19–B29.

Gentner, D. (1982). Why nouns are learned before verbs: Linguistic relativity versus natural partitioning. In S. Kuczaj (Ed.), *Language development: Vol 2, Language, thought, and culture* (pp. 301–334). Hillsdale, NJ: Erlbaum.

Gillette, J., Gleitman, H., Gleitman, L., & Lederer, A. (1999). Human simulations of vocabulary learning. *Cognition, 73,* 135–176.

Gleitman, L. R. (1990). The structural sources of verb meanings. *Language Acquisition, 1,* 3–55.

Goffman, L, & Smith, A. (1999). Development and phonetic differentiation of speech movement patterns. *Journal of Experimental Psychology Human Perception and Performance, 25,* 649–660.

Gold, E. M. (1967). Language identification in the limit. *Information and Control, 16,* 447–474.

Golinkoff, R. M., Mervis, C., & Hirsh-Pasek, K. (1994). Early object labels: The case for a developmental lexical principles framework. *Journal of Child Language, 21,* 125–155.

Gogate, L. J., & Bahrick, L. E. (1998). Intersensory redundancy facilitates learning of arbitrary relations between vowel sounds and objects in 7-month-old infants. *Journal of Experimental Child Psychology, 69,* 133–149.

Gogate, L., Bahrick, L. E., & Watson, J. D. (2000). A study of multimodal motherese: The role of temporal synchrony between verbal labels and gestures. *Child Development, 71,* 878–894.

Gogate, L., & Hollich, G. (in press). Invariance detection within an interactive system: A perceptual gateway to language development. *Psychological Review.*

Gogate, L., Walker-Andrews, A. S., & Bahrick, L. E. (2001). The intersensory origins of word comprehension: An ecological-dynamics systems view. *Developmental Science, 4,* 1–37.

Gomez, R. L., & Gerken, L. (2000). Infant artificial language learning and language acquisition. *Trends in Cognitive Sciences, 4*, 178–186.

Goodell, E. W., & Studdert-Kennedy, M. (1993). Acoustic evidence for the development of gestural coordination in the speech of 2-year-olds: A longitudinal study. *Journal of Speech and Hearing Research, 36*, 707–727.

Kouider, S., Halberda, J., Wood, J., & Carey, S. (2006). Acquisition of English number marking: The singular–plural distinction. *Language Learning and Development, 2*, 1–25.

Hart, B., & Risley, T. (1995). *Meaningful differences in the everyday experiences of young American children*. Baltimore, MD: Paul H. Brookes.

Hirsh-Pasek, K., & Golinkoff, R. M. (1996). *The origins of grammar: Evidence from early language comprehension*. Cambridge, MA: MIT Press.

Hoff, E., & Naigles, L. (2002). How children use input to acquire a lexicon. *Child Development, 73*, 418–433.

Hollich, G., Hirsh-Pasek, K., & Golinkoff, R. M. (2000). Breaking the language barrier: An emergentist coalition model for the origins of word learning. *Monographs of the Society for Research in Child Development, 65* (Serial No. 262).

Hollich, G., Golinkoff, R., & Hirsh-Pasek, K. (2007). Young children associate novel words with complex objects rather than salient parts. *Developmental Psychology, 43*, 1051–1061.

Hollich, G., & Houston, D. (2007). Language development: From speech perception to first words. In A. Slater & M. Lewis (Eds.), *Introduction to infant development* (2nd ed., pp. 170–188). New York: Oxford University Press.

Joanisse, M. F., & Seidenberg, M. S. (2003). Phonology and syntax in specific language impairment: Evidence from a connectionist model. *Brain and Language, 86*, 40–56.

Johnson, E. K., & Jusczyk, P. W. (2001). Word segmentation by 8-month-olds: When speech cues count more than statistics. *Journal of Memory and Language, 44*, 548–567.

Jusczyk, P. W. (1997). *The discovery of spoken language*. Cambridge, MA: MIT Press.

Jusczyk, P. W., & Aslin, R. N. (1995). Infants' detection of the sound patterns of words in fluent speech. *Cognitive Psychology, 29*, 1–23.

Jusczyk, P. W., Cutler, A., & Redanz, N. J. (1993). Infants' preference for the predominant stress patterns of English words. *Child Development, 64*, 675–687.

Jusczyk, P. W., Hohne, E. A., & Bauman, A. (1999). Infant's sensitivity to allophonic cues for word segmentation. *Perception & Psychophysics, 61*, 1465–1476.

Jusczyk, P. W., Houston, D. M., & Newsome, M. (1999). The beginnings of word segmentation in English-learning infants. *Cognitive Psychology, 39*, 159–207.

Kaminski, J., Call, J., & Fischer, J. (2004). Word learning in a domestic dog: Evidence for "fast mapping." *Science, 304*, 1682.

Kaye, K. (1980). Why we don't talk "babytalk" to babies. *Journal of Child Language, 7*, 489–507.

Keller, H. (1903). *The story of my life*. New York: Doubleday

Kirkham, N. Z., Slemmer, J. A., & Johnson, S. P. (2002). Visual statistical learning in infancy: Evidence for a domain general learning mechanism. *Cognition, 83*, B35–B42.

Kuhl, P. K., Coffey-Corina, S., Padden, D., & Dawson, G. (2005). Links between social and linguistic processing of speech in preschool children with autism: behavioral and electrophysiological measures. *Developmental Science, 8*, F1–F12.

Kuhl, P. K., & Miller, J. D. (1975). Speech perception by the chinchilla: Voiced–voiceless distinction in alveolar plosive consonants. *Science, 190*, 69–72.

Kuhl, P. K., Tsao, F. -M., & Liu, H. -M. (2003). Foreign-language experience in infancy: effects of short-term exposure and social interaction on phonetic learning. *Proceedings of the National Academy of Sciences, 100*, 9096–9101.

Leonard, L. (1989). Language learnability and specific language impairment. *Applied Psycholinguistics, 10*, 179–202.

Lippa, R. A. (2002). *Gender, nature, and nurture*. Mahwah, NJ: Erlbaum.

Macken, M. A., & Barton, D. (1980). The acquisition of the voicing contrast in English: a study of voice onset time in word-initial stop consonants. *Journal of Child Language, 7*, 41–74.

Macnamara, J. (1972). Cognitive basis of language learning in infants. *Psychological Review, 79*, 1–13.

Mandel, D. R., Jusczyk, P. W., & Pisoni, D. B. (1995). Infants' recognition of the sound patterns of their own names. *Psychological Science, 6*, 314–317.

Markman, E. (1989). *Categorization and naming in children: Problems of induction*. Cambridge, MA: MIT Press.

Markman, E. M. (1990). Constraints children place on word meanings. *Cognitive Science, 14*(1), 57–77.

Markman, E. M., & Wachtel, G. F. (1988). Children's use of mutual exclusivity to constrain the meanings of words. *Cognitive Psychology, 20*, 121–157.

Mattys, S. L., Jusczyk, P. W., Luce, P. A., & Morgan, J. L. (1999). Phonotactic and prosodic effects on word segmentation in infants. *Cognitive Psychology, 38*, 465–494.

McCune, L. (2008). *How children learn to learn language*. Oxford: Oxford University Press.

Merriman, W. E., & Bowman, L. L. (1989). The mutual exclusivity bias in children's word learning. *Monographs of the Society for Research in Child Development, 4* (Serial No. 220), 1–123.

Mintz, T. (2003). Frequent frames as a cue for grammatical categories in child-directed speech. *Cognition, 90*, 91–117.

Morgan, J. L. (1996). A rhythmic bias in preverbal speech segmentation. *Journal of Memory and Language, 33*, 666–689.

Naigles, L. (1990). Children use syntax to learn verb meanings. *Journal of Child Language, 17*, 357–374.

Nazzi, T., Floccia, C., & Bertoncini, J. (1998). Discrimination of pitch contours by neonates. *Infant Behavior and Development, 21*, 779–784.

Nazzi, T., Jusczyk, P. W., & Johnson, E. K. (2000). Language discrimination by English-learning 5-month-olds. *Journal of Memory and Language, 43*, 1–19.

Nelson, K. (1973). Structure and strategy in learning to talk. *Monographs of the Society for Research in Child Development, 38*(1–2, Serial No. 149).

Nelson, K. (1988). Constraints on word learning? *Cognitive Development, 3*, 221–246.

Oller, D., & Eilers, R. (1982). Similarity of babbling in Spanish- and English-learning babies. *Journal of Child Language, 9*, 565–577.

Pepperberg, I. M., (1999). *The Alex Studies*. Cambridge, MA: Harvard University Press.

Pierrehumbert, J. (2003). Phonetic diversity, statistical learning, and acquisition of phonology. *Language and Speech, 46*, 115–154.

Pine, J. M., Lieven, E. V. M., & Rowland, C. F. (1997). Stylistic variation at the "single word" stage: Relations between maternal speech characteristics and children's vocabulary composition and usage. *Child Development, 68*, 807–819.

Prediger, D. J. (1982). Dimensions underlying Holland's hexagon: Missing link between interests and occupations? *Journal of Vocational Behavior, 21*, 259–287.

Pruden, S. M., Hirsh-Pasek, K., Golinkoff, R., & Hennon, E. A. (2006). The birth of words: Ten-month-olds learn words through perceptual salience. *Child Development, 77*, 266–280.

Rescorla, L. (1989). The Language Development Survey: A screening tool for delayed language in toddlers. *Journal of Speech and Hearing Disorders, 54*, 587–599.

Rizzolatti, G., & Arbib, M. A. (1998). Language within our grasp, *Trends in neurosciences, 21*(5), 188–194.

Robinson, B. F., & Mervis, C. B. (1999). Comparing productive vocabulary measures from the CDI and a systematic diary study. *Journal of Child Language, 26*, 177–185.

Rolls, E. T., & Treves, A. (1998). *Neural networks and brain function*. Oxford: Oxford University Press.

Saffran, J. R. (2001). Words in a sea of sound. *Cognition, 81*, 149–169.

Saffran, J. R., Aslin, R. N., & Newport, E. L. (1996). Statistical learning by 8-month-old infants. *Science, 274*, 1926–1928.

Saffran, J. R., Johnson, E. K., Aslin, R. N., & Newport, E. L. (1999). Statistical learning of tone sequences by human infants and adults. *Cognition, 70*, 27–52.

Savage-Rumbaugh, S., Murphy, J., Sevcik, R. A., Brakke, K. E., Williams, S. L., & Rumbaugh, D. M. (1993). Language comprehension in ape and child. *Monographs of the Society for Research in Child Development, 233*, 1–258.

Saylor, M., & Sabbagh, M. A. (2004). Different kinds of information affect word learning in the preschool years: The case of part-term learning. *Child Development, 75*, 395–408.

Schafer, G., & Plunkett, K. (1998). Rapid word learning by fifteen-month-olds under tightly controlled conditions. *Child Development, 69*, 309–320.

Seidenberg, M. S., & Pettito, L. A. (1979). Signing behavior in apes: A critical review. *Cognition, 7*, 177–215.

Seidl, A., Hollich, G., & Jusczyk, P. W. (2003). Early understanding of subject and object Wh-questions. *Infancy, 4*, 423–436.

Seidl, A., & Johnson, E. (2006). Infant word segmentation revisited: Edge alignment facilitates target extraction. *Developmental Science, 9*, 565–573.

Smith, L. B. (2000). How to learn words: An associative crane. In R. Golinkoff & K Hirsh-Pasek (Eds.), *Breaking the word learning barrier* (pp. 51–80). Oxford: Oxford University Press.

Smith, L., Jones, S., & Landau, B. (1996). Naming in young children: A dumb attentional mechanism? *Cognition, 60*, 143–171.

Speidel, G. E., & Nelson, K. E. (Eds.). (1989). *The many faces of imitation in language learning*. Berlin: Springer-Verlag.

Stern, W., & Stern, C. (1928). *Die Kindersprache*. Darmstadt: Wissenschaftliche Buchgesellschaft.

Swingley, D., & Aslin, R. N. (2007). Lexical competition in young children's word learning. *Cognitive Psychology, 54*, 99–132.

Tamis-LeMonda, C. S., Bornstein, M. H., & Baumwell, L. (2001). Maternal responsiveness and children's achievement of language milestones. *Child Development, 72*, 748–767.

Thiessen, E. D., Hill, E. A., & Saffran, J. R. (2005).Infant-directed speech facilitates word segmentation. *Infancy, 7*, 53–71.

Tincoff, R., & Jusczyk, P. W. (1999). Some beginnings of word comprehension in 6-month-olds. *Psychological Science, 10*, 172–175.

Tomasello, M. (1992). *First verbs: A case study of early grammatical development*. Cambridge: Cambridge University Press.

Tomasello, M. (2000). The social-pragmatic theory of word learning. *Pragmatics, 10*, 401–414.

Tomasello, M., & Akhtar, N. (1995). Two-year-olds use pragmatic cues to differentiate reference to objects and actions. *Cognitive Development, 10*, 201–224.

Tomasello, M., & Barton, M. (1994). Learning words in non-ostensive context. *Developmental Psychology, 30*, 639–650.

Van de Weijer, J. (1998). *Language input for word discovery*. Unpublished PhD thesis, University of Nijmegen, Nijmegen.

Vouloumanos, A., & Werker, J. F. (2004). Tuned to the signal: The privileged status of speech for young infants. *Developmental Science, 7*, 270.

Waxman, S. R., & Booth, A. E. (2001). Seeing pink elephants: Fourteen-month-olds' interpretations of novel nouns and adjectives. *Cognitive Psychology, 43*, 217–242.

Waxman, S. R., & Kosowski, T. D. (1990). Nouns mark category relations: Toddlers' and preschoolers' word-learning biases. *Child Development, 61*, 1461–1473.

Waxman, S. R., & Markow, D. B. (1995). Words as invitations to form categories: Evidence from 12-month-old infants. *Cognitive Psychology, 29*, 257–302.

Werker, J. F., & Tees, R. C. (1984). Cross-language speech perception: Evidence for perceptual reorganization during the first year of life. *Infant Behavior and Development, 7*, 49–63.

Woodward, A. L., & Markman, E. M. (1997). Early word learning. In W. Damon, D. Kuhn, & R. Siegler, (Eds.), *Handbook of child psychology, Vol. 2: Cognition, perception, and language* (pp. 371–420). New York: Wiley.

Xu, F. (1999). Object individuation and object identity in infancy: The role of spatiotemporal information, object property information, and language. *Acta Psychologica, 102*, 113–136.

Xu, F., & Tenenbaum, J. B. (2007). Sensitivity to sampling in Bayesian word learning, *Developmental Science, 10*, 288–297.

Yu, C., & Smith, L. B. (2007). Rapid word learning under uncertainty via cross-situational statistics. *Psychological Science, 18*(5), 414–420.

PART III

Social-Emotional Development

Introduction

This final section contains chapters on long-established research topics such as parent–infant interaction, attachment, peer interaction, emotional development, and temperament. In addition, there are chapters on two topics that tend to receive less attention in texts: the effects of touch and physical contact on infant development, and cultural influences on development.

Infants need caregivers if they are to survive. Beyond this simple point, however, in Chapter 15 Bornstein and Tamis-LeMonda point out that parent–infant interaction serves four particularly important functions; development of social understanding, development of attachment (chapter 16), acquisition of language, and development of emotional regulation (chapter 19). As was pointed out in chapters in Part II, there are important methodological issues that arise when investigating interactions. Many researchers investigate parents' practices, measuring either the content or quality of their parenting. The latter approach often aims to classify parents according to different styles, such as; authoritative, authoritarian, and indulgent-permissive. Although this taxonomy was first applied in the case of older children, it has some applicability to infant–parent interaction. The language parents use with infants is also a key measure that is indicative of both content and quality of parenting. Infant behaviors are also measured in terms of their content and quality. Although there are considerable individual differences, infants are responsive to their parents from the first month, and their behaviors are synchronized, giving all the appearance of a conversation but initially without words on the infant's side. However, the authors argue that the parent–infant dyad is the most meaningful unit of analysis, and go on to outline different approaches to investigation at this level. An important question arising from such analyses is how different forms of parenting impact on infant development. Some accounts take a generalist view, referring to parental properties such as sensitivity and warmth. Others point to specific effects, such as the fact that parents who encourage the infant to look at them, may in the process fail to encourage object exploration. The authors argue that this type of more specific analysis has more explanatory power. It turns out that different parenting styles have specific effects on developmental outcomes, and one popular approach investigates these temporal associations. However, the empirical problem is made more complex by the fact that influences are transactional: although parents' style influences infant behavior and development, the reverse is also true. Additionally, investigation should not be limited to the parent–infant dyad, but should take account of the total ecology, which includes infant effects, parent effects, social support, socioeconomic status, and cultural ideology.

The topic of chapter 16 is infant attachment. Posada and Kaloustian begin by discussing the seminal contributions of Bowlby and Ainsworth that helped formulate the concept of attachment. They note that the original formulations of Bowlby and Ainsworth, while derived from an ethological-evolutionary perspective, also emphasized the idea that infant attachment develops as a function of the nature of interactions between infants and their primary caregivers. Posada and Kaloustian distinguish infant attachment, which refers to the strength of the emotional link between infants and caregivers, from infant attachment behaviors, which refer to the various ways in which infants demonstrate this emotional link. A primary behavioral manifestation of attachment, infant secure-base behavior, is then discussed. Secure-base behavior is seen as reflecting the infant's confidence in the availability and responsiveness of their primary caregiver, and illustrates how infants attempt to balance exploration of their environment with their need for proximity to their primary caregiver. The authors go on to present evidence on the importance of quality of care as the foundation for the quality of infant attachment, with specific reference to caregiver sensitivity to the infant's needs. The chapter continues with discussion of the nature, strengths, and limitations of the methods used to assess individual differences in infant attachment, including both the "strange situation" and q-set procedures. This methodological review also includes a discussion of procedures to assess those aspects of caregiving that are critical to the development of attachment. Posada and Kaloustian then describe how attachment develops over the first few years of life. The four categories of infant attachment (secure, resistant, avoidant, and disorganized) are illustrated, with specific reference to how differences in caregiver behavior relate to differences in patterns of infant attachment. Influences on attachment related aspects of caregiver behavior, such as the caregiver's attachment history and contextual factors such as family stress are also presented. The chapter concludes with a discussion of future research needs in the area of infant attachment.

Interactions with peers become an increasingly important aspect of the infant's life, particularly from the second year onwards. In chapter 17, Ross, Vickar, and Perlman analyze peer interaction in terms of coordinated joint engagement, sensitivity to the goals and intentions of others, appreciating the similarity of self and others, and motivation to engage others. The shift from direct interaction to interaction over a common focus of interest seen in infant–parent interaction (chapter 13) is also evident in peer interaction. Also, the emerging ability to identify others' intentions and goals (chapter 12) is increasingly reflected in peer interactions in the second year, and the ability to identify both self and others as agents leads to understanding of "mine" versus "yours" (here there are links to chapter 10). It is also evident that infants are motivated to interact with others, and increasingly with peers. Within this framework, the authors go on to consider the form of play that emerges between toddlers. Imitation appears to be an important part of peer activity, with toddlers more likely to imitate peers than adults. Prosocial behavior to peers, such as sharing, occurs from 8 months onwards and in the second year sharing seems to be used as a means of making contact with peers. Towards the end of infancy cooperative problem solving emerges. And, of course, friendships emerge from peer interaction. All is not entirely sweetness and light, however. Conflict is also a feature of peer interaction, although it has a relatively infrequent occurrence that arises largely over possession of toys. Even this more negative aspect of peer interaction is liable to have positive developmental outcomes as toddlers increasingly apply rules of possession and rights.

In chapter 18, Stack considers the importance of touch in parent–infant interaction, arguing that this neglected modality is very important in infant development. Animal research indicates that touch has important positive effects on development and resistance to disease, and there is no reason to doubt similar effects in human infants, particularly on the formation of attachment (chapter 16). Additionally, research on parental experience with their newborns indicates that tactile information alone can be used to identify their infant. This emphasis on the importance of touch has led to the use of massage to alleviate problems associated with preterm birth. One speculation is that massage has its effect through stimulating the release of beneficial biochemical compounds and suppressing cortisol release. Although touch is sometimes used alone it often accompanies other forms of input, and serves a range of purposes. Although most research looks at parents' use of touch, infants also use touch, and both partners in the dyad use touch in a way that is responsive to the other. A range of studies demonstrate that touch produces positive affect and can alleviate the negative effects of withdrawal of stimulation in other modalities such as in the still-face procedure. These effects and others lead the author to conclude that studies of interaction that investigate only auditory and visual modalities are liable to miss important aspects of the interaction based in touch. Stack goes on to review evidence of the considerable cross-cultural differences in touch and bodily contact, and to describe the relatively small body of work on fathers' touch. The conclusion is that although much is now known about the important roles of touch in infant development, other areas are relatively unexplored. For instance, we know relatively little about how touch changes in relationship to developmental milestones, or about individual differences in touching. Also, much of the work is as yet descriptive and is in need of a theoretical framework in which to explain the processes through which touch leads to positive outcomes.

In chapter 19, Witherington, Campos, Harriger, Bryan, and Margett present an account of the development of emotion in infancy. Their functionalist approach treats emotions as arising from the way external events have an effect on the individual's progress to particular goals. If an event enhances progress to a goal, positive emotion results, whereas if it interferes with progress, negative emotion results. The authors point out that emotion is a complex, self-organizing system with multiple subcomponents existing both within and outside the individual. They explore the evolution of emotion, suggesting that there is an innate predisposition to rapidly learn to associate certain objects with certain emotions. According to the differentiation account of emotional development, infants begin with one undifferentiated state of excitement, from which specific emotions become progressively differentiated with age. While accepting that differentiation is an important part of the developmental process, the authors argue that early emotions are much more specific than this account would suggest. Furthermore, adopting a functionalist stand-point leads to clear evidence that early emotion systems are quite specific. One of the clear indicators of emotion is the social smile, which emerges around the end of the first month alongside the emergence of synchronized dyadic interaction (chapter 15). Later, when infants come to understand their own agency, anger begins to emerge when their progress towards a goal is frustrated. Additionally, between 6 and 9 months, infants become to show wariness of certain objects. This may arise in part due to cognitive factors: when infants encounter a new object that is discrepant from past experience, wariness results. However, at this point infants also begin to identify others' emotions as referring to objects, and social referencing emerges as a powerful force in the development of emotional responses to objects and situations.

In chapter 20, Wachs and Bates write about the nature of temperament in infancy and its consequences for development. Temperament is not easily defined, although there is general agreement that it refers to a set of traits that appear early in development and remain relatively stable. Accounts vary according to how many dimensions of temperament exist, the number ranging from 5 to 18. However, there appear to be two primary aspects of temperament; *reactivity*, how quickly infants respond to events; and *self-regulation*, the degree to which the infant is able to control emotion and approach/withdrawal. Individual differences in early temperament have been assessed through use of five approaches; interviews, questionnaires, structured laboratory infant observation, naturalistic observation, and measure of brain activity or physiological reactivity. The authors focus primarily on work using questionnaires and laboratory observation. Both approaches have their strengths and weaknesses, and accuracy of measurement of temperament can be improved by using a combination of measures from both approaches. Theories of temperament recognize links between temperament and specific brain structures, and other biological factors include genetic influences, with heritability estimates for temperament higher for twins than nontwins. Although prenatal and neonatal biological factors such as low birth weight, preterm birth, maternal stress, and exposure to toxins are candidate influences on temperament, few consistent relationships with temperament emerge. However, nutritional deficiencies in this period do appear to influence reactivity levels, and a larger number of postnatal factors appear to influence temperament. Turning to psychosocial factors, the authors point out the difficulty in deciding whether parenting style influences infant temperament or vice-versa. It is necessary to conduct longitudinal or intervention studies to tease these possibilities apart. The conclusion from these studies is that infant temperament *is* influenced by characteristics of the psychosocial environment. There are also cross-cultural differences in temperament that may arise due to differences in parenting style, diet, or other biological differences between cultures. The final section of the chapter focuses on the consequences of temperament differences. Infant temperament does not seem to have a very strong influence on parenting style, but this conclusion may change if one adopts a transactional model in which temperament and parenting style interact and change during development. Nor does temperament appear to consistently predict later personality, although this may be due to the relative instability of temperament in infancy. However, infant temperament does appear to predict later behavioral problems.

In the final chapter on culture and infancy, Super and Harkness begin by discussing approaches to conceptualizing what is meant by culture. This is followed by discussion of the various ways in which researchers have studied cultural influences on infant development, including ethnography, social address models, unidimensional models of culture (e.g., individualistic vs. collectivist) and, most recently, the investigation of multidimensional cultural "niches" within which infants and their caregivers function. Super and Harkness then review evidence on the role of culture in the neonatal period, with specific reference to early motor development and emotional expression. This is followed by a detailed presentation of cultural influences on various aspects of development after the neonatal period, including patterns of infant arousal and sleep, motor development, infant performance on standardized tests, Piagetian-based assessments and measures of information processing, and various aspects of early social-emotional development. As part of their presentation of culture and infant social-emotional development the authors present a detailed review of cultural challenges to standard attachment theory (chapter 16), and how culture can influence interpretation of group differences in measures of infant temperament. The chapter concludes with discussion of important future research directions in the study of culture and infant development.

15

Parent–Infant Interaction

Marc H. Bornstein and Catherine S. Tamis-LeMonda

There is no such thing as an infant. (Winnicott, 1965, p. 39)

Introduction

Each year tens of millions of women and men in the world experience the happiness and heartache of becoming new parents. Meaningful parenting begins even before a baby's birth and continues in some form throughout the life of the parent and child – as we all acknowledge, *once a parent, always a parent*. Nonetheless, parenting responsibilities are arguably greatest during infancy, when human beings are most dependent on caregiving and their ability to cope alone is minimal. It has also been contended on evolutionary reasoning that the extended duration of human infancy allows for enhanced parental influence and prolonged learning (Bjorklund, 2007). Thus, infancy is normatively a period of great parental investment; the birth of a child rivets a parent's attention and stirs his or her emotions; and infants alter everything about their parents, beginning with who they are and how they define themselves. Reciprocally, infants profit from parental care: Infancy is the phase of the human life cycle when caregiving is thought to exert significant influences. Infants may be particularly susceptible and responsive to parent-provided experiences, and parent–infant interaction has long been thought to constitute a critical determinant in the development of the individual (Bornstein, 2002a; Collins, Maccoby, Steinberg, Hetherington, & Bornstein, 2000). Thus, parent–infant interactions are the subject of historical and continuing interest (Bornstein & Lamb, 2010; Bremner, 1994; Fogel, 1991; Hrdy, 1999; Parke, 2002).

This chapter surveys basic parent and infant behaviors, their characteristics, their inter-relations, and the contexts in which their interactions are embedded. We begin with a discussion of some of the key functions of parent–infant interactions for the infant's development. We next review methodological approaches to the study of parent–infant interactions and describe behaviors of mothers, fathers, infants, and the dyad that have been considered meaningful indicators of the parent–infant relationship. We then discuss the nature of associations between parenting and infant development – that is, relations as specific or general; the patterning of relations over time; and the extent to which mother–infant versus father–infant associations are similar and/or unique. Finally, we consider the parent–infant relationship in its larger context by examining factors that moderate or mediate the nature and consequences of parent–infant interactions, including characteristics of infants, parents' psychological functioning, social networks, socio-demographic factors, and culture.

Functions of Parent–Infant Interactions

As Winnicott (1965) reminds us, human infants do not and cannot grow up as solitary individuals; parenting constitutes an initial and all-encompassing ecology of infant development. Infants and parents constantly engage in *dyadic interactions* – to which both contribute and through which each alters the other. What essential functions, aside from the basic needs of protection and survival, do parent–infant interactions serve for the developing infant? Four significant functions, among many, are noteworthy: promotion of social understanding, development of attachment, acquisition of language, and the maturity of emotional regulation. We highlight each briefly.

Parent–infant interactions have been referred to as the "cradle of social understanding" (Rochat & Striano, 1999). From birth, babies appear both ready and motivated (albeit in rudimentary form) to communicate and share meaning with others. By 2 months of age, infants engage in complex, highly responsive interactions with their parents (termed "protoconversations"; Bateson, 1979). These interactions are characterized by mutual give-and-take exchanges in the form of coos, gazes, smiles, grunts, and sucks. Through reciprocal engagements with others, especially parents, infants come to develop a sense of shared experience or "intersubjectivity" (Trevarthen, 1993) that over time evolves to greater levels of social and cognitive understanding, including the development of social expectations about others' behaviors in relation to self (Rochat & Striano, 1999). During the first 6 months, infants grow in their sensitivity to the invariant characteristics of their social partners, as they begin to extract information about patterns and routines in face-to-face and other dyadic interactions. These early interactions lay the foundation for further developments in social cognition, including the understanding of self and others as intentional agents. By 9 months, infants demonstrate increased abilities to monitor and coordinate their own perspectives and attention with the perspectives and attention of others (Baldwin & Baird, 1999; Trevarthen, 1979).

A second and related function of parent–infant interaction is its role in the development of infant attachment. According to an evolutionary perspective, the development of attachment in human infants is highly adaptive – infants who sought to maintain proximity to their primary caregivers were more likely to be cared for and protected from potential predators and to survive. Consequently, the proclivity toward attachment became integral to the infant's repertoire of behaviors (Bowlby, 1973). The development of "secure" infant attachment appears to depend on the quality of parent–infant interactions over the course of the first years of life (Ainsworth, 1973). Parents who are attuned to their infants' behavioral and emotional cues and needs are more likely to rear secure infants than are parents who are less sensitive; in turn, secure infants are more likely to develop into prosocial and competent toddlers and children (Sroufe, Egeland, Carlson, & Collins, 2005). Research shows that mothers and fathers can establish equally strong attachment relationships with their infants (Lamb, 2002).

A third function of parent–infant interactions is to ensure the infant's continuous progress toward more mature forms of communication and language (Bloom, 1993; Bornstein, 2000). Parents foster their infants' acquisition of language and communicative skills. For example, parents use sound play with 2-month-olds to selectively reinforce babbling that will foretell speech, and parents' reinforcement of infant sounds facilitates more mature forms of babbling as well as predicts later infant language skills (Goldstein & Schwade, 2010; Goldstein, Schwade, & Bornstein, 2009). Eventually, shared expressions of affect and shared experiences lead to infants and parents sharing experience in speech (Fogel, Messinger, Dickson, & Hsu, 1999). Episodes of joint parent–infant attention provide a prominent context for the acquisition of language (Mundy & Sigman, 2006).

Finally, parent–infant interactions play a prominent role in infants' emotional development – by both heightening emotions in infants as well as helping infants regulate their emotions. From the first days of life, parents support babies' experiences of joy through their facial expressions, vocalizations, and touch, and evoking gazing, smiling, and laughing from their infants (Papoušek & Papoušek, 2002). The progressive escalation of excitement inherent in parent–infant games boosts infants to higher levels of joy than they may achieve on their own (Stern, 1993). In typical theme-and-variation play, caregivers build predictable sequences of behavior and repeat or vary them based on the infant's response, for example, slowly creeping their fingers up the infant's stomach, waiting for the infant's expectant gaze or smile, and then tickling or producing a loud raspberry. It is the infant's growing awareness of contingency in these elementary interactions that adds to feelings of pleasure, in addition to enabling greater tolerance for higher states of stimulation (Roggman, 1991). Beyond affect, parents play an important role in regulating their infant's distress and physiological arousal. Infant emotion regulation is conceptualized as developing within the context of parent–child relationships (Grolnick, McMenamy, & Kurowski, 2005; Tronick, 1989). As very young infants vary their levels of arousal by looking at or away from the parent (Tronick & Weinberg, 1990), a parent's use of visual distractions, as one example, may operate to soothe overly excited infants (Bornstein, Tamis-LeMonda et al., 1992; Thompson, 1994). During later infancy, parent–infant play involves teasing games and rituals that help the infant practice negotiation skills that in turn build more intricate intersubjective understanding (Trevarthen, 1993).

In overview, parent–infant interactions serve multiple cognitive and linguistic, social and emotional functions for the developing infant. Infants acquire social understanding through ongoing, mutually reciprocal interactions with their parents. Sensitive parent–infant interactions also pave the way to secure attachment relationships. In turn, the infant's developing social sense and attachment serve as the foundation and motivation for exploring and learning about the world, healthy social and emotional development, the achievement of language and communication, understanding self and others, and developing positive social relationships.

Methodological Approaches to Studying Parent–Infant Interactions

To find out about parent–infant interactions scientifically entails numerous decisions about which parenting cognitions and practices to assess, how to measure them, and the sorts of analyses that are most suitable to the questions being posed. How are meaningful behaviors in parents, infants, and dyads described, characterized, and quantified?

Cognitions and practices in parents

Parents shape most, if not all, of their infants' experiences and directly influence infant development by their cognitions as well as by their practices. Parenting cognitions include, for example, perceptions about, attitudes toward, and knowledge of parenting and childhood. So, how parents see themselves vis-à-vis infants generally can lead to their expressing one or another kind of affect, thinking, or behavior in infant rearing. How parents construe infancy functions in the same way: Parents who believe that they can or cannot affect infant personality or intelligence can be expected to modify their parenting accordingly. How parents see their own infant has its specific consequences too: Parents who regard their infant as being difficult are less likely to pay attention or respond to their infant's overtures, and their inattentiveness and nonresponsiveness can then foster temperamental difficulties and cognitive shortcomings.

The constellation of everyday parental behaviors with infants is analyzable into a number of domains, and patterns among those behaviors constitute parents' associated styles. Which behaviors in the ongoing stream of gestures, vocalizations, and facial expressions parents display are the most crucial to assess, how are they best evaluated, and in what situations?

Two distinct approaches have been taken to classifying parent–infant interactions. The first emphasizes the *content* of parental practices specifically by focusing on "domains" of engagement. The second emphasizes the *quality* of parental engagements, for example, the extent to which parental behaviors are sensitive to infants' abilities or needs. With respect to content, one useful approach has been to classify parents' behaviors into categories of parenting (which for the infant are experiences). Bornstein (1989a, 2006) described one such system that includes nurturant, social, didactic, and material caregiving. Nurturant caregiving meets the biological, physical, and health requirements of the infant, as when parents provide sustenance, grooming, protection, supervision, and the like. Social caregiving encompasses visual, affective, and physical behaviors parents employ to engage infants in interpersonal exchanges, impart trust and love, help the infant to regulate affect and emotions, and manage and monitor the infant's social relationships. Didactic caregiving is deployed when stimulating the infant to engage and understand the environment outside the dyad, and includes focusing the infant's attention on properties, objects, or events in the immediate surroundings, introducing, mediating, and interpreting the external world, describing and demonstrating, and provoking or providing opportunities to observe, imitate, learn, and the like. Material caregiving consists of how parents provide and organize the infant's physical world in terms of inanimate objects, levels of ambient stimulation, physical safety, and so forth.

Together with language, these categories encompass virtually all of parents' important activities with infants. That is, human infants universally are reared in, influenced by, and adapt to social and physical environments that are characterized by the elements in this taxonomy. Taken as a totality, however, this taxonomy constitutes a varied and demanding set of caregiving tasks. Each element of the parenting taxonomy is conceptually and operationally distinct, although in practice of course parent–infant interaction is intricate, meshed, and multidimensional, and parents regularly engage in combinations of these categories. That is, these different categories of engagement overlap, as when a mother engages in toy play with her infant and alternates between demonstrating how a toy works and engaging her infant through touch, smiles, and face-to-face affective displays. Furthermore, nurturant caregiving seems more scripted and compulsory, to the extent that infant survival depends on the essential activities that comprise this domain; in contrast, social, didactic, and material sorts of caregiving may be more flexible and discretionary – parents vary among themselves in the extent to which they engage in these domains of interaction as well as in the ways they express such behaviors. Of course, these categories of infant caregiving apply to normal parenting of normal infants, and their instantiation or emphasis can be expected to vary with child age, health status, and contextual or cultural setting.

Beyond the contents of these domains of interaction lies the *quality* of parental engagements, sometimes referred to as styles (Bornstein & Zlotnik, 2008). Perhaps the best-known system of parenting styles classifies parents into three main types: authoritative, authoritarian, and indulgent-permissive (Baumrind, 1991; Maccoby & Martin, 1983). Authoritative parents provide clear and firm direction for their children and exercise that clarity through warmth, reason, flexibility, and give-and-take. Authoritarian parents tend to be directive with children, discourage give-and-take, favor punitive measures to maintain or control their children's behavior, and value unquestioning obedience in their exercise of authority. Permissive parents tend to make fewer demands on their children in comparison to other parents, thus allowing their children to regulate their own activities as much as possible. These styles in turn vary along more global dimensions of parental warmth and control, and different parenting styles reflect combinations of high or low levels of these dimensions.

Although Barumrind's taxonomy was developed with parents of older children, rather than infants, aspects of the taxonomy have been applied in various ways to the study of parenting in infancy. Parental "warmth" and "sensitivity" reflect the extent to which the parent is positively and appropriately responsive to the infant's needs and abilities, and this dimension is marked by wide individual differences. Parental responsiveness per se encompasses the contingent, prompt, and appropriate reactions parents display to infant activities (Bornstein, 1989b; Bornstein, Tamis-LeMonda, & Hahn, 2008). Parental responsiveness has attracted attention from infancy researchers for two principal reasons.

First, it reflects faithfully a recurring and significant three-term event sequence in everyday exchanges between infant and parent that involves infant act, parent reaction, and effect on infant. Second, specific kinds of parental responsiveness have been found to exert meaningful predictive influences over a range of domains of infant development, from imbuing effectance and a sense of self to security of attachment to fostering the growth of verbal and cognitive competencies. Infants appear to be especially sensitive to contingencies between their own actions and the reactions of others, and such contingencies are the hallmark of responsive parenting (Goldstein et al., 2009). Empirically, infants who experience contingent responding are more likely to pause after an adult response, engage more regularly in turn taking, and use more speech-like sounds than infants who experience random stimulation (Bloom, 1999). Although the majority of research focuses on mothers' responsiveness, fathers who are responsive during play interactions with their infants have infants who are more persistent and socially communicative (Shannon, Tamis-LeMonda, & Cabrera, 2006). On these accounts, developmentalists since Bowlby (1973) and Ainsworth (1973) have tended to regard positive parental responsiveness to infants – wherever it occurs – as a good thing.

With respect to "control," parents may support their infant's autonomy or interfere, inhibit, or intrude on their infant's interests. Infants of overstimulating or intrusive parents tend to be classified as avoidantly attached, perhaps in an effort to control their level of arousal or in angry response to their parents' inappropriate interactions (Belsky, Rovine, & Taylor, 1984; Isabella & Belsky, 1991; Pederson et al., 1990). A depressed mother, for example, demonstrates a style of interaction marked by intrusiveness, anger, irritation, and rough handling of her infant, a style of engagement that is often received with gaze aversion and avoidance by infants (Dix & Meunier, in press). Maternal intrusiveness is also associated with elevated catecholamine and cortisol levels in infants, a finding that is consistent with the notion that infants of intrusive parents experience more stress and anger (Jones et al., 1997). Moreover, parents who behave in a controlling manner, either by using inappropriate strategies to control their infants' emotions or by not allowing their infants the opportunity to practice self-regulation, may undermine infants' developing capacity for autonomous self-regulation (Grolnick et al., 2005).

A domain of interaction that cuts across both the content and quality of parenting concerns parents' speech to infants. *Language* directed to infants is perhaps the most common feature of parenting, and language serves numerous functions for the infant. Language helps to establish emotional ties between parent and infant, transmit knowledge and promote learning, and socialize the infant into a culture. Notably, mothers and fathers alike modulate their pitch, intonation contours, and utterance length when speaking to their infants, and modifications of speech to infants have been documented in parents from the US, Japan, France, Germany, Italy, and England (Fernald, Taeschner, Dunn, & Papousek, 1989). So-called "child-directed" speech is thought to provoke or potentiate infant attention as well as word recognition and segmentation, and thereby promote infant learning (Papoušek, Papoušek, & Bornstein, 1985; Singh, 2008; Thiessen, Hill, & Saffran, 2005).

In overview, parenting cognitions and practices are displayed as everyday customs with regard to babies and provide important contexts for understanding the nature of infancy. Cognitions and practices thus represent key aspects of the context of childrearing

(Bornstein, 1991; Darling & Steinberg, 1993; Goodnow & Collins, 1990; Miller, 1988). These parenting gambits themselves develop within particular ecologies of social class and culture, and ethnotheorists focus on how cognitions are manifested in particular childrearing practices (Sigel & McGillicudy-DeLisi, 2002; Keller, 2007).

Behaviors in infants

Infant behaviors in parent–infant interactions are also best understood in terms of their content and quality. For example, it is possible to distinguish between infant dyadic versus extradyadic engagements: Dyadic engagements on the part of infants consist of behaviors focused on interpersonal interactions – smiles, coos, and face-to-face episodes with parents or other people – whereas extradyadic engagements concern babies' focus on objects, properties, and events outside the dyad. Parent–infant interactions in infants' first months of life often focus within the dyad, whereas later interactions entail cocommunications about objects and events outside the dyad (Bornstein, Tal, et al., 1992; Bornstein & Tamis-LeMonda, 1990).

With respect to quality, infants' behaviors are responsive to and synchronized with those of their parents. Infants appear to be attuned to their parents from the first weeks of life (Bateson, 1975, 1979; Stern, 1974): They engage in miming of conversation, are emotionally reactive, and play an active role in regulating the ebb and flow of interactions (Beebe, Jaffe, Feldstein, Mays, & Alson, 1985; Crown, Feldstein, Jasnow, Beebe, & Jaffe, 2002; Trevarthen, 1993). Nonetheless, substantial variation exists among infants in terms of their own responsiveness to parental solicitations and abilities at maintaining synchronous interactions. Some infants appear better able to regulate their attention and emotions than others and so engage in more rewarding bouts of joint attention with their caregivers (Raver, 1996). As a specific example, preterm infants often have difficulty regulating engagements with caregivers, as evidenced in increased gaze aversion, decreased joint play, and lower levels of joint attention (Landry, 1995). Some infants exhibit clear, consistent, and responsive cues to changes in their parents' actions, whereas others do not; these early patterns of infant responsiveness set the stage for productive or problematic engagements over the next months and years of life (Kochanska, Forman, & Coy, 1999).

Behaviors of the dyad

Although parent and infant behaviors can be considered separately, the dyad of parent *and* infant is a central and meaningful unit of analysis: The essence of the parent–child relationship is captured by synchronies in the two interacting partners (Fogel & Lyra, 1997). Trevarthen (1993, p. 139) compared parent–infant dyadic communications to a musical duet – the "two performers seek harmony and counterpoint on one beat to create together a melody that becomes a coherent and satisfying narrative of feelings in a time structure that they share completely. In a good performance by two or more musicians each partakes of, or identifies with, the expression of the whole piece, the ensemble." As such, patterned sequences of engagements, comprised of cyclical turn-taking in both parent and infant behaviors, become the focus of investigation.

Logistics of studying parent–infant interactions

Once meaningful forms of behavior have been identified in parents, infants, and the dyad, an appropriate coding strategy for quantifying interactions must be determined. A small number of general approaches are noteworthy; each has inherent strengths and limitations.

Data collection built around molecular procedures is rigorous and powerful and provides precise measures of both behavioral frequency and duration on the basis of their occurrence in the noninterrupted, natural time flow. Computer-video-linked application programs are utilized in such "realtime" coding schemes. As the coder observes the ongoing interaction (typically on prerecorded video), the onset and offset of every instance of each target event is noted. Such data from real-time recording enable the researcher to obtain a rich and highly detailed record of the interaction. From a running record of interactions, it is also possible to evaluate the temporal sequencing of events relative to one another, thereby permitting an examination of conditional probabilities among events of interest. The codependencies between behavioral events can be assessed within and between parents and infants, and changing patterns of codependencies can be evaluated across developmental time (e.g., Cote, Bornstein, Haynes, & Bakeman, 2008). Some disadvantages to such *microanalytic* approaches stem from the time-consuming nature of the coding; depending on the number of events in the coding scheme and the character of those events, it can take many hours to code only a few minutes of parent–infant interaction. A somewhat less time-consuming approach to coding parent–infant behaviors is to use "time-sampling intervals." This procedure entails coding whether a behavior occurred during a predefined interval of time (e.g., whether the infant smiled during each 10-second interval of the interaction). This approach provides data in the form of frequency counts regarding the number of intervals that contained the behavior(s) of interest, but does not yield duration data or information on the sequencing of parent–infant behaviors in real time (Bornstein, 2002b).

An alternative approach uses molar ratings; the coder observes an interaction in whole or in part and, rather than coding specific events, uses a scale to rate the *macroanalytic* impression of parent, infant, or dyad on quantitative or qualitative dimensions (e.g., persistence on a task, responsiveness). This approach to quantifying dyadic interactions is cost-effective and appropriate when the goal is to evaluate parents and/or infants in terms of global dispositions (such as sensitivity). Rating scales have been used, for example, to investigate infant–parent attachment, in which the goal is to describe relations between maternal sensitivity and infant attachment status (e.g., Egeland & Farber, 1984; Seifer, Schiller, Sameroff, Resnick, & Riordan, 1996; Susman-Stillman, Kalkoske, Egeland, & Waldman, 1996). The rating scales used in many contemporary studies of parent–infant interaction build on Ainsworth's (1973) conceptualization of sensitivity, which included awareness of and appropriate responsiveness to infant signals. However, researchers who aim to describe the precise nature of parent–infant interactions, contingencies among parent and infant behaviors, and changes to parent–infant interactions over time may be better served by the microanalytic approach. Moreover, microanalytic approaches yield data that are more "objective" in nature (e.g., number of mother pointing gestures) rather than "subjective" (e.g., how much mothers use gestural communication on qualitative scales).

The Nature of Parent–Infant Associations

In infancy – that is, before children are old enough to enter formal social learning situations, like school, or even informal ones, like playgroups – most of children's experiences stem directly from interactions within the family. Ecology, class, and culture certainly influence individual development from infancy (Bornstein, 1991, 2009), but parents normally are the "final common pathway" to infant oversight and caregiving, development, and stature (Bornstein, 2002a). As a consequence, many social theorists have posited that the parent–infant relationship constructs the crucible for the early and eventual development of individuals in our species. Starting with the premise that parents meaningfully affect the development of infants, two questions regarding the nature of their associations warrant discussion: To what extent are relations between parenting and infant development general or specific? How are the influences of parents on infants, and infants on parents, modeled within and across time?

Generality versus specificity

Classical authorities, including notably psychoanalysts, ethologists, and behavior geneticists, have tended to conceptualize parental behavior as more or less monolithic in nature – as "good," "sensitive," "warm," or "adequate" – despite the wide range of activities parents naturally engage in with infants (e.g., Ainsworth, Blehar, Waters, & Wall, 1978; Mahler, Pine, & Bergman, 1975; Rohner, 1985; Scarr, 1992; Winnicott, 1965). This view assumes in part that parenting reflects personality traits, and that parents therefore behave in consistent ways toward babies across domains of interaction, time, and context (Holden & Miller, 1999). Alternatively, parental activities need not be linked to one another; rather, parents might vary in the constellation and patterns of their activities (Bornstein, 2006). Parents engage their infants in diverse activities, as we have learned, and parents do not necessarily behave in uniform or consistent ways across domains of interaction. Parents who nurture infants more, for example, do not necessarily or automatically engage in more didactics (whether they are US Americans, English, French, Israeli, or Japanese; Bornstein, Azuma, Tamis-LeMonda, & Ogino, 1990; Bornstein & Tamis-LeMonda, 1990; Bornstein, Tamis-LeMonda, Pêcheux, & Rahn, 1991; Bornstein, Toda, Azuma, Tamis-LeMonda, & Ogino, 1990; Dunn, 1977). That is, generally speaking parents' activities do not necessarily covary with one another (nor, it turns out, do those of infants).

An assumption often associated with the monistic view of parenting is that the overall level of parental stimulation affects the infant's overall level of development (see Maccoby

& Martin, 1983). In contrast, the *specificity principle* states that specific experiences parents provide infants at specific times in development exert specific effects over specific aspects of infant development in specific ways (Bornstein, 2006). Contemporary cross-cultural analyses support such a multivariate view of specificity in mother–infant interactions (Bornstein, in preparation). Some specific parent and infant activities correspond to one another, of course, and parents and infants influence one another over time in specific ways. As partners, parents and infants are open to one another's influence from an early period in the infant's life. Indeed, the character and quality of their individual behaviors indicate that parents and their babies are to a certain degree flexible and adaptable. However, parents and infants specialize, and their specializations match; that is, parent–infant interactions can be described as (for the most part) mutually corresponding. So, for example, parents' responses to their infants' communicative overtures might be central to children's early acquisition of language, but exert less influence on the growth of play, motor abilities, or cognition broadly conceived (Tamis-LeMonda & Bornstein, 1994).

To adequately test models of parent–infant specificity, it is important to examine multiple behavioral predictors in parents and multiple outcomes or behaviors in infants. Consider a short-term longitudinal study in which prominent domains of parent–infant engagement were assessed and then mutually analyzed when babies were 2 and 5 months of age (Bornstein & Tamis-LeMonda, 1990). During two home visits, the frequencies of social and didactic forms of parent–infant interaction were evaluated (e.g., face-to-face play vs. toy play), as were parents' and babies' verbal/vocal exchanges. The frequencies of parents' social, didactic, and verbal interactions tended to be unrelated, reinforcing the idea that parents are "specialists" rather than "generalists." Parents who more often encouraged their infants to look at them in interactions did not necessarily encourage their infants to attend to objects or events in the environment; similarly, for infants, looking more at parents was not associated with more environmental exploration. Notably, relations between parents' and infants' activities were highly specific at each age and across these first months of life: Parents who were more social in engaging their infants had infants who more often attended to their parents, and parents who were more didactic in their interactions had infants who attended to the environment and manipulated objects more. In addition, parents' child-directed speech related to their babies' developing nondistress vocalizations.

Similar principles obtain in the infant's second year. Toddlerhood is a time of momentous cognitive growth as reflected in the emergence of language and first expressions of pretense in play. In sequential longitudinal studies, parents and infants were videorecorded during free-play interactions at the start (13 to 14 months) and near the end (20 to 21 months) of the second year. For each contingent response on the part of parents, the target of the response (i.e., what the parent responded to – e.g., a vocalization or play act on the part of the infant) and the content of the response (i.e., *how* the parent responded – e.g., by imitating her infant's vocalization, prompting her infant to engage in a specific play activity) were assessed. In children, two specific outcomes were evaluated – abilities in productive and receptive language and sophistication of play (Tamis-LeMonda & Bornstein, 1994; Tamis-LeMonda, Bornstein, Baumwell, & Damast, 1996). Maternal responsiveness was domain-specific: Responsiveness in the language domain did not relate to responsiveness in the play domain, suggesting that a parent keys into different aspects of their infants' abilities. Moreover, responsiveness to infants' vocalizations (responses that imitated/expanded on children's vocalizations) uniquely predicted children's language, and responsiveness to children's play (responses that prompted further play engagements) uniquely predicted children's play both when they played alone and when children played with their mothers.

The temporal patterning of associations

What patterns of cross-time associations obtain between parent and infant behaviors? The question of timing is distinct from that of generality versus specificity as discussed above. Several models of mutual effects have been identified in infancy research (see Bornstein, 2006; Bradley, Caldwell, & Rock, 1988). These models address the extent to which early and/or later experiences uniquely predict infants' current or later development. Three models define unique effects of one member of the dyad on the other, and one emphasizes their transactional nature. An "early experience" model posits that infants' earlier ("time 1") experiences *uniquely* affect later child development (at "time 2" and beyond); that is, experiences vital to development are early occurring and determinative of later development. In this model, the activity of the parent singularly affects the infant at one time point, and the consequent change in the infant thenceforward endures, independent of later interactions between the parent and infant and independent of whatever individual differences the infant carries into the future. Theoreticians and researchers have long supposed that the child's earliest experiences affect the course of later development (Plato, circa 355 BCE), and data derived from ethology, psychoanalysis, behaviorism, and neuropsychology (like sensitive periods; Bornstein, 1989c) support this model. Empirically, parents encouraging their 2-month-olds to attend to properties, objects, and events in the environment uniquely predicts infants' tactual exploration of objects at 5 months; that is, over and above stability in infant tactual exploration and any contemporaneous 5-month maternal stimulation (Bornstein & Tamis-LeMonda, 1990). Similarly, mothers who attune to changes in their 9-month-old infants' emotional expressions by matching the gradient dimensions of their infants' expressions have toddlers who achieve key developmental milestones in language development sooner, over and above mothers' later attunements (Nicely, Tamis-LeMonda, & Bornstein, 1999).

A second model focuses on the role of the "contemporary environment;" that is, later experiences (at "time 2") uniquely and concomitantly affect development, overriding the effects of earlier experiences (at "time 1"). In this view, parents exert unique influences over their infants only at later points in development and independent of whatever individual differences infants carry forward into their own future. Empirical support for this model typically consists of recovery of functioning from early deprivation (including studies in which malnourished or disadvantaged infants are adopted into advantaged homes), failure of early intervention studies to show long-term effects, and the like (Clarke & Clarke, 1976; Lewis, 1997; Rutter and The English and Romanian Adoptees Study Team, 1998). Empirically, parents' didactic encouragement at 5 months is uniquely associated with infants' visual exploration of the environment, whereas mothers' didactic encouragement at 2 months is not predictive (Bornstein & Tamis-LeMonda, 1990).

A third model combines the first two into a "cumulative/additive/stable environment" view. Cumulative effects presumably emerge from consistent environmental influences. Empirically, maternal didactic encouragement at 2 and at 5 months has been shown to aggregate to account for unique variance in infant nondistress vocalization at 5 months (Bornstein & Tamis-LeMonda, 1990). Although longitudinal data in the first 6 months provide evidence for unique early, unique later, and combined early and late experiential effects between parents and infants, for the most part it is typical for children to be reared in stable environments (Holden & Miller, 1999), so that cumulative experiences are likely (Collins et al., 2000).

These models of parenting effects notwithstanding, the *transaction principle* asserts that experiences shape the characteristics of an individual through time just as, reciprocally, the characteristics of an individual shape his or her experiences. Thus, the importance and pervasiveness of "infant effects" on parents are well recognized (e.g., Bell & Harper, 1977). To a large degree, infants influence which experiences they will be exposed to, as well as how they absorb and interpret those experiences, and, in turn how those experiences ultimately affect them. Infant and parent bring distinctive characteristics to, and infant and parent alike change in distinctive ways as a result of, their mutual interactions; both parent and infant then enter future interactions as "different" individuals. For example, maternal sensitivity does not exert a direct and singular effect on infant attachment security; rather, infant temperament and maternal sensitivity operate in tandem to affect one another and the attachment status of babies (Seifer et al., 1996). In essence, transactional, goodness-of-fit models best explain the development of attachment relationships as they do much else in infant development (Lerner, Theokas, & Bobek, 2005).

In overview, the nature of parent–infant associations appears to be specific rather than general, and different patterns of association between the two ensue over time. Monolithic conceptualizations of parenting fail to acknowledge the range and diversity in parenting content and style, and hence overlook the possibility that different parents emphasize or encourage different modes of engagement and different developmental outcomes in their infants. Even in a particular form of parenting (e.g., contingent responsiveness), parents differ substantially in the ways they express themselves behaviorally: Different parents can be equally "responsive" overall, but still differ in the sorts of activities to which they respond and in the composition of their responsiveness (Bornstein et al., 2008; Bornstein, Tamis-LeMonda, et al., 1992). Different theoretical models define the temporal patterning of parent–infant associations, and it is probable that each model accurately portrays some aspects of parent–infant interactions for some domains of infant development. Whether or not early or later interactions exert unique, combined, or transactional effects depends on the developmental achievement being investigated and the window of time within which that achievement is assessed.

The Ecological Contexts of Parent–Infant Interaction

Our best understanding of parent–infant interaction at present is informed by an ecological view in which multiple factors – some distal, others proximal to parent and infant

– are conceived as contributing to the emergence, ontogenetic course, and eventual character of parent–infant activities. Furthermore, a multivariate systems approach allows us to parse the independent and interdependent roles of these different sources of influence on parent–infant interaction. The origins of variation in parental behaviors are extremely complex, but certain factors seem of particular importance, including characteristics in infants, biological determinants and psychological functioning in parents, and contextual influences, such as family situation and support, socioeconomic status, and culture (Belsky, 1984; Bornstein, 2002a, 2006).

Infant effects

By virtue of their helplessness and "babyish" characteristics, which are structural and universal, infants elicit high levels of attention and nurturance from their parents (Lorenz, 1935/1970). The nature of infancy is change, and normative developments in infancy, even elementary ones such as gaining the ability to stand upright and walk, also influence the nature and quality of parenting (e.g., Campos et al., 2000; Tamis-LeMonda, Adolph, Dimitropolou, & Zack, 2007). However, every infant also develops with his or her own rate and style. The ages at which individual infants achieve developmental milestones vary enormously, just as infants of a given age vary among themselves on nearly every index of development. Infants differ in temperament, emotional regulation, and social style. These individual differences, characteristic of early personality, influence parenting and thereby exert both direct and indirect influences on infant development. For example, infants with more advanced cognitive scores at 14 months have parents who later demonstrate more responsive interactions, even after controlling for parenting characteristics, infant characteristics, and family resources (Lugo-Gil & Tamis-LeMonda, 2008). Others have found that parents of irritable infants engage in less visual and physical contact and are less responsive and involved over time when compared to parents of nonirritable babies (Van den Boom & Hoeksma, 1994). Both normative change and individual differences in infants affect the job parents do. Certainly, dynamic developmental change in the context of individual variation among infants challenges and shapes parenting in every domain of interaction.

Parental biology and psychological functioning

Basic physiology is mobilized to support parenting, and several aspects of mothering are believed initially to arise out of biological processes associated with pregnancy and parturition. For example, pregnancy causes the release of hormones thought to be involved in the development of protective, nurturant, and responsive feelings toward offspring (Rosenblatt, 2002). Prenatal biological characteristics of the parent – age, diet, and stress level – affect postnatal parenting and consequently infant development (Heinicke, 2002). In addition, human beings appear to possess some intuitive knowledge about parenting; that is, some characteristics of parenting may be "wired" into the biological makeup of the species (McGuire, 2003; Papoušek & Papoušek, 2002). For example, parents speak to babies, even though they know that babies cannot understand language and will not reply, and parents even do so in that special vocal register of "child-directed" speech.

Parenting equally draws on transient as well as enduring personality characteristics, including intelligence and personality as well as attitudes toward the parenting role, motivation to become involved with children, and childcare and childrearing knowledge and skills. Some personality characteristics that favor good parenting include well-being, empathic awareness, predictability, responsiveness, and emotional availability. Psychological status can support or inhibit felicitous parent–infant interactions. Parents who feel efficacious and competent in their role as parents are more responsive, more empathic, less punitive, and more appropriate in their developmental expectations (East & Felice, 1996, Schellenbach, Whitman, & Borkowski, 1992). Perceived self-efficacy is likely to affect parenting positively because parents who feel effective vis-à-vis their infants are motivated to engage in further interactions which in turn provide additional opportunities to understand and interact positively and appropriately with their infants. Parenting is also marked by challenging demands, changing and ambiguous criteria, and frequent evaluations, all of which may become overwhelming in the presence of a parent's compromised psychological functioning. For example, depression adversely affects a parent's ability to parent competently. Depressed parents are generally less responsive and communicative with their infants (Albright & Tamis LeMonda, 2002, Cohn, Campbell, Matias, & Hopkins, 1990), more likely to engage in harsh forms of discipline (Dumas & Wekerle, 1995; Jackson, 1993), and less consistent in their structure, or rule enforcement, when compared to nondepressed parents (Goodman & Brumley, 1990). Unsurprisingly, maternal depression adversely affects the synchrony of parent–infant interactions (Zahn-Waxler, Duggal, & Gruber, 2002, 2002), and self-efficacy is found to mediate links among risk factors, depression, and parenting.

Reciprocally, becoming a parent can enhance a person's psychological development, self-confidence, and sense of well-being. Parenting can augment self-esteem and fulfillment and provide ample occasion to test and display diverse competencies. Parents often find interest and derive pleasure in their relationships and activities with their infants. Furthermore, parenting translates into a constellation of new trusts and often affords a unique perspective on the "larger picture" of life.

Social support

Parent–infant interactions are embedded in a nexus of multiple contexts and environments that contribute in critical ways to promote and support infancy (Bronfenbrenner & Morris, 2006). Of particular relevance to the parent–infant relationship is a parent's support network. Social support consists of the people that parents consider important in life, including their spouse or significant other, relatives, friends, and neighbors. These networks may provide coping resources to parents by offering emotional support, advice, guidance, and practical help. Parents with more supportive networks are better able to meet their own needs, and consequently better able to meet the needs of their young children (Cochran & Niego, 2002). Social support can improve parenting satisfaction, affecting the availability of parents to their infants as well as the quality of parent–infant interactions. Social support networks of parents in part determine the quality of parenting, and therefore influence child development indirectly (Belsky, 1984).

As one primary area of support, the quality of the mother–father relationship has been found to relate to parents' sense of competence, family dynamics, parent–infant interactions, and infant outcomes (e.g., Tamis-LeMonda & Cabrera, 1999; Cabrera, Ryan, Mitchell, Shannon, & Tamis-LeMonda, 2008). Parents influence their infants by virtue of their influence on each other. The ways in which mothers and fathers provide support and show respect in parenting, how they work together as a coparenting team, may have far-reaching consequences for infants (Feinberg, 2002). The presence of a supportive partner in the home is associated with consistency in discipline, more patience, and less exhaustion in parents (Furstenberg, Brooks-Gunn, & Chase-Lansdale, 1989; Lamb, Sternberg, & Thompson, 1997) as well as higher levels of sensitivity and greater involvement in fathers (Shannon et al., 2006; Shannon, Tamis-LeMonda, & Margolin, 2005; Tamis-LeMonda, Kahana Kalman, & Yoshikawa, 2009). Moreover, support in the mother–father relationship moderates the effects of infant difficulty on maternal depression and sensitivity (Curtona & Troutman, 1986).

Parental support networks are especially crucial to families living in at-risk circumstances such as poverty (see Powell, volume 2, chapter 13). Often, poorer parents exist with inadequate support networks (McLoyd, 1998); nearly 70% of women on welfare are unmarried when they have their first child (Tamis-LeMonda & Cabrera, 1999). Empirically, social supports moderate relations between poverty and maternal punitiveness, sensitivity, satisfaction, and life stress (Crnic, Greenberg, Robinson, Ragozin, & Basham, 1983; Hashima & Amato, 1994; Miller-Loncar, Erwin, Landry, Smith, & Swank, 1998).

Socioeconomic status

At a more distal level, socioeconomic status (SES) shapes the parent–infant relationship. Parents in different SES groups behave similarly in certain parenting domains; however, SES – perhaps through differential provisions in the environment and education of parents – also orders home circumstances and other attitudes and actions of parents toward infants. In many cases, low SES is considered a risk factor in children's development on account of its detrimental effect on the quality of parent–infant interaction (Dodge, Pettit, & Bates, 1994; McLoyd, Aikens, & Burton, 2006). The numerous negative circumstances associated with poverty are thought to compromise a parent's ability to engage in sensitive, consistent, and involved parenting. Low SES adversely affects parents' psychological functioning and promotes harsh or inconsistent disciplinary practices (Conger, McMarty, Yang, Lahey, & Kropp, 1984; Simons, Whitbeck, Conger, & Wu, 1991). Strong relations between social class and parents' language (e.g., Hoff, Laursen, & Tardif, 2002), specific parenting practices (e.g., Garbarino & Kostelny, 1993; Hart & Risley, 1992), and developmental expectations, theories, and values (e.g., Sameroff & Feil, 1985) have been identified. For fathers specifically, indicators of SES, such as education, income, and employment, are associated with greater sensitivity and/or less detachment toward infants and toddlers (e.g., Shannon et al., 2005; Shannon et al., 2006;

Tamis-LeMonda, Shannon, Cabrera, & Bradley, 2004). A fruitful way of conceptualizing social-class differences in early development was advanced by Kohn (1987), who observed that parents try to inculcate values that will maximize their children's chances of success in the social station in which they are likely to find themselves as mature adults.

Cultural ideology

Cross-cultural investigation shows that virtually all aspects of parenting infants are shaped by culture (Bornstein, 2009). For example, the extent to which parents "play" with their infants as well as their goals in play vary with culture; thus, even the elementary act of a mother demonstrating how a toy works to her infant carries with it cultural meaning (e.g., Bornstein, Haynes, Pascual, Painter, & Galperín, 1999). Parents not only communicate information to their infants about the features of the specific toy, but also convey information about the role of toys and how social partners in a society coconstruct knowledge. According to Göncü, parents' views about the importance of play in children's early development and the extent to which parents actually engage in play with their young children vary across cultures (Göncü & Gaskins, 2007) Middle-class US and Turkish parents think of themselves as play partners for their children and, consistent with such views, participate in frequent pretend play with their children. In contrast, Mayan Indians think of play as exclusively a child's activity, and in line with this belief Mayan parents engage in little or no pretense with their children. Goodnow (2002) observed that parents encounter the prevailing views of their social group both before and after they become parents and often appropriate those views ready-made from the culture at large.

Culture influences parenting practices and patterns (and, in turn, infant development) from a very early age in terms of when and how parents care for their infants and which behaviors parents appreciate and emphasize (Tamis-LeMonda, 2003; Tamis-LeMonda & Kahana Kalman, 2009; Tamis-LeMonda et al., 2008). Reciprocally, infants begin to build their initial knowledge of the world, of persons, and of events during those self-same social exchanges with their parents. Even with generally similar ultimate goals of successful childrearing, cultures often contrast in terms of the types of competencies parents promote in infants, the paths parents follow to instill in infants the desire to achieve those goals, and the developmental timetables parents wish their infants to meet (Adolph, Karasik, & Tamis-LeMonda, 2009; Tamis-LeMonda & McFadden, 2009). Thus, the most basic and concrete features of infant development are affected by culture, as are the most subtle and abstract. Central to a concept of culture, after all, is the expectation that different peoples possess different ideas as well as behave in different ways with respect to childrearing. To the extent that internalized constructs are shaped by culture, parenting views reflect cultural ideologies that parents uphold and transmit to their children. In other words, parents' cognitions implicitly guide parenting practices which in turn affect infant development (Bornstein, 1991; Bornstein et al., 1996; Goodnow, 2002; Goodnow & Collins, 1990; Sigel & McGillicuddy-DeLisi, 2002; Toda, Fogel, & Kawai, 1990). Thus, culture helps to organize the world of parenting because cultural ideas affect parents' sense of self and competence in their role and forms their priorities; in a larger sense, cultural ideas contribute to the "continuity of culture" by helping to define culture and the transmission of cultural information across generations.

In overview, parent–infant interactions do not unfold in a vacuum. Divergent styles of parenting can best be understood in an ecological framework that takes into account infant effects, the parent's own biology and psychological functioning, social supports, social class, and cultural ideology. To interpret meaning in patterns of parent–infant interaction, it is critical to discover how and why parents parent the way they do and to elucidate the values they find to be important.

Conclusions

Parenting is central to childhood, to child development, and to society's long-term investment in children. For new parents, the first years with an infant constitute a period of adjustment and transformation; for infants, interactions with parents constitute critical experiences in development. Moreover, certain enduring psychological characteristics of the individual are believed to arise early in life, and the nature of parent–infant interaction is thought to contribute at least one important source of their development. As a result, parent–infant interactions have often been looked to in attempts to address fundamental questions about human origins and development. A better understanding of the nature of human infants is afforded by examining parent–infant interaction and its consequences in the period of the dyad's initial accommodation – the unique and specific influences of parent on infant and of infant on parent.

Parent–infant interactions command attention for several reasons. First, they are significant in themselves because infancy is a critical period in the life cycle, characterized by noteworthy developments in emotional, social, communicative, and cognitive competencies. Parent–infant interactions serve as the prime context for these early achievements. Second, who infants are, and what they do, influence their social interactions with parents, and so in indirect ways infants affect their own development. Third, the experiences of infancy (separate from continuing postinfancy experiences) are principally provided by parents and may endure, influencing the rate, course, and perhaps eventual resting level of subsequent development. Focus on parent–infant interaction is also portentous for practical reasons. Appreciating factors that affect infant development (as well as those that do not) promises to inform efforts at proper intervention and remediation. Infancy is a time of vulnerability; it is formative in habit formation and development; and it may be foundational for the balance of the life cycle.

As Winnicott (1965) keenly observed, infants cannot exist on their own. Rather, infants can exist only with their caregivers. In turn, infants and caregivers do not exist alone, but are embedded in larger social contexts that include family members, communities, social class, and culture. Moreover, caregivers change in their persons and positions, and infants constantly develop, and each influences the other so that elements of who infants were yesterday, who they are today, and who they will be tomorrow are in constant transformation. To fathom the nature of parenting and parent–infant relationships within families therefore calls for a multivariate and dynamic stance. Only multiple levels of analysis can adequately capture the individual, dyadic, and family unit forces on development and reflect the embeddedness of parent and infant within all relevant extrafamilial systems.

Acknowledgments

This chapter summarizes selected aspects of our research, and portions of the text have appeared in previous scientific publications cited in the references. We thank T. Taylor for assistance. Catherine S. Tamis-LeMonda acknowledges the Center for Research on Culture, Development, and Education, funded by the National Science Foundation.

References

Adolph, K. E., Karasik, L. B., & Tamis-LeMonda, C. S. (2009). Motor skill. In M. H. Bornstein (Ed.), *The handbook of cultural developmental science. Part 1. Domains of development across cultures* (pp. 61–88). New York: Taylor & Francis.

Ainsworth, M. D. S. (1973). The development of infant–parent attachment. In B. M. Caldwell & H. N. Riciutti (Eds.), *Review of child development research* (Vol. 3, pp. 1–94). Chicago: University of Chicago Press.

Ainsworth, M. D. S., Blehar, M. C., Waters, E., & Wall, S. (1978). *Patterns of attachment: A psychological study of the strange situation.* Hillsdale, NJ: Erlbaum.

Albright, M. B., & Tamis-LeMonda, C. S. (2002). Maternal depressive symptoms in relation to dimensions of parenting in low-income mothers. *Applied Developmental Science, 6,* 24–34.

Baldwin, D. A., & Baird, J. A. (1999). Early perception of social contingencies and interpersonal intentional inference. In P. Rochat (Ed.), *Early social cognition* (pp. 189–214). Mahwah, NJ: Erlbaum.

Bateson, M. C. (1975). Parent–infant exchanges: The epigenesis of conversational interaction. In D. Aronson & R. W. Rieber (Eds.), *Annals of the New York Academy of Sciences: Developmental psycholinguistics and communication disorders* (Vol. 263, pp. 101–113). New York: New York Academy of Sciences.

Bateson, M. C. (1979). "The epigenesis of conversational interaction": A personal account of research development. In M. Bullowa (Ed.), *Before speech: The beginning of human communication* (pp. 63–77). New York: Cambridge University Press.

Baumrind, D. (1991). Effective parenting during the early adolescent transition. In P. A. Cowan & E. M. Hetherington (Eds.), *Family transitions. Advances in family research series* (pp. 111–163). Hillsdale, NJ: Erlbaum.

Beebe, B., Jaffe, J., Feldstein, S., Mays, K., & Alson, D. (1985). Interpersonal timing: The application of an adult dialogue model to parent–infant vocal and kinesic interactions. In T. M. Field & N. Fox (Eds.), *Social perception in infants* (pp. 217–247). Norwood, NJ: Ablex.

Bell, R. Q., & Harper, L. (1977). *Child effects on adults.* Hillsdale, NJ: Erlbaum.

Belsky, J. (1984). The determinants of parenting: A process model. *Child Development, 55,* 83–96.

Belsky, J., Rovine, M., & Taylor, D. G. (1984). The Pennsylvania infant and family development project III: The origins of individual differences in infant–parent attachment: Maternal and infant contributions. *Child Development, 55,* 718–728.

Bjorklund, D. F. (2007). *Why youth is not wasted on the young: Immaturity in human development*. Malden, MA: Blackwell.

Bloom, L. (1993). *The transition from infancy to language*. New York: Cambridge University Press.

Bloom, L. (1999). Language acquisition in its developmental context. In W. Damon, D. Kuhn & R. S. Siegler, (Eds.), *Handbook of child psychology: Vol. 2, Cognition, perception, and language* (5th ed., pp. 309–370). New York: Wiley.

Bornstein, M. H. (1989a). Between caretakers and their young: Two modes of interaction and their consequences for cognitive growth. In M. H. Bornstein & J. S. Bruner (Eds.), *Interaction in human development* (pp. 197–214). Hillsdale, NJ: Erlbaum.

Bornstein, M. H. (Ed.). (1989b). *Maternal responsiveness: Characteristics and consequences*. San Francisco: Jossey-Bass.

Bornstein, M. H. (1989c). Sensitive periods in development: Structural characteristics and causal interpretations. *Psychological Bulletin, 105*, 179–197.

Bornstein, M. H. (Ed.). (1991). *Cultural approaches to parenting*. Hillsdale, NJ: Erlbaum.

Bornstein, M. H. (2000). Infant into conversant: Language and nonlanguage processes in developing early communication. In N. Budwig, I. Z. Uzgiris, & J. V. Wertsch (Eds.), *Communication: An arena of development* (pp. 109–129). Stamford, CT: Ablex.

Bornstein, M. H. (2002a). Parenting infants. In M. H. Bornstein (Ed.), *Handbook of parenting: Vol. 1, Children and parenting* (2nd ed., pp. 3–43). Mahwah, NJ: Erlbaum.

Bornstein, M. H. (2002b). Measurement variability in infant and maternal behavioral assessment. *Infant Behavior and Development, 25*, 413–432.

Bornstein, M. H. (2006). Parenting science and practice. In I. E. Sigel & K. A. Renninger, W. Damon, & R. M. Lerner (Eds.), *Handbook of child psychology: Vol. 4, Child psychology and practice* (6th ed., pp. 893–949). New York: Wiley.

Bornstein, M. H. (Ed.). (2009). *The handbook of cultural developmental science. Part 1. Domains of development across cultures. Part 2. Development in different places on earth*. New York: Taylor & Francis.

Bornstein, M. H. (in preparation). Infancy, parenting, and culture. *National Institute of Child Health and Human Development*.

Bornstein, M. H., Azuma, H., Tamis-LeMonda, C. S., & Ogino, M. (1990). Parent and infant parent activity and interaction in Japan and in the United States: I. A comparative macroanalysis of naturalistic exchanges. *International Journal of Behavioral Development, 13*, 267–287.

Bornstein, M. H., Haynes, O. M., Pascual, L., Painter, K. M., & Galperín, C. (1999). Play in two societies: Pervasiveness of process, specificity of structure. *Child Development, 70*, 317–331.

Bornstein, M. H., & Lamb, M. E. (2010). *Development in infancy: An introduction* (5th ed.). New York: Taylor & Francis.

Bornstein, M. H., Tal, J., Rahn, C., Galperín, C. Z., Pêcheux, M-G., Lamour, M., … Tamis-LeMonda, C. S. (1992). Functional analysis of the contents of maternal speech to infants of 5 and 13 months in four cultures: Argentina, France, Japan, and the United States. *Developmental Psychology, 28*, 593–603.

Bornstein, M. H., & Tamis-LeMonda, C. S. (1990). Activities and interactions of parents and their firstborn infants in the first six months of life: Covariation, stability, continuity, correspondence, and prediction. *Child Development, 61*, 1206–1217.

Bornstein, M. H., Tamis-LeMonda, C. S., & Hahn, C.-S. (2008). Maternal responsiveness to very young children at three ages: Longitudinal analysis of a multidimensional modular and specific parenting construct. *Developmental Psychology, 44*, 867–874.

Bornstein, M. H., Tamis-LeMonda, C. S., Pascual, L., Haynes, M. O., Painter, K. M., Galperin, C. Z., & Pêcheux, M-G. (1996). Ideas about parenting in Argentina, France, and the United States. *International Journal of Behavioral Development, 19*, 347–367.

Bornstein, M. H., Tamis-LeMonda, C. S., Pêcheux, M.-G., & Rahn, C. (1991). Infant and parent activity and interaction in France and in the United States: A comparative study. *International Journal of Behavioral Development, 14*, 21–43.

Bornstein, M. H., Tamis-LeMonda, C. S., Tal, J., Ludemann, P., Toda, S., Rahn, C. W., ... Vardi, D. (1992). Maternal responsiveness to infants in three societies: The United States, France, and Japan. *Child Development, 63*, 808–821.

Bornstein, M. H., Toda, S., Azuma, H., Tamis-LeMonda, C. S., & Ogino, M. (1990). Parents and infant activity and interaction in Japan and in the United States: II. A comparative microanalysis of naturalistic interactions focused on the organization of infant attention. *International Journal of Behavioural Development, 13*, 289–308.

Bornstein, M. H., & Zlotnik, D. (2008). Parenting styles and their effects. In M. M. Haith & J. B. Benson (Eds.), *Encyclopedia of infant and early childhood development* (pp. 496–509). San Diego, CA: Academic.

Bowlby, J. (1973). *Attachment and loss.* New York: Basic Books.

Bradley, R. H., Caldwell, B. M., & Rock, S. L. (1988). Home environment and school performance: A ten-year follow-up and examination of three models of environmental action. *Child Development, 59*, 852–867.

Bradley, R.H., & Whiteside-Mansell, L. (1997). Children in poverty. In R.T. Ammerman & M. Hersen (Eds.), *Handbook of prevention and treatment with children and adolescents* (pp. 13–58). New York: Wiley.

Bremner, J. G. (1994). *Infancy* (2nd ed.). Malden, MA: Blackwell Publishers.

Bronfenbrenner, U., & Morris, P. A. (2006). The bioecological model of human development. In R. M. Lerner (Ed.), W. Damon (Series Ed.), *Handbook of child psychology: Vol. 1, Theoretical models of human development* (6th ed., pp. 793–828). New York: Wiley.

Cabrera, N. J., Ryan, R. M., Mitchell, S. J., Shannon, J. D., & Tamis-LeMonda, C. S. (2008). Low-income, nonresident father involvement with their toddlers: Variation by fathers. *Journal of Family Psychology, 22*, 643–647.

Campos, J. J., Anderson, D. I., Barbu-Roth, M. A., Hubbard, E. M., Hertenstein, M. J., Witherington, D. (2000). Travel broadens the mind. *Infancy, 1*, 149–219.

Clarke, A. M., & Clarke, A. D. B. (Eds.). (1976). *Early experience: Myth and evidence.* New York: Free Press.

Cochran, M., & Niego, S. (2002). Parenting and social networks. In M. H. Bornstein (Ed.), *Handbook of parenting: Vol. 4, Applied parenting* (2nd ed., pp. 123–148). Mahwah, NJ: Erlbaum.

Cohn, J. F., Campbell, S. B., Matias, R., & Hopkins, J. (1990). Face-to-face interactions of postpartum depressed and nondepressed parent–infant pairs at 2 months. *Developmental Psychology, 26*, 15–23.

Collins, W. A., Maccoby, E. E., Steinberg, L., Hetherington, E. M., & Bornstein, M. H. (2000). Contemporary research on parenting: The case for nature *and* nurture. *American Psychologist, 55*, 218–232.

Conger, R. D., McMarty, J., Yang, R., Lahey, B., & Kropp, J. (1984). Perception of child, child rearing values, and emotional distress as mediating links between environmental stressors and observed maternal behavior. *Child Development, 55*, 2234–2247.

Cote, L. R., Bornstein, M. H., Haynes, O. M., & Bakeman, R. (2008). Mother–infant person- and object-directed interactions in Latino immigrant families: A comparative approach. *Infancy, 13*, 338–365.

Crnic, K. A., Greenberg, M. T., Robinson, N. M., Ragozin, A. S., & Basham, R. B. (1983). Effects of stress and social support on parents and premature and full-term infants. *Child Development, 54*, 209–217.

Crown, C. L., Feldstein, S., Jasnow, M. D., Beebe, B., & Jaffe, J. (2002). The cross-modal coordination of interpersonal timing: Six-week-old infants. *Journal of Psycholinguistic Research, 31,* 1–23.

Curtona, C. E., & Troutman, B. R. (1986). Social support, infant temperament, and parenting self-efficacy: A mediational model of postpartum depression. *Child Development, 57,* 1507–1518.

Darling, N., & Steinberg, L. D. (1993). Parenting style as context: An integrative model. *Psychological Bulletin, 113,* 487–496.

Dix, T., & Meunier, L. N. (2009). Depressive symptoms and parenting competence: An analysis of 13 regulatory processes. *Developmental Review, 29,* 45–68.

Dodge, K. A., Pettit, G. S., & Bates, J. E. (1994). Socializing mediators of the relation between socioeconomic status and child conduct problems. *Child Development, 65,* 649–665.

Dumas, J. E., & Wekerle, C. (1995). Maternal reports of child behaviors and personal distress as predictors of dysfunctional parenting. *Development and Psychopathology, 7,* 465–479.

Dunn, J. B. (1977). Patterns of early interaction: Continuities and consequences. In H. R. Schaffer (Ed.), *Studies in parent–infant interaction* (pp. 438–456). London: Academic.

East, P. L., & Felice, M. E. (1996). *Adolescent pregnancy and parenting: Findings from a racially diverse sample.* Mahwah, NJ: Erlbaum.

Egeland, B., & Farber, E. A. (1984). Infant–parent attachment: Factors related to its development and changes over time. *Child Development, 55,* 753–771.

Feinberg, M. E. (2002). Coparenting and the transition to parenthood: A framework for prevention. *Clinical Child and Family Psychology Review, 5,* 173–195.

Fernald, A., Taeschner, T., Dunn, J., & Papousek, M. (1989). A cross-language study of prosodic modifications in mothers. *Journal of Child Language, 16,* 477–501.

Fogel, A. (1991). *Infancy: Infant, family, and society* (2nd ed.). St. Paul, MN: West Publishing.

Fogel, A., & Lyra, M. C. D. P. (1997). Dynamics of development in relationships. In F. Masterpasqua & P. A. Perna (Eds.), *The psychological meaning of chaos: Translating theory into practice* (pp. 75–94). Washington, DC: American Psychological Association.

Fogel, A., Messinger, D. S., Dickson, K. L., & Hsu, H.-C. (1999). Posture and gaze in early parent–infant communication: Synchronization of developmental trajectories. *Developmental Science, 2,* 325–332.

Furstenberg, F. F., Brooks-Gunn, J., & Chase-Lansdale, P. L. (1989). Teenaged pregnancy and childbearing. *American Psychologist, 44,* 313–320.

Garbarino, J., & Kostelny, K. (1993). Neighborhood and community influences on parenting. In T. Luster & L. Okagaki (Eds.), *Parenting: An ecological perspective* (pp. 203–236). Hillsdale, NJ: Erlbaum.

Goldstein, M. H., & Schwade, J. A. (2010). From birds to words: Perception of structure in social interactions guides vocal development and language learning. In M. S. Blumberg, J. H. Freeman & S. R. Robinson (Eds.), *The Oxford handbook of developmental and comparative neuroscience* (pp. 708–729). New York: Oxford University Press.

Goldstein, M. H., Schwade, J. A., & Bornstein, M. H. (2009). The value of vocalizing: Five-month-old infants associate their own noncry vocalizations with responses from caregivers. *Child Development, 80,* 636–644.

Göncü, A., & Gaskins, S. (Eds.). (2007). *Play and development: Evolutionary, sociocultural, and functional perspectives.* Mahwah, NJ: Erlbaum.

Goodman, S., & Brumley, E. (1990). Schizophrenic and depressed women: Relational deficits in parenting. *Developmental Psychology, 26,* 31–39.

Goodnow, J. J. (2002). Parents' knowledge and expectations: Using what we know. In M. H. Bornstein (Ed.), *Handbook of parenting: Vol. 3, Status and social conditions of parenting* (2nd ed., pp. 439–460). Mahwah, NJ: Erlbaum.

Goodnow, J. J., & Collins, W. A. (1990). *Development according to parents: The nature, sources, and consequences of parents' ideas.* Hillsdale, NJ: Erlbaum.

Grolnick, W. S., McMenamy, J. M., & Kurowski, C. O. (2005). Emotional self-regulation in infancy and toddlerhood. In L. Balter & C. S. Tamis-Lemonda (Eds.), *Child psychology: A handbook of contemporary issues* (2nd ed., pp. 3–26). Philadelphia: Psychology Press.

Harkness, S., & Super, C. M. (2002). Culture and parenting. In M. H. Bornstein (Ed.), *Handbook of parenting: Vol. 2, Biology and ecology of parenting* (2nd ed., pp. 253–280). Mahwah, NJ: Erlbaum.

Hart, B., & Risley, T. R. (1992). American parenting of language-learning children: Persisting differences in family-child interactions observed in natural home environments. *Developmental Psychology, 28,* 1096–1105.

Hashima, P. Y., & Amato, P. R. (1994). Poverty, social support, and parental behavior. *Child Development, 65,* 394–403.

Heinicke, C. M. (2002). The transition to parenting. In M. H. Bornstein (Ed.), *Handbook of parenting: Vol. 3, Status and social conditions of parenting* (2nd ed., pp. 363–388). Mahwah, NJ: Erlbaum.

Hoff, E., Laursen, B., & Tardif, T. (2002). Socioeconomic status and parenting. In M. H. Bornstein (Ed.), *Handbook of parenting. Vol. 2, Biology and ecology of parenting* (2nd ed., pp. 231–252). Mahwah, NJ: Erlbaum.

Holden, G. W., & Miller, P. C. (1999). Enduring and different: A meta-analysis of the similarity in parents' child rearing. *Psychological Bulletin, 125,* 223–254.

Hrdy, S. B. (1999). *Parent nature: A history of parents, infants, and natural selection.* New York: Pantheon.

Isabella, R. A., & Belsky, J. (1991). Interactional synchrony and the origins of infant–parent attachment: A replication study. *Child Development, 62,* 373–384.

Jackson, A. (1993). Black, single, working parents in poverty: Preferences for employment, well-being, and perceptions of preschool-age children. *Social Work, 38,* 26–34.

Jones, N. A., Field, T., Fox, N. A., Davalos, M., Malphurs, J., Carraway, K., Schanberg, S., & Kuhn, C. (1997). Infants of intrusive and withdrawn parents. *Infant Behavior and Development, 20,* 175–186.

Keller, H. (2007). *Cultures of infancy.* Mahwah, NJ: Erlbaum.

Kochanska, G., Forman, D. R., & Coy, K. C. (1999). Implications of the parent–child relationship in infancy for socialization in the second year of life. *Infant Behavior and Development, 22,* 249–265.

Kohn, M. L. (1987). Cross national research as an analytic strategy. *American Sociological Review, 52,* 713–731.

Lamb, M. E. (2002). Infant–father attachments and their impact on child development. In C.S. Tamis-LeMonda & N. Cabrera (Eds.), *Handbook of father involvement: Multidisciplinary perspectives* (pp. 93–117). Mahwah, NJ: Erlbaum.

Lamb, M., Sternberg, K., & Thompson, R. (1997). The effects of divorce and custody arrangements on children's behavior, development, and adjustment. *Family and Conciliation Courts Review, 35,* 393–404.

Landry, S.H. (1995). The development of joint attention in premature low birthweight infants. Effects of early medial complications and maternal attention-directing behaviors. In C. Moore & P.J. Dunham (Eds.), *Joint attention: Its origins and role in development* (pp. 223–250). Hillsdale, NJ: Erlbaum.

Lerner, R. M., Theokas, C., & Bobek, D. L. (2005). Concepts and theories of human development: Contemporary dimensions. In M. H. Bornstein & M. E. Lamb (Eds.), *Developmental science: An advanced textbook* (pp. 3–44). Mahwah, NJ: Erlbaum.

Lewis, M. (1997). *Altering fate: Why the past does not predict the future*. New York: Guilford Press.

Lorenz, K. (1935/1970). *Studies in animal and human behavior* (R. Martin, Trans.). London: Methuen.

Lugo-Gil, J., & Tamis-LeMonda, C. S. (2008). Family resources and parenting quality: Links to children's cognitive development across the first three years. *Child Development, 79*, 1065–1085.

Maccoby, E. E., & Martin, J. A. (1983). Socialization in the context of the family: Parent–child interaction. In M. Hetherington (Ed.), *Handbook of child psychology* (Vol. *10*, pp. 1–103). New York: Wiley.

Mahler, M., Pine, A., & Bergman, F. (1975). *The psychological birth of the human infant*. New York: Basic Books.

McGuire, S. (2003). The heritability of parenting. *Parenting: Science and Practice, 3*, 73–94.

McLoyd, V. C. (1998). Children in poverty: Development, public policy, and practice. In I. E. Sigel & K. A. Renninger (Eds.), W. Damon (Series Ed.), *Handbook of child psychology: Vol. 4, Child psychology in practice* (5th ed., pp. 135–208). New York: Wiley.

McLoyd, V. C., Aikens, N. L., & Burton, L. M. (2006). Childhood poverty, policy, and practice. In K. A. Renninger, I. E. Sigel, & W. Damon, *Handbook of child psychology: Vol. 4, Child psychology in practice* (2nd ed., pp. 700–775). Hoboken, NJ: Wiley.

Miller, S. A. (1988). Parents beliefs about their children's cognitive development. *Child Development, 59*, 259–285.

Miller-Loncar, C. L., Erwin, L. J., Landry, S. H., Smith, K. E., & Swank, P. R. (1998). Characteristics of social support networks of low socioeconomic status African American, Anglo American, and Mexican American parents of full-term and pre-term infants. *Journal of Community Psychology, 26*, 131–143.

Mundy, P., & Sigman, M. (2006). Joint attention, social competence and developmental psychopathology. In D. Cicchetti & D. Cohen (Eds.), *Developmental psychopathology: Vol. 1, Theory and methods* (2nd ed., pp. 293–332). Hoboken, NJ: Wiley.

Nicely, P., Tamis-LeMonda, C. S., & Bornstein, M. H. (1999). Parents' attuned responses to infant affect expressivity promote earlier achievement of language milestones. *Infant Behavior and Development, 22*, 557–568.

Papoušek, H., & Papoušek, M. (2002). Intuitive parenting. In M. H. Bornstein (Ed.), *Handbook of parenting: Vol. 2, Biology and ecology of parenting* (2nd ed., pp. 183–203). Mahwah, NJ: Erlbaum.

Papoušek, H., Papoušek, M., & Bornstein, M. (1985). The naturalistic vocal environment of young infants: On the significance of homogeneity and variability in parental speech. In T. Fields & N. Fox (Eds.), *Social perception in infants* (pp. 269–298). Norwood, NJ: Ablex.

Parke, R. D. (2002). Fathers and families. In M. H. Bornstein (Ed.), *Handbook of parenting Vol. 3, Status and social conditions of parenting* (2ne ed., pp. 27–73). Mahwah, NJ: Erlbaum.

Pederson, D. R., Moran, G., Sitko, C., Campbell, K., Ghesquire, K., & Acton, H. (1990). Maternal sensitivity and the security of infant-parent attachment: A Q-sort study. *Child Development, 58*, 1974–1983.

Plato (circa 355 bce/1970). *The laws* (T. J. Saunders, Trans.). Harmondsworth, UK: Penguin.

Raver, C. C. (1996). Success at catching and keeping toddlers' attention: An examination of joint attention among low-income parents and their 2-year olds. *Early Development and Parenting, 5*, 225–236.

Rochat, P., & Striano, T. (1999). Social-cognitive development in the first year. In P. Rochat (Ed.), *Early social cognition* (pp. 3–34). Mahwah, NJ: Erlbaum.

Roggman, L. A. (1991). Assessing social interactions of parents and infants through play. In C. E. Schaefer, K. Gitlin & A. Sandgrund (Eds.), *Play diagnosis and assessment* (pp. 427–462). New York: Wiley.

Rohner, R. (1985). *The warmth dimension.* Beverly Hills, CA: Sage Publications.

Rosenblatt, J. S. (2002). Hormonal basis of parenting in mammals. In M. H. Bornstein (Ed.), *Handbook of parenting: Vol. 2, Biology and ecology of parenting* (2nd ed., pp. 31–60). Mahwah, NJ: Erlbaum.

Rutter, M., & The English and Romanian Adoptees Study Team (1998). Developmental catch-up and delay, following adoption after severe global early privation. *Journal of Child Psychology and Psychiatry, 39,* 465–476.

Sameroff, A. J., & Feil, L. A. (1985). Parental concepts of development. In I. E. Sigel (Ed.), *Parent belief systems: The psychological consequences for children* (pp. 83–105). Hillsdale, NJ: Erlbaum.

Scarr, S. (1992). Developmental theories for the 1990s: Development and individual differences. *Child Development, 63,* 1–19.

Schellenbach, C. J., Whitman, T. L., & Borkowski, J. G. (1992). Toward an integrative model of adolescent parenting. *Human Development, 35,* 81–99.

Seifer, R., Schiller, M., Sameroff, A. J., Resnick, S., Riordan, K. (1996). Attachment, maternal sensitivity, and infant temperament during the first year of life. *Developmental Psychology, 32,* 12–25.

Shannon, J. D., Tamis-LeMonda, C. S., & Cabrera, N. J. (2006). Fathering in infancy: Mutuality and stability between 8 and 16 months. *Parenting: Science and Practice, 6,* 167–188.

Shannon, J.D., Tamis-LeMonda, C. S., & Margolin, A. (2005). Father involvement in infancy: Influences of past and current relationships. *Infancy, 8,* 21–41.

Sigel, I. E., & McGillicuddy-De Lisi (2002). Parental beliefs and cognitions: The dynamic belief systems model. In M. H. Bornstein (Ed.), *Handbook of parenting: Vol 3, Status and social conditions of parenting* (2nd ed., pp. 485–508). Mahwah, NJ: Erlbaum.

Simons, R. L., Whitbeck, L. B., Conger, R. D., &Wu, C. -I. (1991). Intergenerational transmission of harsh parenting. *Developmental Psychology, 27,* 159–171.

Singh, L. (2008). Influences of high and low variability on infant word recognition. *Cognition, 106,* 833–870.

Sroufe, L. A., Egeland, B., Carlson, E. A., & Collins, W. A. (2005). *The development of the person: The Minnesota study of risk and adaptation from birth to adulthood.* New York: Guilford Publications.

Stern, D. N. (1974). Parent and infant at play: The dyadic interaction involving facial, vocal, & gaze behaviors. In M. Lewis & L. Rosenblum (Eds.), *The effect of the infant on its caregiver* (pp. 187–211). New York: Wiley.

Stern, D. N. (1993). The role of feelings for an interpersonal self. In U. Neisser (Ed.), *The perceived self: Ecological and interpersonal sources of self-knowledge* (pp. 205–215). Cambridge: Cambridge University Press.

Susman-Stillman, A., Kalkoske, M., Egeland, B., & Waldman I. (1996). Infant temperament and maternal sensitivity as predictors of attachment security. *Infant Behavior and Development, 19,* 33–47.

Tamis-LeMonda, C. S. (2003). Cultural perspectives on the "what?" and "whys?" of parenting. *Human Development, 46,* 319–327.

Tamis-LeMonda, C. S., Adolph, K. E., Dimitropolou, K. A., & Zack, E. (2007). "No! Don't! Stop!": Mothers' words for impending danger. *Parenting: Science and Practice, 7,* 1–25.

Tamis-LeMonda, C. S., & Bornstein, M. H. (1994). Specificity in parent-toddler language-play relations across the second year. *Developmental Psychology, 30,* 283–292.

Tamis-LeMonda, C. S., Bornstein, M. H., Baumwell, L., & Damast, A. M. (1996). Sensitivity in parenting interactions across the first two years: Influences on children's language and play. *Early Development and Parenting, 5,* 173–183.

Tamis-LeMonda, C. S., & Cabrera, N. (1999). Perspectives on father involvement: Research and policy. *Social Policy Report, Society for Research in Child Development, 13,* 1–25.

Tamis-LeMonda, C. S., & Kahana Kalman, R. K. (2009). Mothers' views at the transition to a new baby: Variation across ethnic groups. *Parenting: Science and Practice, 9*(1&2), 36–55.

Tamis-LeMonda, C. S., & McFadden, D. (2009). The United States. In M. H. Bornstein (Ed.), *The handbook of cross-cultural developmental science: Vol. 2, Human development in different places on earth* (pp. 299–322). New York: Psychology Press/Taylor & Francis.

Tamis-LeMonda, C. S., Shannon, J. D., Cabrera, N., & Bradley, B. (2004). Mothers and fathers at play with their 2- and 3-year olds. *Child Development, 75*, 1806–1820.

Tamis-LeMonda, C. S., Way, N., Hughes, D., Yoshikawa, H., Kahana Kalman, R. K., & Niwa, E. (2008). Parents' goals for children: The dynamic coexistence of individualism and collectivism in cultures and individuals. *Social Development, 17*, 183–209.

Tamis-LeMonda, C. S., Kahana Kalman, R. K., & Yoshikawa, H. (2009). Father involvement in immigrant and ethnically diverse families from the prenatal period to the second year: Prediction and mediating mechanisms. *Sex Roles, 60*, 496–509.

Thiessen, E. D., Hill, E. A., & Saffran, J. R. (2005). Infant-directed speech facilitates word segmentation. *Infancy, 7*, 53–71.

Thompson, R. A. (1994). Emotional regulation: A theme in search of definition. In N. A. Fox (Ed.), The development of emotion regulation: Biological and behavioral aspects. *Monographs of the Society for Research in Child Development, 59*, (2–3 Serial No. 240), 25–52.

Toda, S., Fogel, A., & Kawai, M. (1990). Maternal speech to three-month-old infants in the United States and Japan. *Journal of Child Language, 17*, 279–294.

Trevarthen, C. (1979). Communication and cooperation in early infancy: A description of primary intersubjectivity. In M. M. Bullowa (Ed.), *Before speech: The beginning of interpersonal communication* (pp. 321–347). New York: Cambridge University Press.

Trevarthen, C. (1993). The self born in intersubjectivity: The psychology of an infant communicating. In U. Neisser (Ed.), *The perceived self* (pp. 121–173). New York: Cambridge University Press.

Tronick, E. Z. (1989). Emotions and emotional communication in infants. *American Psychologist, 44*, 112–119.

Tronick, E. Z., & Weinberg, M. K. (1990, April). *The stability of regulation behaviors.* Paper presented at the biennial meeting of the International Conference on Infant Studies, Montreal.

Van den Boom, D., & Hoeksma, J. (1994). The effect of infant irritability on parent–infant interaction: A growth curve analysis. *Developmental Psychology, 30*, 581–590.

Winnicott, D. W. (1965). *The maturational processes and the facilitating environment: Studies in the theory of emotional development.* New York: International Universities Press.

Zahn-Waxler, C., Duggal, S., & Gruber, R. (2002). Parental psychopathology. In M. H. Bornstein (Ed.), *Handbook of parenting: Vol. 4, Applied Parenting* (2nd ed., pp. 295–327). Mahwah, NJ: Erlbaum.

16

Attachment in Infancy

Germán Posada and Garene Kaloustian

Introduction

Attachment theory is concerned with the development of child–caregiver(s) relationship(s) and the role those relationships play in future intimate relationships and individual development. Judged by the sheer amount of empirical work it has guided and organized, and the broad range of extensions and applications that it has inspired, attachment theory could be deemed successful. Yet, despite its usefulness in describing and explaining relationship phenomena, the theory is a work in progress, for which the overall framework proposed by John Bowlby and the seminal empirical work on individual differences conducted by Mary Ainsworth remain central to our understanding of current theoretical, methodological, and application efforts. The foundations of attachment theory are the joint product of Bowlby's efforts to explain children's emotional response to separation from and/or loss of mother and the impact that such experiences may have on personality development, and Ainsworth's account of differences in the quality of infant–mother relationships in Uganda and Baltimore.

The focus of this chapter is on child–mother attachment relationships during infancy. This developmental period is perhaps the one with the largest research output involving child–mother attachment relationships. This chapter will cover central theoretical and methodological issues in attachment research that are deemed essential to understand both the theory and current research efforts. It is not, however, an exhaustive review of studies on the topic. In this chapter we will briefly introduce the work of Bowlby and Ainsworth, and will describe some key characteristics of their approach and constructs necessary to understand the theory. Next, we present the most used methodological tools when assessing infant attachment security and maternal sensitivity. We will then discuss the issue of normative development. Bowlby's evolutionary rationale will be presented, and his normative model of development will be described. Next, we will present the study of individual differences in the development of infant–mother attachment relation-ships, with an emphasis on quality of care as a key factor to account for such differences and the factors that impact quality of care. Last, we will briefly discuss important issues that remain to be investigated.

John Bowlby

A British psychoanalyst, John Bowlby, was interested in the study of personality and the influence that the child–mother relationship may have on personality development. Intellectually curious, and with support from some of his mentors, he was alerted, during his training years, to the importance of parenting and actual family interaction patterns in understanding the difficulties and problems children had (Bowlby, 1946, 1949). Contrary to psychoanalytic theory of the day, Bowlby became convinced of the important effects of real life experiences on development. In attempting to explain children's strong emotional reaction when separated from their parents he put together a theoretical per-spective that sought to keep important insights Freud had provided regarding the child–mother relationship, but framed them in the context of modern evolutionary theory and ethology. In addition, Bowlby used both control systems theory and cognitive develop-ment theory to account for normative changes in the development of attachment, the construction of mental representations about attachment experiences, and the mental dynamics (e.g., issues associated with the storage and retrieval of information) associated with attachment-related clinical problems.

With an appetite for testing his ideas with empirical data, Bowlby organized informa-tion collected by himself and colleagues (e.g., Ainsworth, 1963, 1967; Bowlby, 1958; Bowlby, Robertson, & Rosenbluth, 1952; Harlow, 1958, 1961; Harlow & Harlow, 1962; Shaffer & Emerson, 1964; Yarrow, 1963) and put together his now famous trilogy "Attachment," "Separation," and "Loss." The ideas stated there regarding the centrality of relationships in development have been at the forefront of explanations regarding the nature of the child–mother tie.

Mary Ainsworth

Mary Ainsworth was a clinical psychologist with an expertise in assessment. While in London in the 1950s, she worked with Bowlby and became familiar with his ideas (Bretherton, 1992). With her husband, she traveled to Uganda, where she conducted the first empirical observational-longitudinal study on infant–mother attachment relation-ships (Ainsworth, 1967). Her findings included information on both normative and individual differences that was pivotal to Bowlby's theoretical perspective and to her own interest in the variation of quality in infant–mother relationships. In addition, results hinted at the importance of maternal care and the potential impact of variations in the quality of such care on infants' feelings of security (Ainsworth, 1967; Bretherton, 1992).

Subsequently, in her seminal Baltimore study, she detailed the development of indi-vidual differences in attachment relationships during the first year of an infant's life (Ainsworth, Blehar, Waters, & Walls, 1978). Both infant and maternal behavior were carefully, systematically, and extensively observed and described. This study provided the basis for a surge of research on individual variation in attachment. Ainsworth's studies not only corroborated many of Bowlby's key ideas, but were instrumental in shaping the theory, providing both key concepts and methodological tools that permeate all current research activities on the topic.

Some Key Characteristics of Attachment Theory

A fundamental feature of the Bowlby–Ainsworth perspective is the role attributed to real-life experiences in relationships. According to Bowlby, it is in the context of interactions that infants develop preference for, organize their behavior around, and become attached to their principal caregivers. It is important to emphasize that Bowlby did not consider the organization of an attachment behavioral system and the development of attachment simply as the outcome of learning. From the beginning the interaction between inborn biases in infants' behavioral equipment, and continuous experience in infant–caregiver transactions, are key to the eventual organization and development of attachment. Experience is essential but so are the characteristics of the infant, who is not a blank slate at birth. Furthermore, interaction experience provides the raw materials for children's representations of attachment relationships later on, and for the maintenance or change of such representations. Bowlby's emphasis on real-life interaction experience was a point of departure from traditional psychoanalytic theory at the time he proposed his account.

Another distinctive feature of the Bowlby–Ainsworth approach is the framing of the phenomenon being explained, that is, child–mother attachment relationships, in the context of evolutionary theory. Bowlby proposed that these relationships exist because they have been selected for in the course of human evolution, due to the survival advantages they provide. Bowlby further elaborated a notion of instinct that allowed him to explain the apparent purposefulness of attachment behavior. Using control systems theory, he distinguished between the causation and function of attachment behavior. Activation of the attachment behavioral system is intensified in conditions of pain, fatigue, and fear and reduced by proximity and/or contact with the attachment figure. The biological function of attachment behavior is that of protection and diminishing the risk of harm to the individual (Bowlby, 1988). The predictable outcome of attachment behaviors (e.g., crying, sucking, orienting, smiling, and clinging) is that of bringing the infant's caregiver(s) into close proximity.

It is relevant to mention Bowlby's use of information originating in ethology about the formation of social bonds in other species. Based on information on offspring–mother interactions in nonhuman primates (e.g., chimpanzees, gorillas, orangutans, and rhesus), in conjunction with information pertaining to humans, Bowlby (1982) conceptualized attachment relationships at the level of the species as an outcome of evolution. Ethological and evolutionary theories provided Bowlby not only with a range of concepts, but also a framework in which to place child–parent relationships. Introducing an evolutionary biological approach has profound implications for our understanding and research on attachment relationships. Hypotheses about the universality and the context-specificity of these relationships, inborn biases, contextual support needed, and types of learning that operate are important research issues to be tackled to explicate how these relationships are put together and what kinds of impact they are expected to have.

Another important feature introduced by the Bowlby–Ainsworth framework is its prospective approach. Bowlby (1982) described patterns of behavior and interaction that are established early in infancy and extrapolated forward to discern functionally similar later patterns of response. This prospective approach has required the gathering of developmental data in very young infants, and following them up as behavioral organization develops and their interactions with significant others are coorganized. Ainsworth's research (Ainsworth, 1967; Ainsworth et al., 1978) and the Minnesota longitudinal study (e.g., Sroufe, 1983; Sroufe, Egeland, & Kreutzer, 1990; Sroufe, Egeland, Carlson, & Collins, 2005; E. Waters, Wippman, & Sroufe, 1979; E. Waters, Merrick, Treboux, Crowell, & Albersheim, 2000) best illustrate this approach. However, although deemed as essential, this prospective longitudinal strategy has not been frequently used in research (Sroufe, 2002).

Central Constructs

Attachment and attachment behavior

Attachment is an emotional tie that an infant constructs and elaborates with his principal caregiver(s)[1] in the context of everyday interactions (Bowlby, 1982, 1988; Ainsworth, 1969). This bond is specific in that it is directed towards a particular individual, is long-lasting, and ties the two individuals together across contexts. Attachment is distinct from attachment behavior. While attachment refers to the emotional bond, and to a strong predisposition to seek proximity to and contact with a specific individual, *attachment behavior* is concerned with the diverse behavioral manifestations that allow the individual to achieve the desired proximity and contact. Importantly, attachment is conceptually different from dependency. While the latter tends to have negative connotations when used in the context of relationships (e.g., clinginess), attachment does not. On the contrary, attachment enables children to move out, to explore, and to learn (Bowlby, 1982).

A key concept is that of the *attachment behavioral system*. In replacing Freud's theory of instinct and trying to account for the apparently purposeful and complex behavior in infants, Bowlby used control systems theory to propose an instinctual model based on an inherited potential to organize an attachment behavioral system. Specifically, he proposed that behavioral elements in the infant's repertoire that once were separate, such as crying, sucking, smiling, clinging, and following, become organized into a system whose set goal is proximity to the mother figure, given that infants are raised within the environment of evolutionary adaptedness. What allows the system to function in a seemingly purposive way (achieving the set goal) is feedback. Feedback refers to the process of continuously receiving and collating information about the effects of behavioral performance. This information is compared to the system's goal to determine whether, and if so what, further action is required. The system is versatile in that different behavioral outputs can be used successfully in achieving the goal of proximity. For example, an infant could crawl to mother, call her, cling to her, or use any combination of behaviors. The development of such a behavioral system requires environmental support, that is, a caregiving system. Further, its particular organization will vary depending on the specific interaction experiences encountered in that environment. In addition to offering a new way to think about the origins and organization of infant–caregiver relationships, this new conceptualization had important methodological implications. Rather than sheer behavioral output, as assessed by frequency counts or behavioral intensity, the emphasis becomes the organization of behavior and the efficiency of the system in achieving the set goal.

Secure-base behavior

The *secure-base phenomenon* concept proposed by Ainsworth captures Bowlby's notion that while attachment ties the child to his mother, it also enables him to explore his surroundings. Ainsworth (1967) coined the term *secure-base behavior* in the course of her longitudinal naturalistic observations of attachment development in rural Uganda. On reviewing her field notes, Ainsworth noticed that infants "do not always stay close to the mothers but rather make little excursions away from her, exploring other objects and interacting with other people, but returning to the mother from time to time" (Ainsworth, 1967, p. 345). As described, the secure-base phenomenon refers to the apparent purposeful balance between proximity seeking and exploration away from an attachment figure at different times and across contexts. The attachment figure is used as a haven of safety when needed, and also as a base from which to venture into the world.

Security

Attachment *security* refers to a child's confidence in his mother's availability and responsiveness. The organization of a child's secure-base behavior is the basis for inferring how secure he feels when exploring his surroundings and retreating to her. More specifically, securely attached infants are those who: (a) exhibit skillful secure-base use; (b) participate in smooth exchanges with mother; (c) respond more positively to being picked up and held by mother; (d) respond less negatively to being put down; (e) cry less when mother leaves the room and are more positive in greeting her when she enters; (f) enjoy bodily contact and tend to respond cheerfully to being put down; and (g) tend to move off into independent exploratory play (Ainsworth et al., 1978). In addition, these infants are less angry with mother than are insecure infants, and by year one they comply with maternal demands more readily than do insecure infants.

Internal working models

Integral to the notion of behavioral system is the concept of *working models*. These refer to the internal representations of the relationship environment and self an individual builds through his repeated experiences with caregivers. Those representations incorporate the child's adaptations to and expectations about his caregiving environment. In describing the organization of behavioral systems, Bowlby asserted the centrality of devising plans to achieve the behavioral system set goal. Working models are important in that they assist individuals in coming up with plans to attain the set goal. Specifically, Bowlby proposed that during the first 8 or so months of life, it is likely that an infant does not make a planned attempt to bring about the conditions that terminate his attachment behavior. However, during the last part of his first year and during his second and third years the child becomes more skillful and knowledgeable as to the conditions that make him feel secure, and begins to plan his behavior so that those conditions are met. Aware of early cognitive limitations, Bowlby suggested that infants create a primitive cognitive map, that is, a representation of their relationship with mother. Initially, those maps are about mother moving in a specific spatial and temporal layout. These representations are based on interactions and are expected to be elaborated through relationship experience and cognitive development. The use of language and other representational systems plays an increasingly important role, as infants become toddlers and eventually preschoolers. Bowlby argued that for simple as well as for complex plans, and for the intercoordination of plans, accurate, efficient, and up-to-date working models of the environment and of the self were necessary if they were to be useful. Importantly, Bowlby called those representations internal *working* models to emphasize the fact that they are not static pictures of the environment and self, but dynamic organizations, stable and yet open to change depending on experience and context.

Quality of care

Caregiver *quality of care* plays a central role in attachment theory and research. Bowlby (1982) suggested that a caregiving system complementary to the attachment behavioral system is necessary for attachment relationships to develop. Infants develop an attachment to those persons who provide care on a regular basis. With her emphasis on individual differences in attachment relationships, Ainsworth (1967; Ainsworth et al., 1978) further elaborated the construct of care. She concluded that it was not the quantity but the quality of care that mattered most in accounting for the different types of infant–mother relationships. In addition to specific maternal behaviors observed during infant–mother interactions, Ainsworth conceptualized a model of care proposing four general domains of behavior to describe the main features of maternal care influencing attachment security: sensitivity–insensitivity; cooperation–interference; acceptance–rejection, and accessibility–ignoring. Those four domains turned out to be highly intercorrelated and the overall quality of maternal care was subsumed under the label of *sensitivity*.

Sensitivity–insensitivity to an infant's signals and communications refers to a mother's ability to perceive her baby's signals, interpret them correctly, and respond to them appropriately and promptly. Cooperation–interference with a baby's ongoing behavior refers to a mother's ability to respect her baby as a separate individual, to see things from the baby's perspective, and to intervene in the baby's activities in a skillful and collaborative manner so that the baby does not experience it as interfering. Acceptance–rejection of the baby's needs refers to the balance between a mother's positive and negative feelings about the restrictions her baby's needs place on her, and the extent to which she is able to resolve those negative feelings and not let them permeate her interactions with the infant. Accessibility–ignoring refers to a mother's ability to notice and attend to her baby's signals despite demands from other sources on her attention.

Predominant Methodologies

The strange situation

Ainsworth's strange situation (Ainsworth & Wittig, 1969) is the most frequently used laboratory procedure to assess individual differences in infant–mother attachment relationships, and more specifically infant attachment security. It is an economical and practical procedure that lasts about 22 minutes or so and consists of 8 episodes (see Table 16.1), and is typically used with infants between 12 and 18 months of age. Four scales, proximity seeking, contact maintenance, avoidance, and resistance are used to rate an infant's behavior, especially during reunion episodes. The scores an infant obtains in each scale are used to come up with the way he or she patterns his or her behavior throughout the procedure. Based on their behavioral organization, infants are classified in one of 3

Table 16.1 Strange situation episodes.

Episode – Time	
1 – 30 seconds	Research associate brings infant and mother into a room containing toys and two chairs.
2 – 3 minutes	Researcher associate leaves. Mother and infant stay in the room, the infant can play with the toys and mother has been instructed to be responsive if infant initiates interaction.
3 – 3 minutes	Stranger walks in, remains silent for 1 minute, talks to mother, during the second minute, and then talks and/or plays with the infant for the third minute.
4 – 3 minutes (max.)	Mother leaves room and the infant remains with the stranger. If the infant is too upset and the stranger cannot soothe him, the episode is cut short.
5 – 3 minutes	Mother returns and greets baby. The stranger leaves unobtrusively.
6 – 3 minutes (max.)	Mother leaves and the infant is alone in the room. If the infant is too upset the episode is cut short.
7 – 3minutes	Stranger returns; if the infant continues to be upset and the stranger cannot soothe him, the episode is cut short and mother comes back into the room.
8 – 3 minutes	Mother returns and greets baby. The stranger leaves unobtrusively.

initial groups: Secure, anxious/avoidant, and anxious/resistant. Then, they are rated and classified on disorganization (a description of each of these terms will be given later in this chapter). The validity of the strange situation has been documented empirically (Ainsworth et al., 1978; Vaughn & Waters, 1990).

The utilization of the strange situation was such during the late-1970s and 1980s that it became synonymous with attachment research (Bretherton, 1985). The reasons are diverse, but certainly the careful and strong validation empirical effort by Ainsworth is key. Further, the strange situation provided a means to assess the quality of infant security in his relationship with mother by evaluating the organization of behavior, shifting the focus away from assessment of individual behaviors that had been found to be ineffective in capturing the complexity of the phenomenon under study (E. Waters, 1978). Yet, paradoxically, the efficiency, economy, (as compared to conducting naturalistic obser-vations a la Ainsworth), and success of the strange situation has contibuted to keep researchers away from studying the development of attachment relationships during the second year of life and beyond in naturalistic settings.

The Attachment Q-Set

Partly in response to the aforementioned situation, E. Waters and Deane (1985) devel-oped the Attachment Q-Set (AQS) as an economical alternative to Ainsworth's natural-istic observational methodology, one that allows for efficient descriptions of secure-base behavior in infants and children, and affords more analytical alternatives. Revised and in its third version (E. Waters, 1995), the AQS has emerged as an alternative tool to assess attachment relationships during infancy and early childhood (van IJzendoorn, Vereijken, Bakermans-Kranenburg, & Riksen-Walraven, 2004). As developed, the AQS allows researchers to describe the functioning of the attachment behavior control system and assesses how characteristic secure-base behavior is during infant/child–caregiver interac-tions in naturalistic settings.

The AQS can be used with children between 1 and 5 years (Pederson & Moran, 1995, 1996; Posada et al., 1999; Posada, Carbonell, Alzate, & Plata, 2004; Symons, Clark, Isaksen, & Marshall, 1998; Vaughn & Waters, 1990; Vereijken, Riksen-Walraven, & Kondo-Ikemura, 1997). It consists of 90 descriptive items. Most items refer to behavior in context, and tap different aspects of the secure-base phenomenon, though there also are some filler items. After observing an infant interacting with his mother, researchers use the items to describe child behavior by placing them in 9 piles from most characteristic to least characteristic of the infant. To determine whether an infant's behavior is organ-ized in ways similar to the secure-base phenomenon, his q-description is correlated with a theoretical description that indicates optimal use of the caregiver as a secure base. The higher the correlation the more an infant's behavior is organized in ways that resemble the secure-base phenomenon.

Supporting the validity of the AQS van IJzendoorn and colleagues (2004) presented a meta-analysis of 139 q-sort studies. These authors conclude that the AQS, as used by trained observers, is a valid tool for assessing the organization of attachment behavior, but suggest caution is needed when using AQS data provided by mothers. However, research in regard to maternal report data has demonstrated that the key issue, as with any other methodology, is that of training those who will report on *what* and *how* they are to do it. Thus, Teti and McGourty (1996), and Posada et al., (1999) showed that mothers, like any other observer, can provide valid and useful information when trained and assisted properly. Handing the AQS to untrained mothers to report on their children's behavior, with just a few instructions may be time convenient, but it is a risky business as far as the quality of data gathered is concerned, much as it would be when collecting data from untrained observers.

Assessment of caregiving

Ainsworth's scales. Most research on the association between caregiving and attachment security has been based on Ainsworth's construct of sensitivity and the scale she proposed to assess it. The degree of similarity to her assessment approach has varied from study to study, with some investigators using a conceptualization close to Ainsworth's while others use a notion removed from the one she offered (e.g., maternal self-efficacy as defined by her attribution style and mood state Donovan & Leavitt, 1989). In part this is because Ainsworth's evaluation of maternal care was based upon many hours of naturalistic observation during the first year, and no abbreviated procedure has been devised, as it was for infants' secure-base behavior. As noted earlier, Ainsworth provided ratings for four highly intercorrelated dimensions of maternal characteristics: sensitivity–insensitivity, acceptance–rejection, cooperation–interference, and accessibility–ignoring (Ainsworth et al., 1978). The use of the 9-point scales proposed by Ainsworth, Bell, and Stayton (1974) to assess these dimensions requires a good deal of insight, familiarization, and knowledge about a mother's behavior, and this is in turn depends on good detailed observations. Up to the present no study has sampled maternal behavior, or for that matter infant behavior, as extensively as Ainsworth

The Maternal Behavior Q-Set (MBQS). Much like the AQS, the MBQS (Pederson & Moran, 1995) was proposed as an economical descriptive alternative to Ainsworth's caregiving scales. It allows researchers to describe the quality of maternal care and its support of an infant's attachment behavioral system. The MBQS also permits researchers to obtain more objective and easier to replicate descriptions of maternal behavior during infant–mother interactions. Although the MBQS has mainly been used with infants (Pederson et al., 1990; Pederson & Moran, 1995, 1996; Pederson, Gleason, Moran, & Bento, 1998), it also has been used with older children (e.g., Posada et al., 1999) [2]. It consists of 90 items about maternal behavior based on Ainsworth's conceptualization. One of its great advantages is the operationalization of Ainsworth's sensitivity, cooperation, availability, and acceptance constructs.

After observing a mother interacting with her infant, researchers describe maternal behavior by placing the 90 items into 9 piles from the most characteristic to the least characteristic of the mother. To determine whether a mother's behavior is organized in ways similar to the hypothetically sensitive mother, her q-description is correlated with a theoretical description that indicates optimal sensitive caregiving. The higher the correlation the more a mother's behavior is organized in ways that resemble a sensitive mother.

The validity of the MBQS has been documented in a series of studies by Pederson, Moran, and colleagues (e.g., Moran, Pederson, Pettit, & Krupka, 1992; Pederson & Moran, 1995, 1996; Pederson et al., 1990; Pederson et al., 1998) and Posada and colleagues (e.g., Posada et al., 1999; Posada et al., 2002; Posada et al., 2004). More recently, the MBQS has been revised. The newer version mainly includes items that directly describe the infant's experiences by focusing on mother's behavior during interactions with her infant, rather than identifying sensitive mothers, and utilizes descriptions of maternal behavior that would distinguish avoidant from ambivalent relationships.

The Development of Attachment

Bowlby was interested in explaining children's reactions to separation from and loss of the mother figure, and the potential effects that such experiences may have on individual development. Observations conducted in the Hampstead Nurseries by Freud and Burlingham (1943), as well as those systematically conducted by Robertson on hospitalized children (Bowlby, Robertson, & Rosenbluth, 1952) led Bowlby to pose that young children's response (from 6 months of age on) to separation and loss of the mother figure consists of three phases, protest, despair, and detachment.

Specifically, children's initial reaction to separation from mother is marked by behavior that indicates their displeasure and anger. During this first phase, the young child is severely distressed as shown by loud crying, throwing things and himself around, rejecting objects offered to him, and looking eagerly for any signs of mother's returning. If the separation is long enough, and the "protest" does not bring back their mother, children begin to look uninterested in their environment, apathetic, and sad, and their protest behaviors subside. During the second phase, despair, the child remains concerned about his mother. However, the active motor movements of the previous phase decrease, the child may cry monotonously or intermittently, becomes withdrawn and makes little or no demands on people. Bowlby (1982) suggested that the child's behavior seems to indicate he is becoming increasingly hopeless about mother's return and that he appears to be in a state of deep mourning. During the last phase, detachment, the child shows more interest in his environment, no longer rejects other figures, accepts their care, food and objects and may even be sociable. However, when seeing his mother the behaviors characteristic of attachment are absent. There is no special greeting and no clinging, the child seems distant, and no tears are expressed at separation; mother is no longer treated as a distinctive special figure and the child seems to have lost his interest in mother.

Why do children react in such a manner if separated from mother? In explaining children's response to separation from and loss of mother, Bowlby built developmental attachment theory. The answer Bowlby formulated was that such an emotional reaction takes place because children are attached to and want to be close to their mother.

Attachment in infancy

Children are not born emotionally attached to their mother. Rather, Bowlby proposed a model for the development of attachment relationships during the first 3 years of life. At first, different elements in the behavioral repertoire of the neonate serve to bring and/or maintain his mother in close proximity. Initially, crying, sucking, looking, and somewhat later smiling, clinging, and following have the predictable outcome of bringing mothers and/or caregiving figures closer or into physical contact with the baby. Through learning, practice, and feedback from mother, during daily interactions that become more and more familiar, those once separated behaviors become organized into the attachment behavioral system. This behavioral system is readily observable during the second half of the first year and certainly by the end of the infant's first year of life when infants, once they become mobile, exhibit the secure-base phenomenon in both everyday circumstances and emergency situations (Posada et al., 1999).

To account for the existence of such a system, Bowlby proposed an evolutionary rationale, discarding Freud's economic model of energies and proposing a new instinctual model. Specifically, as noted earlier, Bowlby (1982) framed attachment as a species-characteristic product and proposed a rationale for the existence of attachment relationships in the context of modern evolutionary theory. He offered an explanation that included the survival advantages that proximity seeking and physical contact afforded during the course of human evolution. Infants who sought and maintained some degree of proximity to and/or contact with their caregivers were more likely to survive than those who did not. The biological function of attachment behavior, protection, although most obvious during infancy and childhood, can be observed throughout the life cycle.

Bowlby (1982) further proposed that, by virtue of our primate heritage, human infants are endowed with learning biases and predispositions that make it likely that they will put together an attachment behavioral system, as long as they are exposed to a caring environment. To support his reasoning, Bowlby reviewed and used available evidence concerning offspring–mother relationships in each of the great ape species.

A testable hypothesis derived from such a rationale is that all human infants have the capacity to construct secure-base relationships in the context of interactions with caregivers. That is, across cultures all infants exposed to ordinary parental care will organize their behavior in interactions with caregivers in ways that resemble the secure-base phenomenon. However, despite being at the core of Bowlby and Ainsworth's' theoretical foundations, and, also, at the center of theoretical debates (Chao, 2001; Gjerde, 2001; Kondo-Ikemura, 2001; Posada & Jacobs, 2001; Rothbaum, Weisz, Pott, Miyake, & Morelli, 2000, 2001; van IJzendoorn & Sagi, 2001; E. Waters & Cummings, 2000), very little research work on the cross-cultural generality of secure-base behavior has been conducted. Empirical tests of this hypothesis are important to help resolve discussions and semantic disputes regarding the ubiquity of attachment relationships.

In the only explicit study of the cross-cultural generality of secure-base behavior, Posada and colleagues (1995) collected information about secure-base behavior at home in infants and children from seven different countries representing a variety of cultures. Specifically, data was collected in China, Colombia, Germany, Israel, Japan, Norway, and the United States. Using a methodology (i.e., the attachment q-set) that does not presuppose the existence of the secure-base phenomenon in children's behavioral reper- toire, descriptions of infants' and children's behavior during interactions with mother at home indicated that secure-base behavior was evident in all samples studied.

This study, in conjunction with other research reports based on samples from specific cultures (Ainsworth, 1967; Anderson, 1972; Posada et al., 2004; Symons et al., 1998; Vereijken, Riksen-Walraven, & Kondo-Ikemura, 1997), provides support for the idea that secure-base behavior characterizes infant and child behavior when interacting with mother in naturalistic settings. These studies have opened the door for further exploration of the relationships between hypothesized propensities and cultural and social contexts. For example, even if secure-base behavior turns out to be characteristic of children's behavioral repertoire in diverse cultural contexts, its specific forms and patterning may not be the same. What has been selected for in evolution appears to be a propensity to organize a secure-base behavioral system within the context of child–mother interactions. What remains to be established is the flexibility (range) and the impact of context (e.g., cultural) in the construction of attachment relationships and the secure-base phenomenon (for addi- tional discussion of issues involving culture and attachment see chapter 21 this volume).

Furthermore, existing research has barely included developmental considerations as far as changes over time in secure-base behavior are concerned. This issue is key when study- ing the cross-cultural generality hypothesis. Specific cultural influences may be more limited during the first 2 years of life, when most research has taken place. The impact of specific cultural influences on secure-base behavior may be more obvious once the acquisition of language and representation is in full motion and new channels of influence in child–parent relationships are open. Even if common across cultures, secure-base relationships may be organized, impacted, and used differently, depending on the specific cultural mandates of the group as the child grows older. Little if anything is known about this.

Normative issues

As evinced by their behavior (e.g., crying stops when picked up by anyone), newborns' do not seem to prefer one caregiver over another. One of Bowlby's key contributions was to conceptualize and describe the process of attachment in the making. It takes time for secure-base relationships to develop and consolidate. Based on available empirical evi- dence Bowlby (1982) suggested a four-phase model of attachment development.

During the first phase, *Orientation and signals with limited discrimination of figure*, which occurs during the first 2 or 3 months of a baby's life, the infant reacts in charac- teristic ways to people around him. He orients towards anyone around him, using track- ing eye movements, reaching, grasping, and eventually smiling. The key characteristic of this phase is that the infant exhibits limited ability to discriminate one person from another and does not seem to prefer anyone. While the infant's ability to discriminate is initially limited to auditory and olfactory stimuli, the capacity to discriminate one person from another is hypothesized to increase as interactions with caregivers become a fixture of a child's experiences.

The second phase, *Orientation and signals directed towards one or more discriminated figure(s)* is hypothesized to last from 2 or 3 to about 6 or 7 months of age, and indicates the beginning of an infant's preference for certain figure(s). The infant continues to behave in the same friendly way towards adults around him, but now this response is more obvious when the baby interacts with regular caregivers. Ainsworth (1967) presented evidence for differential crying (crying when mom left the room and ceasing of crying when held by mother) and smiling (smiling more easily and fully with mother than a stranger) as early as 9 and 10 weeks respectively. It is very likely that everyday infant–mother interaction episodes during these first months breed familiarity, and from familiarity preference arises (E. Waters, Kondo-Ikemura, Posada, & Richters, 1991). Patterns of infant–mother interaction bias the baby and not only allow him to discriminate, but also to prefer those individuals that provide care. At this point the infant has moved from very limited discrimination of main caregiver(s) to familiarity and preference for those who care for him. Daily infant–mother behavioral exchanges, in interaction with characteristics of both the neonate's sensory and behavioral equipment and mother's behavior, shape the secure-base relationship in the making.

The third phase, *Maintenance of proximity to a discriminated figure by means of locomotion as well as signals,* indicates the infant's clear preference for his mother-figure. This phase was proposed to begin at 6 or 7 months of age and last until about 2.5 years of age. Soon after the infant acquires mobility, he could be observed to implement the secure-base phenomenon. Certainly, by age 1 year, secure-base behavior is observable. It is very likely that during the first 6 months of life, experience or practice establishes the foundations of the secure-base phenomenon: The baby signals, mother comes close and joins the child in interaction, either cooperating with his behavior and vocalizations or easing the discomfort and stress the infant is experiencing. The caregiver expands the child's activities in time and space, and/or restructures his behavior and context so that the infant is now comfortable and/or can reengage his surroundings. These exchanges are likely to provide the behavioral and sensory substrates for the rapid appearance of the secure-base phenomenon soon after the child develops locomotion.

As described, the process of attachment development thus far can be succinctly stated as going from interaction, to familiarity and preference, to attachment. Even though it could be said that in the third phase the infant is attached, it would be a mistake to think that little more occurs in this phase. As with any developmental phenomenon, the appearance of a secure-base relationship does not mean mastery. Infant–mother interaction continues to be fundamental in supporting and consolidating the quality of the relationship thus far constructed. The infant continues to expand his spatial and temporal limits in regard to his comings and goings from mother. The latter continues to be the matrix upon which the child organizes his behavior. Through interaction practice the secure-base relationship is consolidated. Importantly, towards the end of the second year of infancy, with the advent of language and symbolic representation on the child's part, new avenues of influence and modes of communication enter and transform the relationship.

Formation of a goal-corrected partnership is the fourth phase that Bowlby (1982) proposed. The main feature here is the child's incipient ability to gain perspective about the attachment figure(s) as an independent being with her own goals. By the same token the child becomes more insightful about his mother's feelings and motives. The more the child is able to do so, the more flexible and complex a relationship develops. In that sense Bowlby labeled it a partnership.

Individual differences in attachment relationships

Although all children form attachment relationships with their main caregivers, not all relationships are equal. They vary in their quality. That is, not all relationships are equal. Investigating the effects of weaning and separation from mother in Uganda, Ainsworth (1967) sketched both normative as well as individual differences in the development of infant–mother relationships. Her findings provided a first glance into the process of attachment formation. Her rich descriptions of infants' attachment behaviors (e.g., crying, smiling, greeting, burying their face, and following, among others), coining of the secure-base phenomenon, and her observations of maternal behavior (e.g., enjoyment of breastfeeding, amount and quality of care, excellence as an informant about her infant, being affectionate), provided her with the foundations and hypotheses she systematically tested in Baltimore.

In the Baltimore study Ainsworth launched the field of individual differences in the study of infant–mother attachment relationships. Her findings about the different patterns of behavior organization during interaction with mother permeate essentially all subsequent research on the topic. Ainsworth used a naturalistic longitudinal study of 23 infant–mother dyads, followed during the first year of the infants' lives. The study involved frequent and intensive observations of infant–mother interactions at home. Dyads were visited at home at 3 weeks of age, and every 3 weeks thereafter, for 4 hours until the infants were 1 year old. At 12 months infants were brought to a laboratory setting where each infant was observed in a series of episodes involving interaction with, separation from, and reunion with mother. The laboratory procedure was labeled the *strange situation*.

Meticulous analysis of the configuration and patterning of infants' behavior during the entire strange situation procedure, but especially during the reunion episodes, led Ainsworth to separate infants into secure, anxious/avoidant, and anxious/resistant/ambivalent groups. Ainsworth construed the differences between the groups in terms of security when using mother as a secure base. Two of these groups, "A" (avoidant) and "C," (resistant) are considered as consisting of infants in anxious/insecure attachment relationships with their mothers; "B," infants are those in secure relationships (Ainsworth et al., 1978).

Secure infants (group B) are able to use their mother as a secure base for exploration in the novel room. If distressed during separation, they seek proximity and contact with mother during reunion, and contact is effective in promptly reducing distress. If not openly distressed by separation, the baby responds to mother with active greeting and interaction during reunion episodes. There is little or no tendency to avoid, to resist, or to be angry with mother upon reunion. While secure infants may or may not be distressed during the separation episodes, when distressed it is clear that the infant wants his mother, even though he may be somewhat consoled by the stranger in the room. Although secure infants tend to be friendly with the stranger when in mother's presence, they are clearly more interested in contact and interaction with their mother than with the stranger.

Anxiously avoidant infants (group A) exhibit little affective sharing with mother in the strange situation and readily separate to explore toys. They treat the stranger much as they treat their mothers, and are affiliative with the stranger in mother's absence; they show little preference for mother. "A" infants show active avoidance of proximity, contact, or interaction with mother in reunion episodes. The baby looks, turns, or moves away, and ignores his mother when she returns. Alternatively he greets her casually. If there is approach, the infant mixes his welcoming with avoidance. If the baby is picked up by mother, there is little or no tendency to cling or resist being put down. During separation episodes, the baby is typically not distressed. If there is distress it seems to be due to having been left alone, for it tends to be alleviated when the stranger returns and there is little or no stranger avoidance.

Anxious-resistant infants in group C (also labeled anxious-ambivalent) display poverty of exploration even in preseparation episodes; they seem wary of novel situations and of the stranger. These infants are likely to be very distressed upon separation and are not easily calmed by the stranger. Upon reunion, babies in group C also are not easily calmed by mother's return. They may show proximity seeking and contact mixed with resistance (hitting, squirming, or rejecting toys offered by their mother); alternatively, they may continue to cry and fuss or show extreme passivity. Babies in this group show no or little tendency to ignore their mother during the reunion episodes. Upon reunion, C infants are likely to seek proximity and contact, but proximity and contact are not effective in calming them down as shown by their resistance and inability to be soothed. Ainsworth proposed that these infants may show general maladaptive behavior in the strange situation because they tend to be angrier than infants in the other groups.

Based on subsequent research, Main and Solomon (1986, 1990) proposed a fourth classification group "D" (disorganized/disoriented), which is assigned in addition to an alternate best-fitting category of A, B, or C. Although considered to be anxiously attached, D group infants cannot maintain a clear and coherent strategy in the organization of their attachment behavior. Infants classified into this group, exhibit behavior that lacks a readily observable goal, purpose, or explanation. The most characteristic theme in the list of behaviors these infants demonstrate is that of disorganization or an observed contradiction in movement patterns. A lack of orientation to the immediate environment is also characteristic of these children. Indices of disorganization and disorientation include: sequential and/or simultaneous display of contradictory behavior patterns; undirected, misdirected, incomplete, and interrupted movements and expressions; stereotypy, asymmetrical movements, mistimed movements, and anomalous postures; freezing, stilling, and slowed movements and expressions; and direct indices of apprehension regarding the parent.

At the heart of the infant groups reported by Ainsworth and colleagues (1978) is their significant association with child behavior organization during interaction with mothers at home. That is, the patterning of behavior at home predicts behavior organization in the laboratory procedure. There are two important points to highlight here. *First*, it is the organization of behavior that is predicted and not individual behaviors. Discrete behaviors were not found to be associated in home and laboratory contexts. For example, in the case of crying, while securely attached infants were found to cry the least at home, they may or may not have cried in the strange situation. On the other hand, anxiously attached babies who cried the least (avoidant) or a lot (resistant) in the strange situation were the infants who cried the most at home during both the first and fourth quarter of their first year, and were not distinguishable from each other in terms of crying (Ainsworth et al., 1978).

Second, the validity of the strange situation attachment classification system rests on the demonstration of an association between patterns of secure-base behavior organization at home and in the laboratory. Ainsworth assigned meaning to an infant's behavior in the strange situation based on her findings about different *patterns* of interaction she had observed at home (Ainsworth & Marvin, 1995). The numerous studies that followed Ainsworth's research that have used the strange situation procedure are based on her demonstration of the link between home and laboratory behavior organization. This kind of extensive validity information regarding home behavior is not available yet for the disorganized/disoriented group.

Quality of care and individual differences in attachment security

A core aspect of Bowlby and Ainsworth's theory is concerned with the role of a main caregiver as a secure base from which an infant can organize his behavior, derive security, explore, and learn about the environment (e.g., Ainsworth, 1969, 1991; Ainsworth et al., 1974; Ainsworth et al., 1978; Bowlby, 1982, 1988). In an effort to account for the different outcomes in the organization of infants' secure-base behavior, Ainsworth focused on characteristics of mothers' caregiving during interactions with their baby. Findings from her Baltimore study (Ainsworth et al., 1978) indicated that many aspects of caregiving behavior were significantly related to an infant's quality of attachment at 12 months.

In this study Ainsworth collected detailed information on specific maternal behavior such as responsiveness to infant crying, behavior relevant to separation and reunion, close bodily contact, face-to-face interactions, feeding, and behavior relevant to child obedience (e.g., frequency of physical interventions). As described earlier, Ainsworth rated mothers on four broader categories of behavior, sensitivity–insensitivity, cooperation–interference, acceptance–rejection, accessibility–ignoring. Each category was found to be highly and significantly related to the organization of attachment behavior in the strange situation (e.g., the effect size of the association sensitivity–security amounted to a .78 correlation). Ainsworth's identification of those four dimensions as important aspects of infant care has provided a valuable framework for empirical research on this issue. Her model of early care has served as the theoretical foundation for empirical studies investigating the factors that account for individual differences in infants' organization of secure-base behavior (e.g., Cox, Owen, Henderson, & Margand, 1992; Grossmann, Grossmann, Spangler, Suess, & Unzner, 1985; NIHCD, Early Child Care Research Network, 2006; Pederson & Moran, 1995; Posada et al., 2004; Smith & Pederson, 1988).

A meta-analysis of 66 studies conducted by de Wolff and van IJzendoorn (1997) reported a correlation coefficient of .24 for studies that investigated the relationship between sensitivity and security, assessing the constructs in similar ways to Ainsworth. Those findings are remarkable, especially in consideration of the fact that most studies subsequent to the work of Ainsworth have drastically reduced the window of observation time and situations, and thus, perhaps, the representativeness of the phenomena being observed. Specifically, most research has observed maternal behavior and scored maternal sensitivity once in contrived situations, and for periods usually lasting under an hour. Low correlations can reflect measurement problems rather than weak effects. Ainsworth's many hours of naturalistic observations throughout the first year afforded a better assessment of maternal sensitivity and child behavior than the less extensive, structured observations and narrowly focused measures typical of most subsequent studies. Indeed, the results of more recent studies conducted in different laboratories by Pederson, Moran and colleagues (e.g., Moran et al., 1992; Pederson & Moran, 1995, 1996; Pederson et al., 1998; Pederson et al., 1990) and Posada and colleagues (e.g., Posada et al., 1999; Posada et al., 2002; Posada et al., 2004) that involve observations and measures more akin to Ainsworth's have yielded comparable results (sensitivity–security correlation coefficients between .40–.61). Clearly, the issue of effect size in research on maternal care and infant security requires further study, with special attention to construct definitions, observational strategies, sampling of behavior, and measurement issues. In the meantime, even small correlations should not be dismissed out of hand in contexts where they can be projected through large numbers of events or interactions to produce important effects (Abelson, 1985).

Individual differences in sensitivity

Since the empirical evidence available indicates that sensitivity plays an important role in infant security outcomes, an obvious question to pose is concerned with the factors that may be impacting maternal sensitive behavior. To account for individual differences in maternal sensitivity, attachment researchers have turned their attention to caregivers' current conceptualizations of their own attachment relationships, and to concurrent living circumstances surrounding the infant–mother dyad.

Research focusing on the caregivers' current representations of attachment relationships experienced a surge during the past 25 years due to the development of the Adult Attachment Interview (AAI; George, Kaplan, & Main, 1984; Main, Kaplan, & Cassidy, 1985). The AAI is a semistructured interview that asks for descriptions of early relationships and attachment-related events (Crowell, Fraley, & Shaver, 1999). It also asks for the adult's views of how those relationships and events have impacted her or his adult personality. It is presumed that individuals' verbal accounts reflect their current state of mind regarding attachment. The transcript of the interview is scored using rating scales for the individual's child–parent relationship experiences and her/his style of discourse, that is, how experiences are described and the ability to provide an integrated, believable, and coherent account of those experiences and their meaning. Based on these interviews individuals are classified in one of four groups, secure (autonomous), dismissing, preoccupied, and unresolved. The last three are considered insecure representations or conceptualizations of attachment relationships.

Overall, studies investigating the association between mothers' AAI classifications and their infants' strange situation classifications have reported significant levels of correspondence, especially when the match is restricted to the secure–insecure distinction.

Results for father–infant dyads are similar, although the levels of correspondence are not as high as those for mothers (e.g., Ainsworth & Eichberg, 1991; Fonagy, Steele, & Steele, 1991; Levine, Tuber, Slade, & Ward, 1991; Main et al., 1985; van IJzendoorn, Kranenburg, Zwart-Woudstra, van Busschbach, & Lambermon, 1991). However, these findings do not address the issue of whether attachment representations indeed are related to individual differences in sensitive caregiving behavior, and the relevant empirical literature on the issue using the AAI is limited and not always consistent. A study by Pederson and colleagues (1998) demonstrated that maternal representations of attachment were significantly associated with maternal sensitivity, and that sensitivity mediated the associations between maternal and infant classifications. In contrast, studies by Ward and Carlson (1995) and Atkinson et al. (2005) found evidence that does not support the role of maternal sensitivity as a mediator. These results may reflect the multidetermined nature of parenting or of quality of maternal care (see chapter 15 this volume for a discussion of this issue). More research is needed to test the hypothesis that maternal current attachment representations and sensitivity are significantly related and to determine their contributions to infant attachment security (Atkinson et al., 2005; Raval et al., 2001).

In addition to mental representations of attachment some researchers have studied characteristics of the context where the infant–mother dyad lives. The assumption underlying this research is that the quality of care and of attachment relationships are also impacted by features of a dyad's ecology. For example, if stressful circumstances are a constant feature of the dyad's context, this can adversely impact maternal sensitivity, which in turn affects the quality of infant–mother relationships. Supporting the validity of this notion, one set of findings has shown that the marital climate is associated with attachment security in expected ways. Specifically, findings indicate that infant–mother secure attachments were more likely to occur in families in which husbands and wives were highly satisfied with their marriages, had higher marital adjustment, and experienced less marital conflict. Similarly, infant insecure attachments have been found to be associated with low marital adjustment and high marital conflict (Belsky, 1999; Glober-Tippelt & Huerkamp, 1998; Goldberg & Easterbrooks, 1984; Howes & Markman, 1989; Isabella & Belsky, 1985).

Attachment security has also been related in expected ways to stressors associated with low socio-economic status (SES) conditions (e.g., De Wolff & van IJzendoorn, 1997; Diener, Nievar, & Wright, 2003; Posada et al., 1999). Similarly, other studies have demonstrated that changes in child security are associated with an increase or decrease of stressful events in family living conditions (Egeland & Farber, 1984; Vaughn, Egeland, Sroufe, & Waters, 1979; Vondra, Hommerding, & Shaw, 1999; E. Waters & Valenzuela, 1999).

Overall however, studies directly and specifically addressing the association between context characteristics and maternal sensitivity are few and sorely needed. In general, studies on the issue have been conducted with older children and results show that negative emotions from the couple's relationship and other context-related characteristics (e.g., stress) have adverse effects on the mother–child relationship, particularly in the domains of maternal emotional availability and sensitivity to her child's needs and signals (Cummings & Davies, 2002; Frosch, Mangelsdorf, & McHale, 2000; Pianta, Sroufe, & Egeland, 1989; Stevenson-Hinde & Shouldice, 1995).

Future Directions

A look at the research field in infant attachment relationships after Ainsworth's ethological studies provides a clear picture: Numerous studies on attachment relationships have been conducted in the laboratory using the strange situation. Most of these have investigated hypothesized associations between infant attachment security and socialization outcomes, assessed either concurrently or at a later time (Thompson, 1998, 2000). Most of those studies report significant associations between security and the outcome variables studied (Cohn, 1990; Easterbrooks, Biesecker, & Lyons-Ruth, 2000; Elicker, Englund, & Sroufe, 1992; Erickson, Sroufe, & Egeland 1985; Greenberg, Speltz, & DeKlyen, 1993; Harrison & Ungerer, 2002; Izard & Abe, 2004; Kochanska, Aksan, & Carlson, 2005; Lieberman, 1977; Main & Weston, 1981; Matas, Arend, & Sroufe, 1978; NIHCD Early Child Care Research Network, 2006; Pastor, 1981; Turner 1991; Warren, Huston, Egeland, & Sroufe, 1997). Yet, as some authors have stated (e.g., Thompson 1998; E. Waters, Posada, Crowell, & Lay, 1993), it is not yet clear how infant security is linked to socialization outcomes, because most of the studies do not explicitly address the issue of mechanisms and processes accounting for such associations. At present we have a network of correlates that need to be accounted for by further research.

Paradoxically, longitudinal studies in naturalistic settings, the kind of studies that gave rise to and consolidated attachment theory and research, have been set aside for the most part. Ainsworth herself lamented the lack of observational studies (Ainsworth, 1991), and deemed field research essential to study what actually transpires in infant/child–caregiver exchanges (Ainsworth & Marvin, 1995). This is more than a lapse or an oversight. Studies in naturalistic settings are expensive as far as time, personnel, money, and effort are concerned. Issues of design and measurement are complex as the target is organization of behavior and the efficiency of a behavioral system, and not simply frequency counts or ratings of intensity of behavior. Yet, it is just this kind of Ainsworth-type study that is necessary to expand the descriptive base on which attachment research stands. Naturalistic and longitudinal studies will allow us to begin to delineate the developmental course of attachment relationships during the second year of an infant's life and beyond. For example, little is known about infant–mother interactions, either from the infant or mother's behavioral perspective, during the second year of life at the level of detail offered by Ainsworth for the first year of life.

Given the breadth and success of research on attachment why emphasize or even bring up such issues? One answer involves the importance of investigating attachment relationships as the child develops. If attachment theory is to be a developmental account, it needs to detail the time course of child–mother relationships. Childhood is a time of rapid change and acquisition of new capacities and skills. Even though Bowlby (1982) proposed that the third phase of attachment development lasts from approximately 6 or 7 months to the middle of the third year, and that during this phase an infant expresses a clear preference for main caregivers and uses them as a secure base, little else is known about the details of infant–mother exchanges and their transformations. It would be foolish to think that the phenomenon appears readymade. E. Waters et al. (1991) suggested that after the appearance of the secure-base phenomenon by the second half of the first year, a consolidation phase takes place, where the infant refines and becomes more skillful in his use of mother as a secure base. Further, those authors suggest that separation distress decreases as the child achieves a better grasp of the time and spatial considerations of his surroundings. Although provocative, there are no normative or individual differences data on these issues. This is no trivial matter. Assessments of security as the child grows older are typically based on the strange situation groups for infants. Researchers make conceptual and rational decisions about how to classify older children using new coding systems, rarely checking the latter against descriptive information on child–mother relationships and child secure-base use in real-life environments. The manifestations of security–insecurity are likely to vary as the child grows older, changes, and avails himself of new motor, linguistic, and cognitive tools to achieve his relationships goals, particularly as attachment figures modify their approach when taking into consideration the child's new capabilities. The changing nature of infant–mother relationships, even in the phase of continuity, needs to be documented if we are to understand the transformations and continuities of those relationships.

The same reasoning applies to the study of the provision of secure-base support. Ainsworth and colleagues (1978) illustrated clearly that the study of quality of care during the first year of life needed to include changes implemented by mothers as their infants grew older. Thus, during the first trimester of life, an important dimension of maternal behavior is related to face-to-face encounters, which by the final quarter of the first year are not as salient as before. By the same token, issues related to infant obedience become relevant and were explicitly considered during the fourth quarter (Ainsworth et al., 1978). It is difficult not to envisage a transformed maternal behavioral output with a more mobile infant, who begins to use language and more clearly expresses his emotions and wants. This requires a different kind of monitoring than the one used during the first year. Similarly, it is likely that support of exploration differs from before since the child has new means of learning, and it may become more challenging to balance infant–mother interaction with other tasks now that the infant is moving about. How attachment figures handle their rapidly changing infant and how able they are to establish and maintain smooth exchanges with him is likely to impact the quality of their attachment relationship (Posada et al., 1999; Posada et al., 2004).

Also, in view of the increasing importance of language as the infant develops, research on the interface of behavior and incipient language and representation is sorely needed as it is crucial to understand the basic structure of representations regarding attachment relationships. Similarly, we will be better equipped to grasp the organization of attachment internal working models by gathering information as to how caregivers support and help their infants understand and go about child–parent relationship issues in different ways; for example, how attachment figures and infants coconstruct interaction experiences and their meaning. Mother–infant interaction is a central mechanism in the developmental course of secure-base relationships and continues to be so later in infancy during the second year and beyond. This kind of research is necessary and validates Bowlby's insight and emphasis on real-life experience as a key factor to understand individual development in relationships.

Furthermore, questions remain about the continuity–discontinuity of attachment relationships, and about the integration of various attachment relationships and of attachment relationships with other domains of functioning (i.e., how attachment is influenced by and how it contributes to other developmental areas). Such questions cannot be well addressed until we gather information about how infants and their caregivers interact with each other, how they react when separated and when reunited, and how infants use caregivers as a secure base from which to explore during the latter part of infancy and hereafter.

Conclusions

Much has been learned about attachment relationships thanks to the framework offered by Bowlby and Ainsworth. Such a conceptual perspective has stimulated research and theoretical formulations that allow us to more clearly comprehend relationship phenomena at different points in the lifespan. At the same time, we need to view their propositions as an initial approach to account for a phenomenon that still requires much attention, even during infancy, to become a truly developmental theory. Of particular importance is the need to specify the details of these relationships during the later part of infancy and beyond. Much work has been done in consolidating many of Bowlby and Ainsworth's insights, in clarifying cognitive aspects implicated in attachment relationships (Bretherton, 1993; Bretherton, 2005; Bretherton, & Munholland, 2008; Main et al., 1985; H.S. Waters, Rodrigues, & Ridgeway, 1998; H. S. Waters & Waters, 2006), and in establishing a network of correlates. Yet, much empirical work remains to be completed before we attain a clear picture of the developmental course of attachment relationships after the first year of life. The ethological work that served Bowlby and Ainsworth so well has not been implemented and used fruitfully on a regular basis by the generations of attachment researchers that have followed them. The task at hand is enormous, as is Bowlby and Ainsworth's legacy.

Notes

1. We use the word mother to denote main caregivers, as women tend to be the principal caregiver for infants. Also, we use "he" to denote the infant to avoid awkward or unclear sentence constructions.
2. Recently, Posada, Kaloustian, Richmond, & Moreno (2007) have presented evidence for the validity of a new q-sort tool to describe caregiver's behavior in naturalistic settings in dyads with preschool-age children.

References

Abelson, R. P. (1985). A variance explanation paradox: When little is a lot. *Psychological Bulletin*, *97*, 129–133.

Ainsworth, M. D. S. (1963). The development of infant–mother interaction among the Ganda. In B. M. Foss (Ed.), *Determinants of infant behavior* (Vol. 2, pp. 67–104). London: Methuen.

Ainsworth, M. D. S. (1967). *Infancy in Uganda*. Baltimore: Johns Hopkins University Press.

Ainsworth, M. D. S. (1969). Object relations, dependency, and attachment: A theoretical review of the infant–mother relationship. *Child Development, 40*, 969–1025.

Ainsworth, M. D. S. (1991). Attachment and other affectional bonds across the life cycle. In C. Murray Parkes, J. Stevenson-Hinde, & P. Marris (Eds.), *Attachment across the life cycle*, pp. 33–49. London: Tavistock/Routledge.

Ainsworth, M. D. S., Bell, S. M., & Stayton D. F. (1974). Infant–mother attachment and social development: Socialization as a product of reciprocal responsiveness to signals. In M. P. M. Richards (Ed.), *The integration of a child into a social world* (pp. 99–135). New York: Cambridge University Press.

Ainsworth, M. D. S., Blehar, M. C., Waters, E., & Wall, S. (1978). *Patterns of attachment*. Hillsdale, NJ: Erlbaum.

Ainsworth, M. D. S., & Eichberg, C. G. (1991). Effects on infant–mother attachment of mother's unresolved loss of an attachment figure or other traumatic experience. In C. Murray Parkes, J. Stevenson-Hinde, & P. Marris (Eds.), *Attachment across the life cycle* (pp. 161–183). London: Tavistock/Routledge.

Ainsworth, M. D. S., & Marvin, R. S. (1995). On the shaping of attachment theory and research: An interview with Mary D. S. Ainsworth. In E. Waters, B. E. Vaughn, G. Posada, & K. Kondo-Ikemura (Eds.), Caregiving, cultural, and cognitive perspectives on secure-base behavior and working models. New growing points of attachment theory and research (pp. 3–21). *Monographs of the Society for Research in Child Development, 60*(2–3, Serial No. 244).

Ainsworth, M. D. S., & Wittig, B. A. (1969). Attachment and exploratory behavior of one-year-olds in a Strange Situation. In B. M. Foss (Ed.), *Determinants of Infant Behaviour IV*. London: Methuen; Baltimore: Johns Hopkins University Press.

Anderson, J. (1972). Attachment behavior out of doors. In N. G. Blurton-Jones (Ed.), *Ethological studies of child behavior* (pp. 199–215). London: Cambridge University Press.

Atkinson, L., Raval, V., Benoit, D., Poulton, L., Gleason, K., Goldberg, S., Pederson, D., Moran, G., Myhal, N., Zwiers, M., & Leung, E. (2005). On the relations between maternal state of mind and sensitivity in the prediction of infant attachment security. *Developmental Psychology, 41*, 42–53.

Belsky, J. (1999). Interactional and contextual determinants of attachment security. In J. Cassidy & P. R. Shaver (Eds.), *Handbook of attachment: Theory, research and clinical applications* (pp. 249–264). New York: Guilford Press.

Bowlby, J. (1946). *Forty-four juvenile thieves; their characters and home-life*. Oxford: Bailliere, Tindall & Cox.

Bowlby, J. (1949). The study and reduction of group tensions in the family. *Human Relations. 2*, 123–128.

Bowlby, J. (1958). The nature of a child's tie to his mother. *International Journal of Psychoanalysis, 39*, 350–373.

Bowlby, J. (1982). *Attachment and loss: Vol. I, Attachment*. New York: Basic Books.

Bowlby, J. (1988). *A Secure-base*. New York: Basic Books.

Bowlby, J., Robertson, J., & Rosenbluth, D. (1952). A two-year-old goes to the hospital. *The Psychoanalytic Study of the Child. 7*, 82–94.

Bretherton, I. (1985). Attachment theory: Retrospect and prospect. In I. Bretherton, & E. Waters (Eds.), Growing points of attachment theory and research (pp. 3–35). *Monographs of the Society for Research in Child Development, 50*(1–2, Serial No. 209).

Bretherton, I. (1992). The origins of attachment theory: John Bowlby and Mary Ainsworth. *Developmental Psychology, 28*, 759–775.

Bretherton, I. (1993). From dialogue to internal working models: The co-construction of self in relationships. In C. Nelson (Ed.), *The Minnesota Symposia on Child Psychology: Vol. 26. Memory and affect in development* (pp. 237–263). Hillsdale, NJ: Erlbaum.

Bretherton, I. (2005). In pursuit of the internal working model construct and its relevance to attachment relationships. In K. E. Grossmann, K. Grossmann, & E. Waters, (Eds.), *Attachment from infancy to adulthood: The major longitudinal studies* (pp. 13–47). New York: Guilford Press.

Bretherton, I., & Munholland, K. (2008). Internal working models in attachment relationships: A construct revisited. In J. Cassidy & P. Shaver (Eds.), *Handbook of attachment: Theory, research, & clinical applications* (2nd ed., pp. 102–130). New York: Guilford Press.

Chao, R. (2001). Integrating culture and attachment. *American Psychologist, 56,* 822–823.

Cohn, D. A. (1990). Child–mother attachment of six-year-olds and social competence at school. *Child Development, 61,* 152–162.

Cox, M. J., Owen, M. T., Henderson, V.K., & Margand, N. A. (1992). Prediction of infant–father and infant–mother attachment. *Developmental Psychology, 28,* 474–483.

Crowell, J. A., Fraley, R. C., & Shaver, P. R. (1999). Measurement of individual differences in adolescent and adult attachment. In J. Cassidy & P. R. Shaver (Eds.), *Handbook of Attachment: Theory, Research, and Clinical Applications* (pp. 434–465). New York: Guilford Press.

Cummings, E. M., & Davies, P. T. (2002). Effects of marital conflict on children: Recent advances and emerging themes: In process-oriented research. *Journal of Child Psychology and Psychiatry, 43,* 31–63.

De Wolff, M. S., & van IJzendoorn, M. H. (1997). Sensitivity and attachment: A meta-analysis on parental antecedents of infant attachment. *Child Development, 68,* 571–591.

Diener, M. L., Nievar, M. A., & Wright, C. (2003). Attachment security among mothers and their young children living in poverty: Associations with maternal, child, and contextual characteristics. *Merrill-Palmer Quarterly, 49,* 154–182.

Donovan, W. L., & Leavitt, L. A. (1989). Maternal self-efficacy and infant attachment: Integrating physiology, perceptions, and behavior. *Child Development, 60,* 460–472.

Easterbrooks, M. A., Biesecker, G., & Lyons-Ruth, K. (2000). Infancy predictors of emotional availability in middle childhood: The roles of attachment security and maternal depressive symptomatology. *Attachment and Human Development, 2,* 170–187.

Egeland, B., & Farber, E. A. (1984). Infant–mother attachment: Factors related to its development and changes over time. *Child Development, 55,* 753–771.

Elicker, J., Englund, M., & Sroufe, L. A. (1992). Predicting peer competence and peer relationships in childhood from early parent–child relationships. In R. D. Parke & G. W. Ladd (Eds.), *Family–peer relationships: Modes of linkage* (pp. 77–106). Hillsdale, NJ: Erlbaum.

Erickson, M. F., Sroufe, L. A., & Egeland, B. (1985). The relationship between quality of attachment and behavior problems in preschool in a high-risk sample. In I. Bretherton & E. Waters (Eds.), Growing points in attachment theory and research (pp. 147–197). *Monographs of the Society for Research in Child Development 50* (1–2, Serial No. 209).

Fonagy, P., Steele, H., & Steele, M. (1991). Maternal representations of attachment during pregnancy predict the organization of infant–mother attachment at one year of age. *Child Development, 62,* 5, 891–905.

Freud A., & Burlingham, D. T. (1943). *War and children.* New York: Medical War Books.

Frosch, C. A., Mangelsdorf, S. C., & McHale, J. L. (2000). Marital behavior and the security of preschooler–parent attachment relationships. *Journal of Family Psychology, 14,* 144–161.

George, C., Kaplan, N., & Main, M. (1984). *The adult attachment interview.* Unpublished manuscript, University of California, Berkeley.

George, C., & Solomon, J. (1999). Attachment and care giving. In J. Cassidy & P. R. Shaver (Eds.), *Handbook of attachment: Theory, research, and clinical applications* (pp. 649–670). New York: The Guilford Press.

Gjerde, P. (2001). Attachment, culture, and amae. *American Psychologist, 56*, 826–827.

Glober-Tippelt, G. S., & Huerkamp, M. (1998). Relationship change at the transition to parenthood and security of infant–mother attachment. *International Journal of Behavioral Development, 22*, 633–655.

Goldberg, W. A., & Easterbrooks, M. A. (1984). Role of marital quality in toddler development. *Developmental Psychology, 20*, 504–514.

Greenberg, M. T., Speltz, M. L., & DeKlyen, M. (1993). The role of attachment in the early development of disruptive behavior problems. *Development and Psychopathology, 5*(1–2), 191–213.

Grossmann, K., Grossmann, K. E., Spangler, G., Suess, G., & Unzner, L. (1985). Maternal sensitivity and newborns' orientation responses as related to quality of attachment in Northern Germany. In I. Bretherton & E. Waters (Eds.), Growing points of attachment theory and research (pp. 233–256). *Monographs of the Society for Research in Child Development, 50*(1–2, Serial No. 209).

Harlow, H. F. (1958). The nature of love. *American Psychologist. 13*, 673–685.

Harlow, H. F. (1961). The development of affectional patterns in infant monkeys. In B. M. Foss (Ed.), *Determinants of infant behavior I*. New York: Wiley.

Harlow, H. F., & Harlow, M. K. (1962). The effect of rearing conditions on behavior. *Bulletin of the Menninger Clinic, 26*, 213–224.

Harrison, L. J., & Ungerer, J. A. (2002). Maternal employment and infant–mother attachment security at 12 months post-partum. *Developmental Psychology, 38*, 758–773.

Howes, P., & Markman, H. J. (1989). Marital quality and child functioning: A longitudinal investigation. *Child Development, 60*, 5, 1044–1051.

Isabella, R., & Belsky, J. (1985). Marital change during the transition to parenthood and security of infant–parent attachment. *Journal of Family Issues, 6*, 505–522.

Izard, C. E., & Abe, J. A. (2004). Developmental changes in facial expressions of emotions in the strange situation during the second year of life. *Emotion, 4*, 251–265.

Kochanska, G., Aksan, N., & Carlson, J. J. (2005). Temperament, relationships, and young children's receptive cooperation with their parents. *Developmental Psychology, 41*, 648–660.

Kondo-Ikemura, K. (2001). Insufficient evidence. *American Psychologist, 56*, 825–826.

Levine, L. V., Tuber, S. B., Slade, H., & Ward, M. J. (1991). Mothers' mental representations and their relationship to mother–infant attachment. *Bulletin of the Menninger Clinic, 55*, 4, 454–469.

Lieberman, A. F. (1977). Preschoolers' competence with a peer: Relations with attachment and peer experience. *Child Development, 48*, 1277–1287.

Main, M., Kaplan, N., & Cassidy, J. (1985). Security in infancy, childhood, and adulthood: A move to the level of representation. In I. Bretherton & E. Waters (Eds.), Growing points of attachment theory and research (pp. 66–106). *Monographs of the Society for Research in Child Development, 50*(1–2, Serial No. 209).

Main, M., & Solomon, J. (1986). Discovery of a new, insecure disorganized/disoriented attachment pattern. In M. Yogman & T. B. Brazelton (Eds.), *Affective Development in Infancy* (pp. 95–124). Norwood, NJ: Ablex.

Main, M., & Solomon, J. (1990). Procedures for identifying infants as disorganized/disoriented during the Ainsworth Strange Situation. In M. T. Greenberg, D. Cicchetti, & E. M. Cummings (Eds.), *Attachment in the preschool years* (pp. 121–160). Chicago: University of Chicago Press.

Main, M., & Weston, D. R. (1981). The quality of the toddler's relationship to mother and to father: Related to conflict behavior and the readiness to establish new relationships. *Child Development, 52*, 932–940.

Matas, L., Arend, R. A., & Sroufe, L. A. (1978). Continuity of adaptation in the second year: The relation between quality of attachment and later competence. *Child Development, 49*, 547–556.

Moran, G., Pederson, D. R., Pettit, P., & Krupka, A. (1992). Maternal sensitivity and infant–mother attachment in a developmentally delayed sample. *Infant Behavior and Development, 15*, 427–442.

NIHCD Early Child Care Research Network (2006). Infant–mother attachment classification: Risk and protection in relations to changing maternal caregiving quality. *Developmental Psychology, 42*, 38–58.

Pastor, D. L. (1981). The quality of mother–infant attachment and its relationships to toddlers' initial sociability with peers. *Developmental Psychology, 17*, 326–335.

Pederson, D. R., Gleason, K. E., Moran, G., & Bento, S. (1998). Maternal attachment representations, maternal sensitivity, and the infant–mother attachment relationship. *Developmental Psychology, 34*, 925–933.

Pederson. D. R., & Moran, G. (1995). A categorical description of infant–mother relationships in the home and its relation to Q-sort measures of infant–mother interaction. In E. Waters, B. E. Vaughn, G. Posada, & K. Kondo-Ikemura (Eds.), Care giving, cultural, and cognitive perspectives on secure-base behavior and working models: New growing points of attachment theory and research (pp. 111 132). *Monographs of the Society for Research in Child Development, 60*(2–3, Serial No. 244).

Pederson, D. R., & Moran, G. (1996). Expressions of the attachment relationship outside of the strange situation. *Child Development, 67*, 915–927.

Pederson, D. R., Moran, G., Sitko, C., Campbell, K., Ghesquire, K., & Acton, H. (1990). Maternal sensitivity and the security of infant–mother attachment: A Q-sort study. *Child Development, 61*, 1974–1983.

Pianta, R. C., Sroufe, L. A., & Egeland, B. (1989). Continuity and discontinuity in maternal sensitivity at 6, 24, and 42 months in a high-risk sample. *Child Development, 60*, 481–487.

Posada, G., Carbonell, O. A., Alzate, G., & Plata, S. J. (2004). Through Colombian lenses: Ethnographic and conventional analyses of maternal care and their associations with secure base behavior. *Developmental Psychology, 40*, 323 333.

Posada, G., Kaloustian, G., Richmond, M., & Moreno, A. (2007). Maternal secure base support and preschoolers' secure base behavior in natural environments. *Journal of Attachment and Human Development, 4*, 393–411.

Posada, G., Gao, Y., Fang, W., Posada, R., Tascon, M., Schöelmerich, A., … Synnevaag, B. (1995). The secure-base phenomenon across cultures: Children's behavior, mothers' preferences, and experts' concepts. In E. Waters, B. Vaughn, G. Posada, and K. Kondo-Ikemura (Eds.), Care giving, cultural, and cognitive perspectives on secure-base behavior and working models: New growing points of attachment theory and research (pp. 27–48). *Monographs of the Society for Research in Child Development, 60*(2–3, Serial No. 244).

Posada, G., & Jacobs, A. (2001). Child–other attachment relationships and culture. *American Psychologist, 56*, 821–822.

Posada, G., Jacobs, A., Carbonell, O. A, Alzate, G., Bustamante, M. R., & Arenas, A. (1999). Maternal care and attachment security in ordinary and emergency contexts. *Developmental Psychology, 35*, 1379–1388.

Posada, G., Jacobs, A., Richmond, M., Carbonell, O. A., Alzate, G., Bustamante, M. R., & Quiceno, J. (2002). Maternal care giving and infant security in two cultures. *Developmental Psychology, 38*, 1, 67–78.

Raval, V., Goldberg, S., Atkinson, L., Benoit, D., Myhal, N., Poulton, L., & Zwiers, M. (2001). Maternal attachment, maternal responsiveness and infant attachment. *Infant Behavior & Development, 24,* 281–304.

Rothbaum, F., Weisz, J., Pott, M., Miyake, K., & Morelli, G. (2000). Attachment and culture. *American Psychologist, 55,* 1093–1104.

Rothbaum, F., Weisz, J., Pott, M., Miyake, K., & Morelli, G. (2001). Attachment and culture. *American Psychologist, 56,* 827–829.

Shaffer, H. R., & Emerson, P. E. (1964). The development of social attachments in infancy. *Monographs of the Society for Research in Child Development, 29*(Serial No. 94).

Smith, P. B., & Pederson, D. R. (1988). Maternal sensitivity and patterns of infant–mother attachment. *Child Development, 59,* 1097–1101.

Sroufe, L. A. (1983). Infant–caregiver attachment and patterns of adaptation in preschool: The roots of maladaptation and competence. In M. Perlmutter (Ed.), *Minnesota symposium in child psychology* (Vol. *16,* pp. 41–81). Hillsdale, NJ: Erlbaum.

Sroufe, L. A. (2002). From infant attachment to promotion of adolescent autonomy: Prospective, longitudinal data on the role of parents in development. In J. G. Borkowski, S. L. Ramey, M. Bristol-Power (Eds.), *Parenting and the Child's World* (pp. 187–202). Mahwah, NJ: Lawrence Erlbaum Associates.

Sroufe, L. A., Egeland, B., Carlson, E. A., & Collins, W. A. (2005). *The development of the person.* New York: Guilford Press.

Sroufe, L. A., Egeland, B., & Kreutzer, T. (1990). The fate of early experience following developmental change: Longitudinal approaches to individual adaptation in childhood. *Child Development, 61,* 1363–1373.

Stevenson-Hinde, J., & Shouldice, A. (1995). Maternal interactions and self-reports related to attachment classifications at 4.5 years. *Child Development, 66,* 583–596.

Symons, D., Clark, S., Isaksen, G., & Marshall, J. (1998). Stability of Q-sort attachment security from age two to five. *Infant Behavior and Development, 21,* 785–792.

Teti, D. M., & McGourty, S. (1996). Using mothers versus trained observers in assessing children's secure base behavior: Theoretical and methodological considerations. *Child Development, 67,* 597–605.

Thompson, R. A. (1998). Early sociopersonality development. In N. Eisenberg (Ed.), W. Damon (Series Ed.), *Handbook of child psychology: Vol. 3. Social, emotional, and personality development* (5th ed., pp. 25–104). New York: Wiley.

Thompson, R. A. (2000). The legacy of early attachments. *Child Development, 71,* 145–152.

Turner, P. J. (1991). Relations between attachment, gender, and behavior with peers in preschool. *Child Development, 62,* 1475–1488.

van IJzendoorn, M. H., Kranenburg, M. J., Zwart-Woudstra, H. A., van Busschbach, A. M., & Lambermon, M. W. (1991). Parental attachment and children's socio-emotional development: Some findings on the validity of the adult attachment interview in the Netherlands. *International Journal of Behavioral Development,* 375–394.

van IJzendoorn, M. H., & Sagi, A. (1999). Cross-Cultural patterns of attachment. In J. Cassidy, & P. R. Shaver (Eds.), *Handbook of Attachment* (pp. 713–734). New York: Guilford Press.

van IJzendoorn, M., & Sagi, A. (2001). Cultural blindness or selective inattention. *American Psychologist, 56,* 824–825.

van IJzendoorn, M. H., Vereijken, C. M., Bakermans-Kranenburg, M. J., & Riksen-Walraven, J. M. (2004). Assessing attachment security with the attachment q-sort: Meta-analytic evidence for the validity of the observer AQS. *Child Development, 75,* 1188–1213.

Vaughn, B., Egeland, B., Sroufe, A., & Waters, E. (1979). Individual differences in infant–mother attachment at twelve and eighteen months: Stability and change in families under stress. *Child Development, 50,* 971–975.

Vaughn, B. E., & Waters, E. (1990). Attachment behavior at home and in the laboratory: Q-sort observations and strange situation classifications of one-year-olds. *Child Development, 61,* 1965–1973.

Vereijken, C., Riksen-Walraven, J., & Kondo-Ikemura, K. (1997). Maternal sensitivity and infant attachment security in Japan: A longitudinal study. *International Journal of Behavioral Development, 21,* 35–49.

Vondra, J. I., Hommerding, K. D., & Shaw, D. S. (1999). Stability and change in infant attachment in a low income sample (pp. 119–144). *Monographs of the Society for Research in Child Development. 64*(3 Serial No. 258).

Ward, M. J., & Carlson, E. A. (1995). Associations among adult attachment representations, maternal sensitivity, and infant–mother attachment in a sample of adolescent mothers. *Child Development, 66,* 69–79.

Warren, S. L., Huston, L., Egeland, B., & Sroufe, L. A. (1997). Child and adolescent anxiety disorders and early attachment. *Journal of the Academy of Child and Adolescent Psychiatry, 36,* 637–644.

Waters, E. (1978). The stability of individual differences in infant–mother attachment. *Child Development, 49,* 483–494.

Waters, E. (1995). The attachment Q-set (version 3). In E. Waters, B. Vaughn, G. Posada, & K. Kondo-Ikemura (Eds.), Care giving, cultural, and cognitive perspectives on secure-base behavior and working models: New growing points of attachment theory and research (pp. 234–246). *Monographs of the Society for Research in Child Development, 60*(2–3, Serial No. 244).

Waters, E., & Cummings, E. M. (2000). A secure base from which to explore close relationships. *Child Development, 71,* 164–172.

Waters, E., & Deane K. (1985). Defining and assessing individual differences in attachment relationships: Q-methodology and the organization of behavior in infancy and early childhood. In I. Bretherton, & E. Waters (Eds.), Growing points of attachment theory and research (pp. 41–65), *Monographs of the Society for Research in Child Development, 50*(1–2, Serial No. 209).

Waters, E., Kondo-Ikemura, K., Posada, G., & Richters, J. E. (1991). Learning to love: Mechanisms and milestones. In M. R. Gunnar & L. A. Sroufe (Eds.), *Self processes and development. Minnesota symposia on child psychology* (Vol. 23, pp. 217–255). Hillsdale, NJ: Erlbaum.

Waters, E., Merrick, S., Treboux, D., Crowell, J., & Albersheim, L. (2000). Attachment security in infancy and early adulthood: A twenty-year longitudinal study. *Child Development, 71,* 684–689.

Waters, E., Posada, G., Crowell, J., & Lay, K. L. (1993). Is attachment theory ready to contribute to our understanding of disruptive behavior problems? *Development and Psychopathology, 5,* 215–224.

Waters, H. S., Rodrigues, L. M., & Ridgeway, D. (1998). Cognitive underpinnings of narrative attachment assessment. *Journal of Experimental Child Psychology, 71,* 211–234.

Waters E., & Valenzuela, M. (1999). Explaining disorganized attachment: Clues from research on mild-to-moderately undernourished children in Chile. In J. Solomon & C. George (Eds.), *Attachment Disorganization* (pp. 265–287). New York: Guildford Press.

Waters, H. S., & Waters, E. (2006). The attachment working models concept: Among other things, we build script-like representations of secure base experiences. *Attachment and Human Development, 8,* 185–197.

Waters, E., Wippman, J., & Sroufe, L. A. (1979). Attachment, positive affect, and competence in the peer group: Two studies in construct validation. *Child Development, 50,* 821–829.

Yarrow, L. J. (1963). Research in dimensions of early maternal care. *Merrill-Palmer Quarterly, 9,* 101–114.

17

Early Social Cognitive Skills at Play in Toddlers' Peer Interactions

Hildy Ross, Marcia Vickar, and Michal Perlman

Introduction

When infants and toddlers play with peers, they meet both social and social-cognitive challenges that are not present in other relationships; together they assume full responsibility for maintaining interaction, which they do not do with attentive adults, and they convey and understand the meanings that guide their play without benefit of language. Therefore, it is surprising that interest in the development of infant peer competence and early relationships has waxed and waned so dramatically over the decades. Foundational observational work began in the 1930s, under the careful hands of Charlotte Buhler (1933), Katherine Bridges (1933), Maria Maudry (Maudry & Nekula, 1939), and Mary Shirley (1933), which indicated that infants and toddlers showed early interest in peers. Dramatic increases in both cooperative and conflictual peer interaction toward the end of the second year of life were also noted. Such studies should have provided the impetus for continuing research, but few followed that lead in the decades ahead. Then a revival occurred beginning in the 1970s, with publications by Carol Eckerman (Eckerman, Whatley, & Kutz, 1975), Ned Mueller (Mueller & Lucus, 1975), Wanda Bronson (Bronson, 1975) and others. At that time the earlier work was rediscovered and built upon with observational studies that charted the gradual development of infant and toddler social skills. As we reviewed work on peer relationships, we found ourselves focused on findings from that time period; although some researchers continue to examine infant peer interactions (notably, Celia Brownell and Dale Hay), interest has, more generally, seemingly waned once more.

At the same time, developmental psychologists have turned attention to a set of infant and toddler social skills that could provide important links to analyzing early social abilities found in peer interaction. The current focus on (1) coordinated joint engagement; (2) sensitivity to the goals and intentions of others; (3) appreciating the similarity of self and others; and (4) motivation to engage others provides a set of interrelated constructs that has captured both theoretical and empirical attention in the current decade. By our reading, such concepts have a great deal to offer to the understanding of the development of social interaction, particularly in the second year of life. Moreover, toddlers' relationships with agemates could provide an important domain within which these developing social-cognitive skills are put into action. The social-cognitive skills that have been recently discovered are strikingly similar to those displayed with peers; however, direct evidence linking these domains is largely lacking. As we survey the evidence on cooperative play, prosocial behavior, conflict, and friendship in infant peer relationships, we draw attention to the ways in which four early social-cognitive skills are demonstrated.

Coordinated joint engagement

Trevarthen and Hubley (1978) coined the phrase "secondary intersubjectivity" to mark an early transition from an interest in others ("primary intersubjectivity") to a state of coordinated interest with others in an external topic. Behaviors such as looking where others look or point and pointing to direct others' attention characterize this new state of joint attention, and increasingly, children are able both to follow adults' pointing and to direct others' attention though their own pointing, giving and showing between 9 and 13 months (e.g., Carpender, Nagell, & Tomasello, 1998). Adamson and Bakeman (1984) directly observed infants' abilities to attend both to their social partners (either mothers or peers) and to the objects with which they and their partners were engaged. As might be expected, infants' active coordination of attention to others and objects was observed less frequently with peers than with mothers; however, the extent to which this could be attributed to an adults' attentive fostering of such states is unknown. What is more interesting is that changes in infants' abilities seemed to follow roughly the same timetables with both mothers and peers – gradual increases before 12 months, and more dramatic shifts between 12 and 15months of age.

Sensitivity to goals and intentions

The end of the first year of life also begins a transition in infants' sensitivity to the goals and intentions of others (Agnetta & Rochat, 2004; Gergely, Nadasdy, Csibra, & Bro, 1995). Baldwin and her colleagues have shown that infants perceive everyday human actions, such as reaching for and retrieving a towel from the floor, as a sequence of hierarchically organized goal-directed segments; a still-frame pause placed in the midst of an actor's goal attainment draws more attention from 10-month-olds than one that occurs after the completion of a goal or a subgoal in the sequence (Baldwin, Baird, Saylor, & Clark, 2001). Similarly, between 9 and 12 months of age, infants begin to distinguish purposeful from accidental actions and between the goals of specific adult actions; for example, toddlers wait less patiently for adults who tease them by purposefully withholding an attractive toy, than for those who appear to be unable to give it to them (Behne, Carpenter, & Tomasello, 2005). Most convincingly, 14-month-olds analyze adults' goals and selectively imitate actions in relation to those goals (Gergley, Bekkering, & Kiraly, 2002; Meltzoff, 1988). Eckerman and her colleagues (e.g., Eckerman & Didow, 1996) draw attention to the central importance of imitation for peer interaction and to toddlers' growing proficiency and enthusiasm for imitative play in the second year of life.

Similarities between self and others

Moore (2006) outlines important developments in toddlers' abilities to regard the self as an object from an outside perspective, and to simultaneously realize the subjectivity of others. Accordingly, toddlers come to recognize both self and other as agents that are at once independent and interdependent. Shared intentionality, it is argued, may be possible only when such distinctions are understood (Brownell & Kopp, 2007). Self–other mapping is also regarded as critical for imitation, where the similarity between perceptions of others' actions and the experience of one's own actions is required (Rogers & Williams, 2006). Asendorph and Baudonniere (1993) provided direct evidence of associations between self-awareness and synchrony with peers among 19-month-olds. In interaction with peers, toddlers also show evidence of understanding what belongs to self and other, and recognize the entitlement of owners and possessors when property disputes arise (Bakeman & Brownell, 1992; Conant, 1991). The mutual adherence to reciprocal rights of entitlement provides evidence of an additional domain in which parallels between self ("mine") and others ("yours") are demonstrated.

Motivation to engage other

Tomasello, Carpenter, Call, Behne, and Moll (2005) make explicit the role of the motivational element in toddlers' eagerness to engage in interaction with people. One source of evidence is found in children's active signaling to adults when game-like interaction is interrupted. Infants have been shown not only to engage actively in games with adult partners, but also to signal their desire for continued involvement when games are interrupted by the adult (Ross & Lollis, 1987; Warneken, Chen, & Tomasello, 2006). Infants as young as 9 months signal their desire for continuing involvement by vocalizing, alternating their gaze from toy to adult, or pointing. More explicit signals such as showing or giving the toy, and even taking the adult's turn and then waiting for continuing involvement increase in frequency up to 18 months, when most game interruptions include references to both the adult and the objects of common engagement (Ross & Lollis, 1987). Toddler peers also invent games to play with one another, and sometimes signal their desire for mutual involvement in ways that are similar to the actions toddlers use with adult play partners (Goldman & Ross, 1978; Ross, 1982a). It is also clear that infants are not equally likely to seek interaction with all other potential play partners; the motivation to engage others is importantly moderated by the emergence of specific relationships with others including early peer friendships (e.g., Howes, 1988; Ross & Lollis, 1989).

Within peer interaction, children are roughly equal in social skills and observations of their accomplishments can be attributed to the children themselves. Studying the social exchanges of very young children requires ingenuity and significant methodological rigor. In each of the sections that follow, we provide a detailed description of the methods and findings of at least one study as an example of how conclusions are drawn in the areas we cover.

Toddler–Peer Cooperative Play

With the resurgence of interest in early peer interaction, Carol Eckerman and colleagues (Eckerman et al., 1975) reestablished that young infants were interested in and capable of interacting with peers – even those they met for the first time. Infants between 10 months and 2 years, finding themselves in an unfamiliar toy-stocked playroom, played often with the toys, but also smiled, vocalized, and imitated their newly met peers. In 2-year-olds, social play with the peer exceeded children's interaction with their mothers and their solitary play with the toys. Eckerman et al. (1975, p. 48) point to the importance of "the integration of activities with toys and people during the second year of life." A second early observer of toddler peers, Ned Mueller, also assigned a seminal role to toys in bringing toddlers together and fostering their interest in one another. His observations were of a small playgroup of toddler boys who met twice weekly early in their second year of life (Mueller & Lucas, 1975; Mueller & Rich, 1976). Mueller noted that the toys, or, more specifically, what the children did with the toys, drew virtually the entire group of toddlers together to repeat the interesting actions of the peer and reproduce the effects of those actions on the toys. Later, these clusters of children provided the occasions for more coordinated, often raucous interaction. Imitation played a role from the earliest playgroup gatherings, and a small set of repeated games established themselves among the toddlers.

Early games with peers

Barbara Goldman and Hildy Ross extended the early work with a closer examination of toddler–peer games (Goldman & Ross, 1978; Ross, 1982a;). In games, each toddler has a role to play and interaction proceeds as the children repeat their roles, alternating turns with one another. The toddlers coordinated game roles in three different ways, role relations were equally: imitative; complementary (e.g., placing a block into one's own mouth; removing the block from the peer); or reciprocal (e.g., throwing and retrieving a ball, and then reversing those roles). Up to 60% of peer dyads, meeting for only 24 minutes, were able to use the toys available to them to create games to play together (Ross, 1982a). Moreover, toddlers who were well-acquainted with one another engaged more often in extended coordinated interactions than did those who met less regularly (Mueller & Brenner, 1977).

More interesting than the frequencies were the skills evident in the children who played games together. For a game to begin, both children had to signal and recognize that their actions constituted a game, with turns to be repeated and game actions serving primarily to further their mutual engagement. The toddlers indicated their interest in play when they first performed an action while the peer watched and then paused and looked toward the peer, waiting for a response. Toddlers responded to such overtures 42% of the time, and if a response did occur, the originator was likely to continue the play to a third turn (63% of the time), and responding remained above 70% for games of up to 10 turns (Ross, 1982a). Turn-alternation signals during the course of a game also indicated the children's motivation to continue the play. Children commonly looked to the peer and waited immobile once their own turn was completed, or alternated their gaze between the peer and the object featured in the game when peers delayed in taking their turns. Toddlers also vocalized, pointed, and sometimes verbally urged their partners on. In ball games children were observed to back away with arms extended, or to pat the floor between outstretched legs as they waited for the partner to return the ball to them. After prolonged waits, children would sometimes retake their own turns, and wait once more for the partner's reengagement (Goldman & Ross, 1978).

This work in the 1970s showed that toddlers were motivated to engage with peers, and demonstrated an early ability to coordinate their peer play and toy play. They appear to understand one another's intentions and sometimes explicitly signal their own goals of mutual play. The children regulated their interaction with peers in imitative, complementary, and reciprocal games that showed abilities to mutually coordinate their own actions with those of their agemates. Although complementary and reciprocal play would later become the hallmark of toddler–peer friendships (Howes, 1988), the study of imitation played a greater role in unfolding the development of toddler peer interaction.

Peer imitation

The very nature of imitation requires a partner to observe and to interact with, and the connections these mutual interactions can create make imitation a social device. While a great deal of infant interaction involves caregivers, young children are also involved in imitative exchanges with similar-aged peers. Eckerman and Didow (1996) examined the reciprocal imitations of nonverbal behavior between infant peers at intervals between 16 and 32 months. Overall, imitation increased as a function of age; however, a marked acceleration in the frequency and diversity of imitation occurred in nearly all of the pairs at some time between 16 and 28 months. This created an imitative pattern in their play with one another, and once an imitative pattern had emerged, other social activities increased, especially when the nonverbal imitations took the form of imitative games. Specifically, with the pattern of imitation in place, children were better able to coordinate behavior with one another, both topically and temporally, and to direct their peers' actions by requesting positive, and objecting to negative, behaviors. With explicit verbal directions, children both express their own goals for peer interaction and regulate each other's participation.

Using imitation, infants are able to gain the attention of their partners, engage them in an interaction lasting two or more turns, and direct their peer's behavior regarding their intentions for the interaction or game. Coordinating actions with others may be supported by developing abilities to share attention to objects and other's actions from the end of the first and into the second year of life (Eckerman, Davis, & Didow, 1989). Additionally the act of imitating another's actions allows for a connection with a peer and may facilitate further peer interactions to a greater degree than nonimitative actions would.

Toddlers also appear to have special status as effective models for both younger and aged-matched peers (Ryalls, Gul, & Ryalls, 2000). Ryalls et al. (2000) had 14-, 16-, and 18-month-olds observe either an adult or an agemate perform sequences of actions (e.g. putting a stuffed animal to bed). Toddlers were more likely to imitate their peers than the adult models, both immediately and after a one week delay. The greater similarity between peers could facilitate greater attention to the actions being performed. More than this, imitation is one of the most effective tools that toddlers have for coordinated activities with one another. In contrast, adults largely bear responsibility for maintaining adult–toddler interaction. Thus, toddlers may imitate their peers more readily than adults because imitation is a well-practiced means through which young children connect with one another.

Taking peer modeling one step further, Hanna and Meltzoff (1993) first trained a 14-month-old 'expert peer' to demonstrate actions with five novel toys to 14 to 18-month-old infants. In two other control conditions either the peer merely played with the novel objects, or an adult experimenter played with the child who was then shown the toys. After a five minute delay the infants with the peer model performed significantly more target actions with the novel objects than children in either of the control conditions. In two subsequent experiments using a similar procedure, children in the peer model condition outperformed the other children after delays of 48 hours in laboratory, home, and daycare settings. These findings suggest that children can not only imitate behavior produced by their peers but they can retain this information over a delay and generalize imitation across settings. Thus peer models are effective at gaining the attention of and engaging other children in their actions with objects.

In order to imitate, a child must recognize correspondences between the other's actions (her hand is waving) and their own bodies (this is my hand) and put them into action (my hand can wave). Essentially, imitation requires an understanding of the relation of self and other and of the correspondence between one's own action and the actions of another person (Meltzoff & Moore, 1999; Rogers & Pennington, 1991; see chapter 11 this volume). Asendorph and Baudonniere (1993) observed peer interactions of dyads who could either recognize themselves in a mirror or not. The authors found that imitative actions with peers occurred in those dyads that were able to recognize themselves but not in pairs without self-recognition abilities. The authors suggested that along with self-recognition comes the recognition of others as distinct individuals. Moreover, imitative interactions may help infants to recognize both the distinctions and relations between themselves and others. Additionally, Forman, Aksan, and Kochanska (2004) found a link between 14- and 35-month-old children's willingness to imitate and measures of conscience and empathy, again suggesting a relation between imitation and understanding others. Thus it appears that the development of self–other understanding may coincide with, or perhaps even support, imitative interactions with peers.

Overall imitation is an integral process in infancy coinciding with numerous other developmental abilities. With imitation, infants are able to initiate social interactions (through joint engagement) maintain social interactions (through imitative games, directing attention) and better understand their peer partner's intentions and similarities to the self. Although games and imitation have been studied most often, these are not the only way in which toddlers' positive interactions give evidence of mutual engagement and understanding. Peers also share with and comfort their agemates, and join forces to solve problems together.

Prosocial peer interactions

Very young children display prosocial behaviors that are intentional towards their peers. Chief among these are children's sharing and responsiveness to others' distress. Spontaneous sharing of food or objects with adults occurs as early as 8 to 12 months of age and 18-month-olds share with their parents, peers, and strangers (Rheingold, Hay, & West, 1976). Throughout the second year of life, children appear to share as a means of establishing contact with their peers, drawing attention to their own toys by offering or giving them to a peer, and requesting that peers share their own possessions. This suggests a motivation to engage with others in this prosocial way. Hay, Castle, Davies, Demetriou, and Stimson (1999) observed toddler friends playing at home. Sharing occurred in virtually all of the pairs, with children offering, giving, and adding objects to an array of toys that the peer was playing with more often than they took toys from one another. There was early evidence that 1-year-olds were more likely than 2-year-olds to share in response to a peer's desire for an object (Hay, Caplan, Castle, and Stimson, 1991); however, that finding may reflect occasions when the youngest children relinquished toys that their peers attempted to grab from them. Subsequent research suggested no age differences in sharing when peers expressed their interest in children's possessions by pointing or reaching towards them (Hay et al., 1999). Children's early understanding of the meaning of overt gestures that signal another person's desire for an object is probably one more step in the process of learning more generally about the mental state of desire and of the relation between desire and action (Harris, 2006). What does change with age is children's responsiveness to the resources that are available to them. Two-year-olds shared most often (and more than younger children in any context) when there were plenty of toys and identical toys available; 1-year-olds were not similarly "rational" in their decisions to share with others (Hay et al., 1991). Thus, 2-year-old children maximized their positive peer contact when the cost to them was minimal.

Sharing with peers is also associated with the children's later ability to recognize and respond to the distress of their friends (Hay et al., 1999). Sensitivity to a friend's distress is less frequently observed than sharing toys (Demetriou & Hay, 2004; Hay et al., 1999; Lamb & Zakhireh, 1997) and suggests complex skills including an understanding of others' emotions and intentions and the ability to understand others' reactions as they succeed or fail in achieving their own goals (Meltzoff, Gopnik, & Repacholi, 1999). Prior to the middle of the second year of life, infants recognize the distress of others, but respond largely by becoming distressed themselves (e.g., Zahn-Waxler, Radke-Yarrow, Wagner, & Chapman, 1992). Later, they are more active in offering comfort and help, probably reflecting a growing understanding that others' distress is different from their own and that they could take steps to alleviate it. However, toddlers do not necessarily use this knowledge to help their peers. Although toddlers' positive responses to the distress of their friends increases between 18 and 24 months, they also begin to differentiate their responses, at times responding sympathetically, but also frequently displaying negative behaviors towards distressed friends (Demetriou and Hay, 2004; Zahn-Waxler et al., 1992). Interestingly, toddlers are more responsive to the distress they cause their friends than to distress with other origins; however, they react both by offering comfort and help and by further aggravating the distress that they caused in the first place (Demetriou and Hay, 2004).

There is also evidence that context influences children's responsiveness to their peers' distress. In childcare settings children have been observed to respond relatively infrequently to peer distress. For example, Lamb and Zakhireh (1997) found that peers responded prosocially to only 3% of distress episodes they observed in daycare settings. In contrast, nearly half of toddlers observed interacting with a friend in their homes responded to peer distress by approaching, distracting, or offering comfort or assistance on at least one occasion (Demetriou & Hay, 2004; Hay et al., 1999). The relative indifference to peer distress in the group context may constitute an early form of diffusion of responsibility whereby children in childcare centers come to expect that others, particularly their caregivers, will comfort crying children.

Sharing, especially sharing when others need or request something from you, is both cooperative and sensitive to others' intentions. Sharing is a prosocial means of establishing joint attention to objects, but becomes more sensitive to the availability of resources over the second year. Comforting others in distress appears to be less frequent, with children seemingly deferring such responsibilities to others. Nonetheless, the transition from reacting with one's own distress to more active attempts to alleviate the distress of others, as well as children' sensitivity to their own actions as causes of another's distress, probably reflects children's growing differentiation between self and other.

Cooperative Problem Solving

The ability to coordinate activities with another and to solve problems together provides additional evidence of toddlers' social cognitive skills. Key among these are understanding the separation of self and other, knowledge of the desires, goals, and intentions of others and an ability to act upon these inferences about others. Celia Brownell and her colleagues have been instrumental in linking these social cognitive abilities to coordinated problem solving among young children (Brownell & Carriger, 1990; Brownell, Ramani, & Zerwas, 2006). In one study children were presented with a toy dog encased in a Plexiglas container (Brownell et al., 2006). Two handles, if pulled simultaneously by the two children, activated the dog. Pairs of children aged 19, 23, and 27 months were first trained on the task and then observed to see if they would coordinate their behavior toward a common goal or attempt to carry out the task without reference to the peer. Although the majority of children at each age were able to act jointly to activate the toy, the older pairs did so more frequently, and were more sensitive to the whereabouts and current interest of their peers. Indeed Brownell et al. (2006) concluded that the coordination achieved by the youngest group was coincidental, whereas that of the older children indicated their abilities to understand one another's intentions and to adopt and achieve joint goals in their interactions. This interpretation is supported by associations between the children's performance on this task and their abilities to establish joint attention with an adult (by following the direction of pointing), and linguistic indicators (pronoun and verb usage) of both self–other differentiation and of understanding goals. In an earlier study, the children's success on a similar peer cooperation task was associated with their imitative abilities with adult models (Brownell & Carriger, 1990). These direct associations provide strong support for the relationship between toddlers' social-cognitive achievements and their abilities to interact with their peers.

We would, however, quibble with the exact age placement of toddlers' abilities to adopt joint goals, favoring the view that 18- and 19-month-olds are able to do so, both in the cooperative tasks, and in other imitative and game-like situations. To establish that the 19-month-old coordinations were coincidental, Brownell and colleagues require a comparison with baseline probabilities (i.e., a direct comparison of the probability of pulling given that the peer was touching a handle with the probability of pulling when the peer was not doing so). Without this explicit comparison, our reading of the data is that the youngest children were coordinating their behavior with a peer, just not as fluently, frequently, or as skillfully as their slightly older counterparts. Furthermore, children in this age group are more likely to coordinate behavior with peers around goals of their own devising than around goals provided for them by a researcher in relation to the material at hand. In an earlier peer study (Ross, 1982a), toddlers of ages 15, 18, 21 and 24 months were successfully taught a set of complementary games that they could play with peers, and then brought together, with the game toys present. These children rarely played the games they were taught. Rather, they invented new game roles, signaled their partners to join in the play, and played games with one another. The 18-month-olds, in particular, played ball, put blocks on and off a child's chest, played peek-a-boo behind a chair, imitated actions with a mirror, put blocks into a pail or banged them together and so on. They were as adept as the older children in doing so; however, the 15-month-olds more rarely achieved the coordination required for peer games. The uniqueness and variety of game actions suggests that the coordination achieved was based on the children's sensitivity to one another's goals, and motivations to play together; the games were a means of doing so. In some sense, the goal of toddler–peer games is to play together, and the game roles provide a means of doing so; in the problem-solving tasks the goal is to activate a toy, and the means is the coordinated actions of the two children. This distinction might also be significant in explaining differences in toddlers' cooperation.

Toddler–Peer Conflict

Early conflict, like cooperative interaction, reflects transitions in toddlers' social-cognitive development. Importantly, in their conflict, as in more positive forms of interaction, toddlers coordinate attention to others and to their playthings, show understanding of intentions, and appear eager to interact with others. Only a minority of conflicts between young children involves the use of physical force or hostile aggression; rather, conflicting goals present a problem for young children – most commonly, antagonists want control of the same plaything at the same time. Opposition provides the basic structure of conflict (Emery, 1992; Ross & Conant, 1992), and an oppositional structure may facilitate, rather than impede, young children's abilities to respond to their peers' behavior as well as to read their apparent intentions.

The development of early conflict over possessions

Dale Hay and Hildy Ross (1982) identified conflicts in pairs of 21-month-old toddlers as occurring "when one child's actions are met with protest, resistance or retaliation" from another (p. 107). In laboratory observations over four consecutive days, nearly all toddlers engaged in conflict, but conflicts were brief and occupied less than 6% of the children's time together. Consistent with other studies, the vast majority of toddlers' fights involved toys (88% in this instance). Hay and Ross argued that toddler–peer conflict, despite its focus on access to property, is inherently social – that it involves patterned sequences of interaction, explicitly communicative gestures and speech, and both antecedents and consequences that are meaningfully related to the antagonists' social goals. More than half of the children's conflict moves involved some form of communication that indicated, though words or gestures, their interest in a toy held by the other. The majority of conflicts began communicatively and ended when one toddler wrested a toy from the other's possession. Indeed, the children's tugging and resisting was more powerful in ending a dispute in their favor when accompanied by speech that made their claims explicit. The toddlers' speech also was meaningfully related to their conflict roles: attackers clarified just what they wanted by naming the toy, defenders attempted to stop others' actions that were designed to take their possessions (protesting "no" or "don't"), and both laid claim to the legitimacy of their own entitlement (proclaiming the toy to be "mine"). Beyond this, the majority of children's object struggles betrayed other signs of interpersonal as well as object-related concerns. The toddlers struggled over toys when duplicates were available nearby and often showed limited interest in the spoils of their victories, turning attention instead to the next object that attracted the peer's interest.

Understanding the potential place of early conflict in toddlers' interactions with their peers led naturally to investigations that traced the early development of social conflict, that sought to understand the role of early conflict in infant and toddler relationships, and that examined links between conflicts in the early years and later development. Studies of infants in the first 9 months of life provide generally consistent evidence of the lack of interpersonal conflict in their early contacts with peers (Bridges, 1933; Eckerman et al., 1975; Hay, Nash & Pederson, 1983; Vandell, Wilson, & Buchanan, 1980). In a laboratory study of pairs of unacquainted 6-month-olds, Hay et al. (1983) report that the babies did touch toys that others were playing with, but they did not struggle with one another for possession. Indeed, Bridges (1933, p. 43) described 9- and 10-month-old babies as "indifferent" to peers' attempts to take their toys; according to her close observations of children who lived together in a Montreal foundling home, children take things from one another based on their momentary interest in the object, and "scarcely struggle at all for the possession of anything." Bridges' observations change quite dramatically within the next 2 months: By 11 to 12 months infants are described as being far more possessive about objects; they cry and struggle when others attempt to take things from them, and toys in the possession of others become more attractive to the 1-year-old. To what should we attribute the beginnings of property conflicts at the end of the first year? Infants show earlier separate interest in toys and in others, including peers; however, property conflicts do not begin until a time when they are also able to coordinate their engagement with others and objects of joint attention. Thus, it is tempting to regard conflicts over possessions as an early manifestation of secondary intersubjectivity, as indicated by infants' growing abilities to coordinate their social and nonsocial worlds in peer conflicts over objects.

Toddlers' conflicts with their agemates grow more frequent during the second year (Bridges, 1933; Bronson, 1981; Caplan, Vespo, Pederson, & Hay, 1991; Eckerman et al., 1975; Holmberg, 1980). Although access to objects continues to be the preponderant issue of contention, scarce resources do not lead to any greater likelihood of property disputes, providing further corroboration of the social nature of conflict throughout the second year (Caplan et al., 1991). Toddlers between 18 and 30 months also defend their own possessions in reaction to a friend's apparent intentions to take things from them; when a peer reaches or gestures toward things that a toddler possesses, most react by protesting or withdrawing the object prior to the peer's assault (Hay, Castle, & Davies, 2000; Ross, Lollis, & Elliott, 1982). The ability to interpret another's reaching toward an object you hold appears to be a clear manifestation of early abilities to understand and to act upon the intentions of another person.

Rules of entitlement in toddler conflict

Moral concerns and cultural rules are also apparent in nascent form as toddlers fight with their peers. This is most apparent with respect to early property disputes, where principles of ownership and possession constrain the children's actions and influence the outcomes of their conflicts. Property conflicts may also provide the basis for learning about rules of entitlement. Ownership is the central principle governing property, in that owners are entitled to possess and use their property, to exclude others from using their property, and to destroy their property or transfer ownership to others (Snare, 1972). In this sense ownership sets social priorities between individuals concerning control over things owned. Possessors also have rights, but these are generally more limited in scope and subordinate to the rights of owners. Possession rights, however, might be important for young children because possession is a visible, concrete state, whereas ownership is more abstract and must be inferred rather than directly observed (Friedman & Neary, 2008). Thus, it might be the case that understanding ownership derives from an earlier understanding of rights related to possession. As early as 6 months, when two babies are interested in and contact the same toy, the original possessors were more likely to retain than to cede it to their peers, in the virtual absence of conflict or distress (Hay et al.,

1983). The fact that this occurs in more than 70% of the episodes of mutual contact suggests the power of possession very early in life.

Toddlers who have had contact with a toy for a longer period of time are more likely to win object conflicts than those who have more recently picked up the toy (Bronson, 1981). Additionally, 18-month-olds are more likely to gain possession of another's toy if they themselves had the toy in their own possession earlier (Bakeman & Brownlee, 1982). Bakeman and Brownlee argue that winning may result both from children's accepting and respecting the rights of prior possession, or from the more vigorous assaults of earlier possessors within such struggles. They suggested that a more definitive assessment of children's accepting the property rights of others would come from evidence that the new possessor was less likely to resist the onslaught of the peer who wished to regain possession. Their original observations were of classrooms of toddlers (at 18 months) and preschoolers (who averaged 44 months) and, indeed, they found that preschoolers were less likely to resist the attempts of their peers to take objects from them if the assaults came from prior possessors; toddlers did not do so. Unfortunately, the very large age gap between the children in the two classes makes it impossible to determine when children accept the rights of others in such disputes, or to link this social accomplishment with the understanding of self and other that might underpin it. Despite the significance of Bakeman and Brownlee's original findings, subsequent research has not clarified the development and acceptance of rights of prior possession. It may be that the early abilities of infants and toddlers to retain possession when they either simultaneously contact or jointly struggle over objects leads to the development of mutually accepted rules governing rights of possessors.

Ownership rights are also evident in the conduct and outcomes of early conflicts (Conant, 1991). To establish "ownership," Conant had two mothers remove a toy from a gift box, and give it to their own 24-month-old child. After a short play period, the toys were replaced by new toys, given to the children in the same way. Other children had experience playing with the same four toys, two at a time, but they were not given by parents but rather placed on the floor of the playroom. Then all four toys were placed in the center of the room and the children played freely for 6 minutes. During free play, children whose ownership was established were less likely to play with the toys together than children who originally found the same toys placed on the floor of the playroom. When ownership was not established, children more often offered, reached for, or played jointly with the toys and they were more likely to have conflicts over the toys than owners. Furthermore, when conflicts did arise between children whose ownership was established, those who owned the particular toys were more likely to proclaim their ownership verbally ("mine" or "my toy"), regardless of who currently possessed the toy. They also won more conflicts over toys that they owned, again, regardless of who possessed the toy at the beginning of the dispute. Thus 2-year-olds, who had been given a "gift" along with those who witnessed a gift being given to another, behaved in ways consistent with the recognition of the entitlement conferred on owners. As with the observations of Bakeman and Brownlee (1982), these behavioral differences between owners and nonowners cannot be unambiguously attributed to either one. However, the fact that ownership had an impact on the joint behavior of the children regardless of who had an object before a dispute began indicates that 2-year-olds adopt principles similar to the cultural rules that give priority to ownership over possession.

Interestingly, toddlers' claims to property, which become fluent at 24 months, and increase in frequency to peak at 2.5 years, also include recognition of the entitlement rights of others (Hay, 2006). With the word "yours," they attribute ownership to their friends, and children who claim property as their own were also more likely to recognize the ownership of their friends, in that the frequency with which the children proclaimed their own ownership (saying "mine") was correlated with how often they acknowledged their peers' ownership (using "yours"). Furthermore, the use of personal pronouns was associated both with children's aggression (children claimed ownership as they grabbed things from their friends) and, more interestingly, with their inclination to share. Indeed, Hay (2006, p. 50) proposes that "the ability to think about what is 'mine' and 'yours' marks a very early step in the development of constructive approaches to the inevitable conflicts that occur between peers." Consistent with this, Conant's (1991) observations of less conflict between peers whose ownership is established than those who play with undesignated toys, suggests further that conflict might be avoided when children know who owns what. Toddler property rules take the ideas of self–other differentiation one step beyond what has so far been claimed: in the resolution of their property disputes children display evidence of their emerging understanding of the principles that differentiate the entitlement of self and the entitlement of others. The fact that such rights are reciprocal also evidences the similarity of self and other in their relations to property.

The good, the bad, and the ugly

While it is normative for 2-year-olds to take toys from their peers, or even to occasionally hit or kick them, it is rare for them to engage frequently in aggressive behavior (Calkins, Gill, Johnson, & Smith, 1999; Hay et al., 2000; Hay & Ross, 1982; Rubin, Hastings, Chen, Stewart, &, McNichol, 1998; NICHD ECCRN, 2004). Note, however, that conflict and personal aggression are related activities: Rubin et al. found a strong correlation between angry aggression and conflict initiation and Hay et al. found that personal aggression was related to defensive reactions to peers' attempts to take toys. At the same time, conflict is also associated with more positive peer interaction.

Caplan et al. (1991) report that a majority of toddlers' property conflicts occur in the context of immediately preceding positive interaction and that close to half are followed by children showing toys or cooperating in their use with peers. Moreover, recent evidence suggests that early in the second year of life, positive peer-directed behavior is associated with children's attempts to take things from their peers (Williams, Ontai, & Mastergeorge, 2007). Analyses of interaction observed in toddler groups identified three factors – sociability, peer refusal, and passive avoidance. Taking toys from peers loaded on the sociability factor along with smiles, imitation, play initiations, and responsiveness to the initiations of others. Thus children's early property conflict appears to be part and parcel of their desire to interact with peers. Parallel relationships are found in the third and fourth years of life. Children who engage in more sophisticated play involving complementary, reciprocal, and cooperative pretend at age 2.5 use instrumental aggression but less hostile aggression with peers than preschoolers (Howes & Matheson, 1992). Finally, toddlers' use of possessive pronouns to claim rights over their own property was correlated with the use of force in grabbing or assaulting friends and the use of force was associated with the children's sharing; however, associations over a 6-month period, to a time when children's talk to peers was more common, suggest that earlier use of "mine" predicted sharing but not further forceful conflict (Hay, 2006).

In contrast, children who are hostile and aggressive with peers tend to react angrily when their goals are frustrated (Calkins et al., 1999; Rubin, Burgess, Hastings, & Dwyer, 2003). They bang at barriers that prevent their reaching desirable toys and do not regulate their own emotional reactions by self-soothing or turning to their mothers in the way that other toddlers do when frustrated. Children whose aggression at age 2 years is low or moderate, tend to desist in their use of aggression with age; in contrast, those who are both aggressive and who lack abilities to regulate emotions as toddlers persist in their use of aggression with peers in the preschool years (Rubin et al., 2003); additionally, highly aggressive subgroups of toddlers are persistently aggressive into middle childhood (NICHD ECCRN, 2004). Thus, there are serious negative consequences for those easily frustrated and highly aggressive toddlers. High levels of personal aggression are also associated with toddlers' defensive actions when others reach for their toys (Hay et al., 2000). These children appear to recognize the intentions of their agemates, but their inability to regulate their own emotional reactions focuses their attention on their own goals. Their motivation to engage with peers is subordinated to their own unregulated desires. Aggressive toddlers may recognize peers' goals and intentions, but interpret others' actions as impediments to their own objectives in a way that is reminiscent of older aggressive boys who make unusually negative attributions for the behavior of their peers (Dodge & Frame, 1983; Dodge & Somberg, 1987). As third graders, highly aggressive toddlers have academic difficulties, are identified as having significant behavior problems, and experience poor relationships with parents, teachers, and agemates (NICHD ECCRN, 2004). Thus, whereas conflict may be normative for toddlers, and property conflict may serve as a means of establishing relationships with others, high levels of aggression and conflict may be early signs of persistent behavior problems.

Establishing Special Relationships with Peers

The social cognitive achievements of the first years of life are put to good use in the gradual development of competence in interacting with peers. However, it could be argued that even more is required of young children: that is, the formation of specific relationships with particular others. As Paul Harris (2006, p. 813) has argued in relation to 4-year-olds: "the child surely faces questions about what particular people are like as opposed to people in general – questions about the personality, skills and reliability of specific individuals." Decades of research on attachment clearly establish that specific relationships are formed with parents and that the qualities of parent–child interaction are related to the nature of the attachment. Additionally, some of the earliest peer work by Anna Freud detailed the extent to which children deprived of parenting by their wartime evacuation or by the deaths of their parents in the Holocaust developed strong and dependent relationships with their agemates (Freud & Burlingham, 1944; Freud & Dann, 1951). But, do infants and toddlers, reared in more normal circumstances, differentiate among their peers and, if so, do they forge specific relationships with agemates?

As infants and toddlers cannot nominate their friends or enemies, as older children do, researchers need to establish criteria for defining early peer relationships from the way children interact together. By our definition, relationships with others require emergent properties; children both engage in more interaction with specific others, and such preferences are not general (everyone does not choose the same friend); rather specific relationship qualities emerge from the joint interaction that cannot be fully accounted for by the positive or negative characteristics that these children commonly display with or elicit from others (Ross, Conant, Cheyne, & Alevizos, 1992).

With this approach, Ross et al. (1992) examined relationships in two groups of six kibbutz-reared toddlers. With approximately 40 hours of observation in each group, there were close to 1,300 initiations of peer interaction in total. From these data, differential relationships were identified for each child within both toddler groups; each had specific preferred partners and directed behavior more often to one or two others than to the remaining group members. Importantly, the relationships identified by this method were mutual; reciprocal rather than unilateral preferences were the rule.

The kibbutz children had spent nearly all of their days with one another from early infancy; however, preferential and reciprocal relationships also develop in toddlers who spend much less time together than is typical for children reared together in a kibbutz. Based on a Canadian sample, Ross and Lollis (1989) observed the gradual development, over time, of specific relationships between 20- or 30-month-olds. The children met with one another in pairs, alternating between each of their homes, in a way that might occur naturally when mothers decide to bring their toddlers together for what is now known as a "play date." Preferences were possible to determine because each child had two, rather than one peer partner, a minimal condition for determining if specific relationships are formed (Kenny & Lavoie, 1985). The four pairs within each group met 18 times over a 4-month period. The children's tendencies to initiate interaction were consistent across partners, but the extent to which their interactions continued once initiated were characteristic of each relationship. In this case, relationship effects were observed for episodes of positive interaction and for peer games. Relationships did not emerge all at once, but strong, consistent, and reciprocal preferences were found for both age groups in the second half of the play sessions. It appears that, with repeated interaction, children were better able to interpret the communicative and game overtures of their peers. With emerging preferences, toddlers moderated their general desires to engage with others, forming specific positive relationships selectively. Although relationships developed over time, time spent together did not account for the quality of relationships that the children formed with one another; peer relationships were distinctive, even though children spent the same amount of time with each partner as the study progressed. The positive qualities that defined these reciprocal relationships suggest that the toddlers were developing friendships with young agemates.

A more direct approach to studying children's earliest friendships comes from a remarkable set of studies by Carolee Howes (1983, 1988). Friends, by her definition, were children who responded to at least half of the overtures that they received from one another, who were observed in complementary or reciprocal games, and who shared at least one positive affective exchange. Friendships identified by these criteria were also verified by teachers' judgments. In her initial study, Howes observed two daycare groups, one with 7 infants and the other with 8 toddlers over a 1-year period. Multiplying these numbers out, there were 21 possible pairs in the infant group, and 28 among the toddlers, but friendships were selective at both ages. In the infant group, five of the seven children had at least one friend, and one child met the friendship criteria with two others. Once friendships were formed, they continued throughout the observations. Among the toddlers, 10 friendships were found, with all children having at least one friend, and 5 having two or more friends. In this case, 60% of the friendships persisted.

The selectiveness and stability of early friendships were found again in a much larger sample that continued daycare observations over a period of 3 years (Howes, 1988). Infants and toddlers were once again found to form friendships and to be discriminating in doing so. Within stable peer groups the vast majority of children who had been friends in their second year of life, remained friends 1 year later. Children did lose friends over the year, however, when peers moved to other centers and classrooms. Although children did make new friends over time, keeping and losing friends in this way had a serious impact on their social interaction with peers. Toddlers who kept a higher proportion of friendships into the preschool period engaged more readily in complementary and reciprocal interaction, cooperated in pretend play, entered the peer group more easily, and eventually received higher sociometric ratings from their peers. Children whose friends moved away engaged in less pretend play in the subsequent year and those whose friendships ended while the peer remained in the group were rated as more difficult and less social by their teachers. Thus there are large payoffs for children's very early friendships in terms of the possibilities for interaction with agemates, the development of competence in peer play, and peer acceptance. Children who remained in the peer group once their friends had departed were found to be less competent in their interaction with remaining peers in subsequent years, and those moving on to other centers were found to be more competent if they moved along with familiar children from their daycare groups.

Howes (1988, p. 57) explains that "for toddlers, experience with particular peers in stable peer groups facilitates mastery of social interaction skills . . . The presymbolic nature of toddler peer interaction appears to be dependent on peer familiarity. For toddlers, this requires many months of sustained contact . . . Toddlers are more dependent on idiosyncratic routines for play than are preschoolers, whose mastery of spoken or signed languages permits more general communication and play." This assessment is supported by evidence of the tendency of toddler pairs to repeat the same games and conflicts with one another (Mueller & Rich, 1976; Ross, 1982b) but not with other peer partners, with whom they develop other characteristic forms of interaction. These observations suggest that stable relationships enable preverbal toddlers to understand better the goals and interactive intentions of their agemates. We would also expect that coordinated peer interaction, especially in sustained relationships, highlights the similarity of one's own actions and desires to those of one's agemates, and so fosters the recognition of the subjectivity of others more effectively than does interaction with adults.

Conflict in peer friendships

Toddler friendships share many of the positive qualities that define friends at other ages, and, like later friendships, contain a mixture of competent positive engagement and conflict. Howes (1983, 1988), for example, integrated conflict behavior as part of her definition of friendship, in that children's responsiveness to both the positive and negative initiations of their peers was required for children to be identified as friends. She specified that a sequence of behavior in which a child hits a peer and takes her toy followed by a protest and hit from the victim is rated as complementary and reciprocal in much the same way as a sequence in which one child offers a toy to another who takes it and offers it back to the initiating peer (Howes, 1988). More pertinent, however, is the observation that friends more often took toys or aggressed against one another than did nonfriends, and that those children who would later cease to be friends were more aggressive with one another than those whose friendships remained intact (Howes, 1983). Among kibbutz toddler groups, where friendships were identified based on emergent preferences, dyadic relationships showed reciprocity in children's selectively initiating and engaging in conflict as well as playing positively with one another (Ross et al., 1992). Thus conflict was part of the more positive relationships children forged with their friends. It is likely that the mixture of conflict and positive engagement persists for some time in children's peer groups, as preschoolers also are most likely to fight with their friends (Green, 1933; Hartup, Laursen, Stewart, & Estenson, 1988; Hinde, Titmus, Eason, & Tamplin, 1985). In group settings friendships bring children together, and conflict arises more often as a result. At the same time, conflicts between preschool friends are more mitigated and less hostile (Hartup et al., 1988). As conflict ensues within children's valued relationships, it may be constrained by the positive feelings that prevail within the dyad, and the desire to continue to maintain positive relationships and joint engagement with those that the children like best. Such constraint is also likely to enhance the contribution of conflicts to the nexus of children's developing social skills.

Conclusions and Future Directions

Our conclusions tend toward hypotheses that build upon the two pillars of research in early peer engagement and recent activity concerning toddlers' emerging social-cognitive skills. Research and theory in both domains would benefit from links that could elucidate their relationships to one another. Here we suggest several directions for future research.

Coordinated joint engagement is seen in nearly every aspect of toddler peer interaction. Toddlers' imitation, sharing, games and conflicts involve interpersonal interactions that utilize toys and other objects in a variety of different ways. The emergence of these activities occurs close in time to infants' tested abilities for joint attention and coordinated engagement with others; however, empirical verification of the links between social-cognitive skills entailed in peer interaction are not well established. At the same time, the skills that toddlers show as they engage others in play present a broader array of potentially related manifestations of infant and toddler social abilities than have been examined in the more cognitive literature. Thus attention to early peer interaction could expand our understanding of the range and extent of social-cognitive abilities found in early life, and examining infant peer interaction in light of key social-cognitive abilities will contribute to our understanding of early peer interactions.

Children's emerging abilities to *understand others' goals and intentions* are also seen in early peer interaction. Objects are offered and withdrawn in response to peers' displayed interest, and games and imitative exchanges rest on understanding that others would like to play and to play in certain ways. Clearly some goals ("I want that toy you are holding") are easier to understand than others, and some children respond more willingly to what others want. Interesting links could be sought that focus on whether the communication and understanding of intentions develops in concert across various forms of peer interaction. The extent to which these are linked to developments in children's apprehension of others' internal states, most particularly their desires, should be examined.

Toddler social interaction with peers also illustrates their developing abilities to both *differentiate and relate self and other*. Mirror self-recognition shows understanding of self, but early pronoun use with peers indicates recognition of others as well. Children's property and property conflicts show more explicitly how self and other are coordinated, and early recognition that others have rights to what belongs to them is surely an advanced form of understanding priorities associated with self and others. As imitation is taken as a classic example of self–other differentiation and coordination, it would be useful to examine relationships between these domains in children's interactions with peers. Toddlers may be more likely to differentiate themselves from adults, but more likely to see the subjectivity of their peers.

Finally, children's *willingness to engage others* is recognized throughout the peer literature. It is perhaps surprising the number of studies that have challenged infants and toddlers to interact with total strangers and found them willing to do so. Importantly, the peer literature makes clear that infants and toddlers can also be selective in their sociability and that, within friendships, interaction is not only more frequent but also more sophisticated. Just as children's social-cognitive skills contribute to their abilities to interact with one another, stable friendships appear to impact children's social skills over time. These intriguing findings suggest that parents, childcare providers, and other adults who manage children's social experiences should pay closer attention to and support the friendships of very young children. Perhaps the practice in child care centers of moving children from one class to another based on their age needs to be reconsidered. Moving a cohort of children together may be advantageous because it would allow them to maintain their early friendships. Along similar lines, parents may be able to buffer the potential negative impact on their child of losing a friend in school by maintaining his or her contact with a child who has moved. Such an emphasis on friendships between 1- and 2-year-old children may be novel but it is supported by the limited existing research.

In sum, there is evidence that very young children engage in fairly complex social behaviors and are sensitive to a number of contextual factors (e.g., whether duplicate toys are available, familiarity with a peer and many others). Much remains to be studied about the quality, stability, and meaning of early peer interactions. However, it is clear that they are measurable and that they matter. Linking children's early behaviors with their cognitive underpinnings will be especially important in future research in this area.

References

Adamson, L. B., & Bakeman, R. (1984). Coordinating attention to people and objects in mother–child and child–peer interaction. *Child Development, 55*, 1278–1289.

Agnetta, B., & Rochat, P. (2004). Imitative games by 9-, 14-, and 18-month-old infants. *Infancy, 6*, 1–36.

Asendorph, J. B., & Baudonniere, P. (1993). Self-awareness and other-awareness: Mirror self-recognition and synchronic imitation among unfamiliar peers. *Developmental Psychology, 29*, 88–95.

Bakeman, R., & Brownlee, J. R. (1982). Social rules governing object conflicts in toddlers and preschoolers. In K. R. Rubin & H. S. Ross (Eds.), *Peer relationships and social skills in childhood* (pp. 99–112). New York: Springer-Verlag.

Baldwin, D. A., Baird, J. A., Saylor, M. A., & Clark, M. A. (2001). Infants parse dynamic action. *Child Development, 72*, 708–717.

Behne, T., Carpenter, M., & Tomasello, M. (2005). One-year-olds comprehend the communicative intentions behind gestures in a hiding game. *Developmental Science, 8*, 492–499.

Bridges, K. M. B. (1933). A study of social development in early infancy. *Child Development, 4*, 36–49.

Bronson, W. C. (1975). Developments in behavior with age mates during the second year of life. In M. Lewis & L. A. Rosenblum (Eds.), *Friendship and peer relations*. New York: Wiley.

Bronson, W. C. (1981). *Toddlers' behaviors with agemates: Issues of interaction, cognition, and affect.* Norton, NJ: Ablex.

Brownell, C. A., & Carriger, M. S. (1990). Changes in cooperation and self–other differentiation during the second year. *Child Development, 61*, 1164–1174.

Brownell, C. A., & Kopp, C. B. (2007). Transitions in toddler socioemotional development: Behavior, understanding and relationships, In C. A. Brownell & C. B. Kopp (Eds.), *Socioemotional development in the toddler years: Transitions and transformations* (pp. 1–39). New York: Guilford Press.

Brownell, C. A., Ramani, G. B., & Zerwas, S. (2006). Becoming a social partner with peers: Cooperation and social understanding in one- and two-year-olds. *Child Development, 77*, 803–821.

Buhler, C. (1933). The social behavior of children. In C. A. Murchison (Ed.), *A handbook of child psychology* (Vol. *1*, pp. 374–416). New York: Russell & Russell.

Calkins, S. D., Gill, K. L., Johnson, M. C., & Smith, C. L. (1999). Emotional reactivity and emotion regulation strategies as predictors of social behavior with peers during toddlerhood. *Social Development, 8*, 310–334.

Caplan, M., Vespo, J. E., Pederson, J., & Hay, D. F. (1991). Conflict and its resolution in small groups of one- and two-year-olds. *Child Development, 62*, 1513–1524.

Carpender, M., Nagell, K., & Tomasello, M. (1998). Social cognition, joint attention, and communicative competence from 9 to 15 months of age. *Monographs of the Society for Research in Child Development, 63*(4, Serial No. 255).

Conant, C. L. (1991). *The influence of toy ownership on toddler peer interaction*. Doctoral dissertation, University of Waterloo.

Demetriou, H., & Hay, D. F. (2004). Toddlers' reactions to the distress of familiar peers: The importance of context. *Infancy, 6*, 299–319.

Dodge, K. A., & Frame, C. L. (1983). Social cognitive biases and deficits in aggressive boys. *Child Development, 53*, 620–635.

Dodge, K. A., & Somberg, D. R. (1987). Hostile attributional biases among aggressive boys are exacerbated under conditions of threats to the self. *Child Development, 58*, 213–224.

Eckerman, C. O., Davis, C. C., & Didow, S. M. (1989). Toddlers' emerging ways of achieving social coordinations with a peer. *Child Development, 60*, 440–453.

Eckerman, C. O., & Didow, S. M. (1996). Nonverbal imitation and toddlers' mastery of verbal means of achieving coordinated action. *Developmental Psychology, 32*, 141–152.

Eckerman, C. O., Whately, J. L., & Kutz, S. L. (1975). Growth of social play with peers during the second year of life. *Developmental Psychology, 11*, 42–49.

Emery, R. E. (1992). Family conflicts and their developmental implications: A conceptual analysis of meanings for the structure of relationships. In C. U. Shantz and W. W. Hartup (Eds.), *Conflict in child and adolescent development* (pp. 270–298). Cambridge: Cambridge University Press.

Forman, D. R., Aksan, N., & Kochanska, G. (2004). Toddlers' responsive imitation predicts preschool-age conscience. *Psychological Science, 15*(10), 699–704.

Freud A., & Burlingham, D. (1944). *Infants without families*. New York: International University Press.

Freud, A., & Dann, S. (1951). An experiment in group upbringing. *The Psychoanalytic Study of the Child, 6*, 127–168.

Friedman, O., & Neary, K. R. (2008). Determining who owns what: Do children infer ownership from first possession? *Cognition, 107*, 829–849.

Gergely, G., Bekkering, H., & Kiraly, I. (2002). Rational imitation in preverbal infants. *Nature, 415*, 755–756.

Gergley, G., Nadasdy, Z., Csibra, G., & Bro, S. (1995). Taking the intentional stance at 12 months of age. *Cognition, 56*, 165–193.

Goldman, B. D. and Ross, H. S. (1978). Social skills in action: An analysis of early peer games. In J. Glick and A. Clarke-Stewart (Eds.), *Studies in social and cognitive development, Vol. 1. The development of social understanding* (pp. 177–212). New York: Gardner Press.

Green, E. H. (1933). Friendship and quarrels among preschool children. *Child Development, 4*, 237–252.

Hanna, E., & Meltzoff, A. N. (1993). Peer imitation by toddlers in laboratory, home, and day-care contexts: Implications for social learning and memory. *Developmental Psychology, 29*, 701–710.

Harris, P. L. (2006). Social cognition. In, D. Kuhn, R. S. Siegler, W. Damon, & R. M. Lerner (Eds.), *Handbook of child psychology: Vol 2, Cognition, perception, and language* (6th ed., pp. 811–858). Hoboken, NJ: Wiley.

Hartup, W. W., Laursen, B., Stewart, M. I., & Estenson, A. (1988). Conflict and the friendship relations of young children. *Child Development, 59*, 1590–1600.

Hay, D. F. (2006). Yours and mine: Toddlers' talk about possessions with familiar peers. *British Journal of Developmental Psychology, 24*, 39–52.

Hay, D. F., Caplan, M., Castle, J., & Stimson, C. A. (1991). Does sharing become increasingly "rational" in the second year of life? *Developmental Psychology, 27*, 987–994.

Hay, D. F., Castle, J., & Davies, L. (2000). Toddlers' use of force against familiar peers: A precursor of more serious aggression? *Child Development, 71*, 457–467.

Hay, D. F., Castle, J., Davies, L., Demetriou, H., & Stimson, C. A. (1999). Prosocial action in very early childhood. *Journal of Child Psychology and Psychiatry, 40*, 905–916.

Hay, D. F., Nash, A., & Pedersen, J. (1983). Interaction between six-month-old peers. *Child Development, 54,* 557–562.

Hay, D. F., & Ross, H. S. (1982). The social nature of early conflict. *Child Development, 53,* 105–113.

Hinde, R. A., Titmus, G., Eason, D., & Tamplin, A. (1985). Incidence of "friendships" and behavior with strong associates versus nonassociates in preschoolers. *Child Development, 54,* 1041–1053.

Holmberg, M. C. (1980). The development of social interchange patterns from 12 to 42 months. *Child Development, 51,* 448–456.

Howes, C. (1983). Patterns of friendship. *Child Development, 54,* 1041–1053.

Howes, C. H. (1988). Peer interaction among toddlers. *Monographs of the Society for Research in Child Development, 53*(1, 217).

Howes, C., & Matheson, C. C. (1992). Sequences in the development of competent play with peers: Social and social pretend play. *Developmental Psychology, 28,* 961–974.

Kenny, D. A., & Lavoie, L. (1985). The social relations model. In L. Berkowitz (Ed.), *Advances in experimental social psychology* (Vol. *19,* pp. 141–182). New York: Academic Press.

Lamb, S., & Zakhireh, B. (1997). Toddlers' attention to the distress of peers in the daycare setting. *Early Education and Development, 8*(2), 105–118.

Maudry, M., & Nekula, M. (1939). Social relations between children of the same age during the first two years of life. *Journal of Genetic Psychology, 54,* 193–215.

Meltzoff, A. N. (1988). Infant imitation after a 1-week delay: Long-term memory for novel acts and multiple stimuli. *Developmental Psychology, 24,* 470–476.

Meltzoff, A. N., Gopnik, A., & Repacholi, B. M. (1999). Toddlers' understanding of intentions, desires and emotions: Explorations of the dark ages. In P. D. Zelazo, J. W. Astington, & D. R. Olsen (Eds.). *Developing theories of intention: Social understanding and self control* (pp. 17–41). Mahwah, NJ: Erlbaum.

Meltzoff, A. N., & Moore, M. K. (1999). Persons and representation: Why infant imitation is important for theories of human development. In J. Nadel & G. Butterworth (Eds.), *Imitation in Infancy,* (pp. 9–35). Cambridge: Cambridge University Press.

Moore, C. (2006). *The development of commonsense psychology.* Mahwah, NJ: Erlbaum.

Mueller, E., & Brenner, J. (1977). The origins of social skills and interaction among playgroup toddlers. *Child Development, 48,* 854–861.

Mueller, E., & Lucus, J. A. (1975). A developmental analysis of peer interaction among toddlers. In M. Lewis & L. Rosenblum (Eds.), *Friendship and peer relations* (pp. 223–257). New York: Wiley.

Mueller, E., & Rich, A. (1976). Clustering and socially directed behaviours in a playgroup of one-year-old boys. *Journal of Child Psychology and Psychiatry, 17,* 315–322.

NICHD ECCRN (2004). Trajectories of physical aggression from toddlerhood to middle child-hood. *Monographs of the Society for Research in Child Development, 69*(4, 278).

Rheingold, H. L., Hay, D. F., & West, M. J. (1976). Sharing in the second year of life. *Child Development, 47,* 1148–1158.

Rogers, S. J., & Pennington, B. F. (1991). A theoretical approach to the deficits in infantile autism. *Development and Psychopathology, 107,* 147–161.

Rogers, S. J., & Williams, J. H. G. (Eds.). (2006). *Imitation and the social mind.* New York: Guilford Press.

Ross, H. S. (1982a). The establishment of social games among toddlers. *Developmental Psychology, 18,* 509–518.

Ross, H. S. (1982b). Toddler peer relations: Differentiation of games and conflicts. *Canadian Journal of Behavioural Science, 14,* 364–379.

Ross, H. S., & Conant, C. L. (1992). The social structure of early conflict: Interaction, relationships, and alliances. In C. Shantz & W. W. Hartup (Eds.), *Conflict in child and adolescent development* (pp. 153–185). Cambridge: Cambridge University Press.

Ross, H. S., Conant, C. L., Cheyne, J. A., and Alevizos, E. (1992). Relationships and alliance among kibbutz-reared toddlers. *Social Development, 1,* 1–13.

Ross, H. S., and Lollis, S. P. (1987). Communication within infant social games. *Developmental Psychology, 23,* 241–248.

Ross, H. S., and Lollis, S. P. (1989). A social relations analysis of toddler peer relationships. *Child Development, 60,* 1082–1091.

Ross, H. S., Lollis, S. P., & Elliott, C. (1982). Toddler–peer communication. In K. H. Rubin and H. S. Ross (Eds.), *Peer relationships and social skills in childhood* (pp. 73–98). New York: Springer-Verlag.

Rubin, K. H., Burgess, K. B., Hastings, P. D., & Dwyer, K. M. (2003). Predicting preschoolers' externalizing behaviors from toddler temperament, conflict, and maternal negativity. *Developmental Psychology, 39,* 164–176.

Rubin, K. H., Hastings, P., Chen, X., Stewart, S., & McNichol, K. (1998). Intrapersonal and maternal correlates of aggression, conflicts, and externalizing problems in toddlers. *Child Development, 69,* 1614–1629.

Ryalls, B. O., Gul, R. E., & Ryalls, K. R. (2000). Infant imitation of peer and adult models: Evidence for a peer model advantage. *Merrill-Palmer Quarterly, 46,* 188–202.

Shirley, M. (1933). *The first two years: A study of twenty five babies* (Vol. 11). Minneapolis: University of Minnesota Press.

Snare, F. (1972). The concept of property. *American Philosophical Quarterly, 9,* 200–206.

Tomasello, M., Carpenter, M., Call, J., Behne, T., & Moll, H. (2005). Understanding and sharing intentions: The origins of cultural cognition. *Behavioral and Brain Sciences, 28,* 675–735.

Trevarthen, C., & Hubley, P. (1978). Secondary intersubjectivity: Confidence, confiding and acts of meaning in the first year. In A. Lock (Ed.), *Action, gesture, and symbol* (pp. 183–229). London: Academic Press.

Vandell, D. L., Wilson, K. S., & Buchanan, N. R. (1980). Peer interaction in the first year of life: An examination of its structure, content, and sensitivity to toys. *Child Development, 51,* 481–488.

Warneken, F., Chen, F., & Tomasello, M. (2006). Cooperative activities in young children and chimpanzees. *Child Development, 77,* 640–663.

Williams, S. T., Ontai, L. L., & Mastergeorge, A. M. (2007). Reformulating infant and toddler social competence with peers. *Infant Behavior and Development, 30,* 353–365.

Zahn-Waxler, C., Radke-Yarrow, M., Wagner, E., & Chapman, M. (1992). Development of concern for others. *Developmental Psychology, 28,* 126–136.

18

Touch and Physical Contact during Infancy: Discovering the Richness of the Forgotten Sense

Dale M. Stack

it has always fascinated me that two of the earliest sensory experiences in fetal development, touch and pain, are also the experiences that help us stay in contact with life until life ends. (Fanslow, 1984, p. 183)

Overview

The primary goals of this chapter are to provide a detailed overview of the research regarding touch and development, and to bring the reader up to date with the current status of the field and important directions since the first edition of this handbook. The emphasis will be on touch as it occurs in a social context; between an infant and another person, usually the caregiver. It is important to note that in most of the literature reviewed it is the mother who is the participant; there have been fewer studies conducted with fathers to date. One objective of the present chapter is to underscore the importance of parental (particularly maternal) touch in early social and emotional development, specifically focusing on its role(s) in social contexts and communication. The goal is to provide evidence for the contributions of parental/adult touch to early interactions and the developing relationship, and to highlight the role of infant touch that has emerged in recent research. Although it is important to note that these contributions extend into cognition and perception by providing the context within which to practice and learn new skills, a discussion of these domains is beyond the scope of the chapter. Studies that bear on the contributions of parental, adult, and infant touch to early interactions and the developing relationship, and how touch is used in different ways depending on the interactive context or modalities of communication available to parents, are summarized. A second objective is to draw together some of the diverse lines of research on touch and physical contact and integrate these findings into an emerging body of literature underscoring the importance of touch and physical contact and, simultaneously, pointing to emerging directions of investigation. Emphasis is placed on the first year of the healthy, typically developing infant's life. Special attention is given to the first 6 months because it is well researched, and dyadic communication and face-to-face interactions are prominent during this period.

The parent–infant relationship is the first relationship to develop for the infant. It provides the building blocks for socio-emotional development and future relationships, and is a primary means to communicate, teach, and learn. Parent–infant interactions are a central context for the developing relationship to grow and are important in and of themselves. Early interactions reveal information about infants' social communication (e.g., Kaye, 1982), regulatory responses (e.g., Field, Vega-Lahr, Scafidi, & Goldstein, 1986), and development of social expectations (e.g., Cohn & Tronick, 1983), among other domains. Nonverbal communication is particularly important given that infants are largely preverbal before 12 months of age. Contact behaviors such as touch have been found to be integral features of emotional communication between mothers and infants, and higher levels of touch are related to secure positive attachment (Ainsworth, Blehar, Waters, & Wall, 1978; Bowlby, 1969). Early contact also aids in helping infants regulate their emotions. Consequently, there are essential roles for physical contact, touching, and gesture, as critical means of communication (Stack, 2001, 2004; Hertenstein, Verkamp, Kerestes, & Holmes, 2006) and in the organization and expression of emotions. Emotional displays are also among the first cues used by infants to make sense of human actions. Social communication and the regulation of emotion experiences are two adaptive functions of emotion expressions that are covered in this chapter. Notably, the role that parents play is an important one: parents are able to interpret their infants' behavior and attribute meaning to it, providing the basis for communication to unfold, and as Papousek (2007) contends, this implicit communicative competence is remarkable.

Since the publication of the prior volume of the *Blackwell Handbook of Infant Development*, research in the area of touch during infancy has grown. Significant progress has been made in animal models and mechanisms for handling effects, benefits of massage for human infants, understanding the mechanisms and functions of touch, defining and extending the role(s) that touch plays, and discovering more about parental touch with infants, at different ages and under different contexts. Touch is also included more in interaction studies and even studied on its own. While still sparse, we see the beginnings of investigations of infant touch and the relationship of touching behaviors to other modalities, as well as direct and indirect links from touch to other domains of development.

Importance of Touch

The somaesthetic system (kinesthetic and cutaneous processes) is the earliest sensory system to develop in the human embryo (Maurer & Maurer, 1988; Montagu, 1971), followed by the vestibular, auditory, and visual systems (Gottlieb, 1983). Given that the skin is the largest sensory system in the body, the fact that its capacities are among the most basic, and the fact that this system matures early, it seems reasonable to expect that the somaesthetic system plays a fundamental role in development. Somesthesis collectively includes kinesthetic sensitivity, referring to spatial position and movement information derived from mechanical stimulation of the muscles and joints, and cutaneous sensitivity, referring to the sensitivity of the skin to touch, pressure, temperature, or pain (Klatzky & Lederman, 1987; Schiffman, 1982). For purposes of the current chapter, the emphasis is on cutaneous sensitivity, specifically the infant's sensitivity and responsivity to human touching. However, because it is difficult to separate the tactile from the kinesthetic component, the use of the term "touch" refers to both components. Along with its early developmental timing, it is known that fetuses respond to vibroacoustic stimulation while developing in the womb (e.g., Kisilevsky, Fearon, & Muir, 1998; Kisilevsky & Low, 1998; Kisilevsky, Muir, & Low, 1992; Lecanuet, Fifer, Krasnegor, & Smotherman, 1995; Lecanuet, Granier-Deferre, & Bushnel, 1989), that touch/pressure is one of the first sensations newborns experience (e.g., Maurer & Maurer, 1988; Schiffman, 1982), and that infants use touch or "haptics" to explore objects manually and orally (Bushnell & Boudreau, 1991; Stack & Tsonis, 1999; Hernandez-Reif, Field & Diego, 2004).

Although the size of the system and its early development suggest a system of fundamental importance, the volume of research specifically associated with the tactile modality remains rather scant and diverse, albeit growing. This growth is reflected in the fact that the importance of touch with infants has been given more research attention in scientific journals and in book volumes (e.g., Field, 1995; Field, 2004; Stack, 2001, 2004), in early childhood education (e.g., Caulfield, 2001), and its importance has reached the popular press literature, evidenced by a number of books on the early years (e.g., Brazelton, 1994), touching (e.g., Field, 2001; Heller, 1997) and infant massage (e.g., McClure, 1989; Kluck-Ebbin, 2004). The importance of touch also extends to nonhuman species.

Importance of touch for nonhuman species

Evidence for the importance of tactile stimulation for normal development of nonhuman species is well established. Harlow's (1959) classic work with rhesus monkeys demonstrated that contact was more important than reducing the feeding drive for the development of social attachment. Other examples of the importance of tactile stimulation include the survival functions of maternal washing of the young (Montagu, 1971) and the specific beneficial effects of handling on survival (Hamnett, 1921, 1922), growth, development, and resistance to disease (Denenberg, 1968), as well as increased activity and exploratory behavior (Denenberg, 1969; Levine, Haltmeyer, & Karas, 1967). Neonatal handling in rats has been shown to lead to a number of changes in central nervous system (CNS) reward systems; those systems involved in pleasure, reward, feeding, and response to stress (Silveira, Portella, Clemente, Gamaro, & Dalmaz, 2005).

Tactile stimulation has also been shown to play a role in the development of affiliative behaviors, along with social stimulation from littermates and odor from the nest (Melo et al., 2006). Moreover, external tactile stimulation in newborn rat pups has been demonstrated to have long-term beneficial effects on adult spatial working memory (Zhang & Cai, 2008).

Research with rat pups has shown that a mother's licking and grooming of her pup regulates its growth (Kuhn & Schanberg, 1998; Schanberg & Field, 1987). Hofer (1993) has investigated this important regulatory function in his work on separation and its effects. He demonstrated that the mother regulates her infant rat pup's physiology and behavior, and that there is a sensory foundation to the mother–infant bond. J. M. Stern (1989, 1990, 1996, 1997) contends that rat pups impel their mothers to nurture them, largely in the form of tactile stimulation. Schanberg and colleagues (e.g., Kuhn & Schanberg, 1998) have shown that maternal separation, even for just one hour, produces a decrease in the enzyme ornithine decarboxylase, an enzyme necessary for growth. They have also shown that this change is directly related to the lack of a specific form of tactile stimulation enacted on the pup by the mother, maternal licking (Schanberg & Field, 1987). Recently, Kaffman and Meaney (2007) in their review demonstrated that during a critical period of development in rodents (namely the first week of life), the frequency of licking and grooming by the mother plays an important role in shaping neurodevelopment, and there is evidence for these changes to persist and to be lifelong. However, not only does handling render physiological changes to the pup but it also modifies maternal care (e.g., once reunited with pups, sustained increases in licking, grooming, and arched-back nursing are demonstrated), making it difficult to know which one or both is responsible for the effects of handling and their sequelae. According to Kaffman and Meaney, while there is still research to be done, increasing evidence supports the possibility that it is changes in maternal tactile stimulation during the first week of the rat pup's life that mediate the long-term consequences of handling.

Studies such as those above underscore the importance of parental care and parent–infant interactions even in rat pups and provide unequivocal evidence for the importance of tactile stimulation. Results from primate and rodent models have also implicated physical contact and touch (tactile stimulation) as significant concomitants of the infant's ability to regulate its own responses to stress (Levine, 1956, 1960; Levine & Stanton, 1990), and maternal behavior and proximity are considered the most important regulatory factors (Levine, 1994). Moreover, the dopamine system can be changed with tactile stimulation; that is, the increased locomotor activity in response to amphetamine can be reversed by tactile stimulation in artificially reared rats (Lovic, Fleming, & Fletcher, 2006).

Research with primates adds to the growing literature underscoring the importance of touch. For example, rhesus monkeys spend their first month of life in physical contact or proximal contact with their mothers, and subsequently use their mothers as secure bases to explore and interact, developing complex social networks over time (Suomi, 2005, 2006). Chimpanzee mothers have been shown to cradle their infants 66% of the time and more cradling was shown in 1-month-olds (approx. 80%) versus 2- and 3-month-olds (Bard et al., 2005). Moreover, investigations of nonverbal communication in nonhuman primates such as the rhesus monkey reveal that tactile stimulation is at the root of such activities as grooming, play, and sexual and aggressive episodes, continuing in the form of rough-and-tumble play (Suomi, 1997).

Importance of touch for human infants

Touch is of central importance to human infants. Just as in animal and rodent models (e.g., Weller & Feldman, 2003; Liu et al., 1997), maternal separation has been shown to have adverse effects and negative sequelae, however touch and contact (i.e., handling) can alter the adverse effects during periods of maternal separation, and positively impact emotion regulatory abilities. Observations on maternal deprivation of human infants and the lack of tactile stimulation also underscored the value of tactile contact (Provence & Lipton, 1962; Spitz & Wolf, 1946). In these classic studies, there were reports of catastrophic effects on infants who were deprived of mothering for lengthy periods of time and institutionalized infants who were only given the essential care with no extra attention from staff (Provence & Lipton, 1962; Spitz & Wolf, 1946). This work, at least in part, led to more systematic work on maternal attachment, bonding, and deprivation. For example, physical and social stimulation, in addition to nutrition, were noted as key determinants of development in Ames' (1997) study on children from Romanian orphanages adopted to Canada; these were noted to be in short supply in these orphanages and there was minimal interaction with adults or between children.

Owing to methodological limitations, results from past studies cannot answer the question of the necessity of touch for optimal development of the human organism. However, results from many studies have led researchers to advocate that tactile stimulation is essential to psychological and physical health (e.g., Frank, 1957; Jones & Yarbrough, 1985; Montagu, 1986). Research in the last 10 years (e.g., Field, 2002; Rutter & English and Romanian Adoptees Study Team, 1998) is indicative that in extreme forms limited touch affects children's growth and development, and there is an accumulating literature on massage that implicates touch in benefits for infant growth. Moreover, Hofer (2006) argues that there are hidden regulators and psychobiological roots that underlie attachment and explain the stressful nature of early maternal separation, with implications for long-term effects on development across the lifespan.

Despite advances and the acknowledged importance of tactile stimulation, the specific contribution of tactile stimulation to early development (e.g., first year of life) remains relatively undefined. There is evidence to suggest that touch is involved in regulation (e.g., Brazelton, 1990; Montagu, 1986) and soothing (Birns, Blank, & Bridger, 1966; Korner & Thoman, 1972; Byrne & Horowitz, 1981), control of arousal (behavioral state, i.e., maintaining alertness, reducing drowsiness etc.), modulating the overall level of stimulation (Koester, Papousek, & Papousek, 1989) and inducing changes in behavioral state (e.g., Barrera & Maurer, 1981; Muir & Field, 1979), as well as communication and exploration (see below).

Past studies of tactile stimulation have focused, to a large extent, on its potential for aiding the physical or perceptual development of high-risk infants. Recently, we have seen increased attention to touching in the social sphere in both typically developing and high-risk infants, its role in regulation and communication, and understanding the mechanisms for touch effects.

Physical Contact between Parent and Newborn: The Benefits of Touch

The socialization of human newborns and their parents, that first relationship, begins early, even in the womb. Physical contact between parent(s) and their newborn, immediately following the birth as well as several months later, has received some research attention. Beyond its survival value, contact and affection between mother and infant are likely to serve the infant's developing social and emotional needs. One aspect of research on the role of maternal contact with her newborn has examined whether there are commonalities in how mothers touch their newborns (e.g., Carlsson et al., 1978; de Chateau, 1976; Klaus, Kennell, Plumb, & Zuelke, 1970; Rubin, 1963; Trevathan, 1981). For example, Rubin reported that mothers follow a specific pattern of touching when first handling their newborns, beginning by using their fingertips then full palms to examine first the infant's extremities, and then the trunk. Klaus et al. not only confirmed Rubin's findings but also found that mothers of preterm infants follow the same pattern, but at a slower rate. Fathers have also been shown to display this pattern of touching (Yogman, 1982), although they take longer to show the progression. In contrast, Trevathan disputes the argument favoring a species-typical pattern of touching, as she found no evidence of an invariant pattern of maternal tactile behavior. Consistent with Trevathan, Tulman (1985) compared mothers and unfamiliar nursing students' initial handling of newborns; she found differences between the groups but it was the students rather than the mothers who followed the typical pattern reported in the literature.

Kaitz and colleagues (Kaitz, Lapidot, Bronner, & Eidelman, 1992; Kaitz, Meirov, Landman, & Eidelman, 1993) demonstrated that mothers are uniquely sensitive to their newborns through the tactile sense. They were able to show that mothers could recognize their own baby between 5 and 79 hours after delivery by stroking the dorsal surface of their infant's hand, and this was without the added benefit of visual, auditory, or olfactory cues. Their findings suggest that mothers learn the special tactile characteristics of their infant during the course of routine contact and interaction.

Observations of parents' first contacts with their newborns reveal the use of touch as integral and seemingly central to those first communications. In a study investigating the effects of maternal contact, Carlsson et al. (1978) found that extended body contact between mother and newborn immediately after delivery was related to an increase in what the authors refer to as affective components of maternal nursing behavior observed 2 to 4 days later; that is, increased contact behaviors such as rubbing, rocking, touching, and holding were shown during nursing and there were fewer noncontact behaviors. The authors substantiated the claim of Klaus, Jerauld, Kreger, McAlpine, Steffa, and Kennell (1972) that events occurring immediately after birth influence subsequent maternal behavior. Along similar lines, de Chateau (1976) examined the influence of a close, natural contact between mothers and their newborns after delivery who were given 10 to

15 minutes of extra contact during the first postpartum hour on later behavior at 3 days and 3 months. Mothers with extra contact experience showed more holding, encompassing, looking "en face," and less cleaning behaviors at 36 hours than mothers given opportunities to provide only routine care. Infants with extra contact smiled more and cried less at the 3-month observation. Beyond maternal contact and its longer-term effects, Fransson, Karlsson, and Nilsson (2005) demonstrated the importance of physical contact for temperature regulation in newborns.

Incorporating a different means to capture the early touching behaviors occurring between mothers and their newborns, Robin (1982) analyzed videotapes of maternal tactile contacts in the days following birth, looking at both fullterm and preterm neonate–mother dyads. Findings indicated that utilitarian contacts (e.g., wiping the infant's mouth, cleaning, winding, etc.) were the most frequent in an 8-minute observation period which included feeding, followed closely by face and hand contacts. Neither birth order, term, nor infant age seemed to distinguish the frequency of these contacts; however, a greater frequency of maternal tactile contacts was shown with female infants. Taken together, what is clear from these studies is that there are diverse roles for touching in the newborn period and that the sense of touch holds meaning for both parent and infant.

Massage

Beyond contact at birth, infants' responses to the complexity of naturally occurring patterns of touch provided to them by adults are also reflected in infant massage. According to Field (1998), touch therapies, and particularly massage therapy, were primary forms of medicine before the advent of the pharmaceutical age and they date back to at least 1800 BCE. Leboyer (1976) graphically illustrates an East Indian body massage lasting 30 minutes completed daily on infants up to 6 months of age. Leboyer's premise is that infants' bodies crave touch. Although his work was descriptive with no experimental manipulations undertaken, the technique of body massage is designed to relieve tension and anxiety, facilitate relaxation, and in infant massage, transmit love from the caregiver to the infant.

There is some support for massage and tactile stimulation as having positive effects and being successful in facilitating activity in the fetus (e.g., by giving pregnant women foot and hand massage, Diego, Field, & Hernandez-Reif, 2004), and growth in the newborn, particularly with the preterm infant (e.g., Rose, Schmidt, Riese, & Bridger, 1980; Scafidi et al., 1986; Solkoff, Yaffe, Weintraub, & Blase, 1969). For example, weight gain and caloric intake in premature infants have been shown to increase with tactile stimulation (e.g., Helders, Cats, & Debast, 1989; Phillips & Moses, 1996; Scafidi et al., 1990; Watt, 1990; White & Labarba, 1976), energy expenditure has been shown to decrease (Lahat, Mimouni, Ashbel, & Dollberg, 2007), while temperature increases have been shown with massage (Diego, Field, & Hernandez-Reif, 2008). Notably, moderate versus light pressure massage has been shown to produce greater weight gain, and those who received moderate touch appeared to be more relaxed and less aroused as measured by such indicators as sleep state, fussiness, crying, and movement (Field, Diego,

Hernandez-Reif, Deeds, & Figuereido, 2006). In addition to a 47% greater weight gain for preterm infants given tactile stimulation, Scafidi et al. (1986) demonstrated that treated infants spent more time in awake and active states, showed more mature behaviors on the Brazelton scale (NBAS), and were discharged from hospital 6 days earlier. In Phillips and Moses' (1996) study, massaged infants maintained a calmer state and were less irritable.

In a review of 24 studies on the effects of supplemental stimulation on premature infants, Harrison (1985) found evidence to support the positive effects of extra tactile stimulation as well as extra auditory, gustatory, and visual stimulation. Beneficial effects included those mentioned above, as well as decreased irritability, and more advanced social and neurological development. However, she also noted a number of limitations to the studies (e.g., small samples, wide variation in samples). In her more recent review of tactile stimulation (comforting touch and massage) of preterm infants in neonatal intensive care units (NICU), Harrison (2001) argues that the literature on NICU infants demonstrates that they receive an abundance of procedural touch (to which infants often show adverse reactions), but very little nurturing or comforting touch (e.g., soothing). Short- and long-term supplemental tactile interventions of stroking or gentle touch, moderate stroking/massage, and stroking/massage combined with kinesthetic or vestibular stimulation have shown varying positive effects, particularly with infants who are physiologically stable. Gentle touch may be safe with physiologically fragile infants and they may be able to tolerate this form of tactile stimulation best. However, determining when infants are ready for the different forms of stimulation is important.

Recently, Diego et al. (2008) showed that massage on preterm infants in the nursery led to short term increases in vagal activity and gastric motility, suggesting that increased vagal activity and motility may be at the root of understanding the relationship between massage therapy and weight gain. The increased oxytocin levels following massage may be linked to anti-stress-like effects according to Uvnas-Moberg (2004), underscoring the role that oxytocin might play as the underlying mechanism integrating massage, relaxation, and well-being. In their review of massage therapy effects in the last decade, Field, Diego, and Hernandez-Reif (2007) provide evidence that pregnancy massage reduces prematurity and that infant massage increases weight in preterm babies. In addition, while they argue that stimulating pressure receptors under the skin activates certain events such as stimulation of the vagus, increased serotonin and dopamine, decreased cortisol, and that it alters brain activity, research is warranted to discover the pathways that connect these processes. In their review of prenatal depression effects on the fetus and newborn, Field, Diego, and Hernandez-Reif (2006) suggest that moderate pressure massage can alleviate the effects typically demonstrated in newborns of depressed mothers (e.g., prematurity, elevated cortisol, lower vagal tone, etc.). Similarly, O'Higgins, Roberts, and Glover (2008) showed that, in postnatal depressed mothers, outcomes for both mother and infant were better on some indices in those that received massage.

Another practice that is tactile in nature is kangaroo care or skin-to-skin holding, where the preterm infant is held on the parent's chest under the clothing. It originated in Bogota, Columbia in the 1970s and was introduced to American NICUs in the late 1980s (Gale, 1998). It involves the naked baby being placed prone on the mother's bare chest and covered with a warm blanket on the back (Moore, Anderson, & Bergman, 2007). Its positive effects seem to be primarily in the physiologic domain (heart rate, respiration rate, oxygen saturation, thermoregulation; e.g., Anderson, 1995), however there is evidence to suggest benefits on breastfeeding outcomes (Anderson, Chiu, Morrison, Burkhammer, & Ludington-Hoe, 2004), pain response (Johnston et al., in press), attachment, and crying (Moore et al., 2007), some evidence for improved development (Ludington-Hoe & Swinth, 1996), and positive effects on family interaction, proximity and touch (Feldman, Weller, Sirota, & Eidelman, 2003) and on sleep-wake cyclicity, arousal modulation, and sustained exploration (Feldman, Eidelman, Sirota, & Weller, 2002). However, the range in methodological rigor and quality and the number of studies assessing specific outcomes, limits conclusions (Moore et al., 2007). Consequently, more research is warranted to determine the efficacy of skin-to-skin contact and with whom it is both effective and appropriate.

Whether specific regimens of tactile stimulation or massage have beneficial effects on the fullterm neonate is not clear. According to Field (1998), massage therapists suggest that there are beneficial effects (e.g., reducing stress responses, reducing pain, helping to induce sleep), however there is little data to support these claims. Underdown, Barlow, Chung, and Stewart-Brown (2006) argue that there is no evidence to support growth effects in low-risk infants and only some evidence supporting beneficial effects on mother–infant interaction, sleep, relaxation, crying, and stress hormones. Koniak-Griffin and Ludington-Hoe (1987) found paradoxical effects in their examination of the effects of unimodal and multimodal stimulation (e.g., more optimal performance was demonstrated by the control infants on the Brazelton Neonatal Behavior Assessment Scale). More recently, Ferber, Laudon, Kuint, Weller, & Zisapel (2002) showed positive effects of a bedtime massage on fullterm infants' growth rates, activity-rest cycles and melatonin rhythms during the night a few months later. Reissland and Burghart (1987) discuss the importance of massage in Mithila (South Asia), where women are expected to massage their infants daily. Some of the assumed benefits include hardening bone structure, enhancing movement and coordination, and even instilling fearlessness.

It is still not clear from these studies what beneficial effects these handling and massage practices have on socio-emotional development and on the parent–infant relationship. However, what is clear is that it is a daily routine where parent and infant spend circumscribed amounts of time together. While there are limitations, it appears from these studies that positive effects may be observed on the whole family system, rather than solely impacting on the infant.

Physical Contact beyond the Newborn Period: Adult–Infant Touching in Social Contexts

Investigations of the role of touch in early interactions have had a rather short history. In past studies of social interactions during infancy, the focus was on the more distal behavioral indices of gaze and affect to the relative exclusion of touch and gesture. Yet mothers (and fathers) commonly employ touch during face-to-face interactions and play, along with their vocal and visual expressions. During face-to-face interactions, the infant and adult (primarily the mother) are seated at eye-level to each other during a series of brief interaction periods. Caregivers interact spontaneously, using their facial, vocal and tactile expressions, while infants respond to and even initiate interactions. Face-to-face interactions have been one of the primary means used to study the infant's social communication (Kaye & Fogel, 1980), emotional expressions and responses to stressful episodes (Field, Vega-Lahr, Scafidi, & Goldstein, 1986), and the development of social expectations (Cohn & Tronick, 1983). However, typically, researchers have analyzed maternal and infant facial and vocal behavior, but not touch, despite the fact that incidental reports reveal that *maternal* touch occurs during 33% to 61% of brief interaction periods (e.g., Field, 1984; Kaye & Fogel, 1980; Symons & Moran, 1987), and *infant* touch occurs 85% of the time (Moszkowski & Stack, 2007). Other measures such as posture (Fogel, Dedo, & McEwen, 1992), manual hand actions (Toda & Fogel, 1993) and gesture (Stack & Arnold, 1998) have also been documented. Contextual features such as location during play, position, inclination of position, proximity of contact etc., are other examples of what appear to be important factors in influencing the infant's engagement during face-to-face play (e.g., Lavelli & Fogel, 1998; Stack, Arnold, Girouard, & Welburn, 1999).

Touching during mother–infant interactions: Face-to-face still-face studies

The still-face procedure (Tronick, Als, Adamson, Wise, & Brazelton, 1978), a modification of the face-to-face procedure, has proven to be a valuable tool to examine the role of touching. The mother–infant interaction is divided into three brief periods (90–120 sec). In period 1, mothers interact normally, using facial expression, voice, and touch (Normal), in period 2 they assume a neutral, nonresponsive still face and provide neither vocal nor tactile stimulation (SF), and in period 3 they resume Normal interaction (Reunion). During the SF, compared to Normal periods, infants typically decrease gazing and smiling at mothers (Gusella, Muir, & Tronick, 1988; Lamb, Morrison, & Malkin, 1987; Mayes & Carter, 1990), increase neutral to negative affect, and increase vocalizing (Ellsworth, Muir, & Hains, 1993; Stack & Muir, 1990). This dramatic effect has been replicated numerous times and in various ways (see Adamson & Frick, 2003 for an overview and history). The still-face procedure continues its popularity in the literature noted by the number of recent studies using the procedure (e.g., Montirosso, Borgatti, Trojan, Zanini, & Tronick, 2009; Hsu & Sung, 2008; Legerstee & Markova, 2007; Field, Hernandez-Reif, Diego, Feijo et al., 2007; Moore, Oates, Goodwin, & Hobson, 2008; Lowe, Handmaker, & Aragon, 2006; Cleveland, Kobiella, & Striano, 2006; Merin, Young, Ozonoff, & Rogers, 2007; Weinberg, Olson, Beeghly, & Tronick, 2006) and has revealed important discoveries. Attempts to explain its dramatic effects continue, and more research is warranted to extricate and disentangle the effect. In addition, new applications figure prominently in the literature (e.g., Tronick, 2003; Muir & Lee, 2003; Cohn, 2003; Frick & Adamson, 2003; Haley & Stansbury, 2003; Tronick et al., 2005; Jean & Stack, 2009). However, it is important to note that most studies using the still-face do not include touch (either mother or child) as a measure.

In those studies that have measured touch, there are particular roles that the still-face has played in revealing important touch effects. For example, Gusella et al. (1988) compared the responses during SF periods between groups of infants where some infants received maternal touch in the preceding Normal period, and others received only maternal face and voice. They found that 3-month-olds exhibited the still-face effect only when maternal touching was part of the prior Normal periods and their attention declined over time without the tactile stimulation. According to Gusella et al. this suggests that maternal touch during the Normal periods facilitated the maintenance of attention in these very young infants such that a SF effect could be shown in the experimental group. In the control group, attention remained stable throughout the periods when touch was included in the Normal periods, but attention showed a steady decline without touch.

Field et al. (1986) compared responses of 4-month-olds to a SF episode with those to a separation sequence and reported that the infants found the SF sequence more stressful (e.g., more motor activity, gaze aversion, distress brow, crying, and less smiling). More maternal tactile-kinesthetic behavior was shown following the SF period indicating that maternal proximal and comforting behaviors were potentiated. These findings support the view that infants are sensitive to maternal cues, and suggest both the soothing role and communicative nature of touching.

Studies examining infants' responsiveness to their mother's touch and their sensitivity to touch when other forms of stimulation are absent provide important insight into why mothers use touch during the first 6 months of life. By comparing a standard SF with one where mothers could touch during the SF period (still-face with touch), Stack and Muir (1990) showed that by adding touch infants were not distressed, they showed increased smiling, and they maintained the high levels of gaze that are typical in Normal interactions. This new role for touch in moderating the SF effect has been replicated a number of times (e.g., Peláez-Nogueras, Field, Hossain, & Pickens, 1996; Stack & LePage, 1996; Stack & Muir, 1992). Moreover, Stack and Muir (1992) demonstrated that it was the tactile and not the visual stimulation from the adults' hands that was responsible for the effects. Through the still-face procedure, infants' sensitivity to changes in their mothers' touch has been demonstrated by providing mothers with different verbal instructions (Stack & LePage, 1996; Stack & Muir, 1990, 1992; Stack & Arnold, 1998). For example, mothers can use touch to elicit specific behaviors from their infants (e.g., maximize their infants' smiling; Stack & LePage, 1996; shift infants' attention to their mothers' hands; Stack & Muir, 1992). Using a still-face with touch procedure and making comparisons to a no-change control group, Stack and Arnold (1998) examined how touch and gesture alone are used to obtain specific infant responses. They found that infants are sensitive to changes in maternal touch and hand gestures and that, when instructed, mothers appear successful in eliciting specific behaviors from their infants using only nonverbal channels of communication. For example, maternal touch and hand gestures attracted infants' attention to their mothers' faces even when the face was still and expressionless. During the period where mothers were instructed to engage their infants in a playful interaction, infants in the experimental group smiled more relative to the control group.

Arnold and Stack (Arnold, Brouillette, & Stack, 1996; Arnold, 2002) subsequently took an important step by comparing face-to-face interactions under two conditions:

unimodal (touch-only) and multimodal (all modalities) including two additional control groups with 3.5- and 5.5-month-old infants and their mothers. Among numerous results, they found that mothers changed their touching and gesturing as a function of the instructions provided. For example, during the touch-only conditions, mothers touched their infants the most (and gestured least) when asked to relax and calm their infants, and demonstrated less touching and more gesturing during the attention-to-face period. Infant behaviors were different across periods in both conditions indicating that mothers were successful in eliciting behavior reflective of, for example, positive arousal.

It is important to note that for the Stack and LePage (1996) and Stack and Arnold (1998) studies, changes in maternal touch were inferred on the basis of changes in infants' behavior. The actual patterns and types of touching were not directly measured. Since then, Stack and colleagues have examined some of the specific changes in maternal touching using the Caregiver–Infant Touch Scale (e.g., Stack, LePage, Hains, & Muir, 1996; Stack, 2001; Stack, 2004) and changes in infant touching using the Infant Touch Scale (Moszkowski & Stack, 2007; Moszkowski, Stack, & Chiarella, 2009; Moszkowski, Stack, Girouard, et al., 2009). Some of these findings are described in the section on patterns of touching during social interactions.

Consistent with the findings on maternal touch modulating the SF effect, Jean and Stack (2009) used the typical still-face procedure and demonstrated the influence of maternal behaviors during the inter-period interval (or transition period) between the SF and Reunion Normal periods on infants' behavior during the Reunion period. Mothers used these brief transition periods to regulate their infants, and the amount and quality of the regulatory behaviors shown during the transition between the SF and Reunion Normal periods were related to maternal touch in the Reunion period. That is, maternal regulatory behavior in the transition period following the SF and infant fretting during the Reunion period predicted the amount of maternal nurturing touch in the Reunion period. These findings imply the critical regulatory role that the transition periods play and underscore the regulatory role of touch. In a subsequent study with groups of 5-month-old fullterm and very low birth weight (VLBW) preterm infants, Millman, Jean, and Stack (2009) compared maternal touching and infants' self-regulating abilities during a still-face procedure. Increased self-comforting, attention-seeking, and escape behaviors were shown by both fullterm and VLBW preterm infants during the SF period, while only fullterm infants showed increased self-comforting regulatory behavior during the Reunion period. Furthermore, mothers used more attention-getting touch during the Normal period while more nurturing and playful touch was shown during the Reunion period. Moreover, mothers of fullterm infants increased their amount of nurturing touching when their infants exhibited distress during the SF. Similarly, the regulatory effects of touch on infants' stress responses have been shown during inoculations of infants at 2 and 6 months (Jahromi, Putnam, & Stifter, 2004); maternal touching was associated with less crying at 2 months, and at both 2 and 6 months, the combination of holding/rocking and vocalizing was effective at reducing crying.

LePage (1998; LePage & Stack, 1997) used a modification of the still-face with touch procedure and investigated infants' abilities to perceive a tactile contingency (or the lack of contingency) during social interactions. While infants in the contingent condition were reinforced for gazing at the experimenter's neutral face with standardized tactile stimulation (still-face interaction with touch as the reinforcer), infants in the noncontingent condition received the same tactile stimulation as their matched counterparts regardless of their behaviors. All infants in the contingent condition learned the contingency. For example, their level of gazing at the experimenter's face was higher, and gazing away was lower, relative to infants in the noncontingent condition. It was thus demonstrated that 4- and 7-month-olds could perceive and learn a contingent relationship presented through the tactile modality during social adult–infant interactions, underscoring that infants of this age are both sensitive to and reinforced by touch.

Taken together, results from these studies underscore infants' responsiveness and sensitivity to maternal touch, highlight the prevalence of touch during interactions, and demonstrate the value of the face-to-face and SF procedures in revealing the role(s) for touch.

Touch and multiple modalities

While the still-face with touch studies were essential to isolating the contribution of touch to mother–infant interchange, information is typically multimodally specified for the developing infant. Several studies have addressed touch (directly or indirectly) through procedures that either do not use the still-face procedure or that attempt to bring together multiple behavioral actions in some unified way. For example, Roedell and Slaby (1977) explored 24-week-old infants' preferences for three adults who interacted in different ways. One adult (distal) smiled, talked, sang, and made facial expressions; another (proximal) carried, rocked, bounced, patted, and stroked the infant but remained silent with a neutral face; and a third (neutral) was silent, unresponsive, and made no eye-contact. Over a 3-week period, infants increased their time spent near the distal adult while no changes were made to the proximal and neutral adults, and infants chose to look more at the distal than at the proximal adult. However, results were limited by the lack of natural social interaction (Stack & Muir, 1990): there were no measures of affect, the adult was not permitted to maintain eye-contact in the proximal condition, and the infant did not need to establish eye-contact with the proximal adult to receive stimulation.

It has also been shown that rhythmic touch is preferred over nonrhythmic touch in dyads (Peláez-Nogueras, 1995), and infants are more responsive when touch is added to face and voice (Peláez-Nogueras, Gewirtz, et al., 1996). In addition, Perez and Gewirtz (2004) in their study assessing three types of tactile stimulation at two different levels of tactile pressure found that infants preferred intense stroking the most and intense poking the least.

Parent–infant games that involve much touching and physical contact (such as pat-a-cake, lap games, tickle games, I'm gonna get you games, finger walking games, even bouncing games and "horsey" games) have also been demonstrated to elicit positive responses from infants (e.g., Wolff, 1963; D. N. Stern, 1985; Fogel, Hsu, Shapiro, Nelson-Goens, & Secrist, 2006). In a study examining distinct types of infant smiles and their relation to the social context in which they typically occur, Dickson, Walker, and Fogel (1997) coded for four types of smiles using the Baby FACS coding scheme during parent–infant interactions. They found that it was physical play that included tactile stimulation that elicited the most play smiles (45% of the time), and these play smiles occurred less often during object play, vocal play, and book reading. Along similar lines, Fogel, Hsu, et al., (2006) found longer durations and higher amplitudes of smiling during tickle compared to peek-a-boo games.

In their examination of infant affective and behavioral states across a series of conditions (i.e., normal play, baby can only see mother, baby can only hear mother, baby can only feel mother's touch, baby is alone), Brown and Tronick (in preparation, cited in Tronick, 1995) found that the lowest levels of infant fussing and crying were displayed in the touch-only condition. Interestingly, they also showed a low level of scanning, high levels of object attention, and less smiling than during the normal and face-only conditions. Consistent with Stack and colleagues' findings (e.g., Stack & Muir, 1990, 1992; Stack & LePage, 1996; Stack & Arnold, 1998), touching had calming effects on the infants, reflected in their decreased fretting, and seemed to permit an openness to the stimulation, reflected in high levels of attention and continued smiling. On the basis of these findings and others, Tronick (1989, 1995) suggests that touch is a component of the mutual regulatory process of the caregiver-infant dyad, and he contends that touch may serve a regulatory function.

Moreno, Posada, and Goldyn (2006) directly examined the regulatory functions of touch by linking the quality of parent–infant touch and the regulatory effects on the infant. In their study of fullterm infants there were two conditions of face-to-face interaction, one in which they could touch their infants and one in which they could not. Quality of touch and coregulation were coded. Results indicated that there was more symmetrical coregulation when touch was prohibited, and affectionate touch was inversely related to infant activity level while stimulating touch was directly related to infant activity level. The authors raise the importance of considering context, and stress the limits of their quality of touch measure and the structured nature of the procedure that was used. In Jean and Stack's (2009) aforementioned study, they demonstrated that the quality of maternal regulatory behavior (and not infant fretting during the SF period) during the transition period between the SF and the Reunion periods influenced the amount of nurturing touch mothers provided to their infants in the Reunion period.

There are other relationships that have been posited between touch and emotion and regulation. The soothing function of touch directly links touching to emotional regulation, and it is already known that emotions play a critical part in infants' evaluation of their goals (Tronick, 1989). It has also been proposed that touch is a mode of communication (e.g., Fisher, Rytting, & Heslin, 1976). However, within the large literature on emotional communication, it is striking that touch has received little attention (Beyette, Atkinson, & Kendall, 1989). With a few exceptions (e.g., Jean & Stack, 2009; Hertenstein & Campos, 2001), studies in the infant social interaction literature have not been specifically designed to explore these relationships directly and systematically. Hertenstein and Campos attempted to examine the effects of touch on infants' emotion by varying the tactile stimulation provided to infants while they sat on their mothers' laps and were presented with objects. They showed that specific qualities of touch (i.e., tension increase condition, where the mother was instructed to tighten her grip around her infant's torso with her fingers for a brief period) reliably elicited negative expression from infants, however, they were not successful with the touch quality that was expected to elicit positive expressions. The challenges in the emotion field are not new: expression may not reflect the underlying emotion, but a lack of expression does not translate to an absence of an underlying emotion. Increased emphasis on coding and integrating touch and gesture is warranted in order to understand more fully their roles in communication.

The importance of multiple measures and the examination of patterns of responses from mothers and infants have been underscored. Previously, emphasis was placed on facial expressions with the result that attention to touch, gestures, postural changes, vocalizations, and the relations between measures has been inadequate (Tronick, 1989). According to Toda and Fogel (1993), "emotional" responses in young infants cannot be judged entirely from the face but must involve the whole body and the patterns of temporally organized action in a context (Fogel et al., 1992). In their study with 6-month-olds, Weinberg and Tronick (1994) examined multiple modalities including infants' gaze, vocalizations, gestures, facial expressions, self-regulatory and withdrawal behaviors. They found evidence for behavioral clusters or "affective configurations" that they argued conveyed information about the infant's state and intentions.

Taken together, interaction studies have provided important insights and have advanced what we know about the young infant's sensitivity to manipulations in facial, vocal and now tactile expressions, underscoring the complexity and sophistication of mother–infant dyadic interactions, and the importance of including measures of touch. Moreover, through these studies, an abundance of findings with important contributions have been revealed. Results from these studies highlight infants' sensitivity to maternal behavior, in particular their sensitivity to their mothers' touch. Most importantly, these studies have provided evidence for a functional context for touch that is not limited to the regulation of distress.

Patterns of Touching: Evidence for Exploratory, Regulatory, and Communicative Functions

Patterns of touching during social interactions: Maternal

While the importance of the above-mentioned studies is not in question, the functions and adaptability of touch were largely inferred based on evidence taken from infant responses to their caregivers, rather than direct measures of caregiver touch. Even in those studies where touch has been directly assessed, the measures have largely been the duration of all touching (e.g., Gusella et al., 1988) or they have been intensity levels (e.g., Stack & Muir, 1990). All touch may not be used or interpreted similarly; different types of touch and the way touch is applied may have different meanings.

To illustrate, Stack, LePage, Hains, and Muir (1996; Stack, 2001) developed the Caregiver–Infant Touch Scale to measure types of touch and associated quantitative characteristics (e.g., intensity, speed) in social contexts such as mother–infant play, and to examine changes across age. Following a period of natural face-to-face interaction mothers and their 5.5-month-old infants participated in three SF with touch periods: (1) normal touch, (2) touch to maximize infant smiling, and (3) touch restricted to one area of the body. There was a baseline comparison group also included who received four periods of natural face-to-face interaction. Specific patterns or profiles of touching were shown across perturbation period. For example, when asked to maximize infant smiling, mothers used more active types of touch (lifting, tickling), used more surface area, and greater intensity and speed. During the SF period where mothers were asked to touch their babies in only one area, there was increased stroking and far less shaking. Touching was also less intense, and most types of touch during this period were executed more slowly. Thus, the more tactilely active profile was revealed during the period where smiling was maximized. This finding supports the notion of heightened activity during playful interactions. From these results it is clear that mother's profiles of touching during brief interactions change as a function of experimenter instruction, suggesting that what was being communicated through the touch was different.

Jean, Stack, and Fogel (2008) examined maternal touch using the Caregiver–Infant Touch Scale in a longitudinal sample of mothers and their infants of 1, 3, and 5 months during both face-to-face lap and floor play contexts. Mothers changed their touching as a function of age and interaction context. That is, while touching was consistently high, maternal touch decreased from 1 to 3 months. Furthermore, there was more touching during the lap than the floor context. Across age and context, static touch was used the most, and mothers used more lifting compared to squeezing, tickling, and shaking. More static touch was used at 5 compared to 3 months, and more stroking was used at 1 and 5 months of age. More lifting in the floor context was used with 3-month-olds, while in the lap context mothers used more stroking at 1 month and more tickling at 5 months. In both contexts, nurturing touch, such as stroking and patting, decreased over age. Results from this study illustrate the beginnings of how maternal touch evolves across infant age and context.

Several other studies have also demonstrated that mothers use different types of touch during interactions with their infants (e.g., Ferber, Feldman, & Makhoul, 2008; Harrison & Woods, 1991; Polan & Ward, 1994). For example, Ferber et al. examined the development of maternal touch during natural caregiving and mother–child play using 9 different types of touch that were aggregated into the 3 global touch categories of affectionate, stimulating, and instrumental. While affectionate and stimulating touch decreased during the second half year of life, dyadic reciprocity increased. Jean and Stack (2009) took an important step by measuring the functions of touch. They developed the Functions of Touch Scale (FTS), a systematic observational measure used to assess the functions of maternal touch while taking into consideration other modalities of verbal and nonverbal communication such as mothers' verbalizations and infants' emotional displays and attention. They found that the attention-getting function of touch increased in the first Normal period of the SF while the nurturing function of touch increased in the Reunion period. Furthermore, in both the Normal and Reunion periods it was the playful function of touch that predicted infants' smiling, while it was the nurturing function of touch that predicted infants' fretting. Moreover, as described in the *face-to-face still-face studies* discussed earlier, infants' distress level influenced the functions of touch and the regulatory behaviors employed by mothers.

These findings suggest that simple touch duration is not a sufficient index to characterize adult behavior – qualitative and quantitative variations in touching occur for a variety of reasons and are important to measure and describe. What is also clear is that mothers use different patterns of touching for different functions.

Patterns of touching during social interactions: Infant

While research on maternal touching is still sparse, albeit growing, even less research has been conducted on infant touch. Yet, infants use touch to explore their environments and themselves, self-comfort and regulate, and communicate. Most studies on infant touch have investigated how infants physically explore their proximal and distal environments and learn about object properties (Stack & Tsonis, 1999; Bushnell & Boudreau, 1991), typically termed haptic exploration. When infants are very young, they explore objects orally by mouthing them rather than exploring with their hands and fingers. Yet, beyond exploration of their physical environments, infants use touch in social contexts to learn about themselves and others. However, few studies have included measurements of infants' tactile or manual behaviors during early social exchanges between mothers and their infants (Murray & Trevarthen, 1985; Trevarthen, 1986; Toda & Fogel, 1993). Toda and Fogel demonstrated that infants' self-touch, grasping, and touching of their clothes, and the infant seat increased during the SF period, implying that touching behaviors are important to examine and may serve a regulatory function. Similarly, Landau, Shusel, Eshel, and Ben-Aaron (2003), in their kibbutz study of mother–child and metaplet–child touch during picture book and Duplo tasks, found evidence for self-touch as a mode of self-regulation. However, given the paucity of studies and the lack of specificity, it remains the case that little is known about the types of touch infants use, how they use touch to fulfill different functions, and under what conditions.

Recently, Moszkowski and Stack (2007) conducted a study that systematically examined the qualitative and quantitative components of infant touching: the types, locations, and duration of touch. Using a still-face procedure with fullterm 5.5-month-olds, they demonstrated that infants' touching varied as a function of their mothers' availability. During the SF period when mothers were unavailable, infants touched themselves more and used more active, reactive, and soothing touching behaviors (e.g., stroke, finger, pat, pull). In contrast, during the Normal periods when mothers were available for interaction, they touched their mothers and used more passive touch (static touch). This study was an important first step in delineating the regulatory, exploratory, and communicative roles for infant touch and Moszkowski and Stack developed a methodology for measuring infant touch. However, functions of touch were only indirectly examined. A subsequent study (Moszkowski, Stack, & Chiarella, 2009) established new ground by more directly measuring the functions of touch and examining how touch co-occurs with infant gaze and affect. The functions of infant touch and the way in which the functions were organized with gaze and affect varied depending on the interactive period. For example, infants demonstrated more regulatory and exploratory touch during the SF period: passive touch cooccurred with gaze at mothers during the Normal periods while soothing and reactive touch cooccurred with gaze away from mothers during the SF period.

Finally, Moszkowski and Stack's infant touch work was extended to a population of depressed and nondepressed mothers of 4-month-olds (Moszkowski, Stack, Girouard, et al., 2009) where they examined infants' touching behaviors during periods of maternal emotional unavailability (SF) and physical unavailability (separation procedure). During the separation procedure (SP; Field et al., 1986), mothers were physically absent for a brief perturbation period and were concealed behind a curtain just outside the testing area within which the infant was securely fastened in the infant seat. When mothers were unavailable, infants exhibited more patting and pulling. In addition, during both the SF and SP periods, infants of depressed mothers used more reactive types of touch (such as grabbing, pulling). Similarly, Herrera, Reissland, and Shepherd (2004) found that infants of depressed mothers touched their mothers and toys less and touched themselves more.

While there are few studies examining touch in *infants* of depressed mothers, results from touching in depressed *mothers* add to this picture. It has been shown that positive touch stimulation enhances positive affect and attention in infants of depressed mothers (Peláez-Nogueras, Field, et al., 1996). Paradoxically, in their study of parenting stress, depression, and anxiety and its relationship to behavior during interactions, Fergus, Schmidt, and Pickens (1998) found that it was those mothers who reported more symptoms of depression who touched their infants more relative to nondepressed mothers. However, the pattern of interaction was more intrusive and over-stimulatory in nature. As they reported, more poking and tickling were used and these symptomatic mothers (mild to moderate levels of depressive symptoms) attempted more attention-getting strategies such as finger snapping. Similarly, Cohn and Tronick (1989) described depressed mothers as using more poking and jabbing with their infants; these touching behaviors were associated with negative affect and gaze aversion on the part of infants. Herrera et al., (2004) found that depressed mothers restrained their infants more by lifting them, and Stepakoff (2000) found that they showed more object-mediated and less affectionate touch. Combined, these studies point to the importance of types of touch and converge to suggest that touch might be an important parenting component.

Taken together, the findings from patterns of mother and infant touch reveal that both mothers and infants use different touching behaviors depending on context and age, that there are specific functions that maternal and infant touch serve during interactions, that these vary across interaction periods, birth status, and age, and that infant touch is organized with other behaviors during interactions. Touch is clearly an integral part of mother–infant interactions and results underscore the importance of touch for communication, exploration, and regulation. Consequently, parental and infant touch behaviors are important measures to include in still-face and interaction studies.

Touching in the Cultural Context and Father–Infant Touch

To this point the focus has largely been with mother–infant touching. Observing variations and similarities in parental touching in different cultures and across mothers and fathers are also important avenues to explore. Studying parenting-in-culture is important to developmental investigations (Bornstein, 1991). Parents across the world have ways with which they have both learned and developed to rear their children and to teach them to become a part of the culture. There also seem to be both culture-specific and culture-universal parenting activities. It is not surprising then that ways of touching and the amount of physical contact between parent (mother vs. father) and infant can be different across culture and across parent in some studies, as well as levels of affection and how affection is expressed.

The benefits of close physical contact, in the forms of touching, holding, and carrying practices have been underscored (e.g., Solter, 2001). It has also been demonstrated that different cultural groups engage in different *styles* of touching (Fogel, Toda, & Kawai, 1988; Franco, Fogel, Messinger, & Frazier, 1996). For example, differences in the type and timing of Japanese mothers' behavior toward their infants were reflected in a higher probability of facial expressions and vocalizations being interspersed with touches and looming upper-body movements (Fogel et al., 1988), and when infants shifted their gaze from away to toward the mother, Japanese mothers were more likely to respond with increased touch. American mothers provided largely facial and vocal displays to their infants and placed their faces closer to the infants', using few hand displays. Interestingly, there were no differences in the amount of touching – mothers from both cultures touched their infants about 50% of the time. However, in a longitudinal study of American and Japanese dyads over the first year of life, Kawakami, Takai-Kawakami, and Kanaya (1994) found that American dyads engaged in interactions more often and American mothers touched their infants more. Comparing Hispanic and Anglo mothers living in the United States, Franco et al. (1996) demonstrated that while mothers from both groups reported touching their infants daily it was the Hispanic mothers who reported higher frequencies of touching, affection, and skin-to-skin contact. Observations of free play revealed that Hispanic mothers showed more close touch (e.g., resting against mother, body contact, tight hugs) as well as more close and affectionate touch, relative to Anglo mothers who showed more distal touch (e.g., playing at a distance, extended arms, etc.). No overall differences in the amount of mother–infant touch were observed during the interactions. The fact that Franco et al.'s results revealed no differences in overall touching between mothers and their infants implies in their view that touch is an integral component of early interactions, even in cultures who have different attitudes about affection and touching. Notably, attributions to situations involving touch have been shown to be different between Latinos and Anglo-Americans (Albert & Ha, 2004).

Ritualized behaviors form part of the developing relationship between parent and infant (Casati, 1991). Childcare routines also differ across cultures and social groups. Whether and for how long a relationship is tactile differs as a function of culture and such factors as age of the child. For example, Sigman and Wachs (1991) studied families in Kenya and in Egypt. They found that amount of physical contact declined from 18 to 27 months and then increased from 27 to 29 months. In another culture, Konner (1976) showed that !Kung infants were in physical bodily contact with someone 75% of the time during their first 3 to 6 months of life. The Fore of New Guinea, considered at the human evolution stage of protoagricultural, have their infants in direct physical contact with them during infancy; from being carried on their mothers' backs, to being on their laps, they are in constant skin-to-skin contact and can feed and suckle on demand (Barnett, 2005 based on Sorenson, 1976). There are also many cultures and places in the world where massage is a part of the daily routine (e.g., Bedouin Arabs, Gujarati of Western India, Maori of New Zealand; Barnett, 2005). Caregiving practices may also benefit the infant in critical ways (e.g., the Manta Pouch used by Quechua mothers of Peru that buffers their infants against high altitude; Tronick, Thomas, & Daltabuit, 1994).

While the majority of studies conducted to date have involved mothers or female adults, especially those that address touch, there is an accumulating literature on fathers (e.g., Allen & Daly, 2002). It is known that fathers engage in more vigorous, physically stimulating play with their infants (e.g., Arco, 1983; Hewlett, 1987; Parke & O'Leary, 1976; Yogman, 1982; Forbes, Cohn, Allen, & Lewinsohn, 2004), that fathers are potentially important attachment figures (Belsky, 1999), and it is believed by some that their style of play serves to create a critical means for the development of attachment (e.g., Lamb, 1981).

Using the still-face paradigm with mothers and fathers with their infants at 3 and 6 months, Forbes et al., (2004) demonstrated that during the Normal period mothers showed more positive affect and fathers used more physical play, however, parents did not engage in physical play with boys more than with girls. In their still-face study with 4-month-olds, Braungart-Rieker, Garwood, Powers, and Notaro (1998) found stability in infants' affect and regulatory behaviors, and both parents were equally sensitive. In their follow-up study (Braungart-Rieker, Garwood, Powers, & Wang, 2001), they found that 4-month-old infants' regulatory behaviors and parent sensitivity were related to attachment groups at 1 year for mothers, but not for fathers. Unfortunately, neither of these studies included measures of touch, apart from one category for infant self-regulation (self-comfort). Jean, Moszkowski, Girouard, and Stack (2005) included systematic measurement of touch in their still-face study, and found that there were no differences in the overall duration and frequency of touch used between mothers and fathers. While there were some differences in the types and combinations as well as locations of touch between mothers and fathers (e.g., mothers used more stimulating touch such as lifting for longer while fathers grabbed for longer; during the Normal period, stroking of the face was greater for fathers while tickling of the trunk was greater for mothers), mothers and fathers were as sensitive and responsive to their infants' needs.

In a study with low birth weight infants, fathers' patterns of touching with their 3-month-olds were shown to vary widely with regard to total amount of touching, and the areas touched most frequently were shoulders, back, torso, and face (Goebel, 2002). Moreover, patting, lifting, and passive contact were the most frequent types of touch used by fathers; only 10% of fathers' touch was considered nurturing, yet contact with many areas of the body with different types of touch occurred 70% of the time, and approximately half of the time touch was of moderate intensity. While the author argues on the basis of these results that fathers touch differently than mothers, no direct comparison of mothers' touch was included in the study design. Examining dual-career parents during face-to-face interactions with their 8-month-olds, Field et al. (1987) demonstrated that in addition to smiling and vocalizing more, mothers touched their infants more than fathers, resulting in greater infant smiling and motor activity. Similar effects were shown in a triadic interaction context, taking place in the home environment (Zaslow, Pederson, Suwalsky, Cain, & Fivel, 1985).

There have also been a few studies of fathers' touching with their infants in different cultures. For example, Hewlett (1987) observed the Aka pygmies of the tropical forest region of southern Central African Republic. While fathers held their infants substantially less than mothers, several patterns emerged. Fathers' holding was often context-specific (e.g., leisure time). Interestingly, however, it was the Aka fathers who were more likely to engage in minor physical play such as tickling and bouncing with their infants. Aka fathers did not engage in the vigorous type of play characteristic of American fathers. In their observations of Italian fathers, New and Benigni (1987) described fathers' interactions with their infants as more distal rather than proximal, involving more looking and talking. Fathers' touches were described as awkward and brief, and holding by the father was often limited to times when the mother was preparing for feeding. Their physical contact typically included tickling and poking.

Feldman, Masalha, and Alony (2006) examined microregulatory patterns of family interactions at 5 and 33 months of age in an effort to determine whether pathways to toddlers' self-regulation were different as a function of culture. They compared Israeli and Palestinian families (mother, father, infant) in a number of behaviors, including contact and touch at 5 months during a mother–infant, father–infant, and triadic naturalistic interaction in the home environment. For Palestinian infants 83% of the time was spent in physical contact (laps, in arms; proximity position) while for Israeli infants 74% of the time was spent in the face-to-face position. Physical contact between the couple was higher for the Palestinian families, while direct touching of the infant was higher for the Israeli parents. Touching by both parents was higher when they were looking at their infant, when their infant was looking at them, and when the infant was in the face-to-face position. Infant touching was also higher in the face-to-face position and when infants were looking at their parents. While affectionate touching by fathers was more common during high positive affect states, maternal affectionate touch was equally common during neutral and high positive affect states but low during states of withdrawn affect. Similarly, in their study examining the contribution of skin-to-skin care in Israeli families mentioned earlier in this chapter, Feldman, Weller, Sirota, and Eidelman (2003) found no differences in the total amount of touch between mothers and fathers and their premature babies. However, mothers provided more affectionate touch when infants were in neutral affective states while fathers touched more during positive affective states. In general, touch occurred most when infants were free of physical constraint and when parent and infant were in shared visual contact.

The characteristics of holding and play in different cultures can also be a means of revealing some aspects of physical touch and affection during parent–infant interchange. In a study describing Indian (New Delhi) mothers' and fathers' holding patterns, Roopnarine, Talukder, Jain, Joshi, and Srivastav (1990) found that mothers held their babies more than fathers, were also more likely to pick them up, to feed and comfort them while holding, and to display affection while holding. Tickling and lap bouncing were rare occurrences between Indian parents and their infants. However, peek-a-boo play was more common between mothers and infants. Finally, the infants themselves were more likely to vocalize to, smile at, and follow their mothers compared to fathers, but there was no difference in the amount of touch or approach behaviors to mothers and fathers. In a study of traditional and nontraditional families in Sweden, Lamb, Frodi, Hwang, Frodi, and Steinberg (1982) found that, in addition to other maternal effects, mothers held their 8-month-olds more than fathers regardless of caretaking or sex role.

Finally, Taiwanese mothers were shown to hold their infants more than fathers while fathers engaged in more rough play (Sun & Roopnarine, 1996).

Taken together, findings from this brief overview of some of the cross-culture findings have shown that touch is important and even intrinsic to other cultures. It can also be used differently in some contexts (e.g., holding patterns, pouches, swaddling) or be more frequent. More research with fathers is warranted, particularly pertaining to fathers' use and styles of touching during interactions, and the implications that different amounts, styles, or patterns might have for specific domains, such as emotion regulation, and for later development. The results converge to suggest that touching is used to bring people together, for closeness and intimacy, proximity and play, as well as for survival purposes in environments that require it.

Conclusions: Challenges and Directions

There remain many important pursuits in our quest to reveal the richness and unravel the mysteries and challenges of the sense of touch. Several questions and pivotal issues raised in the 2001 volume remain and new ones have surfaced. One significant theme to emerge from the current review of the literature is that there is abundant converging evidence to support the importance of touch and highlight its various facets. Touch is a diverse and adaptable modality, a modality that, while often used alone, also accompanies other modalities and channels of communication. It is used frequently in the first year of life in human and nonhuman species and it serves a multitude of purposes. The literature also underscores that the tactile modality provides an important means for parents and infants to maintain a connection with each other (as well as to the environment and to the self). It illustrates the flexibility and adaptability of touch but, as well, the adaptability of the communication system – both partners modify their behavior, to adjust and compensate for the situation. Both are responsive to each other. It is clear that mothers, fathers, and infants use touch, and this is the case across a variety of cultures, and that patterns of touching may be different.

More is known about how facial, vocal, and tactile components are used together during interactions, although further research is necessary to determine how they are used to achieve goals, and, if they do convey messages, how this is accomplished. How touching is integrated with the other communication channels that are available warrants continued investigation. Although understanding each component's discrete and independent role is important, the context within which touching occurs is important too, and the context within which much of early development occurs is social and multimodal. This includes vocalizing, affect, and gaze. Context shapes meaning (Jones & Yarbrough, 1985) and is considered by some to be the "mortar" of caregiver–infant communication (Hertenstein, 2002); what accompanies a touch behavior is important to impart meaning and the same behavior may have different meanings depending on the context. Studying verbal and nonverbal communication as inseparable phenomena when they occur together is what Jones and LeBaron (2002) label an integrated approach. However, examining, coding, and understanding the communication event or interaction sequence as a whole, is made far more difficult when studying multidimensional interactions, and interactions that include touch. This is an important direction for research on touch. Other directions to address the roles of context and understanding meaning include: manipulating context; integrating both microscopic and global measures; using naturalistic and experimental paradigms; integrating studies of different cultures to find the potential universality of meaning in some touch and to assess cultural similarities and differences; emphasizing the nature of mutual or coactive influences; and developing improved technology (software) to integrate measures.

More research on touching at different ages and under varied contexts is warranted, as well as expansion beyond mothers to fathers, siblings, peers, and other significant figures. The use of different paradigms and procedures is advantageous and innovations in measurement are critical. For example, testing different paradigms where emotions vary or specifically inducing an emotion and then examining touch on the part of the infant and caregiver, would uniquely contribute to expanding our knowledge and to developing conceptual and empirical models. Studies that tie touch and emotion and attention together and examine the regulatory roles for touch are warranted, and these types of studies raise important challenges. For example, the issue of expression and emotionality is debated in the emotional competence literature; by examining behavior such as affective expressions, it is difficult to determine what emotion the infant is experiencing and whether the underlying emotion is being captured by the behavior being coded. Physiological measures would be a helpful addition. More emphasis on positive touch could also be valuable, in light of Hertenstein and Campos' (2001) role for positive touch in the elicitation of emotionality, and in light of the regulatory role for touch and its success in eliciting smiling (e.g., Jean & Stack, 2009; Moszkowski & Stack, 2007; Moszkowski, Stack, & Chiarella, 2009; Moszkowski, Stack, Girouard, et al. 2009; Stack, 2001; Stack & Arnold, 1998; Stack & LePage, 1996). At the same time, there is little research on negative touch.

Technology has advanced and extends beyond video recorded interactions to software that permits coding of multiple behaviors, merging and integration of behaviors that are time synchronized, cooccurrence and sequential analysis, and integration with physiological measurement. This enables, among other things, emphasis of mutual or coactive influences from both parent and infants. While we have made progress in measuring types and more recently functions of touch, much remains to be done in order to demonstrate more fully the communicative nature and other roles that touch serves. Moreover, research efforts need to be directed to some of the more quantitative components of touch such as extent and speed. Indeed, while certainly systematic, detailed, and directly related to progress, behavioral coding systems are limited in the ways that they can measure such quantitative components of touching as intensity. Along similar lines, clustering touch with other behaviors to formulate constellations of behavior, styles, or expressions of communicative meaning, and then subsequently validating these in independent studies, would advance our understanding of touch, as well as its relation to emotion and communication, its measurement, and its potential mechanisms. Exploring the mechanisms that underlie the effects of touch is also essential.

Another domain in which progress has been made since the last volume is in the area of touch and development. The field has started to move beyond maternal touch to include infant and caregiver touch. Longitudinal studies on touching behavior over time, while still rare, have commenced, and studies examining the patterns of touching between parents and their infants within and across cultures have been published. These studies have remained largely in the descriptive realm and in the short term, and need to move toward addressing functions and mechanisms, and these over the longer term. The long-term implications of touching (or the absence of it) are notably lacking, outside of the literature on massage. Furthermore, models that conceptualize the functions and meaning of touch during development are practically nonexistent. Consequently, studies designed to address aspects of a theoretically driven model or tenets of socio-emotional development, do not exist.

Individual differences in touching have yet to be explored in depth. In addition, how touch changes as infants get older in connection with particular milestones of development deserves attention (Muir, 2002; Stack, 2001). Throughout the first few years of life, the infant (and its parents) are developing, changing, and adjusting. It is important to pursue and be aware of how development itself plays a role in the changes we see related to touch, physical contact, and affection (e.g., locomotor ability, language, referential communication etc; also, fine motor abilities and haptic exploration). Moreover, exploring caregiver and child touch beyond infancy and into preschooler and early childhood is warranted.

Finally, issues related to measurement of touch continue. Touch is inherently relational. The act of tickling is a good example of its relational nature. Tickling is interesting because it is not possible to tickle oneself – that is, respond with laughter to the tickling. The laughter evoked by tickling appears to depend entirely upon the social situation. The act of stroking and the strokability of the infant (allowing someone to touch him/her) are inherent in touch and are also relational measures. Similarly, to experience hugging demands a partner (D. N. Stern, 1985). Each of these examples makes clear the relational and bidirectional nature, but an important challenge is to determine a systematic means of measuring the touching that occurs and beyond this, to ascertain its meaning, all within the dyad rather than the individual. A dynamic perspective would view the dyad as developing together thus making it irrelevant, and even inappropriate, to attempt to divide the communicative process into the sender and receiver of the message. Process is considered primordial and the history and future of the dyad are important considerations. For example, Fogel and Garvey's (2007) metaphor in dynamic systems of "aliveness" in communication goes beyond a static model to one that embraces dynamically changing communication, focusing on the three related components of coregulation, ordinary variability, and innovation. What is studied over time is the coordinated coaction in the ongoing relationship, underscoring the coconstruction and the innovation in communication that embodies the continuous process model (see Fogel, Garvey, et al., 2006; Fogel, Hsu, et al., 2006).

The future is an exciting one. While there are many unresolved questions and issues to pursue, research is at a point where cutting edge issues are surfacing, studies are accumulating, and findings are converging. There is much to discover, reveal, and integrate into existing research and theory. We are on the cusp of discovering more about the way touch works its influence, and social interactions provide rich and fertile ground from which to study its multiple roles and impact during the first years of life and beyond.

Indeed, touch offers us a rich world to discover, and one that has implications for a variety of fields of inquiry. It is also a privileged field for promising interactions and convergence across a number of disciplines.

Acknowledgments

This chapter was written with the support of the Social Sciences and Humanities Research Council of Canada (SSHRC) and Fonds Quebecois de la Recherche sur la societe et la culture (FQRSC). The author expresses her gratitude to Yves Beaulieu for his detailed comments on an earlier version of this chapter, and to Gavin Bremner for his thorough review. Appreciation is also extended to Jesse Burns, Sabrina Chiarella, Joleen Coirazza, Julie Coutya, Irene Mantis, Tara Millman, and Kimberly Watson for their help with literature searches, library work, and preparation of the final version of the chapter.

References

Adamson, L. B., & Frick, J. E. (2003). The still face: A history of a shared experimental paradigm. *Infancy, 4,* 451–473.

Ainsworth, M. D. S., Blehar, M. C., Waters, E., & Wall, S. (1978). *Patterns of attachment: A psychological study of the strange situation.* Hillsdale, NJ: Erlbaum.

Albert, R. D., & Ha, I. A. (2004). Latino/Anglo-American differences in attributions to situations involving touch and silence. *International Journal of Intercultural Relations, 28,* 253–280.

Allen, S., & Daly, K. (2002). The effects of father involvement: A summary of the research evidence. *Newsletter of the Father Involvement Initiative, 1,* 1–11.

Ames, E. (1997). *The development of Romanian children adopted into Canada: Final report.* Burnaby: Simon Fraser University.

Anderson, G. C. (1995). Touch and the kangaroo care methods. In T. M. Field (Ed.), *Touch in early development* (pp. 35–51). Mahwah, NJ: Erlbaum.

Anderson, G. C., Chiu, S.-H., Morrison, B., Burkhammer, M., & Ludington-Hoe, S. (2004). Skin-to-skin care for breastfeeding difficulties postbirth. In Field, T. (Ed), *Touch and massage in early child development* (pp. 115–136). San Francisco: Johnson & Johnson Pediatric Institute.

Arco, C. M. (1983). Infant reactions to natural and manipulated temporal patterns of paternal communication. *Infant Behavior and Development, 6,* 391–399.

Arnold, S. (2002). *Maternal tactile-gestural stimulation and infants' nonverbal behaviors during early mother–infant face-to-face interactions: Contextual, age and birth status effects.* Unpublished doctoral dissertation, Concordia University, Montreal, Quebec, Canada.

Arnold, S. L., Brouillette, J., & Stack, D. M. (1996, August). *Changes in maternal and infant behavior as a function of instructional manipulations during unimodal and multimodal interactions.* Poster session presented at the biennial meeting of the International Society for the Study of Behavioral Development, Quebec City, Canada.

Bard, K. A., Myowa-Yamakoshi, M., Tomonaga, M., Tanaka, M., Costall, A., & Matsuzawa, T. (2005). Group differences in the mutual gaze of chimpanzees (Pan troglodytes). *Developmental Psychology, 41,* 616–624.

Barnett, L. (2005). Keep in touch: The importance of touch in infant development. *Infant Observation, 8,* 115–123.

Barrera, M. E., & Maurer, D. (1981). The perception of facial expressions by the three-month-old. *Child Development, 52,* 203–206.

Belsky, J. (1999). Interactional and contextual determinants of attachment security. In J. Cassidy & P. Shaver (Eds.), *Handbook of attachment theory and research* (pp. 249–264). New York: Guilford Press.

Beyette, M. E., Atkinson, M. L., & Kendall, S. (1989, June). *Emotional communication by touch.* Poster presented at the Canadian Psychological Association Annual Convention, Halifax, Nova Scotia.

Birns, B., Blank, M., & Bridger, W. H. (1966). The effectiveness of various soothing techniques on human neonates. *Psychosomatic Medicine, 28,* 316–322.

Bornstein, M. H. (1991). Approaches to parenting in culture. In M. H. Bornstein (Ed.), *Cultural approaches to parenting* (pp. 3–19). Hillsdale, NJ: Erlbaum.

Bowlby, J. (1969). *Attachment and loss.* (Vol. *1*). New York: Basic Books.

Braungart-Rieker, J., Garwood, M. M., Powers, B. P., & Notaro, P. C. (1998). Infant affect and affect regulation during the still-face paradigm with mothers and fathers: The role of infant characteristics and parental sensitivity. *Developmental Psychology, 34,* 1428–1437.

Braungart-Rieker, J. M., Garwood, M. M., Powers, B. P., & Wang, X. (2001). Parental sensitivity, infant affect, and affect regulation: Predictors of later attachment. *Child Development, 72,* 252–270.

Brazelton, T. B. (1990). Touch as a touchstone: Summary of the round table. In K. E. Barnard & T. B. Brazelton (Eds.). *Touch: The foundation of experience.* Madison, CT: International Universities Press.

Brazelton, T. B. (1994). *Touchpoints: Your child's emotional and behavioral development.* New York: Da Capo Press.

Bushnell, E. W., & Boudreau, P. R. (1991). The development of haptic perception during infancy. In M. A. Heller & W. Schiff (Eds.), *The psychology of touch.* Hillsdale, NJ: Erlbaum.

Byrne, J. M., & Horowitz, F. D. (1981). Rocking as a soothing intervention: The influence of direction and type of movement. *Infant Behavior and Development, 4,* 207–218.

Carlsson, S. G., Fagerberg, H., Horneman, G., Hwang, C.-P., Larsson, K., Rodholm, M., et al. (1978). Effects of amount of contact between mother and child on the mother's nursing behavior. *Developmental Psychobiology, 11,* 143–150.

Casati, I. (1991). Hugging and embracing; kisses given, kisses received. Preludes to tenderness between infant and adult. *Early Child Development and Care, 67,* 1–15.

Caulfield, R. (2001). Beneficial effects of tactile stimulation on early development. *Early Childhood Education Journal, 27,* 255–257.

Cleveland, A., Kobiella, A., & Striano, T. (2006). Intention or expression? Four-month-olds' reactions to a sudden still-face. *Infant Behavior & Development, 29,* 299–307.

Cohn, J. F. (2003). Additional components of the still-face effect: Commentary on Adamson and Frick. *Infancy, 4,* 493–497.

Cohn, J. F., & Tronick, E. Z. (1983). Three-month-old infants' reaction to simulated maternal depression. *Child Development, 54,* 185–193.

Cohn, J. F., & Tronick, E. Z. (1989). Specificity of infants' response to mothers' affective behavior. *Journal of the American Academy of Child and Adolescent Psychiatry, 28,* 242–248.

de Chateau, P. (1976). The influence of early contact on maternal and infant behavior on primiparae. *Birth and the Family Journal, 3,* 149–155.

Denenberg, V. H. (1968). A consideration of the usefulness of the critical period hypothesis as applied to the stimulation of rodents in infancy. In G. Newton and S. Levine (Eds.), *Early experience and behavior.* Springfield, IL: Charles C. Thomas.

Denenberg, V. H. (1969). The effects of early experience. In E. S. E. Hafez (Ed.), *The behavior of domestic animals* (2nd ed.). London: Baillure, Tindall and Cox.

Dickson, K. L., Walker, H., & Fogel, A. (1997). The relationship between smile type and play type during parent–infant play. *Developmental Psychology, 33,* 925–933.

Diego, M., Field, T., & Hernandez-Reif, M. (2004). Fetal responses to foot and hand massage of pregnant women. In T. Field (Ed.), *Touch and massage in early child development* (pp. 49–81). San Francisco: Johnson & Johnson Pediatric Institute.

Diego, M., Field, T., & Hernandez-Reif, M. (2008). Temperature increases in preterm infants during massage therapy. *Infant Behavior & Development, 31,* 149–152.

Diego, M., Field, T., Hernandez-Reif, M., Deeds, O., Ascencio, A., & Begert, G. (2008). Preterm infant massage elicits consistent increases in vagal activity and gastric motility that are associated with greater weight gain. *Acta Paediatrica, 96,* 1588–1591.

Ellsworth, C. P., Muir, D. W., & Hains, S. M. H. (1993). Social competence and person–object differentiation: An analysis of the still-face effect. *Developmental Psychology, 29,* 63–73.

Fanslow, C. (1984). Touch and the elderly. In C. C. Brown (Ed.), *The many facets of touch* (pp. 183–189). Skillman, NJ: Johnson & Johnson Baby Products Co.

Feldman, R., Eidelman, A. I., Sirota, I., & Weller, A. (2002). Comparison of skin-to-skin (kangaroo) and traditional care: Parenting outcomes and preterm infant development. *Pediatrics, 110,* 16–26.

Feldman, R., Masalha, S., & Alony, D. (2006). Microregulatory patterns of family interactions: Cultural pathways to toddlers' self-regulation. *Journal of Family Psychology, 20,* 614–623.

Feldman, R., Weller, A., Sirota, L., & Eidelman, A. I. (2003). Testing a family intervention hypothesis: The contribution of mother–infant skin-to-skin contact (kangaroo care) to family interaction and touch. *Journal of Family Psychology, 17,* 94–107.

Ferber, S. G., Feldman, R., & Makhoul, I. R. (2008). The development of maternal touch across the first year of life. *Early Human Development, 84,* 363–370.

Ferber, S. G., Laudon, M., Kuint, J., Weller, A., & Zisapel, N. (2002). Massage therapy by mothers enhances the adjustment of circadian rhythms to the nocturnal period in full-term infants. *Journal of Developmental & Behavioral Pediatrics, 23,* 410–415.

Fergus, E. L., Schmidt, J., & Pickens, J. (1998, April). *Touch during mother–infant interactions: The effects of parenting stress, depression and anxiety.* Poster session presented at the biennial meeting of the International Society of Infant Studies, Atlanta, GA.

Field, T. M. (1984). Early interactions between infants and their postpartum depressed mothers. *Infant Behavior and Development, 7,* 517–522.

Field, T. M. (Ed.). (1995). *Touch in early development* . Hillsdale, NJ: Erlbaum.

Field, T. M. (1998). Touch therapy effects on development. *International Journal of Behavioral Development, 22,* 779–797.

Field, T. M. (Ed.). (2001). *Touch.* Boston, MA: MIT Press.

Field, T. M. (2002). Infants' need for touch. *Human Development, 45,* 100–103.

Field, T. M. (Ed.). (2004). *Touch and massage in early development.* San Francisco: Johnson & Johnson Pediatric Institute.

Field, T., Diego, M., & Hernandez-Reif, M. (2006). Prenatal depression effects on the fetus and newborn, a review. *Infant Behavior and Development, 29,* 445–455.

Field, T., Diego, M., & Hernandez-Reif, M. (2007). Massage therapy research. *Developmental Review, 27,* 75–89.

Field, T., Diego, M. A., Hernandez-Reif, M., Deeds, O., & Figuereido, B. (2006). Moderate versus light pressure massage therapy leads to greater weight gain in preterm infants. *Infant Behavior & Development, 29,* 574–578.

Field, T., Hernandez-Reif, M., Diego, M., Feijo, L., Vera, Y., Gil, K., et al. (2007). Responses to animate and inanimate faces by infants of depressed mothers. *Early Child Development and Care, 177,* 533–539.

Field, T., Vega-Lahr, N., Goldstein, S., & Scafidi, F. (1987). Interaction behavior of infants and their dual-career parents. *Infant Behavior and Development, 10,* 371–377.

Field, T. M., Vega-Lahr, N., Scafidi, F., & Goldstein, S. (1986). Effects of maternal unavailability on mother–infant interactions. *Infant Behavior and Development, 9,* 473–478.

Fisher, J. D., Rytting, M., & Heslin, R. (1976). Hands touching hands: Affective and evaluative effects of an interpersonal touch. *Sociometry, 39,* 416–421.

Fogel, A., Dedo, J., & McEwen, I. (1992). Effect of postural position and reaching on gaze during mother–infant face-to-face interaction. *Infant Behavior and Development, 15,* 231–244.

Fogel, A., & Garvey, A. (2007). Alive communication. *Infant Behaviour and Development, 30,* 251–257.

Fogel, A., Garvey, A., Hsu, H.-C., West-Stroming, D. (2006). *Change processes in relationships: A relational-historical research approach.* New York: Cambridge University Press.

Fogel, A., Hsu, H. C., Shapiro, A. F., Nelson-Goens, C. G., & Secrist, C. (2006). Effects of normal and perturbed social play on the duration and amplitude of different types of infant smiles. *Developmental Psychology, 42,* 459–473.

Fogel, A., Toda, S., & Kawai, M. (1988). Mother–infant face-to-face interaction in Japan and the United States: A laboratory comparison using 3-month-old infants. *Developmental Psychology, 24,* 398–406.

Forbes, E. E., Cohn, J. F., Allen, N. B., & Lewinsohn, P. M. (2004). Infant affect during parent–infant interaction at 3 and 6 months: Differences between mothers and fathers and influence of parent history of depression. *Infancy, 5,* 61–84.

Franco, F., Fogel, A., Messinger, D. S., & Frazier, C. A. (1996). Cultural differences in physical contact between Hispanic and Anglo mother–infant dyads living in the United States. *Early Development and Parenting, 5,* 119–127.

Frank, L. K. (1957). Tactile communication. *Genetic Psychology Monographs, 56,* 209–255.

Fransson, A.-L., Karlsson, H., & Nilsson, K. (2005). Temperature variation in newborn babies: Importance of physical contact with the mother. *Archives of Disease in Childhood: Fetal and Neonatal Edition, 90,* F500–F504.

Frick, J. E., & Adamson, L. B. (2003). One still-face, many visions. *Infancy, 4,* 499–501.

Gale, G. (1998). Kangaroo care. *Neonatal Network, 17,* 69–71.

Goebel, P. W. (2002). Fathers' touch in low birthweight infants. *Dissertation Abstracts International: Section B: The Sciences and Engineering, 62,* 3553.

Gottlieb, G. (1983). The psychobiological approach to developmental issues. In M. M. Haith and J. J. Campos (Eds.), *Handbook of child psychology* (Vol. 2, pp. 1–26). New York: Wiley.

Gusella, J. L., Muir, D. W., & Tronick, E. Z. (1988). The effect of manipulating maternal behavior during an interaction of 3- and 6-month olds' affect and attention. *Child Development, 59,* 1111–1124.

Haley, D. W., & Stansbury, K. (2003). Infant stress and parent responsiveness: Regulation of physiology and behavior during still-face and reunion. *Child Development, 74,* 1534–1546.

Hamnett, F. S. (1921). Studies in the thyroid apparatus. *American Journal of Physiology, 56,* 196–204.

Hamnett, F. S. (1922). Studies of the thyroid apparatus. *Endocrinology, 6,* 221–229.

Harlow, H. F. (1959). Love in infant monkeys. *Scientific American, 200,* 68.

Harrison, L. (1985). Effects of early supplemental stimulation programs for premature infants: Review of the literature. *Maternal Child Nursing Journal, 14,* 69–90.

Harrison, L. (2001). The use of comforting touch and massage to reduce stress for preterm infants in the neonatal intensive care unit. *Newborn and Infant Nursing Reviews, 1*, 235–241.

Harrison, L. L., & Woods, S. (1991). Early parental touch and pretem infants. *Journal of Obstetric, Gynecologic, and Neonatal Nursing, 20*, 299–306.

Helders, P. J. M., Cats, B. P., & Debast, S. (1989). Effect of a tactile stimulation/range-finding programme on the development of VLBW-neonates during the first year of life. *Child Care, Health and Development, 15*, 369–380.

Heller, S. (1997). *The vital touch*. New York: Henry Holt.

Hernandez-Reif, M., Field, T., & Diego, M. (2004). Differential sucking by neonates of depressed versus non-depressed mothers. *Infant Behavior and Development, 27*, 465–476.

Herrera, E., Reissland, N., & Shepherd, J. (2004). Maternal touch and maternal child-directed speech: Effects of depressed mood in the postnatal period. *Journal of Affective Disorders, 81*, 29–39.

Hertenstein, M. J. (2002). Touch: Its communicative functions in infancy. *Human Development, 45*, 70–94.

Hertenstein, M. J., & Campos, J. J. (2001). Emotion regulation via maternal touch. *Infancy, 2*, 549–566.

Hertenstein, M. J., Verkamp, J. M., Kerestes, A. M., & Holmes, R. M. (2006). The communicative functions of touch in humans, nonhuman primates and rates: A review and synthesis of empirical research. *Genetic, Social, and General Psychology Monographs, 132*, 5–94.

Hewlett, B. S. (1987). Intimate fathers: Patterns of paternal holding among Aka Pygmies. In M. E. Lamb (Ed.), *The father's role: Cross-cultural perspectives* (pp. 295–330). Hillsdale, NJ: Erlbaum.

Hofer, M. (1993). Developmental roles of timing in the mother–infant interaction. In G. Turkewitz and D. A. Devenny (Eds.), *Developmental time and timing* (pp. 211–231). Hillsdale, NJ: Erlbaum.

Hofer, M. A. (2006). Psychobiological roots of early attachment. *Current Directions in Psychological Science, 15*, 84–88.

Hsu, H.-C., & Sung, J. (2008). Separation anxiety in first-time mothers: Infant behavioral reactivity and maternal parenting self-efficacy as contributors. *Infant Behavior & Development, 31*, 294–301.

Jahromi, L. B., Putnam, S. P., & Stifter, C. A. (2004). Maternal regulation of infant reactivity from 2 to 6 months. *Developmental Psychology, 40*, 477–487.

Jean, A., Moszkowski, R., Girouard, N., & Stack, D. M. (2005, April). *The quality of mother–infant and father–infant face-to-face interactions: Parental touching behavior across interaction contexts*. Poster presented at the Biennial Meeting of the Society for Research in Child Development, Atlanta, GA.

Jean, A., & Stack, D. M. (2009). Functions of maternal touch and infants' affect during face-to-face interactions: New directions for the still-face. *Infant Behavior and Development, 32*, 123–128.

Jean, A., Stack, D. M., & Fogel, A. (2008). A longitudinal investigation of maternal touching across the first six months of life: Age and context effects. *Infant Behavior and Development, 32*, 344–349.

Johnston, C. C., Filion, F., Campbell-Yeo, M., Goulet, C., Bell, L., McNaughton, K., et al. (in press). Enhanced kangaroo mother care for heel lance in preterm neonates: a crossover trial. *Journal of Perinatology, 29*, 51–56.

Jones, S. E., & LeBaron, C. D. (2002). Research on the relationship between verbal and nonverbal communication: Emerging integrations. *Journal of Communication, 52*, 499–521.

Jones, S. E., & Yarbrough, A. E. (1985). A naturalistic study of the meanings of touch. *Communication Monographs, 52*, 19–56.

Kaffman, A., & Meaney, M. J. (2007). Neurodevelopmental sequelae of postnatal maternal care in rodents: Clinical and research implications of molecular insights. *Journal of Child Psychology and Psychiatry, 48,* 224–244.

Kaitz, M., Lapidot, P., Bronner, R., & Eidelman, A. I. (1992). Parturient women can recognize their infant by touch. *Developmental Psychology, 28,* 35–39.

Kaitz, M., Meirov, H., Landman, I., & Eidelman, A. I. (1993). Infant recognition by tactile cues. *Infant Behavior and Development, 16,* 333–341.

Kawakami, K., Takai-Kawakami, K., & Kanaya, Y. (1994). A longitudinal study of Japanese and American mother–infant interactions. *Psychologia: An International Journal of Psychology in the Orient, 37,* 18–29.

Kaye, K. (1982). *The mental and social life of babies: How parents create persons.* Chicago, IL: University of Chicago Press.

Kaye, K., & Fogel, A. (1980). The temporal structure of face-to-face communication between mothers and infants. *Developmental Psychology, 16,* 454–464.

Kisilevsky, B. S., Fearon, I., & Muir, D. W. (1998). Fetuses differentiate vibroacoustic stimuli. *Infant Behavior and Development, 21,* 25–46.

Kisilevsky, B. S., & Low, J. A. (1998). Human fetal behavior: 100 years of study. *Developmental Review, 18,* 1–29.

Kisilevsky, B. S., Muir, D. W., & Low, J. A. (1992). Maturation of human fetal responses to vibroacoustic stimulation. *Child Development, 63,* 1497–1508.

Klatzky, R. L., & Lederman, S. (1987). The intelligent hand. In G. H. Bower (Ed.), *The psychology of learning and motivation* (pp. 121–151). San Diego: Academic Press.

Klaus, M., Jerauld, R., Kreger, N., McAlpine, W., Steffa, M., & Kennell, J. (1972). Maternal attachment: Importance of the first post-partum days. *New England Journal of Medicine, 286,* 460–463.

Klaus, M. H., Kennell, J. H., Plumb, N., & Zuelke, S. (1970). Human maternal behavior at the first contact with her young. *Pediatrics, 46,* 187–192.

Kluck-Ebbin, M. R. (2004). *Hands on baby massage.* New York: Running Press.

Koester, L. S., Papousek, H., & Papousek, M. (1989). Patterns of rhythmic stimulation by mothers with three-month-olds: A cross-modal comparison. *International Journal of Behavioral Development, 12,* 143–154.

Koniak-Griffin, D., & Ludington-Hoe, S. (1987). Paradoxical effects of stimulation on normal neonates. *Infant Behavior and Development, 10,* 261–277.

Konner, M. J. (1976). Maternal care, infant behavior and development among the !Kung. In R. B. Lee & I. DeVore (Eds.), *Kalahari hunter-gatherers: Studies of the !Kung San and their neighbors* (pp. 218–245). Cambridge, MA: Harvard University Press.

Korner, A. F., & Thoman, E. B. (1972). The relative efficacy of contact and vestibular-proprioceptive stimulation in soothing neonates. *Child Development, 43,* 443–453.

Kuhn, C. M., & Schanberg, S. M. (1998). Responses to maternal separation: Mechanisms and mediators. *International Journal of Developmental Neuroscience, 16,* 261–270.

Lahat, S., Mimouni, F. B., Ashbel, G., & Dollberg, S. (2007). Energy expenditure in growing preterm infants receiving massage therapy. *Journal of the American College of Nutrition, 26,* 356–359.

Lamb, M. E. (1981). *The role of the father in child development* (Rev. Ed.). New York: Wiley.

Lamb, M. E., Frodi, A. M., Hwang, C.-P., Frodi, M., & Steinberg, J. (1982). Mother– and father–infant interaction involving play and holding in traditional and nontraditional Swedish families. *Developmental Psychology, 18,* 215–221.

Lamb, M. E., Morrison, D. C., & Malkin, C. M. (1987). The development of infant social expectations in face-to-face interaction: A longitudinal study. *Merrill-Palmer Quarterly, 33,* 241–254.

Landau, R., Shusel, R., Eshel, Y., & Ben-Aaron, M., (2003). Mother–child and metapelet–child touch behavior with three-year-old kibbutz children in two contexts. *Infant Mental Health Journal, 24,* 529–546.

Lavelli, M., & Fogel, A. (1998, April). *Developmental changes in early mother–infant face-to-face communication.* Poster session presented at the biennial meeting of the International Conference on Infant Studies, Atlanta, Georgia.

Leboyer, F. (1976). *Loving hands.* New York: Alfred A. Knopf.

Lecanuet, J.-P., Fifer, W. P., Krasnegor, N. A., & Smotherman, W. P. (1995). *Fetal development: A psychobiological perspective.* Hillsdale, NJ: Erlbaum.

Lecanuet, J. P., Granier-Deferre, C., & Bushnel, M. C. (1989). Differential fetal auditory reactiveness as a function of stimulus characteristics and states. *Seminars in Perinatology, 13,* 421–429.

Legerstee, M., & Markova, G. (2007). Intentions make a difference: Infant responses to still-face and modified still-face conditions. *Infant Behavior & Development, 30,* 232–250.

LePage, D. E. (1998). *Four-and 7-month-old infants' sensitivities to contingency during face-to-face social interactions.* Unpublished doctoral dissertation, Concordia University, Montreal, Quebec, Canada.

LePage, D. E., & Stack, D. M. (1997, April). *Four- and seven-month-old infants' abilities to detect tactile contingencies in a face-to-face context.* Poster session presented at the biennial meeting of the Society for Research in Child Development, Washington, DC.

Levine, S. (1956). A further study of infantile handling and adult avoidance learning. *Journal of Personality, 25,* 70–80.

Levine, S. (1960). Stimulation in infancy. *Scientific American, 202,* 80.

Levine, S. (1994). The ontogeny of the hypothalamic-pituitary-adrenal axis: The influence of maternal factors. *Annals of the New York Academy of Sciences, 746,* 275–288.

Levine, S., Haltmeyer, G. C., Karas, G. G. (1967). Physiological and behavioral effects of infantile stimulation. *Physiology & Behavior, 2,* 55–59.

Levine, S., & Stanton, M. E. (1990). The hormonal consequences of mother–infant contact. In K. E. Barnard & T. B. Brazelton (Eds.), *Touch: The foundation of experience.* Clinical Infant Reports, (no. 4), Johnson & Johnson Pediatric Round Table X. Madison, CT: International University Press.

Liu, D., Diorio, J., Tannenbaum, B., Caldji, C., Francis, D., Freedman, A., et al. (1997). Maternal care, hippocampal glucocorticoid receptors, and hypothalamic-pituitary-adrenal responses to stress. *Science, 277,* 1659–1662.

Lovic, V., Fleming, A. S., & Fletcher, P. J. (2006). Early Life tactile stimulation changes adult rat responsiveness to amphetamine. *Psychopharmacology, 84,* 497–503.

Lowe, J., Handmaker, N., & Aragon, C. (2006). Impact of mother interactive style on infant affect among babies exposed to alcohol in utero. *Infant Mental Health Journal, 27,* 371–382.

Ludington-Hoe, S. M., & Swinth, J. Y. (1996). Developmental aspects of kangaroo care. *Journal of Obstetric, Gynecologic, and Neonatal Nursing, 25,* 691–703.

Maurer, D., & Maurer, C. (1988). *The world of the newborn.* New York: Basic Books.

Mayes, L. C., & Carter, A. S. (1990). Emerging social regulatory capacities as seen in the still-face situation. *Child Development, 61,* 754–763.

McClure, V. S. (1989). *Infant massage: A handbook for loving parents.* New York: Bantam.

Melo, A. I., Lovic, V., Gonzalez, A., Madden, M., Sinopoli, K., & Fleming, A. S. (2006). Maternal and littermate deprivation disrupts maternal behavior and social-learning of food preference in adulthood: Tactile stimulation, nest odor, and social rearing prevent these effects. *Developmental Psychobiology, 48,* 209–219.

Merin, N., Young, G. S., Ozonoff, S., & Rogers, S. J. (2007). Visual fixation patterns during reciprocal social interaction distinguish a subgroup of 6-month-old infants at risk for autism from comparison infants. *Journal of Autism and Developmental Disorders, 37*, 108–121.

Millman, T. P., Jean, A., & Stack, D. M. (2009, April). *Infants' self-regulating abilities and maternal touch: Examining the impact of birth status and reaction to the still-face period.* Poster presented at the Biennial Meeting of the Society for Research in Child Development, Denver, CO.

Montagu, A. (1971). *Touching: The human significance of the skin.* New York: Columbia University Press.

Montagu, A. (1986). *Touching: The human significance of the skin* (3rd ed.). New York: Harper and Row Publishers.

Montirosso, R., Borgatti, R., Trojan, S., Zanini, R., & Tronick, E. (2009). A comparison of dyadic interactions and coping with still-face in healthy pre-term and full-term infants. *British Journal of Developmental Psychology*, doi 10.1348/026151009X416429.

Moore, E. R., Anderson, G. C., & Bergman, N. (2007, July 18). Early skin-to-skin contact for mothers and their healthy newborn infants. *Cochrane database of systematic reviews, 3*, CD003519.

Moore, D. G., Oates, J. M., Goodwin, J., & Hobson, R. P. (2008). Behavior of mothers and infants with and without Down syndrome during the still-face procedure. *Infancy, 13*, 75–89.

Moreno, A. J., Posada, G. E., & Goldyn, D. T. (2006). Presence and quality of touch influence coregulation in mother–infant dyads. *Infancy, 9*, 1–20.

Moszkowski, R. J., & Stack, D. M. (2007). Infant touching behavior during mother–infant face-to-face interactions. *Infant and Child Development, 16*, 307–319.

Moszkowski, R. M., Stack, D. M., & Chiarella, S. (2009). Infant touch with gaze and affective behaviors during mother–infant still-face interactions: Co-occurrence and functions of touch. *Infant Behavior and Development, 32*, 392–403.

Moszkowski, R. M., Stack, D. M., Girouard, N., Field, T. M., Hernandez-Reif, M., & Diego, M. (2009). Touching behaviors of infants of depressed mothers during normal and perturbed interactions. *Infant Behavior and Development, 32*, 183–194.

Muir, D. W. (2002). Adult communications with infants through touch: The forgotten sense. *Human Development, 45*, 95–99.

Muir, D., & Field, J. (1979). Newborn infants orient to sounds. *Child Development, 50*, 431–436.

Muir, D., & Lee, K. (2003). The still-face effect: Methodological issues and new applications. *Infancy, 4*, 483–491.

Murray, L., & Trevarthen, C. (1985). Emotional regulation of interactions between two-month-olds and their mothers. In T. M. Field, & N. A. Fox (Eds.), *Social perception in infants* (pp. 177–197). Norwood, NJ: Ablex.

New, R. S., & Benigni, L. (1987). Italian fathers and infants: Cultural constraints on paternal behavior. In M. E. Lamb (Ed.), *The father's role: Cross-cultural perspectives* (pp. 139–167). Hillsdale, NJ: Erlbaum.

O'Higgins, M., Roberts, I. St-J., & Glover, V. (2008). Postnatal depression and mother and infant outcomes after infant massage. *Journal of Affective Disorders, 109*, 189–192.

Papousek, M. (2007). Communication in early infancy: An arena of intersubjective learning. *Infant Behavior & Development, 30*, 258–266.

Parke, R. D., & O'Leary, S. (1976). Family interaction in the newborn period: Some findings, some observations and some unresolved issues. In K. Riegan & J. Meacham (Eds.), *The developing individual in a changing world.* The Hague: Mouton.

Peláez-Nogueras, M. (1995, March). *Rhythmic and nonrhythmic touch during mother–infant interactions*. Poster session presented at the biennial meeting of the Society for Research in Child Development, Indianapolis, IN.

Peláez-Nogueras, M., Field, T. M., Hossain, Z., & Pickens, J. (1996). Depressed mothers' touching increases infants' positive affect and attention in still-face interactions. *Child Development, 67*, 1780–1792.

Peláez-Nogueras, M., Gewirtz, J. L., Field, T., Cigales, M., Malphurs, J., Clasky, S., et al. (1996). Infants' preference for touch stimulation in face-to-face interactions. *Journal of Applied Developmental Psychology, 17*, 199–213.

Perez, H., & Gewirtz, J. L. (2004). Maternal touch effects on infant behavior. In T. Field (Ed), *Touch and massage in early child development* (pp. 39–48). San Francisco: Johnson and Johnson Pediatrics Institute.

Phillips, R. B., & Moses, H. A. (1996). Skin hunger effects on preterm neonates. *The Transdisciplinary Journal, 6*, 39–49.

Polan, H. J., & Ward, M. J. (1994). Role of the mother's touch in failure to thrive: A preliminary investigation. *Journal of the American Child and Adolescent Psychiatry, 33*, 1098–1105.

Provence, S., & Lipton, R. C. (1962). *Infants in institutions*. New York: International Universities Press.

Reissland, N., & Burghart, R. (1987). The role of massage in South Asia: Child health and development. *Social Science and Medicine, 25*, 231–239.

Robin, M. (1982). Neonate–mother interaction: Tactile contacts in the days following birth. *Early Child Development and Care, 9*, 221–236.

Roedell, W. C., & Slaby, R. G. (1977). The role of distal and proximal interaction in infant social preference formation. *Developmental Psychology, 13*, 266–273.

Roopnarine, J. L., Talukder, E., Jain, D., Joshi, P., & Srivastav, P. (1990). Characteristics of holding, patterns of play, and social behaviors between parents and infants in New Delhi, India. *Developmental Psychology, 26*, 667–673.

Rose, S. A., Schmidt, K., Riese, M. L., & Bridger, W. H. (1980). Effects of prematurity and early intervention on responsivity to tactual stimuli: A comparison of pre-term and full-term infants. *Child Development, 51*, 416–425.

Rubin, R. (1963). Maternal touch. *Nursing Outlook, 11*, 328–331.

Rutter, M., & English and Romanian Adoptees (ERA) Study Team (1998). Developmental catch-up, and deficit, following adoption after severe early privation. *Journal of Child Psychology and Psychiatry, 39*, 465–476.

Scafidi, F. A., Field, T. M., Schanberg, S. M., Bauer, C. R., Tucci, K., Roberts, J., et al. (1990). Massage stimulates growth in preterm infants: A replication. *Infant Behavior and Development, 13*, 167–188.

Scafidi, F. A., Field, T. M., Schanberg, S. M., Bauer, C. R., Vega-Lahr, N., Garcia, R., et al. (1986). Effects of tactile/ kinesthetic stimulation on the clinical course and sleep/wake behavior of preterm neonates. *Infant Behavior and Development, 9*, 91–105.

Schanberg, S. M., & Field, T. M. (1987). Sensory deprivation stress and supplemental stimulation in the rat pup and preterm human. *Child Development, 58*, 1431–1447.

Schiffman, H. R. (1982). *Sensation and perception* (2nd ed.). New York: Wiley.

Sigman, M., & Wachs, T. D. (1991). Structure, continuity, and nutritional correlates of caregiver behavior patterns in Kenya and Egypt. In M. H. Bornstein (Ed.), *Cultural approaches to parenting* (pp. 123–137). Hillsdale, NJ: Erlbaum.

Silveira, P. P., Portella, A. K., Clemente, Z., Gamaro, G. D., & Dalmaz, C. (2005). The effect of neonatal handling on adult feeding behavior is not an anxiety-like behavior. *International Journal of Developmental Neuroscience, 23*, 93–99.

Solkoff, N., Yaffe, S., Weintraub, D., & Blase, B. (1969). Effects of handling on the subsequent developments of premature infants. *Developmental Psychology, 1*, 765–768.

Solter, A. (2001). Hold me! The importance of physical contact with infants. *Journal of Prenatal & Perinatal Psychology & Health, 15*, 193–205.

Sorenson, R. (1976). *The edge of the forest.* Washington, DC: Smithsonian Institute Press.

Spitz, R. A., & Wolf, K. M. (1946). Anaclitic depression: An inquiry into the genesis of psychiatric conditions in early childhood. *The Psychoanalytic Study of the Child, 2*, 313–342.

Stack, D. M. (2001). The salience of touch and physical contact during infancy: Unraveling some of the mysteries of the somesthetic sense. In G. Bremner & A. Fogel (Eds.), *Blackwell handbook of infant development* (pp. 351–378). Oxford: Blackwell.

Stack, D. M. (2004). Touching during mother–infant interactions. In T. Field (Ed.), *Touch and massage in early child development* (pp. 49–81). San Francisco: Johnson and Johnson Pediatrics Institute.

Stack, D. M., & Arnold, S. L. (1998). Changes in mothers' touch and hand gestures influence infant behavior during face-to-face interchanges. *Infant Behavior and Development, 21*, 451–468.

Stack, D. M., Arnold, S. L., Girouard, N., & Welburn, B. (1999, April). *Infants' reactions to maternal unavailability in very low birth weight preterm and fullterm infants.* Paper presented at the biennial meeting of the Society for Research in Child Development, Albuquerque, New Mexico.

Stack, D. M., & LePage, D. E. (1996). Infants' sensitivity to manipulations of maternal touch during face-to-face interactions. *Social Development, 5*, 41–55.

Stack, D. M., LePage, D. E., Hains, S. M., & Muir, D. W. (1996, April). Qualitative changes in maternal touch as a function of instructional condition during face-to-face social interactions [Abstract]. *Infant Behavior and Development, 19*, 761.

Stack, D. M., & Muir, D. W. (1990). Tactile stimulation as a component of social interchange: New interpretations for the still-face effect. *British Journal of Developmental Psychology, 8*, 131–145.

Stack, D. M., & Muir, D. W. (1992). Adult tactile stimulation during face-to-face interactions modulates 5-month-olds' affect and attention. *Child Development, 63*, 1509–1525.

Stack, D. M., & Tsonis, M. (1999). Infants' haptic perception of texture in the presence and absence of visual cues. *British Journal of Developmental Psychology, 17*, 97–110.

Stepakoff, S. A. (2000). *Mother–infant tactile communication at four months: Effects of infant gender, maternal ethnicity, and maternal depression.* Unpublished doctoral dissertation, St. John's University, New York.

Stern, D. N. (1985). *The interpersonal world of the infant: A view from psychoanalysis and developmental psychology.* New York: Basic Books.

Stern, J. M. (1989). Maternal behavior: Sensory, hormonal, and neural determinants. In F. R. Brush & S. Levine (Eds.), *Psychoendocrinology* (pp. 105–226). New York: Academic Press.

Stern, J. M. (1990). Multisensory regulation of maternal behavior and masculine sexual behavior: A revised view. *Neuroscience and Biobehavioral Reviews, 14*, 183–200.

Stern, J. M. (1996). Somatosensation and maternal care in Norway rats. In J. S. Rosenblatt & C. T. Snowden (Eds.), *Evolution, mechanisms, and adaptive significance of parental care. Advances in the study of behavior* (Vol. 25, pp. 243–294). New York: Academic Press.

Stern, J. M. (1997). Offspring-induced nurturance: Animal–human parallels. *Developmental Psychobiology, 31*, 19–37.

Sun, L.-C, & Roopnarine, J. L. (1996). Mother–infant, father–infant interaction and involvement in childcare and household labor among Taiwanese families. *Infant Behavior and Development, 19*, 121–129.

Suomi, S. (1997). Nonverbal communication in nonhuman primates: Implications for the emergence of culture. In U. Segerstråle & P. Molnár (Eds.), *Nonverbal communication: Where nature meets culture* (pp. 131–146). Mahwah, NJ: Erlbaum.

Suomi, S. J. (2005). Mother–infant attachment, peer relationships, and the development of social networks in rhesus monkeys. *Human Development, 48*, 67–79.

Suomi, S. J. (2006). Risk, resilience, and gene x environment interactions in Rhesus monkeys. *Annals of the New York Academy of Sciences, 1094*, 52–62.

Symons, D. K., & Moran, G. (1987). The behavioral dynamics of mutual responsiveness in early face-to-face mother–infant interactions. *Child Development, 58*, 1488–1495.

Toda, S., & Fogel, A. (1993). Infant response to the still-face situation at 3 and 6 months. *Developmental Psychology, 29*, 532–538.

Trevarthen, C. (1986). Form, significance and psychological potential of hand gestures in infants. In J. L. Nespoulos, P. Perron, & A. Roch Lecours (Eds.), *The Biological Foundation of Gestures: Motor and Semiotic Aspects* (pp. 149–202). Cambridge, MA: MIT Press.

Trevathan, W. R. (1981). Maternal touch at first contact with the newborn infant. *Developmental Psychobiology, 14*, 549–558.

Tronick, E. Z. (1989). Emotions and emotional communication in infants. *American Psychologist, 44*, 112–119.

Tronick, E. Z. (1995). Touch in mother–infant interaction. In T. M. Field (Ed.), *Touch in early development* (pp. 53–65). Mahwah, NJ: Erlbaum.

Tronick, E. Z. (2003). Things still to be done on the still-face effect. *Infancy, 4*, 475–482.

Tronick, E. Z., Als, H., Adamson, L., Wise, S., & Brazelton, T. B. (1978). The infant's response to entrapment between contradictory messages in face-to-face interactions. *Journal of the American Academy of Child Psychiatry, 17*, 1–13.

Tronick, E. Z., Messinger, D. S., Weinberg, M. K., Lester, B. M., LaGasse, L., Seifer, R., et al. (2005). Cocaine exposure is associated with subtle compromises of infants' and mothers' social-emotional behavior and dyadic features of their interaction in the face-to-face still-face paradigm. *Developmental Psychology, 41*, 711–722.

Tronick, E. Z., Thomas, R. B., & Daltabuit, M. (1994). The quechua manta pouch: A caretaking practice for buffering the Peruvian infant against the multiple stressors of high altitude. *Child Development, 65*, 1005–1013.

Tulman, L. J. (1985). Mother's and unrelated persons' initial handling of newborn infants. *Nursing Research, 34*, 205–210.

Underdown, A., Barlow, J., Chung, V., & Stewart-Brown, S., (2006, Oct. 18). Massage intervention for promoting mental and physical health in infants aged under six months. *Cochrane database of systematic reviews, 4*, CD005038.

Uvnas-Moberg, K. (2004). Massage, relaxation and well-being: A possible role for oxytocin as an integrative principle? In T. Field (Ed.), *Touch and massage in early child development* (pp. 191–208). San Francisco: Johnson & Johnson Pediatric Institute.

Watt, J. (1990). Interaction, intervention, and development in small-for-gestational-age infants. *Infant Behavior and Development, 13*, 273–286.

Weinberg, M. K., Olson, K. L., Beeghly, M., & Tronick, E. Z. (2006). Making up is hard to do, especially for mothers with high levels of depressive symptoms and their infant sons. *Journal of Child Psychology and Psychiatry, 47*, 670–683.

Weinberg, M. K., & Tronick, E. Z. (1994). Beyond the face: An empirical study of infant affective configurations of facial, vocal, gestural, and regulatory behaviors. *Child Development, 65*, 1503–1515.

Weller, A., & Feldman, R. (2003). Emotion regulation and touch in infants: The role of cholecystokinin and opioids. *Peptides, 24*, 779–788.

White, J. L., & Labarba, R. C. (1976). The effects of tactile and kinesthetic stimulation on neonatal development in the premature infant. *Developmental Psychobiology, 9*, 569–577.

Wolff, P. H. (1963). Observations on the early development of smiling. In B. M. Foss (Ed.), *Determinants of infant behavior II* (pp. 113–138). London: Methuen & Co.

Yogman, M. W. (1982). Development of the father–infant relationship. In H. F. Fitzgerald, B. M. Lester & M. W. Yogman (Eds.), *Theory and research in behavioral pediatrics* (Vol. *1*, pp. 221–279). New York: Plenum Press.

Zaslow, M. J., Pederson, F. A., Suwalsky, J. T. D., Cain, R. L., & Fivel, M. (1985). The early resumption of employment by mothers: Implications for parent–infant interaction. *Journal of Applied Developmental Psychology, 6*, 1–16.

Zhang, M., & Cai, J. X. (2008). Neonatal tactile stimulation enhances spatial working memory, prefrontal long-term potentiation, and D1 receptor activation in adult rats. *Neurobiology of Learning and Memory, 89*, 397–406.

19

Emotion and its Development in Infancy

David C. Witherington, Joseph J. Campos, Jennifer A. Harriger, Cheryl Bryan, and Tessa E. Margett

A Perspective on the Nature of Emotion

From a phenomenological standpoint, emotions are internal feeling states, states over which we seemingly have little control and which frequently disrupt and disorganize our behavior. These internal states manifest themselves in outward "expressions," through the face, voice, and the actions we perform. Such a view of emotion at one time dominated scientific conceptualizations of the phenomenon, but in the last 25 years, a new conceptualization of emotion has emerged, one which treats emotions as adaptive, relational processes which function to regulate our exchanges with the world (Barrett & Campos, 1987; Campos, Campos, & Barrett, 1989; Witherington, Campos, & Hertenstein, 2001; Witherington & Crichton, 2007). From the standpoint of this functionalist perspective, emotion is not just a feeling state because it powerfully affects both one's own behavior and the behavior of others. Feeling states are the internal, subjective, experiential components of emotion. While feelings are a crucial facet of emotion, they are not its core; they are not what determines everything else about the emotion process (Frijda, 1986).

As detailed more explicitly in Witherington et al. (2001), the functionalist approach to emotion argues that emotions reach out to the social and physical world. Emotions are *relational*, resulting from the impact of events on what the person is trying to do. They emerge neither from the self nor from the environment but from the fusion of external event and internal intent. When self and world clash, creating problems which require steps to address, negative emotions such as anger and fear occur. When self and world suddenly coordinate effectively, creating smooth progress to a goal, positive emotions, such as joy, relief, love, triumph, etc., emerge. In brief, emotions are processes through which an individual attempts to establish, alter, or maintain her/his relation to the environment on matters of significance to the individual (Campos et al., 1989; Witherington et al., 2001). Emotions are organized around the functions they serve, with specific behaviors, facial and vocal configurations, and physiological activities acquiring emotional meaning only in terms of the role they play in person–environment transactions. A smile, therefore, can serve many masters, as Kagan (1971) put it; in context, it can as readily be in the service of scorn as of joy.

What makes an interaction emotional?

From the functionalist perspective, the most unambiguous feature distinguishing emotion from the nonemotion is *personal significance* – that is, the value, importance, or relevance of the transaction for the person. How does significance arise in the relationship between an organism and its environment? One way is through goal relevance: if an event is congruent or incongruent with one's goals, emotion is generated (Frijda, 1986; Lazarus, 1991). Another way is through social signals (Campos et al., 1989). The emotional signals from others, such as their smiles, coos, frowns, laughs, sneers, can imbue the actions we perform with affective significance, as when the scream from a mother upon seeing her baby reach for a light socket renders the light socket frightening for the child. The significance of one's transaction with the world assumes different patterns and functions depending on the nature of relation between person and event. Emotions like joy or relief come from congruence between a person's goals and events and function to maintain such congruence. Emotions like anger and sadness come from goal–event incongruence. Both anger and sadness involve frustrating encounters with an obstacle to goal attainment, but in anger the functional possibility of overcoming the obstacle – and hence the incongruence – exists. When goal restoration is deemed unattainable, sadness ensues. In fear, the relation of an event to one's goals involves a particular goal – that of personal security; the event is a threat to one's safety, well-being, or status, and fear functions to remove the individual from the threat.

Whatever the specific nature of exchange between person and event, it is at the level of relation between the two that the emotion process resides (Frijda, 1986; Lazarus, 1991). Events in themselves do not intrinsically generate emotion but must always be considered in relation to an individual to understand the generation of emotion, for the same event can acquire a different emotional meaning the moment it is linked, for example, to a different goal or striving of the individual. The meaning of an event also depends on what a person can do, or thinks she/he can do, in relation to the event. Having the means available to eliminate an obstacle can mean the difference between whether anger or sadness arises in the context of goal frustration. Thus, understanding the generation of emotion depends on a simultaneous integration of event, the person's goals and strivings, and the action repertoire available to the person for evaluating and regulating her/his relation to the event.

Multiple Component Processes and Emotional Development

As we have argued, the emotion process sits at the interface of relationship between person and event. Construed in this way, emotion is a complex system comprised of multiple subsystems or components, both within and outside of the organism (Camras & Witherington, 2005; Fogel et al., 1992; Saarni, Campos, Camras, & Witherington, 2006; Witherington et al., 2001). These subsystems/components include organismic variables like our goals, the evaluations (appraisals) we make of situations as we relate them to our goals, the instrumental and expressive actions we use to maintain or change our relation to the environment, as well as extraorganismic variables like the situations themselves that impact our goals. Emotions are built up out of the relations that exist among these components of the process. Each component (e.g., appraisals, goals, instrumental actions, situational contexts) is an important part of the emotion process, but none is more privileged than any other when explaining how emotion is generated. This point – that emotion is *irreducible* to any of the subsystems that give rise to it – is a cornerstone of the dynamic systems approach to emotion and its development (Camras & Witherington, 2005; Witherington & Crichton, 2007). In recent years, the dynamic systems approach has complemented and extended the functionalist perspective by specifically articulating the nature of *development* in emotional processes, a topic not as thoroughly elaborated in functionalist accounts. If the emotion process consists of multiple, interrelated components, then emotional development stems from systematic changes in the interactions among these components (Camras & Witherington, 2005; Fogel et al., 1992). Both individual developments of particular components themselves (e.g., the development of expressive patterns in the face) and interactions among components (changes in the way an individual relates goals to particular events) establish organizational changes in emotion; to understand emotional development, therefore, requires an assessment of how the components of emotion interact to produce behavior at different levels of developmental organization, from birth forward (M. D. Lewis, 2000; M. D. Lewis & Granic, 1999; Mascolo & Griffin, 1998).

Just as no one component serves as criterion for emotion in its mature form, no one component of the emotion process serves as criterion for either a given developmental level of organization in emotion or a transition between levels of organization in development. Thus, characterizing the emotional life of a 4-month-old – as distinct from an 8-month-old – requires more than simply knowing the child's appraisal skills, because event appraisals necessarily depend on the actions available to the infant for engaging the event (Campos, Mumme, Kermoian, & Campos, 1994). We must also know the action repertoire available to the 4-month-old. However, this is only half the picture, for we must also know about the world in which the 4-month-old resides, the social and physical contexts in which the infant is embedded. Both the emergence in real time of any given emotion and the organizational transformation in developmental time of emotion systems are thus multiply determined, a function not of the system's components themselves but of the relations that form among these parts of the system (Dickson, Fogel, & Messinger, 1998; M. D. Lewis, 2000).

As active, self-organizing processes, emotions take root directly in activity geared toward adaptation in the world. When reorganization occurs in this adaptation, in the way a person relates to her environment, emotional development takes place (Campos et al., 1994; Griffin & Mascolo, 1998; Thompson, 1993). The period of infancy is marked by a series of major qualitative changes in infants' relationship to their world, and in the process, their emotional lives change remarkably over the first 2 years of life.

In this chapter, we will focus on four major periods of transition in the relationship between infants and their environment and on how each of these transitional periods specifically maps onto qualitative reorganization in the emotional world of the infant. Between the first and second month, infants begin to systematically engage with their social environment – through the emergence of the social smile and coordinated patterns of affect sharing via face-to-face interaction with their caregivers – in what amounts to a "social birth" of the infant (Rochat & Striano, 1999). Subsequent to this period, infants, beginning around 3 to 4 months, begin to refocus much of their attention to the world of objects and away from dyadic communication. Between 6 and 9 months, infants undergo a third qualitative reorganization in development, marked by the emergence of a newfound wariness in their engagement with the world, both social and object. Finally, at the end of the first year, between 9 and 12 months, infants graduate to a new level of social interaction, moving from the purely dyadic affective sharing patterns of earlier development to triadic forms of sharing in which the caregiver–infant dyad now communicate about people and things outside the dyad. However, before moving into these transitional periods, we will first establish some phylogenetic and postnatal ontogenetic starting points in emotion for the human infant.

Phylogenetic Starting Points for Emotional Development

It is very difficult to infer the operation of evolutionary factors in emotion (Haig & Durrant, 2000; Ketelaar & Ellis, 2000). In general, we can infer an evolutionary role in emotion when as many as possible of the following criteria are met: (1) universality of manifestation across cultures; (2) presence very early in ontogeny; (3) presence later in ontogeny in the absence of experience (e.g., the smile in blind infants); (4) evidence for underlying brain organization and circuitry that make possible a phenomenon when such brain circuits do not depend upon experience for their organization; and (5) apparent adaptive value in the sense that appropriate responding to certain situations results in the person surviving to pass along her/his genes. Using some of these criteria as a guide, and operating under the assumption that human evolution has been made possible largely by the development of flexibility rather than rigidity of responding, we will describe a number of ways in which we believe that evolutionary processes could play a role in explaining emotional development.

In general terms, humans seem to have evolved an overall capacity for emotion. The potential role of evolution in emotion, however, does not likely extend to specific event–emotion linkages. For example, in some cultures eating insects is considered a delicacy; in others, it is repulsive. Although what is repulsive differs across cultures, disgust is nonetheless universal, so long as the event–person relation involves an appreciation of contamination and a rejection of oral incorporation (Rozin & Fallon, 1987). Universality thus characterizes emotions at an abstract – but not specific – level of person–event transaction.

Nonetheless, there are some specific aspects of the emotion process for which evolutionary factors seem to play a role. Behavioral flexibility is not limitless. Even if one does not always or generally see an angry face when someone is expressing anger, it seems very likely that *elements* of such a facial display are *more likely* in a state of anger than elements of a facial display communicating sadness or joy. Such constraints on response were alluded to by Darwin (1872/1965) in his principle of serviceable associated habits. This principle states that we show certain facial movements and not others when in a given emotional state because such movements in the past served very specific adaptive functions. In anger, for instance, the narrowing of the eyes and elevation of the cheek served a protective function of minimizing the surface of the eye that could be injured in potential combat. The baring of teeth was adaptive as a preparation for biting in attack. The fixed stare was adaptive in keeping prey or adversaries in view for the purpose of monitoring their behavior. Over evolutionary time, as a function of their likely adaptive value, these responses gradually became readily shown in states of anger. Similar considerations apply to the serviceable habits in fear, disgust, joy, and so on.

The idea that elements of emotion phenomena evolved, not whole response patterning, can also be applied to the stimuli that are associated with emotion generation. Evolutionary factors may be responsible for the close link between relatively simple *featural* parameters of stimulation and the generation of aspects of emotion. Tinbergen (1948, 1951), for example, exposed goslings to displays where, if moved in one direction, the leading edge of the display had the long-necked shaped of a goose but if moved in the opposite direction, the leading edge had the short-necked shape of a hawk. Tinbergen observed that goslings exhibited scurrying, fear-like reactions when exposed to the overhead movement of the hawk-like shape but not to the overhead movement of the goose-like shape. Subsequent studies used a dark triangle the base of which was presented vertically, such that, when moved in one direction, the base of the triangle appeared first, and when moved in the opposite direction, the apex appeared first (reviewed in Schneirla, 1965). Although this stimulus lacked any fit to an evolutionarily derived template of a potential predator, the base-appearing-first presentation led to scurrying in the goslings studied; but the apex-appearing-first display did not. Schneirla (1965) proposed that the scurrying-inducing element was the rate of change of stimulation, not the hawk or goose shape of the stimulus. When the rate of change is abrupt (as in the short-necked hawk stimulus or the base of the triangle), scurrying occurs. When the rate of change is gradual (as in the goose neck or the apex of the triangle), scurrying is lacking. Schneirla thus concluded that the goslings were sensitive to the relatively simple parameter of rate of change of stimulation, and not to the complex gestalt of goose or hawk.

Recent research on neonatal preferences for human faces underscores the idea that evolution is more likely to entrain responsiveness to lower-order parameters of stimulation, not higher-order patterned wholes. Being attuned to faces is considered a major key to the establishment of many aspects of socioemotional development, yet work by Turati and colleagues has demonstrated that newborns come into this world not preferring faces *qua* faces but instead being responsive to certain lower level, non-face-specific stimulus factors which just happen to be typical of human faces (Cassia, Turati, & Simion, 2004; de Heering et al., 2008; Turati, 2004; Turati, Simion, Milani, & Umilta, 2002). In particular, newborns prefer stimuli with up-down asymmetry – stimuli that involve more featural elements in the upper than in the lower portion of the configuration. That faces happen to be top-heavy may well account for newborn's preferential attention to them;

when a bottom-heavy face-like stimulus is contrasted with a top-heavy, non-face-like stimulus, newborns prefer to look at the latter (Turati, 2004).

In addition to evolution's potential role in establishing the significance of certain featural parameters of stimulation, there is now abundant evidence that evolutionary factors affect learning by influencing how quickly a stimulus is linked to emotion, how enduring the learning is, and how strong is the emotion that occurs following an encounter between a person and an event. The fact that some emotions can be learned more quickly and retained in more enduring fashion to certain stimuli but not others is called "biological preparedness for learning." Cook and Mineka (1990; Mineka & Cook, 1993), for example, have demonstrated how laboratory-reared monkeys who had never been exposed to a snake or to a flower, and who initially showed no wariness to either stimulus quickly learned lasting avoidance responses to the snake but not to the flower. Similar preparedness has been demonstrated for taste stimuli (when these are associated with subsequent nausea, but not shock, Garcia & Koelling, 1966), for fear and joy faces (when used to signal electric shock, fear faces produce physiological responses much more resistant to extinction than do joy faces, Ohman, 1993), and for appetitive responses such as learning to suck for sugary substances (Lipsitt, 1986).

Typically, emotional displays are only effective in a social context if they are perceived and acted upon by another (Fridlund, 1997). From this viewpoint, evolution must necessarily play a role not only in the production of expressions, but also in the reception of others' emotional displays. Researchers have demonstrated that infants, in their first days and even first hours of life, can imitate certain facial displays such as tongue protrusions and pursed lips (e.g., Meltzoff & Moore 1977, 1983; see chapter 11 this volume), although, some have argued, not robustly and not always replicably (Anisfeld, 1991). Over the first few months of life, imitation becomes increasingly prominent in the life of the infant (Uzgiris & Hunt, 1975). Many researchers have interpreted the existence of imitation as a "meeting of the minds" between modeler and caregiver (e.g., Gopnik & Meltzoff, 1997), such that the infant can feel what the modeler is feeling (e.g., joy when seeing a smile). From both an evolutionary and a functionalist perspective on emotions, what is important is not that the infant feels a like emotion, but that the infant can predict the future behavior of the emoting person (Fridlund, 1997). Regardless of which stance one takes on the issue of feeling, some (e.g., Hoffman, 2000) have pointed out that motor mimicry and imitation form the basis for empathy and ultimately prosocial and moral development. An important study has shown that rhesus monkeys less than 2 months of age respond appropriately to the social signals of conspecifics even when reared in the absence of social experience. For instance, infant rhesus monkeys show marked avoidance reactions to the presentation of a staring, immobile, face; on the other hand, the same monkeys approach a figure engaging in lipsmacking behavior (Kenney, Mason, & Hill, 1979).

The evolutionarily based tendency toward motor mimicry may account for these findings. If a staring figure creates through response matching a momentary state of immobility and this immobility feeds information to the brain that is assimilated into representations of prior aggressive actions by the perceiver, such feedback, then, would generate a "meaning" to the perception of a stare, and lead to the assumption of avoidance responses. Similarly, perception of lipsmacking may result in reproduction in some way of lipsmacks by the perceiver monkey. If the feedback to the brain from such imitative lipsmacks is assimilated to actions such as feeding, the "meaning" of the lipsmack would then be positive, and result in approach behaviors. Motor mimicry, evident in the human and nonhuman primate in very early life without social learning, is an important building block for generating complex emotional meanings, such as those so critically provided to conspecifics by social signals.

Postnatal Ontogenetic Starting Points for Emotional Development

Evolution both prepares the infant for various organism–environment transactions that result in emotions and establishes very general constraints on the manifestation of emotions. However, evolutionary factors offer relatively limited insight into the actual changes that take place as emotion develops. As a result, the nature and course of emotional organization in infancy and beyond is specifically discovered through an examination of ontogenesis.

What are the starting points in the ontogenesis of emotion? What level of organization characterizes the newborn's emotional repertoire? One very widespread view, accepted by many cognitive and psychoanalytic theorists, is that the newborn is capable of manifesting only one emotion – a diffuse state of excitement, perhaps "tinged with unpleasure" (Bridges, 1932; Spitz, 1965). Only gradually, through a process of differentiation, do qualitatively distinct emotions develop from this initial, undifferentiated state. At about 4 weeks of age, for example, the emotion of distress, characterized by a more clearly negative expressiveness, differentiates out of excitement. At 6 weeks, the emotion of joy branches off from excitement, at 4 months anger differentiates out of distress, at 6 months disgust springs off from anger, and, at 8 months, fear becomes evident. According to Bridges (1932) and others, this differentiation of discrete emotions from an originally diffuse arousal state constitutes a basic principle of emotional development.

Variants of Bridges' differentiation view persist to this day. Camras (1992; see also Oster, Hegley, & Nagel, 1992), for example, has reported that infant facial patterns of distress–pain, anger, and sadness – patterns often interpreted as reflecting discrete emotional states (e.g., Izard, 1991) – frequently co-occur under a variety of circumstances designed to elicit only anger, only sadness, or only distress. Given these observations, Camras argued that anger and sadness expressions in the first year constitute intensity differences, not qualitatively distinct reactions, in an undifferentiated "unhappiness" or distress reaction. Even in infants as old as 11 months, evidence for distinct facial patterns of fear and anger, specific to distinct fear- and anger-eliciting contexts, is largely absent, although other components of the emotion process, such as infants' nonfacial behavior (e.g., body posturing, instrumental behaviors like swatting at something, looking behavior like gaze aversion), show clear evidence of differentiation and situational specificity (Camras, Oster, Bakeman, Meng, Ujiie, & Campos, 2007).

Work by Bennett, Bendersky, and Lewis (2002, 2005) has documented in a large sample of infants the relative lack of situational specificity in infants' facial patterning of emotion at 4 months and the increasing specificity and differentiation of response to situation by 12 months. Employing 5 different emotion-eliciting contexts, each designed to target a qualitatively distinct emotional response (e.g., an arm restraint context to elicit anger, a jack-in-the-box context to elicit surprise), Bennett et al. (2002) found no evidence that specific facial expressions of negative emotion (fear vs. disgust vs. anger vs. sadness) were more prevalent in response to predicted eliciting contexts than in response to other contexts. Sadness expressions, for example, were the most common expression produced in response to a sour taste – a (predicted) disgust-eliciting context. Only joy facial patterns demonstrated situational specificity at 4 months, most common in the joy-eliciting context of tickling and least common across other eliciting contexts (Bennett et al., 2002). By 12 months, increasing situational specificity of facial expressions was evident in the sample for all contexts but the fear-eliciting situation (masked stranger), suggesting a progressive differentiation in the organization of situational context and facial patterning across the first year of life (Bennett et al., 2005).

Although differentiation certainly characterizes many aspects of emotional development, emotional organization as a whole seems far more articulated than many differentiation accounts suggest. Anger and sadness expressions in 4-month-olds, for example, in response to having a goal blocked, are differentiated at the level of physiological response, with anger expressions accompanied by increased heart rate and sadness accompanied by increased cortisol, but not vice versa (Lewis & Ramsay, 2005; Lewis, Ramsay, & Sullivan, 2006). The work of Weinberg and Tronick (1994) has revealed a number of distinct positive and negative affect patterns in the repertoire of 6-month-olds. Examining patterns of coherence across different modes of expressive and instrumental actions – such as facial displays, vocalizations, gestures, postural orientation, and gaze behavior – Weinberg and Tronick reported the presence of four distinct affect configurations. A "Social Engagement" configuration involved infant facial expressions of joy and positive vocalizations coupled with gazing at the mother and the mouthing of hands or feet. Infants also exhibited an "Object Engagement" configuration, involving gazing at and the mouthing of objects, general scanning activity of the room, and facial expressions of interest, as well as distinct organizations of "Passive Withdrawal," involving fussy vocalizations, sad facial expressions, and indicators of stress such as hiccupping and spitting up, and "Active Protest," involving angry expressions, scanning behavior, crying, attempts to escape, as well as fussy vocalizations and stress indicators.

Each of the configurations Weinberg and Tronick (1994) identified serves a specific function with respect to the infant's relation to the world. As their labels suggest, Social Engagement functions to establish and maintain contact with social others, Object Engagement focuses the infant on object exploration, Passive Withdrawal serves to disengage or withdraw the infant from interaction, and Active Protest functions to engage the infant in efforts to eliminate an obstacle. More recently, Yale, Messinger, Cobo-Lewis, and Delgado (2003) have extended Weinberg and Tronick's work on the concordance between infant facial expressions and other behavioral components of emotion, such as vocalizations, gazing patterns, and posture. Unlike Weinberg and Tronick, who specifically started with infant facial expressions and related these expressions to other behavioral components, Yale et al. examined the full range of potential relationships among infants' gazing to mothers' faces, vocalizations, and facial expressions in a longitudinal assessment of 3- and 6-month-olds. Results revealed coordinated organization of both positive and negative facial expressions with gazing to mother and with vocalizations, although vocalizations were not independently coordinated with gazing patterns. This coordinated organization was evident at both ages, though the specific coordination between positive and negative facial expressions and gazing patterns strengthened from 3 to 6 months.

If we approach the study of younger infants from a functionalist standpoint, we see evidence not for an undifferentiated state of excitement or distress but for more specific emotion systems (Sroufe, 1979, 1996). Under conditions of loss of support, the neonate will typically startle and draw her/his arms around the chest in what functions as a protective embrace (Peiper, 1963). This pattern of response contrasts sharply with the head withdrawal, arm flailing, and pushing behavior we see in neonates whose nostrils have been inadvertently occluded during breast feeding; these infants do not clasp in protective fashion but instead implement actions that function however crudely as a defensive attack on the condition of respiratory occlusion (Gunther, 1961; Lipsitt, 1976). Yet another functionally distinct pattern of behavior surfaces when neonates encounter bitter tasting substances; in this context, the infant retracts her/his lips and often extends her/his tongue in a facial action that functions to reject or orally discharge the offending substance (Steiner, 1979). In each of these cases, we see patterns of behavior that, when considered in relation to specific events, serve distinct functions of protection, obstacle removal, and rejection. Even the neonate, therefore, has an action repertoire sufficiently differentiated to deal with distinct forms of aversive stimulation.

Like Sroufe (1979, 1996), we argue for the presence of some distinct, precursor emotion organizations in the neonatal period, rather than for nothing but undifferentiated arousal. However, this in no way undermines the importance of a process like differentiation for the characterization of emotional development. Processes of differentiation transform aspects of the emotion process, such as facial expressions, instrumental actions, and evaluations, from more global, homogenous organizations to specific, increasingly heterogeneous ones, but they do so with respect to distinct proto-emotion systems (Sroufe, 1996). An example from Buhler (1930) aptly demonstrates the differentiation process with respect to the proto-anger system evident in the neonate. Buhler observed that young infants, when having their noses wiped, responded with undirected, whole body movement; their arms and legs would move wildly without necessarily contacting the hand of the individual wiping their noses. Later in development, infants increasingly coordinated their arm movements to push aside the hand and resist having their noses wiped. By 8 months, infants began to prepare for nose wiping by swiping at the hand before it could reach their noses. Thus, in this example, the relational meaning of infants' action in the context of nose wiping – obstacle removal – provides a continuity in the organization of infant–environment transactions, but the specific properties of infant action in relation to an obstacle undergo increasing differentiation with development.

The Emergence of Social Smiling and Dyadic Coordination

In the first few weeks of life, infants, although attuned to many aspects of their environment, are not particularly socially engaged with the world of people around them (Rochat,

2001), prompting some to liken the infant in the neonatal period to an "externalized fetus" (Prechtl, 1984). Sander (1964) has argued that the main task facing caregiver and infant in the first weeks is primarily physiological in nature, revolving around the establishment of feeding, quieting, sleep and arousal regulatory patterns. This all changes by 2 months in what amounts to a "2 month revolution" (Rochat, 2001) with the emergence of the social smile and systematic, highly regulated exchanges of affect sharing between caregiver and infant.

The social smile is a response the infant begins to show between 4 and 6 weeks of age (Sroufe & Waters, 1976; Wolff, 1987). This event is powerful for parents and bystanders alike to witness, and devastating when it is manifested abnormally (as with Down Syndrome infants, see Emde, Katz, & Thorpe, 1978). Neonatal smiles, unlike the social smiles of older infants, seem unrelated to external stimulation and are termed endogenous. These endogenous smiles occur predominantly during REM sleep or when the neonate is drowsy, although recent evidence suggests that full blown smiling does also occur during wakeful, alert states (Dondi et al., 2007; Emde, Gaensbauer, & Harmon, 1976; Emde & Koenig, 1969; Messinger et al., 2002; Wolff, 1987). Over the first few weeks of life, full blown smiling becomes more frequent during alert states and begins to be exogenously oriented, elicited, that is, by external stimulation, first tactile, then auditory, then visual (Messinger & Fogel, 2007; Sroufe & Waters, 1976; Wolff, 1987). Smiling, however, does not become specific to social others and integrated into patterns of interpersonal interaction until 4 to 6 weeks.

Around the same time as the social smile emerges, there emerges a new pattern of coordinated emotion sharing between caregiver and infant (Stern, 1985; Tronick, 1989), involving synchronous dyadic interaction in what Trevarthen (1979) has termed "primary intersubjectivity." Lavelli and Fogel (2002, 2005) have longitudinally charted this qualitative reorganization in the relationship between infant and caregiver, specifically demonstrating how social smiles emerge during a time when infants' gazing patterns at their mothers' faces become more systematic and in conjunction with mothers' increasing psychological engagement of the infant via talking and smiling. In the first month, infants' gazes at their mothers lacked emotional engagement, involving minimal motor activity and neutral facial expressions. However, in the second month, infants began to temporally coordinate bouts of concentrated attention (involving brow knitting and visual fixation), smiling and cooing vocalizations while gazing at their mothers. Coincident with this new level of coordination was a transition in mothers' interaction patterns with their infants, from more neutral expressions in the first month to increasingly coordinated patterns of talking and smiling expressions during the second month. In the second and third months, increasing coordination at a dyadic level occurred, as mothers' talking/smiling patterns became increasingly coordinated with infants' smiling and cooing (Lavelli & Fogel, 2005).

Specific factors in the interaction of caregiver and infant in turn shape the forms that infant smiling behavior assumes (Dickson, Walker, & Fogel, 1997). At the start of face-to-face interaction with their mothers, young infants predominantly exhibit smiles that only involve a lip corner raise – which may index a less aroused, more cautious engagement (Messinger & Fogel, 2007). But these smiles typically flower into full-blown Duchenne smiles – involving both lip and cheek raise/eye constriction actions such that the infant is smiling with both her mouth and with her eyes – as the interaction progresses (Dickson et al., 1997; Messinger, Fogel, & Dickson, 1999). These Duchenne smiles, with or without an opened mouth, are especially prominent when infants' mothers smile at them in the midst of mutual regard and seem to index the infants' positive emotional engagement with their mothers (Messinger, Fogel, & Dickson, 2001; Messinger & Fogel, 2007). Different types of mother–infant interaction are associated with different smile configurations. During peek-a-boo, for example, smiles involving just a raise of the lip are more typical than Duchenne smiles (Fogel, Nelson-Goens, Hsu, & Shapiro, 2000). During tickling games, Duchenne smiles are common, especially when the infant is actually being tickled. Duchenne smiles accompanied by an open mouth, indexing a more heightened level of positive emotional engagement, become increasingly likely as the games extend in time (Fogel et al., 2000; Messinger & Fogel, 2007). Developmentally, infants show significant increases between 1 and 6 months in the frequency with which they display Duchenne smiles, relative to smiles without eye constriction, when engaged with smiling mothers (Messinger et al., 2001).

Increased Attention to the World of Objects

Between 2 and 6 months, the time infants spend in face-to-face dyadic interaction decreases, whereas their time spent interacting with physical objects increases (Trevarthen, 1979; Trevarthen & Hubley, 1978; Rochat, 2001). During this time period, advances in infants' postural control and manual exploratory capabilities seem to usher in a new orientation for infants, toward the world of objects (Rochat, 2001). Coincident with this increased immersion in the world of objects are qualitative changes in the development of anger. M. Lewis, Alessandri, and Sullivan et al. (1990) have hypothesized that development in means–ends ability explains this link, arguing that the more infants know about how their own activity relates to the world, the greater the likelihood of their demonstrating discrete states of anger under circumstances where their means to achieving an end are blocked (see also Campos, Barrett, Lamb, Goldsmith, & Stenberg, 1983; Izard, 1978; M. Lewis, 1993). In other words, once infants understand how their causal activity affects the environment, they have at their disposal a greater flexibility of goal implementation. Goal blockage then represents for the means–ends infant a potentially remediable state of affairs; thus, anger has a crucial place in infants' lives as a motivator of goal implementation through the removal of obstructions to those goals. In the absence of such means–ends understanding, an expression of anger "makes little adaptive sense" (M. Lewis, 1993, p. 151).

M. Lewis et al. (1990) have demonstrated discrete facial patterns of anger in infants as young as 2 months in response to a learned contingency task in which infants' arm-pulling actions activated an audiovisual stimulus. Blockage or interruption of the learned efficacy of the arm-pull action – captured in the extinction phase of the task when arm-pulls no longer activated the stimulus – provided a context of frustration for the infants, which Lewis et al. characterized as "loss of control" and "violation of expectancy." Two-month-olds, during this extinction phase, increased their rate of arm-pulling and displayed facial expressions of anger. These infants, however, needed to have established for them, through supported learning, an artificially induced contingency between their arm-pulls and activation of the stimulus in order to show anger during extinction. Infants in a control condition, who experienced a period of noncontingent stimulation followed by an extinction phase of no stimulation, showed no change in anger displays from phase to phase at 2 months. At 4 months, however, infants in this control condition did display increases in anger displays during extinction (M. Lewis et al., 1990), which may reflect their increased orientation to the external world (the stimulation no longer needs to be contingent on their action). By 4 months, too, infants in contingency learning contexts show organizational coordination across behavioral and autonomic components of anger during extinction (M. Lewis, Hitchcock, & Sullivan, 2004).

We have already cited evidence from Buhler (1930) of a developmental sequence in infants' anger under conditions of having their noses wiped: as neonates, they respond in undifferentiated, globally distressed fashion, but by 3 to 4 months they exhibit specific, coordinated movements functioning to push aside the hand and thereby resist having their noses wiped. Work by Stenberg and Campos (1990) on the development of anger-expressive patterning in 1-, 4-, and 7-month-old infants further underscores this developmental sequence. In their study, anger was generated by gently holding the infant's arms but preventing them from readily moving, and the infant's facial and vocal expressions, as well as their instrumental behaviors, were recorded. The study yielded three important findings.

First, infants showed intense negativity in emotional reaction at every age tested. Facially, their reactions were neither diffuse nor uncoordinated and quickly became coordinated into an anger-like pattern between 1 and 4 months of age. More specifically, infants' facial displays showed few components related to fear, disgust, sadness, or other negative emotions. At 1 month, the components shown were mostly, though not exclusively, those associated with anger: The infants lowered their brows and drew them together and they elevated their cheeks. However, they also showed two facial components that indicated incomplete, partially diffuse organization of facial movements. In one, they closed their eyes, rather than narrowed them (as would be expected in an anger encounter), displaying a more general distress pattern. In the second, they stuck their tongues out, rather than pulling the corners of the mouth back. Although they also vocalized negatively, 1-month-olds did not specifically target their expressions at anything relevant in the environment, looking instead all over the room in a relatively diffuse manner.

By 4 months, infants' facial actions were more organized, with the eyes showing the expectable narrowing (rather than closing), and the oral region the prototypical pulled-back appearance. Moreover, the infants directed their facial movements toward the site of the frustration – the hands of the experimenter holding the infants' arms – suggesting that the emotional state had a target or an aim. The voice, too, showed a greater coordination with the face. It was as if the facial movements were in the service of vocalizing, because in general the vocalizations that were observed followed rather than preceded the facial patterning.

At 7 months, reorganization took place, not in the face or the voice, but in the targeting component of the emotion. The infants directed their expressions both to the frustrating experimenter, as well as to the mother (who was a bystander in the testing procedure). Indeed, they vocalized only when looking at the person frustrating their movements, or at their bystander mothers. In effect, by 7 months infants showed significant signs of anger targeted toward people, meaning that anger had now become socially targeted.

From Impulsiveness to Wariness: The Emergence of Fear

Anyone who has observed infants will notice a major transition in the second half of their first year, between 6 and 9 months. New objects, which previous to this period were readily explored, are now initially regarded with caution (Scarr & Salapatek, 1970). Infants begin to show wariness and distress both in the presence of strangers and in the absence of their primary caregivers (Emde et al., 1976; Scarr & Salapatek, 1970; Spitz, 1965). Edges with a drop-off become sources of threat as locomoting infants begin to steadfastly avoid them (Campos, Hiatt, Ramsay, Henderson, & Svejda, 1978; Campos, Bertenthal, & Kermoian, 1992). Prior to this period, certain forms of fear may be evident but in more isolated, context-specific circumstances. Many mothers, for example, report a period of early stranger distress in infants between 3 and 6 months – a reaction that is not as strong, as consistent, or as independent of context as the reaction will be later. Similarly, some observers, such as Stayton, Ainsworth, & Main (1973), report a spurt in negative reactions to separation at 5 months of age, but these reactions are observed principally in the home setting. In short, the 6 to 9 month period marks a widespread and robust emergence of fear across multiple contexts.

Cognitive processes such as memory and expectancy have also been implicated in the emergence of fear, especially the fear of strangers. One such process involving memory development is the principle of discrepancy from the familiar (e.g., Hebb, 1946, 1949; McCall & McGhee, 1977). Stimuli or events that moderately diverge from an infant's past experience, that require some degree of effort to incorporate into memory ("effortful assimilation"), but that nonetheless ultimately comply with memory, are said to result in positive emotion such as joy (Kagan, 1971). Events that actively conflict with infant memory – familiar in some respects but discrepant enough to prove incompatible with past experience – produce negative emotion such as fear, whereas highly familiar events that readily match memory provoke much less interest and even boredom from the infant (McCall & McGhee, 1977).

In infancy, discrepancy from the familiar follows a two-step developmental sequence. In the infant's first 6 months or so, discrepancy takes the form of basic event recognition. Infants simply assess an event as matching or not matching their previous experience; in effect, their processing maps onto the question, "Have I encountered this event before or not?" (Schaffer, 1974). The emergence of infant distress to an unresponsive, expressionless mother supports a discrepancy framework of explanation. Beginning around 3 months, infants cry and protest when their mothers simulate depression during face-to-face interaction (Cohn & Tronick, 1983). Around this time, infants begin to demonstrate marked sensitivity to routines and specific contingencies in dyadic interaction, suggesting that between 2 and 4 months infants establish expectations for how primary caretakers should interact with them (Rochat, Querido, & Striano, 1999). Thus, by 3 months of age, a stiff-faced, unresponsive mother conflicts with most infants' past experience, thereby generating negative affect.

Between 6 and 9 months, infants move beyond mere recognition in memory to rudimentary levels of recall (Carver & Bauer, 2001; Herbert, Gross, & Hayne, 2006; Schaffer, 1974; see chapter 8 this volume). Infants' processing of discrepancy consequently assumes a new form and establishes the basis for stranger distress. Although infants as young as 3 months recognize strangers as unfamiliar (Bronson, 1972), between 6 and 9 months infants no longer rate a stranger as simply unfamiliar but as *different from* their mothers, in effect asking the question "How does this event compare or relate to my other experiences?" (Schaffer, 1974). In general, the transition in discrepancy processing from recognition of familiarity to active comparison of events with stored memories reflects a shift from sequential to simultaneous processing. In the first 6 months, infants process events in isolation from other events and never contrast the processing of a current event with other event representations in their memory store. But after 6 months simultaneous processing becomes evident, in which infants compare/contrast discrepant events with stored representations of similar but different events (Schaffer, 1974).

Discrepancy processes, however, are insufficient for explaining fear development. For example, the same event for the same infant can generate markedly different emotions depending on various contextual factors. Ten-month-olds, when presented with their mothers wearing a mask, invariably smile, and frequently laugh when the presentation occurs at home, but show much less positive affect to the same event conducted in the lab; similarly, a stranger's approach elicits greater heart rate acceleration in the lab than in the infant's home (Sroufe, Waters, & Matas, 1974). These results and others like them suggest that the specific quality of an infant's emotion depends on much more than an event and its discrepancy from past experience (M. Lewis & Goldberg, 1969; Sroufe et al., 1974; Stechler & Carpenter, 1967).

From a functionalist perspective, we must approach cognitive factors like discrepancy from the standpoint of relational meaning patterns in emotion and ultimately embed these "cold" cognitions within a motivational context of the infant's goals and strivings. Separation and stranger distress, for example, may emerge as a consequence of specific expectations infants have for how social others should behave when communicating with them (Bower, 1977). With the emergence of primary intersubjectivity at 2 to 3 months, infants and their primary caregivers gradually coconstruct unique modes of communicating and sharing emotion with one another, consisting of specific and routinized sequences of facial signaling, vocalizing, gesturing, body orientation, and tactile contact. These communication modes have powerful regulatory effects on infant arousal levels and emotional state (Tronick, 1989). Eventually, infants come to expect these specific forms of communication in the context of social interaction. Infants for whom these expectations are consolidated will encounter a rather dramatic violation of expectancy when a stranger interacts with them; similarly, when separated from the primary caregiver, these same infants will be without an important source of emotional regulation via the loss of a significant communicational partner. Work by Bigelow and Rochat (2006; see also Bigelow, 1998) has, in fact, confirmed that infants as young as 2 months have already begun to establish sensitivity to the kinds of social contingencies present in interactions with their own mothers and are maximally responsive to strangers whose interaction pattern of contingency mirrors that of their mothers. Infants' sensitivity continues to develop and become better organized between 2 and 6 months. By couching the emergence of stranger and separation distress in the context of infant–caregiver communication patterns and their regulatory consequences, we can see why, for example, infants are most likely to react with distress when a stranger tries to interact with them but rarely ever show distress to the mere presence of a stranger (Schaffer, 1971).

From Dyad to Triad: Relating the Worlds of People and Objects

Beginning around 9 months, infants show signs of systematically relating people's attention and emotions to objects and events in the environment in what Rochat (2001) has called the "9 month revolution." At this time, infants' interactive exchanges with their caregivers start to extend beyond the realm of dyadic interaction to triadic interaction, a process termed "secondary intersubjectivity" (Trevarthen & Hubley, 1978). This process specifically involves infants' using information from a dyadic partner to guide their actions toward objects and events outside the dyad and is evident in the phenomenon of joint attention, comprising of such skills as following others' pointing and gazing as well as gesturing via point and gaze to direct others' attention to objects (Bakeman & Adamson, 1984; Carpenter, Nagell, & Tomasello, 1998). In effect, infants between 9 and 12 months begin to share attention and emotion with their caregivers *about* a third event – such as an object in the environment or another person – and to understand that others' emotional displays and gaze patterns can refer to people and events outside the caregiver–infant dyad (Bates, 1979).

Social referencing is perhaps the emotional cornerstone of secondary intersubjectivity. As a clear example of appraisal in infancy, social referencing involves evaluations of situations that directly affect infants' goals and strivings and makes use of expressive behavior via the face, voice, and gesture. Infants who socially reference use the facial, vocal, and gestural affective displays of others to evaluate ambiguous events and to regulate subsequent action in relation to those events (Campos & Stenberg, 1981). This process relies on the infant's being able to relate the meaning conveyed by a social other to an event whose meaning is not clear-cut – such as the presence of a novel toy, the approach of a stranger, or the drop-off of a support surface on the visual cliff. Infants as young as 9 months do indeed relate the general positive or negative affective meaning, conveyed by social others to ambiguous people/events, and adjust their responses to the person/event accordingly. If, for example, a mother displays fear in relation to the drop-off edge of the visual cliff, infants rarely cross the cliff to their mothers, but in the context of a happy display from the mother, infants readily cross (Sorce, Emde, Campos, & Klinnert, 1985). Similarly, infants are less friendly with strangers and inhibit their play with strange toys when their mothers react to the events with negative facial signals and vocalizations than when reacting with neutral or positive emotional displays (Boccia & Campos, 1989;

Feinman & Lewis, 1983; Gunnar & Stone, 1984; Hornick, Risenhoover, & Gunnar, 1987; Mumme, Fernald, & Herrera, 1996).

A current point of contention in the social referencing literature surrounds the relative effectiveness of face versus voice in signaling emotion to the infant (Saarni, Campos, Camras, & Witherington, 2006). Evidence exists demonstrating the potency of facial signals alone in guiding infant behavior (e.g., Sorce et al., 1985) and the greater potency of facial as opposed to vocal signals (Mumme et al., 1996). Evidence also exists, however, demonstrating the greater potency of vocal as opposed to facial signals (Vaish & Striano, 2004).

Recent work in the realm of social referencing has also investigated infants' ability to identify the particular referent of an emotion signal – knowing, for example, that mother's fear display is directed at the light socket rather than at the table close by. By 12 months, infants show clear signs of being able to link another person's emotional signals to specific targets or events (Hertenstein & Campos, 2004; Moses, Baldwin, Rosicky, & Tidball, 2001; Mumme & Fernald, 2003). Less clear-cut is the 12-month-old's ability to use the different meanings attendant on specific emotions to guide their behavior in relation to an object or event, for example, being able to distinguish the meaning conveyed by anger and the meaning conveyed by sadness as opposed to simply treating these emotions as generally "negative." Sorce et al. (1985) found support for this kind of "affect specificity" (Saarni et al., 2006) in 12-month-olds when mothers signaled fear versus sad facial expressions to their infants on a modified visual cliff, with virtually all infants avoiding the drop-off when fear was signaled but only two-thirds of the infants avoiding when sadness was signaled. Bingham, Campos, & Emde (1987), however, found no differences in 13- to 15-month-olds' doll play when the doll's arm falling off was paired with an experimenter's vocal and facial messages of fear, sadness, disgust, and anger. Infants in their study did avoid playing with the doll more when presented with negative messages as opposed to positive ones (e.g., joy) and played more with the doll when presented with positive messages as opposed to negative ones, but failed to differentiate in their play behavior among different negative messages (Saarni et al., 2006). A recent study, consistent with Bingham et al.'s work, found some evidence for affect specificity in 16- to 18-month-olds but not in 12- to 14-month-olds (Gendler-Martin, Witherington, & Edwards, 2008).

Conclusion

Emotions are multifaceted processes, and explaining their development requires a multifaceted approach. Emotion as a process is comprised of many components – both intra- and extraorganismic – all of which contribute to its organization at any given time and to transformations in its organization across development. Characterizing emotion in terms of its components and their interactions affords us insight into the nature of the developmental process itself. We fully capture emotional development, in turn, when we derive from this multicomponential analysis a synthetic rendering of person–environment relations across development. Such a thorough synthesis as yet eludes the study of emotion in any period of development. Even at the basic level of identifying coherent patterning in infant emotion, as evidenced in the work of Weinberg and Tronick (1994) and Yale et al. (2003), the field is sorely lacking. More research needs to simply focus on establishing this patterning across multiple environmental contexts and across levels of development in infancy. Still, by treating emotion in relational terms, as the outgrowth of evaluations and actions in physical and social contexts, we know where to tap critical transition points in emotional development. It is at points in development when the person's relation to her/his environment is fundamentally altered that we know the person's emotional life will reorganize.

For the infant, we have outlined four periods during infancy that involve fundamental reorganization in infants' relation to their world. We want to stress that each of these periods, in turn, involves significant changes in infant motor development, changes which themselves potentially mark major reorganizations in the infant's emotional stance toward the world, giving rise to new sets of experiences. The emergence, for example, of smooth pursuit eye tracking developmentally coincides with the emergence of the social smile. The emergence of visually guided reaching and grasping coincides with infants' refocused attention to the world of objects and anger development. Independent standing and walking coincide with developments in social referencing. The importance of these motor milestones for organizing the infant's stance toward the world rests not in the acts themselves but in the experiential consequences they generate, in the way the acquisition of these new skills fundamentally alters the infant's relationship to her world. Though theoretical speculation abounds, relatively little research to date has mined the potential of these important developmental transitions (Biringen, Emde, Campos, & Appelbaum, 1995; M. D. Lewis, 1993; Witherington, 1999).

An exception to this arrives in research on how crawling relates to transformations in the emotional world of the infant. Research with human infants on the "visual cliff" (Walk & Gibson, 1961), for example, has consistently demonstrated a link between the emergence of fear of heights between 7 and 9 months and experience with self-produced locomotion. It does not matter whether this self-produced movement experience is gained through "naturally" occurring hands-and-knees crawling or through "artificial" means, as when prelocomotor infants are given walkers to move around in: once infants gain a few weeks of experience actively moving themselves in the world, they begin to systematically avoid drop-offs (Bertenthal & Campos, 1990; Bertenthal, Campos, & Barrett, 1984; Campos, Bertenthal, et al., 1992; Campos et al., 1978). It is the nature of the experience that self-produced movement generates – new ways of perceiving the world through new means of acting upon the world – that is key to the relationship.

Crawling and the experience it generates affect the emotional life of the infant in other profound ways. Through crawling and the newfound autonomy it provides, infants can not only entertain new goals but also more fully explore existing goals. Caregivers, in turn, must regulate the infant's newfound opportunities for exploration to ensure their infants' safety, which impacts communication patterns between caregiver and infant. Major increases in infants' displays of anger and temper tantrums follow crawling onset (Campos, Kermoian, et al., 1992; Chen, Green, & Gustafson, 2009). Once infants begin to crawl, caregivers themselves target more positive affect toward infant exploration and the discovery of new events and situations. At the same time, caregivers begin to assign a more sophisticated intentionality to their infants and treat them as more responsible for their actions. This change, coupled with the increased chance for a mobile infant to encounter dangerous situations, produces a substantial increase in parental targeting of fear and anger to their infants once crawling begins (Campos, Kermoian, et al., 1992; Chen et al., 2009; Zumbahlen & Crawley, 1996).

In short, the onset of crawling, a basic action component of the process of relating to the world, prompts the need for fundamental reorganization in the infant's emotional life, both at the level of infant affectivity and at the level of the emotional climate in which the infant resides. Once infants begin to crawl, their goals, evaluations, expectations, and interactions with others undergo major transition in conjunction with the new adaptive demands they face. The organization of the infant's emotional life consequently assumes new forms as various components of the emotion process reestablish stable interaction with one another. Future work in infancy needs to systematically explore other motoric transitions and their relationship to emotional development – from reaching and sitting to standing and walking – in order to move the field toward increasingly process-oriented accounts for emotional development.

With each motoric transition, infants establish more effective means of meaningfully interacting with the social and physical world. New means of action fundamentally alter the manner in which infants implement their existing goals/strivings and establish for the infant new sets of goals, as well. In essence, emotional development in infancy revolves around systematic changes in the way infants regulate their goal-directed activity, their significant engagement with the people and things that surround them. At every point in development, then, emotion can be viewed from the standpoint of its regulatory effects on person–environment relations. We must establish what the person is trying to do to understand anything about her/his emotional stance toward the world. It is at this level – the level of infants regulating their relation to the world – that the fundamental and most significant properties of infant emotional development will be discovered.

References

Anisfeld, M. (1991). Neonatal imitation. *Developmental Review, 11*, 60–97.

Bakeman, R., & Adamson, L. (1984). Coordinating attention to people and objects in mother–infant and peer–infant interaction. *Child Development, 55*, 1278–1289.

Barrett, K. C., & Campos, J. J. (1987). Perspectives on emotional development: II. A functionalist approach to emotions. In J. D. Osofsky (Ed.), *Handbook of infant development* (2nd ed., pp. 555–578). New York: Wiley.

Bates, E. (1979). Intentions, conventions, and symbols. In E. Bates, L. Bennigni, I. Bretherton, L. Camaioni, & V. Volterra (Eds.), *The emergence of symbols: Cognition and communication in infancy* (pp. 33–68). New York: Academic Press.

Bennett, D. S., Bendersky, M., & Lewis, M. (2002). Facial expressivity at 4 months: A context by expression analysis. *Infancy, 3*, 97–113.

Bennett, D. S., Bendersky, M., & Lewis, M. (2005). Does the organization of emotional expression change over time? Facial expressivity from 4 to 12 months. *Infancy, 8*, 167–187.

Bertenthal, B., & Campos, J. J. (1990). A systems approach to the organizing effects of self-produced locomotion during infancy. In C. Rovee-Collier & L. P. Lipsitt (Eds.), *Advances in infancy research* (Vol. 6, pp. 1–60). Norwood, NJ: Ablex.

Bertenthal, B. I., Campos, J. J., & Barrett, K. C. (1984). Self-produced locomotion: An organizer of emotional, cognitive, and social development in infancy. In R. Emde & R. Harmon (Eds.), *Continuities and discontinuities in development* (pp. 175–210). New York: Plenum.

Bigelow, A. E. (1998). Infants' sensitivity to familiar imperfect contingencies in social interaction. *Infant Behavior & Development, 21*, 149–162.

Bigelow, A. E., & Rochat, P. (2006). Two-month-old infants' sensitivity to social contingency in mother–infant and stranger–infant interaction. *Infancy, 9*, 313–325.

Bingham, R., Campos, J., & Emde, R. (1987, April). *Negative emotions in a social relationship context.* Paper presented at the Biennial Meeting of the Society for Research in Child Development, Baltimore, MD.

Biringen, Z., Emde, R. N., Campos, J. J., & Appelbaum, M. I. (1995). Affective reorganization in the infant, the mother, and the dyad: The role of upright locomotion and its timing. *Child Development, 66*, 499–514.

Boccia, M., & Campos, J. J. (1989). Maternal emotional signals, social referencing, and infants' reactions to strangers. In N. Eisenberg (Ed.), *New directions for child development* (Vol. 44, pp. 25–49). San Francisco: Jossey-Bass.

Bower, T. G. R. (1977). *A primer of infant development.* San Francisco: W. H. Freeman.

Bridges, K. (1932). Emotional development in early infancy. *Child Development, 3*, 324–341.

Bronson, G. W. (1972). Infants' reactions to unfamiliar persons and novel objects. *Monographs of the Society for Research in Child Development, 37*(3, Serial No. 148).

Buhler, C. (1930). *The first year of life.* New York: Day Press.

Campos, J. J., Barrett, K. C., Lamb, M. E., Goldsmith, H. H., & Stenberg, C. (1983). Socio-emotional development. In P. H. Mussen (Series Ed.) & M. Haith & J. J. Campos (Vol. Eds.), *Handbook of child psychology: Vol. 2. Infancy and developmental psychobiology* (4th ed., pp. 783–915). New York: Wiley.

Campos, J. J., Bertenthal, B. I., & Kermoian, R. (1992). Early experience and emotional development: The emergence of wariness of heights. *Psychological Science, 3*, 61–64.

Campos, J. J., Campos, R. G., & Barrett, K. C. (1989). Emergent themes in the study of emotional development and emotion regulation. *Developmental Psychology, 25*, 394–402.

Campos, J. J., Hiatt, S., Ramsay, D., Henderson, C., & Svejda, M. (1978). The emergence of fear on the visual cliff. In M. Lewis & L. Rosenblum (Eds.), *The development of affect* (pp. 149–182). New York: Plenum.

Campos, J. J., Kermoian, R., & Zumbahlen, M. (1992). Socioemotional transformations in the family system following infant crawling onset. In N. Eisenberg & R. A. Fabes (Eds.), *New directions for child development: Emotion and its regulation in early development, 55* (pp. 25–40). San Francisco: Jossey-Bass.

Campos, J. J., Mumme, D. L., Kermoian, R., & Campos, R. G. (1994). A functionalist perspective on the nature of emotion. In N. Fox (Ed.), *The development of emotion regulation: Biological and behavioral considerations* (pp. 284–303). Monographs of the Society for Research in Child Development, 59 (2–3, Serial No. 240).

Campos, J. J., & Stenberg, C. R. (1981). Perception, appraisal, and emotion: The onset of social referencing. In M. E. Lamb & L. R. Sherrod (Eds.), *Infant social cognition: Empirical and theoretical considerations* (pp. 273–314). Hillsdale, NJ: Erlbaum.

Camras, L. A. (1992). Expressive development and basic emotions. *Cognition and Emotion, 6*, 269–283.

Camras, L. A., Oster, H., Bakeman, R., Meng, Z., Ujiie, T., & Campos, J. J. (2007). Do infants show distinct negative facial expressions for fear and anger? Emotional expression in 11-month-old European American, Chinese, and Japanese infants. *Infancy, 11*, 131–155.

Camras, L. A., & Witherington, D. C. (2005). Dynamical systems approaches to emotional development. *Developmental Review, 25*, 328–350.

Carpenter, M., Nagell, K., & Tomasello, M. (1998). Social cognition, joint attention, and communicative competence. *Monographs of the Society for Research in Child Development, 63*(4).

Carver, L. J., & Bauer, P. J. (2001). The dawning of a past: The emergence of long-term explicit memory in infancy. *Journal of Experimental Psychology: General, 130*, 726–745.

Cassia, V. M., Turati, C., & Simion, F. (2004). Can a non specific bias toward top-heavy patterns explain newborns' face preference? *Psychological Science, 15*, 379–383.

Chen, X., Green, J. A., & Gustafson, G. E. (2009). Development of vocal protests from 3 to 18 months. *Infancy, 14*, 44–59.

Cohn, J. F., & Tronick, E. Z. (1983). Three-month-old infants' reaction to simulated maternal depression. *Child Development, 54*, 185–193.

Cook, M., & Mineka, S. (1990). Selective associations in the observational conditioning of fear in rhesus monkeys. *Journal of Experimental Psychology: Animal Behavior Processes, 16*, 372–389.

Darwin, C. (1965). *The expression of the emotions in man and animals.* Chicago: University of Chicago Press. (Original work published 1872.)

De Heering, A., Turati, C., Rossion, B., Bulf, H., Goffaux, V., & Simion, F. (2008). Newborns' face recognition is based on spatial frequencies below 0.5 cycles per degree. *Cognition, 106*, 444–454.

Dickson, K. L., Fogel, A., & Messinger, D. (1998). The development of emotion from a social process view. In M. F. Mascolo & S. Griffin (Eds.), *What develops in emotional development?* (pp. 253–271). New York: Plenum Press.

Dickson, K. L., Walker, H., & Fogel, A. (1997). The relationship between smile type and play type during parent–infant play. *Developmental Psychology, 33*, 925–933.

Dondi, M., Messinger, D., Colle, M., Tabasso, A., Simion, F., Barba, B. D., et al. (2007). A new perspective on neonatal smiling: Differences between the judgments of expert coders and naïve observers. *Infancy, 12*, 235–255.

Emde, R. N., Gaensbauer, T., & Harmon, R. J. (1976). Emotional expression in infancy: A biobehavioral study. *Psychological Issues Monograph Series, 10* (No. 37), 1–198.

Emde, R. N., Katz, E. L., & Thorpe, J. K. (1978). Emotional expression in infancy: II. Early deviations in Down's syndrome. In M. Lewis & L. A. Rosenblum (Eds.), *The development of affect* (pp. 351–360). New York: Plenum.

Emde, R. N., & Koenig, K. (1969). Neonatal smiling and rapid eye movement states. *Journal of American Academic Child Psychiatry, 8*, 57–67.

Feinman, S., & Lewis, M. (1983). Social referencing at ten months: A second-order effect on infants' responses to strangers. *Child Development, 54*, 878–887.

Fogel, A., Nelson-Goens, G. C., Hsu, H., & Shapiro, A. F. (2000). Do different infant smiles reflect different positive emotions? *Social Development, 9*, 497–520.

Fogel, A., Nwokah, E., Dedo, J. Y., Messinger, D., Dickson, K. L., Matusov, E., & Holt, S. A. (1992). Social process theory of emotion: A dynamic systems approach. *Social Development, 1*, 122–142.

Fridlund, A. J. (1997). The new ethology of human facial expressions. In J. A. Russell & J. M. Fernandez-Dols (Eds.), *The psychology of facial expression* (pp. 103–129). Cambridge: Cambridge University Press.

Frijda, N. (1986). *The emotions.* Cambridge: Cambridge University Press.

Garcia, J., & Koelling, R. A. (1966). Relation of cue to consequence in avoidance learning. *Psychonomic Science, 4,* 123–124.

Gendler-Martin, N., Witherington, D. C., & Edwards, A. (2008). The development of affect specificity in infants' use of emotion cues. *Infancy, 13*(5), 456–468.

Gopnik, A., & Meltzoff, A. N. (1997). *Words, thoughts, and theories.* Cambridge, MA: MIT Press.

Griffin, S., & Mascolo, M. F. (1998). On the nature, development, and functions of emotions. In M. F. Mascolo & S. Griffin (Eds.), *What develops in emotional development?* (pp. 3–27). New York: Plenum Press.

Gunnar, M., & Stone, C. (1984). The effects of positive maternal affect on infants responses to pleasant, ambiguous, and fear-provoking toys. *Child Development, 55,* 1231–1236.

Gunther, M. (1961). Infant behavior at the breast. In B. Foss (Ed.), *Determinants of infant behavior* (Vol. *1*, pp. 37–44). London: Methuen.

Haig, B., & Durrant, R. (2000). Theory evaluation in evolutionary psychology. *Psychological Inquiry, 11,* 34–38.

Hebb, D. O. (1946). On the nature of fear. *Psychological Review, 53,* 88–106.

Hebb, D. O. (1949). *The organization of behavior: A neuropsychological theory.* New York: Wiley.

Herbert, J., Gross, J., & Hayne, H. (2006). Age-related changes in deferred imitation between 6 and 9 months of age. *Infant Behavior & Development, 29,* 136–139.

Hertenstein, M., & Campos, J. (2004). The retention effects of an adult's emotional displays on infant behavior. *Child Development, 75,* 595–613.

Hoffman, M. L. (2000). *Empathy and moral development: Implications for caring and justice.* Cambridge: Cambridge University Press.

Hornick, R., Risenhoover, N., & Gunnar, M. (1987). The effects of maternal positive, neutral, and negative affective communications in infant responses to new toys. *Child Development, 58,* 937–944.

Izard, C. (1978). On the ontogenesis of emotions and emotion-cognition relationships in infancy. In M. Lewis & L. A. Rosenblum (Eds.), *The development of affect* (pp. 389–413). New York: Plenum.

Izard, C. E. (1991). *The psychology of emotions.* New York: Plenum Press.

Kagan, J. (1971). *Change and continuity in infancy.* New York: Wiley.

Kenney, M., Mason, W., & Hill, S. (1979). Effects of age, objects, and visual experience on affective responses of rhesus monkeys to strangers. *Developmental Psychology, 15,* 176–184.

Ketelaar, T., & Ellis, B. J. (2000). Are evolutionary explanations unfalsifiable? Evolutionary psychology and the Lakatosian philosophy of science. *Psychological Inquiry, 11,* 1–21.

Lavelli, M., & Fogel, A. (2002). Developmental changes in mother–infant face-to-face communication: Birth to 3 months. *Developmental Psychology, 38,* 288–305.

Lavelli, M., & Fogel, A. (2005). Developmental changes in the relationship between the infant's attention and emotion during early face-to-face communication. The 2-month transition. *Developmental Psychology, 41,* 265–280.

Lazarus, R. S. (1991). *Emotion and adaptation.* New York: Oxford University Press.

Lewis, M. (1993). The emergence of human emotions. In M. Lewis & J. M. Haviland (Eds.), *Handbook of emotions* (pp. 223–235). New York: Guilford Press.

Lewis, M., Alessandri, S. M., & Sullivan, M. W. (1990). Violation of expectancy, loss of control, and anger expressions in young infants. *Developmental Psychology, 26,* 745–751.

Lewis, M., & Goldberg, S. (1969). The acquisition and violation of expectancy: An experimental paradigm. *Journal of Experimental Child Psychology, 7,* 70–80.

Lewis, M., Hitchcock, D. F. A., & Sullivan, M. W. (2004). Physiological and emotional reactivity to learning and frustration. *Infancy, 6,* 121–143.

Lewis, M., & Ramsay, D. (2005). Infant emotional and cortisol responses to goal blockage. *Child Development, 76,* 518–530.

Lewis, M., Ramsay, D. S., & Sullivan, M. W. (2006). The relation of ANS and HPA activation to infant anger and sadness response to goal blockage. *Developmental Psychobiology, 48,* 397–405.

Lewis, M. D. (1993). Emotion–cognition interactions in early infant development. *Cognition and Emotion, 7,* 145–170.

Lewis, M. D. (2000). Emotional self-organization at three time scales. In M. D. Lewis & I. Granic (Eds.), *Emotion, development, and self-organization: Dynamic systems approaches to emotional development* (pp. 37–69). Cambridge: Cambridge University Press.

Lewis, M. D., & Granic, I. (1999). Self-organization of cognition–emotion interactions. In T. Dalgleish & M. Power (Eds.), *Handbook of cognition and emotion* (pp. 683–701). New York: Wiley.

Lipsitt, L. P. (1976). Developmental psychobiology comes of age: A discussion. In L. P. Lipsitt (Ed.), *Developmental psychobiology: The significance of infancy* (pp. 109–127). Hillsdale, NJ: Erlbaum.

Lipsitt, L. P. (1986). Toward understanding the hedonic nature of infancy. In L. P. Lipsitt & J. H. Cantor (Eds.), *Experimental child psychologist: Essays and experiments in honor of Charles C. Spiker* (pp. 97–109). Hillsdale, NJ: Erlbaum.

Mascolo, M. F., & Griffin, S. (1998). Alternative trajectories in the development of anger-related appraisals. In M. F. Mascolo & S. Griffin (Eds.), *What develops in emotional development?* (pp. 219–249). New York: Plenum Press.

McCall, R. B., & McGhee, P. E. (1977). The discrepancy hypothesis of attention and affect in infants. In I. C. Uzgiris & F. Weizmann (Eds.), *The structuring of experience* (pp. 179–210). New York: Plenum.

Meltzoff, A. N., & Moore, M. K. (1977). Imitation of facial and manual gestures by human neonates. *Science, 198,* 75–78.

Meltzoff, A. N., & Moore, M. K. (1983). Newborn infants imitate adult facial gestures. *Child Development, 54,* 702–709.

Messinger, D., Dondi, M., Nelson-Goens, G. C., Beghi, A., Fogel, A., & Simion, F. (2002). How sleeping neonates smile. *Developmental Science, 5,* 48–54.

Messinger, D., & Fogel, A. (2007). The interactive development of social smiling. In R. V. Kail (Ed.), *Advances in child development and behavior,* (Vol. 35, pp. 327–366). Amsterdam: Elsevier

Messinger, D. S., Fogel, A., & Dickson, K. L. (1999). What's in a smile? *Developmental Psychology, 35,* 701–708.

Messinger, D. S., Fogel, A., & Dickson, K. L. (2001). All smiles are positive, but some smiles are more positive than others. *Developmental Psychology, 37,* 642–653.

Mineka, S., & Cook, M. (1993). Mechanisms involved in the observational conditioning of fear. *Journal of Experimental Psychology: General, 122,* 23–38.

Moses, L., Baldwin, D., Rosicky, J., & Tidball, G. (2001). Evidence for referential understanding in the emotions domain at twelve and eighteen months. *Child Development, 72,* 718–735.

Mumme, D., & Fernald, A. (2003). The infant as onlookers: Learning from emotional reactions observed in a television scenario. *Child Development, 74*(1), 221–237.

Mumme, D. L., Fernald, A., & Herrera, C. (1996). Infants' responses to facial and vocal emotional signals in a social referencing paradigm. *Child Development, 67,* 3219–3237.

Ohman, A. (1993). Stimulus prepotency and fear learning: Data and theory. In N. Birbaumer & A. Ohman (Eds.), *The structure of emotion: Psychophysiological, cognitive and clinical aspects.* Göttingen: Hogrefe & Huber Publishers.

Oster, H., Hegley, D., & Nagel, L. (1992). Adult judgments and fine-grained analysis of infant facial expressions. *Developmental Psychology, 28,* 1115–1131.

Peiper, A. (1963). *Cerebral function in infancy and childhood.* New York: Consultants Bureau.

Prechtl, H. F. R. (1984). *Continuity of neural functions: From prenatal to postnatal life.* Oxford: Blackwell Scientific Publications.

Rochat, P. (2001). *The infant's world.* Cambridge, MA: Harvard University Press.

Rochat, P., Querido, J. G., & Striano, T. (1999). Emerging sensitivity to the timing and structure of protoconversation in early infancy. *Developmental Psychology, 35*, 950–957.

Rochat. P., & Striano, T. (1999). Social-cognitive development in the first year. In P. Rochat (Ed.), *Early social cognition: Understanding others in the first months of life* (pp. 3–34). Mahwah, NJ: Erlbaum.

Rozin, P., & Fallon, A. E. (1987). A perspective on disgust. *Psychological Review, 94*, 23–41.

Saarni, C., Campos, J. J., Camras, L. A., & Witherington, D. (2006). Emotional development: Action, communication, and understanding. In W. Damon & R. M. Lerner (Series Eds.) & N. Eisenberg (Vol. Ed.), *Handbook of child psychology: Vol. 3. Social, emotional and personality development* (6th ed., pp. 226–299). New York: Wiley.

Sander, L. (1964). Adaptive relationships in early mother–child interaction. *Journal of the American Academy of Child Psychiatry, 3*, 231–264.

Scarr, S., & Salapatek, P. (1970). Patterns of fear development during infancy. *Merrill-Palmer Quarterly, 16*, 53–90.

Schaffer, H. R. (1971). *The growth of sociability.* Baltimore: Penguin.

Schaffer, H. R. (1974). Cognitive components of the infant's response to strangers. In M. Lewis & L. A. Rosenblum (Eds.), *The origins of fear* (pp. 11–24). New York: Wiley.

Schneirla, T. C. (1965). Aspects of stimulation and organization in approach/withdrawal processes underlying vertebrate behavioral development. In D. S. Lehrman, R. A. Hinde, & E. Shaw (Eds.), *Advances in the study of behavior* (Vol. *1*, pp. 1–74). New York: Academic Press.

Sorce, J. F., Emde, R. N., Campos, J. J., & Klinnert, M. D. (1985). Maternal emotional signaling: Its effect on the visual cliff behavior of 1-year-olds. *Developmental Psychology, 21*, 195–200.

Spitz, R. (1965). *The first year of life.* New York: International Universities Press.

Sroufe, L. A. (1979). Socioemotional development. In J. D. Osofsky (Ed.), *Handbook of infant development* (pp. 462–516). New York: Wiley.

Sroufe, L. A. (1996). *Emotional development: The organization of emotional life in the early years.* Cambridge: Cambridge University Press.

Sroufe, L. A., & Waters, E. (1976). The ontogenesis of smiling and laughter: A perspective on the organization of development in infancy. *Psychological Review, 83*, 173–189.

Sroufe, L. A., Waters, E., & Matas, L. (1974). Contextual determinants of infant affective response. In M. Lewis & L. A. Rosenblum (Eds.), *The origins of fear* (pp. 49–72). New York: Wiley.

Stayton, D. J., Ainsworth, M. D. S., & Main, M. B. (1973). Development of separation behavior in the first year of life: Protest, following, and greeting. *Developmental Psychology, 9*, 213–225.

Stechler, G., & Carpenter, G. (1967). A viewpoint on early affective development. In J. Hellmuth (Ed.), *The exceptional infant* (Vol. *1*, pp. 163–190). Seattle: Special Child Publications.

Steiner, J. E. (1979). Human facial expressions in response to taste and smell stimulation. In H. W. Reese & L. P. Lipsitt (Eds.), *Advances in child development and behavior* (Vol. *13*, pp. 257–295). New York: Academic Press.

Stenberg, C. R., & Campos, J. J. (1990). The development of anger expressions in infancy. In N. L. Stein, B. Leventhal, & T. Trabasso (Eds.), *Psychological and biological approaches to emotion* (pp. 297–310). Hillsdale, NJ: Erlbaum.

Stern, D. (1985). *The interpersonal world of the infant.* New York: Basic Books.

Thompson, R. A. (1993). Socioemotional development: Enduring issues and new challenges. *Developmental Review, 13*, 372–402.

Tinbergen, N. (1948). Social releasers and the experimental method required for their study. *Wilson Bulletin, 60,* 6–52.

Tinbergen, N. (1951). *The study of instinct.* Oxford: Clarendon Press.

Trevarthen, C. (1979). Communication and cooperation in early infancy: A description of primary intersubjectivity. In M. Bullowa (Ed.), *Before speech: The beginnings of interpersonal communication* (pp. 321–347). Cambridge: Cambridge University Press.

Trevarthen, C., & Hubley, P. (1978). Secondary intersubjectivity: Confidence, confiders, and acts of meaning in the first year of life. In A. Lock (Ed.), *Action, gesture and symbol: The emergence of language* (pp. 183–229). New York: Academic Press.

Tronick, E. (1989). Emotions and emotional communication in infants. *American Psychologist, 44,* 112–119.

Turati, C. (2004). Why faces are not special to newborns: An alternative account of the face preference. *Current Directions in Psychological Science, 13,* 5–8.

Turati, C., Simion, F., Milani, I., & Umilta, C. (2002). Newborns' preference for faces: What is crucial? *Developmental Psychology, 38,* 875–882.

Uzgiris, I. C., & Hunt, J. McV. (1975). *Assessment in infancy: Ordinal scales of psychological development.* Urbana: University of Illinois Press.

Vaish, A., & Striano, T. (2004). Is visual reference necessary? Contributions of facial versus vocal cues in 12-month-olds' social referencing behavior. *Developmental Science, 7,* 261–269.

Walk, R. D., & Gibson, E. J. (1961). A comparative and analytical study of visual depth perception. *Psychological Monographs, 75*(15, Whole No. 519).

Weinberg, M. K., & Tronick, E. Z. (1994). Beyond the face: An empirical study of infant affective configurations of facial, vocal, gestural, and regulatory behaviors. *Child Development, 65,* 1503–1515.

Witherington, D. C. (1999). Visually-guided reaching and the development of anger in infancy (Doctoral dissertation, University of California, Berkeley, 1998). *Dissertation Abstracts International: Section B: The Sciences & Engineering, 59*(8–B), 4514.

Witherington, D. C., Campos, J. J., & Hertenstein, M. J. (2001). Principles of emotion and its development. In G. Bremner & A. Fogel (Eds.), *Blackwell handbook of infant development* (pp. 427–464). Oxford: Blackwell.

Witherington, D. C., & Crichton, J. A. (2007). Frameworks for understanding emotions and their development: Functionalist and dynamic systems approaches. *Emotion, 7,* 628–637.

Wolff, P. H. (1987). *The development of behavioral states and the expression of emotions in early infancy.* Chicago: University of Chicago Press.

Yale, M. E., Messinger, D. S., Cobo-Lewis, A. B., & Delgado, C. F. (2003). The temporal coordination of early infant communication. *Developmental Psychology, 39,* 815–824.

Zumbahlen, M., & Crawley, A. (1996, April). *Infants' early referential behavior in prohibition contexts: The emergence of social referencing?* Paper presented at the meetings of the International Conference on Infant Studies, Providence, RI.

20

Temperament

Theodore D. Wachs and John E. Bates

This chapter focuses on the nature and consequences of temperament during the first several years of life. Topics include definitions, dimensions, and measurement of temperament, brain and temperament, biological and nonbiological influences, and temperament and parenting, personality, and adjustment.

The Definition and Dimensions of Temperament

Definitional issues

The concept of temperament has been traced back over 2000 years (Kagan, 1994). In spite of this long history there is, at present, no commonly accepted, precise definition of the term temperament (Nigg, 2006; Wachs, 2006). Temperament has been defined as behavioral style or the "how" of behavior, as individual differences in the experience and expression of emotionality, as individual differences in arousability, or as constitutionally based differences in reactivity and self-regulation (Rothbart & Bates, 2006; Zentner & Bates, 2008). Some view temperament as a dimensional construct – quantitative differences between individuals – while others view it as a categorical construct – qualitative, typological differences between individuals (Woodward, Lenzenweger, Kagan, Snidman, & Arcus, 2000).

Despite the multiple definitions of temperament there is a general consensus on the major features that define it: Temperament is a multidimensional array of traits that are early appearing, relatively stable and, while biologically rooted, are also sensitive to variation in the child's environment (Bates, 1989; Else-Quest, Hyde, Goldsmith & Hulle, 2006; Wachs & Bates, 2001). Although this "working definition" promotes communication among temperament researchers it is nevertheless ambiguous. For example, the criterion "early appearing" is not well defined. While individual differences in behavior patterns that fit the defining criteria for temperament can be detected in the first week of life (Riese, 1987; Wachs, Pollitt, Cueto, & Jacoby, 2004), other behavioral patterns commonly included as exemplars of temperament such as effortful control, may not appear until the second year or later (Rothbart & Bates, 1998).

Further, the criteria defining temperament (early appearing, relatively stable, biologically rooted but sensitive to the environment) also can apply to cognitive (e.g., selective attention) or motivational traits (e.g., persistence). For example, it has been proposed that there are two major domains of temperament (Rothbart & Bates, 2006). *Reactivity* refers to how quickly or strongly infants react to stimuli and whether an infant's emotional response to stimuli is primarily positive or negative. *Self-regulation* refers to the mechanisms through which the child controls their emotional or approach/withdrawal responses. Conceptually, temperament traits involving self-regulation should be more likely to share dimensional characteristics with other nontemperament domains than traits involving reactivity (e.g., the dimensional characteristics of attention as temperament may well overlap with the dimensional characteristics of attention as cognition – Wachs, 2006). Although this hypothesis has not yet been tested, Lemery, Essex, & Smider (2002) provide an example of how trait boundaries might be tested. Specifically, they had experts rate items from different scales to determine if individual items were more representative of individual differences in temperament or another domain, namely behavioral problems.

Dimensional issues

Thomas and Chess (1986) proposed nine separate temperament dimensions. While recent research has not supported the validity of the original Thomas and Chess nine-dimensional model (Rothbart & Bates, 2006), there is no clear consensus on the issue of number of individual dimensions of temperament (Wachs, 2006). For example, Ball, Pelco, Havill, and Reed-Victor (2001) reported a five-dimensional structure, while Putnam, Gartstein, and Rothbart (2006) identified as many as 18 temperament dimensions, although some of this may reflect similar dimensions with different names (Rothbart, Ahadi, & Evans, 2000).

One approach to deal with this issue has been to use exploratory or confirmatory factor analyses procedures. For example, Putnam, Gartstein, and Rothbart (2006) reduced their 18 scales to three broad domains of temperament: *surgency-extraversion*, composed of positive anticipation, activity level, and sensation seeking; (b) *negative affectivity*, defined by fear, anger-frustration, and social discomfort; (c) *effortful control*, which includes inhibitory control, attentional focusing, and perceptual sensitivity. One issue with factorial approaches is that the particular higher-order factor depends on the particular lower-order scales analyzed. A second issue is that the number of identified dimensions can vary as a function of analytic technique or sample characteristics (Ball et al., 2001; Shiner and Caspi, 2003). Finally, factors can reflect very different domains but have common underlying mechanisms (Wolfe & Bell, 2007). For example, conceptually distinct temperament and cognitive-processing activities might share common neural structures such as the limbic system (Nigg, 2006). Purely statistical approaches are unlikely to resolve the question of the number of behavioral dimensions that constitute temperament. It also is important to remember that temperament variables are hypothetical constructs – provisional tools for describing natural phenomena – not real entities in themselves.

Measurement of Temperament

Five approaches to assessing individual differences in early temperament have been developed: (1) structured or semistructured interviews; (2) questionnaires; (3) observation of infant behavior in structured laboratory situations; (4) naturalistic observations of infant's unstructured behavior; and (5) recordings of infant brain activity or physiological reactivity. Currently there has been relatively little systematic development of either interview or naturalistic observational approaches. Neural assessments based on brain electrical activity (e.g., evoked potentials – Fox, Henderson, Marshall, Nichols, & Ghera, 2005; also see chapter 9 this volume) are becoming increasingly prominent, but their scope, at present, is too limited for detailed coverage (Bishop, Spence, & McDonald, 2003). Hence, we will focus primarily on questionnaires and laboratory observations.

Parent report measures

In a prior review (Wachs & Bates, 2001) the following four conclusions were drawn:

1 The strengths of parent report measures include ease of administration and built-in aggregation, since caregivers usually base their ratings on many experiences with their child.
2 Concerns have been raised as to whether parent report measures are assessing parental emotional characteristics or expectancies about their child, rather than child temperament. However, there is increasing agreement that, while parent report measures do contain subjective components, these measures also contain a substantial objective component that does accurately assess child temperament.

   Subsequent reviews and research appearing after our earlier review support conclusions 1 and 2 with regard to the positive features of parental report measures and their subjective–objective nature (Bishop et al., 2003; Rothbart & Bates, 2006; Shiner & Caspi, 2003). For example, a number of studies have shown evidence for congruence between maternal report measures and objective laboratory-based assessments on negative emotionality measures (Hane, Fox, Polak-Toste, Ghera, & Guner, 2006), particularly after 12 months of age (Carnicero, Pérez-López, Del Carmen, & Martínez-Fuentes, 2000), when mothers are lower in sensitivity (Leerkes & Crockenberg, 2003) and when laboratory assessments are aggregated (Forman et al., 2003). Further, some evidence suggests that the so-called "bias" aspects of parent report measures may actually reflect reality. For example, a difficult temperament infant can accentuate maternal depression (Murray, Stanley, Hooper, King, & Fiori-Cowley, 1996), so associations between maternal depression and temperament ratings of her infant may reflect reality and not simply reporting bias.

3   Correlations between temperament ratings by mothers versus either observers or daycare/preschool personnel ratings are modest, often in the .30s- to mid-.40s (Wachs & Bates, 2001). Modest correlations between parent and observer ratings may reflect parents having greater experience with their child's behavior and thus basing their ratings on a more representative database, while modest correlations between parent and preschool teacher/daycare provider ratings may result from children showing different facets of temperament in home and day-care center contexts. Bates and Novosad (2005) have also suggested that individual temperament items may have different meanings for parents and childcare personnel.

4   Agreement between parents is higher (r range: .50-.60) but not as strong as might be expected. Suggested interpretations included children behaving differently for each parent, mother and fathers having different amounts of contact with their children, or using different rating criteria. Recent findings continue to show moderate interparent agreement on most ratings of specific dimensions of temperament in the early years of life (Hagekull & Bohlin, 2003; Pesonen, Raikkonen, Kajantie, et al., 2006), particularly for negative emotionality (Putnam et al., 2006). Nevertheless, there is still insufficient research to fully elucidate the meanings of parental reports.

Laboratory assessment procedures

Laboratory assessments involve presenting infants with a series of structured situations (e.g., The Lab-TAB Procedure; Rothbart, Derryberry, & Hershey, 2000; The Louisville Temperament Assessment Battery-LTAB; Matheny & Phillips, 2001). Infants' reactions are subsequently coded into specific dimensions of temperament, like inhibition or reactivity (e.g., Kagan, Snidman, Kahn, & Towsley. 2007). Infant temperament has also been coded during structured cognitive assessment procedures using the Bayley Infant Behavior Record (e.g., Guerin, Gottfried, Oliver, & Thomas, 2003).

Based on several recent reviews the following conclusions can be drawn concerning laboratory assessment procedures (Bishop et al., 2003; Rothbart & Bates, 2006; Shiner & Caspi, 2003):

1   Laboratory assessments of temperament have the advantages of allowing control of extraneous or nontemperament contextual factors, and of allowing detailed analysis of behavior, including time course and intensity.

2   Drawbacks of laboratory assessments include the need for experienced raters, the time-intensive nature of laboratory assessments, limits on what can be observed in such constrained situations or in brief periods of time, and the increased probability of missing rarely occurring but important infant behaviors.

Three recent papers have suggested alternative approaches to assessing temperament using laboratory assessment procedures. Putnam and Stifter (2005) noted that infants' reluctance to approach novel or complex stimuli in a laboratory assessment is typically

interpreted as reflecting high inhibition. However, failure to approach could also be interpreted as reflecting low approach rather than high inhibition. By integrating measures of
affect and approach Putnam and Stifter (2005) showed that failure to approach novel or
complex stimuli combined with high negative affectivity was a more accurate indicator
of individual differences in inhibition than just failure to approach; failure to approach
combined with low levels of negative affect was more characteristic of infants who were
low in approach but were not highly inhibited.

Kochanska (2001) and Forman et al. (2003) assessed atypical infant emotional
reactions, such as positive affect in laboratory situations designed to elicit negative
affect and negative emotions in situations designed to elicit positive affect. Emotional
atypicality was moderately stable over a 3-month period and infants who showed more
distress in contexts designed to elicit positive affect were also found to have less secure
attachments.

Finally, laboratory assessments typically focus on individual (mean) differences in the
level of temperament. However, when infants are assessed across a variety of situations,
it is also possible to measure intraindividual differences in temperament variability (IIV),
using standard deviation scores. Based on the different testing situations comprising the
LTAB, Wachs, Kanashiro, and Gurkas (2008) measured individual differences in IIV.
IIV scores were found to be early appearing, moderately stable between 3 and 12 months
and sensitive to infant nutritional status.

Improving the measurement of temperament

The accuracy of both parent report and laboratory procedures can be improved by the
use of aggregation, assessing common dimensions of temperament using different measurement approaches at the same point in time (Shiner & Caspi, 2003; Rothbart & Bates,
2006). For example, infant activity level could be measured using a combination of parent
report, coding of child activity in a structured laboratory situation, and actometer readings
in daycare or at home. Alternatively, standard parental and laboratory temperament
assessments could be combined with physiological measures. Aggregation can also be
carried out across time, although it may be difficult to get parental cooperation for
repeated laboratory visits within a short time period.

Brain Development and Temperament

Temperament dimensions have been linked to specific brain structures. Examples are
shown in Table 20.1. The nature of these links depends on the development of brain
systems. Individual differences in temperament cannot be clearly observed until the relevant brain systems become functional. A key example is the relatively late maturation
during infancy of the anterior attentional system (Rothbart & Bates, 2006), which is a
crucial component of effortful control.

Table 20.1   Examples of brain areas related to dimensions of temperament.*

Temperament dimension	Relevant brain areas
Behavioral inhibition (e.g., fear or withdrawal to novel or unfamiliar stimuli	Amygdala, Lateral prefrontal cortex, Superior parietal cortex of the posterior attention system.
Approach (e.g., surgency)	Basolateral amygdala, Lateral hypothalamus, Nucleus accumbens, Orbitofrontal cortex.
Effortful Control	Anterior cingulate cortex, basal ganglia, dorsolateral prefrontal cortex, ventromedial orbitofrontal cortex.

*For details see reviews by: Fox et al., 2005; Henderson & Wachs, 2007; Rothbart & Bates, 2006.

Individual differences in temperament also are linked to variations in brain function. Higher behavioral inhibition has been associated with increased activation of the right frontal cortex whereas higher approach or positive affect have been related to increased left frontal cortex activation (Buss et al., 2003; Fox et al., 2005; Schmidt, 2008). Similarly, differences in the serotonin neurotransmitter system have been linked to inhibition traits, whereas differences in the dopamine system are thought to mediate approach traits (Reif & Lesch, 2003; Rothbart & Bates, 2006). Individual differences in temperament can also reflect variability in activation of the parasympathetic and sympathetic branches of the autonomic nervous system, as measured by cardiac vagal tone (Porter, Wouden-Miller, Silva, & Porter, 2003), skin conductance (Scarpa, Raine, Venables, & Mednick, 1997) and facial temperature asymmetries (Boyce et al., 2002).

Individual differences in the functioning of the Hypothalamic-Pituitary-Adrenal axis (HPA), as measured by cortisol, have also been linked to individual differences in early temperament. Studies have shown that aspects of inhibition such as shyness (de Haan, Gunnar, Tout, Hart, & Stansbury, 1998) or fearfulness (Goldsmith, Lemery, Aksan, & Buss, 2000; Watamura, Donzella, Alwin, & Gunnar, 2003) are related to higher infant or toddler cortisol levels. Links between cortisol and anger proneness or effortful control are less consistent (van Bakel, & Riksen-Walraven, 2004; Watamura et al., 2003), perhaps reflecting age-limited associations (Watamura, Donzella, Kertes, & Gunnar, 2004). In addition, relations between cortisol levels and temperament may be bidirectional, as seen in evidence showing that infant inhibition at 14 months is related to higher cortisol levels at 4 years of age (Schmidt et al., 1997).

Brain–temperament links are best understood using a systems framework (Henderson & Wachs, 2007; Reif & Lesch, 2003). What is critical is not the functioning of a specific brain area or function, but rather the degree and nature of coordination among different brain areas or brain functions. Thus, individual differences in temperament can be viewed as reflecting the balance between the behavioral approach and behavioral inhibition brain systems, (Gray, 1991), or the interaction between brain structures involved in reactivity versus those involved in effortful control (Rothbart, Derryberry, & Posner, 1994). For example, the behavioral consequences of input from brain areas like the amygdala which are involved in reactivity will vary depending on input from midline frontal cortical areas involved in regulation (Pezawas et al., 2005). Similarly, emotional processing activity by the anterior cingulate cortex partly depends on dopamine input from the basal ganglia (Rothbart & Bates, 2006), while contributions of the dopamine system to individual differences in approach motivation partly depends on level of inhibitory serotonin activity (Reif & Lesch, 2003). Consistent with a systems framework, specific brain temperament associations may also vary depending on nonneural moderating influences such as chronological age (Calkins, Fox, & Marshall, 1996; Kagan et al., 2007) or infant attachment status (Vermeer & van Ijzendoorn, 2006).

Other Biological Influences on Individual Differences in Temperament

Genetic influences

Reviews have consistently shown genetic influences upon individual differences in infant and toddler activity, emotionality, inhibition, reactivity, persistence, and sociability (Goldsmith et al., 2000; Roisman & Fraley, 2006; Wachs & Bates, 2001). The heritability of temperament (percentage of variability in temperament accounted for by genetic influences) is in the moderate range (e.g., .20 to .35), and the nature and extent of genetic influences appear to depend on which temperament dimension is assessed, individual age and population characteristics. For example, in our prior review we reported that there was a lower genetic influence upon positive emotionality than upon negative emotionality, and heritability estimates of temperament were higher in twins than in nontwins and were lower during the first few months of life. Recent evidence also indicates that heritability may vary depending on infant's age (Nigg, 2006; Saudino, 2005), and depending upon whether maternal report measures or structured observational assessments are used (Roisman & Fraley, 2006).

In our previous review we also reported findings indicating that genes may influence the stability of temperament, whereas changes in temperament appear to be due either to environmental influences or to the joint operation of both genetic and environmental influences. While generally confirming these conclusions, recent findings also suggest that gene expression itself may change over time. Changes in gene expression can mean that even if heritability is similar at different ages for a given temperament trait, over time the nature of underlying genetic influences on temperament may change (Saudino, 2005).

In addition to behavioral-genetic studies there is a small literature on the molecular genetics of temperament. Some studies report that individual variability in inhibition is associated with individual polymorphisms in the 5-HTT serotonin transporter gene (Auerbach, Faroy, Ebstein, Kahana, & Levine, 2001; Hayden et al., 2007). However, not all studies find this association (Schmidt, Fox, Rubin, Hu, & Hamer, 2002). Such inconsistencies have been attributed to moderation of the expression of temperament related genes by rearing conditions (Propper & Moore, 2006) or by interactions between different genes (Lakatos et al., 2003). In addition, there may be specificity of gene action. For example, while variability in the DRD4 dopamine receptor gene has been linked to individual differences in activity level (Auerbach et al., 2001) DRD4 polymorphisms are unrelated to individual differences in inhibition (Schmidt et al., 2002) or self-regulation (Sheese, Voelker, Rothbart, & Posner, 2007).

Pre- and neonatal biological influences

Likely candidates for pre or neonatal biological influences on temperament are those that have the potential to influence fetal brain development. These include low birth weight or preterm birth, environmental toxins, and maternal prenatal stress hormone levels or nutritional status. With some exceptions, evidence for most of these influences is both scant and inconsistent. Inconsistencies may reflect the influence of other biological or nonbiological factors that act to moderate relations between prenatal influences and temperament.

Preterm birth and low birth weight. As shown in Table 20.2 relations between preterm birth or low birth weight and infant temperament are not consistent. This may reflect the operation of moderating factors such as the extent of prenatal growth retardation (Halpern & Garcia-Coll, 2000; Pesonen, Raikkonen, Strandberg, et al., 2006), postnatal infant zinc status (Black et al., 2004) and the degree to which the preterm or low birth weight infant is also at risk for biomedical problems that covary with preterm birth (e.g., intraventricular hemorrhage: Garcia-Coll, Halpern, Vohr, Seifer, & Oh, 1992).

Exposure to toxins. Prenatal exposure to toxins can involve either maternal exposure to environmental pollutants or maternal substance abuse. The overwhelming majority of pre- and postnatal behavioral toxicology studies involve cognitive outcomes (Hubbs-Tait, Nation, Krebs, & Bellinger, 2005). However, in one study prenatal lead exposure was related to reduced infant attention to novel stimuli (Plusquellec et al., 2007). While prenatal exposure to methylmercury has been linked to increased activity in school age children, detailed statistical analysis suggests that this association may be a chance finding (Myers et al., 2003). As shown in Table 20.2, relations between infant temperament and maternal use of illegal drugs during pregnancy are inconsistent, and probably reflect the complexity of biomedical and psychosocial risk factors that are linked to maternal substance abuse (Weiss, Jonn-Seed, & Harris-Muhell, 2007).

Maternal stress and hormone levels during pregnancy. Stress during pregnancy raises maternal cortisol levels, which in turn are thought to influence fetal brain development (Weinstock, 2005). However, as seen in Table 20.1, findings relating maternal stress or stress hormones to infant temperament are both limited and inconsistent. Inconsistencies may reflect moderating influences such as when during pregnancy maternal stress exposure occurred (Davis et al., 2007).

Table 20.2 Relations between infant temperament and prenatal influences.

Prenatal influence	Findings
Preterm birth or low birth weight.	Preterm infants characterized as less difficult, less sociable, less active–reactive, showing lower approach, having a lower threshold or a more positive mood than full-terms (Garcia-Coll et al., 1992; Newman et al., 1997b; Sajaniemi, Salokorpi, & vonWendt, 1998).
	Small body size at birth related to higher levels of negative affect at 5 years of age (Pesonen, Raikkonen, Kajantie, et al., 2006).
	Small for gestational (SGA) full-term infants rated as higher in fear and negative affect than appropriate for gestational age (AGA) term infants (Pesonen, Raikkonen, Strandberg, et al., 2006).
	SGA preterm infants show lower stability of temperament over time than AGA full-term or preterm infants (Gennaro, Medoff, & Lotas, 1992; Riese, 1992).
	No relation between infant temperament and low birth weight (Riese, 1994; Wachs et al., 2005), or weight for gestational age (Gorman, Lourie & Choudhury, 2001; Robson & Cline, 1998).
Maternal prenatal illegal drug use.	Maternal use of illegal drugs unrelated to variability in infant temperament (Sheinkopf et al., 2006).
	Maternal substance abuse negatively related to infant distractibility (Weiss et al., 2007).
	Maternal substance abuse associated with higher levels of infant negative affect (Das, 2001).
	Maternal substance abuse related to reduced levels of both positive and negative affect in infancy (Alessandri, Sullivan, Imaizumi, & Lewis, 1993).
Maternal prenatal stress or stress hormones.	Relations between prenatal maternal stress and postnatal infant temperament are nonsignificant (Davis et al., 2007) or, when significant show relatively small effect sizes (Huizink, Robles De Medina, Mulder, Visser, & Buitelaar, 2002).
	Continuity of maternal stress from the prenatal period to 6 months postnatally predicts 6-months infant negative reactivity (Pesonen, Raikkonen, Strandberg, et al., 2005).
	Higher levels of maternal cortisol associated with extreme stress are related to maternal ratings of infants as distress-prone (Brand, Engel, Canfield, & Yehuda, 2006).
	Non-significant relations between prenatal maternal hormonal levels and infant (Gutteling et al., 2005) or preschooler temperament (Susman, Schmeelk, Ponirakis, & Gariepy (2001).
	Baseline infant fetal heart rate or changes in fetal heart rate when mothers are involved in a short-term mild stress task are related to higher infant motor reactivity and positive affect, but are unrelated to negative emotional reactivity assessed at 4 months (Werner et al., 2007).

Pre- and neonatal nutritional influences.   The literature on pre- or neonatal nutrition and temperament, while small, is more consistent, particularly regarding iron deficiency. Prenatal (Vaughn, Brown, & Carter, 1986) and neonatal iron deficiency (Tamura et al., 2002; Wachs et al., 2005) have been associated with lower infant alertness, lower soothability when distressed, lower self-regulation, and greater negative emotionality. Less adequate neonatal iron status is also associated with reduced variability in reactivity to objects and persons in the environment (Wachs et al., 2008). In addition, lower reactivity to aversive stimuli and poor state control was found for neonates whose mothers had low vitamin B6 status (McCullough et al., 1990), while poorer maternal zinc status during pregnancy has been linked to lower fetal activity levels (Merialdi, Caulfield, Zavaleta, Figueroa, & DiPietro, 1999).

Postnatal biological influences

Postnatal biological influences on infant temperament again include exposure to environmental toxins, and nutrition.

Exposure to toxins.   Higher levels of body lead in infancy are associated with higher levels of withdrawal (Mendelsohn et al., 1998; Wasserman, Staghezza-Jaramillo, Shrout, Popovac, & Graziano, 1998) and lower levels of emotion regulation (Mendelsohn et al., 1998) and activity (Padich, Dietrich, & Pearson, 1985). In addition, exposure to environmental contaminants in breast milk has been related to reduced infant activity level (Jacobson, Jacobson, & Humphrey, 1990). Evidence further suggests that effects of toxic exposure may be cumulative (Wasserman et al., 1998).

Nutrition.   Evidence does not support a link between breastmilk nutrients and infant temperament (Auestad et al., 2001). However, maternal cortisol levels were positively related to infant fear in breastfed infants, but were unrelated to fear in formula-fed infants (Glynn et al., 2007).

Severely malnourished infants show greater distractibility and lower reactivity, emotional control and activity level, even after receiving nutritional supplementation (Grantham-McGregor, 1995; Meeks-Gardner, Grantham-McGregor, Himes, & Chang, 1999; Simeon & Grantham-McGregor, 1990). Similar to prenatal results, infant and toddler iron deficiency is associated with lower activity and reactivity, and higher inhibition and negative emotionality (Lozoff et al., 2006). Furthermore, poorly nourished infants who received zinc supplementation showed greater responsiveness during social interactions (Ashworth, Morris, Lira, & Grantham-McGregor, 1998), reduced negative affect (Bentley et al., 1997), and higher activity levels (Sazawal et al., 1996).

Gender

Gender can involve both biological and environmental influences. Prior reviews on the question of gender differences in temperament documented inconsistent findings particularly in the first year of life (Martin et al., 1997). The one exception was activity level, with a consistent body of evidence showing that males have a higher activity level than females (Komsi et al., 2006), particularly after the first year of life (Martin et al., 1997). More recently, using meta-analysis procedures, Else-Quest et al., (2006) reported large gender differences in effortful control favoring females. Females tended to be higher than males on approach, positive mood, and shyness, whereas males scored higher on impulsivity and high-intensity pleasure. Confirming prior reviews, males also were higher in activity than females. There were few overall gender differences in negative affect and effect sizes were small for those that were found (males higher in difficulty and intensity, females higher in fear). Although studies in this meta-analysis went from infancy through adolescence, results did not appear to vary by age, suggesting that conclusions on gender differences in temperament apply to the infancy period as well as to older children.

Psychosocial Influences

Given that temperament is regarded as biologically rooted, can we assume that the psychosocial environment primarily influences the behavioral manifestations of temperament? Such an assumption may be problematical, given that environmental characteristics can also influence brain development and the operation of neurotransmitter-hormonal systems (Repetti, Taylor, & Saxbe, 2007).

Most of the studies investigating relations between environment and temperament concern parenting (Putnam, Sanson, & Rothbart, 2002). For example, variability in infant emotionality has been associated with shared parent–infant positive affect, parental responsivity (Kochanska et al., 2004, study 1), maternal sensitivity (Leerkes & Crockenberg, 2003; Pauli-Pott, Mertesacker, Bade, Bauer, & Beckman, 2000) and parental control strategies (Paulussen-Hogeboom, Stams, Hermans, & Peetsma, 2007). Similarly, a meta-analytic review has documented relations between infant temperament and maternal depression (Beck, 2001). However, what these studies do not establish is whether parental rearing styles are influencing the child's temperament or the child's temperament is influencing parental rearing styles. Disentangling the nature of the link between infant temperament and parenting requires either longitudinal or intervention studies.

Longitudinal studies

As shown in Table 20.3, decreases in infant negative emotionality are linked to higher levels of parental sensitivity, involvement, and responsivity. In addition, infant negative emotionality is higher for insecurely attached infants, or for infants living in families where there has been antecedent violence, marital problems, or low maternal social support. In addition, mother–infant synchronous interactions are related to later infant self-regulation, though relations between maternal depression and infant temperament are less consistent.

Table 20.3 Parental influences on infant temperament: Longitudinal findings.

Temperament/parenting dimensions	Findings
Negative emotionality	Lower negative emotionality at 12 months predicted by higher parental sensitivity at 4 & 8 months (Pauli-Pott et al., 2004). Increases in infant's negative emotionality over time associated with lower parental involvement (Belsky, Fish, & Isabella, 1991) and lower parental responsivity to infant distress (Wachs et al., 1993). Reductions in infants' negative emotionality over time related to responsive, sensitive caregiving (Belsky et al., 1991). Secure infant attachment related to reduced negative emotionality; insecure attachment related to higher negative emotionality (Kochanska, 2001).
Inhibition	Highly inhibited infants become less inhibited over time when parents set firm age-appropriate behavioral limits, respond less to infant distress, and are more intrusive. (Arcus, 2001; Park, Belsky, Putnam, & Crnic, 1997). Highly inhibited 2-year-olds show high levels of behavioral inhibition 2 years later if their mothers were overprotective or negative (Rubin et al., 2002), or if they had no daycare experience from birth to 2 years (Fox et al., 2001). More positive mother-child relations and lower maternal power assertion at 22 months predicted higher fearfulness at 33 months (Kochanska, et al., 2007, study 1); parenting assessed between 7 and 15 months was nonpredictive (Kochanska et al., 2007, study 2).
Self-regulation	Higher mother–infant interactional synchrony in the first year predicts higher infant self-regulation at 24 months (Feldman, et al., 1999).
Maternal depression	Prenatal maternal depression or anxiety related to higher infant negative emotional reactivity at 4 months of age (Werner et al, 2007). At 3 months no difference on vagal tone between infants of depressed and nondepressed mothers; by 6 months vagal tone significantly lower for infants of depressed mothers (Propper & Moore, 2006). Maternal depression and social support at 4 months predict 12 month infant withdrawal/fear; maternal depression and social support at 8 months does not predict 12 month temperament (Pauli-Pott et al., 2004). No relation between prenatal maternal depression and infant temperament during the first 6 months (Leerkes & Crockenberg, 2003). Maternal depression at 2 months does not predict changes in infant temperament from 2 to 6 months (McGrath, Records, & Rice, 2008).
Quality of marital relations	Maternal report of physical abuse at time infant was born predicts higher levels of infant difficult temperament at 12 months (Burke, Lee, & O'Campo, 2008). Increases in negative emotionality for infants whose parents have more marital problems (Belsky et al., 1991; Engfer, 1986). Reductions in negative emotionality more likely for infants of mothers with higher levels of social support (Fish, 1997).

As also shown in Table 20.3 decreased infant inhibition is paradoxically associated with higher parental use of firm behavioral limits or power-assertive discipline, and lower maternal responsiveness to infant distress and maternal overprotection and intrusiveness. It has been suggested that inhibited infants who are not overly protected may learn better coping strategies for dealing with minor stresses in the relatively safe environment of the home, compared to inhibited infants who are protected from exposure to minor stressors (Arcus, 2001).

The role of moderators.   Relations between family environment and infant temperament may be moderated by both child and contextual characteristics. Proposed moderators include gender, infant age, family social class, and parental personality characteristics (Putnam et al., 2002). Specific genes also can moderate the influence of family environment on temperament. For example, the relation of parenting quality to infant activity level, impulsivity, and intensity was significantly stronger for infants with the 7 repeat allele form of the D4 dopamine receptor gene than for infants with alternative forms of this gene (Sheese, Voelker, Rothbart, & Posner, 2007). Similarly, infant inhibition can vary as a function of the interaction between the 5HTTLPR serotonin transporter gene and level of social support to the mother (Fox, Henderson, Rubin, Calkins, & Schmidt, 2007).

Infant temperament can also moderate the contributions of the rearing environment to subsequent temperament. For example, Propper & Moore (2006) propose that high reactive infants may be less sensitive to parenting. In contrast, Belsky (2004) proposed that infants with more difficult temperaments may be more sensitive to the environment in general and parenting influences in particular. Evidence is more supportive of the latter hypothesis, with relations between parenting and infant inhibition/fear or self-regulation being stronger for infants high in negative emotionality than for infants who are low on this dimension (Feldman, Greenbaum, & Yirmiya, 1999; Pauli-Pott, Mertesacker, & Beckman, 2004).

Intervention studies

Novosad & Thoman (2003) report that highly fussy infants who were given a "breathing bear" toy, which provided rhythmic stimulation matching the infant's breathing rate showed lower negative emotionality at 7 and 9 months. In a study that also involved highly fussy infants van den Boom (1994) demonstrated that a short-term maternal training program designed to increase mother's sensitivity and responsivity resulted in higher levels of infant sociability and self-regulation, and lower levels of negative emotionality. However, 27 months later, intervention effects had essentially disappeared (van den Boom, 1995). Results from a cognitive intervention program for disadvantaged infants demonstrated differences between intervention and control infants in aspects of self-regulation such as task orientation (MacPhee, Burchinal, & Ramey, 1997). In contrast, findings from a guidance program for mothers of preterm infants indicated no differences in temperament between intervention and control infants (van der Pal et al., 2008). At present there are too few temperament intervention studies available to determine if moderating factors influence which infants benefit from intervention.

Summary conclusions

Evidence from both longitudinal and intervention studies support the hypothesis that infant temperament develops partly in response to psychosocial environmental characteristics. Evidence also suggests that the influence of family environment upon temperament may be moderated by interactions between genes and rearing or between temperament and rearing. The overall pattern of evidence underlines the fact that individual variability in the behavioral manifestations of temperament is due to more than purely biological influences.

Temperament and culture

Differences in infant and toddler temperament in Chinese versus Canadian samples (Chen et al., 1998), US versus Russian (Gartstein, Knyazev, & Slobodskaya, 2005) or Japanese samples (Lewis, Ramsey, & Kawakami, 1993), and US, Spanish, and Chinese samples (Gartstein et al., 2006) have been reported. For example, Chinese infants display higher inhibition to novelty (Chen et al., 1998) and fearfulness than US infants (Gartstein et al., 2006). Cultural characteristics also can influence both the stability and consequences of individual differences in early temperament. Infant temperament patterns that are valued in a given culture show higher stability (Kerr, Lambert, Stattin, & Klackenberg-Larson, 1994). Infants and toddlers whose temperament pattern is not congruent with traits that are valued in their culture are more likely to be viewed negatively (Scheper-Hughes, 1987; Super & Harkness, 1986), and more likely to experience negative parenting, than infants or toddlers whose temperament traits are congruent with cultural values (Chen et al., 1998).

A number of potential mechanisms have been suggested to explain cross-cultural differences in the nature and consequences of infant temperament. These include culturally driven differences in parental rearing strategies, based on what temperament traits are valued in a given culture (Kerr, 2001) or biological influences such as cultural differences in genotype (Lewis, Ramsay, & Kawakami, 1993) or mother's diet during pregnancy (Chisholm 1981). In addition, cultural differences may reflect methodological issues, such as scale items on parent report measures not having the same meaning across cultures.

Consequences of Individual Differences in Temperament

Individual differences in early temperament have been related to a variety of developmental outcomes including *weight gain and risk of obesity* (Wachs, 2008), *failure to thrive* (see chapter 2, vol. II, this work), *susceptibility to infections* (Wilson, Megel, Fredrichs, & McLaughlin 2003), *sleep problems* (Goodnight, Bates, Staples, Pettit, & Dodge, 2007), *cognitive, language and early academic competence* (e.g., Guerin et al., 2003; Stright, Gallagher, & Kelley, 2008; Wolfe & Bell, 2007) and reactivity to intervention programs (Blair, 2002; Velderman, Bakermans-Kranenburg, Juffer, & van IJzendoorn, 2006). However, the vast majority of research on consequences of individual differences in infant and toddler temperament is focused in three areas: parenting, later personality, and later behavior disorders.

Temperament and parenting

As discussed earlier, distinguishing parenting→temperament effects from temperament→ parenting effects is very difficult to do with studies that measure parenting and temperament at the same time point. In their review Putnam et al. (2002) concluded that the overall pattern of evidence on the influence of temperament on parenting is not highly consistent. For example, some studies report no relation between temperament and parenting, while other studies find that difficult temperament is associated with indices of both positive and negative parenting, or that infant irritability may lead to greater parental involvement. Table 20.4 shows a similar inconsistency in relevant studies that appeared after the Putnam et al. review.

Consistent with our earlier discussion, one explanation for inconsistent findings is that moderating factors influence patterns of temperament→parenting relations. Longitudinal findings do not lend support to the Buss & Plomin (1984) hypothesis that the influence of temperament upon parenting occurs primarily for children with extreme temperaments (Guerin et al., 2003). However, studies have shown a pattern of declining involvement by parents of fussy difficult infants as their infants get older (Maccoby, Snow, & Jacklin, 1984; van den Boom & Hoeksma, 1994). Recent evidence has also implicated parental perceptions of their infant's soothability (Ghera, Hane, Malesa, & Fox, 2006) and the quality of parent's marital relationship (Schoppe-Sullivan, Mangelsdorf, Brown, & Sokolowski, 2007) as additional moderators. Similarly, relations between infant temperament and subsequent mother–infant attachment status partly depend on the mother's level of stress reactivity (Ispa, Fine, & Thornburg, 2002), while relations between infant temperament and maternal depression can vary depending on the degree to which mothers are high or low in self-efficacy beliefs about their child-rearing abilities (Cutrona & Troutman, 1986). Parental ability to cope with a difficult temperament infant or the self-efficacy beliefs of parents of difficult temperament infants can also depend on contextual characteristics, such as the level of chaos in the home (Corapci & Wachs, 2002).

These findings suggest that child temperament per se is not a powerful determinant of caregiver childrearing patterns. Having a specific temperament may increase the probability of eliciting certain reactions from caregivers but does not guarantee such linkages, in part because a variety of nontemperament influences can alter the degree to which infant temperament influences parental behavior. In addition, it may also be critical to consider the possibility of transactional bidirectional influences between temperament and parenting. In a transactional model relations between temperament

Table 20.4 Influence of infant temperament upon parenting.

Outcome measure	Findings
Parenting behaviors	Infant temperament assessed at 9 months unrelated to parental emotional reactivity or responsivity between 14 and 45 months (Kochanska et al., 2004, study 2).
	No relation between 4 months infant negative reactivity and 9 months maternal sensitivity (Ghera et al., 2006).
	No relation between 6 months difficult temperament and the slope of parental sensitivity and intrusiveness, repeatedly assessed until the child reached school age (Stright et al., 2008).
	Infant resistance to control in the second year of life related to reduced parental warmth and cognitive stimulation during the preschool period and reduced parental responsivity when the child was school age. Infant fussy difficult temperament related to greater family conflict. Low infant sociability related to reduced family cohesion from 3 to 16 years. (Guerin et al., 2003).
	12 month infant negative withdrawal unrelated to parental negative attitudes or negative parent–child interactions when the child was 9 years of age (Mezulis, Hyde, & Abramson, 2006).
Parental perceptions and choices	Infant manageability assessed at 6 months of age did not predict the age infants were placed in daycare (NICHD, 2003).
	Parent perceptions of infant temperament predicted subsequent objective temperament assessments, suggesting that infants are adjusting their temperament patterns to reflect maternal perceptions rather than the reverse Pauli-Pott et al. (2003).
Maternal depression and mother–infant attachment	Infant difficult temperament increases the risk of subsequent maternal depression (Murray et al., 1996).
	No relation between infant difficult temperament and risk of maternal depression (Edhborg, Seimyr, Lundh, & Widstrom, 2000).
	Individual differences in early fearfulness associated with subsequent proximity seeking and avoidance in the strange situation (Kochanska, 2001; Kochanska & Coy, 2002).
	No relation between early temperament and later differences in attachment status (Laible, Panfile, & Makariev, 2008).

and parenting are not static, given that infant temperament acts to influence parenting behaviors, which in turn influence the subsequent nature of infant temperament: temperament→parenting→temperament (Engfer, 1986; Kochanska, Aksan, & Joy, 2007; Thoman, 1990).

Temperament and later personality

Some personality theorists have hypothesized that personality essentially reflects temperament traits that are expressed differently at different ages, so that we should expect to find linkages between early temperament and the "Big 5" adult personality dimensions: extraversion, agreeableness, conscientiousness, neuroticism, and openness (Halverson, Kohnstamm, & Martin, 1994). For example, early self-regulation and task persistence have been considered as the developmental antecedents of adult conscientiousness (Kohnstamm, Zhang, Slotboom, & Elphick, 1998), while early sociability has been conceptually linked to later adult agreeableness (Hagekull, 1994). Supporting this hypothesis, evidence indicates that infant temperament is heterotypic in nature, such that the behavioral expression of temperament may change over time while the underlying nature of the specific temperament dimension remains constant (Fox et al., 2001; Nigg, 2006). However, although evidence for linkages between child temperament and later personality is accumulating (Shiner & Caspi, 2003), there is still too little evidence for a complete picture, particularly with regard to infant temperament. Some studies show that early temperament dimensions can be classified using the Big 5 framework (Halverson et al., 1994; Kohnstamm, Halverson, Mervielde, & Havill, 1998), but this surface resemblance tells us little about whether these dimensions actually predict similar personality dimensions past infancy.

Evidence from the few relevant longitudinal studies does not offer strong support for hypothesized linkages between specific dimensions of infant temperament and Big 5 personality traits.[1] Some Big 5 dimensions assessed in childhood or adolescence are predicted by conceptually related dimensions of infant temperament (e.g., negative relation between infant resistance to control and adolescent agreeableness: Lanthier & Bates, 1995; positive relation between infant positive affectivity and childhood extraversion: Komsi et al., 2006). However, many predicted associations do not reach statistical significance (Guerin et al., 2003; Hagekull & Bohlin, 2003; Komsi et al., 2006; Lanthier & Bates, 1995). Further, when predicted relations are found the magnitude of associations is often modest at best (Hagekull & Bohlin, 2003; Komsi et al., 2006) and observed relations often do not replicate across ages (Guerin et al., 2003) or across studies (e.g., the relation between infant sociability and later extraversion was significant in the Hagekull & Bohlin study, but was nonsignificant in the Lanthier & Bates findings).

In interpreting the above findings a key issue is the across-time stability of infant and toddler temperament. If measures of temperament are not at least moderately stable from infancy through the preschool period then links between early temperament and personality assessed at later time periods will be tenuous. While significant long-term stability for scores of infants at the extremes of temperament has been documented, only about 25% of infants at the extremes of temperament remain at the extremes when tested as preschoolers (Fox et al., 2001) or in the school age years (Pfiefer et al., 2002). Further, earlier temperament differences between extreme and nonextreme infant groups can attenuate in adolescence (Kagan et al., 2007).

Across the full range of temperament, stability correlations during infancy and from infancy into childhood go from insignificant to high, depending on the age span assessed, with overall stability being best defined as moderate (Guerin et al., 2003; Komsi et al., 2006). Not surprisingly, lower stability is found as the age span from infancy to later measurements of temperament increases. For example, the average 18 months stability of parent temperament ratings on the Early Childhood Behavior Questionnaire was $r = .58$ (Putnam et al., 2006), the average 30 month stability of parent ratings on the Toddler Behavior Assessment Questionnaire was $r = .35$ (Goldsmith, 1996) and the average 7 year stability between corresponding dimensions on the Infant Behavior Questionnaire and the Children's Behavior Questionnaire was $r = .15$ (Rothbart et al., 2000). This pattern is consistent with evidence presented by Lemery et al. (1999), indicating that the pattern of stability found for infant temperament is best described using a simplex model. In a simplex model continuity occurs primarily across adjacent measurement periods, with no direct stability across nonadjacent time periods. The form of a simplex model suggests that stability is short-term rather than long-term, such that any observed relations between infant temperament and later personality may reflect a series of temperament–temperament predictions rather than direct predictions from temperament to personality.

Evidence also indicates that the level of stability will vary across temperament dimensions, with higher stability for measures of negative emotionality (Guerin et al., 2003; Putnam et al., 2006). In addition, parent report measures of temperament show greater stability than laboratory-based assessments (Carnicero et al., 2000; Pauli-Pott, Mertesacker, Bade, Haverkock, & Beckman, 2003). For example, the overall 10 month stability of repeated parent ratings using the Infant Behavior Questionnaire was $r = .46$; corresponding stability correlations over the same time period for four dimensions of infant temperament derived from repeated laboratory assessments yielded an overall $r = .22$ (Rothbart et al., 2000).

Further complicating matters is the question of what mechanisms underlie hypothesized links between early temperament and later personality. A common assumption is that the stability of temperament is the result of stability of neural responses to stimulus input (Schwartz, Wright, Shin, Kagan, & Rauch, 2003), perhaps reflecting stable genetic influences. However, as noted earlier, gene expression can change over time. There is also evidence that variability in the stability of temperament can be influenced by intervening contextual characteristics (Propper & Moore, 2006; Wachs, 1994). For example, changes in the across-time stability of infant temperament have been shown to occur as a function of the nature of parental rearing styles (Arcus, 2001; Rubin, Burgess, & Hastings, 2002) and whether or not the infant was in daycare (Fox et al., 2001). Without taking account of such intervening experiences conclusions about the stability or instability of infant temperament, or relations between infant temperament and later personality will be incomplete.

Given the issues reviewed above the conceptual rationale for postulating specific links between infant temperament and later personality may not be as strong as initially proposed. While theoretically intriguing, at present the overall pattern of evidence does not support an assumption that infant temperament and later personality are robustly linked together. Nevertheless, from about age 3, temperament is more stable (Lemery et al., 1999) and shows stronger links to personality (Rothbart & Bates, 2006).

Temperament and adjustment

Much of the interest in temperament has stemmed from its potential to predict and explain the origins of differences in behavioral adjustment (Thomas & Chess, 1986). Does infant temperament predict later behavior problems? Probably yes. A relatively large number of studies do show temperament-adjustment predictions, certainly from early childhood, and possibly from infancy (Rothbart & Bates, 2006). Further, a fairly robust pattern of findings indicates that the nature of temperament-adjustment predictions fits a *differential linkage* pattern (Rothbart & Bates, 1998, 2006).

The differential linkage pattern suggests that particular behavior problems represent homologous extensions of particular dimensions of temperament. Specifically, although early temperamental fearfulness (novelty distress) is not always associated with later problems, when it is linked, fearfulness is more strongly linked to internalizing problems (e.g., anxiety-type problems). Viewed as an homologous extension, the link between early fearfulness and later anxiety seems conceptually straightforward. In contrast, early temperamental unmanageability (impulsivity, resistance to control) is most strongly linked to later externalizing problems (e.g., aggression and noncompliance). Viewed as an homologous extension, this link again seems conceptually straightforward. Early temperamental negative emotionality (the core of what is called difficult temperament) is linked to both internalizing and externalizing problems. Given that both internalizing and externalizing behavior patterns involve negative emotionality, this link seems conceptually meaningful as well. Although not all studies show differential linkage and the links are of moderate size, especially when predicting from infancy, this pattern has been frequently replicated (Crockenberg, Leerkes, & Barrig-Jo, 2008; Rothbart & Bates, 2006).

The meaningfulness of the differential linkage pattern has been questioned on methodological grounds. As much of the evidence involves parental ratings of both temperament and behavior problems, there is the possibility that some form of parental bias accounts for the across-time correlations. While there is little doubt that there is some bias in parental ratings, there does not appear to be major confounding of findings by parental bias. Even if the temperament-adjustment correlations were mostly due to bias, in order to account for differential linkage the bias would need to be precisely differentiated. Further, similar findings emerge when temperament and adjustment are measured using different sources. For example, parents' ratings of temperament predict later teacher ratings of adjustment (e.g., Bates, Pettit, Dodge, & Ridge, 1998; Guerin, Gottfried, & Thomas, 1997), and, experimenter's ratings of temperament predict later parent and teacher adjustment ratings (Caspi, Henry, McGee, Moffitt, & Silva, 1995).

A second methodological concern is that temperament-adjustment correlations are an artifact of the similarity of content in the two kinds of rating scales (content contamination: Sanson, Prior, & Kyrios, 1990). While content similarities do occur, content contamination does not appear to be a major concern. If temperament dimensions are inherent parts of behavioral adjustment, and if the differential linkage model of continuity from temperament to adjustment is correct, it would be both hard and theoretically counterproductive to completely avoid content similarity. Further, a number of studies have removed temperament items that overlap with adjustment scales or vice versa, and this only slightly attenuates the temperament adjustment linkages (Lemery et al., 2002; Lengua, West, & Sandler, 1998). Further, at least one study has shown that interventions that change parental perceptions of child adjustment do not necessarily change their perceptions of child temperament (Sheeber, 1995). While it is hard to quarrel with efforts to refine measurement, issues of bias or "contamination" do not seem to explain away the evidence for continuity from temperament to adjustment.

Assuming that predictions from early temperament to later adjustment are real, the question becomes what developmental processes explain the links. One potential model involves an increasing continuity of temperament, which gradually becomes a stable core to behavioral adjustment. This model is consistent with longitudinal findings. Across the first 2 years of life continuity of temperament appears to occur primarily between adjacent time periods, such that any continuity between nonadjacent time periods depends on the nature or level of the intervening temperament factor. However, from 24 months of age on, the increasing stability of temperament reflects the appearance of a common underlying stable core of temperament factors that cut across ages (Lemery et al., 1999).

A second model involves child temperament evoking negative reactions from others which then produces adjustment problems (Rothbart & Bates, 1998, 2006). For example, a poorly self-regulated child evokes parental hostility, which leads to child anger and defensiveness. In a third model, the child's temperament leads to active selection of environments that in turn, promote adjustment problems (Rothbart & Bates, 1998, 2006). For example, an unadaptable, fearful child seeks safe, comforting environments, which leads to failures to master challenges and thus, to further fear and withdrawal.

While such models are theoretically plausible there is too little research demonstrating such processes. Part of this may have to do with the limited correlations between early temperament and later adjustment – typically ranging from small to medium in size. This suggests that linear effects of temperament upon adjustment, whether highly direct or somewhat indirect via transactions with the environment, are only part of the story. As theory has long suggested, there may be nonlinear, interactive effects of temperament and environment upon adjustment.

Over the past 10 years, there has been an explosion of research on temperament-environment interactions. One example is seen in a recent study (Bradley & Corwyn, 2008), which shows that externalizing behaviors were reduced for difficult temperament children whose parents were sensitive or involved the child in cognitively stimulating activities; these parenting patterns did not predict similar reductions in externalizing behavior for children with easy temperaments.

A second example is derived from the work of Kochanska (1991), who has hypothesized that inhibited and uninhibited infants may be more sensitive to different types of parental rearing styles. Kochanska and colleagues (Kochanska, 1991, 1995, 1997; Kochanska et al., 2007) have shown that temperamentally fearful young children develop a more internalized conscience when they are disciplined in relatively gentle, rather than harsh ways, whereas fearless children's conscience development is not strongly related to gentle versus harsh discipline. Theoretically, harsh discipline arouses anxiety in fearful children, which prevents them from internalizing regulatory messages from the discipline encounter. In contrast, temperamentally fearless children develop more advanced signs of conscience when their mothers maintain strong positive relationships with them. Theoretically, fearless children become socialized through desire to maintain positive, rewarding relationships. Although replication is needed, these findings support experimental refinements of parent training treatments for young children with behavior problems, given that some children with oppositional problems are fairly high on anxiety whereas others are not (detailed reviews of temperament–environment interactions are found in Bates & Pettit, 2007 and Rothbart & Bates, 2006).

Compared to findings on temperament–environment interactions, there have been fewer studies testing whether one temperament characteristic moderates the developmental influence of another temperament characteristic (temperament–temperament moderation). However, there is evidence that children high on negative emotionality are less likely to show behavior problems if they are also high on effortful control (Eisenberg et al., 2001). In addition, there are also a few studies of more complex interactive relations where more than one temperament trait interacts with environmental characteristics. One intriguing example is the 3-way interaction finding of Crockenberg and Leerkes (2005) that infants who were high in both activity in response to novelty and distress to novelty, and who experienced high levels of daycare, had more internalizing problems compared to those who were not high on both temperament variables.

Overall, current findings indicate that early temperament does predict later behavior problems, with the pattern one of differential linkage. As behavioral adjustment differences result from a gradually accumulating product of multiple influences, ultimately, empirical models will need to show how temperament and environment moderate one another in a series of developmental steps.

Conclusions and Future Directions

There is increasing consensus on the definition, dimensions, development, and consequences of individual differences in infant temperament. The measurement of infant temperament has grown increasingly sophisticated, but greater use of aggregation procedures, across reporters, time, and measurement techniques could further increase precision in the assessment of individual differences in temperament. The greater sophistication of neural assessments will undoubtedly lead to greater understanding of temperament–brain relations. Future progress in this area will especially depend on advances in understanding of coordination among different brain systems, as these influence the behavioral manifestations and development of early temperament. Given amazing progress in the area of molecular genetics, we also would expect a corresponding increase in our knowledge of the genetic basis of temperament. However, in our rush to explore genetic contributions, we should not ignore other biological factors, such as exposure to environmental toxins or nutritional deficiencies, which can also directly influence both brain and genetic contributions to temperament. Finally, empirical research has increasingly shown that temperament and environment interact and moderate each other's effects. Future research needs to establish the particular temperament–environment interactions that have been emerging, to extend our knowledge of temperament–temperament interactions, and to explore the ways in which early and later social-emotional outcomes develop as a function of complex arrays of multiple temperament and multiple environmental characteristics.

Note

1. In our previous review (Wachs & Bates, 2001) we included longitudinal results from the Fels and the Dunedin studies. We choose not to include these studies in this review because many of the personality outcome measures in the Fels study do not clearly fit into the Big 5 structure and the earliest assessment of temperament in the Dunedin study occurred at age 3 years. Including the results from these studies in the present review would not have changed our overall conclusions.

References

Alessandri, S., Sullivan, M., Imaizumi, S., & Lewis, M. (1993). Learning and emotional responsivity in cocaine-exposed infants. *Developmental Psychology, 29,* 989–997.

Arcus, D. (2001). Inhibited and uninhibited children: Biology in the social context. In T. D. Wachs & D. Kohnstamm (Eds.), *Temperament in context* (pp. 43–60). Hillsdale, NJ: Erlbaum.

Ashworth, A., Morris, S., Lira, P., & Grantham-McGregor, S. (1998). Zinc supplementation, mental development and behaviour in low birth weight term infants in northeast Brazil. *European Journal of Clinical Nutrition, 52,* 223–227.

Auerbach, J., Faroy, M., Ebstein, R., Kahana, M., & Levine, J. (2001). The association of the dopamine D4 receptor gene (DRD4) and the serotonin transporter promoter gene (5 HTTL–PR) with temperament in 12 month old infants. *Journal of Child Psychology and Psychiatry, 42,* 777–783.

Auestad, N., Halter, R., Hall, R., Blatter, M., Bogle, M., Burks, W., et al. (2001). Growth and development in term infants fed long-chain polyunsaturated fatty acids: A double-masked, randomized, parallel, prospective, multivariate study. *Pediatrics, 108,* 372–381.

Ball, C., Pelco, L., Havill, V., & Reed-Victor, E. (2001). Confirmatory factor analysis of the Temperament Assessment Battery for Children Revised. *Journal of Psychoeducational Assessment, 19,* 365–379.

Bates, J. (1989). Concepts and measures of temperament. In G. A. Kohnstamm, J. E. Bates, & M. K. Rothbart (Eds.), *Temperament in childhood* (pp. 3–26). New York: Wiley.

Bates, J., & Novosad, C. (2005). Measurement of individual difference constructs in child development or taking aim at movement targets. In D. Teti. (Ed.), *Handbook of research methods in developmental science* (pp. 103–122). Malden MA: Blackwell.

Bates, J., & Pettit, G. (2007). Temperament, parenting and socialization. In J. Grusec & P. Hastings (Eds.), *Handbook of socialization* (pp. 153–177). New York: Guilford.

Bates, J., Pettit, G., Dodge, K., & Ridge, B. (1998). The interaction of temperamental resistance to control and restrictive parenting in the development of externalizing behavior. *Developmental Psychology, 34,* 982–995.

Beck, C. (2001). Predictors of postpartum depression. *Nursing Research, 50*, 275–285.

Belsky, J. (2004). Differential susceptibility to rearing influence: An evolutionary hypothesis and some evidence. In B. Ellis & D. Bjorklund (Eds.), *Origins of the social mind: Evolutionary psychology and child development* (pp. 139–163). New York: Guilford.

Belsky, J., Fish, M., & Isabella, R. (1991). Continuity and discontinuity in infant negative and positive emotionality. *Developmental Psychology, 27*, 421–431.

Bentley, M., Caulfield, L., Ram, M., Santizo, C., Hurtado, E., Rivera, J., et al. (1997). Zinc supplementation effects the activity patterns of rural Guatemalan infants. *Journal of Nutrition, 127*, 1333–1338.

Bishop, G., Spence, S., & McDonald, C. (2003). Can parents and teachers provide a reliable and valid report of behavioral inhibition. *Child Development, 74*, 1899–1917.

Black, M., Sazawal, S., Black, R., Khosla, S., Kumar, J., & Menon, V. (2004). Cognitive and motor development among small-for-gestational-age infants: Impact of zinc supplementation, birth weight, and caregiving practices. *Pediatrics, 113*, 1297–1305.

Blair, C. (2002). Early intervention for low birth weight preterm infants: The role of negative emotionality in the specification of effects. *Development and Psychopathology, 14*, 311–332.

Boyce, W., Essex, M., Alkon, A., Smider, N., Pickrell, T., & Kagan, J. (2002). Temperament, tympanum and temperature, *Child Development, 73*, 718–733.

Bradley, R., & Corwyn, R. (2008). Infant temperament, parenting and externalizing behavior in first grade: A test of the differential susceptibility hypothesis. *Journal of Child Psychology and Psychiatry, 49*, 124–131.

Brand, S., Engel, S., Canfield, R., & Yehuda, R. (2006). The effect of maternal PTSD following in utero trauma exposure on behavior and temperament in the 9-month-old infant. In R. Yehuda (Ed.), *Psychobiology of posttraumatic stress disorders: A decade of progress* (Vol. *1071*, pp. 454–458). Malden, MA: Blackwell.

Burke, J., Lee, L., & O'Campo, P. (2008). An exploration of maternal intimate partner violence experiences and infant general health and temperament. *Maternal Child Health Journal, 12*, 172–179.

Buss, A., & Plomin, R. (1984). *Temperament: Early developing personality traits.* Hillsdale, NJ: Erlbaum.

Buss, K., Malmstadt Schumacher, J., Dolski, I., Kalin, N., Goldsmith, H., & Davidson, R. (2003). Right frontal brain activity, cortisol, and withdrawal behavior in 6-month-old infants. *Behavioral Neuroscience, 117*, 11–20.

Calkins, S., Fox, N., & Marshall, T. (1996). Behavioral and physiological antecedents of inhibited and uninhibited behaviour. *Child Development, 67*(2), 523–540.

Carnicero, J., Pérez-López, J., Del Carmen,M., & Martínez-Fuentes, M. (2000). *European Journal of Personality, 14*, 21–37.

Caspi, A., Henry, B., McGee, R., Moffitt, T., & Silva, P. (1995). Temperamental origins of child and adolescent behavior problems: From age three to age fifteen. *Child Development, 66*, 55–68.

Chen, X., Hastings, P., Rubin, K., Chen, H., Cen, G., & Stewart, S. (1998). Child rearing attitudes and behavioral inhibition in Chinese and Canadian toddlers. *Developmental Psychology, 34*, 677–686.

Chisholm, J. (1981). Prenatal influences on Aboriginal-White Australian differences in neonatal irritability. *Ethnology and Sociobiology, 2*, 67–73.

Corapci, F., & Wachs, T. D. (2002). Does parental mood or efficacy mediate the influence of environmental chaos upon parenting behavior? *Merrill-Palmer Quarterly, 48*, 182–201.

Crockenberg, S., & Leerkes, E. (2005). Infant temperament moderates associations between child-care type and quantity and externalizing and internalizing behaviors at 2½ years. *Infant Behavior and Development, 28*, 20–35.

Crockenberg, S., Leerkes, E., & Barrig-Jo, P. (2008). Predicting aggressive behavior in the third year from infant reactivity and regulation as moderated by maternal behavior. *Development and Psychopathology, 20*, 37–54.

Cutrona, C., & Troutman, B. (1986). Social support, infant temperament and parenting self–efficacy. *Child Development, 57*, 1507–1518.

Das, R. (2001). Maternal substance use and mother–infant feeding interactions. *Infant Mental Health Journal, 22*, 497–511.

Davis, E., Glynn, L., Schetter, C., Hobel, C., Chicz-Demet, A., & Sandman, C. (2007). Prenatal exposure to maternal depression and cortisol influences infant temperament. *Journal of the American Academy of Child & Adolescent Psychiatry, 46*(6), 737–746.

de Haan, M., Gunnar, M., Tout, K., Hart, J., & Stansbury, K. (1998). Familiar and novel contexts yield different associations between cortisol and behavior among 2-year-old children. *Developmental Psychobiology, 33*, 93–101.

Edhborg, M., Seimyr, L., Lundh, W., & Widstrom, A., (2000). Fussy child – difficult parenthood? Comparisons between families with a "depressed" mother and non-depressed mother 2 months postpartum. *Journal of Reproductive and Infant Psychology, 18*, 226–238.

Eisenberg, N., Cumberland, A., Spinrad, T., Fabes, R., Shephard, S., Reiser, M., et al. (2001). The relations of regulation and emotionality to children's externalizing and internalizing problem behavior. *Child Development, 72*, 1112–1134.

Else-Quest, N., Hyde, J., Goldsmith, H., & Hulle, C. (2006). Gender differences in temperament: A meta-analysis *Psychological Bulletin, 132*(1), 33–72.

Engfer, A. (1986). Antecedents of perceived behavior problems in infancy. In G. Kohnstamm (Ed.), *Temperament discussed* (pp. 165–180). Lisse: Swets & Zeitlinger.

Feldman, R., Greenbaum, C., & Yirmiya, N. (1999). Mother–infant affect synchrony as an antecedent of the emergence of self-control. *Developmental Psychology, 35*, 223–231.

Fish, M. (1997, April). *Stability and change in infant temperament.* Paper presented to the Society for Research in Child Development, Washington, DC.

Forman, D., O'Hara, M., Larsen, K., Coy, K., Gorman, L., & Stuart, S. (2003). Infant emotionality: Observational methods and the validity of maternal reports. *Infancy, 4*, 541–565.

Fox, N., Hane, A., & Pine, D. (2007). Plasticity for affective neurocircuitry. *Current Directions in Psychological Science, 16*, 1–5.

Fox, N., Henderson, H., Marshall, P., Nichols, K., & Ghera, M. (2005). Behavioral inhibition: Linking biology and behavior within a developmental framework. *Annual Review of Psychology, 56*, 235–262.

Fox, N., Henderson, H., Rubin, K., Calkins, S., & Schmidt, L. (2001). Continuity and discontinuity of behavioral inhibition and exuberance. *Child Development, 72*, 1–21.

Garcia-Coll, C., Halpern, L., Vohr, B., Seifer, R., & Oh, W. (1992). Stability and correlates of change of early temperament in preterm and full term infants. *Infant Behavior and Development, 15*, 137–153.

Gartstein, M., Gonzalel, C., Carranza, J., Ahadi, S., Ye, R., Rothbart, M. & Yang, S. (2006). Studying cross-cultural differences in the development of infant temperament: People's Republic of China, The United States of America and Spain. *Child Psychiatry and Human Development, 37*, 145–161.

Gartstein, M., Knyazev, G., & Slobodskaya, H. (2005). Cross-cultural differences in the structure of infant temperament: United States of America (US) and Russia. *Infant and Behavior and Development, 28*, 54–61.

Gennaro, S., Medoff, B., & Lotas, M. (1992). Perinatal factors in infant temperament. *Nursing Research, 41*, 375–377.

Ghera, M., Hane, A., Malesa, E., & Fox, N. (2006). The role of infant soothability in the relation between infant negativity and maternal sensitivity. *Infant Behavior and Development, 29*, 289–293.

Glynn, L., Davis, E., Schetter, C., Chicz-DeMet, A., Hobel, C., & Sandman, C. (2007). Postnatal maternal cortisol levels predict temperament in healthy breastfed infants. *Early Human Development, 83*, 675–681.

Goldsmith, H. (1996). Studying temperament via construction of the Toddler Behavior Assessment Questionnaire. *Child Development, 67*, 218–235.

Goldsmith, H., Lemery, K., Aksan, N., & Buss, K. (2000). Temperamental substrates of personality development. In V Molfese & D Molfese (Eds.), *Temperament and personality development across the life span* (pp. 1–32). Mahwah, NJ: Erlbaum.

Goodnight, J., Bates, J., Staples, A., Pettit, G., & Dodge, K. (2007). Temperament resistance to control increases the association between sleep problems and externalizing behavior development. *Journal of Family Psychology, 21*(1), 39–48.

Gorman, K., Lourie, A., & Choudhury, N. (2001). Differential patterns of development: The interaction of birth weight, temperament, and maternal behavior. *Journal of Developmental & Behavioral Pediatrics, 22*, 366–375.

Grantham-McGregor, S. (1995). A review of studies of the effect of severe malnutrition on mental development. *Journal of Nutrition, Supplement, 125*, 2233S–2238S.

Gray, J. (1991). The neuropsychology of temperament. In J. Strelau & A. Angleitner (Eds.), *Explorations in temperament: International perspectives on theory and measurement* (pp. 105–128). New York: Plenum Press.

Guerin, D., Gottfried, A., Oliver, P., & Thomas, C. (2003). *Temperament: Infancy through Adolescence*. New York: Kluwer Academic Press.

Guerin, D., Gottfried, A., & Thomas, C. (1997). Difficult temperament and behavior problems: A longitudinal study from 1.5 to 12 years. *International Journal of Behavioral Development, 21*, 71–90.

Gutteling, B., de Weerth, C., Willemsen-Swinkels, S., Huizink, A., Mulder, E., Visser, G. H. et al., (2005). The effects of prenatal stress on temperament and problem behavior of 27-month-old toddlers. *European Child & Adolescent Psychiatry, 14*(1), 41–51.

Hagekull, B. (1994). Infant temperament and early childhood functioning. In C. Halverson, G. Kohnstamm, & R. Martin (Eds.), *The developing structure of temperament and personality from infancy to adulthood* (pp. 227–240). Hillsdale, NJ: Erlbaum.

Hagekull, B., & Bohlin, G. (2003). Early temperament and attachment as predictors of the five factor model of personality. *Attachment and Human Development, 5*, 2–18.

Halpern, L., & Garcia-Coll, C. (2000). Temperament of small-for-gestational-age and appropriate-for-gestational-age infants across the first year of life. *Merrill-Palmer Quarterly, 46*, 738–765.

Halverson, C., Kohnstamm, D., & Martin, R. (1994). *The developing structure of temperament and personality from infancy to childhood*. Hillsdale, NJ: Erlbaum.

Hane, A., Fox, N., Polak-Toste, C., Ghera, M., & Guner, B. (2006). Contextual basis of maternal perceptions of infant temperament. *Developmental Psychology, 42*, 1077–1088.

Hayden, E., Dougherty, L., Maloney, B., Durbin, C., Olino, T., Nurnberger, J., et al. (2007). Temperamental fearfulness in childhood and the serotonin promoter region polymorphism. *Psychiatric Genetics, 17*, 135–142.

Henderson, H., & Wachs, T. D. (2007). Temperament theory and the study of cognition–emotion interactions across development. *Developmental Review, 27*, 396–427.

Hubbs-Tait, L., Nation, J., Krebs, N., & Bellinger, D. (2005). Neurotoxicants, micronutrients, and social environments: Individual and combined effects on children's development. *Psychological Science in the Public Interest, 6*(3), 57–121.

Huizink, A., Robles De Medina, P., Mulder, E., Visser, G., & Buitelaar, J. (2002). Psychological measures of prenatal stress as predictors of infant temperament. *Journal of the American Academy of Child & Adolescent Psychiatry, 41*(9), 1078–1085.

Ispa, J., Fine, M., & Thornburg, K. (2002). Maternal personality as a moderator of relations between difficult infant temperament and attachment security in low-income families. *Infant Mental Health Journal, 23*, 130–144.

Jacobson, J., Jacobson, S., & Humphrey, H. (1990). Effects of exposure to PCBs and related compounds on growth and activity in children. *Neurotoxicology and Teratology, 12*, 319–326.

Kagan, J. (1994). On the nature of emotion. *Monographs of the Society for Research in Child Development, 59*, 7–24.

Kagan, J., Snidman, N., Kahn, V., & Towsley, S. (2007). The preservation of two infant temperaments into adolescence. *Monographs of the Society for Research in Child Development, 287*(Serial No. 72).

Kerr, M. (2001). Culture as a context for temperament. In T. D. Wachs & G. Kohnstamm. *Temperament in context* (pp. 139–152). Hillsdale, NJ: Erlbaum.

Kerr, M., Lambert, W., Stattin, H., & Klackenberg-Larson, I. (1994). Stability of inhibition in a Swedish longitudinal sample. *Child Development, 65*, 138–146.

Kochanska, G. (1991). Socialization and temperament in the development of guilt and conscience. *Child Development, 62*, 1379–1392.

Kochanska, G. (1995). Children's temperament, mothers' discipline, and security of attachment: Multiple pathways to emerging internalization. *Child Development, 66*, 597–615.

Kochanska, G. (1997). Multiple pathways to conscience for children with different temperaments: From toddlerhood to age 5. *Developmental Psychology, 33*, 228–240.

Kochanska, G. (2001). Emotional development in children with different attachment histories. *Child Development, 72*, 474–490.

Kochanska, G., Aksan, N., & Joy, M. (2007). Child fearfulness as a moderator of parenting in early socialization. *Developmental Psychology, 43*, 222–237.

Kochanska, G., & Coy, K. (2002). Child emotionality and maternal responsiveness as predictors of reunion behaviors in the strange situation. *Child Development, 73*, 228–240.

Kochanska, G., Friesenborg, A., Lange, L., & Martel, M. (2004). Parents personality and infant's temperament as contributors to their emerging relationship. *Journal of Personality and Social Psychology, 86*, 744–759.

Kohnstamm, G., Halverson, C., Mervielde, I., & Havill, V. (Eds.). (1998). *Parental descriptions of child personality*. Hillsdale, NJ: Erlbaum.

Kohnstamm, G., Zhang, Y., Slotboom, A., & Elphick, E. (1998). A developmental integration of conscientiousness from childhood to adulthood. In G. Kohnstamm, C. Halverson, I. Mervielde, & V. Havill (Eds.), *Parental descriptions of child personality* (pp. 65–84). Hillsdale, NJ: Erlbaum.

Komsi, N., Räikkönen, K., Pesonen, A., Heinonen, K., Keskivaara, P., Järvenpää, A. et al. (2006). Continuity of temperament from infancy to middle childhood. *Infant Behavior & Development, 29*, 494–508.

Laible, D., Panfile, T., & Makariev, D. (2008). The quality and frequency of mother–toddler conflict: Links with attachment and temperament. *Child Development, 79*, 426–443.

Lakatos, K., Nemoda, Z., Birkas, E., Ronai, Z., Kovacs, E., & Ney, K. (2003). Association of the D3 dopamine receptor gene and serotonin transporter polymorphisms with infants' response to novelty. *Molecular Psychiatry, 8*, 90–97.

Lanthier, R., & Bates, J. (1995, May). *Infancy era predictors of the Big 5 personality dimensions in adolescence*. Paper presented to the Midwestern Psychological Association, Chicago, IL.

Leerkes, E., & Crockenberg, S. (2003). The impact of maternal characteristics and sensitivity on the concordance between maternal reports and laboratory observations of infant negative emotionality. *Infancy, 4*, 517–539.

Lemery, K., Essex, M., & Smider, N. (2002). Revealing the relation between temperament and behavior problem. *Child Development, 73*, 867–882.

Lemery, K., Goldsmith, H., Klinnert, M., & Mraszek, D. (1999). Developmental models of infant and childhood temperament. *Developmental Psychology, 35,* 189–204.

Lengua, L., West, S., & Sandler, I. (1998). Temperament as a predictor of symptomatology in children: Addressing contamination of measures. *Child Development, 69,* 164–181.

Lewis, M., Ramsey, D., & Kawakami, K. (1993). Differences between Japanese infants and Caucasian American infants in the behavioral and cortisol response to inoculation. *Child Development, 64,* 1722–1731.

Lozoff, B., Beard, J., Connor, J., Felt, B., Georgieff, M., & Schallert, T. (2006). Long-lasting neural and behavioral effects of iron deficiency in infancy. *Nutrition Reviews, 64,* s34–s44.

Maccoby, E., Snow, M., & Jacklin, C. (1984). Children's disposition and mother child interactions at 12 and 18 months. *Developmental Psychology, 20,* 459–472.

MacPhee, D., Burchinal, M., & Ramey, C. (1997). *Individual differences in response to intervention.* Paper presented to the Society for Research in Child Development. April, Washington, DC.

Martin, R., Wisenbaker, J., Baker, J., & Huttenen, M. (1997). Gender differences in temperament at six months and five years. *Infant Behavior and Development, 20,* 339–347.

Matheny, A., & Phillips, K. (2001). Temperament and context: Correlates of home environment with temperament continuity and change, newborn to 30 months. In T.D. Wachs & G. Kohnstamm (Eds.), *Temperament in context* (pp. 81–102). Hillsdale, NJ: Erlbaum.

McCullough, A., Kirksey, A., Wachs, T. D., McCabe, G., Bassily, N., Bishry, Z., et al. (1990). Vitamin B-6 status of Egyptian mothers: Relation to infant behavior and maternal infant interactions. *American Journal of Clinical Nutrition, 51,* 1067–1074.

McGrath, J., Records, K., & Rice, M. (2008). Maternal depression and infant temperament characteristics. *Infant Behavior & Development, 31,* 71–80.

Meeks-Gardner, J., Grantham-McGregor, S., Himes, J., & Chang, S. (1999). Behaviour and development of stunted and nonstunted Jamaican children. *Journal of Child Psychology and Psychiatry, 5,* 819–827.

Mendelsohn, A., Dreyer, B., Fierman, A., Rosen, C., Legano, L., Kruger, H., et al. (1998). Low-level lead exposure and behavior in early childhood. *Pediatrics, 101,* 464–465.

Merialdi, M., Caulfield, L., Zavaleta, N., Figueroa, A., & DiPietro, J. (1999). Adding zinc to prenatal iron and folate tablets improves fetal neurobehavioral development. *American Journal of Obstetrics and Gynecology, 180,* 483–490.

Mezulis, A., Hyde, J., & Abramson, L. (2006). The developmental origins of cognitive vulnerability to depression: Temperament, parenting, and negative life events in childhood as contributors to negative cognitive style. *Developmental Psychology, 42,* 1012–1025.

Murray, L., Stanley, C., Hooper, R., King, F., & Fiori-Cowley, A. (1996). The role of infant factors in postnatal depression and mother–infant interactions. *Developmental Medicine and Child Neurology, 38,* 109–119.

Myers, G., Davidson, P., Cox, C., Shamlaye, C., Palumbo, D., Cerrichiari, E., et al. (2003). Prenatal methylmercury exposure from ocean fish consumption in the Seychelles child development study. *The Lancet, 361,* 1686–1692.

Newman, D., O'Callaghan, M., Harvey, J., Tudehope, D., Gray, P., Burns, Y., et al. (1997). Characteristics at four months follow-up of infants born small for gestational age. *Early Human Development, 49,* 169–181.

NICHD Early Child Care Research Network (2003). Does amount of time spent in child care predict socioemotional adjustment during the transition to kindergarten? *Child Development, 74,* 451–477.

Nigg, J. (2006). Temperament and developmental psychopathology. *Journal of Child Psychology and Psychiatry, 47,* 395–422.

Novosad, C., & Thoman, E. (2003). The breathing bear: An intervention for crying babies and their mothers. *Journal of Developmental & Behavioral Pediatrics, 24,* 89–95.

Padich, R., Dietrich, K., & Pearson, D. (1985). Attention activity level on lead exposure at 18 months. *Environmental Research, 38,* 137–143.

Park, S., Belsky, J., Putnam, S., & Crnic, K. (1997). Infant emotionality, parenting and 3 year inhibition. *Developmental Psychology, 33,* 218–227.

Pauli-Pott, U., Mertesacker, B., Bade, U., Bauer, C., & Beckman, D. (2000). Contexts of relations of infant negative emotionality to caregiver's reactivity/sensitivity. *Infant Behavior & Development, 23,* 23–39.

Pauli-Pott, U., Mertesacker, B., Bade, U., Haverkock, A., & Beckman, D. (2003). Parental perceptions and infant temperament development. *Infant Behavior & Development, 26,* 27–48.

Pauli-Pott, U., Mertesacker, B., & Beckman, D. (2004). Predicting the development of infant emotionality from maternal characteristics. *Development and Psychopathology, 16,* 19–42.

Paulussen-Hoogeboom, M., Stams, G., Hermans, J., & Peetsma, T. (2007). Child negative emotionality and parenting from infancy to preschool: A meta-analytic review. *Developmental Psychology, 43,* 438–453.

Pesonen, A., Raikkonen, K., Kajantie, E., Heinonen, K., Strandberg, T., & Jarvenpaa, A. (2006). Fetal programming of temperamental negative affectivity among children born healthy at term. *Developmental Psychobiology, 48,* 633–643.

Pesonen, A., Raikkonen, K., Strandberg, T., & Jarvenpaa, A. (2005). Continuity of maternal stress from the pre- to the postnatal period: Associations with infant's positive, negative and overall temperamental reactivity. *Infant Behavior and Development, 28,* 36–47.

Pesonen, A., Raikkonen, K., Strandberg, T., & Jarvenpaa, A. (2006). Do gestational age and weight for gestational age predict concordance in parental perceptions of infant temperament? *Journal of Pediatric Psychology, 31,* 331–336.

Pezawas, L., Meyer-Lindenberg, A., Drabant, E., Verchinski, B., Munoz, K., Kolachana, B., et al. (2005). 5-HTTLPR polymorphism impacts human cingulate-amygdala interactions: A genetic susceptibility mechanism for depression. *Nature Neuroscience, 8,* 828–834.

Pfeifer, M., Holdsmith, H., Davidson, R., & Rickman, M. (2002). Continuity and change in inhibited and uninhibited children. *Child Development, 73,* 1474–1485.

Plusquellec, P., Muckle, G., Dewailly, E., Ayotte, P., Jacobson, S. W., & Jacobson, J. L. (2007). The relation of low-level prenatal lead exposure to behavioral indicators of attention in Inuit infants in Arctic Quebec. *Neurtoxicology & Teratology, 29,* 527–537.

Porter, C., Wouden-Miller, M., Silva, S., & Porter, A. (2003). Marital harmony and conflict: Links to infants' emotional regulation and cardiac vagal tone. *Infancy, 4,* 297–307.

Propper, C., & Moore, G. A. (2006). The influence of parenting on infant emotionality: A multilevel psychobiological perspective. *Developmental Review, 26,* 427–460.

Putnam, S., Gartstein, M., & Rothbart, M. (2006). Measurement of fine-grained aspects of toddler temperament: The Early Childhood Behavior Questionnaire. *Infant Behavior and Development, 29,* 386–401.

Putnam, S., Sanson, A., & Rothbart, M. (2002). Child temperament and parenting. In M. Bornstein (Ed.), *Handbook of parenting* (Vol. *1,* 2nd ed., pp. 255–277). Mahwah, NJ: Erlbaum.

Putnam, S., & Stifter, C. (2005). Behavioral approach-inhibition in toddlers: Prediction from infancy, positive and negative affective components, and relations with behaviour problems. *Child Development, 76,* 212–226.

Reif, A., & Lesch, K. (2003). Toward a molecular architecture of personality. *Behavioural Brain Research, 139,* 1–20.

Repetti. R., Taylor, S., & Saxbe, D. (2007). The influence of early socialization experiences on the development of biological systems. In J. Grusec & P. Hastings (Eds.), *Handbook of socialization* (pp. 124–152). New York: Guilford.

Riese, M. (1987). Longitudinal assessment of temperament from birth to two years. *Infant Behavior and Development, 10,* 347–363.

Riese, M. (1992). Temperament prediction for neonate twins: Relation to size for gestational age in same-sex pairs. *Acta Geneticae Medicae et Gemellologiae: Twin Research, 41,* 123–135.

Riese, M. (1994). Discordant twin pairs: The relation between gestational age and neonatal temperament differences in co-twins. *Acta Geneticae Medicae et Gemellologiae: Twin Research, 43,* 165–173.

Robson, A., & Cline, B. (1998). Developmental consequences of intrauterine growth retardation. *Infant Behavior and Development, 21,* 331–344.

Roisman, G., & Fraley, R. (2006). The limits of genetic influence: A behavior genetic analysis of infant–caregiver relationship quality of temperament. *Child Development, 77,* 1656–1667.

Rothbart, M., Ahadi, S., & Evans, D. (2000). Temperament and personality: Origins and outcomes. *Journal of Personality and Social Psychology, 78,* 122–135.

Rothbart, M., & Bates, J. (1998). Temperament. In N. Eisenberg (Ed.), *Handbook of child psychology: Vol. 3. Social, emotional, and personality development* (5th ed., pp. 105–176). New York: Wiley.

Rothbart, M., & Bates, J. (2006). Temperament. In N. Eisenberg, N. Damon, & R. Lerner (Eds.), *Handbook of child psychology: Vol. 3, Social, emotional, and personality development* (6th ed., pp. 99–166). Hoboken, NJ: Wiley.

Rothbart, M., Derryberry, D., & Hershey, K. (2000). Temperament stability: Infancy to seven years. In V. Molfese & D. Molfese (Eds.), *Temperament and personality development across the life span* (pp. 85–120). Mahwah, NJ: Erlbaum.

Rothbart, M., Derryberry, D., & Posner, M. (1994). A psychobiological approach to the development of temperament. In J. Bates & T. D. Wachs (Eds.), *Temperament: Individual differences at the interface of biology and behavior* (pp. 82–116). Washington, DC: American Psychological Association.

Rubin, K., Burgess, K., & Hastings, P. (2002). Stability and social-behavioral consequences of toddlers' inhibited temperament and parenting behaviors. *Child Development, 73,* 483–495.

Sajaniemi, N., Salokorpi, T., & vonWendt, L. (1998). Temperament profiles and their role in neurodevelopmental assessed pre-term children at two years of age. *European Child and Adolescent Psychiatry, 7,* 145–152.

Sanson, A., Prior, M., & Kyrios, M. (1990). Contamination of measures in temperament research. *Merrill-Palmer Quarterly, 36,* 179–192.

Saudino, K. (2005). Behavioral genetics and child temperament. *Journal of Developmental and Behavioral Pediatrics, 26,* 214–223.

Sazawal, S., Bently, M., Black, R., Dhingra, P., George, S., & Bhan, M. (1996). Effect of zinc supplementation on observed activity in low socioeconomic Indian preschool children. *Pediatrics, 98,* 1132–1137.

Scarpa, A., Raine, A., Venables, P., & Mednick, S. (1997). Heart rate and skin conductance in behaviorally inhibited Mauritian children. *Journal of Abnormal Psychology, 106,* 182–190.

Scheper-Hughes, N. (1987). Culture, scarcity and maternal thinking. In N. Scheper–Hughes (Ed.), *Child survival* (pp. 187–208). Reidel: Dordrecht.

Schmidt, L. (2008). Patterns of second-by-second resting frontal brain (EEG) asymmetry and their relation to heart rate and temperament in 9-month-old human infants. *Personality and Individual Differences, 44,* 219–225.

Schmidt, L., Fox, N., Rubin, K., Hu, S., & Hamer, D. (2002). Molecular genetics of shyness and aggression in preschoolers. *Personality and Individual Differences, 33,* 227–238.

Schmidt, L., Fox, N., Rubin, K., Sternberg, E., Gold, P., Smith, C., et al. (1997). Behavioral and neuroendocrine responses in shy children. *Developmental Psychobiology, 30,* 127–140.

Schoppe-Sullivan, S., Mangelsdorf, S., Brown, G., & Sokolowski, M. (2007). Goodness-of-fit in family context: Infant temperament, marital quality and early coparenting behaviour. *Infant Behavior and Development, 30,* 82–96.

Schwartz, C., Wright, C., Shin, L., Kagan, J., & Rauch, S. (2003). Inhibited and uninhibited infants "grown up": Adult amygdalar response to novelty. *Science, 300,* 1952–1953.

Sheeber, L. (1995). Empirical dissociations between temperament and behavior problems. *Merrill-Palmer Quarterly, 41,* 554–561.

Sheese, B., Voelker, P., Rothbart, M., & Posner, M. (2007). Parenting quality interacts with genetic variation in dopamine receptor D4 to influence temperament in early childhood. *Development and Psychopathology, 19,* 1039–1046.

Sheinkopf, S., Lester, B., LaGasse, L., Seifer, R., Bauer, C., Shankaran S., et al. (2006). Interactions between maternal characteristics and neonatal behavior in the prediction of parenting stress and perception of infant temperament. *Journal of Pediatric Psychology, 31,* 27–40.

Shiner, R., & Caspi, A. (2003). Personality differences in childhood and adolescence: measurement, development and consequences. *Journal of Child Psychology and Psychiatry, 44,* 2–32.

Simeon, D., & Grantham-McGregor, S. (1990). Nutritional deficiencies and children's behavior and mental development. *Nutrition Research Review, 3,* 1–24.

Stright, A., Gallagher, K., & Kelley, K. (2008). Infant temperament moderates relations between maternal parenting in early childhood and children's adjustment in first grade. *Child Development, 79,* 186–200.

Super, C., & Harkness, S. (1986). Temperament, development and culture. In R. Plomin & J. Dunn (Eds.), *The study of temperament* (pp. 131–150). Hillsdale, NJ: Erlbaum.

Susman, E., Schmeelk, K., Ponirakis, A., & Gariepy, J. (2001). Maternal prenatal, postpartum and concurrent stressors and temperament in 3-year olds. *Development and Psychopathology, 13,* 629–652.

Tamura, T., Goldenberg, M., Hou, J., Johnston, K., Cliver, S., Ramey, S., et al. (2002). Cord serum ferritin concentrations and mental and psychomotor development of children at five years of age. *Journal of Pediatrics, 140,* 165–170.

Thoman, E. (1990). Sleeping and waking states of infants. *Neuroscience and Biobehavioral Reviews, 14,* 93–107.

Thomas, A., & Chess, S. (1986). The New York longitudinal study: From infancy to early adult life. In R. Plomin & J. Dunn (Eds.), *The study of temperament* (pp. 39–52). Hillsdale, NJ: Erlbaum.

van Bakel, H., & Riksen-Walraven, J. (2004). Stress reactivity in 15-month-old infants: Links with infant temperament, cognitive competence, and attachment security. *Developmental Psychobiology, 44,* 157–167.

Van den Boom, D. (1994). The influence of temperament and mothering on attachment and exploration: An experimental manipulation of sensitive responsiveness among lower-class mothers and irritable infants. *Child Development, 65,* 1457–1477.

Van den Boom, D. (1995). Do first year intervention effects endure: Follow-up during toddlerhood of a sample of Dutch irritable infants. *Child Development, 66,* 1798–1816.

Van den Boom, D., & Hoeksma, J. (1994). The effect of infant irritability on mother infant interaction. *Developmental Psychology, 30,* 581–590.

van der Pal, S., Maguire, C., Le Cessie, S., Veen, S., Wit, J., Walther, F., et al. (2008). Parental stress and child behavior and temperament in the first year after the newborn individualized developmental care and assessment program. *Journal of Early Intervention, 30,* 102–115.

Vaughn, J., Brown, J., & Carter, J. (1986). The effects of maternal anemia on infant behavior. *Journal of the National Medical Association, 78,* 963–968.

Velderman, M., Bakermans-Kranenburg, M., Juffer, F., & van IJzendoorn, M. (2006). Effects of attachment-based interviews of maternal sensitivity and infant attachment. *Journal of Family Psychology, 20,* 266–274.

Vermeer, H., & van IJzendoorn, M. (2006). Children's elevated cortisol levels at daycare: A review and meta-analysis. *Early Childhood Research, 21,* 390–401.

Wachs, T. D. (1994). Fit, context and the transition between temperament and personality. In C. J. Halverson, G. A. Kohnstamm, & R. P. Martin (Eds.), *The developing structure of temperament and personality from infancy to adulthood* (pp. 209–220). Hillsdale, NJ: Erlbaum.

Wachs, T. D. (2006). The nature, etiology and consequences of individual differences in temperament. In T. LeMonda & L. Balter (Eds.), *Child psychology: A handbook of contemporary issues* (2nd ed., pp. 27–52). New York: Garland.

Wachs T. D. (2008). Multiple influences on children's nutritional deficiencies: A systems perspective. *Physiology and Behavior, 94*, 48–60.

Wachs, T. D., & Bates, J. (2001). Temperament. In G. Bremner & A. Fogel, (Eds.), *Blackwell handbook of infant development* (pp. 465–501). Malden, MA: Blackwell.

Wachs, T. D., Bishry, Z., Sobhy, A., McCabe, G., Shaheen, F., & Galal, O. (1993). Relation of rearing environment to adaptive behavior of Egyptian toddlers. *Child Development, 67*, 586–604.

Wachs, T. D., Kanashiro, H., & Gurkas, P. (2008). Intra-individual variability in infancy: Structure, stability and nutritional correlates. *Developmental Psychobiology, 50*, 217–231.

Wachs, T. D., Pollitt, E., Cueto, S., & Jacoby, E. (2004). Structure and cross-contextual stability of neonatal temperament. *Infant Behavior & Development, 27*, 382–396.

Wachs T. D., Pollitt, E., Cueto, S., Jacoby, E., & Creed-Kanashiro, H. (2005). Relation of neonatal iron status to individual variability in neonatal temperament. *Developmental Psychobiology, 46*, 141–153.

Wasserman, G., Staghezza-Jaramillo, B., Shrout, P., Popovac, D., & Graziano, J. (1998). The effect of lead exposure on behavior problems in preschool children. *American Journal of Public Health, 88*, 481–486.

Watamura, S., Donzella, B., Alwin, J., & Gunnar, M. (2003). Morning-to-afternoon increases in cortisol concentrations for infants and toddlers at child care. *Child Development, 74*, 1006–1020.

Watamura, S., Donzella, B., Kertes, D., & Gunnar, M. (2004). Developmental changes in baseline cortisol activity in early childhood: Relations with napping and effortful control. *Developmental Psychobiology, 125*, 125–133.

Weinstock, M. (2005).The potential influence of maternal stress hormones on development and mental health of the offspring. *Brain, Behavior, and Immunity, 19*, 296–308.

Weiss, S., Jonn-Seed, M., & Harris-Muhell, C. (2007). The contribution of fetal drug exposure to temperament. *Journal of Child Psychology and Psychiatry, 48*, 773–784.

Werner, E., Myers, M., Fifer, W., Cheng, B., Fang, Y., Allen, R., et al. (2007). Prenatal predictors of infant temperament. *Developmental Psychobiology, 49*, 474–484.

Wilson, M., Megel, M., Fredrichs, A., & McLaughlin, P. (2003). Physiologic and behavioral responses to stress, temperament, and incidence of infection and atopic disorders in the first year of life: A pilot study. *Journal of Pediatric Nursing, 18*, 257–266.

Wolfe, C., & Bell, M. (2007). The integration of cognition and emotion during infancy and early childhood: Regulatory processes associated with the development of working memory. *Brain and Cognition, 65*, 3–13.

Woodward, S., Lenzenweger, M., Kagan, J., Snidman, N., & Arcus, D. (2000). Taxonic structure of infant reactivity: Evidence from a taxometric perspective. *Psychological Science, 11*, 296–301.

Zentner, M., & Bates, J. (2008). Child temperament: An integrative review of concepts, research programs and measures. *European Journal of Developmental Psychology, 2*, 7–37.

21

Culture and Infancy

Charles M. Super and Sara Harkness

Just over a quarter-century ago, a chapter entitled "Behavioral development in infancy," written by the first author of the present chapter, was published in the *Handbook of Cross-cultural Human Development* (Super, 1981). At that time, the state of research on infants in other cultural settings, particularly non-Western and premodern ones, was such that a comprehensive review of the existing literature could be accommodated in a single chapter. The focus of that review was primarily descriptive: "assembling reports of infant behavioral development in non-Euro-American societies, especially in the first year of life" (Super, 1981, p. 181). Much has changed in developmental research since that time, including a shift from cross-cultural research as a focal enterprise to the recognition of cultural perspectives by mainstream publications whose primary focus is development, not context. Correspondingly, there have been new approaches to the concept of culture. The *Handbook* mentioned above was edited by a team of cross-cultural psychologists and anthropologists who had worked closely together for many years, and who shared a set of assumptions about what "culture" is. Developmental scientists today, in contrast, have an array of theoretical frameworks for understanding culture, including ones formulated by psychologists who do not share the intellectual heritage of earlier discussions in anthropology. In this chapter, we first address the question of how culture is currently conceptualized, followed by a selective review of research on culture and infancy.

Culture in Developmental Research

The concept of culture, like person-related concepts such as personality and intelligence, seems self-evident until examined more closely. There is also a special ambiguity about culture as being internal or external: Do individuals live in a culture, or does culture reside in the individual? Although debate surrounding this question is part of culture's intellectual history (D'Andrade, 1987; Harkness, 1992), the external version of culture has always been implicitly recognized as a kind of shorthand. People do not live in "cultures" per se; rather – as anthropologist Thomas Weisner (1996) puts it – they live in "cultural places." Such places can be characterized in terms of the "way of life" of the inhabitants, including shared internal representations and motivations as well as their manifestations in behavior, language, social organization, and physical artifacts.

Anyone who observes other cultural places is likely to be amazed at human adaptability in a wide range of developmental environments. This is particularly striking with regard to infants, who seem to be able to cope successfully with any number of rearing conditions, ranging from imposed immobility due to swaddling to complete freedom of movement, and from nursing on demand to being fed on a strict schedule. Observations such as these have been the basis for the growing research literature on culture and infancy. Despite the accumulating information on variability in behavior and context, however, basic questions remain: What is the core developmental agenda of infancy? How is infant development affected by culturally constructed environments? Is there one basic developmental pathway during infancy, or do differing cultural contexts create their own distinctive pathways? The research to be reviewed here generally starts from one of several approaches to these questions.

The *ethnographic approach* to the study of culture and infancy, with roots in anthropology dating back to the early twentieth century, focuses on the particulars of a single cultural group and the local integration of those features into a compelling whole. Culture in this classical sense is seen as a super-organic phenomenon, characteristic of an identified group and shared by individual members of that group. Everyday interactions and responses to interviews are treated as primary data, often supplemented in developmental work with more formal tests and questionnaires that are used in aggregate to describe the thoughts, feelings, and behavior patterns of that cultural community. At their best, such ethnographic works provide sufficient detail to document developmental phenomena and also to convey its integration with the larger culture. On the other hand, the descriptive demands of ethnography are often so great that developmental work is slighted and lacks clear connection to the mass of cultural material.

The *social address* approach, common in cross-cultural psychology, entails comparing groups from two or more cultures on some features of behavior. By far the most common comparison in the infant literature is between a North American (or European) sample and one that is non-Western. Although this approach has made substantial contributions to knowledge about cultural variability in development, it often suffers from a lack of contextual information that could help explain the observed differences. Sometimes explanations are offered based on general observations about the society but, by definition, social address studies do not measure the environment itself.

Perhaps in response to this dilemma, psychologists interested in culture and human development have in recent years frequently turned to *unidimensional models* of cultural variation. The most common approach contrasts "individualistic" (or "independent") societies and "collectivistic" (or "interdependent") ones; usually educated Western populations are contrasted with non-Western, traditional, or rural groups. The theoretical and procedural parsimony of a unidimensional model for understanding large-scale differences in societies and individual development is attractive in that it reduces the "degrees of freedom" to a manageable lot, while still picking up some variance across diverse measures of developmental interest. The simplicity is also a profound limitation, however, in that the model essentially bypasses measurement of the environment. Thus all cultures labeled collectivist are assumed to be essentially the same (Hermans & Kempen, 1998; Kağitçibaşi, 1980). When results belie this assumption, as they often do, the researcher has little recourse but to redefine the original prototypes or search for other, noncultural sources of difference (Harkness, 2008). Not surprisingly, most anthropologists consider this approach contradictory to the basic concept of "culture."

None of the above approaches fully addresses the need for systematic attention to the child's culturally structured environment in combination with equally focused study of the child. As a possible solution, several empirically oriented developmentalists have derived models to represent the *culturally structured niches* of infancy and childhood (Worthman, 2010). They include Weisner's (2002) "ecocultural niche," Worthman's (2003) "developmental microniche," and Super and Harkness' (1986, 1999, 2002) "developmental niche." Specifically, we have found it useful to parse the infants' developmental niche into three interacting subsystems: (1) physical and social settings – who is there, how the physical space influences behavior; (2) customs and practices of child rearing – inherited and adapted ways of carrying, feeding, stimulating, entertaining, educating, and protecting the infant; and (3) the psychology of the caretakers, particularly parental ethnotheories[1] of child development and parenting, which play a directive role in actual practices. The developmental niche functions as an integrated whole, though selected aspects of the niche such as parental ethnotheories and practices have been used by a variety of studies of infant development across cultures.

Recognizing the challenges of integrating cultural and developmental findings, we now review specific aspects of infant development in global perspective. We start with behavior during the neonatal period.

Culture and Neonatal Development

The ecology of newborn development

Virtually all of the cross-cultural research on newborn behavior (leaving aside medical status, which is not covered here – see volume 2, chapter 1) comes from the network of colleagues using Brazelton's Neonatal Behavioral Assessment Scales (NBAS; Brazelton & Nugent, 1995). Surveying this work, one gets a sense of the extraordinary array of circumstances into which the human newborn arrives and to which the newborn adapts: rainforest and frozen tundra; prosperous fishing village on stilts and poverty-stricken shanty town on a mountainside; high in the Andes and below sea level in the Netherlands. As a group, human newborns show the same startle to sudden noise, the same yawn and stretch and, under the right circumstances, the same bright-eyed focus on their mother's face. On the other hand, our species' adaptability at birth produces a broad array of small

Table 21.1   Examples of specific routes of cultural influence on newborn behavior.

Routes of cultural influences	References
Maternal diet and nutritional status	de Costa & Griew, 1982; Wachs, Pollitt, Cueto, Jacoby, & Creed-Kanashiro, 2005
Pregnancy spacing	Brazelton, Tryphonopoulou, & Lester, 1979
Maternal age	Quack Loetscher, Selvin, Zimmermann, & Abrams, 2007
Prenatal maternal workload	Tuntiseranee, Geater, Chongsuvivatwong, & Koranantakul, 1998
Maternal psychological stress and social supports	de Weerth, van Hees, & Buitelaar, 2003
Beliefs about pregnancy and related taboos and prescriptions	Newton & Newton, 1972
Obstetric and perinatal traditions and institutions	Atkin et al., 1991; Horowitz et al., 1977; Laughlin, 1992
Settings available for examination of the neonate	deVries & Super, 1979; Wachs, Pollitt, Cueto, & Jacoby, 2004

but interesting group differences, as virtually every comparative study indicates. Babies born to rural mothers in Southern India, for example, behave differently from those born to middle-class mothers in Israel or to Peruvian mothers high in the Andes, and they elicit different responses from their caretakers (Nugent, Lester, & Brazelton, 1989). Those differences from the moment of birth and subsequent trajectories of adaptation are an important part of the global perspective on human development.

Many factors have been identified as influencing neonatal status (Bell, 1963); some examples are shown in Table 21.1. Because so many of these influences are part of, or directly result from, cultural features, constructing "matched" samples for comparisons across cultural groups would often eliminate representativeness. One could not, for example, balance on parity in representative samples from urban China, with its one-child policy, and Saudi Arabia, with an average fertility rate of 3.89. Thus, even though a sample's geographic or ethnic origin is often used for reporting results or organizing the literature, this by itself tells us little about underlying factors. Further, as people move about the globe they take aspects of their culture as well as their genes with them, and the intricacies of rearing an infant are probably among the last domains to acculturate. Examination of the newborn may once have been heralded as an assessment free of cultural influences, but it can no longer be viewed that way. With this observation in mind, we now review two groups of studies which report on infants in two different parts of the world and on different areas of neonatal performance.

Newborn motor skills in Africa

The behavioral status of non-Western newborns first captured scientific interest through the reports of Géber and Dean (1957), who conducted neurological examinations of over

100 newborns in hospitals in Kampala, Uganda. The researchers concluded that African babies were at a more advanced state of development than were newborn Europeans. African precocity was said to be most evident in a lesser degree of flexion in muscle tone, advanced control of the head, and the frequent absence of reflexes that normally disappear in Euro-American populations only after 6 to 10 weeks of age. However, there proved to be significant flaws in this work (Super, 1981; Warren, 1972), and subsequent studies of African newborns have failed to replicate the claim of neurological precocity (e.g., Freedman, 1974; Keefer, Dixon, Tronick, & Brazelton, 1991; Konner, 1972; Super & Harkness, 2009; Vouilloux, 1959; Warren & Parkin, 1974).

In contrast to this clear conclusion regarding the absence of neurological differences at birth, there are recurring, if not entirely consistent, reports of superior performance by African infants and infants of African descent in some aspects of motor behavior and muscle strength, such as hand-to-mouth activity, general muscle tone, postural control, or briskness of the walking reflex or other reflexes (e.g., Garcia Coll, Sepkoski, & Lester, 1981; Géber & Dean, 1957; Hopkins, 1976; Lester & Brazelton, 1981; Rosser & Randolph, 1989; Super & Harkness, 2009). In a particularly sophisticated assessment, Keefer and colleagues (Keefer, Tronick, Dixon, & Brazelton, 1982) examined Gusii infants in an agricultural community of Western Kenya on days 2, 5, and 10, and concluded that the "Gusii infants have more [muscle] tone and better control of it than their American counterparts" (p. 758). However, these authors go on to comment that traditional scoring of the "qualitative difference in motor tone and quantitative difference in motor maturity did not characterize all the motor performance of the Gusii," and that the specificity of the motor differences fails to support the concept of "general motor precocity in African newborn." It is also important to note that specific behavioral differences are generally not replicated from one study to the next, further suggesting caution in accepting an overly general explanation.

Although most cross-cultural studies of newborn behavior also describe infants' basic medical status, we learn little else about them other than their social address. The few exceptions identify culturally organized differences in the treatment of newborns that begin almost immediately after birth and might, therefore, affect performance within a few days, when assessments are typically carried out. For example, massage of newborns and vigorous application of oil are common traditions in many African groups (Super & Harkness, 2009; Thairu & Pelto, 2008) and for some of the African diaspora (Hopkins, 1976; Moscardino, Nwobu, & Axia, 2006; Rabain-Jamin & Wornham, 1990). Such procedures are known to reduce levels of cortisol (Acolet et al., 1993), and to have other immediate physiological effects that are likely to influence motor performance (Field et al., 2004).

Although it is difficult to evaluate how much such differences in early experience might contribute to the African findings, it is interesting to compare Landers' (1989) results from South India, where vigorous massage is common in the opening days of life, to reports by Keefer (Keefer et al., 1982) and Lester (Lester & Brazelton, 1981) on African, African-American, and Euro-American samples. Even though the Indian infants were born to mothers with a history of poor health and nutrition and performed less than optimally on most NBAS scoring clusters, their good motor scores were generally closer to the African and African-American results than to those of the Euro-Americans.

Newborn emotional reactivity in Asia

The first published report on the newborn behavior of Asian infants was by the Freedmans (Freedman & Freedman, 1969), using the Cambridge Neonatal Scales, a precursor to the NBAS. Examining Chinese-American and Euro-American infants on the second day of life, the researchers found the two groups essentially equal in sensory development, CNS maturity, motor development, and social responsiveness. However, the Chinese-American infants showed less activity and distress when placed on their stomachs or when a cloth was placed to cover the nose. Freedman replicated and expanded this work with data from Japanese-American infants in Hawaii, an additional Chinese-American sample in Chicago, and a group of Navajo who, he argued, are closely related genetically to the other Asian groups (Freedman, 1974). Chisholm (1983) replicated Freedman's findings of lower irritability and more self-quieting among Navajo newborns. Similarly, Muret-Wagstaff and Moore (1989) compared Hmong and Euro-American newborns in Minnesota and found the Asian infants to be less irritable (on days 1 and 3 but not 7). The Hmong mothers also averaged close to the maximum score on the Ainsworth Maternal Sensitivity Scale, the authors note, an attribute which is often found to be related to lower irritability.

Looking for a broader ontogenetic explanation for his Navajo findings, Chisholm (1983) found that maternal blood pressure during the middle trimester of pregnancy correlated highly with neonatal irritability. This finding has been replicated in Malay, Chinese, Tamil (Chisholm, Woodson, & da Costa Woodson, 1978), and Euro-American infants (Korner, Gabby, & Kraemer, 1980). In these studies, maternal blood pressure was a better predictor of neonatal irritability than the social address or ethnicity; this may explain why other investigators have found no reliable differences in irritability between Hawaiian infants of Japanese descent and a group of African- and Euro-American new-borns in Providence, RI (Rosenblith & Anderson-Huntington, 1975), or between Mayan newborns in rural Guatemala and Euro-American newborns in Kansas (Sellers, Klein, Sellers, Lechtig, & Yarbrough, 1971).

Infant Development beyond the Neonatal Period

States of arousal and sleep

Level of arousal is a critical factor in infant testing, and is immediately evident to caretakers – crying, sleeping, and calm engagement are primary signals of the infant's homeostatic needs. Arousal states are also a fundamental arena of development in their own right. Given the strong biological perspective with which state behavior is usually viewed, one might reasonably expect the same parameters of state development in diverse rearing environments (Scher et al., 1995). As in other domains, however, accommodations to the environment are too easily taken for granted within any single context (McKenna, 2000).

Patterns of arousal are influenced by the level of stimulation individuals receive, and cultures vary dramatically in the kind and amount of stimulation provided to infants (Brazelton, Tronick, Lechtig, Lasky, & Klein, 1977; deVries & Super, 1979; Landers,

1989). As the infant matures, parents' ethnotheories about cognitive development, affective expression, and relations within the family quickly shape patterns of social interaction, which is a primary moderator of state. Other subsystems of the developmental niche are influential as well. Vertical posture while riding on a caretaker's back or hip, for example, is more conducive to calm alertness than lying horizontally in a playpen or inclined in an infant seat, in part because vertical posture stimulates the production of adrenal hormones that influence attentional processes (Gregg, Haffner, & Korner, 1976). Kipsigis infants in rural Kenya spend approximately 50% more time in the vertical position than do US infants (Super & Harkness, 1994a). Feeding patterns also are intimately linked to the regulation of state, and these vary substantially across cultures: In contrast to the 4-hour cycle of six feeds per day common in the US, rural Kipsigis infants have been observed to average over 20 bouts of nursing per day during the first 4 months (Super & Harkness, 1982b); among the !Kung San the figure is even greater (Konner & Worthman, 1980).

The sleep–wake cycle is more salient to parents and caretakers than are gradations in alertness, and strategies for managing infants' sleep are quite varied. They result from cultural traditions, parental beliefs, and contemporary family ecology, and can become a point of stress or pleasure (Welles-Nyström, 2005; Wolf, Lozoff, Latz, & Paludetto, 1996; Yovsi & Keller, 2007). In the rural African context, infants typically fall asleep on their own but while in a caretaker's arms or strapped to a caretaker's back (Konner, 1976; Super & Harkness, 1982b). Reports from both Korea (Harkness et al., 2007) and Japan (Caudill & Weinstein, 1969) also highlight physical proximity during transition to sleep, but in contrast to the African examples, the procedure is often a deliberate and time-consuming process by the mother, requiring her to hold the baby in her arms until he falls asleep.

The largest reported difference in amount of sleep – approximately 2 hours per day at 6 months of age – is between two samples that might otherwise appear very similar: middle-class families in the Netherlands and the Northeast US (Super, Blom, Ranade, Londhe, & Harkness, 2010; Super et al., 1996). This difference is attributed to parental ethnotheories and practices that promote restful regularity in one case and stimulation for development, especially cognitive development, in the other (Harkness et al., 2007). Notably for its developmental implications, almost all the sleep difference consists of additional "quiet" sleep by the Dutch, a state that involves distinctive patterns of centrally regulated physiological and hormonal activity.

Sleep data are also available from the Kipsigis of rural Kenya, where Super and Harkness (1982b) found little difference in the total amount of sleep or in measures of sustained wakefulness. However, the Kipsigis infant, breastfed on demand and sleeping at the mother's side at night, averaged about 4 hours as the longest period of sustained sleep throughout the first months after birth, compared to an increase from 4 to 8 hours over that period in the US.

Motor development

It is probably not coincidental that advancements in gross motor behavior – sitting, crawling, walking – were an early focus of inquiry historically and also cross-culturally:

these behaviors are easy to observe and demonstrate high face validity (see chapter 5, this volume). The cross-cultural differences in typical age at mastery for specific items can be substantial. For example, Lim, Chan, and Yoong (1994) found that more than a quarter of the Denver Developmental Screening Test items differed by more than 10% in the average age of attainment across cultural subgroups. Further, the developmental sequence of related items (such as rolling from back to stomach and stomach to back) can shift (Mead & MacGregor, 1951; Nelson, Yu, Wong, Wong, & Yim, 2004).

Early comparative work on motor milestones was dominated by concern with "African infant precocity," especially following Géber and Dean's (1957) claim of neonatal differences. Most of the studies reported elevated average developmental quotients (DQ), as high as 130, over the first year of life (e.g. Leiderman, Babu, Kagia, Kraemer, & Leiderman, 1973; Vouilloux, 1959), but many also suffered serious methodological shortcomings, like the initial newborn work (Warren, 1972). Eventually, it was demonstrated through item analysis that African motor precocity was not uniform across domains. Rather, advances were most evident in items testing the progression to sitting and walking. In contrast, US and European infants have been found to excel in prone behaviors, such as crawling (e.g., Falmagne, 1962; J. E. Kilbride & Kilbride, 1975; Konner, 1976; Super, 1976).

At the same time, it was recognized that patterns of advancement and delay are matched by the presence (or absence) of explicit teaching and exercising by mothers and siblings. These practices have been reported in nearly 20 studies across East, West, and Southern Africa (e.g., Ainsworth, 1967; Faladé, 1955; LeVine & LeVine, 1966; Super, 1976; Varkevisser, 1973). In addition to explicit practice, other aspects of traditional African child care, such as carrying on the back or hip, provide frequent exercise for muscles of the trunk and pelvic girdle, which are involved in sitting and walking, as well as vestibular stimulation. These traditional practices are mentioned in most ethnographies of village life in sub-Saharan Africa (e.g. Gottlieb, 2004; LeVine et al., 1994) and contrast with traditional Euro-American practices, which include significantly more opportunity, in a playpen or crib, to practice prone behaviors. There are reports of both less and greater advancement in more urban or "modernizing" samples (e.g. Géber & Dean, 1958; Leiderman et al., 1973), but examination of specific, developmentally relevant practices revealed the mediating role of particular experiences in promoting (or not) specific motor behaviors (Super, 1976, 1981).

This interpretation of "African infant precocity" is supported by experimental evidence from Euro-American samples that demonstrates a causal relationship between deliberate, anticipatory exercise of walking, sitting, and crawling and acceleration of their development (N. A. Zelazo, Zelazo, Cohen, & Zelazo, 1993; P. R. Zelazo, 1976). There is also experimental evidence that both passive exercise and high levels of vestibular stimulation promote the development of gross motor behaviors in infants (e.g. Clark, Kreutzberg, & Chee, 1977).

Cognitive development

Studying cognitive development, unlike motor development, requires an abstraction from concrete behaviors to identify the competencies of interest. In comparative research the task of abstraction is especially complex, as there may be alternative expressions of the same internal competence. Similarly, there may be different forms of environmental support for mental development. For example, if the opportunity to explore variety is needed, can it be provided equally as well by interaction with older siblings in an unchanging setting, as by a physically complex but minimally social home?

Standardized testing.   Measures of cognitive development as found in tests such as the Bayley Scales show at least as much sensitivity to experience as do motor behaviors (Leiderman et al., 1973; Lim et al., 1994; Werner, Bierman, & French, 1971). As with the motor results, studies that identify differences in specific behavioral items and relate them to ethnographic observations of particular care practices are the most helpful (e.g., J. E. Kilbride & Kilbride, 1975; Leiderman & Leiderman, 1974). A similar pattern of relationship between early verbal interaction and average performance on language items in standardized tests is found when comparing regional and ethnic groups within Africa (Agiobu-Kemmer, 1984; Aina & Morakinyo, 2005; Harkness, Super, Barry, Zeitlin, & Long, 2009), as well as in comparisons between the US and Japan (Arai, Ishikawa, & Toshima, 1958; Caudill & Frost, 1974). Generalization to lasting differences in underlying cognitive and linguistic competence appears unwarranted.

Piagetian approaches.   The interplay of internal mental structures and physical reality was the focus of Piaget's well-known work, and his constructionist approach is particularly open to comparative studies. The most thorough reports come from the Ivory Coast, where infants in a rural agricultural village of the Baoulé people were observed, and tested with Piagetian scales (Dasen, Inhelder, Lavallée, & Retschitzki, 1978). The primary finding was a "remarkable similarity" (p. 125) in unstructured play with objects when Baoulé and French infants were compared, even though "toys" in the Baoulé village were minimal and adults did not use objects to mediate social interaction as much as Western parents typically do. With regard to formal testing, the authors found that depending on the cognitive outcome assessed, Baoulé infants were generally either slightly advanced (e.g., tasks involving use of objects as tools), or on par (e.g. object permanence tasks), when compared to French norms. Konner (1972, 1976) in Botswana, and Goldberg (1977) in Zambia reported the same pattern for Piagetian test items, namely occasional differences in timing reflecting variability in culturally structured opportunities for exploration. Most importantly from a theoretical perspective, none of these relatively minor differences altered the sequence of substage accomplishment.

Information processing measures.   Laboratory studies of infants' attention to various stimuli have been a major source of knowledge about early cognitive development (see chapters 2 and 4, this volume). The limited evidence from non-Western settings demonstrates a similarity in basic processes. Lécuyer and Tano (1990) studied the rate of visual habituation in French and Ivorian infants from 3 to 8 months, and found expected age effects but no sample differences. Kennedy et al. (2008) replicated the well-known novelty effect, but demonstrated a delay in its reliable appearance related to malnutrition. An increase in attention to discrepant models of the human face and/or figure between the first and second year in US samples (Kagan, Kearsley, & Zelazo, 1978) was replicated with Mayan subjects in rural Mexico (Finley, Kagan, & Layne, 1972), !Kung San infants in Botswana (Konner, 1973), and Ladino babies in Guatemalan villages (Sellers, Klein, Kagan, & Minton, 1972). Such findings suggest that long-term memory develops in a similar way in these diverse samples during the second year (Carver & Bauer, 2001; Kagan, 1971; Kagan et al., 1978). However, although US studies indicate that these processes do not emerge until around 11 months, the limited cross-cultural data during the first year are inconclusive, and the upswing may occur as early as 6 months in Japanese infants (M. Takahashi, 1973, pers. comm. cited in Super, 1981).

Emotional development

Social distress.   "Stranger anxiety" and distress to maternal departure emerge toward the end of the first year in Western samples and are generally interpreted to reflect an emerging ability to engage and utilize long-term memory. The comparative data are impressive in the similarity of their initial timing. Kagan and his colleagues (Kagan, 1976; Kagan et al., 1978) have assembled reports of US infants, Ladino and Mayan Guatemalans, !Kung San in the Kalahari Desert, and Israeli infants reared in group homes in a kibbutz. In every sample, infants showed little crying at maternal departure until around 7 or 8 months, when the likelihood rises steeply to a peak shortly after the first birthday, and then declines. Very similar timing has been found in a Bangladeshi community suffering very high rates of malnutrition and disease (Super, Guldan, Ahmed, & Zeitlin, 2010). Relatedly, "fear of strangers" is reported to emerge with parallel timing among Navajo (Chisholm, 1983) and Ivorian infants (Dasen et al., 1978).

However, in contrast to the similarity in timing for the rise of distress, the overall rate of crying and the rate of disappearance with age vary dramatically among these samples. At the peak distress period around 12 months, nearly all US and !Kung San infant show distress, compared to about 65% among the Mayan and Israeli infants. This response has largely disappeared by 24 months in the latter two groups, whereas nearly half the !Kung San and US infants still become distressed. The nearly exclusive maternal care practices of the latter groups appear to intensify and extend the reaction to maternal departure, whereas customs of shared infant care in Guatemala and the Israeli kibbutzim make for less discrepancy and associated distress.

Social smiling.   Smiling, which can be seen fleetingly in the newborn period, increases dramatically from the second month to a peak at about four months in the US (Wolff, 1963), diverse Israeli samples (Gewirtz, 1965), the !Kung San (Konner, 1973), the Baganda of Uganda (P. L. Kilbride & Kilbride, 1974), and Japan (M. Takahashi, 1974). The similarity in rise supports the argument that reliable social smiling has underpinnings in a broad neurological shift at around 4 months of age (Kagan, 1971). However, as the smiling curve peaks, there are already substantial differences in the absolute rate of smiling. Rural Kipsigis infants were observed to smile at least once during 20% of their waking minutes (Super & Harkness, 1982a), about four times the rate for rural Navajo (Chisholm, 1983). Studies from Africa, Europe, the Middle East, and the US report smiling rates within this range of 5% to 20% (Super, 1981), with increasing divergence in subsequent months (Camras et al., 1998; Landau, 1977).

Vocalization.   Infant vocalization shows a similar pattern, starting with a considerable increase in frequency around four months of age. As initially summarized (Super, 1981) and confirmed in more recent reports, 4-month-old infants spontaneously vocalize in about half of their observed waking minutes in middle-class US and European samples, and about one-third to one-half less in rural areas of East and West Africa, and in urban Japan (e.g. Bornstein, Tamis-LeMonda, Pêcheux, & Rahn, 1991; Chisholm, 1983; Hewlett, Lamb, Shannon, Leyendecker, & Schölmerich, 1998). The fact that US, French, and some other European infants vocalize at up to twice the rate of infants from a variety of other cultures calls into question the generalizability of Euro-American findings regarding the development and correlates of early vocal development (Euro-American findings on early vocal development are reviewed chapter 14, this volume). Further, even within a "Western" comparison, Rebelsky (1972) reports a decline in mother–infant mutual vocalization in the Netherlands from 2 to 12 weeks, in contrast to an increase in the US.

Complex social interactions.   From such simple and universal acts as smiling and vocalizing, infants and caretakers quickly build complex, developmentally supportive, and culturally meaningful scripts of social interaction. A number of recent reports on social interaction patterns focus on group differences. Vigil (2002), for example, highlights that Chinese immigrant mothers are more likely to direct their infants' attention, whereas British mothers are more likely to follow their infants' lead. This difference was mediated in part by the manipulation of objects by the caretaker, a behavior found by others to play a significant role in cultural differences in infant interaction (Bornstein, Cote, & Venuti, 2001; Fernald & Morikawa, 1993; Rabain-Jamin, 1989). Other subtle but deeply important differences in interactions have been noted in studies of early language acquisition, regarding both who the actors are (e.g. Rabain-Jamin, Maynard, & Greenfield, 2003; Whaley, Sigman, Beckwith, Cohen, & Espinosa, 2002), and how they manage joint attention and semantic contingency (e.g. Childers, Vaughan, & Burquest, 2007; Harkness, 1988). Keller (2007) has integrated several of these features in tracing alternate pathways for development of the self in individualistic versus collectivistic cultures.

However, a number of reports also have noted similarities in developing social interactions. For example Rabain-Jamin and Sabeau-Jouannet (1997) noted high rates of expressive communication in French and Wolof-speaking Senegalese mother–infant pairs, even in the context of large stylistic differences. Similarly, Bornstein and colleagues (Bornstein et al., 2008) noted adaptive levels of emotional availability in urban and rural regions of Argentina, Italy, and the US despite average differences in some measures.

Understanding the patterns of social interaction that emerge in divergent settings requires information about cultural meaning systems. Of particular importance are studies that draw on ethnographic information, especially parental ethnotheories, to understand maternal behavior and interaction with infants (e.g., Bornstein et al., 1992; Holloway & Minami, 1996). For example, a primary goal of the traditional Japanese mother, as presented by Caudill and others, is to help her infant, thought to be an innately separate being, become integrated into the fabric of social life in the family and, by anticipation, into the larger society (Caudill, 1972; Caudill & Frost, 1974; Schooler, 1996). She therefore encourages a close and solicitous relationship with the purpose of rearing a passive and contented baby. She spends more time with her infant than comparison mothers in the US, and provides more soothing, lulling, and rocking. The American mother, in contrast, is more concerned with assisting her infant's emerging independence, and with facilitating individual activity, assertiveness, and self-direction. Correspondingly, she provides more stimulation, especially through distal interactions and verbal exchanges.

Caudill's work included an examination of change in the context of immigration. It demonstrates the power of both home and host cultures, as the behavior of Japanese-American mothers and their infants – such as smiling and vocalizing – was roughly halfway between that observed for Japanese and US mothers in Caudill's original study (Caudill & Weinstein, 1969). The current literature expands this paradigm to include a broader array of ages, cultures, and interaction domains. For the most part, this body of research also demonstrates strong continuity of beliefs and practices and, to a lesser degree, of daily activities and settings across the experience of immigration (e.g. Bornstein & Cote, 2001; Cabrera, Shannon, West, & Brooks-Gunn, 2006; Leyendecker, Harwood, Lamb, & Schölmerich, 2002; Meléndez, 2005; Moscardino et al., 2006; Rabain-Jamin, 1994).

Attachment

Nowhere has comparative work so engaged central issues of theory as in the study of attachment. Bowlby's theory, along with Ainsworth's elaboration and research operationalization, are well known and described elsewhere in this volume (see chapter 16, this volume). Explorations of this model in other cultural contexts were undertaken surprisingly quickly. Leiderman and Leiderman (1974) examined the claim that an attachment bond could be established with only a single figure (e.g., the mother), and found in their East African sample that the "polymatric" care provided by siblings was not pathological and indeed conferred some adaptive advantages. Fox (1977) came to a similar conclusion for kibbutz children in Israel, echoing Rabin's classic work on "multiple mothering" (Rabin, 1958). Nevertheless, subsequent work in Israel, focused on other aspects of the theory, tends to support key aspects of the classical attachment postulates (Gardner, Lamb, Thompson, & Sagi, 1986; Sagi, 1990; Sagi, Van IJzendoorn, & Koren-Karie, 1991).

Conceptual challenges to attachment theory.   Harwood, Miller, and Irizarry (1995) were among the first to explore locally defined meanings and culturally shaped behavioral manifestations of attachment. They found, for example, that attachment security was considered by Puerto Rican mothers to rest on a balance between "calm, respectful attentiveness" and "positive engagement in interpersonal relationships," not the more familiar (to attachment researchers) balance of autonomy and relatedness. Further, Puerto Rican mothers included anticipating their babies' needs as part of sensitive mothering (Harwood, 1992). The ethnotheories of Puerto Rican mothers form an important contrast with standard attachment concepts, and demonstrate the role of such beliefs in directing maternal behavior. Of particular importance for developmental theory, the consequences of parental behavior proved to follow more from local ideas than from standard attachment theory. For example, Carlson and Harwood (2003) demonstrated that among middle-class Puerto Rican families, high physical control was related to *greater* likelihood of secure attachment, the opposite of findings in their Euro-American sample, and in contrast to the traditional attachment literature.

As the cross-cultural literature on attachment has accumulated, a general critique of the theory and its operationalization has also emerged. This critique is partly based on an analysis of the theory's own cultural base. Rothbaum, Weisz, Pott, Miyake, & Morelli, (2000) call into question the assumptions that sensitivity can be expressed only in distal responsiveness (rather than proximal anticipation), and that the purpose of a secure base is only autonomous exploration and individuation (rather than also including social accommodation and interdependence). LeVine and Norman (2001/2008, pp. 129) more generally fault the Bowlby–Ainsworth model as "positing species universals in the optimal pattern of attachment [with] no explicit place for cultural variations other than as 'suboptimal,' maladaptive, or pathogenic."

Empirical challenges.   There is also a body of empirical findings that challenge the traditional view of infant attachment. LeVine and Norman (2001/2008) focus on the apparently anomalous distribution of attachment styles found in two German studies: 49% "anxious-avoidant" (type "A") in the Grossmann's original Bielefeld study (Grossmann, Grossmann, Huber, & Wartner, 1981), and 42% in East Berlin (Ahnert, Meischner, & Schmidt, 2000), compared to Ainsworth's landmark Baltimore study showing 20% in that category (Ainsworth, Blehar, Waters, & Wall, 1978). LeVine and Norman draw on ethnographic evidence to suggest that the "type-A" response pattern in the Strange Situation is in fact quite consistent with North German infant care focused on self-reliance and frequent solitude. LeVine and Norman conclude that the results should be viewed as cultural learning, or enculturation.

Asian results pose a different challenge. K. Takahashi (1986), reporting on Japanese infants, found that by standard criteria all of the 32% of the sample who were not "securely attached" (Type B) would be classified as "anxious-resistant" (Type C), whereas the avoidant "A" pattern, dominant in the Bielefeld study, was entirely absent. Jin (2005) reported similar findings in Korea. Rothbaum and colleagues (Rothbaum & Morelli, 2005; Rothbaum et al., 2000) reject the idea that Japanese infants are truly insecure in their attachment. Drawing on both ethnographic and theoretical work, these authors demonstrate that key concepts in attachment theory do not correspond to the meaning systems of Japanese parents and Japanese society, and conclude that fundamental tenets of the theory cannot be universal.

Morelli, Tronick, Gewirtz, & Kurtines (1991) take the critique further and propose dropping altogether the "continuous care and contact model." They suggest replacing this model with one that focuses on the allocation of material and psychological resources, which are constrained by "a multiplicity of factors including evolved capacities and motivations, cultural beliefs and practices, residence patterns, and situational factors." The authors see three universal goals for parents – "child survival and eventual reproduction, economic self-sufficiency, and enculturation" (p. 74) – which can be met in a variety of ways. They present evidence from the Efe of the Ituri forest in Zaire to suggest that there is no single prototype of early care, and the variety of observed patterns can be understood only as highly complex adaptations to the presenting realities.

Not all attachment researchers have been convinced by these cultural critiques. Van IJzendoorn and Kroonenberg (1988) conducted a widely cited meta-analysis of secure-attachment classifications from 32 studies in 8 counties. While noting a tendency for A classifications to be relatively more prevalent in European countries, and for the C type to prevail in Israel and Japan, the authors nevertheless observed that the within-country variation was larger than that between countries, and concluded that the results constitute evidence for the cross-cultural validity of the Strange Situation procedure. Other theorists share the cultural critique of ethnocentrically defined of key constructs, such as "sensitivity," but do not consider that different manifestations invalidate the original ideas. Posada and colleagues, in particular, argue that naturalistic observations can help illuminate local expressions (Posada, Carbonell, Alzate, & Plata, 2004; Posada et al., 2002), and van IJzendoorn, Bakermans-Kranenburg, and Sagi-Schwartz (2006) have proposed a model of human universality and cultural specificity, similar to language, to encompass the growing comparative literature.

Temperament

Temperament theory is unique in that a cultural perspective was introduced early in the field's own development. This understanding of systematic differences in environmental demands contributed to the early reconceptualization of "the difficult infant" to the more contextually defined issue of "goodness of fit" (Korn & Gannon, 1983; Super & Harkness, 1994b). Multiple studies of "culture and temperament" have reported group differences in parents' ratings of their infant's temperament (e.g., Axia, Prior, & Carelli, 1992; deVries & Sameroff, 1984; Gartstein, Slobodskaya, & Kinsht, 2003). Ironically, given the initial impetus of temperament studies, much of the comparative research ended with mean differences, and studies of the correlates and consequences of temperamental variation in non-Western contexts are rare. The few available examples suggest powerful effects of temperament on the ecology of caretaking (Winn, Tronick, & Morelli, 1989) and on survival during periods of drought (deVries, 1994).

The cultural basis of parental ratings.   Cross-cultural findings highlight the ways in which parental (and professional) ratings of infant temperament reflect culturally based concepts. Consider a newborn who holds his head up, neck straight, apparently looking around. To an American mother this behavior revealed that her son was "alert and attentive." On the other hand a Kipsigis mother from rural Kenya would focus her interpretation around the integrity and smoothness of the motor act (Super & Harkness, 2009). In many ways Kipsigis mothers' understanding of behavioral organization was similar to US mothers', but their judgments also highlighted energetic activity and motor integrity, as well as the effect of unique local contexts such as carrying the infant on the back during most of the day (Super & Harkness, 1994a).

Shwalb, Shwalb, & Shoji (1994) have also found culturally specific organization in Japanese mothers' ratings of temperament using a locally generated questionnaire. For example, one factor at 6 months was labeled "stability/gentleness" by Japanese mothers, which was separate from the more familiar "intensity." When Japanese mothers used concepts that corresponded more directly to standard temperament dimensions they often saw those concepts in items not likely to be similarly grouped by US mothers. For example, "bending backward when embraced" and "expressing anger viscerally" both indicated "intensity" to the Japanese mothers, as they both consisted of negative emotional expression. Not surprisingly, then, Nakagawa and Sukigara (2005) were unable to replicate the US factor structure of the Infant Behavior Questionnaire (Garstein & Rothbart, 2003), and when they asked Japanese mothers to sort the questionnaire's behavioral items into its 14 *a priori* categories, the results were dramatic. Nearly half of the infant behaviors belonging to the dimension of Activity Level, for example, were considered by Japanese mothers to represent instead Distress to Limitations. Apparently these mothers were working from a different cultural model of how infants should self-regulate, a finding that resonates with the discussion by Rothbaum and colleagues of culturally defined competence and dependence in attachment studies (Rothbaum et al., 2000).

The cultural basis of parental ratings raises a particular difficulty in interpreting average group differences, the mainstay of cross-cultural temperament studies. The traditional approach to understanding group differences in parental reports identifies three potential explanations: (1) different parental expectations or values regarding behavior, leading to a bias in reporting; (2) different parental behaviors, leading to different child behaviors; (3) true differences in the "constitutional" basis of behavioral style (Hsu, 1981; Prior, Kyrios, & Oberklaid, 1986; Super & Harkness, 1994b). When it can be demonstrated that parents share a common meaning system, even if different cultural backgrounds shade connotation, then this triad of interpretations may work satisfactorily for direct comparison of *a priori* measures. In this situation such explanations can help researchers understand the kind of subtle structural differences suggested by Gartstein's findings in Russia (Gartstein, Knyazev, & Slobodskaya, 2005; Gartstein et al., 2003), or her demonstration of group similarities in accord with predictions from individualism/collectivism theory (Gartstein et al., 2006). If, on the other hand, nearly half of the items are "incorrectly" assigned, as Nakagawa and Sukigara's (2005) results suggest, then a comparison of averages of standard summaries would be uninterpretable.

Objective assessment procedures.   Parental questionnaires are not the only way to assess temperament (see chapter 20, this volume). Kagan's extensive work on behavioral inhibition began with laboratory observations of Chinese and non-Chinese infants in Boston (Kagan et al., 1978; Kagan, Snidman, Arcus, & Reznick, 1994). In both that context and in a later study with 4-month-olds in Beijing (Kagan, Arcus, et al., 1994), Chinese infants typically displayed a pattern of high basal heart rate and wariness to the unfamiliar, as do the most inhibited quartile of Euro-American infants. Largely on this basis, and citing the neonatal findings by Freedman & Freedman (1969), Kagan suggested that genetic dispositions may contribute to behavioral differences observed in the behavior of children of Asian and European origin (Kagan, Arcus et al., 1994; Kagan & Fox, 2006). It is evident, though, that the parallel is at best a partial one: Asians do not generally have the narrow faces and blue eyes characteristic of inhibited Euro-American children, characteristics that Kagan viewed as being biologically linked to an inhibited temperament (Kagan, Snidman, et al., 1994).

Camras and colleagues have used the "arm restraint" and other paradigms to induce negative emotions in the laboratory, as indicated by facial expression and other behaviors (Camras et al., 2007; Camras, Oster, Campos, Miyake, & Bradshaw, 1992). Although the authors' primary interest lay elsewhere, they reported that even within the first year Japanese and Chinese infants were subtly different in their emotional reactions, compared to Euro-American infants. For example, at 5 months of age, US infants were quicker to show negative facial expression. Similarly, Rosmus, Johnston, Chan-Yip, & Yang (2000) found that Chinese-Canadians, compared to Euro-Canadians, became more upset in response to routine pediatric inoculation at two months. In contrast, Kisilevsky and colleagues (Kisilevsky et al., 1998) used the "still face" procedure to elicit mild upset, and found Chinese and Canadian infants to show quite similar patterns of response (the exception being a longer latency to smile among the Chinese). Finally, in a study by Lewis, Ramsay, & Kawakami (1993), Euro-American infants showed more intense overt reactions to inoculation at 4 months than did Japanese infants, but the Japanese infants had greater cortisol responses.

Overall, the picture seems familiar at first: two groups with different social addresses – "Asian" and "Euro-North-American" in this case – have infants who usually present distinct patterns of behavior, which are generalized to a broad dimension of contrast already familiar in the Western literature, and there are parallel newborn findings, often interpreted to indicate a genetic basis for the differences. Unlike the opening scene of the "African Infant Precocity" story, however, we already have a good deal of relevant information about maternal beliefs and caretaking interactions. By and large this information suggests an environmental contribution: traditional Japanese and Chinese infant care is close and protected, focused on maintaining calm and anticipating distress in order to prevent it.

Interestingly, the growing body of relevant genetic information only complicates the picture. There are several versions of a specific gene (called DRD4) that influences the density of receptors in the brain for the neurotransmitter dopamine. Longer versions of the gene (with multiple repeats of the key sequence) have been associated with the personality trait called sensation seeking, greater risk of attention-deficit/hyperactivity disorder, and low levels of inhibition (Congdon, Lesch, & Canli, 2008), as well as greater developmental sensitivity to certain qualities of the caretaking environment (Propper, Willoughby, Halpern, Carbone, & Cox, 2007; Sheese, Voelker, Rothbart, & Posner, 2007). East Asian populations have very few individuals, about 6%, with the long, 7-repeat version of DRD4. North American native groups such as the Cheyenne and Pima, whose ancestors migrated across the Bering Straits from East Asia, average 26%, or about four times as high, a result in line with the hypothesis of novelty seeking in migrant groups (Chen, Burton, Greenberger, & Dmitrieva, 1999). It follows that native North American groups should be relatively uninhibited. Further, because only 16% of Euro-American population show the 7-repeat alleles, there should be *fewer* uninhibited infants than in the Native American groups. But this is clearly not the pattern of reactivity reported by the Freedmans, who place Native American newborns next to their Chinese sample, and in contrast to the Euro-Americans. Thus, with regard to at least this particular gene, the search for a simple gene–temperament link as an explanation of population differences in the development of reactivity and emotion regulation is unlikely to yield satisfying results.

Conclusions and Future Directions

Several patterns emerge from this selective review. One confirms expectations based on the Euro-American literature regarding infancy's developmental agenda. It underlines similarities in change, and often the timing of change, in the global diversity of settings. The cognitive mastery of physical reality moves predictably through its early phases, and motor skills to explore that reality appear at roughly comparable times. The elements of social interaction, with ready smiles and vocal exchange, emerge at 4 months. A surge in memory function follows several months later, and at the same time the emotional link to caretakers becomes compelling.

A cultural pattern, complementing the developmental one, emphasizes the adaptive and learning aspects of infancy. Going beyond results from monocultural studies, cross-cultural results illustrate how, from the beginning, infants learn about and learn from their environments. Skills that are supported, encouraged, and practiced emerge earlier and become stronger than others, and as skills emerge they engage the physical and social environments in increasingly complex ways. The concept of *culturally structured* environments for learning is becoming part of the developmental perspective. There is no dominant framework for that integration at present, but what was once an interdisciplinary barrier is becoming thinner and more flexible.

Finally, there are patterns in the research literature that suggest valuable strategies for the next quarter-century. A weakness of some early work was to assume that construct validity travels as easily as do measurement instruments. It is a sign of progress that more studies now assume less, and include such diverse procedures as psychometric replication and the exploration of local meanings. Relatedly, the drive to identify variation in behavior as a dependent variable has too often yielded evidence of group differences with only a social address to hang them on. Fortunately, the ethnographic interests and skills of cross-cultural researchers are increasing, and it seems that as infant research is becoming a more global enterprise, a dual focus on culture and development is becoming more normative. One further glimpse of the future may be seen in the recent introduction of molecular genetics into infant research. If it is more true than trivial that everything we are is the result of gene–environment interaction, then studies of culture and infancy will continue to offer an essential paradigm for developmental research.

Note

1. Parental ethnotheories are culturally constructed ideas about children's behavior and development, about the family, and about parenting; they are often implicit, they have strong motivational properties, and they are hierarchically integrated with each other and with other cultural themes and models (Harkness & Super, 1992, 1996; Harkness, Super, & Keefer, 1992).

References

Acolet, D., Modi, N., Giannakoulopoulos, X., Bond, C., Weg, W., Clow, A., et al. (1993). Changes in plasma cortisol and catecholamine concentrations in response to massage in preterm infants. *Archives of disease in childhood, 68*(1 Spec No), 29–31, 1468–2044.

Agiobu-Kemmer, I. (1984). Cognitive and affective aspects of infant development. In H. V. Curran (Ed.), *Nigerian children: Developmental perspectives* (pp. 74–117). Boston: Routledge and Kegan Paul.

Ahnert, L., Meischner, T., & Schmidt, A. (2000). Maternal sensitivity and attachment in East German and Russian family networks. In P. M. Crittenden & A. H. Claussen (Eds.), *The organization of attachment relationships: Maturation, culture, and context* (pp. 61–74). New York: Cambridge University Press.

Aina, O. F., & Morakinyo, O. (2005). Normative data on mental and motor development in Nigerian children. *West African Journal Of Medicine, 24*(2), 151–156.

Ainsworth, M. D. S. (1967). *Infancy in Uganda: Infant care and the growth of love*. Baltimore: Johns Hopkins Press.

Ainsworth, M. D. S., Blehar, M. C., Waters, E., & Wall, S. (1978). *Patterns of attachment: A psychological study of the Strange Situation*. Hillsdale, NJ: Erlbaum.

Arai, S., Ishikawa, J., & Toshima, K. (1958). Développement psychomoteur des enfants Japonais. *Revue de Neuropsychiatrie Infantile et d'Hygiène Mentale de l'Enfance, 6*, 262–269.

Atkin, L. C., Olvera, M. D. C., Givaudan, M., Landeros, G., Nugent, J. K., Lester, B. M., et al. (1991). Neonatal behavior and maternal perceptions of urban Mexican infants. In J. K. Nugent, B. M. Lester, & T. B. Brazelton (Eds.), *The cultural context of infancy, Vol. 2: Multicultural and interdisciplinary approaches to parent–infant relations* (pp. 201–236). Westport, CT: Ablex.

Axia, G., Prior, M., & Carelli, M. G. (1992). Cultural influences on temperament: A comparison of Italian, Italo-Australian, and Anglo-Australian toddlers. *Australian Psychologist, 27*(1), 52–56.

Bell, R. Q. (1963). Some factors to be controlled in studies of the behavior of newborns. *Biologia Neonatorum. Neo-Natal Studies, 5*, 200–214.

Bornstein, M. H., & Cote, L. R. (2001). Mother-infant interaction and acculturation: I. Behavioural comparisons in Japanese American and South American families. *International Journal of Behavioral Development, 25*(6), 549–563.

Bornstein, M. H., Cote, L. R., & Venuti, P. (2001). Parenting beliefs and behaviors in Northern and Southern groups of Italian mothers and young infants. *Journal of Family Psychology, 15*(4), 663–675.

Bornstein, M. H., Putnick, D. L., Heslington, M., Gini, M., Suwalsky, J. T. D., Venuti, P., et al. (2008). Mother-child emotional availability in ecological perspective: Three countries, two regions, two genders. *Developmental Psychology, 44*(3), 666–680.

Bornstein, M. H., Tamis-LeMonda, C. S., Pêcheux, M.-G., & Rahn, C. W. (1991). Mother and infant activity and interaction in France and in the United States: A comparative study. *International Journal of Behavioral Development, 14*(1), 21–43.

Bornstein, M. H., Tamis-LeMonda, C. S., Tal, J., Ludemann, P., Toda, S., Rahn, C. W., et al. (1992). Maternal responsiveness to infants in three societies: The United States, France, and Japan. *Child Development, 63*, 808–821.

Brazelton, T. B., & Nugent, J. K. (1995). *Neonatal Behavioral Assessment Scale* (3rd ed.). London: Mac Keith.

Brazelton, T. B., Tronick, E. Z., Lechtig, A., Lasky, R. E., & Klein, R. E. (1977). The behavior of nutritionally deprived Guatemalan infants. *Developmental Medicine & Child Neurology, 19*, 364–372.

Brazelton, T. B., Tryphonopoulou, Y., & Lester, B. M. (1979). A comparative study of the behavior of Greek neonates. *Pediatrics, 63*(2), 279–285.

Cabrera, N. J., Shannon, J. D., West, J., & Brooks-Gunn, J. (2006). Parental interactions with Latino infants: Variation by country of origin and English proficiency. *Child Development, 77*(5), 1190–1207.

Camras, L. A., Oster, H., Bakeman, R., Meng, Z., Ujiie, T., & Campos, J. J. (2007). Do infants show distinct negative facial expressions for fear and anger? Emotional expression in 11-month-old European American, Chinese, and Japanese Infants. *Infancy, 11*(2), 131–155.

Camras, L. A., Oster, H., Campos, J., Campos, R., Ujiie, T., Miyake, K., et al. (1998). Production of emotional facial expressions in European American, Japanese, and Chinese infants. *Developmental Psychology, 34*(4), 616–628.

Camras, L. A., Oster, H., Campos, J. J., Miyake, K., & Bradshaw, D. (1992). Japanese and American infants' responses to arm restraint. *Developmental Psychology, 28*(4), 578–583.

Carlson, V. J., & Harwood, R. L. (2003). Attachment, culture, and the caregiving system: The cultural patterning of everyday experiences among Anglo and Puerto Rican mother-infant pairs. *Infant Mental Health Journal, 24*(1), 53–73.

Carver, L. J., & Bauer, P. J. (2001). The dawning of a past: The emergence of long-term explicit memory in infancy. *Journal of Experimental Psychology, 130*(4), 726–745.

Caudill, W. (1972). Tiny dramas: Vocal communication between mother and infant in Japanese and American families. In W. P. Lebra (Ed.), *Mental health research in Asia and the Pacific* (Vol. 2, pp. 45–48). Honolulu: East-West Center Press. Reprinted in G. Handel (Ed.), (1988), *Childhood Socialization* (pp. 49–72). Hawthorne, NY: Aldine de Gruyter.

Caudill, W., & Frost, L. (1974). A comparison of maternal care and infant behavior in Japanese-American, American, and Japanese families. In W. P. Lebra (Ed.), *Mental health research in Asia and the Pacific* (Vol. 3, pp. 4–15). Honolulu: East-West Center Press.

Caudill, W., & Weinstein, H. (1969). Maternal care and infant behavior in Japan and America. *Psychiatry, 32*, 12–43.

Chen, C., Burton, M., Greenberger, E., & Dmitrieva, J. (1999). Population migration and the variation of dopamine D4 receptor (DRD4) allele frequencies around the globe. *Evolution and Human Behavior, 20*(5), 309–324.

Childers, J. B., Vaughan, J., & Burquest, D. A. (2007). Joint attention and word learning in Ngas-speaking toddlers in Nigeria. *Journal of Child Language, 34*(2), 199–225.

Chisholm, J. S. (1983). *Navajo infancy: An ethnological study of child development.* Albuquerque: University of New Mexico Press.

Chisholm, J. S., Woodson, R. H., & da Costa Woodson, E. M. (1978). Maternal blood pressure in pregnancy and newborn irritability. *Early Human Development, 2*(2), 171–178.

Clark, D. L., Kreutzberg, J. R., & Chee, F. K. W. (1977). Vestibular stimulation influence on motor development in infants. *Science, 196*, 1228–1229.

Congdon, E., Lesch, K. P., & Canli, T. (2008). Analysis of DRD4 and DAT polymorphisms and behavioral inhibition in healthy adults: Implications for impulsivity. *American Journal of Medical Genetics. Part B, Neuropsychiatric Genetics: The Official Publication of The International Society of Psychiatric Genetics, 147B*(1), 27–32.

D'Andrade, R. G. (1987). A folk model of the mind. In D. Holland & N. Quinn (Eds.), *Cultural models in language and thought* (pp. 112–148). New York: Cambridge University Press.

Dasen, P., Inhelder, B., Lavallée, M., & Retschitzki, J. (1978). *Naissance de l'intelligence chez l'enfant baoulé de Côte d'Ivoire.* Berne: Hans Huber.

de Costa, C., & Griew, A. R. (1982). Effects of betel chewing on pregnancy outcome. *The Australian & New Zealand Journal of Obstetrics & Gynaecology, 22*(1), 22–24.

de Weerth, C., van Hees, Y., & Buitelaar, J. K. (2003). Prenatal maternal cortisol levels and infant behavior during the first 5 months. *Early Human Development, 74*(2), 139–151.

deVries, M. W. (1994). Kids in context: Temperament in cross-cultural perspective. In W. B. Carey & S. C. McDevitt (Eds.), *Prevention and early intervention: Individual differences as risk factors for the mental health of children: A festschrift for Stella Chess and Alexander Thomas* (pp. 126–139). Philadelphia: Brunner/Mazel.

deVries, M. W., & Sameroff, A. J. (1984). Culture and temperament: Influence on infant temperament in three East African societies. *Journal of Orthopsychiatry, 43*, 92–101.

deVries, M. W., & Super, C. M. (1979). Contextual influences on the Brazelton Neonatal Behavioral Assessment Scale and implications for its cross-cultural use. In A. J. Sameroff (Ed.), *Organization and stability of newborn behavior: A commentary on the Brazelton Neonatal Behavioral Assessment Scale. Monographs of the Society for Research in Child Development 43*(Serial No. 177).

Faladé, S. (1955). *Le développement psychomoteur du jeune africain originaire du Sénégal au cours de sa première anée.* Paris: Foulon.

Falmagne, J.-D. (1962). Étude comparative du développement psychomoteur pendant les six premiers mois de 105 nourrissons blancs (Bruxelles) et 78 nourrissons noirs (Johannesburg). *Mémoirs de L'Academie Royale des Sciences d'Outre-Mer. Classes des Sciences Naturelle et Médicales, 13*(5).

Fernald, A., & Morikawa, H. (1993). Common themes and cultural variations in Japanese and American mothers' speech to infants. *Child Development, 64*(3), 637–656.

Field, T., Hernandez-Reif, M., Diego, M., Feijo, L., Vera, Y., & Gil, K. (2004). Massage therapy by parents improves early growth and development. *Infant Behavior & Development, 27*(4), 435–442.

Finley, G. E., Kagan, J., & Layne, O. (1972). Development of young children's attention to normal and distorted stimuli: A cross-cultural study. *Developmental Psychology, 6*(2), 288–292.

Fox, N. (1977). Attachment of kibbutz infants to mother and metapelet. *Child Development, 48*, 1228–1239.

Freedman, D. G. (1974). *Human infancy: An evolutionary perspective.* Hillsdale, NJ: Erlbaum.

Freedman, D. G., & Freedman, N. C. (1969). Behavioral differences between Chinese-American and European-American newborns. *Nature, 224*, 1227.

Garcia Coll, C. T., Sepkoski, C., & Lester, B. M. (1981). Cultural and biomedical correlates of neonatal behavior. *Developmental Psychobiology, 14*, 147–154.

Gardner, W., Lamb, M. E., Thompson, R. A., & Sagi, A. (1986). On individual differences in Strange Situation behavior: Categorical and continuous measurements systems in a cross-cultural data set. *Infant Behavior & Development, 9*(3), 355–375.

Gartstein, M. A., Gonzalez, C., Carranza, J. A., Ahadi, S. A., Ye, R., Rothbart, M. K., et al. (2006). Studying cross-cultural differences in the development of infant temperament: People's Republic of China, the United States of America, and Spain. *Child Psychiatry & Human Development, 37*(2), 145–161.

Gartstein, M. A., Knyazev, G. G., & Slobodskaya, H. R. (2005). Cross-cultural differences in the structure of infant temperament: United States of America (US) and Russia. *Infant Behavior & Development, 28*(1), 54–61.

Garstein, M. A., & Rothbart, M. K. (2003). Studying infant temperament via the Infant Behavior Questionnaire. *Child Development, 26*(1), 64–86.

Gartstein, M. A., Slobodskaya, H. R., & Kinsht, I. A. (2003). Cross-cultural differences in temperament in the first year of life: United States of America and Russia. *International Journal of Behavioral Development, 27*(4), 316–328.

Géber, M., & Dean, R. F. (1957). The state of development of newborn African children. *Lancet, 272*(1), 1216–1219.

Géber, M., & Dean, R. F. (1958). Psychomotor development in African children: The effects of social class and the need for improved tests. *Bulletin of the World Health Organization*, *18*(3), 471–476.

Gewirtz, J. L. (1965). The course of infant smiling in four child-rearing environments in Israel. In B. A. Foss (Ed.), *Determinants of infant behavior*. London: Methuen.

Goldberg, S. (1977). Infant development and mother–infant interaction in urban Zambia. In P. H. Leiderman, S. R. Tulkin & A. Rosenfeld (Eds.), *Culture and infancy: Variations in the human experience*. New York: Academic Press.

Gottlieb, A. (2004). *The afterlife is where we come from*. Chicago: University of Chicago Press.

Gregg, C. L., Haffner, M. E., & Korner, A. F. (1976). The relative efficacy of vestibular-proprioceptive stimulation and the upright position in enhancing visual pursuit in neonates. *Child Development*, *47*, 309–314.

Grossmann, K. E., Grossmann, K., Huber, F., & Wartner, U. (1981). German children's behavior towards their mothers at 12 months and their fathers at 18 months in Ainsworth's Strange Situation. *International Journal of Behavioral Development*, *4*(2), 157–181.

Harkness, S. (1988). The cultural construction of semantic contingency in mother-child speech. *Language Sciences*, *10*(1), 53–67.

Harkness, S. (1992). Human development in psychological anthropology. In T. Schwartz, G. M. White & C. A. Lutz (Eds.), *New directions in psychological anthropology* (pp. 102–121). New York: Cambridge University Press.

Harkness, S. (2008). Human development in cultural context. One pathway or many? (Essay review of *Cultures of infancy* by Heidi Keller). *Human Development*, *51*, 283–289.

Harkness, S., & Super, C. M. (1992). Parental ethnotheories in action. In I. Sigel, A. V. McGillicuddy-DeLisi & J. Goodnow (Eds.), *Parental belief systems: The psychological consequences for children* (2nd ed., pp. 373–392). Hillsdale, NJ: Erlbaum.

Harkness, S., & Super, C. M. (1996). Introduction. In S. Harkness & C. M. Super (Eds.), *Parents' cultural belief systems: Their origins, expressions, and consequences* (pp. 1–23). New York: Guilford Press.

Harkness, S., Super, C. M., Barry, O., Zeitlin, M., & Long, J. (2009). Assessing the environment of children's learning: The developmental niche in Africa. In E. Grigorenko (Ed.), *Multicultural psychoeducational assessment* (pp.133–155). New York: Springer.

Harkness, S., Super, C. M., & Keefer, C. H. (1992). Learning to be an American parent: How cultural models gain directive force. In R. G. D'Andrade & C. Strauss (Eds.), *Human motives and cultural models* (pp. 163–178). New York: Cambridge University Press.

Harkness, S., Super, C. M., Moscardino, U., Rha, J.-H., Blom, M. J. M., Huitrón, B., et al. (2007). Cultural models and developmental agendas: Implications for arousal and self-regulation in early infancy. *Journal of Developmental Processes*, *1*(2).

Harwood, R. (1992). The influence of culturally derived values on Anglo and Puerto Rican mothers' perceptions of attachment behavior. *Child Development*, *63*, 822–839.

Harwood, R. L., Miller, J. G., & Irizarry, N. L. (1995). *Culture and attachment: Perceptions of the child in context*. New York: Guilford Press.

Hermans, H. J. M., & Kempen, H. J. G. (1998). Moving cultures: The perilous problems of cultural dichotomies in a globalizing society. *American Psychologist*, *53*(10), 1111–1120.

Hewlett, B. S., Lamb, M. E., Shannon, D., Leyendecker, B., & Schölmerich, A. (1998). Culture and early infancy among central African foragers and farmers. *Developmental Psychology*, *34*(4), 653–661.

Holloway, S. D., & Minami, M. (1996). Production and reproduction of culture: The dynamic role of mothers and children in early socialization. In D. W. Shwalb & B. J. Shwalb (Eds.), *Japanese childrearing: Two generations of scholarship* (pp. 164–176). New York: Guilford Press.

Hopkins, B. (1976). Culturally determined patterns of handling the human infant. *Journal of Human Movement Studies, 2*, 1–27.

Horowitz, F. D., Ashton, J., Culp, R., Gaddis, E., Levin, S., & Reichmann, B. (1977). The effects of obstetrical medication on the behavior of Israeli newborn infants and some comparisons with Uruguayan and American infants. *Child Development, 48*, 1607–1623.

Hsu, C.-C. (1981). The temperamental characteristics of Chinese babies. *Child Development, 52*(4), 1337–1340.

Jin, M. K. (2005). *A cross-cultural study of infant attachment patterns in Korea and the United States: Associations among infant temperament, maternal personality, separation anxiety and depression.* ProQuest Information & Learning, US.

Kagan, J. (1971). *Change and continuity in infancy.* New York: Wiley.

Kagan, J. (1976). Emergent themes in human development. *American Scientist, 64*, 186–196.

Kagan, J., Arcus, D., Snidman, N., Feng, W. Y., Hendler, J., & Greene, S. (1994). Reactivity in infants: A cross-national comparison. *Developmental Psychology, 30*(3), 342–345.

Kagan, J., & Fox, N. A. (2006). Biology, culture, and temperamental biases. In N. Eisenberg, W. Damon, & R. M. Lerner (Eds.), *Handbook of child psychology: Vol. 3, Social, emotional, and personality development* (6th ed., pp. 167–225). Chichester: Wiley.

Kagan, J., Kearsley, R. B., & Zelazo, P. R. (1978). *Infancy: Its place in human development.* Cambridge, MA: Harvard University Press.

Kagan, J., Snidman, N., Arcus, D., & Reznick, J. S. (1994). *Galen's prophecy: Temperament in human nature.* Cambridge, MA: Harvard University Press.

Kağıtçıbaşi, Ç. (1980). Individualism and collectivism. In J. W. Berry, M. H. Segall & Ç. Kağıtçıbaşi (Eds.), *Handbook of cross-cultural psychology: Vol. 3 Social behavior and applications* (pp. 1–50). Boston: Allyn and Bacon.

Keefer, C. H., Dixon, S., Tronick, E. Z., & Brazelton, T. B. (1991). Cultural mediation between newborn behavior and later development: Implications for methodology in cross-cultural research. In J. K. Nugent, B. M. Lester & T. B. Brazelton (Eds.), *The cultural context of infancy, Vol. 2: Multicultural and interdisciplinary approaches to parent–infant relations* (pp. 39–61). Westport, CT: Ablex.

Keefer, C. H., Tronick, E. Z., Dixon, S., & Brazelton, T. B. (1982). Specific differences in motor performance between Gusii and American newborns and a modification of the Neonatal Behavioral Assessment Scale. *Child Development, 53*(3), 754–759.

Keller, H. (2007). *Cultures of infancy.* Mahwah, NJ: Erlbaum.

Kennedy, T., Thomas, D. G., Woltamo, T., Abebe, Y., Hubbs-Tait, L., Sykova, V., et al. (2008). Growth and visual information processing in infants in Southern Ethiopia. *Journal of Applied Developmental Psychology, 29*(2), 129–140.

Kilbride, J. E., & Kilbride, P. L. (1975). Sitting and smiling behavior of Baganda infants: The influence of culturally constituted experience. *Journal of Cross-Cultural Psychology, 6*, 88–107.

Kilbride, P. L., & Kilbride, J. E. (1974). Sociocultural factors and the early manifestation of sociability behavior among Baganda infants. *Ethos, 2*, 296–314.

Kisilevsky, B. S., Hains, S. M. J., Lee, K., Muir, D. W., Xu, F., Fu, G., et al. (1998). The still-face effect in Chinese and Canadian 3- to 6-month-old infants. *Developmental Psychology, 34*(4), 629–639.

Konner, M. J. (1972). Aspects of the developmental ethology of a foraging people. In N. G. Blurton Jones (Ed.), *Ethological studies of child behavior.* Cambridge: Cambridge University Press.

Konner, M. J. (1973). *Infants of a foraging people.* Unpublished PhD dissertation, Harvard University, Cambridge, MA.

Konner, M. J. (1976). Maternal care, infant behavior and development among the !Kung. In R. Lee & I. DeVore (Eds.), *Kalahari hunter-gatherers.* Cambridge, MA: Harvard University Press.

Konner, M. J., & Worthman, C. (1980). Nursing frequency, gonadal function, and birth spacing among !Kung hunter-gatherers. *Science, 207*(4432), 788–791.

Korn, S. J., & Gannon, S. (1983). Temperament, cultural variation and behavior disorder in preschool children. *Child Psychiatry and Human Development, 13*(4), 203–212.

Korner, A. F., Gabby, T., & Kraemer, H. C. (1980). Relation between prenatal maternal blood pressure and infant irritability. *Early Human Development, 4*(1), 35–39.

Landau, R. (1977). Spontaneous and elicited smiles and vocalizations of infants in four Israeli environments. *Developmental Psychology, 13*(4), 389–400.

Landers, C. (1989). A psychobiological study of infant development in South India. In J. K. Nugent, B. M. Lester & T. B. Brazelton (Eds.), *The cultural context of infancy: Vol. 1, Biology, culture, and infant development* (pp. 169–207). Westport, CT: Ablex.

Laughlin, C. D. (1992). Pre- and peri-natal anthropology: II. The puerperium in cross-cultural perspective. *Journal of Prenatal & Perinatal Psychology & Health, 7*(1), 23–60.

Lécuyer, R., & Tano, J. (1990). Vitesse d'habituation visuelle chez des bébés ivoiriens et français. *International Journal of Psychology, 25*(3), 337–342.

Leiderman, P. H., Babu, B., Kagia, J., Kraemer, H. C., & Leiderman, G. F. (1973). African infant precocity and some social influences during the first year. *Nature, 242,* 247–249.

Leiderman, P. H., & Leiderman, G. F. (1974). Affective and cognitive consequences of polymatric infant care in the East African Highlands. In A. D. Pick (Ed.), *Minnesota symposium on child psychology* (Vol. 8). Minneapolis: University of Minnesota Press.

Lester, B. M., & Brazelton, T. B. (1981). Cross-cultural assessment of neonatal behavior. In D. A. Wagner & H. W. Stevenson (Eds.), *Cultural perspectives on child development* (pp. 20–53). San Francisco: Freeman.

LeVine, R. A., Dixon, S., LeVine, S., Richman, A., Leiderman, P. H., Keefer, C. H., et al. (1994). *Child care and culture: Lessons from Africa.* New York: Cambridge University Press.

LeVine, R. A., & LeVine, B. B. (1966). *Nyansongo: A Gusii community in Kenya.* New York: Wiley.

LeVine, R. A., & Norman, K. (2001/2008). The infant's acquisition of culture: Early attachment reexamined in anthropological perspective. In H. Mathews & C. Moore (Eds.), *The psychology of cultural experience* (pp. 83–104). New York: Cambridge University Press. Reprinted as Attachment in anthropological perspective, in R. A. LeVine & R. S. New (Eds.), *Anthropology and child development: A cross-cultural reader* (pp. 127–142). Malden, MA: Blackwell.

Lewis, M., Ramsay, D. S., & Kawakami, K. (1993). Differences between Japanese infants and Caucasian American infants in behavioral and cortisol response to inoculation. *Child Development, 64*(6), 1722–1731.

Leyendecker, B., Harwood, R. L., Lamb, M. E., & Schölmerich, A. (2002). Mothers' socialization goals and evaluations of desirable and undesirable everyday situations in two diverse cultural groups. *International Journal of Behavioral Development, 26*(3), 248–258.

Lim, H. C., Chan, T., & Yoong, T. (1994). Standardisation and adaptation of the Denver Developmental Screening Test (DDST) and Denver II for use in Singapore children. *Singapore Medical Journal, 35*(2), 156–160.

McKenna, J. J. (2000). Cultural influences on infant and childhood sleep biology, and the science that studies it: Toward a more inclusive paradigm. In G. M. Loughlin, J. L. Caroll & C. L. Marcus (Eds.), *Sleep and breathing in children: A developmental approach* (pp. 99–130). New York: Marcel Dekker.

Mead, M., & MacGregor, F. C. (1951). *Growth and culture.* New York: Putnam.

Meléndez, L. (2005). Parental beliefs and practices around early self-regulation: The impact of culture and immigration. *Infants & Young Children, 18*(2), 136–146.

Morelli, G. A., Tronick, E. Z., Gewirtz, J. L., & Kurtines, W. M. (1991). Efe multiple caretaking and attachment. In *Intersections with attachment.* (pp. 41–51). Hillsdale, NJ: Erlbaum.

Moscardino, U., Nwobu, O., & Axia, G. (2006). Cultural beliefs and practices related to infant health and development among Nigerian immigrant mothers in Italy. *Journal of Reproductive and Infant Psychology, 24*(3), 241–255.

Muret-Wagstaff, S., & Moore, S. G. (1989). The Hmong in America: Infant behavior and rearing practices. In J. K. Nugent, B. M. Lester & T. B. Brazelton (Eds.), *The cultural context of infancy: Vol. 1, Biology, culture, and infant development* (pp. 319–339). Westport, CT: Ablex.

Nakagawa, A., & Sukigara, M. (2005). How are cultural differences in the interpretation of infant behavior reflected in the Japanese Revised Infant Behavior Questionnaire? *Japanese Journal of Educational Psychology, 53*(4), 491–503.

Nelson, E. A., Yu, L. M., Wong, D., Wong, H. Y., & Yim, L. (2004). Rolling over in infants: Age, ethnicity, and cultural differences. *Developmental Medicine and Child Neurology, 46*(10), 706–709.

Newton, N., & Newton, M. (1972). Childbirth in cross-cultural perspective. In J. B. Howells (Ed.), *Modern perspectives in psycho-obstetrics.* (pp. 83–132). New York: Bruner/Mazel.

Nugent, J. K., Lester, B. M., & Brazelton, T. B. (1989). *The cultural context of infancy: Vol. 1, Biology, culture, and infant development.* Norwood, NJ: Ablex.

Posada, G., Carbonell, O. A., Alzate, G., & Plata, S. J. (2004). Through Colombian lenses: Ethnographic and conventional analyses of maternal care and their associations with secure base behavior. *Developmental Psychology, 40*(4), 508–518.

Posada, G., Jacobs, A., Richmond, M. K., Carbonell, O. A., Alzate, G., Bustamante, M. R., et al. (2002). Maternal caregiving and infant security in two cultures. *Developmental Psychology, 38*(1), 67–78.

Prior, M. R., Kyrios, M., & Oberklaid, F. (1986). Temperament in Australian, American, Chinese, and Greek infants: Some issues and directions for future research. *Journal of Cross Cultural Psychology, 17*(4), 455–474.

Propper, C., Willoughby, M., Halpern, C. T., Carbone, M. A., & Cox, M. (2007). Parenting quality, DRD4, and the prediction of externalizing and internalizing behaviors in early childhood. *Developmental Psychobiology, 49*(6), 619–632.

Quack Loetscher, K. C., Selvin, S., Zimmermann, R., & Abrams, B. (2007). Ethnic-cultural background, maternal body size and pregnancy outcomes in a diverse Swiss cohort. *Women & Health, 45*(2), 25–40.

Rabain-Jamin, J. (1989). Culture and early social interactions: The example of mother-infant object play in African and native French families. *European Journal of Psychology of Education, 4*(2), 295–305.

Rabain-Jamin, J. (1994). Language and socialization of the child in African families living in France. In P. M. Greenfield & R. R. Cocking (Eds.), *Cross-cultural roots of minority child development* (pp. 147–166). Hillsdale, NJ: Erlbaum.

Rabain-Jamin, J., Maynard, A. E., & Greenfield, P. (2003). Implications of sibling caregiving for sibling relations and teaching interactions in two cultures. *Ethos, 31*(2), 204–231.

Rabain-Jamin, J., & Sabeau-Jouannet, E. (1997). Maternal speech to 4-month-old infants in two cultures: Wolof and French. *International Journal of Behavioral Development, 20*(3), 425–451.

Rabain-Jamin, J., & Wornham, W. L. (1990). Transformations des conduites de maternage et des pratiques de soin chez les femmes migrantes originaires d'Afrique de l'Ouest [Changes in maternal behavior and care practices in migrant women from Western Africa]. *La Psychiatrie de L'enfant, 33*(1), 287–319.

Rabin, A. I. (1958). Behavioral research in collective settlements in Israel: 6 Infants and children under conditions of "intermittent" mothering in the kibbutz. *American Journal of Orthopsychiatry, 28*, 577–584.

Rebelsky, F. (1973). First discussant's comments: Cross-cultural studies of mother–infant interaction: Description and consequence. *Human Development*, *15*(2), 128–130.

Rosenblith, J. F., & Anderson-Huntington, R. B. (1975). Defensive reactions to stimulation of the nasal and oral regions in newborns: Relations to state. In J. F. Bosma & J. Showacre (Eds.), *Development of upper respiratory anatomy and function: Implications for sudden infant death syndrome*. Publication NIH 75–941. Bethesda: Department of Health, Education, and Welfare.

Rosmus, C., Johnston, C. C. l., Chan-Yip, A., & Yang, F. (2000). Pain response in Chinese and non-Chinese Canadian infants: Is there a difference? *Social Science & Medicine*, *51*(2), 175–184.

Rosser, P. L., & Randolph, S. M. (1989). Black American infants: The Howard University normative study. In J. K. Nugent, B. M. Lester & T. B. Brazelton (Eds.), *The cultural context of infancy: Vol. 1, Biology, culture, and infant development* (pp. 133–165). Westport, CT: Ablex.

Rothbaum, F., & Morelli, G. (2005). Attachment and culture: Bridging relativism and universalism. In W. Friedlmeier, P. Chakkarath & B. Schwarz (Eds.), *Culture and human development: The importance of cross-cultural research for the social sciences* (pp. 99–123). Mahwah, NJ: Psychology Press/Erlbaum.

Rothbaum, F., Weisz, J., Pott, M., Miyake, K., & Morelli, G. (2000). Attachment and culture: Security in the United States and Japan. *American Psychologist*, *55*(10), 1093–1104.

Sagi, A. (1990). Attachment theory and research from a cross-cultural perspective. *Human Development*, *33*(1), 10–22.

Sagi, A., Van IJzendoorn, M. H., & Koren-Karie, N. (1991). Primary appraisal of the Strange Situation: A cross-cultural analysis of preseparation episodes. *Developmental Psychology*, *27*(4), 587–596.

Scher, A., Tirosh, E., Jaffe, M., Rubin, L., Sadeh, A., & Lavie, P. (1995). Sleep patterns of infants and young children in Israel. *International Journal of Behavioral Development*, *18*(4), 701–711.

Schooler, C. (1996). William Caudill and the reproduction of culture: Infant, child, and maternal behavior in Japan and the United States. In D. W. Shwalb & B. J. Shwalb (Eds.), *Japanese childrearing: Two generations of scholarship* (pp. 139–163). New York: Guilford Press.

Sellers, M. J., Klein, R. E., Kagan, J., & Minton, C. (1972). Developmental determinants of attention: A cross-cultural replication. *Developmental Psychology*, *6*(1), 185.

Sellers, M. J., Klein, R. E., Sellers, S., Lechtig, A., & Yarbrough, C. (1971). *Medición de infantos reién nacidos en una muestra rural de Guatemala usando la escala de Brazelton*. Guatemala City: División de Desarrollo Human, Instituto de Nutrición de Centro America y Panama.

Sheese, B. E., Voelker, P. M., Rothbart, M. K., & Posner, M. I. (2007). Parenting quality interacts with genetic variation in dopamine receptor D4 to influence temperament in early childhood. *Development and Psychopathology*, *19*(4), 1039–1046.

Shwalb, B. J., Shwalb, D. W., & Shoji, J. (1994). Structure and dimensions of maternal perceptions of Japanese infant temperament. *Developmental Psychology*, *30*(2), 131–141.

Super, C. M. (1976). Environmental effects on motor development: The case of African infant precocity. *Developmental Medicine and Child Neurology*, *18*, 561–567.

Super, C. M. (1981). Behavioral development in infancy. In R. H. Munroe, R. L. Munroe & B. B. Whiting (Eds.), *Handbook of Cross-cultural Human Development* (pp. 181–270). New York: Garland Press.

Super, C. M., Blom, M. J. M., Ranade, N., Londhe, R., & Harkness, S. (2010). *Culture and the architecture of infant sleep*. Manuscript submitted for publication.

Super, C. M., Guldan, G. S., Ahmed, N. U., & Zeitlin, M. (2010). *The emergence of separation protest is robust under conditions of severe developmental stress*. Manuscript submitted for publication.

Super, C. M., & Harkness, S. (1982a). The development of affect in infancy and early childhood. In D. A. Wagner & H. W. Stevenson (Eds.), *Cultural perspectives on child development* (pp. 1–19). San Francisco: Freeman.

Super, C. M., & Harkness, S. (1982b). The infant's niche in rural Kenya and metropolitan America. In L. L. Adler (Ed.), *Cross-cultural research at issue* (pp. 47–56). New York: Academic Press.

Super, C. M., & Harkness, S. (1986). The developmental niche: A conceptualization at the interface of child and culture. *International Journal of Behavioral Development*, *9*, 545–569.

Super, C. M., & Harkness, S. (1994a). The cultural regulation of temperament–environment interactions. *Researching Early Childhood*, *2*(1), 59–84.

Super, C. M., & Harkness, S. (1994b). Temperament and the developmental niche. In W. B. Carey & S. A. McDevitt (Eds.), *Prevention and early intervention: Individual differences as risk factors for the mental health of children – a Festschrift for Stella Chess and Alexander Thomas* (pp. 15–25). New York: Brunner/Mazel.

Super, C. M., & Harkness, S. (1999). The environment as culture in developmental research. In T. Wachs & S. Friedman (Eds.), *Measurement of the environment in developmental research* (pp. 279–323). Washington, DC: American Psychological Association.

Super, C. M., & Harkness, S. (2002). Culture structures the environment for development. *Human Development*, *45*(4), 270–274.

Super, C. M., & Harkness, S. (2009). The developmental niche of the newborn in rural Kenya. In J. K. Nugent, B. Petrauskas & T. B. Brazelton (Eds.), *The newborn as a person: Enabling healthy infant development worldwide* (pp. 85–97). New York: Wiley.

Super, C. M., Harkness, S., van Tijen, N., van der Vlugt, E., Dykstra, J., & Fintelman, M. (1996). The three Rs of Dutch child rearing and the socialization of infant arousal. In S. Harkness & C. M. Super (Eds.), *Parents' cultural belief systems: Their origins, expressions, and consequences* (pp. 447–466). New York: Guilford Press.

Takahashi, K. (1986). Examining the strange-situation procedure with Japanese mothers and 12-month-old infants. *Developmental Psychology*, *22*(2), 265–270.

Takahashi, M. (1973). The cross-sectional study of infants' smiling, attention, reaching, and crying responses to the facial models. *Japanese Journal of Psychology*, *44*, 124–134.

Takahashi, M. (1974). The longitudinal study of infants' smiling responses in relation to neonatal spontaneous smiles. *Japanese Journal of Psychology*, *45*, 256–267.

Thairu, L., & Pelto, G. (2008). Newborn care practices in Pemba Island (Tanzania) and their implications for newborn health and survival. *Maternal and Child Nutrition*, *4*(3), 194–208.

Tuntiseranee, P., Geater, A., Chongsuvivatwong, V., & Kor-anantakul, O. (1998). The effect of heavy maternal workload on fetal growth retardation and preterm delivery. A study among southern Thai women. *Journal of Occupational and Environmental Medicine/American College of Occupational and Environmental Medicine*, *40*(11), 1013–1021.

van IJzendoorn, M. H., & Kroonenberg, P. M. (1988). Cross-cultural patterns of attachment: A meta-analysis of the strange situation. *Child Development*, *59*(1), 147–156.

van IJzendoorn, M. H., Bakermans-Kranenburg, M. J., & Sagi-Schwartz, A. (2006). Attachment across diverse sociocultural contexts: The limits of universality. In K. H. Rubin & O. B. Chung (Eds.), *Parenting beliefs, behaviors, and parent-child relations: A cross-cultural perspective* (pp. 107–142). New York: Taylor & Francis.

Varkevisser, C. M. (1973). *Socialization in a changing society: Sukuma childhood in rural and urban Mwanza, Tanzania*. Den Haag: Center for the Study of Education in Changing Societies.

Vigil, D. C. (2002). Cultural variations in attention regulation: A comparative analysis of British and Chinese populations. *International Journal of Language & Communication Disorders*, *37*(4), 433–458.

Vouilloux, P. D. (1959). Étude de las psychomotoricité d'enfants africains au Cameroun: Test de Gesell et reflexes archaïques. *Journal de la Societé des Africainists*, *29*, 11–18.

Wachs, T. D., Pollitt, E., Cueto, S., & Jacoby, E. (2004). Structure and cross-contextual stability of neonatal temperament. *Infant Behavior & Development*, *27*(3), 382–396.

Wachs, T. D., Pollitt, E., Cueto, S., Jacoby, E., & Creed-Kanashiro, H. (2005). Relation of neonatal iron status to individual variability in neonatal temperament. *Developmental Psychobiology*, *46*(2), 141–153.

Warren, N. (1972). African infant precocity. *Psychological bulletin*, *78*, 353–367.

Warren, N., & Parkin, J. M. (1974). A neurological and behavioral comparison of African and European newborns in Uganda. *Child Development*, *45*, 966–971.

Weisner, T. S. (1996). Why ethnography should be the most important method in the study of human development. In A. Colby, R. Jessor & R. Shweder (Eds.), *Ethnography and human development: Context and meaning in social inquiry* (pp. 305–324). Chicago: University of Chicago Press.

Weisner, T. S. (2002). Ecocultural understanding of children's developmental pathways. *Human Development*, *45*(4), 275–281.

Welles-Nyström, B. (2005). Co-sleeping as a window into Swedish culture: Considerations of gender and health care. *Scandinavian Journal of Caring Sciences*, *19*(4), 354–360.

Werner, E. E., Bierman, J. M., & French, F. E. (1971). *The children of Kauai: A longitudinal study from the prenatal period to age ten*. Honolulu: University of Hawaii Press.

Whaley, S. E., Sigman, M., Beckwith, L., Cohen, S. E., & Espinosa, M. P. (2002). Infant caregiver interaction in Kenya and the United States: The importance of multiple caregivers and adequate comparison samples. *Journal of Cross-Cultural Psychology*, *33*(3), 236–247.

Winn, S., Tronick, E. Z., & Morelli, G. A. (1989). The infant and the group: A look at Efe caretaking practices in Zaire. In J. K. Nugent, B. M. Lester & T. B. Brazelton (Eds.), *The cultural context of infancy: Vol. 1, Biology, culture, and infant development* (pp. 87–109). Westport, CT: Ablex.

Wolf, A. W., Lozoff, B., Latz, S., & Paludetto, R. (1996). Parental theories in the management of young children's sleep in Japan, Italy, and the United States. In S. Harkness & C. M. Super (Eds.), *Parents' cultural belief systems: Their origins, expressions, and consequences* (pp. 364–384). New York: Guilford Press.

Wolff, P. H. (1963). Observations on the early development of smiling. In B. A. Foss (Ed.), *Determinants of infant behavior* (Vol. 2). New York: Wiley.

Worthman, C. (2003). Energetics, sociality, and human reproduction: Life history theory in real life. In K. W. Wachter & R. A. Bulatao (Eds.), *Offspring: Human fertility behavior in biodemographic perspective* (pp. 289–321). Washington, DC: National Academies Press.

Worthman, C. (2010, in press). The ecology of human development: Evolving models for cultural psychology. *Journal of Cross-cultural Psychology*.

Yovsi, R. D., & Keller, H. (2007). The architecture of cosleeping among wage-earning and subsistence farming Cameroonian Nso families. *Ethos*, *35*(1), 65–84.

Zelazo, N. A., Zelazo, P. R., Cohen, K. M., & Zelazo, P. D. (1993). Specificity of practice effects on elementary neuromotor patterns. *Developmental Psychology*, *29*(4), 686–691.

Zelazo, P. R. (1976). From reflexive to instrumental behavior. In L. P. Lipsitt (Ed.), *Developmental psychobiology: The significance of infancy*. Hillsdale, NJ: Erlbaum.

Author Index

Subject Index

A not B search error, 228–34
   action history, 230–1
   competing systems account, 234
   connectionist model, 232–3, 237
   locations as places of concealment, 230
   memory interference, 228–9
   neurophysiological account, 231–2
   problem-solving analyses, 233–4, 237
   role of action, 228
   spatial analyses, 229–30
AAI (Adult Attachment Interview), 499–500
ABR (auditory brainstem response), 103, 104
acoustic stimuli, 87, 104, 126
action, 36–7, 167–96
   A not B search error, 228
   bimanual coordination, 181–3
   and the brain, 172
   and cognition, 169
   complex systems, 169, 172–5, 179–80
   connection to environment, 168
   context-conditioned variability, 171
   degrees of freedom (DFs), 170–1, 172,
      173, 174, 175
   dynamic systems, 168–9
   ecological mechanism, 168, 176–7
   environmental perception, 167–9, 172–3,
      176–7
   goal-directed, 168, 178–81, 376, 377, 378,
      511

intentions, 380–1
interlimb coordination, 182
and knowledge, 235
and language, 195
link to communication, 195, 414
mass spring systems, 173–5
nonlinearities, 171, 172
and perception, 175, 176–7, 205, 236–7,
   326, 330
planning of, 195–6
purposeful vs. accidental, 511–12
reaching/grasping, 37, 177–84
realization of a potential, 168
reasons to study, 168–9
search error, 228, 230–1
selective attention, 122, 123
self-organization, 169, 172, 173
self-produced, 326–30
sensori-motor development, 42
social context, 195
visual perception, 70–1
visually guided, 296
walking, 169, 170, 185–91
see also affordances; cooperative coordinated
   action
active intermodal mapping (AIM) theory, 62,
   355–6
activity-dependent processes, 296, 299, 300,
   310

Contents of Volume 2